THE GUINNESS BOOK OF RECORDS
1987

EDITOR

Alan Russell

EDITORIAL ADVISOR

Norris D. McWhirter

GUINNESS BOOKS

THE STORY BEHIND THE GUINNESS BOOK

On Saturday 10 November 1951, Sir Hugh Beaver (1890–1967) was out shooting on The North Slob, by the river Slaney in County Wexford in the south-east of Ireland. Some golden plover were missed by the party. That evening at Castlebridge House it was realized that it was not possible to confirm in reference books whether or not the golden plover was Europe's fastest game bird.

In August 1954 argument arose as to whether grouse were even faster. Sir Hugh, managing director of Guinness, thought that there must be numerous other questions debated nightly in the 81,400 pubs in

Britain and in Ireland, but there was no book with which to settle arguments about records.

On 12 September 1954, Sir Hugh invited Norris and Ross McWhirter to see if their fact and figure agency in London could help. An office was set up at 107 Fleet

— Norris McWhirter —

Street, London EC4 and work began on the first 198 page edition, the first copy of which was bound by the printers on 27 August 1955. Before Christmas *The Guinness Book of Records* was No. 1 on the bestsellers list and it has occupied this position every year since, except in 1957 and 1959 when it was not republished.

The first US edition appeared in New York in 1956 followed by editions in French (1962) and German (1963). In 1967 there were first editions in Japanese, Spanish, Danish and Norwegian, while the following year editions were pub-

lished in Swedish, Finnish and Italian. In the 'seventies there followed Dutch (1971); Portuguese (1974); Czechoslovak (1976); Hebrew, Serbo-Croat and Icelandic (all in 1977) and Slovenian (1978). In the 1980's translations into Greek, Indonesian, Chinese, Turkish, Hindi, Malay, Polish and Arabic brought the total to 233 editions in 26 languages.

In November 1974 the *Guinness Book of Records* earned its own place in the Guinness Book by becoming the top selling copyright book in publishing history with sales of 23.9 million. By 1986 global sales had risen to more than 53 million, which is equivalent to 118 stacks each as high as Mount Everest.

On 31 March 1986, having edited the book for 32 years, Norris McWhirter handed over the editorship to Alan Russell.

**President
Guinness PLC
October 1986**
The Rt Hon the Earl of Iveagh.

THE EDITOR WRITES

The world of record breaking is forever changing and for the first time in the history of the *Guinness Book of Records* the Editor has changed too. Norris McWhirter, Co-founder and Editor for thirty two years, twenty one of them with his twin brother Ross, has retired. Having made the book the world's leading authority on records, he is remaining as an advisor on the subject material that he has spent most of his life studying. I am immensely grateful for his guidance.

A change in editorship does not, however, mean a change in our policy governing the chronicling of records. We are still inclined to publish only those which are outstanding achievements, newly significant in having become the subject of widespread and preferably international competitiveness, or which improve upon previous records.

Inevitably, some record holders have gained their titles with lesser achievements than their predecessors. On 21 Feb 1986 at 12.15 Greenwich Mean Time, Shigechiyo Izumi died at his home in Asan, Japan at the authenticated age of 120 years 237 days. The world's oldest living person, the new title holder, is only 113!

In the animal kingdom, the only Tahltan bear dogs in existence last

The last photograph taken of Shigechiyo Izumi.

year both died, thus making the breed extinct. The title of rarest breed now goes to 76 Chinooks.

Most records though are broken because they better the previous extremity and some of them are impossible to chronicle with complete accuracy. In the scientific

Alan Russell

world, Pioneer 10, the most distant man-made object, is already beyond our solar system and in the time it has taken you to read this sentence—about 10 seconds—has travelled another $84\frac{1}{2}$ miles, breaking its own record all the time.

When it comes to sport, year after year the record barriers are pushed further and further. As well as the latest information on the World Cup and the Commonwealth Games, this edition also records the limits reached in over 100 other sports—from Bridge to Boardsailing, Croquet to Caving, and Snooker to Sumo Wrestling.

Nearly every activity associated with record breaking has a set of rules. If that activity is one controlled by a recognised world or national governing body, that body should be consulted and involved in ratifying it. If there is no such body, then potential claimants are advised to contact my editorial department for guidance.

Even though we reserve the right not to publish any record, potential record breakers have our best wishes for future attempts to further the frontiers.

Six people who have achieved greatness in the field of record breaking have been invited into what has been described as 'the most exclusive club in the world'— The Guinness Book Of Records Hall Of Fame. In a television programme specially made by the BBC and presented by David Frost on 17 May, the recipients, who are featured overleaf, received their gold medals from Norris McWhirter.

I can never think of Norris without thinking of 'The Story Behind The Guinness Book' told by Lord Iveagh on the opposite page. Reading that reminds me of another piece of information you ought to know. The Golden Plover is not Europe's fastest game bird even though, in level flight, it can reach a speed of 60 miles per hour. The European and World record belongs to . . . why don't you look it up? It's in the book!

EDITOR

Alan Russell

OCTOBER 1986
THE GUINNESS BOOK OF RECORDS
33 LONDON ROAD
ENFIELD, MIDDLESEX EN2 6DJ
ENGLAND

1986 HALL OF FAME

Joseph Kittinger
UNITED STATES OF AMERICA

On a research project in the U.S. Air Force, he successfully completed the longest ever delayed parachute drop of 4 minutes 36 seconds from a height of 19.5 miles.

Paul McCartney
GREAT BRITAIN

His unparalleled contribution to popular music both as a composer and as a performer includes 43 one million sellers, 67 gold discs and "Yesterday" the most recorded song ever written.

Billie-Jean King
UNITED STATES OF AMERICA

In a Wimbledon career from 1961 to 1983, she played 265 matches of which she emerged victorious in 224: a performance surpassing that of any other female player; and gained an unrivalled total of 20 titles.

Vesna Vulovic
YUGOSLAVIA

Her extraordinary story of survival stretched the limits of human endurance when she plunged to earth without a parachute from a DC9 aircraft which exploded at 33,330 feet or 10,610 metres.

Sir Ranulph Fiennes, Bt.
GREAT BRITAIN

In a lifetime dedicated to exploration, his achievements include the first polar circumnavigation of the earth by surface travel, during which he visited both Poles and recorded the fastest crossing of both the Arctic and Antarctic.

THE INAUGURAL MEMBERS OF

THE GUINNESS BOOK OF RECORDS HALL OF FAME

who were presented with their awards

on 17 MAY 1986

by

NORRIS McWHIRTER

on a

BBC Television Programme

presented by

DAVID FROST

Vernon Craig
UNITED STATES OF AMERICA

His remarkable achievements in the conquest of pain, including a firewalk on a temperature of 1494°F or 812°C, defy scientific analysis.

CONTENTS

CHAPTER ONE

THE

HUMAN BEING

TALLEST GIANTS

The true height of human giants is frequently obscured by exaggeration and commercial dishonesty. The only admissible evidence on the actual height of giants is that collected this century under impartial medical supervision. Unfortunately medical authors themselves are not guiltless in including fanciful, as opposed to measured, heights.

The assertion that Goliath of Gath (*c.* 1060 BC) stood 6 cubits and a span (9 ft 6½ in *290 cm*) suggests a confusion of units or some over-zealous exaggeration by the Hebrew chroniclers. The Jewish historian Flavius Josephus (born AD 37/38, died *c.* AD 100) and some of the manuscripts of the Septuagint (the earliest Greek translation of the Old Testament) attribute to Goliath the wholly credible height of 4 Greek cubits and a span (6 ft 10 in *208 cm*).

Giants exhibited in circuses and exhibitions are routinely under contract not to be measured and are, almost traditionally, billed by their promoters at heights up to 18 in *45 cm* in excess of their true heights.

An extreme case of exaggeration concerned Siah Khān ibn Kashmir Khān (b. 1913) of Bushehr (Bushire), Iran. Prof. D. H. Fuchs showed photographs of him at a meeting of the Society of Physicians in Vienna, Austria, in January 1935, claiming that he was 320 cm *10 ft 6 in* tall. Later, when Siah Khān entered the Imperial Hospital in Teheran for an operation, it was revealed that his actual height was a full metre less at 220 cm *7 ft 2.6 in.*

World *All-time*

Modern opinion is that the tallest recorded man of whom there is irrefutable evidence was the pre-acromegalic giant Robert Pershing Wadlow, born at 6.30 a.m. on 22 Feb 1918 in Alton, Illinois, USA.

Weighing 8½ lb *3,85 kg* at birth, the abnormal growth of Robert Wadlow started at the age of 2 following a double hernia operation. His height progressed as follows:

Age in Years	Height		Weight lb	kg
5	5' 4"	*163 cm*	105	*48*
8	6' 0"	*183 cm*	169	*77*
9	6' 2½"	*189 cm*	180	*82*
10	6' 5"	*196 cm*	210	*95*
11	6' 7"	*200 cm*	—	—
12	6' 10½"	*210 cm*	—	—
13	7' 1¾"	*218 cm*	255	*116*
14	7' 5"	*226 cm*	301	*137*
15	7' 8"	*234 cm*	355	*161*
16	7' 10½"	*240 cm*	374	*170*
17	8' 0½"	*245 cm*	315[1]	*143*
18	8' 3½"	*253 cm*	—	—
19	8' 5½"	*258 cm*	480	*218*
20	8' 6¾"	*261 cm*	—	—
21	8' 8½"	*265 cm*	491	*223*
22.4[2]	8' 11"	*272 cm*	439	*199*

[1] *Following severe influenza and infection of the foot.*
[2] *Wadlow was still growing during his terminal illness.*

Dr C. M. Charles, Associate Professor of Anatomy at Washington University's School of Medicine in St Louis, Missouri and Dr Cyril MacBryde measured Robert Wadlow at 272 cm *8 ft 11.1 in* in St Louis on 27 June 1940. Wadlow died 18 days later in a hotel, at 1.30 a.m. on 15 July 1940, in Manistee, Michigan as a result of cellulitis (inflammation of cellular tissue) of the right ankle aggravated by a brace, which had been poorly fitted only a week earlier.

He was buried in Oakwood Cemetery, Alton, Illinois in a coffin measuring 10 ft 9 in *328 cm* in length, 32 in *81 cm* wide and 30 in *76 cm* deep.

Britain's tallest man Chris Greener at 7 ft 6¼ in *229 cm* displays the moustache of John Roy before the hair-raising accident that cost John his record breaking title (*see p. 16*). (Rex Features)

His greatest recorded weight was 35 st 1 lb *222,71 kg*, on his 21st birthday, and he weighed 31 st 5 lb *199 kg* at the time of his death. His shoes were size 37AA (18½ in *47 cm* long) and his hands measured 12¾ in *32,4 cm* from the wrist to the tip of the middle finger (*cf.* the depth of this page at 11¼ in *28,5 cm*). He wore a size 25 ring.

His arm span was 9 ft 5¾ in *288 cm* and his peak daily food consumption attained 8000 calories. At the age of 9 he was able to carry his father, Harold F. Wadlow (d. Sept 1967) later Mayor of Alton, who stood 5 ft 11 in *180 cm* and weighed 170 lb *77 kg*, up the stairs of the family home. His last words were 'The doctor says I won't get home for the . . . celebrations' (a reference to his paternal grandparents golden wedding).

GIANT LEAGUE

The only other men for whom heights of 8 ft *244 cm* or more have been reliably reported are the nine listed below. In seven cases, gigantism was followed by acromegaly, a disorder which causes an enlargement of the nose, lips, tongue, lower jaw, hands and feet, due to renewed activity by an already swollen pituitary gland, which is located at the base of the brain.

John F. Carroll (1932–69) of Buffalo, New York State, USA [1] 8 ft 7¾ in *263,5 cm*.

John William Rogan (1871–1905), a negro of Gallatin, Tennessee, USA [2] 8 ft 6 in *259,1 cm*.

Väinö Myllyrinne (1909–63) of Helsinki, Finland [3] 8 ft 3 in *251,4 cm*.

Don Koehler (1925–81) of Denton, Montana, USA [4] 8 ft 2 in *248,9 cm*, latterly lived in Chicago.

Bernard Coyne (1897–1921) of Anthon, Iowa USA [5] 8 ft 2 in *248,9 cm*.

Patrick Cotter O'Brien (1760–1806) of Kinsale, County Cork, Ireland [6] 8 ft 1 in *246 cm*.

'Constantine' (1872–1902) of Reutlingen, West Germany [7] 8 ft 0.8 in *245,8 cm*.

Gabriel Estevao Monjane (b. 1944–fl. 1986) of Monjacaze, Mozambique [8] c. 8 ft 0¾ in *245,7 cm*.

Sulaimān 'Ali Nashnush (b. 1943–fl. 1986) of Tripoli, Libya [9] 8 ft 0.4 in *245 cm*.

[1] *Severe kypho-scoliosis (two dimensional spinal curvature). The figure represents his height with assumed normal spinal curvature, calculated from a standing height of 8 ft 0 in 244 cm, measured on 14 Oct 1959. His standing height was 7 ft 8½ in 234 cm shortly before his death.*
[2] *Measured in a sitting position. Unable to stand owing to ankylosis (stiffening of the joints through the formation of adhesions) of the knees and hips. Weighed only 175 lb 79 kg.*
[3] *Stood 7 ft 3½ in 222 cm at the age of 21 years. Experienced a second phase of growth in his late thirties and measured 8 ft 1.2 in 246,8 cm at the time of his death.*
[4] *Spinal curvature reduced his standing height to c. 7 ft 10 in 238,4 cm. Abnormal growth started at the age of 10. He had a twin sister who is 5 ft 9 in 175 cm tall. His father was 6 ft 2 in 187 cm and his mother 5 ft 10 in 177 cm.*
[5] *Eunuchoidal giant (Daddy long-legs syndrome). Rejected by Army in 1918 when 7 ft 9 in 236 cm. Still growing at time of death.*
[6] *Revised height based on skeletal remeasurement in 1975.*
[7] *Eunuchoidal. Height estimated, as both legs were amputated after they turned gangrenous. He claimed a height of 8 ft 6 in 259 cm.*
[8] *Eunuchoidal. Measured 7 ft 5 in 226 cm at the age of 16 and 7 ft 10 in 238,7 cm in Dec 1965. Latest measurement taken in May 1967. Has not been anthropometrically assessed since joining a Portuguese circus (billed height 265 cm 8 ft 8½ in). Now suffering from pronounced scoliosis.*
[9] *Operation to correct abnormal growth successfully carried out in Rome in 1960.*

Living
Muhammad Aalam Channa (b. Sehwan, 1956), who works as an attendant at the shrine of Lal Shahbaz Qalandar in Pakistan assumed the role of the world's tallest man in 1981 with the death of Don Koehler. A height of 8 ft 2¾ in *251 cm* attributed to him, proved in 1984 to be exaggerated and he is now believed to be 239 cm *7 ft 10 in*. The only two living giants with a stature greater than 8 feet *244 cm* are thus Monjane and Nashnush (see table above).

The tallest teenage giant still growing is Kazim Hussein (b. 1968) of Baghdad, Iraq, who was 2,26 m *7 ft 5 in* in Feb 1985. He had grown 7,6 cm *3 in* in the previous 12 months.

England
The tallest Englishman ever recorded was William Bradley (1787–1820), born in Market Weighton, Humberside. He stood 7 ft 9 in *236 cm*. John Middleton (1578–1623), the famous Childe of Hale, from near Liverpool, was credited with a height of 9 ft 3 in *282 cm* but a life-size impression of his right hand (length 11½ in *29,2 cm*, *cf.* Wadlow's 12¾ in *32,4 cm*) painted on a panel in Brasenose College, Oxford indicates his true stature was nearer 7 ft 8 in *233,6 cm*. Albert Brough (1871–1919), a publican of Nottingham, reached a height of 7 ft 7½ in *232 cm*. Frederick Kempster (1889–1918) of Bayswater, London, was reported to have measured 8 ft 4½ in *255 cm* at the time of his death, but photographic evidence suggests that his height was 7 ft 8½ in *235 cm*. He measured 234 cm *7 ft 8.1 in* in 1913. Henry Daglish, who stood 7 ft 7 in *231 cm* died in Upper Stratton, Wiltshire, on 16 March 1951, aged 25. The much-publicised Edward (Ted) Evans (1924–58) of Englefield Green, Surrey, was reputed to be 9 ft 3 in *282 cm* but actually stood 7 ft 8½ in *235 cm*.

The tallest fully mobile man now living in Great Britain is Christopher Paul Greener (b. New Brighton, Merseyside, 21 Nov 1943) of Hayes, Kent, who measures 7 ft 6¼ in *229 cm* (weight 26 st *165 kg*). Terence Keenan (b. 1942) of Rock Ferry, Merseyside measured 7 ft 6 in *229 cm* in 1968, but is confined to a wheelchair owing to a leg condition. His abnormal growth began at the age of 17 when he was only 5 ft 4 in *163 cm* tall.

Scotland
The tallest Scotsman, and the tallest recorded 'true' (non-pathological) giant, was Angus Macaskill (1825–63), born on the island of Berneray, in the Sound of Harris, in the Western Isles. He stood 7 ft 9 in *236 cm* and died in St Anns', on Cape Breton Island, Nova Scotia, Canada. Lambert Quételet (1796–1874), a Belgian anthropometrist, considered that a Scotsman named MacQuail, known as 'the Scotch Giant', stood 8 ft 3 in *251 cm*. He served in the famous regiment of giants of Frederick William I (1688–1740), King of Prussia. His skeleton, now in the Staatliche Museum zu Berlin, East Germany, measures 220 cm *7 ft 2.6 in*. Sam McDonald (1762–1802) of Lairg in Sutherland, was reputed to be 8 ft *244 cm* tall but actually stood 6 ft 10 in *208 cm*. William Olding (b. 1914–fl. 1942) of Glasgow measured 7 ft 6½ in *230 cm* (weight 366 lb *166 kg*).

The tallest Scotsman now living is George Gracie (b. 1938) of Forth, Lanark, Strathclyde. He stands 7 ft 3 in *221 cm* and weighs 32 st *203 kg*. His brother Hugh (b. 1941) is 7 ft 0½ in *215 cm*.

Wales
The tallest Welshman on record was William Evans (1599–1634) of Gwent, then Monmouthshire, who was porter to King James I. He stood 7 ft 6 in *228,6 cm*.

Ireland
The tallest Irishman was the 8 ft 1 in *246 cm* tall Patrick Cotter O'Brien (1760–1806), born in Kinsale, County Cork. He died at Hotwells, Bristol (See table column one).

Twins
The tallest twins (identical) ever recorded are Michael and James Lanier (b. 27 Nov 1969) of Troy, Michigan, USA who both measure 7 ft 4 in *223,5 cm*. Britain's tallest twins are Jonathan and Mark Carratt (b. 11 June 1955) of Maltby, South Yorkshire who are 6 ft 8 in *203,2 cm* and 6 ft 9 in *205,7 cm* respectively. David and John Moore (b. 29 Mar 1963) of Erith, Kent both measure 6 ft 8¼ in *203,8 cm*.

TALLEST GIANTESSES

World *All-time*
Giantesses are rarer than giants but their heights are still spectacular. The tallest woman in history was the acromegalic giantess Zeng Jinlian (pronounced San Chunglin) (b. 26 June 1964) of Yujiang village in the Bright Moon Commune, Hunan Province, central China. She began to grow abnormally from the age of 4 months and stood 156 cm *5 ft 1½ in* before her 4th birthday (*cf.* 162,5 cm *5 ft 4 in* for Robert Wadlow at the age of 5) and 217 cm *7 ft 1½ in* when she was 13. Her hands measured 25,5 cm *10 in* and her feet 35,5 cm *14 in* in length. She could not stand erect, due to scoliosis, but was 247 cm *8 ft 1¼ in* long when she died on 13 Feb 1982. Her parents are 163 cm *5 ft 4 in* and 156 cm *5 ft 1½ in* while her brother was 158 cm *5 ft 2¼ in* as an 18 year old.

Living
The tallest living woman is Sandy Allen (b. 18 June 1955, Chicago) of Niagara Falls, Ontario, Canada. On 14 July 1977 she underwent a pituitary gland operation, which inhibited further growth at 7 ft 7¼ in *231,7 cm*. A 6½ lb *2,95 kg* baby, her acromegalic growth began soon after birth. She now weighs 33 st *209,5 kg* and takes a size 16EEE American shoe (= 14½ UK or 50PP Continental).

United Kingdom
The tallest woman in British medical history was Jane ('Ginny') Bunford, born on 26 July 1895 at Bartley Green, Northfield, Birmingham, England. Her abnormal growth started at the age of 11 following a head injury, and on her 13th birthday she measured 6 ft 6 in *198 cm*. Shortly before her death on 1 April 1922 she stood 7 ft 7 in *231 cm* tall, but she had severe kyphoscoliosis. She was the tallest woman on record and but for her spinal curvature would have stood about 7 ft 11 in *241 cm*. Her skeleton, now preserved in the Anatomical Museum in the Medical School at Birmingham University, has a mounted height of 7 ft 4 in *223,5 cm*.

Tallest couple
Anna Hanen Swan (1846–88) of Nova Scotia, Canada, was billed at 8 ft 1 in *246 cm* but actually measured 7 ft 5½ in *227 cm*. In London on 17 June 1871 she married Martin van Buren Bates (1845–1919) of Whitesburg, Letcher County, Kentucky, USA, who stood 7 ft 2½ in *219 cm* making them the tallest married couple on record.

SHORTEST DWARFS

The strictures which apply to giants apply equally to dwarfs, except that exaggeration gives way to understatement. In the same way as 9 ft *274 cm* may be regarded as the limit towards which the tallest giants tend, so 23 in *58 cm* must be regarded as the limit towards which the shortest mature dwarfs tend (*cf.* the average length of new-born babies is 18–20 in *46–50 cm*). In the case of child dwarfs their *ages* are often enhanced by their agents or managers.

There are many forms of human dwarfism, but those suffering from ateleiosis (midgets) are generally the shortest. They have essentially normal proportions but suffer from growth hormone deficiency. Such dwarfs tended to be even shorter at a time when human stature was

Male All-time

The shortest recorded adult male dwarf was Calvin Phillips, born on 14 Jan 1791 in Bridgewater, Massachusetts, USA. He weighed 2 lb *907 g* at birth and stopped growing at the age of 5. When he was 19 he measured 26½ in *67 cm* tall and weighed 12 lb *5,4 kg* with his clothes on. He died two years later, in April 1812, from progeria, a rare disorder characterised by dwarfism and premature senility.

The most famous midget in history was Charles Sherwood Stratton, *alias* 'General Tom Thumb', born on 4 Jan 1838. When he got into the clutches of the circus proprietor Mr Barnum his birth date was changed to 4 Jan 1832 so that when billed at 30½ in *77 cm* at the age of 18 he was in fact 12. He died in his birthplace of Bridgeport, Connecticut, USA of apoplexy on 15 July 1883 aged 45 (not 51) and was 3 ft 4 in *102 cm*.

William E. Jackson, *alias* 'Major Mite', born on 2 Oct 1864 in Dunedin, New Zealand, measured 9 in *23 cm* long and weighed 12 oz *340 g* at birth. In November 1880 he stood 21 in *53 cm* and weighed 9 lb *4 kg*. He died in New York City, NY, USA, on 9 Dec 1900, when he measured 27 in *69 cm*.

Living

The world's shortest known mobile living adult human is Antonio Ferreira (b. 1943), a rachitic dwarf of Arcozelo, Portugal who measures 75 cm *29½ in*. He is a professional drummer. In July 1982 an unconfirmed height of 28 in *71 cm* was reported for a chicken farmer named Ghucam Ahmed Dar living near Srinagar in Kashmir, India.

United Kingdom

The shortest mature human ever recorded in Britain was Miss Joyce Carpenter (b. 21 Dec 1929), a rachitic dwarf of Charford, Hereford & Worcester, who stood 29 in *74 cm* tall and weighed 30 lb *13,60 kg*. She died on 7 Aug 1973 aged 43. Hopkins Hopkins (1737–54) of Llantrisant, Mid-Glamorgan who suffered from progeria, was 31 in *79 cm* tall. He weighed 19 lb *8,62 kg* at the age of 7 and 13 lb *6 kg* at the time of his death. There are an estimated 2000 people of severely restricted growth (i.e. under 4 ft 8 in *142 cm*), living in Britain today.

The shortest adult living in Britain is Michael Henbury-Ballan (b. 26 Nov 1958) of Bassett, Southampton, who is 37 in *94 cm* tall and weighs 5½ st *35 kg*. A 5 lb 14 oz *2,66 kg* baby, he stopped growing at the age of 13 years. His fraternal twin brother Malcolm is 5 ft 9 in *175 cm* tall and weighs 11 st 7 lb *73 kg*.

Twins

The shortest twins ever recorded were the primordial dwarfs Matjus and Bela Matina (b. 1903–*fl.* 1935) of Budapest, Hungary who later became naturalised Americans. They both measured 30 in *76 cm*. The world's shortest living twins are John and Greg Rice (b. 3 Dec 1951) of Maitland, Florida, USA who both measure 34 in *86,3 cm*.

Oldest

There are only two centenarian dwarfs on record. The older was Hungarian-born Miss Susanna Bokoyni ('Princess Susanna') of Newton, New Jersey, USA who died aged 105 years on 24 Aug 1984. She was 3 ft 4 in *101 cm* tall and weighed 37 lb *16,78 kg*. The other was Miss Anne Clowes of Matlock, Derbyshire, who died on 5 Aug 1784 aged 103 years. She was 3 ft 9 in *114 cm* tall and weighed 48 lb *21,7 kg*.

Most variable stature

Adam Rainer, born in Graz, Austria, in 1899,

---

generally shorter due to lower nutritional standards.

World *All-time*

The shortest mature human of whom there is independent evidence was Pauline Musters ('Princess Pauline'), a Dutch midget. She was born at Ossendrecht, on 26 Feb 1876 and measured 30 cm *11.8 in* at birth. At the age of 9 she was 55 cm *21.65 in* tall and weighed only 1,5 kg *3 lb 5 oz*. She died on 1 Mar 1895 in New York City, NY, USA, at the age of 19, of pneumonia, with meningitis, her heart weakened from alcoholic excesses. Although she was billed at 48 cm *19 in*, she had earlier been medically measured to be 59 cm *23.2 in* tall. A *post mortem* examination showed her to be exactly 61 cm *24 in* (there was some elongation after death). Her mature weight varied from 3,4–4 kg *7½–9 lb* and her 'vital statistics' were 47–48–43 cm *18½–19–17 in*, which suggests she was overweight.

In 1938 a height of 19 in *48 cm* was attributed to Paul Del Rio (b. Madrid, Spain, 1920) by *Life Magazine* when he visited Hollywood, but the fact that his presence created no great impression among other dwarfs in the film capital and that he weighed as much as 12 lb *5,4 kg* suggests that he was closer to 26 in *66 cm* tall.

In 1979 a height of 50 cm *19.68 in* and a weight of 4 lb 6 oz *1,98 kg* were reported for a nine-year-old Greek girl named Stamatoula (b. Sept 1969 length 15 cm *5.9 in*). When she died on 22 Aug 1985 at the Lyrion Convent, Athens, she measured 67 cm *26.4 in* and weighed 5 kg *11 lbs*. The child, believed to be the survivor of twins, suffered from Seckel's 'bird-face' syndrome.

Antonio Ferreira (*above*), the world's shortest authenticated living human showing his 'entyre' height at 29½ in *75 cm*. (Gamma Presse Agence)

(*Below*) 'Nelson, The Little Man' poses with Richard L. Finkler (US) in the indoor market place in Santa Domingo, Dominican Republic. He is reported to be between 30 and 32 years of age and stands 24–26 in *61–66 cm* short, but his true height has not been measured.

measured 118 cm *3 ft 10.45 in* at the age of 21. But then he suddenly started growing at a rapid rate, and by 1931 he had reached 218 cm *7 ft 1¾ in*. He became so weak as a result that he was bed-ridden for the rest of his life. At the time of his death on 4 Mar 1950 aged 51 he measured 234 cm *7 ft 8 in* and was the only person in medical history to have been both a dwarf and a giant.

Lord Adare (4th Earl of Dunraven and Mount-Earl, b. 12 Feb 1841, d. 14 June 1926) recorded that the Scots-born medium Daniel Home (b. 1833) could elongate his body 11 in *28 cm*.

Most disparate couple *Britain*
Nigel Wilks (6 ft 6 in *198 cm*) of Kingston upon Hull, Humberside married Beverly Russell (4 ft *122 cm*), both aged 21, on 30 June 1984. Their son Daniel, 9 lb 5 oz *4,22 kg*, was born on 22 Mar 1986.

TRIBES

Tallest
The tallest major tribe in the world is the Tutsi (also known as Watussi) (pop. *c.* 10,000), Nilotic herdsmen of Rwanda and Burundi, Central Africa where the average adult height (males) is more than 6 ft *183 cm*. The Tehuelches of Patagonia, long regarded as of gigantic stature (*i.e.* 7–8 ft *213–244 cm*), have in fact an average height (males) of 5 ft 10 in *177 cm*. The Montenegrins of Yugoslavia, with a male average of 5 ft 10 in *177 cm* (in the town of Trebinje the average height is 6 ft *183 cm*), compare with the men of Sutherland, at 5 ft 9½ in *176,5 cm*. In 1912 the average height of the men living in Balmaclellan, in the Kircudbright district of Dumfries and Galloway was reported to be 5 ft 10.4 in *179 cm*.

Shortest
The smallest pygmies are the Mbuti, with an average height of 4 ft 6 in *137 cm* for men and 4 ft 5 in *135 cm* for women, with some groups averaging only 4 ft 4 in *132 cm* for men and 4 ft 1 in *124 cm* for women. They live in the forests near the river Ituri in Zaïre.

WEIGHT

Heaviest men *World*
The heaviest human in recorded medical history was alleged to be Jon Brower Minnoch (b. 29 Sept 1941) of Bainbridge Island, Washington, USA, who was carried on planking by a rescue team into the University Hospital, Seattle in March 1978. Dr Robert Schwartz, his endocrinological consultant, estimated, by extrapolating his intake and elmination rates, that he was 'probably more' than 1400 lb *635 kg* (100 st). His highest actually recorded bodyweight was 975 lb *442 kg* in September 1976. To roll him over in his hospital bed it took 13 attendants. After nearly 2 years on a 1200 calorie per day diet he was discharged at 476 lb *216 kg* (34 st). He had to be readmitted in October 1981 having reportedly regained 200 lb *91 kg* (over 14 st) in 7 days. He died on 10 Sept 1983. This former taxi-cab driver stood 6 ft 1 in *1,85 m* tall. He was 400 lb *181 kg* in 1963, and 700 lb *317 kg* in 1966.

Living
The heaviest living man is T. J. Albert Jackson (b. 22 lb *9,97 kg* Kent Nicholson), also known as 'Fat Albert' of Canton, Mississippi, USA (see Table). He was recently recorded at 891 lb *404 kg*. Albert Pernitsch of Grafkorn, Austria (see right) also claims to be the world's heaviest man, but the greatest weight recorded for him so far is 880 lb *399 kg*.

Great Britain
The heaviest recorded man in Great Britain was

Motorcycle fanatics John and Greg Rice, the world's shortest twins, whose aggregate height of 68 in *173 cm* would just qualify them for the Metropolitan Police Force.

Peter Yarnall of East Ham, London, who died on 30 March 1984 aged 34 years. He was 5 ft 10 in *177,8 cm* tall and weighed 59 st *374 kg*. His coffin measured 7 ft 4 in *2,23 m* in length, 4 ft *1,22 m* across and had a depth of 2 ft 9 in *83,8 cm*.

Only two other British men had a recorded weight of more than 50 st *317,5 kg*. One of them was William Campbell (b. Glasgow 1856) who died on 16 June 1878 when a publican at High Bridge, Newcastle upon Tyne, Tyne and Wear. He was 6 ft 3 in *190 cm* tall and weighed 53 st 8 lb *340 kg* with an 85 in *216 cm* waist and a 96 in *244 cm* chest. The other was the celebrated Daniel Lambert (1770–1809) of Stamford, Lincolnshire. He stood 5 ft 11 in *180 cm* tall and weighed 52 st 11 lb *335 kg* shortly before his death and had a girth of more than 92 in *233 cm*.

Britain's heaviest man is the 6 ft 11 in *210,8 cm* tall professional wrestler Martin Ruane ('Giant Haystacks') (b. Camberwell, London 1946) of Manchester. A 14 lb *6,35 kg* baby he weighed 25 st *158,7 kg* at the age of 18 years and 32 st *203 kg* when he was 25. His weight now fluctuates between 41 st *260 kg* and 43 st *273 kg* but he once claimed to have tipped the scales at 50 st *317 kg*.

Ireland
The heaviest Irishman is reputed to have been Roger Byrne, who was buried in Rosenallis,

County Laoighis (Leix), on 14 Mar 1804. He died in his 54th year and his coffin and its contents weighed 52 st *330 kg*. Roly McIntyre (b. 1955) of Kesh, Fermanagh, Northern Ireland scaled a peak 42 st 4 lb *268,5 kg* in April 1983 (see Slimming, p. 10).

Heaviest women *World*
The heaviest woman ever recorded was the late Mrs Percy Pearl Washington, 46 who died in hospital in Milwaukee, on 9 Oct 1972. The hospital scales registered only up to 800 lb (57 st 2 lb) *362,8 kg* but she was believed to weigh about 880 lb (62 st 12 lb) *399,1 kg*. The previous feminine weight record had been set 84 years earlier at 850 lb (60 st 10 lb) *385 kg* although a wholly unsubstantiated report exists of a woman Mrs Ida Maitland (1898–1932) of Springfield, Mississippi, USA, who reputedly weighed 65 st 1 lb (911 lb) *413,2 kg*.

A more reliable and better documented case was that of Mrs Flora Mae Jackson (*née* King), a 5 ft 9 in *175 cm* Negress born in 1930 at Shuqualak, Mississippi, USA. She weighed 10 lb *4,5 kg* at birth, 19 st 1 lb (267 lb) *121 kg* at the age of 11,

The only others for whom weights of more than 60 st (840 lb) *381 kg* have been reported are the 10 listed below:				
	lb	st	lb	kg
Michael Walker *née* Francis Lang (b. 1934) USA (6 ft 2 in *188 cm*)[1]	est. 1187	84	11	538
Robert Earl Hughes (1926–58) USA (6 ft 0½ in *184 cm*)	1069	76	5	485
Mohamed Naaman (b 1946) Kenya (6 ft 0 in *182 cm*)[2]	1055	75	5	478
Mills Darden (1798–1857) USA (7 ft 6 in *229 cm*)	1020	72	12	462
John Hanson Craig (1856–94) USA (6 ft 5 in *195 cm*)[3]	907	64	11	411
Arthur Knorr (1914–60) USA (6 ft 1 in *185 cm*)[4]	900	64	4	408
T. J. Albert Jackson (b. 1941) Canton, Mississippi, USA (6 ft 4 in *193 cm*)	891	63	9	404
Albert Pernitsch (b. 1956) of Grafkorn, Austria (5 ft 9 in *175 cm*)[5]	880	62	12	399
Toubi (b. 1946) Cameroon	857½	61	3½	389
T. A. Valenzuela (1895–1937) Mexico (5 ft 11 in *180 cm*)	850	60	10	385

[1] *Reduced to 369 lb 167 kg by Feb. 1980. Peak weight was only estimated in 1971.*
[2] *Reported in Aug 1984 to have reduced to 770 lb 349 kg.*
[3] *Won $1000 in a 'Bonny Baby' contest in New York City in 1858.*
[4] *Gained 300 lb 136 kg in the last 6 months of his life.*
[5] *His left arm tattoo proclaims 'Nobody is perfect'. In July 1984 his girth was 200 cm 78¾ in.*

44 st 5 lb (621 lb) *282 kg* at 25 and 60 st (840 lb) *381 kg* shortly before her death in Meridian, Mississippi, on 9 Dec 1965. She was known in show business as 'Baby Flo'.

Great Britain and Ireland

The heaviest woman ever recorded in Great Britain was a Cypriot patient (unnamed) admitted to the Royal Free Hospital in Hampstead, London in c. 1975. After her death the intrigued undertaker took the hearse over a weighbridge, loaded and unloaded, so revealing, after making an allowance for the coffin, a weight of 46 stone *292 kg*.

Heaviest twins

The heaviest twins in the world were Billy Leon (1946–79) and Benny Loyd (b. 7 Dec 1946) McCrary *alias* McGuire of Hendersonville, North Carolina, USA, who in November 1978 were weighed at 743 lb (53 st 1 lb) *337 kg* (Billy) and 723 lb (51 st 9 lb) *328 kg* (Benny) and had 84 in *213 cm* waists. As professional tag wrestling performers they were *billed* at weights up to 770 lb *349 kg*. Billy died at Niagara Falls, Ontario, Canada on 13 July 1979 after a mini-motorcycle accident.

Lightest *World*

The lightest adult human on record was Lucia Zarate (b. San Carlos, Mexico 2 Jan 1863, d. October 1889), an emaciated Mexican ateleiotic dwarf of 26½ in *67 cm*, who weighed 2,125 kg *4.7 lb* at the age of 17. She 'fattened up' to 13 lb *5,9 kg* by her 20th birthday. At birth she weighed 2½ lb *1,1 kg*. The lightest adult ever recorded in the United Kingdom was Hopkins Hopkins (Shortest dwarfs, see p. 8).

The thinnest recorded adults of normal height are those suffering from Simmonds' Disease (Hypophyseal cachexia). Losses up to 65 per cent of the original body-weight have been recorded in females, with a 'low' of 3 st 3 lb *20 kg* in the case of Emma Shaller (b. St Louis, Missouri 8 July 1868, d. 4 Oct 1890), who stood 5 ft 2 in *157 cm*. Edward C. Hagner (1892–1962), *alias* Eddie Masher (USA) is alleged to have weighed only 3 st 6 lb *22 kg* at a height of 5 ft 7 in *170 cm*. He was also known as 'the Skeleton Dude'. In August 1825 the biceps measurement of Claude-Ambroise Seurat (b. 10 Apr 1797, d. 6 Apr 1826) of Troyes, France was 4 in *10 cm* and the distance between his back and his chest was less than 3 in *7.6 cm*. According to one report he stood 5 ft 7½ in *171 cm* and weighed 5 st 8 lb *35 kg*, but in another account was described as 5 ft 4 in *163 cm* and only 2 st 8 lb *16 kg*. It was recorded that the American exhibitionist Rosa Lee Plemons (b. 1873) weighed 27 lb *12 kg* at the age of 18.

In July 1977 the death was reported of an 83 year old woman in Mexborough, South Yorkshire who scaled only 2 st 5 lb *15 kg* (height not recorded).

Lightest *Great Britain*

Robert Thorn (b. 1842) of March, Cambridgeshire weighed 49 lb *22 kg* at the age of 32. He was 4 ft 6 in *137 cm* tall and had a 27 in *68 cm* chest (expanded) and 4½ in *11.4 cm* biceps.

Slimming *Men*

The greatest slimming feat with published details was that of William J. Cobb (b. 1926), *alias* 'Happy Humphrey', a professional wrestler of Augusta, Georgia, USA. It was reported in July 1965 that he had reduced from 57 st 4 lb *364 kg* to 16 st 8 lb *105 kg*, a loss of 40 st 11 lb *259 kg* in 32 months. His waist measurement declined from 101 to 44 in *256 to 112 cm*. In October 1973 it was reported that 'Happy' was back to his normal weight of 31 st or 432 lb *196 kg*. By July 1979 Jon Brower Minnoch

(1941–83) (see p. 9) had reduced to 476 lb *216 kg* (34 st); if his estimated peak weight was authentic, this indicated a weight loss of 924 lb *419 kg* (66 st) in 2 years, an average of 8.8 lb *3,99 kg* per week.

Roly McIntyre (b. 1952) (see Heaviest Men) reduced from 42 st 4 lb *268,5 kg* to 13 st 5 lb *84,8 kg* from April 1983 to Feb 1985. Paul M. Kimelman, 23, of Pittsburgh, Pennsylvania, USA reduced from 487 lb (34 st 11 lb) *215,9 kg* to 130 lb (9 st 4 lb) *59 kg* between 31 Dec 1966 and 3 Aug 1967. Richard Stephens of Birmingham, Alabama, USA slimmed from 467 lb (33 st 5 lb) *211,8 kg* to 305¾ lb (21 st 11¾ lb) *138,6 kg* in 157 days from 12 Apr to 16 Sept 1985. Ron Allen (b. 1947) sweated off 21½ lb *9,7 kg* of his 250 lb *113,4 kg* in Nashville, Tennessee, USA in 24 hr in Aug 1984.

Women

The US circus fat lady Mrs Celesta Geyer (b. 1901), *alias* Dolly Dimples, reduced from 553 lb *251 kg* to 152 lb *69 kg* in 1950–51, a loss of 401 lb *182 kg* in 14 months. Her vital statistics diminished *pari passu* from 79–84–84 in *200–213–213 cm* to a *svelte* 34–28–36 in *86–71–91 cm*. Her book 'How I lost 400 lbs' was not a best-seller because of the difficulty of would-be readers identifying themselves with the dress-making and other problems of losing more than 28 st *178 kg* when 4 ft 11 in *150 cm* tall. In December 1967 she was reportedly down to 7 st 12 lb *50 kg*. In February 1951 Mrs Gertrude Levandowski (b. 1893) of Burnips, Michigan, USA successfully underwent a protracted operation for the removal of a cyst which subsequently reduced her weight from 44 st *280 kg* to 22 st *140 kg* (See also p. 21).

The feminine champion in Britain was Mrs Dolly Wager (b. 1933) of Charlton, London, who, between September 1971 and 22 May 1973 reduced from 31 st 7 lb *200 kg* to 11 st *69,8 kg* so losing 20 st 7 lb *130 kg* with Weight Watchers.

Weight gaining

The reported record for gaining weight was set by Jon Minnoch (see p. 9) when in October 1981 he was readmitted to University Hospital, Seattle, Washington State, USA having regained 200 lb *91 kg* in 7 days. Miss Doris James of San Francisco, California, USA is alleged to have gained 23 st 3 lb *147 kg* in the 12 months before her death in August 1965, aged 38, at a weight of 48 st 3 lb *306 kg*. She was only 5 ft 2 in *157 cm* tall.

Greatest differential

The greatest weight differential recorded for a married couple is c. 1300 lb *589 kg* (92 st 12 lb) in the case of Jon Brower Minnoch (see p. 9) and his 110 lb *50 kg* (7 st 12 lb) wife Jeannette in March 1978. She bore him two sons. The UK record is held by Martin Ruane (see p. 9) and his 7½ st *47,6 kg* wife Rita, where their weight differential was at times 42½ st *270 kg*. They have three sons.

2. ORIGINS

EARLIEST MAN

Earliest *Primate*

The first primates appeared in the Palaeocene epoch about 69,000,000 years ago. The earliest members of the sub-order Anthropoidea are known from both Africa and South America in the early Oligocene, 34–30 million years ago, when the two infra-orders, Platyrrhini and Catarrhini from the New and Old Worlds respectively were already distinct.

Earliest *Hominid*

Characteristics typical of the Hominidae such as the large brain and bipedal locomotion do not appear until much later. The earliest undoubted hominid relic found is an Australopithecine jaw bone with two molars 2 in *5 cm* in length found by Kiptalam Chepboi near Lake Baringo, Kenya in Feb 1984 and dated at 4 million years by associated fossils and 5.6–5.4 million years through rock correlation by K-Ar dating.

The most complete of the earliest hominid skeletons is that of 'Lucy' (forty per cent complete) found by Dr Donald C. Johanson and T. Gray at Locality 162 by the Awash river, Hadar, in the Afar region of Ethiopia on 30 Nov 1974. She was estimated to be c. 40 years old when she died 3 million years ago, and she was 3½ ft *106 cm* tall.

Parallel tracks of hominid footprints extending over 80 ft *24 m* were discovered at Laetoli, Tanzania in 1978, first by Paul Abell, in volcanic ash dating to 3.5 million years ago. The height of the smallest of the seemingly 3 individuals was estimated to be 120 cm *4 ft 7 in*.

Earliest genus *Homo*

The earliest species of the genus *Homo* is *Homo habilis* or 'Handy Man' so named by Prof. Raymond Arthur Dart (b. Australia 1893) in 1964. The greatest age attributed to fossils of this genus is 1.9 million years for the skull KNM-ER (Kenya National Museum-East Rudolf) 1470 discovered in 1972 by Bernard Ngeneo at Koobi Fora by Lake Turkana, North Kenya. It was reconstructed by Dr Meave Leakey (née Epps).

The earliest stone tools are abraded core-choppers dating from c. 2.5 million years. They were found at Hadar, Ethiopia in 1976 by Hélène Roche (France). Finger (as opposed to fist) -held quartz dicers found by Roche close to the Hadar site by the Gona river are also dated to c. 2.5 million years.

Earliest *Homo erectus*

The earliest *Homo erectus* (upright man), the species directly ancestral to *Homo sapiens*, was discovered by Kamoya Kimen on the surface at the site of Nariokotome III to the west of Lake Turkana, Kenya in 1984. The skeleton of a 12-year old boy is the most complete of this species ever found; only a few small pieces are missing.

Great Britain

The earliest but disputed evidence for the presence of hominids in Great Britain dates from c. 400,000 BC. Five worked flint artefacts showing features normally attributed to human workmanship were found in cave deposits near Westbury-sub-Mendip, Somerset, and described in 1975 by Michael J. Bishop. The oldest definite human remains ever found in Britain are pieces of a brain case from a specimen of *Homo sapiens*, recovered in June 1935 and March 1936 by Dr

Alvan T. Marston from the Boyn Hill terrace in the Barnfield Pit, near Swanscombe, northern Kent. The remains were associated with a middle Acheulian tool culture and probably date to the Holsteinian interglacial (230,000 BC). Three hominid teeth, mandible fragments and a vertebra were found in Pontnewydd Cave, Lower Elwy Valley, North Wales from October 1980. They were dated by the Thorium/Uranium disequilibrium method to a little over 200,000 years.

3. LONGEVITY

No single subject is more obscured by vanity, deceit, falsehood and deliberate fraud than the extremes of human longevity. Extreme claims are generally made on behalf of the very aged rather than *by* them.

Many hundreds of claims throughout history have been made for persons living well into their second century and some, insulting to the intelligence, for people living even into their third. Centenarians surviving beyond their 113th year are in fact of the extremest rarity and the present absolute proven limit of human longevity does not yet admit of anyone living to celebrate any birthday after their 120th.

The most reliably pedigreed large group of people in the world, the British peerage, has, after ten centuries, produced only three centenarian peers, but only two reached their 101st birthdays. However, this is possibly not unconnected with the extreme draughtiness of many of their residences and the amount of lead in their game.

Several celebrated super-centenarians (over 110 years) are believed to have been double lives (father and son, relations with the same names or successive bearers of a title). The most famous example is Christian Jakobsen Drackenberg allegedly born in Stavanger, Norway on 18 Nov 1626 and died in Aarhus, Denmark aged seemingly 145 years 326 days on 9 Oct 1772. A number of instances have been commercially sponsored, while a fourth category of recent claims are those made for political ends, such as

Shigechiyo Izumi, the world's oldest proven human, who died on 21 February 1986 at the remarkable age of 120 years 237 days.

AUTHENTIC NATIONAL LONGEVITY RECORDS

	Years	Days		Born		Died	
Japan	120	237	Shigechiyo Izumi	29 June	1865	21 Feb	1986
United States[1]	113	273	Fannie Thomas	24 Apr	1867	22 Jan	1981
Canada[2]	113	124	Pierre Joubert	15 July	1701	16 Nov	1814
United Kingdom[3]	113	+	Anna Eliza Williams (Mrs) (*née* Davies)	2 June	1873	*fl.* 2 June	1986
Spain[4]	112	228	Josefa Salas Mateo	14 July	1860	27 Feb	1973
France	112	66	Augustine Teissier (Sister Julia)	2 Jan	1869	9 Mar	1981
Morocco	>112		El Hadj Mohammed el Mokri (Grand Vizier)		1844	16 Sept	1957
Poland	112	+	Roswlia Mielczarek (Mrs)		1868	7 Jan	1981
Ireland	111	327	The Hon. Katherine Plunket	22 Nov	1820	14 Oct	1932
Australia	111	235	Jane Piercy (Mrs)	2 Sept	1869	3 May	1981
South Africa[5]	111	151	Johanna Booyson	17 Jan	1857	16 June	1968
Czechoslovakia	111	+	Marie Bernatkova	22 Oct	1857	*fl.* Oct	1968
Channel Islands							
(Guernsey)	110	321	Margaret Ann Neve (*née* Harvey)	18 May	1792	4 April	1903
Northern Ireland	110	234	Elizabeth Watkins (Mrs)	10 Mar	1863	31 Oct	1973
Sweden	110	200+	Wilhelmine Sande (Mrs)	24 Oct	1874	*fl.* 12 May	1985
Yugoslavia	110	150+	Demitrius Philipovitch	9 Mar	1818	*fl.* Aug	1928
Netherlands[6]	110	141	Gerada Hurenkamp-Bosgoed	5 Jan	1870	25 May	1980
Greece[7]	110	+	Lambrini Tsiatoura (Mrs)		1870	19 Feb	1981
USSR[8]	110	+	Khasako Dzugayev	7 Aug	1860	*fl.* Aug	1970
Italy	110	+	Dimiana Sette (Sig)		1884	25 Feb	1985
Norway[9]	109	208	Marie Olsen (Mrs)	1 May	1850	24 Nov	1959
Tasmania (State of)	109	179	Mary Ann Crow (Mrs)	2 Feb	1836	31 July	1945
Scotland[10]	109	14	Rachel MacArthur (Mrs)	26 Nov	1827	10 Dec	1936
Belgium	108	327	Mathilda Vertommen-Hellemans	12 Aug	1868	4 July	1977
Germany[11]	108	128	Luise Schwarz	27 Sept	1849	2 Feb	1958
Iceland	108	45	Halldóra Bjarndóttir	14 Oct	1873	28 Nov	1981
Portugal[12]	108	+	Maria Luisa Jorge	7 June	1859	*fl.* July	1967
Finland	109	182	Andrei Akaki Kuznetsoff	17 Oct	1873	*fl.* 17 Apr	1983
Malaysia	106	+	Hassan Bin Yusoff	14 Aug	1865	*fl.* Jan	1972
Luxembourg	105	228	Nicolas Wiscourt	31 Dec	1872	17 Aug	1978

[1] *Ex-slave Mrs Martha Graham died at Fayetteville, North Carolina on 25 June 1959 reputedly aged 117 or 118. Census researches by Eckler show that she was seemingly born in Dec 1844 and hence aged 114 years 6 months. Mrs Rena Glover Brailsford died in Summerton, South Carolina, USA on 6 Dec 1977 reputedly aged 118 years. Mrs Rosario Reina Vasquez who died in California on 2 Sept 1980 was reputedly born in Sonora, Mexico on 3 June 1866, which would make her 114 years 93 days. The 1900 US Federal Census for Crawfish Springs Militia District of Walker County, Georgia, records an age of 77 for a Mark Thrash. If the Mark Thrash (reputedly born in Georgia in December 1822) who died near Chattanooga, Tennessee on 17 Dec 1943 was he, and the age attributed was accurate, then he would have survived for 121 years.*

[2] *Mrs Ellen Carroll died in North River, Newfoundland, Canada on 8 Dec 1943, reputedly aged 115 years 49 days. Research is underway on the Ontario 1881 Census records on the claim of David Trumble to have been b. 15 Dec 1867.*

[3] *London-born Miss Isabella Shepheard was allegedly 115 years old when she died at St Asaph, Clwyd, North Wales, on 20 Nov 1948, but her actual age was believed to have been 109 years 90 days. Charles Alfred Nunez Arnold died in Liverpool on 15 Nov 1941 reputedly aged 112 years 66 days based on a baptismal claim (London, 10 Sept 1829). Mrs Elizabeth Cornish (née Veale) who was baptised at Stratton, Cornwall on 10 Mar 1691/2 was reputedly baptized on 16 Oct 1578, 113 years 4 months earlier.*

[4] *Snr Benita Medrana of Avila died on 28 Jan 1979 allegedly aged 114 years 335 days.*

[5] *Mrs Susan Johanna Deporter of Port Elizabeth, South Africa, was reputedly 114 years old when she died on 4 Aug 1954. Mrs Sarah Lawrence, Cape Town, South Africa was reputedly 112 on 3 June 1968.*

[6] *Thomas Peters was recorded to have been born on 6 Apr 1745 in Leeuwarden and died aged 111 years 354 days on 26 Mar 1857 in Arnhem.*

[7] *The claim that Liakon Efdokia died 17 Jan 1982 aged 119 years 13 days is not substantiated by the censuses of 1971 or 1981. Birth registration before 1920 was fragmentary.*

[8] *There are allegedly 21,700 centenarians in USSR (cf. 7000 in USA). Of these 21,000 are ascribed to the Georgian SSR i.e. one in every 232. In July 1962 it was reported that 128, mostly male, were in the one village of Medini.*

[9] *Mrs W. Sande was born in present-day Norway.*

[10] *Lachlen McDonald died 7 June 1858 in Harris, Outer Hebrides, was recorded as being '110 years' on his death certificate.*

[11] *West Germany: An unnamed female died in 1979 aged 112 years and an unnamed male died, aged also 112 years in 1969. The Austrian record is 108 years (female d. 1975) and the Swiss record is also 108 years (female d. 1967).*

[12] *Senhora Jesuina da Conceicao of Lisbon was reputedly 113 years old when she died on 10 June 1965.*

Note: *fl.* is the abbreviation for *floruit*, Latin for he (or she) was living at the relevant date.

the 100 citizens of the Russian Soviet Federative Socialist Republic (population about 132,000,000 at mid-1967) claimed in March 1960 to be between 120 and 156. From data on documented centenarians, actuaries have shown that only one 115-year life can be expected in 2100 million lives (*cf.* world population was estimated to be *c.* 4925 million at mid-1986).

The height of credulity was reached on 5 May 1933, when a news agency gullibly filed a story from China with a Peking date-line that Li Chung-yun, the 'oldest man on Earth', born in 1680, had just died aged 256 years (*sic*).

The most extreme case of longevity recently claimed in the USSR has been 168 years for Shirali 'Baba' Mislimov of Barzavu, Azerbaijan, who died on 2 Sept 1973 and was reputedly born on 26 Mar 1805. No interview of this man was ever permitted to any Western journalist or scientist. He was said to have celebrated the 100th birthday of his third wife Hartun, in 1966, and that of one of his grandchildren in August 1973. It was reported in 1954 that in the Abkhasian Republic of Georgia, USSR, where aged citizens are invested with an almost saint-like status, 2.58 per cent of the population was aged over 90—24 times the proportion in the USA.

Dr Zhores Aleksandrovich Medvedev, (b. Tbilisi, 14 Nov 1925), the expelled Soviet gerontologist, in Washington DC, on 30 Apr 1974 referring to USSR claims stated 'The whole phenomenon looks like a falsification' adding 'He [Stalin] liked the idea that [other] Georgians lived to be a 100 or more.' 'Local officials tried hard to find more and more cases for Stalin.' He points out (a) the *average* life-span in the regions claiming the highest incidence of centenarians is lower than the USSR average and (b) in contrast to the rest of the world, the incidence of centenarians claimed in the Caucasus had declined rapidly from 8000 in 1950 to 4500 in 1970. Dr Medvedev, in December 1977, put the *proven* limit in the USSR as low as 108 years.

It was announced in February 1984 that the 1982 Census in China revealed only 2450 centenarians of whom two thirds were women. In the US the mid-1983 figure was 32,000. Birth and death registration however became complete only in 1933 but was only 30.9 per cent by 1915.

Oldest authentic centenarian *World*

The greatest *authenticated* age to which any human has ever lived is a unique 120 years 237 days in the case of Shigechiyo Izumi of Asan on Tokunoshima an island 820 miles *1320 km* SW of Tokyo, Japan. He was born at Asan on 29 June 1865 and recorded as a 6-year-old in Japan's first census of 1871. He died at his home at 12.15 GMT on 21 Feb 1986 after developing pneumonia.

Living

The oldest living person after Mr Izumi's death has not been certainly established. Probably the oldest is 113 year old Mrs Mamie Eva Keith (*née* Walter) born at Anna, Illinois, USA on 22 Mar 1873.

Oldest authentic centenarian *Great Britain*

The United Kingdom has an estimated population of some 4000 centenarians of whom only 22 per cent are male. While husbands have a better chance than bachelors, it appears that spinsters have a better chance than wives in reaching 100 years! The only UK citizens with birth and death certificates more than 112 years apart have been Miss Alice Stevenson (1861–1973) (112 years 39 days), Miss Janetta Jane Thomas (1869–1982) (112 years 35 days) and Mrs Anna Williams of Tuxedo Old People's Home, Swansea, West Glamorgan, who became the proven oldest ever European on 16 Jan 1986 when 112 years 229 days (see Table, page 11). Britain's oldest proven man has been John Mosley Turner (b. 15 June 1856), who died on 22 Mar 1968 aged 111 years 281 days. In April 1706 a John Bailes was buried at All Saints Church, Northampton, having apparently been baptised on 20 Aug 1592. If these two John Bailes were the same person, he would have been 113 years 8 months. Britain's oldest living man is the former miner John Evans (b. 19 Aug 1877) of Swansea, who on 19 Mar 1986 had a pacemaker fitted, at the age of 108.

The first recorded case in the UK of three siblings being centenarians occurred on 26 Nov 1982 when Miss Frances Adams MSc reached her 100th birthday. Her brother was Dr John Andrew Adams (1867–1967) and her sister Dr Elizabeth Hart (*née* Adams) (1876–1977). The family came from Omagh, Co Tyrone, Northern Ireland.

Oldest quadruplets

The world's oldest quads are the Ottman quads of Munich, West Germany—Adolf, Anne-Marie, Emma and Elisabeth. They celebrated their 74th birthday on 5 May 1986.

Oldest triplets

The longest-lived triplets on record were Faith, Hope and Charity Caughlin born at Marlboro, Massachusetts, USA on 27 Mar 1868. The first to die was Mrs (Ellen) Hope Daniels aged 93 on 2 Mar 1962.

Oldest twins *World and Great Britain*

The oldest recorded twins were Eli Shadrack and John Meshak Phipps (b. 14 Feb 1803, Affinghton, Virginia, USA). Eli died at Hennessey, Oklahoma on 23 Feb 1911 aged 108 years 9 days on which day John was still living in Shenandoah, Iowa. On 17 June 1984, identical twin sisters, Mildred Widman Philippi and Mary Widman Franzini of St. Louis, Missouri, USA celebrated their 104th birthday. Mildred died on 4 May 1985, 44 days short of the twins' would-be 105th birthday. The chances of identical twins both reaching 100 are now probably about one in 500 million. The oldest twins on record in Great Britain have been the Bean twins Robert, of Birkenhead, Merseyside and Mary (later Mrs Simpson) of Etton, Cambridgeshire who celebrated their 100th birthday on 19 Oct 1973. Robert died before the end of 1973.

Most reigns

The greatest number of reigns during which any English subject could have lived is ten. A person born on the day (11 April) that Henry VI was deposed in 1471 had to live to only the comparatively modest age of 87 years 7 months and 6 days to see the accession of Elizabeth I on 17 Nov 1558. Such a person could have been Thomas Carn of London, reputedly born in 1471 and died 28 Jan 1578 in his 107th year.

Last 18th-century link

The last Briton with 18th-century paternity was Miss Alice J. Grigg of Belvedere, Kent (d. 28 Apr 1970) whose father William was born on 26 Oct 1799.

Oldest mummy

Mummification (from the Persian word *mām*, wax) dates from 2600 BC or the 4th dynasty of the Egyptian pharaohs. The oldest surviving mummy is of *Wati*, a court musician of *c.* 2400 BC from the tomb of Nefer in Saqqâra, Egypt found in 1944.

4. REPRODUCTIVITY

MOTHERHOOD

Most children *World*

The greatest officially recorded number of children produced by a mother is 69 by the first of the two wives of Feodor Vassilyev (b. 1707– *fl.* 1782), a peasant from Shuya, 150 miles *241 km* east of Moscow. In 27 confinements she gave birth to 16 pairs of twins, 7 sets of triplets and 4 sets of quadruplets. The case was reported by the Monastery of Nikolskiy on 27 Feb 1782 to Moscow. At least 67 survived infancy. Empress Ekaterina II (The Great) (1762–96) was reputed to have evinced interest. The children, of whom almost all survived to their majority, were born in the period *c.* 1725–65.

Currently the world's most prolific mother is reported to be Leontina Albina (*née* Espinosa) (b. 1925) of San Antonio, Chile, who in 1981 produced her 55th and last child. Her husband Gerardo Secunda Albina (variously Alvina) (b. 1921) states that he was married in Argentina in 1943 and they had 5 sets of triplets (all boys) before coming to Chile. 'Only' 40 (24 boys and 16 girls) survive. Eleven were lost in an earthquake thus indicating the truth about the many other children born earlier than those born in Chile.

Great Britain

The British record is seemingly held by Elizabeth, wife of John Mott married in 1676 of Monks Kirby, Warwickshire, who produced 42 live-born children. She died in 1720, 44 years later. According to an inscription on a gravestone in Conway Church cemetery, Gwynedd, North Wales, Nicholas Hookes (d. 27 Mar 1637) was the 41st child of his mother Alice Hookes, but further details are lacking. It has not been possible to corroborate or refute this report. Mrs Elizabeth Greenhille (d. 1681) of Abbot's Langley, Hertfordshire is alleged to have produced 39 children (32 daughters, 7 sons) in a record 38 confinements. Her son Thomas was author of 'Art of Embalming' (1705).

Great Britain's champion mothers of today are

(*Right*) Megan Sue Austin who was unique in having 19 living direct ascendants (see p. 14). (*Below*) Matthew Stork with his five ascendants culminating with Mrs Ann Weirick, his great-great-great grandmother who was only 88 when he was born (see p. 14).

believed to be Mrs Margaret McNaught (b. 1923), of Balsall Heath, Birmingham (12 boys and 10 girls, all single births) and Mrs Mabel Constable (b. 1920), of Long Itchington, Warwickshire who also has had 22 children including a set of triplets and two sets of twins.

Ireland's champion is Mrs Catherine Scott (b. 4 July 1914), who bore an authenticated total of 24 children.

Oldest mother *World*

Medical literature contains extreme but unauthenticated cases of septuagenarian mothers, such as Mrs Ellen Ellis, aged 72, of Four Crosses, Clwyd, who allegedly produced a still-born 13th child on 15 May 1776 in her 46th year of marriage. Many very late maternities will be cover-ups for illegitimate grandchildren. The oldest recorded mother for whom the evidence satisfied medical verification was Mrs Ruth Alice Kistler (*née* Taylor), formerly Mrs Shepard (1899–1982), of Portland, Oregon, USA. A birth certificate indicates that she gave birth to a daughter, Suzan, at Glendale, near Los Angeles, California, on 18 Oct 1956, when her age was 57 years 129 days. After her death a person purporting to be a relative alleged for an unknown motive that Mrs Kistler had 'changed the birth date'.

Great Britain

The oldest British mother reliably recorded is Mrs Winifred Wilson (*née* Stanley) of Eccles, Greater Manchester. She was born in Wolverhampton on 11 Nov 1881 or 1882 and had her tenth child, a daughter Shirley, on 14 Nov 1936, when aged 54 or 55 years and 3 days. She died aged 91 or 92 in January 1974. At Southampton, on 10 Feb 1916, Mrs Elizabeth Pearce gave birth to a son when aged 54 years 40 days. According to a report in the *Lancet* (1867) a woman aged 62 gave birth to triplets. She had previously had 10 children.

Ireland

The oldest Irish mother recorded was Mrs Mary Higgins of Cork, County Cork (b. 7 Jan 1876) who gave birth to a daughter, Patricia, on 17 Mar 1931 when aged 55 years 69 days.

MULTIPLE BIRTHS

Lightest twins

The lightest recorded birthweight for a pair of surviving twins has been 2 lb 3 oz *992 g* in the case of Mary 16 oz *453 g* and Margaret 19 oz *538 g* born to Mrs Florence Stimson, Queens Road, Old Fletton, Peterborough, England, delivered by Dr Macaulay on 16 Aug 1931. Margaret is now Mrs M. J. Hurst.

'Siamese' twins

Conjoined twins derived the name 'Siamese' from the celebrated Chang and Eng Bunker (known in Thailand as Chan and In) born at Meklong, on 11 May 1811 of Chinese parents. They were joined by a cartilaginous band at the chest and married in April 1843 the Misses Sarah and Adelaide Yates of Wilkes County, North Carolina, USA and fathered ten and twelve children respectively. They died within three hours of each other on 17 Jan 1874, aged 62. The only known British example to reach maturity were the pygopagus twins Daisy and Violet Hilton born in Brighton, East Sussex, on 5 Feb 1908, who were joined at the buttocks. They died in Charlotte, North Carolina, USA, on 5 Jan 1969, aged 60 from Hong Kong flu. The earliest successful separation of Siamese twins was performed on xiphopagus girls joined at the sternum at Mt Sinai Hospital, Cleveland, Ohio by Dr Jac S. Geller on 14 Dec 1952.

The rarest form of conjoined twins is Dicephales tetrabrachius dipus (two heads, four arms and two legs) of which only three examples are known today. They are the pair Masha and Dasha born in the USSR on 4 Jan 1950, an unnamed pair separated in a 10-hour operation in Washington, DC, USA on 23 June 1977, and Fonda Michelle and Shannon Elaine Beaver of Forest City, North Carolina, USA born on 9 Feb 1980. The only known British example were the 'Scottish brothers', who were born near Glasgow in 1490. They were brought to the Court of King James IV of Scotland in 1491, and lived under the king's patronage for the rest of his reign. They died in 1518 aged 28 years, one brother succumbing five days before the other, who 'moaned piteously as he crept about the castle gardens, carrying with him the dead body of the brother from whom only death could separate him and to whom death would again join him'.

The oldest surviving unseparated twins are the craniopagus pair Yvonne and Yvette Jones (b. 1949) of Los Angeles, California, USA whose heads are fused together at the crown. They have rejected an operation to separate them.

Most twins *Geographically*

In Chungchon, South Korea it was reported in September 1981 that there was unaccountably 38 pairs in only 275 families—the highest ever recorded ratio.

Fastest triplet birth

The fastest recorded natural birth of triplets has been 2 minutes in the case of Mrs James E. Duck of Memphis, Tennessee (Bradley, Christopher and Carmon) on 21 Mar 1977.

Quindecaplets

It was announced by Dr Gennaro Montanino of Rome that he had removed the foetuses of 10 girls and 5 boys from the womb of a 35-year-old housewife on 22 July 1971. A fertility drug was responsible for this unique and unsurpassed instance of quindecaplets.

Longest and shortest pregnancy

Claims up to 413 days have been widely reported but accurate data are bedevilled by the increasing use of oral contraceptive pills which is a cause of amenorrhoea. The *US Medical Investigator* of 27 Dec 1884 reported a case of 15 months 20 days and the *Histoire de l'Academie* of 1751 the most extreme case of 36 months. In the pre-pill era English law has accepted pregnancies with extremes of 174 days (*Clark* v. *Clark*, 1939) and 349 days (*Hadlum* v. *Hadlum*, 1949). Ernestine Hudgins was born weighing 17 oz *482 g* 18 weeks premature in San Diego, California, USA on 8 Feb 1983. This has been equalled by Alexander McGlade born in Middlesbrough, Cleveland, on 10 May 1986 at the same weight.

DESCENDANTS

In polygamous countries, the number of a person's descendants can become incalculable. The last Sharifian Emperor of Morocco, Moulay Ismail (1672–1727), known as 'The Bloodthirsty', was reputed to have fathered a total of 525 sons and 342 daughters by 1703 and a 700th son in 1721.

In April 1984 the death was reported of Adam Borntrager, aged 96, of Medford, Wisconsin, USA who had had 707 direct descendants of whom all but 32 were living. The total comprised 11 children, 115 grand, 529 great-grand and 20 great-great grandchildren. The family is of the Amish Mennonite sect who eschew cars, telephones, electric light and higher education.

Mrs Sarah Crawshaw (d. 25 Dec 1844) left 397

The world's largest convention of twins staged at Twinsberg, Ohio, USA on 3–4 Aug 1985. The photograph shows less than a quarter of the final attendance of 1181 sets.

descendants according to her gravestone in Stones Church, Ripponden, Halifax, West Yorkshire.

Multiple great-grandparents

The report in 1983 that Jane Kau Pung (1877–1982) had left 4 great-great-great-great-grandchildren has proved to be incorrect. She in fact proved to be one of many cases of great-great-great-grandparents. Of these cases the youngest person to learn that their great-granddaughter had become a grandmother was Mrs Ann V. Weirick (1888–1978) of Paxtonville, Pennsylvania, USA, who received news of her great-great-great-grandson Matthew Stork (b. 9 Sept 1976) when aged only 88. She died on 6 Jan 1978. Britain's youngest 3 greats grandmother is Mrs Violet Lewis (b. June 1885) of Southampton.

Most living ascendants

Megan Sue Austin (b. 16 May 1982) of Bar Harbor, Maine, USA, had a full set of grandparents and great-grandparents and five great-great-grandparents, making 19 direct ascendants.

BABIES

Heaviest *World*

The heaviest viable babies on record, of normal parentage, were boys of 22 lb 8 oz *10,2 kg* born to Sig Carmelina Fedele of Aversa, Italy in September 1955 and by caesarian section to Mrs Christina Samane at Sipetu Hospital, Transkei, South Africa on 24 May 1982. The latter boy named Sithandive weighed 77 lb *34,9 kg* at 16

months. Mrs Anna Bates *née* Swan (1846–88), the 7 ft 5½ in *227 cm* Canadian giantess (see also p. 7), gave birth to a boy weighing 23 lb 12 oz *10,77 kg* (length 30 in *76 cm*) at her home in Seville, Ohio, USA on 19 Jan 1879, but the baby died less than 24 hours later. Her first child, an 18 lb *8,16 kg* girl (length 24 in *61 cm*) was still-born when she was delivered in 1872. On 9 Jan 1891 Mrs Florentin Ortega of Buenos Aires, Argentina produced a still-born boy weighing 25 lb *11,3 kg*. In May 1939 a deformed baby weighing 29 lb 4 oz *13,26 kg* was born in a hospital at Effingham, Illinois, USA, but died two hours later.

Heaviest *United Kingdom*

The greatest recorded live birth weight in the United Kingdom is 21 lb *9,53 kg* for a child born on Christmas Day, 1852. It was reported in a letter to the *British Medical Journal* (1 Feb 1879) from a doctor in Torpoint, Cornwall. The only other reported birth weight in excess of 20 lb *9,07 kg* is 20 lb 2 oz *9,13 kg* for a boy born to a 33-year-old schoolmistress in Crewe, Cheshire, on 12 Nov 1884 with a 14¼ in *36,8 cm* chest.

Most bouncing baby

The most bouncing baby on record was probably James Weir (1819–21) who, according to his headstone in Cambushnethan, Old Parish Cemetery, Wishaw, Strathclyde, Scotland was 8 st or 112 lb *50,8 kg* at 13 months, 3 ft 4 in *1,01 m* in height and 39 in *99 cm* in girth. Brazil's 'super-baby' Veridiano dos Santos (b. 1978) weighed 143 lb *64,8 kg* aged 5. Therese Parentean, who died in Rouyn, Quebec, Canada on 11 May 1936 aged 9 years, weighed 24 st 4 lb *154 kg*. (*cf.* 27 st *171 kg* for Robert Earl Hughes at the age of ten [see Table p. 9 and Chest measurements, p. 15]).

Lightest

The lowest birth weight recorded for a surviving infant, of which there is definite evidence, is 10 oz *283 g* in the case of Mrs Marian Taggart *née* Chapman (b. 5 June 1938, d. 31 May 1983) who was born six weeks premature in South

Shields, Tyne and Wear. She was born unattended (length 12¼ in *31 cm*) and was nursed by Dr D. A. Shearer, who fed her hourly for the first 30 hours with brandy, glucose and water through a fountain-pen filler. At three weeks she weighed 1 lb 13 oz *821 g* and by her first birthday 13 lb 14 oz *6,29 kg*. Her weight on her 21st birthday was 7 st 8 lb *48,08 kg*. The smallest viable baby reported from the United States has been Jacqueline Benson born at Palatine, Illinois, on 20 Feb 1936, weighing 12 oz *340 g*.

A weight of 8 oz *227 g* was reported on 20 Mar 1938 for a baby born prematurely to Mrs John Womack, after she had been knocked down by a lorry in East St Louis, Illinois, USA. The baby was taken alive to St Mary's Hospital, but died a few hours later. On 23 Feb 1952 it was reported that a 6 oz *170 g* baby only 6½ in *17 cm* long lived for 12 hours in a hospital in Indianapolis, Indiana, USA. A twin was still-born. Megan, born to Jim and Edith Burnett at Queen Mother's Hospital, Glasgow on 6 Sept 1985, measured 10.2 in *25,9 cm*—shorter than the depth of this page. She weighed 16.5 oz *470 g*.

Coincident birthdates

The only verified example of a family producing five single children with coincident birthdays is that of Catherine (1952); Carol (1953); Charles (1956); Claudia (1961) and Cecilia (1966), born to Ralph and Carolyn Cummins of Clintwood, Virginia, USA, all on 20 February. The random odds against five single siblings sharing a birthdate would be one in 17,797,577,730—almost 4 times the world's population.

The three children of the Henriksen family of Andenes, Norway, Heidi (b. 1960); Olav (b. 1964) and Lief-Martin (b. 1968) all celebrate their birthday infrequently, because these all fall on Leap Day – February 29. Ralph Bertram Williams was born on 4 July 1982 in Wilmington, North Carolina, USA. His father, grandfather and, in 1876, his great-grandfather were also born on 4 July.

Most southerly birth

Emilio Marcos Palma (Argentina) born 7 Jan 1978 at the Sargento Cabral Base, Antarctica is the only infant who can claim to be the first born on any continent. The mother was flown from Argentina at governmental expense.

Test tube baby *Earliest*

Louise Brown (5 lb 12 oz *2,6 kg*) was delivered by Caesarian section from Lesley Brown, 31, in Oldham General Hospital, Lancashire, at 11.47 p.m. on 25 July 1978. She was externally conceived on 10 Nov 1977.

5. PHYSIOLOGY AND ANATOMY

Hydrogen (63 per cent) and oxygen (25.5 per cent) constitute the commonest of the 24 elements in the human body. In 1972 four more trace elements were added—fluorine, silicon, tin and vanadium. The 'essentiality' of nickel has not yet been finally pronounced upon.

BONES

Longest

Excluding a variable number of sesamoids, there are 206 bones in the human body. The thigh bone or *femur* is the longest. It constitutes usually 27½ per cent of a person's stature, and may be expected to be 19¾ in *50 cm* long in a 6 ft *183 cm*-tall man. The longest recorded bone was the femur of the German giant Constantine, who died in Mons, Belgium, on 30 Mar 1902, aged 30 (see p. 7). It measured 76 cm *29.9 in.* The femur of Robert Wadlow, the tallest man ever recorded, measured an estimated 29½ in *75 cm*.

Smallest

The *stapes* or stirrup bone, one of the three auditory ossicles in the middle ear, is the smallest human bone, measuring from 2,6 to 3,4 mm *0.10* to *0.17 in* in length and weighing from 2,0 to 4,3 mg *0.03 to 0.065 g*.

MUSCLES

Largest

Muscles normally account for 40 per cent of the body weight and the bulkiest of the 639 muscles in the human body is the *gluteus maximus* or buttock muscle, which extends the thigh.

Smallest

The smallest muscle is the *stapedius*, which controls the *stapes* (see above), an auditory ossicle in the middle ear, and which is less than 1/20th of an inch *0,127 cm* long.

Smallest waists

Queen Catherine de Medici (1519–89) decreed a waist measurement of 13 in *33 cm* for ladies of the French Court. This was at a time when females were more diminutive. The smallest recorded waist among women of normal stature in the 20th century is a reputed 13 in *33 cm* in the case of the French actress Mlle Polaire (1881–1939) and Mrs Ethel Granger (1905–82) of Peterborough, Cambs, who reduced from a natural 22 in *56 cm* over the period 1929–39.

Largest chest measurements

The largest chest measurements are among endomorphs (those with a tendency towards globularity). In the extreme case of Hughes (see Table p. 9) this was reportedly 124 in *315 cm*, but in the light of his known height and weight a figure of 104 in *264 cm* would be more supportable. George Macaree (formerly Britain's heaviest man) has a chest measurement of 75 in *190,5 cm* (waist 70 in *177,8 cm*), at a bodyweight of 31 st *196,8 kg* (height 5 ft 10 in *177,8 cm*) and Martin Ruane (see p. 9) has a

chest measurement of 73 in *185,4 cm* (waist 68 in *172,7 cm*). Among muscular subjects (meso-morphs) of normal height *expanded* chest measurements above 56 in *142 cm* are extremely rare. Vasili Alexeyev (b. 1942), the 6 ft 1¼ in *186 cm* Russian super-heavyweight weight-lifting champion, had a 60½ in *153,6 cm* chest at his top weight of 350 lb *158,7 kg*. Arnold Schwarzenne-ger (b. 1948) of Graz, Austria, the 6 ft 1 in *185 cm* former Mr Universe and 'the most perfectly developed man in the history of the world', had a chest measurement of 57 in *145 cm* (bicep 22 in *55,8 cm*) at his best bodyweight of 235 lb *107 kg*. The American power lifter Gary Aprahamian (b. 2 Feb 1962, d. 23 Aug 1984) the first man to achieve a cold (not pumped) bicep measurement over 25 in *63,5 cm* with 25⅜ in *64,4 cm* had a normal chest measurement of 61 in *155 cm*. He weighed 365 lb *165 kg*.

Longest necks

The maximum measured extension of the neck by the successive fitting of copper coils, as practised by the Padaung or Kareni people of Burma, is 15¾ in *40 cm*.

BRAIN AND BRAIN POWER

Largest

The brain of an average adult male (*i.e.* 20–55 years) weighs 1424 g *3 lb 2.2 oz*, decreasing gradually to 1395 g *3 lb 1.1 oz* with advancing age. The heaviest non-diseased brain on record was that of Ivan Sergeyvich Turgenev (1818–83), the Russian author. His brain weighed 2012 g *4 lb 6.9 oz*.

Human brains are getting heavier. Examination of post-mortem records shows that the average

A giraffe-necked mother of the Padaung tribe in Burma with 19 copper neck coils. (Christine Osborne)

male brain weight has increased from 1372 g *3 lb 0.4 oz* in 1860 to 1424 g *3 lb 2.2 oz* today. Women's brains have also put on weight, from 1242 g *2 lb 11.8 oz* to 1265 g *2 lb 12.6 oz* and in recent years have been growing almost as fast as men's.

Prof Marian Diamond of the University of California at Berkeley, California, USA, announced on 13 Feb 1985 that the neuron to glial cell ratio in Section 39 of the brain of Albert Einstein (1879–1955) was 1.12 as opposed to the standard 1.936—a difference of 72.8 per cent.

Smallest
The lightest 'normal' or non-atrophied brain on record was one weighing 1096 g *2 lb 6.7 oz* reported by Dr P. Davis and Prof E. Wright of King's College Hospital, London in 1977. It belonged to a 31 year old woman.

Highest IQ
Intelligence quotients or IQ's comprise the subject's mental age divided by his chronological or actual age multiplied by 100 such that an 8 year old more gifted than an average 16 year old would have an IQ of $\frac{16}{8} \times 100 = 200$. The highest childhood score has been achieved by Marilyn Mach vos Savant of St. Louis, Missouri, USA who as a 10-year-old achieved a ceiling score for 23-year-olds thus giving her an IQ of 228.

In adult High IQ clubs admission requirements are not on IQ points but are gauged in percentiles. An IQ exhibited by 1 person in 10,000 for instance coincides with 158 on the Stanford-Binet scale but 187 on the Cattell scale. The most elite ultra High IQ Society is the Mega Society with 26 members with percentiles of 99.9999 or 1 in a million. The topmost scorer in the Mega admission test, devised by its founder Ronald K. Hoeflin, has been 46 out of 48 by Marilyn Mach vos Savant superceding the 43 of Jeff Ward.

The three members who have scored 197 on the Stanford Binet scale are Christopher Philip Harding (born Keynsham, England, 1944) of Rockhampton, Queensland, Australia, Dr Ferris Eugene Alger (b. Des Moines, Iowa, 1913) of New Hope, Pennsylvania, USA and Dr Johannes Dougles Veldhuis (b. Hamilton, Ontario, Canada, 1949) of Charlottesville, Virginia, USA.

The highest IQ published for a national population is 111 for the Japanese. For those born in 1960–61 a figure of 115 has been published. At least 10 per cent of their whole population has an IQ > 130.

Human computer
The fastest extraction of a 13th root from a 100 digit number is in 1 min 28.8 sec by Willem

Klein (b. 1912, Netherlands) on 7 Apr 1981 at the National Laboratory for High Energy Physics (KEK), Tsukuba, Japan. Mrs Shakuntala Devi of India demonstrated the multiplication of two 13-digit numbers 7,686,369,774,870 × 2,465,099,745,779 picked at random by the Computer Department of Imperial College, London on 18 June 1980, in 28 sec. Her correct answer was 18,947,668,177,995,426,462,773,730. An eminent mathematical writer has questioned the conditions under which this was apparently achieved and predicts that it would be impossible for her to replicate such a feat under highly rigorous surveillance.

Some experts on calculating prodigies refuse to give credence to the above—largely on the grounds that it is so vastly superior to the calculating feats of any other invigilated prodigy.

Human memory
Bhandanta Vicitsara recited 16,000 pages of Bhuddist canonical texts in Rangoon, Burma in May 1974. Rare instances of eidetic memory—the ability to re-project and hence 'visually' recall material—are known to science.

Creighton Carvello (see below) memorised a random sequence of 6 separate packs (312) of cards on a single sighting with only 4 errors including an all correct straight run of 139 cards at the New Marske Institute Club, Cleveland, England on 21 Mar 1985. On 21 July 1985 on the Kyodo TV programme 'Guinness Book of World Records '85' in Japan, he achieved the rarer accomplishment of only 24 errors with 6 packs shuffled together.

The greatest number of places of π
All India Radio broadcast in its *Weekly Roundup* on 5 July 1981 part of a recording made earlier that day of Rajan Srinivasen Mahadevan, 23, in the process of reciting 'pi' from memory (in English) to 31,811 places in 3 hr 49 min (incl. 26 min of breaks) at the Lion Seva Mandir, Mangalore. His rate was 156.7 digits per minute. Mr Mahadevan has explained to the Editor that he learns each digit separately and acquires a 'feeling', when he is able to recall the number at will. The British record is 20,013 by Creighton Carvello (see above) on 27 June 1980 in 9 hr 10 min at Saltscar Comprehensive School, Redcar, Cleveland, England. Note: It is only the *approximation* of π at $^{22}/_7$ which recurs after its sixth decimal place and can, of course, be recited *ad nauseam*. The true value is a string of random numbers fiendishly difficult to memorise. The average ability for memorizing random numbers is barely more than 7.

Mike Solomons, the proud owner of Britain's longest moustache which measures 33 in *83,8 cm*.

HANDS, FEET AND HAIR
Touch sensitivity
The extreme sensitivity of the fingers is such that a vibration with a movement of 0.02 of a micron can be detected.

Most fingers and toes
At an inquest held on a baby at Shoreditch, East London on 16 Sept 1921 it was reported that the boy had 14 fingers and 15 toes.

Least toes
The 'lobster claw syndrome' exhibited by the two-toed Wadomo tribe of the Zambesi valley, Zimbabwe and the Kalanga tribe of the eastern Kalahari desert, Botswana is hereditary *via* a single mutated gene.

Longest finger nails
The longest finger nails ever reported are those of Shridhar Chillal, (b. 1937) of Poona, India. The aggregate measurement, on 8 Apr 1985, was 143 in *363,2 cm* for the 5 nails on his left hand (thumb 34½ in *87,6 cm*). He last cut his nails in 1952.

Longest hair
Swami Pandarasannadhi, the head of the Tirudaduturai monastery, Tanjore district, Madras, India was reported in 1949 to have hair 26 ft *7,92 m* in length. From photographs it appears that he was afflicted with the disease Plica caudiformis, in which the hair becomes matted and crusted as a result of neglect. The length of hair of Miss Skuldfrid Sjorgren (b. Stockholm) was reported from Toronto, Canada in 1927 to have reached twice her height at 10 ft 6 in *3,20 m*. The hair of Georgia Sabrantke (b. 10 Jan 1943) of West Germany was measured to be 9 ft 8½ in *296 cm* on 6 Mar 1986.

Strongest hair
In a test on BBC TV *Record Breakers* on 9 Sept 1984 a hair from the head of Miss Pham Thy Lan broke at a strain of 178 g *6¼ oz*.

Longest beard
The longest beard preserved was that of Hans N. Langseth (b. 1846 near Eidsroll, Norway) which measured 17½ ft *5,33 m* at the time of his burial at Kensett, Iowa in 1927 after 15 years residence in the United States. The beard was presented to the Smithsonian Institution, Washington, DC in 1967. Richard Latter (b. Pembury, Kent, 1831) of Tunbridge Wells, Kent, who died in 1914 aged 83, reputedly had a beard 16 ft *4,87 m* long but contemporary independent corroboration is lacking and photographic evidence indicates this figure was exaggerated. The beard of the bearded lady Janice Deveree (b. Bracken Co., Kentucky, USA, 1842) was measured at 14 in *36 cm* in 1884. The beard of Mlle Helene Antonia of Liège, Belgium, a 17th century exhibitionist was said to have reached her hips.

Longest moustache
The longest moustache on record was that of Masuriya Din (b. 1908), a Brahmin of the Partabgarh district in Uttar Pradesh, India. It grew to an extended span of 8 ft 6 in *2,59 m* between 1949 and 1962. Karna Ram Bheel (b. 1928) was granted permission by a New Delhi prison governor in February 1979 to keep his 7 ft 10 in *238 cm* moustache grown since 1949 during his life sentence. The moustache of Birger Pellas (b. 21 Sept 1934) of Malmö, Sweden, grown since 1973, reached 2,64 m *8 ft 8 in* on 8 Jan 1986. The longest moustache in Great Britain has been that of Mr John Roy (b. 14 Jan 1910), of Weeley, near Clacton, Essex. It attained a peak span of 74½ in *189 cm* between 1939 and when measured on the BBC TV

'Nationwide' programme on 2 Apr 1976 but he accidentally sat on it in the bath in 1984 and chopped off 2 ft *61 cm*. He then took 2 ft *61 cm* off the other side to even the moustache. The current UK champion is Mike Solomons of Long Ditton, Surrey with 33 in *83,8 cm* as of 24 Mar 1986.

DENTITION

Earliest
The first deciduous or milk teeth normally appear in infants at 5–8 months, these being the mandibular and maxillary first incisors. There are many records of children born with teeth, the most distinguished example being Prince Louis Dieudonné, later Louis XIV of France, who was born with two teeth on 5 Sept 1638. Molars usually appear at 24 months, but in Pindborg's case published in Denmark in 1970, a 6-week premature baby was documented with 8 natal teeth of which 4 were in the molar region.

Most
Cases of the growth in late life of a third set of teeth have been recorded several times. A reference to a case in France of a fourth dentition, known as Lison's case, was published in 1896. A triple row of teeth was noted in 1680 by Albertus Hellwigius.

Most dedicated dentist
Brother Giovanni Battista Orsenigo of the Ospedale Fatebenefratelli, Rome, Italy, a religious dentist, conserved all the teeth he extracted in three enormous cases during the time he exercised his profession from 1868 to 1904. In 1903 the number was counted and found to be 2,000,744 teeth, indicating an average of 185 a day.

Most valuable tooth
In 1816 a tooth belonging to Sir Isaac Newton (1643–1727) was sold in London for £730. It was purchased by a nobleman who had it set in a ring which he wore constantly.

OPTICS

Smallest visible object
The resolving power of the human eye is 0.0003 of a radian or an arc of one minute ($\frac{1}{60}$th of a degree), which corresponds to 100 microns at 10 in. A micron is a thousandth of a millimetre, hence 100 microns is 0.003937, or less than four thousandths, of an inch. The human eye can, however, detect a bright light source shining through an aperture only 3 to 4 microns across.

Colour sensitivity
The unaided human eye, under the best possible viewing conditions, comparing large areas of colour, in good illumination, using both eyes, can distinguish 10,000,000 different colour surfaces. The most accurate photo-electric spectrophotometers possess a precision probably only 40 per cent as good as this. About 7.5 per cent of men and 0.1 per cent of women are colour blind. The most extreme form, monochromatic vision, is very rare. The highest recorded rate of red-green colour blindness is in Czechoslovakia and the lowest rate among Fijians and Brazilian Indians.

VOICE

Highest and lowest
The highest and lowest recorded notes attained by the human voice before this century were a staccato E in *alt altissimo* (e[iv]) by Ellen Beach Yaw (US) (1869–1947) in Carnegie Hall, New York, on 19 Jan 1896, and an A$_1$ (55 Hz (cycles per sec)) by Kasper Foster (1617–73). Madeleine

Marie Robin (1918–60) the French operatic coloratura could produce and sustain the B above high C in the Lucia mad scene in *Lucia di Lammermoor*. Since 1950 singers have achieved high and low notes far beyond the hitherto accepted extremes. However, notes at the bass and treble extremities of the register tend to lack harmonics and are of little musical value. Frl Marita Gunther, trained by Alfred Wolfsohn, has covered the range of the piano from the lowest note, A$_{\text{II}}$ to c^v. Of this range of 7$\frac{1}{4}$ octaves, six octaves were considered to be of musical value. Mr Roy Hart, also trained by Wolfsohn, has reached notes below the range of the piano. Barry Girard of Canton, Ohio in May 1975 reached the e (4340 Hz) above the piano's top note. The highest note put into song is G^{iv} first occurring in *Popoli di Tessaglia* by Mozart. The lowest vocal note in the classical repetoire is in Mozart's *Il Seraglio* by Osmin who descends to low D (73.4 Hz). Dan Britton reached the 4th E below middle C at 20.6 Hz at Anoka County Fair, Maryland, USA on 31 July 1984. Stefan Zucker sang A in *alt altissimo* for 3.8 sec in the tenor role of Salvini in the première of Bellini's *Adelson e Salvini* in New York, USA on 12 Sept 1972.

Greatest range
The normal intelligible outdoor range of the male human voice in still air is 200 yd *180 m*. The *silbo*, the whistled language of the Spanish-speaking Canary Island of La Gomera, is intelligible across the valleys, under ideal conditions, at five miles *8 km*. There is a recorded case, under freak acoustic conditions, of the human voice being detectable at a distance of 10$\frac{1}{2}$ miles *17 km* across still water at night. It was said that Mills Darden (see table page 9) could be heard 6 miles *9 km* away when he bellowed at the top of his voice.

Because of their more optimal frequency, female screams tend to higher readings on decibel meters than male bellows. The annual World Shouting Championship record is 112.4 dBA by Anthony Fieldhouse on 9 Sept 1984 at Scarborough. The highest scientifically measured emission has been one of 123.2 dBA by the screaming of Neil Stephenson of Newcastle-upon-Tyne, Tyne and Wear on 18 May 1985.

Lowest detectable sound
The intensity of noise or sound is measured in terms of pressure. The pressure of the quietest sound that can be detected by a person of normal hearing at the most sensitive frequency of *c.* 2750 Hz is 2×10^{-5} pascal. One tenth of the logarithm to this standard provides a unit termed a decibel (dBA). A noise of 30 decibels is negligible.

Highest noise levels
Prolonged noise above 150 decibels will cause immediate permanent deafness while above 192 dBA a lethal over-pressure shock wave can be formed. Equivalent continuous sound levels (LEQ) above 90 dBA are impermissible in factories, but this compares with 125 emitted by racing cars, 130 (amplified music) and 170 (some toy guns).

Highest detectable pitch
The upper limit of hearing by the human ear has long been regarded as 20,000 Hz (cycles per sec), although it has been alleged that children with asthma can detect sounds of 30,000 Hz. Bats emit pulses at up to 90,000 Hz. It was announced in February 1964 that experiments in the USSR had conclusively proved that oscillations as high as 200,000 Hz can be detected if the oscillator is pressed against the skull.

Yorkshire Television's speedy commentator John Helm, whose Aldershot to York City recitation took just 26 seconds and included the other 90 Football League Clubs. (Yorkshire Television)

Fastest talker
Few people are able to speak *articulately* at a sustained speed above 300 words per min. The fastest broadcaster has been regarded as Gerry Wilmot (b. Victoria, BC, Canada, 6 Oct 1914) the ice hockey commentator in the post-World War II period. Raymond Glendenning (1907–74), the BBC horseracing commentator, once spoke 176 words in 30 sec while commentating on a greyhound race. In public life the highest speed recorded is a 327 words per min burst in a speech made in December 1961 by John Fitzgerald Kennedy (1917–63), then President of the United States. Results of tests by a radio station on John Moschitta (USA) in March 1983 at a rate of 534 in 58 sec or 552 words per min were intelligible. John Helm of Yorkshire TV can recite the 92 Football League clubs in 26 sec.

BLOOD

Blood groups
The preponderance of one blood group varies greatly from one locality to another. On a world basis Group O is the most common (46 per cent), but in some areas, for example Norway, Group A predominates.

The full description of the commonest sub-group in Britain is O MsNs, P+, Rr, Lu(a−), K−, Le(a−b+), Fy(a+b+), Jk(a+b+), which occurs in one in every 270 people.

The rarest blood group on the ABO system, one of 14 systems, is AB, which occurs in less than 3 per cent of persons in the British Isles. The rarest type in the world is a type of Bombay blood (sub-type h-h) found so far only in a Czechoslovak nurse in 1961 and in a brother (Rh positive) and sister (Rh negative) named Jalbert in Massachusetts, USA reported in February 1968.

Richest natural resources
Joe Thomas of Detroit, Michigan, USA was reported in August 1970 to have the highest known count of Anti-Lewis B, the rare blood antibody. A US biological supply firm pays him $1500 per quart *1,13 l*. The Internal Revenue regard this income as a taxable liquid asset.

Champion plasmapheresis blood donor
Since 1966 Allen Doster, a self-employed beautician, has (to April 1986) donated 1800 US pints *851,76 l* at Roswell Park Memorial Institute, New York, USA as a plasmapheresis donor. The present-day normal limit on donations is 5 pints per annum. A 50-year-old haemophiliac Warren C. Jyrich required 2400 donor units *1080 l* of blood when undergoing open heart surgery at the Michael Reese Hospital, Chicago, USA in December 1970.

Largest vein
The largest vein in the human body is the *inferior vena cava*, which returns most of the blood from the body below the level of the heart.

Most alcoholic subject
California University Medical School, Los Angeles reported in December 1982 the case of a confused 24-year-old female, who was shown to have a blood alcohol level of 1510 mg per 100 ml—nearly 19 times the UK driving limit and triple the normally lethal limit. After two days she discharged herself.

The United Kingdom's legal limit for motorists is 80 mg of alcohol per 100 ml of blood. The hitherto recorded highest figure in medical literature of 656 mg per 100 ml was submerged when the late Samuel Riley (b. 1922) of Sefton Park, Merseyside, was found by a disbelieving pathologist to have a level of 1220 mg on 28 Mar 1979. He had expired in his flat and had been an inspector at the plant of a well-known motor manufacturer.

BODY TEMPERATURE

Highest body temperature
Willie Jones, a 52 year old black, was admitted to Grady Memorial Hospital, Atlanta, Georgia on 10 July 1980 with heat stroke on a day when the temperature reached 90° F *32,2° C* with 44% humidity. His temperature was found to be 46,5° C *115.7° F*. After 24 days he was discharged 'at prior baseline status'.

Lowest body temperature
There are two recorded cases of patients surviving body temperatures as low as 60.8° F *16,0° C*. Dorothy Mae Stevens, (1929–74) was found in an alley in Chicago, Illinois on 1 Feb 1951 and Vickie Mary Davis aged 2 years 1 month in an unheated house in Marshalltown, Iowa on 21 Jan 1956, both with this temperature. People may die of hypothermia with body temperatures of 95.0° F *35,0° C*.

ILLNESS AND DISEASE

Commonest disease
The commonest non-contagious disease in the world is periodontal disease, such as gingivitis, which subclinically afflicts some 80 per cent of the US population. In Great Britain 13 per cent of people have lost all their teeth before they are 21 years old. During their lifetime few completely escape its effects. Infestation with pinworm (*Enterobius vermicularis*) approaches 100 per cent in some tropical areas of the world.

The commonest contagious disease in the world is coryza (acute nasopharyngitis) or the common cold. Only 872,000 working days were reportedly lost as a result of this illness in Great Britain between mid-1981 and mid-1982, since absences of less than three days were not reported. The greatest reported loss of working time in Britain is from neurotic disorders, which accounted for 27,384,700, or 7.59 per cent, of the total of 361,015,100 days lost from mid 1982 to mid 1983.

The most resistant recorded case to being infected at the Medical Research Council Common Cold Unit, Salisbury, Wiltshire is J. Brophy, who has had one mild reaction in 24 visits.

Rarest disease
Medical literature periodically records hitherto undescribed diseases. A disease as yet undescribed but predicted by a Norwegian doctor is podocytoma of the kidney—a tumour of the epithelial cells lining the glomerulus of the kidney.

The last case of endemic smallpox was recorded in Ali Maow Maalin in Merka, Somalia on 26 Oct 1977. Paul Braddon of Rusper, West Sussex was reported on 2 Aug 1983 to be the first case to contract malaria in Britain for more than 35 years.

Kuru, or laughing sickness, afflicts only the Fore tribe of eastern New Guinea and is 100 per cent fatal. This was formally attributed to the cannibalistic practice of eating human brains.

The rarest fatal diseases in England and Wales have been those from which the last deaths (all males) were all recorded more than 40 years ago—yellow fever (1930), cholera nostras (1928) and bubonic plague (1926).

Most infectious disease
The most infectious of all diseases is the pneumonic form of plague, as evidenced by the Black Death of 1347–51. It has a mortality rate of about 99.99 per cent.

AIDS (Acquired immune-deficiency syndrome), was first recognised in 1978, though it has similarities with an outbreak of African swine fever in Haiti which has been known since 1909. The virus was first identified in Jan 1983 at the Pasteur Institute, Paris by Luc Montagnier, Françoise Barré-Sinoussi and Jean-Claude Chermann as a Human T-lymphotrophic virus Type III (HTLV III). A US patent was granted to Prof Robert Gallo at the National Cancer Institute, Bethesda, Maryland for HTLV III in May 1985.

Highest mortality
Rabies in humans has been regarded as uniformly fatal when associated with the hydrophobia symptom. A 25-year-old woman, Candida de Sousa Barbosa of Rio de Janeiro, Brazil, after surgery by Dr Max Karpin, was believed to be the first ever survivor of the disease in November 1968. Some sources prefer the case of Matthew Winkler, 6, who, on 10 Oct 1970, survived a bite by a rabid bat.

Leading cause of death
The leading cause of death in industrialised countries is arteriosclerosis (thickening of the arterial wall) which underlies much coronary and cerebrovascular disease. Deaths from diseases of the circulatory system totalled 278,849 in England and Wales in 1984.

Most notorious carrier
The most publicised of all typhoid carriers has been Mary Mallon, known as Typhoid Mary, of New York City, NY, USA. She was the source of nine outbreaks, notably that of 1903. She was placed under permanent detention from 1915 until her death in 1938. A still anonymous dairy farmer from Camden, N.Y. was the source of 409 cases (40 fatal) in August 1909.

Parkinson's disease
The most protracted case of Parkinson's disease (named after 'An Essay on the Shaking Palsy' of 1817 by Dr James Parkinson (1755–1824) for which the earliest treatments were not published until 1946, is 62 years in the case of Frederick G. Humphries (d. 23 Feb 1985) of Croydon, London. His symptoms were detected in 1923.

MEDICAL EXTREMES

Heart stoppage
The longest recorded heart stoppage is a minimum of 3 hr 40 min in the case of Miss Jean Jawbone, 20, who was revived by a team of 26, using peritoneal dialysis, in the Health Sciences Centre, Winnipeg, Manitoba, Canada on 8 Jan 1977. The 'Mammalian diving reflex' can be triggered in humans falling into water cooler than 70° F *21° C*. In February 1974 Vegard Slettmoen, 5, fell through the ice on the river Nitselv, Norway. He was found 40 min later 2,5 m *8 ft* down but was revived in Akershus Central Hospital without brain-damage.

The longest recorded interval in a *post mortem* birth was one of 84 days in the case of a baby girl delivered on 5 July 1983 from a clinically dead woman in Roanoke, Virginia, who had been kept on life support since suffering a seizure in April.

Pulse rates
A normal adult pulse rate is 70–72 beats per min at rest for males and 78–82 for females. Rates increase to 200 or more during violent exercise and drop to as low as 12 in the extreme cases of Dorothy Mae Stevens (see Lowest body temperature, column 1), and Jean Hilliard (b. 1962) of Fosston, Minnesota, USA on 20 Dec 1980.

Longest coma
The longest recorded coma was that undergone by Elaine Esposito (b. 3 Dec 1934) of Tarpon Springs, Florida, USA. She never stirred since an appendicectomy on 6 Aug 1941, when she was 6, in Chicago, Illinois, USA, and died on 25 Nov 1978 aged 43 years 357 days, having been in a coma for 37 years 111 days.

Longest dream
Dreaming sleep is characterised by rapid eye movements known as REM discovered in 1953 by William Dement of the University of Chicago. The longest recorded period of REM is one of 2 hr 23 min on 15 Feb 1967 at the department of Psychology, University of Illinois, Chicago on Bill Carskadon, who had had his previous sleep interrupted. In July 1984 The Sleep Research Centre, Haifa, Israel recorded nil REM in a 33-year-old male who had a shrapnel brain injury.

Largest stone
The largest stone or vesical calculus reported in medical literature was one of 13 lb 14 oz *6,29 kg* removed from an 80-year-old woman by Dr Humphrey Arthure at Charing Cross Hospital, London, on 29 Dec 1952.

Longest in iron lung
The longest recorded period in an 'iron lung' is 37 years 58 days by Mrs Laurel Nisbet (b. 17 Nov 1912) of La Crescenta, California, USA, who died on 22 Aug 1985. She had been in an 'iron lung' continuously since 25 June 1948. The longest survival in an 'iron lung' in Britain has been 30 years by Denis Atkin in Lodge Moor Hospital, Sheffield, South Yorkshire. Mr John Prestwich (b. 24 Nov 1938) of Kings Langley, Hertfordshire has been dependent on a negative pressure respirator since 24 Nov 1955. Paul Bates of Horsham, West Sussex, was harnessed to a mechanical positive pressure respirator on 13 Aug 1954. From continuous respiration, he has received an estimated 237,374,528 respirations *via* his trachea up to 1 May 1986.

Fastest nerve impulses
The results of experiments published in 1966 have shown that the fastest messages transmitted

FIRE WALKER

The highest temperature recorded by pyrometer for the coals in any fire walk was 1494°F *812°C* for a walk by 'Komar' (Vernon E. Craig) of Wooster, Ohio at the International Festival of Yoga and Esoteric Sciences, Maidenhead, Berks on 14 Aug 1976.

GUINNESS BOOK OF RECORDS HALL OF FAME

1986

by the human nervous system travel as fast as 180 mph *288 km/h*. With advancing age impulses are carried 15 per cent more slowly.

Fastest reactions

The fastest recorded apparent reaction times recorded for sprinters at the 1980 Olympic Games were 120/1000ths of a second for Romy Müller (GDR) in the women's 200 metre semi-final and 124/1000ths for Wilbert Greaves (GB) in the 110 m hurdles heats. Both may have been anticipatory. These compare with 11/1000ths for the cockroach *Periplaneta americana*.

Most voracious fire breathers and extinguishers

Reg Morris blew a flame from his mouth to a distance of 27 ft *8,23 m* igniting a bonfire, at The Castle Working Men's Club, Brownhills, West Midlands on 5 Nov 1983. On 11 May 1985, Gerry Mawdsley of Westhoughton, Lancashire, extinguished 13,115 torches of flame successively in his mouth in 2 hr at Blackrod, Lancashire. On 13 Feb 1982 at the 'Six Bells' Stoke Poges, Bucks, Jean Leggett set a female record of 6607.

Fire-eater Jean Leggett (*above*) whose female record for fire eating 6607 torches is less than half that of human fire extinguisher Gerry Mawdsley (*below*) who quenched 13,115 torches of flame in his mouth.

Human salamanders

The highest dry-air temperature endured by naked men in the US Air Force experiments in 1960 was 400°F *204,4°C* and for heavily clothed men 500°F *260°C*. Steaks require only 325°F *162,8°C*. Temperatures of 140°C *284°F* have been found quite bearable in *Sauna* baths.

Thirty five people from the Sawau tribe on the island of Beqa in the Fijian group participated in a firewalk with the temperature over 1000°F *537°C* on 18 May 1982. There is an annual fire walk during the feast of St Constantine each May in Aghia Eleni, northern Greece.

Swallowing

The worst reported case of compulsive swallowing was an insane female Mrs H. aged 42, who complained of a 'slight abdominal pain'. She proved to have 2533 objects, including 947 bent pins, in her stomach. These were removed by Drs Chalk and Foucar in June 1927 at the Ontario Hospital, Canada. The heaviest object extracted from a human stomach has been a 5 lb 3 oz *2,53 kg* ball of hair in Swain's case from a 20-year-old female compulsive swallower in the South Devon and East Cornwall Hospital, England on 30 Mar 1895.

Sword

Edward Benjamin 'Count Desmond' (b. 1941 of Binghamton, NY, USA) swallowed thirteen 23 in *58,4 cm* long blades to below his xiphisternum and injured himself in the process. *This category has now been retired and no further claims will be entertained.*

Hiccoughing

The longest recorded attack of hiccoughs or

singultus is that which afflicted Charles Osborne (b. 1894) of Anthon, Iowa, USA, for 60 years from 1922. He contracted it when slaughtering a hog and has hiccoughed about 430 million times in the interim period. He was unable to find a cure, but led a reasonably normal life in which he had two wives and fathered eight children. He did admit, however, that he could not keep in his false teeth. In Feb 1985 he was reported to be down to 10 hics per minute from his earlier high of 40.

Sneezing

The most chronic sneezing fit ever recorded is that of Donna Griffiths (b. 1969) of Pershore, Hereford & Worcester. She started sneezing on 13 Jan 1981 and surpassed the previous duration record of 194 days on 27 July 1981. She sneezed an estimated million times in the first 365 days. She achieved her first sneeze-free day on 16 Sept 1983—the 978th day. The highest speed at which expelled particles have ever been measured to travel is 103.6 mph *167 km/h.*

Snoring *Loudest*

The highest measured sound level recorded by any chronic snorer is a peak of 87.5 decibels at Hever Castle, Kent in the early hours of 28 June 1984. Melvyn Switzer of Totton, Hants was 1 ft *30 cm* from the meter. His wife Julie is deaf in one ear. A sagging pharynx is associated with snoring.

Yawning

In Lee's case, reported in 1888, a 15-year-old female patient yawned continuously for a period of 5 weeks.

Sleeplessness

Researches indicate that on the Circadian cycle for the majority peak efficiency is attained between 8 and 9 p.m. and the low point comes at 4 a.m. The longest recorded period for which a person has voluntarily gone without sleep is 449 hr (18 days 17 hr) by Mrs Maureen Weston of Peterborough, Cambs in a rocking chair marathon on 14 Apr–2 May 1977. Though she tended to hallucinate toward the end of this surely ill-advised test, she surprisingly suffered no lasting ill-effects. Victims of the very rare condition chronic colestites (total insomnia) have been known to go without definable sleep for many years. Jesus de Frutos (b. 1925) of Segovia, Spain asserts that he has only dozed since 1954.

Motionlessness

The longest that anyone has continuously remained motionless is 13 hr by Willie Nugent, 38, at *The Guinness World of Records* permanent exhibition at the Trocadero, Piccadilly, London, on 24 June 1985. The longest recorded case of involuntarily being made to stand to attention was when Corporal Everett D. Reamer of the 60th Coast Artillery Regiment AA Battery F, USA FFE was so punished in Camp No 1, Osaka, Japan for 132 consecutive hours from 8.00 am, 15 Aug until 8.00 pm 20 Aug 1944.

Fasting

Most humans experience considerable discomfort after an abstinence from food for even 12 hr but this often passes off after 24–48 hr. Records claimed unless there is unremitting medical surveillance are inadmissible. The longest period for which anyone has gone without solid food is 382 days by Angus Barbieri (b. 1940) of Tayport, Fife, who lived on tea, coffee, water, soda water and vitamins in Maryfield Hospital, Dundee, Angus, from June 1965 to July 1966. His weight declined from 33 st 10 lb *214,1 kg* to 12 st 10 lb *80,74 kg.*

Hunger strike

The longest recorded hunger strike was one of 94 days by John and Peter Crowley, Thomas Donovan, Michael Burke, Michael O'Reilly, Christopher Upton, John Power, Joseph Kenny and Seán Hennessy in Cork Prison, Ireland, from 11 Aug to 12 Nov 1920. These nine survivors from 12 prisoners owed their lives to expert medical attention and an appeal by the nationalist leader Arthur Griffith (1872–1922). The longest recorded hunger strike in a British gaol is 385 days from 28 June 1972 to 18 July 1973 by Denis Galer Goodwin in Wakefield Prison, West Yorkshire protesting his innocence of a rape charge. He was fed by tube orally.

The longest recorded case of survival without food *and* water is 18 days by Andreas Mihavecz, 18, of Bregenz, Austria who was put into a holding cell on 1 Apr 1979 in a local government building in Höchst, Austria but was totally forgotten by the police. On 18 Apr 1979 he was discovered close to death having had neither food nor water. He had been a passenger in a crashed car.

Underwater

The world record for voluntarily staying underwater is 13 min 42.5 sec by Robert Foster, aged 32, an electronics technician of Richmond, California, who stayed under 10 ft *3,05 m* of water in the swimming pool of the Bermuda Palms Motel at San Rafael, California, USA, on 15 Mar 1959. He hyperventilated with oxygen for 30 min before his descent. (See also Heart Stoppage, p. 18.)

g forces

The acceleration g, due to gravity, is 32 ft 1.05 in per sec per sec *978,02 cm/sec²* at sea-level at the Equator. A *sustained* acceleration of 25 g was withstood in a dry capsule during astronautic research by Dr Carter Collins of California, USA. The highest g value endured on a water-braked rocket sled is 82.6 g for 0.04 of a sec by Eli L. Beeding Jr. at Holloman Air Force Base, New Mexico, USA, on 16 May 1958. He was put in hospital for 3 days. A man who fell off a 185 ft *56,39 m* cliff (before 1963) has survived a *momentary* g of 209 in decelerating from 68 mph *109 km/h* to stationary in 0.015 of a sec.

The racing driver David Purley GM (1945–1985) survived a deceleration from 108 mph *173 km/h* to zero in 26 in *66 cm* in a crash at Silverstone on 13 July 1977 which involved a force of 179.8 g. He suffered 29 fractures, 3 dislocations and 6 heart stoppages.

A land diver of Pentecost Island, New Hebrides dived from a platform 81 ft 3 in *24,76 m* high with liana vines attached to his ankles on 15 May 1982. The body speed was 50 ft *15,24 m* per sec 34 mph *54 km/h.* The jerk transmitted a momentary g force in excess of 110.

Electric shock *Highest voltage*

People in aircraft in thunder clouds may be at 30 million volts relative to the earth without harm. In some 'bare hand' laboratory work in France experimenters in insulated cabins have experienced 5 million volts. People walking on nylon carpets on dry days may go up to 10,000 volts relative to earth and yet experience only mild shocks. Contact with exposed high tension power lines with system voltages of 765,000 have occurred in the US and at up to 400,000 in the UK. A person in contact with earth via ladders, dinghy masts, crane jibs etc, normally suffer instant death due to a heavy current arc or flashover flowing through the body. That shocks received from high tension cables by Brian Latasa (230,000 volts in Griffith Park, Los Angeles on 9 Nov 1967) and Harry F. McGrew (340,000 volts in Huntington Canyon, Utah on 7 Oct 1977) were non-lethal underlines their

idiosyncratic nature when compared with the mere 2,500 volts used in 1890 for judicial electrocution.

Isolation

The longest recorded period for which any volunteer has been able to withstand total deprivation of all sensory stimulation (sight, hearing and touch) is 92 hr, recorded in 1962 at Lancaster Moor Hospital, Lancashire.

Pill-taking

The highest recorded total of pills swallowed by a patient is 500,689 between 9 June 1967 and 31 Jan 1986 by C. H. A. Kilner (b. 1926) of Bindura, Zimbabwe, following a successful operation to remove a cancerous pancreas on 26 May 1966.

Most injections

The diabetic Mrs Evelyn Ruth Winder (b. 1921) of Invercargill, New Zealand gave an estimated 57,838 insulin injections to herself over 55 years to May 1986.

Most tattoos

The seeming ultimate in being tattooed is represented by Wilfred Hardy of Huthwaite, Nottinghamshire, England. Not content with a perilous approach to within 4 per cent of totality, he has been tattooed on the inside of his cheek, his tongue, gums and eyebrows. Walter Stiglitz of North Plainfield, New Jersey, USA in March 1984 claimed 5457 separate tattoos by six artists. Britain's most decorated woman is Rusty Field (b. 1944) of Norfolk, who after 12 years under the needle of Mr Bill Skuse, has come within 15 per cent of totality. He stated he always had designs on her. Both the 1980 and 1981 World's Most Beautiful Tattooed Lady Contest in the US were won by Susan James (GB) (b. 1959).

OPERATIONS

Longest

The most protracted reported operation, for surgical as opposed to medical control purposes, has been one of 96 hr performed on Mrs Gertrude Levandowski (see also p. 10) during the period 4–8 Feb 1951. The patient suffered from a weak heart and the surgeons had to exercise the utmost caution during the operation. The 'slowest' operation on record is one on the feet of Mrs Doreen Scott of Derby, England on 20 Nov 1981. She had been waiting since 10 March 1952—19 years 8 months.

Most

Padmabhushan Dr M. C. Modi, a pioneer of mass eye surgery in India since 1943, has performed as many as 833 cataract operations in a single working day.

Dr Robert B. McClure (b. 1901) of Toronto, Canada performed a career total of 20,423 major operations in 1924–78.

Joseph Ascough (b. 1935) of Nottingham, England underwent his 333rd operation (for the removal of papillomas from his wind pipe) on 24 April 1986. These wart-like growths which impede breathing first formed when he was 18 months old.

Oldest subject

The greatest recorded age at which a person has been subjected to an operation is 111 years 105 days in the case of James Henry Brett, Jr (b. 25 July 1849, d. 10 Feb 1961) of Houston, Texas, USA. He underwent a hip operation on 7 Nov 1960. The oldest age established in Britain was the case of Miss Mary Wright (b. 28 Feb 1862) who died during a thigh operation at Boston, Lincolnshire on 22 Apr 1971 aged 109 years 53 days.

Heart transplant

Earliest and longest surviving

The first human heart transplant operation was performed on Louis Washkansky, aged 55, at the Groote Schuur Hospital, Cape Town, South Africa, between 1.00 a.m. and 6 a.m., on 3 Dec 1967, by a team of 30 headed by Prof. Christiaan Neethling Barnard (b. Beaufort West, South Africa, 8 Oct 1922). The donor was Miss Denise Ann Darvall, aged 25. Washkansky lived for 18 days. The longest surviving heart transplantee has been Emmanuel Vitria, of Marseilles, France (b. 24 Jan 1920) who received the heart of a 20 year old man on 27 Nov 1968 and entered the 18th year of his new life in 1985. Britain's longest-surviving heart transplant patient was Keith Castle (1927–85) of Battersea, London who died 5 years 310 days after his transplant on 18 Aug 1979 at Papworth Hospital, Cambridge.

Hollie Roffey (b. 20 July 1984) underwent a heart transplant aged a record 10 days in a 5½ hr operation by Mr Magdi Yacoub at the National Heart Hospital, London on 30 July. She died after 18 days, on 17 August.

The first transplantee to give birth was Betsy Sneith, 23, with a baby girl Sierra (7 lb 10 oz *3,45 kg*) at Stanford University, California on 17 Sept 1984. She had received a donor heart in February 1980.

Artificial heart

On 1–2 Dec 1982 at the Utah Medical Center, Salt Lake City, Utah, USA, Dr Barney B. Clark, 61 of Des Moines, Wisconsin, USA received an artificial heart. The surgeon was Dr William C. De Vries. The heart was a Jarvik Mark 7 designed by Dr Robert K. Jarvik. Dr Clark died on 23 Mar 1983, 112 days later.

Earliest kidney transplant

R. H. Lawler (b. 1895) (USA) performed the first homo transplantation of the kidney in the human in 1950. The longest survival, as between identical twins, has been 20 years.

Earliest appendicectomy

The earliest recorded successful appendix operation was performed in 1736 by Claudius Amyand (1680–1740). He was Serjeant Surgeon to King George II (reigned 1727–60).

Earliest anaesthesia

The earliest recorded operation under general anaesthesia was for the removal of a cyst from the neck of James Venable by Dr Crawford Williamson Long (1815–78), using diethyl ether $(C_2H_5)_2O$, in Jefferson, Georgia, USA, on 30 Mar 1842. The earliest amputation under an anaesthetic in Great Britain was by Dr William Scott and Dr James McLauchlan at the Dumfries and Galloway Infirmary, Scotland on 19 Dec 1846.

Most durable cancer patient

The most extreme recorded case of survival from diagnosed cancer is that of Mrs Winona Mildred Melick (*née* Douglass) (b. 22 Oct 1876) of Long Beach, California. She had four cancer operations in 1918, 1933, 1966 and 1968 but died from pneumonia on 28 Dec 1981, 67 days after her 105th birthday.

Laryngectomy

On 24 July 1924 John I. Poole of Plymouth, Devon after diagnosis of carcinoma, then aged 33 underwent total laryngectomy in Edinburgh. He died on 19 June 1979 after surviving nearly 55 years as a 'neck-breather'. Mr F. B. Harvey of Plymouth, Devon has been a neck-breather since 1929.

Fastest amputation

The shortest time recorded for a leg amputation in the pre-anaesthetic era was 13–15 sec by Napoleon's chief surgeon Dominique Larrey. There could have been no ligation.

Largest tumour

The largest tumour ever recorded was Spohn's case of an ovarian cyst weighing 328 lb (23 st 6 lb) *148,7 kg* from a woman in Texas, USA in 1905. She recovered fully. The most extreme case reported in Britain was of a cyst weighing 298 lb (21 st 4 lb) *135 kg* removed from a woman in England in 1846. The patient did not survive.

Surgical instruments

The largest surgical instruments are robot retractors used in abdominal surgery introduced by Abbey Surgical Instruments of Chingford, Essex in 1968 and weighing 11 lb *5 kg*. Some bronchoscopic forceps measure 60 cm *23½ in* in length. The smallest are Elliot's eye trephine, which has a blade 0.078 in *0,20 cm* in diameter and 'straight' stapes picks with a needle-type tip or blade of 0,3 mm *0.013 in* long.

PSYCHIC FORCES

Extra-sensory perception

The two most extreme published examples of ESP in scientific literature have been those of the Reiss case of a 26 year old female at Hunter College, New York State, USA in 1936 and of Pavel Stepánek (Czechoslovakia) in 1967–68. The importance which might be attached to their cases was diminished by subsequent developments. The Reiss subject refused to undergo any further tests under stricter conditions. When Stepánek was retested at Edinburgh University with plastic cards he 'failed to display any clairvoyant ability'. Much smaller departures from the laws of probability have however been displayed in less extreme cases carried out under strict conditions.

Fifty-one year old Joseph Ascough who can still smile after averaging over six operations a year since he was born.

Most durable ghosts

Ghosts are not immortal and, according to the *Gazetteer of British Ghosts*, seem to deteriorate after 400 years. The most outstanding exception to their normal 'half-life' would be the ghosts of Roman soldiers thrice reported still marching through the cellars of the Treasurer's House, York Minister after nearly 19 centuries. The book's author, Peter Underwood, states that Britain has more reported ghosts per square mile than any other country with Borley Rectory near Long Melford, Suffolk the site of unrivalled activity between 1863 and its destruction by fire in 1939. Andrew M. Green, author of *Ghost Hunting, A Practical Guide* claims to possess the only known letter from a *poltergeist*.

Rusty Field the world's most tattooed lady with her former husband who spent more than 20 years decorating her body with over 2500 designs. (Rex Features)

CHAPTER TWO

THE

LIVING WORLD

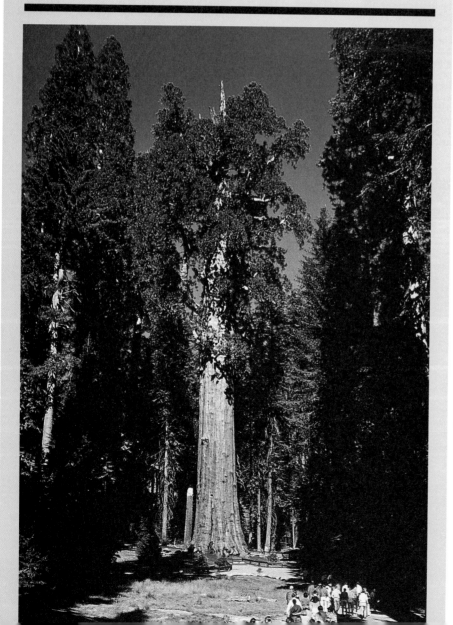

Note—Guinness Superlatives Ltd has published a specialist volume entitled *The Guinness Book of Animal Facts and Feats* (3rd Edition) by Gerald L. Wood (price £8.95). This work treats the dimensions and performances of the Classes of the Animal Kingdom in greater detail, giving also the sources and authorities for much of the material in this chapter.

Largest and heaviest

The largest and heaviest animal in the world is the female Blue or Sulphur-bottom whale (*Balaenoptera musculus*), also called Sibbald's rorqual (see table). The longest specimen ever recorded was a female landed at the Compania Argentina de Pesca, Grytviken, South Georgia in 1909 which measured 107 Norwegian fot *33,58 m 110 ft 2¼ in* in length. During summer months an average-sized specimen consumes up to 3 million calories per day. The tongue and heart of the 190 tonne *187 ton* female (see Table pp. 24–5) taken by the *Slava* whaling fleet in the Southern Ocean on 20 Mar 1947 weighed 4.22 tons *4,29 tonnes* and 1540 lb *698,5 kg* respectively.

The low frequency pulses made by blue whales when communicating with each other have been measured up to 188 dB making them the loudest sounds emitted by any living source. They have been detected 850 km *530 miles* away.

Heaviest brain

The Sperm whale (*Physeter macrocephalus*) has the heaviest brain of any living animal. The brain of a 49 ft *14,93 m* bull processed aboard the Japanese factory ship *Nissin Maru No. 1* in the Antarctic on 11 Dec 1949 weighed 9,2 kg *20.24 lb* compared with 6,9 kg *15.38 lb* for a 90 ft *27 m* Blue whale. The heaviest brain recorded for an elephant was an exceptional 16.5 lb *7,5 kg* in the case of a diseased 1.94 ton *1,95 tonne* Asiatic cow (*cf.* 9¼–12 lb *4,2–5,4 kg* for an adult bull African elephant).

Largest eye

The Giant squid (*Architeuthis* sp.) has the largest eye of any living animal. The ocular diameter may exceed 38 cm *15 in* (*cf.* 30 cm *11.81 in* for a 33⅓ long-playing record and 12 cm *4.72 in* for a large blue whale).

Largest egg

The largest egg laid by any known animal was that of the Elephant bird (*Aepyornis maximus*) which lived in southern Madagascar until *c.* AD 900. One example preserved in the British Museum (Natural History) measures 85,6 cm *33.7 in* round the long axis with a circumference of 72,3 cm *28.5 in*, giving a capacity of 8,88 litres *2.35 gal* or equivalent to 180–185 hen's eggs. It weighed about 27 lb *12,2 kg* when full.

The largest egg of any living animal is that of the Whale shark (*Rhincodon typus*). One egg case measuring 12 in by 5.5 in by 3.5 in *30 × 14 × 9 cm* was picked up on 29 June 1953 at a depth of 31 fathoms (186 ft *56,6 m*) in the Gulf of Mexico 130 miles *209 km* south of Port Isabel, Texas, USA. The egg contained a perfect embryo of a Whale shark 13.78 in *35 cm* long.

Longest gestation

The viviparous Alpine black salamander (*Salamandra atra*) has a gestation period of up to 38 months at altitudes above 1400 m *4600 ft* in the Swiss Alps, but this drops to 24–26 months at lower altitudes.

The 'General Sherman' tree in California, the most massive living thing on Earth. Although over 2500 years old, its annual growth rate has been measured at almost a millimeter ($\frac{1}{125}$th inch)—the volume contained in a tree 30 cm *1 ft* in diameter and 15 m *49.2 ft* tall (see p. 47). (National Park Service, USA)

Fastest and slowest growth

The fastest growth in the Animal Kingdom is that of the blue whale calf (see Table and above). A barely visible ovum weighing a fraction of a milligramme (*0.000035 oz*) grows to a weight of *c*. 26 tons *26 tonnes* in 22¾ months, made up of 10¾ months gestation and the first 12 months of life. This is equivalent to an increase of 30,000 million-fold. The slowest growth is that of the deep-sea clam *Tindaria callistiformis* of the North Atlantic, which takes *c*. 100 years to reach a length of 8 mm *0.31 in*.

Highest altitude

In April 1967 NASA reported that bacteria had been discovered at an altitude of 135,000 ft (25.56 miles) *41 100 m*.

Greatest size difference between sexes (Dimorphism)

The largest female marine worms of the species *Bonellia viridis* are at least 100 million times heavier than the smallest males. The female is up to 100 cm *39.3 in* long against the miserable 1,0 mm *0.04 in* of the male.

Most monogamous

The male Klipspringer (*Oreotragus oreotragus*) a small antelope found in eastern and southern Africa rarely strays more than 5 m *16¼ ft* from its mate during their lifetime together.

Highest g force

The highest force encountered in nature is the 400 g *averaged* by the Click beetle *Athous haemorrhoidalis* (a common British species) when 'jack-knifing' into the air to escape predators. One example measuring 12 mm *0.47 in* in length and weighing 40 mg *0.00014 oz* which jumped to a height of 30 cm *11¾ in* was calculated to have 'endured' a peak brain deceleration of 2300 g at the end of the movement.

Internal temperatures

The highest average mammalian blood temperature is that of the Xoloitzcuintli or Mexican hairless dog with 104° F *40,0° C*. That of the dromedary *Camelus dromedarius* reaches 41° C *105.8° F* at the end of a hot day. The lowest mammalian blood temperature is that of the Spiny anteater (Echidna), (*Tachyglossus aculeatus*), a monotreme found in Australia and New Guinea, with a normal range of 72°–87° F *22,2°–24,4° C*. The ice worm of Alaska has an internal temperature of − 10° C *14° F*.

Most prodigious eater

The most phenomenal eating machine in nature is the larva of the Polyphemus moth (*Antheraea polyphemus*) of North America which, in the first 48 hours of its life, consumes an amount equal to 86,000 times its own birthweight. In human terms, this would be equivalent to a 7 lb *3,17 kg* baby taking in 269 tons *273 tonnes* of nourishment!

Heaviest ambergris

The heaviest piece of ambergris (a solid substance formed in the intestine of the Sperm whale) on record was a 1003 lb *455 kg* lump recovered from a Sperm whale (*Physeter macrocephalus*) caught off Tasmania on 24 Dec 1912. It was later sold in London for £23,000, equivalent in 1986 to more than £500,000.

Most valuable

The most valuable animals in cash terms are thoroughbred racehorses. It was announced in August 1983 that *Shareef Dancer* (see Chap. 12 Horseracing) had been syndicated by his owner Sheikh Maktoum al Maktoum for $40 million (*£26 million*). The most valuable zoo exhibit is the Giant panda (*Ailuropoda melanoleuca*), 'Chu-

Lin' (b. Sept 1982) of Madrid Zoo, Spain. It was the first cub in Europe to be valued at more than £1 million. The most valuable marine exhibits are 'Orky' and 'Corky', the world's only captive breeding pair of killer whales (*Orcinus orca*) at Marineland, Palos Verdes, Los Angeles. In 1985 they were valued at $2,000,000 (*then £1,650,000*).

1. MAMMALS

Mammalia

Largest and heaviest *British waters*

The largest blue whale ever recorded in the waters of Great Britain was probably an 88 ft *26,8 m* specimen killed near the Bunaveneader station in Harris in the Western Isles, Scotland in 1904. In Dec 1851 the carcase of a blue whale measuring 94 ft 9 in *28,87 m* in length (girth 42 ft *13,7 m*) was brought into Bantry harbour, Co. Cork, Ireland after it had been found floating dead in the sea. A specimen stranded on the west coast of Lewis, Western Isles, Scotland in *c*. 1870 was credited with a length of 105 ft *32 m* but the carcase was cut up by the local people before the length could be verified. The length was probably exaggerated or taken along the curve of the body instead of in a straight line from the tip of the snout to the notch in the flukes. Four blue whales have been stranded on British coasts since 1913, at least two of them after being harpooned by whalers. The last occurrence (*c*. 60 ft *18 m*) was at Wick, Highland, Scotland on 15 Oct 1923.

Blue whales inhabit the colder seas and migrate to warmer waters in the winter for breeding. Observations made in the Antarctic in 1947–8 showed that a blue whale can maintain a speed of 20 knots (23 mph *37 km/h*) for 10 min when frightened. It has been calculated that a 90 ft *27 m* blue whale travelling at 20 knots *37 km/h* would develop 520 hp *527 cv*. Newborn calves measure 6,5–8,6 m *21 ft 3½ in–28 ft 6 in* in length and weigh up to 3000 kg *2.95 tons*.

It has been estimated that there are about 12,000 blue whales roaming the world's oceans today as a result of over-fishing. This compares with a peak estimate of *c*. 220,000 in the past. The species has been protected *de jure* since 1967, although non-member countries of the International Whaling Commission. *e.g.* Panama and Taiwan, are not bound by this agreement. A world-wide ban on commercial whaling is due to come into effect this year (1986) but Iceland and S. Korea intend to carry on taking 200 whales annually for 'scientific purposes' until 1990 and the Philippines say they will continue whaling until 1988.

Deepest dive

The greatest *recorded* depth to which a whale has dived is 620 fathoms (3720 ft *1134 m*) by a 47 ft *14,32 m* bull sperm whale (*Physeter macrocephalus*) found with its jaw entangled with a submarine cable running between Santa Elena, Ecuador and Chorillos, Peru, on 14 Oct 1955. At this depth the whale withstood a pressure of 1680 lb/in² *11583 kPa* of body surface. On 25 Aug 1969 another bull sperm whale was killed 100 miles *160 km* south of Durban after it had surfaced from a dive lasting 1 hr 52 min, and inside its stomach were found two small sharks which had been swallowed about an hour earlier. These were later identified as *Scymnodon* sp., a species found only on the sea floor. At this point from land the depth of water is in excess of 1646 fathoms (10,476 ft *3193 m*) for a radius of 30–40 miles *48–64 km*, which now suggests that the Sperm whale sometimes descends to a depth of

over 10,000 ft *3000 m* when seeking food and is limited by pressure of time rather than by pressure of pressure.

Largest on land *World*

(*See also Table*) The largest living land animal is the African bush elephant (*Loxodonta africana*). The average adult bull stands 10 ft 6 in *3,2 m* at the shoulder and weighs 5.6 tons *5,7 tonnes*. The largest specimen ever recorded, and the largest land animal of modern times, was a bull shot 25 miles *40 km* north-north-east of Mucusso, southern Angola on 7 Nov 1974. Lying on its side this elephant measured 13 ft 8 in *4,16 m* in a projected line from the highest point of the shoulder to the base of the forefoot, indicating that its standing height must have been about 13 ft *3,96 m*. Other measurements included an overall length of 35 ft *10,67 m* (tip of extended trunk to tip of extended tail) and a forefoot circumference of 5 ft 11 in *1,80 m*. The weight was computed to be 26,998 lb (12.05 tons, *12,24 tonnes*).

Largest on land *Britain*

The largest wild mammal in the British Isles is the Red deer (*Cervus elaphus*). A full-grown stag stands 3 ft 8 in *1,11 m* at the shoulder and weighs 230–250 lb *104–113 kg*. The heaviest ever recorded was probably a stag killed at Glenfiddich, Banff, Scotland in 1831, which weighed 525 lb *238 kg*. The heaviest park Red deer on record was a stag weighing 476 lb *215 kg* (height at shoulder 4 ft 6 in *1,37 m*) killed at Woburn, Bedfordshire in 1836. The so-called wild pony (*Equus caballus*) may weigh up to 700 lb *320 kg* but there are no truly feral populations living today.

Smallest *Land*

(*See also Table*) The Kitti's hog-nosed bat (*Craseonycteris thonglongyai*) or Bumblebee bat, is now restricted to a few caves near the forestry station at Ban Sai Yoke on the Kwae Noi River, Kanchanaburi, Thailand. A new hydro-electric project is endangering the species. Mature specimens (both sexes) have a wing span of *c*. 160 mm *6.29 in* and weigh 1,75–2 g *0.062–0.071 oz*. The smallest mammal found in the British Isles is the European pygmy shrew (*Sorex minutus*). Mature specimens have a head and body length of 43–64 mm *1.69–2.5 in*, a tail length of 31–46 mm *1.22–1.81 in* and weigh between 2,4 and 6,1 g *0.084 and 0.213 oz*.

Smallest *Marine*

The smallest totally marine mammal in terms of weight is probably Commerson's dolphin (*Cephalorhynchus commersoni*) also known as Le Jacobite, which is found in the waters off the southern tip of South America. In one series of six adult specimens the weights ranged from 23 kg *50.7 lb* to 35 kg *77.1 lb*. The Sea otter (*Enhydra lutris*) of the north Pacific is of comparable size (55–81.4 lb *25–38,5 kg*), but this species sometimes comes ashore during storms.

Rarest

A number of mammals are known only from a single or holotype specimen including Garrido's hutia (*Capromys garridoi*) known only from a single specimen collected on the islet of Cayo Maja, off southern Cuba in April 1967. In 1979 zoologists uncovered the first evidence that the Bali leopard (*Panthera pardus balica*) still existed on the island. On 19 Jan 1984 the Wild Life Service in Tasmania announced that a Tasmanian wolf had been sighted in July 1982.

Britain's rarest native mammal is the Large mouse-eared bat (*Myotis myotis*) (see p. 28).

Longest lived

No other mammal can match the extreme proven 120 years attained by Man (*Homo sapiens*) (see

Mammals continued

pp. 11 and 12). It is probable that the closest approach is made by the Asiatic elephant (*Elephas maximus*). The greatest age that has been verified with absolute certainty is 81 years in the case of Nepal's royal elephant 'Prem Prased', who died in Katmandu on 27 Feb 1985. The longest lived marine mammal is Baird's beaked whale (*Berardius bairdii*) which has a maximum life-span of *c.* 70 years.

Highest living

The highest living wild mammal in the world is probably the Yak (*Bos grunniens*), of Tibet and the Szechwanese Alps, China, which occasionally climbs to an altitude of 20,000 ft *6100 m* when foraging.

Largest herds

The largest herds on record were those of the Springbok (*Antidorcas marsupialis*) during migration across the plains of the western parts of southern Africa in the 19th century. In 1849 John (later Sir John) Fraser observed a *trekbokken* that took three days to pass through the settlement of Beaufort West, Cape Province. Another herd seen moving near Nels Poortje, Cape Province in 1888 was estimated to contain 100,000,000 head, although 10,000,000 is probably a more realistic figure. A herd estimated to be 15 miles *24 km* wide and more than 100 miles *160 km* long was reported from Karree Kloof, Orange River, South Africa in July 1896.

The largest concentration of wild mammals found living anywhere in the world today is that of the Mexican free-tailed Bat (*Tadarida brasiliensis*) in Bracken Cave, San Antonio, Texas, USA, where up to twenty million animals assemble after migration.

> The world's largest and heaviest living creature, the Blue whale, which can attain a length of 110 ft *33,5 m* and a weight of up to 174 tons/tonnes. Alongside it, the world's largest baby, a blue whale calf.
> (Artwork: Matthew Hillier, FSIAD)

	Largest/Heaviest	Longest/Tallest
WHOLE ANIMAL KINGDOM	190 tonnes Blue whale (*Balaenoptera musculus*); female 27,6 m *90½ ft* long caught by Soviet ship *Slava* in Antarctica, 1947	180 ft *55 m* Bootlace worm (*Lineus longissimus*); St Andrews, Fife, Scotland, 1864
MAMMALS	Land Mammal: est. 12,24 tonnes African bush elephant (*Loxodonta africana*) Angola, 1974	20 ft *6,09 m* Giraffe (*Giraffa camelopardalis tippelskirchi*) from Kenya. 'George' d. Chester Zoo, 22 July 1969
BIRDS	345 lb *156,5 kg* Ostrich (*Struthio c. camelus*). Up to 9 ft *2,7 m* tall North Africa	Largest wing span 11 ft 11 in *3,63 m* Wandering albatross (*Diomedea exulans*) Tasman Sea, 18 Sept 1965
REPTILES	> 2 tonnes, 28 ft 4 in *8,63 m* Norman River, Australia, July 1957, Salt-water crocodile (*Crocodylus porosus*)	10 m *32 ft 9 in* Reticulated python (*Python reticulatus*) Celebes, 1912
SNAKES	Nearly 500 lb *227 kg* Anaconda (*Eunectes murinus*) girth 44 in *111 cm*, length 27 ft 9 in *8,45 m* Brazil, *c.* 1960	Of venomous species 18 ft 9 in *5,71 m* King Cobra (*Ophiophagus hannah*) or Hamadryad, Malaya 1937 (d. London Zoo)
AMPHIBIANS	143 lb *65 kg* Chinese giant salamander (*Andrias davidianus*) Hunan Province	5 ft 11 in *180 cm* length (see left)
FISHES	42.4 tons *43 tonnes* Whale shark (*Rhincodon typus*) Koh Chik, Gulf of Siam 1919. Length 60¾ ft *18,5 m*	(Of freshwater fish) 720 lb *327 kg* European catfish (*Siluris glanis*) 15 ft *4,6 m*, Dneiper River, USSR, *c.* 1856.
ARACHNIDS	'Nearly 3 oz *85 g*' Lasiodora klugi; Manaos, Brazil 1945	10.6 in *270 mm* legspan. *Lasiodora sp.*; Puraque, W. Brazil 1973
CRUSTACEANS	44 lb 6 oz *20,14 kg* North Atlantic lobster (*Homarus americanus*) overall length 3½ ft *1,06 m* Nova Scotia, 11 Feb 1977	> 12 ft *3,65 m* claw span Giant spider crab (*Macrocheira kaempferi*) Eastern Japan
INSECTS	3.5 oz *100 g* Goliath beetle (*Goliathus giganteus*) equatorial Africa	13 in *330 mm* female Giant stick insect (*Pharnacia serratipes*) Indonesia
MOLLUSCS	2 tons/tonnes Atlantic Giant squid (*Architeuthis dux*) Thimble Tickle Bay, Newfoundland, 2 Nov 1878	57 ft (*17,37 m* Giant squid (*Architeuthis longimanus*) Tentacle 49 ft *14,93 m*, New Zealand, 1887

THE ANIMAL KINGDOM

Smallest/Lightest	Fastest	Longest Lived	Commonest	Rarest
0.008 in *0,2 mm* long Hairy-winged beetles (family *Ptiliidae*) and battledore-wing fairy flies (family *Myrmaridae*)	350 km/h *217 mph* Peregrine falcon (*Falco peregrinus*) during stoop. Germany 1963–7	c. 220 years Ocean quahog (*Arctica islandica*). Example with 220 annual growth rings reported from mid-Atlantic, 1982	Nematodes sea worms. Est. populaton 4×10^{25} *cf.* Est. total of all living things on Earth of 3×10^{33}	A member of species known only from a single specimen or holotype.
0.062–0.071 oz *1,75–2,0 g* Kitti's hog-nosed bat (*Craseonycteris thonglongyai*), Thailand	60–63 mph *96–101 km/h* Cheetah (*Acionyx jubatus*)	120 years Man (see p 11) *Homo sapiens* 1865–fl. 1985	House mouse (*Mus musculus*): distribution embraces all continents	Single Tasmanian wolf or thylacine (*Thyalacine cynocephalus*) positively identified after a 46 year void, Tasmania, July 1982 by a wildlife ranger. Last captured specimen d. 7 Sept. 1936.
0.056 oz *1,6 g* male Bee humming-bird (*Mellisuga helenae*) Cuba, Caribbean. Overall length 57 mm 2¼ in	*Level flight (air speed):* 106.2 mph *171 km/h* White throated spinetailed swift (*Hirundapus caudacutus*) USSR, 1942	80 + years male Greater sulphur-crested cockatoo (*Cacatua galerita*) London Zoo 1925–82. Fully mature when acquired.	In the wild: 10,000 million Red-billed quelea (*Quelea quelea*) sub-Saharan Africa	Yellow-fronted bowerbird (*Amblyornis flavifrons*) one male sighting from 1895 to 1981
0.7 in 18 mm Gecko (*Sphaerodactylus parthenopion*) British Virgin Islands, 1964	On land: 18 mph *29 km/h* Six-lined racerunner (*Cnemidophorus sexlineatus*) South Carolina, 1941	152 + years male Marion's tortoise *Geochelone sumeiriei*; Mauritius, d. 1918	Sea snake (*Astrotia stokesii*) found *en masse* from Arabia sea to south western Pacific	Holotype—Dwarf chameleon (*Evoluticanda tuberculata*), Madagascar
4.7 in *11,9 cm* Thread snake (*Leptotyphlops bilineata*), West Indies	7 mph *11 km/h* Black mamba (*Dendroaspis polylepsis*) Tanzania April 1906	40 years 3 months, Common Boa (*Boa c. constrictor*) named 'Popeye', Philadelphia Zoo, USA, d. April 1977	(see above) In May 1929 a coiled mass of these sea snakes in the Malacca Straits measured 60 miles *96 km*	Keel-scaled boa (*Casarea dussumieri*) of Round Island, western India Ocean has total population of 58 (1982).
8,5–12,4 mm *0.33–0.48 in* Arrow-poison frog (*Smithnillus limbatus*) Cuba	c. 18 mph *29 km/h* take-off speed by champions in frog leaping contests	c. 55 years Japanese giant salamander (*Andrias japonicus*) 1826–1881, Amsterdam Zoo, Netherlands	Marine toad (*Bufo marinus*) world-wide distribution. Female may ovulate 35,000 eggs in a year	Israel painted frog (*Discoglossus nigriventer*) Lake Huleh—5 since 1940
0.00014 oz *4 mg* Dwarf pygmy goby (*Pandaka pygmaea*) Luzon, Philippines. Males 7,5–9,9 mm *0.28–0.38* long. Up to 7150 per oz.	Est. 68 mph *109 km/h* Sailfish *Istiophorus platypterus*, Long Key, Florida	82 years Lake sturgeon (*Acipenser fulvescens*) based on annuli; Lake Winnebago, Wisconsin, USA, 1951–54	Deep-sea bristlemouth (*Cyclothone elongata*) 3 in *76 mm* long; world-wide	Holotypes (see above)
0.016 in *0,43 mm* male *Patu marplesi*; Western Samoa, 1956	c. 10 mph *16 km/h*, Sun spiders genus solpuga. Middle East and African deserts	c. 28 years female *Mygalomorphae* (tarantula) Mexico c. 1923–1951	Crab spiders (family *Thomisidae*) are common with worldwide distribution	Trapdoor spider (genus *Liphistius*) south-east Asia
0.01 in *0.25 mm*, Water flea (genus *Alonella*) northern Europe	18 mph *28 km/h* Lobsters *H. vulgaris* and *Polinurus vulgaris* when leaping backwards	c. 50 years North American lobster (see left)	650 million tonnes krill (*Euphausia superba*) of the southern oceans. A 10 million tonne swarm was tracked in March 1981	Holotypes (see above)
See above: Smallest in Whole Animal Kingdom	36 mph *58 km/h* Deer bot-fly (*Cephenemyia pratti*)	47 years Splendour beetle (*Buprestidae aurulenta*) Prittlewell, Essex 1936–83	Springtails (Order Collembola) attain densities of 5000 per ft² or 54 000/m²	(Butterfly) Only 2 specimens of the Eight spotted skipper (*Dalla octomaculata*) of Costa Rica, found since 1900. Many holotypes exist
0.02 in *0,5 mm* diameter univalve shell *Ammonicera rota*; British waters	(Of snails) 55 yd *50,3 m* per hour. Common garden snail *Helix aspersa*. Some species 23 in *58 cm* per hour	See above: Longest lived Whole Animal Kingdom	Sea hare (*Tethys californicus*) can lay a million eggs in a day	Prices up to $12,000 have been offered by conchologists for examples of *Conus cypraea*

Longest and shortest gestation periods

The longest of all mammalian gestation periods is that of the Asiatic elephant (*Elephas maximus*), with an average of 609 days or just over 20 months and a maximum of 760 days—more than two and half times that of a human. By 1981 only *c.* 35,000 survived. The gestation period of the American opossum (*Didelphis marsupialis*), also called the Virginian opossum, is normally 12–13 days but may be as short as 8 days.

The gestation periods of the rare Water opossum or Yapok (*Chironectes minimus*) and the American opossum (*Didelphis marsupialis*), also called the Virginian opossum both of central and northern South America and the Eastern native cat (*Dasyurus viverrinus*) of Australia are all normally 12–13 days but they can be as short as 8 days.

Largest litter

The greatest number of young born to a *wild* mammal at a single birth is 31 (30 of which survived) in the case of the Tail-less tenrec (*Tenrec ecaudatus*) found in Madagascar and the Comoro Islands. The normal litter size is 12–15, although females can suckle up to 24.

Youngest breeder

The Streaked tenrec (*Hemicentetes semispinosus*) of Madagascar is weaned after only 5 days, and females can breed 3–4 weeks after birth.

SPEED

Fastest *World*

(*See also Table*) The fastest of all land animals over a short distance (*i.e.* up to 600 yd *549 m*) is the Cheetah or Hunting leopard (*Acinonyx jubatus*) of the open plains of East Africa, Iran, Turkmenia and Afghanistan, with a probable maximum speed of 60–63 mph *96–101 km/h* over suitably level ground. Speeds of 71, 84 and even 90 mph, *114, 135 and 145 km/h* have been claimed for this animal, but these figures must be considered exaggerated. Tests in London in 1937 showed that on an oval greyhound track over 345 yd *316 m* a female cheetah's average speed over three runs was 43.4 mph *69,8 km/h* (*cf.* 43.26 mph *69,6 km/h* for the fastest racehorse), but this specimen was not running flat out and had great difficulty negotiating the bends. The fastest land animal over a sustained distance (*i.e.* 1000 yd *914 m* or more) is the Pronghorn antelope (*Antilocapra americana*) of the western United States. Specimens have been observed to travel at 35 mph for 4 miles *56 km/h for 6 km*, at 42 mph for 1 mile *67 km/h for 1,6 km* and 55 mph for half a mile *88,5 km/h for 0,8 km*.

Fastest *Marine*

The fastest marine mammal is the Killer whale (Orcinus orca). On 12 Oct 1958 a bull measuring an estimated 20–25 ft *6,10–7,62 m* in length was timed at 30 knots (34.5 mph *55,5 km/h*) in the E. Pacific. Speeds of up to 30 knots in short bursts have also been reported for Dall's porpoise (*Phocoenoides dalli*).

Fastest *Britain*

The fastest British land mammal over a sustained distance is the Roe deer (*Capreolus capreolus*), which can cruise at 25–30 mph *40–48 km/h* for more than 20 miles *32 km*, with occasional bursts of up to 40 mph *64 km/h*.

On 19 Oct 1970 a frightened runaway Red deer (*Cervus elaphus*) registered a speed of 42 mph *67,5 km/h* on a police radar trap as it charged through a street in Stalybridge, Greater Manchester.

Slowest and sleepiest

The slowest moving land mammal is the Ai or Three-toed sloth (*Bradypus tridactylus*) of tropical America. The average ground speed is 6–8 ft *1,83–2,44 m* a minute (0.068–0.098 mph *0,109–0,158 km/h*), but in the trees it can 'accelerate' to 15 ft *4,57 m* a minute (0.17 mph *0,272 km/h*) (*cf.* these figures with the 0.03 mph *0,05 km/h* of the common garden snail and the 0.17 mph *0,27 km/h* of the giant tortoise). The slowest swimming marine mammal is the Sea otter (*Enhydra lutris*) which has a top speed of *c.* 6 mph *9,6 km/h*. Some sloths (*Bradypodidae*) sleep up to 20 hr per day.

CARNIVORES

Largest land *World*

The largest living terrestrial carnivore is the Kodiak bear (*Ursus arctos middendorffi*), which is found on Kodiak Island and the adjacent Afognak and Shuyak islands in the Gulf of Alaska, USA. The average adult male has a nose to tail length of 8 ft *2,4 m* (tail about 4 in *10 cm*), stands 52 in *132 cm* at the shoulder and weighs between 1050 and 1175 lb *476–533 kg*. In 1894 a weight of 1656 lb *751 kg* was recorded for a male shot at English Bay, Kodiak Island, whose *stretched* skin measured 13 ft 6 in *4,11 m* from the tip of the nose to the root of the tail. This weight was exceeded by a 'cage-fat' male in the

Cheyenne Mountain Zoological Park, Colorado Springs, Colorado, USA which scaled 1670 lb *757 kg* at the time of its death on 22 Sept 1955. In 1981 an unconfirmed weight of over 2000 lb *907 kg* was reported for a Peninsula giant bear (*Ursus a. gyas*) from Alaska on exhibition at the Space Farms Zoological Park at Beemerville, New Jersey, USA.

Weights in excess of 2000 lb *907 kg* have also been reported for the Polar bear (*Ursus maritimus*), but the average adult male weighs 850–900 lb *386–408 kg* and measures 7¾ ft *2,4 m* nose to tail. In 1960 a Polar bear allegedly weighing 2210 lb *1002 kg* before skinning was shot at the polar entrance to Kotzebue Sound, north-west Alaska. The mounted specimen has a standing height of 11 ft 1¼ in *3,38 m*.

Largest land *Britain*

The largest land carnivore found in Britain is the Badger (*Meles meles*). The average adult boar (sows are slightly smaller) measures 3 ft *90 cm* in length—including a 4 in *10 cm* tail—and weighs 27 lb *12,3 kg* in the early spring and 32 lb *14,5 kg* at the end of the summer when it is in 'grease'. In December 1952 a boar weighing exactly 60 lb *27,2 kg* was killed near Rotherham, South Yorkshire.

Largest marine

The largest toothed mammal ever recorded is the Sperm whale (*Physeter macrocephalus*), also called the Cachalot. The largest accurately measured specimen on record was a 67 ft 11 in *20,7 m* bull captured off the Kurile Islands, north-west Pacific, by a USSR whaling fleet in the summer of 1950 but bulls of much larger size have been reported. The 5 m *16 ft 4¾ in* long lower jaw preserved in the British Museum (Natural History) indicates the Sperm whale can reach 84 ft *25,6 m* in length. Thirteen cachalots have been stranded on British coasts since 1913. The largest, a bull measuring 61 ft 5 in *19 m*, was washed ashore at Birchington, Kent on 18 Oct 1914. Another bull estimated at 65 ft *19,8 m* but badly decomposed was stranded at Derryloughan, Co. Galway, Ireland on 2 Jan 1952.

Smallest

The smallest living member of the order Carnivora is the Least weasel (*Mustela rixosa*), also called the Dwarf weasel, which is circumpolar in distribution. Four races are recognised, the smallest of which is *M. r. pygmaea* of Siberia. Mature specimens have an overall length of 177–207 mm *6.96–8.14 in* and weigh between 35 and 70 g *1¼–2½ oz*.

Largest feline

The largest member of the cat family (Felidae) is the protected long-furred Siberian tiger (*Panthera tigris altaica*), also called the Amur or Manchurian tiger. Adult males average 10 ft 4 in *3,15 m* in length (nose to tip of extended tail), stand 39–42 in *99–107 cm* at the shoulder and weigh about 585 lb *265 kg*. In 1950 a male weighing 384 kg *846.5 lb* was shot in the Sikhote Alin Mts, Maritime Territory, USSR. In November 1967 David H. Hasinger of Philadelphia, USA shot an outsized Indian tiger (*Panthera tigris tigris*) in northern Uttar Pradesh which measured 10 ft 7 in *3,22 m* between pegs (11 ft 1 in *3,37 m* over the curves) and weighed 857 lb *388,7 kg* (*cf.* 9 ft 3 in *2,82 m* and 420 lb *190 kg* for average adult male). It is now on display in the US Museum of Natural History, Smithsonian Institution, Washington, DC.

The largest 'Big Cat' presently in captivity is an adult male Litigon (an Indian lion/Tigon cross) named 'Cubanacan' at Alipore Zoological Gardens, Calcutta, India, who is believed to weigh at least 800 lb *363 kg*. This animal stands 52 in *1,32 m* at the shoulder (*cf.* 44 in *1,11 m* for the lion 'Simba') and measures a record 11 ft 6 in *2,5 m* in total length.

The average adult African lion (*Panthera leo*) measures 9 ft *2,7 m* overall, stands 36–38 in *91–97 cm* at the shoulder and weighs 400–410 lb *181–185 kg*. The heaviest wild specimen on record was one weighing 690 lb *313 kg* shot by Mr Lennox Anderson just outside Hectorspruit in the eastern Transvaal, South Africa in 1936. In July 1970 a weight of 826 lb *375 kg* was reported for a black-maned lion named 'Simba' (b. Dublin Zoo, 1959) at Colchester Zoo, Essex. He died on 16 Jan 1973 at the now defunct Knaresborough Zoo, North Yorkshire, where his stuffed body had been on display.

Smallest feline

The smallest member of the cat family is the Rusty-spotted cat (*Felis rubiginosa*) of southern India and Sri Lanka. The average adult male has an overall length of 25–28 in *64–71 cm* (tail 9–10 in *23–25 cm*) and weighs about 3 lb *1,35 kg*.

PINNIPEDS (Seals, Sea-lions and Walruses)

Largest *World*

The largest of the 34 known species of pinniped is the Southern elephant seal (*Mirounga leonina*), which inhabits the sub-Antarctic islands. Adult bulls average 16½ ft *5 m* in length (tip of inflated snout to the extremities of the outstretched tail flippers), 12 ft *3,7 m* in maximum bodily girth and weigh about 5000 lb (2.18 tons *2268 kg*). The largest accurately measured specimen on record was a bull killed in Possession Bay, South Georgia on 28 Feb 1913 which measured 21 ft 4 in *6,5 m* after flensing (original length about 22½ ft *6,85 m*) and probably weighed at least 4 tons/*tonnes*. There are old records of bulls measuring 25–30 ft *7,62–9,14 m* and even 35 ft *10,66 m* but these figures must be considered exaggerated. Adult cows are much smaller, averaging 3 m *10 ft* in length and weighing about 680 kg *1500 lb*.

Largest *British*

The largest pinniped among British fauna is the Grey seal (*Halichoerus grypus*), also called the Atlantic seal. In one sample taken during the breeding season at the Farne Islands, Northumberland the heaviest (a male) weighed 310 kg *683½ lb* (length from nose to tip of flippers 2,45 m *8 ft 0½ in*.)

Smallest *World*

The smallest pinnipeds are the Ringed seal

Champion sprinter of the Animal Kingdom, the Cheetah or hunting leopard, which can reach a speed of 63 mph *101 km/h* (Artwork: Matthew Hillier, FSIAD)

(*Phoca hispida*) of the Arctic and the closely-related Baikal seal (*P. sibirica*) of Lake Baykal and the Caspian seal (*P. caspica*) of the Caspian Sea, USSR. Adult specimens (males) measure up to 5 ft 6 in *1,67 m* in length and reach a maximum weight of 280 lb *127 kg*. Females are about two-thirds this size.

Smallest *British*
Britain's smallest pinniped is the Common seal (*Phoca vitulina*). Adult males measure 1,5–1,85 m *4 ft 11 in–6 ft 0¼ in* in length and weigh up to 105 kg *231 lb*. Females are four-fifths this size.

Most abundant
The most abundant species of pinniped is the Crabeater seal (*Lobodon carcinophagus*) of Antarctica. In 1978 the total population was believed to be nearly 15,000,000.

Rarest
The last reliable sighting of the Caribbean or West Indian monk seal (*Monachus tropicalis*) was on Serranilla Bank off the coast of Mexico's Yucatan peninsula in 1952. In 1974 two seals were sighted near Cay Verde and Cay Burro, SE Bahamas, but a search in 1979 found nothing. It has been suggested that they may have been Californian sea-lions (*Zalophus californianus*) which had escaped from captivity and have been recorded in the Gulf of Mexico on several occasions.

Fastest and deepest
The highest swimming speed recorded for a pinniped is a 40 km/h *25 mph* short spurt by a Californian sea-lion (*Zalophus californianus*). The fastest-moving pinniped on land is the crabeater seal (*Lobodon carcinophagus*) which has been timed at speeds up to 19 km/h *11.8 mph*. The deepest dive recorded for a pinniped is 630 m *2067 ft* by a female northern elephant seal (*Mirounga anguistirostris*) off Ano Nuevo Point, California, USA on 1 Mar 1983. At this depth the seal withstood a pressure of 6335 kPa *919 lb/in²* of body area. The much larger bulls of this species can probably dive even deeper.

Longest lived
A female Grey seal (*Halichoerus grypus*) shot at Shunni Wick in the Shetland Islands on 23 Apr 1969 was believed to be 'at least 46 years old' based on a count of dentine rings. The captive record is an estimated 43 years for a bull grey seal 'Jacob' held in Skansen Zoo (1901–42).

BATS

Largest *World*
The only flying mammals are bats (order Chiroptera), of which there are about *c.* 950 living species. That with the greatest wing span is the Bismarck flying fox (*Pteropus neohiberni-*

cus) of the Bismarck Archipelago and New Guinea. One specimen preserved in the American Museum of Natural History has a wing spread of 165 cm *5 ft 5 in* but some unmeasured bats probably reach 183 cm *6 ft.*

Largest *Britain*
The largest bat found in Britain (15 species) is the very rare Large mouse-eared bat (*Myotis myotis*). Mature specimens have a wing span of 355–450 mm *13.97–17.71 in* and weigh up to 45 g *1.58 oz* in the case of females).

Smallest *World*
For details of Kitti's hog-nosed bat see p. 24 and 25.

Smallest *Britain*
The smallest native British bat is the Pipistrelle (*Pipistrellus pipistrellus*). Mature specimens have a wing span of 190–250 mm *7.48–9.84 in* and weigh between 3 and 8 g *0.1–0.28 oz.*

Rarest *World*
At least three species of bat are known only from the single holotype. They are: the Small-toothed fruit bat (*Neopteryx frosti*) from Tamalanti, West Celebes (1938/39); *Paracoelops megalotis* from Vinh, Vietnam (1945); and *Latidens salimalii* from the High Wavy Mountains, southern India (1948).

Rarest *Britain*
The rarest bat on the British list is now the Large mouse-eared bat (*Myotis myotis*) of southern England. In February 1986 a single 13 year old male was reported from Sussex but a small colony was then reported near Melbury, Dorset.

Fastest
Because of the great practical difficulties few data on bat speeds have been published. The greatest velocity attributed to a bat is 32 mph *51 km/h* in the case of a Mexican free-tailed bat (*Tadarida brasiliensis*), but this may have been wind-assisted. In one American experiment using an artificial mine tunnel and 17 different kinds of bat, only four of them managed to exceed 13 mph *20,8 km/h* in level flight.

Longest lived
The greatest age reliably reported for a bat is 31 years 5 months for an Indian flying fox (*Pteropus giganteus*) which died at London Zoo on 11 Jan 1979.

Highest detectable pitch
Because of their ultrasonic echolocation bats have the most acute hearing of any terrestrial animal. Vampire bats (*Desmodontidae*) and Fruit bats (*Pteropodidae*) can hear frequencies as high as 120–210 kHz (*cf.* 20 kHz for the adult human limit but 280 kHz for the Common dolphin (*Delphinus delphis*)).

PRIMATES

Largest
The largest living primate is the Mountain gorilla (*Gorilla gorilla berengei*) of the volcanic mountain ranges of W Rwanda, SW Uganda and E Zaïre. The average adult male stands 5 ft 9 in *1,75 m* tall (including crest) and weighs about 430 lb *195 kg*. The greatest height (top of crest to heel) recorded for a gorilla is 195 cm

6 ft 4¾ in for a male collected by a German expedition at Alimbongo, N Kivu on 16 May 1938.

The heaviest gorilla ever kept in captivity was a male of the mountain race named 'N'gagi', who died in San Diego Zoo, California, USA on 12 January 1944 aged 18 years. He scaled 683 lb *310 kg* at his heaviest in 1943, and weighed 636 lb *288 kg* at the time of his death. He was 5 ft 7¾ in *1,72 m* tall and boasted a record chest measurement of 78 in *198 cm.*

Smallest
The smallest known primate is the rare Pen-tailed shrew (*Ptilocercus lowii*) of Malaysia, Sumatra and Borneo. Adult specimens have a total length of 230–330 mm *9–13 in* (head and body 100–140 mm *3.93–5.51in*, tail 130–190 mm *5.1–7.5 in*) and weigh 35–50 g *1.23–1.76 oz*. The Pygmy marmoset (*Cebuella pygmaea*) of the Upper Amazon Basin and the Lesser mouse-lemur (*Microcebus murinus*) of Madagascar are also of comparable length but heavier, adults weighing 50–75 g *1.76–2.64 oz* and 45–80 g *1.58–2.82 oz* respectively.

Rarest
The rarest primate is the Hairy-eared dwarf lemur (*Allocebus trichotis*) of Madagascar which, until fairly recently, was known only from the holotype and three skins. In 1966, however, a live example was found on the east coast near Mananara.

Longest lived
The greatest irrefutable age reported for a non-human primate is *c.* 59 years in the case of a male Orang-utan (*Pongo pygmaeus*) named 'Guas', who died in Philadelphia Zoological Garden, Pennsylvania, USA on 9 Feb 1977. When he was received on 1 May 1931 he was at least 13 years of age. The oldest Chimpanzee (*Pan troglodytes*) on record was a male named 'Jimmy' at Seneca Zoo, Rochester, N.Y., USA, who died on 17 Sept 1985 aged 55 years 6 months. The famous Western Lowland gorilla 'Massa' (b. July 1931) died on 30 Dec 1984 aged 53 years 5 months.

Strength
In 1924 'Boma', a 165 lb *74,80 kg* male chimpanzee at Bronx Zoo, New York, NY, USA recorded a right-handed pull (feet braced) of 847 lb *384 kg* on a dynamometer (*cf.* 210 lb *95 kg* for a man of the same weight). On another occasion an adult female chimpanzee named 'Suzette' (estimated weight 135 lb *61 kg*) at the same zoo registered a right-handed pull of 1260 lb *572 kg* while in a rage. A record from the USA of a 100 lb *45 kg* chimpanzee achieving a two-handed dead lift of 600 lb *272 kg* with ease suggests that a male gorilla could with training raise 2000 lb *907 kg*.

MONKEYS

Largest
The only species of monkey reliably credited with weights of more than 100 lb *45 kg* is the Mandrill (*Mandrillus sphinx*) of equatorial West Africa. The greatest reliable weight recorded is 119 lb *54 kg* for a captive male but an unconfirmed weight of 130 lb *59 kg* has been reported. (Adult females are about half the size of males).

The most devoted couple in the animal world, the female (*left*) and male (*right*) Klipspringer antelope who never stray more than 5 metres from one another

Smallest

The smallest known monkey is the Pygmy marmoset (*Cebuella pygmaea*) of the Upper Amazon Basin (see Primate Smallest).

Oldest

The world's oldest living monkey is a male White-throated capuchin (*Cebus capucinus*) called 'Bobo' owned by Dr Raymond T. Bartus of the American Cyanamid Company in Pearl River, NY, USA, who celebrated his 50th birthday in 1985.

Rarest

The rarest living monkey is the Golden lion tamarin (*Leontopithecus rosalia*) of south-east Brazil. In 1980 there were less than 100 of these animals left, all of them in the São João basin in the State of Rio de Janeiro, and the species could well be extinct in the wild by 1990.

RODENTS

Largest

The world's largest rodent is the Capybara (*Hydrochoerus hydrochaeris*), also called the Carpincho or Water hog, which is found in tropical South America. Mature specimens have a head and body length of 3¼–4½ ft *0,99–1,4 m* and weigh up to 250 lb *113 kg* (cage-fat specimen). Britain's largest rodent is now the Coypu (*Myocastor coypus*) also known as the Nutria, which was introduced from Argentina by East Anglian fur-breeders in 1929. Three years later, the first escapes were recorded and by 1960 at least 200,000 coypus were living in East Anglia. About 80 per cent were killed by the winter of 1963 and a government campaign of extermination has reduced the population to *c.* 4000 animals and a target date of 1990 has been set for the complete eradication of the species in Britain. Adult males measure 30–36 in *76–91 cm* in length (including short tail) and weigh up to 28 lb *13 kg* in the wild state (40 lb *18 kg* in captivity).

Smallest

The smallest known rodent is the Northern Pygmy mouse (*Baiomys taylori*) of central Mexico and southern Arizona and Texas, USA, which measures up to 109 mm *4.3 in* in total length and weighs 7–8 g *0.24–0.28 oz*. Britain's smallest rodent is the Old World harvest mouse (*Micromys minutus*), which measures up to 135 mm *5.3 in* in total length and weighs 7–10 g *0.24–0.35 oz*.

Rarest

The rarest rodent in the world is probably the Little earth hutia (*Capromys sanfelipensis*) of Juan Garcia Cay, an islet off southern Cuba. It has not been recorded since its discovery in 1970.

Longest lived

The greatest reliable age reported for a rodent is 27 years 3 months for a Sumatran crested porcupine (*Hystrix brachyura*) which died in National Zoological Park, Washington DC, USA, on 12 Jan 1965.

Fastest breeder

The female Meadow vole (*Microtus agrestis*) found in Britain, can reproduce from the age of 25 days and have up to 17 litters of 6–8 young in a year.

The world's largest species of monkey, the Mandrill of West Africa which has attained a weight of 119 lb *54 kg* (Zoological Society of London)

INSECTIVORES

Largest

The largest insectivore is the Moon rat (*Echinosorex gymnurus*), also known as Raffles' gymnure, which is found in Burma, Thailand, Malaysia, Sumatra and Borneo. Mature specimens have a head and body length of 265–445 mm *10.43–17.52 in*, a tail measuring 200–210 mm *7.87–8.26 in* and weigh up to 1400 g *3.08 lb*. The European hedgehog (*Erinaceus europaeus*) is much shorter in overall length (196–298 mm *7.71–11.73 in*), but well-fed examples have been known to scale as much as 1900 g *4.19 lb*. Although the much larger Anteaters (family Tachyglossidae and Myrmecophagidae) feed on termites and other soft-bodied insects they are not insectivores, but belong to the orders Monotremata and Edentata, ('without teeth').

Smallest

The smallest insectivore is Savi's white-toothed pygmy shrew (*Suncus etruscus*), also called the Etruscan shrew, which is found along the coast of the northern Mediterranean and southwards to Cape Province, South Africa. Mature specimens have a head and body length of 36–52 mm *1.32–2.04 in*, a tail length of 24–29 mm *0.94–*

1.14 in and weigh between 1,5 and 2,5 g *0.052 and 0.09 oz*.

Longest lived

The greatest reliable age recorded for an insectivore is 16+ years for a Lesser hedgehog-tenrec (*Echinops telfairi*), which was born in Amsterdam Zoo, Netherlands in 1966 and was later sent to Jersey Zoo. It died on 27 Nov 1982.

ANTELOPES

Largest

The largest of all antelopes is the rare Giant eland (*Tragelaphus derbianus*), of West and Central Africa, which may surpass 2000 lb *907 kg*. The Common eland (*T. oryx*) of East

throughout their lives. (*Left:* Anthony Bannister/OXFORD SCIENTIFIC FILMS, *right:* Peter Steyn/ARDEA)

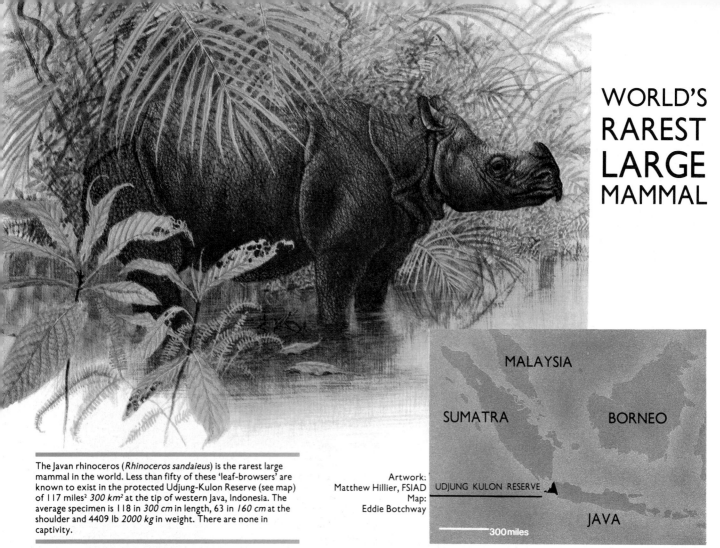

MALAYSIA

SUMATRA

BORNEO

Artwork:
Matthew Hillier, FSIAD
Map:
Eddie Botchway

UDJUNG KULON RESERVE

JAVA

300 miles

The Javan rhinoceros (*Rhinoceros sandaieus*) is the rarest large mammal in the world. Less than fifty of these 'leaf-browsers' are known to exist in the protected Udjung-Kulon Reserve (see map) of 117 miles² *300 km²* at the tip of western Java, Indonesia. The average specimen is 118 in *300 cm* in length, 63 in *160 cm* at the shoulder and 4409 lb *2000 kg* in weight. There are none in captivity.

and South Africa has the same shoulder height of up to 5 ft 10 in *1,78 m* but is not quite so massive, although there is one record of a 5 ft 5 in *1,65 m* bull shot in Nyasaland (now Malawi) in *c.* 1937 which weighed 2078 lb *943 kg*.

Smallest

The smallest known antelope is the Royal antelope (*Neotragus pygmaeus*) of West Africa. Mature specimens measure 10–12 in *25–31 cm* at the shoulder and weigh only 7–8 lb *3–3,6 kg* which is the size of a large Brown hare (*Lepus europaeus*). Salt's dik-dik (*Madoqua saltina*) of NE Ethiopia and Somalia weighs only 5–6 lb *2,2–2,7 kg* when adult, but this species stands about 14 in *35,5 cm* at the withers.

Rarest

The rarest antelope is the Arabian oryx (*Oryx leucoryx*) which until very recently had not been reported in the wild since 1972 when 3 were killed and 4 others captured on the Jiddat-al Harasis plateau, South Oman. On 31 Jan 1982 ten individuals, nine of them born and bred at San Diego Zoo, California, USA, were released into the open desert in South Oman under the protection of a nomadic tribe. Since then 6 young have been born in the wild and by Jan 1985 there were 25 animals in the herd. Another release has also been carried out in Jordan.

Oldest

The greatest reliable age recorded for an antelope is 25 years 4 months for an Addax (*Addax nasomaculatus*) which died in Brookfield Zoo, Chicago, Illinois, USA on 15 Oct 1960.

DEER

Largest

The largest deer is the Alaskan moose (*Alces*

alces gigas). Adult bulls average 6 ft *1,83 m* at the shoulder and weigh *c.* 1100 lb *500 kg*. A bull standing 7 ft 8 in *2,34 m* between pegs and weighing an estimated 1800 lb *816 kg* was shot on the Yukon River in the Yukon Territory, Canada in September 1897. Unconfirmed measurements up to 8 ft 6 in *2,59 m* at the shoulder and estimated weights up to 2600 lb *1180 kg* have been claimed. The record antler span or 'rack' is 78½ in *199 cm*.

Smallest

The smallest true deer (family Cervidae) is the Northern pudu (*Pudu mephistopheles*) of Ecuador and Colombia. Mature specimens measure 13–14 in *33–35 cm* at the shoulder and weigh 16–18 lb *7,2–8,1 kg*. The smallest ruminant is the Lesser Malay chevrotain (*Tragulus javanicus*) of SE Asia, Sumatra and Borneo. Adult specimens measure 8–10 in *20–25 cm* at the shoulder and weigh 6–7 lb, *2,7–3,2 kg*.

Rarest

The rarest deer in the world is Fea's muntjac (*Muntiacus feae*), which until recently, was known only from two specimens collected on the borders of S Burma and W Thailand. In December 1977 a female was received at Dusit Zoo, Bangkok, followed by 2 females in 1981 and 3 males and 3 females from Xizang, Tibet, SW China in Feb 1982–Apr 1983.

Oldest

The greatest reliable age recorded for a deer is 26 years 8 months for a Red deer (*Cervus elaphus scoticus*) which died in Milwaukee Zoo, Wisconsin, USA on 28 June 1954.

MARSUPIALS

Largest

The largest of all marsupials is the Red kangaroo

(*Macropus rufus*) of central, southern and eastern Australia. Adult males stand up to 7 feet *2,13 m* tall, weigh up to 175 lb *79 kg* and measure up to 9 ft 6 in *2,9 m* along the curves of the body.

Smallest

The smallest known marsupial is the very rare Ingram's planigale (*Planigale ingrami = P. subtilissima*), a flat-skulled mouse found only in north-west Australia. Adult males have a head and body length of 45 mm *1.77 in*, a tail length of 50 mm *2 in* and weigh about 4 g *0.14 oz*.

Longest lived

The greatest reliable age recorded for a marsupial is 26 years 0 months 22 days for a Common Wombat (*Vombatus ursinus*) which died in London Zoo on 20 Apr 1906.

Fastest speed, highest and longest jumps

The highest speed recorded for a marsupial is 40 mph *64 km/h* for a young female Eastern grey kangaroo (*Macropus giganteus*). The greatest height cleared by a hunted kangaroo is 10 ft 6 in *3,20 m* over a pile of timber and during the course of a chase in January 1951 a female Red kangaroo made a series of bounds which included one of 42 ft *12,80 m*. There is also an unconfirmed report of an Eastern grey kangaroo jumping nearly 13,5 m *44 ft 8½ in* on the flat.

TUSKS

Longest

The longest recorded elephant tusks (excluding prehistoric examples) are a pair from Zaïre preserved in the National Collection of Heads and Horns kept by the New York Zoological Society in Bronx Park, New York City, NY, USA. The right tusk measures 11 ft 5½ in *3,49 m* along the outside curve and the left 11 ft *3,35 m*.

Their combined weight is 293 lb *133 kg*. A single tusk of 11 ft 6 in *3,5 m* has been reported. Ivory rose from $2.30 to $34/lb in 1970–80.

Heaviest
The heaviest recorded tusks are a pair in the British Museum (Natural History) which were collected from an aged bull shot by an Arab with a muzzle-loading gun at the foot of Mt Kilimanjaro, Kenya in 1897. They originally weighed 240 lb *109 kg* (length 10 ft 2½ in *3,11 m*) and 225 lb *102 kg* (length 10 ft 5½ in *3,18 m*) respectively, giving a total weight of 465 lb *211 kg*, but their combined weight today is 440½ lb *200 kg*.

The greatest weight ever recorded for an elephant tusk is 117 kg *258 lb* for a specimen collected in Benin, West Africa and exhibited at the Paris Exposition in 1900.

HORNS

Longest
The longest horns grown by any living animal are those of the Water buffalo (*Bubalus arnee* = *B. bubalis*) of India. One huge bull shot in 1955 had horns measuring 13 ft 11 in *4,24 m* from tip to tip along the outside curve across the forehead. The longest single horn on record was one measuring 81¼ in *206 cm* on the outside curve found on a specimen of domestic Ankole cattle (Bos taurus) near Lake Ngami, Botswana. The largest spread recorded for a Texas longhorn steer is 10 ft 6 in *3,2 m* owned by the Hermitage Museum, Big Springs, Texas, USA.

HORSES AND PONIES
The world's horse population is estimated to be 75,000,000.

Largest
The largest horse ever recorded was a 19.2 hand (6 ft 6 in *1,98 m*) pure-bred red-roan Belgian (Brabant) stallion named 'Brooklyn Supreme' (1928–48) owned by C. G. Good of Ogden, Iowa, USA which weighed 3200 lb 1.42 tons *1,44 tonnes* at his heaviest in 1938 and had a chest girth of 102 in *259 cm*.

In April 1973 a weight of 3218 lb *1459 kg* was reported for a 18.2 hands (6 ft 2 in *1,88 m*) Belgian (Brabant) mare named 'Wilma du Bos' (foaled 15 July 1966) shortly before she was shipped from Antwerp to her new owner, Mrs Virgie Arden of Reno, Nevada, USA, but at the time she was heavily in foal (maximum girth 12 ft *3,65 m*). When this horse arrived in New York she scaled 3086 lb *1399 kg*, but after she had foaled her weight returned to her normal 2400–2500 lb *1088–1134 kg*. The British weight record is held by the 17.2-hand (5 ft 10 in *1,78 m*) Shire stallion 'Honest Tom 5123' (foaled in 1884), owned by James Forshaw of Littleport, Cambridgeshire, which scaled 2912 lb *1325 kg* in 1891. This poundage may have been exceeded by another huge Shire stallion named 'Great Britain 978', bred by Henry Bultitaft of Ely, Cambridgeshire in 1876, but no weight details are available. In 1888 this horse was sold to Phineas T. Barnum, the American showman, for exhibition purposes.

The heaviest horse living in Britain today is the 17.2 hands (5 ft 10 in *1,78 m*) champion Percheron stallion 'Pinchbeck Union Crest' (foaled 27 Jan 1964), whose weight fluctuates between 2520 lb *1143 kg* and 2632 lb *1194 kg*.

Tallest
The tallest documented horse on record was the Shire gelding named 'Sampson' (later renamed 'Mammoth') bred by Thomas Cleaver of Toddington Mills, Bedfordshire. This horse (foaled in 1846) measured 21.2½ hands (7 ft 2½ in *2,19 m*) in 1850 and was later said to have weighed

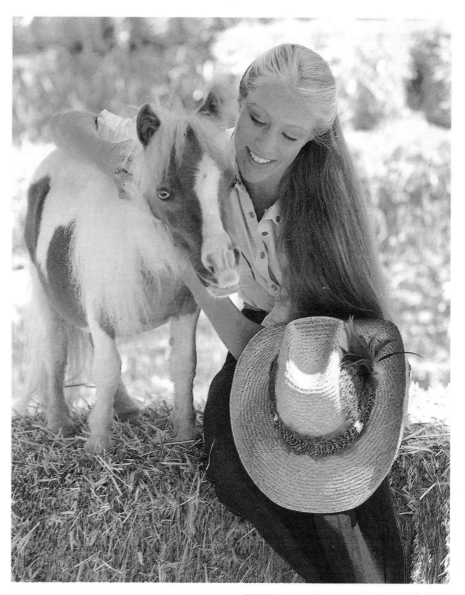

'Smidget', a superlative representative of the world's smallest breed of horse, the Falabella of Argentina. She stands only 21 in *53 cm* tall.

30 cwt 3360 lb *1524 kg*. Britain's tallest living horse is the 19.1½ hand (6 ft 5½ in *1,97 m*) Shire gelding 'Goliath' (foaled 1977) owned by Young & Company's Brewery of Wandsworth, London.

Smallest
The smallest breed of horse is the Falabella of Argentina which was developed over a period of 70 years by inbreeding and crossing a small group of undersized horses originally discovered in the southern part of the country. Most adult specimens stand less than 30 in *76 cm* and average 80–100 lb *36–45 kg*. The smallest mature horse bred by Julio Falabella of Recco de Roca before he died in 1981 was a mare which stood 15 in *38 cm* and weighed 26¼ lb *11,9 kg*. Dr T. H. Hamison of the Circle Veterinary Center, Spartenburg, South Carolina on 30 Nov 1975 certified that the stallion 'Little Pumpkin' (foaled 15 Apr 1973) owned by J. C. Williams Jr. of Della Terra Mini Horse Farm, Inman, South Carolina, USA stood 14 in *35,5 cm* and weighed 20 lb *9,07 kg*.

Oldest
The greatest reliable age recorded for a horse is 62 years in the case of 'Old Billy' (foaled 1760), believed to be a cross between a Cleveland and Eastern blood, who was bred by Mr Edward Robinson of Wild Grave Farm in Woolston, Lancashire. In 1762 or 1763 he was sold to the

Mersey and Irwell Navigation Company and remained with them in a working capacity (*i.e.* marshalling and towing barges) until 1819 when he was retired to a farm at Latchford, near Warrington, where he died on 27 Nov 1822. The skull of this horse is preserved in the Manchester Museum, and his stuffed head, (fitted with false teeth), is now on display in the Bedford Museum. The greatest reliable age recorded for a pony is 54 years for a stallion owned by a farmer in Central France (*fl.* 1919). A moorland pony named 'Joey' owned by June and Rosie Osborne of the Glebe Equestrian Centre, Wickham Bishops, Essex, was still alive and healthy in 1986 aged 42 years. The greatest age recorded for a thoroughbred racehorse is 42 years in the case of the chestnut gelding 'Tango Duke' (foaled 1935), owned by Mrs Carmen J. Koper of Barongarook, Victoria, Australia. The horse died on 25 Jan 1978.

Strongest *draught*
The greatest load ever hauled by a pair of draught-horses was allegedly one weighing 144 short tons (130.9 tonnes) which two Shires with

'Joey', who at 42 years is believed to be the oldest pony in Britain, pictured with his owners June and Rosie Osborne (see p. 31). (Gerald L. Wood FZS)

a combined weight of 3500 lb *1587 kg* pulled on a sledge litter for a distance of 440 yd *402 m* along a frozen road at the Nester Estate near Ewen, Michigan, USA on 26 Feb 1893, but this tonnage was exaggerated. The load, which comprised 50 logs of white pine scaling 36 055 board feet, actually weighed in the region of 53 short tons *42,3 tonnes*. On 23 Apr 1924 a Shire gelding named 'Vulcan', owned by Liverpool Corporation, registered a pull equal to a starting load of 29 tons *29,47 tonnes* on a dynamometer at the British Empire Exhibition at Wembley, and a pair of Shires *easily* pulled a starting load of 50 tons *51 tonnes*, the maximum registered on the dynamometer.

DOGS

Guinness Superlatives has published a more specialist book *The Guinness Book of Pet Records* (£7.95) by Gerald L. Wood.

UK dog population 6,000,000 (1986 estimate) compared with 50,200,000 for the USA).

Largest

The heaviest breed of domestic dog (*Canis familiaris*) is the St Bernard. The heaviest recorded example is 'Benedictine Jr Schwarzwald Hof', owned by Thomas and Anne Irwin of Grand Rapids, Michigan, USA. He was whelped in 1982 and weighed 22 st 2 lb *140,6 kg* on 3 Dec 1984 (height at shoulder 39 in *99 cm*). The heaviest dog ever recorded in Britain was 'Heidan Dark Blue' (whelped 23 Apr 1978) also called 'Jason', a St Bernard owned by Nicol Plummer of Skeffington, Leics. In December 1981 he reached a peak 21 st 10¾ lb *138,23 kg* (shoulder height 34 in *86,3 cm*) but by January 1983 he was down to 15 st *95,25 kg* after being put on a diet. Shortly before his death on 4 Nov 1983 he scaled 14 st 10 lb *93,4 kg*.

Tallest

The tallest breeds of dog are the Great Dane and the Irish wolfhound, both of which can exceed 39 in *99 cm* at the shoulder. In the case of the Great Dane the extreme recorded example was 'Shamgret Danzas' (whelped in 1975), owned by Mr and Mrs Peter Comley of Milton Keynes, Bucks. He stood 41½ in *105,4 cm* or 42 in *106,6 cm* when his hackles went up and weighed up to 17 st *108 kg*. He died on 16 Oct 1984. The Irish wolfhound 'Broadbridge Michael' (1920–29), owned by Mrs Mary Beynon of Sutton-at-Hone, Kent, stood 39½ in *100,3 cm* at the age of 2 years.

Smallest

The world's smallest breeds of dog are the Yorkshire terrier, the Chihuahua and the Toy poodle, *miniature* versions of which have been known to weigh less than 16 oz *453 g* when adult.

The smallest mature dog on record was a

matchbox-sized Yorkshire terrier owned by Mr Arthur F. Marples of Blackburn, Lancs, a former editor of the magazine *Our Dogs*. This tiny atom, which died in 1945 aged nearly two years, stood 2½ in *6,3 cm* at the shoulder and measured 3¾ in *9,5 cm* from the tip of its nose to the root of its tail. Its weight was an incredible 4 oz *113 g!*

Oldest

Most dogs live between 8 and 15 years, and authentic records of dogs living over 20 years are rare. The greatest reliable age recorded for a dog is 29 years 5 months for an Australian cattle-dog named 'Bluey', owned by Mr Les Hall of Rochester, Victoria, Australia. The dog was obtained as a puppy in 1910 and worked among cattle and sheep for nearly 20 years. He was put to sleep on 14 Nov 1939. The British record is 27 years 313 days for a Welsh collie named 'Taffy' owned by Mrs Evelyn Brown of Forge Farm, West Bromwich, W. Midlands. He was whelped on 2 Apr 1952 and died on 9 Feb 1980.

Strength and endurance

The greatest load ever shifted by a dog was 6400½ lb *2905 kg* of railroad steel pulled by a 176 lb *80 kg* St Bernard named 'Ryettes Brandy Bear' at Bothell, Washington, USA on 21 July 1978. The 4-year-old dog, owned by Douglas Alexander of Monroe, Washington, pulled the weight on a four-wheeled carrier across a

One of only 76 Chinooks remaining in the world. None of them live outside the USA. (Barbara A. Martin)

concrete surface for a distance of 15 ft *4,57 m* in less than 90 sec. Ten days earlier the same dog had moved 6600 lb *2993 kg*, but was 5 in *12,7 cm* short of the 15 ft *4,5 m* minimum distance when the 90 seconds were up. The strongest dog in the world in terms of most proportionate weight hauled is 'Barbara-Allen's Dark Hans', a 97 lb *44 kg* Newfoundland, who pulled 5045½ lb *2289 kg* (= 52 lb *23,5 kg* per lb *0,45 kg* body weight) across a cement surface at Bothell on 20 July 1979. The dog, owned by Miss Terri Dickinson of Kenmore, Washington, was only 12 months old when he made the attempt. The record time for the annual 1049 mile *1688 km* sled race from Anchorage to Nome, Alaska (inaugurated 1973) is 11 days 15 hr 6 min by Susan Butcher's team of dogs in the 1986 race.

Rarest

The world's rarest breed of dog is the Chinook, which was developed originally in New Hampshire, USA, in the early 1900's for use as a sled dog. Even at the height of its popularity this breed numbered less than 300, and by 1966 the population had dropped to 125. Twelve years later there were only 28 Chinooks left, but since then the population has more than doubled thanks to the efforts of the Chinook Owners' Association. In September 1985 a litter of six puppies was born in New York, bringing the total to 76, all of them in the USA.

Guide dog

The longest period of *active service* reported for a guide dog is 13 years 2 months in the case of a Labrador-retriever bitch named 'Polly' (whelped 10 Oct 1956), owned by Miss Rose Resnick of San Rafael, California, USA. The dog was put to sleep on 15 Dec 1971.

Largest litter

The largest recorded litter of puppies is one of 23 thrown on 19 June 1944 by 'Lena', an American foxhound bitch owned by Commander W. N. Ely of Ambler, Pennsylvania, USA. All survived. On 6–7 Feb 1975 'Careless Ann', a St Bernard, owned by Robert and Alice Rodden of Lebanon, Missouri, USA also produced a litter of 23, 14 of which survived. The British record is held by 'Settrina Baroness Medina', (d. 1983) an Irish Red Setter owned by Mgr M. J. Buckley, Director of the Wood Hall Centre, Wetherby, West Yorkshire. The bitch gave birth to 22 puppies, 15 of which survived, on 10 Jan 1974.

Most prolific

The greatest sire of all time was the champion greyhound 'Low Pressure', nicknamed 'Timmy', whelped in September 1957 and owned by Mrs Bruna Amhurst of Regent's Park, London. From December 1961 until his death on 27 Nov 1969 he fathered 2414 registered puppies, with at least 600 others unregistered.

Most valuable

In 1907 Mrs Clarice Ashton Cross of Ascot, Berkshire turned down an offer of £32,000 (equivalent to £865,000 today!) from the American financier and industrialist J. Pierpont Morgan for her famous Pekingese 'Ch. Ch'êrh of Alderbourne' (1904-*fl.* 1914). Mr Morgan then came back with an 'open' cheque, but again she turned him down.

The largest legacy devoted to a dog was by Miss Ella Wendel of New York who 'left' her standard poodle named 'Toby' £15 million in 1931.

Highest and longest jump

The canine 'high jump' record for a leap and a scramble over a smooth wooden wall (without any ribs or other aids) is held by a German shepherd dog named 'Max of Pangoula', who scaled an 11 ft 5½ in *3,48 m* wall, at Chikurubi prison's dog training school near Harare, Zimbabwe on 18 Mar 1980. His trainer was Chief Prison Officer Alec Mann. 'Young Sabre', another German shepherd dog, handled by Cpl David Smith scaled a ribbed wall with regulation shallow slats to a height of 11 ft 8 in *3,55 m* at RAF Newton, Nottinghamshire on 17 July 1981. The longest recorded canine long jump was one of 30 ft *9,14 m* by a greyhound named 'Bang' whilst coursing a hare at Brecon Lodge, Gloucestershire in 1849. He cleared a 4 ft 6 in *1,4 m* gate and landed on a hard road.

Ratting

The greatest ratter of all time was a 26 lb *11,8 kg* 'bull and terrier' dog named 'Billy'. During the five-year period 1820–24 he despatched 4000 rats in 17 hr in matches, a remarkable feat considering that he was blind in one eye. His most notable feat was the killing of 100 rats in 5 min 30 sec at the cockpit in Tufton St, Westminster, London on 23 Apr 1825. He died on 23 Feb 1829 aged 13 yrs. James Searle's famous 'bull and terrier' bitch 'Jenny Lind' was another outstanding ratter. On 12 July 1853 she was backed to kill 500 rats in under 3 hr at 'The Beehive' in Old Crosshall St, Liverpool, and completed the job in 1 hr 36 min.

Tracking

The greatest tracking feat on record was performed by a Dobermann Pinscher named 'Sauer', trained by Detective-Sergeant Herbert Kruger. In 1925 he tracked a stock-thief 100 miles *160 km* across the Great Karroo, South Africa by scent alone. In 1923 a collie dog named 'Bobbie', lost by his owners while they were on holiday in Wolcott, Indiana, USA, turned up at the family home in Silverton, Oregon 6 months later, after covering a distance of some 2000 miles *3200 km*. The dog, later identified by householders who had looked over him along the route, had apparently travelled back through the states of Illinois, Iowa, Nebraska and Colorado, before crossing the Rocky Mountains in the depths of winter.

Top show dogs

The greatest number of Challenge Certificates won by a dog is the 78 compiled by the famous chow chow 'Ch. U'Kwong King Solomon' (whelped 21 June 1968). Owned and bred by Mrs Joan Egerton of Bramhall, Cheshire, 'Solly' won his first CC at the Cheshire Agricultural Society Championship Show on 4 June 1969, and his 78th CC was awarded at the City of Birmingham Championship Show on 4 Sept 1976. He died on 3 April 1978. The greatest number of 'Best-in-Show' awards won by any dog in all-breed shows is the 203 compiled by the Scottish terrier bitch 'Ch. Braeburn's Close Encounter' (whelped 22 Oct 1978) up to 10 Mar 1985. She is owned by Sonnie Novick of Plantation Acres, Florida, USA.

Show Largest World

At the Ladies Kennel Association Show (LKA) held at the Birmingham National Exhibition Centre on 14–15 Dec 1984 there were 21,212 entries and a total of 14,611 dogs exhibited.

Top trainer

The most successful dog trainer in the world is Mrs Barbara Woodhouse of Rickmansworth, Hertfordshire, who has trained 19,000 dogs to obey the basic commands during the period 1951 to her retirement in 1985. The fastest dog trainer is Mr Armand Rabuttinio of Aston, Pennsylvania, USA. His highest total for a single day (9 am–6 pm) is 132 dogs at a training marathon held at Upland, Pennsylvania on 12 June 1982.

Drug sniffing

The greatest drug-sniffing dog on record was a golden retriever named 'Trep' (whelped 1969), owned by former policeman Tom Kazo of Dade County, Miami, Florida, USA. During the 5-year period 1973–77 'Agent K9–3', as he was also known, sniffed out $63 million (*then £36 million*) worth of narcotics. His owner said he would retire his pet, who could detect 16 different drugs, when he reached the magic $100 million (*then £57 million*) mark, but it is not known whether Trep achieved this target. The only drug-sniffing dog with a 100 per cent arrest record was a German shepherd of the US Army called 'General'. During the period April 1974 to March 1976 this canine detective and his handler, SP4 Michael R. Harris of the 591st Military Police Company in Fort Bliss, Texas, carried out 220 searches for narcotics, arrested 220 people for possession and uncovered 330 caches of drugs. The German shepherd 'Blue' of the Los Angeles Police Department was reported in January 1986 to have assisted in apprehending 253 suspected felons.

CATS

(*UK cat population 5,300,000 (1985 estimate) compared with 46,300,000 for the USA*)

Largest

In the majority of domestic cats (*Felis catus*), the average weight of the male (tom) at maturity is 6.2 lb *2,81 kg*, compared to 5.4 lb *2,45 kg* for the adult female or queen. Neuters and spays average out somewhat heavier. The heaviest domestic cat on record is a ten year old neutered male tabby named 'Himmy' owned by Thomas Vyse of Redlynch, Cairns, Queensland, Australia. On 14 Jan 1986 he weighed 21,3 kg *46 lb 15¼ oz* (neck 15 in *38,1 cm*, waist 33 in *83,8 cm*, length 38 in *96,52 cm*). The heaviest cat ever recorded in Britain was an 11-year-old male tabby called 'Poppa' owned by Miss Gwladys Cooper of Newport, Gwent, S. Wales. He scaled 44½ lb *20,19 kg* in Nov 1984 and died on 25 June 1985. The largest of the 330 breeds of cat is the ragdoll with males weighing 15–20 lb *6,8–9,07 kg*.

Smallest

The smallest breed of domestic cat is the Singapura or 'Drain Cat' of Singapore. Adult males average 6 lb *2,72 kg* in weight and adult females 4 lb *1,81 kg*. A male Siamese cross named 'Ebony-Eb-Honey Cat' owned by Miss Angelina Johnston of Boise, Idaho, USA tipped the scales at only 1 lb 12 oz *0,79 kg* in February 1984 when aged 23 months.

Oldest

Cats are generally longer-lived than dogs. Information on this subject is often obscured by two or more cats bearing the same nickname in succession. The oldest cat ever recorded was probably the tabby 'Puss', owned by Mrs T. Holway of Clayhidon, Devon who celebrated his 36th birthday on 28 Nov 1939 and died the next day. A more recent and better-documented case was that of the female tabby 'Ma', owned by Mrs Alice St George Moore of Drewsteignton, Devon. This cat was put to sleep on 5 Nov 1957 aged 34.

Largest kindle

The largest litter ever recorded was one of 19 kittens (4 stillborn) delivered by Caesarean section to 'Tarawood Antigone', a 4-year-old brown Burmese, on 7 Aug 1970. Her owner, Mrs Valerie Gane of Church Westcote, Kingham, Oxfordshire, said the result was a mis-mating with a half-Siamese. Of the 15 survivors, 14 were males and one female.

The largest live litter (all of which survived) was one of 14 kittens born in December 1974 to a Persian cat named 'Bluebell', owned by Mrs Elenore Dawson of Wellington, Cape Province, South Africa.

Most prolific

The greatest number of kittens produced by a cat during her breeding life was 420 in the case of a tabby named 'Dusty' (b. 1935) living in Bonham, Texas, USA. She gave birth to her last kindle (a single kitten) on 12 June 1952. The British record is held by another tabby named 'Tippy' of Kingston-upon-Hull, Humberside, who produced her 343rd kitten in June 1933 when aged 21 years.

Richest and most valuable

When Mrs Grace Alma Patterson of Joplin, Missouri, USA died in January 1978 she left her entire estate worth $250,000 (*then £131,000*) to her 18 lb *8,16 kg* white alley cat 'Charlie Chan'. When the cat dies the estate, which includes a three-bedroom house, a 7 acre *2,9 ha* pet cemetery and a collection of valuable antiques, will be auctioned off and the proceeds donated to local and national humane societies. In 1967 Miss Elspeth Sellar of Grafham, Surrey turned down an offer of 2000 guineas (£2100) from an American breeder for her international champion copper-eyed white Persian tom 'Coylum Marcus' (b. 28 Mar 1965) who died on 14 Apr 1978.

Best climber

On 6 Sept 1950 a four-month-old kitten belong-

LARGEST PET LITTERS

Animal/Breed	Date	No.	Owner
CAT *Burmese/Siamese*	7.8.1970	15[1]	Mrs Valerie Gane, Church Westcote, Kingham, Oxfordshire.
DOG *American Foxhound*	19.6.1944	23[2]	Cdr W. N. Ely, Ambler, Pennsylvania, USA.
DOG *St Bernard*	6/7.2.1975	23[3]	R. and A. Rodden, Lebanon, Missouri, USA.
RABBIT *New Zealand White*	1978	24	Joseph Filek, Sydney, Cape Breton, Nova Scotia, Canada.
GUINEA PIG (CAVY)	1972	12	Laboratory Specimen.
HAMSTER *Golden*	28.2.1974	26[4]	L. and S. Miller, Baton Rouge, Louisiana, USA.
MOUSE *House*	12.2.1982	34[5]	Marion Ogilvie, Blackpool, Lancs.
GERBIL *Mongolian*	5.1983	14	Sharon Kirkman, Bulwell, Nottingham.
GERBIL *Mongolian*	1960's	15[6]	George Meares, geneticist-owner gerbil breeding farm, St Petersburg, Florida, USA.

[1] 4 still born [2] all survived [3] 14 survived [4] 18 killed by mother [5] 33 survived [6] Uses special food formula

CAGED PET LONGEVITY The greatest recorded ages for commonly kept pets

Animal/Species	Name, Owner etc.	Years	Months
HAMSTER Golden	...Reported 1984 Cambridge, England	19	—
RABBIT	...Flopsy caught 6 Aug 1964 d. 29 June 1983 (owner Mrs. L. B. Walker) Longford, Tasmania	18	10¾
GUINEA PIG	...Snowball Died: 14 Feb 1979 (owner, M. A. Wall) Bingham, Notts.	14	10½
GERBIL Mongolian	...Sahara fl. May 1981 (owner Aaron Milstone) Lathrap Village, Michigan, USA	8	1
MOUSE House	...Fritzy fl. Apr 1985 (owner West House School, Edgbaston, Birmingham)	7	6
RAT Common	...Died: c. 1924 Philadelphia, Pennsylvania, USA.	5	8

ing to Josephine Aufdenblatten of Geneva, Switzerland, followed a group of climbers up to the top of the 14,691 ft *4,478 m* Matterhorn in the Alps.

Mousing champion
The greatest mouser on record is a female tortoiseshell named 'Towser' (b. 21 Apr 1963) owned by Glenturret Distillery Ltd near Crieff, Tayside, Scotland who notched up her 25,716th kill by her 23rd birthday. She averages 3 mice per day.

RABBITS AND HARES

Largest
The largest breed of domestic rabbit (*Oryctolagus cuniculus*) is the Flemish Giant. Adults weigh 7–8,5 kg *15.4–18.7 lb* (average toe to toe length when fully stretched 36 in *91 cm*), but weights up to 25 lb *11,3 kg* have been reliably reported

for this breed. The largest British breed is the Giant Rabbit (British). Adults regularly weigh 12–15 lb *5,4–6,8 kg*, and examples over 20 lb *9 kg* have been recorded. In April 1980 a five month old French lop doe weighing 12 kg *26.45 lb* was exhibited at the Reus Fair, NE Spain.

The heaviest recorded wild rabbit (av. weight 3½ lb *1,58 kg*) was one of 8 lb 4 oz *3,74 kg*, killed by Norman Wilkie of Markinch, Fife, Scotland while ferreting on 20 Nov 1982.

Smallest
The smallest breeds of domestic rabbit are the Netherland Dwarf and the Polish, both of which have a weight range of 2–2½ lb *0,9–1,13 kg* when fully grown. In 1975 Jacques Bouloc of Coulommiere, France, announced a new cross of the above breeds which weighed 396 g *14 oz*.

Most prolific
The most prolific domestic breeds are the New Zealand white and the Californian. Does produce 5–6 litters a year, each containing 8–12 kittens during their breeding life (*cf.* five litters and three to seven young for the wild rabbit).

Longest ears
The longest ears are found in the Lop family where measurements exceeding 30 in *76 cm* have been recorded for the French variety.

Largest Hare
In November 1956 a Brown hare (*Lepus europaeus*) weighing 15 lb 1 oz *6,83 kg* was shot near Welford, Northamptonshire. The average adult weight is 8 lb *3,62 kg*

2. BIRDS

Aves

Largest *Ratite*
The largest living bird is the North African ostrich (*Struthio camelus camelus*), which is found in reduced numbers south of the Atlas Mountains from Upper Senegal and Niger across to the Sudan and central Ethiopia (*see Table* pp. 24–25).

The red-billed quelea (shown here life-size) is not only the commonest wild bird in the world but also the most destructive, posing a serious threat to the growers of cereal crops in many African countries. It has been estimated that the population of this 20 g *0.70 oz* bird that breeds three or four times a year and whose eggs hatch in 12 days, exceeds 10,000 million.

Largest *Carinate*

The heaviest flying bird or carinate is the Kori bustard or Paauw (*Otis kori*) of East and South Africa. Weights up to 40 lb *18 kg* have been reliably reported for cock birds shot in South Africa. The Mute swan (*Cygnus olor*), which is resident in Britain, can also reach 40 lb *18 kg* on occasion, and there is a record from Poland of a cob weighing 22,5 kg *49.5 lb* which could not fly. The heaviest bird of prey is the Andean condor (*Vultur gryphus*), adult males averaging 20–25 lb *9,09–11,3 kg*. A weight of 31 lb *14,1 kg* has been claimed for an outsize male Californian condor (*Gymnogyps californianus*) now preserved in the California Academy of Sciences, Los Angeles. This species is appreciably smaller than the Andean condor and rarely exceeds 23 lb *10,4 kg*.

Largest wing span

The Wandering albatross (*Diomedea exulans*) of the southern oceans has the largest wing span of any living bird (*see Table*). The only other bird reliably credited with a wingspread in excess of 11 ft *3,35 m* is the vulture-like Marabou stork (*Leptoptilus crumeniferus*) of Africa. In 1934 a freakish measurement of 13 ft 4 in *4,06 m* was reported for a male shot in Central Africa, but this species rarely exceeds 9 ft *2,43 m*.

Smallest *World*

The smallest bird in the world is the male Bee hummingbird (*Mellisuga helenae*) of Cuba and the Isle of Pines (*see Table*). The smallest bird of prey is the 35 g *1.23 g* White-fronted falconet (*Microhierax latifrons*) of NW Borneo which is sparrow-sized. The smallest sea bird is the Least storm petrel (*Halocyptena microsoma*), which breeds on many of the small islands in the Gulf of California, NW Mexico. Adult specimens average 140 mm *5½ in* in total length and weigh *c.* 28 g *1 oz*.

(Artwork: Matthew Hillier FSIAD)

Smallest *Great Britain*

The smallest regularly-breeding British bird is the Goldcrest (*Regulus regulus*), also known as the Golden crested wren or Kinglet. Adult specimens measure 90 mm *3.5 in* total length and weigh between 3,8 and 4,5 g *0.108* and *0.127 oz*.

Most abundant *Wild*

The most abundant species of wild bird is the Red-billed quelea (*Quelea quelea*) (*see Table*). The most abundant sea bird is probably Wilson's storm-petrel (*Oceanites oceanicus*) of the Antarctic. No population estimates have been published, but the number must run into hundreds of millions. Britain's most abundant sea-bird is the Common guillemot (*Uria aalge*) with an estimated 577,000 breeding pairs in 1969–70.

Most abundant *Domestic*

The most abundant species of domesticated bird is the Chicken, the domesticated form of the wild Red jungle fowl (*Gallus gallus*) of south-east Asia. In 1984 there were believed to be about 4,500,000,000 in the world, or about one chicken for every member of the human race. The fowl stock in Britain was estimated at 120,826,000 in 1984, producing 469,150,000 chicks annually.

Most abundant *Great Britain*

The commonest nesting birds found in Great Britain are the House sparrow (*Passer domesticus*), the starling (*Sturnus vulgaris*) and the chaffinch (*Fringilla coelebs*), all of which have a peak breeding population in excess of 5 million pairs. Between 1964 and 1974 the population of the Wren (*Troglodytes troglodytes*) increased tenfold after a series of mild winters, and at the end of this period there were an estimated 10 million pairs. This bird, however, is severely affected by very cold weather and suffered heavy losses during bad winters of 1981–2 and 1985–6. It was estimated in 1984 that 250,000 pigeon fanciers owned an average of 40 racing pigeons per loft, making a population of *c.* 10 million in Great Britain.

Rarest *World*

Because of the practical difficulties involved in assessing bird populations in the wild, it is virtually impossible to establish the identity of the world's rarest living bird (*see Table*). The strongest contenders must be the Ooaa (*Moho braccatus*) of Kauai, Hawaiian Islands, which was down to a single pair in 1980 and the protected Dusky seaside sparrow (*Ammospiza nigrescens*) of Disneyworld's Discovery Island in Florida, USA with only 2 males in 1985. The world's rarest bird of prey is the Californian vulture (*Vultur californianus*). In Jan 1986 there were only 7 in the wild, plus 20 in captivity.

Rarest *Great Britain*

According to the British Ornithologists' Union there are more than 40 species of birds which have been recorded only once in the British Isles—most of them since the end of the Second World War in 1945. That which has not recurred for the longest period is the Black-capped petrel (*Pterodroma hasitata*), of the West Indies. A specimen was caught alive on a heath at Southacre, near Swaffham, Norfolk in March or April 1850. On 28–29 May 1979 an Aleutian tern (*Sterna aleutica*) was sighted on the Farne Islands, Northumberland. This bird breeds on the coasts of Alaska and eastern Siberia, and until then had never been recorded outside the N. Pacific. The most tenuously established British bird is the Snowy owl (*Nyctea scandiaca*). During the period 1967–75 one pair bred regularly on Fetlar, Shetland Isles and reared a total of 21 young, but soon afterwards the old male took off for an unknown destination, having driven off all the young males, and left the females without a mate. On 19–22 April 1979 an adult male was seen on Fair Isle some 80 miles *129 km* further south, but it did not find its way to Fetlar. Since 1983 seven females have been sighted, but no males were in evidence. In 1916, an English vicar stole the eggs of the last White-tailed sea eagle (*Haliaeetus albicilla*) on

Formerly a regular visitor to the Shetlands, Orkneys and Hebrides, only 31 Snowy owls have been sighted since 1967. (Brian Hawkes/Aquila).

Skye. Ten years after their re-introduction from Norway, the first hatchlings in Scotland for 69 years appeared in June 1985.

Fastest and slowest flying

The fastest flying bird in level flight is the White-throated spine-tailed swift (*Hirundapus caudacutus*) (*see Table*). The slowest flying bird is the American woodcock (*Scolopax minor*), which has been timed at 5 mph *8 km/h* without sinking.

The bird which presents the hunter with the greatest difficulty is the Red-breasted merganser (*Mergus serrator*). On 29 May 1960 a specimen flushed from the Kukpuk River, Cape Thompson, northern Alaska, USA by a light aircraft recorded an air speed of 80 mph *128 km/h* in level flight for nearly 13 sec before turning aside. The Spur-winged goose (*Plectropterus gambiensis*) has been timed at 88 mph *142 km/h* in an escape dive.

Fastest and slowest wing beat

The fastest recorded wing beat of any bird is

that of the Horned sungem (*Heliactin cornuta*) of tropical South America with a rate of 90 beats a second. Large vultures (Vulturidae) sometimes exhibit a flapping rate as low as one beat per sec, and condors can cruise on air currents for up to 60 miles *96 km* without beating their wings once.

Longest lived

The greatest irrefutable age reported for any bird is 80 + years (*see Table*). The British record is 68 + years in the case of a female European eagle-owl (*Bubo bubo*) which was still alive in 1899. In 1964 the death was reported of a male Andean Condor called 'Kuzya' at Moscow Zoo, USSR aged 70 + years. This bird was already fully grown when it was received in 1892.

Eggs *Largest*

The largest egg produced by any living bird is that of the ostrich (*Struthio camelus*). The average example measures 6–8 in *15–20 cm* in length, 4–6 in *10–15 cm* in diameter and weighs 3.63–3.88 lb *1,65–1,78 kg* (equal to the volume of two dozen hen's eggs). It requires about 40 min for boiling. The shell, though $\frac{1}{16}$ in *1,5 mm* thick, can support the weight of a 20 st *127 kg* man. The largest egg laid by any bird on the British list is that of the Mute swan (*Cygnus olor*), which measures 4.3–4.9 in *109–124 mm* in length and between 2.8 and 3.1 in *71–78,5 mm* in diameter. The weight is 12–13 oz *340–368 g*.

Eggs *Smallest*

The smallest egg laid by any bird is that of the Vervain hummingbird (*Mellisuga minima*) of Jamaica. Two specimens measuring less than 10 mm *0.39 in* in length weighed 0,365 g *0.0128 oz* and 0,375 g *0.0132 oz* respectively (*cf* 0,5 g *0.017 oz* for the Bee hummingbird). The smallest egg laid by a bird on the British list is that of the Goldcrest (*Regulus regulus*), which measures 12,2–14,5 mm *0.48–0.57 in* in length and between 9,4 and 9,9 mm *0.37 and 0.39 in* in diameter with a weight of 0,6 g *0.021 oz*. Eggs emitted from the oviduct before maturity, known as 'sports', are not reckoned to be of significance in discussion of relative sizes.

Incubation *Longest and shortest*

The longest normal incubation period is that of the Wandering albatross (*Diomedea exulans*), with a normal range of 75–82 days. There is an isolated case of an egg of the Mallee fowl (*Leipoa ocellata*) of Australia taking 90 days to hatch against its normal incubation of 62 days. The shortest incubation period is the 10 days of the Great spotted woodpecker (*Dendrocopus major*) and the Blackbilled cuckoo (*Coccyzus erythropthalmus*). The idlest of cock birds include hummingbirds (family Trochilidae), Eider duck (*Somateria mollissima*) and Golden pheasant (*Chrysolophus pictus*) among whom the hen bird does 100 per cent of the incubation, whereas the female Common kiwi (*Apteryx australis*) leaves this to the male for 75–80 days.

Longest flights

The greatest distance covered by a ringed bird is 14,000 miles *22 530 km* by an Arctic tern (*Sterna paradisea*), which was banded as a nestling on 5 July 1955 in the Kandalaksha Sanctuary on the White Sea coast and was captured alive by a fisherman 8 miles *13 km* south of Fremantle, Western Australia on 16 May 1956. The bird had flown south via the Atlantic Ocean and then circled Africa before crossing the Indian Ocean. It did not survive to make the return journey.

Highest flying

The highest acceptable altitude recorded for a bird is just over 27,000 ft *8230 m* for 30 Whooper swans (*Cygnus cygnus*) flying in from Iceland to winter at Lough Foyle, Northern Ireland. They were spotted by an airline pilot over the Outer Hebrides on 9 Dec 1967, and the height was also confirmed by air traffic control in Northern Ireland after the swans had been picked up on radar.

Most airborne

The most aerial of all birds is the Sooty tern (*Sterna fuscata*) which, after leaving the nesting grounds, remains continuously aloft for 3 or 4 years before returning to the breeding grounds. The most aerial land bird is the Common swift (*Apus apus*) which remains 'airborne' for 2–3 years until it is mature enough to breed.

Fastest swimmer

The fastest swimming bird is the Gentoo penguin (*Pygoscelis papua*) which has a maximum burst speed of *c.* 17 mph *27,4 km/h*. The deepest diving bird is the Emperor penguin (*Aptenodytes forsteri*) of the Antarctic which can reach a depth of 265 m *870 ft* and remain submerged for up to 18 min.

Vision *Most acute*

Birds of prey (Falconiformes) have the keenest eyesight in the avian world, and their visual acuity is at least 8–10 times stronger than that of human vision. The Golden eagle (*Aquila chrysaetos*) can detect an 18 in *46 cm* long hare at a range of 2 miles *3,2 km* in good light and against a contrasting background, and a Peregrine falcon (*Falco peregrinus*) can spot a pigeon at a range of over 5 miles *8 km*.

g force *Highest*

Recent American scientific experiments have revealed that the beak of the Red-headed woodpecker (*Melanerpes erythrocephalus*) hits the bark of a tree with an impact velocity of 13 mph *20,9 km/h*. This means that when the head snaps back the brain is subject to a deceleration of about 10 g.

Feathers *Longest*

The longest feathers grown by any bird are those of the Phoenix fowl or Onagadori (a strain of Red junglefowl *Gallus gallus*) which has been bred in south-western Japan since the mid 17th century. In 1972 a tail covert measuring 10,6 m *34 ft 9¼ in* was reported for a rooster owned by Masasha Kubota of Kochi, Shikoku. Among

flying birds the two central pairs of tail feathers of Reeve's pheasant (*Syrmaticus reevesi*) of central and northern China can exceed 8 ft *2,43 m*. They serve as an escape brake.

Feathers *Most*

In a series of 'feather counts' on various species of bird a Whistling swan (*Cygnus columbianus*) was found to have 25,216 feathers, 20,177 of which were on the head and neck. The Ruby-throated hummingbird (*Archilochus colubris*) has only 940.

Longest bill

The longest bill grown by any bird in proportion to its body size is that of the male Toco toucan (*Ramphastos toco*) of eastern S. America. It accounts for 20 cm *7.87 in* of the bird's total length of 66 cm *25.98 in*.

Earliest and latest cuckoo

It is unlikely that the Cuckoo (*Culculus canorus*) has ever been *heard and seen* in Britain earlier than 2 Mar, on which date one was observed under acceptable conditions by Mr William A. Haynes of Trinder Road, Wantage, Oxfordshire in 1972. The two latest dates are 16 Dec 1912 at Anstey's Cove, Torquay, Devon and 26 Dec 1897 or 1898 in Cheshire.

Champion bird-spotter

The world's leading bird-spotter or 'twitcher' is Norman Chesterfield (b. 8 Mar 1913) of Wheatley, Ontario, Canada. By 23 Apr 1986 he had logged exactly 6220 of the 9016 known species. The British life list record is 450 by Ron Johns of Slough, Bucks, and the British year list record is 329 by Stephen Webb of Chelmsford, Essex in 1980 who drove 40,000 miles *64 000 km* and spent about 150 days in the field to achieve his record. The greatest number of species spotted in a 24 hr period is 290 by three Kenyan birdwatchers on 23–24 Nov 1984.

Nests *Largest*

The largest bird's nest on record is one 9½ ft *2,9 m* wide and 20 ft *6 m* deep built by a pair of Bald eagles (*Haliaeetus leucocephalus*) and possibly their successors near St Petersburg, Florida, USA reported in 1963. It weighed more than 3 tons/*tonnes*. The Golden eagle (*Aquila chrysaetos*) also constructs huge nests, and one 15 ft *4,57 m* deep was reported from Scotland in 1954. It had been in use for 45 years. The incubation mounds built by the Mallee fowl (*Leipoa ocellata*) of Australia are much larger, having been measured up to 15 ft *4,57 m* in height and 35 ft *10,6 m* across. The nest site may involve the mounding of matter weighing 300 tonnes *295 tons*.

DOMESTICATED BIRDS

Chicken *Heaviest*

The heaviest breed of chicken is the White Sully which Mr Grant Sullens of West Point, California, USA developed over a period of 7 years by crossing and re-crossing from large Rhode Island Reds with other varieties. One monstrous rooster named 'Weirdo' reportedly weighed 22 lb *10 kg* in January 1973, and was so aggressive that he had already killed two cats and crippled a dog which came too close. The largest chicken reported in Britain was a 17 lb 3 oz *7,78 kg* Cobb capon bred by Mr Henry Ransom of Brancaster Staithe, Dorset and weighed in December 1982.

Chicken flying *for distance*
The record distance flown by a chicken is 310 ft 6 in *94,64 m* by *Shorisha* owned by Morimitzu Meura at Hammatzu, Japan on 8 Mar 1981. Hens are better fliers than cocks.

Turkey *Heaviest*
The greatest dressed weight recorded for a turkey (*Meleagris gallapavo*) is 78 lb 14¾ oz *35,8 kg* for a stag reared by Dale Turkeys of Caynham, Shropshire. It won the annual 'heaviest turkey' competition in London on 15 Dec 1982. Turkeys were introduced into Britain *via* Spain from Mexico in 1549.

Turkey *Most expensive*
The highest price reached at auction (auctioneer Christopher Norton) for a turkey was the £3500 paid by Ray Argrave of West Butchers, for a 77 lb 6¼ oz *35,1 kg* stag at the Annual British Turkey Federation/Nitrovit Ltd Heaviest Turkey Competition at Smithfield Market, London on 9 Dec 1985.

Longest lived
The longest lived domesticated bird (excluding the ostrich) is the domestic goose (*Anser anser domesticus*) which normally lives about 25 years. On 16 Dec 1976 a gander named 'George' owned by Mrs Florence Hull of Thornton, Lancashire, died aged 49 years 8 months. He was hatched out in April 1927. The longest lived small cagebird is the canary (*Serinus canaria*). The oldest example on record was a 34-year-old cock bird named 'Joey' owned by Mrs K. Ross of Hull. The bird was purchased in Calabar, Nigeria in 1941 and died on 8 Apr 1975. The oldest budgerigar (*Melopsittacus undulatus*) was a hen bird named 'Charlie' owned by Miss J. Dinsey of Stonebridge, London. She died on 20 June 1977 aged 29 years 2 months.

Most talkative
The world's most talkative bird is a female African grey parrot (*Psittacus erythacus*) named 'Prudle', owned by Mrs Lyn Logue of Seaford, Sussex, which won the 'Best talking parrot-like bird' title at the National Cage and Aviary Bird Show in London each December for 12 consecutive years (1965–76). Prudle, who has a vocabulary of nearly 800 words, was taken from a nest at Jinja, Uganda in 1958. She retired undefeated.

3. REPTILES

Reptilia

(Crocodiles, snakes, turtles, tortoises and lizards.)

Largest and heaviest
The largest reptile in the world is the Estuarine or Salt-water crocodile (*Crocodylus porosus*) of south-east Asia, northern Australia, New Guinea, the Malay archipelago and the Solomon Islands (*see Table* pp. 24–25).

Smallest
The smallest known species of reptile is believed to be *Sphaerodactylus parthenopion*, a tiny gecko found only on the island of Virgin Gorda, one of the British Virgin Islands, in the West Indies (*see Table*). It is possible that another gecko, *Sphaerodactylus elasmorhynchus*, may be even smaller. The only known specimen was an apparently mature female with a snout-vent length of 17 mm *0.67 in* and a tail the same measurement found on 15 March 1966 among the roots of a tree in the western part of the Massif de la Hotte in Haiti.

The smallest reptile found in Britain is the Viviparous or Common lizard (*Lacerta vivipara*). Adult specimens have an overall length of 118–178 mm *4.64–7.01 in* weighing 8–15 g *0.28–0.53 oz*.

Fastest
The highest speed measured for any reptile on land is 18 mph *29 km/h* for a Six-lined racerunner (*Cnemidophorus sexlineatus*) (*see Table*). The highest speed claimed for any reptile in water is 22 mph *35 km/h* by a frightened Pacific leatherback turtle (see below).

Lizards *Largest*
The largest of all lizards is the Komodo monitor or Ora (*Varanus komodoensis*), a dragonlike reptile found on the Indonesian islands of Komodo, Rintja, Padar and Flores. Adult males average 225 cm *7 ft 5 in* in length and weigh about 59 kg *130 lb*. Lengths up to 30 ft *9,14 m* (*sic*) have been claimed for this species, but the largest specimen to be accurately measured was a male presented to an American zoologist in 1928 by the Sultan of Bima which taped 3,05 m *10 ft 0.8 in*. In 1937 this animal was put on display in St Louis Zoological Gardens, Missouri, USA for a short period. It then measured 10 ft 2 in *3,10 m* in length and weighed 365 lb *166 kg*. The longest lizard in the world is the slender Salvadori monitor (*Varanus salvadori*) of New Guinea which has been reliably measured up to 15 ft 7 in *4,75 m*.

Lizards *Oldest*
The greatest age recorded for a lizard is more than 54 years for a male Slow worm (*Anguis fragilis*) kept in the Zoological Museum in Copenhagen, Denmark from 1892 until 1946.

Chelonians *Largest*
The largest living chelonian is the Pacific leatherback turtle (*Dermochelys coriacea schlegelii*). The greatest weight reliably recorded is 1908 lb *865 kg* for a male captured off Monterey, California, USA on 29 Aug 1961 measuring 8 ft 4 in *2,54 m* overall. The largest chelonian found in British waters is the Atlantic leatherback turtle (*Dermochelys coriacea coriacea*). A male which drowned off Crail, Fifeshire, Scotland measured 6 ft 4 in *1,93 m* in total length and weighed 772 lb *350 kg*.

The largest living tortoise is *Geochelone gigantea* of the Indian Ocean islands of Aldabra, Mauritius, and the Seychelles (introduced 1874). A male named 'Marmaduke' received at London Zoo in 1951 recorded a peak weight of 616 lb *279 kg* before his death on 27 Jan 1963.

Chelonians *Longest lived*
The greatest authentic age recorded for a tortoise is 152+ years for a male Marion's tortoise (*Testudo sumeirii*) brought from the Seychelles to Mauritius in 1766 by the Chevalier de Fresne, who presented it to the Port Louis army garrison. This specimen (it went blind in 1908) was accidentally killed in 1918. When the famous Royal Tongan tortoise 'Tu'malilia' (believed to be a specimen of *Testudo radiata*) died on 19 May 1966 it was reputed to be over 200 years old, having been presented to the then King of Tonga by Captain James Cook (1728–79) on 22 Oct 1773, but this record may well have been conflated between two (or more) overlapping residents. The greatest proven age of a continuously observed tortoise is 116+ years for a Mediterranean spur-thighed tortoise (*Testudo graeca*) (*see Table*).

Chelonians *Slowest moving*
In a recent 'speed' test carried out in the Seychelles a male giant tortoise (*Geochelone gigantea*) could only cover 5 yd *4,57 m* in 43.5 sec (0.23 mph *0,37 km/h*) despite the enticement of a female. The National Tortoise Championship record is 18 ft *5,48 m* up a 1:12 gradient in 43.7 sec, 0.28 mph *0,45 km/h* by 'Charlie' at Tickhill, South Yorkshire on 2 July 1977.

SNAKES

Longest *World*
The longest of all snakes (average adult length) is the Reticulated python (*Python reticulatus*) of south-east Asia, Indonesia and the Philippines (*see Table*).

Longest *In captivity*
The longest (and heaviest) snake ever held in captivity was a female Reticulated python (*Python reticulatus*) named 'Colossus' who died in Highland Park Zoo, Pennsylvania, USA on 15 Apr 1963. She measured 28 ft 6 in *8,68 m* in length, and scaled 320 lb *145 kg* at her heaviest. Another female reticulated python 'Cassius', owned by Adrian Nyoka of the now defunct Knaresborough Zoo, N. Yorkshire measured about 25 ft 6 in *7,77 m* at the time of her death on 3 Apr 1980. She yielded a 29 ft *8,84 m* skin.

Longest *British*
The longest snake found in Britian is the Grass snake (*Natrix natrix*), which is found throughout southern England, parts of Wales and in Dumfries and Galloway, Scotland. The longest accurately measured specimen was probably a female killed in South Wales in 1887 which measured 1775 mm *5 ft 10 in*.

Shortest
The shortest known snake is the Thread snake *Leptotyphlops bilineata*, which is found on the islands of Martinique, Barbados and St Lucia in the West Indies (*see Table*).

The skin of a Reticulated python, the longest of all snakes which can measure 10 m *32 ft 9 in* (David Roberts).

Heaviest

The heaviest snake is the Anaconda (*Eunectes murinus*) (*see Table*). The heaviest venomous snake is the Eastern diamond-back rattlesnake (*Crotalus adamanteus*) of the south-eastern United States. One specimen measuring 7 ft 9 in *2,36 m* in length weighed 34 lb *15 kg*. Less reliable lengths up to 8 ft 9 in *2,66 m* and weights up to 40 lb *18 kg* have been reported. In February 1973 a posthumous weight of 28 lb *12,75 kg* was reported for a 14 ft 5 in *4,39 m* long King cobra (*Ophiophagus hannah*) at New York Zoological Park (Bronx Zoo).

Oldest

The greatest irrefutable age recorded for a snake is 40 years 3 months and 14 days for a male Common boa (*Boa constrictor constrictor*) (*see Table*).

Fastest moving

The fastest moving land snake is probably the slender Black mamba (*Dendroaspis polylepis*) (*see Table*). A speed of 10–12 mph *16–19 km/h* may be possible for short bursts over level ground. The British grass snake (*Natrix natrix*) has a maximum speed of 4.2 mph *6,8 km/h*.

Most venomous *World*

The world's most venomous snake is the sea snake *Hydrophis belcheri* which has a venom one hundred times as toxic as that of the Australian taipan (*Oxyuranus scutellatus*). The snake abounds round Ashmore Reef in the Timor Sea, off the coast of North West Australia. The most venomous land snake is the 2 m *6 ft 6 in* long Inland taipan (*Oxyuranus microlepidotus*) of the Diamantina River and Cooper's Creek drainage bases in Channel County, Queensland which has a venom nine times as toxic as that of the Tiger snake (*Notechis scutatus*) of South Australia and Tasmania. One specimen yielded 110 mg *0.00385 oz* of venom after milking, a quantity sufficient to kill 218,000 mice. On the Amami Islands in the Ryukyu group, SW Japan there is an incidence of one snakebite case per 500 people per annum from the aggressive Okinawa habu (*Trimeresurus flavavirdes*). With modern treatments mortality is now only 3 per cent.

Most venomous *Britain*

The only venomous snake in Britain is the adder (*Vipera berus*). Since 1890 ten people have died after being bitten by this snake, including six children. The most recently recorded death was on 1 July 1975 when a 5-year-old was bitten at Callander, Central Scotland and died 44 hr later. The longest-recorded specimen was a female measuring 43½ in *110,5 cm* which was killed by Graham Perkins of Paradise Farm, Pontrilas, Hereford & Worcester in August 1977.

Venomous *Longest and Shortest*

The longest venomous snake in the world is the King cobra (*Ophiophagus hannah*) (*see Table*). The shortest venomous snake is the Spotted dwarf adder (*Bitis paucisquamata*) of Little Namaqualand, South West Africa, with adults averaging 9 in *228 mm* in length.

Longest fangs

The longest fangs of any snake are those of the highly venomous Gaboon viper (*Bitis gabonica*) of tropical Africa. In a 6 ft *1,83 m* long specimen they measured 50 mm *1.96 in*. On 12 Feb 1963 a Gaboon viper bit itself to death in the Philadelphia Zoological Gardens, Philadelphia, Pennsylvania, USA. Keepers found the dead snake with its fangs deeply embedded in its own back.

Rarest

The rarest snake in the world is the Keel-scaled boa (*see Table*). The rarest snake of Britain's 3

indigenous species is the Smooth snake (*Coronella austriaca*) of southern England. In the early 1960s a localised population of the harmless *Elaphe longissima* found in southern Europe and Asia Minor, established itself in the Colwyn Bay area, North Wales following the escape of a gravid female from captivity.

4. AMPHIBIANS

Amphibia

Largest *World*

The largest species of amphibian is the Chinese giant salamander (*Andrias davidianus*), which lives in the cold mountain streams and marshy areas of north-eastern, central and southern China (*see Table* pp. 24–25).

Largest *Britain*

The heaviest British amphibian is the Common toad (*Bufo bufo*) of which a female has been weighed at 118 g *4.16 oz*.

The longest is the Warty or Great crested newt (*Triturus cristatus*). One female specimen collected at Hampton, Greater London measured 162 mm *6.37 in* in total length.

'Colossus' Britain's largest captive frog proving to be quite a handful for his owner, Steve Crabtree of Southsea, Hants.

Smallest *World and Britain*

The smallest species of amphibian is the frog *Sminthillus limbatus*, found only in Cuba (*see Table*). The smallest amphibian found in Britain is the Palmate newt (*Triturus helveticus*). Adult specimens measure 7,5–9,2 cm *2.95–3.62 in* in total length and weigh up to 2,39 g *0.083 oz*. The Natterjack or Running toad (*Bufo calamita*) has a maximum snout-vent length of only 80 mm *3.14 in* (female) but it is a bulkier animal.

Longest lived

The greatest authentic age recorded for an amphibian is 55 years for a Japanese giant salamander (*Andrias japonicus*) (*see Table*).

Rarest *World and Britain*

The rarest amphibian in the world is the Israel painted frog (*Discoglossus nigriventer*) (*see Table*). Britain's rarest amphibian is the Natterjack toad (see above). In 1983 the total population

was estimated at 20,000, a third of them living among the sand dunes between Southport and Liverpool.

Highest and lowest

The greatest altitude at which an amphibian has been found is 8000 m *26,246 ft* for a Common toad collected in the Himalayas. This species has also been found at a depth of 340 m *1115 ft* in a coal mine.

Most poisonous

The most active known poison is the batrachotoxin derived from the skin secretions of the Golden dart-poison frog (*Phyllobates terribilis*) of western Colombia, South America, which is at least 20 times more toxic than that of any other known dart-poison frog. An average adult specimen contains enough poison (1100 mg *0.038 oz*) to kill 2200 people.

Newt *Largest world*

The largest newt in the world is the Pleurodele or Ribbed newt (*Pleurodeles waltl*), which is found in Morocco and on the Iberian Peninsula. Specimens measuring up to 40 cm *15.74 in* in total length and weighing over 1 lb *450 g* have been reliably reported.

Newt *Smallest world*

The smallest newt in the world is believed to be the Striped newt (*Notophthalmus perstriatus*) of the south-eastern United States. Adult specimens average 51 mm *2.01 in* in total length.

Frog *Largest World*

The largest known frog is the rare Goliath frog (*Conraua goliath*) of Cameroun and Equatorial Guinea. A female weighing 3306 g *7 lb 4.5 oz* was caught in the River Mbia, Equatorial Guinea on 23 Aug 1960. It had a snout-vent length of 34 cm *13.38 in* and measured 81,5 cm *32.08 in* overall with legs extended. A slightly longer female (35,6 cm *14 in*) collected in the same river in December 1966 weighed 3100 g *6 lb 13¼ oz*.

Frog *Largest Britain*

The largest frog found in Britain is the *introduced* Marsh frog (*Rana r. ridibunda*). Adult males have been measured up to 96 mm *3.77 in* snout-vent, and adult females up to 133 mm *5.25 in*, the weight ranging from 60 to 95 g *1.7–3 oz*.

The largest captive frog living in Britain today is a male African bull frog (*Pyxicephalus adspersus*) named 'Colossus' (b. 1978) owned by Mr Steve Crabtree of Southsea, Hants. It has a snout-vent length of 8¾ in *22,2 cm*, a girth of 18 in *45,7 cm* and weighs 4 lb 3 oz *1,89 kg*.

Longest jump

(*Competition Frog Jumps are invariably triple jumps*). The record for three consecutive leaps is 10,3 m *33 ft 5¼ in* by a female South African sharp-nosed frog (*Ptychadena oxyrhynchus*) named 'Santjie' at a frog Derby held at Lurula Natal Spa, Paulpietersburg, Natal on 21 May 1977. The record at the famous annual Calaveras Jumping Jubilee at Angels Camp, California is 21 ft 1½ in *6,43 m* by Janet Seiber's 'Weird Harold' on 20 May 1985. 'Santjie' would have been ineligible because Calaveras entrants must measure at least 4 in *10,16 cm* 'stem to stern'.

Toad *Largest World*

The most massive toad in the world is probably the Marine toad (*Bufo marinus*) of tropical South America. An enormous female collected on 24 Nov 1965 at Miraflores Vaupes, Colombia and later exhibited in the Reptile House at Bronx Zoo, New York City, USA had a snout-vent length of 23,8 cm *9.37 in* and weighed 1302 g *2 lb 11¼ oz* at the time of its death in 1967.

Toad *Largest Britain*

The largest toad and heaviest amphibian found in Britain is the Common toad (*Bufo bufo*). An outsized female collected in Kent with a snout–vent length 99 mm *3.89 in* weighed 118 g *4.16 oz.*

Toad *Smallest World*

The smallest toad in the world is *Bufo beiranus*, first discovered in *c.* 1906 near Beira, Mozambique, East Africa. Adult specimens have a maximum recorded snout–vent length of 24 mm *0.94 in*.

5. FISHES

Agnatha, Gnathostomata

Largest marine *World*

The largest fish in the world is the rare plankton-feeding Whale shark (*Rhincodon typus*), which is found in the warmer areas of the Atlantic, Pacific and Indian Oceans. It is not, however, the largest marine animal, since it is smaller than the larger species of whales (mammals) (*see Table* pp. 24–25). The largest carnivorous fish (excluding plankton eaters) is the comparatively rare Great white shark (*Carcharodon carcharias*), also called the 'Maneater', which ranges from the tropics to temperate zone waters. Females are larger than males. A 21 ft *6,4 m* male caught off Castillo de Cojimar, Cuba in May 1945 weighed 7302 lb *3312 kg*. A 21 ft 4 in *6,5 m* female was caught near Hobart, Tasmania in June 1983 but weighed 4500 lb *2040 kg.*

The longest of the bony or 'true' fishes (Pisces) is the Oarfish (*Regalecus glesne*), also called the 'King of the Herrings', which has a worldwide distribution. In *c.* 1885 a 25 ft *7,6 m* long example weighing 600 lb *272 kg* was caught by fishermen off Pemaquid Point, Maine, USA. Another oarfish, seen swimming off Asbury Park, New Jersey by a team of scientists from the Sandy Hook Marine Laboratory on 18 July 1963, was estimated to measure 50 ft *15,2 m* in length. The heaviest bony fish in the world is the Ocean sunfish (*Mola mola*), which is found in all tropical, sub-tropical and temperate waters. On 18 Sept 1908 a huge specimen was accidentally struck by the SS *Fiona* off Bird Island about 40 miles *65 km* from Sydney, New South Wales, Australia and towed to Port Jackson. It measured 14 ft *4,26 m* between the anal and dorsal fins and weighed 4927 lb *2235 kg.*

Britain

The largest fish ever recorded in the waters of the British Isles was a 36 ft 6 in *11,12 m* Basking shark (*Cetorhinus maximus*) washed ashore at Brighton, East Sussex in 1806. It weighed an estimated 8 tons/*tonnes.* The largest bony fish found in British waters is the Ocean sunfish (*Mola mola*). A specimen weighing 800 lb *363 kg* stranded near Montrose, Scotland on 14 Dec 1960 was sent to the Marine Research Institute in Aberdeen.

Largest freshwater *World*

The largest fish which spends its whole life in fresh or brackish water is the rare Pa beuk or Pla buk (*Pangasianodon gigas*) (*see Table*). This size *was* exceeded by the European catfish or Wels (*Silurus glanis*) in earlier times (in the 19th century lengths up to 15 ft *4,57 m* and weights up to 720 lb *336,3 kg* were reported for Russian specimens), but today anything over 6 ft *1,83 m* and 200 lb *91 kg* is considered large. The Arapaima (*Arapaima glanis*), also called the Pirarucu, found in the Amazon and other South American rivers and often claimed to be the largest freshwater

fish, averaged 6½ ft *2 m* and 150 lb *68 kg*. The largest 'authentically recorded' measured 8 ft 1½ in *2,48 m* in length and weighed 325 lb *147 kg*. It was caught in the Rio Negro, Brazil in 1836. In September 1978, a Nile perch (*Lates niloticus*) weighing 416 lb *188,6 kg* was netted in the eastern part of Lake Victoria, Kenya.

Largest freshwater *Britain*

The largest fish ever caught in a British river was a Common sturgeon (*Acipenser sturio*) weighing 507½ lb *230 kg* and measuring 9 ft *2,74 m*, which was accidentally netted in the Severn at Lydney, Gloucestershire on 1 June 1937. Larger specimens have been taken at sea—notably one weighing 700 lb *317 kg* and 10 ft 5 in *3,18 m* long netted by the trawler *Ben Urie* off Orkney and landed on 18 Oct 1956.

Smallest

The shortest and lightest freshwater fish is the Dwarf pygmy goby (*Pandaka pygmaea*) (*see table*). The shortest recorded marine fish—and the shortest known vertebrate—is the Dwarf goby *Trimmatom nanus* of the Chagos Archipelago, central Indian Ocean. In one series of 92 specimens collected by the 1978–9 Joint Services Chagos Research Expedition of the British Armed Forces the adult males averaged 8,6 mm *0.338 in* in length and the adult females 8,9 mm *0.35 in*. The lightest of all vertebrates and the smallest catch possible for any fisherman is the Dwarf goby *Schindleria praematurus* from Samoa which measures 12–19 mm *0.47–0.74 in*. Mature specimens have been known to weigh only 2 mg, which is equivalent to *17,750 to the oz.* The smallest British marine fish is Guillet's goby (*Lebutus guilleti*) which does not exceed 24 mm *0.94 in*. It has been recorded from the English Channel, the west coast of Ireland and the Irish Sea. The smallest known shark is the Long-faced dwarf shark (*Squaliolus laticaudus*) of the western Pacific which does not exceed 150 mm *5.9 in*.

The world's smallest commercial fish is the now endangered Sinarapan (*Mistichthys luzonensis*), a goby found only in Lake Buhi, Luzon. Adult males measure 10–13 mm *0.39–0.51 in* in length, and a dried 1 lb *454 g* fish cake contains about 70,000 of them!

Fastest

The cosmopolitan sailfish (*Istiophorus platypterus*) is generally considered to be the fastest species of fish, although the practical difficulties of measurement make data extremely difficult to secure. A figure of 68 mph *109 km/h* (100 yd *91 m* in 3 sec) has been cited for one off Long Key, Florida, USA. The swordfish (*Xiphias gladius*) has also been credited with very high speeds, but the evidence is based mainly on bills that have been found deeply embedded in ships' timbers. A speed of 50 knots (57.6 mph *92,7 km/h*) has been calculated from a penetration of 22 in *56 cm* by a bill into a piece of timber, but 30–35 knots (35–40 mph *56–64 km/h*) is the most conceded by some experts. A Wahoo (*Acanthocybium solandri*), 1,1 m *43 in* in length is capable of attaining a speed of 77 km/h *47.8 mph*.

Longest lived

Aquaria are of too recent origin to be able to establish with certainty which species of fish can be regarded as being the longest lived. Early indications are, however, that it may be the Lake sturgeon (*Acipenser fulvescens*) of North America (*see Table*). In July 1974 a growth ring count of 228 years (*sic*) was reported for a female Koi fish, a form of fancy carp, named 'Hanako' living in a pond in Higashi Shirakawa, Gifu Prefecture, Japan, but the greatest authoritatively accepted age for this species is 'more than

50 years'. In 1948 the death was reported of an 88-year-old female European eel (*Anguilla anguilla*) named 'Putte' in the aquarium at Halsingborg Museum, southern Sweden. She was allegedly born in the Sargasso Sea, North Atlantic in 1860, and was caught in a river as a three year old elver.

Oldest goldfish

Goldfish (*Carassius auratus*) have been reported to live for over 40 years in China. The British record is held by a specimen named 'Fred' owned by Mr A. R. Wilson of Worthing, Sussex, which died on 1 Aug 1980, aged 41 years.

Shortest lived

The shortest-lived fishes are probably certain species of the sub-order Cyprinodontei (Killifish) found in Africa and South America which normally live about eight months.

Most abundant

The most abundant species of fish in the world is probably the 3 in *76 mm* long deep-sea Bristlemouth *Cyclothone elongata* which has a worldwide distribution.

Deepest

The greatest depth from which a fish has been recovered is 8300 m *27,230 ft* in the Puerto Rico Trench (27,488 ft *8366 m*) in the Atlantic by Dr Gilbert L. Voss of the US research vessel *John Elliott* who took a 6½ in *16,5 cm* long *Bassogigas profundissimus* in April 1970. It was only the fifth such brotulid ever caught. Dr Jacques Picard and Lieutenant Don Walsh, US Navy, reported they saw a sole-like fish about 1 ft *33 cm* long (tentatively identified as *Chascanopsetta lugubris*) from the bathyscaphe *Trieste* at a depth of 35,810 ft *10 915 m* in the Challenger Deep (Marianas Trench) in the western Pacific on 24 Jan 1960. This sighting, however, has been questioned by some authorities, who still regard the brotulids of the genus *Bassogigas* as the deepest-living vertebrates.

Most and least eggs

The Ocean sunfish (*Mola mola*) produces up to 300,000,000 eggs, each of them measuring about 0.05 in *1,3 mm* in diameter at a single spawning. The egg yield of the Tooth carp *Jordanella floridae* of Florida, USA is only *c.* 20 over a period of several days.

Most valuable

The world's most valuable fish is the Russian sturgeon (*Huso huso*). One 2706 lb *1227 kg* female caught in the Tikhaya Sosna River in 1924 yielded 541 lb *245 kg* of best quality caviare which would be worth £123,000 on today's market.

Dr Takayaki Hosogi, the owner of a 7 year old 35 in *89 cm* long fancy carp called 'Fujitavo', which won the All-Japan Koi Championship on 1 Mar 1982, has since refused an offer of £69,400 for this specimen.

Most venomous

The most venomous fish in the world are the Stonefish (*Synanceidae*) of the tropical waters of the Indo-Pacific, and in particular *Synanceja horrida* which has the largest venom glands of any known fish. Direct contact with the spines of its fins, which contain a strong neurotoxic poison, often proves fatal.

Most electric

The most powerful electric fish is the Electric eel (*Electrophorus electricus*), which is found in the rivers of Brazil, Colombia, Venezuela and Peru. An average sized specimen can discharge 400 volts at 1 ampere, but measurements up to 650 volts have been recorded.

6. STARFISHES

Asteroidea

Largest
The largest of the 1600 known species of starfish in terms of total arm span is the very fragile brisingid *Midgardia xandaros*. A specimen collected by the Texas A & M University research vessel *Alaminos* in the southern part of the Gulf of Mexico in the late summer of 1968, measured 1380 mm *54.33 in* tip to tip, but the diameter of its disc was only 26 mm *1.02 in*. Its dry weight was 70 g *2.46 oz*. The heaviest species of starfish is the five-armed *Thromidia catalai* of the Western Pacific. One specimen collected off Ilot Amedee, New Caledonia on 14 Sept 1969 and later deposited in Noumea Aquarium weighed an estimated 6 kg *13.2 lb* (total arm span 630 mm *24.8 in*). The largest starfish found in British waters is the Spiny starfish (*Marthasterias glacialis*). In January 1979 Jonathon MacNeil of the Isle of Barra, Western Isles, found a specimen on the beach which originally spanned 30 in *76,2 cm*.

Smallest
The smallest known starfish is the asterinid sea star *Patiriella parvivipara* discovered by Wolfgang Zeidler on the west coast of the Eyre peninsula, S. Australia in 1975. It has a maximum radius of only 4,7 mm *0.18 in* and a diameter of less than 9 mm *0.35 in*.

Deepest
The greatest depth from which a starfish has been recovered is 7584 m *24,881 ft* for a specimen of *Porcellanaster ivanovi* collected by the USSR research ship *Vityaz* in the Marianas Trench, in the West Pacific c. 1962.

7. ARACHNIDS

Arachnida

SPIDERS (order Araneae)

Largest *World*
The world's largest known spiders in terms of leg-span are the bulky theraphosid spiders of the genera *Lasiodora* and *Grammostola* of Brazil, and *Theraphosa* of NE South America, all of which have been credited with leg spans in excess of 10 in *250 mm* (*see Table* pp. 24–25).

The miniscule starfish from the west coast of Australia—seen here 3 times its natural size.

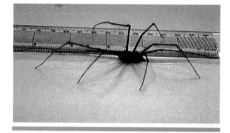

The 5.5 in *139 mm* Cardinal spider found by Evan and Lyndsay Jarrett wandering in their home in Marston Meysey, Wiltshire. (Evan Jarrett).

Largest *Britain*
Of the 617 known British species of spider covering an estimated population of over 500,000,000,000, the Cardinal spider (*Tegenaria gigantea*) of Southern England has the greatest leg span. In October 1985 Mrs Lyndsay Jarrett of Marston Meysey, Wiltshire collected an outsized female in her home which had a span of 5.5 in *139 mm*. The well-known 'Daddy Longlegs' spider (*Pholcus phalangioides*) rarely exceeds 4½ in *114 mm* in leg span, but one outsized specimen collected in England measured 6 in *15,2 cm* across. The heaviest spider found in Britain is the orb weaver *Araneus quadratus*. On 10 Sept 1979 a female weighing 2,25 g *0.079 oz* was collected at Lavington, Sussex by J. R. Parker.

Smallest *World and Britain*
The smallest known spider is *Patu marplesi* (family Symphytognathidae) of Western Samoa (*see Table*).

Britain's smallest spider is the extremely rare money spider *Clyphesis cottonae* found only in a swamp near Beaulieu Road Station, Hampshire and on Thursley Common, Surrey. Adult specimens of both sexes have a body length of 1 mm *0.039 in*.

Rarest
The most elusive of all spiders are the rare Trapdoor spiders of the genus *Liphistius,* which are found in south-east Asia (*see Table*). The most elusive spiders in Britain are the four species which are known only from the holotype specimen. These are the jumping spiders *Salticus mutabilis* (1 male Bloxworth, Dorset, 1860) and *Heliophanus melinus* (1 female Bloxworth, 1870); the Crab spider *Philodromus buxi* (1 female Bloxworth pre-1879); and the Cobweb spider *Robertus insignis* (1 male Norwich, 1906).

Commonest *World and Britain*
For world's commonest see Table. The commonest spider in Britain is the orb weaver *Araneus diadematus*, which has been recorded from all but four counties of Great Britain and Ireland.

Longest lived
The longest lived of all spiders are the primitive *Mygalomorphae* (tarantulas and allied species) (*see Table*). The longest-lived British spider is probably the Purse web spider (*Atypus affinis*). One specimen was kept in a greenhouse for nine years.

Largest and smallest webs
The largest webs are the aerial ones spun by the tropical orb weavers of the genus *Nephila,* which have been measured up to 18 ft 9¾ in *573 cm* in circumference. The smallest webs are spun by spiders such as *Glyphesis cottonae*, (see above) which cover about 0.75 in² *480 mm²*.

Most venomous
The most venomous spiders in the world are the Brazilian wandering spiders of the genus *Pho-*

neutria, and particularly *P. fera,* which has the most active neurotoxic venom of any living spider. These large and highly aggressive creatures frequently enter human dwellings and hide in clothing or shoes. When disturbed they bite furiously several times, and hundreds of accidents involving these species are reported annually. Fortunately an effective antivenin is available, and when deaths do occur they are usually children under the age of seven.

8. CRUSTACEANS

Crustacea

(Crabs, lobsters, shrimps, prawns, crayfish, barnacles, water fleas, fish lice, woodlice, sandhoppers, krill, etc.)

Largest *World*
The largest of all crustaceans (although not the heaviest) is the Sanschouo or Giant spider crab (*Macrocheira kaempferi*), also called the Stilt crab, which is found in deep waters off the south-eastern coast of Japan (*see Table* pp. 24–25).

Largest *Britain*
The largest crustacean found in British waters is the Common or European lobster (*Homarus vulgaris*), which averages 2–3 lb *900–1360 g*. In June 1931 an outsized specimen weighing 20½ lb *5,80 kg* and measuring 4 ft 1½ in *1,26 m* in total length, was caught in a caisson during the construction of No. 3 jetty at Fowey, Cornwall. Its crushing claw weighed 2 lb 10 oz *1188 g* after the meat had been removed. The largest crab found in British waters is the Edible or Great crab (*Cancer pagurus*). In 1895 a crab measuring 11 in *279 mm* across the shell and weighing 14 lb *6,35 kg* was caught off the coast of Cornwall.

Smallest
The smallest known crustaceans are water fleas of the genus *Alonella*, which may measure less than 0,25 mm *0.0098 in* in length (*see Table*). They are found in British waters.

Longest lived
The longest lived of all crustaceans is the American lobster (*Homarus americanus*) (*see Table*).

Vertical distribution
The greatest depth from which a crustacean has been recovered is 10 500 m *34,450 ft* for *live* amphipods from the Challenger Deep, Marianas Trench, West Pacific by the US research vessel *Thomas Washington* in November 1980. Amphipods and isopods have also been collected in the Ecuadorean Andes at a height of 13,300 ft *4053 m*.

9. INSECTS

Insecta

Heaviest *World*
The heaviest insects in the world are the Goliath beetles (family *Scarabaeidae*) of equatorial Africa. The largest members of the group are *Goliathus regius* and *Goliathus goliathus* (= *giganteus*) (*see Table* pp. 24–25).

Heaviest *Britain*
The heaviest insect found in Britain is the Stag beetle (*Lucanus cervus*) which is widely distributed over southern England. The largest specimen on record was a male collected at Sheerness, Kent, in 1871 and now preserved in the British Museum (Natural History), London, which

measures 87,4 mm *3.04 in* in length (body plus mandibles) and probably weighed over 6 g *0.21 oz* when alive.

Rarest
It has recently been estimated that there may be 30 million species of insect—more than all other classes put together. Thousands are known only from a single or type specimen.

BUTTERFLIES AND MOTHS (order Lepidoptera)

Largest *World*
The largest known butterfly is the protected Queen Alexandra's birdwing (*Ornithoptera alexandrae*) which is restricted to the Popondetta Plain in Papua New Guinea. Females may have a wing span exceeding 280 mm *11.02 in* and weigh over 25 g *0.88 oz*. The largest moth in the world (although not the heaviest) is the Hercules moth (*Cosdinoscera hercules*) of tropical Australia and New Guinea. A wing area of up to 40.8 in² *263,2 cm²* and a wing span of 280 mm *11 in* have been recorded. In 1948 an unconfirmed measurement of 360 mm *14.17 in* was reported for a female captured near the post office at the coastal town of Innisfail, Queensland, Australia now in the Oberthur collection. The rare Owlet moth (*Thysania agrippina*) of Brazil has been measured up to 12.16 in *308 mm* wing span in the case of a female taken in 1934 and now in the collection of John G. Powers in Ontario, Canada.

Largest *Britain*
The largest (but not the heaviest) of the 21,000 species of insect found in Britain is the very rare Death's head hawkmoth (*Acherontia atropos*). One female found dead in a garden at Tiverton, Devon, in 1931 had a wing span of 5.75 in *145 mm* and weighed nearly 3 g *0.10 oz*. The largest butterfly found in Britain is the Monarch butterfly (*Danaus plexippus*), also called the Milkweed or Black-veined brown butterfly, a rare vagrant which breeds in the southern United States and Central America. It has a wing span of up to 5 in *127 mm* and weighs about 1 g *0.04 oz*. The largest *native* butterfly is the Swallowtail (*Papilio machaon britannicus*), females of which have a wing span up to 100 mm *3.93 in*. This species is now confined to fens in Suffolk, Cambridgeshire and the Norfolk Broads.

Smallest *World and Britain*
The smallest of the 140,000 known species of Lepidoptera are the moths *Johanssonia acetosea* found in Britain, and *Stigmella ridiculosa* from the Canary Islands, which have a wing span of *c.* 2 mm *0.08 in* with a similar body length. The world's smallest known butterfly is the Dwarf blue (*Brephidium barberae*) of South Africa. It has a wing span of 14 mm *0.55 in*. The smallest butterfly found in Britain is the Small blue (*Cupido minimus*), which has a wing span of 19–25 mm *0.75–1.0 in*.

Rarest *World and Britain*
The birdwing butterfly *Ornithopteria* (= *Troides*) *allottei* of Bougainville, Solomon Islands, is known from less than a dozen specimens. A male from the collection of C. Rousseau Decelle was auctioned for £750 in Paris on 24 Oct 1966.

The rarest British butterfly (59 species) is the Chequered Skipper (*Carterocephalus palaemon*) which is confined to a small number of sites in western Scotland. The Large blue (*Maculinea arion*) was officially declared extinct in 1979, but was re-introduced in June 1983 when 93 larvae were imported from Sweden.

Most acute sense of smell
The most acute sense of smell exhibited in nature is that of the male Emperor moth (*Eudia pavonia*) which, according to German experiments in 1961, can detect the sex attractant of the virgin female at the almost unbelievable range of 11 km *6.8 miles* upwind. This scent has been identified as one of the higher alcohols ($C_{16}H_{29}OH$), of which the female carries less than 0,0001 mg.

Longest
The longest insect in the world is the giant stick-insect *Pharnacia serratipes* of Indonesia (*see Table*). The longest known beetle (excluding antennae) is the Hercules beetle (*Dynastes hercules*) of Central and South America, which has been measured up to 190 mm *7.48 in*. More than half the length however, is taken up by the prothoracic horn.

Smallest *World*
The smallest insects recorded so far are the 'Hairy-winged' beetles of the family Ptiliidae (= Trichopterygidae) and the 'Battledore-wing fairy flies' (parasitic wasps) of the family Myrmaridae (*see Table*). They are smaller than some of the protozoa (single-celled animals). The male Bloodsucking banded louse *Enderleinellus zonatus*, ungorged, and the parasitic wasp (*Caraphractus cinctus*) may each weigh as little as 0,005 mg, or *5,670,000 to an oz*. The eggs of the latter each weigh 0,0002 mg, or *141,750,000 to an oz*.

Commonest
The most numerous of all insects are Springtails (Order Collembola), which have a wide geographical range (*see Table*).

Fastest flying
Experiments have proved that the widely publicised claim by an American entomologist in 1926 that the Deer bot-fly *Cephenemyia pratti* could attain a speed of 818 mph *1316 km/h* (*sic*) was wildly exaggerated. If true it would have generated a supersonic 'pop'! Acceptable modern experiments have now established that the highest maintainable airspeed of any insect, including the Deer bot-fly, is 24 mph *39 km/h*, rising to a maximum of 36 mph *58 km/h* for short bursts (*see Table*).

Longest lived
The longest-lived insects are the Splendour beetles (*Buprestidae*) (*see Table*). On 27 May 1983 a *Buprestis aurulenta* appeared from the staircase timber in the home of Mr W. Euston of Prittlewell, Southend-on-Sea, Essex after 47 years as a larva.

Loudest
The loudest of all insects is the male cicada (family Cicadidae). At 7400 pulses/min its tymbal organs produce a noise (officially described by the United States Department of Agriculture as 'Tsh-ee-EEEE-e-ou') detectable more than a quarter of a mile *400 m* distant. The only British species is the very rare Mountain cicada (*Cicadetta montana*), which is confined to the New Forest area in Hampshire.

Toughest
According to experiments carried out by Prof. H. E. Hinton at Bristol University, the larva of the chironomid fly *Polypedilum vanderplanki* can tolerate temperatures ranging from −270°C to 102°C *−454°F to 215.6°F*, and is the most advanced organism so far known that can be totally dehydrated.

Largest locust swarm
The greatest swarm of Desert locusts (*Schistocera gregaria*) ever recorded was one covering an estimated 2000 miles² *5180 km²* observed crossing the Red Sea in 1889. Such a swarm must have contained about 250,000,000,000 insects weighing about 500,000 tons *508 000 tonnes*. In 1958 in Somalia a swarm of *c* 60,000 million covering a measured 1000 km² *400 miles²* was estimated to be devouring *c* 120,000 tons of biomass daily.

Fastest wing beat
The fastest wing beat of any insect under natural conditions is 62,760 per min by a tiny midge of the genus *Forcipomyia*. In experiments with truncated wings at a temperature of 37° C *98.6° F* the rate increased to 133,080 beats/min. The muscular contraction–expansion cycle in 0.00045 or 1/2218th of a sec, further represents the fastest muscle movement ever measured.

Slowest wing beat
The slowest wing beat of any insect is 300 per min by the Swallowtail butterfly (*Papilio machaon britannica*). The average is 460–636 per min.

Hive record
The greatest reported amount of wild honey ever extracted from a single hive is 549 lb *249,02 kg* recorded by A. D. Wilkes of Cairns, Queensland, Australia in the 11 months Feb–Dec 1983.

Dragonflies *Largest and smallest*
The largest dragonfly in the world is *Megaloprepus caeruleata* of Central and South America, which has been measured up to 191 mm *7.52 in* across the wings and 120 mm *4.72 in* in body length. The largest dragonfly found in Britain is *Anax imperator*, which has a wing span measurement of up to 106 mm *4.17 in*. The smallest British dragonfly is *Lestes dryas*, which has a wing span of 20–25 mm *0.78–0.98 in*.

Flea *Largest*
The largest known flea is *Hystrichopsylla schefferi*, which was described from a single specimen taken from the nest of a Mountain beaver (*Aplodontia rufa*) at Puyallup, Washington, USA in 1913. Females measure up to 8 mm *0.31 in* in length which is the diameter of a pencil. The largest flea (61 species) found in Britain is the Mole and Vole flea (*H. talpae*)—females measured to 6 mm *0.23 in*.

Flea *Longest jump*
The champion jumper among fleas is the Common flea (*Pulex irritans*). In one American experiment carried out in 1910 a specimen allowed to leap at will performed a long jump of 13 in *330 mm* and a high jump of 7¾ in *197 mm*. In jumping 130 times its own height a flea subjects itself to a force of 200 g. Siphonapterologists recognise 1830 varieties.

10. CENTIPEDES

Chilopoda

Longest
The longest known species of centipede is a large variant of the widely distributed *Scolopendra morsitans*, found on the Andaman Islands, Bay of Bengal. Specimens have been measured up to 13 in *330 mm* in length and 1½ in *38 mm* in breadth. The longest centipede found in Britain is *Haplophilus subterraneus*, which has been measured up to 70 mm *2.75 in* in length and 1,4 mm *0.05 in* across the body. On 1 Nov 1973 Mr Ian Howgate sighted an uncollected specimen on the run in St Albans, Herts, estimated to be at least 4½ in *114 mm* long.

Shortest
The shortest recorded centipede is an unidentified species which measures only 5 mm *0.19 in*.

The shortest centipede found in Britain is *Lithobius dubosequi*, which measures up to 9,5 mm *0.374 in* in length.

Most legs

The centipede with the greatest number of legs is *Himantarum gabrielis* of southern Europe which has 171–177 pairs when adult.

Fastest

The fastest centipede is probably *Scrutigera coleoptrata* of southern Europe which can travel at 1.1 mph *1,8 km/h*.

11. MILLIPEDES

Diplopoda

Longest

The longest known species of millipede are *Graphidostreptus gigas* of Africa and *Scaphistostreptus seychellarum* of the Seychelles in the Indian Ocean, both of which have been measured up to 280 mm *11.02 in* in length and 20 mm *0.78 in* in diameter. The longest millipede found in Britain is *Cylindroiulus londinensis* which measures up to 50 mm *1.96 in.*

Shortest

The shortest millipede in the world is the British species *Polyxenus lagurus*, which measures 2,1–4,0 mm *0.082–0.15 in.*

Most legs

The greatest number of legs reported for a millipede is 375 pairs (750 legs) for *Illacme plenipes* of California, USA.

12. SEGMENTED WORMS

Annelida

Longest

The longest known species of earthworm is *Microchaetus rappi* (= *M. microchaetus*) of South Africa. In *c.* 1937 a giant measuring 22 ft *6,70 m* in length when naturally extended and 0.78 in *20 mm* in diameter was collected in the Transvaal. The longest segmented worm found in Britain is the King rag worm (*Nereis virens*). On 19 Oct 1975 a specimen measuring 44 in *111,7 cm* when fully extended was collected by Mr James Sawyer at Hauxley Bay, Northumberland. On 5 Nov 1982 the mutilated body of an earthworm measuring 5 ft 1 in *155 cm* in length was found in a garden in Herne Bay, Kent, but it was discarded before it could be identified.

Shortest

The shortest known segmented worm is *Chaetogaster annandalei*, which measures less than 0,5 mm *0.019 in* in length.

Worm charming

At the third international worm charming championship held in Blackawton, Devon, on 22 Mar 1986, a Round Table team led by Mr Bob Benn of Dartmouth coaxed 149 worms from a square metre of soil in 15 minutes.

13. MOLLUSCS

Mollusca

(Squids, octopuses, shellfish, snails, etc.)

Largest squid

The largest known invertebrate is the Atlantic giant squid *Architeuthis dux* (*see Table* pp. 24–25). The largest squid ever recorded in British waters was an *Architeuthis monachus* found at the head of Whalefirth Voe, Shetland on 2 Oct 1959 which measured 24 ft *7,31 m* in total length.

Largest octopus

The largest octopus known to science is *Octopus apollyon* of the coastal waters of the North Pacific. One huge individual caught single-handed by skin-diver Donald E. Hagen in Lower Hoods Canal, Puget Sound, Washington, USA on 18 Feb 1973 had a relaxed radial spread of 23 ft *7,01 m* and weighed 118 lb 10 oz *53,8 kg*. In November 1896 the remains of an unknown animal weighing an estimated 6–7 tons/*tonnes* were found on a beach near St Augustine, Florida, USA. Tissue samples were later sent to the US National Museum in Washington, DC, and in 1970 they were *positively* identified as belonging to a giant form of octopus (*Octopus giganteus*). Some experts, however, do not agree with this assessment because there was no evidence of tentacles or a beak and they believe the decomposing carcase was more probably that of a large whale, shark—or even an elephant! The largest octopus found in British waters is the Common octopus (*Octopus vulgaris*). It may span 7 ft *2,13 m* and weigh more than 10 lb *4,5 kg.*

Longest lived mollusc

The longest lived mollusc is the Ocean Quahog (*Artica islandica*) (*see Table*).

SHELLS

Largest

The largest of all existing bivalve shells is the marine Giant clam *Tridacna gigas*, which is found on the Indo-Pacific coral reefs. A specimen measuring 110 cm *43.3 in* in length and weighing 333 kg *734 lb* collected off Ishigaki Island, Okinawa, Japan, was found in 1956 but not formally measured until Aug 1984 by Dr Shomei Shirai. The largest bivalve shell found in British waters is the Fan mussel (*Pinna fragilis*). One specimen found at Tor Bay, Devon measured 37 cm *14.56 in* in length and 20 cm *7.87 in* in breadth at the hind end.

Smallest

The smallest shell is the univalve *Ammonicera rota*, which measures 0,5 mm *0.02 in* in diameter (*see Table*). The smallest bivalve shell also found in British waters is the coinshell *Neolepton sykesi*, which has an average length of 1,2 mm *0.047 in.* This species is only known from a few examples collected off Guernsey, Channel Islands and West Ireland.

Most Expensive Shell and Rarest

For details of most expensive shell see table.

GASTROPODS

Largest

The largest known gastropod is the Trumpet or Baler conch (*Syrinx aruanus*) of Australia. One outsized specimen collected off Western Australia in 1979 and now owned by Don Pisor (who bought it from a fisherman in Kaoh-siung, Taiwan in November 1979) of San Diego, California, USA measures 77,2 cm *30.39 in* in length and has a maximum girth of 101 cm *39.76 in.* It weighed nearly 40 lb *18,14 kg* when alive.

The largest known land gastropod is the African giant snail (*Achatina* sp.). 'Gee Geronimo' found by Christopher Hudson (1955–79) of Hove, E. Sussex, measured 15½ in *39,3 cm* from snout to tail, (shell length 10¾ in *27,3 cm*) in December 1978 and weighed exactly 2 lb *900 g*. The snail

was collected in Sierra Leone in June 1976 where shell lengths up to 14 in *35,5 cm* have been reliably reported.

The largest land snail found in Britain is the Roman or Edible snail (*Helix pomatia*), which measures up to 4 in *10 cm* in overall length and weighs up to 3 oz *85 g*. The smallest British land snail is *Punctum pygmaeum*, which has a shell measuring 0.023–0.035 in *0,6–0,9 mm* by 0.047–0.059 in, *1,2–1,5 mm.*

Speed

The fastest-moving species of land snail is probably the common garden snail (*Helix aspersa*) (*see Table*).

14. RIBBON WORMS

Nemertina

Longest

The longest of the 550 recorded species of ribbon worms, also called nemertines (or nemerteans), is the 'Boot-lace worm' (*Lineus longissimus*), which is found in the shallow waters of the North Sea (*see Table* pp. 24–25).

15. JELLYFISHES AND CORALS

Cnidaria

Largest and smallest jellyfish

The largest jellyfish is the Arctic giant jellyfish (*Cyanea capillata arctica*) of the north-western Atlantic. One washed up in Massachusetts Bay had a bell diameter of 7 ft 6 in *2,28 m* and tentacles stretching 120 ft *36,5 m*. The largest cnidarian found in British waters is the rare 'Lion's mane' jellyfish (*Cyanea capillata*), also known as the Common sea blubber. One specimen measured at St Andrew's Marine Laboratory, Fife, Scotland had a bell diameter of 91 cm *35.8 in* and tentacles stretching over 13,7 m *45 ft*. Some true jellyfishes have a bell diameter of less than 20 mm *0.78 in.*

Most venomous

The most venomous cnidarian is the Australian sea wasp (*Chironex fleckeri*) which carries a cardio-toxic venom similar in strength to that found in the Asiatic cobra. These box jellyfish have caused the deaths of 66 people off the coast of Queensland, Australia since 1880. Victims die within 1–3 min if medical aid is not available. A most effective defence is women's panty hose, outsize versions of which are now worn by Queensland lifesavers at surf carnivals.

Coral

The world's greatest stony coral structure is the Great Barrier Reef off Queensland, north east Australia. It stretches 1260 miles *2028 km* and covers 80,000 miles² *207 000 km²*.

The world's largest reported discrete coral is a stony colony of *Galaxea fascicularis* found in Sakiyama Bay off Irimote Island, Okinawa on 7 Aug 1982 by Dr Shohei Shirai. It measured more than 16 m *52½ ft* overall.

16. SPONGES

Porifera

Largest

The largest known sponge is the barrel-shaped

Loggerhead sponge (*Spheciospongia vesparium*) of the West Indies and the waters off Florida, USA. Individuals measure up to 3 ft 6 in *105 cm* in height and 3 ft *91 cm* in diameter. Neptune's cup or goblet (*Poterion patera*) of Indonesia grows to 4 ft *120 cm* in height, but it is a less bulky animal. In 1909 a Wool sponge (*Hippospongia canaliculatta*) measuring 6 ft *183 cm* in circumference was collected off the Bahama Islands. When first taken from the water it weighed between 80 and 90 lb *36 and 41 kg* but after it had been dried and relieved of all excrescences it scaled 12 lb *5,44 kg* (this sponge is now preserved in the US National Museum, Washington, DC, USA).

Smallest

The smallest known sponge is the widely distributed *Leucosolenia blanca*, which measures 3 mm *0.11 in* in height when fully grown.

Deepest

Sponges have been recovered from depths of up to 18,500 ft *5637 m.*

The 110 cm *43.3 in* long Giant clam shell, the largest in the world which took 28 years to be formally ratified.

---

17. EXTINCT ANIMALS

Longest *World*

The longest dinosaurs so far recorded are some of the attenuated diplodocids ('double beams') of the Late Jurassic (160 million years ago) of western North America, south Central China, Mongolia and Tanzania. A composite reconstruction of a *Diplodocus carnegii* in the Carnegie Museum of Natural History in Pittsburgh, Pennsylvania, USA, measures 87 ft 6 in *26,6 m* in total length—head and neck 22 ft *6,7 m*, body 15 ft *4,5 m*, tail 50 ft *15,2 m*—and has a mounted height of 11 ft 9 in *3,58 m* at the pelvis, the highest point on the body, but this lightweight giant (discovered in Albany County, Wyoming, in 1899) only scaled an estimated 5 tonnes/*tons* based on the mid-shaft circumferences of the long-bones. In the summer of 1972 the remains of a huge barosaur were discovered in the Dry Mesa Quarry of the Uncompahgre Plateau, western Colorado, USA. From the evidence of the bones already collected, including 8 ft *2,4 m* long matching scapula blades (the articulation for the forelimbs) this diplodocid, nicknamed 'Supersaurus' ('super lizard'), measured an estimated 145 ft *44 m* in overall length, thus making it the longest vertebrate ever recorded.

Longest *Britain*

Britain's longest dinosaur was *Cetiosaurus oxoniensis* ('whale lizard'), which roamed across southern England about 150 million years ago. It measured up to 68 ft 6 in *20,88 m* in total length.

Heaviest *World*

The heaviest land vertebrates of all times were probably the brachiosaurids ('arm lizards') of the Late Jurassic (160 million years ago) of Tanzania, South Africa, Algeria, Portugal, Korea and the south-western USA. A brachiosaurid nicknamed 'Ultrasaurus' ('ultra lizard'), discovered in the Dry Mesa Quarry (see above) in 1979, which had scapula blades measuring 8 ft 10 in *2,69 m* and 9 ft *2,74 m* long respectively, must have scaled at least 40 tonnes *39.3 tons*, while *Brachiosaurus ataliensis* from Portugal may have been even heavier.

Heaviest *Britain*

Britain's heaviest dinosaur was *Cetiosaurus oxoniensis* (see above), which weighed up to 25 tonnes *24.59 tons*.

Largest land predator

The largest of the flesh-eating dinosaurs was probably *Tyrannosaurus rex* ('king tyrant lizard'), which stalked across what are now the States of Montana and Wyoming in the USA and part of China during the Late Cretaceous (about 75 million years ago). No complete skeleton of this carnosaur has ever been discovered, but a composite skeleton in the American Museum of Natural History, New York City, has a bipedal height of 18 ft 6 in *5,6 m* (total length 34 ft *10,4 m*). This specimen weighed an estimated 4,5 tonnes/*tons* when alive. The upper jaw bone (maxilla) of another *T. rex* preserved in the University of California, Berkeley, is 30 per cent bigger than the one in the American Museum of Natural History, and it has been calculated that the owner of this jaw must have measured *c.* 44 ft *13,4 m* in total length (estimated weight *c.* 8 tonnes/*tons*). *Tarbosaurus efremovi* ('alarming lizard'), its Mongolian counterpart, measured up to 46 ft *14 m* overall (bipedal height 20 ft *6,1 m*), but this carnosaur had a proportionately longer tail than *T. rex* and was less heavily built.

Smallest dinosaurs

The smallest dinosaurs so far recorded are the chicken-sized Compsognathus ('pretty jaw') of southern West Germany and south-east France, and an undescribed plant-eating fabrosaurid from Colorado, USA, both of which measured 75 cm *29.5 in* from the snout to the tip of the tail.

Longest trackway

In 1983 a series of four *Apatosaurus* (= *Brontosaurus*) trackways which ran parallel for a distance of over 215 m *705 ft* were recorded from 145 million year-old Jurassic strata in south-east Colorado, USA.

Fastest dinosaurs

Trackways can be used to estimate dinosaur speeds, and one from the Lower Cretaceous of Texas discovered in 1981 indicated that a carnivorous dinosaur had been moving at 40 km/h *25 mph*. Some of the Ornithomimids (ostrich dinosaurs) were even faster, and the 220 lb *100 kg Dromiceiomimus* ('emu mimic') of the Late Cretaceous (about 140 million years ago) of southern Alberta, Canada, could probably outsprint an ostrich, which has a top speed of 45 mph *72 km/h.*

Largest dinosaur footprints

In 1932 the gigantic footprints of a large bipedal hadrosaurid (duckbill) measuring 1,36 m *53.5 in* in length and 81 cm *31.8 in* in diameter were discovered at Salt Lake City, Utah, USA, and other reports from Colorado and Utah refer to footprints 95–100 cm *37·4–39.4 in* in diameter. Footprints attributed to the largest brachiosaurids also range up to 100 cm *39.3 in* in diameter for the hind feet, and the Korean *Ultrasaurus tabriensis* has yielded prints measuring 1,15 m *45.28 in* in diameter.

Most brainless

Stegosaurus ('plated reptile'), which measured up to 30 ft *9 m* in total length had a walnut-sized brain weighing only 2½ oz *70g*, which represented 0.004 of 1 per cent of its computed body weight of 1¾ tons/*tonnes.* (*cf.* 0.074 of 1 per cent for an elephant and 1.88 per cent for a human). It roamed widely across the Northern Hemisphere about 150,000,000 years ago.

Largest dinosaur eggs

The largest known dinosaur eggs are those of *Hypselosaurus priscus*, ('high ridge lizard'), a 40 ft *12,19 m* long titanosaurid which lived about 80,000,000 years ago. Some examples found in the valley of the Durance near Aix-en-Provence, southern France in October 1961 would have had, uncrushed, a length of 12 in *300 mm* and a diameter of 10 in *255 mm* (capacity 5.8 pints *3,3 l*).

Largest flying creature

The largest flying creature is the pterosaur *Quetzalcoatlus northropi* ('feathered serpent') which glided over what is now the state of Texas, USA and Alberta, Canada about 65 million years ago. Partial remains discovered in Big Bend National Park, West Texas in 1971 indicate that this reptile must have had a wing span of 11–12 m *36–39 ft* and weighed about *86 kg* 190 lb.

Largest marine reptile

The largest marine reptile ever recorded was *Stretosaurus macromerus*, a short-necked pliosaur from the Kimmeridge Clay of Stretham, Cambridgeshire and Oxfordshire.

A mandible found at Cumnor, Oxfordshire and now in the University Museum, Oxford has a restored length of over 3 m *9 ft 10 in* and must have belonged to a reptile measuring at least 46 ft *14 m* in total length. *Kronosaurus queenslandicus*, another pliosaur from Australia, was also of comparable size, and a complete skeleton in the Museum of Comparative Zoology at Harvard University, Cambridge, Massachusetts, USA measures 42 ft *12,8 m* in total length.

Largest crocodile

The largest known crocodile was *Deinosuchus riograndensis*, which lived in the lakes and swamps of what is now the state of Texas, USA about 75,000,000 years ago. Fragmentary remains discovered in Big Bend National Park, West Texas, indicate a hypothetical length of 16 m *52 ft 6 in*, compared with the 12–14 m *39.3–45.9 ft* of the *Sarcosuchus imperator* of Niger. The huge gavial *Rhamphosuchus*, which lived in what is now northern India about 2,000,000 years ago, was even longer reaching 60 ft *18,3 m*, but it was not so heavily built.

Largest chelonians

The largest prehistoric chelonian was *Stupendemys geographicus*, a pelomedusid turtle which lived about 5,000,000 years ago. Fossil remains discovered by Harvard University palaeontologists in Northern Venezuela in 1972 indicate that this turtle had a carapace (shell) measuring 218–230 cm *7 ft 2 in–7 ft 6½ in* in mid-line length and measured 3 m *9 ft 10 in* in overall length. It had a computed weight of 4500 lb *2041 kg* in life.

Largest tortoise

The largest prehistoric tortoise was probably *Geochelone* (= *Colossochelys*) *atlas*, which lived in what is now northern India, Burma, Java, the Celebes and Timor about 2 million years ago. In 1923 the fossil remains of a specimen with a carapace 5 ft 11 in *180 cm* long (7 ft 4 in *223 cm* over the curve) and 2 ft 11 in *89 cm* high were discovered near Chandigarh in the Siwalik Hills. This animal had a total length of 8 ft *2,44 m* and is computed to have weighed 2100 lb *852 kg* when it was alive. Recently the fossil remains of other giant tortoises (*Geochelone*) have been found in Florida and Texas, USA.

Longest snake

The longest prehistoric snake was the python-like *Gigantophis garstini*, which inhabited what is now Egypt some 55,000,000 years ago. Parts of a spinal column and a small piece of jaw discovered at Fayum in the Western Desert indicate a length of *c.* 37 ft *11 m*. Another fossil giant snake, *Madtsoia bai* from Patagonia, S. America, measured *c.* 10 m *33 ft* in length, comparable with the longest constrictors living today.

Largest amphibian

The largest amphibian ever recorded was the gharial-like *Prionosuchus plummeri* which lived 230,000,000 years ago. In 1972 the fragmented remains of a specimen measuring an estimated 9 m *30 ft* in life, were discovered in North Brazil.

Largest fish

No prehistoric fish larger than living species has yet been discovered. The claim that the Great shark (*Carcharodon megalodon*), which abounded in Miocene seas some 15,000,000 years ago, measured 80 ft *24 m* in length, based on ratios from fossil teeth has now been shown to be in error. The modern estimate is that this shark did not exceed 43 ft *13,1 m*.

Largest insect

The largest prehistoric insect was the dragonfly *Meganeura monyi*, which lived about 280,000,000 years ago. Fossil remains (*i.e.* impressions of wings) discovered at Commentry, central France, indicate a wing extending up to 70 cm *27.5 in*.

Britain's largest dragonfly was *Pupus diluculum* (family *Meganeuridae*), which is only known from a wing impression found on a lump of coal in Bolsover colliery, Derbyshire in July 1978. It had an estimated wing span of 50–60 cm *19.68–23.62 in* and lived about 300,000,000 years ago, making it the oldest flying creature so far recorded.

Largest bird

The largest prehistoric bird was the flightless *Dromornis stirtoni*, a huge emu-like creature which lived in central Australia 11,000,000 years ago. Fossil leg bones found near Alice Springs in 1974 indicate that the bird must have stood *c.* 10 ft *3 m* in height and weighed *c.* 1100 lb *500 kg*. The giant moa *Dinornis maximus* of New Zealand was even taller, attaining a maximum height of 12 ft *3,6 m* but it only weighed about 500 lb *227 kg*.

The largest known flying bird was the giant teraton *Argentavis magnificens* which lived in Argentina about 6 million years ago. Fossil remains discovered at a site 100 miles *160 km* west of Buenos Aires in 1979 indicate that this gigantic vulture had a wing span of 7,0–7,6 m *23–25 ft* and weighed about 120 kg *265 lb*.

Largest mammals

The largest land mammal ever recorded was *Paraceratherium* (= *Baluchitherium*), a long-necked hornless rhinoceros which roamed across western Asia and Europe (Yugoslavia) about 35 million years ago. A restoration in the American

Museum of Natural History, New York measures 17 ft 9 in *5,41 m* to the top of the shoulder hump and 37 ft *11,27 m* in total length, and this particular specimen must have weighed about 20 tonnes/tons in the flesh. The bones of this gigantic browser were first discovered in the Bugti Hills in east Baluchistan, Pakistan in 1907–8.

The largest marine mammal was the serpentine *Basilosaurus* (*Zeuglodon*) *cetoides*, which swam in the seas over what are now the American states of Arkansas and Alabama 50 million years ago. It measured up to 70 ft *21,3 m* in length.

Largest mammoth

The largest prehistoric elephant was the Steppe mammoth *Mammuthus* (*Parelephas*) *trogontherii*, which roamed over what is now central Europe a million years ago. A fragmentary skeleton found in Mosbach, West Germany indicates a shoulder height of 4,5 m *14 ft 9 in*.

Tusks *Longest*

The longest tusks of any prehistoric animal were those of the Straight-tusked elephant *Palaeoloxodon antiquus germanicus*, which lived in northern Germany about 300,000 years ago. The average length in adult bulls was 5 m *16 ft 5 in*. A single tusk of a Woolly mammoth (*Mammuthus primigenius*) preserved in the Franzens Museum at Brno, Czechoslovakia measures 5,02 m *16 ft 5⅓ in* along the outside curve. In *c.* August 1933, a single tusk of an Imperial mammoth (*Mammuthus imperator*) measuring 16 + ft *4,87 + m* (anterior end missing) was unearthed near Post, Gorza County, Texas, USA. In 1934 this tusk was presented to the American Museum of Natural History in New York City, NY, USA.

Tusks *Heaviest*

The heaviest single fossil tusk on record is one weighing 150 kg *330 lb* with a maximum circumference of 35 in *89 cm* now preserved in the Museo Civico di Storia Naturale, Milan, Italy. The specimen (in two pieces) measures 11 ft 9 in *3,58 m* in length.

The heaviest recorded fossil tusks are a pair belonging to a 13 ft 4 in *4,06 m* tall Columbian mammoth (*Mammuthus columbi*) in the State Museum, Lincoln, Nebraska, USA which have a combined weight of 498 lb *226 kg* and measure 13 ft 9 in *4,21 m* and 13 ft 7 in *4,14 m* respectively. They were found near Campbell, Nebraska in April 1915.

Antlers *Greatest span*

The prehistoric Giant deer (*Megaceros giganteus*), which lived in northern Europe and northern Asia as recently as 8000 BC, had the longest horns of any known animal. One specimen recovered from an Irish bog had greatly palmated antlers measuring 14 ft *4,3 m* across.

EARLIEST OF THEIR TYPES

Type	Scientific name and year of discovery	Location	Estimated years before present
Primate	Unnamed ape (May 1979)	Padaung Hills, Burma	40,000,000
Primate	Lemur	Indonesia	70,000,000
Primate	Tarsier-like	Madagascar	70,000,000
Social insect	*Sphecomyrma freyi* (1967)	New Jersey, USA	110,000,000
Bird	*Archaeopteryx lithographica* (1861)	Bavaria, W. Germany	150,000,000
Moth	*Archaeolepis* (1985)	Dorset coast, England	180,000,000
Mammal	*Megazostrodon* (1966)	Thaba-ea-Litau, Lesotho	190,000,000
Reptile	Unnamed (insectivory) 1972	Kentucky, USA	310,000,000
Amphibian	*Ichthyostega* (first quadruped)	Greenland	350,000,000
Spider	*Palaeostenzia crassipes*	Tayside, Scotland	370,000,000
Insect	*Rhyniella procursor*	Tayside, Scotland	370,000,000
Fish	*Branchiostoma*	Canada	550,000,000
Crustacean	*Karagassiema* (12 legged)	Sayan Mts, USSR	*c.* 650,000,000
Metazoans	Bore hole tracks	Zambia	1,000,000,000
Eukaryotes	(c. Sept 1983)	Tianjin, China	1,800,000,000
Microfossils	Carbonaceous microspheroids	'North Pole', Western Australia	3,500,000,000

Note: Free Oxygen began forming in the Earth's atmosphere about 2300 million years ago.

PLANT KINGDOM

Plantea

PLANTS

The medicinal value of plants was known to Neanderthal man *c.* 60,000 BC. The world's oldest garden has yet to be identified but is probably that of a Chinese temple. The world's oldest Botanical Garden is that at Pisa dating from 1543. Britain's oldest is the Botanic Garden, Oxford founded as a Physic Garden in 1621.

Oldest living thing

'King Clone', the oldest known clone of the

creosote plant (*Larrea tridentata*) found in south west California, was estimated in February 1980 by Prof. Frank C. Vasek to be 11,700 years old. It is possible that crustose lichens in excess of 500 mm *19.6 in* in diameter may be as old. In 1981 it was estimated that Antarctic lichens of more than 100 mm *3.9 in* in diameter are at least 10,000 years old. The oldest known pot-plant is the succulent *Fockea crispa* potted by Baron Jacquin (1728–1817) at the Schönbrunn gardens, Vienna *c.* 1801.

Rarest

Plants thought to be extinct are rediscovered each year and there are thus many plants of which specimens are known in but a single locality. The small pink blossoms of *Presidio manzanita* survive in a single specimen reported in June 1978 at an undisclosed site in California. *Pennantia baylisiana*, a tree found in 1945 on Three Kings Island, off New Zealand, only exists as a female and cannot fruit. In May 1983 it was reported that there was a sole surviving specimen of the Lady's slipper orchid (*Cypripedium calceolus*). *Sporastatia cinerea*, a new genus of alpine lichen for Britain was found in Choire Garbh snowfield in the Cairngorm Scotland in 1982.

Northernmost

The Yellow poppy (*Papaver radicatum*) and the Arctic willow (*Salix arctica*) survive, the latter in an extremely stunted form, on the northernmost land (83° N).

Southernmost

Lichens resembling *Rhinodina frigida* have been found in Moraine Canyon in 86° 09′ S 157° 30′ W in 1971 and in the Horlick Mountain area, Antarctica in 86° 09′ S 131° 14′ W in 1965. The southernmost recorded flowering plant is the Antarctic Hair grass (*Deschampsia antarctica*) which was found in latitude 68° 21′ S on Refuge Island, Antarctica on 11 Mar 1981.

Highest

The greatest certain altitude at which any flowering plants have been found is 21,000 ft *6400 m* on Kamet (25,447 ft *7756 m*) by N. D. Jayal in 1955. They were *Ermania himalayensis* and *Ranunculus lobatus*.

Roots

The greatest reported depth to which roots have penetrated is a calculated 400 ft *120 m* in the case of a wild fig tree at Echo Caves, near Ohrigstad, East Transvaal, South Africa. An elm tree root of at least 360 ft *110 m* was reported from Auchencraig, Largs, Strathclyde *c.* 1950. A single Winter rye plant (*Secale cereale*) has been shown to produce 387 miles *622,8 km* of roots in 1.83 ft³ *0,051 m³* of earth.

Worst weeds

The most intransigent weed is the mat-forming water weed *Salvinia auriculata*, found in Africa. It was detected on the filling of Kariba Lake in May 1959 and within 11 months had choked an area of 77 miles² *199 km²* rising by 1963 to 387 miles² *1002 km²*. The world's worst land weeds are regarded as Purple nut sedge, Bermuda grass, Barnyard grass, Jungle-rice, goose grass, Johnson grass, Guinea grass, Cogon grass and lantana. The most damaging and widespread cereal weeds in Britain are the wild oats *Avena fatua* and *A. ludoviciana*. Their seeds can withstand temperatures of 240° F *115,6° C* for 15 min and remain viable.

The largest weed in Britain is the giant hogweed *Heracleum manteggazzianum* which established itself from seeds brought from the Caucasas before 1862. It grows to over 12 ft *3,65 m* in height.

Most spreading plant

The greatest area covered by a single clonal growth is that of the wild Box huckleberry (*Gaylussacia brachyera*), a mat-forming evergreen shrub first reported in 1796. A colony covering about 100 acres, was found on 18 July 1920 near the Juniata River, Pennsylvania. It has been estimated that this colony began 13,000 years ago.

Longest Philodendron

A Philodendron over 654 ft *199 m* in length grows in the home of Mr M. J. Linhart in Thornton, Leicestershire.

Longest Passion plant

In November 1974 a Passion plant, fed by a hormone by Dennis and Patti Carlson, was reported to have grown to a length of 600 ft *182 m* at Blaine, Minnesota, USA.

Largest aspidistra

The aspidistra (*Aspidistra elatior*) was introduced to Britain as a parlour palm from Japan and China in 1822. The biggest in the world (*pace* Gracie Fields) belongs to Cliff Evans of Kiora, Moruya, NSW, Australia. In April 1983 it measured 56 in *142 cm*. The biggest aspidistra in Britain is one 50 in *127 cm* tall with more than 500 leaves spanning 5 ft *1,52 m* grown by Gertie James in Staveley, Chesterfield.

Earliest flower

The oldest fossil of a flowering plant with palm-like imprints was found in Colorado, USA, in 1953 and dated about 65,000,000 years old.

Largest cactus

The largest of all cacti is the saguaro (*Cereus giganteus* or *Carnegiea gigantea*), found in Arizona, south-eastern California, USA and Sonora, Mexico. The green fluted column is surmounted by candelabra-like branches rising to a height of 16 m *52 ft 6 in* in the case of a specimen measured on the boundary of the Saguaro National Monument, Arizona. They have waxy white blooms which are followed by edible crimson fruit. An armless cactus 78 ft *24 m* in height was measured in April 1978 by Hube Yates in Cave Creek, Arizona.

HEDGES

Tallest hedge *World*

The world's tallest hedge is the Meikleour beech hedge in Perthshire, Scotland. It was planted in 1746 and has now attained a trimmed height of 85 ft *26 m*. It is 600 yd *550 m* long. Some of its trees now exceed 120 ft *36,5 m*.

Tallest hedge *Yew*

The tallest yew hedge in the world is in Earl Bathurst's Park, Cirencester, Gloucestershire. It was planted in 1720, runs for 170 yd *155 m*, reaches 36 ft *11 m*, is 15 ft *4,5 m* thick at its base and takes 20 man-days to trim.

Tallest hedge *Box*

The tallest box hedge is 35 ft *10,7 m* in height at Birr Castle, Offaly, Ireland dating from the 18th century.

SEAWEED

Longest *Seaweed*

Claims made that the seaweed off Tierra del Fuego, South America, grows to 600 ft *182,5 m* and even to 1000 ft *305 m* in length have gained currency. More recent and more reliable records indicate that the longest species of seaweed is the Pacific giant kelp (*Macrocystis pyrifera*), which does not exceed 196 ft *60 m* in length. It can grow 45 cm *18 in* in a day. The longest of the 700 species of British seaweed is the Brown seaweed *Chorda filum* which grows up to a length of 20 ft *6,10 m*. The Japanese *Sargassum muticum* introduced *c.* 1970 can grow to 30 ft *9,0 m*.

Deepest *Seaweed*

The greatest depth at which plant life has been found is 884 ft *269 m* by Mark and Diane Littler (USA) off San Salvadore Island, Bahamas in October 1984. These maroon coloured algae survived though 99.9995 per cent of sunlight was filtered out.

Mosses

The smallest of mosses is the pygmy moss (*Ephemerum*) and the longest is the brook moss (*Fontinalis*), which forms streamers up to 3 ft *91 cm* long in flowing water.

VINES & VINEYARDS

Largest Vine

This was planted in 1842 at Carpinteria, California, USA. By 1900 it was yielding more than 9 tons/*tonnes* of grapes in some years, and averaging 7 tons/*tonnes* per year. It died in 1920. Britain's largest vine (1898–1964) was at Kippen, Stirling with a girth, measured in 1956, of 5 ft *1,52 m*. England's largest vine is the Great Vine, planted in 1768 at Hampton Court, Greater London. Its girth is 85 in *215,9 cm* with branches up to 114 ft *34,7 m* long and an average yield of 703 lb *318,8 kg*. In 1983 Leslie Stringer of Dartford, Kent obtained a yield of 1015½ lb *460,6 kg* from a vine from Banstead, Surrey planted in 1962. A single bunch of grapes (Red Thomson seedless) weighing 9400 grammes

The rare Bolivian *Puya raimondii* whose 35 ft *10,7 mm* panicle, which emerges after about 150 years, makes it the world's largest and slowest flowering herb. *See p. 46.* (Photo by Mulford B. Foster, Orlando, Florida and reproduced with the assistance of the Bromeliad society).

20 lb 11½ oz were weighed in Santiago, Chile in May 1984.

Most northerly and southerly vineyards

A vineyard at Sabile, Latvia, USSR is just north of Lat. 57° N. The most northerly commercial vineyard in Britain is that at Renishaw hall, Derbyshire with 2600 vines. It lies in Lat. 53° 18′ N. The most southerly commercial vineyard is operated by Moorilla Estates Pty Ltd at Berridale, Tasmania in Lat. 42° 47′ S.

BLOOMS AND FLOWERS

Largest bloom *World*

The mottled orange-brown and white parasitic Stinking corpse lily (*Rafflesia arnoldii*) has the largest of all blooms. These attach themselves to the cissus vines of the jungle in south-east Asia and measure up to 3 ft *91 cm* across and ¾ inch *1,9 cm* thick, and attain a weight of 15 lb *7 kg*. The spathe and spadix of the less massive green and purple flower of *Amorphophallus titanum* of Sumatra may attain a length of more than 1,5 m *5 ft*.

The largest known inflorescence is that of *Puya raimondii*, a rare Bolivian plant with an erect panicle (diameter 8 ft *2,4 m*) which emerges to a height of 35 ft *10,7 m*. Each of these bears up to 8000 white blooms (see also Slowest-flowering plant below). The flower-spike of an agave was in 1974 measured to be 52 ft *15,8 m* long in Berkeley, California.

The world's largest blossoming plant is the giant Chinese wisteria at Sierra Madre, California, USA. It was planted in 1892 and now has branches 500 ft *152 m* long. It covers nearly an acre, weighs 225 tons *228 tonnes* and has an estimated 1,500,000 blossoms during its blossoming period of five weeks, when up to 30,000 people pay admission to visit it.

Largest bloom *Great Britain*

The largest bloom of any indigenous British flowering plant is that of the wild white water lily (*Nymphaea alba*), which measures 6 in *15 cm* across. Other species bear much larger inflorescences such as the 19 in *48 cm* diameter sunflower (*Helianthus annuus*) flower head measured for Mrs Lena Filipchuk of Burnaby, British Columbia, Canada on 15 Oct 1984.

Smallest flowering and fruiting plant

The floating flowering aquatic duckweed *Wolffia angusta* of Australia described in 1980 is only 0,6 mm 1/42 *of an inch* in length and 0.33 mm 1/85 *of an inch* in width. It weighs about 0,00015 g *1/190,000 of an oz*, its fruit resembling a miniscule

Dr Julian Steyermark whose world-beating collection of plants numbers 137,000.

fig weighs 0.00007 g or 400,000 to the oz. The smallest land plant regularly flowering in Britain is the chaffweed (*Cetunculus minimus*), a single seed of which weighs 0,00003 of a gramme.

Smallest plant

The smallest 'plant' is a uni-cellular alga and is listed under Protista smallest (see p. 50).

Most valuable

The Burpee Co $10,000 prize offered in 1954 for the first all-white marigold was won on 12 Aug 1975 by Alice Vonk of Sully, Iowa, USA.

Fastest growth

The case of a *Hesperogucca whipplei* of the family Liliaceae growing 12 ft *3,65 m* in 14 days was reported from Tresco Abbey, Isles of Scilly in July 1978.

Slowest flowering plant

The slowest flowering of all plants is the rare *Puya raimondii*, the largest of all herbs, discovered in Bolivia in 1870. The panicle emerges after about 150 years of the plant's life. It then dies. (See also above under Largest blooms.) Some agaves, erroneously called Century plants, first flower after 40 years.

Champion plant collector

Dr Julian A. Steyermark of the Herbario Nacional, Caracas, Venezuela, had by September 1985, made an unrivalled total of 137,000 collections of which 132,000 were solo.

Largest wreath

The largest wreath constructed was the wreath built by The Gothenburg Florists at Liseberg Amusement Park, Sweden, completed on 4 Sept 1982. It measured 20,83 m *68 ft 4 in* in diameter and weighed 1980 kg (*1.95 tons*).

Longest daisy chain

The longest daisy chain, made in 7 hr, was one of 6980 ft 7 in *2,12 km* by villagers of Good Easter, Chelmsford, Essex on 27 May 1985. The team is limited to 16.

Orchid *Largest and Tallest*

The largest of all orchids is *Grammatophyllum speciosum*, native to Malaysia. Specimens have been recorded up to 25 ft *7,62 m* in height. The largest orchid flower is that of *Phragmipedium caudatum*, found in tropical areas of America. Its petals are up to 18 in *46 cm* long, giving it a maximum outstretched diameter of 3 ft *91 cm*. The flower is, however, much less bulky than that of the Stinking corpse lily (see above). The tallest free-standing orchid is *Grammatophyllum speciosum* (see above). *Galeola foliata* may attain 49 ft *15 m* on decaying rainforest trees in Queensland, Australia.

The first flowering in Britain of *Grammatophyllum wallisii* from Mindanao, Philippines at Burnham Nurseries, Kingsteignton, Devon in 1982 produced 557 flowers.

Orchid *Smallest*

The smallest orchid is *Platystele jungermannoides*, found in Central America. Its flowers are 1 mm *0.04 in* across.

Orchid *Highest priced*

The highest price ever paid for an orchid is 1150 guineas (£1,207.50), paid by Baron Schröder to Sanders of St Albans for an *Odontoglossum crispum* (variety *pittianum*) at an auction by Protheroe & Morris of Bow Lane, London, on 22 Mar 1906. A Cymbidium orchid called Rosanna Pinkie was sold in the United States for $4500 (*then £1600*) in 1952.

Largest rhododendron

The largest species of rhododendron is the

(Artwork: Pam Stephens)

SLIMMERS NIGHTMARE
741 *calories per lb*

SLIMMERS FRIEND
73 *calories per lb*

scarlet *Rhododendron arboreum*, examples of which reach a height of 65 ft *19,8 m* on Mt Japfu, Nagaland, India. The cross-section of the trunk of a *Rhododendron giganteum*, reputedly 90 ft *27,43 m* high from Yunnan, China is preserved at Inverewe Garden, Highland. The largest in the United Kingdom is one 25 ft *7,60 m* tall and 272 ft *82,90 m* in circumference at Government House, Hillsborough, Co. Down. A specimen 35 ft *10,65 m* high and 3 ft 3 in *99 cm* in circumference has been measured at Tregothan, Truro, Cornwall.

Largest rose tree
A 'Lady Banks' rose tree at Tombstone, Arizona, USA, has a trunk 40 in *101 cm* thick, stands 9 ft *2,74 m* high and covers an area of 5380 ft² *499 m²* supported by 68 posts and several thousand feet of piping. This enables 150 people to be seated under the arbour. The cutting came from Scotland in 1884.

FRUITS AND VEGETABLES
Most and least nutritive
An analysis of the 38 commonly eaten raw (as opposed to dried) fruits shows that the one with the highest calorific value is avocado (*Persea americana*), with 741 calories per edible pound or *163 cals per 100 gr*. That with the lowest value is cucumber with 73 calories per pound *16 cals per 100 gr*. Avocados probably originated in Central and South America and contain also vitamins A, C, and E and 2.2 per cent protein.

Chilli
The tallest chilli plant was one of 6,6 m *21 ft 7 in* grown by Shri Kishan Joshi of Almora, India in 1981.

Melon
A watermelon weighing 200 lb *90,7 kg* was reported by Grace's Garden in April 1980. The growers were Ivan and Lloyd Bright of Hope, Arkansas, USA.

Peach *Largest*
The largest peach reported in Britain is one of 14½ oz *411 g* 12 in *30,4 cm* in August 1984 from a 26-year-old Italian tree grown by Mrs Jean Bird of London SW6.

Pineapple *Largest*
A pineapple weighing 17 lb 8 oz *7,96 kg* was harvested by Dole Philippines Inc at South Cotabato, Philippines in November 1984. Pineapples up to 13 kg *28.6 lb* were reported in 1978 from Tarauaca, Brazil.

Potato
A record display of 369 varieties of potato (*Solanum tuberosum*) was mounted on *BBC Record Breakers* by Donald MacLean on 16 Sept 1984.

HERBS
Herbs are not botanically defined but consist of plants whose leaves or roots are of culinary or medicinal value. The most heavily consumed is coriander *Coriandrum sativum*. It is used in curry powder, confectionery, in bread and in gin.

FERNS
Largest
The largest of all the more than 6000 species of fern is the tree fern (*Alsophila excelsa*) of Norfolk Island, in the South Pacific, which attains a height of up to 60 ft *18,28 m*.

The highest recorded in Britain is bracken *Pteridium aquilinum* over 16 ft *4,8 m* in Ruislip, Middlesex in 1970.

The 'Lady Banks' in Arizona—the ultimate rose tree pruner's problem.

Smallest
The world's smallest ferns are *Hecistopteris pumila*, found in Central America, and *Azolla caroliniana*, which is native to the United States and has fronds down to ½ in *12 mm*.

GRASSES
Commonest
The world's commonest grass is *Cynodon dactylon* or Bermuda grass. The 'Callie' hybrid, selected in 1966, grows as much as 6 in *15,2 cm* a day and stolons reach 18 ft *5,5 m* in length.

Fastest growing
Some species of the 45 genera of bamboo have been measured to grow at up to 36 in *91 cm* per day (0.00002 mph *0,00003 km/h*).

Tallest
A Thorney bamboo culm (*Bambusa arundinacea*) felled at Pattazhi, Travancore, India in November 1904 measured 121½ ft *37,0 m*. The tallest of the 160 grasses found in Great Britain is the common reed (*Phragmites communis*), which reaches a height of 9 ft 9 in *2,97 m*.

Shortest
The shortest grass native to Great Britain is the very rare sand bent (*Mibora minima*) from Anglesey, Gwynedd which has a maximum growing height of under 6 in *15 cm*.

LEAVES
Largest *World*
The largest leaves of any plant belong to the Raffia palm (*Raphia raffia*) of the Mascarene Islands, in the Indian Ocean and the Amazonian bamboo palm (*R. toedigera*) of South America, whose leaf blades may measure up to 65 ft *19,81 m* in length with petioles up to 13 ft *3,96 m*.

The largest undivided leaf is that of *Alocasia macrorrhiza*, found in Sabah, East Malaysia. One found in 1966 was 9 ft 11 in *3,02 m* long and 6 ft 3½ in *1,92 m* wide, with a unilateral area of 34.2 ft² *3,17 m²*.

Largest *Great Britain*
The largest leaves to be found in outdoor plants in Great Britain are those of *Gunnera manicata* from Brazil with leaves 6–10 ft *1,82–3,04 m* across on prickly stems 5–8 ft *1,52–2,43 m* long.

Fourteen-leafed clover
A fourteen-leafed white clover (*Trifolium repens*) was found by Randy Farland near Sioux Falls, South Dakota, USA on 16 June 1975.

SEEDS
Largest
The largest seed in the world is that of the double coconut or Coco de Mer (*Lodoicea seychellarum*), the single-seeded fruit of which may weigh 40 lb *18 kg*. This grows only in the Seychelles, in the Indian Ocean.

Smallest
The smallest seeds are those of *Epiphytic* orchids, at 35,000,000 to the oz (*cf.* grass pollens at up to 6,000,000,000 grains/oz). A single plant of the American ragweed can generate 8,000,000,000 pollen grains in five hours.

Most viable
The most protracted claim for the viability of seeds is that made for the Arctic lupin (*Lupinus arcticus*) found in frozen silt at Miller Creek in the Yukon, Canada in July 1954 by Harold Schmidt. The seeds were germinated in 1966 and were dated by the radiocarbon method of associated material to at least 8000 BC and more probably to 13,000 BC.

Most conquering conker
The highest recorded battle honours for an untreated conker (fruit of the Common horsechestnut or *Aesculus hippocastanum*) is a 'five thousander plus', which won the BBC Conker Conquest in 1954. A professor of botany has however opined that this heroic specimen might well have been a 'ringer', probably an ivory or tagua nut (*Phytelephas macrocarpa*). The *Guinness Book of Records* will not publish any category for the largest collection of conkers for fear that trees might suffer wholesale damage

TREES AND WOOD
Most massive tree
The most massive living thing on Earth is the biggest known Giant Sequoia (*Sequoiadendron giganteum*) named the 'General Sherman', standing 274.9 ft *83,8 m* tall, in the Sequoia National Park, California, USA. It has a true girth of 114.6 ft *34,9 m* (1980) (at 5 ft *1,52 m* above the ground). The 'General Sherman' has been estimated to contain the equivalent of 600,120 board feet of timber, sufficient to make 5,000,000,000 matches. The foliage is bluegreen, and the red-brown tan bark may be up to 24 in *61 cm* thick in parts. Estimates (1981) place its weight, including its root system, at 6000 long tons *6100 tonnes* but the timber is light (18 lb/ft³ *288,3 kg/m³*) and a 1985 estimate suggests nearer 2500 tons/tonnes. The largest known petrified tree is one of this species with a 295 ft *89,9 m* trunk near Coaldale, Nevada, USA.

The seed of a 'big tree' weighs only 1/6000th of an oz *4,7 mg*. Its growth at maturity may therefore represent an increase in weight of 1,300,000 million-fold.

The tree canopy covering the greatest area is the

RECORD DIMENSIONS AND WEIGHTS FOR FRUIT VEGETABLES AND FLOWERS GROWN IN THE UNITED KINGDOM

Many data subsequent to 1958 come from the annual *Garden News* and Phostrogen Ltd. Giant Vegetable and Fruit Contest and the Super Sunflower Contest.

APPLE	3 lb 1 oz	1,357 kg	V. Loveridge	Ross-on-Wye, Hereford & Worcester	1965
ARTICHOKE	8 lb	3,625 kg	A. R. Lawson	Tollerton, North Yorkshire	1964
BEETROOT	29 lb	13,154 kg	F. A. Pulley	Maidstone, Kent	1964
BROAD BEAN	23⅜ in	59,3 cm	T. Currie	Jedburgh, Borders	1963
	23⅜ in	59,3 cm	Mrs M. Adrian	Irvine, Strathclyde	1982
BROCCOLI	28 lb 14¾ oz	13,100 kg	J. T. Cooke	Funtington, W. Sussex	1964
BRUSSELS SPROUT[1]	16 lb 1 oz	7,285 kg	E. E. Jenkins	Shipston-on-Stour, Warwickshire	1974
CABBAGE[2]	114 lb 3 oz	51,8 kg	P. G. Barton	Cleckheaton, W. Yorkshire	1977
CARROT[3]	10 lb 4 oz	4,649 kg	E. Stone	East Woodyates, Wiltshire	1984
CAULIFLOWER	52 lb 11½ oz	23,900 kg	J. T. Cooke	Funtington, W. Sussex	1966
CELERY	35 lb	15,875 kg	C. Bowcock	Willaston, Merseyside	1973
CUCUMBER[4]	13 lb 10⅞ oz (indoor)	6,201 kg	A. Emery	Rochester, Kent	1984
	8 lb 4 oz (outdoor)	3,740 kg	C. Bowcock	Willaston, Merseyside	1973
	43½ in	110 cm	A. C. Rayment	Chelmsford, Essex	1984
DAHLIA[5]	10 ft 5 in	3,17 m	R. Lond	Diss, Norfolk	1985
DWARF BEAN	17½ in	43,4 cm	C. Bowcock	Willaston, Merseyside	1973
GLADIOLUS	8 ft 4½ in	2,55 m	A. Breed	Melrose, Roxburgh, Borders	1981
GOOSEBERRY	2.06 oz	58,5 g	A. Dingle	Macclesfield, Cheshire	1978
GOURD	196 lb	88,900 kg	J. Leathes	Herringfleet Hall, Suffolk	1846
GRAPEFRUIT*[6]	3 lb 11 oz	1,673 kg	Willington G.C.	Willington, Bedfordshire	1986
HOLLYHOCK	24 ft 3 in	7,39 m	W. P. Walshe	Eastbourne, E. Sussex	1961
KALE[7]	12 ft tall	3,65 m	B. T. Newton	Mullion, Cornwall	1950
LEEK	9 lb 5½ oz	4,235 kg	C. Bowcock	Willaston, Merseyside	1973
LEEK, POT	117.82 in³	1930 cm³	G. Brownlees	Brandon, Durham	1984
LEMON[8]	4 lb 11 oz	2,13 kg	Pershore College	Pershore, Worcestershire	1986
LETTUCE	25 lb	11,335 kg	C. Bowcock	Willaston, Merseyside	1974
LUPIN*	6 ft 0½ in	1,84 m	J. Lawlor	New Malden, Surrey	1971
MANGOLD	54½ lb	24,720 kg	P. F. Scott	Sutton, Humberside	1971
MARROW	105 lb 8 oz	47,85 kg	D. C. Payne	Tewkesbury, Glos.	1982
MUSHROOM[9]	54 in circum.	1,37 m	—	Hasketon, Suffolk	1957
ONION[10]	7 lb 11¾ oz	3,508 kg	W. Rodger	Crail, Fife	1984
PARSNIP[11]	10 lb 8½ oz	4,776 kg	C. Moore	Peacehaven, E. Sussex	1980
PEAPOD	10⅛ in	25,7 cm	T. Currie	Jedburgh, Borders	1964
PEAR[12]	2 lb 10½ oz	1,200 kg	Mrs. K. Loines	Hythe, Hampshire	1973
PETUNIA*	8 ft 4 in	2,53 m	G. A. Warner	Dunfermline, Fife	1978
POTATO[13]	7 lb 1 oz	3,200 kg	J. H. East	Spalding, Lincolnshire	1963
	7 lb 1 oz	3,200 kg	J. P. Busby	Atherstone, Warwickshire	1982
PUMPKIN[14]	444 lb	201,4 kg	R. A. Butcher	Stockbridge, Hampshire	1984
RADISH[15]	17 lb	7,711 kg	K. Ayliffe	Brecon, Powys	1976
RED CABBAGE	42 lb	19,05 kg	R. Straw	Staveley, Derbyshire	1925
RHUBARB	5 lb 14 oz	2,665 kg	E. Stone	East Woolgates, Wiltshire	1985
RUNNER BEAN	39 in long	99 cm	Mrs. E. Huxley	Churton, Cheshire	1976
SAVOY CABBAGE	38 lb 8 oz	17,450 kg	W. H. Neil	Retford, Nottinghamshire	1966
SHALLOT*	2 lb 12 oz (47 bulbs)	1,245 kg	M. Silverstoff	Falmouth, Cornwall	1977
STRAWBERRY	8.17 oz	231 g	G. Anderson	Folkestone, Kent	1983
SUGAR BEET[16]	30 lb 10 oz	13,9 kg	K. McLean	Meldreth, Hertfordshire	1984
SUNFLOWER[17]	23 ft 6½ in tall	7,17 m	F. Kelland	Exeter, Devon	1976
SWEDE	48 lb 12 oz	22,11 kg	A. Foster	Alnwick, Northumberland	1980
TOMATO[18]	4 lb 5½ oz	1,970 kg	R. G. Burrows	Huddersfield, Yorkshire	1985
TOMATO PLANT[19]	45 ft 9½ in (length)	13,96 m	Chosen Hill School	Gloucester, Glos.	1981
TOMATO TRUSS	20 lb 4 oz	9,175 kg	C. Bowcock	Willaston, Merseyside	1973
TURNIP[20]	35 lb 4 oz	15,975 kg	C. W. Butler	Nafferton, Humberside	1972

[1] A Brussels Sprout plant measuring 11 ft 8 in 3,55 m was grown by Ralph G. Sadler of Watchbury Farm, Barford, Warwickshire on 6 July 1978.

[2] The Swalwell, County Durham Red Cabbage of 1865 grown by William Collingwood (d. 8 Oct 1867) reputedly weighed 123 lb 55,7 kg and was 259 in 6,57 m in circumference.

[3] A specimen of 7 kg 15 lb 7 oz was grown by Miss I. G. Scott of Nelson, New Zealand in October 1978.

[4] A 17 kg 37 lb 4 oz monster was grown by Mrs Eileen Chappel at Nudgee, Qld, Australia in the 6 months before it was weighed on 29 Apr 1985. A Vietnamese variety 6 ft 1,83 m long was reported by L. Szabo of Debrecen, Hungary in September 1976.

[5] A 16 ft 5 in 5,0 m dahlia was grown by Sam and Pat Barnes of Chattahoochee, Florida, USA in 1982.

[6] A 6 lb 8½ oz 2,966 kg specimen was weighed for Joshua and Allison Sosnow in Tucson, Arizona, USA on 21 Dec 1984.

[7] F. Doven of Mt Lawley, Australia grew a kale measuring 4,16 m 13 ft 7½ in in 1982.

[8] An 8 lb 8 oz 3,88 kg lemon with a 29½ in 74,9 cm girth was grown by Charlotte and Donald Knutzen of Whittier, California, USA in August 1983.

[9] Same size reported by J. Coombes at Mark, Somerset on 28 July 1965. In September 1968 one weighing 18 lb 10 oz 8,425 kg was reported from Whidbey I. Washington, USA. A specimen of the edible Termitomyces titanicus found near Kitwe, Zambia on 18 Dec 1978 measured 26 in 63 cm in diameter and weighed 5.5 lb 2,5 kg. A mushroom of 'nearly 100 lb' and 20 in 51 cm thick was reported from Potenza, Italy on 30 Oct 1985.

[10] An onion of 7½ lb 3,4 kg was grown by Nelson W. Hope of Cardiff, California in 1965 with a girth of 26 in 66 cm. Its original gross weight was reputedly 8 lb 3,62 kg.

[11] One 60 in 152 cm long was reported by M. Zaninovich of Waneroo W. Australia.

[12] A specimen weighing 1,405 kg 3.09 lb was harvested on 10 May 1979 at Messrs K. & R. Yeomans, Arding, Armidale, NSW, Australia.

[13] One weighing 18 lb 4 oz 8,275 kg reported dug up by Thomas Siddal in his garden in Chester on 17 Feb 1795. A yield of 515 lb 233,5 kg from a 2¾ lb parent seed by Bowcock planted in April 1977. Six tubers weighing 54 lb 8 oz 24,72 kg by Alan Nunn of Rhodes, Greater Manchester were reported on 18 Sept 1949.

[14] A pumpkin (C. maxima) of 612 lb 277,6 kg (135 in 3,42 m girth) grown by Norman Gallagher of Chalen, Washington, USA won the Half Moon Bay Pumpkin Festival at San Francisco, California USA on 8 Oct 1984.

[15] A radish of 27 lb 12,25 kg and 27⅓ in 69,8 cm long was grown by Ron Whitford in Wollongong, Australia in Nov 1985.

[16] One weighing 45½ lb 20,63 kg was grown by R. Meyer of Brawley, California in 1974.

[17] A sunflower of 7,38 m 24 ft 2½ in was grown by Martien Heijms of Oirschot, The Netherlands in 1983.

[18] Grace's Gardens reported a 6 lb 8 oz 2,94 kg tomato grown by Clarence Daily of Monona, Wisconsin in 1977.

[19] Gordon Graham of Edmond, Oklahoma, has grown a tomato plant of 52 ft 15,85 m in April 1985.

[20] A 73 lb 33,1 kg turnip was reported in Dec. 1768 and one of 51 lb 23,1 kg from Alaska in 1981.

* Not in official contest.

The heaviest orange ever reported is one weighing 5 lb 8 oz 2,50 kg exhibited in Nelspruit, South Africa on 19 June 1981. It was the size of a human head but was stolen.

---

great Banyan *Ficus benghalensis* in the Indian Botanical Garden, Calcutta with 1775 prop or supporting roots and a circumference of 1350 ft *412 m*. It covers overall some 3 acres *1,2 ha* and dates from *ante* 1787.

Greatest girth *World*

El Arbol del Tule, in the state of Oaxaca, in Mexico is a 135 ft *41 m* tall Montezuma cypress (*Taxodium mucronatum*) with a girth of 117.6 ft *35,8 m* at a height of 5 ft *1,52 m* above the ground in 1982. A figure of 167 ft *51 m* in circumference was reported for the pollarded European chestnut (*Castanea sativa*) known as the 'Tree of the 100 Horses' (Castagno di Cento Cavalli) on Mount Etna, Sicily, Italy in 1972 and measurements up to 180 ft *54,5 m* have been attributed to Baobab trees (*Adansonia digitata*).

Greatest girth *Britain*

The tree of greatest girth in Britain is a sweet ('Spanish') chestnut (*Castanea sativa*) in the grounds of Canford School, Nr. Wimborne, Dorset, with a bole 43 ft 9 in *13,33 m* in circumference. The largest-girthed living British oak is one at Bowthorpe Farm near Bourne, south Lincolnshire, measured in September 1973 to be 39 ft 1 in *11,91 m*. The largest 'maiden' (i.e. not pollarded) oak is the Majesty Oak at Fredville Park, near Nonington, Kent, with a girth of 38 ft 1 in *11,60 m* (1973). The largest yew with a clear bole at 5 ft *1,52 m* is 35 ft 5 in *10,79 m* at Ulcombe Church, Kent.

Fastest growing

Discounting bamboo, which is not botanically classified as a tree, but as a woody grass, the fastest rate of growth recorded is 35 ft 3 in *10,74 m* in 13 months by an *Albizzia falcata* planted on 17 June 1974 in Sabah, Malaysia. The youngest recorded age for a tree to reach 100 ft *30,48 m* is 64 months for one of the species planted on 24 Feb 1975, also in Sabah.

Slowest growing

The speed of growth of trees depends largely upon conditions, although some species, such as box and yew, are always slow-growing. The extreme is represented by a specimen of Sitka spruce which required 98 years to grow to 11 in *28 cm* tall with a diameter of less than 1 in *2,5 cm* on the Arctic tree-line. The growing of miniature trees or *bonsai* is an oriental cult mentioned as early as *c.* 1320.

Tallest *World*

The tallest tree ever measured was a Douglas Fir *Pseudotsuga menziesii* in Lynn Valley, British Columbia, Canada in 1902. It stood 415 ft *126,5 m*. According to the researches of Dr A. C. Carder (Canada) the closest measured rivals to this champion have been:

ft	m	
393	119,7	The Mineral Douglas fir *Pseudotsuga menziesii*, Washington State, USA, 1905
380	115,8	Nisqually fir *Pseudotsuga menziesii*, Nisqually River, Washington State, 1899
375	114,3	Cornthwaite Mountain ash *Eucalyptus regnans*, Thorpdale, Victoria, Australia, 1880
*367.8	112,1	'Tallest Tree', Redwood Creek *Sequoia sempervirens*, Humboldt County, California, USA, 1963
367.6	112	Coast redwood *Sequoia sempervirens*, Guerneville, California, USA, 1873

* Tallest standing tree in the world. Crown dying back. Height last re-estimated at 362 ft *110,3 m* in 1972.

Currently the tallest standing broadleaf tree is a Mountain ash in the Styx Valley, Tasmania at 325 ft *99 m*.

Tallest *Great Britain*

The tallest trees in Great Britain are a Grand fir (*Abies grandis*) at Strone, Cairndow, Strathclyde, and Douglas firs at The Hermitage, Perth, and in Moniac Glen, Inverness. In June 1985 all

TALLEST TREES IN THE BRITISH ISLES By species

		ft	m
ALDER (Italian)	Westonbirt, Gloucester	98	30
ALDER (Common)	Ashburnham Park, East Sussex	105	32
ASH	Old Roar Ghyll, St. Leonards, East Sussex	135	41
BEECH	Beaufront Castle, Northumberland	144	44
BEECH (Copper)	Chart Park Golf Course, Dorking, Surrey	124	38
BIRCH (Swedish)	Taymouth Castle	110	29
CEDAR (Blue Atlas)	Brockhampton Pk, Hereford & Worcs	125	38
CEDAR (of Lebanon)	Leaton Knolls, Shropshire	140	42
CHESTNUT (Horse)	Ashford Chase, Hampshire	130	39
CHESTNUT (Sweet)	Godinton Park, Kent	122	37
CYPRESS (Lawson)	Endsleigh, Devon	133	40
CYPRESS (Leyland)	Bicton, Devon	118	36
CYPRESS (Monterey)	Bicton, Devon	124	38
DOUGLAS FIR	The Hermitage, Perth, Tayside	200+	61+
ELM[1] (Huntingdon)	Howlett's Park Zoo, Kent	132	40
ELM[1] (Smooth Leaf)	North Inch, Perth, Tayside	132	40
ELM (Wych)[1]	Rossie Priory, Tayside	138	42
EUCALYPTUS (Blue Gum)	Glencormack, Co. Wicklow	144	44
GRAND FIR	Strone, Cairndow, Strathclyde	203	62
GINKGO	Linton Park (Maidstone), Kent	98	30
HEMLOCK (Western)	Murthly Castle, Tayside	170	52
HOLLY	Ashburnham Park, East Sussex	80	24
HORNBEAM	Wrest Park, Bedfordshire	105	32
LARCH (European)	Glenlee, Dumfries & Galloway	150	46
LARCH (Japanese)	Blair Castle, Tayside	123	37
LIME	Duncombe Park, North Yorkshire	150	45
METASEQUOIA	Leonardslee, Sussex	95	29
MONKEY PUZZLE	Lochnaw, Dumfries & Galloway	95	29
OAK (Common)	Leeds Castle, Kent	135	41
OAK (Sessile)	Whitfield Ho., Hereford & Worcs	140	42
OAK (Red)	Cowdray Park, West Sussex	115	35
OAK (Turkey)	Knightshayes, Devon	138	42
PEAR	Borde Hill, West Sussex	64	19
PINE (Corsican)	Adhurst, St. Mary, Hampshire	150	46
PLANE	Bryanston, Dorset	156	48
POPLAR (Black Italian)	Fairlawne, Kent	150	46
POPLAR (Black, native)	Longnor Hall, Shropshire	124	37
POPLAR (Lombardy)	Marble Hill, Twickenham, G. London	130	39
REDWOOD (Coast)	Bodnant, Gwynedd	148	45
SILVER FIR	Arninglas Ho, Strathclyde	176	54
SPRUCE (Sitka)	River Findhorn, Nairn	195	59
SYCAMORE	Lennoxlove, Lothian	132	40
TULIP-TREE	Taplow House, Buckinghamshire	120	36
WALNUT	Gayhurst, Newport Pagnell, Buckinghamshire	80	24
WALNUT (Black)	Bisham Abbey, Buckinghamshire	118	36
WELLINGTONIA	Castle Leod, Easter Ross, Highland	167	51
WILD SERVICE	Gatton Manor, Surrey	87	26
WILLOW (Weeping)	Ashford Chase, Hampshire	79	24
WINGNUT (Caucasian)	Abbotsbury, Dorset	115	35
YEW	Close Walks, Midhurst, West Sussex	95	29

[1] It was estimated in 1980 that more than 17 million of the 23 million elms in southern England had since 1968 been killed by the fungus that causes Dutch elm disease Ceratocystis ulmi.

This 126 ft *38,4 m* Douglas Fir christmas tree erected in Lantana, Florida, in December 1984 was decorated with 15,100 lights, 0.5 mile *0.8 km* of garland, 1050 coloured balls, 250 snowflakes, 225 red bows and supported a 6 ft *1,83 m* high illuminated silver star.

were 200–203 ft *61–62 m*. Only the Strone Grand fir can be measured from both sides. At 203 ft *62 m* and still making visible annual increase, this is the best claimant. The tallest in England is a Douglas fir (*Pseudotsuga taxifolia*) measured at 174 ft *53,0 m* at Broadwood, Dunster, Somerset. The tallest measured in Northern Ireland is a Giant Sequoia (*Sequoiadendron giganteum*), measured in 1983 to be 164 ft *50 m* tall at Caledon Castle, County Tyrone. The tallest in Wales is a Grand Fir (*Abies grandis*) at Leighton Park, Powys (pl. 1886) measured in 1982 to be 190 ft *58 m*.

Tallest *Ireland*

The tallest tree in Ireland is a Sitka spruce (*Picea sitchensis*) 166 ft *50,59 m* tall at Curraghmore, Waterford, measured in March 1974.

Tallest Christmas tree

The world's tallest cut Christmas tree was a 221 ft *67,36 m* tall Douglas fir (*Pseudotsuga taxifolia*) erected at Northgate Shopping Center, Seattle, Washington in December 1950. The tallest Christmas tree erected in Britain was the 85 ft 3¼ in *25,98 m* long spruce from Norway erected for the Canterbury Cathedral appeal on the South Bank, London on 20 Nov 1975.

Oldest tree *World*

The oldest recorded tree was a Bristlecone pine (*Pinus longaeva*) designated WPN-114, which grew at 10,750 ft *3275 m* above sea-level on the north-east face of Mt Wheeler, E. Nevada, USA. It was found to be 5100 years old. The oldest known *living* tree is the Bristlecone pine named *Methuselah* at 10,000 ft *3050 m* in the California side of the White Mountains confirmed as 4600 years old. In March 1974 it was reported that this tree had produced 48 live seedlings. Dendrochronologists estimate the *potential* life-span of a bristlecone pine at nearly 5500 years, but that of a California Big Tree (*Sequoia giganteum*) at perhaps 6000 years. No single cell lives more than 30 years. A report in March 1976 stated that some enormous specimens of Japanese cedar (*Cryptomeria japonica*) had been dated by carbon-14 to 5200 BC.

Oldest tree *Great Britain*

Of all British trees that with the longest life is the yew (*Taxus baccata*), for which a maximum age well in excess of 1000 years is usually conceded. The oldest known is the Fortingall Yew near Aberfeldy, Tayside, part of which still grows. In 1777 this tree was over 50 ft *15,24 m* in girth and it cannot be much less than 2500 years old today. The 1500 years attributed by the Royal Archeological Society to the Eastham yew in Wirral is possible but many are very much bigger and older.

Earliest species

The earliest species of tree still surviving is the Maiden-hair tree (*Ginkgo biloba*) of Chekiang, China, which first appeared about 160,000,000 years ago, during the Jurassic era. It was 'rediscovered' by Kaempfer (Netherlands) in 1690 and reached England *c.* 1754. It has been grown in Japan since *c.* 1100 where it was known as *ginkyō* ('silver apricot') and is now known as *icho*.

Most leaves

Little work has been done on the laborious task of establishing which species has most leaves. A large oak has perhaps 250,000 but a Cypress may have some 45–50 million leaf scales.

Remotest

The tree remotest from any other tree was the one at an oasis in the Ténéré Desert, Niger Republic. In February 1960 it survived being rammed by a lorry driven by a Frenchman. There were no other trees within 50 km *31 miles*.

The tree was transplanted and it is now in the Museum at Niamey, Niger.

Most expensive
The highest price ever paid for a tree is $51,000 (*then £18,214*) for a single Starkspur Golden Delicious apple tree from near Yakima, Washington, USA, bought by a nursery in Missouri in 1959.

Largest forest *World*
The largest afforested areas in the world are the vast coniferous forests of the northern USSR, lying mainly between latitude 55° N, and the Arctic Circle. The total wooded area amounts to 2,700,000,000 acres *1100 million ha* (25 per cent of the world's forests), of which 38 per cent is Siberian larch. The USSR is 34 per cent afforested.

Largest forest *Great Britain*
The largest forest in England is Kielder Forest (72,336 acres *29 273 ha*), in Northumberland. The largest forest in Wales is the Coed Morgannwg (Forest of Glamorgan) (42,555 acres *17 221 ha*). Scotland's most extensive forest is the Glen Trool Forest (51,376 acres *20 791 ha*) in Kirkcudbright, Dumfries & Galloway. The United Kingdom is 7 per cent afforested.

Longest avenue of trees
The longest avenue of trees has been the now partly felled private avenue of 1750 beeches in Savernake Forest near Marlborough, Wiltshire. It measured 3.25 miles *5,23 km*.

Wood *Heaviest*
The heaviest of all woods is Black ironwood (*Olea laurifolia*), also called South African ironwood, with a specific gravity of up to 1.49, and weighing up to 93 lb/ft³ *1490 kg/m³*. The heaviest British wood is boxwood (*Buxus sempervirens*) with an extreme of 64 lb/ft³ *1025 kg/m³*.

Wood *Lightest*
The lightest wood is *Aeschynomene hispida*, found in Cuba, which has a specific gravity of 0.044 and a weight of only 2¾ lb/ft³ *44 kg/m³*. The wood of the Balsa tree (*Ochroma pyramidale*) is of very variable density—between 2½ and 24 lb/ft³ *40 and 384 kg/m³*. The density of cork is 15 lb/ft³ *240 kg/m³*.

KINGDOM PROTISTA

PROTISTA
Protista were first discovered in 1676 by Antonie van Leeuwenhoek of Delft (1632–1723), a Dutch microscopist. Among Protista are characteristics common to both plants and animals. The more plant-like are termed Protophyta (protophytes), including unicellular algae, and the more animal-like are placed in the phylum Protozoa (protozoans), including amoeba and flagellates.

Largest
The largest protozoans in terms of volume, which are known to have existed were calcareous foraminifera (Foraminiferida) belonging to the genus *Nummulites*, a species of which, in the Middle Eocene rocks of Turkey, attained 22 cm *8.6 in* in diameter. The largest existing protozoan, a species of the fan-shaped *Stannophyllum* (Xenophyophorida), can exceed this in length (25 cm *9.8 in* has been recorded) but not in volume.

Smallest
The smallest of all protophytes is the marine microflagellate alga *Micromonas pusilla*, with a diameter of less than 2 microns or micrometres (2 × 10⁻⁶ m) or *0.00008 in*.

Fastest moving
The protozoan *Monas stigmatica* has been measured to move a distance equivalent to 40 times its own length in a second. No human can cover even seven times his own length in a second.

Fastest reproduction
The protozoan *Glaucoma*, which reproduces by binary fission, divides as frequently as every three hours. Thus in the course of a day it could become a 'six greats grandparent' and the progenitor of 510 descendants.

KINGDOM FUNGI

Largest
Martin Mortenson, a science teacher at Dodgeland Junior High, Reeseville, Wisconsin, USA, found a puff ball (*Calvatia gigantea*) 76½ in *194,3 cm* in circumference in 1985. A 72 lb *32,6 kg* example of the edible mushroom (*Polyporus frondosus*) was reported by Joseph Opple near Solon, Ohio in September 1976.

The largest officially recorded tree fungus was a specimen of *Oxyporus* (*Fomes*) *nobilissimus*, measuring 56 in *142 cm* by 37 in *94 cm* and weighing at least 300 lb *136 kg* found by J. Hisey in Washington State, USA, in 1946. The largest recorded in the United Kingdom is an ash fungus (*Fomes fraxineus*) measuring 50 in by 15 in *127 cm* by *38 cm* wide, found by the forester A. D. C. LeSueur on a tree at Waddesdon, Buckinghamshire, in 1954.

Most poisonous toadstool
The yellowish-olive death cap (*Amanita phalloides*) is regarded as the world's most poisonous fungus. It is found in England. From six to fifteen hours after tasting, the effects are vomiting, delirium, collapse and death. Among its victims was Cardinal Giulio de' Medici, Pope Clement VII (b. 1478) on 25 Sept 1534.

The Registrar General's Report states that between 1920 and 1950 there were 39 fatalities from fungus poisoning in the United Kingdom. As the poisonous types are mostly *Amanita* varieties, it is reasonable to assume that the deaths were predominantly due to *Amanita phalloides*. The most recent fatality was probably in 1960.

Aeroflora
Fungi were once classified in the subkingdom Protophyta of the Kingdom Protista. The highest total fungal spore count was 161,037 per m³ near Cardiff on 21 July 1971. A plant tree pollen count of 2160 per m³ was recorded near London on 9 May 1971. The lowest counts of airborne allergens are nil. The highest recorded grass pollen count in Britain was one of 2824 per m³ recorded at Aberystwyth on 29 June 1961.

KINGDOM PROCARYOTA

Earliest life form
In June 1980 Prof J. William Schopf announced the discovery of thread-like cellular remnants built by blue-green algae or bacteria-like organisms in calcareous stromatolites dated to 3500 million years old in the 'North Pole' region of northern Western Australia.

The earliest life-form reported from Britain is *Kakabekia barghoorniana*, a microorganism similar in form to an orange slice, found near Harlech, Gwynedd, Wales in 1964 and dated to 2000 million years ago.

BACTERIA
Antonie van Leeuwenhoek (1632–1723) was the first to observe bacteria in 1675. The largest of the bacteria is the sulphur bacterium *Beggiatoa mirabilis*, which is from 16 to 45 microns in width and which may form filaments several millimetres long.

The bacteria *Thermoactinomyces vulgaris* have been found alive in cores of mud taken from the bottom of Windermere, Cumbria, England which have been dated to 1500 years before the present.

Smallest free-living entity
The smallest of all free-living organisms are pleuro-pneumonia-like organisms (PPLO) of the *Mycoplasma*. One of these, *Mycoplasma laidlawii*, first discovered in sewage in 1936, has a diameter during its early existence of only 100 millimicrons, or 0.000004 in. Examples of the strain known as H.39 have a maximum diameter of 300 millimicrons and weigh an estimated 1.0 × 10⁻¹⁶ gramme. Thus a 190 tonne Blue whale would weigh 1.9 × 10²⁴ or 1.9 quadrillion times as much.

Highest
In April 1967 the US National Aeronautics and Space Administration reported that bacteria had been discovered at an altitude of 135,000 ft (25.56 miles) *41 100 m*.

Longest lived
The oldest deposits from which living bacteria are claimed to have been extracted are salt layers near Irkutsk, USSR, dating from about 600,000,000 years ago, but the discovery was not accepted internationally. The US Dry Valley Drilling Project in Antarctica claimed resuscitated rod-shaped bacteria from caves up to a million years old.

Fastest
The rod-shaped bacillus *Bdellovibrio bacteriovorus*, by means of a polar flagellum rotating 100 times/sec, can move 50 times its own length of 2 µm per second. This would be the equivalent of a human sprinter reaching 200 mph *320 km/h* or a swimmer crossing the Channel in 6 min.

Toughest
The bacterium *Micrococcus radiodurans* can withstand atomic radiation of 6.5 million röntgens or 10,000 times that fatal to the average man. In March 1983 John Barras (University of Oregon, USA) reported bacteria from sulfurous sea bed vents thriving at 306°C *583°F* in the East Pacific Rise at Lat. 21°N.

VIRUSES

Largest
Dmitriy Ivanovsky (1864–1920) first reported filterable objects in 1892 but Martinus Willem Beijerink (1851–1931) first confirmed the nature of viruses in 1898. These are now defined as aggregates of two of more types of chemical (including either DNA or RNA) which are infectious and potentially pathogenic. The longest known is the rod-shaped *Citrus tristeza* virus with particles measuring 200 × 10 nm (1 nanometer = 1 × 10⁻⁹ m).

Smallest
The smallest known viruses are the nucleoprotein plant viruses such as the satellite of tobacco *necrosis virus* with spherical particles 17 nm in diameter. A putative new infectious submicroscopic organism but without nucleic acid, named

a 'prion', was announced from the University of California in February 1982. Viroids (RNA cores without protein coating) are much smaller than viruses. They were discovered by Theodor O. Diener (USA) in February 1972. Dr Rohwer of Bethesda, Maryland, USA stated in September 1984 that scrapie-specific protein was smaller than the concept of a 'yet to be identified prion'.

PARKS, ZOOS, OCEANARIA AND AQUARIA

PARKS

Largest *World*

The world's largest park is the Wood Buffalo National Park in Alberta, Canada (established 1922), which has an area of 11,172,000 acres (17,560 miles² *45 480 km²*).

Largest *Britain*

The largest National Park in Great Britain is the Lake District National Park which has an area of 866 miles² *2240 km²*. The largest private park in the United Kingdom is Woburn Park (3000 acres *1200 ha*), near Woburn Abbey, the seat of the Dukes of Bedford.

ZOOS

Largest game reserve

It has been estimated that throughout the world there are some 500 zoos with an estimated annual attendance of 330,000,000. The largest zoological reserve in the world has been the Etosha Reserve, Namibia established in 1907 with an area which grew to 38,427 miles² *99 525 km²*.

Oldest

The earliest known collection of animals was that set up by Shulgi, a 3rd dynasty ruler of Ur in 2094–2097 BC at Puzurish in south-east Iraq. The oldest known zoo is that at Schönbrunn, Vienna, Austria, built in 1752 by the Holy Roman Emperor Franz I for his wife Maria Theresa. The oldest existing privately owned zoo in the world is that of the Zoological Society of London, founded in 1826. Its collection, housed partly in Regent's Park, London (36 acres *14,5 ha*) and partly at Whipsnade Park, Bedfordshire (541 acres *219 ha*) (opened 23 May 1931), is the most comprehensive in the United Kingdom. The stocktaking on 1 Jan 1986 accounted for a total of 9797 specimens. These comprised 2486 mammals, 2013 birds, 568 reptiles and amphibians, an estimated total of 1430 fish and an estimated total of 3300 invertebrates. Locusts, ants and bees are excluded from these figures. The record annual attendances are 3,031,571 in 1950 for Regent's Park and 756,758 in 1961 for Whipsnade.

OCEANARIA

Earliest and largest

The world's first oceanarium is Marineland of Florida, opened in 1938 at a site 18 miles *29 km* south of St Augustine, Florida, USA. Up to 5,800,000 gal *26,3 million litres* of sea-water are pumped daily through two major tanks, one rectangular (100 ft *30,48 m* long by 40 ft *12,19 m* wide by 18 ft *5,48 m* deep) containing 375,000 gal *1,7 million litres*, and one circular (233 ft *71 m* in circumference and 12 ft *3,65 m* deep) containing 330,000 gal *1,5 million litres*. The tanks are seascaped, including coral reefs and even a

Hanna-Barbera's Marineland at Palos Verdes (*above*) which boasts the largest saltwater tank with a capacity of 530,000 gal 2,4 million litres. (*Below*) Diving in the world's largest aquarium tanks at the newly opened Monterey Bay Aquarium in California, USA.

shipwreck. The salt water tank at Hanna-Barbera's Marineland, located at Palos Verdes, California, USA is 251½ ft *76,65 m* in circumference and 22 ft *6,7 m* deep, with a capacity of 530,000 gal *2,4 million litres*. The total capacity of this whole oceanarium is 2,080,000 gal *9,4 million litres*. Their killer whale 'Orky' at 14,000 lb *6350 kg* is the largest in captivity.

AQUARIA

Largest aquarium

The world's largest aquarium, as opposed to fish farm, is the $40 million Monterey Bay Aquarium, California, USA opened on 2 Oct 1985. The two biggest tanks hold 335,000 and 326,000 US gallons.

CHAPTER THREE

THE

NATURAL
WORLD

The Sogne Fjord in Norway which stretches 183 km *113.7 miles* in length and 4,75 km *3 miles* in width. *See p. 56.* (HUSMO FOTO).

See p. 56.

THE EARTH

The Earth is not a true sphere, but flattened at the poles and hence an oblate spheroid. The polar diameter of the Earth (7899.806 miles *12 713,505 km*) is 26.575 miles *42,769 km* less than the equatorial diameter (7926.381 miles *12 756,274 km*). The Earth has a pear shaped asymmetry with the north polar radius being 148 ft *45 m* longer than the south polar radius. There is also a slight ellipticity of the equator since its long axis (about longitude 37° W) is 522 ft *159 m* greater than the short axis. The greatest departures from the reference ellipsoid are a protuberance of 240 ft *73 m* in the area of Papua New Guinea and a depression of 344 ft *105 m* south of Sri Lanka, in the Indian Ocean.

The greatest circumference of the Earth, at the equator, is 24,901.46 miles *40 075,02 km*, compared with 24,859.73 miles *40 007,86 km* at the meridian. The area of the surface is estimated to be 196,937,400 miles^2 *510 065 600 km^2*. The period of axial rotation, *i.e.* the true sidereal day, is 23 hr 56 min 4.0996 sec, mean time.

The mass of the Earth was first assessed by Dr Nevil Maskelyne (1732–1811) in Perthshire, Scotland in 1774. The modern value is 5,880,000,000,000,000,000,000 tons *5,974 × 10^{21} tonnes* and its density is 5.515 times that of water. The volume is an estimated 259,875,300,000 miles^3 *1 083 207 000 000 km^3*. The Earth picks up cosmic dust but estimates vary widely with 30,000 tons/*tonnes* a year being the upper limit. Modern theory is that the Earth has an outer shell or lithosphere 50 miles *80 km* thick, then an outer and inner rock layer or mantle extending 1745 miles *2809 km* deep, beneath which there is an iron rich core of radius 2164 miles *3482 km*. If the iron rich core theory is correct, iron would be the most abundant element in the Earth. At the centre of the core the estimated density is 13.09 g/cm^3; the temperature 4500°C and the pressure 23,600 tons f/in^2 or 364 GPa.

1. NATURAL PHENOMENA

EARTHQUAKES

(Note: Seismologists record all dates with the year *first*, based not on local time but on Greenwich Mean Time).

Greatest *World*

It is estimated that each year there are some 500,000 detectable seismic or micro-seismic disturbances of which 100,000 can be felt and 1000 cause damage. The deepest recorded hypocentres are of 720 km *447 miles* in Indonesia in 1933, 1934 and 1943.

An inherent limitation in the widely used Gutenberg–Richter scale (published in 1954) precludes its usefulness when extended to the relative strengths of the strongest earthquakes ever recorded. The scale was named after Dr Beno Gutenberg (1889–1960) and Dr Charles Robert Richter (1900–1985). Its use of surface-wave magnitudes, based on amplitudes of waves of a period of 20 sec, results in the 'damping' of any increase in amplitude where fault ruptures break over a length much above 60 km *37 miles*. These however provenly may reach a length of 800 to 1000 km *500–620 miles*. This 'overload' or 'saturation effect' has resulted in the adoption since 1977 of the Kanamori scale for comparing the most massive earthquakes. Magnitudes are there defined in terms of energy release using the concept of the seismic moment, devised by K-Aki in 1966. Thus the most massive instrumentally recorded earthquake has been the

PROGRESSIVE LIST OF THE WORLD'S STRONGEST INSTRUMENTALLY RECORDED EARTHQUAKES

Kanamori Scale Magnitudes M_s	Gutenberg–Richter Scale Magnitude M_w	Where $M_s = \frac{2}{3}(\log_{10}E - 11.8)$ and $M_w = \frac{2}{3}[\log_{10}(2E \times 10^4) - 10.7]$ Where E = energy released in dyne/cm		
8.8	8.6	Colombia coast	1906 Jan 31
(8.6)	8.6	Assam, India	1950 Aug 15
9.0	(8¼)	Kamchatka, USSR	1952 Nov 4
9.1	(8.3)	Andreanol, Aleutian Is., USA	1957 Mar 9
9.5	(8.3)	Lebu, Chile	1960 May 22

cataclysmic Lebu shock south of Concepción, Chile on 1960 May 22 estimated at 10^{26} ergs. While this uniquely rates a magnitude of 9.5 on the Kanamori scale, it ranks in only equal 4th place (with the 1922 Chilean earthquake) at Magnitude 8.3 on the Gutenberg–Richter scale. For the removal of doubt the progressive records on the two scales are shown in the table above.

Worst death roll *World*
The greatest chronicled loss of life occurred in the earthquake which rocked every city of the Near East and Eastern Mediterranean c. July 1201. Contemporary accounts estimate the loss of life at 1,100,000. Less uncertain is the figure of 830,000 fatalities in prolonged quake (*ti chen*) in the Shensi, Shansi and Honan provinces of China, of 1556 Feb 2, (new style) (Jan 23 os). The highest death roll in modern times has been in the Tangshan 'quake (Mag. 8.2) in Eastern China on 1976 July 27 (local time was 3 a.m. July 28). A first figure published on 4 Jan 1977 revealed 655,237 killed, later adjusted to 750,000. On 22 Nov 1979 the New China News Agency unaccountably reduced the death toll to 242,000. As late as Jan 1982 the site of the city was still a prohibited area. The greatest material damage was in the 'quake on the Kwanto plain, Japan, of 1923 Sept 1 (Mag. 8.2, epicentre in Lat. 35° 15′ N, Long. 139° 30′ E). In Sagami Bay the sea-bottom in one area sank 400 m *1310 ft*. The official total of persons killed and missing in the *Shinsai* or great 'quake and the resultant fires was 142,807. In Tōkyō and Yokohama 575,000 dwellings were destroyed. The cost of the damage was estimated at £1000 million (now £17,000 million). It has however been estimated that a 7.5 magnitude shock (G-R scale) 30 miles *48 km* north of Los Angeles would result in damage estimated at $75,000 million.

Worst death roll *Great Britain and Ireland*
The total of the undisputed death roll for Great Britain is two—an apprentice, Thomas Grey, struck by falling masonry from Christ's Hospital Church, near Newgate, London at 6 p.m. on 6 Apr 1580. Mabel Everet of about the same age died of injuries 4 days later.

The East Anglian or Colchester earthquake of 1884 Apr 22 (9.18 a.m.) (epicentres Lat. 51° 48′ N, Long. 0° 53′ E, and Lat. 51° 51′ N, Long. 0° 55′ E) caused damage estimated at more than £12,000 to 1250 buildings. Langenhoe Church was wrecked. Windows and doors were rattled over an area of 53,000 miles² *137 250 km²* and the shock was felt in Exeter and Ostend, Belgium. It has been estimated to have been of magnitude 5.2 on the Richter scale. Researches by Andrew Phillips of the Colchester Institute in 1984 have dispelled every indication that *any* fatalities or even serious injury can be attributed to this shock.

The highest instrumentally measured magnitude is 6.0 for the Dogger Bank event of 7 June 1931. The strongest Scottish tremor occurred at Inverness at 10.45 p.m. on 1816 Aug 13, and was felt over an area of 50,000 miles² *130 000 km²*. The strongest Welsh tremor occurred in Swansea at 9.45 a.m. on 1906 June 27 (epicentre Lat. 51° 38′ N, Long. 4° W). It was felt over an area of 37,800 miles² *97 900 km²*.

No earthquake with its epicentre in Ireland has ever been instrumentally measured, though the effects of the North Wales shock of 19 July 1984 (mag. 5 to 5.5) dislocated traffic lights in Dublin. However, there was a shock in August 1734 which damaged 100 dwellings and five churches.

VOLCANOES

The total number of known active volcanoes in the world is 850 of which many are submarine. The greatest active concentration is in Indonesia, where 77 of its 167 volcanoes have erupted within historic times. The name volcano derives from the now dormant Vulcano Island (from the God of fire Vulcanus) in the Mediterranean.

Greatest eruption
The total volume of matter discharged in the eruption of Tambora, a volcano on the island of Sumbawa, in Indonesia, 5–7 Apr 1815, was 150–180 km³. The energy of this 1395 mph *2245 km/h* eruption, which lowered the height of the island by 4100 ft *1250 m* from 13,450 ft *4100 m* to 9350 ft *2850 m*, was 8.4×10^{19} joules. A crater seven miles *11 km* in diameter was formed. Some 90,000 were killed or died of famine. This compares with a probable 60–65 km³ ejected by Santoríni and 20 km³ ejected by Krakatoa (see below). The internal pressure at Tambora has been estimated at 3270 kg/cm² or 20.76 tons/in².

The ejecta in the Taupo eruption in New Zealand c. AD 130 have been estimated at 30,000 million tonnes/*tons* of pumice moving at one time at 400 mph *700 km/h*. It flattened 16 000 km² *6180 miles²* (over 26 times the devastated area of Mt. St. Helens). Less than 20 per cent of the 14×10^9 tonnes of pumice ejected in this most violent of all documented volcanic events fell within 200 km *125 miles* of the vent.

Longest lava flow
The longest lava flow in historic times, known as *pahoehoe* (twisted cord-like solidifications), is that from the eruption of Laki in 1783 in south-east Iceland which flowed 65–70 km *40.5–43.5 miles*. The largest known pre-historic flow is the Roza basalt flow in North America c. 15 million years ago, which had an unsurpassed length (480 km *300 miles*), area (40 000 km² *15,400 miles²*) and volume (1250 km³ *300 miles³*).

Greatest explosion
The greatest explosion (possibly since Santoríni in the Aegean Sea 1626 ± 1 BC) occurred at c. 10 a.m. (local time), or 3.00 a.m. GMT, on 27 Aug 1883, with an eruption of Krakatoa, an island (then 18 miles² *47 km²*) in the Sunda Strait, between Sumatra and Java, in Indonesia. A total of 163 villages were wiped out, and 36,380 people killed by the wave it caused. Rocks were thrown 34 miles *55 km* high and dust fell 3313 miles *5330 km* away 10 days later. The explosion was recorded four hours later on

Mauna Loa in Hawaii, the world's largest active volcano, erupted as recently as April 1984. (Colorific).

the island of Rodrigues, 2968 miles *4776 km* away, as 'the roar of heavy guns' and was heard over 1/13th part of the surface of the globe. This explosion estimated to have had about 26 times the power of the greatest H-bomb test (by the USSR) was still only a fifth part of the Santoríni cataclysm.

Highest *Extinct*
The highest extinct volcano in the world is Cerro Aconcagua (stone sentinel) (22,834 ft *6960 m*) on the Argentine side of the Andes. It was first climbed on 14 Jan 1897 by Mathias Zurbriggen; the highest summit climbed until 12 June 1907.

Highest *Dormant*
The highest dormant volcano is Volcán Llullaillaco (22,057 ft *6723 m*), on the frontier between Chile and Argentina.

Largest and highest *Active*
The highest volcano regarded as active is Volcán Antofalla (6450 m *21,162 ft*), in Argentina, though a more definite claim is made for Volcán Guayatiri or Guallatiri (19,882 ft *6060 m*), in Chile, which erupted in 1959. The world's largest active volcano is Mauna Loa (13,677 ft *4168 m*), Hawaii which erupted in 1975 and in April 1984.

Northernmost and southernmost
The northernmost volcano is Beeren Berg (7470 ft *2276 m*) on the island of Jan Mayen (71° 05′ N) in the Greenland Sea. It erupted on 20 Sept 1970 and the island's 39 inhabitants (all male) had to be evacuated. It was possibly discovered by Henry Hudson in 1607 or 1608, but definitely visited by Jan Jacobsz May (Netherlands) in 1614. It was annexed by Norway on 8 May 1929. The Ostenso seamount (5825 ft *1775 m*) 346 miles *556 km* from the

North Pole in Lat. 85° 10′ N, Long. 133° W was volcanic. The most southerly known active volcano is Mount Erebus (12,450 ft *3795 m*) on Ross Island (77° 35′ S), in Antarctica. It was discovered on 28 Jan 1841 by the expedition of Captain (later Rear-Admiral Sir) James Clark Ross, RN (1800–62), and first climbed at 10 a.m. on 10 Mar 1908 by a British party of five, led by Professor (later Lieut.-Col. Sir) Tannatt William Edgeworth David (1858–1934).

Largest crater

The world's largest *caldera* or volcano crater is that of Toba, north central Sumatra, Indonesia covering 685 miles² *1775 km²*.

GEYSERS

Tallest *World*

The Waimangu (Maori, *black water*) geyser, in New Zealand, erupted to a height in excess of 1500 ft *457 m* in 1904, but has not been active since it erupted violently at 6.20 a.m. on 1 Apr 1917 and killed 4 people. Currently the world's tallest active geyser is the US National Parks' Service Steamboat Geyser, in Yellowstone National Park, which from 1962 to 1969 erupted with intervals ranging from 5 days to 10 months to a height of 250–380 ft *76–115 m*. The greatest measured water discharge has been 825,000 gal *37 850 hl* by the Giant Geyser, also in Yellowstone National Park, Wyoming, which has been dormant since 1955. The *Geysir* ('gusher') near Mount Hekla in south-central Iceland, from which all others have been named, spurts, on occasions, to 180 ft *55 m*, while the adjacent Strokkur, reactivated by drilling in 1963, spurts at 10–15 min intervals.

2. WEATHER

The meteorological records given below necessarily relate largely to the last 140–160 years, since data before that time are both sparse and often unreliable. Reliable registering thermometers were introduced as recently as *c.* 1820.

The longest continuous observations have been maintained at the Radcliffe Observatory, Oxford since 1815 though discontinuous records have enabled the Chinese to assert that 903 BC was a very bad winter.

Palaeo-entomological evidence is that there was a southern European climate in England *c.* 90,000 BC, while in *c.* 6000 BC the mean summer temperature reached 67° F *19,4° C*, or 6 deg F *3,3 deg C* higher than at the present. It is believed that 1.2 million years ago the world's air temperature averaged 95° F *35° C*. The earliest authentic recording of British weather relates to the period 26 Aug–17 Sept 55 BC. The earliest reliably known hot summer was in AD 664 during our driest-ever century and the earliest known severe winter was that of AD 763–4. In 1683–4 there was frost in London from November to April. Frosts were recorded during August in the period 1668–89.

Most equable temperature

The location with the most equable recorded temperature over a short period is Garapan, on Saipan, in the Mariana Islands, Pacific Ocean. During the nine years from 1927 to 1935, inclusive, the lowest temperature recorded was 19,6° C *67.3° F* on 30 Jan 1934 and the highest was 31,4° C *88.5° F* on 9 Sept 1931, giving an extreme range of 11,8 deg C *21.2 deg F*. Between 1911 and 1966 the Brazilian off-shore island of Fernando de Noronha had a minimum temperature of 18,6° C *65.5° F* on 17 Nov 1913 and a maximum of 32,0° C *89.6° F* on 2 Mar 1965, an extreme range of 13,4 deg C *24.1 deg F*.

Greatest temperature ranges

The greatest recorded temperature ranges in the world are around the Siberian 'cold pole' in the eastern USSR. Temperatures in Verkhoyansk (67° 33′ N, 133° 23′ E) have ranged 192 deg F *106,7 deg C* from −94° F *−70° C* (unofficial) to 98° F *36,7° C*. The greatest temperature variation recorded in a day is 100 deg F *55,5 deg C* (a fall from 44° F *6,7° C* to −56° F *−48,8° C*) at Browning, Montana, USA, on 23–24 Jan 1916. The most freakish rise was 49 deg F *27,2 deg C* in 2 min at Spearfish, South Dakota, from

−4° F *−20° C* at 7.30 a.m. to 45° F *7,2° C* at 7.32 a.m. on 22 Jan 1943. The British record is 29 deg C *52.2 deg F* (*−7° C 19.4° F* to 22° C *71.6° F*) at Tummel Bridge, Tayside on 9 May 1978.

Longest freeze

The longest recorded unremitting freeze in the British Isles was one of 40 days at the Great Dun Fell radio station, Appleby, Cumbria, from 23 Jan to 3 Mar 1986. Less rigorous early data includes a frost from 5 Dec 1607 to 14 Feb 1608 and a 91-day frost on Dartmoor, Devon in 1854–5. No temperature lower than 34° F *1° C* has ever been recorded on Bishop Rock, Isles of Scilly.

Upper atmosphere

The lowest temperature ever recorded in the atmosphere is −143° C *−225.4° F* at an altitude of about 50–60 miles *80,5–96,5 km*, during noctilucent cloud research above Kronogård, Sweden, from 27 July to 7 Aug 1963. A jet stream moving at 408 mph *656 km/h* at 154,200 ft *47 000 m* (29.2 miles *46 km*) was recorded by Skua rocket above South Uist, Outer Hebrides, Scotland on 13 Dec 1967.

Thickest ice

The greatest recorded thickness of ice is 2.97 miles (15,670 ft) *4776 m* measured by radio echo soundings from a U.S. Antarctic Research aircraft at 69° 9′ 38″ S 135° 20′ 25″ E 400 km *250 miles* from the coast in Wilkes Land on 4 Jan 1975.

Deepest permafrost

The deepest recorded permafrost is more than 4500 ft *1370 m* reported from the upper reaches of the Viluy River, Siberia, USSR in February 1982.

Most recent White Christmas and Frost Fair

London has experienced seven 'White' or snowing Christmas Days since 1900. These have been 1906, 1917 (slight), 1923 (slight), 1927, 1938, 1956 (slight) and 1970. These were more frequent in the 19th century and even more so before the

---

I. HIGHEST SHADE TEMPERATURE: *World* 136.4° F *58° C* al'Azīzīyah, Libya, (alt. 367 ft *111 m*) 13.9.1922 *UK & Ireland* 98.2° F *36,77° C* Raunds, Northants; Epsom, Surrey and Canterbury, Kent 9.8.1911(a)

2. LOWEST SCREEN TEMPERATURE: *World* −128.6° F *−89,2° C* Vostok, Antarctica, 21.7.1983 (b). *UK & Ireland* −17° F *−27,2° C* 11.2.1895 and −27,2° C *−17° F* 10.1.1982 both Braemar, Grampian, Scotland (c)

3. GREATEST RAINFALL (24 hours): *World* 73.62 in *1870 mm*, Cilaos, La Réunion, Indian Ocean, 15–16.3.1952 (d) *UK & Ireland* 11.00 in *279 mm*, Martinstown, Dorset, 18–19.7.1955

4. GREATEST RAINFALL (Calendar Month): *World* 366.14 in *9299 mm*, Cherrapunji, Meghalaya, India, July 1861 *UK & Ireland* 56.54 in *1436 mm*, Llyn Llydau, Snowdon, Gwynedd, October 1909

4. GREATEST RAINFALL (12 months): *World* 1041.78 in *26 461 mm*, Cherrapunji, Meghalaya, 1.8.1860–31.7.1861 *UK & Ireland* 257.0 in *6527 mm*, Sprinkling Tarn, Cumbria, in 1954 (e)

4. WETTEST PLACE (Annual mean): *World* Tutunendo, Colombia annual av. 11770 mm *463.4 in.* *UK & Ireland* Styhead Tarn (1600 ft *487 m*), Cumbria, 172.9 in *4391 mm*

5. GREATEST SNOWFALL (f) (12 months): *World* 1224.5 in *31 102 mm*, Paradise, Mt Rainier, Washington, USA 19.2.1971 to 18.2.1972 *UK & Ireland* 60 in *1524 mm* Upper Teesdale and Denbighshire Hills, Clwyd, Wales, 1947

6. MAXIMUM SUNSHINE: (g) *World* >97 per cent (over 4300 hours), eastern Sahara, annual average *UK & Ireland* 78.3 per cent (382 hours) Pendennis Castle, Falmouth, Cornwall, June 1925

7. MINIMUM SUNSHINE: *World* Nil at North Pole—for winter stretches of 186 days *UK & Ireland* Nil in a month at Westminster, London, in December 1890 (h)

8. BAROMETRIC PRESSURE (Highest): *World* 1083.8 mb. (*32.00 in*), Agata, Siberia, USSR (alt. 862 ft *262 m*), 31.12.1968. *UK & Ireland* 1054.7 mb. (*31.15 in*), Aberdeen, 31.1.1902

9. BAROMETRIC PRESSURE (Lowest): **(j)** *World* 870 mb (*25.69 in*), 300 miles *482 km* west of Guam, Pacific Ocean, in Lat. 16°44′ N, Long. 137°46′ E. 12.10.1979 *UK & Ireland* 925.5 mb (*27.33 in*), Ochtertyre, near Crieff, Tayside, 26.1.1884

10. HIGHEST SURFACE WIND-SPEED: (k) *World* 231 mph *371 km/h*, Mt. Washington (6288 ft *1916 m*), New Hampshire, USA 12.4.1934 *UK & Ireland* 172 mph *278 km/h* (150 knots), Cairn Gorm Summit (4084 ft *1245 m*), 20.3.1986 (l)

11. THUNDER-DAYS (Year): **(m)** *World* 322 days, Bogor (formerly Buitenzorg), Java, Indonesia (average, 1916–19) *UK & Ireland* 38 days, Stonyhurst, Lancashire, 1912 and Huddersfield, West Yorkshire, 1967

12. HOTTEST PLACE (Annual mean): **(n)** *World* Dallol, Ethiopia, 94° F *34,4° C* (1960–66) *UK & Ireland* Penzance, Cornwall, and Isles of Scilly, both 52.7° F *11,5° C*, average 1931–60

13. COLDEST PLACE (Extrapolated annual mean): *World* Polus Nedostupnosti, Pole of Cold (78° S., 96° E.), Antarctica, −72° F *−57,8° C* Coldest measured mean: −70° F *−56,6° C* Plateau Station, Antarctica *UK & Ireland* Braemar, Grampian 6,34° C *43.41° F* (1952–81)

14. MOST RAINY DAYS (Year): *World* Mt. Wai-'ale-'ale (5148 ft *1569 m*), Kauai, Hawaii, up to 350 per annum *UK & Ireland* Ballynahinch, Galway, 309 days in 1923

15. DRIEST PLACE (Annual mean): *World* Nil—in the Desierto de Atacama, near Calama, Chile *UK & Ireland* St Osyth, Lee Wick Farm, Essex, 20.2 in *513 mm* (1964–82) (o)

15. LONGEST DROUGHT: *World c.* 400 years to 1971 Desierto de Atacama, Chile *UK & Ireland* 73 days Mile End, Greater London, 4.3 to 15.5.1893 (p)

16. HEAVIEST HAILSTONES: (q) *World* 1.67 lb *750 g* (7½ in *19 cm* diameter, 17½ in *44,45 cm* circumference), Coffeyville, Kansas, USA 3.9.1970 *UK and Ireland* 5 oz *141 g*, Horsham, West Sussex, 5.9.1958

17. LONGEST SEA LEVEL FOGS (Visibility less than 1000 yd *914,4 m*); *World* Fogs persist for weeks on the Grand Banks, Newfoundland, Canada, and the average is more than 120 days per year *UK & Ireland* London duration record was 26.11 to 1.12.1948 and 5.12 to 9.12.1952 (both 4 days 18 hours)

18. WINDIEST PLACE: *World* The Commonwealth Bay, George V Coast, Antarctica, where gales reach 200 mph *320 km/h UK & Ireland* Tiree, Strathclyde (89 ft *27 m*); annual average 17.4 mph *28 km/h*. Fair Isle (1974–78) returned 20.6 mph *33,1 km/h*

change of the calendar, which, by removing 3–13 Sept brought forward all dates subsequent to 2 Sept 1752 by 11 days. The last of the nine recorded Frost Fairs held on the Thames since 1564/65 was from December 1813 to 26 Jan 1814.

Most intense rainfall

Difficulties attend rainfall readings for very short periods but the figure of 1.50 in *38,1 mm* in 1 min at Barst, Guadeloupe on 26 Nov 1970, is regarded as the most intense recorded in modern times. The cloudburst of 'near 2 ft *609 mm* in less than a quarter of half an hour' at Oxford on the afternoon of 31 May (Old Style) 1682 is regarded as unacademically recorded. The most intense rainfall in Britain recorded to modern standards has been 2.0 in *51 mm* in 12 min at Wisbech, Cambridgeshire on 27 June 1970.

Falsest St. Swithin's Days

The legend that the weather on St. Swithin's Day, celebrated on 15 July (Old and New Style) since AD 912, determines the rainfall for the next 40 days is one which has long persisted. There was a brilliant 13½ hr sunshine in London on 15 July 1924, but 30 of the next 40 days were wet. On 15 July 1913 there was a 15-hr downpour, yet it rained on only 9 of the subsequent 40 days in London.

Best and worst British summers

According to Prof. Gordon Manley's survey over the period 1728–1978 the best (*i.e.* driest and hottest) British summer was that of 1976 and the worst (*i.e.* wettest and coldest) that of 1879. Temperatures of >32° C (89.8° F) were recorded on 13 consecutive days (25 June–7 July 1976) within Great Britain including 7 such consecutive days in Cheltenham (1–7 July), where 35,9° C *96.6° F* was reached on 3 July. In 1983 there were 40 days > 80°F *26,6° C* in Britain between 3 July–31 Aug including 17 consecutively (3–19 July). London experienced its hottest month (July) since records began in 1840.

Humidity and discomfort

Human comfort or discomfort depends not merely on temperature but on the combination of temperature, humidity, radiation and windspeed. The United States Weather Bureau uses a Temperature-Humidity Index, which equals two-fifths of the sum of the dry and wet bulb thermometer readings plus 15. A THI of 98.2 has been twice recorded in Death Valley, California—on 27 July 1966 (119° F and 31 per cent) and on 12 Aug 1970 (117° F and 37 per cent). A person driving at 45 mph *72 km/h* in a car without a windscreen in a temperature of −45° F *−42,7° C* would, by the chill factor, experience the equivalent of −125° F *−87,2° C,* *i.e.* within 3.5 deg F *2,0 deg C* of the world record.

Largest mirage

The largest mirage on record was that sighted in the Arctic at 83° N 103° W by Donald B. MacMillan in 1913. This type of mirage known as the Fata Morgana appeared as the same 'Hills, valleys, snow-capped peaks extending through at least 120 degrees of the horizon' that Peary had misidentified as Crocker Land 6 years earlier. On 17 July 1939 a mirage of Snaefells Jokull (4715 ft *1437 m*) on Iceland was seen from the sea at a distance of 335–350 miles *539–563 km.*

Longest lasting rainbow

A rainbow lasting over 3 hours was reported from the coastal border of Gwynedd and Clwyd, North Wales on 14 Aug 1979.

Lightning

The visible length of lightning strokes varies greatly. In mountainous regions, when clouds are very low, the flash may be less than 300 ft *91 m* long. In flat country with very high clouds, a cloud-to-earth flash may measure 4 miles *6 km* though in the most extreme cases such flashes have been measured at 20 miles *32 km.* The intensely bright central core of the lightning channel is extremely narrow. Some authorities suggest that its diameter is as little as half an inch *1,27 cm.* This core is surrounded by a 'corona envelope' (glow discharge) which may measure 10–20 ft *3–6 m* in diameter.

Footnotes to weather map and table

(a) The 100.5° F *38,6° C* reported from Tonbridge, Kent was a non-standard exposure and is estimated to be equivalent of 97–98° F *36–36,7° C*
(b) Vostok is 11,220 ft *3419 m* above sea-level. The coldest permanently inhabited place is the Siberian village of Oymyakon (pop. 600) (63° 16′ N., 143° 15′ E.), (2300 ft *700 m*) in the USSR where the temperature reached − 96° F *− 71,1° C* in 1964.
(c) The −23° F *−30,5° C* at Blackadder, Borders, on 4 Dec 1879, and the −20° F *−28,9° C* at Grantown-on-Spey on 24 Feb 1955, were not standard exposures.
The lowest official temperature in England is − 15° F *− 26,1° C* at Newport, Shropshire on 10 Jan 1982.
The lowest maximum temperature for a day was − 19,1° C *− 2.3° F* at Braemar on 10 Jan 1982.
(d) This is equal to 7435 tons *7554 tonnes* of rain per acre. Elevation 1200 m *3937 ft.*
(e) The record for Ireland is 145.4 in *3921 mm* near Derriana Lough, County Kerry in 1948.
(f) The record for a single snow storm is 189 in *4800 mm* at Mt. Shasta, Ski Bowl, California, and for 24 hr, 76 in *1930 mm* at Silver Lake, Colorado, USA on 14–15 April 1921. The greatest depth of snow on the ground was 27 ft 7 in *8407 mm* at Helen Lake, Mount Lassen in April 1983. London's earliest recorded snow was on 25 Sept 1885, and the latest on 27 May 1821. Less reliable reports suggest snow on 12 Sept 1658 (Old Style) and on 12 June 1791.
(g) St Petersburg, Florida, USA, recorded 768 consecutive sunny days from 9 Feb 1967 to 17 March 1969.
(h) The south-eastern end of the village of Lochranza, Isle of Arran, Strathclyde is in shadow of mountains from 18 Nov to 8 Feb each winter.
(j) The USS *Repose,* a hospital ship, recorded 25.55 in *856 mb* in the eye of a typhoon in 25° 35′ N 128° 20′ E off Okinawa on 16 Sept 1945.
(k) The highest speed yet measured in a tornado is 280 mph *450 km/h* at Wichita Falls, Texas, USA on 2 Apr 1958.
(l) The figure of 177.2 mph *285,2 km/h* at RAF Saxa Vord, Unst, in the Shetlands, Scotland, on 16 Feb 1962, was not recorded with standard equipment. British tornadoes may reach 180 mph *290 km/h.* There were gales of great severity on 15 Jan 1362 and 26 Nov 1703.
(m) Between Lat. 35° N and 35° S. there are some 3200 thunderstorms each 12 night-time hours, some of which can be heard at a range of 18 miles *29 km.*
(n) In Death Valley, California, USA, maximum temperatures of over 120° F *48,9° C* were recorded on 43 consecutive days—6 July to 17 Aug 1917. At Marble Bar, Western Australia (maximum 121° F *49,4° C*) 160 consecutive days with maximum temperatures of over 100° F *37,8° C* were recorded—31 Oct 1923 to 7 Apr 1924. At Wyndham, Western Australia, the temperature reached 90° F *32,2° C* or more on 333 days in 1946.
(o) The lowest rainfall recorded in a single year was 9.29 in *23,6 cm* at one station in Margate, Kent in 1921.
(p) The longest drought in Scotland was one of 38 days at Port William, Dumfries & Galloway on 3 Apr to 10 May 1938.
(q) Much heavier hailstones are sometimes reported. These are usually not single but coalesced stones. An ice block of 1–2 kg *35–70 oz.* was reputed at Withington, Manchester on 2 Apr 1973. The *Canton Evening News* reported on 14 Apr 1981 5 killed and 225 injured by a hailstorm with stones weighing up to 30 lb *13,6 kg* (sic).
(r) Lower visibilities occur at higher altitudes. Ben Nevis is reputedly in cloud 300 days per year.

PROGRESSIVE RECORDINGS OF EXTREME HIGH TEMPERATURES WORLD WIDE

127.4° F	53,0° C	Ouargla, Algeria	27 Aug	1884
130° F	54,4° C	Amos, California, USA	17 Aug	1885
130° F	54,4° C	Mammoth Tank, California, USA	17 Aug	1885
134° F	56,7° C	Death Valley, California, USA	10 July	1913
136.4° F	58,0° C	Al'Aziziyah (el-Azizia), Libya*	13 Sept	1922

Obtained by the US National Geographical Society but not officially recognised by the Libyan Ministry of Communications.

A reading of 140° F 60° C at Delta, Mexico, in August 1953 is not now accepted because of over-exposure to roof radiation. The official Mexican record of 136.4° F 58,0° C at San Luis, Sonora on 11 Aug 1933 is not internationally accepted.

A freak heat flash reported from Coimbra, Portugal, in September 1933 said to have caused the temperature to rise to 70° C 158° F for 120 sec is apocryphal.

PROGRESSIVE RECORDINGS OF EXTREME LOW TEMPERATURES WORLD WIDE

−73° F	−58,3° C	Floeberg Bay, Ellesmere I., Canada		1852[1]
−90.4° F	−68° C	Verkhoyansk, Siberia, USSR	3 Jan	1885
−90.4° F	−68° C	Verkhoyansk, Siberia, USSR	5 & 7 Feb	1892
−90.4° F	−68° C	Oymyakon, Siberia, USSR[2]	6 Feb	1933
−100.4° F	−73,5° C	South Pole, Antarctica	11 May	1957
−102.1° F	−74,5° C	South Pole, Antarctica	17 Sept	1957
−109.1° F	−78,34° C	Sovietskaya, Antarctica	2 May	1958
−113.3° F	−80,7° C	Vostok, Antarctica	15 June	1958
−114.1° F	−81,2° C	Sovietskaya, Antarctica	19 June	1958
−117.4° F	−83,0° C	Sovietskaya, Antarctica	25 June	1958
−122.4° F	−85,7° C	Vostok, Antarctica	7-8 Aug	1958
−124.1° F	−86,7° C	Sovietskaya, Antarctica	9 Aug	1958
−125.3° F	−87,4° C	Vostok, Antarctica	25 Aug	1958
−126.9° F	−88,3° C	Vostok, Antarctica	24 Aug	1960
−128.6° F	−89,2° C	Vostok, Antactica	21 July	1983

[1] *The earliest recorded occasion that mercury froze (at −40° F or −40° C) was by M. V. Lomonosov, near Moscow c. 1750.*
[2] *Population in 1986 reported to be 4000—the world's coldest inhabited place.*

The speed of a discharge varies from 100 to 1000 miles/sec *160–1600 km/sec* for the downward leader track, and reaches up to 87,000 miles/sec *140 000 km/sec* (nearly half the speed of light) for the powerful return stroke. In Britain there is an average of 6 strikes/mile² per annum or 3,7 per km² and an average of 4200 per annum over London alone. Every few million strokes there is a giant discharge, in which the cloud-to-earth and return strokes flash from and to the top of the thunder clouds. In these 'positive giants' energy of up to 3000 million joules (3 × 10¹⁶ ergs) has been recorded. The temperature reaches about 30,000° C, which is more than five times greater than that of the surface of the Sun.

Highest waterspout

The highest waterspout of which there is a reliable record was one observed on 16 May 1898 off Eden, New South Wales, Australia. A theodolite reading from the shore gave its height as 5014 ft *1528 m*. It was about 10 ft *3 m* in diameter. The Spithead waterspout off Ryde, Isle of Wight on 21 Aug 1878 was measured by sextant to be 'about a mile' or *600 m* in height. A waterspout moved around Tor Bay, Devon on 17 Sept 1969 which, according to press estimates, was 1000 ft *300 m* in height.

Cloud extremes

The highest standard cloud form is cirrus, averaging 27,000 ft *8250 m* and above, but the rare nacreous or mother-of-pearl formation sometimes reaches nearly 80,000 ft *24 000 m* (see also Noctilucent clouds, Chapter 4). Cirrus cloud at 26,500 ft *8075 m* contains unfrozen but super-cooled water at −31° F *−35° C*. The lowest is stratus, below 3500 ft *1066 m*. The cloud form with the greatest vertical range is cumulo-nimbus, which has been observed to reach a height of nearly 68,000 ft *20 000 m* in the tropics.

Tornadoes (see also Accidents and Disasters Chap 11)

Britain's strongest tornado was at Southsea, Portsmouth on 14 Dec 1810 (Force 8 on the Meaden-TORRO scale). The Newmarket tornado (Force 6) of 3 Jan 1978 caused property damage estimated at up to £1,000,000. On 23 Nov 1981, 58 tornadoes were reported in one day from Anglesey to Eastern England.

3. STRUCTURE AND DIMENSIONS

OCEANS

Largest

The area of the Earth covered by sea is estimated to be 139,670,000 miles² *361 740 000 km²* or 70.92 per cent of the total surface. The mean depth of the hydrosphere was once estimated to be 12,450 ft *3795 m*, but recent surveys suggest a lower estimate, of 11,660 ft *3554 m*. The total weight of the water is estimated to be 1.3 × 10¹⁸ tons, or 0.022 per cent of the Earth's total weight. The volume of the oceans is estimated to be 308,400,000 miles³ *1 285 600 000 km³* compared to 8,400,000 miles³ *35 000 000 km³* of fresh water.

The largest ocean in the world is the Pacific. Excluding adjacent seas, it represents 45.8 per cent of the world's oceans and covers 64,186,300 miles² *166 240 000 km²* in area. The average depth is 12,925 ft *3939 m*. The shortest navigable trans-Pacific distance from Guayaquil, Ecuador to Bangkok, Thailand is 10,905 miles *17 550 km*.

Deepest *World*

The deepest part of the ocean was first pinpointed in 1951 by HM Survey Ship *Challenger* in the Marianas Trench in the Pacific Ocean. The depth was measured by sounding and published as 5960 fathoms (35,760 ft *10 900 m*). Subsequent visits have resulted in slightly deeper measurements by multi-beam sonar now refined to 5973 fathoms (35,840 ft *10,924 m*) or 6.79 miles *10,92 km* made by the Japanese research vessel *Takuyo* on 17–19 Feb 1984 in Lat 11° 22' 24" N Long 142° 35' 30" E. On 23 Jan 1960 the US Navy bathyscaphe *Trieste* descended to the bottom which is 5490 ft *1673 m*. A metal object, say a pound ball of steel, dropped into water above this trench would take nearly 64 min to fall to the sea-bed 6.79 miles *10,92 km* below, where hydrostatic pressure is over 18,000 lb/in² *1250 bars*.

Deepest *British waters*

The deepest point in the territorial waters of the United Kingdom is an areas 6 cables (*1100 m*)

off the island of Raasay, Highland, in the Inner Sound at Lat. 57° 30' 33" N, Long. 5° 57' 27" W. A depth of 1038 ft (173 fathoms, *316 m*) was found in December 1959 by HMS *Yarnton* (Lt-Cdr A. C. F. David, RN.)

Largest sea

The largest of the world's seas is the South China Sea, with an area of 1,148,500 miles² *2 974 600 km²*. The Malayan Sea, comprising the waters between the Indian Ocean and the South Pacific, south of the Chinese mainland covering 3,144,000 miles² *8 142 900 km²* is not now an entity accepted by the International Hydrographic Bureau.

Largest gulf

The largest gulf in the world is the Gulf of Mexico, with an area of 580,000 miles² *1 500 000 km²* and a shoreline of 3100 miles *4990 km* from Cape Sable, Florida, USA, to Cabo Catoche, Mexico.

Largest bay

The largest bay in the world measured by shoreline length is Hudson Bay, northern Canada, with a shoreline of 7623 miles *12 268 km* and with an area of 317,500 miles² *822 300 km²*. The area of the Bay of Bengal is however 839,000 miles² *2 172 000 km²*. Great Britain's largest bay is Cardigan Bay which has a 140 mile *225 km* long shoreline and measures 72 miles *116 km* across from the Lleyn Peninsula, Gwynedd to St David's Head, Dyfed in Wales.

Longest fjords and sea lochs *World*

The world's longest fjord is the Nordvest Fjord arm of the Scoresby Sund in eastern Greenland, which extends inland 195 miles *313 km* from the sea. The longest of Norwegian fjords is the Sogne Fjord, which extends 183 km *113.7 miles* inland from Sygnefest to the head of the Lusterfjord arm at Skjolden. It averages barely 4,75 km *3 miles* in width and has a deepest point of 1245 m *4085 ft*. If measured from Huglo along the Bømlafjord to the head of the Sørfjord arm at Odda, Hardangerfjorden can also be said to extend 183 km *113.7 miles*. The longest Danish fjord is Limfjorden (100 miles *160 km* long).

Longest sea loch *Great Britain*

Scotland's longest sea loch is Loch Fyne, which extends 42 miles *67,5 km* inland into Strathclyde.

Highest seamount

The highest known submarine mountain, or seamount, is one discovered in 1953 near the Tonga Trench, between Samoa and New Zealand. It rises 28,500 ft *8690 m* from the sea bed, with its summit 1200 ft *365 m* below the surface.

Remotest spot from land

The world's most distant point from land is a spot in the South Pacific, approximately 48° 30' S, 125° 30' W, which is about 1660 miles *2670 km* from the nearest points of land, namely Pitcairn Island, Ducie Island and Cape Dart, Antarctica. Centred on this spot, therefore, is a circle of water with an area of about 8,657,000 miles² *22 421 500 km²*—about 7000 miles² *18 000 km²* larger than the USSR, the world's largest country (see Chapter 11).

Most southerly

The most southerly part of the oceans is 85° 34' S, 154° W, at the snout of the Robert Scott Glacier, 305 miles *490 km* from the South Pole.

Longest voyage

The longest possible great circle sea voyage is one of 19,860 miles *31 960 km* from a point 150 miles *240 km* west of Karachi, Pakistan to a point 200 miles *320 km* north of Uka' Kamchatka *via* the Mozambique Channel, Drake Passage and Bering Sea.

Sea temperature

The temperature of the water at the surface of the sea varies from −2° C 28.5° F in the White Sea to 35,6° C 96° F in the shallow areas of the Persian Gulf in summer. Ice-focused solar rays have been known to heat lake water to nearly 80° F 26,8° C. The normal Red Sea temperature is 22° C 71.6° F. The highest temperature recorded in the ocean is 759° F 404° C, measured by an American research submarine some 300 miles 480 km off the American west coast, in an expedition under the direction of Prof. Jack Diamond, Oregon State University, USA. Remote probes measured the temperature of the spring which was kept from vapourising by the weight of water above it.

STRAITS

Longest

The longest straits in the world are the Tatarskiy Proliv or Tartar Straits between Sakhalin Island and the USSR mainland running from the Sea of Japan to Sakhalinsky Zaliv : 800 km 497 miles, thus marginally longer than the Malacca Straits.

Broadest

The broadest named straits in the world are the Davis Straits between Greenland and Baffin Island with a minimum width of 210 miles 338 km. The Drake Passage between the Diego Ramirez Islands, Chile and the South Shetland Islands is 710 miles 1140 km across.

Narrowest

The narrowest navigable straits are those between the Aegean island of Euboea and the mainland of Greece. The gap is only 45 yd 40 m wide at Khalkis. The Seil Sound, Strathclyde, Scotland, narrows to a point only 20 ft 6 m wide where the Clachan bridge joins the island of Seil to the mainland and said to span the Atlantic.

WAVES

Highest

The highest officially recorded sea wave was measured by Lt Frederic Margraff USN from the USS Ramapo proceeding from Manila, Philippines, to San Diego, California, USA, on the night of 6–7 Feb 1933, during a 68-knot (78.3 mph 126 km/h) hurricane. The wave was calculated to be 112 ft 34 m from trough to crest. The highest instrumentally measured wave was one 86 ft 26,2 m high, recorded by the British ship Weather Reporter, in the North Atlantic on 30 Dec 1972 in Lat. 59° N, Long. 19° W. It has been calculated on the statistics of the Stationary Random Theory that one wave in more than 300,000 may exceed the average by a factor of 4.

On 9 July 1958 a landslip caused a 100 mph 160 km/h wave to wash 1720 ft 524 m high along the fjord-like Lituya Bay, Alaska, USA.

Highest seismic wave

The highest estimated height of a tsunami (often wrongly called a tidal wave) was one of 85 m 278 ft, which appeared off Ishigaki Island, Ryukyu Chain on 24 Apr 1771. It tossed a 750 ton block of coral more than 2,5 km 1.3 miles. Tsunami (a Japanese word meaning nami, a wave; tsu, overflowing) have been observed to travel at 490 mph 790 km/h.

Evidence for a 1000 ft 300 m ocean wave breaking on the southern shore of Lanai, Hawaiian Islands was reported on 4 Dec 1984. This occurred about 100 000 years ago due to a meteorite, a volcanic eruption or a submarine landslide.

CURRENTS

Greatest

The greatest current in the oceans of the world is the Antarctic Circumpolar Current or West Wind Drift Current which was measured in 1969 in the Drake Passage between South America and Antarctica to be flowing at a rate of 9500 million ft³ 270 000 000 m³ per sec—nearly treble that of the Gulf Stream. Its width ranges from 185 to 1240 miles 300–2000 km and has a proven surface flow rate of $\frac{4}{10}$ of a knot 0,75 km/h.

Strongest

The world's strongest currents are the Nakwakto Rapids, Slingsby Channel, British Columbia, Canada (Lat. 51° 05′ N, Long. 127° 30′ W) where the flow rate may reach 16.0 knots 29,6 km/h. The fastest current in British territorial waters is 10.7 knots 19,8 km/h in the Pentland Firth between the Orkney Islands and Caithness.

GREATEST TIDES

Extreme tides are due to lunar and solar gravitational forces affected by their perigee, perihelion and syzygies. Barometric and wind effects can superimpose an added 'surge' element. Coastal and sea-floor configurations can accentuate these forces. The normal interval between tides is 12 hr 25 min.

World

The greatest tides in the world occur in the Bay of Fundy, which divides the peninsula of Nova Scotia, Canada, from the United States' north-easternmost state of Maine and the Canadian province of New Brunswick. Burncoat Head in the Minas Basin, Nova Scotia, has the greatest mean spring range with 47.5 ft 14,50 m. A range of 54⅓ ft 16,6 m was recorded at springs in Leaf Basin in 1953. Tahiti experiences virtually no tide.

Great Britain

The place with the greatest mean spring range in Great Britain is Beachley, on the Severn, with a range of 40.7 ft 12,40 m, compared with the British Isles' average of 15 ft 4,57 m. Prior to 1933 tides as high as 28.9 ft 8,80 m above and 22.3 ft 6.80 m below datum (total range 51.2 ft 15,60 m) were recorded at Avonmouth though an extreme range of 52.2 ft 15,90 m for Beachley was officially accepted. In 1883 a freak tide of greater range was reported from Chepstow, Gwent.

ICEBERGS

Largest and tallest

The largest iceberg on record was an Antarctic tabular 'berg of over 12,000 miles² 31 000 km² (208 miles 335 km long and 60 miles 97 km wide and thus larger than Belgium) sighted 150 miles 240 km west of Scott Island, in the South Pacific Ocean, by the USS Glacier on 12 Nov 1956. The 200 ft 61 m thick Arctic ice island T.1 (140 miles² 360 km²) (discovered in 1946) was tracked for 17 years. The tallest iceberg measured was one of 550 ft 167 m reported off western Greenland by the US icebreaker East Wind in 1958.

Most southerly Arctic

The most southerly Arctic iceberg was sighted in the Atlantic by a USN weather patrol in Lat. 28° 44′ N, Long. 48° 42′ W in April 1935. The southernmost iceberg reported in British home waters was one sighted 60 miles 96 km from Smith's Knoll, on the Dogger Bank, in the North Sea.

Most northerly Antarctic

The most northerly Antarctic iceberg was a remnant sighted in the Atlantic by the ship Dochra in Lat. 26° 30′ S, Long. 25° 40′ W, on 30 Apr 1894.

LAND

There is satisfactory evidence that at one time the Earth's land surface comprised a single primeval continent of 80 million miles² 2×10^8 km², now termed Pangaea, and that this split about 190 million years ago, during the Jurassic period, into two super-continents,

Rockall, Britain's remotest islet which is 191 miles 307 km west of St Kilda in the Western Isles. See p. 58.

termed Laurasia (Eurasia, Greenland and Northern America) and Gondwanaland (Africa, Arabia, India, South America, Oceania and Antarctica) and named after Gondwana, India, which itself split 120 million years ago. The South Pole was apparently in the area of the Sahara as recently as the Ordovician period of c. 450 million years ago.

ROCKS

The age of the Earth is generally considered to be within the range of 4450 ± 50 million years, by analogy with directly measured ages of meteorites and of the moon. However, no rocks of this great age have yet been found on the Earth since geological processes have presumably destroyed them.

Oldest *World*

The greatest reported age for any scientifically dated rock is 3800 ± 100 million years for granite gneiss rock found near Granite Falls in the Minnesota river valley, USA as measured by the lead-isotope and rubidium-uranium methods by the US Geological Survey and announced on 26 Jan 1975. These metamorphic samples compare with the Amîtsoq gneiss from Godthaab, Greenland unreservedly accepted to be between 3700 and 3750 million years. Zirconium silicate crystals from Mt Narrayer, Australia were dated to 4200 million years (1983).

Oldest *Great Britain*

The original volcanic products from which were formed the gneiss and granulite rocks of the Scourian complex in the north west Highlands and the Western Isles were crystallized 2800 million years ago.

Largest

The largest isolated monolith in the world is the 1237 ft *377 m* high Mount Augustus (3627 ft *1105 m* above sea-level), discovered on 3 June 1858, 200 miles *320 km* east of Carnarvon, Western Australia. It is an upfaulted monoclinal gritty conglomerate 5 miles *8 km* long and 2 miles *3 km* across and thus twice the size of the celebrated monolithic arkose Ayer's Rock (1100 ft *335 m*), 250 miles *400 km* south-west of Alice Springs, in Northern Territory, Australia. It was estimated in 1940 that La Gran Piedra, a volcanic plug in the Sierra Maestra, Cuba weighs 61,355 tons/*tonnes*.

CONTINENTS

Largest

Of the Earth's surface 41.25% or 81,200,000 miles^2 *210 400 000 km^2* is covered by continental masses of which only about two-thirds of 29.08% of the Earth's surface (57,270,000 miles^2 *148 328 000 km^2*) is land above water, with a mean height of 2480 ft *756 m* above sea-level. The Eurasian land mass is the largest, with an area (including islands) of 20,733,000 miles^2 *53 698 000 km^2*. The Afro-Eurasian land mass, separated artificially only by the Suez Canal covers an area of 32,704,000 miles^2 *84 702 000 km^2* or 57.1% of the Earth's landmass.

Smallest

The smallest is the Australian mainland, with an area of 2,941,526 miles^2 *7 618 493 km^2*, which, together with Tasmania, New Zealand, New Guinea and the Pacific Islands, is described sometimes as Oceania.

Land remotest from the sea *World*

There is an as yet unpinpointed spot in the Dzoosotoyn Elisen (desert), northern Xinjiang Uygur Zizhiqu (Sin Kiang), China's most north westerly province, that is more than 1500 miles

2400 km from the open sea in any direction. The nearest large city to this point is Urümqi (Urümchi) to its south.

Land remotest from the sea *Great Britain*

The point furthest from the sea in Great Britain is a point near Meriden, West Midlands, England, which is 72½ miles *117 km* equidistant from the Severn Bridge, the Dee and Mersey estuaries and the Welland estuary in the Wash. The equivalent point in Scotland is in the Forest of Atholl, north-west Tayside 40½ miles *65 km* equidistant from the head of Loch Leven, Inverness Firth and the Firth of Tay.

Peninsula

The world's largest peninsula is Arabia, with an area of about 1,250,000 miles^2 *3 250 000 km^2*.

ISLANDS

Largest *World*

Discounting Australia, which is usually regarded as a continental land mass, the largest island in the world is Greenland (renamed Kalaallit Nunaat 1 May 1979), with an area of about 840,000 miles^2 *2 175 000 km^2*. There is evidence that Greenland is in fact several islands overlaid by an ice cap without which it would have an area of 650,000 miles^2 *1 680 000 km^2*.

Largest *Great Britain*

The mainland of Great Britain is the eighth largest in the world, with an area of 84,186 miles^2 *218 024 km^2*. It stretches 603½ miles *971 km* from Dunnet Head in the north to Lizard Point in the south and 287½ miles *463 km* across from Porthaflod, Dyfed to Lowestoft, Suffolk. The island of Ireland (32,594 miles^2 *84 418 km^2*) is the 20th largest in the world.

Freshwater

The largest island surrounded by fresh water is the Ilha de Marajó (18,500 miles^2 *48 000 km^2*), in the mouth of the River Amazon, Brazil. The world's largest inland island (*i.e.* land surrounded by rivers) is Ilha do Bananal, Brazil (7000 miles^2 *18 130 km^2*). The largest island in a lake is Manitoulin Island (1068 miles^2 *2766 km^2*) in the Canadian (Ontario) section of Lake Huron. The largest lake island in Great Britain is Inchmurrin in Loch Lomond, Strathclyde/Central, Scotland with an area of 284 acres *115 ha*.

Remotest *World uninhabited*

The remotest island in the world is Bouvet Øya (formerly Liverpool Island), discovered in the South Atlantic by J. B. C. Bouvet de Lozier on 1 Jan 1739, and first landed on by Capt. George Norris on 16 Dec 1825. Its position is 54° 26′ S, 3° 24′ E. This uninhabited Norwegian dependency is about 1050 miles *1700 km* from the nearest land—the uninhabited Queen Maud Land coast of eastern Antarctica.

Remotest *World inhabited*

The remotest inhabited island in the world is Tristan da Cunha, discovered in the South Atlantic by Tristao da Cunha, a Portuguese admiral, in March 1506. It has an area of 38 miles^2 *98 km^2* (habitable area 12 miles^2 *31 km^2*) and was annexed by the United Kingdom on 14 Aug 1816. After evacuation in 1961 (due to volcanic activity) 198 islanders returned in November 1963. The nearest inhabited land is the island of St Helena, 1320 miles *2120 km* to the north-east. The nearest continent, Africa, is 1700 miles *2735 km* away.

Remotest *Great Britain*

The remotest of the British islets is Rockall 191 miles *307 km* west of St Kilda, Western Isles. This 70 ft *21 m* high rock measuring 83 ft *25 m* across was not formally annexed until 18 Sept

1955. The remotest British island which has ever been inhabited is North Rona which is 44 miles *70,8 km* from the next nearest land at Cape Wrath and the Butt of Lewis. It was evacuated c. 1844. Muckle Flugga, off Unst, in the Shetlands, is the northernmost inhabited with a population of 3 (1971) and is in a latitude north of southern Greenland. Just to the north of it is the rock of Out Stack in Lat. 60° 51′ 35.7″ N.

Highest rock pinnacle

The world's highest rock pinnacle is Ball's Pyramid near Lord Howe Island, Pacific which is 1843 ft *561 m* high, but has a base axis of only 200 m *220 yd*. It was first scaled in 1965.

Northernmost land

On 26 July 1978 Uffe Petersen of the Danish Geodetic Institute observed the islet of OOdaq Ø 30 m *100 ft* across, 1,36 km *1478 yd* north of Kaffeklubben Ø off Pearyland, Greenland in Lat. 83° 40′ 32.5″ N, Long, 30° 40′ 10.1″ W. The island is 706,4 km *438.9 miles* from the North Pole.

Southernmost land

The South Pole, unlike the North Pole, is on land. The Amundsen–Scott South Polar station was built there at an altitude of 9370 ft *2855 m* in 1957. It is drifting bodily with the ice cap 27–30 ft *8–9 m* per annum in the direction 43° W and was replaced by a new structure in 1975.

Greatest archipelago

The world's greatest archipelago is the 3500 mile *5600 km* long crescent of more than 13,000 islands which forms Indonesia.

Newest

The world's newest island is the lava islet of Fukuto Kuokanoba near Iwo Jima in the Pacific reported in Jan 1986. It measures 650 × 450 m *2132 × 1476 ft* and is 12 m *40 ft* above sea level.

Largest atoll

The largest atoll in the world is Kwajalein in the Marshall Islands, in the central Pacific Ocean. Its slender 176 mile *283 km* long coral reef encloses a lagoon of 1100 miles^2 *2850 km^2*. The atoll with the largest land area is Christmas Atoll, in the Line Islands, in the central Pacific Ocean. It has an area of 248 miles^2 *642 km^2* of which 125 miles^2 *323 km^2* is land. Its principal settlement, London, is only 2½ miles *4,0 km* distant from Paris.

Longest reef

The longest reef is the Great Barrier Reef off Queensland, north-eastern Australia, which is 1260 statute miles *2027 km* in length. Between 1959 and 1971 a large section between Cooktown and Townsville was destroyed by the proliferation of the Crown of Thorns starfish (*Acanthaster planci*).

DEPRESSIONS

Deepest *World*

The deepest depression so far discovered is the bed rock in the Bentley sub-glacial trench, Antarctica at 2538 m *8326 ft* below sea level. The greatest submarine depression is a large area of the floor of the north-west Pacific which has an average depth of 15,000 ft *4570 m*. The deepest exposed depression on land is the shore surrounding the Dead Sea, now 400 m *1312 ft* below sea-level. The deepest point on the bed of this saltiest of all lakes is 728 m *2388 ft* below sea level. The deepest part of the bed of Lake Baykal in Siberia, USSR, is 4872 ft *1485 m* below sea-level.

Deepest *Great Britain*

The lowest lying area in Great Britain is in the

Holme Fen area of the Great Ouse, in Cambridgeshire, at 9 ft *2,75 m* below sea-level. The deepest depression in England is the bed of part of Windermere, 94 ft *28,65 m* below sea-level, and in Scotland the bed of Loch Morar, Highland 987 ft *300,8 m* below sea-level.

Largest

The largest exposed depression in the world is the Caspian Sea basin in the Azerbaydzhani, Russian, Kazakh and Turkmen Republics of the USSR and northern Iran (Persia). It is more than 200,000 miles² *518 000 km²* of which 143,550 miles² *371 800 km²* is lake area. The preponderant land area of the depression is the Prikaspiyskaya Nizmennost', lying around the northern third of the lake and stretching inland for a distance of up to 280 miles *450 km*.

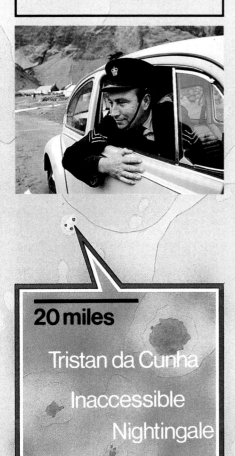

THE REMOTEST INHABITED ISLAND *Tristan da Cunha*

20 miles

Tristan da Cunha

Inaccessible

Nightingale

Sergeant Albert Glass of the Tristan da Cunha Police Force is a direct descendant of the founder of the community. Together with the other 197 inhabitants of the island, his nearest next door neighbours are 1320 miles *2120 km* away. (Map: Eddie Botchway. Picture: The Sunday Times).

CAVES

Longest

The most extensive cave system in the world is that under the Mammoth Cave National Park, Kentucky, USA first discovered in 1799. On 9 Sept 1972 an exploration group led by Dr John P. Wilcox completed a connection, pioneered by Mrs Patricia Crowther on 30 Aug between the Flint Ridge Cave system and the Mammoth Cave system, so making a combined system with a total mapped passageway length which is now over 530 km */330 miles*. The longest cave system in Great Britain is the Ease Gill system which now has 52.4 km *32.5 miles* of explored passage.

Largest cavern

The world's largest cave chamber is the Sarawak Chamber, Lubang Nasib Bagus, in the Gunung Mulu National Park, Sarawak discovered and surveyed by the 1980 British–Malaysian Mulu Expedition. Its length is 700 m *2300 ft*; and its average width is 300 m *980 ft* and it is nowhere less than 70 m *230 ft* high. It would be large enough to garage 7500 buses.

Longest stalactite

The longest known stalactite in the world is a wall-supported column extending 195 ft *59 m* from roof to floor in the Cueva de Nerja, near Málaga, Spain. Probably the longest free-hanging stalactite is one of 7 m *23 ft* in the Poll an Ionain cave in County Clare, Ireland. The tallest cave column is probably the 128 ft *39 m* high Flying Dragon Pillar in Nine Dragons Cave (Daji Dong), Guizhou, China.

Tallest stalagmite

The tallest known stalagmite in the world is La Grande Stalagmite in the Aven Armand cave, Lozère, France, which has attained a height of 98 ft *29 m* from the cave floor. It was found in September 1897.

DEEPEST CAVES BY COUNTRIES
These depths are subject to continuous revisions.

Depth			
m	Ft		
1535	5036	Réseau Jean Bernard	France
1370	4495	Snieznaja Piezcziera	USSR
1338	4390	Puerta de Illamina	Spain
1252	4108	Sistema Huautla	Mexico
1219	3999	Schwersystem	Austria
1208	3964	Complesso Fighiera Carchia	Italy
1007	3304	Anou Ifflis	Algeria
920	3018	Jama u Vjetrena brda	Yugoslavia
878	2880	Holloch	Switzerland
768	2520	Jaskinia Sniezna	Poland
751	2464	Ghar Parau, Zagros	Iran
308	1010	Ogof Ffynnon Ddu	Wales
214	702	Giant's Hole System	England
179	587	Reyfad Pot	N Ireland
140	459	Carrowmore Cavern	Rep. of Ireland

MOUNTAINS

Highest *World*

An eastern Himalayan peak of 29,028 ft *8848 m* above sea-level on the Tibet–Nepal border (in an area first designated Chu-mu-lang-ma on a map of 1717) was discovered to be the world's highest mountain in 1852 by the Survey Department of the Government of India, from theodolite readings taken in 1849 and 1850. In 1860 its height was computed to be 29,002 ft *8840 m*. On 25 July 1973 the Chinese announced a height of 8848,1 m or *29,029 ft 3 in*. In practice the altitude can only be justified as 29,028 ft ± 10 feet or a mean *8848 m*. The 5½ mile *8,85 km* high peak was named Mount Everest after Col. Sir George

Everest, CB. (1790–1866), formerly Surveyor-General of India. Other names for Everest are: Sagarmatha (Nepalese), Qomolongma (Chinese) and Mi-ti Gu-ti Cha-pu Long-na (Tibetan). After a total loss of 11 lives since the first reconnaissance in 1921, Everest was finally conquered at 11.30 a.m. on 29 May 1953. (For details of ascents, see under Mountaineering in Chapter 12.) The mountain whose summit is farthest from the Earth's centre is the Andean peak of Chimborazo (20,561 ft *6267 m*), 98 miles *158 km* south of the equator in Ecuador, South America. Its summit is 7057 ft *2150 m* further from the Earth's centre than the summit of Mt Everest. The highest mountain on the equator is Volcán Cayambe (19,285 ft *5878 m*), Ecuador, in Long. 77° 58′ W. A mountaineer atop the summit would be moving at 1671 km/h *1038 mph* relative to the Earth's centre due to the Earth's rotation.

Highest *Insular*

The highest insular mountain in the world is Puncak Jayak (formerly Puncak Sukarno, formerly Carstensz Pyramide) in Irian Jaya, Indonesia, once Netherlands New Guinea. A survey by the Australian Universities' Expedition in 1973 yielded a height of 4884 m *16,023 ft*. Ngga Pula now 4861 m *15,950 ft* was in 1936 possibly *c.* 4910 m *c. 16,110 ft* before the melting of its snow cap.

Highest *UK and Ireland*

The highest mountain in the United Kingdom is Ben Nevis (4406 ft *1343 m* excluding the 12 ft *3,65 m* cairn), 4¼ miles *6,85 km* south-east of Fort William, Highland, Scotland. It was climbed before 1720 but though acclaimed the highest in 1790 was not confirmed to be higher than Ben Macdhui (4300 ft *1310 m*) until 1847. In 1834 Ben Macdhui and Ben Nevis (Gaelic, *Beinn Nibheis*) (first reference, 1778) were respectively quoted as 4570 ft *1393 m* and 4370 ft *1332 m*. The highest mountain in England is Scafell Pike (3210 ft *978 m*) in Cumbria; in Wales is Snowdon (*Yr Wyddfa*) (3560 ft *1085 m*) in Gwynedd; and in the island of Ireland is Carrauntual (3414 ft *1041 m*) in County Kerry.

There is some evidence that, before being ground down by the ice-cap, mountains in the Loch Bà area of the Isle of Mull, Strathclyde were 15,000 ft *4575 m* above sea-level.

Highest *Peaks over 3000 ft* 915 m

There are 577 peaks and tops over 3000 ft *915 m* in the whole British Isles and 165 peaks and 136 tops in Scotland higher than England's highest point, Scafell Pike. The highest mountain off the mainland is Sgùrr Alasdair (3309 ft *1008 m*) on Skye named after Alexander (Gaelic, *Alasdair*) Nicolson, who made the first ascent in 1873.

Highest unclimbed

The highest unclimbed mountain is now only the 31st highest—Zemu Gap Peak (25,526 ft *7780 m*) in the Sikkim Himalaya.

Largest

The world's tallest mountain measured from its submarine base (3280 fathoms *6000 m*) in the Hawaiian Trough to peak is Mauna Kea (Mountain White) on the island of Hawaii, with a combined height of 33,476 ft *10 203 m* of which 13,796 ft *4205 m* are above sea-level. Another mountain whose dimensions, but not height, exceed those of Mount Everest is the volcanic Hawaiian peak of Mauna Loa (Mountain Long) at 13,680 ft *4170 m*. The axes of its elliptical base, 16,322 ft *4975 m* below sea-level, have been estimated at 74 miles *119 m* and 53 miles *85 km*. It should be noted that Cerro

The daunting North Face of Puncak Jayak the world's tallest insular mountain with a height of 4884 m *16,023 ft. See p. 59.* (Ian Allsion).

Aconcagua (22,834 ft *6960 m*) is more than 38,800 ft *11 826 m* above the 16,000 ft *4875 m* deep Pacific abyssal plain or 42,834 ft *13 055 m* above the Peru-Chile Trench which is 180 miles *290 km* distant in the South Pacific.

Greatest ranges
The world's greatest land mountain range is the Himalaya-Karakoram, which contains 96 of the world's 109 peaks of over 24,000 ft *7315 m*. Himalaya derives from the sanskrit *him*, snow; *alaya*, home. The greatest of all mountain ranges is, however, the submarine Indian/East Pacific Oceans Cordillera extending 19,200 miles *30 900 km* from the Gulf of Aden to the Gulf of California by way of the seabed between Australia and Antarctica with an average height of 8000 ft *2430 km* above the base ocean depth.

Longest lines of sight
Vatnajökull (6952 ft *2118 m*), Iceland has been seen by refracted light from the Faeroe Islands 340 miles *550 km* distant. In Alaska Mt McKinley (20,320 ft *6193 m*) has been sighted from Mt Sanford (16,237 ft *4949 m*) from a distance of 230 miles *370 km*. McKinley, so named in 1896, was called Denali (Great One) in the Athabascan language.

Greatest plateau
The most extensive high plateau in the world is the Tibetan Plateau in Central Asia. The average altitude is 16,000 ft *4875 m* and the area is 77,000 miles² *200 000 km²*.

Sheerest wall
Mount Rakaposhi (25,498 ft *7772 m*) rises 5,99 vertical kilometres *19,652 ft* from the Hunza

The 1260 mile *2027 km* Great Barrier Reef off Queensland, Australia—the longest in the world. *See p. 58.* (Daily Telegraph).

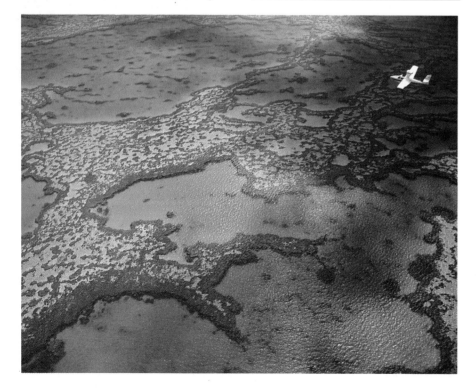

Valley, Pakistan in 10 horizontal kilometres *32,808 ft* with an overall gradient of 31°.

The 3200 ft *975 m* wide northwest face of Half Dome, Yosemite, California, USA is 2200 ft *670 m* high but nowhere departs more than 7 degrees from the vertical. It was first climbed (Class VI) in 5 days in July 1957 by Royal Robbins, Jerry Gallwas and Mike Sherrick.

Highest halites
Along the northern shores of the Gulf of Mexico for 725 miles *1160 km* there exists 330 subterranean 'mountains' of salt, some of which rise more than 60,000 ft *18 300 m* from bed rock and appear as the low salt domes first discovered in 1862.

Lowest hill
The official map of Seria, Brunei shows an artificial hillock named Bukit Thompson by the 13th hole on the Panaga Golf Course at 15 ft *4,5 m*.

WATERFALLS

Highest
The highest waterfall (as opposed to vaporized 'Bridal Veil') in the world is the Salto Angel in Venezuela, on a branch of the River Carrao, an upper tributary of the Caroni with a total drop of 3212 ft *979 m*—the longest single drop is 2648 ft *807 m*. They were named for the United States pilot James (Jimmy) Angel (died 8 Dec 1956), who had crashed nearby on 9 Oct 1937. The falls, known by the Indians as Cherun-Meru, were first reported by Ernesto Sanchez La Cruz in 1910.

Highest *United Kingdom*
The tallest waterfall in the United Kingdom is Eas a'Chùal Aluinn, from Glas Bheinn (2541 ft *774 m*), Highland, Scotland, with a drop of 658 ft *200 m*. England's highest fall above ground is Caldron (or Cauldron) Snout, on the Tees, with a fall of 200 ft *60 m* in 450 ft *135 m* of cataracts, but no sheer leap. It is on the border of Durham and Cumbria. The cascade in the Gaping Gill Cave descends 365 ft *111 m*. The highest Welsh waterfall is the Pistyll-y-Llyn on the Powys-Dyfed border which exceeds 300 ft *90 m* in descent.

Highest *Ireland*
The highest falls in Ireland are the Powerscourt Falls (350 ft *106 m*), on the River Dargle, County Wicklow.

Greatest
On the basis of the average annual flow, the greatest waterfalls in the world are the Boyoma (formerly Stanley) Falls in Zaïre with 600,000 cusec *17 000 m³/sec*. The peak flow of the Guaíra (Salto das Sete Quedas) on the Alto Paraná river between Brazil and Paraguay at times attained a peak flow rate of 1,750,000 cusec *50 000 m³/sec*. The completion of the Itaipu dam in 1982 ended this claim to fame.

It has been calculated that, when some 5,500,000 years ago the Mediterranean basins began to be filled from the Atlantic through the Straits of Gibraltar, a waterfall 26 times greater than the Guaíra and perhaps 800 m *2625 ft* high was formed.

Widest
The widest waterfalls in the world are the Khône Falls (50–70 ft *15–21 m* high) in Laos, with a width of 6.7 miles *10,8 km* and a flood flow of 1,500,000 cusec *42 500 m³/sec*.

RIVERS

Longest *World*
The two longest rivers in the world are the

Amazon (*Amazonas*), flowing into the South Atlantic, and the Nile (*Bahr-el-Nil*) flowing into the Mediterranean. Which is the longer is more a matter of definition than simple measurement.

The true source of the Amazon was discovered in 1953 to be a stream named Huarco, deriving from the Misuie Glacier (5400 m *17,715 ft*) in the Arequipa Andes of Peru. This stream progressively becomes the Toro then the Santiago then the Apurimac, which in turn is known as the Ene and then the Tambo before its confluence with the Amazon prime tributary the Ucayali. The length of the Amazon from this source to the South Atlantic *via* the Canal do Norte was measured in 1969 to be 4007 miles *6448 km* (usually quoted to the rounded off figure of 4000 miles *6437 km*).

If, however, a vessel navigating down the river follows the 'arm' (carrying 10% of the river's water) to the south of Ilha de Marajó through the Furo Tajapuru and Furo dos Macacos into the Pará, the total length of the water-course becomes 4195 miles 6750 km. The Rio Pará is not however a tributary of the Amazon, being hydrologically part of the basin of the Tocantins which however itself flows into the Bahia de Marajó and out into the South Atlantic.

The length of the Nile watercourse, as surveyed by M. Devroey (Belgium) before the loss of a few miles of meanders due to the formation of Lake Nasser, behind the Aswan High Dam, was 4145 miles *6670 km*. This course is unitary from a hydrological standpoint and runs from the source in Burundi of the Luvironza branch of the Kagera feeder of the Victoria Nyanza *via* the White Nile (*Bahrel-Jebel*) to the delta in the Mediterranean.

Longest *Great Britain*

The longest river in Great Britain is the Severn, which empties into the Bristol Channel and is 220 miles *354 km* long. Its basin extends over 4409 miles² *11 419 km²*. It rises in north-western Powys and flows through Shropshire, Hereford & Worcester, Gloucestershire and Avon and has a record 17 tributaries. The longest river *wholly* in England is the Thames, which is 215 miles, *346 km* long to the Nore. Its remotest source is at Seven Springs, Gloucestershire, whence the River Churn joins the other head waters. The source of the Thames proper is Trewsbury Mead, Coates, Cirencester, Gloucestershire. The basin measures 3841 miles² *9948 km²*. The Yorkshire Ouse's 11 tributaries aggregate 629 miles *1012 km*.

The longest river wholly in Wales is the Usk, with a length of 65 miles *104,5 km*. It rises on the border of Dyféd and Powys and flows out via Gwent into the Severn Estuary. The longest river in Scotland is the Tay, with Dundee, Tayside, on the shore of the estuary. It is 117 miles *188 km* long from the source of its remotest head-stream, the River Tummel, Tayside and has the greatest volume of any river in Great Britain, with a flow of up to 49,000 cusecs *1387 m³* per sec. Of Scottish rivers the Tweed and the Clyde have most tributaries with 11 each.

Longest *Ireland*

The longest river in Ireland is the Shannon, which is longer than any river in Great Britain. It rises 258 ft *78,6 m* above sea-level, in County Cavan, and flows through a series of loughs to Limerick. It is 240 miles *386 km* long, including the 56 mile *90 km* long estuary to Loop Head. The basin area is 6060 miles² *15 695 km²*.

Shortest river

The world's shortest named river is the D River, Lincoln City, Oregon, USA which connects

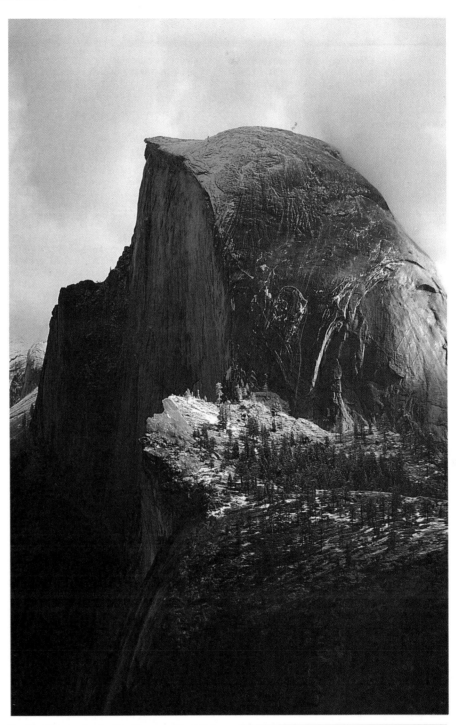

Devil's Lake to the Pacific Ocean and is 440 ft *134 m* long at low tide.

Largest basin and longest tributary

The largest river basin in the world is that drained by the Amazon (4007 miles *6448 km*). It covers about 2,720,000 miles² *7 045 000 km²*. It has about 15,000 tributaries and subtributaries, of which four are more than 1000 miles *1609 km* long. These include the Madeira, the longest of all tributaries, with a length of 2100 miles *3380 km*, which is surpassed by only 14 rivers in the whole world.

Longest sub-tributary

The longest sub-tributary is the Pilcomayo (1000 miles *1609 km* long) in South America. It is a tributary of the Paraguay (1500 miles *2415 km* long), which is itself a tributary of the Paraña (2500 miles *4025 km*).

The near perpendicular northwest face of Half Dome, Yosemite, California. (Bruce Coleman).

Longest estuary

The world's longest estuary is that of the often frozen Ob', in the northern USSR, at 550 miles *885 km*. It is up to 50 miles *80 km* wide.

Largest delta

The world's largest delta is that created by the Ganga (Ganges) and Brahmaputra in Bangla Desh (formerly East Pakistan) and West Bengal, India. It covers an area of 30,000 miles² *75 000 km²*.

Greatest flow

The greatest flow of any river in the world is that of the Amazon, which discharges an average of 4,200,000 cusec *120 000 m³/sec* into the Atlantic Ocean, rising to more than 7,000,000 cusec *200 000 m³/sec* in full flood. The lowest 900 miles *1450 km* of the Amazon average 300 ft *90 m* in depth.

Submarine river

In 1952 a submarine river 250 miles *400 km* wide, known as the Cromwell current, was discovered flowing eastward 300 ft *90 m* below the surface of the Pacific for 3500 miles *5625 km* along the equator. Its volume is 1000 times that of the Mississippi.

Subterranean river

In August 1958 a crypto-river was tracked by radio isotopes flowing under the Nile with 6 times its mean annual flow or 500,000 million m³ *20 million million ft³*.

Largest swamp

The world's largest tract of swamp is in the basin of the Pripet or Pripyat River—a tributary of the Dnieper in the USSR. These swamps cover an estimated area of 18,125 miles² *46 950 km²*.

RIVER BORES

World

The bore on the Ch'ient'ang'kian (Hang-chou-fe) in eastern China is the most remarkable of the 60 in the world. At spring tides the wave attains a height of up to 25 ft *7,5 m* and a speed of 13–15 knots *24–27 km/h*. It is heard advancing at a range of 14 miles *22 km*. The annual downstream flood wave on the Mekong sometimes reaches a height of 46 ft *14 m*. The greatest volume of any tidal bore is that of the Canal do Norte (10 miles *16 km* wide) in the mouth of the Amazon.

Great Britain

The most notable of the 8 river bores in the United Kingdom is that on the Severn, which attained a measured height of 9¼ ft *2,8 m* on 15 Oct 1966 downstream of Stonebench, and a speed of 13 mph *20 km/h*. It travels from Framilode towards Gloucester.

LAKES AND INLAND SEAS

Largest *World*

The largest inland sea or lake in the world is the Kaspiskoye More (Caspian Sea) in the southern USSR and Iran (Persia). It is 760 miles *1225 km* long and its total area is 139,000 miles² *360 700 km²*. Of the total area some 55,280 miles² *143 200 km²* (38.6 per cent) is in Iran, where it is named the Darya-ye-Khazar. Its maximum depth is 1025 m *3360 ft* and its surface is 28,5 m *93 ft* below sea-level. Its estimated volume is 21,500 miles³ *89 600 km³* of saline water. Its surface has varied between 32 m *105 ft* (11th century) and 22 m *72 ft* (early 19th century) below sea level. The USSR Government plan to reverse the flow of the upper Pechora River from flowing north to the Barents Sea by blasting a 70 mile *112 km* long canal with nuclear explosives into the south-flowing Kolva river so that *via* the Kama and Volga rivers the Caspian will be replenished.

Lake in a lake

The largest lake in a lake is Manitou Lake (41.09 miles² *106,42 km²*) on the world's largest lake island Manitoulin Island (1068 miles² *2766 km²*) in the Canadian part of Lake Huron. It contains itself a number of islands.

Underground lake

Reputedly the world's largest underground lake is the Lost Sea 300 ft *91 m* subterranean in the Craighead Caverns, Sweetwater, Tennessee, USA measuring 4½ acres *1,8 ha* and discovered in 1905.

Freshwater lake *World*

The freshwater lake with the greatest surface area is Lake Superior, one of the Great Lakes of North America. The total area is 31,800 miles² *82 350 km²*, of which 20,700 miles² *53 600 km²* are in Minnesota, Wisconsin and Michigan, USA and 11,100 miles² *27 750 km²* in Ontario, Canada. It is 600 ft *182 m* above sea-level. The freshwater lake with the greatest volume is Baykal with an estimated volume of 5520 miles³ *23 000 km³*.

Freshwater lake *United Kingdom*

The largest lake in the United Kingdom is Lough Neagh (48 ft *14,60 m* above sea-level) in Northern Ireland. It is 18 miles *28,9 km* long and 11 miles *17,7 km* wide and has an area of 147.39 miles² *381,73 km²*. Its extreme depth is 102 ft *31 m*.

Freshwater lakes or lochs *Great Britain*

The largest lake in Great Britain, and the largest inland loch in Scotland is Loch Lomond (23 ft *7,0 m* above sea-level), which is 22.64 miles *36,44 km* long and has a surface area of 27.45 miles² *70,04 km²*. It is situated in the Strathclyde and Central regions and its greatest depth is 623 ft *190 m*. The lake or loch with the greatest volume is however Loch Ness with 262,845,000,000 ft³ *7 443 000 000 m³*. The longest lake or loch is Loch Ness which measures 24.23 miles *38,99 km*. The three arms of the Y-shaped Loch Awe aggregate, however, 25.47 miles *40,99 km*. The largest lake in England is Windermere, in the county of Cumbria. It is 10½ miles *17 km* long and has a surface area of 5.69 miles² *14,74 km²*. Its greatest depth is 219 ft *66,75 m* in the northern half. The largest *natural* lake in Wales is Llyn Tegid, with an area

A spectacular view of the Grand Canyon in Arizona, home of the world's largest gorge. (Robert Harding).

Sand dunes in the Saharan sand sea of Isaouane-n-Tifernine which can have a wavelength of nearly 3 miles *5 km* and a height of 1410 ft *430 m*. (Robert Harding).

of 1.69 miles² *4,38 km²*, although it should be noted that the largest lake in Wales is that formed by the reservoir at Lake Vyrnwy, where the total surface area is 1120 acres *453,25 ha.*

Freshwater lakes or loughs *Republic of Ireland*
The largest lough in the Republic of Ireland is Lough Corrib in the counties of Mayo and Galway. It measures 27 miles *43,5 km* in length and is 7 miles *11,25 km* across at its widest point with a total surface area of 41,616 acres (65.0 miles² *168 km²*).

Largest lagoon
The largest lagoon in the world is Lagoa dos Patos in southernmost Brazil. It is 158 miles *254 km* long and extends over 4110 miles² *10 645 km²*.

Deepest *World*
The deepest lake in the world is Ozero (Lake) Baykal in central Siberia, USSR. It is 385 miles *620 km* long and between 20 and 46 miles *32–74 km* wide. In 1957 the lake's Olkhon Crevice was measured to be 1940 m *6365 ft* deep and hence 1485 m *4872 ft* below sea-level (see p. 59).

Deepest *Great Britain*
The deepest lake in Great Britain is the 10.30 mile *16,57 km* long Loch Morar, in Highland. Its surface is 30 ft *9 m* above sea-level and its extreme depth 1017 ft *310 m*. England's deepest lake is Wast Water (258 ft *78 m*), in Cumbria. The lake with the greatest mean depth is Loch Ness with *c.* 426 ft *130 m*.

Highest *World*
The highest steam-navigated lake in the world is Lago Titicaca (maximum depth 1214 ft *370 m*), with an area of about 3200 miles² *8285 km²* (1850 miles² *4790 km²* in Peru, 1350 miles² *3495 km²* in Bolivia), in South America. It is 130 miles *209 km* long and is situated at 12,506 ft *3811 m* above sea-level. There is an unnamed glacial lake near Everest at 19,300 ft *5880 m*. Tibet's largest lake Nam Tso of 722 miles² *1956 km²* is at 15,060 ft *4578 m*.

Highest *United Kingdom*
The highest lake in the United Kingdom is the 1.9 acre *0,76 ha* Lochan Buidhe at 3600 ft *1097 m* above sea-level in the Cairngorm Mountains, Scotland. England's highest is Broad Crag Tarn (2746 ft *837 m* above sea-level) on Scafell Pike, Cumbria and the highest named freshwater in Wales is The Frogs Pool, a tarn near the summit of Carnedd Llywelyn, Gwynedd at *c.* 2725 ft *830 m*.

OTHER FEATURES

Desert *Largest*
Nearly an eighth of the world's land surface is arid with a rainfall of less than 25 cm *9.8 in* per annum. The Sahara in N. Africa is the largest in the world. At its greatest length it is 3200 miles *5150 km* from east to west. From north to south it is between 800 and 1400 miles *1275 and 2250 km*. The area covered by the desert is about 3,250,000 miles² *8 400 000 km²*. The land level varies from 436 ft *132 m* below sea-level in the Qattâra Depression, Egypt, to the mountain Emi Koussi (11,204 ft *3415 m*) in Chad. The diurnal temperature range in the western Sahara may be more than 80° F or *45° C.*

Sand dunes
The world's highest measured sand dunes are those in the Saharan sand sea of Isaouane-n-Tifernine of east central Algeria in Lat. 26° 42′ N, Long. 6° 43′ E. They have a wave-length of near 3 miles *5 km* and attain a height of 1410 ft *430 m*.

Gorge *Largest*
The largest land gorge in the world is the Grand Canyon on the Colorado River in north-central Arizona, USA. It extends from Marble Gorge to the Grand Wash Cliffs, over a distance of 217 miles *349 km*. It varies in width from 4 to 13 miles *6–20 km* and is some 5300 ft *1615 m* deep. The submarine Labrador Basin canyon is *c.* 2150 miles *3440 km* long.

Gorge *Deepest*
The deepest canyon is El Cañón de Colca, Peru reported in 1929 which is 3223 m *10,574 ft* deep. It was first traversed by the Polish Expedition CANOANDES '79 kayak team on 12 May–14 June 1981. A stretch of the Kali River in central Nepal flows 18,000 ft *5485 m* below its flanking summits of the Dhaulagiri and Annapurna groups. The deepest submarine canyon yet discovered is one 25 miles *40 km* south of Esperance, Western Australia, which is 6000 ft *1800 m* deep and 20 miles *32 km* wide.

Cliffs *Highest*
The highest sea cliffs yet pinpointed anywhere in the world are those on the north coast of east Moloka'i, Hawaii near Umilehi Point, which descend 3300 ft *1005 m* to the sea at an average gradient of >55°. The west face of Thor Peak, Baffin Island, Canada allowed an abseiling or rappelling record of 3250 ft *990 m* by Steve Holmes (USA) in July 1982. The highest cliffs in North West Europe are those on the north coast of Achill Island, in County Mayo, Ireland, which are 2192 ft *668 m* sheer above the sea at Croaghan. The highest cliffs in the United Kingdom are the 1300 ft *396 m* Conachair cliffs on St Kilda, Western Isles (1397 ft *425 m*). The highest sheer sea cliffs on the mainland of Great Britain are at Clo Mor, 3 miles *4,8 km* south-east of Cape Wrath, Highland, Scotland which drop 921 ft *280,7 m*. England's highest cliff (gradient >45°) is Great Hangman Hill, near Combe Martin, in North Devon, which descends from 1043 ft *318 m* to the sea in 984 ft *300 m*, the last 700 ft *213 m* of which is sheer.

Natural arch *Longest*
The longest natural arch in the world is the Landscape Arch in the Arches National Park, 25 miles *40 km* north of Moab, Utah, USA. This natural sandstone arch spans 291 ft *88 m* and is set about 100 ft *30 m* above the canyon floor. In one place erosion has narrowed its section to 6 ft *1,82 m*. Larger, however, is the Rainbow Bridge, Utah discovered on 14 Aug 1909 with a span of 278 ft *84,7 m* but more than 22 ft *6,7 m* wide.

Natural bridge *Highest*
The highest natural arch is the sandstone arch 25 miles *40 km* WNW of K'ashih, Sinkiang, China, estimated in 1947 to be nearly 1000 ft *312 m* tall with a span of about 150 ft *45 m*.

Longest glaciers
It is estimated that 6,020,000 miles² *15 600 000 km²*, or 10½ per cent of the Earth's land surface, is permanently glaciated. The world's longest known glacier is the Lambert Glacier, discovered by an Australian aircraft crew in Australian Antarctic Territory in 1956–7. It is up to 40 miles *64 km* wide and, with its upper section, known as the Mellor Glacier, it measures at least 250 miles *402 km* in length. With the Fisher Glacier limb, the Lambert forms a continuous ice passage about 320 miles *514 km* long. The longest Himalayan glacier is the Siachen (47 miles *75,6 km*) in the Karakoram range, though the Hispar and Biafo combine to form an ice passage 76 miles *122 km* long. The fastest moving major glacier is the Quarayaq in Greenland flowing 20–24 m *65–80 ft* per day.

Greatest avalanches
The greatest natural avalanches, though rarely observed, occur in the Himalaya but no estimates of their volume had been published. It was estimated that 3,500,000 m³ *120 000 000 ft³* of snow fell in an avalanche in the Italian Alps in 1885. The 250 mph *400 km/h* avalanche triggered by the Mount St. Helens eruption in Washington on 18 May 1979 was estimated to measure 2800 million m³ *96,000 million ft³* (see Disasters, Chapter 11).

CHAPTER FOUR

THE

UNIVERSE & SPACE

A colour composite of comet Halley made from three photographic plates exposed on the United Kingdom 1,2 m Schmidt telescope in Australia on the night of 12 Mar 1986. *See p. 66.* (Royal Observatory, Edinburgh).

See p. 66.

LIGHT-YEAR—that distance travelled by light (speed 186,282.397 miles/sec *299 792,458 km/s* or 670,616,629.2 mph *1 079 252 848,8 km/h in vacuo*) in one tropical year (365.24219878 mean solar days at January 0,12 hours Ephemeris time in AD 1900) and is 5,878,499,814,000 miles *9 460 528 405 000 km.* The unit was first used in March 1888 and fixed at this constant in October 1983.

MAGNITUDE—a measure of stellar brightness such that the light of a star of any magnitude bears a ratio of 2.511886 to that of a star of the next magnitude. Thus a fifth magnitude star is 2.511886 times as bright, while one of the first magnitude is exactly 100 (or 2.511886^5) times as bright, as a sixth magnitude star. In the case of such exceptionally bright bodies as Sirius, Venus, the Moon (magnitude -12.71) or the Sun (magnitude -26.78), the magnitude is expressed as a minus quantity.

PROPER MOTION—that component of a star's motion in space which, at right angles to the line of sight, constitutes an apparent change of position of the star in the celestial sphere.

The universe is the entirety of space, matter and anti-matter. An appreciation of its magnitude is best grasped by working outward from the Earth, through the Solar System which is revolving around the centre of the Milky Way once in each 237,000,000 years, at a speed of 492,000 mph *792 000 km/h* and has a velocity of 44,700 mph *72 000 km/h* relative to stars in our immediate region and then on to the remotest extra-galactic nebulae and quasars.

METEOROIDS

Meteoroids are of cometary or asteroidal origin. A meteor is the light phenomenon caused by the entry of a meteoroid into the Earth's atmosphere.

Meteor shower

The greatest meteor 'shower' on record occurred on the night of 16–17 Nov 1966, when the Leonid meteors (which recur every $33\frac{1}{4}$ years) were visible between western North America and eastern USSR. It was calculated that meteors passed over Arizona, USA, at a rate of 2300 per min for a period of 20 min from 5 a.m. on 17 Nov 1966.

METEORITES

When a meteoroid penetrates to the Earth's surface, the remnant which could be either aerolite (stony) or siderite (metallic) is described as a meteorite. This occurs about 150 times per year over the whole land surface of the Earth. Although the chances of being struck are deemed negligible, the most anxious time of day for meteorophobes is 3 p.m.

Oldest
The oldest dated meteorites are from the Allende fall in Chihuahua, Mexico on 8 Feb 1969 dating back to 4610 million years.

It was reported in August 1978 that dust grains in the Murchison meteorite which fell in Australia in September 1969 also pre-date the formation of the Solar System 4600 million years ago.

Largest *World*
There was a mysterious explosion of $12\frac{1}{2}$ megatons in Lat. 60° 55′ N, Long. 101° 57′ E, in the basin of the Podkamennaya Tunguska river, 40 miles north of Vanavar, in Siberia, USSR, at 00 hrs 17 min 11 sec UT on 30 June 1908. The cause was variously attributed to a meteorite (1927), a comet (1930), a nuclear explosion (1961) and to anti-matter (1965). This devastated an area of about 1500 miles² *3885 km²* and the shock was felt as far as 1000 km (more than *600 miles*) away. The theory is now favoured that this was the terminal flare of stony debris from a comet, possibly Encke's comet, at altitude of only 6 km *or less than 20,000 ft.* A similar event may have occurred over the Isle of Axholm, Humberside a few thousand years before. A stony meteorite with a diameter of 10 km *6.2 miles* striking the Earth at 25 km/sec *55,925 mph* would generate an explosive energy equivalent to 100 million megatons. Such events should not be expected to recur more than once in 75 million years.

The largest known meteorite is one found in 1920 at Hoba West, near Grootfontein in southwest Africa. This is a block 9 ft *2,75 m* long by 8 ft *2,43 m* broad, estimated to be 132,000 lb (59 tons/*tonnes*). The largest meteorite exhibited by any museum is the 'Tent' meteorite, weighing 68,085 lb (30.39 tons *30 883 kg*) found in 1897 near Cape York, on the west coast of Greenland, by the expedition of Commander (later Rear-Admiral) Robert Edwin Peary (1856–1920). It was known to the Eskimos as the Abnighito and is now exhibited in the Hayden Planetarium in New York City, NY, USA. The largest piece of stony meteorite recovered is a piece of 1770 kg *3902 lb* part of a 4 tonne shower which struck Jilin (formerly Kirin), China on 8 Mar 1976. In historic times, the only recorded person injured by a meteorite has been Mrs E. H. Hodges of Sylacanga, Alaska, USA. On 30 Nov 1954 a 9 lb *4 kg* stone went through her roof.

Largest *United Kingdom and Ireland*
The heaviest of the 22 meteorites known to have fallen on the British Isles since 1623 was one weighing at least 102 lb *46,25 kg* (largest piece 17 lb 6 oz *7,88 kg*), which fell at 4.12 p.m. on 24 Dec 1965 at Barwell, Leicestershire. Scotland's largest recorded meteorite fell in Strathmore, Tayside on 3 Dec 1917. It weighed $22\frac{1}{4}$ lb *10,09 kg* and was the largest of four stones totalling 29 lb 6 oz *13,324 kg*. The largest recorded meteorite to fall in Ireland was the Limerick Stone of 65 lb *29,5 kg*, part of a shower weighing more than 106 lb *48 kg* which fell near Adare, County Limerick, on 10 Sept 1813. The larger of the two recorded meteorites to land in Wales was one weighing 28 oz *794 g* of which a piece weighing $25\frac{1}{2}$ oz *723 g* went through the roof of the Prince Llewellyn Hotel in Beddgelert, Gwynedd, shortly before 3.15 a.m. on 21 Sept 1949. Debris from the Bovedy Fall in N. Ireland in 1969 spread over 50 miles *80 km.*

Largest craters
It has been estimated that some 2000 asteroid-Earth collisions have occurred in the last 600 million years. A total of 102 collision sites or astroblemes have been recognised. A crater 150 miles *241 km* in diameter and $\frac{1}{2}$ mile *805 m* deep has been postulated in Wilkes Land, Antarctica since 1962. It would be caused by a 13,000 million ton meteorite striking at 44,000 mph *70 811 km/h.* USSR scientists reported in December 1970 an astrobleme with a 60 mile *95 km* diameter and a maximum depth of 1300 ft *400 m* in the basin of the River Popigai. There is a possible crater-like formation or astrobleme 275 miles *442,5 km* in diameter on the eastern shore of the Hudson Bay, Canada, where the Nastapoka Islands are just off the coast.

The largest proven crater is the Coon Butte or Barringer crater, discovered in 1891 near Canyon Diablo, Winslow, northern Arizona, USA. It is 4150 ft *1265 m* in diameter and now about 575 ft *175 m* deep, with a parapet rising 130–155 ft *40–48 m* above the surrounding plain. It has been estimated that an iron-nickel mass with a diameter of 200–260 ft *61–79 m* and weighing about 2,000,000 tons/*tonnes* gouged this crater in *c.* 25,000 BC. Evidence was published in 1963 discounting a meteoric origin for the crypto-volcanic Vredefort Ring (diameter 26 miles *41,8 km*), to the south-west of Johannesburg, South Africa, but this has now been re-asserted. The New Quebec (formerly the Chubb) 'Crater', first sighted on 20 June 1943 in northern Ungava, Canada, is 1325 ft *404 m* deep and measures 6.8 miles *10,9 km* round its rim.

Fireball *Brightest*
The brightest fireball ever photographically recorded was by Dr Zdenek Ceplecha over Sumava, Czechoslovakia on 4 Dec 1974 with a momentary magnitude of −22 or 10,000 times brighter than a full Moon.

Tektites
The largest tektite of which details have been published has been of 3,2 kg *7.04 lb* found in 1932 at Muong Nong, Saravane Province, Laos and now in the Paris Museum.

AURORAE

Most frequent
Polar lights, known since 1560 as Aurora Borealis or Northern Lights in the northern hemisphere and since 1773 as Aurora Australis in the southern hemisphere, are caused by electrical solar discharges in the upper atmosphere and occur most frequently in high latitudes. Aurorae are visible at some time on *every* clear dark night in the polar areas within 20 degrees of the magnetic poles. The extreme height of aurorae has been measured at 1000 km *620 miles,* while the lowest may descend to 72,5 km *45 miles.* Reliable figures exist only from 1952, since when the record high and low number of nights of auroral displays in Shetland (geomagnetic Lat. 63°) has been 203 (1957) and 58 (1965). The most recent great display in north-west Europe was that of 4–5 Sept 1958.

Lowest latitudes
Extreme cases of displays in very low latitudes are Cuzco, Peru (2 Aug 1744); Honolulu, Hawaii (1 Sept 1859) and questionably Singapore (25 Sept 1909).

Noctilucent clouds
Regular observations (at heights of *c.* 52 miles *85 km*) in Western Europe date only from 1964, since when the record high and low number of nights on which these phenomena have been observed have been 41 (1974) and 15 (1970).

THE MOON

The Earth's closest neighbour in space and only natural satellite is the Moon, at a mean distance of 238,855 statute miles *384 400 km* centre-to-centre or 233,812 miles *376 284 km* surface-to-surface. In the present century the closest approach (smallest perigee) was 216,398 miles *348 259 km* surface-to-surface or 221,441 miles *356 375 km* centre-to-centre on 4 January 1912, and the farthest distance (largest apogee) was 247,675 miles *398 598 km* surface-to-surface or 252,718 miles *406 711 km* centre-to-centre on 2 March 1984. The Moon was only a few Earth radii distant during the 'Gerstenkorn period' 3900 million years ago. It has a diameter of 2159.3 miles *3475,0 km* and has a mass of 7.23×10^{19} tons *7,35 × 10¹⁹ tonnes* with a mean density of 3.342. The average orbital speed is 2287 mph *3680 km/h.* The first direct hit on the Moon was achieved at 2 min 24 sec after midnight (Moscow time) on 14 Sept 1959, by the Soviet space probe *Luna II* near the *Mare Serenitatis.* The first photographic images of the hidden side were collected by the USSR's *Luna III* from 6.30 a.m. on 7 Oct 1959, from a range of up to 43,750 miles *70 400 km* and transmitted to the Earth from a distance of 470 000 km *292,000 miles.* The oldest of the Moon material brought back to Earth by the *Apollo* programme crews has been soil dated to 4720 million years.

Crater *Largest and deepest*
Only 59 per cent of the Moon's surface is directly visible from the Earth because it is in 'captured rotation', *i.e.* the period of rotation is equal to the period of orbit. The largest wholly visible crater is the walled plain Bailly, towards the Moon's South Pole, which is 183 miles *295 km* across, with walls rising to 14,000 ft *4250 m.* The Orientale Basin, partly on the averted side, measures more than 600 miles *965 km* in diameter. The deepest crater is the Newton crater, with a floor estimated to be between 23,000 and 29,000 ft *7000–8850 m* below its rim and 14,000 ft *2250 m* below the level of the plain outside. The brightest directly visible spot on the Moon is *Aristarchus.*

Highest mountains
In the absence of a sea level, lunar altitudes are measured relative to an adopted reference sphere of radius 1738,000 km or *1079.943 miles.* Thus the greatest elevation attained on this basis by any of the 12 US astronauts has been 7830 m *25,688 ft* on the Descartes Highlands by Capt. John Watts Young USN and Major Charles M. Duke Jr on 27 Apr 1972.

Temperature extremes
When the Sun is overhead the temperature on the lunar equator reaches 243°F *117,2°C* (31 deg F *17,2 deg C* above the boiling point of water). By sunset the temperature is 58°F *14,4°C* but after nightfall it sinks to −261°F *−162,7°C.*

THE SUN

Distance extremes
The Earth's 66,620 mph *107 210 km/h* orbit of 584,017,800 miles *939 885 500 km* around the Sun is elliptical, hence our distance from the Sun varies. The orbital speed varies between

65,520 mph *105 450 km/h* (minimum) and 67,750 mph *109 030 km/h*. The average distance of the Sun is 1.000 000 230 astronomical units or 92,955,829 miles *149 597 906 km.*

The closest approach (perihelion) is 91,402,000 miles *147 097 000 km* and the farthest departure (aphelion) is 94,510,000 miles *152 099 000 km.*

Temperature and dimensions
The Sun has a central temperature of about 15 400 000 K, a core pressure of 1,650,000,000 tons/in^2 25,4 PPa and uses up 4,000,000 tons/ *tonnes* of hydrogen per sec, thus providing a luminosity of 3×10^{27} candlepower, with an intensity of 1,500,000 candles/in^2 *1 530 000 candelas.* The Sun has the stellar classification of a 'yellow dwarf' and, although its density is only 1.407 times that of water, its mass is 332,946 times as much as that of the Earth. It has a mean diameter of 865,270 miles *1 392 520 km.* The Sun with a mass of 1.958×10^{27} tons *$1,989 \times 10^{27}$ tonnes* represents more than 99 per cent of the total mass of the Solar System but will exhaust its energy in 10,000 million years.

Sunspots *Largest*
To be visible to the *protected* naked eye, a sunspot must cover about one two-thousandth part of the Sun's disc and thus have an area of about 500,000,000 miles^2 *1300 million km^2.* The largest sunspot occurred in the Sun's southern hemisphere on 8 Apr 1947. Its area was about 7000 million miles^2 *18 000 million km^2* with an extreme longitude of 187,000 miles *300 000 km* and an extreme latitude of 90,000 miles *145 000 km.* Sunspots appear darker because they are more than 1500 deg C cooler than the rest of the Sun's surface temperature of 5525° C. The largest observed solar prominence was one protruding 365,000 miles *588 000 km,* photographed on 19 Dec 1973 during the 3rd and final manned Skylab mission. In October 1957 a smoothed sunspot count showed 263, the highest recorded index since records started in 1755 (*cf.* previous record of 239 in May 1778). In 1943 one sunspot lasted for 200 days from June to December.

ECLIPSES

Earliest recorded
For the Middle East, lunar eclipses have been extrapolated to 3450 BC and solar ones to 4200 BC. No centre of the path of totality for a solar eclipse crossed London for the 575 years from 20 Mar 1140 to 3 May 1715. On 14 June 2151 at 18.25 GMT the eclipse will be 99 per cent total in central London but total in Sheffield and Norfolk. The most recent occasion when a line of totality of a solar eclipse crossed Great Britain was on 29 June 1927 for 24.5 sec at 6.23 a.m. at West Hartlepool, Cleveland and the next instance will clip the coast at St Just, Cornwall at 10.10 a.m. on Wednesday 11 Aug 1999. On 30 June 1954 a total eclipse was witnessed from Unst, Shetland Islands but the centre of the path of totality was to the north.

Longest duration
The maximum *possible* duration of an eclipse of the Sun is 7 min 31 sec. The longest actually *measured* was on 20 June 1955 (7 min 8 sec), seen from the Philippines. One of 7 min 29 sec should occur in mid-Atlantic on 16 July 2186, which will then be the longest for 1469 years. The longest possible in the British Isles is 5 min 30 sec. That of 15 June 885 lasted nearly 5 min, as will that of 20 July 2381 in the Borders area. Durations can be extended by observers being airborne as on 30 June 1973 when an eclipse was 'extended' to 72 min aboard *Concorde.* An annular eclipse may last for 12 min 24 sec. The longest totality of any lunar eclipse is 104 min. This has occurred many times.

Most and least frequent
The highest number of eclipses possible in a year is seven, as in 1935, when there were five solar and two lunar eclipses; or four solar and three lunar eclipses, as occurred in 1982. The lowest possible number in a year is two, both of which must be solar, as in 1944 and 1969.

COMETS

Earliest recorded
The earliest records of comets date from the 7th century BC. The speeds of the estimated 2,000,000 comets vary from 700 mph *1125 km/h* in outer space to 1,250,000 mph *2 000 000 km/h* when near the Sun. The successive appearances of Halley's Comet have been traced back to 467 BC. It was first depicted in the Nuremberg Chronicle of AD 684. The first prediction of its return by Edmund Halley (1656–1742) proved true on Christmas Day 1758, 16 years after his death. On 13–14 Mar 1986, the European satellite Giotto (launched 2 July 1985) penetrated to within 335 miles *540 km* of the nucleus of Halley's comet. It was established that this was 9.3 miles *15 km* in length and velvet black in colour.

Sir William Herschel who on 13 March 1781 discovered the planet Uranus using a telescope in his back garden. (Mary Evans).

Closest approach
On 1 July 1770, Lexell's Comet, travelling at a speed of 23.9 miles/sec *38,5 km/sec* (relative to the Sun), came within 745,000 miles *1 200 000 km* of the Earth. However, the Earth is believed to have passed through the tail of Halley's Comet, most recently on 19 May 1910.

Largest
The tail of the brightest of all comets, the Great Comet of 1843, trailed for 205,000,000 miles *330 million km.* The bow shock of Holmes Comet of 1892 once measured 1,500,000 miles *2 400 000 km* in diameter.

Shortest period
Of all the recorded periodic comets (these are members of the Solar System), the one which most frequently returns is Encke's Comet, first identified in 1786. Its period of 1206 days (3.3 years) is the shortest established. Not one of its 53 returns (including 1983) has been missed by astronomers. Now increasingly faint, it is expected to 'die' by February 1994. The most frequently observed comets are Schwassmann–Wachmann I, Kopff and Oterma which can be observed every year between Mars and Jupiter.

Longest period
At the other extreme is Delavan's Comet of 1914, whose path was not accurately determined. It is not expected to return for perhaps 24 million years.

PLANETS

Largest
The nine major planets (including the Earth) are bodies within the Solar System and which revolve round the Sun in definite orbits. The search for Planet X continues. Jupiter, with an equatorial diameter of 88,846 miles *142 984 km* and a polar diameter of 83,082 miles *133 708 km* is the largest of the nine major planets, with a mass 317.83 times, and a volume 1321.4 times that of the Earth. It also has the shortest period of rotation resulting in a Jovian day of only 9 hr 50 min 30.003 sec in the equatorial zone.

Smallest and coldest
The smallest and coldest planet is Pluto, with its partner Charon, announced on 22 June 1978 which have an estimated surface temperature of $-360°$ F $-220°$ C (100 deg F *53 deg C* above absolute zero). Their mean distance from the Sun is 3,674,488,000 miles *5 913 514 000 km* and their period of revolution is 248.54 years. The diameter is *c.* 3000 km *1860 miles* and the mass is about 1/470th of that of the Earth. Pluto was first recorded by Clyde William Tombaugh (b. 4 Feb 1906) at Lowell Observatory, Flagstaff, Arizona, USA, on 18 Feb 1930 from photographs taken on 23 and 29 Jan and announced on 13 Mar. Because of its orbital eccentricity Pluto moved closer to the Sun than Neptune between 23 Jan 1979 and 15 Mar 1999.

Fastest
Mercury, which orbits the Sun at an average distance of 35,983,100 miles *57 909 200 km,* has a period of revolution of 87.9686 days, so giving the highest average speed in orbit of 107,030 mph *172 248 km/h.*

Hottest
For Venus a surface temperature of 462° C *864° F* has been estimated from measurements made from the USSR *Venera* and US Pioneer Cytherean surface probes. Venus has a canyon 4 miles *6,4 km* deep and 250 miles *402 km* long 1000 miles *1609 km* south of Venusian equator.

Nearest
The fellow planet closest to the Earth is Venus, which is, at times, about 25,700,000 miles *41 360 000 km* inside the Earth's orbit, compared with Mars's closest approach of 34,600,000 miles *55 680 000 km* outside the Earth's orbit. Mars, known since 1965 to be cratered, has temperatures ranging from 85° F *29,4° C* to $-190°$ F $-123°$ C.

Surface features
By far the highest and most spectacular is Olympus Mons (formerly Nix Olympica) in the Tharsis region of Mars with a diameter of 500–600 km *310–370 miles* and a height of 26 ± 3 km *75,450–95,150 ft* above the surrounding plain.

Brightest and faintest
Viewed from the Earth, by far the brightest of the five planets visible to the naked eye is Venus,

with a maximum magnitude of −4.4. Uranus, the first to be discovered by telescope when it was sighted by Sir William Herschel from his garden at 19, New King St., Bath on 13 Mar 1781, is only marginally visible with a magnitude 5.5. The faintest is Pluto, with magnitude of 15.0.

Densest and least dense
Earth is the densest planet with an average figure of 5.515 times that of water, whilst Saturn has an average density only about one-eighth of this value or 0.687 times that of water.

Conjunctions
The most dramatic recorded conjunction (coming together) of the other seven principal members of the Solar System (Sun, Moon, Mercury, Venus, Mars, Jupiter and Saturn) occurred on 5 Feb 1962, when 16° covered all seven during an eclipse in the Pacific area. It is possible that the seven-fold conjunction of September 1186 spanned only 12°. The next notable conjunction will take place on 5 May 2000.

SATELLITES

Most
Of the nine major planets, all but Venus and Mercury have satellites. The planet with the most is probably Saturn with at least 17 satellites. The Earth and Pluto are the only planets with a single satellite. The distance from their parent planets varies from the 5827 miles *9377 km* of *Phobos* from the centre of Mars to the 14,700,000 miles *23 700 000 km* of Jupiter's outer satellite *Sinope* (Jupiter IX). The Solar System has a total of 54 established satellites.

Largest and smallest
The largest and heaviest satellite is *Ganymede* (Jupiter III), which is 2.017 times heavier than our own Moon and has a diameter of 5262 km *3270 miles*. The smallest satellite is *Leda* (Jupiter XIII) with a diameter of less than 15 km *9,3 miles*. The Uranian satellite 1986 U7 found by *Voyager 2* is estimated to have a diameter of 15 km *9.3 miles*.

CLOSE ENCOUNTERS OF THE SPACE KIND

Pioneer 10, beyond our own solar system and the most distant man-made object carries a plaque (*right*) to communicate with possible interstellar humanoids on any planet outside our own solar system. The plaque shows our solar system and where the spacecraft came from, and how our sun is related to pulsars whose rates are given in digital code (relative to the time of relaxation of the hydrogen atom). *See Table p. 69.*

(Artwork: Paul Doherty/Plaque: NASA).

Largest asteroids

In the belt which lies between Mars and Jupiter, there are some 45,000 (3357 numbered to Jan 1986) minor planets or asteroids which are, for the most part, too small to yield to diameter measurement. The largest and first discovered (by G. Piazzi at Palermo, Sicily on 1 Jan 1801) of these is *Ceres*, with a diameter of 588 miles *946 km*. The only one visible to the naked eye is asteroid 4 *Vesta* (diameter 318 miles *512 km*) discovered on 29 Mar 1807 by Dr Heinrich Wilhelm Olbers (1758–1840), a German amateur astronomer. The closest measured approach to the Earth by an asteroid was 485,000 miles *780 000 km* in the case of *Hermes* on 30 Oct 1937 (asteroid now lost). The most distant detected is 2060 *Chiron*, found between Saturn and Uranus on 18–19 Oct 1977, by Charles T. Kowal from the Hale Observatory, California, USA.

STARS

Largest and most massive

The variable star Eta Carinae which is 9100 light years distance in the Carina Nebula in our own Galaxy has a mass at least 200 times greater than our own Sun. The object R136a in the Tarantula Nebula, an appendage of the Large Magellanic Cloud, which was assessed to have a mass 2100 times greater than the Sun is now known to be a small compact cluster of at least eight bright stars, each with a mass up to 100 times that of the Sun. However, Betelgeux (top left star of Orion) has a diameter of 700 million km *400 million miles* or about 500 times greater than the Sun. In 1978 it was found to be surrounded not only by a dust 'shell' but also an outer tenuous gas halo up to 5.3×10^{11} miles $8,5 \times 10^{11}$ *km* in diameter, that is over 1100 times the diameter of the star. The light left Betelgeux in AD 1680.

Smallest and lightest

A mass of 0.014 that of the Sun is estimated for the very faint star RG 0058.8-2807 which was discovered by I. Neill Reid and Gerard Gilmore using the U.K. Schmidt telescope and was announced in April 1983. The white dwarf star L362-81 has an estimated diameter of 3500 miles *5600 km* or only 0.0040 that of the Sun.

Brightest

Sirius A (*Alpha Canis Majoris*), also known as the Dog Star, is apparently the brightest star of the 5776 stars of naked eye visibility in the heavens, with an apparent magnitude of −1.46. It is in the constellation *Canis Major* and is visible in the winter months of the northern hemisphere, being due south at midnight on the last day of the year. The Sirius system is 8.64 light-years distant and has a luminosity 26 times as much as that of the Sun. It has a diameter of 1,450,000 miles *2,33 million km* and a mass of 4.20×10^{27} tons $4,26 \times 10^{27}$ *tonnes*. The faint white dwarf companion Sirius B has a diameter of only 6000 miles *10 000 km* but is 350,000 times heavier than the Earth. Sirius will reach a maximum of −1.67 in *c.* AD 61,000.

Farthest

The Solar System, with its Sun's nine principal planets, 54 satellites, asteroids and comets was estimated in 1982 to be 28,000 light-years from the centre of the lens-shaped Milky Way galaxy (diameter 70,000 light-years) so that the most distant stars in our galaxy are estimated to be 63,000 light-years distant.

Nearest

Excepting the special case of our own Sun (*q.v.* above) the nearest star is the very faint *Proxima Centauri*, discovered in 1915, which is 4.22 light-years (24,800,000,000,000 miles *4,00 × 10¹³ km*) away. The nearest 'star' visible to the naked eye is the southern hemisphere binary *Alpha Centauri*, or *Rigel Kentaurus* (4.35 light-years distant), with an apparant magnitude of − 0.29. It was discovered by Nicolas L. da Lacaille (1713–62) in *c.* 1752. In AD 29,700 this binary will reach a minimum distance of 2.84 light years and will appear as the second brightest 'star' with an apparent mag. of −1.20.

Most and least luminous

If all the stars could be viewed at the same distance the most luminous would be the variable ETA Carinae (see Most Massive Star) which now has a total luminosity 6,500,000 times that of the Sun but at its peak brightness in 1843 was at least ten times more luminous than this. The visually brightest star is the hypergiant Cygnus OB2 No. 12 which is 5900 light years distance in our own Galaxy and which has an absolute visual magnitude of −9.9 and is therefore visually 810,000 times brighter than the Sun. This brightness may be matched by the supergiant IV b 59 in the nearby galaxy Messier 101 but this depends on the distance adopted for this galaxy (estimates vary between 15,600,000 and 19,700,000 light years). The variable η Carinae in *c.* 1840 was perhaps visually 4 million times more luminous than the Sun. The faintest star detected is the recently discovered RG 0058.8–2807 (see Lightest Star) which has a total luminosity only 0.00021 that of the Sun and an absolute visual magnitude of 20.2 so that the visual brightness is less than one millionth that of the Sun.

Brightest supernova

Supernovae, or temporary 'stars' which flare and then fade, occur perhaps five times in 1000 years in our galaxy. The brightest 'star' ever seen by historic man is believed to be the supernova SN 1006 in April 1006 near *Beta Lupi* which flared for 2 years and attained a magnitude of −9 to −10. It is now believed to be the radio source G.327.6 + 14.5 nearly 3000 light-years distant.

Constellations

The largest of the 89 constellations is *Hydra* (the Sea Serpent), which covers 1,302.844 deg² or 6.3 per cent of the hemisphere and contains at least 68 stars visible to the naked eye (to 5.5 mag.). The constellation *Centaurus* (Centaur), ranking ninth in area embraces however at least 94 such stars. The smallest constellation is *Crux Australis* (Southern Cross) with an area of 68.477 deg²

PROGRESSIVE RECORDS OF THE MOST DISTANT MEASURED HEAVENLY BODIES

The possible existence of galaxies external to our own Milky Way system was mooted in 1789 by Sir William Herschel (1738–1822). These extra-galactic nebulae were first termed 'island universes'. Sir John Herschel (1792–1871) opined as early as 1835 that some might be more than 250,000,000,000 million miles distant. The first direct measurement of any body outside our Solar System was in 1838. Distances in the table below are based on a Hubble *constant* of 60 km/s⁻¹ Mpc⁻¹ and assume that the edge of the observable Universe is at a distance of 16,300 million light years.

Estimated Distance in Light Years[1]	Object	Method	Astronomers	Observatory	Date
about 6 (now 11.08)	61 Cygni	Parallax	F. Bessel	Königsberg, Germany	1838
> 20 (now 26)	Vega	Parallax	F. G. W. Struve	Dorpat (now Tartu), Estonia	1840
c. 200	Limit	Parallax			by 1900
750,000 (now 2.15 m)[2]	Galaxy M31	Cepheid variable	E. P. Hubble (1889–1953)	Mt. Wilson, Cal., USA	1923
900,000 (now 2.15 m)[2]	Galaxy M31	Cepheid variable	E. P. Hubble	Mt. Wilson, Cal., USA	1924

Millions of Light Years	Recession Speed % of *c*	Object	Red shift[3]	Astronomers	Observatory	Date
c. 200	1.3	NGC 7619		M. L. Humason	Mt. Wilson, Cal., USA	early 1928
> 2100	13.3	Ursa Major No. 2		Humason & E. P. Hubble	Mt. Wilson, Cal., USA	by 1936[4]
5300	32.6	Cluster 1448	0.403		Palomar, Cal., USA	1956
5900	36.2	3C 295 in Boötes	0.461	R. Minkowski	Palomar, Cal., USA	June 1960
6700	41.0	QSO 3C 147	0.545	M. Schmidt & T. A. Matthews	Palomar, Cal., USA	Feb 1964[5]
13,100	80.1	QSO 3C 9	2.01	M. Schmidt	Palomar, Cal., USA	April 1965
c. 13,200	81.3	QSO 0106 × 01	2.11	E. M. Burbridge *et al.*	Palomar, Cal., USA	Dec 1965
13,300	81.4	QSO 1116 + 12	2.12	C. R. Lynds & A. N. Stockton	Steward, Ariz., USA	March 1966
				M. Schmidt	Palomar, Cal., USA	March 1966
13,400	82.4	QSO Pks 0237 − 23	2.22	H. C. Arp *et al.*	Palomar, Cal., USA	Dec 1966
13,600	83.7	QSO 4C 25.05	2.36	E. T. Olsen & M. Schmidt	Palomar, Cal., USA	Dec 1967[6]
14,300	87.5	QSO 4C 05.34	2.88	R. Lynds & D. Wills	Kitt Peak, Arizona, USA	March 1970
14,700	90.2	QSO OH 471	3.40	R. F. Carswell & P. A. Strittmatter	Steward, Ariz., USA	March 1973
14,800	90.7	QSO OQ 172	3.53	E. J. Wampler *et al.*	Lick, Cal., USA	May 1973
14,900	91.6	QSO Pks 2000 − 330	3.78	B. A. Peterson *et al.*	Siding Spring, NSW, Australia	April 1982

Note: *c* is the notation for the speed of light. (see p. 64). [1] *Term first utilised in March 1888.* [2] *Re-estimate by G. de Vaucouleurs in Dec 1983.* [3] *Discovered by Vesto Slipher (1875–1969) from Flagstaff, Arizona, USA 1920. Redshift, denoted by z, is the measure of the speed of recession indicated by the ratio resulting from the subtraction of the rest wavelength of an emission line from the observed wavelength divided by the rest wavelength.* [4] *In 1934 Hubble opined that the observable horizon would be 3000 m light-years.* [5] *In Dec 1963 Dr I. S. Shklovsky's (USSR) suggestion that QSO 3C2 was more distant was subsequently confirmed with a value of 0.612 c.* [6] *In Oct 1968 Dr Margaret Burbidge (GB) published a tentative redshift of 2.38 for QSO 5C 2.56.*

PROGRESSIVE ROCKET ALTITUDE RECORDS

Height in miles	Height in km	Rocket	Place	Launch	Date
0.71	1,14	A 3 in 7,62 cm rocket	near London, England	April	1750
1.24	2	Reinhold Tiling[1] (Germany) solid fuel rocket	Osnabruck, Germany	April	1931
3.1	5	GIRD-X liquid fuel (USSR)	USSR	25 Nov	1933
8.1	13	USSR 'Stratosphere' rocket	USSR		1935
52.46	84,42	A.4 rocket (Germany)[2]	Peenemünde, Germany	3 Oct	1942
c. 85	c. 136	A.4 rocket (Germany)[2]	Heidelager, Poland	early	1944
118	190	A.4 rocket (Germany)[2]	Heidelager, Poland	mid	1944
244	392,6	V-2/W.A.C. Corporal (2-stage) Bumper No. 5 (USA)	White Sands, NM, USA	24 Feb	1949
318	512	Geophysical rocket V-5-V (USSR)	Tyuratam, USSR		1950–52
682	1097	Jupiter C (USA)	Cape Canaveral, Florida, USA	20 Sept	1956
>800	>1300	ICBM test flight R-7 (USSR)	Tyuratam, USSR	Aug	1957
>2700	>4345	Farside No. 5 (4-stage) (USA)	Eniwetok Atoll	20 Oct	1957
70,700	113 770	Pioneer 1-B Lunar Probe (USA)	Cape Canaveral, Florida, USA	11 Oct	1958
215,300,000*	346 480 000	Luna 1 or Mechta (USSR)	Tyuratam, USSR	2 Jan	1959
242,000,000*	389 450 000	Mars 1 (USSR)	USSR	1 Nov	1962
3,372,000,000[3]	5 426 000 000	Pioneer 10 (USA) (see pages 67, 70)	Kennedy Space Center, Cape Canaveral, Florida, USA	2 Mar	1972

Apogee in solar orbit. [1] *There is some evidence that Tiling may shortly after have reached 9500 m (5.90 miles) with a solid fuel rocket at Wangerooge, East Friesian Islands, W. Germany.* [2] *The A4 was latterly referred to as the V2 rocket, a code for second revenge weapon (vergeltungswaffe) following upon the V1 'flying bomb'.* [3] *At 1.30 a.m. on 13 June 1983 Pioneer 10 crossed the orbit of Neptune at a distance of 2,845 million miles 4580 million km. In Oct 1986 it will cross Pluto's mean orbit so leaving the Solar System. It will be more distant than the furthest extension of Pluto's orbit in April 1989 and will continue at 49 000 km/h 30,450 mph towards the edge of the heliosphere (solar magetosphere) and the heliopause (zone of 'solar wind'). In AD 34 593 it will make its nearest approach to the 12th nearest star Ross 248, 10.3 light-years distant. Its peak speed has been 27 miles/sec 97,200 mph 156 400 km/h. The strength of the signal still receivable is now down to 10^{-18} of a watt. However before AD 1991 Voyager I, travelling faster, will surpass Pioneer 10 in remoteness from Earth.*

compared with the 41,252.96 deg^2 of the whole sky.

Stellar planets
The first direct evidence of a planet-like companion was announced in Jan 1985 by D. McCarthy Jr, F. J. Law and R. G. Probst (US). It is an object in orbit 1000 million km *600 million miles* from the very faint red dwarf star Van Biesbroeck 8 (VB8), 21 light-years distant in Ophiuchus.

Longest name
The longest name for any star is *Shurnarkabtishashutu*, the Arabic for 'under the southern horn of the bull'.

Black Holes
This term for a star that has undergone complete gravitational collapse was first used by Prof John Archibald Wheeler at an Institute for Space Studies meeting in New York City on 29 Dec 1967.

The first tentative identification of a Black Hole was announced in December 1972 in the binary-star X-ray source Cygnus X-1. The best candidate is now LMC X-3 of 10 solar masses and 180,000 light-years distant reported in Jan 1983. The critical size has been estimated to be as low as a diameter of 3.67 miles *5,90 km*. In early 1978 supermassive Black Holes were suggested with a mass of 100 million suns or 2×10^{35} tonnes. One at the centre of the Seyfert galaxy, NGC 4151 in Canes Venatici, was estimated by Michael Preston (GB) in Oct 1983 to be of between 50–100 million solar masses.

THE UNIVERSE

Outside the Milky Way galaxy, which is part of the so-called Local Group of galaxies moving at a speed of 1,400,000 mph *2 300 000 km/h* relative to the microwave background radiation in a direction offset 44° from the centre of the Virgo cluster, there exist 10,000 million other galaxies. The largest discrete object in the Universe is a bent filament of galaxies in the constellations Pisces and Cetus, announced by Jack O. Burns and David Batuski of the University of New Mexico, Albuquerque, in May 1984 measuring 730 million light years.

Farthest visible object
The remotest heavenly body visible with the *naked eye* is the Great Galaxy in *Andromeda* (Mag. 3.47), known as Messier 31. It was first noted by the German Simon Marius (1570–1624). This is a rotating nebula in spiral form, and its distance from the Earth is about 2,150,000 light-years, or *c* 12,600,000,000,000,000,000 miles *20,3 × 10^{18} km* and is moving towards us. It is just possible however that, under ideal seeing conditions, Messier 33, the Spiral in Triangulum (Mag. 5.79), can be glimpsed by the naked eye of keen-sighted people at a distance of 2,360,000 light years.

Quasars
An occultation of 3C-273, observed from Australia on 5 Aug 1962, enabled the existence of quasi-stellar radio sources ('quasars' or QSO's) to be announced by Maarten Schmidt (b. Netherlands 1929). The red shift proved to be z = 0.158. Quasars have immensely high luminosity for bodies so distant and of such small diameter. It was announced in May 1983 that the quasar S5 0014 + 81 had a visual luminosity 1.1×10^{15} times greater than that of the Sun. The first double quasar (0957 + 56) among 1500 known quasars, was announced in May 1980.

Pulsars
The earliest observation of a pulsating radio source or 'pulsar' CP 1919 (now PSR 1919 + 21) by Dr Jocelyn Bell Burnell was announced from the Mullard Radio Astronomy Observatory, Cambridgeshire, England, on 24 Feb 1968. It had been detected on 28 Nov 1967. The fastest spinning is pulsar 1937 + 214 which is in the region of the minor constellation Vulpecula (The Fox) 16,000 light years distant. It has a pulse period of 1.557806449 milli-sec and a spin-down rate of 1.0511×10^{-19} sec/sec. However, the most *accurate* stellar clock is the second fastest pulsar PSR 1953 + 29 which has a spin-down rate of only 1×10^{-20} sec/sec.

Remotest object
Both the interpretation of the very large redshifts exhibited by quasars and the estimation of equivalent distances remain controversial. The record redshift of z = 3.78 for quasar PKS 2000 − 330 (see Table) has been interpreted as indicating proximity to the 'observable horizon' at 16,300 million light years, which is 96,000,000,000,000,000,000,000 miles *1,54 × 10^{23} km*. It was announced in Aug 1985 that the most distant known galaxy, which is associated with the quasar PKS 1614 + 051 in Hercules, has a redshift of 3.218 (equal to a recession speed 89.4% of that of light). The 3 K background radiation or primordial hiss discovered in 1965 by Arno Penzias and Robert Wilson of Bell Laboratories appears to be moving at a velocity of 99.9998 per cent *c*.

Age of the Universe
For the age of the Universe a value of 15 ± 3 aeons or gigayears (an aeon or gigayear being 1000 million years) is obtained from cosmochronology and nucleochronology. Based on the presently accepted Friedman models of the Universe with zero cosmological constant then

The immediate aftermath of the explosion of *Challenger 51L* that caused the worst human disaster in space flight history. (SIPA PRESS).

the equivalent Hubble ratio is about 60 km/s/ Mpc which compares to the most likely experimental value of 80 km s^{-1} Mpc^{-1}. In 1973 an *ex nihilo* creation was postulated by Edward P. Tryon (US). Modified versions of the Inflationary Model, originally introduced by Alan Guth (US) in 1981, now rival the 'Big Bang' theory of creation.

ROCKETRY AND MISSILES

Earliest uses
War rockets, propelled by a charcoal-saltpetre-sulphur gun-powder, were described by Tseng Kung Liang of China in 1042. These early rockets became known in Europe by 1258. The pioneer of military rocketry in Britain was Col. Sir William Congreve, Bt., MP (1772–1828), Comptroller of the Royal Laboratory, Woolwich, Greater London and Inspector of Military Machines, whose 'six-pound *2,72 kg* rocket' was developed to a range of 2000 yd *1825m* by 1805 and first used by the Royal Navy against Boulogne, France on 8 Oct 1806.

The first launching of a liquid-fuelled rocket (patented 14 July 1914) was by Dr Robert Hutchings Goddard (1882–1945) of the United States, at Auburn, Massachusetts, USA, on 16 Mar 1926, when his rocket reached an altitude of 41 ft *12,5 m* and travelled a distance of 184 ft *56 m*. The USSR's earliest rocket was the semi-liquid fuelled GIRD-IX (Gruppa Izucheniya Reaktivnogo Dvizheniya) begun in 1931 and tested on 17 Aug 1933.

Longest ranges
On 16 Mar 1962, Nikita Khrushchyov, then Prime Minister of the USSR, claimed in Moscow that the USSR possessed a 'global rocket' with a range of 30 000 km (*about 19,000 miles*) i.e. more than the Earth's semi-circumference and therefore capable of hitting any target from either direction.

Most powerful *World*
It has been suggested that the USSR lunar booster which blew up at Tyuratam in the summer (3 July) of 1969 had a thrust of 10–14 million lb *4,5–6,35 million kg*. There is some evidence of the launch of a USSR 'G' class lunar booster, larger than the US Saturn V, on 11 May 1973.

The most powerful rocket that has been publicised is the Saturn V, used for the Project Apollo and Skylab programmes on which development began in January 1962, at the John F. Kennedy Space Center, Merritt Island, Florida, USA. The rocket is 363 ft 8 in *110,85 m* tall, with a payload of 74 783 kg *73.60 tons* in the case of *Skylab I*, and gulps 13.4 tons *13,6 tonnes* of propellant per sec for 2½ min (2010 tons *2042 tonnes*). Stage I (S-IC) is 138 ft *42,06 m* tall and is powered by five Rocketdyne F-1 engines, using liquid oxygen (LOX) and kerosene, each delivering 1,514,000 lb *686 680 kg* thrust. Stage II (S-II) is powered by five LOX and liquid hydrogen Rocketdyne J-2 engines with a total thrust of 1,141,453 lb *517 759 kg* while Stage III (designated S-IVB) is powered by a single 228,290 lb *103 550 kg* thrust J-2 engine. The whole assembly generates 175,600,000 hp and weighs up to 7,600,000 lb (3393 tons *3447 tonnes*) fully loaded in the case of *Apollo 17*. It,was first launched on 9 Nov 1967, from Cape Canaveral (then Kennedy), Florida.

Highest velocity
The first space vehicle to achieve the Third Cosmic velocity sufficient to break out of the Solar System was *Pioneeer 10* (see table p. 69). The Atlas SLV-3C launcher with a modified Centaur D second stage and a Thiokol Te-364-4 third stage left the Earth at an unprecedented 32,114 mph *51 682 km/h* on 2 Mar 1972. The highest recorded velocity of any space vehicle has been 240 000 km/h *149,125 mph* in the case of the US-German solar probe *Helios B* launched on 15 Jan 1976.

Ion rockets
Speeds of up to 100,000 mph *160 000 km/h* are envisaged for rockets powered by an ion discharge. An ion thruster has been maintained for 9715 hours (404 days 19 hrs) at the Lewis Research Center in Cleveland, Ohio, USA. Ion rockets were first used in flight by NASA's SERT I rocket launched on 20 July 1964.

SPACE FLIGHT
The physical laws controlling the flight of artificial satellites were first propounded by Sir Isaac Newton (1642–1727) in his *Philosophiae Naturalis Principia Mathematica* ('Mathematical Principles of Natural Philosophy'), begun in March 1686 and first published in the summer of 1687. The first artificial satellite was successfully put into orbit at an altitude of 142/588 miles *228,5/946 km* and a velocity of more than 17,750 mph *28 565 km/h* from Tyuratam, a site located 170 miles *275 km* east of the Aral Sea on the night of 4 Oct 1957. This spherical satellite *Sputnik* ('Fellow Traveller') *1*, officially designated 'Satellite 1957 Alpha 2', weighed 83,6 kg *184.3 lb*, with a diameter of 58 cm *22.8 in*, and its lifetime is believed to have been 92 days, ending on 4 Jan 1958. It was designed under the direction of former Gulag prisoner Dr Sergey Pavlovich Korolyov (1907–66).

Earliest successful manned satellite
The first successful manned space flight began at 9.07 a.m. (Moscow time), or 6.07 a.m. GMT, on 12 Apr 1961. Cosmonaut Flight Major (later Colonel) Yuriy Alekseyevich Gagarin (born 9 Mar 1934) completed a single orbit of the Earth in 89.34 min in the 4.65 ton *4,72 tonnes* space vehicle *Vostok* ('East') 1. The take-off was from Tyuratam in Kazakhstan, and the landing was 108 min later near the village of Smelovka, near Engels, in the Saratov region of the USSR. The maximum speed was 17,560 mph *28 260 km/h* and the maximum altitude 327 km *203.2 miles* in a flight of 40 868,6 km *25,394.5 miles*. Colonel Gagarin, invested a Hero of the Soviet Union and awarded the Order of Lenin and the Gold Star Medal, was killed in a jet plane crash near Moscow on 27 Mar 1968.

First woman in space
The first woman to orbit the Earth was Junior Lieutenant (now Lt-Col Eng) Valentina Vladimirovna Tereshkova (b. 6 Mar 1937), who was launched in *Vostok 6* from Tyuratam, USSR, at 9.30 a.m. GMT on 16 June 1963, and landed at 8.16 a.m. on 19 June, after a flight of 2 days 22 hr 42 min, during which she completed over 48 orbits (1,225,000 miles *1 971 000 km*) and passed momentarily within 3 miles *48 km* of *Vostok 5*.

In flight fatality
Col. Vladimir Mikhailovich Komarov (b. 16 Mar 1927) was launched in *Soyuz* ('Union') *1* at 00.35 a.m. GMT on 23 Apr 1967. The spacecraft was in orbit for about 25½ hr but he impacted on the final descent due to parachute failure and was the first man undisputedly known to have died during space flight. The greatest number to perish in any of the 116 attempted space flights to date is seven (five men and two women) aboard the ill-fated *Challenger* 51L on 28 Jan 1986 when an explosion occurred 73 sec after lift off, at a height of 14 326 m *47,000 ft*.

First 'walk' in space
Lt-Col (now Maj-Gen) Aleksey A. Leonov (b. 20 May 1934) from *Voskhod 2* was the first to engage in 'extra vehicular activity' on 18 Mar 1965. Capt Bruce McCandless II (b. 8 Jun 1937) USN, from the space shuttle *Challenger*, was the first to engage in untethered EVA, at an altitude of 164 miles *264 km* above Hawaii, on 7 Feb 1984. His MMU (Manned Maneuvering Unit) back-pack cost $15 million to develop.

Longest manned space flight
The longest time spent in space is 236 days 22 hr 50 min, by Dr Oleg Y. Atkov (b. 9 May 1949), Leonid D. Kizim (b. 5 Aug 1941) and Vladimir A. Solovyev (b. 11 Nov 1946) on board Soyuz T10. They were launched on 8 Feb 1984.

Astronaut *Oldest and youngest*
The oldest of the 127 people in space has been Karl G. Henize (US) aged 58 while on the 19th Space Shuttle mission aboard the *Challenger* on 29 Jul 1985. The youngest has been Major (later Col) Gherman Stepanovich Titov (b. 11 Sept 1935), who was aged 25 years 329 days when launched in *Vostok 2* on 6 Aug 1961.

Most journeys
Capt John Watts Young (b. 24 Sept 1930) (USN ret) completed his sixth space flight on 8 Dec 1983 when he relinquished command of *Columbia* STS 9/Spacelab after a space career of 34 days 19 hr 42 min 13 sec.

Duration record on the Moon
The crew of *Apollo 17* collected a record 253 lb *114,8 kg* of rock and soil during their 22 hr 5 min 'extra-vehicular activity'. They were Capt Eugene A. Cernan, USN (b. Chicago, 14 Mar 1934) and Dr Harrison H. (Jack) Schmitt (b. Santa Rosa, New Mexico, 3 July 1935) who became the 12th man on the moon. The crew were on the lunar surface for 74 hr 59 min during this longest of lunar missions which took 12 days 13 hr 51 min on 7–19 Dec 1972.

First extra-terrestrial vehicle
The first wheeled vehicle landed on the Moon was *Lunakhod I* which began its Earth-controlled travels on 17 Nov 1970. It moved a total of 10,54 km *6.54 miles* on gradients up to 30° in the Mare Imbrium and did not become non-functioning until 4 Oct 1971. The lunar speed and distance record was set by the *Apollo 16* Rover with 11.2 mph *18km/h* downhill and 22.4 miles *33,8 km*.

Closest approach to the Sun by a rocket
The research spacecraft *Helios B* approached within 27 million miles *43,4 million km* of the Sun, carrying both US and West German instrumentation on 16 Apr 1976.

Largest space object
The heaviest object orbited is the Saturn V third stage with *Apollo 15* (space craft) which, prior to trans-lunar injection in parking orbit weighed 140 512 kg *138.29 tons*. The 442 lb *200 kg* US RAE (radio astronomy explorer) B or *Explorer 49* launched on 10 June 1973 has, however, antennae 1500 ft 415 m from tip to tip.

Most expensive project
The total cost of the US manned space programme up to and including the lunar mission of *Apollo 17* has been estimated to be $25,541,400,000 (then £9,823,150,000). The first 15 years of the USSR space programme from 1958 to September 1973 has been estimated to have cost $45,000 million. The cost of the NASA Shuttle programme was $9.9 billion (*£4350 million*) to the launch of *Columbia* on 12 Apr 1981.

CHAPTER FIVE

THE
SCIENTIFIC
WORLD

Colleen McHegan of the Museum of Natural History in New York, USA compares her one carat diamond ring to 'The Brazilian Princess', the 21,327 carat topaz that is the world's largest cut precious stone. (AP: Martin Lederhandler).

All known matter in, on and beyond the Earth is made up of chemical elements. It is estimated that there are 10^{87} electrons in the known universe. The total of naturally-occurring elements so far detected is 94, comprising, at ordinary temperatures, two liquids, 11 gases and 81 solids. The so-called 'fourth state' of matter is plasma, when negatively charged electrons and positively-charged ions are in flux.

1. ELEMENTS

Lightest and heaviest sub-nuclear particles

By April 1984 the existence of 30 'stable' particles, 53 meson resonance multiplets and 48 baryon resonance multiplets was accepted, representing the eventual discovery of 242 particles

and an equal number of anti-particles. The heaviest 'stable' particle fully accepted is the neutral weak gauge boson, the Z°, of mass 92.9 ± 1.6 GeV which was first detected in May 1983 by the UA1 Collaboration, CERN, Geneva, Switzerland using the 540 GeV Super Proton Synchrotron proton-antiproton beam collider. The heaviest hadron is the upsilon (45) meson resonance of mass 10577 ± 1 MeV and lifetime 3×10^{-23} sec, which consists of a bottom or beauty quark and its anti-quark, and which was first identified in April 1980 by two groups using the Cornell electron storage ring facilities at Cornell University, Ithaca, New York, USA. Sub-atomic concepts require that the masses of the graviton, photon, and neutrino should all be zero. Based on the sensitivities of various cosmological theories, upper limits for the masses of these particles are $7,6 \times 10^{-67}$ g for the graviton; $3,0 \times 10^{-53}$ g for the photon and $1,4 \times 10^{-32}$ g for the neutrino (cf. $9,10953 \times 10^{-28}$ g for the mass of an electron.)

Newest particles

It was announced in July 1984 that the UA1 Collaboration, CERN, Geneva, Switzerland had obtained tentative evidence for the existence of the sixth flavour of quark, the top or truth quark, of mass about 40 GeV. In October 1984 two groups using the Cornell University electron storage ring facilities identified two higher mass states of a combination of a bottom or beauty quark and its anti-quark, known as the upsilon (5S) and (6S) meson resonances of mass 10.86 GeV and 11.02 GeV and lifetimes 6×10^{-24} sec and 9×10^{-24} sec respectively.

The discovery in July 1984 by the Crystal Ball Collaboration, Hamburg, West Germany, of a particle of mass 8.32 GeV known as the 'zeta', and which was associated with the existence of the important theoretical particle known as the Higgs boson, has not been confirmed.

Most and least stable

Experiments in 1982 to 1984 have confirmed that the proton definitely has a lifetime in excess of 1×10^{30} years compared to theoretical predictions based on the 'grand unified theory' which suggests that the lifetime may be less than 1×10^{34} years. The least stable or shortest lived particles are the two baryon resonances N(2220) and N(2600), both 1.6×10^{-24} sec.

Substance smelliest

The most evil smelling substance, of the 17,000 smells so far classified, must be a matter of opinion but ethyl mercaptan (C_2H_5SH) and butyl seleno-mercaptan (C_4H_9SeH), are powerful claimants, each with a smell reminiscent of a combination of rotting cabbage, garlic, onions and sewer gas.

Most expensive perfume

The retail prices of the most expensive perfumes tend to be fixed at public relations rather than economic levels. The Chicago-based firm Jōvan marketed from March 1984 a cologne called Andron which contains a trace of the attractant pheromone androstenol which has a cost of $2750 (£2381) per oz or $97 (£84) per gramme.

Most potent poison

The rickettsial disease, Q-fever can be instituted by a *single* organism but is only fatal in 1 in 1000 cases. About 10 organisms of *Francisella tularenesis* (formerly *Pasteurella tularenesis*) can institute tularaemia variously called alkali disease, Francis disease or deerfly fever, and this is fatal in upwards of 10 cases in 1000.

Most powerful nerve gas

VX, 300 times more toxic than phosgene ($COCl_2$) used in World War I, was developed at the Chemical Defence Experimental Establishment, Porton Down, Wiltshire in 1952. Patents were applied for in 1962 and published in February 1974 showing it to be Ethyl S-2-diisopropylaminoethylmethylphosphonothiolate. The lethal dosage is 10 mg-minute/m^3 airborne or 0,3 mg orally.

THE 109 ELEMENTS

There are 94 naturally-occurring elements comprising, at ordinary temperatures, two liquids, 11 gases, 72 metals and nine other solids. To date the discovery of a further 15 transuranic elements (Elements 95 to 109) has been claimed of which 10 are undisputed.

Category	Name	Symbol	Discovery of Element	Record
Commonest (lithosphere)	Oxygen	O	1771 Scheele (Germany-Sweden)	46.60% by weight
Commonest (atmosphere)	Nitrogen	N	1772 Rutherford (GB)	78.09% by volume
Commonest (extra-terrestrial)	Hydrogen	H	1776 Cavendish (GB)	90% of all matter
Rarest (of the 94)	Astatine	At	1940 Corson (US) et al.	1/100th oz 0,35 g in Earth's crust
Lightest	Hydrogen	H	1776 Cavendish (GB)	0.005612 lb/ft³ 0,00008989 g/cm³
Lightest (Metal)	Lithium	Li	1817 Arfwedson (Sweden)	33.30 lb/ft³ 0.5334 g/cm³
Densest	Osmium	Os	1804 Tennant (GB)	1410 lb/ft³ 22,59 g/cm³
Heaviest (Gas)	Radon	Rn	1900 Dorn (Germany)	0.6274 lb/ft³ 0.01005 g/cm³ at 0° C
Newest[1]	Unniloctium	Uno	1984 G. Munzenberg et al. (W. Germany) and at Dubna Research Institute, Moscow, USSR	Element 108
Purest[2]	Helium	⁴He	1868 Lockyer (GB) & Janssen (France)	2 parts in 10¹⁵ (1978)
Hardest	Carbon	C	— prehistoric	Diamond allotrope, Knoop value 8400
Most Expensive	Californium	Cf	1950 Seaborg (US) et al.	Sold in 1970 for $10 per µg
Most Stable[3]	Tellurium	¹²⁸Te	1782 von Reichenstein (Austria)	Half-life of 1.5 × 10²⁴ years
Least Stable	Lithium (isotope 5)	Li 5	1817 Arfwedson (Sweden)	Lifetime of 4.4 × 10⁻²² sec.
Most Isotopes	Xenon	Xe	1898 Ramsay & Travers (GB)	36
	Caesium	Cs	1860 Bunsen & Kirchoff (Germ.)	36
Least Isotopes	Hydrogen	H	1776 Cavendish (GB)	3 (confirmed)
Most Ductile	Gold	Au	ante 3000 BC	1 oz drawn to 43 miles 1 g/2,4 km
Highest Tensile Strength	Boron	B	1808 Gay-Lussac & Thenard (France) & H. Davy (GB)	3.9 × 10⁶ lb f/in² 26,8 GPa
Lowest Melting/Boiling Point (non-metallic)[2,4]	Helium	⁴He	1868 Lockyer (GB) & Janssen (France)	−272,375° C under pressure (2532 kPa) and −268,928° C
Lowest Melting/Boiling Point (metallic)	Mercury	Hg	— protohistoric	−38.836° C/356.661° C
Highest Melting/Boiling Point (non-metallic)	Carbon (carbyne 6)	C	prehistoric[4]	3530° C/3870° C
Highest Melting/Boiling Point (metallic)[5]	Tungsten	W	1783 J. J. & F. d'Elhuyar (Spain)	3420° C and 5730° C
Largest Expansion (negative)	Plutonium	Pu	1940 Seaborg (US) et al.	−5.8 × 10⁻⁵ cm/cm/deg C between 450–480° C (Delta prime allotrope disc. 1953)
Lowest Expansion (positive)	Carbon (diamond)	C	— prehistoric	1.0 × 10⁻⁶ cm/cm/deg C (at 20° C)
Highest Expansion (metal)	Caesium	Cs	1860 Bunsen & Kirchoff (Germ.)	9.7 × 10⁻⁵ cm/cm/deg C (at 20° C)
Highest Expansion (solid)	Neon	Ne	1898 Ramsay & Travers (GB)	1.94 × 10⁻³ cm/cm/deg C at −248.59° C
Most Toxic	Radium	²²⁴Ra	1898 The Curies & Bemont (France)	Naturally occurring isotope 17,000 × more toxic than plutonium 239

[1] Provisional IUPAC name. A single atom of Une (Element 109) was created by bombardment of bismuth with iron ions at the GSI laboratory, Dormstadt, W. Germany on 29 Aug 1982. It had the highest atomic number (element 109) and the highest atomic mass (266).
[2] Identified on Earth by Ramsay (GB) in 1895.
[3] Double beta decay estimate. Alpha particle record is Samarium 148 at 8 × 10¹⁵ years and Beta particle record is Cadmium 113 at 9 × 10¹⁵ years.
[4] Monatomic hydrogen H is expected to be a non-liquifiable superfluid gas.
[5] The carbyne forms of carbon were discovered by A. E. Goresy and G. Donnay (USA) and A. M. Sladkov and Yu. P. Koudrayatsev (USSR) in 1968.

Most absorbent substance

The US Department of Agriculture Research Service announced on 18 Aug 1974 that 'H-span' or Super Slurper composed of one half starch derivative and one fourth each of acrylamide and acrylic acid can, when treated with iron, retain water 1300 times its own weight.

Finest powder

The ultimate in fine powder is solid helium which was first postulated to be a monatomic powder as early as 1964.

2. DRINK AND DRUGS

As from 1 Jan 1981 the strength of spirits has been expressed only in terms of percentage volume of alcohol at 20° C. Absolute or '100% vol' alcohol was formerly expressed to be 75.35 degrees over proof or 75.35° OP. In the USA proof is double the actual percentage of alcohol by volume at 60° F 15,6° C such that absolute alcohol is 200 per cent proof spirit. 'Hangovers' are said to be aggravated by the presence of such toxic congenerics as amyl alcohol ($C_5H_{11}OH$).

Most alcoholic

During independence (1918–40) the Estonian Liquor Monopoly marketed 98 per cent potato alcohol (196 proof US). In 31 US states *Everclear* 190 proof or 95% vol alcohol, is marketed by the American Distilling Co 'primarily as a base for home-made cordials'. Royal Navy rum, intro-duced in 1655, was 40° OP (79% vol) before 1948, but was reduced to 4.5° UP (under proof) or 46% vol, before its abolition on 31 July 1970. Full strength Pusser's naval rum was again sold by E. D. & F. Man from 1984.

Oldest wine

The oldest datable wine has been an amphora salvaged and drunk by Capt. Jacques Cousteau from the wreck of a Greek trader sunk in the Mediterranean c 230 BC. A wine jar recovered in Rome has been found to bear the label 'Q. Lutatio C. Mario Cos' meaning that it was produced in the consulship of Q. Lutatius and C. Marius i.e. in 102 BC. A bottle of 1748 Rudesheimer Rosewein was auctioned at Christie's, London for £260 on 6 Dec 1979.

Beer *Strongest world*

The strongest beer as measured by original gravity is the German EKU Kulminatur Urtyp hell 28 with 1131.7° and 13.52% alcohol by volume. The world's most alcoholic beer is Samichlaus Bier brewed by Brauerai Hürlimann of Zürich, Switzerland. It is 13.70 per cent alcohol by volume at 20° C with an original gravity of 1117.8°.

Beer *Strongest Great Britain*

The strongest regularly brewed beer in Britain is Thomas Hardy's brewed by Eldridge Pope & Co at their Dorchester Brewery, Dorset. It has an alcoholic content of 12.48 per cent by volume at 60° F and an original gravity of 1125.8°.

Beer *Weakest*

The weakest liquid ever marketed as beer was a sweet Ersatz beer which was brewed in Germany by Sunner, Colne-Kalk, in 1918. It had an original gravity of 1000.96° and a strength 1/30th that of the weakest beer now obtainable in the U.K.

Most expensive wine

The highest price paid for any bottle has been £105,000 for a 1787 Château Lafite claret sold to Christopher Forbes (USA) at Christie's, London on 5 Dec 1985. The price was affected insofar as the bottle was initialled by Thomas Jefferson (1743–1826), 3rd President of the United States.

Greatest wine auction and wine tasting

The largest single sale of wine was conducted by Christie's of King Street, St James's, London on 10–11 July 1974 at Quaglino's Ballroom, London when 2325 lots comprising 432,000 bottles realised £962,190. The largest ever reported wine-tasting was that staged by the Wine Institute at St Francis Hotel, San Francisco, California on 17 July 1980 with 125 pourers, 90 openers and a consumption of 3000 bottles.

Most expensive spirits

The most expensive bottle of spirits at auction is £780 for a magnum of *Grande Armée Fine Champagne Cognac, 1811* at Christie's Geneva on 13 Nov 1978. *Grande Fine Champagne Cognac, Biscuit du Boucher 1811* retails at 18,000 F (now £1667) a bottle at Fauchon. In Britain *Hennessy Private Reserve Grande Champagne* retails for £120 (including VAT) for a standard bottle.

Largest bottles

The largest bottle normally used in the wine and spirit trade is the Jeroboam (equal to 4 bottles of champagne or, rarely, of brandy and from 5 to 6½ bottles of claret according to whether blown or moulded) and the Double Magnum (equal, since c. 1934 to 4 bottles of claret or, more rarely, red Burgundy). A complete set of Champagne bottles would consist of a ¼ bottle, through the ½ bottle, bottle, magnum, Jeroboam, Rehoboam, Methuselah, Salmanazer and Balthazar, to the Nebuchadnezzar, which has a capacity of 16 litres 28.14 pt, and is equivalent to 20 bottles. In May 1958 a 5 ft 152 cm tall sherry bottle with a capacity of 20½ Imperial gal 93,19 litres was blown in Stoke-on-Trent, Staffordshire. This bottle, with the capacity of 131 normal bottles, was named an 'Adelaide'.

Smallest bottles

The smallest and meanest bottles of liquor now sold are White Horse bottles of Scotch whisky containing 1,3 millilitres or 22 minims at 33p a bottle or £2.16 per 'case' of 12.

Bottle collections

The largest reported collection of unduplicated miniature bottles is one of 26,794 by April 1986 owned by David L. Maund of Upham, Hampshire.

The largest reported collection of distilled spirits or liqueurs in any bar is 1722 unduplicated labels collected by Ian Boasman at Bistro French, Avenham Street, Preston, Lancashire audited in May 1986.

The world's greatest collection of whisky bottles is one of 3100 unduplicated labels assembled by Sig Edward Giaccone at his Whiskyteca, Salo, Lake Garda, Italy.

Champagne cork flight

The longest distance for a champagne cork to fly from an untreated and unheated bottle 4 ft 1,22 m from level ground is 105 ft 9 in 32,23 m by Peter Kirby at Idlewild Park, Reno, Nevada, USA on 4 July 1981.

Most powerful drugs

The most powerful commonly available drug is d-Lysergic Acid Diethylamide tartrate (LSD-25, $C_{20}H_{25}N_3O$) first produced in 1938 for common cold research and as a hallucinogen by Dr Albert Hoffman (Swiss) on 16–19 Apr 1943. The most potent analgesic drug is the morphine-like R33799 confirmed in 1978 to have almost 12,000 times the potency of morphine. Interferon was reported available for $10 US per millionth of a microgramme.

Most lethal man-made chemical

TCDD (2,3,7,8-tetrachlorodibenzo-p-dioxin), discovered in 1872, is admitted to be 150,000 times more deadly than cyanide at 3.1×10^{-9} moles/kg.

Most prescribed drug

The top-selling prescription drug in the world is the anti-ulcer drug Tagamet marketed by Smithkline-Beckman of Philadelphia, USA. The sales in 1981 were estimated at $800 million. The most prescribed drug in the United Kingdom is the tranquilliser Valium with over 1 million users.

3. PHOTOGRAPHY

CAMERAS

Earliest

The earliest veiled reference to a photograph on glass taken in a camera was in a letter from Joseph Nicéphore Niépce (1765–1833), a French scientist dated 19 July 1822. It was a photograph of a copper engraving of Pope Pius VII taken at Gras, near Chalon-sur-Saône and it was rediscovered in London in Feb 1952 by the photo-historian Helmut Gernsheim after six years research. The earliest photograph taken in England was one of a diamond-paned window in Laycock (or Lacock) Abbey, Wiltshire, taken in August 1835 by William Henry Fox Talbot, MP (1800–77), the inventor of the negative-positive process. The negative of this was donated to the Science Museum, London in 1937 by his granddaughter Matilda. The world's earliest aerial photograph was taken in 1858 by Gaspard Félix Tournachon (1820–1910), alias Nadar, from a balloon near Villacoublay, on the outskirts of Paris, France.

Largest

The largest and most expensive industrial camera ever built is the 27 ton/tonne Rolls Royce camera now owned by BPCC Graphics Ltd of Derby, England commissioned in 1956. It measures 8 ft 10 in 2,69 m high, 8 ft 3 in 2,51 m wide and 46 ft 14,02 m in length. The lens is a 63 in 160 cm f 16 Cooke Apochromatic. In 1986 it was still in full use.

Smallest

Apart from cameras built for intra-cardiac surgery and espionage, the smallest camera that has been marketed is the circular Japanese 'Petal' camera with a diameter of 1.14 in 2,9 cm and a thickness of 0.65 in 1,65 cm. It has a focal length of 12 mm 0.47 in. The BBC TV programme Record Breakers showed prints from this camera on 3 Dec 1974.

Fastest

A camera for fusion research built by the Rutherford-Appleton Laboratory at Essex University, Colchester, England and designed by Dr Tom Hall can register images at a rate of 3000 million per sec.

Most expensive camera

The most expensive complete range of camera equipment in the world is that of Nikon of Tokyo, Japan, who marketed in April 1985 their complete range of 25 cameras with 128 lenses and 523 accessories. Fox Talbot of London quoted £123,573 excluding VAT. The highest auction price for an antique camera is £21,000 for a J. B. Dancer stereo camera, patented in 1856 and sold at Christie's, South Kensington on 12 Oct 1977.

Longest Negative

On 22 June 1985 Robert J. Paluzzi using a 16 in 40,6 cm Century Cirkut camera captured a 200 degree view of Las Vegas in a single shot. The resulting negative measured 9 ft 274 cm by 16 in 40,6 cm.

4. TELESCOPES

Earliest

Although there is evidence that early Arabian scientists understood something of the magnifying power of lenses, their first use to form a telescope has been attributed to Roger Bacon (c. 1214–92) in England. The prototype of modern refracting telescopes was that completed by Johannes Lippershey for the Netherlands government on 2 Oct 1608.

Largest Reflector World

The largest telescope in the world is the altazimuth mounted 6 m 236.2 in telescope sited on Mount Semirodriki, near Zelenchukskaya in the Caucasus Mountains, USSR, at an altitude of 6830 ft 2080 m. Work on the mirror, weighing 70 tons/tonnes was not completed until the summer of 1974. Regular observations were begun on 7 Feb 1976 after 16 years work. The weight of the 42 m 138 ft high assembly is 840 tonnes 827 tons. Being the most powerful of all telescopes its range, which includes the location of objects down to the 25th magnitude, represents the limits of the observable Universe. Its light-gathering power would enable it to detect the light from a candle at a distance of 15,000 miles 24 000 km.

On 12 Sept 1985, work started on the W. M. Keck 10 metre 393.7 inch reflector for Caltech and the University of California on Mauna Kea, Hawaii. It is due to be completed by 1989 and will comprise 36 independently controlled fitting hexagonal mirrors.

Note: The attachment of an electronic charge-coupled device (CCD) increases the 'light-grasp' of a telescope by a factor up to 100 fold. Thus a 200 in 508 cm telescope achieves the light gathering capacity of a 1000 inch 25,4 m telescope.

A photograph of the contact print of the world's longest negative showing the Las Vegas skyline with photographer Bob Paluzzi.

Largest *Reflector Great Britain*

The largest British (and European) reflector is the Isaac Newton 100 in *254 cm* reflector formerly installed (1969–78) at the Royal Greenwich Observatory, Herstmonceux Castle, East Sussex. It was built in Newcastle upon Tyne, Tyne and Wear, weighs 92 tons *93,5 tonnes*, cost £641,000 and was inaugurated on 1 Dec 1967. It has been dismantled and re-erected on the 2423 m *7949 ft* high Roque de los Muchachos, La Palma, Canary Islands and became operational in February 1984. It is hoped that the William Herschel 4,2 m *167.3 in* reflector will also become operational at this new Northern Hemisphere Observatory in 1988.

Largest *Refractor*

The largest refracting (*i.e.* magnification by lenses) telescope in the world is the 62 ft *18,90 m* long 40 in *101,6 cm* telescope completed in 1897 at the Yerkes Observatory, Williams Bay, Wisconsin, and belonging to the University of Chicago, Illinois, USA. In 1900 a 125 cm *49.2 in* refractor 54,85 m *180 ft* in length was built for the Paris Exposition but its optical performance was too poor to justify attempts to use it. The largest in the British Isles is the 28 in *71,1 cm* at the Royal Greenwich Observatory (then in London) completed in 1894.

Radio *Largest steerable dish*

Radio waves of extra-terrestrial origin were first detected by Karl Jansky of Bell Telephone Laboratories, Holmdel, New Jersey, USA using a 100 ft *30,48 m* long shortwave rotatable antenna in 1932. The world's largest trainable dish-type radio telescope is the 100 m *328 ft* diameter, 3000 ton *3048 tonnes* assembly at the Max Planck Institute for Radio Astronomy of Bonn in the Effelsberger Valley, W. Germany; it became operative in May 1971. The cost of the installation begun in November 1967 was 36,920,000 DM (*then £6,150,000*).

Radio *Largest dish*

The world's largest dish radio telescope is the partially-steerable ionospheric assembly built over a natural bowl at Arecibo, Puerto Rico, completed in November 1963 at a cost of about $9,000,000 (*then £3.75 million*). The dish has a diameter of 1000 ft *304,8 m* and covers 18½ acres *7,48 ha*. Its sensitivity was raised by a factor of 1000 and its range to the edge of the observable Universe at some 15,000 million light-years by the fitting of new aluminium plates at a cost of $8.8 million. Rededication was on 16 Nov 1974. The RATAN-600 radio telescope completed in the Northern Caucasus, USSR in 1976 has 895 metal mirror panels mounted in a circle 576 m *1890 ft* across.

Radio *Largest World*

The world's largest radio telescopic installation is the US National Science Foundation VLA (Very Large Array). It is Y-shaped with each arm 13 miles *20,9 km* long with 27 mobile antennae (each of 25 m *82 ft* diameter) on rails. It is 50 miles *80 km* west of Socorro in the Plains of San Augustin, New Mexico, and was dedicated on 10 Oct 1980 at a cost of $78 million (*now £41 million*).

A computer-linked very long base-line array of 25 m *82 ft* radio telescopes stretched over 4200 km *2600 miles* on Latitude 49.3° N has been planned by the Canadian Astronomical Society.

Radio *Largest Great Britain*

The British Science Research Council 5 km radio telescope at Lord's Bridge, Cambridgeshire operated by the Mullard Radio Astronomy Observatory of Cambridge University utilises eight mobile 42 ft *12,80 m* rail-borne computer-controlled dish aerials, equivalent to a single steerable dish 5 km *3 miles 188 yd* in diameter. The project cost more than £2,100,000 and was completed in 1973.

Solar

The world's largest solar telescope is the 480 ft *146,30 m* long McMath telescope at Kitt Peak National Observatory near Tucson, Arizona, USA. It has a focal length of 300 ft *91,44 m* and an 80 in *2,03 m* heliostat mirror. It was completed in 1962 and produces an image measuring 33 in *83,8 cm* in diameter.

Observatory *Highest*

The highest altitude observatory in the world is the University of Denver's High Altitude Observatory at an altitude of 14,100 ft *4297 m*, opened in 1973. The principal instrument is a 24 in *60,48 cm* Ealing Beck reflecting telescope.

Observatory *Oldest*

The oldest astronomical observatory building extant in the world is 'Tower of the Winds' used by Andronichus of Cyrrhos in Athens, Greece *c.* 70 BC, and equipped with sundials and clepsydra.

Planetaria *World*

The ancestor of the planetarium is the rotatable Gottorp Globe, built by Andreas Busch in Denmark between 1654 and 1664 to the orders of Olearius, court mathematician to Duke Frederick III of Holstein. It is 34.6 ft *10,54 m* in circumference, weighs nearly 3½ tons/*tonnes* and is now preserved in Leningrad, USSR. The stars were painted on the inside. The earliest optical installation was not until 1923 in the Deutsches Museum, Munich, by Zeiss of Jena, Germany. The world's largest planetarium is in Moscow, USSR, and has a diameter of 82½ ft *25,15 m*.

Planetaria *Great Britain*

The United Kingdom's first planetarium was opened at Madame Tussaud's, Marylebone Road, London, on 19 Mar 1958. Accurate images of 8900 stars (some below naked eye magnitude) are able to be projected on the 70 ft *21,33 m* high copper dome.

Space Telescope

The first space observatory was the Orbiting Solar observatory 0504 launched on 18 Oct 1967. The largest will be the $1.2 billion NASA Space Telescope of 11 tonnes *10.8 tons* and 13,1 m *43 ft* in overall length with a 94.5 inch *240 cm* reflector originally scheduled to be placed in orbit at *c.* 480 km *300 miles* altitude aboard the US Space Shuttle *Atlantis* in August 1986.

5. NUMEROLOGY

In dealing with large numbers, scientists use the notation of 10 raised to various powers to eliminate a profusion of noughts. For example, 19,160,000,000,000 miles would be written 1.916×10^{13} miles. Similarly, a very small number, for example 0,0000154324 of a gram, would be written $1,54324 \times 10^{-5}$. Of the prefixes used before numbers the smallest is 'tredo' from the Danish tredyvo *for 30, indicating 10^{-30} of a unit, and the highest is 'dea' (Greek, deca, ten), symbol D, indicating ten groups of 3 zeros 10^{30} or a quintillion (UK) or a nonillion (US).*

Highest numbers

The highest lexicographically accepted named number in the system of successive powers of ten is the centillion, first recorded in 1852. It is the hundredth power of a million, or one followed by 600 noughts. The highest named number outside the decimal notation is the Buddhist *asankhyeya*, which is equal to 10^{140}.

The number 10^{100} is designated a Googol. The term was devised by Dr Edward Kasner (US) (d. 1955). Ten raised to the power of a Googol is described as a Googolplex. Some conception of the magnitude of such numbers can be gained when it is said that the number of electrons in some models of the observable Universe does not exceed 10^{87}.

The highest number ever used in a mathematical proof is a bounding value published in 1977 and known as Graham's number. It concerns bichromatic hypercubes and is inexpressible without the special 'arrow' notation, devised by Knuth in 1976, extended to 64 layers. Mr Candelaria ('the only man infinity fears') of Loma Linda, California has devised a Large Number Denomination System concluding with a milli-decilli-fiveillionillion.

Prime numbers

A prime number is any positive integer (excluding 1) having no integral factors other than itself and unity, *e.g.* 2, 3, 5, 7 or 11. The lowest prime number is thus 2. The highest known prime number is $2^{216,091} - 1$ discovered in Sept 1985 by analysts using a Cray X-MP/24 computer at Chevron Geosciences Co. in Houston, Texas, USA. It is the 30th known Marsenne prime, and contains 65,050 digits. The lowest non-prime or composite (excluding 1) number is 4.

Perfect numbers

A number is said to be perfect if it is equal to the sum of its divisors other than itself, *e.g.* $1 + 2 + 4 + 7 + 14 = 28$. The lowest perfect number is 6 (= 1 + 2 + 3). The highest known and the 30th so far discovered, is $(2^{216,091} - 1) \times 2^{216,090}$. It is a consequence of the highest known prime (see above).

Most innumerate

The most innumerate people are the Nambiquara of the north west Matto Grosso of Brazil who lack any system of numbers. They do however have a verb which means 'they are two alike'.

Most accurate and most inaccurate version of 'pi'

The greatest number of decimal places to which *pi* (π) has been calculated is 16,777,216 by Yasumasu Kanada and Y. Tamura (Japan), after 30 hours on the main frame computer in Tokyo University on 24 July 1985. The published value to two million places, in what has been described as the world's most boring 300 page book, was 3.141592653589793 . . . (omitting the next 1,999,975 places) . . . 1457297909. In 1897 the General Assembly of Indiana enacted in House Bill No. 246 that *pi* was *de jure* 4.

Earliest measures

The earliest known measure of weight is the *beqa* of the Amratian period of Egyptian civilisation *c.* 3800 BC found at Naqada, Egypt. The weights are cylindrical with rounded ends from 188,7 to 211,2 g *6.65–7.45 oz*. The unit of length used by the megalithic tomb-builders in Britain *c.* 3500 BC appears to have been 2.72 ± 0.003 ft *82,90 cm ± 0.09 cm*. This was deduced by Prof. Alexander Thom (b. 1894) in 1966.

Time measure *Longest*

The longest measure of time is the *kalpa* in Hindu chronology. It is equivalent to 4320 million years. In astronomy a cosmic year is the period of rotation of the sun around the centre

GEMS

of the Milky Way galaxy, *i.e.* 225 million years. In the Late Cretaceous Period of *c.* 85 million years ago the Earth rotated faster so resulting in 370.3 days per year while in Cambrian times some 600 million years ago there is evidence that the year contained 425 days.

Time measure *Shortest*

Owing to variations in the length of a day, which is estimated to be increasing irregularly at the average rate of about a milli-second per century due to the Moon's tidal drag, the second has been redefined. Instead of being 1/86,400th part of a mean solar day, it has, since 1960, been reckoned as 1/31,556,925,9747th part of the solar (or tropical) year at AD 1900, January 0. 12 hr, Ephemeris time. In 1958 the second of Ephemeris time was computed to be equivalent to 9,192,631,770 ± 20 cycles of the radiation corresponding to the transition of a caesium 133 atom when unperturbed by exterior fields. The greatest diurnal change recorded has been 10 milliseconds on 8 Aug 1972 due to the most violent solar storm recorded in 370 years of observations.

The accuracy of the caesium beam frequency standard approaches 8 parts in 10^{14} compared to 2 parts in 10^{13} for the methane-stabilised helium-neon laser and 6 parts in 10^{13} for the hydrogen maser.

6. GEMS AND OTHER PRECIOUS MATERIALS

PRECIOUS STONE RECORDS

Note: The carat was standardised at 205 mg in 1877. The metric carat of 200 mg was introduced in 1914.

DIAMOND *(first recorded in India c. 300 BC recognized as pure crystallised carbon in 1796)*
Largest 3106 metric carats (over 1¼ lb)—*The Cullinan*, found by Mr Gray on 25 Jan 1905 in the Premier Mine, Pretoria, South Africa.
The first synthetic diamonds were produced by Prof H. T. Hall at the General Electric Research Laboratories, USA on 16 Dec 1954. In Feb 1984 a Tass report from Leningrad, USSR announced that the Institute of High Frequency Currents had produced an artificial diamond weighing 4½ lb *2,04 kg*.
Largest Cut Stone 530.2 metric carats of 74 facets. Cleaved from *The Cullinan* in 1908, by Jak Asscher of Amsterdam and polished by Henri Koe known as *The Star of Africa* or Cullinan I and now in the Royal Sceptre. The Cullinan II is of 317.40 carats. Third on the list of the 55 diamonds of more than 100 ct is the Great Mogul of 280 old carats lost in the sack of Delhi in 1739 and arguably the most valuable object ever lost. In Nov 1984 the Zale Corporation of New York announced that it may be feasible to cut their pale yellow 890 ct uncut stone from Africa into a 550–600 ct cut stone.
Other Records Diamond is the *hardest* known naturally-occurring substance, with 5 times the indentation hardness of the next hardest mineral, corundum (Al_2O_3). The peak hardness value on the Knoop scale is 8400 compared with an average diamond of 7000. The rarest colour for diamond is blood red. The largest example is a flawless 5.05 ct stone found in Lichtenburg, S. Africa in 1927 and now in a private collection in the U.S. The diamond per carat record price of $113,000 was set by the 41.3 ct 'Polar Star' bought in Geneva for £2,100,000 on 21 Nov 1980 by Mr Razeen Salih.
The 42.92 ct Terestchenko blue diamond was auctioned at Christie's, Geneva on 14 Nov 1984 for $4,580,000. The largest blue diamond is the 45.85 ct Copenhagen Blue.
The Argyle field, Western Australia yielded 6.2 million carats in 1983 and 5.7 million in 1984 and is now the most prolific in the world.

EMERALD *(green beryl)* $[Be_3Al_2(SiO_3)_6]$
Largest Cut Stone 86,136 carat natural beryl Gleim emerald. Found in Carnaiba, Brazil, Aug 1974. Carved by Richard Chan (Hong Kong). Appraised at $1,292,000 (£718,000) in 1982.
Other Records $520,000 (then £305,000) paid for an 18.35 ct gem emerald ring sold at Sotheby Parke Bernet, New York, in Apr 1977.

SAPPHIRE *(corundum any colour but red)* (Al_2O_3)
Largest 2302 carat stone found at Anakie, Queensland, Australia, in *c.* 1935, now a 1318 carat head of President Abraham Lincoln (1809–65).

(*Left*) The world's smallest cut diamond at 0,00063 carats compared with a match head. (*Right*) The 'Liberty Bell' ruby—the world's largest. (Franklin Berger).

Largest Cut Stone 1444 carat black star stone carved from 2097 carats in 1953–5 into a bust of General Dwight David Eisenhower (1890–1969).
Note: both the sapphire busts are in the custody of the Kazanjian Foundation of Los Angeles, California, USA. Auction record for a single stone was set by a step-cut sapphire of 66.03 carats at £579,300 from the Rockefeller collection at Sotheby's Zurich on 8 May 1980.

RUBY *(red corundum)* (Al_2O_3)
Largest In July 1985 the jeweller James Kazanjian of Beverly Hills, California, displayed a 5½ inch *14 cm* tall 8500 carat ruby carved into the Liberty Bell.
Largest Cut Stone 1184 carat natural gem stone of Burmese origin. The largest star ruby is the 650 carat Vidyaraj ruby in Bangalore, India.
Other Records Since 1955 rubies have been the world's most precious gem attaining a record carat price of $100,639 (*then £46,600*) at Christie's sale in Geneva in November 1979 in the case of a 4.12 carat caspian-shaped ruby.

The ability to make corundum prisms for laser technology up to over 12 in *30 cm* in length seems to have little bearing on the market for natural gems.

OTHER PRECIOUS MATERIALS

PEARL
(Molluscan consecretion)
14 lb 1 oz *6,37 kg* 9½ in *24 cm* long by 5½ in *14 cm* in diameter—*Pearl of Laotze*
Found: At Palawan, Philippines, 7 May 1934 in shell of giant clam.
Present location: The property of Wilburn Dowell Cobb from 1936 until his death, it was valued at $4,080,000 in July 1971. On 15 May 1980 it was bought at auction in San Francisco by Peter Hoffman, a jeweller of Beverly Hills, California for $200,000 (*then £85,000*). An appraisal for the owners (Peter

Hoffman and Victor Barbish) in May 1982 by the San Francisco Gem Laboratory suggested a value of $32,640,000.

The largest black pearl 18,1 mm *0.7 in* in diameter was found in Namarai Bay, Fuji Island on 26 Jan 1984 by Yasuhiro Tokito.

OPAL
(SiO_2nH_2O)
220 troy oz (yellow-orange).
Found: Coober Pedy, South Australia.
Present location: The Olympic Australis (17,700 carats) found in Aug 1956 owned by Altmann & Cherny Pty Ltd is on public display in Melbourne and is valued at $1.8 million (US). An opal containing much 'potch' (colourless material) named the Desert Flame was found at Andamooka, South Australia. The 34,215 carat mass first reported in Sept 1969 was broken up and auctioned off on 29 Aug 1978.

ROCK CRYSTAL (QUARTZ)
SiO_2
Ball: 106¾ lb *40,48 kg* 12⅜ in *32,7 cm* diameter, the *Warner* sphere
Found: Burma, (originally a 1000 lb *450 kg* piece).
Present location: US National Museum, in Washington, DC.

TOPAZ
$Al_2SiO_4(F,OH)_2$
'Brazilian Princess' 21,327 carat 221 facets.
Found: Light blue: from Brazil.
Present location: American Museum of Natural History, New York City from 10 Dec 1985. Valued at $1,066,350 or $50 per carat. Cut from a 75 lb *334 kg* crystal. World's largest facetted stone.

AMBER
(Coniferous fossil resin)
33 lb 10 oz *15,25 kg*.
Found: Reputedly from Burma acquired in 1860.
Present location: Bought by John Charles Bowing (d. 1893) for £300 in Canton, China. Natural History Museum, London, since 1940.

The 733 carat Star of Queensland, the largest star sapphire ever cut. (Franklin Berger).

NEPHRITE JADE

$Ca_2(Mg, Fe)_5(Si_4O_{11})_2(OH)_2$
Boulder of 143 tons/*tonnes* and 21,300 ft³ *603 m³*
Found: In China. Reported 17 Sept 1978.
Present location: Jadeite $Na_2O.Al_2O_3 4SiO_2$ can be almost any colour excepting red or blue. The largest known example has been a block weighing 33 tons from Burma.

MARBLE

(*Metamorphosed* $CaCO_3$)
90 tons/*tonnes* (single slab)
Found: Quarried at Yule, Colorado, USA.
Present location: A piece of over 45 tons/*tonnes* was dressed from this slab for the coping stone of the Tomb of the Unknown Soldier in Arlington National Cemetery, Virginia, USA.

NUGGETS—GOLD (Au)

7560 oz (472¼ lb *214,32 kg*) (reef gold) *Holtermann Nugget*
Found: Beyers & Holtermann Star of Hope Gold Mining Co., Hill End, NSW, Australia, 19 Oct 1872.
Present location: The Holtermann nugget contained some 220 lb *99,8 kg* of gold in a 630 lb *285,7 kg* slab of slate. The purest large nugget was the *Welcome Stranger*, found at Moliagul, Victoria, Australia, which yielded 2248 troy oz *69,92 kg* of pure gold from 2280¼ oz *70,92 kg*.

SILVER (Ag)

2750 lb troy *Found:* Sonora, Mexico.
Present location: Appropriated by the Spanish Government before 1821.

OTHER GEM RECORDS:

Largest Crystal of Gem Quality
A 520,000 carat (2 cwt 5 lb *103,8 kg*) aquamarine, $[Be_3Al_2(SiO_3)_6]$ found near Marambaia, Brazil in 1910. Yielded over 200,000 carats of gem quality cut stones.

Rarest and commonest mineral
The world's rarest mineral cannot be certainly established. The total known amount of scotlandite ($PbSO_3$) comprises only a few tens of milligrams. Though probably found in the 19th century in Leadhills, Strathclyde, this first naturally occurring yellowish sulphite was only certainly identified in 1978 by Dr R. S. W. Braithwaite.

The world's commonest mineral is silicate of calcium, iron magnesium and manganese collectively known as olivine.

Densest Gem Mineral
Stibiotantalite $[(SbO)_2(Ta,Nb)_2O_6]$ a rare brownish-yellow mineral found in San Diego County, California, has a density of 7.46. The alloy platiniridium has a density of 22.0.

Smallest Brilliant Cut Diamond
A 57 facet diamond of 0.00063 carat (0.126 mg) *0,53 mm 0.02 in* by Gebroeders Van Den Wouwer of Antwerp, Belgium.

Largest Crystal
A 380 000 kg *187 tons* beryl ($Be_3Al_2Si_6O_{18}$) measuring 18 m *59 ft* long and 3,5 m *11½ ft* in diameter was recorded at Malakialina, Malagasy in 1976.

Newest Gemstones
Tanzanite was discovered in Tanzania in 1969. It reached $1200 (*then £670*) per carat in 1977. The deep purple Royal Lavalite found in Hotazel, South Africa by Randy Polk of Phoenix, Arizona reached $1300 (*then £840*) per carat in 1982.

7. PHYSICAL EXTREMES

Terrestrial

Temperature *Highest*

The highest man-made temperatures yet attained are those produced in the centre of a thermonuclear fusion bomb, which are of the order of 300,000,000 – 400,000,000° C. Of controllable temperatures, the highest effective laboratory figure reported is 82 million degrees C at the Princeton Plasma Physics Laboratory, USA in the fusion research PLT (Princeton Large Torus) in May 1980. A figure of 3000 million °C was reportedly achieved in the USSR with Ogra injection-mirror equipment in *c.* 1962.

Temperature *Lowest*

The lowest temperature reached is 3×10^{-8} Kelvin above absolute zero attained in a two stage nuclear demagnetisation cryostat at Espoo, Finland by the team led by Prof. Olli V. Loúnasmaa (b. 1930) and announced in June

1984. Absolute or thermodynamic temperatures are defined in terms of ratios rather than as differences reckoned from the unattainable absolute zero, which on the Kelvin scale is $-273,15°$ C or $-459.67°$ F. Thus the lowest temperature ever attained is 1 in 9.1×10^9 of the melting point of ice (0° C or 273.15 K or 32° F). Tokyo University's Institute of Solid State Physics announced on 15 Feb 1983 that a team led by Prof. Kazuo Ono had attained a temperature within 0.00003 of a degree of absolute zero at which molecular motion ceases.

Smallest Thermometer

Dr Frederich Sachs, a biophysicist at the State University of New York at Buffalo, has developed an ultra-microthermometer for measuring the temperature of single living cells. The tip is one micron in diameter, about one fiftieth the diameter of a human hair.

Highest pressures

The highest sustained laboratory pressures yet reported are of 1.72 megabars (11,000 tons force/in² *160 GPa*) achieved in the giant hydraulic diamond-faced press at the Carnegie Institution's Geophysical Laboratory, Washington DC reported in June 1978. This laboratory announced solid hydrogen achieved at 57 kilobars pressure on 2 Mar 1979. If created, metallic hydrogen is expected to be silvery white but soft with a density of 1.1 g/cm³. The pressure required for the transition is estimated by H. K. Mao and P. M. Bell to be 1 megabar at 25°C. Using dynamic methods and impact speeds of up to 18,000 mph *29 000 km/h*, momentary pressures of 75,000,000 atmospheres (490,000 tons/in² *7000 GPa*) were reported from the United States in 1958.

Highest velocity

The highest velocity at which any solid visible object has been projected is 150 km/sec *335,000 mph* in the case of a plastic disc at the Naval Research Laboratory, Washington DC, reported in August 1980.

Finest balance

The most accurate balance in the world is the Sartorius Model 4108 manufactured in Göttingen, W. Germany, which can weigh objects of up to 0,5 g to an accuracy of 0,01 μg or 0,00000001 g which is equivalent to little more than one sixtieth of the weight of the ink on this full stop.

Largest bubble chamber

The largest bubble chamber in the world is the $7 million (*then £2.5 million*) installation completed in October 1973 at Weston, Illinois. It is 15 ft *4,57 m* in diameter and contains 7259 gal *33 000 litres* of liquid hydrogen at a temperature of −247°C with a super conducting magnet of 3 tesla.

Fastest centrifuge

Ultra-centrifuges were invented by Theodor Svedberg (b. 30 Aug 1884) (Sweden) in 1923. The highest man-made rotary speed ever achieved and the fastest speed of any earthbound object is 4500 mph *7250 km/h* by a swirling tapered 6 in *15,2 cm* carbon fibre rod in a vacuum at Birmingham University, England reported on 24 Jan 1975.

Finest cut

The $13 million Large Optics Diamond Turning Machine at the Lawrence Livermore National Laboratory, California was reported in June 1983 to be able to sever a human hair 3000 times lengthwise.

Longest echo

The longest recorded echo in any building in

Great Britain is one of 15 sec following the closing of the door of the Chapel of the Mausoleum, Hamilton, Strathclyde built in 1840–55.

Most powerful electric current

The most powerful electric current generated is that from the Zeus capacitor at the Los Alamos Scientific Laboratory, New Mexico, USA. If fired simultaneously the 4032 capacitors would produce for a few microseconds twice as much current as that generated elsewhere on Earth.

Hottest flame

The hottest flame that can be produced is from carbon subnitride (C_4N_2) which at one atmosphere pressure is calculated to reach 5261 K.

Highest measured frequency

The highest *directly* measured frequency is a visible yellow-green light at 520.2068085 terahertz (a terahertz being a million million hertz or cycles per second) for the o-component of the 17–1 P(62) transition line of iodine 127. The highest measured frequency determined by precision metrology is a green light at 582.491703 terahertz for the b_{21} component of the R(15) 43–0 transition line of iodine 127. However with the decision on the 20 October 1983 by the Conférence Générale des Poids et Mesures (CGPM) to exactly define the metre (m) in terms of the velocity of light (c) such that 'the metre is the length of the path travelled by light in vacuum during a time interval of 1/299,792,458 of a second' then frequency (f) and wavelength (λ) are exactly interchangeable through the relationship $f\lambda = c$.

Lowest friction

The lowest coefficient of static and dynamic friction of any solid is 0.02, in the case of polytetrafluoroethylene ($[C_2F_4]_n$), called PTFE—equivalent to wet ice on wet ice. It was first manufactured in quantity by E. I. du Pont de Nemours & Co Inc in 1943, and is marketed from the USA as Teflon. In the United Kingdom it is marketed by ICI as Fluon. In the centrifuge at the University of Virginia a 30 lb *13,60 kg* rotor magnetically supported has been spun at 1000 rev/sec in a vacuum of 10^{-6} mm of mercury pressure. It loses only one revolution per second per day, thus spinning for years.

Smallest hole

A hole of 40 Å (4×10^{-6} mm) was shown visually using a JEM 100C electron microscope and Quantel Electronics devices at the Dept. of Metallurgy, Oxford on 28 Oct. 1979. To find such a hole is equivalent to finding a pinhead in a haystack with sides of 1.2 miles *1,93 km*. An electron microscope beam on a sample of sodium beta-alumina at the University of Illinois, USA, in May 1983 accidentally bored a hole 2×10^{-9} m in diameter.

Most powerful laser beams

The first illumination of another celestial body was achieved on 9 May 1962, when a beam of light was successfully reflected from the Moon by the use of a laser (light amplification by stimulated emission of radiation) attached to a 48 in *121,9 cm* telescope at Massachusetts Institute of Technology, Cambridge, Massachusetts, USA. The spot was estimated to be 4 miles *6,4 km* in diameter on the Moon. The device was propounded in 1958 by Dr Charles Hard Townes (born 1915) of the USA. Such a flash for 1/5000th of a second can bore a hole through a diamond by vaporisation at 10,000°C, produced by 2×10^{23} photons. The 'Shiva' laser was reported at the Lawrence Livermore Laboratory, California to be concentrating 2.6×10^{13} watts into a pinhead-sized target for 9.5×10^{-11} sec in a test on 18 May 1978.

Brightest light

The brightest steady artificial light sources are 'laser' beams with an intensity exceeding the Sun's 1,500,000 candles/in² *232 500 candelas/ cm²* by a factor of well in excess of 1000. In May 1969 the USSR Academy of Sciences announced blast waves travelling through a luminous plasma of inert gases heated to 90,000 K. The flare-up for up to 3 micro-seconds shone at 50,000 times the brightness of the Sun *viz.* 75,000 million candles/in² *11 625 million candelas/cm²*. Of continuously burning sources, the most powerful is a 313 kW high-pressure argon arc lamp of 1,200,000 candle-power, completed by Vortek Industries Ltd of Vancouver, BC, Canada in March 1984.

The synchrotron radiation from a 4 × 0.5 in *100 × 2,5 mm* slit in the SPEAR high energy physics plant at the end of the 2 mile *3,2 km* long Stanford Linear Accelerator, California, USA has been described as the world's most powerful light beam.

The most powerful searchlight ever developed was one produced during the 1939–45 war by the General Electric Company Ltd at the Hirst Research Centre in Wembley, Greater London. It had a consumption of 600 kW and gave an arc luminance of 300,000 candles/in² *46 500 candelas/cm²* and a maximum beam intensity of 2,700,000,000 candles from its parabolic mirror (diameter 10 ft *3,04 m*).

Shortest light pulse

Charles Z. Shank and colleagues of the AT & T Laboratories in New Jersey, USA achieved a light pulse of 8 femtoseconds (8 × 10⁻¹⁵ sec) announced in April 1985. The pulse comprised only 4 or 5 wavelengths of visible light or 2.4 micrometres long.

Most durable light

The average bulb lasts for 750–1000 hr. There is some evidence that a 5 watt carbide filament bulb made by the Shelby Electric Co and presented by Mr Bernell in the Fire Department, Livermore, south Alameda County, California was first shedding light in 1901.

Heaviest magnet

The heaviest magnet in the world is one measuring 60 m *196 ft* in diameter, with a weight of 36,000 tons/*tonnes* for the 10 GeV synchrophasotron in the Joint Institute for Nuclear Research at Dubna, near Moscow, USSR.

Magnetic fields *Strongest and weakest*

The strongest continuous magnetic field strength achieved has been one of 33,6 teslas at the Francis Bitter National Magnet Laboratory, Massachusetts Institute of Technology, Cambridge, Massachusetts, USA on 20 March 1986 employing a hybrid magnet with holmium pole pieces which enhanced the central field. The weakest magnetic field measured is one of 8 × 10⁻¹⁵ tesla in the heavily shielded room at the Francis Bitter National Magnet Laboratory. It is used for research by Dr David Cohen into the very weak magnetic field generated in the heart and brain.

Most powerful microscope

The world's most powerful microscope is the scanning tunnelling microscope invented at the IBM Zürich research laboratory in 1981. It has the magnifying ability of 100 million and is capable of resolving down to one hundredth the diameter of an atom (3 × 10⁻¹⁰). The lightest high power microscope in the world is the 1200 × McArthur Microscope made in Cambridge, England and weighing 9 oz *255 g*.

Dr. Albert Crewe (b. 1927 in U.K.) of the University of Chicago is projecting a scanning electron microscope by 1986 capable of seeing between atoms.

The Stanford Linear Accelerator in California—home of the world's most powerful light beam. (Science Photo Library).

Loudest noise

The loudest noise created in a laboratory is 210 decibels or 400,000 acoustic watts reported by NASA from a 48 ft *14,63 m* steel and concrete test bed with 60 ft *18,3 m* deep foundations at Huntsville, Alabama, USA in October 1965. Holes could be bored in solid material by this means. and the audible range has been put at 100 miles *161 km*.

Smallest microphone

Prof Ibrahim Kavrak of Bogazici University, Istanbul, Turkey, developed a microphone for a new technique of pressure measurement in fluid flow in 1967. It has a frequency response of 10 Hz to 10 KHz and measures 1,5 mm × 0,76 mm *0.06 in × 0.03 in*.

Highest note

The highest note yet attained is one of 60,000 megahertz (60 GHz) (60,000 million vibrations/ sec), generated by a 'laser' beam striking a sapphire crystal at the Massachusetts Institute of Technology in Cambridge, Massachusetts, USA, in September 1964.

Most powerful particle accelerator

The 2 kilometre *6562 ft* diameter proton synchrotron at the Fermi National Accelerator Laboratory east of Batavia, Illinois, USA is the highest energy 'atom-smasher' in the world. On 14 May 1976 an energy of 500 billion (5 × 10¹¹) electron volts was attained. On 13 Oct 1985 a centre of mass energy of 1.6 Tera electron volts (1.6 × 10¹² electron volts) was achieved by colliding together beams of protons and antiprotons. This involves 1000 super-conducting magnets maintained at a temperature of −452°F *−268,8°C* by means of the world's largest 4500 litre *990 gal* per hour helium liquefying plant which began operating on 18 Apr 1980.

The aim of CERN (*Conseil Européan pour la Recherche*) to collide beams of protons and antiprotons in their Super Proton Synchroton (SPS) near Geneva, Switzerland at 270 GeV × 2 = 540 GeV was achieved at 4.55 a.m. on 10 July 1981. This was the equivalent of striking a fixed target with protons at 150 TeV or 150 000 GeV.

The US Department of Energy set up a study for a $5 billion Super Superconductivity Collider (SSC) 1995 with two 20 TeV proton and antiproton colliding beams on 16 Aug 1983. If 8 tesla magnets were used the diameter would be 19,6 km *12.1 miles* but with 3 tesla magnets this would be 52,3 km *32.5 miles*.

Quietest place

The 'dead room', measuring 35 ft by 28 ft *10,67 × 8,50 m* in the Bell Telephone System laboratory at Murray Hill, New Jersey, USA, is the most anechoic room in the world, eliminating 99.98 per cent of reflected sound.

Sharpest objects and smallest tubes

The sharpest objects yet made are glass micropipette tubes used in intracellular work on living cells. Techniques developed and applied by Prof Kenneth T. Brown and Dale G. Flaming of the Department of Physiology, University of California, San Francisco achieved by 1977 bevelled tips with an outer diameter of 0.02 μm and 0.01 μm inner diameter. The latter is smaller than the smallest known nickel tubing by a factor of 340 and is 6500 times thinner than human hair.

Highest vacuum

The highest (or 'hardest') vacuums obtained in scientific research are of the order of 10⁻¹⁴ torr at the IBM Thomas J. Watson Research Center, Yorktown Heights, New York, USA in October 1976 in a cryogenic system with temperatures down to −269°C *−452°F*. This is equivalent to depopulating (baseball-sized) molecules from 1 metre apart to 80 km apart or from 1 yard to 50 miles.

Lowest viscosity

The California Institute of Technology, USA announced on 1 Dec 1957 that there was no measurable viscosity, *i.e.* perfect flow, in liquid helium II, which exists only at temperatures close to absolute zero (−273,15°C or −459.67°F).

Highest voltage

The highest potential difference ever obtained in a laboratory has been 32 ± 1.5 million volts by the National Electrostatics Corporation at Oak Ridge, Tennessee, USA on 17 May 1979.

CHAPTER SIX

THE
ARTS
& ENTERTAINMENT

Jean-Michel Jarre (born 24 Aug 1948), the French composer and musician who created an original score for his live performance in . . .

. . . Downtown Houston, Texas, USA, that incorporated lasers, fireworks, computers and sky lighting before a world record audience of 1.3 million people. *See page 91.*

Earliest *World*

Evidence of Palaeolithic art was first found in 1833 at Veyrier, 3 miles *5 km* south-west of Geneva, Switzerland when François Mayor (1779–1854) found two harpoon-like objects decorated with geometric figures. The oldest known dated examples come from La Ferrassie, near Les Eyzies in the Périgord, France, in layers dated to *c* 25,000 BC. Blocks of stone were found with engraved animals and female symbols; some of the blocks also had symbols painted in red ochre. Pieces of ochre with ground facets have been found at Lake Mungo, NSW, Australia, in a context *ante* 30,000 BC but there is no evidence whether these were used for body-painting or art.

Largest World *All time*

Panorama of the Mississippi, completed by John Banvard (1815–91) in 1846, showing the river for 1200 miles *1930 km* in a strip probably 5000 ft *1525 m* long and 12 ft *3,65 m* wide, was the largest painting in the world, with an area of more than 1.3 acres *0,52 ha*. The painting is believed to have been destroyed when the rolls of canvas, stored in a barn at Cold Spring Harbor, Long Island, New York State, USA, caught fire shortly before Banvard's death on 16 May 1891.

Existing

A larger painting, now only partially in existence, is *The Battle of Gettysburg*, completed in 1883, after 2½ years of work, by Paul Philippoteaux (France) and 16 assistants. The painting was 410 ft *125 m* long, 70 ft *21,3 m* high and weighed 5.36 tons *5,45 tonnes*. It depicts the climax of the Battle of Gettysburg, in southern Pennsylvania, USA, on 3 July 1863. In 1964 the painting was bought by Joe King of Winston-Salem, North Carolina, USA after being stored by E. W. McConnell in a Chicago warehouse since 1933. In 1964, owing to deterioration, the sky was trimmed down so decreasing the area. Jackson Bailey's *Life of Christ* exhibited by Religious Art Institute of America Inc. of Atlanta, Georgia comprises 50 panels 11 × 20 ft *3,35 × 6,09 m* and was completed in 1968–70 with an area of 11,000 ft² *1022 m²*.

Kimiko Hibino (b. 1942) completed a painting of over 800 species of the Animal Kingdom on a canvas 3 km *1.86 miles* and 2.2 m *7.2 ft* wide. On 27 Oct 1985, it was unveiled with the help of 3,000 volunteers along the bank of the Tamagawa River in Tokyo.

'Old Master'

The largest 'Old Master' is *Il Paradiso*, painted on canvas between 1587 and 1590 by Jacopo Robusti, *alias* Tintoretto (1518–94), and his son Domenico (1565–1637) on the east wall of the Sala del Maggior Consiglio in the Palazzo Ducale (Doge's Palace) in Venice, Italy. The work is 22 m *72 ft 2 in* long and 7 m *22 ft 11½ in* high and contains some 350 human figures.

Largest *Great Britain*

The largest painting in Great Britain is the giant oval *Triumph of Peace and Liberty* by Sir James Thornhill (1676–1734), on the ceiling of the Painted Hall in the Royal Naval College, Greenwich. It measures 106 ft *32,3 m* by 51 ft *15,4 m* and took 20 years (1707–1727) to complete.

Most valuable

The 'Mona Lisa' (*La Gioconda*) by Leonardo da Vinci (1452–1519) in the Louvre, Paris, was assessed for insurance purposes at the highest ever figure of $100,000,000 (*then £35.7 million*) for its move for exhibition in Washington, DC, and New York City, NY, USA, from 14 Dec 1962 to 12 Mar 1963. However, insurance was not concluded because the cost of the closest security precautions was less than that of the premiums. It was painted in *c.* 1503–7 and measures 77 × 53 cm *30.5 × 20.9 in.* It is believed to portray either Mona (short for Madonna) Lisa Gherardini, the wife of Francesco del Giocondo of Florence, or Constanza d'Avalos, coincidently nicknamed La Gioconda, mistress of Guiliano de Medici. Francis I, King of France, bought the painting for his bathroom in 1517 for 4000 gold florins or 92 oz *15,30 kg* of gold worth some £220,000 (mid-1984). Dr Pulitzer claims the Louvre have a painting of Constanza by Leonardo while his Swiss syndicate have the Mona Lisa proper in London first bought from Florence by William Blaker.

Largest poster
The largest recorded poster was one measuring 40,24 × 51,47 m   *132 × 168ft 10 in*   (2071 m² *22,292 ft²*) constructed by students of Osaka Gakun University, Osaka, Japan on 7 Oct 1984. The record price for a poster is £62,000 for an advertisement for the 1902 Vienna Exhibition by Koloman Moser (b. Vienna 30 Mar 1868—d. 18 Oct 1918) sold at Christie's, South Kensington, London on 1 April 1985.

HIGHEST PRICE

Auction price *World*
The highest price ever bid at a public auction for any painting is £7,500,000 for *The Adoration of the Magi* by Andrea Mantegna (1431–1506), sold for the Marquess of Northampton at Christie's, London on 18 April 1985 and bought by the J. Paul Getty Museum of Malibu, California. The auctioneer was Hon. Patrick Lindsay (1931–1986). With an 8 per cent buyer's premium, this amounts to £8,100,000. In Dec 1985 it was strongly suggested that the painting may have been by the artist's son Francesco.

By A Woman Artist
The highest price ever paid for a painting by a female artist is $1,100,000 (*then £705,000*), at Christie's, New York on 17 May 1983, for *Reading Le Figaro* by Mary Cassatt (b. Pennsylvania, USA, 1844–d. 1926). She worked mainly from Paris.

Abstract
The auction record for an abstract painting is £1,512,000 for *Composition with Red, Blue and Yellow* painted in 1930 by Piet Mondrian (1872–1944) at Christies, London on 27 June 1983. The purchaser was Shigeki Kameyama.

Miniature portrait
The highest price ever paid for a portrait miniature is the £75,000 given by an anonymous buyer at a sale held by Sotheby's, London on 24 Mar 1980 for a miniature of Jane Broughton, aged 21, painted on vellum by Nicholas Hilliard (1547–1619) in 1574. The painted surface measures 1.65 in *42 mm* in diameter.

Modern painting
The record bid at auction for an impressionist painting is $9,900,000 (£7.9 million) for *Landscape with Rising Sun* by Van Gogh (1853–1890) from the estate of the late Mrs Florence J. Gould (d. 1983) by an anonymous private collector at Sotheby Park Bernet, New York City on 25 Apr 1985. The hammer price was $9 million and the buyer's premium was 10 per cent of that.

Living artist *World*
The highest price at auction for a work by a living artist is £1,451,612 (*then $1,819,596*) for 'Two Women' (22 × 28 in *56 × 71 cm*) by Willem de Kooning (b. 24 April 1904) the Dutchborn American at Christie's, New York on 2 Nov 1984. The $1,950,000 paid for the two canvasses *Two Brothers* (1905) and *Seated Harlequin* (1922) by Pablo Diego José Francisco

de Paula Juan Nepomuceno Crispín Crispiano de la Santisima Trinidad Ruiz y Picasso (1881–1973) of Spain, bought by the Basle City Government from the Staechelin Foundation in Dec 1967 were even more expensive if inflation is allowed for.

British and Irish
The highest price for any painting by a living United Kingdom born artist is $350,000 (*then £167,000*) for the painting *Triptych* (in memory of George Dyer) by Francis Bacon (b. Dublin, Ireland, 1909, then part of the United Kingdom) sold on 18 May 1981 at Christie's, New York City, USA.

Print
The record price for a print at auction was £561,600 for a 1655 print of *Christ Presented to the People* by Rembrandt at Christie's, London on 5 Dec 1985 sold by Chatsworth Settlement Trustees.

Drawing
The highest price ever paid for any drawing is £3,546,000 for a study of an apostle's head and hand for the Transfiguration in the Vatican by Raphael (Raffaello Santi 1483–1520) and sold for the 11th Duke of Devonshire (b. 1920) at Christie's, London on 3 July 1984.

Most prolific painter
Picasso was the most prolific of all painters in a career which lasted 78 years. It has been estimated that Picasso produced about 13,500 paintings or designs, 100,000 prints or engravings, 34,000 book illustrations and 300 sculptures or ceramics. His life-time *oeuvre* has been valued at £500 million. Morris Katz (b. 1932) of Greenwich Village, New York City is the most prolific painter of saleable portraits in the world. His sales total as of 5 Mar 1986 was 153,629. Described as the 'King of Schlock Art', he sells his paintings 'cheap and often'. On the NBC 'Today' TV programme in Nov 1985 Katz demonstrated he could paint at a rate of 2.64 ft² *0,25 m²* per min.

Most repetitious painter
Antonio Bin of Paris has painted the *Mona Lisa* on some 300 occasions. These sell for up to £1000 apiece.

Oldest and youngest RA
The oldest ever Royal Academician has been

The flamingo pink plastic tutus surrounding three of the eleven islands in Florida—part of the world's largest 'Work of Art'. *See page 80.* (Randy Taylor: Sygma).

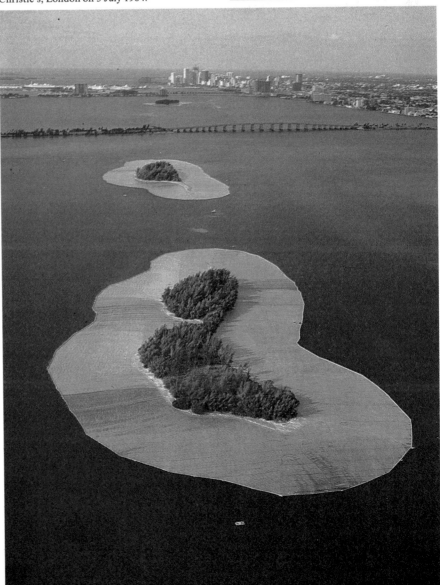

HIGHEST PRICE PAINTINGS   PROGRESSIVE RECORDS

Price	Equivalent 1986 Value	Painter, title, sold by and sold to	Date
£6500	£265,670	Antonio Correggio's *The Magdalen Reading* (in fact spurious) to Elector Friedrich Augustus II of Saxony.	1746
£8500	£319,050	Raphael's *The Sistine Madonna* (1513–14) from Piacenza to Elector Friedrich Augustus II of Saxony.	1759
£16,000	£362,000	Van Eycks' *Adoration of the Lamb*, 6 outer panels of Ghent altarpiece by Edward Solby to the Government of Prussia.	1821
£24,600*	£816,000	Murillo's *The Immaculate Conception* by estate of Marshal Soult to the Louvre (against Czar Nicholas I) in Paris.	1852
£70,000	£3,595,000	Raphael's *Ansidei Madonna* (1506) from Perugia by the 8th Duke of Marlborough to the National Gallery.	1885
£100,000	£5,208,000	Raphael's *The Colonna Altarpiece* (1503–05) from Perugia by Seldemeyer to J. Pierpont Morgan.	1901
£102,880	£4,090,000	Van Dyck's *Elena Grimaldi-Cattaneo* (portrait) by Knoedler to Peter Widener (1834–1915).	1906
£102,880	£3,068,000	Rembrandt's *The Mill* by 6th Marquess of Lansdowne to Peter Widener.	1911
£116,500	£3,877,000	Raphael's smaller *Panshanger Madonna* by Joseph (later Baron) Duveen (1869–1939) to Peter Widener.	1913
£310,400	£10,267,000	Leonardo da Vinci's *Benois Madonna* (c. 1477) to Czar Nicholas II in Paris.	1914
£821,429*	£6,660,000	Rembrandt's *Aristotle Contemplating the Bust of Homer* by estate of Mr and Mrs Alfred W. Erickson to New York Metropolitan Museum of Art.	1961
£1,785,714	£10,780,000	Leonardo da Vinci's *Ginevra de' Benci* (c. 1475) by Prince Franz Josef II of Liechtenstein to National Gallery of Art, Washington DC, USA.	1967
£2,310,000*	£11,628,000	Velázquez's *Portrait of Juan de Pareja* by the Earl of Radnor to the Wildenstein Gallery, New York.	1970
£2,729,000*	£4,185,000	Turner's *Juliet and Her Nurse* by Trustees of Whitney Museum, New York to undisclosed bidder at Sotheby Park Bernet, New York.	1980
£7,470,500*	£8,315,000	Turner's *Seascape: Folkestone* from estate of Lord Clark (1903–83) to Leggatt's of London for an unknown buyer.	1984
£8,100,000*	£8,505,000	Mantegna's *The Adoration of the Magi* by the Marquess of Northampton to the J. Paul Getty Museum, Malibu, California.	1985

* Indicates price at auction, otherwise prices were by private treaty.

(Thomas) Sidney Cooper cvo, who died on 8 Feb 1902 aged 98 yr 136 days, having exhibited 266 paintings over the record span of 69 consecutive years (1833–1902). The youngest ever RA has been Mary Moser (1744–1819) (later Mrs Hugh Lloyd), who was elected on the foundation of the Royal Academy in 1768 when aged 24.

Youngest exhibitor

The youngest ever exhibitor at the Royal Academy of Arts Annual Summer Exhibition has been Lewis Melville 'Gino' Lyons (b. 30 Apr 1962). His *Trees and Monkeys* was painted on 4 June 1965, submitted on 17 Mar 1967 and exhibited to the public on 29 Apr 1967.

Largest galleries

The world's largest art gallery is the Winter Palace and the neighbouring Hermitage in Leningrad, USSR. One has to walk 15 miles *24 km* to visit each of the 322 galleries, which house nearly 3,000,000 works of art and objects of archaeological interest. The world's largest modern art museum is the Georges Pompidou

National Centre for Art and Culture, Beauborg, opened in Paris in 1977 with 17 700 m² *183,000 ft²* of floor space. The most heavily endowed is the J. Paul Getty Museum, Malibu, California with an initial £700,000,000 in Jan 1974 and now £104 million p.a. for acquisitions. It has 38 galleries.

Finest brush

The finest standard brush sold is the 000 in Series 7 by Winsor and Newton known as a 'triple goose'. It is made of 150–200 Kolinsky sable hairs weighing 15 mg *0.000529 oz*.

MURALS

Earliest

The earliest known murals on man-made walls are the clay relief leopards at Çatal Hüyük in southern Anatolia, Turkey, discovered by James Malaart at level VII in 1961 and dating from *c.* 6200 BC.

Largest

The world's largest 'mural' was unveiled in 44

colours on the 30 storey Villa Regina condominium, Biscayne Bay, Miami, Florida on 14 Mar 1984 covering 300,000 ft² *27 870 m²*. The longest recorded continuous mural was one stretching 1509.8 ft *460,2 m* on the wall surrounding the Aotea Centre construction site in Auckland, NZ 'painted' by over 3000 members of the Auckland Star Jellybeans Club in 6 hours on 8 Sept 1985. It covered an area of 14,861 ft² *1380,6 m². Future entries for this category will be assessed on overall area only.*

Largest mosaic

The world's largest mosaic is on the walls of the central library of the Universidad Nacional Autónoma de Mexico, Mexico City. There are four walls, the two largest measuring 12,949 ft² *1203 m²* each representing the pre-Hispanic past. The largest Roman mosaic in Britain is the Woodchester Pavement, Gloucestershire of *c.* AD 325, excavated in 1793, now re-covered with protective earth. It measures 47 ft *14,3 m* square comprising 1½ million tesserae. A brilliant total reconstruction was carried out by Robert and John Woodward in 1973–1982.

'WORK OF ART'

Largest

The largest work of art ever perpetrated was the wrapping in 1983 of 11 islands in Biscayne Bay, Florida, USA in flamingo pink plastic tutus by Christo's 6,500,000 ft² *603 000 m²* work entitled 'Surrounded Islands'.

The intricate pattern of the Woodchester Pavement in Gloucestershire which comprises 1½ million tesserac. (J. B. Blossom).

2. SCULPTURE

Earliest *World*

A piece of ox rib found in 1973 at Pech de l'Aze, Dordogne, France in an early Middle Palaeolithic layer of the Riss glaciation *c.* 105,000 BC has several engraved lines on one side, thought to be possibly intentional. A churingo or curved ivory plaque rubbed with red ochre from the Middle Palaeolithic Mousterian site at Tata, Hungary has been dated to 100,000 BC by the thorium/uranium method. The earliest known example of sculpture is a 2½ in *6,3 cm* long figure of a horse carved from mammoth ivory dated to *c.* 28,000 BC and found in the Vogelherd cave in south-west Germany.

Great Britain

The earliest example of an engraving found in Britain is of a horse's head on a piece of rib-bone from Robin Hood Cave, Creswell Crag,

Derbyshire. It dates from the Upper Palaeolithic period (*c.* 15,000 to 10,000 BC). The earliest Scottish rock carving from Lagalochan, Strathclyde dates from *c.* 3000 BC.

Most expensive *World and Ancient*

The highest price for a sculpture is $3,900,000 (*then £2,400,000*) paid by private treaty in London in early 1977 by The J. Paul Getty Museum, Malibu, California for a 4th century BC bronze statue of a youth attributed to the school of Lysippus. It was found by fishermen on the seabed off Faro, Italy in 1963.

Living sculptor

The highest price paid for the work of a living sculptor is the $1,265,000 (*then £702,780*) given at Sotheby Parke Bernet, New York on 21 May 1982 for the 75 in *190,5 cm* long elmwood *Reclining figure* by Henry Moore, OM, CH, (b. Castleford, West Yorkshire, 30 July 1898).

Largest

The world's largest sculptures are the mounted figures of Jefferson Davis (1808–89), Gen Robert Edward Lee (1807–70) and Gen Thomas Jonathan ('Stonewall') Jackson (1824–63), covering 1.33 acres *0,5 ha* on the face of Stone Mountain, near Atlanta, Georgia. They are 90 ft *27,4 m* high. Roy Faulkner was on the mountain face for 8 years 174 days with a thermo-jet torch working with the sculptor Walker Kirtland Hancock and other helpers from 12 Sept 1963 to 3 Mar 1972. If completed the world's largest sculpture will be that of the Indian chief Tashunca-Uitco (*c.* 1849–77), known as Crazy Horse, of the Oglala tribe of the Dakota or Nadowessioux (Sioux) group. The sculpture was begun on 3 June 1948 near Mount Rushmore, South Dakota, USA. A projected 563 ft *171,6 m* high and 641 ft *195 m* long, it was the uncompleted life work of one man, Korczak Ziółkowski (1908–82). The horse's nostril is 50 ft *15,2 m* deep and 35 ft *10,7 m* in diameter. In 1984 another 200,000 tons of granite blasted off the mountain face brought the total to 7.8 million tons.

Ground figures

In the Nazca Desert, 300 km *185 miles* south of Lima, Peru there are straight lines (one more than 7 miles *11,2 km* long), geometric shapes and shapes of plants and animals drawn on the ground sometime between 100 BC and AD 600 for an uncertain but probably religious, astronomical, or even economic, purpose by a not precisely identified civilization. They were first detected from the air in *c.* 1928 and have also been described as the world's longest works of art.

Hill figures

In August 1968, a 330 ft *100 m* tall figure was found on a hill above Tarapacá, Chile.

The largest human hill carving in Britain is the 'Long Man' of Wilmington, East Sussex, 226 ft *68 m* in length. The oldest of all White Horses in Britain is the Uffington White Horse in Oxfordshire, dating from the late Iron Age (*c.* 150 BC) and measuring 374 ft *114 m* from nose to tail and 120 ft *36 m* high.

Most massive mobile

The most massive mobile is *White Cascade* weighing 8 tons/*tonnes* and measuring 100 ft *30,48 m* from top to bottom installed on 24–25 May 1976 at the Federal Reserve Bank of Philadelphia, Pennsylvania, USA. It was designed by Alexander Calder (1898–1976), whose first mobiles were exhibited in Paris in 1932 and whose *Big Crinkley* sold for a record £555,572 at Sotheby's, New York on 10 May 1984.

3. LANGUAGE AND LITERATURE

Earliest

The ability to speak is believed to be dependent upon physiological changes in the height of the larynx between *Homo erectus* and *Homo sapiens sapiens* as developed *c.* 45,000 BC. The earliest written language discovered has been on Yangshao culture pottery from Paa-t'o, near Xi'an (Sian) in the Shanxi (Shensi) province of China found in 1962. This bears proto-characters for the numbers 5, 7 and 8 and has been dated to 5000–4000 BC. The earliest dated pictographs are on clay tablets from Nippur, southern Iraq from a level equivalent to Uruk V/VI and dated in 1979 to *c.* 3400 BC. Tokens or tallies from Tepe Asiab and Ganji-I-Dareh Tepe in Iran have however been dated to 8500 BC. The earliest known piece of English writing (*c.* 630 AD) is a fragment of Irish uncial script in an ecclesiastical history sold for £75,000 by the Folger Shakespeare Library, Washington DC to the British Rail Pension Fund at Sotheby's, London on 25 June 1985.

Oldest

The written language with the longest continuous history is Chinese extending over more than 6000 years from the Yangshao culture (see above) to the present day.

Oldest words in English

It was first suggested in 1979 that languages ancestral to English and to Latvian (both Indo-European) split *c.* 3500 BC. Research shortly to be published will indicate that about 40 words of a pre-Indo-European substrate survive in English *e.g.* apple (apal), bad (bad), gold (gol) and tin (tin).

Commonest language

Today's world total of languages and dialects still spoken is about 5000 of which some 845 come from India. The language spoken by more people than any other is Northern Chinese, or Mandarin, by an estimated 68 per cent of the population, hence 695 million people in 1983. The so-called national language (*Guóyŭ*) is a standardised form of Northern Chinese (*Běifanghuà*) as spoken in the Peking area. This was alphabetised into *zhùyīn fùhào* of 37 letters in 1913 by Wa Chih-hui (1865–1953). On 11 Feb 1938 the *Hanyu-Pinyin-Fang'an* system, which is a phonetic pronunciation guide, was introduced. The next most commonly spoken language and the most widespread is English, by an estimated 400,000,000 in mid-1981. English is spoken by 10 per cent or more of the population in 45 sovereign countries.

In Great Britain and Ireland there are six indigenous tongues: English, Cornish, Scots Gaelic, Welsh, Irish Gaelic, and Romany (Gipsy). Of these English is, of course, predominant. Mr Edward (Ned) Maddrell (1877–1974) of Glen Chass, Port St Mary, Isle of Man, died as the last islander whose professed tongue was Manx. Cornish, of which there are now some 300 students, came within an ace of extinction. A dictionary was published in 1887, four years before the death of the then last fluent speaker John Davey. A novel by Melville and Kitty Bennetto 'An Gurun Wosek a Geltya' was published in Nov 1984. In the Channel Islands, apart from Jersey and Guernsey *normand*, there survive words of Sarkese or *Sèrtchais* in which the Parable of the Sower, as recited by some fishermen, was noted and published by Prince Louis Lucien Bonaparte (1813–91) in 1862.

Most complex

The following extremes of complexity have been noted: Chippewa, the North American Indian language of Minnesota, USA, has the most verb forms with up to 6000; Tillamook, the North American Indian language of Oregon, USA, has the most prefixes with 30; Tabassaran, a language in Daghestan, USSR, uses the most noun cases with 35, while Eskimaux use 63 forms of the present tense and simple nouns have as many as 252 inflections. In Chinese the 40 volume *Chung-wén Tà Tz'u-tién* dictionary lists 49,905 characters. *The Dictionary of Chinese Characters* (Sichuan and Huber) in 8 volumes will contain 20 million characters when completed in 1989. The fourth tone of 'i' has 84 meanings, varying as widely as 'dress', 'hiccough' and 'licentious'. The written language provides 92 different characters of 'i⁴'. The most complex written character in Chinese is that representing *xiè* consisting of 64 strokes meaning 'talkative'. The most complex in current use is *yù* with 32 strokes meaning to urge or implore.

Most and least irregular verbs

Esperanto was first published by its inventor Dr Ludwig Zamenhof (1859–1917) of Warsaw in 1887 without irregular verbs and is now estimated (by text book sales) to have a million speakers. The even earlier interlanguage Volapük, invented by Johann Martin Schleyer (1831–1912), also has absolutely regular configuration. The Turkish language has a single irregular verb—*olmak*, to be. According to *The Morphology and Syntax of Present-day English* by Prof. Olu Tomori, English has 283 irregular verbs of which 30 are merely formed with prefixes.

Rarest and commonest sounds

The rarest speech sound is probably the sound written ř in Czech which occurs in very few languages and is the last sound mastered by Czech children. In the southern Bushman language !xo there is a click articulated with both lips, which is written ʘ. The *l* sound in the Arabic word *Allah*, in some contexts, is pronounced uniquely in that language. The commonest sound is the vowel *a* (as in the English father); no language is known to be without it.

Literature, smallest

The *Great Soviet Encyclopaedia* states that only one word of Khazar survives—*oqurüm*, meaning 'I have read'.

Vocabulary

The English language contains about 490,000 words plus another 300,000 technical terms, the most in any language, but it is doubtful if any individual uses more than 60,000. Those in Great Britain who have undergone a full 16 years of education use perhaps 5000 words in speech and up to 10,000 words in written communications. The membership of the International Society for Philosophical Enquiry (no admission for IQ's below 148) have an average vocabulary of 36,250 words.

Greatest linguist

If the yardstick of ability to speak with fluency and reasonable accuracy is adhered to, it is doubtful whether any human could maintain fluency in more than 20–25 languages concurrently or achieve fluency in more than 40 in a lifetime.

The most multi-lingual living person in the world is Georges Henri Schmidt (b. Strasbourg, France, 28 Dec 1914), the Chief of the UN Terminology Section in 1965–71. The 1975 edition of *Who's Who in the United Nations*, listed 'only' 19 languages because he was then unable to find time to 'revive' his former fluency in 12 others. Powell Alexander Janulus (b. 1939) has worked with 41 languages in the Provincial Court of British Columbia, Vancouver, Canada. Britain's greatest linguist is George Campbell (b. 9 Aug 1912), who is retired from the BBC Overseas Service where he *worked* with 54 languages.

Historically the greatest linguists have been proclaimed as Cardinal Mezzofanti (1774–1849) (fluent in 26 or 27), Professor Rask (1787–1832), Sir John Bowring (1792–1872) and Dr Harold Williams of New Zealand (1876–1928), who were all fluent in 28 languages.

ALPHABET

Earliest
The earliest example of alphabetic writing has been found at Ugarit (now Ras Sharma), Syria dated to *c.* 1450 BC. It comprised a tablet of 32 cuneiform letters.

The oldest letter is 'O', unchanged in shape since its adoption in the Phoenician alphabet *c.* 1300 BC. The newest letters added to the English alphabet, are 'j' and 'v' which are of post-Shakespearean use *c.* 1630. Formerly they were used only as variants of 'i' and 'u'. There are 65 alphabets now in use.

Longest and shortest
The language with most letters is Cambodian with 72 (including useless ones) and Rotokas in central Bougainville Island has least with 11 (just a, b, e, g, i, k, o, p, ř, t and u).

Most and least consonants and vowels
The language with most distinct consonantal sounds is that of the Ubykhs in the Caucasus, with 80–85, and that with least is Rotokas, which has only 6 consonants. The language with the most vowels is Sedang, a central Vietnamese language with 55 distinguishable vowel sounds and that with the least is the Caucasian language Abkhazian with two. The record in written English for consecutive vowels is 6 in the musical term *euouae*. The Estonian word jäääärne, meaning the edge of the ice, has the same 4 consecutively. The name of a language in Pará State, Brazil consists solely of 7 vowels—uoiauai. The English word 'latchstring' has 6 consecutive letters which are consonants, but the Georgian word gvprtskvnis (he is feeling us) has 8 separately pronounced consonants.

Largest letters
The largest permanent letters in the world are the giant 600 ft *183 m* letters spelling READYMIX on the ground in the Nullarbor near East Balladonia, Western Australia. This was constructed in December 1971.

Smallest Letters
The 16 letters MOLECULAR DEVICES have been etched into a salt crystal by an electron beam so that the strokes were only 2 to 3 nm (10^{-9}) wide—the width of 20 hydrogen atoms. This was done by Michael Isaacson at Cornell University, Ithaca, NY, USA in February 1982.

WORDS

Longest words *World*
Lengthy concatenations and some compound or agglutinative words or nonce words are or have been written in the closed up style of a single word e.g. the 182 letter fricassee of 17 sweet and sour ingredients in Aristophanes' comedy *The Ecclesiazusae* in the 4th century BC. A compound 'word' of 195 sanskrit characters (which transliterates into 428 letters in the Roman alphabet) describing the region near Kanci, Tamil Nadu,

India appears in a 16th century work by Tirumalāmbā, Queen of Vijayanagara.

English
The longest word in the Oxford English Dictionary is floccipaucinihilipilification (alternatively spelt in hyphenated form with 'n' in seventh place), with 29 letters, meaning 'the action of estimating as worthless', first used in 1741, and later by Sir Walter Scott (1771–1832). Webster's Third International Dictionary lists among its 450,000 entries: pneumonoultramicroscopicsilicovolcanoconiosises (47 letters) the plural of a lung disease contracted by some miners.

The longest regularly formed English word is praetertranssubstantiationalistically (37 letters), used by Mark McShane in his 1963 novel *Untimely Ripped*. The medical term hepaticocholangiocholecystenterostomies (39 letters) refers to the surgical creations of new communications between gallbladders and hepatic ducts and between intestines and gallbladders. The longest words in common use are disproportionableness and incomprehensibilities (21 letters). Interdenominationalism (22 letters) is found in Webster's Dictionary and hence perhaps interdenominationalistically (28 letters) is permissible. Simon Proctor of Maidstone, Kent has compiled 15,592 lesser words (excluding plurals) from its 28 letters.

A plasmid of bacterial DNA whose systematic name contains over 200,000 letters—the world's longest scientific name. (Science Photo Library).

Longest palindromes
The longest known palindromic word is *saippuakivikauppias* (19 letters), the Finnish word for a dealer in lye (*i.e.* caustic soda). The longest in the English language is *redivider* (9 letters). The nine-letter word, *Malayalam*, is a proper noun given to the language of the Malayali people in Kerala, southern India while *Kanakanak* near Dillingham, Alaska is a 9 lettered palindromic place-name. The contrived chemical term *detartrated* has 11 letters. Some baptismal fonts in Greece and Turkey bear the circular 25 letter inscription NIΨON ANOMHMATA MH MONAN OΨIN meaning 'wash (my) sins not only (my) face'. This appears at St Mary's Church, Nottingham, St Paul's, Woldingham, Surrey and other

churches. The longest palindromic composition devised is one of 65,000 words completed by Edward Benbow of Bewdley, Hereford & Worcs. in January 1983. It begins 'Rae hits Eb, sire. Eb . . .' and hence predictably ends '. . . . Beer is best, I hear'

Longest scientific name
The systematic name for deoxyribonucleicacid of the human mitochondria, contains 16,569 nucleotide residues and is thus *c.* 207,000 letters long. It was published in key form in *Nature* on 9 Apr 1981.

Longest anagrams
The longest non-scientific English words which can form anagrams are the 18-letter transpositions 'conservationalists' and 'conversationalists'. The longest scientific transposals are cholecystoduodenostomy/duodenocholecystostomy and hydropneumopericardium/pneumohydropericardium each of 22 letters.

John S. Koch of Ontario, Canada has found a five letter word with 34 anagrams and a four letter word with 25—these are 'steam' and 'seat'.

Longest abbreviation
The longest known abbreviation is S.K.O.M.K.H.P.K.J.C.D.P.W.B., the initials of the Syarikat Kerjasama Orang-orang Melayu Kerajaan Hilir Perak Kerana Jimat Cermat Dan Pinjam-meminjam Wang Berhad. This is the Malay name for The Cooperative Company of the Lower State of Perak Government's Malay People for Money Savings and Loans Ltd., in Teluk Anson, Perak, West Malaysia (formerly Malaya). The abbreviation for this abbreviation is Skomk. The 55-letter full name of Los Angeles (El Pueblo de Nuestra Señora la Reina de los Angeles de Porciuncula) is abbreviated to LA or 3.63 per cent of its length.

Longest Acronym
The longest acronym is NIIOMTPLABOPARM-BETZHELBETRABSBOMONIMONKONOTDTEKHSTRO-MONT with 56 letters (54 in cyrillic) in the *Concise Dictionary of Soviet Terminology* meaning: The laboratory for shuttering, reinforcement, concrete and ferroconcrete operations for composite-monolithic and monolithic constructions of the Department of the Technology of Building—assembly operations of the Scientific Research Institute of the Organisation for building mechanisation and technical aid of the Academy of Building and Architecture of the USSR.

Commonest words and letters
In written English the most frequently used words are in order: the, of, and, to, a, in, that, is, I, it, for *and* as. The most used in conversation is I. The commonest letter is 'e' and the commonest initial letter is 'T'.

Most meanings
The most over-worked word in English is the word *set* which has 58 noun uses, 126 verbal uses and 10 as a participial adjective.

Most succinct word
The most challenging word for any lexicographer to define briefly is the Fuegian (southernmost Argentina and Chile) word 'mamihlapinatapai' meaning 'looking at each other hoping that either will offer to do something which both parties desire but are unwilling to do'.

Most synonyms
The condition of being inebriated has more synonyms than any other condition or object. Delacourt Press of New York City, USA has published a selection of 1224 from 2241 compiled by Paul Dickson of Garrett Park, Maryland, USA.

Most homophones

The most homophonous sounds in English are *air* and *sol* which, according to the researches of Dora Newhouse of Los Angeles, both have 38 homophones. The homonym with most variant spellings is *Air* with Aire, are, Ayer, Ayr, Ayre, err, e'er, ere, eyre and heir.

Most accents

Accents were introduced in French in the reign of Louis XIII (1601–43). The word with most accents is *hétérogénéité*, meaning heterogeneity. An atoll in the Pacific Ocean 320 miles *516 km* east-south-east of Tahiti is named Héréhérétué. An example of a Hungarian word with 6 accents is *újjáépítésére* meaning 'for its reconstruction'.

Shortest pangram (holoalphabetic sentence)

Pangrammists who endeavour to produce meaningful sentences of minimal length utilizing all the letters in the alphabet have now attained the ultimate of 26 letter brevity. Michael Jones of Chicago, Illinois, compiled in 1984 the sentence to describe the situation in which a wryneck woodpecker from the grasslands of Africa climbed up the side of a male bovid which is grazing on sacred Muslim-owned land. viz: 'Veldt jynx grimps waqf zho buck'.

PERSONAL NAMES

Earliest

The earliest personal name which has survived is seemingly that of a predynastic king of Upper Egypt *ante* 3050 BC, who is indicated by the hieroglyphic sign for a scorpion. It has been suggested that the name should be read as Sekhen. The earliest known name of any resident of Britain is Divitiacus, King of the Suessiones, the Gaulish ruler of the Kent area *c.* 100 BC under the name Prydhain. Scotland, unlike England, was never fully conquered by the Roman occupiers (AD 43–410). Calgācus (b. *c.* AD 40), who led the final resistance in Scotland was the earliest native whose name has been recorded.

Longest pedigree

The only non-Royal English pedigree that can with certainty show a clear pre-Conquest descent is that of the Arden family. Shakespeare's mother was a Mary Arden. It is claimed on behalf of the Clan Mackay that their clan can be traced to Loarn, the Irish invader of south west Pictland, now Argyll, *c.* AD 501.

Longest single name

The longest Christian or given name on record is one of 622 letters given by Mr Scott Roaul Sör-Lökken of Missoula, Montana, USA to his daughter Miss S. Ellen Georgianna Sör Lökken (b. 1979). The 'S' stands for a 598 letter name designed to throw a monkey wrench into the computers of federal bureaucracy. She is known as 'Snow Owl' for short or 'Oli' for shorter.

Longest personal name *World*

The longest name appearing on a birth certificate is that of Rhoshandiatellyneshiaunneveshenk Koyaanfsquatsiuty Williams born to Mr and Mrs James L. Williams in Beaumont, Texas, USA on 12 Sept 1984. On 5 Oct 1984 the father filed an amendment which expanded his daughter's first name to 1,019 letters and the middle name to 36 letters.

United Kingdom

The longest surname in the United Kingdom was the six-barrelled one borne by the late Major L.S.D.O.F. (Leone Sextus Denys Oswolf Fraudatifilius) Tollemache-Tollemache-de Orellana-Plantagenet-Tollemache-Tollemache, who was born on 12 June 1884 and died of pneumonia in

---

WORLD'S LONGEST WORDS

JAPANESE[1]
Chi-n-chi-ku-ri-n (12 letters)
—a very short person (slang)

SPANISH
Superextraordinarisimo (22 letters)
—extraordinary

FRENCH[2]
Anticonstitutionnellement (25 letters)
—anticonstitutionally.
Anthropoclimatologiquement[2] (26 letters)
—anthropoclimatologically

CROATIAN
Prijestolonasljednikovica (25 letters)
—wife of an heir apparent.

ITALIAN
Precipitevolissimevolmente (26 letters)
—as fast as possible.

PORTUGUESE
inconstitucionalissimamente (27 letters)
—with the highest degree of unconstitutionality.

ICELANDIC
Hæstaréttarmálaflutningsmaður (29 letters)
—supreme court barrister

RUSSIAN
ryentgyenoelyektrokardiografichyeskogo (33 Cyrillic letters, transliterating as 38)
—of the radioelectrocardiographic.

HUNGARIAN
Megszentségtelenithetetlenségeskedéseitekért (44 letters)
—for your unprofaneable actions.

TURKISH[5]
Cekoslovakyalılastıramadıklarımızdanmıymissiniz (47 letters)
—'are you not of that group of persons that we were said to be unable to Czechoslovakianise?'

DUTCH[5]
Kindercarnavalsoptochtvoorberei-dingswerkzaamheden (49 letters)
—preparation activities for a children's carnival procession

MOHAWK[3]
tkanuhstasrihsranuhwe'tsraaksahsrakaratattsrayeri' (50 letters)
—the praising of the evil of the liking of the finding of the house is right.

GERMAN[4][5]
Donaudampfschiffahrtselectrizitaetenhaupt betriebswerkbauunterbeamtengesellschaft (80 letters)
—The club for subordinate officials of the head office management of the Danube steamboat electrical services (Name of a pre-war club in Vienna).

SWEDISH[5]
Spårvagnsaktiebolags skensmutsskjutarefack förenings-personal beklädnadsmagasins förrådsförvaltaren (94 letters)
—Manager of the depot for the supply of uniforms to the personnel of the track cleaners' union of the tramway company.

[1] Patent applications sometimes harbour long compound 'words'. An extreme example is one of 13 kana which transliterates to the 40 letter Kyūkitsürohekimenfuchakunenryōsekisanryō meaning 'the accumulated amount of fuel condensed on the wall face of the air intake passage'.
[2] Not accepted by *savants* to be an acceptable French word.
[3] Lengthy concatenations are a feature of Mohawk. Above is an example.
[4] The longest dictionary word in every day usage is Kraftfahrzeu-greparaturwerkstätten (33 letters or 34 if the ä is written as ae) meaning motor vehicle repair shops (or service garages).
[5] Agglutinative words are only limited by imagination and are not found in standard dictionaries. The first 100 letter such word was published in 1975 by the late Eric Rosenthal in Afrikaans.

France on 20 Feb 1917. Of non-repetitious surnames, the last example of a five-barrelled one was that of the Lady Caroline Jemima Temple-Nugent-Chandos-Brydges-Grenville (1858–1946). The longest single English surname is Featherstonehaugh (17 letters), correctly pronounced on occasions (but improbably on the correct occasion) Featherstonehaw or Feston-haw or Fessonhay or Freestonhugh or Feerston-haw or Fanshaw.

Scotland

In Scotland the surname nin (feminine of mac) Achinmacdholicachinskerray (29 letters) was recorded in an 18th century parish register.

Most Christian names

The great-great-grandson of Carlos III of Spain, Don Alfonso de Borbón y Borbón (1866–1934) had 94 Christian names of which several were lengthened by hyphenation.

John and Margaret Nelson of Chesterfield, Derbyshire, gave their daughter Tracey Nelson (b. 31 Dec 1985) a total of 139 other Christian names.

Shortest

The commonest single-letter surname is O, prevalent in Korea, but with 52 examples in US phone books (1973–81) and 12 in Belgium. This name causes most distress to those concerned with the prevention of cruelty to computers. Every other letter, except Q, has been traced in US phone books (used as a surname) by A. Ross Eckler. There are two one-lettered Burmese names E (calm), pronounced aye and U (egg), pronounced Oo. U *before* the name means 'uncle'. There exist among the 47,000,000 names on the Dept. of Health & Social Security index 6 examples of a one-lettered surname. Their identity has not been disclosed, but they are 'A', 'B', 'J', 'N', 'O' and 'X'. Two-letter British surnames include By and On and have recently been joined by Oy, Za and others. The Christian name 'A' has been used for 5 generations in the Lincoln Taber family of Fingringhoe, Essex.

Commonest family name *World*

The commonest family name in the world is the Chinese name Chang which is borne, according to estimates, by between 9.7 and 12.1 per cent of the Chinese population, so indicating even on the lower estimate that there are at least some 104 million Changs—more than the entire population of all but 7 of the 170 other sovereign countries of the world.

English

The commonest surname in the English-speaking world is Smith. The most recent published count showed 659,050 nationally insured Smiths in Great Britain, of whom 10,102 were plain John Smith and another 19,502 were John (plus one or more given names) Smith. Including uninsured persons there were over 800,000 Smiths in England and Wales alone, of whom 81,493 were called A. Smith. There were an estimated 2,382,509 Smiths in the USA in 1973. It is no secret that by 1984 there were some 90,000 Singhs in Britain—the name means 'in secret'.

'Macs'

There are, however, estimated to be 1,600,000 persons in Britain with M', Mc or Mac (Gaelic genitive of 'son') as part of their surnames. The commonest of these is Macdonald which accounts for about 55,000 of the Scottish population.

Commonest first names

From the latest available data (to Sept 1984) birth registrations for England and Wales at the General Register Office at St Catherine's House,

Kingsway, London, the most favoured first forename choice of parents from the classless samples of over 9000 entries bearing the (easily) commonest surname of Smith are (with phonetic variations allowed): boys Matthew, closely followed by Christopher, then Daniel, Stephen and Michael. For girls Gemma (including Jemma) ahead of Claire, Sarah, Emma and Laura. This survey was carried out by C. V. Appleton. From 1196 to at least 1925 William and John were first and second.

Most versions
Mr Edward A. Nedelcov of Regina, Saskatchewan, Canada has collected 1023 versions of the spelling of his family name since January 1960. Mzilikazi of Zululand (b. *c.* 1795) had his name chronicled in 325 spellings, according to researches by Dr R. Kent Rasmussen.

Most Changed
Excluding members of the royal family the living monogamous woman who has most times changed her name is Lady Home of the Hirsel formerly Lady Douglass-Home; Countess of Home; Lady Dunglass and originally Miss Elizabeth Alington.

Most contrived name
In the United States the determination to derive commercial or other benefit from being the last listing in the local telephone book has resulted in self-given names, starting with up to 9 z's—an extreme example being Zachary Zzzzzzzzzra in the San Francisco book. The alpha and omega of Britain's 82 directories are Mrs Maude E. Aab of Hull, Humberside and the Zzzzzz Coffee Shop in Gray's Inn Road, London WC1.

PLACE-NAMES

Earliest
The world's earliest place names are pre-Sumerian e.g. Kish, Ur and Attara. The earliest recorded British place-name is Belerion, the Penwith peninsula of Cornwall, referred to as such by Pytheas of Massilia in *c.* 308 BC. The name Salakee on St Mary's, Isles of Scilly is however arguably of a pre Indo-European substrate meaning *tin island*. There are reasons to contend that Leicester (Roman, Ligora Castrum) contains an element reflecting its founding by the Western Mediterranean navigators, the Ligurians, as early as *c.* 1200 BC. The earliest distinctive name for what is now Great Britain was Albion by Himilco *c.* 500 BC. The oldest name among England's 46 counties is Kent, first mentioned in its Roman form of Cantium (from the Celtic *canto,* meaning a rim, *i.e.* a coastal district) from the same circumnavigation by Pytheas. The earliest mention of England is the form *Angelcymn,* which appeared in the Anglo-Saxon Chronicle in AD. 880.

Longest *World*
The official name for Bangkok, the capital city of Thailand, is Krungtep Mahanakhon. The full name is however: Krungthep Mahanakhon Bovorn Ratanakosin Mahintharayutthaya Mahadilokpop Noparatratchathani Burirom Udomratchanivetmahasathan Amornpiman Avatarnsathit Sakkathattiyavisnukarmprasit (167 letters) which in its most scholarly transliteration emerges with 175 letters. The longest place-name now in use is Taumatawhakatangihangakoauauotamatea-(turipukakapikimaungahoronuku)pokaiwhen-uakitanatahu, the unofficial 85-letter version of the name of a hill (1002 ft *305 m* above sea-level) in the Southern Hawke's Bay district of North Island, New Zealand. This Maori name means 'the hill whereon was played the flute of Tamatea, circumnavigator of lands, for his lady love'. The official version has 57 letters (1 to 36

and 65 to 85). Cauaiauaia in Angola, has 9 consecutive vowel letters.

Great Britain
The longest place-name in the United Kingdom is the concocted 58-letter version of Llanfair-pwllgwyngyll/gogerychwyrndrobwllllantysil-iogogogoch, which is translated: 'St Mary's Church by the pool of the white hazel trees, near the rapid whirlpool, by the red cave of the Church of St Tysilio'. This is the name used for the reopened (April 1973) village railway station in Anglesey, Gwynedd, Wales, but the *official* name consists of only the first 20 letters of what the Welsh would regard as a 51 letter word since 'll' and 'ch' may be regarded as one. The longest Welsh place-name listed in the Ordnance Survey Gazetteer is Lower Llanfihangel-y-Creuddyn (26 letters), a village near Aberystwyth, Dyfed. For commercial rather than toponymic reasons the proprietors of the Fairbourne Steam Railway, near Barmouth, North Wales have posted a 67 letter long name on a station board 64 ft *19,5 m* long. It reads Gorsafawddachaidraigd-danheddogleddollonpenrhynarevrdraethcere-digion though the 'll' should read 'l' making 66 letters or 65 if 'ch' is regarded as a single letter.

England
The longest single-word (unhyphenated) place-name in England is Blakehopeburnhaugh, a hamlet between Byrness and Rochester in Northumberland, of 18 letters. The nearby Cottonshopeburnfoot (19 letters) is locally rendered as one word though not by the Ordnance Survey. The hyphenated Sutton-under-Whites-tonecliffe, North Yorkshire has 27 letters on the Ordnance Survey but with the insertion of 'the' and the dropping of the final 'e' 29 letters in the Post Office List. The longest parish name is Saint Mary le More and All Hallows with Saint Leonard and Saint Peter, Wallingford (68 letters) in Oxfordshire formed on 5 Apr 1971.

Scotland
The longest single-word place-name in Scotland is Coignafeuinternich in Inverness-shire. Kirk-cudbrightshire (also 18 letters) became merged into Dumfries and Galloway on 16 May 1975. A 12-acre *5 ha* loch 9 miles *14 km* west of Stornoway on Lewis, Western Isles is named Loch Airidh Mhic Fhionnlaidh Dhuibh (31 letters).

Ireland
The longest place-name in Ireland is Muckan-aghederdauhaulia (22 letters), 4 miles *6 km* from Costello in Camus Bay, County Galway. The name means 'soft place between two seas'.

Shortest
The shortest place names in the world are the French village of Y (population 143), so named since 1241, the Danish village Å on the island Fyn, the Norwegian village of Å (pronounced 'Aw'), the Swedish place Å in Vikholandet, U in the Caroline Islands, Pacific Ocean; and the Japanese town of Sosei which is alternatively called Aioi or O. There was once a '6' in West Virginia, USA. The shortest place-names in Great Britain are the two-lettered places of Ae (population 199 in 1961) Dumfries and Galloway; Oa on the island of Islay, Strathclyde and Bu on Wyre, Orkney Islands. In the Shetland Islands there are skerries called Ve and two stacks called Aa. The island of Iona was originally I. The River E flows into the southern end of Loch Mhór, Invernessshire, and O Brook flows on Dartmoor, Devon. The shortest place-name in Ireland is Ta (or Lady's Island) Lough, a sea-inlet on the coast of County Wexford. Tievelough, in County Donegal, is also called Ea.

Most spellings
The spelling of the Dutch town of Leeuwarden

has been recorded in 225 versions since AD 1046. Bromesberrow, Hereford and Worcester, is recorded in 161 spellings since the 10th century as reported by local historian Lester Steynor.

PRINTED TEXT AND BOOKS

Oldest printed
The oldest surviving printed work is the Dharani scroll or *sutra* from wooden printing blocks found in the foundations of the Pulguk Sa pagoda, Kyŏngju, South Korea, on 14 Oct 1966. It has been dated no later than AD 704. It was claimed in November 1973 that a 28-page book of Tang dynasty poems at Yonsei University, Korea was printed from metal type *c.* 1160.

Oldest mechanically printed
It is widely accepted that the earliest mechanically printed full length book was the 42-line Gutenberg Bible, printed in Mainz, West Germany, in *c.* 1454 by Johann Gensfleisch zur Laden, called 'zu Gutenberg' (*c.* 1398–*c.* 1468). Work on water marks published in 1967 indicates a copy of a surviving printed 'Donatus' Latin grammar was made from paper in *c.* 1450. The earliest exactly dated printed work is the Psalter completed on 14 Aug 1457 by Johann Fust (*c.* 1400–66) and Peter Schöffer (1425–1502), who had been Gutenberg's chief assistant. The earliest printing by William Caxton (*c.* 1422–1491) though undated would appear to be *The Recuyel of the Historyes of Troye* in Cologne in late 1473 to spring 1474.

Book *Largest*
The largest book in the world is the *Super Book* measuring 9 ft × 10 ft 2⅛ in *2,74 × 3,07 m* weighing 557 lb *252,6 kg* consisting of 300 pages published in Denver, Colorado, USA in 1976.

Publication *Largest*
The largest publication in the world is the 1112 volume set of *British Parliamentary Papers* published by the Irish University Press in 1968–72. A complete set weighs 3¼ tons *3,3 tonnes*, costs £53,500 and would take 6 years to read at 10 hours per day. The production involved the death of 34,000 Indian goats, and the use of £15,000 worth of gold ingots. The total print is 500 sets and the price per set in 1984 was £42,000.

Dictionary *Largest*
Deutches Wörterbuch started by Jacob and Wilhelm Grimm in 1854 was completed in 34,519 pages and 33 volumes in 1971. Today's price is DM5456.97 (*now £1428*). The largest English language dictionary is the 12-volume Royal quarto *The Oxford English Dictionary* of 15,487 pages published between 1884 and 1928 with a first supplement of 963 pages in 1933. Of the 4-volume supplement, edited by R. W. Burchfield, the final (Se-Z) volume and the Bibliography was published in 1986. The work contains 414,825 words, 1,827,306 illustrative quotations and reputedly 227,779,589 letters and figures, 63.8 times more than the Bible. The greatest outside contributor has been Marghanita Laski with 175,000 quotations since 1958.

The New Grove Dictionary of Music and Musicians edited by Stanley Sadie CBE (b. 30 Oct 1930), published in 20 volumes by Macmillan's in February 1981 contains over 22 million words and 4500 illustrations and is the largest specialist dictionary yet published. The price in 1985 is £1100.

Book *Smallest*
The smallest marketed bound printed book with cursive material is one printed on 22 gsm paper measuring 1 mm × 1 mm 1/25 × 1/25 *in*, comprising the children's story *Old King Cole!* and published

in 85 copies in March 1985 by The Gleniffer Press of Paisley, Scotland. The pages can only be turned (with care) by the use of a needle.

Novel *Longest*
The longest important novel ever published is *Les hommes de bonne volonté* by Louis Henri Jean Farigoule (b. 26 Aug 1885), *alias* Jules Romains, of France, in 27 volumes in 1932–46. The English version *Men of Good Will* was published in 14 volumes in 1933–46 as a 'novel-cycle'. The 4959 page edition published by Peter Davies Ltd has an estimated 2,070,000 words excluding a 100 page index. The novel *Tokuga-Wa Ieyasu* by Sohachi Yamaoka has been serialised in Japanese daily newspapers since 1951. Now completed it will require nearly 40 volumes in book form.

Encyclopaedias *Earliest*
The earliest known encyclopaedia was compiled by Speusippus (*post* 408–*c.* 338 BC) a nephew of Plato, in Athens *c.* 370 BC. The earliest encyclo-paedia compiled by a Briton was *Liber exerptionum* by the Scottish monk Richard (d. 1173) at St Victor's Abbey, Paris *c.* 1140.

Encyclopaedia *Largest*
The largest encyclopaedia is *La Enciclopedia Universal Ilustrada Europeo-Americana* (J. Espasa & Sons, Madrid and Barcelona) totalling 105,000 pages and an annual supplement since 1935 comprising 165,200,000 words. The number of volumes in the set in August 1983 was 104, and the price is $2325 (*£1660*).

Encyclopaedia *Most comprehensive*
The most comprehensive English language encyclopaedia is the *Encyclopaedia Britannica*, first published in Edinburgh, Scotland, in December 1768–1771. A group of booksellers in the United States acquired reprint rights in 1898 and completed ownership in 1899. In 1943 the *Britannica* was given to the University of Chicago, Illinois, USA. The current 30-volume 15th edition contains 33,141 pages and 43,000,000 words from 4277 contributors. It is now edited in Chicago and in London.

Index *Longest*
The Tenth Collective Index of *Chemical Abstracts* completed in June 1983 contains 23,948,253 entries in 131,445 pages and 75 volumes, and weighs 380 lb *172,3 kg*.

MAPS
The oldest known map of any kind is a clay tablet depicting the river Euphrates flowing through northern Mesopotamia, Iraq, dated *c.* 3800 BC. The earliest surviving product of English map-making is the Anglo Saxon *mappa mundi*, known as the Cottonian manuscript from the late 10th century. The earliest printed map in the world is one of western China dated to 1115. The earliest printed map of Britain was Ptolemy's outline printed in Bologna, Italy in 1477.

A *Giant Relief Map of California*, weighing 38.4 tons *39 tonnes*, was displayed in the Ferry Building, San Francisco from 1924 until 1962. Now in storage, it measures 450 × 18 ft *137,1 × 5,48 m*.

HIGHEST PRICES

Most expensive work of art
The highest price paid for any book or any work of art was £8,140,000 for the 226 leaf manuscript *The Gospel Book of Henry the Lion, Duke of Saxony* at Sotheby's, London on 6 Dec. 1983. The book, 13½ × 10 in *34,3 × 25,4 cm*, was illuminated by the monk Herimann in *c.* 1170 at Helmershansen Abbey with 41 full page illustra-

tions, and was bought by Hans Kraus for the Hermann Abs consortium.

Printed Book *Highest Price*
The highest price ever paid for a printed book is $2,400,000 (*then £1,265,000*) for one of the only 21 complete known copies of the Gutenberg Bible, printed in Mainz, W. Germany in *c.* 1454. It was bought from the Carl and Lily Pforzheimer Foundation by Texas University in a sale arranged by Quaritch of London in New York on 9 June 1978. The most expensive new book is the reproduction of the full set of ornithological prints *The Birds of America* by John James Audubon (1785–1851) by Abbeville Press, USA for $15,000.

Broadsheet *Highest Price*
The highest price ever paid for a broadsheet has been $412,500 (*then £264,500*) for one of the 22 known copies of *The Declaration of Independence*, printed in Philadelphia in 1776 by Samuel T. Freeman & Co, and sold to the Chapin Library, Williams College, Williamstown, Massachusetts, USA at Christie's, New York City on 22 Apr 1983.

A page from one of only 21 known copies of the Gutenburg Bible—the world's highest priced printed book. (Cambridge University Press).

Musical manuscript
The highest price ever paid for a complete manuscript is £2.2 million by Armand Hammer at Christie's, London on 12 Dec 1980 for Leonardo da Vinci's 36-page Codex Leicester illustrated manuscript on cosmology compiled in *c.* 1507. It was sold by the trustees of the Holkham estate.

The auction record for a musical manuscript is £330,000 for *The Rite of Spring* by Igor F. Stravinsky (1882–1971), by Otto Haas for the Paul Sacher Collection in Basel, Switzerland at Sotheby's, London on 11 Nov 1982.

Atlas *Highest Price*
The highest price paid for an atlas is £340,000 for a Gerardus Mercator atlas of *c.* 1571 of Europe, sold at Sotheby's, London, on 13 Mar 1979.

BIBLE

Oldest
The oldest leather and papyrus Dead Sea Scrolls

were discovered in Cave 4 near Qumran in 1952. They comprise fragments of Exodus and Samuel I dating to *c.* 225–200 BC. The oldest known bible is the *Codex Vaticanus* written in Greek *ante* AD 350 and preserved in the Vatican Museum, Rome. The earliest complete Bible *printed* in English was one edited by Miles Coverdale, Bishop of Exeter (*c.* 1488–1569), while living in Antwerp, and printed in 1535. William Tyndale's New Testament in English had, however, been printed in Cologne and in Worms, Germany in 1525 while John Wycliffe's first manuscript translation dates from 1382.

Longest and shortest books
The longest book in the Authorized version of the Bible is the Book of Psalms, while the longest book including prose is the Book of the Prophet Isaiah, with 66 chapters. The shortest is the Third Epistle of John, with 294 words in 14 verses. The Second Epistle of John has only 13 verses but 298 words.

Longest and shortest psalm and verse
Of the 150 Psalms, the longest is the 119th, with 176 verses, and the shortest is the 117th, with two verses. The shortest verse in the Authorised Version (King James) of the Bible is verse 35 of Chapter XI of the Gospel according to St. John, consisting of the two words 'Jesus wept'. The longest is verse 9 of Chapter VIII of the Book of Esther, which extends to a 90-word description of the Persian empire.

Total letters and words, longest name
The total number of letters in the Bible is 3,566,480. The total number of words depends on the method of counting hyphenated words, but is usually given as between 773,692 and 773,746. The word 'and' according to Colin McKay Wilson of the Salvation Army appears 46,227 times. The longest personal name in the Bible is the 18 letter Maher-shalal-hash-baz, the symbolic name of the second son of Isaiah (Isaiah, Chapter VIII, verses 1 and 3). The caption of Psalm 22, however, contains a Hebrew title sometimes rendered Al-'Ayyeleth Hash-Shahar (20 letters).

DIARIES AND LETTERS

Longest diary
The diary of Edward Robb Ellis (b. 1911) of New York City begun in 1927 is estimated after 55 years to run to 15 million words. The diary of T. C. Baskerville of Chorlton-cum-Hardy, Manchester, maintained since 1939 comprises an estimated 5,300,000 words in 149 volumes occupying 33,000 pages. Col Ernest Loftus CBE of Harare, Zimbabwe began his daily diary on 4 May 1896 at the age of 12 and has thus completed 90 years.

Letters *Longest*
The longest personal letter based on a word count is one of 1,402,344 words started on 3 Jan 1982 by Alan Foreman of Erith, Kent, England and posted to his wife Janet on 25 Jan 1984.

To an editor *Longest*
The Upper Dauphin Sentinel of Pennsylvania, USA published a letter of 25,513 words over 8 issues from August to November 1979, written by John Sultzbaugh of Lykens, Pennsylvania.

Most
David Green, a solicitor, of Castle Morris, Dyfed had 112 letters published in the main correspondence columns of *The Times* by March 1986. His record year was 1972 with 12.

Correspondence *Shortest*
The shortest correspondence on record was that between Victor Marie Hugo (1802–85) and his publisher Hurst and Blackett in 1862. The

The indefatigable David Green who has had 112 letters published in *The Times* (*see page 85*).

author was on holiday and anxious to know how his new novel *Les Misérables* was selling. He wrote '?'. The reply was '!'.

The shortest letter to *The Times* was a letter comprising the single abbreviated symbol 'Dr²?' in the interrogative from R. S. Cookson of London NW11, on 30 July 1984, in a correspondence on the correct form of recording a plurality of academic doctorates. On 8 Jan 1986 a letter from a 7 year old girl responding to an appeal for any survivor bearing a particularly rare name. It read 'Sir, Yours faithfully Caroline Sophia Kerenhappuch Parkes'.

Most personal mail
The highest confirmed mail received by any private citizen in a year is 900,000 letters by the baseball star Hank Aaron reported by the US Postal Department in June 1974. About a third were letters of hate engendered by his bettering of 'Babe' Ruth's career record for 'home runs' set in 1927. (See Chap. 12.)

Pen pals *Most durable*
The longest sustained correspondence on record is one of 75 years from 11 Nov 1904 between Mrs Ida McDougall of Tasmania, Australia and Miss R. Norton of Sevenoaks, Kent until Mrs McDougall's death on 24 Dec 1979.

Birthday card *Most parsimonious*
Mrs Amelia Finch (b. 18 Apr 1912) of Lakehurst, New Jersey, USA and Mr Paul E. Warburgh (b. 1 Feb 1902) of Huntington, New York have been exchanging the same card since 1 Feb 1927.

Christmas cards
The greatest number of personal Christmas cards sent out is believed to be 62,824 by Mrs Werner Erhard of San Francisco, California in December 1975. Many must have been to unilateral acquaintances. The earliest known Christmas card was sent out by Sir Henry Cole (1808–82) in 1843 but did not become an annual ritual until 1862.

AUTOGRAPHS AND SIGNATURES
Earliest
The earliest surviving examples of an autograph are those made by scribes on cuneiform clay tablets from Tell Abu Ṣalābīkh, Iraq dated to the early Dynastic III A *c.* 2600 BC. A scribe named 'a-du' has added 'dub-sar' after his name thus translating to 'Adu, scribe'. The earliest surviving signature on a papyrus is that of the scribe Amen-'aa dated to the Egyptian middle kingdom which began in *c.* 2130 BC and which is in the Leningrad Museum, USSR. A signum exists for William I (the Conqueror) *c.* 1070. The earliest English sovereign whose handwriting is known to have survived is Edward III (1327–77). The earliest full signature extant is that of Richard II (dated 26 July 1386). The Magna Carta does not bear even the mark of King John (reigned 1199–1216), but carries only his seal affixed on 19 June 1215.

Most expensive
The highest price ever paid on the open market for a single autograph letter signed is $100,000 (*then £45,500*), paid on 18 Oct 1979 at a Charles Hamilton auction in New York City for a brief receipt signed by the Gloucestershire-born Button Gwinnett (1732–77), one of the 56 signatories of the United States' Declaration of Independence of 1776.

The highest price paid for a signed autograph letter of a living person is $12,500 (*then £5430*) at the Hamilton Galleries on 22 Jan 1981 for a letter from President Ronald Reagan praising Frank Sinatra.

A record $4250 (*then £2500*) was paid at a Hamilton sale on 12 Aug 1982 by Barry D Hoffman for the signed portrait of Al Capone (1899–1947).

Most valuable
Only one example of the signature of Christopher Marlowe (1564–93) is known. It is in the Kent County Archives on a Will of 1583. It is estimated that a seventh Shakespearean signature, should it ever come to light, might realise at least £1 million at auction.

A 3-dimensional card; the design is based on the first ever Christmas card printed in 1843 and sent out by Sir Henry Cole. (From the collection of Christmas Archives International).

AUTHORS
Most prolific
The champion of the goose quill era was Józef Ignacy Kraszewski (1812–87) of Poland who produced more than 600 volumes of novels and historical works. Until recently very high productivity had been attributed to Frank Richards, alias Charles Hamilton, (1875–1961) with up to 80,000 words a week in 1913 including the whole of the periodicals *Gem* (founded 1907) and *Magnet* (1908–40). In 1984 George Samways (b. 1894) asserted that Hamilton used him and others as 'ghost-writers'.

Soho Tokutomi (1863–1957) wrote the history *Kinsei Nippon Kokuminshi* in 100 volumes of 42,468 pages and 19,452,952 letters in 35 years.

Most novels
The greatest number of novels published by an authoress is 904 by Kathleen Lindsay (Mrs Mary Faulkner) (1903–73) of Somerset West, Cape Province, South Africa. She wrote under two other married names and 8 pen names. Baboorao Arnalkar (b. 9 June 1907) of Maharashtra State, India between 1936 and 1984 has published 1092 short mystery stories in book form and several non-fiction books.

After receiving a probable record 743 rejection slips the British novelist John Creasey MBE (1908–73), under his own name and 25 *noms de plume* had 564 books totalling more than 40,000,000 words published from 1932 to his death on 9 June 1973. The British authoress with the greatest total of full-length titles was Ursula Harvey Bloom (Mrs A. C. G. Robinson, formerly Mrs Denham-Cookes 1892–1984), who reached 560 in 1976, starting in 1924 with *The Great Beginning* and including the best sellers *The Ring Tree* (novel) and *The Rose of Norfolk* (non-fiction). Enid Mary Blyton (1898–1968) (Mrs Darrell Waters) completed 600 titles of children's stories, many of them brief, with 59 in the single year 1955. She was translated into a record 128 languages.

Most text books
Britain's most successful writer of text books is the ex-schoolmaster Ronald Ridout (b. 23 July 1916) who between 1948 and April 1986 had 499 titles published with sales of 84,800,000. His *The First English Workbook* has sold 5,135,000.

The annual aggregate sales of all titles by Louis Alexander of Haslemere, Surrey, reached 4,573,000 in the year 1977.

Highest paid
In 1958 Mrs Deborah Schneider of Minneapolis, Minnesota, USA, wrote 25 words to complete a sentence in a competition for the best blurb for Plymouth cars. She won from about 1,400,000 entrants the prize of $500 (*then £178*) every month for life. On normal life expectations she would have collected $12,000 (*£4285*) per word. No known anthology includes Mrs Schneider's deathless prose but it is in her deed box at her bank 'Only to be opened after death'. She passed $6000 a word by 1983.

Greatest advance
The greatest advances paid for any book is $5,000,000 (*then £3,430,000*) for *Whirlwind* by James Clavell at auction in New York City on 11 Jan 1986 to William Morrow & Co and Avon Books.

Top selling
It was announced on 13 Mar 1953 that 672,058,000 copies of the works of Generalissimo Stalin (born Yózef Vissarionovich Dzhugashvili) (1879–1953), had been sold or distributed in 101 languages.

Currently the top-selling authoress is Barbara Cartland with global sales of over 400,000,000 for 418 titles in 17 languages. In 1985 she published 26 titles.

The all-time estimate of book sales by Erle Stanley Gardner (1889–1970) (US) to 1 Jan 1986 is 319,034,707 copies in 37 languages. The top selling lady crime writer has been Dame Agatha Christie (*née* Miller) (later Lady Mallowan) (1890–1976) whose 87 crime novels sold an estimated 300,000,000 in 103 languages. *Sleeping Murder* was published posthumously in 1977.

Biography *Longest*
The longest biography in publishing history is that of Sir Winston Churchill by his son Randolph (4832 pages) and Martin Gilbert (13,830 pages) to date comprising some 8,214,000 words. George Simenon (b. 1903) wrote 22 autobiographical books from 1972.

Most rejections
The greatest recorded number of publishers' rejections for a manuscript is 223 (by March 1986) for the 130,000 word manuscript *World Government Crusade* written in 1966 by Gilbert Young (b. 1906) of Bath, England. The record for rejections before publication (and wide acclaim) is 69 from 55 publishers in the case of Prof. Steven Goldberg's *The Inevitability of Patriarchy*.

Authoress *Oldest*
The oldest authoress in the world was Mrs Alice Pollock (*née* Wykeham-Martin) (1868–1971), of Haslemere, Surrey, whose book *Portrait of My Victorian Youth* (Johnson Publications) was published in March 1971 when she was aged 102 years 8 months.

Literary luncheons
Literary luncheons were inaugurated by Christina Foyle (Mrs Ronald Batty) in Oct 1930 at the Old Holborn Restaurant, London. Attendances were over 1500 at the Grosvenor House, Park Lane, London at lunches for Mistinguett (1873–1956) and Dr Edvard Benes (1884–1948) in 1938.

Literary gestation *Longest*
The standard German dictionary *Deutsches Wörterbuch*, begun by the brothers Grimm in 1854, was finished in 1971. *Acta Sanctorum* begun by Jean Bolland in 1643, arranged according to saints' days, reached the month of November in 1925 and an introduction for December was published in 1940. Oxford University Press received back their proofs of *Constable's Presentments* from the Dugdale Society in Dec 1984. They had been sent out for correction 35 years earlier in Dec 1949.

Poet Laureate *Youngest and oldest*
The youngest Poet Laureate was Laurence Eusden (1688–1730), who received the bays on 24 Dec 1718 at the age of 30 years and 3 months. The greatest age at which a poet has succeeded is 73 in the case of William Wordsworth (1770–1850) on 6 Apr 1843. The longest lived Laureate was John Masefield, OM, who died on 12 May 1967, aged 88 years 345 days. The longest which any poet has worn the laurel is 41 years 322 days, in the case of Alfred (later the 1st Lord) Tennyson (1809–92), who was appointed on 19 Nov 1850 and died in office on 6 Oct 1892.

Poem *Longest*
The lengthiest poem ever published has been the Kirghiz folk epic *Manas*, which appeared in printed form in 1958 but which has never been translated into English. It runs to 'more than 500,000 lines'. Short translated passages appear in *The Elek Book of Oriental Verse*.

The longest poem ever written in the English language is one on the life of King Alfred by John Fitchett (1766–1838) of Liverpool which ran to 129,807 lines and took 40 years to write. His editor Robert Riscoe added the concluding 2585 lines.

Roger Brien's (b. Montreal, 1910) *Prométhée— dialogue des vivants et des morts* runs to 456,047 lines written in 1964–81. Brien has written another 497,000 lines of French poetry in over 90 published works.

Poem *Most successful*
If by Joseph Rudyard Kipling (1865–1936), first published in 1910 has been translated into 27 languages and according to Kipling 'anthologized to weariness'.

HIGHEST PRINTINGS
World
The world's most widely distributed book is the Bible, which has been translated into 286 languages and portions of it into a further 1522 languages. This compares with 222 languages for Lenin. It has been estimated that between 1815 and 1975 some 2,500,000,000 copies were printed of which 1,500,000,000 were handled by Bible Societies. *The English Good News Bible*, translation of the New Testament (which is copyright of The Bible Society), sold 80,000,000 copies in the period 1976–80.

The King James version is not copyright but at least 14 copyrights exist on other versions. The oldest publisher of Bibles is the Cambridge University Press which began with the Geneva version in 1591.

It has been reported that 800,000,000 copies of the red-covered booklet *Quotations from the Works of Mao Tse-tung* were sold or distributed between June 1966, when possession became virtually mandatory in China, and September 1971 when their promoter Marshal Lin Piao died in an air crash.

It is believed that in the USA Van Antwerp Bragg and Co. printed some 60 million copies of the 1879 edition of *The McGuffey Reader*, compiled by Henry Vail in the pre-copyright era for distribution to public schools.

The total disposal through non-commercial channels by Jehovah's Witnesses of *The Truth That Leads to Eternal Life* published by the Watchtower Bible and Tract Society of Brooklyn, New York, on 8 May 1968, reached 105,685,818 in 116 languages by May 1986.

BEST SELLING BOOKS
Excluding versions of the Bible, the world's all-time best selling copyright book is the *Guinness Book of Records* first published in September 1955 by the Guinness Brewery and edited by Norris Dewar McWhirter (b. 12 Aug 1925) and his twin brother Alan Ross McWhirter (k. 27 Nov 1975).

Best Seller Lists
The *Sunday Times* best seller list (which excludes books published annually) was first published on 14 Apr 1974. *The Country Diary of an Edwardian Lady* (Michael Joseph, Webb & Bower) held No 1 position for 64 weeks up to the paper's 10 month closure which started on 30 Nov 1978. Its global sales in 13 languages reached 2,634,150 copies by May 1986. The longest duration on the *New York Times* best sellers' list (founded 1935) is 'A Light in the Attic' by Shelby Silverstein (b. 1932) which on 10 Jan 1985 had its 112th week on the lists.

Fiction
The novel with the highest sales has been *Valley*

Author Frederick Forsyth whose novel *The Fourth Protocol* earned him over £3 million in advances. (Monitor).

of the Dolls (first published March 1966) by Jacqueline Susann (Mrs Irving Mansfield) (1921–74) with a world-wide total of 27,465,000 to 1 May 1985. In the first 6 months Bantam sold 6.8 million. In the United Kingdom the highest print order has been 3,000,000 by Penguin Books Ltd. for their paperback edition of *Lady Chatterley's Lover*, by D. H. (David Herbert) Lawrence (1885–1930). The total sales to May 1986 were 4,685,000. Alistair Stuart MacLean (b. Scotland, April 1922) between 1955 and 1986 wrote 29 books of which the sales of 20 have exceeded a million copies and 13 have been filmed. *The Cruel Sea* by Nicholas Monsarrat (1910–79) published in 1951 by Cassell, reached sales of 1,200,000 in its *original* edition.

Publisher *Fastest*
The fastest time in which a book has been published is less than 24 hours by Corgi Books from receipt of final manuscript to finished copies, in the case of John Lisners' *The House of Horrors* a 223 page paperback on the mass murderer in North London Dennis Nilsen sentenced to life imprisonment at 4.23 pm on 4 Nov 1983. (See Crime, Chapter 11.)

Seller *Slowest*
The accolade for the world's slowest selling book (known in US publishing as slooow-sellers) probably belongs to David Wilkins's Translation of the New Testament from Coptic into Latin published by Oxford University Press in 1716 in 500 copies. Selling an average of one each 139 days, it remained in print for 191 years.

PUBLISHERS AND PRINTERS
Oldest Publisher
Cambridge University Press has a continuous history of printing and publishing since 1584. The University received Royal Letters Patent to print and sell all manner of books on 20 July 1534.

In 1978 the Oxford University Press celebrated the 500th anniversary of the printing of the first book in the City of Oxford in 1478. This was before OUP was itself in existence.

Prolific Publisher
In terms of new titles per annum Britain's most prolific publisher in 1985 was Cambridge University Press with 840. The UK published a

record 52,994 book titles in 1985 of which a record 11,740 were reprints.

Largest Printer *World*

The largest printers in the world are R. R. Donnelley & Sons Co. of Chicago, Illinois, USA. The company, founded in 1864, has plants in 15 main centres, turning out $1,814,000,000 (*£1500 million*) worth of work per year. More than 133,000 tons of inks and 1,645,000 tons of paper and board are consumed every year.

The largest printer under one roof is the United States Government Printing Office (founded 1860) in Washington, DC, USA. The Superintendent of Documents sold in 1984 almost $60 million (*£50 million*) worth of US governmental publications every year and maintains an inventory of over 17,200 titles in print.

Print order

The initial print order for the 54th Automobile Association Members' Handbook (1986–7) was 4,800,000 copies—stacked one on top of each other, 33 times the height of Ben Nevis. The total print since 1908 has been 86,700,000. It is currently printed by web offset by Petty & Sons of Leeds.

The aggregate print of The Highway Code (instituted 1931) reached 90,000,000 after 50 years in mid-1981.

LIBRARIES

Largest *World*

The largest library in the world is the United States Library of Congress (founded on 24 Apr 1800), on Capitol Hill, Washington, DC. By 1986 it contained 90 million items, including 20 million volumes and pamphlets. The buildings contain 64.6 acres *26.14 ha* of floor space and contain 532 miles *856 km* of shelving. The James Madison Memorial Building was dedicated in April 1980 and has 34.5 acres *14 ha* of floor space.

One of the many reading rooms at the British Library, the largest library in the UK which houses 15.5 million volumes.

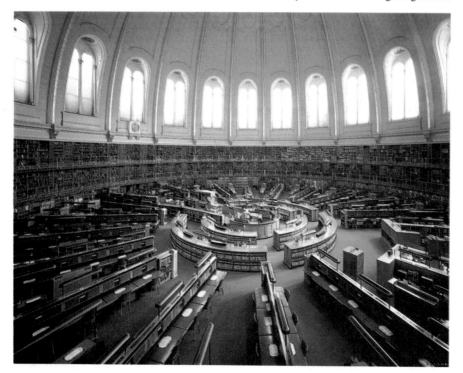

The largest non-statutory library in the world is the New York Public Library (founded 1895) on Fifth Avenue with a floor space of 525,276 ft² *48 800 m²* and 88 miles *141,6 km* of shelving. Its collection including 81 branch libraries embraces 11,949,333 volumes, 14,466,478 manuscripts and 363,679 maps.

The greatest personal library ever amassed was that of Sir Thomas Phillipps. Dispersal began in 1886. The residue was bought largely unseen by the brothers Lionel Robinson CBE MC and Philip Robinson for £100,000. Sales began on 1 July 1946.

Great Britain

The largest library in the United Kingdom is the British Library, dispersed among more than 20 buildings in London and a 60 acre *24,3 ha* site at Boston Spa, West Yorkshire, with a total staff of some 2500. The Library contains over 15.5 million volumes. Stock increases involve over 8 miles *12,8 km* of new shelving annually. The Newspaper Library at Colindale, North London, opened in 1932, has 562,300 volumes and parcels comprising 70,000 different titles on 22 miles *35,4 km* of shelving. The Document Supply Centre in West Yorkshire (shelf capacity 98 miles *157,7 km*) runs the largest library interlending operation in the world; it handles annually nearly 3 million requests from other libraries (UK and overseas) for items they do not hold in stock. The National Sound Archive holds 1,000,000 discs and 50,000 hours of recorded tape. The largest public library in Europe is the extended Mitchell Library, North Street, Glasgow with a floor area of 538,200 ft² *50 000 m²* or 12.3 acres *4,9 ha* and an ultimate capacity for 4,000,000 volumes. The Mitchell also houses Europe's largest public reference library.

Overdue books

The most overdue book taken out by a known borrower was one reported on 7 Dec 1968, checked out in 1823 from the University of Cincinnati Medical Library on Febrile Diseases (London, 1805 by Dr J. Currie). This was returned by the borrower's great-grandson

Richard Dodd. The fine calculated to be $2264 (*then £1102 10s*) was waived.

Museums *Oldest*

The oldest museum in the world is the Ashmolean Museum in Oxford built in 1679–83 and named after the collector Elias Ashmole (1617–1692). Since 1924 it has housed an exhibition of historic scientific instruments.

Museums *Largest*

The largest single museum in the world is the American Museum of Natural History on 77th to 81st Streets and Central Park West, New York City, NY, USA. Founded in 1874, it comprises 19 interconnected buildings with 23 acres *9 ha* of floor space.

The world's largest complex of museums is the Smithsonian Institution comprising 13 museums with 5600 employees. The largest and the most visited museum in the United Kingdom is the British Museum (founded in 1753), which was opened to the public in 1759. The main building in Bloomsbury, London, was built in 1823 and has a total floor area of 17.57 acres *7,11 ha*. In 1985, 4,142,092 people passed through its doors.

Most popular

The highest attendance for any museum is that at the Smithsonian Air and Space Museum, Washington DC opened in July 1976. The record-setting day in 1984 at 118,437 required the doors to be temporarily closed.

NEWSPAPERS

Oldest *World*

A copy has survived of a news pamphlet published in Cologne, West Germany in 1470. The oldest existing newspaper in the world is the Swedish official journal *Post och Inrikes Tidningar*, founded in 1645. It is published by the Royal Swedish Academy of Letters. The oldest existing commercial newspaper is the *Haarlems Dagblad/Oprechte Haarlemsche Courant*, published in Haarlem, in the Netherlands. The *Courant* was first issued as the *Weeckelycke Courante van Europa* on 8 Jan 1656 and a copy of issue No. 1 survives.

United Kingdom

The newspaper with the earliest origins in the United Kingdom is *Berrow's Worcester Journal* (originally the *Worcester Post Man*), published in Worcester. It was traditionally founded in 1690 and has appeared weekly since June 1709. No complete file exists. The earliest date of foundation for any British newspaper published under the same title is the *Stamford Mercury*, printed since 1712 and traditionally even 1695. The *London Gazette* (originally the *Oxford Gazette*) was first published on 16 Nov 1665. The oldest Sunday newspaper is *The Observer*, first issued on 4 Dec 1791.

Newspapers *Largest and smallest*

The most massive single issue of a newspaper was the 7½ lb *3,40 kg New York Times* of Sunday 17 Oct 1965. It comprised 15 sections with a total of 946 pages, including about 1,200,000 lines of advertising. The largest page size ever used has been 51 in × 35 in *130 cm × 89 cm* for *The Constellation*, printed in 1859 by George Roberts as part of the Fourth of July celebrations in New York City, NY, USA. The *Worcestershire Chronicle* was the largest British newspaper. A surviving issue of 16 Feb 1859 measures 32¼ in × 22½ in *82 cm × 57 cm*. The smallest original page size has been 3 × 3¾ in *7,6 × 9,5 cm* of the *Daily Banner* (25 cents per month) of Roseberg, Oregon, USA, issues of which, dated 1 and 2 Feb 1876, survive. The *Answers to Correspond-*

ents published by Messrs Carr & Co, Paternoster Square, London in 1888 was 3½ × 4½ in *9 × 11 cm*. The British Library Newspaper Library has the *Watford News and Advertiser* of 1 Apr 1899 measuring 2.9 × 3.9 in *7,5 × 10 cm*.

Most expensive

Britain's most expensive paper is *The Sunday Times* at 50p (or 10s 0d in the money prior to 15 Feb 1971), or double the price of the original 1955 fully bound edition of the *Guinness Book of Records*.

The United States has 1692 English-language daily newspapers at 1 May 1985 with a combined net paid circulation of 62,000,000 copies per day. The peak year for US newspapers was 1910, when there were 2202. The leading newspaper readers in the world are the people of Sweden, where 580 newspapers are sold for each 1000 compared with the UK figure of 410.

Editorship *Longest*

Sir Etienne Dupuch OBE of Nassau, Bahamas, editor of the *Tribune* since 1 Apr 1919 entered his 66th year in the chair on 1 Apr 1984. The longest editorship of any United Kingdom national newspaper has been more than 59 years by C. P. Scott (1846–1932) of the (then *Manchester*) *Guardian*, who was appointed aged 25 in 1877 and died on 1 Jan 1932.

Most durable feature

The longest lasting feature in the British national press from one pen was *Your Stars* by Edward Lyndoe. It ran from Oct 1933 to 1982 in *The Sunday People*. Frank Lowe contributed a weekly natural history column to the *Bolton Evening News* every week from 4 Feb 1926 to his death on 26 Oct 1985. Albert E. Pool (b. 1909) has been a part-time journalist for the *Lincolnshire and South Humberside* (formerly *The Hull*) *Times* since March 1923 until the demise of the paper on 26 July 1985.

Biggest headline

Torells School, Grays, Essex reproduced the front page of their local newspaper, the *Thurrock Gazette*, in a blown up edition comprising 11,664 sheets of A1 paper measuring 180 × 270 ft *54,86 × 82,29 m* staked out on 4 July 1984. The headline was 3 ft *91,4 cm* deep.

Most syndicated columnist

The world's most syndicated columnist is Ann Landers, 67 whose numbers of newspapers in 30 years has now surpassed 1,000 with an estimated readership of 85 million.

Longest lived strip

The most durable newspaper comic strip has been the Katzenjammer Kids (Hans and Fritz) created by Rudolph Dirks and first published in the *New York Journal* on 12 Dec 1897 and perpetuated by his son John. The earliest strip was The Yellow Kid, which first appeared in the New York *Journal* on 18 Oct 1896. The most widely syndicated is *Peanuts* by Charlie Schulz appearing in 1514 newspapers in 26 languages starting in October 1950.

Most misprints

The record for misprints in *The Times* was set on 22 Aug 1978 when on page 19 there were 97 in 5½ single column inches. The passage concerned 'Pop' (Pope) Paul VI.

Most durable advertiser

The Jos Neel Co, a clothing store in Macon, Georgia, USA (founded 1880) has run an 'ad' in the *Macon Telegraph* every day in the upper left corner of page 2 since 22 Feb 1889 or 35,405 times to Feb 1986.

CIRCULATION

Earliest 1,000,000

The first newspaper to achieve a circulation of 1,000,000 was *Le Petit Journal*, published in Paris, France, which reached this figure in 1886, when selling at 5 centimes. The *Daily Mail* first reached a million on 2 Mar 1900.

Highest *World*

The highest circulation for any newspaper in the world is that for the *Yomiuri Shimbun* (founded 1874) of Japan which attained a figure of 14,134,187 copies on 1 April 1986. This is achieved by totalling the figures for editions published in various centres with a morning figure of 9,167,000 and an evening figure of 4,966,887. It reaches 38 per cent of Japan's 34 million households. It has a staff of 3060 and 436 bureaux. *Trud*, the Soviet trade union daily, is printed in 53 cities in 15.4 million copies of which only 70,000 are bought at newsstands.

Great Britain

The highest circulation of any single newspaper in Britain is that of the Sunday newspaper *The News of the World*, printed at Wapping, London E1. Single issues have attained a sale of 9,000,000 copies with an estimated readership of more than 19,000,000. The paper first appeared on 1 Oct 1843, and surpassed the million mark in 1905. The latest sales figure is 5,103,164 copies per issue (average for 1 July to 31 Dec 1985), with an estimated readership of 13,024,000.

The highest net sale of any daily newspaper in the United Kingdom is that of *The Sun,* founded in London in 1964. The latest sales figure is 4,125,480 (1 July to 31 Dec 1985), with an estimated readership of 11,623,000.

Most read

The national newspaper which achieves the closest to a saturation circulation is *The Sunday Post*, established in Glasgow in 1914. In 1985 its estimated readership in Scotland of 2,653,000 represented 65 per cent of the entire population aged 15 and over. The *Arran Banner* (founded March 1974) has a readership of 97+ per cent on Britain's seventh largest off-shore island.

PERIODICALS

Oldest *World*

The oldest continuing periodical in the world is *Philosophical Transactions of the Royal Society*, published in London, which first appeared on 6 Mar 1665.

Great Britain

The bi-monthly *The Gospel Magazine* has been published since 1766. Curtis's *Botanical Magazine* has been in continuous publication since 1 Feb 1787, as several 'parts' a year forming a series of continuously numbered volumes. Britain's oldest weekly periodical is *Lancet* first published in 1823. The *Scots Magazine* began publication in 1739 and ran till 1826, and with three breaks has been produced continuously since 1924.

Largest circulations *World*

The largest circulation of any weekly periodical is that of *TV Guide* (USA) which in 1974 became the first magazine in history to sell a billion (1000 million) copies in a year. The weekly average for July–December 1985 was 16,898,697. In its 39 basic international editions *The Reader's Digest* (established February 1922) circulates 28,000,000 copies monthly in 15 languages, including a United States edition of more than 16,250,000 copies and a United Kingdom edition (established 1939) of 1,506,031 copies (av. January–December 1985).

Parade, the syndicated Sunday newspaper colour magazine, is distributed with 135 newspapers every Sunday. The current circulation is 25,153,000 (April 1985). Britain's highest circulation Sunday colour supplement is the *News of the World's SunDay* at 5,103,164 (1985).

Great Britain

The highest circulation of any periodical in Great Britain is that of the *Radio Times* (instituted on 28 Sept 1923). The average weekly sale for July–December 1985 was 3,224,038 copies with a readership of 9,790,000. The highest sale of any issue was 10,283,911 copies for the Christmas issue of 1986. *TV Times* averaged sales of 3,166,546 in the period July–Dec 1985 with an estimated readership of 9,981,000 (July–Dec 1985).

Annual

Old Moore's Almanack has been published annually since 1697, when it first appeared as a broadsheet, by Dr Francis Moore (1657–1715) of Southwark, London to advertise his 'physiks'. The annual sale certified by its publishers W. Foulsham & Co. Ltd of Slough, England is 1 million copies and its aggregate sale is estimated to be in excess of 108 million.

CROSSWORDS

First

The earliest known crossword was a 9 by 9 Double Diamond published in *St Nicholas* for September 1875 in New York City, USA. This was discovered by Dr Kenneth Miller of Newcastle upon Tyne, England inventor of the colour crossword in 1983. The first crossword published in a British newspaper was one furnished by C. W. Shepherd in the *Sunday Express* of 2 Nov 1924. However a 25 letter acrostic of Roman provenance was discovered on a wall in Cirencester, England in 1868.

Largest

The world's largest published crossword has been one compiled by Robert Trucot of Québec, Canada. It comprised 82,951 squares, contained 12,489 clues across and 13,125 down and covered 38.28 ft² *3,55 m²*.

Fastest and slowest solution

The fastest recorded time for completing *The Times* crossword under test conditions is 3 min 45.0 sec by Roy Dean, 43 of Bromley, London in the BBC 'Today' radio studio on 19 Dec 1970. Dr John Sykes won the *Times* championship 8 times between 1972 and 1985. In May 1966 *The Times* of London received an announcement from a Fijian woman that she had just succeeded in completing their crossword No. 673 in the issue of 4 Apr 1932.

Most durable compilers

Adrian Bell (1901–1980) of Barsham, Suffolk contributed a record 4520 crosswords to *The Times* from 2 Jan 1930 until his death. R. J. Baddock of Plymouth (b. 30 Oct 1894) has been a regular contributor to national newspapers since 13 Aug 1926. The most prolific compiler is Roger F. Squires of Ironbridge, Shropshire, who compiles 35 published puzzles single-handedly each week. His total output to August 1985 was over 25,000.

ADVERTISING RATES

The highest ever price for a single page has been $327,230 (£272,691) for a four-colour back cover in *Parade* (circulation 25.2 million per week) in April 1985 (see above). The record for a four colour inside page is $284,560 (£182,430) in *Parade* (in April 1985). The advertising revenue from the November 1982 US edition of *The Reader's Digest* was a peak $14,716,551 (*then £9,495,000*).

The highest expenditure ever incurred on a single advertisement in a periodical is $3,200,000 (*£1,600,000*) by Gulf and Western Industries on 5 Feb 1979 for insertions in *Time* Magazine (US and selected overseas editions). The British record is some £100,000 for a 20-page colour supplement by Woolworths in the *Radio Times* of 16 Nov 1972. The rate for a single page in *SunDay* magazine is £27,500, and £55,000 for a centre spread (April 1986). The world's highest newspaper advertising rate is 37,350,000 Yen (*£144,210*) for a full page in the morning edition and 30,825,000 Yen (*£119,000*) for the evening edition of the *Yomiuri Shimbun* of Tokyo (April 1986). The highest rate in Britain is a full page in *The Sunday Express* at £33,600 (May 1985).

The imposing Grand Court organ in the Wanamaker Store in Philadelphia, USA, the largest functional organ in the world, with over 30,000 pipes and a six-tiered keyboard.

4. MUSIC

Published by Guinness Books at £11.95 net.

Origins

Whistles and flutes made from perforated phalange bones have been found at Upper Palaeolithic sites of the Aurignacian period (*c.* 25,000–22,000 BC) *e.g.* at Istallóskö, Hungary and in Molodova, USSR. The world's earliest surviving musical notation dates from *c.* 1800 BC. A heptatonic scale deciphered from a clay tablet by Dr Duchesne-Guillemin in 1966–7 was found at a site in Nippur, Sumer, now Iraq. An Assyrian love song also *c.* 1800 BC to an Ugaritic god from a tablet of notation and lyric was reconstructed for an 11 string lyre at the University of California, Berkeley on 6 Mar 1974. Musical history is, however, able to be traced back to the 3rd millennium BC, when the yellow bell (*huang chung*) had a recognised standard musical tone in Chinese temple music.

INSTRUMENTS

Piano *Earliest*
The earliest pianoforte in existence is one built in Florence, Italy, in 1720 by Bartolommeo Cristofori (1655–1731) of Padua, and now preserved in the Metropolitan Museum of Art, New York City.

Piano *Grandest*
The grandest grand piano was one of 1¼ tons/ *tonnes* 11 ft 8 in *3,55 m* in length made by Chas. H. Challen & Son Ltd of London in 1935. The longest bass string measured 9 ft 11 in *3,02 m* with a tensile of 30 tons/*tonnes*.

Piano *Most Expensive*
The highest price ever paid for a piano is $390,000 (*then £177,273*) at Sotheby Parke Bernet, New York City on 26 Mar 1980 for a Steinway grand of *c.* 1888 sold by the Martin Beck Theatre. It was bought by a non-pianist.

Organ largest *World*
The largest and loudest musical instrument ever constructed is the now only partially functional Auditorium Organ in Atlantic City, New Jersey, USA. Completed in 1930, this heroic instrument had two consoles (one with seven manuals and another movable one with five), 1477 stop controls and 33,112 pipes ranging in tone from $\frac{3}{16}$ of an inch *4,7 mm* to the 64 ft *19,5 m* tone. It had the volume of 25 brass bands, with a range of seven octaves. The world's largest fully functional organ is the six manual 30,067 pipe Grand Court Organ installed in the Wanamaker Store, Philadelphia, Pennsylvania, USA in 1911 and enlarged between then and 1930. It has a 64 ft *19,5 m* tone gravissima pipe. The world's largest church organ is that in Passau Cathedral, Germany. It was completed in 1928 by D. F. Steinmeyer & Co and has 16,000 pipes and five manuals. The world's most powerful electronic organ is the 5000 watt Royal V. Rodgers organ, designed by Virgil Fox with 465 speakers installed by Orient Shoji Co in Chuo-ku, Tokyo, Japan in June 1983. The chapel organ at West Point US Military Academy, NY has, since 1911, been expanded from 2406 to 18,200 pipes.

Great Britain
The largest organ in Great Britain is that completed in Liverpool Anglican Cathedral on 18 Oct 1926, with two five-manual consoles of which only one is now in use, and 9704 speaking pipes (originally 10,936) ranging from tones ¾ in to 32 ft *1,9 cm to 9,75 m*.

Loudest organ stop
The loudest organ stop in the world is the Ophicleide stop of the Grand Great in the Solo Organ in the Atlantic City Auditorium (see above). It is operated by a pressure of 100 in *254 cm* of water (3½ lb/in² *24 kPa*) and has a pure trumpet note of ear-splitting volume, more than six times the volume of the loudest locomotive whistles.

Musicians *Most Durable*
Elsie Maude Stanley Hall (1877–1976) gave piano recitals for 90 years giving her final concert in Rustenburg. Transvaal, South Africa aged 97. Charles Bridgeman (1779–1873) of All Saints Parish Church, Hertford, England, who was appointed organist in 1792, was still playing 81 years later in 1873. Norwegian pianist Reidar Thommesen (1889–1986) played over 30 hours a week in theatre cafés when a nonagenarian.

Brass instrument *Largest*
The largest recorded brass instrument is a tuba standing 7½ ft *2,28 m* tall, with 39 ft *11,8 m* of tubing and a bell 3 ft 4 in *1 m* across. This

contrabass tuba was constructed for a world tour by the band of John Philip Sousa (1854–1932), the United States composer, in *c.* 1896–8. It is now owned by a circus promoter in South Africa.

Horns *Longest Alphorn*
The longest alphorn is one of 24,02 m *78 ft 9½ in* weighing 83 kg *183 lb* built from spruce by Swiss-born Peter Wutherich, 65, of Boise, Idaho. It took over a year and a half to complete.

Stringed instrument *Largest*
The largest movable stringed instrument ever constructed was a pantaleon with 270 strings stretched over 50 ft² *4,6 m²* used by George Noel in 1767. The greatest number of musicians required to operate a single instrument was the six required to play the gigantic orchestrion, known as the Apollonicon, built in 1816 and played until 1840.

Guitar *Largest and Most Expensive*
The largest and presumably also the loudest playable guitar in the world is one 14 ft 3¼ in *4,35 m* tall, and 309 lb *140 kg* in weight, built by Joe Kovacic of Lado Musical Inc., Scarborough, Ontario, Canada. The most expensive standard sized guitar is the German chittara battente by Jacob Stadler, dated 1624, which was sold for £10,500 at Christie's, London on 12 June 1974.

Double bass *Largest and Most players*
The largest double bass ever constructed was one 14 ft *4,26 m* tall, built in 1924 in Ironia, New Jersey, USA by Arthur K. Ferris, allegedly on orders from the Archangel Gabriel. It weighed 11.6 cwt. *590 kg* with a sound box 8 ft *2,43 m* across, and had leathern strings totalling 104 ft *31,7 m*. Its low notes could be felt rather than heard. On 27 June 1984 5 members of 'Bass Ten' from Bournemouth, Dorset bowed and 6 fingered a double bass simultaneously in a rendition of Monti's *Czardas* at Hever Castle, Kent.

'Cello *Most valuable*
The highest ever auction price for a violoncello is £145,000 at Sotheby's, London on 8 Nov 1978 for a Stradivari made in Cremona, Italy in 1710.

Violin *Most valuable*
The Lady Blunt Stradivarius violin of 1721 failed at £820,000 to reach its undisclosed 'reserve' at Sotheby's, London on 14 Nov 1985. The highest ever price *paid* at auction for a violin or any musical instrument is £396,000 for La Cathédrale Stradivari dated 1707 at Sotheby's, London on 22 Nov 1984. Some 700 of the 1116 violins by Stradivarius (1644–1737) have survived. His Alarol violin was confirmed by Jacques Francais to have been sold by private treaty by W. E. Hill for $1.2 million (*then £600,000*) to a Singaporean.

Violinist *Underwater*
The pioneer violinist to surmount the problems of playing the violin underwater was Mark Gottlieb. Submerged in Evergreen State College swimming bath in Olympia, Washington, USA in March 1975 he gave a submarine rendition of Handel's *Water Music*. His most intractable problem was his underwater *détaché*. On 7 Oct 1979 the first underwater quartet performed in the *Challenge the Guinness* TV show on Channel 7 in Tokyo, Japan.

Most durable fiddlers
Rolland S. Tapley retired as a violinist from the Boston Symphony Orchestra after playing for a reputedly unrivalled 58 years from February 1920 to 27 Aug 1978. Otto E. Funk, 62, walked 4165 miles *6702 km* from New York City to San Francisco, California playing his Hopf violin every step of the way westward. He arrived on 16 June 1929 after 183 days on the road.

The world's longest alphorn whose sound takes 70.6 milliseconds to emerge from the bowl after entry from the mouthpiece.

Drum *Largest*
The largest drum ever constructed was one 12 ft *3,65 m* in diameter weighing 600 lb *272 kg* for the Boston World Peace Jubilee of 1872.

Highest and lowest notes
The extremes of orchestral instruments (excluding the organ) range between a handbell tuned to g^v (6272 cycles/sec) and the sub-contrabass clarinet, which can reach C_{11} or 16.4 cycles/sec. The highest note on a standard pianoforte is c^v (4186 cycles/sec), which is also the violinist's limit. In 1873 a sub double bassoon able to reach $B_{111}\#$ or 14.6 cycles/sec was constructed but no surviving specimen is known. The extremes for the organ are g^{vi} (the sixth G above middle C) (12,544 cycles/sec) and C_{111} (8.12 cycles/sec) obtainable from ¾ in *1,9 cm* and 64 ft *19,5 m* pipes respectively.

Easiest and most difficult instruments
The American Music Conference announced in September 1977 that the easiest instrument is the ukulele, and the most difficult are the French horn and the oboe, which latter has been described as 'the ill woodwind that no-one blows good'.

ORCHESTRAS
Largest *Orchestra*
The most massive orchestra ever assembled was one of 20,100 at the Ullevaal Stadium, Oslo, of Norges Musikkorps Forbund bands from all Norway on 28 June 1964. On 17 June 1872, Johann Strauss the younger (1825–99) conducted an orchestra of 987 pieces supported by a choir of 20,000, at the World Peace Jubilee in Boston, Massachusetts, USA. The number of first violinists was 400.

Marching band
The largest marching band on record was one of 4524 including 1342 majorettes under direction of Danny Kaye at Dodger stadium, Los Angeles on 15 Apr 1985. The longest recorded musical march is one of 61 km *37.9 miles* from Lillehammer to Hamar, Norway in 15 hours when, on 10 May 1980, 26 of 35 members of the Trondheim Brass Band survived the playing of 135 marches.

Most Durable
The Cork Symphony Orchestra has performed

under the baton of Dr Aloys Fleischmann for 52 seasons (1935–86).

Most successful bands
Most British Open Brass band Championship titles (inst. 1853) have been won by the Black Dyke Mills Band which has won 22 times from 1862 to 1974 including three consecutive wins in 1972–4. The most successful pipe band is the Shotts & Dykehead Caledonian Pipe Band with their 10th world title in August 1980.

Greatest attendance *Classical*
The greatest attendance at any classical concert has been 400,000 for the Boston Pops Orchestra, conducted by Arthur Fiedler (1895–1979) at the Hatch Memorial Shell, Boston, Massachusetts, USA on 4 July 1976. At the 1978 concert the 83-year-old conductor was presented with a testimonial bearing a record 500,000 signatures.

Pop Festival
The greatest claimed attendance at a Pop Festival has been 600,000 for the 'Summer Jam' at Watkins Glen, New York, USA, on Sunday 29 July 1973 of whom about 150,000 actually paid. There were 12 'sound towers'. The attendance at the third Pop Festival at East Afton Farm, Freshwater, Isle of Wight, England on 30 Aug 1970 was claimed by its promoters, Fiery Creations, to be 400,000.

Single Performer
The largest paying audience ever attracted by a solo performer is an estimated 175,000 in the Maracaña Stadium, Rio de Janeiro, Brazil to hear Frank Sinatra (b. 1915) on 26 Jan 1980. Jean-Michel Jarre entertained an estimated 1.3 million at downtown Houston, Texas, USA at a free concert on 5 Apr 1986.

Greatest Choir
Excluding 'sing alongs' by stadium crowds, the greatest choir is one of 60,000 which sang in unison as a finale of a choral contest among 160,000 participants in Breslau, Germany on 2 Aug 1937.

COMPOSERS
Most prolific
The most prolific composer of all time was probably Georg Philipp Telemann (1681–1767) of Germany. He composed 12 complete sets of services (one cantata every Sunday) for a year, 78 services for special occasions, 40 operas, 600 to 700 orchestral suites, 44 Passions, plus concertos and chamber music. The most prolific symphonist was Johann Melchior Molter (*c.* 1695–1765) of Germany who wrote 169. Joseph Haydn (1732–1809) of Austria wrote 108 num-

bered symphonies many of which are regularly played today.

Most rapid

Among composers of the classical period the most prolific was Wolfgang Amadeus Mozart (1756–91) of Austria, who wrote *c.* 1000 operas, operettas, symphonies, violin sonatas, divertimenti, serenades, motets, concertos for piano and many other instruments, string quartets, other chamber music, masses and litanies, of which only 70 were published before he died aged 35. His opera *The Clemency of Titus* (1791) was written in 18 days and three symphonic masterpieces, *Symphony No. 39 in E flat major, Symphony No. 40 in G minor* and the *Jupiter Symphony No. 41 in C major,* were reputedly written in the space of 42 days in 1788. His overture *Don Giovanni* was written in full score at one sitting in Prague in 1787 and finished on the day of its opening performance.

Longest symphony

The longest of all single classical symphonies is the orchestral symphony No. 3 in D minor by Gustav Mahler (1860–1911) of Austria. This work, composed in 1896, requires a contralto, a women's and boys' choir in addition to a full orchestra. A full performance requires 1 hr 40 min, of which the first movement alone takes between 30 and 36 min. The Symphony No. 2 (the Gothic, or No. 1), composed in 1919–22 by Havergal Brian (1876–1972) was played by over 800 performers (4 brass bands) in the Victoria Hall, Hanley, Staffordshire on 21 May 1978 (conductor Trevor Stokes). A recent broadcast required 1 hr 45½ min. Brian wrote an even vaster work based on Shelley's 'Prometheus Unbound' lasting 4 hr 11 min but the full score has been missing since 1961. The symphony *Victory at Sea* written by Richard Rodgers and arranged by Robert Russell Bennett for NBC TV in 1952 lasted for 13 hr.

Longest piano composition

The longest continuous non-repetitious piano piece ever published has been 'The Well-Tuned Piano' by La Monte Young first presented by the Dia Art Foundation at the Concert Hall, Harrison St, New York City on 28 Feb 1980. The piece lasted 4 hr 12 min 10 sec. *Symphonic Variations,* composed by Kaikhosru Shapurji Sorabji (b. 1892) into 500 pages of close manuscript in 3 volumes in the 1930's, would last for 6 hours at the prescribed tempo.

Longest silence

The longest interval between the known composition of a major composer, and its performance in the manner intended, is from 3 Mar 1791 until 9 Oct 1982 (over 191 years), in the case of Mozart's *Organ Piece for a Clock,* a fugue fantasy in F minor (K 608), arranged by the organ builders Wm Hill & Son and Norman & Beard Ltd at Glyndebourne, East Sussex.

HIGHEST PAID MUSICIANS

Pianist

Wladziu Valentino Liberace (b. West Allis, Wisconsin, USA, 16 May 1917) has earned more than $2 million each 26 week season with a peak of $138,000 (*then £49,285*) for a single night's performance at Madison Square Garden, New York City, USA in 1954. The highest paid classical concert pianist was Ignace Jan Paderewski (1860–1941), Prime Minister of Poland (1919–20), who accumulated a fortune estimated at $5,000,000, of which $500,000 (*then £110,000*) was earned in a single season in 1922–23. The *nouveau riche* wife of a US industrialist once required him to play in her house behind a curtain. For concerts Artur Rubinstein (1887–

1982), between 1937 and 1976, commanded 70 per cent of the gross.

Greatest Span

Sergei Vassilievitch Rachmaninov (1873–1943) had a span of 12 white notes and could play a left hand chord of C, E♭, G, C, G.

Singer *Most Successful*

Of great fortunes earned by singers, the highest on record are those of Enrico Caruso (1873–1921), the Italian tenor, whose estate was about $9,000,000 (*then £1,875,000*) and the Italian-Spanish coloratura soprano Amelita Galli-Curci (1889–1963), who received about $3,000,000 (*£750,000*). In 1850, up to $653 was paid for a single seat at the concerts given in the United States by Johanna ('Jenny') Maria Lind, later Mrs Otto Goldschmidt (1820–87), the 'Swedish Nightingale'. She had a range from g to e^{III} of which the middle register is still regarded as unrivalled. The tenor Count John Francis McCormack (1884–1945) of Ireland gave up to 10 concerts to capacity audiences in a single season in New York City.

David Bowie drew a fee of $1.5 million (*then £960,000*) for a single show at the US Festival in Glen Helen Regional Park, San Bernardino County, California on 26 May 1983. The 4 man Van Halen rock band attracted a matching fee. The total attendance at Michael Jackson's 'Victory Tour' in the United States, July–Dec 1984, brought in a tour gross revenue of $81 million (*then £67.5 million*).

The most successful concert tour was that of Bruce Springsteen beginning in April 1984, which grossed an estimated $117 million. It ended with 4 nights in the Los Angeles Memorial Coliseum (capacity 85,000) with a gross of $5.8 million.

Worst

While no agreement exists as to the identity of history's greatest singer, there is unanimity on the worst. The excursions of the soprano Florence Foster Jenkins (1868–1944) into lieder and even high coloratura culminated on 25 Oct 1944 in her sell-out concert at the Carnegie Hall, New York, USA. The diva's (already high) high F was said to have been made higher in 1943 by a crash in a taxi. It is one of the tragedies of musicology that Madame Jenkins' *Clavelitos,* accompanied by Cosme McMoon, was never recorded for posterity.

OPERA

Longest

The longest of commonly performed operas is *Die Meistersinger von Nürnberg* by Wilhelm Richard Wagner (1813–83) of Germany. A normal uncut performance of this opera as performed by the Sadler's Wells company between 24 Aug and 19 Sept 1968 entailed 5 hr 15 min of music. *The Heretics* by Gabriel von Wayditch (1888–1969) a Hungarian-American, is orchestrated for 110 pieces and lasts 8½ hr.

Shortest

The shortest opera published was *The Deliverance of Theseus* by Darius Milhaud (b. 4 Sept 1892) first performed in 1928 which lasts for 7 min 27 sec.

Aria

The longest single aria, in the sense of an operatic solo, is Brünnhilde's immolation scene in Wagner's *Gotterdammerung*. A well-known recording of this has been precisely timed at 14 min 46 sec.

Opera houses *Largest*

The largest opera house in the world is the

Metropolitan Opera House, Lincoln Center, New York City, NY, USA, completed in September 1966 at a cost of $45,700,000 (*then £16,320,000*). It has a capacity of 3800 seats in an auditorium 451 ft *137 m* deep. The stage is 234 ft *71 m* wide and 146 ft *44,5 m* deep. The tallest opera house is one housed in a 42-storey building on Wacker Drive in Chicago, Illinois, USA.

Most tiers

The Teatro della Scala (La Scala) in Milan, Italy, shares with the Bolshoi Theatre in Moscow, USSR, the distinction of having the greatest number of tiers. Each has six, with the topmost being nicknamed the *Galiorka* by Russians.

Opera singers *Youngest and Oldest*

The youngest opera singer in the world has been Jeanette Gloria La Bianca, born in Buffalo, New York on 12 May 1934, who sang Rosina in *The Barber of Seville* at the Teatro dell'Opera, Rome, on 8 May 1950 aged 15 years 361 days, having appeared as Gilda in *Rigoletto* at Velletri 45 days earlier. Ginetta La Bianca was taught by Lucia Carlino and managed by Angelo Carlino. The tenor Giovanni Martinelli sang Emperor Altoum in *Turandot* in Seattle, Washington, USA on 4 Feb 1967 when aged 81.

Danshi Toyotake (b. 1 Aug 1891) has been singing *Gidayu* for 86 years.

Longest encore

The longest operatic encore, listed in the *Concise Oxford Dictionary of Opera,* was of the entire opera Cimarosa's' *Il Matrimonio Segreto* at its première in 1792. This was at the command of the Austro-Hungarian Emperor Leopold II (1790–92).

It was reported on 5 July 1983 that Placido Domingo received 83 curtain calls and was applauded for 1 hr 30 min after singing the lead in Puccini's *La Boheme* at the State Opera House in Vienna, Austria.

SONG

Oldest

The oldest known song is the *shaduf* chant, which has been sung since time immemorial by irrigation workers on the man-powered pivoted-rod bucket raisers of the Nile water mills (or *saqiyas*) in Egypt. The oldest known harmonized music performed today is the English song *Sumer is icumen in* which dates from *c.* 1240.

National anthems

The oldest national anthem is the *Kimigayo* of Japan, in which the words date from the 9th century. The anthem of Greece constitutes the first four verses of the Solomos poem, which has 158 stanzas. The shortest anthems are those of Japan, Jordan and San Marino, each with only four lines. Of the 23 wordless national anthems the oldest is that of Spain dating from 1770.

Longest rendering

'God Save the King' was played non-stop 16 or 17 times by a German military band on the platform of Rathenau Railway Station, Brandenburg, on the morning of 9 Feb 1909. The reason was that King Edward VII was struggling inside the train with the uniform of a German Field-Marshal before he could emerge.

Top songs of all time

The most frequently sung songs in English are *Happy Birthday to You* (based on the original *Good morning to all*), by Mildred and Patty S. Hill of New York (published in 1935 and in copyright until 2010); *For He's a Jolly Good Fellow* (originally the French *Malbrouk*), known at least as early as 1781, and *Auld Lang Syne* (originally the Strathspey *I fee'd a Lad at Michaelmass*), some words of which were written by Robert Burns (1759–96). *Happy Birthday* was sung in space by the Apollo IX astronauts on 8 Mar 1969.

Top selling sheet music

Sales of three non-copyright pieces are known to have exceeded 20,000,000 namely *The Old Folks at Home* by Stephen Foster (1855), *Listen to the Mocking Bird* (1855) and *The Blue Danube* (1867). Of copyright material the two topsellers are *Let Me Call You Sweetheart* (1910, by Whitson and Friedman) and *Till We Meet Again* (1918, by Egan and Whiting) each with some 6,000,000 by 1967. Other huge sellers have been *St Louis Blues*, *Stardust* and *Tea for Two*.

SONGWRITER
Most successful

In terms of sales of single records, the most successful of all song writers has been Paul McCartney (see also Recorded Sound, p. 96–97) formerly of the Beatles and now of Wings. Between 1962 and 1 Jan 1978 he wrote jointly or solo 43 songs which sold a million or more.

GUINNESS BOOK OF RECORDS HALL OF FAME

1986

Eurovision Contest

In the 29 contests since 1956 Luxembourg has won outright 5 times (1961–65–72–73–83). France has won 4 outright (1958–60–62–77) and shared 1 (1969). The UK won in 1967 (Sandie Shaw, *Puppet On A String*), 1976 (Brotherhood of Man, *Save Your Kisses For Me*), 1981 (Bucks Fizz, *Making Your Mind Up*) and shared in 1969 (Lulu, *Boom, Bang-a-Bang*). Norway twice scored zero with Jahn Teigan with *Mil etter mil* (1980) and Finn Kalvik with *Aldri i livet* (1981), but won the contest in 1985 with Bobbysox and *Let it Swing*.

HYMNS

Earliest

There are more than 950,000 Christian hymns in existence. The music and parts of the text of a hymn in the *Oxyrhynchus Papyri* from the 2nd century are the earliest known hymnody. The earliest exactly datable hymn is the *Heyr Himna Smíóur* (*Hear, the maker of heaven*) from 1208 by the Icelandic bard and chieftain Kolbeinn Tumason (1173–1208).

Longest and shortest

The longest hymn is *Hora novissima tempora pessima sunt; vigilemus* by Bernard of Cluny (12th century), which runs to 2966 lines. In English the longest is *The Sands of Time are sinking* by Mrs Anne Ross Cousin, née Cundell (1824–1906), which is in full 152 lines, though only 32 lines in the Methodist Hymn Book. The shortest hymn is the single verse in Long Metre *Be Present at our Table Lord*, anon., but attributed to 'J. Leland'.

Most prolific hymnists

Mrs Frances (Fanny) Jane Van Alstyne née

Crosby (1820–1915) (USA) wrote 8500 hymns although she had been blinded at the age of 6 weeks. She is reputed to have knocked off one hymn in 15 min. Charles Wesley (1707–88) wrote about 6000 hymns. In the seventh (1950) edition of *Hymns Ancient and Modern* the works of John Mason Neale (1818–66) appear 56 times.

BELLS

Oldest *World*

The oldest bell in the world is the tintinnabulum found in the Babylonian Palace of Nimrod in 1849 by Mr (later Sir) Austen Henry Layard (1817–94) dating from *c.* 1100 BC. The oldest known tower bell is one in Pisa, Italy dated MCVI (1106).

Great Britain

The fragile hand bell known as the Black or Iron Bell of St. Patrick is dated *c.* AD 450. The oldest tower bell in Great Britain is one of 1 cwt *50 kg* at St Botolph, Hardham, Sussex still in use but dated *ante* 1100. The oldest inscribed bell is the Gargate bell at Caversfield church, Oxfordshire and is dated *c.* 1200–1210. The oldest *dated* bell in England is one hanging in Lissett church, near Bridlington, Humberside discovered in October 1972 to bear the date MCCLIIII (1254).

Heaviest *World*

The heaviest bell in the world is the Tsar Kolokol, cast on 25 Nov 1735 in Moscow, USSR. It weighs 193 tons *196 tonnes*, measures 5,9 m *19 ft 4¼ in* diameter and 5,87 m *19 ft 3 in* high, and its greatest thickness is 24 in *60 cm*. The bell is cracked, and a fragment, weighing about 11 tons/*tonnes* was broken from it. The bell has stood, unrung, on a platform in the Kremlin, in Moscow, since 1836.

The heaviest bell in use is the Mingun bell, weighing 55,555 viss or *90.52 tons* with a diameter of 16 ft 8½ in *5,09 m* at the lip, in Mandalay, Burma, which is struck by a teak boom from the outside. It was cast at Mingun late in the reign of King Bodawpaya (1782–1819). The heaviest swinging bell in the world is the Petersglocke in the South-West tower of Cologne Cathedral, Germany, cast in 1923 with a diameter of 3,40 m *11 ft 1¾ in* weighing 25,4 tonnes *25.0 tons*.

Great Britain

The heaviest bell hung in Great Britain is 'Great Paul' in the south-west tower of St Paul's Cathedral, London, cast in 1881. It weighs 16 tons 14 cwt 2 qrs 19 lb net *17 002 kg* and has a diameter of 9 ft 6½ in *2,90 m* and sounds note E-flat. 'Big Ben', the hour bell in the clock tower of the House of Commons, was cast in 1858 and weighs 13 tons 10 cwt 3 qrs 15 lb *13 761 kg*. It is the most broadcast bell in the world and is note E.

Ringing Peals

A ringing peal is defined as a diatonic 'ring' of five or more bells hung for full-circle change ringing. Of 5500 rings so hung only 70 are outside the United Kingdom and Ireland. The heaviest ring in the world is that of 13 bells cast in 1938–39 for the Anglican Cathedral, Liverpool. The total bell weight is 16½ tons *16,76 tonnes* of which Emmanuel, the tenor bell note A, weighs 82 cwt 11 lb *4170,8 kg*.

Carillon *Largest*

The largest carillon (minimum of 23 bells) in the world is the Laura Spelman Rockefeller Memorial carillon in Riverside Church, New York City, USA with 74 bells weighing 102 tons. The bourdon, giving the note lower C, weighs 40,926 lb *18 563 kg*. This 18.27 ton bell, cast in England, with a diameter of 10 ft 2 in *3,09 cm* is the largest *tuned* bell in the world.

Heaviest

The heaviest carillon in Great Britain is in St Nicholas Church, Aberdeen, Scotland. It consists of 48 bells, the total weight of which is 25 tons 8 cwt 2 qrs 13 lb *25 838 kg*. The bourdon bell weighs 4 tons 9 cwt 3 qrs 26 lb *4571 kg* and is the note G-sharp.

Bell ringing

Eight bells have been rung to their full 'extent' (40,320 unrepeated changes of Plain Bob Major) only once without relays. This took place in a bell foundry at Loughborough, Leicestershire, beginning at 6.52 a.m. on 27 July 1963 and ending at 12.50 a.m. on 28 July, after 17 hr 58 min. The peal was composed by Kenneth Lewis of Altrincham, Greater Manchester, and the eight ringers were conducted by Robert B. Smith, aged 25, of Marple, Greater Manchester. Theoretically it would take 37 years 355 days to ring 12 bells (maximus) to their full extent of 479,001,600 changes. The greatest number of peals (minimum of 5040 changes, all in tower bells) rung in a year is 209 by Mark William Marshall of Ashford, Kent in 1973. The late George E. Fearn rang 2666 peals from 1928 to May 1974. Matthew Lakin (1801–1899) was a regular bell-ringer at Tetney Church near Grimsby for 84 years.

5. THEATRE

Origins

Theatre in Europe has its origins in Greek drama performed in honour of a god, usually Dionysus. The earliest amphitheatres date from the 5th century BC and the largest of all known is one at Megalopolis in central Greece, where the auditorium reached a height of 75 ft *23 m* and had a capacity of 17,000. The first stone-built theatre in Rome erected in 55 BC could accommodate 40,000 spectators.

Oldest *World*

The oldest indoor theatre in the world is the Teatro Olimpico in Vicenza, Italy. Designed in the Roman style by Andrea di Pietro, *alias* Palladio (1508–80), it was begun three months before his death and finished by his pupil Vicenzo Scamozzi (1552–1616) in 1583. It is preserved today in its original form.

Great Britain

The earliest London theatre was James Burbage's 'The Theatre', built in 1576 near Finsbury Fields, London. The oldest theatre still in use in Great Britain is The Royal, Bristol. The foundation stone was laid on 30 Nov 1764, and the theatre was opened on 30 May 1766 with a 'Concert of Music and a Specimen of Rhetorick'. The City Varieties Music Hall, Leeds was a singing room in 1762 and so claims to outdate the Theatre Royal. Actors were legally rogues and vagabonds until the passing of the Vagrancy Act in 1824. The oldest amateur dramatic society is the Old Stagers inaugurated in Canterbury, Kent in 1841. They have performed in every year except the years of World War I and II.

Largest *World*

The world's largest building used for theatre is the National People's Congress Building (*Ren min da hui tang*) on the west side of Tian an men Square, Peking, China. It was completed in 1959 and covers an area of 12.9 acres *5,2 ha*. The theatre seats 10,000 and is occasionally used as such as in 1964 for the play 'The East is Red'. The highest capacity purpose-built theatre is the Perth Entertainment Centre, Western Australia completed at a cost of $A 8.3 million (*then £4.2 million*) in November 1976 with 8003 seats. The stage area is 12,000 ft² *1148 m²*.

Great Britain

The highest capacity theatre is the Odeon, Hammersmith, Greater London, with 3483 seats. The largest theatre stage in Great Britain is the Opera House in Blackpool, Lancashire. It was re-built in July 1939 and has seats for 2975 people. Behind the 45 ft *14 m* wide proscenium arch, the stage is 110 ft *33 m* high, 60 ft *18 m* deep and 100 ft *30 m* wide, and there is dressing room accommodation for 200 artistes.

Britain's largest open air theatre is at Scarborough, North Yorkshire opened in 1932 with a seating capacity of 7000 plus standing room for 9000 and a 182 ft *55 m* long stage.

Smallest

The smallest regularly operated professional theatre in the world is the Piccolo in Juliusstrasse, Hamburg, West Germany. It was founded in 1970 and has a maximum capacity of 30 seats.

Largest amphitheatre

The largest amphitheatre ever built is the Flavian amphitheatre or Colosseum of Rome, Italy, completed in AD 80. Covering 5 acres *2 ha* and with a capacity of 87,000, it has a maximum length of 612 ft *187 m* and maximum width of 515 ft *175 m*.

Largest stage

The largest stage in the world is in the Ziegfeld Room Reno, Nevada with 176 ft *53,6 m* passerelle, three main lifts each capable of raising 1200 show girls (64¼ tons *65,3 tonnes*), two 62½ ft *19,1 m* circumference turntables and 800 spotlights.

Dame Anna Neagle, DBE who played the lead role in *Charlie Girl* for 2062 performances. (Pictorial Press).

Longest runs

The longest continuous run of any show in the world is *The Mousetrap* by Dame Agatha Mary Clarissa Christie, DBE (née Miller, later Lady Mallowan) (1890–1976). This thriller opened on 25 Nov 1952, at the Ambassadors Theatre (capacity 453) and moved after 8862 performances 'down the road' to St Martin's Theatre on 25 Mar 1974. The 30th Anniversary performance on 25 Nov 1982 was the 12,481st. The Vicksburg Theatre Guild of Vicksburg, Mississippi, USA have been playing the melodrama *Gold in the Hills*, by J. Frank Davis discontinuously but every season since 1936.

Revue

The greatest number of performances of any theatrical presentation is 45,051 (to 9 Aug 1985) in the case of *The Golden Horseshoe Revue*—a show staged at Disneyland Park, Anaheim, California, USA. It started on 16 July 1955 and has been seen by 16 million people. The three main performers Fulton Burley, Dick Hardwick and Betty Taylor play as many as five houses a day in a routine lasting 45 min.

Broadway

The long-run record for any Broadway show was set on 29 Sept 1983 with the 3389th performance of *Chorus Line*. It opened on 25 July 1975 and had been seen by an estimated 22,300,000 people with a box office receipt of $260 million. The off-Broadway musical show *The Fantasticks* by Tom Jones and Harvey Schmidt achieved its 10,500th performance at the Sullivan Street Playhouse, Greenwich Village, New York City on 30 July 1985. It has been played in a record 8681 productions in 67 countries.

Musical shows

The longest-running musical show ever performed in Britain was *The Black and White Minstrel Show* later *Magic of the Minstrels*. The aggregate but discontinuous number of performances was 6464 with a total attendance of 7,794,552. The show opened at the Victoria Palace, London on 25 May 1962 and closed on 4 Nov 1972. It re-opened for a season in June 1973 at the New Victoria and finally closed on 8 Dec 1973.

Jesus Christ Superstar, which opened at Palace Theatre, London on 8 Aug 1972, closed on 23 Aug 1980 after 3357 performances having played to 2 million people with box office receipts of £7 million. By 1984 it had been produced in 37 other countries.

Comedy

The British record for long running comedy is set by *No Sex Please We're British* which reaches its 6000th performance in its 15th year in 1986, having opened at The Strand Theatre on 3 June 1971 and transferred to the Garrick Theatre on 18 Jan 1982. It's director Allan Davis has had his name in lights from the start.

Shortest runs *World*

The shortest run on record was that of *The Intimate Revue* at the Duchess Theatre, London, on 11 Mar 1930. Anything which could go wrong did. With scene changes taking up to 20 min apiece, the management scrapped seven scenes to get the finale on before midnight. The run was described as 'half a performance'.

Broadway

The opening and closing nights of many Broadway shows have coincided. Spectacular failures are known as 'turkeys' of which there were 11 in 1978–79. *Frankenstein*, which opened and closed on Broadway on 4 Jan 1981, lost an estimated $2 million but *A Doll's Life* (23–26 Sept 1982) lost close to $4 million.

Attendance *Lowest*

The ultimate in low attendances was in December 1983 when the comedy *Bag* in Grantham, Lincolnshire opened to a nil attendance.

Broadway producer *Youngest*

Margo Feiden (Margo Eden) (b. New York, 2 Dec 1944) produced the musical *Peter Pan*, which opened on 3 Apr 1961 when she was 16 years 5 months old. She wrote *Out Brief Candle*, which opened on 18 Aug 1962. She is now a leading art dealer.

One-man shows

The longest run of one-man shows is 849 by Victor Borge (b. Copenhagen, 3 Jan 1909) in his *Comedy in Music* from 2 Oct 1953 to 21 Jan 1956 at the Golden Theater, Broadway, New York City. The world aggregate record for one-man shows is 1700 performances of *Brief Lives* by Roy Dotrice (b. Guernsey, 26 May 1923) including 400 straight at the Mayfair Theatre, London ending on 20 July 1974. He was on stage for more than 2½ hr per performance of this 17th century monologue and required 3 hr for make up and 1 hr for removal of make-up so aggregating 40 weeks in the chair.

Actors and actresses *Most durable*

Kanmi Fujiyama (b. 1929) played the lead role in 10,288 performances by the comedy company Sochiku Shikigeki from Nov 1966 to June 1983. Dame Anna Neagle, DBE (b. 20 Oct 1904) played the lead role in *Charlie Girl* at the Adelphi Theatre, London for 2062 of 2202 performances between 15 Dec 1965 and 27 Mar 1971. She played the role a further 327 times in 327 performances in Australasia. Frances Etheridge has played Lizzie, the housekeeper, in *Gold in the Hills* (see Longest Runs) more than 660 times over a span of 47 years since 1936. Jack Howarth MBE (1896–1984) was an actor on the stage and in television for 76 years from 1907 until his last appearance after 23 years as Albert Tatlock in *Coronation Street* on 25 Jan 1984.

Most roles

The greatest recorded number of theatrical, film and television roles is 3350 from 1951 to May 1985 by Jan Leighton (US).

Longest play

The longest recorded theatrical production has been 'The Acting Life' staged in the Tom Mann Theatre, Sydney, Australia on 17–18 Mar 1984 with a cast of 10. The production required 19½ hours or 21 hours with intervals.

Shakespeare

The first all-amateur company to have staged all 37 of Shakespeare's plays was The Southsea Shakespeare Actors, Hampshire, England (founded 1947) in October 1966 when, under their amateur director, K. Edmonds Gateley MBE, they presented *Cymbeline*. The longest is *Hamlet* with 4042 lines and 29,551 words. Of Shakespeare's 1277 speaking parts the longest is Hamlet with 11,610 words.

Chorus line *Longest*

The longest chorus line in performing history were up to 120 in some of the early Ziegfeld's Follies. In the finale of *Chorus Line* on the night of 29 Sept 1983 when it broke the record as the longest-running Broadway show ever, 332 top-hatted 'strutters' performed on stage.

Cabaret *Highest fee*

The highest paid entertainer is Dolly Parton with up to $400,000 (£333,000) per live concert. Johnny Carson's fee for the non-televised Sears Roebuck Centenary Gala in Oct 1984 was set at 1 million dollars (£833,000).

Ice shows

Holiday on Ice Production Inc, founded by Morris Chalfen in 1945, stages the world's most costly live entertainment with up to seven productions playing simultaneously in several of 75 countries drawing 20,000,000 spectators paying $40 million (£33.3 million) in a year. The total skating and other staff exceeds 900. The most prolific producer of Ice Shows was Gerald Palmer (1908–83) with 137 since 1945 including 34 consecutive shows at Empire Pool, Wembley, London with attendances up to 850,000. Hazel Wendy Jolly (b. 1933) has appeared in the Wembley Winter Pantomime for 27 years.

Most ardent theatregoers

Dr H. Howard Hughes (b. 1902) Professor Emeritus of Texas Wesleyan College, Fort Worth, Texas, has attended 5512 shows in the period 1956–83. Britain's leading 'first nighter' Edward Sutro MC (1900–78) saw 3000 first night productions in 1916–56 and possibly more than 5000 in his 60 years of theatre-going. The highest precisely recorded number of theatre attendances in Britain is 3687 shows in 33 years from 28 Mar 1953 to 28 Mar 1986 by John Iles of Salisbury, Wiltshire. He estimates he has travelled 151,642 miles *244 043 km* and seen 186,955 performers in 9655 hours (over 57 weeks) inside theatres.

Arts Festival

The world's largest arts festival is the annual Edinburgh Festival Fringe (instituted in 1959). In 1983, 454 groups gave 6886 performances of 875 shows between 21 Aug and 10 Sept. Prof. Gerald Berkowitz of Northern Illinois University, USA attended a record 145 separate performances at the 1979 Festival from 15 Aug–8 Sept.

Fashion shows

The most prolific producer and most durable commentator of fashion shows is Adalene Ross of San Francisco, California with totals over 4702 in both categories to mid-1986.

Professional wrestling

The professional wrestler who has received most for a single bout has been Kanii Antonio Inoki of Japan on 26 Jun 1976. He received $2 million for the drawn wrestler v boxer bout against Muhammad Ali in the Budokan Arena, Tokyo. Lou Thesz has won 7 of the world's many 'world' titles. 'Fabulous' Moolah won major US women's alliance titles over the longest span starting in 1956. The heaviest ever wrestler has been William J. Cobb of Macon, Georgia, USA (b. 1926), who was billed in 1962 as the 802 lb *363 kg* (57 st 4 lb) 'Happy' Humphrey. Ed 'Strangler' Lewis (1890–1966) *né* Robert H. Friedrich, fought 6200 bouts in 44 years losing only 33 matches. He won world titles in 1921, 1922, 1928 and 1931–32. See also Ch 12 Heaviest Sportsmen.

6. RECORDED SOUND

Origins

The gramophone (phonograph) was first *conceived* by Charles Cros (1842–88) a French poet and scientist, who described his idea in sealed papers deposited in the French Academy of Sciences on 30 Apr 1877. However the realisation of a practical device was first *achieved* by Thomas Alva Edison (1847–1931) of the USA. The first successful wax cylinder machine was constructed by his mechanic, John Kruesi on 4–6 Dec 1877, demonstrated on 7 Dec and patented

Dolly Parton, the highest paid 'live' entertainer the world has ever known. (Pictorial Press). (*Below*) Part of the world's largest arts festival, The Edinburgh Fringe—seen here in action in front of St Giles Cathedral on the Royal Mile. (Scottish Tourist Board).

The Beatles whose many achievements include the accolade 'Most successful group of all-time'.

on 19 Feb 1878. The horizontal disc was introduced by Emile Berliner (1851–1929).

Recordings *Earliest*

The earliest birthdate of anyone whose voice is recorded is Alfred, first Baron Tennyson (born 6 Aug 1809). The earliest born singer was Peter Schram, the Danish baritone of whom a cylinder was made in the role of Don Giovanni on his 70th birthday on 5 Sept 1889.

Tape Recording

Magnetic recording was invented by Valdemar Poulsen (1869–1942) of Denmark with his steel wire Telegraphone in 1898 (US Pat. No. 661619). Fritz Pfleumer (German patent 500900) introduced tape in 1928. Tapes were first used at the Blattner Studios, Elstree, Hertfordshire in 1929. Plastic tapes were devised by BASF of Germany in 1932–35, but were not marketed until 1950 by Recording Associates of New York. In April 1983 Olympic Optical Industry Co. of Japan marketed a micro-cassette recorder 10,7 ×

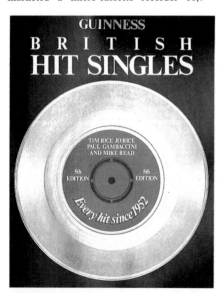

GUINNESS BOOKS ALSO PUBLISH THE GUINNESS BOOK OF BRITISH HIT ALBUMS (EDITION 2), HITS OF THE 60'S, 500 NO I HITS AND THE GUINNESS HITS CHALLENGE.

5,1 × 1,4 cm *4.2 × 2 × 0.55 in* weighing 125 g *4.4 oz.*

Records *Oldest*

The BBC record library contains over 1,000,000 records, including 5250 with no known matrix. The oldest records in the library are white wax cylinders dating from 1888. The earliest commercial disc recording was manufactured in 1895.

Record *Smallest*

The smallest functional gramophone record is one 1⅜ in *3,5 cm* in diameter of 'God Save the King' of which 250 were made by HMV Record Co in 1924.

Phonographic Identification

Dr Arthur B. Lintgen (b. 1932) of Rydal, Pennsylvania, USA has an as yet unique and proven ability to identify the music on phonograph records purely by visual inspection without hearing a note.

Jazz records *Earliest*

The earliest jazz record made was *Indiana* and *The Dark Town Strutters Ball*, recorded for the Columbia label in New York City, NY, USA, on or about 30 Jan 1917, by the Original Dixieland Jazz Band, led by Dominick (Nick) James La Rocca (1889–1961). This was released on 31 May 1917. The first jazz record to be released was the ODJB's *Livery Stable Blues* (recorded 24 Feb), backed by *The Dixie Jass Band One-Step* (recorded 26 Feb), released by Victor on 7 Mar 1917.

Solo recording artist *Most successful*

No independently audited figures have ever been published for Elvis Aron Presley (1935–77). In view of Presley's worldwide tally of over 170 major hits on singles and over 80 top-selling albums from 1956 continuing after his death, it may be assumed that it was he who must have succeeded Bing Crosby as the top-selling solo artist of all-time. CBS Records reported in August 1983 that sales of albums by Julio Iglesias (b. 1943) in 6 languages had surpassed 100,000,000.

On 9 June 1960 the Hollywood Chamber of Commerce presented Harry Lillis (*alias* Bing) Crosby, Jr (1904–77) with a platinum disc to commemorate the alleged sale of 200,000,000 records from the 2600 singles and 125 albums he had recorded. On 15 Sept 1970 he received a second platinum disc when Decca claimed a sale of 300,650,000 discs. No independently audited figures of his global life-time sales from his royalty reports have ever been published and experts regard figures as high as this before the industry became highly developed as exaggerated.

Group *Most successful*

The singers with the greatest sales of any group have been the Beatles. This group from Liverpool, Merseyside, comprised George Harrison, MBE (b. 25 Feb 1943), John Ono (formerly John Winston) Lennon, MBE (b. 9 Oct 1940–k. 8 Dec 1980), James Paul McCartney, MBE (b. 18 June 1942) and Richard Starkey, MBE *alias* Ringo Starr (b. 7 July 1940). The all-time Beatles sales by May 1985 have been estimated by EMI at over 1000 million discs and tapes.

All 4 ex-Beatles sold many million further records as solo artists. Since their break-up in 1970, it is estimated that the most successful group in the world in terms of record sales is the Swedish foursome ABBA (Agnetha Faltskog, Anni-Frid Lyngstad, Bjorn Ulvaeus and Benny Andersson) with a total of 215 million discs and tapes by May 1985.

Golden discs *Earliest*

The earliest recorded piece eventually to aggregate a total sale of a million copies were performances by Enrico Caruso (b. Naples, Italy, 1873, and d. 2 Aug 1921) of the aria *Vesti la giubba* (*On with the Motley*) from the opera *I Pagliacci* by Ruggiero Leoncavallo (1858–1919), the earliest version of which was recorded with piano on 12 Nov 1902. The first single recording to surpass the million mark was Alma Gluck's *Carry me back to old Virginny* on the Red Seal Victor label on the 12-inch *30,48 cm* single faced (later backed) record 74420. The first actual golden disc was one sprayed by RCA Victor for the US trombonist and band-leader Alton 'Glenn' Miller (1904–44) for his *Chattanooga Choo Choo* on 10 Feb 1942.

Golden discs *Most*

The only *audited* measure of gold, platinum and multiplatinum singles and albums within the United States, is certification by the Recording Industry Association of America introduced 14 Mar 1958. Out of the 2,582 RIAA awards made to 1 Jan 1985, The Beatles with 47 (plus one with Billy Preston) have most for a group. McCartney has 27 more awards outside the group and with Wings (including one with Stevie Wonder and one with Michael Jackson). The most awards to an individual is 51 to Elvis Presley (1935–77) spanning 1958 to 1 Jan 1986. Globally however Presley's total of million-selling singles has been authoritatively put at 'approaching 80'.

Song *Most recorded*

Three songs have each been recorded over 1000 times—*Yesterday* written by Paul McCartney and John Lennon (see above) with 1600 versions between 1965 and 1 Jan 1986; *Tie A Yellow Ribbon Round the old Oak Tree* written by Irwin Levine and L. Russell Brown with more than 1200 from 1973 to 1 Apr 1985; and *My Way*, music by Jacques Revaux and the late Claude François and the English lyrics by Paul Anka (b. Ottawa, 30 July 1941).

UK TOP 10 BEST SELLING SINGLES

Figures supplied by Gallup

1. **Do They Know Its Christmas** BAND AID
2. **Mull Of Kintyre** WINGS
3. **Rivers Of Babylon/Brown Girl In The Ring** BONEY M
4. **You're The One That I Want** JOHN TRAVOLTA & OLIVIA NEWTON JOHN
5. **Relax** FRANKIE GOES TO HOLLYWOOD
6. **I Just Called To Say I Love You** STEVIE WONDER
7. **Two Tribes** FRANKIE GOES TO HOLLYWOOD
8. **She Loves You** THE BEATLES
9. **I Want To Hold Your Hand** THE BEATLES
10. **Mary's Boy Child** BONEY M

Number 13 in this chart would be WHITE CHRISTMAS by *BING CROSBY*. Sales figures from its release until the inception of the Singles charts in 1952 are not recorded, therefore not expressing accurately the popularity of this single.

Recordings *Most*

Miss Lata Mangeshker (b. 1928) between 1948 and 1985 has reportedly recorded not less than 30,000 solo, duet and chorus backed songs in 20 Indian languages. She frequently had 5 sessions in a day and has 'backed' more than 2000 films.

Biggest sellers *Singles*

The greatest seller of any gramophone record to date is *White Christmas* by Irving Berlin (b. Israel Bailin, at Tyumen, Russia, 11 May 1888) with 30,000,000 for the Crosby single (recorded 29 May 1942) and more than 100,000,000 in other versions. The highest claim for any 'pop' record is an unaudited 25,000,000 for *Rock Around the Clock*, copyrighted in 1953 by James E. Myers under the name Jimmy DeKnight and the late Max C. Freedmann and recorded on 12 Apr 1954 by Bill Haley (1927–1981) and the Comets. The top-selling British record of all-time is *I Want to Hold Your Hand* by the Beatles, released in 1963, with world sales of over 13,000,000. The top selling single of all time in the United Kingdom is *Do They Know It's Christmas* written and produced by Bob Geldof and Midge Ure with 31.6 million by May 1986 with a further 7¾ million world wide. The profits were in aid of the Ethiopian Famine Relief Fund and are now estimated to be over £60 million.

Biggest sellers *Albums*

The best selling album of all time is *Thriller* by Michael Joseph Jackson (b. Gary, Indiana, 29 Aug 1958) with global sales of 38.5 million copies by 1 Aug 1985. The best selling album by British performers is considered to be *Dark Side Of The Moon* recorded by Pink Floyd (Dave Gilmour, Nick Mason, Roger Waters, and Rick Wright), in June 1972–January 1973 in London, with sales of over 17 million by May 1985.

The charts—*US Singles*

Singles record charts were first published by *Billboard* on 20 July 1940 when the No. 1 was *I'll Never Smile Again* by Tommy Dorsey (b. 19 Nov 1905, d. 26 Nov 1956). Three discs have stayed top for a record 13 consecutive weeks—*Frenesi* by Artie Shaw from December 1940; *I've Heard that Song Before* by Harry James from February 1943 and *Goodnight Irene* by Gordon Jenkins and the Weavers from August 1950. *Tainted Love* by Soft Cell stayed on the chart for 43 consecutive weeks from January 1982. The Beatles have had most No. 1 records (21) and Elvis Presley has had most hit singles on Billboard's Hot 100—149 from 1956 to May 1986.

US Albums

Billboard first published an album chart on 15 Mar 1945 when the No. 1 was *King Cole Trio* featuring Nat 'King' Cole (b. 17 Mar 1919, d. 15 Feb 1965). *South Pacific* was No. 1 for 69 weeks (non-consecutive) from May 1949. *Dark Side of The Moon* by Pink Floyd enjoyed its 621st week on the *Billboard* charts in May 1986. The Beatles had most No. 1's (15) and Presley most hit albums (93 from 1956 to May 1986).

UK Singles

Singles record charts were first published in Britain on 14 Nov 1952 by *New Musical Express*. *I Believe* by Frankie Laine (b. 30 Mar 1913) held No. 1 position for 18 weeks (non-consecutive) from April 1953, with *Rose Marie* by Slim Whitman (b. 20 Jan 1924) the consecutive record holder with 11 weeks from July 1955. The longest stay has been the 122 weeks of *My Way* by Francis Albert Sinatra (b. 12 Dec 1917) in 10 separate runs from 2 Apr 1969 into 1984. The record for an uninterrupted stay is 56 weeks for Engelbert Humperdinck's *Release Me* from 26 Jan 1967. The Beatles and Presley hold the record for most No. 1 hits with 17 each, with Presley having an overall record of 106 hits in the UK singles chart from 1956 to May 1985.

UK Albums

The first British album chart was published on 8 Nov 1958 by *Melody Maker*. The first No. 1 LP was the film soundtrack *South Pacific* which held the position for a record 70 consecutive weeks and eventually accumulated a record 115 weeks at No. 1. The album with the most total weeks on chart is *Bat Out Of Hell* by Meat Loaf with 384 weeks by early 1986. The Beatles have had most No. 1 albums—12; and Elvis Presley the most hit albums—90.

Albums *Fastest selling*

The fastest selling record of all time is *John Fitzgerald Kennedy—A Memorial Album* (Premium Albums), recorded on 22 Nov 1963, the day of Mr Kennedy's assassination, which sold 4,000,000 copies at 99 cents (*then 35 p*) in six days (7–12 Dec 1963), thus ironically beating the previous speed record set by the satirical LP *The First Family* in 1962–3. The fastest selling British record is the Beatles' double album *The Beatles* (Apple) with 'nearly 2 million' in its first week in November 1968.

Richard Clayderman (b. Philippe Pages, 1954) of France is reputed to have sold 25 million LP's in the 3 years to Jan 1983 for which he collected 127 gold and 23 platinum records.

Advance sales

The greatest advance sale was 2,100,000 for *Can't Buy Me Love* by the Beatles, released in the United States on 16 Mar 1964. The Beatles also equalled their British record of 1,000,000 advance sales, set by *I Want to Hold Your Hand* (Parlophone transferred to Apple, Aug 1968) on 29 Nov 1963, with this same record on 20 Mar 1964. The UK record for advance sales of an LP is 1,000,000 for the Epic album *Super Trouper* by ABBA released in November 1980.

Pop Group *Loudest*

The amplification at *The Who* concert at Charlton Athletic Football Ground, London on 31 May 1976 provided by a Tasco PA System had a total power of 76,000 watts from eighty 800 W Crown DC 300 A Amplifiers and twenty 600 W Phase Linear 200's. The readings at 50 m *164 ft* from the front of the sound system were 120 db. Sound engineer Rob Cowlyn with Duran Duran claimed that the audience's level of anticipatory screaming in Australia in November 1983 exceeded 120 dB *before* the group came on stage. The US group Manowar, a heavy metal rock band, claim to have measured a reading of 160 dB in October 1984 is unsupportable. *Exposure to high noise levels is known to cause PSH—Permanent Shift of Hearing or partial up to total instant deafness.*

Grammy Awards

The record number of Grammy awards in a year is 8 by Michael Joseph Jackson in 1984 (see also *Biggest Seller Albums*). The all-time record is 25 by the orchestral conductor Sir Georg Solti KBE (b. Budapest, 21 Oct 1912) which he has won since 1958.

7. Cinema

FILMS

Origins

The earliest motion pictures ever taken were by Louis Aimé Augustin Le Prince (1842–1890). He was attested to have achieved dim moving

Bat Out Of Hell by Meatloaf stayed in the UK album charts for a record 384 weeks. (London Features International).

outlines on a whitewashed wall at the Institute for the Deaf, Washington Heights, New York, USA as early as 1885–87. The earliest surviving film (sensitized 2⅛ in *53,9 mm* wide paper roll) is from his camera, patented in Britain on 16 Nov 1888, taken in early October 1888 of the garden of his father-in-law, Joseph Whitley in Roundhay, Leeds, West Yorkshire at 10 to 12 frames per second. The first commercial presentation of *motion pictures* was at Holland Bros' Kinetoscope Parlour at 1155 Broadway, New York City on 14 April 1894. Viewers could see 5 films for 25 cents or 10 for 50 cents from a double row of Kinetoscopes developed by William Kennedy Laurie Dickson (1860–1935) assistant to Thomas Alva Edison (1847–1931) in 1889–91. The earliest publicly presented film on a *screen* was *La Sortie de Ouvriers de l'Usine Lumière* probably shot in August or September 1894 in Lyon, France. It was exhibited at 44 Rue de Rennes, Paris on 22 Mar 1895 by the Lumière Brothers, Auguste Marie Louis Nicholas (1862–1954) and Louis Jean (1864–1948).

Earliest 'Talkie'

The earliest sound-on-film motion picture was achieved by Eugene Augustin Lauste (b. Paris 17 Jan 1857) who patented his process on 11 Aug 1906 and produced a workable system using a string galvanometer in 1910 at Benedict Road, Stockwell, London. The earliest public presentation of sound on film was by the Tri-ergon process at the Alhambra cinema, Berlin, Germany on 17 Sept 1922.

Most expensive film

The highest ever budgeted film has been *Star Trek* which received its world première in Washington D.C. on 6 Dec 1979. Paramount Studios stated that the cost of this space epic directed by Robert Wise and produced by Gene Roddenberry, was $46 million (*then £21 million*). A figure of $60 million has been attributed to *Superman II* but never substantiated.

The biggest flop in cinema history was *Heaven's Gate*. It's losses sent United Artists out of business as an independent studio.

Meryl Streep as she appeared in *Out of Africa* for which she was paid $3 million.

Least expensive film
Cecil Hepworth's highly successful release of 1905 *Rescued by Rover* cost £7.69 (*then $37.40*).

Most expensive film rights
The highest price ever paid for film rights is $9,500,000 (*then £4,950,000*) announced on 20 Jan 1978 by Columbia for *Annie*, the Broadway Musical by Charles Strouse starring Andrea McCardle, Dorothy Loudon and Reid Shelton.

Longest film
The longest film ever premièred was the 48 hr long *The Longest Most Meaningless Movie in the World* in 1970. It was British made and later heavily cut to 90 min.

Highest box office gross
The box office gross championship for films is highly vulnerable to inflated ticket prices. Calculations based on the 1983 value of the dollar shows that *Gone With the Wind* with Clark Gable (1901–1960) and Vivien Leigh (1913–1967) released in 1939 is unsurpassed at $312 million. The highest numerical (as opposed to value) dollar champion is Steven Spielberg's *ET: The Extra-Terrestrial*, released on 11 June 1982, and which by 2 Jan 1983 had grossed $322 million (*then £208 million*).

On 29 May 1983 *The Return of the Jedi* (20th Century Fox) grossed $8,440,105 (*£5,445,200*) for a single day record, and a record $6,219,929 (*£4,013,000*) for its opening day on 25 May 1985.

Largest loss
On 13 May 1981 Steven Bach was fired by United Artists after the loss (shooting, studio overheads and distribution) on *Heaven's Gate* reached $57 million (*£29,000,000*).

Most violent
A study on the portrayal of violence showed the worst film on record was *Red Dawn*, released in the US in 1984, with acts of violence occurring at the rate of 134 per hour (2.23 per min).

Highest earnings *By an actor*
The highest rate of pay in cinema history is that paid to Sylvester Stallone (b. New York City, 6 July 1946) with $12 million for *Rocky IV* plus a, as yet uncomputed, share of box office. In January 1986 Hollywood sources predicted that his salary plus profit share from *Rambo* would reach $20 million. The highest paid actress in 1985 was Meryl Streep (b. Summit, N.J., 1949) with $3 million for her role in *Out of Africa*.

By a Stuntman
Dar Robinson was paid $100,000 (*then £45,500*) for the 1100 ft *335 m* leap from the CN Tower, Toronto in Nov 1979 for *High Point*. His parachute opened at only 300 ft *91 m* above the ground.

Longest Series
Japan's *Tora-San* films have now stretched from *Tora-San I* in August 1968 to *Tora-San XXXII* in 1983 with Kiyoshi Atsumi (b. 1929) starring in each for Shochiku Co.

Character most portrayed
The character most frequently recurring on the screen is Sherlock Holmes, created by Sir Arthur Conan Doyle (1859–1930). Sixty-seven actors portrayed him in 186 films between 1900 and 1984.

Largest studios
The largest complex of film studios in the world are those at Universal City, L.A., California. The Back Lot contains 561 buildings and there are 34 sound stages on the 420 acre *170 ha* site.

Most Prolific Director
Allan Dwan (1885–1981) the Canadian born pioneer directed, from 1909 to the early 'sixties, more than 400 films.

Oscars *Most*
Walter (Walt) Elias Disney (1901–66) won more 'Oscars'—the awards of the United States Academy of Motion Picture Arts and Sciences, instituted on 16 May 1929 and named after Mr Oscar Pierce of Texas, USA—than any other person. The physical count comprises 20 statuettes, and 12 other plaques and certificates including posthumous awards. The only person to win four Oscars in a starring rôle has been Miss Katharine Hepburn, formerly Mrs Ludlow Ogden Smith (b. Hartford, Conn., 9 Nov 1909) in *Morning Glory* (1932–3), *Guess Who's Coming to Dinner* (1967), *The Lion in Winter* (1968) and *On Golden Pond* (1981). She was nominated 12 times. Only 4 actors have won two Oscars in starring rôles—Frederic March in 1931/32 and 1946, Spencer Tracy in 1937 and 1938, Gary Cooper in 1941 and 1952, and Marlon Brando in 1954 and 1972. Edith Head (Mrs Wiard B. Ihnen) (d. 1981) won 8 individual awards for costume design. The film with most awards has been *Ben Hur* (1959) with 11. The film with the highest number of nominations was *All About Eve* (1950) with 14. It won six. The youngest ever winner was Shirley Temple (b. 24 Apr 1928) aged 5 with her honorary Oscar, and the oldest George Burns, (b. 20 Jan 1896) aged 80 for *The Sunshine Boys* in 1976.

Versatility showbusiness awards

The only 3 performers to have won Oscars, Emmy, Tony and Grammy awards have been Helen Hayes (b. 1900) in 1932–1976; Richard Rodgers (1902–1979), composer of musicals and Rita Moreno (b. 1931) in 1961–1977. Barbra Streisand (b. 24 Apr 1942 in Brooklyn, NY) received Oscar, Grammy and Emmy awards in addition to a special 'Star of the Decade' Tony award.

CINEMAS

Earliest

The earliest structure designed and exclusively used for exhibiting projected films is believed to be one erected at the Atlanta Show, Georgia USA in October 1895 to exhibit C. F. Jenkins' phantoscope. The earliest cinema constructed in Great Britain was built without permission at Olympia, London, to house the 'Theatregraph' promoted by Robert William Paul (1869–1943). This was completed by 16 Apr 1896.

Largest *World*

The largest cinema in the world is the Radio City Music Hall, New York City, opened on 27 Dec 1932 with 5945 (now 5882) seats. The Roxy, opened in New York City on 11 March 1927 had 6214 (later 5869) seats but was closed on 29 Mar 1960. Cineplex, opened at the Toronto Eaton Centre, Canada on 19 Apr 1979 has 18 separate theatres with an aggregate capacity of 1700.

Great Britain

Great Britain's largest cinema is the Odeon Theatre, Hammersmith, London, with 3483 seats. The Playhouse, Glasgow had 4235 seats.

Drive-In

The world's largest drive-in cinema is Loew's Open Air at Lynn, Mass., USA with a capacity of 5000 cars. The earliest, at Wilson Boulevard, Camden, New Jersey opened on 6 June 1933.

Most cinemas

San Marino has more cinemas per total population than any other country in the world, with 1 cinema for every 1512 inhabitants. Saudi Arabia (population 8.4 million) has no cinemas. Ascension Island has a record 733 cinema seats for a population of 971 (31 Dec 1981).

Highest cinema going

The Chinese ministry of culture reported in September 1984 that there were 27,000 million cinema attendances in 1983—or nearly 27 per person per annum. The Soviet Union claims to have most cinemas in the world, with 163,400 in 1974, but this includes buildings merely equipped with even 16 mm projectors. The USA has 16,965 actual cinemas (1979). The number of cinemas in the UK reached a peak 4714 in 1944 declining to 1242 screens by May 1985. The average weekly admissions had declined from 33,420,000 in 1944 to 1,221,900 by May 1985.

Biggest screen

The permanently installed cinema screen with the largest area is one of 92 ft 9 in × 70 ft 6 in *28,28 × 21,48 m* installed in the Keong Emas Imax Theatre, Taman Mini Park, Jakarta, Indonesia opened on 20 Apr 1984. It was made by Harkness Screens Ltd at Boreham Wood, Herts. A temporary screen 297 ft × 33 ft *90,5 × 10 m* was used at the 1937 Paris Exposition.

Most films seen

Albert E. Van Schmus (b. 1921) saw 16,945 films in 32 years (1949–1982) as a rater for Motion Picture Association of America Inc.

8. RADIO BROADCASTING

Origins

The earliest description of a radio transmission system was written by Dr Mahlon Loomis (USA) (b. Fulton County, NY, 21 July 1826) on 21 July 1864 and demonstrated between two kites more than 14 miles *22 km* apart at Bear's Den, Loudoun County, Virginia in October 1866. He received US patent No. 129,971 entitled Improvement in Telegraphing on 20 July 1872. He died in 1886.

Earliest patent

The first patent for a system of communication by means of electro-magnetic waves, numbered No. 12039, was granted on 2 June 1896 to the Italian-Irish Marchese Guglielmo Marconi, GCVO (Hon) (1874–1937). A public demonstration of wireless transmission of speech was, however, given in the town square of Murray, Kentucky, USA in 1892 by Nathan B. Stubblefield. He died destitute on 28 March 1928. The first permanent wireless installation was at The Needles on the Isle of Wight, by Marconi's Wireless Telegraph Co., Ltd., in November 1896.

Earliest broadcast *World*

The world's first advertised broadcast was made on 24 Dec 1906 by the Canadian born Prof Reginald Aubrey Fessenden (1868–1932) from the 420 ft *128 m* mast of the National Electric Signalling Company at Brant Rock, Massachusetts, USA. The transmission included Handel's *Largo*. Fessenden had achieved the broadcast of speech as early as November 1900 but this was highly distorted.

Great Britain

The first experimental broadcasting transmitter in Great Britain was set up at the Marconi Works in Chelmsford, Essex, in December 1919, and broadcast a news service in February 1920. The earliest regular broadcast was made from the Marconi transmitter '2MT' at Writtle, Essex, on 14 Feb 1922.

Transatlantic transmissions

The earliest transatlantic wireless signals (the letter S in Morse Code) were received by Marconi, George Stephen Kemp and Percy Paget from a 10 kW station at Poldhu, Cornwall, at Signal Hill, St John's, Newfoundland, Canada, at 12.30 p.m. on 12 Dec 1901. Human speech was first heard across the Atlantic in November 1915 when a transmission from the US Navy station at Arlington, Virginia was received by US radio-telephone engineers on the Eiffel Tower.

Earliest radio-microphones

The radio-microphone, which was in essence also the first 'bug', was devised by Reg Moores (GB) in 1947 and first used on 76 MHz in the ice show *Aladdin* at Brighton Sports Stadium, East Sussex in September 1949.

Longest BBC national broadcast

The longest BBC national broadcast was the reporting of the Coronation of Queen Elizabeth II on 2 June 1953. It began at 10.15 a.m. and finished at 5.30 p.m., after 7 hr 15 min.

Longest continuous broadcast *World*

The longest continuous broadcast (excluding disc-jockeying) has been one of 484 hr (20 days 4 hr) by Larry Norton of WGRQ FM Buffalo, New York, USA on 19 Mar–8 Apr 1981. *No further claims for the above category will be entertained.* Radio Telefís Éireann transmit-

ted an unedited reading of *Ulysses* by James Joyce (1882–1941) for 29 hr 38 min 47 sec on 16–17 July 1982.

Topmost Prize

Mary Buchanan, 15, on WKRQ, Cincinnati, USA won a prize of $25,000 for 40 years (viz $1 million) on 21 Nov 1980.

Brain of Britain Quiz

The youngest person to become 'Brain of Britain' on BBC radio was Anthony Carr, 16, of Anglesey in 1956. The oldest contestant has been the author and translator Hugh Merrick (d. 1981) in his 80th year in August 1977. The record score is 35 by the 1981 winner Peter Barlow of Richmond, Surrey and Peter Bates who won the title in 1984.

Most durable programmes *BBC*

The longest running BBC radio series is *The Week's Good Cause* which began on 24 Jan 1926. The St Francis Leprosy Guild appeal by Cardinal Basil Hume of 27 Jan 1980 raised a record £89,221. The longest running record programme is *Desert Island Discs* which began on 29 Jan 1942 and on which programme only one guest, Arthur Askey CBE, (1900–82) had been stranded a fourth time (on the 1572nd show on 20 Dec 1980). The programme was originally presented by its creator, Roy Plomley, OBE who died on 28 May 1985 having presented 1791 editions. The longest running solo radio feature is *Letter from America* by (Alfred) Alistair Cooke, Hon KBE (b. Salford 20 Nov 1908), first broadcast on 24 Mar 1946. The longest running radio serial is *The Archers* which was created by Godfrey Baseley and was first broadcast on 29 May 1950. Up to May 1986 the signature tune *Barwick Green* had been played over 37,680 times. The only role which has been played without interruption from the start has been that of Philip Archer by Norman Painting OBE (b. Leamington Spa, 23 Apr 1924).

Most heard broadcaster

Larry King has broadcast on network for 27½ hours a week since 30 Jan 1978 from Washington DC on Mutual Broadcasting Systems to all 50 US States (now on 272 Stations).

Earliest antipodal reception

Frank Henry Alfred Walker (b. 11 Nov 1904) on the night of 12 Nov 1924 at Crown Farm, Cuttimore Lane, Walton-on-Thames, Surrey, England, received on his home-made 2 valve receiver on 75 metres, signals from Marconi's yacht *Electra* (call sign ICCM) in Australian waters.

Most assiduous radio ham

Richard C. Spenceley (d. 30 July 1982) of KV4AA at St Thomas, Virgin Islands built his contacts (QSO's) to a record level of 48,100 in 365 days in 1978.

Most stations

The country with the greatest number of radio broadcasting stations is the United States, where there were 9512 authorised broadcast stations as at Apr 1985 made up of both AM (amplitude modulation) and FM (frequency modulation).

Highest listening

The peak recorded listenership on BBC Radio was 30,000,000 adults on 6 June 1950 for the boxing match between Lee Savold (US) and Bruce Woodcock (GB) (b. Doncaster, S. Yorks, 1921).

Highest response

The highest recorded response from a radio show occurred on 27 Nov 1974 when, on a 5 hr talk show on WCAU, Philadelphia, USA, astrologer Howard Sheldon registered a call count of 388,299 calls on the 'Bill Corsair Show'.

Smallest Set
The Toshiba AM-FM RP-1070 with inbuilt loudspeaker measures 9,0 × 5,4 × 1,3 cm *3.5 × 2.1 × 0.5 in* and with battery weighs 70 g *2.5 oz*.

9. TELEVISION

Invention
The invention of television, the instantaneous viewing of distant objects by electrical transmissions, was not an act but a process of successive and inter-dependent discoveries. The first commercial cathode ray tube was introduced in 1897 by Karl Ferdinand Braun (1850–1918), but was not linked to 'electric vision' until 1907 by Prof. Boris Rosing (disappeared 1918) of Russia in St Petersburg (now Leningrad). A. A. Campbell Swinton FRS (1863–1930) published the fundamentals of television transmission on 18 June 1908 in a brief letter to *Nature* entitled 'Distant Electric Vision'. The earliest public demonstration of television was given on 27 Jan 1926 by John Logie Baird (1888–1946) of Scotland, using a development of the mechanical scanning system patented by Paul Gottlieb Nipkow (1860–1940) on 6 Jan 1884. He had achieved the transmission of a Maltese Cross over 10 ft *3,05 m* at 8, Queen's Arcade, Hastings, East Sussex by February 1924 and the first facial image (of William Taynton, 15) at 23, Frith Street on 30 Oct 1925. Taynton had to be bribed with 2s 6d. A patent application for the Iconoscope had been filed on 29 Dec 1923 by Dr Vladimir Kosma Zworykin (1889–1982). It was not issued until 20 Dec 1938. Kenjiro Takayanagi (b. 20 Jan. 1899) succeeded in transmitting a 40-line electronic picture on 25 Dec 1926 with a Braun cathode-ray tube and a Nipkow disc at Hamamatsu Technical College, Japan. Baird launched his first television 'service' via a BBC transmitter on 30 Sept 1929 and marketed the first sets, The Baird Televisors, at £26.25 in May 1930. Public transmissions on 30 lines were made from 22 Aug 1932 until 11 Sept 1935.

The Baird family gravestone (including John Logie, the Television pioneer) in Helensburgh, Strathclyde, Scotland. (J. Urquhart Heron).

Andy Pandy and Teddy, the creation of Mrs Mary Adams, Head of BBC Television Talks Department, who hold the record for the most repeated British children's programme.

Earliest service
The world's first high definition (*i.e.* 405 lines) television broadcasting service was opened from Alexandra Palace, Haringey, London, on 2 Nov 1936, when there were about 100 sets in the United Kingdom. The Chief Engineer was Mr Douglas Birkinshaw. A television station in Berlin, Germany, made a low definition (180 line) transmission from 22 Mar 1935 but the transmitter burnt out in August that year.

Transatlantic transmission
On 9 Feb 1928 the image of J. L. Baird and of a Mrs Howe was transmitted from Station 2 KZ at Coulsdon, Surrey, England to Station 2 CVJ, Hartsdale, NY, USA. The earliest transatlantic transmission by satellite was achieved at 1 a.m. on 11 July 1962, *via* the active satellite *Telstar 1* from Andover, Maine, USA, to Pleumeur Bodou, France. The picture was of Mr Frederick R. Kappell, chairman of the American Telephone and Telegraph Company, which owned the satellite. The first 'live' broadcast was made on 23 July 1962 and the first woman to appear was the *haute couturière*, Ginette Spanier, directrice of Balmain, the next day.

Longest telecast
The longest pre-scheduled telecast on record was a continuous transmission for 163 hr 18 min by GTV 9 of Melbourne, Australia covering the Apollo XI moon mission on 19–26 July 1969. The longest continuous TV transmission under a single director was the KBDI Television Production *Alive* transmitted on Channel 12 in Broomfield, Colorado, USA, on 24–25 Aug 1985 for 24 hr 15 min under the direction of Daniel Salazar.

Video-tape recording *Earliest*
Alexander M. Poniatoff first demonstrated video-tape recording known as Ampex (his initials plus 'ex' for excellence) in 1956. The earliest demonstration of a home video recorder was on 24 June 1963 at the BBC News Studio at Alexandra Palace, London of the Telcan developed by Norman Rutherford and Michael Turner of the Nottingham Electronic Valve Co.

Most durable shows *World*
The world's most durable TV show is NBC's *Meet the Press* first transmitted on 6 Nov 1947 and weekly since 12 Sept 1948, originated by Lawrence E. Spivak, who appeared weekly as either moderator or panel member until 1975. On 1 June 1985 Joe Franklin presented the 21,050th version of his show started in 1951.

Great Britain
Andy Pandy was first transmitted on 11 July 1950 but consisted of repeats of a cycle of 26 shows until 1970. *Come Dancing* was first transmitted on 29 Sept 1950 but is seasonal. *Sooty* was first presented on BBC by its devisor Harry Corbett (born 1918) from 1952 to 1967 and is continued by his son Matthew on ITV. *The Good Old Days* light entertainment ran from 20 July 1953 to 31 Dec 1983. Barney Colehan, MBE, produced all 244 programmes. The *BBC News* was inaugurated in vision on 5 July 1954. Richard Baker OBE read the news from 1954 to Christmas 1982. Of current affairs programmes the weekly BBC *Panorama* was first transmitted on 11 Nov 1953 but has summer breaks, whereas Granada's *What The Papers Say* has been transmitted weekly since 5 Nov 1956. The monthly *Sky at Night* has been presented by Patrick Moore OBE without a break or a miss since 26 Apr 1957. The longest serving TV quizmaster is Bamber Gascoigne of Granada's

University Challenge which has run since 21 Sept 1962. The longest running domestic drama serial is Granada's *Coronation Street* which has run twice weekly since 9 Dec 1960. William Roache had played Ken Barlow without a break since the outset for 25 years by 9 Dec 1985.

Most sets
The US had, by January 1985, 84.8 million TV households, with 32.2 million on Cable TV, 17.8 million on Pay TV and 25 million on Subscription satellite TV, with 3.4 million having video disc or video cassette. The number of homes with colour sets was 71,400,000 (88%) by January 1982. The average number of sets per household surpassed 2.0 in 1982. The number of licences current in the United Kingdom was 18,704,732 on 1 Apr 1986 of which 16,025,336 (85.6 per cent) were for colour sets. Black and white licences became less commonplace than colour in 1976.

TV watching
The National Coalition on TV Violence published an estimate in June 1985 that, by its 16th birthday, the *average* American child will have seen 50,000 TV murders or attempted murders and 200,000 acts of violence. Between the ages of 2 and 11 the average viewing time is 27.3 hours per week. The global total of homes with television surpassed 500 million in 1986 led by the USA with 86.5 million. There are 8250 TV transmitting stations worldwide of which 1149 are in the US. There are 571 TV sets per 1000 people in the USA compared with 348 in Sweden and 330 in Britain.

Greatest audience
The greatest projected number of viewers worldwide for a televised event is 2500 million for the live and recorded transmissions of the XXIIIrd Olympic Games in Los Angeles, California from 27 July to 13 Aug 1984. The American Broadcasting Co airing schedule comprised 187½ hours of coverage on 56 cameras. The estimated viewership for the 'Live Aid' concerts organised by Bob Geldof and Bill Graham, via a record 12 satellites, was 1.6 billion or one third of the world's population. See also chapter 11.

The programme which attracted the highest ever viewership was the *Goodbye, Farewell and Amen* final episode of M*A*S*H (the acronym for Mobile Army Surgical Hospital 4077) transmitted by CBS on 28 Feb 1983 to 60.3 per cent of all households in the United States. It was estimated that some 125 million people tuned in, taking a 77 per cent share of all viewing. The UK record is 39 million for the wedding of TRH the Prince and Princess of Wales in London on 29 July 1981.

Most expensive production
The Winds of War, a seven part Paramount World War II saga, aired by ABC was the most expensive ever TV production costing $42 million over 14 months shooting. The final episode on 13 Feb 1983 attracted a rating of 41.0 per cent (% of total number of viewers), and a share of 56 per cent (% of total sets turned on that were tuned in).

Largest contracts *World*
The highest rate for any TV contract ever signed was one for $7 million (*then £3,100,000*) for 7 hours of transmission by Marie Osmond by NBC announced on 9 Mar 1981. The figure includes talent and production costs.

Currently television's highest-paid performer is John William Carson (b. 23 Oct 1925), the host of *The Tonight Show*. His current NBC contract reportedly calls for annual payment of $5,000,000 (*now £2,275,000*) for his one hour evening show aired four times weekly. The

highest-paid current affairs or news performer is Dan Rather of CBS who reportedly signed an $8 million (*then £4.7 million*) contract for five years from 1982.

Great Britain
The largest contract in British television was one of a reported £9,000,000, inclusive of production expenses, signed by Tom Jones (b. Thomas Jones Woodward, 7 June 1940) of Treforest, Mid Glamorgan, Wales in June 1968 with ABC-TV of the United States and ATV in London for 17 one-hour shows per annum from January 1969 to January 1974.

Highest paid TV performer
Carroll O'Connor, star of *Archie Bunker's Place*, received $275,000 (*£182,500*) for each of 22 episodes in the 1982/83 season totalling $6,050,000 (*£4 million*). Peter Falk (b. 16 Sept 1927), the disarmingly persistent detective *Columbo*, was paid from $300,000 to $350,000 for a single episode of his series of six. Singer Kenny Rogers was reported in February 1983 to have been paid $2 million (*then £1,280,000*) for a single taping of a concert for HBO (Home Box Office) TV Channel. The highest paid newscaster and journalist is Dan Rather of the CBS Nightly News reported in February 1986 to be paid $2,500,000 (*then £1,785,000*) per annum.

Largest TV prizes *World*
On 24 July 1975 WABC-TV, New York City transmitted the first televised Grand Tier draw of the State Lottery in which the winner took the grand prize of $1,000,000 (*now £454,545*). This was however taxable.

Most successful Telethon
The Jerry Lewis Labor Day Telethon on 2 Sept 1984 raised $32,074,566 (*then £26,700,000*) in pledges for the Muscular Dystrophy Association. The Victims of Famine in East Africa and the Sahel appeal raised a record £9,518,736 from 17 July 1984 to 6 Feb 1985.

Biggest sale
The greatest number of episodes of any TV programme ever sold has been 1144 episodes of 'Coronation Street' by Granada Television to CBKST Saskatoon, Saskatchewan, Canada, on 31 May 1971. This constituted 20 days 15 hr 44 min continuous viewing. A further 728 episodes (Jan 1974–Jan 1981) were sold to CBC in August 1982.

Hollywood Television producer Aaron Spelling whose prolific output now includes *Dallas* and *Knots Landing*. (Rex Features).

Most prolific scriptwriter
The most prolific television writer in the world is the Rt Hon Lord Willis known as Ted Willis (b. 13 Jan 1918), who in the period 1949–86 has created 32 series, including the first seven years and 2,250,000 words of *Dixon of Dock Green* which ran from 1955 to 1976, 29 stage plays and 33 feature films. He had 24 plays produced. His total output since 1942 can be estimated at 18,250,000 words.

'Mastermind' Records
Mrs Jennifer Keaveney (on 'The life and work of Edith Nesbit') scored a record 40 points in a 1986 semi-final of this BBC TV series which began on 11 Sept 1972. Sir David Hunt KCMG, OBE won the 'Mastermind Champions' contest on 3 May 1982.

TV Producer
The most prolific TV producer in the world is Aaron Spelling (b. 1928) who, in 29 years from 1956 to 1985, produced more than 1580 TV episodes totalling 2037 hours of air time, as well as 199½ hours of TV movies and 3 feature films. The total 2237 broadcast hours is equal to 12.1 million feet *3688 km* of film and, projected 24 hours a day, it would take 93.4 days—just over 3 months—to screen it all. The average American TV is turned on 6 hours per day. At that rate, Spelling has produced enough film to last 374 days.

Highest TV advertising rates
The highest TV advertising rate has been $550,000 per ½ min (*then £9,166 per sec*) for ABC network prime time during the transmission of Super Bowl XIX on 19 Jan 1985. In Great Britain the peak time weekday 60 sec spot rate (5.40–10.40 p.m.) for Thames Television is £67,375 + VAT (May 1986). The longest run was 7 min 10 sec by Great Universal Stores on Good Morning Britain for £100,000 on 20 Jan 85.

Most takes
The highest number of 'takes' for a TV commercial is 28 in 1973 by Pat Coombs, the comedienne. Her explanation was 'Everytime we came to the punch line I just could not remember the name of the product'.

Commercial records
The highest fee for a 30 sec commercial is $1.5 million paid by Japanese television to 'Boy' George for promoting gin—reported in December 1985.

Largest and Smallest Sets
The Sony Jumbo Tron colour TV screen at the Tsukuba International Exposition '85 near Tokyo in March 1985 measured 80 ft × 150 ft *24,3 m × 45,7 m*.

The Seiko TV-Wrist Watch launched on 23 Dec 1982 in Japan has a 1.2 in *30,5 mm* screen and weighs only 80 g *2.8 oz*. Together with the receiver unit and the headphone set the entire black and white system, costing 108,000 Yen (*then £260*), weighs only 320 g *11,3 oz*. The smallest single-piece TV set is the Casio-Keisanki TV-10 weighing 338 g *11.9 oz* with a 2.7 in *6,85 cm* screen launched in Tokyo in July 1983. The smallest colour TV set is the liquid crystal display (LCD) Japanese Epson launched in 1985 with dimensions of 3 × 6¾ × 1⅛ in *7,6 × 17,1 × 2,8 cm* weighing, with batteries and its 52,800 crystals only 16 oz *453 g*.

Highest definition
A TV system with a 1125 line definition was demonstrated by NHK (Nippon Hoso Kyokai) built by Hitachi and Sony at Brighton, Sussex on 19 Sept 1982.

CHAPTER SEVEN

THE

WORLD'S STRUCTURES

The Dutch flower auction building at Aalsmeer, where over seven million blooms are sold every day in the world's largest commercial building.

EARLIEST STRUCTURES

World

The earliest known human structure is a rough circle of loosely piled lava blocks found on the lowest cultural level at the Lower Palaeolithic site at Olduvai Gorge in Tanzania revealed by Dr Mary Leakey in January 1960. The structure was associated with artifacts and bones on a work-floor, dating to *c.* 1,700,000 BC. The earliest evidence of *buildings* yet discovered is that of 21 huts with hearths or pebble-lined pits and delimited by stake holes found in October 1965 at the Terra Amata site in Nice, France thought to belong to the Acheulian culture of *c.* 400,000 years ago. Excavation carried out between 28 June and 5 July 1966 revealed one hut with palisaded walls with axes of 49 ft *15 m* and 20 ft *6 m*. The oldest free standing structures in the world are now believed to be the megalithic temples at Mgarr and Skorba in Malta and Ggantija in Gozo dating from *c.* 3250 BC. The remains of a stone tower 20 ft *6,1 m* high originally built into the walls of Jericho has been excavated and are dated to 5000 BC. The foundations of the walls themselves have been dated to as early as 8350 BC.

Great Britain

Twelve small stone clusters, associated with broken bones and charcoal in stratum C of the early palaeolithic site at Hoxne, Suffolk may be regarded as Britain's earliest structures dated *c.* 250,000 BC. Remains of the earliest dated stone shelter and cooking pit were discovered in 1967 at Culver Well, Isle of Portland, Dorset (Mesolithic, 5200 BC ± 135). On the Isle of Jura, Argyll, Strathclyde, Scotland a hearth consisting of three linked stone circles has been dated to the Mesolithic period 6013 ± 200 BC. The only original piece of Roman building from the 1st century AD surviving is the bottom 14 ft *4,25 m* of the beacon at Dover, Kent.

Ireland

The earliest known evidence of human occupation in Ireland dates from the Mesolithic period *c.* 7500 at the Carrowmore site in County Sligo. Ireland became enisled or separated from Great Britain *c.* 9050 BC. Nearby there are megalithic burials dated to 3800 ± 80 BC.

1. BUILDINGS FOR WORKING

LARGEST BUILDINGS

Industrial

The largest industrial plant in the world is the Nizhniy Tagil Railroad Car and Tank Plant, 85 miles *136 km* northwest of Sverdlovsk, USSR which has 827 000 m² or 204.3 acres of floor space. It has an annual capacity to produce 2500 T-72 tanks.

Commercial *World*

The greatest ground area covered by any building in the world under one roof is the flower auction building of the Co-operative VBA (Verenigde Bloemenveilingen Aalsmeer), Aalsmeer, Netherlands, which measures 776 × 547 m *2546 × 1794 ft* with a floor surface of 343 277 m² *84.82 acres*. A new extension will increase this to 368 477 m² *91.05 acres* by the end of 1986. The building with the largest cubic capacity in the world is the Boeing Company's main assembly plant at Everett, Washington State, USA completed in 1968 with a capacity of 200 million ft³ *5,6 million m³*.

Great Britain

The largest building in Britain is the Ford Parts Centre at Daventry, Northamptonshire, which measures 1,978 × 780 ft *602 × 237 m* and 1.6 million ft² or 36.7 acres *14,86 ha*. It was opened on 6 Sept 1972 at a cost of nearly £8 million. It employs 1600 people and is fitted with 14,000 fluorescent lights.

Scientific

The most capacious scientific building in the world is the Vehicle Assembly Building (VAB) at Complex 39, the selected site for the final assembly and launching of the Apollo moon spacecraft on the Saturn V rocket, at the John F. Kennedy Space Center (KSC) on Merritt Island, Cape Canaveral, Florida, USA. Construction began in April 1963 by the Ursum Consortium. It is a steel-framed building measuring 716 ft *218 m* in length, 518 ft *158 m* in width and 525 ft *160 m* high. The building contains four bays, each with its own door 460 ft *140 m* high. Its floor area is 343,500 ft² (7.87 acres *3,18 ha*) and its capacity is 129,482,000 ft³ *3 666 500 m³*. The building was 'topped out' on 14 Apr 1965 at a cost of $108,700,000 (*then £38.8 million*).

Administrative

The largest ground area covered by any office building is that of the Pentagon, in Arlington, Virginia, USA. Built to house the US Defense Department's offices it was completed on 15 Jan 1943 and cost an estimated $83,000,000 (*then £20,595,000*). Each of the outermost sides of the Pentagon is 921 ft *281 m* long and the perimeter of the building is about 1500 yd *1370 m*. The five storeys of the building enclose a floor area of 6,500,000 ft² *604 000 m²* (149.2 acres *60,3 ha*). The corridors measure 17 miles *27 km* in length and there are 7748 windows to be cleaned. Twenty nine thousand people work in the building which has over 44,000 telephones connected by 160,000 miles *257 500 km* of cable. Two hundred and twenty staff handle 280,000 calls a day. Two restaurants, six cafeterias and ten snack bars and a staff of 675 form the catering department.

Office

The largest office buildings with the largest rentable space in the world are The World Trade Center in New York City, USA with a total of 4,370,000 ft² *406 000 m²* (100.32 acres *40,6 ha*) in each of the twin towers of which the taller Tower Two (formerly B) is 1362 ft 3¼ in *415,22 m*. The tip of the TV antenna on Tower One is 1710 ft *521,2 m* above street level.

Single office *Great Britain*

The largest single office in the United Kingdom is that of West Midlands Gas at Solihull, built by Spooners (Hull) Ltd in 1962. It now measures 753 ft by 160 ft *230 by 49 m* (2.77 acres *1,12 ha*) in one open plan room accommodating 2170 clerical and managerial workers.

TALLEST BUILDINGS

World

The tallest office building in the world is the Sears Tower, the national headquarters of Sears, Roebuck & Co. in Wacker Drive, Chicago, Illinois with 110 storeys rising to 1454 ft *443 m* and begun in August 1970. Its gross area is 4,400,000 ft² (101.0 acres *40,8 ha*). It was 'topped out' on 4 May 1973. It surpassed the World Trade Center in New York City in height at 2.35 p.m. on 6 Mar 1973 with the first steel column reaching to the 104th storey. The addition of two TV antennae brought the total height to 1559 ft *475,18 m*. The building's population is 16,700 served by 103 elevators and 18 escalators. It has 16,000 windows. Tentative plans for a 169 storey 2300 ft *701 m* tall building, projected to cost $1250 million, for the Chicago Loop, Illinois, USA were published on 27 Oct 1981. Plans for a 150 storey 1670 ft *509 m* tower, entitled Television City, in New York City were unveiled by Donald Trump on 18 Nov 1985.

Great Britain

The tallest office block in Britain and the tallest

The Pentagon, *a paper-pushers paradise*—the world's largest office building.

cantilevered building in the world is the £72 million National Westminster tower block in Bishopsgate, City of London completed in 1979. It has 49 storeys and 3 basement levels, serviced by 21 lifts, and is 600 ft 4 in *183 m* tall. The gross floor area is 636,373 ft² *59,121 m²* (14.6 acres *5,9 ha*). The Canary Wharf development plans in London Docklands includes three office towers of 850 ft *259 m*.

HABITATIONS

Greatest altitude

The highest inhabited buildings in the world are those in the Indian–Tibet border fort of Bāsisi at *c*. 19,700 ft *5988 m*. In April 1961, however, a 3-room dwelling was discovered at 21,650 ft *6600 m* on Cerro Llullaillaco (22,058 ft *6723 m*), on the Argentine–Chile border, believed to date from the late pre-Columbian period *c*. 1480. A settlement on the T'e-li-mo trail in southern Tibet is at an apparent altitude of 19,800 ft *6019 m*.

Northernmost

The most northerly habitation in the world is the Danish Scientific station set up in 1952 in Pearyland, northern Greenland (Kalaalit Nunaat), over 900 miles *1450 km* north of the Arctic Circle. Eskimo hearths dated to before 1000 BC were discovered in Pearyland in 1969. Polar Eskimos were discovered in Inglefield Land, NW Greenland in 1818. The USSR's drifting research station 'North Pole 15', passed within 1¼ miles *2,8 km* of the North Pole in December 1967. The most northerly continuously inhabited place is the Canadian Department of National Defence outpost at Alert on Ellesmere Island, Northwest Territories in Lat. 82° 30′ N, Long. 62° W, set up in 1950.

Southernmost

The most southerly permanent human habitation is the United States' Amundsen–Scott South Polar Station (see Chapter 10) completed in 1957 and replaced in 1975.

The US South Polar Station: 90.00° South, −48,9°C − 56°F. (Science Photo Library).

EMBASSIES AND CIVIC BUILDINGS

Largest
The largest embassy in the world is the USSR embassy on Bei Xiao Jie, Peking, China, in the north-eastern corner of the Northern walled city. The whole 45 acre *18,2 ha* area of the old Orthodox Church mission (established 1728), now known as the *Bei guan*, was handed over to the USSR in 1949. The largest in Great Britain is the United States of America Embassy in Grosvenor Square, London. The Chancery Building, completed in 1960, alone has 600 rooms for a staff of 700 on seven floors with a usable floor area of 255,000 ft² (5.85 acres *2,37 ha*).

Great Britain
The oldest municipal building in Britain is the Exeter Guildhall first referred to in a deed of 1160. The Tudor front was added in 1593.

EXHIBITION CENTRES

Largest *Great Britain*
Britain's largest exhibition centre is the National Exhibition Centre, Birmingham opened in February 1976. Five halls which inter-connect cover 87 180 m² *938,397 ft²* or 21.54 acres with a volume of 1 168 466 m³ or *41.26 million ft³*.

INDUSTRIAL STRUCTURES

Tallest chimneys *World*
The world's tallest chimney is the $5.5 million International Nickel Company's stack 1245 ft 8 in *379,6 m* tall at Copper Cliff, Sudbury, Ontario, Canada, completed in 1970. It was built by Canadian Kellogg Ltd., in 60 days and the diameter tapers from 116.4 ft *35,4 m* at the base to 51.8 ft *15,8 m* at the top. It weighs 38,390 tons *39 006 tonnes* and became operational in 1971. The world's most massive chimney is one of 1148 ft *350 m* at Puentes, Spain, built by M. W. Kellogg Co. It contains 20,600 yd³ *15 750 m³* of concrete and 2.9 million lb *1315 tonnes* of steel and has an internal volume of 6.7 million ft³ *189 720 m³*. Europe's tallest chimney serves the Zasavje thermo-power plant in Trboulje, Yugoslavia completed to 350 metres *1181 ft* on 1 June 1976.

Great Britain
The tallest chimney in Great Britain is one of 850 ft *259 m* at Drax Power Station, North Yorkshire, begun in 1966 and topped out on 16 May 1969. It has an untapered diameter of 87 ft 9 in *26 m* and has the greatest capacity of any chimney. The architects were Clifford Tee & Gale of London. The oldest known industrial chimney in Britain is the Stone Edge Chimney, near Chesterfield, Derbyshire built to a height of 55 ft *16,76 m* ante 1771.

Cooling towers
The largest cooling tower in the world is that adjacent to the nuclear power plant at Uentrop, W. Germany which is 590 ft *179,8 m* tall. It was completed in 1976. The largest in the United Kingdom of the Ferrybridge and Didcot type measure 375 ft *114 m* tall and 300 ft *91 m* across the base.

HANGARS

Largest *World*
The world's largest hanger is Hangar 375 ('Big Texas') at Kelly Air Force Base, San Antonio, Texas, USA completed on 15 Feb 1956. It has 4 doors each 250 ft *76,2 m* wide and 60 ft *18,28 m* high weighing 598 tons/*608 tonnes*. The high bay area measures 2000 × 300 × 90 ft *609,6 × 91,4 × 27,4 m* and is surrounded by a 44 acre *17,8 ha* concrete apron. Delta Air Lines' jet base on a 140 acre *56,6 ha* site at Hartsfield International Airport, Atlanta, Georgia, has 36 acres *14,5 ha* under roof.

Great Britain
The largest hangar building in the United Kingdom is the Britannia Assembly Hall at the former Bristol Aeroplane Company's works at Filton, Avon, now part of British Aerospace. The overall width of the Hall is 1054 ft *321 m* and the overall depth of the centre bay is 420 ft *128 m*. It encloses a floor area of 7½ acres *3,0 ha*. The cubic capacity of the Hall is 33,000,000 ft³ *934 000 m³*. The building was begun in April 1946 and completed by September 1949.

GLASSHOUSE

Largest *Great Britain*
The largest glasshouse in the United Kingdom is one covering 22.5 acres *9,10 ha* owned by Van Heyningen Bros. at Waterham, Herne Bay, Kent completed in October 1982. The crop of 160,000 tomato plants is under 1155 tons of glass.

GRAIN ELEVATOR

Largest
The world's largest single-unit grain elevator is that operated by the C-G-F-Grain Company at Wichita, Kansas, USA. Consisting of a triple row of storage tanks, 123 on each side of the central loading tower or 'head house', the unit is 2,717 ft *828 m* long and 100 ft *30 m* wide. Each tank is 120 ft *37 m* high, with an inside diameter of 30 ft *9 m* giving a total storage capacity of 20,000,000 bushels *7,3 million hl* of wheat. The largest collection of elevators in the world are the 23 at City of Thunder Bay, Ontario, Canada, on Lake Superior with a total capacity of 103.9 million bushels *37,4 million hl*.

SEWAGE WORKS

Largest *World*
The largest single full treatment sewage works in the world is the West-Southwest Treatment Plant, opened in 1940 on a site of 501 acres *203 ha* in Chicago, Illinois, USA. It serves an area containing 2,940,000 people. It treated an average of 835,000,000 US gal *3160 million litres* of wastes per day in 1973. The capacity of its sedimentation and aeration tanks is 1 280 000 m³ *1.6 million yd³*.

Great Britain
The largest full treatment works in Britain and probably in Europe is the Beckton Works which serves a 2,966,000 population and handles a daily flow of 207 million gal *941 million litres* in a tank capacity of 757,000 ft³ *21 400 m³*.

WOODEN BUILDING

Largest
The world's largest buildings in timber are the two US Navy airship hangers built in 1942–3 at Tillamook, Oregon. Now used by the Louisiana-Pacific Corporation as a saw mill they measure 1000 ft long, 170 ft high at the crown and 296 ft wide at the base (*304,8 m × 51,8 m × 90,22 m*) and are worth $6 million (*now £2.7 million*).

AIR-SUPPORTED BUILDING

Largest
The world's largest air-supported roof has been that of the 80,600 capacity octagonal Pontiac Silverdome Stadium, Michigan, USA measuring 522 ft *159 m* in width and 722 ft *220 m* in length. The air pressure was 5 lb/in² *34,4 kPa* supporting the 10 acre *4 ha* translucent 'Fiberglas' roofing. The structural engineers were Geiger-Berger Associates of New York City. The largest standard size air hall was one 860 ft *262 m* long, 140 ft *42,6 m* wide and 65 ft *19,8 m* high. One was first sited at Lima, Ohio, USA, made by Irvin Industries of Stamford, Connecticut, USA.

2. BUILDINGS FOR LIVING

WOODEN BUILDINGS

Oldest
The oldest extant wooden buildings in the world are those comprising the Pagoda, Chumanar gate and the Temple of Horyu (Horyu-ji), at Nara, Japan, dating from *c.* AD 670 and completed in 715. The nearby Daibutsuden, built in 1704–11, once measured 285.4 ft long, 167.3 ft wide and 153.3 ft tall *87 × 51 × 46,75 m*. The present dimensions are 188 × 165.3 × 159.4 ft *57,3 × 50,4 × 48,6 m*.

CASTLES

Earliest *World*
The oldest castle in the world is that at Gomdan, in the Yemen, which originally had 20 storeys and dates from before AD 100.

Great Britain
The oldest stone castle extant in Great Britain is Richmond Castle, Yorkshire, built in *c.* 1075. Iron Age relics from the first century BC or AD have been found in the lower levels of the Dover Castle site.

Ireland
The oldest Irish castle is Ferrycarrig near Wexford dating from *c.* 1180. The oldest castle in Northern Ireland is Carrickfergus Castle, County Antrim, Northern Ireland, which dates from before 1210.

Largest *World, UK and Ireland*
The largest inhabited castle in the world is the Royal residence of Windsor Castle at New Windsor, Berkshire. It is primarily of 12th century construction and is in the form of a waisted parallelogram 1890 ft by 540 ft *576 by 164 m*. The total area of Dover Castle however covers 34 acres *13,75 ha* with a width of 1100 ft *335, 2 m* and a curtain wall of 1800 ft *550 m* or if underground works are taken in, 2300 ft *700 m*. The overall dimensions of Carisbrooke Castle (450 ft by 360 ft *110 by 137 m*), Isle of Wight, if its earthworks are included, are 1350 ft by 825 ft *411 m by 251 m*. The largest castle in Scotland is Edinburgh Castle with a major axis of 1320 ft *402 m* and measuring 3360 ft *1025 m* along its perimeter wall including the Esplanade. The most capacious of all Irish castles is Carrickfergus (see above) but that with the most extensive fortifications is Trim Castle, County Meath, built in *c.* 1205 with a curtain wall 1455 ft *443 m* long.

Forts *Largest*

The largest ancient castle in the world is Hradčany Castle, Prague, Czechoslovakia originating in the 9th century. It is a very oblong irregular polygon with an axis of 570 m *1870 ft* and an average traverse diameter of 128 m *420 ft* with a surface area of 7,28 ha *18 acres*. Fort George, Ardersier, Scotland built in 1748–69 measures 2100 ft *640 m* in length and has an average width of 620 ft *189 m*. The total site covers 42½ acres *17,2 ha*.

Thickest walls

Urnammu's city walls at Ur (now Muqayyar), destroyed by the Elamites in 2006 BC were 27 m *88⅓ ft* thick. The walls of the Great Tower or Donjon of Flint Castle, built in 1277–80 are 23 ft *7,01 m* thick. The largest Norman keep in Britain is that of Colchester Castle measuring 152½ ft *46 m* by 111½ ft *34 m*.

PALACES

Largest *World*

The largest palace in the world is the Imperial Palace (*Gu gong*) in the centre of Peking (*Bei jing*, the northern capital), China, which covers a rectangle 1050 yd by 820 yd *960 by 750 m*, an area of 177.9 acres *72 ha*. The outline survives from the construction of the third Ming Emperor, Yung lo of 1402–24, but due to constant re-arrangements most of the intra-mural buildings are 18th century. These consist of 5 halls and 17 palaces of which the last occupied by the last Empress was the Palace of Accumulated Elegance (*Chu xia gong*) until 1924.

The Palace of Versailles, 23 km *14 miles* southwest of Paris has a facade with 375 windows, 634 yards *580 m* in length. The building, completed in 1682 for Louis XIV occupied over 30,000 workmen under Jules Hardouin-Mansert.

Currently residential

The palace (Istana Nurul Iman) of H.M. the Sultan of Brunei in the capital Bandar Seri Begawan completed in January 1984 at a reported cost of £300 million is the largest in the world with 1788 rooms. The underground garage has to accommodate the Sultan's 110 cars.

Great Britain

The largest palace in the United Kingdom in Royal use is Buckingham Palace, London, so named after its site, bought in 1703 by John Sheffield, the 1st Duke of Buckingham and Normanby (1648–1721). Buckingham House was reconstructed in the Palladian style between 1835 and 1836, following the design of John Nash (1752–1835). The 610 ft *186 m* long East Front was built in 1846 and refaced in 1912. The Palace, which stands in 39 acres *15,8 ha* of garden, has 600 rooms including a ballroom 111 ft *34 m* long. The largest ever Royal palace has been Hampton Court Palace, London, acquired by Henry VIII from Cardinal Wolsey in 1525 and greatly enlarged by the King and later by William III, Anne and George I, whose son George II was its last resident monarch. It covers 4 acres *1,6 ha* of a 669 acre *270,7 ha* site.

Largest moat

The world's largest moats are those which surround the Imperial Palace in Peking (see above). From plans drawn by French sources it appears to measure 54 yd *49 m* wide and have a total length of 3600 yd *3290 m*. The city's moats total in all 23½ miles *38 km*.

FLATS

Largest

The largest blocks of private flats in Britain are

The Wooden Pagoda at Nara, Japan, celebrating this year its 1271st birthday. (Robert Harding).

the Barbican Estate, London, EC2 with 2011 flats on a 40 acre *16 ha* site with covered parking space for 2000 cars. The architects were Chamberlain, Powell and Bon.

Tallest *World*

The tallest block of flats in the world are Lake Point Towers of 70 storeys, and 645 ft *197 m* in Chicago, Illinois, USA.

Great Britain

The tallest residential block in Great Britain is the Shakespeare Tower in the Barbican in the City of London, which has 116 flats on 44 storeys and rises to a height of 419 ft 2½ in *127,77 m* above the street. The first of the three Barbican towers was 'topped out' in May 1971.

Most Expensive

Four flats of at least five bedrooms each at a putative £6 million each were reported by architects YRM to be ready for occupation in late 1987 in Rutland Gate, Kensington, London.

HOTELS

Largest *World*

The hotel with most rooms in the world is the 12 storey Hotel Rossiya in Moscow, USSR, with 3200 rooms providing accomodation for 6,000 guests, opened in 1967. It would thus require more than 8½ years to spend one night in each room. In addition there is a 21 storey 'Presidential' tower in the central courtyard. The hotel employs about 3000 people, and has 93 lifts. The ballroom is reputed to be the world's largest. Muscovites are not permitted as residents while foreigners are charged 16 times more than the very low rate charged to USSR officials. The Izmailovo Hotel complex, opened in July 1980 for the XXIInd Olympic Games in Moscow, was designed to accommodate 9500 people.

The Las Vegas Hilton, Nevada, USA built in 1974–81 has 3174 rooms, 12 international restaurants and a staff of 3600. It has a 10 acre *2,47 ha* rooftop recreation deck and 125,000 ft^2 *11 600 m^2* of convention space.

The Regent Hotel, Royal Leamington Spa, Warwickshire was claimed to be the largest in the world when first opened in 1819 with 100 bedrooms and one bathroom.

Great Britain

The greatest sleeping capacity of any hotel in Great Britain is 1859 in the London Forum Hotel, Cromwell Road, London SW7 with a staff of 419. It was opened in 1973. The Regent Palace Hotel, Piccadilly Circus, London, opened 20 May 1915, has however 225 more rooms totalling 1140. The largest hotel is the Grosvenor House Hotel, Park Lane, London, which was opened in 1929. It is of 8 storeys covering 2½ acres *1 ha* and caters for more than 100,000 visitors per year in 470 rooms. The Great Room is the largest hotel room measuring 181 ft by 131 ft *55 by 40 m* with a height of 23 ft *7 m*. Banquets for 1500 are frequently handled.

The Garvault Hotel in Scotland is more than 16 miles from its nearest competitor. *See p. 106.*

Tallest

The tallest hotel in the world, measured from the street level of its main entrance to the top, is the 741.9 ft *226,1 m* tall 73 storey Westin Stamford in Raffles City, Singapore topped out in March 1985. The $235 million (*£156.66 million*) hotel is operated by Westin Hotel Company and owned by Raffles City Pte Ltd. Their Detroit Plaza measuring from the rear entrance level is however 748 ft *227,9 m* tall. Britain's tallest hotel is the 27 storey 380 ft *132,24 m* tall 907 bedroom London Forum Hotel.

Most remote *Great Britain*

Garvault Hotel, by Kinbrace, Highland, Scotland, is claimed to be the most isolated in mainland Britain being some 16 miles *25,7 km* from its nearest competitor at Forsinard.

Largest lobby

The world's largest hotel lobby is that of The Grand Hotel, Taipei, Taiwan completed on 10 Oct 1973. It measures 47 × 35 m *154 × 114 ft* and is 9,6 m *31½ ft* high.

Most expensive

The world's costliest hotel accommodation was the Royale Suite at $5500 (*£3525*) per day in the Nova Park Elysées, Rue François, Paris which closed on 31 Jan 1985. It had 8 rooms, 7 bathrooms, 3 terraces and a conference room covering 431,5 m² *4644 ft²*. The most expensive hotel suite in Britain is the Royal Suite on the 8th floor of the Hotel Inter-Continental, London W1, at £810 (incl. VAT) (May 1986).

Spas

The largest spa in the world measured by number of available hotel rooms is Vichy, Allier, France, with 14,000 rooms. Spas are named after the watering place in the Liège province of Belgium where hydropathy was developed from 1626. The highest French spa is Baréges, Hautes-Pyrénées, at 4068 ft *1240 m* above sea level.

HOUSING

Largest estate

The largest housing estate in the United Kingdom is the 1670-acre *675 ha* Becontree Estate, on a site of 3000 acres *1214 ha* in Barking and Redbridge, London, built between 1921 and 1929. The total number of homes is 26,822, with an estimated population of nearly 90,000.

New towns

Of the 23 new towns being built in Great Britain that with the largest eventual planned population is Milton Keynes, Buckinghamshire, with a projected 250,000 for 1992.

Largest house *World*

The largest private house in the world is the 250-room Biltmore House in Asheville, North Carolina, USA. It is owned by George and William Cecil, grandsons of George Washington Vanderbilt II (1862–1914). The house was built between 1890 and 1895 in an estate of 119,000 acres *48 160 ha*, at a cost of $4,100,000 (now *£1,708,333*) and now valued at $55,000,000 with 12,000 acres *4856 ha*. The most expensive private house ever built is The Hearst Ranch at San Simeon, California, USA. It was built in 1922–39 for William Randolph Hearst (1863–1951), at a total cost of more than $30,000,000 (*then £6,120,000*). It has more than 100 rooms, a 104 ft *32 m* long heated swimming pool, an 83 ft *25 m* long assembly hall and a garage for 25 limousines. The house required 60 servants to maintain it.

Great Britain

The largest house in Great Britain was Wentworth Woodhouse, near Rotherham, South Yorkshire, formerly the seat of the Earls Fitzwilliam and now a teachers' training college. The main part of the house, built over 300 years ago, has more than 240 rooms with over 1000 windows, and its principal façade is 600 ft *183 m* long. The Royal residence, Sandringham House, Norfolk, has been reported to have had 365 rooms before the demolition of 73 surplus rooms in 1975. The largest house in Ireland is Castletown in County Kildare, owned by the Hon. Desmond Guinness and is the headquarters of the Irish Georgian Society. Scotland's largest house is Hopetoun House, West Lothian, built between 1696 and 1756 with a west façade 675 ft *206 m* long.

Smallest

The smallest house in Britain is the 19th century fisherman's cottage at 22 High Street, Conwy, Gwynedd. It has a 72 in *182 cm* frontage, is 122 in *309 cm* high, 100 in *254 cm* front to back and has two tiny rooms and a staircase. The narrowest known house frontage is of 47 inches *1,19 m* at 50 Stuart Street, Millport, Great Cumbrae, Strathclyde.

The naval veteran of the Battle of Jutland (1916) Alexander Wortley (1900–80) lived his last 20 years in a green painted box in the garden of David Moreau in Langley Park, Buckinghamshire. It measured 5 × 4 × 3 ft *1,5 × 1,2 × 0,91 m* with an extension for his feet—small enough as he said to 'keep women out'. He paid no rent, rates or taxes and did not believe in insurance, pensions or governments.

Most expensive *Houses*

The most expensive private house is The Kenstead Hall with the adjoining Beechwood property in The Bishop's Avenue, Hampstead, London, residence of the late king of Saudi Arabia. It was put on the market for £16 million in August 1982.

Oldest

The oldest house in Britain is Eastry Court near Sandwich, Kent dating from AD 603. Some of the original timbers and stone infill still survives behind its present Georgian façade.

Stately home most visited

The most visited stately home in the United Kingdom in 1985 was Warwick Castle, near Stratford-on-Avon with 640,919 visitors.

Barracks

The oldest purpose built barracks in the world are believed to be Collins Barracks, formerly the Royal Barracks, Dublin, Ireland, completed in 1704 and still in use.

3. BUILDINGS FOR ENTERTAINMENT

STADIUM

Largest *World*

The world's largest stadium is the open Strahov Stadium in Praha (Prague), Czechoslovakia. It was completed in 1934 and can accommodate 240,000 spectators for mass displays of up to 40,000 Sokol gymnasts.

Football

The largest football stadium in the world is the Maracaña Municipal Stadium in Rio de Janeiro, Brazil, where the football ground has a normal capacity of 205,000, of whom 155,000 may be seated. A crowd of 199,854 was accommodated for the World Cup final between Brazil and Uruguay on 16 July 1950. A dry moat, 7ft *2,13 m* wide and more than 5 ft *1,5 m* deep, protects players from spectators and *vice versa*. Britain's most capacious football stadium is Hampden Park, Glasgow opened on 31 Oct 1903 and once surveyed to accommodate 184,000 compared with an attendance of 149,547 on 17 Apr 1937 and the present licensed limit of 74,400.

Covered

The Azteca Stadium, Mexico City, Mexico, opened in 1968, has a capacity of 107,000 of whom nearly all are under cover. The world's

The Louisiana Superdome in New Orleans, USA—the world's biggest all-seater indoor stadium and the venue for the Super Bowl XX between the Chicago 'Bears' and the New England 'Patriots'. (See American Football) (All-Sport).

largest retractable roof is being constructed to cover the 60,000 capacity Toronto Blue Jays new stadium near the CN Tower for completion by August 1988. The diameter will be 207 m *679 ft*.

The largest covered stadium in Britain is the Empire Stadium Wembley, Brent, London, opened in April 1923. It was the scene of the 1948 Olympic Games and the final of the 1966 World Cup. In 1962–3 the capacity under cover was increased to 100,000 of whom 45,000 may be seated. The original cost was £1,250,000.

Largest roof

The transparent acryl glass 'tent' roof over the Munich Olympic Stadium, W. Germany measures 914,940 ft² (21.0 acres *8,5 ha*) in area resting on a steel net supported by masts. The roof of longest span in the world is the 680 ft *207,2 m* diameter of the Louisiana Superdome (see below). The major axis of the elliptical Texas Stadium completed in 1971 at Irving, Texas is however 240 m *787 ft 4 in*.

Indoor

The world's largest indoor stadium is the 13 acre *5,26 ha* $173 million (*then £75 million*) 273 ft *83,2 m* tall Superdome in New Orleans, Louisiana, USA, completed in May 1975. Its maximum seating capacity for conventions is 97,365 or 76,791 for football. Box suites rent for $35,000 excluding the price of admission. A gondola with six 312 in *7,92 m* TV screens produces instant replay.

Ballroom

The dance floor used for championships at Earl's Court Exhibition Hall, Kensington, London extends 256 ft *78 m* in length.

Amusement resort

The world's largest amusement resort is Disney World in 28,000 acres *11 332 ha* of Orange and Osceola counties, 20 miles *32 km* south west of Orlando in central Florida, USA. It was opened on 1 Oct 1971. This $400 million investment attracted a peak 13,221,000 visitors in 1981, annual attendance now exceeds 20 million. The most attended resort is Disneyland, Anaheim, California (opened 1955) which received its 250 millionth visitor on 24 Aug 1985 at 9.52 am.

Largest pleasure beach

The largest pleasure beach in the world is Virginia Beach, Virginia, USA. It has 28 miles *45 km* of beach front on the Atlantic and 10 miles *16 km* of estuary frontage. The area embraces 255 miles² *600 km²* and 134 hotels and motels. The most visited pleasure beach in Britain is at Blackpool, Lancashire which attracts 7 million visitors annually.

Piers *Earliest, longest and most*

A pleasure pier was completed at Great Yarmouth, Norfolk in 1808 but was washed away in 1953. The Old Pier, Weymouth, Dorset dates back to 1812. The longest pleasure pier in the world is Southend Pier at Southend-on-Sea in Essex. It is 1.34 miles *2,15 km* in length. It was first opened in August 1889 with final extensions made in 1929. In 1949–50 the pier had 5,750,000 visitors. The pier railway closed in October 1978.

The resort with most piers is Atlantic City, New Jersey, USA with 6 pre-war and 5 currently. In Britain only Blackpool has three—North, Central and South.

Earliest fair

The earliest major international fair was the Great Exhibition of 1851 in the Crystal Palace, Hyde Park, City of Westminster, London which in 141 days attracted 6,039,195 admissions.

The Crystal Palace in Hyde Park, built specially to house the international fair in 1851. (Bridgeman Art Library).

Largest fair

The largest ever International Fair site was that for the St Louis, Missouri, Louisiana Purchase Exposition which covered 1271.76 acres *514,66 ha*. It also staged the 1904 Olympic Games and drew an attendance of 19,694,855.

Record fair attendance

The record attendance for any fair was 64,218,770 for Expo 70 held on an 815 acre *330 ha* site at Osaka, Japan from March to 13 Sept 1970. It made a profit of 19,439,402,017 yen (*then £22.6 million*).

Big wheel

The original Ferris Wheel, named after its constructor, George W. Ferris (1859–96), was erected in 1893 at the Midway, Chicago, Illinois, at a cost of $385,000 (*then £79,218*). It was 250 ft *76 m* in diameter, 790 ft *240 m* in circumference, weighed 1070 tons *1087 tonnes* and carried 36 cars each seating 60 people, making a total of 2160 passengers. The structure was removed in 1904 to St Louis, Missouri, and was eventually sold as scrap for $1800 (*then £370*). In 1897 a Ferris Wheel with a diameter of 300 ft *91 m* was erected for the Earl's Court Exhibition, London. It had ten 1st-class and 30 2nd-class cars. The largest diameter wheels now operating are 'The Giant Peter' at Himeji Central Park, Himeji City, Hyogo, and that at the city of Tsukuba, both in Japan and with a height of 85 m *278 ft 10 in*. The latter has a capacity for 384 riders.

Fastest and longest switchbacks

The maximum speeds claimed for switchbacks, scenic railways or roller coasters have in the past been exaggerated for commercial reasons. The twin track triple helix American Eagle at Marriott's Great America, Gurnee, Illinois opened on 23 May 1981 has a vertical drop of 147.4 ft *44,92 m* on which a speed of 66.31 mph *106,73 km/h* is reached. The longest roller coaster in the world is *The Beast* at Kings Island near Cincinnati, Ohio, USA. Scientific tests at the

base of its 141 ft *42,98 m* high drop returned a speed of 64.77 mph *104,23 km/h* on 5 Apr 1980. The run of 7400 ft or 1.40 miles *2,25 km* incorporates 800 ft *243,8 m* of tunnels and a 540 degree banked helix. The tallest is the Moonsault Scramble at the Fujikyu Highland Park, nr. Kawaguchi Lake, Japan opened on 24 June 1983. It is 75 m *246 ft* tall (with a speed of 105 km/h *65.2 mph*).

Longest slide

The longest slide in the world is at the Bromley Alpine Slide on Route 11 in Peru, Vermont, USA. This has a length of 4600 ft *1402 m* (0.87 mile) and a vertical drop of 820 ft *250 m*.

Harem largest

The world's most capacious harem is the Winter Harem of the Grand Seraglio at Topaki, Istanbul, Turkey completed in 1589 with 400 rooms. By the time of the deposing of Abdul Hamid II in 1909 the number of *carge* (those who serve) had dwindled from 1200 to 370 odalisques with 127 eunuchs.

Night club *Oldest*

The earliest night club (*boite de nuit*) was 'Le Bal des Anglais' at 6 Rue des Anglais, Paris, 5e France. Founded in 1843 it closed *c.* 1960.

Largest

The largest night club in the world is Gilley's Club (formerly Shelly's) built in 1955 and extended in 1971 on Spencer Highway, Houston, Texas, USA with a seating capacity of 6000 under one roof covering 4 acres *1,6 ha*. In the more classical sense the largest night club in the world is 'The Mikado' in the Akasaka district of Tōkyō, Japan, with a seating capacity of 2000. It is 'manned' by 1250 hostesses. Binoculars are essential to an appreciation of the floor show.

Lowest

The lowest night club is the 'Minus 206' in Tiberias, Israel on the shores of the Sea of Galilee. It is 206 m *676 ft* below sea-level. An

The world's highest restaurant in the world's highest ski resort—Chacaltaya, Bolivia. (South American Pictures).

alternative candidate is 'Outer Limits', opposite the Cow Palace, San Francisco, California which was raided for the 151st time on 1 Aug 1971. It has been called 'The Most Busted Joint' and 'The Slowest to Get the Message'.

Restaurants
The earliest restaurant was opened in 1725 in Calle de Cuchilleros 17, Madrid. Goya, the painter, was a dishwasher there in 1765 when he was 19. The Paris restaurant now serving most 'covers' per day is La Cupole with 2000. The highest restaurant in the world is at the Chacaltaya ski resort, Bolivia at 5340 m *17,519 ft*. The highest in Great Britain is the Ptarmigan Observation Restaurant at 3650 ft *1112 m* above sea-level on Cairngorm (4084 ft *1244 m*) near Aviemore, Highland, Scotland.

PUBLIC HOUSES
Oldest
There are various claimants to the title of the United Kingdom's oldest inn. A foremost claimant is 'The Fighting Cocks', St Albans, Hertfordshire (an 11th century structure on an 8th century site). The timber frame of The Royalist Hotel, Digbeth Street, Stow-on-the-Wold, Gloucestershire has been dated to 1000 years before the present. It was the inn 'The Eagle and the Child' in the 13th century and known to exist in AD 947. An origin as early as AD 560 has been claimed for 'Ye Olde Ferry Boat Inn' at Holywell, Cambridgeshire. There is some evidence that it antedates the local church, built in 980, but the earliest documents are not dated earlier than 1100. There is evidence that the 'Bingley Arms', Bardsey, near Leeds, West Yorkshire, restored and extended in 1738, existed as the 'Priest's Inn' according to Bardsey Church records dated 905.

The oldest pub in Ireland is Grace Neill's Bar, Donaghadee, County Down built in 1611. An inn stood on the site of the Brazen Head Inn, Lower Bridge Street, Dublin since the late 12th century. The present structure dates from 1668.

Largest *World*
The largest beer-selling establishment in the world is the Mathäser, Bayerstrasse 5, München (Munich), West Germany, where the daily sale reaches 84,470 pts *48 000 litres*. It was established in 1829, was demolished in World War II

and re-built by 1955 and now seats 5500 people. The through-put at the Dube beer halls in the Bantu township of Soweto, Johannesburg, South Africa may, however, be higher on some Saturdays when the average consumption of 6000 gal (48,000 pts *27 280 litres*) is far exceeded.

Great Britain
The largest public house in Great Britain is the Courage House, Downham Tavern, Downham

'Dorothy', barmaid of the phone kiosk Wine Bar in The Huddersfield Hotel, West Yorkshire. The smallest bar in the world was granted a licence on 15 May 1985 despite the local Health Department's request for two sinks and the Fire Officer's request for an alternative means of escape!

Way, Bromley, Kent built in 1930. Two large bars (counter length 45 ft *13,7 m*) accommodate 1000 customers with 18–20 staff.

Smallest
The smallest pub in Great Britain is the 17th century 'The Nutshell', Bury St Edmunds, Suffolk with maximum dimensions of 15 ft 10 in by 7 ft 6 in *4,82 × 2,28 m* or 118.74 ft^2 *11,03 m^2*. The bar room in the Earl Grey, Quenington, Gloucestershire measures 116.37 ft^2 *10,81 m^2*.

Longest bars *World*
The world's longest permanent bar is the 340 ft *103,6 m* long bar in Lulu's Roadhouse, Kitchener, Ontario, Canada opened on 3 Apr 1984. The famous Working Men's Club bar at Mildura, Victoria, Australia has a counter 298 ft *90,8 m* in length, served by 27 pumps. Temporary bars have been erected of greater length. The Bar at Erickson's on Burnside Street, Portland, Oregon, in its heyday (1883–1920) possessed a bar which ran continuously around and across the main saloon measuring 684 ft *208,48 m*. The chief bouncer Edward 'Spider' Johnson had an assistant named 'Jumbo' Reilly who weighed 23 stone and said to resemble 'an ill-natured orang-utan'. Beer was 5 cents for 16 fluid ounces.

United Kingdom and Ireland
The longest bar in the United Kingdom with beer pumps is the Long Bar at The Cornwall Coliseum Auditorium at Carlyon Bay, St. Austell, Cornwall measuring 104 ft 4 in *31,8 m* and having 34 dispensers (beer and lager). The longest bar in a pub is of 104 ft 3 in *31,77 m* in The Horse Shoe, Drury Street, Glasgow. The Grand Stand Bar at Galway Racecourse, Ireland completed in 1955, measures 210 ft *64 m*.

Longest tenure
There are no collated records on licensees but the 'Glan-y-Afon Inn', Milwr near Holywell, North Wales had a 418 year long (1559–1977) run within a family which ended with the retirement of Mrs Mary Evans.

Longest name
The pub with the longest name is the 49 letter 'Henry J. Bean's But His Friends All Call Him Hank Bar and Grill', Raphael Street, London SW7.

Shortest name
The public house in the United Kingdom with the shortest name was the 'X' at Westcott, Cullompton, Devon but in October 1983 the name was changed to the 'Merry Harriers'.

Commonest name
The commonest pub name in Britain is 'Red Lion' of which there are probably about 630. Arthur Amos of Bury St Edmunds, Suffolk, has recorded 21,516 differently-named pubs continuously since 1938.

Highest
The highest public house in the United Kingdom is the 'Tan Hill Inn' in North Yorkshire. It is 1732 ft *528 m* above sea-level, on the moorland road between Reeth, North Yorkshire and Brough, Cumbria. The highest pub open the year round is the 'Cat and Fiddle' in Cheshire, near Buxton, Derbyshire at 1690 ft *515 m*. The Snowdon Summit licensed bar and cafeteria is the highest at 3560 ft *1085 m*.

Most visits
Stanley House of Totterdown, Bristol has visited 3308 differently named pubs in Britain by way of public transport only to 1 May 1986. Jimmy Young GM BEM, of Better Pubs Ltd claims to have visited 23,349 different pubs.

4. Towers and Masts

TALLEST STRUCTURES

World

The tallest structure in the world is the guyed Warszawa Radio mast at Konstantynow near Gabin and Płock 60 miles *96 km* north-west of the capital of Poland. It is 646,38 m *2120 ft 8 in* tall or more than four tenths of a mile. The mast was completed on 18 July 1974 and put into operation on 22 July 1974. It was designed by Jan Polak and weighs 550 tons/*tonnes*. The mast is so high that anyone falling off the top would reach their terminal velocity and hence cease to be accelerating before hitting the ground. Work was begun in July 1970 on this tubular steel construction, with its 15 steel guy ropes. It recaptured for Europe a record held in the USA since the Chrysler Building surpassed the Eiffel Tower in 1929.

Great Britain

The tallest structure in the United Kingdom is the Independent Broadcasting Authority's mast north of Horncastle, Lincolnshire completed in 1965 to a height of 1265 ft *385 m* with 7 ft *2,13 m* added by meteorological equipment installed in September 1967. It serves Yorkshire TV and weighs 210 tons.

TALLEST TOWERS

World

The tallest self-supporting tower (as opposed to a guyed mast) in the world is the $44 million CN Tower in Metro Centre, Toronto, Canada, which rises to 1822 ft 1 in *555,33 m*. Excavation began on 12 Feb 1973 for the 130,000 ton/*tonne* structure of reinforced, post-tensioned concrete topped out on 2 Apr 1975. The 416-seat restaurant revolves in the Sky Pod at 1140 ft

347,5 m from which the visibility extends to hills 74½ miles *120 km* distant. Lightning strikes the top about 200 times (30 storms) per annum.

The tallest tower built before the era of television masts is the Eiffel Tower, in Paris, France, designed by Alexandre Gustav Eiffel (1832–1923) for the Paris exhibition and completed on 31 Mar 1889. It was 300,51 m *985 ft 11 in* tall, now extended by a TV antenna to 320,75 m *1052 ft 4 in* and weighs 7340 tonnes *7224 tons*. The maximum sway in high winds is 12,7 cm *5 in*. The whole iron edifice which has 1792 steps, took 2 years, 2 months and 2 days to build and cost 7,799,401 francs 31 centimes.

Great Britain

The tallest self-supported tower in Great Britain is the 1080 ft *329,18 m* tall Independent Broadcasting Authority transmitter at Emley Moor, West Yorkshire, completed in September 1971. The structure, which cost £900,000, has an enclosed room at the 865 ft *263,65 m* level and weighs with its foundations more than 15,000 tons/*tonnes*. The tallest tower of the pre-television era was the New Brighton Tower of 562 ft *171,29 m* built on Merseyside in 1897–1900 and dismantled in 1919–21.

PROGRESSIVE LIST OF HIGHEST STRUCTURES IN GREAT BRITAIN

Feet	Metres		
404	*123*	Salisbury Cathedral Spire	c. 1305–
525	*160*	Lincoln Cathedral	1307–1548
489	*149*	St Paul's Cathedral, London	1315–1561
518.7	*158,1*	Blackpool Tower, Lancashire	1894–
562	*171,29*	New Brighton Tower, Merseyside	1898–1919
820	*250*	GPO Radio Masts, Rugby	1925–
1000*	*304,8*	ITA Mast, Mendlesham, Suffolk	July 1959
1265	*385*	IBA Mast, Emley Moor, West Yorkshire	1965–1969†
1265	*385*	IBA Mast, Belmont, Lincolnshire	1965–
1272	*387,1*	IBA Mast, Belmont, Lincolnshire	Sept. 1967

* ITA masts of the same height followed at Lichfield, Staffordshire; Black Hill, Strathclyde; Caldbeck, Cumbria; and Durris, Grampian.
† Severely damaged by icing and replaced.

5. Bridges

Oldest *World*

Arch construction was understood by the Sumerians as early as 3200 BC and a reference exists to a Nile bridge in 2650 BC. The oldest surviving datable bridge in the world is the slab stone single arch bridge over the River Meles in Smyrna (now Izmir), Turkey, which dates from *c.* 850 BC.

Great Britain

The clapper bridges of Dartmoor and Exmoor (*e.g.* the Tarr Steps over the River Barle, Exmoor, Somerset) are thought to be of prehistoric types although none of the existing examples can be certainly dated. They are made of large slabs of stone placed over boulders. The Romans built stone bridges in England and remains of these have been found at Corbridge (Roman, Corstopitum), Northumberland dating to the 2nd century AD; Chesters, Northumberland and Willowford, Cumbria. Remains of a very early wooden bridge have been found at Aldwinkle, Northamptonshire.

LONGEST

Cable suspension *World*

The world's longest bridge span is the main span of the Humber Estuary Bridge, England at 4626 ft *1410 m*. Work began on 27 July 1972, after a decision announced on 22 Jan 1966. The towers are 162,5 m *533 ft 1⅜ in* tall from datum and are 1⅜ in *36 mm* out of parallel, to allow for the curvature of the Earth. Including the Hessle and the Barton side spans, the bridge stretches 2220 m or 1.37 miles. The bridge was structurally completed on 18 July 1980 at a cost of £96 million and was opened by HM the Queen on 17 July 1981. Tolls, ranging between £1 for cars and £7.50 for heavy vehicles, operative from 4 May 1981, are the highest in Britain. By 1995 the debt is expected to grow to £300 million.

The Mackinac Straits Bridge between Mackinaw City and St Ignace, Michigan, USA, is the longest suspension bridge in the world measured between anchorages (1.58 miles *2543 m*) and has an overall length, including viaducts of the bridge proper measured between abutment bearings, of 3.63 miles *5853,79 m*. It was opened in November 1957 (dedicated 28 June 1958) at a cost of $100 million (*then £35,700,000*) and has a main span of 3800 ft *1158 m*.

The double-deck road-rail Akashi-Kaikyo bridge linking Honshū and Shikoku, Japan is planned to be completed in 1988. The main span will be 5840 ft *1780 m* in length with an overall suspended length with side spans totalling 11,680 ft *3560 m*. Work began on the approaches in October 1978 and the eventual cost is expected to exceed 1000 billion (10¹²) yen.

A PROGRESSIVE RECORD OF THE WORLD'S TALLEST STRUCTURES

Height in ft	m	Structure	Location	Material	Building or Completion Dates
204	*62*	Djoser step pyramid (earliest Pyramid)	Saqqâra, Egypt	Tura limestone casing	*c.* 2650 BC
300.8	*91,7*	Pyramid of Meidum	Meidum, Egypt	Tura limestone casing	*c.* 2600 BC
331.6	*101,1*	Snefru Bent pyramid	Dahshûr, Egypt	Tura limestone casing	*c.* 2600 BC
342	*104*	Snefru North Stone pyramid	Dahshûr, Egypt	Tura limestone casing	*c.* 2600 BC
480.9[1]	*146,5*	Great Pyramid of Cheops (Khufu)	El Gizeh, Egypt	Tura limestone casing	*c.* 2580 BC
525[2]	*160*	Lincoln Cathedral, Central Tower	Lincoln, England	lead sheathed wood	*c.* 1307–1548
489[3]	*149*	St Paul's Cathedral spire	City of London, England	lead sheathed wood	1315–1561
465	*141*	Minster of Notre Dame	Strasbourg, France	Vosges sandstone	1420–1439
502[4]	*153*	St Pierre de Beauvais spire	Beauvais, France	lead sheathed wood	–1568
475	*144*	St Nicholas Church	Hamburg, Germany	stone and iron	1846–1847
485	*147*	Rouen Cathedral spire	Rouen, France	cast iron	1823–1876
513	*156*	Köln Cathedral spires	Cologne, W. Germany	stone	–1880
555[5]	*169*	Washington Monument	Washington, DC, USA	stone	1848–1884
985.9[6]	*300,5*	Eiffel Tower	Paris, France	iron	1887–1889
1046	*318*	Chrysler Building	New York City, USA	steel and concrete	1929–1930
1250[7]	*381*	Empire State Building	New York City, USA	steel and concrete	1929–1930
1572	*479*	KWTV Television Mast	Oklahoma City, USA	steel	Nov 1954
1610[8]	*490*	KSWS Television Mast	Roswell, New Mexico, USA	steel	Dec 1956
1619	*493*	WGAN Television Mast	Portland, Maine, USA	steel	Sept 1959
1676	*510*	KFVS Television Mast	Cape Girardeau, Missouri, USA	steel	June 1960
1749	*533*	WTVM & WRBL Television Mast	Columbus, Georgia, USA	steel	May 1962
1749	*533*	WBIR-TV Mast	Knoxville, Tennessee, USA	steel	Sept 1963
2063	*628*	KTHI-TV Mast	Fargo, North Dakota, USA	steel	Nov 1963
2120.6	*646,38*	Warszawa Radio Mast	Płock, Poland	galvanised steel	22 July 1974

[1] *Original height. With loss of pyramidion (topmost stone) height now 449 ft 6 in 137 m*
[2] *Fell in a storm.*
[3] *Struck by lightning and destroyed 4 June 1561.*
[4] *Fell April 1573, shortly after completion.*
[5] *Sinking at a rate of 0.0047 ft per annum or 5 in 12,7 cm since 1884.*
[6] *Original height. With addition of TV antenna in 1957, now 1052 ft 320,75 m.*
[7] *Original height. With addition of TV tower on 1 May 1951, now 1472 ft 449 m. Exterior is clad in limestone from the Empire Quarry, Indiana.*
[8] *Fell in gale in 1960.*

Plans for a Messina Bridge linking Sicily with the Italian mainland are dependent upon EEC budgets. One preliminary study calls for towers 1000 ft *304,8 m* tall and a span of 10,800 ft *3290 m* or 2.04 miles. The escalating cost of such a project was estimated by 1983 already to have passed the £2000 million mark.

Cantilever *World*
The Quebec Bridge (Pont de Québec) over the St Lawrence River in Canada has the longest cantilever truss span of any in the world— 1800 ft *549 m* between the piers and 3239 ft *987 m* overall. It carries a railway track and 2 carriageways. Begun in 1899, it was finally opened to traffic on 3 Dec 1917 at a cost of 87 lives, and \$Can.22,500,000 (*then £4,623,000*).

Great Britain
The longest cantilever bridge in Great Britain is the Forth Bridge. Its two main spans are 1710 ft *521 m* long. It carries a double railway track over the Firth of Forth 156 ft *47,5 m* above the water level. Work commenced in November 1882 and the first test trains crossed on 22 Jan 1890 after an expenditure of £3 million. It was officially opened on 4 Mar 1890. Of the 4500 workers who built it, 57 were killed in various accidents.

Steel arch *World*
The longest steel arch bridge in the world is the New River Gorge bridge, near Fayetteville, West Virginia, USA, completed in 1977 with a span of 1700 ft *518,2 m*.

Great Britain
The longest steel arch bridge in Great Britain is the Runcorn–Widnes bridge, Cheshire opened on 21 July 1961. It has a span of 1082 ft *329,8 m*.

Floating bridge
The longest floating bridge in the world is the Second Lake Washington Bridge, Seattle, Washington State, USA. Its total length is 12,596 ft *3839 m* and its floating section measures 7518 ft

2291 m (1.42 miles *2,29 km*). It was built at a total cost of \$15,000,000 (*then £5,357,000*) and completed in August 1963.

Covered bridge
The longest covered bridge in the world is that at Hartland, New Brunswick, Canada measuring 1282 ft *390,8 m* overall, completed in 1899.

Railway bridge
The longest railway bridge in the world is the Huey P. Long Bridge, Metairie, Louisiana, USA with a railway section 22,996 ft *7009 m* (4.35 miles *7 km*) long. It was completed on 16 Dec 1935 with a longest span of 790 ft *241 m*. The Yangtse River Bridge, completed in 1968 in Nanking, China is the world's longest combined highway and railway bridge. The rail deck is 6772 m *4.20 miles* and the road deck is 4589 m *2.85 miles*.

Great Britain
The longest railway bridge in Britain is the second Tay Bridge (11,653 ft *3552 m*), Tayside, Scotland opened on 20 June 1887. Of the 85 spans, 74 (length 10,289 ft *3136 m*) are over the waterway. The 878 brick arches of the London Bridge to Deptford Creek viaduct built in 1836 extend for 3¾ miles *6,0 km*.

Longest bridging
The world's longest bridging is the Second Lake Pontchartrain Causeway, completed on 23 Mar 1969, joining Lewisburg and Metairie, Louisiana, USA. It has a length of 126,055 ft *38 422 m* (23.87 miles). It cost \$29,900,000 (*then £12.45 million*) and is 228 ft *69 m* longer than the adjoining First Causeway completed in 1956. The longest railway viaduct in the world is the rockfilled Great Salt Lake Railroad Trestle, carrying the Southern Pacific Railroad 11.85 miles *19 km* across the Great Salt Lake, Utah, USA. It was opened as a pile and trestle bridge on 8 Mar 1904, but converted to rock fill in 1955–60.

The Trans-Canada Highway Bridge at Hartland, New Brunswick, Canada, the longest covered bridge in the world. According to custom, you should cross your fingers, hold your breath and make a wish as you drive through. If you can hold your breath all the way across, your wish will be granted. (Robert Harding).

The longest stone arch bridging in the world is the 3810 ft *1161 m* long Rockville Bridge north of Harrisburg, Pennsylvania, USA, with 48 spans containing 196,000 tons/*tonnes* of stone and completed in 1901.

Widest bridge
The world's widest long-span bridge is the 1650 ft *502,9 m* span Sydney Harbour Bridge, Australia (160 ft *48,8 m* wide). It carries two electric overhead railway tracks, 8 lanes of roadway and a cycle and a footway. It was officially opened on 19 Mar 1932. The Crawford Street Bridge in Providence, Rhode Island, USA, has a width of 1147 ft *350 m*. The River Roch is bridged for a distance of 1460 ft *445 m* where the culvert passes through the centre of Rochdale, Manchester and this is sometimes claimed to be a breadth.

HIGHEST
World
The highest bridge in the world is the bridge over the Royal Gorge of the Arkansas River in Colorado, USA. It is 1053 ft *321 m* above the water level. It is a suspension bridge with a main span of 880 ft *268 m* and was constructed in 6 months, ending on 6 Dec 1929. The highest railway bridge in the world is the single track span at Fades, outside Clermont-Ferrand, France. It was built in 1901–9 with a span of 472 ft *144 m* and is 435 ft *132,5 m* above the River Sioule. The road bridge at the highest

The world famous Sydney Harbour Bridge in Australia—the world's widest with 8 traffic lanes, a cycle and a footway. (Alex Hansen).

altitude in the world, 18 380 ft *5602 m*, is the 30 m *98.4 ft* long Bailey bridge built by Indian Army in Aug 1982 near Khardung La, in Ladakh, India.

Great Britain

The highest railway bridge in Great Britain is the Ballochmyle viaduct over the River Ayr, Strathclyde built 169 ft *51,5 m* over the river bed in 1846–8 with the then world's longest masonry arch span of 181 ft *55,16 m*.

AQUEDUCTS

World longest *Ancient*

The greatest of ancient aqueducts was the Aqueduct of Carthage in Tunisia, which ran 87.6 miles *141 km* from the springs of Zaghouan to Djebel Djougar. It was built by the Romans during the reign of Publius Aelius Hadrianus (AD 117–38). By 1895, 344 arches still survived. Its original capacity has been calculated at 7,000,000 gal *31,8 million litres* per day. The triple-tiered aqueduct Pont du Gard, built in AD 19 near Nîmes, France, is 160 ft *48 m* high. The tallest of the 14 arches of Aguas Livres Aqueduct, built in Lisbon, Portugal, in 1784 is 213 ft 3 in *65 m*.

World longest *Modern*

The world's longest aqueduct, in the modern sense of a water conduit, as opposed to an irrigation canal, is the California State Water Project aqueduct, completed in 1974, to a length of 826 miles *1329 km* of which 385 miles *619 km* is canalised.

Longest *Great Britain*

The longest bridged aqueduct in Britain is the Pont Cysylltau in Clwyd on the Frankton to Llantisilio branch of the Shropshire Union Canal. It is 1007 ft *307 m* long, has 19 arches up to 121 ft *36 m* high above low water on the Dee. It was designed by Thomas Telford (1757–1834) of Scotland, and was opened for use in 1805. The oldest is the Dundas aqueduct on the Avon and Kennet canal near Bath. It was built in 1810 and restored in 1984.

6. CANALS

Earliest *World*

Relics of the oldest canals in the world, dated by archaeologists *c.* 4000 BC, were discovered near Mandali, Iraq early in 1968.

Earliest *Great Britain*

The earliest canals in Britain were first cut by the Romans. In the Midlands the 11 mile *17 km* long Fossdyke Canal between Lincoln and the River Trent at Torksey was built in about AD 65 and was scoured in 1122. Part of it is still in use today. Though the Exeter canal was cut as early as 1564–6, the first wholly artificial major navigation canal in the United Kingdom was the 18½ mile *29,7 km* long canal with 14 locks from Whitecoat Point to Newry, Northern Ireland opened on 28 Mar 1742. The Sankey Navigation Canal in Lancashire, 8 miles *12,8 km* in length, with 10 locks, was opened in November 1757.

Longest *World*

The longest canalised system in the world is the Volga–Baltic Canal opened in April 1965. It runs 1850 miles *2300 km* from Astrakhan up the Volga, *via* Kuybyshev, Gor'kiy and Lake Ladoga, to Leningrad, USSR. The longest canal of the ancient world has been the Grand Canal of China from Peking to Hangchou. It was begun in 540 BC and not completed until 1327 by which time it extended (including canalised river sections) for 1107 miles *1781 km*. The estimated work force *c.* AD 600 reached 5,000,000 on the Pien section. Having been allowed by 1950 to silt up to the point that it was, in no place, more than 6 ft *1,8 m* deep, it is now, however, plied by ships of up to 2000 tons/*tonnes*.

The Beloye More (White Sea) Baltic Canal from Belomorsk to Povenets, in the USSR, is 141 miles *227 km* long with 19 locks It was completed with the use of forced labour in 1933. It cannot accommodate ships of more than 16 ft *5 m* in draught.

The world's longest big ship canal is the Suez Canal linking the Red and Mediterranean Seas, opened on 16 Nov 1869 but inoperative from June 1967 to June 1975. The canal was planned by the French diplomatist Count Ferdinand de Lesseps (1805–94) and work began on 25 Apr 1859. It is 100.6 miles *161,9 km* in length from Port Said lighthouse to Suez Roads and 197 ft *60 m* wide. The construction work force was 8213 men and 368 camels. The largest vessel to transit has been SS *British Progress* a VLCC (Very Large Crude Carrier) of 228 589 tonnes dwt (length 329,66 m *1081.5 ft*; beam 48,68 m *159.7 ft* at a maximum draft of 25,60 m *84 ft*). This was southbound in ballast on 5 July 1976. *USS Shreveport* transited southbound on 15–16 Aug 1984 in a record 7 hr 45 min.

Busiest

The busiest big ship canal is the Panama, first transitted on 15 Aug 1914. In 1974 there were a record 14,304 ocean-going transits. The largest liner to transit is *Queen Elizabeth 2* (66,851 gross tons) on 25 Jan 1980 for a toll of $89,154.62 (*then £38,760*). The ships with the greatest beam to transit have been the *Acadia Forest* and the *Atlantic Forest* of 106.9 ft *32,58 m*. The lowest toll was 36 US cents by the swimmer Richard Halliburton in 1928. The fastest transit has been 2 hr 41 min by the US Navy hydrofoil *Pegasus* on 20 June 1979.

Longest *Great Britain*

Inland Waterways in Great Britain, normally defined as non-tidal (except for a few tidal 'links' on the Thames, Trent and Yorkshire Ouse) rivers and canals, consist of 2394 miles *3852 km* with 110 miles *177 km* being restored. Of this total 2125 miles *3420 km* are inter-linked.

The longest possible journey on the system would be one of 415¾ miles *669 km* and 157 locks from Bedford, on the Great Ouse to near Ripon, North Yorkshire.

Largest seaway

The world's longest artificial seaway is the St Lawrence Seaway (189 miles *304 km* long) along the New York State–Ontario border from Montreal to Lake Ontario, which enables ships up to 222 m *728 ft* long and 8 m *26.2 ft* draught some of which are of 26,000 tons *26 400 tonnes* to sail 2342 miles *3769 km* from the North Atlantic, up the St Lawrence estuary and across the Great Lakes to Duluth, Minnesota, USA, on Lake Superior (602 ft *183 m* above sea level). The project begun in 1954 cost $470,000,000 (*then £168 million*) and was opened on 25 Apr 1959.

Irrigation canal

The longest irrigation canal in the world is the Karakumskiy Kanal, stretching 528 miles *850 km* from Haun-Khan to Ashkhabad, Turkmenistan, USSR. In September 1971 the 'navigable' length reached 280 miles *450 km*. The length of the £370 million project will reach 930 miles *1300 km*.

LOCKS

Largest *World*

The world's largest single lock is the sea lock at Zeebrugge, Belgium measuring 500 × 57 × 23 m *1640 × 187 × 75.4 ft* giving a volume of 655 300 m³ *857,066 yd³*. The Berendrecht Lock,

A satellite's view of the Suez Canal that links the *Red* and the *Med*. The Continent of Africa is on the right. (Daily Telegraph).

Antwerp planned for completion in 1986 will have the same length but a width of 68 m *223 ft* at a depth of 21,5 m *70.5 ft* giving a volume of 731 000 m³ *956,000 yd³*.

Largest *Great Britain*

The largest and deepest lock in the United Kingdom is the Royal Portbury Entrance Lock, Bristol which measures 1200 × 140 ft *366 × 42,7 m* and has a depth of 66 ft *20,2 m*. It was opened in August 1977.

Deepest *World*

The world's deepest lock is the John Day dam lock on the Columbia river, Oregon and Washington, USA completed in 1963. It can raise or lower barges 113 ft *34,4 m* and is served by a 982 ton *998 tonne* gate.

Longest flight

The world's highest lock elevator overcomes a head of 68,58 m *225 ft* at Ronquières on the Charleroi-Brussels Canal, Belgium. The two 236 wheeled caissons each able to carry 1350 tons take 22 min to cover the 1432 m *4698 ft* long ramp. The highest rise of any boat-carrying plane in Britain was the 225 ft *68,6 m* of the 935 ft *285 m* long Hobbacott Down plane on the Bude Canal, Cornwall.

The longest flight of locks in the United Kingdom is on the Worcester and Birmingham Canal at Tardebigge, Hereford and Worcester, where in a 2½ mile *4 km* stretch there are the Tardebigge (30 locks) and Stoke (6 locks) flights which together drop the canal 259 ft *78,9 m*. The flight of locks on the Huddersfield Canal, closed in 1944, on the 7¼ mile *11,6 km* stretch to Marsden numbered 42.

Largest cut

The Gaillard Cut (known as 'the Ditch') on the Panama Canal is 270 ft *82 m* deep between Gold Hill and Contractor's Hill with a bottom width of 500 ft *152 m*. In one day in 1911 as many as 333 dirt trains each carrying 357 tons *363 tonnes* left this site. The total amount of earth excavated for the whole Panama Canal as of 1 Oct 1979 was 666,194,450 yd³ *509 338 960 m³* which total will be raised by the further widening of the Gaillard Cut.

7. DAMS

Earliest

The earliest known dams were those uncovered by the British School of Archaeology in Jerusalem in 1974 at Jawa in Jordan. These stone-faced earth dams are dated to *c.* 3200 BC.

Most massive

Measured by volume, the largest dam in the world is the 98 ft *29,8 m* high New Cornelia Tailings earth-fill dam, on the Ten Mile Wash, Arizona, USA with a volume of 274,015,735 yd³ *209 501 000 m³* completed in 1973 to a length of 6.74 miles *10,85 km*. The Chapetón dam in Argentina is planned to have a volume of 296 200 000 m³ *387,400,000 yd³*.

Largest concrete

The world's largest concrete dam, and the largest concrete structure in the world, is the Grand Coulee Dam on the Columbia River, Washington State, USA. Work on the dam was begun in 1933, it began working on 22 Mar 1941 and was completed in 1942 at a cost of $56 million. It has a crest length of 4173 ft *1272 m* and is 550 ft *167 m* high. It contains 10,585,000 yd³ *8 092 000 m³* of concrete and weighs about 19,285,000 tons *19 595 000 tonnes*. The hydro-electric power plant (now being extended) will have a capacity of 9,780,000 kW.

Highest

The highest dam in the world will be the 335 m *1098 ft* high Rogunsky earth-fill dam across the Vakhsh river, Tadzhikistan, USSR with a crest length of only 2165 ft *660 m*. Building since 1973, the completion date is still unconfirmed. Meanwhile the tallest completed is the 300 m *984 ft* high Narek dam, USSR.

Longest

The 41 m *134.5 ft* high Yacyreta–Apipe dam across the Paraná on the Paraquay–Argentina borders extends for 72 km *44.7 miles*. In the early 17th century an impounding dam of moderate height was built in Lake Hungtze, Kiangsu, China, to a reputed length of 100 km *62 miles*.

The longest sea dam in the world is the Afsluitdijk stretching 20.195 miles *32,5 km* across the mouth of the Zuider Zee in two sections of 1.553 miles *2,499 km* (mainland of North Holland to the Isle of Wieringen) and 18.641 miles *30 km* from Wieringen to Friesland. It has a sea-level width of 293 ft *89 m* and a height of 24 ft 7 in *7,5 m*.

Strongest

The world's strongest structure will be the 242 m *793 ft* high Sayano-Shusenskaya dam on the River Yenisey, USSR which is under construction and designed to bear a load of 18 000 000 tonnes/*tons* from a fully-filled reservoir of 31,300 million m³ *41,000 million yd³* capacity.

United Kingdom

The most massive dam in Britain is the Northumbrian Water Authority's Kielder Dam, 52 m *170 ft* high earth embankment measuring 1140 m *3740 ft* in length and 5 300 000 m³ *6,932,000 yd³*. There are longer low dams or barrages of the valley cut-off type, notably the Hanningfield Dam, Essex, built from July 1952 to August 1956 to a length of 6850 ft *2088 m* and a height of 64.5 ft *19,7 m*. The rock-fill Llyn Brianne Dam, Dyfed is Britain's highest dam reaching 298½ ft *91 m* in Nov 1971. It became operational on 20 July 1972.

Largest reservoir *World*

The most voluminous man-made reservoir is the Kahkovskaya Reservoir, USSR, with a volume of 182 km³ *147,550,000 acre-feet*. The world's largest artificial lake measured by surface area is Lake Volta, Ghana, formed by the Akosombo dam completed in 1965. By 1969 the lake had filled to an area of 3275 miles² *8482 km²* with a shoreline 4500 miles *7250 km* in length.

The completion in 1954 of the Owen Falls Dam near Jinja, Uganda, across the northern exit of the White Nile from the Victoria Nyanza marginally raised the level of that *natural* lake by adding 270 km³ *218,900,000 acre-feet*, and technically turned it into a reservoir with a surface area of 17,169,920 acres *6,9 million ha* (26,828 miles² *69 484 km²*).

The $4 billion Tucurui Dam in Brazil, had, by 1984, converted the Tocantins river into a 1900 km *1180 mile* long chain of lakes.

Largest reservoir *Great Britain*

The most capacious reservoir in Britain is Kielder Water in the North Tyne valley, Northumberland, which filled to 44,000 million gallons *2000 million hl* from 15 Dec 1980 to mid-1982, and which acquired a surface area of 2684 acres *1086 ha* and a perimeter of 27 miles *43,4 km* to become England's second largest lake. Rutland Water has a lesser capacity (27,300 million gallons *124 106 million l*) and a lesser perimeter (24 miles *38,6 km*) but a greater surface area of 3100 acres *1254 ha*. The deepest reservoir in Europe is Loch Morar, Highland, Scotland, with a maximum depth of 1017 ft *310 m* (see also page 63).

The largest wholly artificial reservoir in Great Britain is the Queen Mary Reservoir, built from August 1914 to June 1925, at Littleton, near Staines, Surrey, with an available storage capacity of 8130 million gal *369,6 million hl* and a water area of 707 acres *286 ha*. The length of the perimeter embankment is 20,766 ft *6329 m* (3.93 miles *6,32 km*).

Largest polder

The largest of the five great polders in the old Zuider Zee, Netherlands, will be the 149,000 acre *60 300 ha* (232.8 miles² *602,9 km²*) Markerwaard. Work on the 66 mile *106 km* long surrounding dyke was begun in 1957. The water area remaining after the erection of the 1927–32 dam (20 miles *32 km* in length) is called IJssel Meer, which will have a final area of 487.5 miles² *1262,6 km²*.

Largest levees

The most massive levees ever built are the Mississippi levees begun in 1717 but vastly augmented by the US Federal Government after the disastrous floods of 1927. These extend for 1732 miles *2787 km* along the main river from Cape Girardeau, Missouri, to the Gulf of Mexico and comprise more than 1000 million yd³ *765 million m³* of earthworks. Levees on the tributaries comprise an additional 2000 miles *3200 km*. The Pine Bluff, Arkansas to Venice, Louisiana segment of 650 miles *1046 km* is continuous.

8. TUNNELS

LONGEST

Water supply *World*

The world's longest tunnel of any kind is the New York City West Delaware water supply tunnel, begun in 1937 and completed in 1944. It has a diameter of 13 ft 6 in *4,1 m* and runs for 105 miles *168,9 km* from the Rondout Reservoir into the Hillview Reservoir, on the border of Yonkers and New York City, NY, USA.

Water supply *Great Britain*

The longest water supply tunnel in the United Kingdom is the Kielder Water tunnel system. These tunnels have been driven through the rock to link the Tyne Valley with the Wear Valley. A pipe then passes under the river Wear and the tunnel then proceeds to link up with the Tees Valley. The system is 20.2 miles *32,18 km* in length.

Railway *World*

The world's longest main-line rail tunnel is the 22,2 km (*13 miles 1397 yd*) long Oshimizu Tunnel (Daishimizu) on the Tōkyō–Niigata Joetsu line in central Honshū under the Tanigawa mountain which was holed through on 25 Jan 1979. The cost of the whole project has reached £3150 million.

On 25 Apr 1985 Thomas Stockebrand demonstrated on a model, in which a table-tennis ball was pulled through a 950 m *3116 ft* pipe pneumatically at 646 km/h *1040 mph*, that a railway system could operate at supersonic speeds.

Railway *Great Britain*

Great Britain's longest main-line railway tunnel is the Severn Tunnel (4 miles 628 yd *6 km*), linking Avon and Gwent completed with 76,400,000 bricks between 1873 and 1886.

Sub-aqueous

The 33.46 mile *53,85 km* long Seikan Rail Tunnel has been bored 240 m *787 ft* beneath sea level and 100 m *328 ft* below the sea bed of the Tsugaru Strait between Tappi Saki, Honshū, and Fukushima, Hokkaidō, Japan. Tests started on the sub-aqueous section (14.5 miles *23,3 km*) in 1964 and construction in June 1972. It was holed through on 27 Jan 1983 after a loss of 34 lives. The cost by the finish of tunnelling after 20 years 10 months in March 1985 was 600,000 million yen (about £2500 million).

Subway

The world's longest continuous vehicular tunnel is the Moscow Metro underground railway line from Belyaevo to Medvedkovo. It is c. 30,7 km *19.07 miles* long and was completed in 1978/9.

Road *World*

The longest road tunnel is the 10.14 mile *16,32 km* long two-lane St Gotthard Road Tunnel from Göschenen to Airolo, Switzerland, opened to traffic on 5 Sept 1980. Nineteen lives were lost during the construction which cost Sw Fr 686 million (*then £173.6 million*) since autumn 1969.

Great Britain

The longest road tunnel in the United Kingdom is the Mersey Tunnel, joining Liverpool and Birkenhead, Merseyside. It is 2.13 miles *3,43 km* long, or 2.87 miles *4,62 km* including branch tunnels. Work was begun in December 1925 and it was opened by HM King George V on 18 July 1934. The total cost was £7¾ million. The 36 ft *11 m* wide 4-lane roadway carries nearly 7½ million vehicles a year. The first tube of the second Mersey Tunnel was opened on 24 June 1971.

Largest

The largest diameter road tunnel in the world is that blasted through Yerba Buena Island, San Francisco, California, USA. It is 76 ft *23 m* wide, 58 ft *17 m* high and 540 ft *165 m* long. More than 35,000,000 vehicles pass through on its two decks every year.

Hydro-electric, irrigation or sewerage
World

The longest irrigation tunnel in the world is the 51.5 mile *82,9 km* long Orange-Fish Rivers Tunnel, South Africa, begun in 1967 at an estimated cost of £60 million. The boring was completed in April 1973. The lining to a minimum thickness of 9 inches *23 cm* will give a completed diameter of 17 ft 6 in *5,33 m*. The Majes project in Peru involves 98 km *60.9 miles* of tunnels for hydro-electric and water supply purposes. The dam is at 4200 m *13,780 ft* altitude. The Chicago TARP (Tunnels and Reservoir Plan) in Illinois, USA involves 120 miles *193 km* of sewerage tunnelling.

Bridge-Tunnel

The world's longest bridge-tunnel system is the Chesapeake Bay Bridge-Tunnel, extending 17.65 miles *28,40 km* from Eastern Shore, Virginia Peninsula to Virginia Beach, Virginia, USA. It cost $200,000,000 (*then £71,4 million*) and was completed after 42 months and opened to traffic on 15 Apr 1964. The longest bridged section is Trestle C (4.56 miles *7,34 km* long) and the longest tunnel is the Thimble Shoal Channel Tunnel (1.09 miles *1,75 km*).

Canal tunnels *World*

The world's longest canal tunnel is that on the Rove canal between the port of Marseilles, France and the river Rhône, built in 1912–27. It is 4.53 miles *7,29 km* long, 72 ft *22 m* wide and 50 ft *15 m* high, involving 2¼ million yd³ *1,7 million m³* of excavation.

Great Britain

The longest canal tunnel in Great Britain is the Standedge (more properly Stanedge) Tunnel in West Yorkshire on the Huddersfield Narrow Canal built from 1794 to 4 Apr 1811. It measures 3 miles 418 yd *5,21 km* in length and was closed on 21 Dec 1944. The British canal system has contained 84 tunnels exceeding 30 yd *27,4 m* of which 48 are still open. The longest of these is the 3056 yd *2,79 km* long Blisworth Tunnel on the Grand Union in Northamptonshire. The now closed Huddersfield Narrow Canal is the highest in the United Kingdom, at 638 ft *194 m* above sea-level.

Tunnelling records

The longest unsupported example of a machine-bored tunnel is the Three Rivers Water Tunnel driven 30,769 linear feet *9,37 km* with a 10.5 ft *3,2 m* diameter for the City of Atlanta, Georgia, USA from April 1980 to February 1982. S & M Constructors Inc of Cleveland, Ohio achieved 179 ft *54,5 m* in a day through the granite, schist and gneiss.

The NCB record of 251,4 m *824.8 ft* for a 3,80 m *12½ ft* wide, 2 m *6½ ft* high roadway by a team of 35 pitmen in 5 days was set at West Cannock No 5 Colliery on 30 Mar–3 Apr 1981.

9. SPECIALISED STRUCTURES

Advertising sign Highest *World*

The highest advertising signs in the world are the four Bank of Montreal logos atop the 72 storey 935 ft *285 m* tall First Canadian Place, Toronto. Each sign, built by Claude Neon Industries Ltd, measures 20 × 22 ft *6,09 × 6,70 m* and was lifted by helicopter.

Advertising sign Largest

The most conspicuous sign ever erected was the electric Citroën sign on the Eiffel Tower, Paris. It was switched on on 4 July 1925, and could be seen 24 miles *38 km* away. It was in six colours with 250,000 lamps and 56 miles *90 km* of electric cables. The letter 'N' which terminated the name 'Citroën' between the second and third levels measured 68 ft 5 in *20,8 m* in height. The whole apparatus was taken down after 11 years in 1936. For the largest ground sign see Chapter 6, page 83—Largest letter.

The world's largest neon sign measures 210 ft × 55 ft *64 × 16,7 m* built for Marlboro cigarettes at Hung Hom, Kowloon, Hong Kong in May 1986. It contains 35,000 ft *10 668 m* of neon tubing and weighs approximately 113 tons *114,7 tonnes*. The world's largest reported hoarding is one 44,5 m *146 ft* long and 17,5 m *57 ft 5 in* tall erected by Propaganda Campanella on Route N9, Buenos Aires, Argentina. The largest 'hoarding' in Britain measures 226 ft *68,9 m* by 54 ft *16,5 m* and was produced by Forwardair Ltd. The site is the roof of the Brentford Football Club stand, at its Griffin Park, Middlesex ground which is on the flight path of London, Heathrow airport. Britain's largest illuminated sign is the name NEI NUCLEAR SYSTEMS LTD extending 170 ft 6 in *52 m* installed at their factory in Gateshead, Tyne and Wear, in June 1983. It can be seen from the air at a distance of 20 miles *32 km*.

An interior lit fascia advertising sign in Clearwater, Florida, USA completed by Adco Sign Corp in April 1983 measures 1168 ft 6½ in *356,17 m* in length.

The world's most massive animated sign is reputed to be that outside the Circus Circus Hotel, Reno, Nevada named Topsy, the Clown. It is 127 ft *38,7 m* tall and weighs over 40 tons *40,8 tonnes* with 1.4 miles *2,25 km* of neon tubing. His smile measures 14 ft *4,26 m* across.

Barn Largest

The largest barn in Britain is one at Frindsbury, Kent. Its length is 219 ft *66,7 m* and is still wholly

An aerial view of 'The Studebaker Letters' in Bendix Woods Nature Center, New Carlisle, Indiana, USA. The world's largest living sign is over ½ mile *805 m* long and constructed of 8259 pine trees each 60 ft *18,3 m* tall. The sign was planted as seedlings in 1936 by Mel Neimier, a Studebaker engineer and his 10-year-old son Harry.

Britain's largest hoarding on the roof of the Brentford Football Club stand *and* on the London Heathrow Airport flight path. (S A Parker) *See p. 113.*

roofed. The Ipsden Barn, Oxfordshire, is 385½ ft *117 m* long but 30 ft *9 m* wide (11,565 ft² *1074 m²*). The longest tithe barn in Britain is one measuring 268 ft *81 m* long at Wyke Farm, near Sherborne, Dorset.

Bonfire Largest

The largest recorded bonfire constructed in Britain was the Coronation bonfire using 800 tons *812 tonnes* of timber, 1000 gal *4546 litres* each of petroleum and tar. It was octagonal in shape and built to a height of 120 ft *36,67 m* with a base circumference of 155 ft *47,2 m* tapering to 20 ft *6,1 m* at the summit, on Arrowthwaite Brows at Whitehaven, Cumbria in 1902.

Breakwater Longest *World and Great Britain*

The world's longest breakwater is that which protects the Port of Galveston, Texas, USA. The granite South Breakwater is 6.74 miles *10,85 km* in length.

The longest breakwater in Great Britain is the North Breakwater at Holyhead, Anglesey, Gwynedd which is 7860 ft (1.48 miles *2395 m*) in length and was completed in 1873.

Buildings demolished by Explosives *Largest*

The largest building demolished by explosives has been the 21 storey Traymore Hotel, Atlantic City, New Jersey, USA, on 26 May 1972 by Controlled Demolition Inc of Towson, Maryland. This 600 room hotel had a cubic capacity of 6,495,500 ft³ *181 340 m³*. The tallest chimney ever demolished by explosives was the Matla Power Station chimney, Kriel, South Africa on 19 July 1981. It stood 275 m *902 ft* and was brought down by The Santon (Steeplejack) Co. Ltd of Manchester, England.

The greatest recorded simultaneous smokestack demolition was when 18 were felled at the London Brick Co Coronation Works at Kempston Hardwick, Bedfordshire on 30 Nov 1980 when Mrs Wyn Witherall fired the 100 lb *45,3 kg* of explosives laid by T. W. Robinson & Co.

Cemetery Largest

The world's largest cemetery is that in Leningrad, USSR, which contains over 500,000 of the 1,300,000 victims of the German army's siege of 1941–3. The largest cemetery in the United Kingdom is Brookwood Cemetery, Brookwood, Surrey. It is owned by the London Necropolis Co. and is 500 acres *200 ha* in extent with more than 225,000 interments.

Column Tallest

The tallest columns (as opposed to obelisks) in the world are the 36 fluted pillars 90 ft *27,43 m* tall, of Vermont marble in the colonnade of the Education Building, Albany, New York. Their base diameter is 6½ ft *1,98 m*. The tallest load-bearing stone columns in the world are those measuring 69 ft *21 m* in the Hall of Columns of the Temple of Amun at Karnak, opposite Thebes on the Nile, the ancient capital of Upper Egypt. They were built in the 19th dynasty in the reign of Rameses II in *c.* 1270 BC.

Crematorium Earliest

The oldest crematorium in Britain is one built in 1879 at Woking, Surrey. The first cremation took place there on 26 Mar 1885, the practice having been found legal after the cremation of Iesu Grist Price on Caerlan fields on 13 Jan 1884. The total number of people cremated in Britain since, has been 11,172,452 (to 31 Dec 1985), and the percentage now 68%. The percentage in Japan is 93.4%.

Crematorium Largest

The largest crematorium in the world is at the Nikolo-Arkhangelskoye Cemetery, East Moscow, with 7 twin cremators of British design, completed in March 1972. It has several Halls of Farewell for atheists. Currently, Britain's largest is the City of London Crematorium, E.12, which performed 5395 cremations in 1979. The all-time total of 264,312 at Golders Green Crematorium (since 1902) remains unsurpassed, as does its record 7509 cremations in 1957.

Dock Gate

The world's largest dock gate in regular use is that at the entrance to the Okpo No 1 Dry Dock, Chojé Island, South Korea. It measures 131 m *430 ft* wide and is approximately 14 m *46 ft* high and 10 m *32.8 ft* thick at the base.

Dome Largest *World and Great Britain*

The world's largest dome is the Louisiana Superdome, New Orleans, USA. It has a diameter of 680 ft *207,26 m* (See pages 106–7 for further details.) The largest dome of ancient architecture is that of the Pantheon, built in Rome in AD 112, with a diameter of 142½ ft *43 m*.

The largest dome in Britain is that of the Bell Sports Centre, Perth, Scotland, with a diameter of 222 ft *67 m* designed by D. B. Cockburn and constructed in Baltic whitewood by Muirhead & Sons Ltd of Grangemouth, Central, Scotland.

Door Largest *World*

The largest doors in the world are the four in the Vehicle Assembly Building near Cape Canaveral, Florida, with a height of 460 ft *140 m* (see page 103). The world's heaviest door is that leading to the laser target room at Lawrence Livermore National Laboratory, California. It weighs 321.4 tons *326,5 tonnes*, is up to 8 ft *2,43 m* thick and was installed by Overly.

Door Largest *Great Britain*

The largest doors in Great Britain are those to the Britannia Assembly Hall, at Filton airfield, Avon. The doors are 1035 ft *315 m* in length and 67 ft *20 m* high, divided into three bays each 345 ft *105 m* across. The largest simple hinged door in Britain is that of Ye Old Bull's Head, Beaumaris, Anglesey, Gwynedd, which is 11 ft *3,35 m* wide and 13 ft *3,96 m* high.

Door Oldest

The oldest doors in Britain are those of Hadstock Church, Essex, which date from *c.* 1040 AD and exhibit evidence of Danish workmanship.

Dry dock Largest *World*

The largest dry dock in the world with a maximum shipbuilding capacity of 1,200,000 tons deadweight is the Okpo No 1 Dry Dock, Chojé Island in South Korea. It measures 525 m *1722.4 ft* long by 131 m *430 ft* wide and was completed in 1979.

The largest shipbuilding dry dock in the UK is the Belfast Harbour Commission and Harland and Wolff building dock at Belfast, Northern Ireland. It was excavated by Wimpey's to a length of 1825 ft *556 m* and a width of 305 ft *93 m* and could accommodate tankers of 1,000,000 tons deadweight. Work was begun on 26 Jan 1968 and completed on 30 Nov 1969 and involved the excavation of 400,000 yd³ *306 000 m³*. The dry dock under construction at Port Rashid, Dubai, Persian Gulf, opened in March 1979 measures 1722 × 328 ft *525 × 100 m*.

Earthworks Largest *World*

The largest earthworks in the world carried out prior to the mechanical era were the Linear Earth Boundaries of the Benin Empire in the Bendel state of Nigeria. These were first reported in 1900 and partially surveyed in 1967. In April 1973 it was estimated by Mr Patrick Darling that the total length of the earthworks was probably between 4000 and 8000 miles *6400–12 800 km* with the total amount of earth moved estimated at from 500 to 600 million yd³ *380–460 million m³*.

Earthworks Largest *Great Britain*

The greatest prehistoric earthwork in Britain is Wansdyke, originally Woden's Dyke, which ran 86 miles *138 km* from Portishead, Avon to Inkpen Beacon and Ludgershall, south of Hungerford, Berkshire. It is believed to have been built by the pre-Roman Wessex culture. The most extensive single site earthwork is the Dorset Cursus near Gussage St. Michael, dating from *c.* 1900 BC. The workings are 6 miles *9,7 km* in length, involving an estimated 250,000 yd³

191 000 m³ of excavations. The largest of the Celtic hill-forts is that known as Mew Dun, or Maiden Castle, 2 miles *3 km* SW of Dorchester, Dorset. It covers 115 acres *46,5 ha* and was abandoned shortly after AD 43.

Fence Longest and Highest
The longest fence in the world was the dingo-proof fence enclosing the main sheep areas of Australia. The wire fence is 6 ft *1,8 m* high, 1 ft *30 cm* underground and stretches for 3437 miles *5531 km*. The Queensland State Government discontinued full maintenance in 1982 but 500 km *310 miles* is now being repaired. The world's tallest fences are security screens 20 m *65.6 ft* high erected by Harrop-Allin of Pretoria in November 1981 to keep out Soviet RP67 rocket sabotage missiles from fuel depots and refineries at Sasolburg, South Africa.

Flagstaff Tallest *World*
The tallest flagstaff ever erected was that outside the Oregon Building at the 1915 Panama-Pacific International Exposition in San Francisco, California, USA. Trimmed from a Douglas fir, it stood 299 ft 7 in *91 m* in height and weighed 45 tons *47 tonnes*. The tallest unsupported flag pole in the world is the 282 ft 4 in *86 m* tall steel pole weighing 120,000 lb *54430 kg* erected on 22 Aug 1985 at the Canadian Expo 86 exhibition in Vancouver, British Columbia. It supports a gigantic ice hockey stick 205 ft *62,5 m* in length.

Flagstaff Tallest *Great Britain*
The tallest flagstaff in Great Britain is a 225 ft *68 m* tall Douglas fir staff at Kew, Richmond upon Thames, Greater London. Cut in Canada, it was shipped across the Atlantic and towed up the River Thames on 7 May 1958, to replace the old 214 ft *65 m* tall staff of 1919.

Fountain Tallest *World and Great Britain*
The world's tallest fountain is the Fountain at Fountain Hills, Arizona built at a cost of $1,500,000 for McCulloch Properties Inc. At full pressure of 375 lb/in² *26,3 kg/cm²* and at a rate of 5828 Imp. gal/min *26 500 litres/min* the 560 ft *170 m* tall column of water weighs more than 8 tons/*tonnes*. The nozzle speed achieved by the three 600 hp pumps is 146.7 mph *236 km/h*.

The tallest fountain in Great Britain is the Emperor Fountain at Chatsworth, Bakewell, Derbyshire. When first tested on 1 June 1844, it attained the then unprecedented height of 260 ft *79 m*. Since the war it has not been played to more than 250 ft *76 m* and rarely beyond 180 ft *55 m*.

Garbage dump Biggest
Reclamation Plant No. 1, Fresh Kills, Staten Island, opened in March 1974, is the world's largest sanitary landfill. In its first 4 months 450,000 tons *457 000 tonnes* of refuse from New York City was dumped on the site by 700 barges.

Gasholder Largest *World*
The world's largest gasholder is that at Fontaine l'Eveque, Belgium, where disused mines have been adapted to store up to 500 million m³ *17,650 million ft³* of gas at ordinary pressure. Probably the largest conventional gasholder is that at Wien-Simmering, Vienna, Austria, completed in 1968, with a height of 274 ft 8 in *84 m* and a capacity of 10.59 million ft³ *300 000 m³*.

Gasholder Largest *Great Britain*
The largest gasholder ever constructed in Great Britain is the East Greenwich Gas Works No. 2 Holder built in 1891 with an original capacity for 12,200,000 ft³ *346 000 m³*. As constructed its capacity is 8.9 million ft³ *252 000 m³* with a water tank 303 ft *92 m* in diameter and a full inflated height of 148 ft *45 m*. The No. 1 holder

(capacity 8.6 million ft³ *243 500 m³*) has a height of 200 ft *61 m*. The River Tees Northern Gas Board's 1186 ft *361 m* deep underground storage in use since January 1959 has a capacity of 330,000 ft³ *9300 m³*.

Globe Largest revolving
The world's largest revolving globe is the 21½ ton/*tonnes* 27 ft 11 in *8,50 m* diameter sphere in Babson College Wellesley, Massachusetts, USA completed at a cost of $200,000 (*then £71,425*) in 1956.

Jetty Longest
The longest deep water jetty in the world is the Quai Hermann du Pasquier at Le Havre, France, with a length of 5000 ft *1524 m*. Part of an enclosed basin, it has a constant depth of water of 32 ft *9,8 m* on both sides.

Kitchen *Largest*
The largest kitchen ever set up has been the Indian Government field kitchen set up in April 1973 at Ahmadnagar, Maharashtra in the famine area which daily provided 1.2 million subsistence meals.

Lamp Post *Tallest*
The tallest lighting columns ever erected are four of 63,5 m *208 ft 4 in* made by Petitjean & Cie of Troyes, France and installed by Taylor Woodrow at Sultan Qaboos Sports Complex, Muscat, Oman.

Lighthouse Brightest and Earliest *World*
The £18½ million 100 m *328 ft* tall rock light-house built in 1983–85 40 km *24.8 miles* SW of l'Ile d'Ouessant is visible at 40 nautical miles *74 km*. With reflective clouds at optimal altitude the loom is detectable in Isles of Scilly 105 miles *169 km* distant. The lights with the greatest

An added attraction to the lions at Longleat is the world's longest maze, comprising 16,180 yew trees. *See p. 116.*

range are those 1092 ft *332 m* above the ground on the Empire State Building, New York City, NY, USA. Each of the four-arc mercury bulbs has a rated candlepower of 450,000,000, visible 80 miles *130 km* away on the ground and 300 miles *490 km* away from aircraft. They were switched on on 31 Mar 1956.

Lighthouse Brightest *Great Britain*
The lighthouse in Great Britain with the most powerful light is the shorelight at Strumble Head, near Fishguard, Dyfed. It has an intensity of 6,000,000 candelas. The Irish light with the greatest intensity is Aranmore on Rinrawros Point, County Donegal.

Lighthouse Remotest *Great Britain*
The most remote Trinity House lighthouse is The Smalls, about 16 sea miles (18.4 statute miles *29,6 km*) off the Dyfed coast. The most remote Scottish lighthouse is Sule Skerry, 35 miles *56 km* off shore and 45 miles *72 km* northwest of Dunnet Head, Highland. The most remote Irish light is Blackrock, 9 miles *14 km* off the Mayo coast.

Lighthouse Tallest
The world's tallest lighthouse is the steel tower 348 ft *106 m* tall near Yamashita Park in Yokohama, Japan. It has a power of 600,000 candles and a visibility range of 20 miles *32 km*.

Bishop Rock, Isles of Scilly measures 47,8 m *156.8 ft* high to its helipad. The tallest Scottish lighthouse is the 139 ft *42,3 m* tall North Ronald-say lighthouse, Orkney Islands.

Marquee Largest *World and Great Britain*

The largest tent ever erected was one covering an area of 188,368 ft² *17 500 m²* (4.32 acres *1,7 ha*) put up by the firm of Deuter from Augsburg, W. Germany, for the 1958 'Welcome Expo' in Brussels, Belgium.

The largest marquee in Britain is one made by Piggot Brothers in 1951 and used by the Royal Horticultural Society at their annual show (first held in 1913) in the grounds of the Royal Hospital, Kensington and Chelsea, London. The marquee is 310 ft *94 m* long by 480 ft *146 m* wide and consists of 18¾ miles *30 km* of 36 in *91 cm* wide canvas covering a ground area of 148,800 ft² *13 820 m²*. A tent 435 ft *132,5 m* long was erected in one lift by thirty-five men of the Military Corrective Training Centre, Colchester on 23 July 1980.

The Offshore Europe 1983 exhibition at the Bridge of Don, Showground, Aberdeen, Scotland was housed in 15 contiguous air tents covering 28 400 m² *6.91 acres*.

Maypole

The tallest reported Maypole erected in England was one of Sitka spruce 105 ft 7 in *32,12 m* tall put up in Pelynt, Cornwall on 1 May 1974. The permanent pole at Paganhill, near Stroud, Gloucestershire is 90 ft *27,43 m* tall.

Maze Largest

The oldest dateable representation of a labyrinth is that on a clay tablet from Pylos, Greece from *c.* 1200 BC.

The world's largest hedge maze is that at Longleat, nr Warminster, Wilts, with 1.69 miles *2,72 km* of paths flanked by 16,180 yew trees. It was opened on 6 June 1978 and measures 381 × 187 ft *116 × 57 m*. 'Il Labirinto' at Villa Pisani, Stra, Italy in which Napoleon was 'lost' in 1807 had 4 miles *6,4 km* of pathways.

Menhir *tallest*

The tallest menhir found is the 380 ton Grand Menhir Brisé, now in 4 pieces, which originally stood 69 ft *22 m* high at Locmariaquer, Britanny, France. Britain's tallest is one of 25 ft *7,6 m* at Rudston, Humberside.

Monument Prehistoric *Largest*

Britain's largest megalithic prehistoric monument and largest existing henge are the 28½ acre *11,5 ha* earthworks and stone circles of Avebury, Wiltshire, 'rediscovered' in 1646. The earliest calibrated date in the area of this neolithic site is *c.* 4200 BC. The whole work is 1200 ft *365 m* in diameter with a 40 ft *12 m* ditch around the perimeter and required an estimated 15 million man-hours of work. The henge of Durrington Walls, Wiltshire, obliterated by road building, had a diameter of 1550 ft *472 m*. It was built from *c.* 2500 BC and required some 900,000 man hours.

The largest trilithons exist at Stonehenge, to the south of Salisbury Plain, Wiltshire, with single sarsen blocks weighing over 45 tons/*tonnes* and requiring over 550 men to drag them up a 9° gradient. The earliest stage of the construction of the ditch has been dated to 2800 BC. Whether Stonehenge, which required some 30 million man-years, was a lunar calendar, a temple or an eclipse-predictor is still debated.

Monument Tallest

The world's tallest monument is the stainless steel Gateway to the West Arch in St Louis, Missouri, USA, completed on 28 Oct 1965 to commemorate the westward expansion after the Louisiana Purchase of 1803. It is a sweeping arch spanning 630 ft *192 m* and rising to the same height of 630 ft *192 m* and costing $29,000,000 (*then £10.35 million*). It was designed in 1947 by Eero Saarinen (d. 1961).

The tallest monumental column in the world is that commemorating the battle of San Jacinto (21 Apr 1836), on the bank of the San Jacinto river near Houston, Texas, USA. General Sam Houston (1793–1863) and his force of 743 Texan troops killed 630 Mexicans (out of a total force of 1600) and captured 700 others, for the loss of nine men killed and 30 wounded. Constructed in 1936–9, at a cost of $1,500,000 (*then £372,000*), the tapering column is 570 ft *173 m* tall, 47 ft *14 m* square at the base, and 30 ft *9 m* square at the observation tower, which is surmounted by a star weighing 196.4 tons *199,6 tonnes*. It is built of concrete, faced with buff limestone, and weighs 31,384 tons *31 888 tonnes*.

Monument, Youngest ancient

The newest scheduled ancient monuments are a hexagonal pill box and 48 concrete tank traps south of Christchurch, Dorset built in World War II and protected since 1973.

SEVEN WONDERS OF THE WORLD

The Seven Wonders of the World were first designated by Antipater of Sidon in the 2nd century BC. They included the Pyramids of Giza, built by three Fourth Dynasty Egyptian Pharaohs, Khwfw (Khufu or Cheops), Kha-f-Ra (Khafre, Khefren or Chepren) and Menkaure (Mycerinus) near El Giza (El Gizeh), south-west of El Qâhira (Cairo) in Egypt. The Great Pyramid ('Horizon of Khufu') was finished under Rededef *c.* 2580 BC. Its original height was 480 ft 11 in *146,5 m* (now, since the loss of its topmost stones and the pyramidion, reduced to 449 ft 6 in *137 m*) with a base line of 756 ft *230 m* and thus covering slightly more than 13 acres *5 ha*. It has been estimated that a permanent work force of 4000 required 30 years to manoeuvre into position the 2,300,000 limestone blocks averaging 2½ tons/*tonnes* each, totalling about 5,750,000 tons *5 840 000 tonnes* and a volume of 90,700,000 ft³ *2 568 000 m³*. Some blocks are of 15 tons. A costing exercise published in December 1974, indicated that it would require 405 men 6 years at a cost of $1.13 billion (*then £500 million*).

Of the other six wonders only fragments remain of the Temple of Artemis (Diana) of the Ephesians, built in *c.* 350 BC. at Ephesus, Turkey (destroyed by the Goths in AD 262), and of the Tomb of King Mausolus of Caria, built at Halicarnassus, now Bodrum, Turkey, in *c.* 325 BC. No trace remains of the Hanging Gardens of Semiramis, at Babylon, Iraq *c.* 600 BC; the 40 ft *12 m* tall marble, gold and ivory statue of Zeus (Jupiter), by Phidias (5th century BC) at Olympia, Greece (lost in a fire at Istanbul); the 117 ft *35 m* tall statue by Chares of Lindus of the figure of the god Helios (Apollo) called the Colossus of Rhodes (sculptured 292–280 BC, destroyed by an earthquake in 224 BC); or the 400 ft *122 m* tall world's earliest lighthouse, built by Sostratus of Cnidus (*c.* 270 BC) as a pyramidically shaped tower of white marble, (destroyed by earthquake in AD 1375), on the island of Pharos (Greek, *pharos* = light-house), off the coast of El Iskandariya (Alexandria), Egypt.

Mound Largest *World*

The gravel mound built as a memorial to the Seleucid King Antiochus I (reigned 69–34 BC) on the summit of Nemrud Dagi (8205 ft *2494 m*) south east of Malatya, Eastern Turkey measures 197 ft *59,8 m* tall and covers 7.5 acres *3 ha*.

Mound Largest *United Kingdom*

The largest artificial mound in Europe is Silbury Hill, 6 miles *9,7 km* west of Marlborough, Wiltshire, which involved the moving of an estimated 670,000 tons *681,000 tonnes* of chalk, at a cost of 18 million man-hours to make a cone 130 ft *39 m* high with a base of 5½ acres *2 ha*. Prof. Richard Atkinson in charge of the 1968 excavations showed that it is based on an innermost central mound, similar to contemporary round barrows, and is now dated to 2745 ± 185 BC. The largest long barrow in England is that inside the hill-fort at Maiden Castle (see Earthworks largest GB). It originally had a length of 1800 ft *548 m* and had several enigmatic features such as a ritual pit with pottery, limpet shells, and animal bones, but the date of these is not certain. The longest long barrow containing a megalithic chamber is that at West Kennet (*c.* 2200 BC), near Silbury, measuring 385 ft *117 m* in length.

Naturist resorts

The oldest resort is Der Freilichtpark, Klingberg, W. Germany established in 1903. The largest in the world is the Beau Valley Country Club, Warmbaths, South Africa extending over 4 million m² *988 acres* with up to 20,000 visitors a year. However, 100,000 people visit the smaller centre Helio-Marin at Cap d'Agde, southern France, which covers 90 ha *222 acres*. The term 'nudist camp' is deplored by naturists.

Obelisk (Monolithic) Largest and Oldest

The largest standing obelisk (from the Gk *obeliskos,* skewer or spit) in the world is the obelisk of Tuthmosis III brought from Aswan, Egypt by Emperor Constantius in the spring of AD 357. It was repositioned in the Piazza San Giovanni in Laterane, Rome on 3 Aug 1588. It was once 36 m *118.1 ft* tall but now stands 32,81 m *107.6 ft* and weighs 455 tonnes. The unfinished obelisk, probably commissioned by Queen Hatshepsut *c.* 1490 BC, at Aswan is 41,75 m *136.8 ft* in length and weighs 1168 tonnes/*tons*. The largest obelisk in the United Kingdom is Cleopatra's Needle on the Embankment, London, which at 68 ft 5 in *20,88 m* is the worlds 11th tallest. It weighs 186.3 tons *189,35 tonnes*. It was towed up the Thames from Egypt on 21 Jan 1878 and positioned on 13 Sept. The longest an obelisk has remained *in situ* is that still at Heliopolis, near Cairo, Egypt, erected by Senusret I *c.* 1750 BC.

Pier Longest *World*

The world's longest pier was the Dammam Pier, Saudi Arabia, on the Persian Gulf with an overall length of 6.79 miles *10,93 km*. The work was begun in July 1948 and completed on 15 Mar 1950. The area was subsequently developed by 1980 into the King Abdul Aziz Port with 39 deep water berths.

Pier Longest *Great Britain*

The longest pier in Great Britain is the Bee Ness Jetty, completed in 1930, which stretches 8200 ft *2500 m* along the west bank of the River Medway, 5 to 6 miles *8 to 9,6 km* below Rochester, at Kingsnorth, Kent.

Pyramid Largest

The largest pyramid, and the largest monument ever constructed, is the Quetzacóatl at Cholula de Rivadabia, 63 miles *101 km* south-east of Mexico City, Mexico. It is 177 ft *54 m* tall and its base covers an area of nearly 45 acres *18,2 ha*.

Its total volume has been estimated at 4,300,000 yd³ *3 300 000 m³* compared with 3,360,000 yd³ *2,5 million m³* for the Pyramid of Cheops (*see* Seven Wonders of the World). The pyramid-building era here was between the 2nd and 6th centuries AD.

Pyramid Oldest

The oldest known pyramid is the Djoser step pyramid at Saqqâra, Egypt constructed by Imhotep to a height of 204 ft *62 m* originally with a Tura limestone casing in *c.* 2650 BC. The largest known single block comes from the Third Pyramid (the pyramid of Mycerinus) and weighs 290 tonnes *285 tons*. The oldest New World pyramid is that on the island of La Venta in south-eastern Mexico built by the Olmec people *c.* 800 BC. It stands 100 ft *30 m* tall with a base dimension of 420 ft *128 m*.

Scarecrow

The world's largest scarecrow was built by 'de Binkel' youth club in Creil, Netherlands on 29 June 1985. It was 41.9 ft *12,77 m* tall with a spread of 35.7 ft *10,9 m* and was called *Peuntje*.

Snow Construction *Largest*

The world's largest snow construction is the Ice Palace built in Jan 1986 using 30,000 blocks of ice at St Paul, Minnesota, USA, during the Winter Carnival. Designed and built by Ellerbe Associates Inc, it stood 120 ft *36,5 m* high—the equivalent of a 15-storey building.

Stairs Longest *World*

The world's longest stairway is the service staircase for the Niesenbahn funicular which rises to 2365 m *7759 ft* near Spiez, Switzerland. It has 11,674 steps and a bannister. The stone cut T'ai Chan temple stairs of 6600 steps in the Shantung Mountains, China ascend 4700 feet in 5 miles *1428 m* in *8 km*. The longest spiral staircase is one 1103 ft *336,2 m* deep with 1520 steps installed in the Mapco–White County Coal Mine, Carmi, Illinois, USA by Systems Control Inc in May 1981.

Stairs Longest *Great Britain*

The longest stairs in Britain are those from the transformer gallery to the surface 1065 ft *324 m* in the Cruachan Power Station, Argyll, Scotland. They have 1420 steps and the Work Study Dept. allows 27 min 41.4 sec for the ascent.

Statue Longest

Near Bamiyan, Afghanistan there are the remains of the recumbent Sakya Buddha, built of plastered rubble, which was 'about 1000 ft *305 m*' long and is believed to date from the 3rd or 4th century AD.

Statue Tallest

The tallest full-figure statue in the world is that of 'Motherland', an enormous pre-stressed concrete female figure on Mamayev Hill, outside Volgograd, USSR, designed in 1967 by Yevgenyi Vuchetich, to commemorate victory in the Battle of Stalingrad (1942–3). The statue from its base to the tip of the sword clenched in her right hand measures 270 ft *82,30 m*.

Tidal river barrier

The largest tidal river barrier in the world is the Thames Barrier at Woolwich, London with 9 piers and 10 gates. There are 6 rising sector gates 61 m *200 ft 1¼ in* wide and 4 falling radial gates 31,5 m *103 ft 4 in* wide. The site was chosen in 1971. Costs to the end of 1982 were £400 million.

Tomb Largest

The largest tomb yet discovered is that of Emperor Nintoku (died *c.* AD 428) south of Osaka, Japan. It measures 1594 ft *485 m* long by 1000 ft *305 m* wide by 150 ft *45 m* high.

Right: The world's biggest snowman was constructed between 21–24 Jan 1986 by 8 members of Ski Supertravel in Val-d'Isére, France. It was 23 ft *7 m* tall and weighed more than 15 tons *15,24 tonnes*.

Below: The floodlit Ice Palace, built to celebrate the hundredth Winter Carnival at St Paul, Minnesota, USA, was designed by Ellerbe Associates of Minneapolis and built under the watchful eye of Project Manager Scott Thorpe. (Colorific).

The 9 pier 10 gate tidal barrier at Woolwich, London, is the largest river barrier in the world. (Aspect) *See p. 117.*

Totem pole Tallest

A totem pole 173 ft *52,73 m* tall was raised on 6 June 1973 at Alert Bay, British Columbia, Canada. It tells the story of the Kwakiutl and took 36 man-weeks to carve.

Vats Largest

The largest vat in the world is named 'Strongbow', used by H.P. Bulmer Ltd., the cider makers of Hereford, England. It measures 64½ ft *19,65 m* in height and 75½ ft *23,0 m* in diameter with a capacity of 1,630,000 gallons *74 099 hectolitres.*

The largest wooden wine cask in the world is the Heidelberg Tun completed in 1751 in the cellar of the Friedrichsbau Heidelberg, West Germany. Its capacity is 1855 hectolitres *40,790 gal.* The world's oldest is that in use since 1715 at Hugelet Fils (founded 1639) Riquewihr, Haut-Rhin by the most recent of the 12 generations of the family.

Wall Longest *World*

The Great Wall of China, completed during the reign of Chhin Shih Huang-ti (246–210 BC), has a main line length of 2150 miles *3460 km* with a further 1780 miles *2860 km* of branches and spurs, with a height of from 15 to 39 ft *4,5 to 12 m* and up to 32 ft *9,8 m* thick. It runs from Shanhaikuan, on the Gulf of Pohai, to Yümênkuan and Yang-kuan and was kept in repair up to the 16th century. Some 32 miles *51,5 km* of the Wall have been destroyed since 1966. Part of the wall was blown up to make way for a dam in July 1979. On 6 Mar 1985 a report from China stated that a 5 year long survey proved that the total length had been 9980 km *6200 miles.*

Wall Longest *Great Britain*

The longest of the Roman Walls built in Britain was the 15–20 ft *4,5–6 m* tall Hadrian's Wall, built AD 122–126. It crossed the Tyne-Solway isthmus for 73½ miles *118 km* from Bowness-on-Solway, Cumbria, to Wallsend-on-Tyne, Tyne and Wear, being abandoned in AD 383.

Water tower

The world's tallest water tower is that at Union, New Jersey, USA built in 1965 to a height of 210 ft *64 m* with a capacity of 250,000 gallons *9462 hl.* The tower is owned and operated by the Elizabethtown Water Company.

Waterwheel Largest *World and Great Britain*

The largest waterwheel in the world is the Mohammadieh Noria wheel at Hamah, Syria with a diameter of 131 ft *40 m* dating from Roman times. The Lady Isabella wheel at Laxey, Isle of Man is the largest in the British Isles and was built for draining a lead mine and completed on 27 Sept 1854, and disused since 1929. It has a circumference of 228 ft *69 m,* a diameter of 72½ ft *22 m* and an axle weighing 9 tons/*tonnes.* The largest waterwheel in Britain is the 50 ft 5 in *15,36 m* diameter wheel built in 1870 at Caernarfon, Gwynedd and is owned by the Welsh Industrial and Maritime Museum, based in Cardiff. It worked until 1925 at Dinorwic, Gwynedd and is 5 ft *1,52 m* in width. It is exhibited at the Welsh State Museum, Gilfach Ddu, Llanberis.

Window Largest

The largest sheet of glass ever manufactured was one of 50 m² *538.2 ft²,* or 20 m *65 ft 7 in* by 2,5 m *8 ft 2¼ in,* exhibited by the Saint Gobian Company in France at the *Journées Internationales de Miroiterie* in March 1958. The largest single windows in the world are those in the Palace of Industry and Technology at Rondpoint de la Défense, Paris, with an extreme width of 218 m *715.2 ft* and a maximum height of 50 m *164 ft.*

The record for Pilkington of St Helens, Merseyside is a sheet of 2,5 × 15,2 m *8 ft 2¼ × 49 ft 10¼ in* made for the Festival of Britain in 1951.

Wine cellar

The largest wine cellars in the world are at Paarl, those of the Ko-operative Wijnbouwers Vereeniging, known as KWV, near Cape Town, in the centre of the wine-growing district of South Africa. They cover an area of 25 acres *10 ha* and have a capacity of 30 million gal *136 million litres.* The Cienega Winery of the Almaden Vineyards in Hollister, California, USA covers 4 acres *1,6 ha* and can house 37,300 oak barrels containing 1.83 million gallons of wine.

Ziggurat Largest

The largest ziggurat ever built was by the Elamite King Untash *c.* 1250 BC known as the Ziggurat of Choga Zanbil, 30 km *18.6 miles* from Haft Tepe, Iran. The outer base was 105 × 105 m *344 ft* and the fifth 'box' 28 × 28 m *91.8 ft* nearly 50 m *164 ft* above. The largest surviving ziggurat (from the verb *zaqaru,* to build high) or stage-tower is the Ziggurat of Ur (now Muquyyar, Iraq) with a base 61 × 45,7 m *200 × 150 ft* built to three storeys surmounted by a summit temple. The first and part of the second storeys now survive to a height of 60 ft *18 m.* It was built in the reign of Ur-nammu (*c.* 2113–2096 BC).

10. BORINGS AND MINES

Deepest *World*

Man's deepest penetration into the Earth's crust is a geological exploratory drilling near Zapolarny, Kola peninsula USSR begun in 1970. On 28 Dec 1983 12 000 m *39,370 ft* or 7.45 miles was reached. Progress has understandably greatly slowed to 500 m *1640 ft* per annum as the eventual target of 15 000 m *49,212 ft,* in 1989–90 is neared. The drill bit is mounted on a turbine driven by a mud pump. The temperature at 11 km *6.83 miles* was already 200° C *392° F.*

Deepest *Ocean Drilling*

The deepest recorded drilling into the sea bed by the *Glomar Challenger* of the US Deep Sea Drilling Project is one of 5709 ft *1740 m* off N.W. Spain in 1976. The deepest site is now 7034 m *23,077 ft* below the surface on the western wall of the Marianas Trench (see page 56) in May 1978.

Oil fields

The largest oil field in the world is the Ghawar field, Saudi Arabia developed by ARAMCO which measures 150 miles by 22 miles *240 km by 35 km.*

The Mohammadieh Noria waterwheel on the River Orontes in North Syria—the world's largest with a diameter of 131 ft *40 m.* (Robert Harding).

The area of the designated parts of the UK Continental shelf as at 1 Apr 1975 was 223,550 miles² *579 000 km²* with total recoverable reserves of 3200 million tonnes of oil and 51,000,000 million ft³ *1 443 000 million m³* of gas. Gas was first discovered in the West Sole Field in October 1965 and oil in the Forties Field (Block 22/17) at 11,000 ft *3352 m* from the drilling barge *Sea Quest* on 18 Sept 1970, though a small gasfield was detected near Whitby, N. Yorkshire in 1937. The most productive oil field is expected to be Brent (found in July 1971) where the B platform was installed in August 1976. Production in 1979 reached 350,000 barrels a day and peaked to 850,000 bbd in 1983. The whole UK production in 1979 was 76,415,581 tonnes or 19,558 million Imperial gal. The deepest drilling in British waters is 2400 ft *731 m* in Block 206, west of Shetland by Shell using the drill ship *Petrel* in April 1980.

Gas deposits

The largest gas deposit in the world is at Urengoi, USSR with an eventual production of 200,000 million m³ per year through 6 pipelines from proved reserves of 7,000,000 million m³. The trillionth (10¹²) cubic metre was produced on 23 Apr 1986.

Oil platforms *Largest*

The world's most massive oil platform is the *Statfjord B* Concrete Gravity-base platform built at Stavanger, Norway owned by the Statfjord Group and operated by Mobil Exploration Norway Inc until 31 Dec 1986. Tow-out to its permanent field took place between 1 and 5 Aug 1981 and it was the heaviest object ever moved—816,000 tonnes or 803,000 long tons ballasted weight. The £1.1 billion structure was towed by 8 tugs with a combined power of 115,000 hp. The height of the concrete structure is 204 m *670 ft* and the overall height 271 m *890 ft*. It thus weighs almost three times the weight of each of the towers of the World Trade Centre (290,000 long tons). The world's tallest production platform is the 345 m *1132 ft* tall Shell

The giant-gusher *Statfjord B* oil platform in the North Sea, the biggest in the world.

Cognac platform built in 1976 and placed outside the Mississippi delta in Louisiana, USA.

Gusher Greatest

The greatest wildcat ever recorded blew at Alborz No 5 well, near Qum, Iràn on 26 Aug 1956. The uncontrolled oil gushed to a height of 170 ft *52 m* at 120,000 barrels per day at a pressure of 9000 lb/in² *62 055 kPa*. It was closed after 90 days work by B. Mostofi and Myron

Kinley of Texas, USA. The Lake View No. 1 gusher in California, USA on 15 Mar 1910 may have yielded 125,000 barrels in its first 24 hours.

Oil Spills Greatest

The slick from the Mexican marine blow-out beneath the drilling rig *Ixtoc I* in the Gulf of Campeche, Gulf of Mexico, on 3 June 1979 reached 400 miles *640 km* by 5 Aug 1979. It eventually was capped on 24 Mar 1980 after a loss of 3,000,000 barrels (535,000 tons).

The worst oil spill in history was of 236,000 tons/ *tonnes* of oil from the super-tankers *Atlantic Empress* and *Aegean Captain* when they collided off Tobago on 19 July 1979. The worst oil spill in British waters was from the 118,285 dwt *Torrey Canyon* which struck the Pollard Rock off Land's End on 18 Mar 1967 resulting in a loss of 106,000 tons of oil.

Flare Greatest

The greatest gas fire was that which burnt at Gassi Touil in the Algerian Sahara from noon on 13 Nov 1961 to 9.30 a.m. on 28 Apr 1962. The pillar of flame rose 450 ft *137 m* and the smoke 600 ft *182 m*. It was eventually extinguished by Paul Neal ('Red') Adair (b. 1932), of Houston, Texas, USA, using 550 lb *245 kg* of dynamite. His fee was understood to be about $1,000,000 (*then £357,000*).

Water well Deepest *World*

The world's deepest water bore is the Stensvad Water Well 11-W1 of 7320 ft *2231 m* drilled by the Great Northern Drilling Co. Inc. in Rosebud County, Montana, USA in October–November 1961. The Thermal Power Co. geothermal steam well begun in Sonoma County, California in 1955 is now down to 9029 ft *2752 m*.

Water well Deepest *Great Britain*

The deepest well in Great Britain is a water table well 2842 ft *866 m* deep in the Staffordshire coal measures at Smestow. The deepest artesian well in Britain is that at the White Heather Laundry, Stonebridge Park, Brent, London, bored in 1911 to a depth of 2225 ft *678 m*. The deepest known hand dug well is one dug to 1285 ft *391,6 m* in 1858 to March 1862 on the site of Fitzherbert School, Woodingdean, Brighton, East Sussex.

MINE RECORDS

Earliest *(World)*	41,250 BC ± 1600		Lion Cavern, Haematite (red iron ore)	Ngwenya, Hhohho, Swaziland
Earliest *(GB)*	3390 BC ± 150		Flint	Church Hill, Findon, W. Sussex
Deepest *(World)*[1]	12,391 ft *3777 m* (2.34 miles)		Gold, Western Deep Levels (temp 131°F *55°C*)	Carletonville, South Africa
Deepest *(GB, all-time)*	4132 ft *1259 m*		Coal, Arley Seam, Parsonage Colliery (Feb 1949)	Leigh, Lancashire
(GB, current)	3690 ft *1127 m*		Coal, Bickershaw Colliery	Bickershaw, Lancashire
(Cornwall)	3600 ft *1097 m*		Tin, Williams Shaft, Dolcoath (1910)	Near Camborne, Cornwall
Copper *(deepest, open cast)*	2590 ft *789 m*		Bingham Canyon (began 1904) diameter 2.3 miles *3,7 km*	Utah, USA
Copper *(largest underground)*	356 miles *573 km* tunnels		San Manuel Mine, Magma Copper Co	Arizona, USA
Lead *(largest)*	> 10 per cent of world output		Viburnum Trend	Southeast Missouri, USA
Goldmining *(area)*	> 51 per cent of world output		38 mines of the Witwatersrand Discovery in 1886	South Africa
Gold Mine *(largest world)*[2]	12,100 acres *4900 ha*		East Rand Proprietary Mines Ltd	Boksburg, Transvaal, South Africa
Gold Mine *(largest, GB)*	120,000 fine oz (1854–1914)		Clogau, St David's (disc. 1836)	Gwynedd, Wales
Gold Mine *(richest)*	49.4 million oz		Crown Mines (all-time yield)	Transvaal, South Africa
Iron Mine *(largest)*	20 300 million tonnes rich ore		Lebedinsky (45–65% ore)	Kursk region, USSR
Platinum *(largest)*	1,000,000 oz *28 tonnes* per annum		Rustenberg Group, Impala plant	Springs, South Africa
Tungsten Mine *(largest)*	2000 tonnes per day		Union Carbide Mount Morgan mine	Near Bishop, California, USA
Uranium *(largest)*	5000 tons of uranium oxide		Rio Tinto Zinc open cast pit	Rössing, Namibia, SW Africa
Spoil Dump *(largest, world)*	275 million yd³ *210 million m³*		New Cornelia Tailings	Ten Mile Wash, Arizona, USA
Spoil Dump *(largest, GB)*[3]	114 acre *46 ha* 130 ft *40 m* high		Cutacre Clough Colliery tip (18 million tonnes)	Lancashire
Quarry *(largest, world)*	2.81 miles² *7,21 km²*. 2540 ft *774 m* deep. 3700 million short tons *3355 million tonnes*		Bingham Canyon Copper Mine	Nr. Salt Lake City, Utah, USA
Quarry *(largest, GB)*	500 ft *150 m* deep, 1.6 mile *2,6 km* circumference		Old Delabole Slate Quarry (since c. 1570)	Cornwall
Open Cast Coal Mine	1130 ft *325 m* deep 21 km² *8 mile²* area		Fortuna-Garsdorf (lignite) (began 1955)	Nr. Bergheim, W. Germany
Coal Mine *(oldest, U.K.)*	c. 1822		founded by William Stobart	Wearmouth, near Sunderland, Durham

[1] Sinking began in June 1957. Scheduled to reach 3880 m *12 730 ft* by 1992 with 14 000 ft or 2.65 miles regarded as the limit. No 3 vertical ventilation shaft is the world's deepest shaft at 2948,9 m *9675 ft*. This mine requires 130,000 tons of air per day and refrigeration which uses the energy it would take to make 37,000 short tons of ice. An underground shift comprises 11,150 men. The deepest exploratory coal mining shaft is one reaching 6700 ft *2042 m* near Thorez in the Ukranian Donbas field, USSR in Aug 1983.
[2] The world's most productive gold mine may be Muruntau, Kyzyl Kum, Uzbekistan, USSR. According to one western estimate it produces 80 tonnes of gold in a year. It has been estimated that South Africa has produced in 96 years (1886–1982) 36,400 tons or more than 31 per cent of all gold mined since 3900 BC.
[3] Reclamation plan announced 13 Sept 1982 for 1983–1996.

CHAPTER EIGHT

THE
MECHANICAL
WORLD

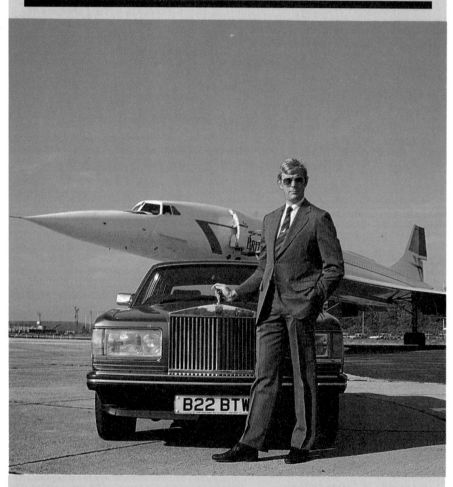

Fred Finn evidently believes in travelling in the best of British—in the sky or on the road. As a supersonic passenger he has no peers having just recorded his 604th *Concorde* flight. *See Aircraft—Personal Aviation Records.* (Executive Travel Magazine).

1. SHIPS

EARLIEST SEA-GOING BOATS

Aborigines are thought to have been able to cross the Torres Strait from New Guinea to Australia, then at least 70 km *43¼ miles* across, as early as 40,000 BC. They are believed to have used double canoes. The earliest surviving 'vessel' is a pinewood dug-out found in Pesse, Netherlands and dated to *c.* 6315 ± 275 BC and now in the Provincial Museum, Assen. The earliest representation of a boat is disputed between possible rock art outlines of mesolithic skin-boats in Høgnipen, Norway (10,000–7750 BC); Minateda, Spain (12,000–3000 BC) and Kobystan, USSR (8000–6000 BC). An 18 in *45 cm* long paddle was found at the Star Carr, North Yorkshire site, described in 1948. It has been dated to *c.* 7600 BC and is now in the Cambridge Museum of Archaeology.

The oldest surviving boat is the 142 ft *43,4 m* long 40 ton Nile boat or Royal Ship of King Cheops buried near the Great Pyramid of Khufu, Egypt *c.* 2515 BC. Its discovery was announced in May 1954 and it has been reassembled in Cairo.

The oldest shipwreck ever found is one of a Cycladic trading vessel located off the islet of Dhókós, near the Greek island of Hydra reported in May 1975 and dated to 2450 BC ± 250.

Earliest power

Propulsion by steam engine was first achieved when in 1783 the Marquis Jouffroy d'Abbans (1751–1832) ascended a reach of the river Saône near Lyon, France, in the 180 ton *182 tonnes* paddle steamer *Pyroscaphe*.

The tug *Charlotte Dundas* was the first successful power-driven vessel. She was a stern paddle-wheel steamer built for the Forth and Clyde Canal, Scotland in 1801–2 by William Syming-ton (1763–1831), using a double-acting condensing engine constructed by James Watt (1736–1819). The screw propeller was invented and patented by the Kent farmer Sir Francis Pettit Smith (1808–71) in 1836.

Oldest vessels

The oldest mechanically propelled boat in the world of certain date is the 48 ton Bristol steam driven dredger or drag-boat *Bertha* of 50 ft *15,42 m*, designed by I. K. Brunel (1806–59) in 1844 and afloat in the custody of the Exeter Maritime Museum, Devon, England. Mr G. H. Pattinson's 40 ft *12,20 m* steam launch *Dolly*, which was raised after 67 years from Ullswater, Cumbria, in 1962 and now on Lake Windermere, also probably dates from the 1840s. The world's oldest active steam ship is the *Skibladner*, which has plied Lake Mjøsa, Norway since 1856. She has had two major refits and was built in Motala, Sweden. The oldest motor vessel afloat in British waters is the *Proven* on the run from the Clyde to the Inner Hebrides. She was built in Norway in 1866. The oldest vessel on *Lloyd's Yacht Register* is the twin screw steam yacht *Esperance* built on the Clyde in 1869 and salvaged from Windermere in 1941.

The oldest square-rigged sailing vessel in the world is the restored SV *Ciudad de Inca*, built near Barcelona, Spain in 1858. She is 125 ft *38,1 m* overall with a grt of 127 tons. She was restored in 1981–82 for operation by the China Clipper Society of Maidstone, Kent.

Earliest turbine

The first turbine ship was the *Turbinia*, built in 1894 at Wallsend-on-Tyne, Tyne and Wear, to the design of the Hon. Sir Charles Parsons, OM, KCB (1854–1931). The *Turbinia* was 100 ft *30,48 m* long and of 44½ tons *45,2 tonnes* displacement with machinery consisting of three steam turbines totalling about 2000 shaft horsepower. At her first public demonstration in 1897 she reached 34.5 knots (39.7 mph *63,9 km/h*).

PASSENGER LINERS

Largest active
The world's largest and the world's longest ever liner is the *Norway* of 70,202.19 grt and 315,66 m *1035 ft 7¼ in* in overall length with a capacity of 2400 passengers. She was built as the *France* in 1961 and renamed after purchase in June 1979 by Knut Kloster of Norway. Her second maiden voyage was from Southampton on 7 May 1980. Britain's largest liner is RMS *Queen Elizabeth 2* of 67,140 gross tons and with an overall length of 963 ft *293 m* completed for the Cunard Line Ltd. in 1969. She set a 'turn round' record of 5 hr 47 min at New York on 21 Nov 1983. Her 1986 World Cruise—New York and return—is for 96 days and costs £97,930 per person in the Penthouse suite.

Largest ever
The RMS *Queen Elizabeth* (finally 82,998 but formerly 83,673 gross tons), of the Cunard fleet, was the largest passenger vessel ever built and had the largest displacement of any liner in the world. She had an overall length of 1031 ft *314 m* and was 118 ft 7 in *36 m* in breadth and was powered by steam turbines which developed 168,000 hp. Her last passenger voyage ended on 15 Nov 1968. In 1970 she was removed to Hong Kong to serve as a floating marine university and renamed *Seawise University*. On 9 Jan 1972 she was fired by 3 simultaneous outbreaks. The gutted hull had been cut up and removed by 1978. *Seawise* was a pun on the owner's initials— C. Y. Tung (1911–1982).

WARSHIPS

Battleships *Largest World*
The largest battleship in service in the world is the 887 ft 9 in *270,6 m* long USS *New Jersey* with a full load displacement of 58,000 tons *58 000 tonnes*. She was the last fire support ship on active service off the Lebanon coast with her nine 16 in guns from 14 Dec 1983 to 26 Feb 1984. The $405 million refit of USS *Iowa* was completed in May 1984. USS *Missouri* and USS *Wisconsin* have also been re-activated. The 16 inch projectiles of 2700 lb *1225 kg* can be fired 23 miles *39 km*.

Largest all-time
The Japanese battleship *Yamato* (completed on 16 Dec 1941 and sunk south-west of Kyūshū, Japan, by US planes on 7 Apr 1945) and *Musashi* (sunk in the Philippine Sea by 11 bombs and 16 torpedoes on 24 Oct 1944) were the largest battleships ever commissioned, each with a full load displacement of 72,809 tons *73 977 tonnes*. With an overall length of 863 ft *263 m*, a beam of 127 ft *38,7 m* and a full load draught of 35½ ft *10,8 m* they mounted nine 460 mm *18.1 in* guns in three triple turrets. Each gun weighed 162 tons *164,6 tonnes* and was 75 ft *22,8 m* in length firing a 3200 lb *1451 kg* projectile.

Largest Great Britain
Britain's largest ever and last battleship was HMS *Vanguard* (1944–1960) with a full load displacement of 51,420 tons *52 245 tonnes* and an overall length of 814 ft *248,1 m*. She mounted eight 15 in *38 cm* guns.

Guns and Armour
The largest guns ever mounted in any of HM ships were the 18 in *45 cm* pieces in the light battle cruiser (later aircraft carrier) HMS *Furious* in 1917. In 1918 they were transferred to the monitors HMS *Lord Clive* and *General Wolfe*. The thickest armour ever carried was in HMS *Inflexible* (completed 1881), measuring 24 in *60 cm* backed by teak up to a maximum thickness of 42 in *106,6 cm*.

Fastest destroyer
The highest speed attained by a destroyer was 45.25 knots (51.84 mph *83,42 km/h*) by the 2830 ton/*tonne* French destroyer *Le Terrible* in 1935. She was built in Blainville and powered by four Yarrow small tube boilers and two Rateau geared turbines giving 100,000 shaft horse-power. She was removed from the active list at the end of 1957.

Earliest launch
On 8 April 1986, the type 22 frigate F98, HMS *Coventry* was launched from the Swan Hunter yard, Tyneside, at 3.45 on a cold, wet and windy morning. Fearing that an industrial dispute might delay the launch, it was brought forward by 12 hours.

AIRCRAFT CARRIERS

Largest *World*
The warships with the largest full load displacement in the world are the Nimitz class US Navy aircraft carriers USS *Dwight D. Eisenhower*, *Carl Vinson* and *Theodore Roosevelt* at 91,487 tons. They are 1092 ft *322,9 m* in length overall with 4½ acres *1,82 ha* of flight deck and have a speed well in excess of 30 knots *56 km/h* from their 4 nuclear-powered 260,000 shp geared steam turbines. They have to be refuelled after about 900,000 miles *1 450 000 km* steaming. Their complement is 6300. The total cost of the *Abraham Lincoln*, laid down at Newport News in December 1984 will exceed $3¼ billion (£2.6 billion), excluding the 90-plus aircraft carried. USS *Enterprise* is, however, 1102 ft *335,8 m* long and thus still the longest warship ever built.

Above: The world's only surviving First Rate Ship-of-the-line, HMS *Victory. See p. 123.*
Below: The USS *New Jersey* takes a rest from her duties as the world's largest battleship in the Long Beach Dockyard in California, USA. (Photo Source).

With 2500 passengers and 600 cars the M/S *Olympia* has in 1986 become the world's largest car ferry.

The Royal Navy's newest aircraft carrier is HMS *Ark Royal*, commissioned in Nov 1984. She has a 550 ft *167,6 m* long flight deck and is 677 ft *206,3 m* long overall, and has a top speed of 28 knots being powered by 4 Rolls Royce Olympus TM3B gas turbines.

Most landings

The greatest number of landings on an aircraft carrier in one day was 602 achieved by Marine Air Group 6 of the United States Pacific Fleet Air Force aboard the USS *Matanikau* on 25 May 1945 between 8 am and 5 pm.

SUBMARINES

Largest *World*

The world's largest submarines are of the USSR Typhoon class code named Oscar. The launch of the first at the secret covered shipyard at Severodvinsk in the White Sea was announced by NATO on 23 Sept 1980. It is believed to have a dived displacement of 30,000 tonnes, measure 170 m *557.6 ft* overall and be armed with twenty SS NX 20 missiles with a 5000 nautical mile *9260 km* range, each with 7 warheads. By 1987 two others building in Leningrad will also be operational, each deploying 140 warheads.

Great Britain

The largest submarines ever built for the Royal Navy are the four atomic-powered nuclear missile R class boats with a surface displacement of 7500 tons *7620 tonnes* and 8400 tons

8534 *tonnes* submerged, a length of 425 ft *129,5 m*, a beam of 33 ft *10 m* and a draught of 30 ft *9,1 m*. The longest submarine patrol ever spent dived and unsupported is 111 days by H.M. Submarine *Warspite* (Cdr. J. G. F. Cooke RN) in the South Atlantic from 25 Nov 1982 to 15 Mar 1983. She sailed 30,804 nautical miles *57 085 km*.

Fastest

The Russian Alfa-Class nuclear-powered submarines have a reported maximum speed of 42 knots *77,8 km/h* plus. With use of titanium steel they are believed to be able to dive to 2500 ft *762 m*. A US spy satelite over Leningrad's naval yard on 8 June 1983 showed they were being lengthened and are now 79.3 m *260.1 ft* long.

Deepest

The two USN vessels able to descend 12,000 ft *3650 m* are the 3-man *Trieste II* (DSV I) of 303 tons dived recommissioned in November 1973 and the DSV 2 (deep submergence vessel) USS *Alvin*. The *Trieste II* was reconstructed from the record-breaking bathyscaphe *Trieste* but without the Krupp-built sphere, which enabled it to descend to 35,820 ft *10 917 m*. (See Chapter 10 Greatest ocean descent).

TANKERS

Largest

The world's largest tanker and ship of any kind is the 564,739 tonnes deadweight *Seawise Giant* completed for C. Y. Tung in 1979. She is 458,45 m *1504 ft* long with a beam of 68,86 m *225 ft 11 in* and has a draught of 24,61 m *80 ft 9 in*. She was lengthened by Nippon Kokan in 1980 by adding an 81 m *265 ft 8 in* midship section.

CARGO VESSELS

Largest

The largest vessel in the world capable of carrying dry cargo is the Liberian ore/oil carrier *World Gala* of 133,748 GT *282,462 dwt* with a length of 1109 ft *338 m* and a beam of 179 ft *54,6 m* completed in 1973. A 365,000 dwt ore carrier being built in Korea for the Norwegian owner Sig Bergesen dy, and is due for delivery in October 1986. The largest British ore/oil carriers are Lombard North Central Leasing's *Rapara* and *Rimula* built in Sweden in 1973 and 1974 of 121,164 GT, *227,412 dwt* with lengths of 332,77 m *1091 ft 9 in*.

Largest whale factory

The largest whale factory ship is the USSR's *Sovietskaya Ukraina* (32,034 gross tons), with a summer deadweight of 46,000 tons *46 738 tonnes* completed in October 1959. She is 217,8 m *714 ft 6 in* in length and 25,8 m *84 ft 7 in* in the beam.

Largest barges

The world's largest RoRo (Roll-on, Roll-off) ships are the four *El Rey* class barges of 16,700 tons and 580 ft *176,78 m* in length. They were built by the FMC Corp of Portland, Oregon, USA, and are operated by Crowley Maritime Corp of San Francisco between Florida and Puerto Rico with tri-level lodging of up to 376 truck-trailers.

Container ship

Shipborne containerisation began in 1955 when the tanker *Ideal X* was converted by Malcom McLean (US). She carried containers only on deck.

The world's largest container ships are the twelve built by United States Lines in Korea in 1984–5. They are capable of carrying 4482 TEU (20ft equivalent units—20 ft *6,1 m* containers.)

Most powerful tugs

The world's most powerful tug is the *Smit Singapore* commissioned in April 1984 by Smit Tak International, of 22,000 horsepower and 189 tons bollard pull at full power. It is 75,20 m *246.72 ft* long and 15,68 m *51.44 ft* wide.

Largest car ferry

The world's largest car and passenger ferry is the 37,800 grt M/S *Olympia* which entered service across the Baltic between Helsinki and Stockholm, Sweden on 28 Apr 1986. Built in Abo, Finland for the Viking Line, she is 177,10 m *581 ft* long, 29 m *95 ft* in the beam and can carry 2500 passengers and 600 cars.

The 9700 dwt 21 knot *Railship II* went into service on the Baltic run in Nov 1984. She can carry 88 20 m *65 ft 7 in* long rail cars, is 186,5 m *611 ft 10 in* overall and was built for HM Gehrckens of Hamburg.

Largest propeller

The world's largest ship propeller is the triple bladed screw of 11,0 m *36 ft 1 in* diameter made by Kawasaki Heavy Industries Ltd on 17 Mar 1982 for the 208,000 ton bulk carrier *Hoei Maru*.

Largest hydrofoil

The world's largest naval hydrofoil is the 212 ft *64,6 m* long *Plainview* (310 tons *314 tonnes* full load), launched by the Lockheed Shipbuilding and Construction Co. at Seattle, Washington, USA on 28 June 1965. She has a service speed of 50 knots (57 mph *92 km/h*). Three 165 ton Supramar PTS 150 Mk III hydrofoils carrying 250 passengers at 40 knots *74 km/h* ply the Malmö–Copenhagen crossing. They were built by Westermoen Hydrofoil Ltd. of Mandal, Norway. A 500 ton wing ground effect vehicle capable of carrying 900 tons has been reported in the USSR.

Largest river boat

The world's largest inland river-boat is the 378 ft *115,2 m* long SS *Admiral* now undergoing a 6 year $26.7 million renovation at St Louis, Missouri as a Mississippi river floating 'entertainment center'.

Fastest building

The fastest-ever building time for a major ship was 4 days 15 hrs in the in the case of the 10,920 ton displacement Robert E. Peory at Kaiser's Yard, Portland, Oregon, USA on 8 Nov (keel laid) to launch on 12 Nov 1942. She was operational on 15 Nov and was No 440 of the fleet of 2742 11.6 knot such liberty ships built in 18 US shipyards from 27 Sept 1941.

Most powerful icebreaker

A 61,000 ton/*tonne* nuclear powered barge-carrying merchantman designed for work along the USSR's Arctic coast was completed in early 1982 and is known to be designed to break ice. The longest purpose-built icebreaker is the 25 000 ton 460 ft *140 m* long *Rossiya*, powered by 75,000 h.p. nuclear engines built in Leningrad and completed in 1985. A new $(Can)500 million, 100,000 hp, 194 m *636 ft* long icebreaker of the Polar Class 8 was ordered by the Canadian government in October 1985.

The largest *converted* icebreaker has been the 1007 ft *306,9 m* long SS *Manhattan* (43,000 shp), which was converted by the Humble Oil Co. into a 150,000 ton *152 407 tonnes* icebreaker with an armoured prow 69 ft 2 in long. She made a double voyage through the North-West Passage in arctic Canada from 24 Aug to 12 Nov 1969. The North-West Passage was first navigated by Roald Amundsen (Norway) in the sealing sloop *Gjöa* on 11 July 1906.

Yacht most expensive

The refit of the £20 million 470 foot *143,2 m* the Saudi Arabian Royal yacht *Abdul Aziz*, built in Denmark, was completed on 22 June 1984 at Vospers Yard, Southampton at a cost of £9 million.

Largest dredger

The world's most powerful dredger is the 468.4 ft *142,7 m* long *Prins der Nederlanden* of 10,586 grt. She can dredge 20,000 tonnes/*tons* of sand from a depth of 35 m *115 ft via* two suction tubes in less than an hour.

Wooden ship

The heaviest wooden ship ever built was the *Richelieu*, 333 ft 8 in *101,70 m* long and of 8534 tons launched in Toulon, France on 3 Dec 1873. HM Battleship *Lord Warden*, completed in 1869, displaced 7940 tons *8060 tonnes*. The longest modern wooden ship ever built was the New York built *Rochambeau* (1867–72) formerly *Dunderberg*. She measured 377 ft 4 in *115 m* overall. It should be noted that the biblical length of Noah's Ark was 300 cubits or, at 18 in *45,7 cm* to a cubit, 450 ft *137 m.*

Largest human powered

The largest human powered ship was the giant Tessarakonteres 3-banked catamaran galley with 4000 rowers built for Ptolemy IV *c.* 210 BC in Alexandria, Egypt. It measured 128 m *420 ft* with up to 8 men to an oar of 38 cubits (17,5 m *57 ft*) in length. The world's longest canoe is the 117 ft *35,7 m* long 20 ton Kauri wood Maori war canoe Nga Toki Matawhaorua built by adzes at Kerikeri Inlet, New Zealand in 1940 for a crew of 70 or more. The 'Snake Boat' Nadubhagóm 135 ft *41,1 m* long from Kerala, Southern India has a crew of 109 rowers and 9 'encouragers'.

Light vessels

The earliest station still marked by a light vessel is the Newarp in the North Sea, off Great Yarmouth in 1791. A Nore Lightvessel was first placed in the Thames estuary in 1732.

SAILING SHIPS

Largest

The largest sailing vessel ever built was the *France II* (5806 gross tons), launched at Bordeaux in 1911. The *France II* was a steel-hulled, five-masted barque (square-rigged on four masts and fore and aft rigged on the aftermost mast). Her hull measured 418 ft *127,4 m* overall. Although principally designed as a sailing vessel with a stump topgallant rig, she was also fitted with two steam engines. She was wrecked off New Caledonia on 13 July 1922. The only seven-masted sailing schooner ever built was the 375.6 ft *114,4 m* long *Thomas W. Lawson* (5218 gross tons) built at Quincy, Massachusetts, USA in 1902 and lost in the English Channel on 15 Dec 1907.

The world's only surviving First Rate Ship-of-the-Line is the Royal Navy's 104-gun battleship HMS *Victory* laid down at Chatham, Kent on 23 July 1759 constructed from the wood of some 2200 oak trees. She bore the body of Admiral Nelson from Gibraltar to Portsmouth arriving 44 days after serving as his victorious flagship at the Battle of Trafalgar on 21 Oct 1805. In 1922 she was moved to No. 2 dock, Portsmouth—site of the world's oldest graving dock. The length of her cordage (both standing and running rigging) is 100,962 ft (19.12 miles *30,77 km.*) See p. 121.

The world's largest sailing vessel in service is the 342 ft *104 m* 4 masted barque *Kruzenshtern* built in *c.* 1933 and used by USSR marine schools of Kaliningrad and Murmansk.

Largest junks

The largest junk on record was the sea-going *Cheng Ho*, flagship of Admiral Cheng Ho's 62 treasure ships, of *c.* 1420, with a displacement of 3100 tons *3150 tonnes* and a length variously estimated up to 538 ft *164 m* and believed to have had 9 masts. A river junk 361 ft *110 m* long, with treadmill-operated paddle-wheels, was recorded in AD 1161. In *c.* AD 280 a floating fortress 600 ft *182,8 m* square, built by Wang Chün on the Yangtze, took part in the Chin-Wu river war. Present-day junks do not, even in the case of the Chiangsu traders, exceed 170 ft *51,8 m* in length.

Longest day's run under sail

The longest day's run calculated for any commercial vessel was one of 462 nautical miles (532.0 statute miles *856,16 km*) by the clipper *Champion of the Seas* (2722 registered tons) of the Liverpool Black Ball Line running before a north-westerly gale in the south Indian Ocean under the command of Capt. Alex. Newlands in 1854. The elapsed time between the fixes was 23 hr 17 min giving an average of 19.97 knots *37,00 km/h* (see Chapter 12 Yachting for sporting record).

Largest sails

Sails are known to have been used for marine propulsion since 3500 BC. The largest spars ever carried were those in HM Battleship *Temeraire*, completed at Chatham, Kent on 31 Aug 1877. She was broken up in 1921. The fore and main yards measured 115 ft *35 m* in length. The foresail contained 5100 ft *1555 m* of canvas, weighing 2 tons *2,03 tonnes* and the total sail area was 25,000 ft² *2322 m²*. HM Battleship *Sultan* was ship-rigged when completed at Chatham, Kent on 10 Oct 1871 and carried

34,100 ft² *3168 m²* of sails plus 15,300 ft² *1421 m²* of stunsails. She was not finally broken up until 1946.

Largest wreck

The largest ship ever wrecked has been the 312,186 dwt VLCC (Very Large Crude Carrier) *Energy Determination* which blew up and broke in two in the Straits of Hormuz on 12 Dec 1979. Her full value was $58 million (*then £26.3 million*). The largest wreck removal was carried out in 1979 by Smit Tak International who removed the remains of the French tanker *Betelgeuse*, 120,000 tons from Bantry Bay, Ireland, within 20 months.

Most massive collision

The closest approach to an irresistible force striking an immovable object occurred on 16 Dec 1977, 22 miles *35 km* off the coast of Southern Africa when the tanker *Venoil* (330,954 dwt) struck her sister ship *Venpet* (330,869 dwt).

Shortest tow

On 17 Aug 1982, by Abidjan, on the Ivory Coast, Capt. B. Nicholson in command of the 8000 hp MV *Dee Service* successfully towed a locking pin to secure the tanker *Philips Enterprise* to a floating pumping station a total distance of 4 in *10,16 cm*.

OCEAN CROSSINGS

Atlantic *Earliest*

The earliest crossing of the Atlantic by a power vessel, as opposed to an auxiliary engined sailing ship, was a 22-day voyage begun in April 1827, from Rotterdam, Netherlands, to the West Indies by the *Curaçao*. She was a 127 ft *38,7 m* wooden paddle boat of 438 tons, built as the *Calpe* in Dover in 1826 and purchased by the Dutch Government for the West Indian mail service. The earliest Atlantic crossing entirely under steam (with intervals for desalting the boilers) was by HMS *Rhadamanthus* from Plymouth to Barbados in 1832. The earliest crossing of the Atlantic under continuous steam power was by the condenser-fitted packet ship *Sirius* (703 tons *714 tonnes*) from Queenstown (now Cóbh), Ireland, to Sandy Hook, New Jersey, USA, in 18 days 10 hr on 4–22 Apr 1838.

Atlantic *Fastest World*

The fastest Atlantic crossing was made by the *United States* (then 51,988, now 38,216 gross tons), former flagship of the United States Lines. On her maiden voyage between 3 and 7 July 1952 from New York City, to Le Havre, France, and Southampton, England, she averaged 35.59 knots, or 40.98 mph *65,95 km/h* for 3 days 10 hr 40 min (6.36 p.m. GMT, 3 July to 5.16 a.m., 7 July) on a route of 2949 nautical miles *5465 km* from the Ambrose Light Vessel to the Bishop Rock Light, Isles of Scilly, Cornwall. During this run, on 6–7 July 1952, she steamed the greatest distance ever covered by any ship in a day's run (24 hr)—868 nautical miles *1609 km*, hence averaging 36.17 knots (41.65 mph *67,02 km/h*). The maximum speed attained from her 240,000 shp engines was 38.32 knots (44.12 mph *71,01 km/h*) on trials on 9–10 June 1952.

Pacific *Fastest*

The fastest crossing of the Pacific Ocean from Yokohama to Long Beach, California (4840 nautical miles *8960 km*) was 6 days 1 hr 27 min (30 June–6 July 1973) by the container ship *Sea-Land Commerce* (50,315 tons) at an average of 33.27 knots (38.31 mph *61,65 km/h*).

Channel crossing *Fastest*

The fastest crossing of the English Channel by a

commercial ferry is 52 min 49 sec from Dover to Calais by Townsend Thorensen's *Pride of Free Enterprise* in a Force 7 Gale on 9 Feb 1982.

HOVERCRAFT (skirted air cushion vehicles)

Earliest

The ACV (air-cushion vehicle) was first made a practical proposition by Sir Christopher Sydney Cockerell, CBE, FRS (b. 4 June 1910), a British engineer who had the idea in 1954, published his Ripplecraft report 1/55 on 25 Oct 1955 and patented it on 12 Dec 1955. The earliest patent relating to air-cushion craft was applied for in 1877 by John I. Thornycroft (1843–1928) of Chiswick, London and the Finn Toivo Kaario developed the idea in 1935. The first flight by a hovercraft was made by the 4 ton/*tonnes* Saunders-Roe SR-N1 at Cowes on 30 May 1959. With a 1500 lb *680 kg* thrust Viper turbojet engine, this craft reached 68 knots *126 km/h* in June 1961. The first hovercraft public service was run across the Dee Estuary by the 60 knot *111 km/h* 24-passenger Vickers-Armstrong VA-3 between July and September 1962.

Largest

The world's largest civil hovercraft is the 305 ton British-built SRN4 Mk III with a capacity of 418 passengers and 60 cars. It is 185 ft *56,38 m* in length, is powered by 4 Bristol Siddeley Marine Proteus engines giving a maximum speed in excess of the permitted cross Channel operating speed of 65 knots.

Fastest warship

The world's fastest warship is the 78 ft *23,7 m* long 100 ton/*tonne* US Navy test vehicle SES-100B. She attained a world record 91.9 knots *103.9 mph* on 25 Jan 1980 on the Chesapeake Bay Test Range, Maryland, USA. The 3000 ton US Navy Large Surface Effect Ship (LSES) was built by Bell Aerospace under contract from the Department of Defense in 1977–81.

Longest flight

The longest hovercraft journey was one of 5000 miles *8047 km* through eight West African countries between 15 Oct 1969 and 3 Jan 1970 by the British Trans-African Hovercraft Expedition.

Highest

The greatest altitude at which a hovercraft is operating is on Lago Titicaca, Peru, where since 1975 an HM2 Hoverferry has been hovering 12,506 ft *3811 m* above sea level.

2. ROAD VEHICLES

COACHING

Before the widespread use of tarred road surfaces from 1845 coaching was slow and hazardous.

'Steamin' Demon, the fastest steam driven car which broke a 79-year-old record in 1985.

The zenith was reached on 13 July 1888 when J. Selby, Esq., drove the 'Old Times' coach 108 miles *173 km* from London to Brighton and back with 8 teams and 14 changes in 7 hr 50 min to average 13.79 mph *22,19 km/h*. Four-horse carriages could maintain a speed of 21¼ mph *34 km/h* for nearly an hour. The *Border Union* stage coach, built *c.* 1825, ran 4 in hand from Edinburgh to London (393 miles *632 km*). When it ceased in 1842, due to competition from railways, the allowed schedule was 42 hr 23 min to average better than 9¼ mph *14,9 km/h*.

John Parker (b. July 1939) drove a mail coach and four 136 miles *218,8 km* from Bristol to London in 17 hr 30 mins on 1–2 Aug 1984. Norwich Union's six teams of greys were changed 11 times. An estimated 1 million people lined the route.

The record for changing a team of four horses by a team of 12 ostlers is 27.69 sec set at Olympia, London on 17 Dec 1984.

The Spies Travelling Company of Denmark on 7 May 1986 organised the longest procession of horse-drawn carriages ever. They transported 810 people in 68 carriages through the woods around Copenhagen to celebrate the coming of Spring. The cavalcade extended for some 920 m *3020 ft* 'nose to tail'.

MOTOR CARS

Most cars

For 1984 it was estimated that the United States, with 168,607,000 vehicles, passed 37.9 per cent of the total world stock of 411,113,000.

Earliest automobiles *Model*

The earliest automobile of which there is record is a two-foot-long steam-powered model constructed by Ferdinand Verbiest (d. 1687) a Belgian Jesuit priest, and described in his *Astronomia Europaea*. His model of 1668 was possibly inspired either by Giovanni Branca's description of a steam turbine, published in his *La Macchina* in 1629, or by writings on 'fire carts' or *Nan Huai-Jen* in the Chu dynasty (*c.* 800 BC).

Earliest automobiles *Passenger-carrying*

The earliest full scale automobile was the first of two military steam tractors, completed at the Paris Arsenal in 1769 by Nicolas-Joseph Cugnot (1725–1804). This reached 2¼ mph *3,6 km/h*. Cugnot's second, larger tractor, completed in May 1771, today survives in the *Conservatoire nationale des arts et métiers* in Paris. The world's first passenger-carrying automobile was a steam-powered road vehicle carrying eight passengers and built by Richard Trevithick (1771–1833). It first ran on 24 Dec 1801 in Camborne, Cornwall.

Earliest automobiles *Internal combustion*

The Swiss Isaac de Rivaz (d. 1828) built a carriage powered by his 'explosion engine' in 1805. The first practical internal-combustion engined vehicle was that built by the Londoner Samuel Brown (Patent 5350, 25 Apr 1826) whose 4 hp *4,05 cv* two cylinder atmospheric gas 88 litre engined carriage climbed Shooters Hill,

Blackheath, Kent in May 1826. Britain's continuous motoring history started in Nov 1894 when Henry Hewetson drove his imported Benz Velo in the south-eastern suburbs of London. The first successful petrol-driven car, the Motorwagen, built by Karl-Friedrich Benz (1844–1929) of Karlsruhe, ran at Mannheim, Germany, in late 1885. It was a 5 cwt *250 kg* 3-wheeler reaching 8–10 mph *13–16 km/h*. Its single cylinder 4-stroke chain-drive engine (bore 91,4 mm, stroke 160 mm) delivered 0.85 hp *0,86 cv* at 200 rpm. It was patented on 29 Jan 1886. Its first 1 km road test was reported in the local newspaper, the *Neue Badische Landeszeitung*, of 4 June 1886, under the news heading 'Miscellaneous'. Two were built in 1885 of which one has been preserved in 'running order' at the Deutsches Museum, Munich.

Registrations *Earliest and Most Expensive*

The world's first plates were probably introduced by the Parisian police in France in 1893. Registration plates were introduced in Britain in 1903. The original A1 plate was secured by the 2nd Earl Russell (1865–1931) for his 12 hp *12,1 cv* Napier. This plate, willed in September 1950 to Mr Trevor T. Laker of Leicester, was sold in August 1959 for £2500 in aid of charity. By April 1986, prices for plates reached £25,000. Licence plate No 3 was reported in Jan 1984 to have been sold at a Hong Kong Government auction for £94,000.

FASTEST CARS (see also p. 125)

Diesel engined

The prototype 230 hp 3 litre Mercedes C 111/3 attained 327,3 km/h *203.3 mph* in tests on the Nardo Circuit, Southern Italy on 5–15 Oct 1978, and in April 1978 averaged 195.398 mph *314,462 km/h* for 12 hours, so covering a world record 2399.76 miles *3773,55 km*.

Rocket powered sleds

The highest speed recorded on ice is 247.93 mph *399,00 km/h* by *Oxygen* driven by Sammy Miller (b. 15 Apr 1945) on Lake George, NY, USA on 15 Feb 1981.

Steam car

On 19 Aug 1985 Robert E. Barber broke the 79-year old record for a steam car driving No 744 *'Steamin' Demon*, built by the Barber-Nichols Engineering Co, 145.607 mph *234,33 km/h* at Bonneville Salt Flats, Utah, USA.

Road cars

Various detuned track cars have been licensed for road use but are not purchasable production models. Manufacturers of very fast and very expensive models understandably limit speed tests to stipulated engine revs. The fastest current manufacturer's *claim* (as opposed to independently road-tested) for any road car is the Vector W2A custom order car from Vector Cars, Venice, California with a 'terminal velocity' in excess of 200 mph *321,8 km/h*. The claimed speed at 7000 rpm by the 1984 Ferrari 308 GTO is 189.5 mph *304,9 km/h*. Aston Martin announced on 1 Mar 1985 the production of 50 Vantage-Zagatos with 432 bhp engines and a speed of 186.4 mph *300 km/h* costing £87,000. The Vantage was first seen in public at the Geneva Show in March 1986, with the first prototype running a month later. The highest ever *tested* speed is 179.9 mph *289,5 km/h* for the Lamborghini Countach LP 500 S in March 1984. The car was kept out of the 'red sector' i.e. at below 7000 rpm. The highest road-tested acceleration reported is 0–60 mph *0–96,5 km/h* in 4.1 sec for an MG Metro 6R4 International Rally Car in 1986.

LARGEST CARS

World

Of cars produced for private road use, the largest has been the Bugatti 'Royale' type 41, known in Britain as the 'Golden Bugatti', of which only six (not seven) were made at Molsheim, France by the Italian Ettore Bugatti, and all survive. First built in 1927, this machine has an 8-cylinder engine of 12,7 litres capacity, and measures over 22 ft *6,7 m* in length. The bonnet is over 7 ft *2 m* long. Of custom built cars the longest is the 16-wheeled 60 ft *18,3 m* long Cadillac limousine 'American Dream' created by Jay Ohrberg Show Cars of Newport Beach, California, USA. It features a swimming pool, hot tub, helipad, satellite dish, crystal chandelier and has 'ample luggage space'.

Largest engines *All-time and current records*

The world's most powerful piston engine car is 'Quad Al.' It was designed and built in 1964 by Jim Lytle and was first shown in May 1965 at the Los Angeles Sports Arena. The car featured four Allison V12 aircraft engines with a total of 6840 in³ *112,087 cc* displacement and 12,000 hp. The car has 4-wheel drive, 8 wheels and tyres, and dual 6-disc clutch assemblies. The wheelbase is 160 in *406,4 cm*, and weighs 5860 lb *2658 kg*. It has 96 spark plugs and 96 exhaust pipes.

The largest car ever used was the 'White Triplex', sponsored by J. H. White of Philadelphia, Pennsylvania, USA. Completed early in 1928, after two years work, the car weighed about 4 tons *4,06 tonnes* and was powered by three Liberty V12 aircraft engines with a total capacity of 81,188 cc, developing 1500 bhp at 2000 rpm. It was used to break the world speed record but crashed at Daytona, Florida, USA on 13 Mar 1929.

Currently the most powerful car on the road is the 6-wheeled Jameson-Merlin, powered by a 27,000 cc 1760 hp Rolls Royce V12 Merlin aero-engine, governed down to a maximum speed of 185 mph *298 km/h*. It has a range of 300 miles *480 km* with tanks of 60 gal *272 litres* capacity. The vehicle weighs 2.65 tons *2,69 tonnes* overall.

Largest engines *Production car*

The highest engine capacity of a production car was 13½ litres *824 in³*, in the case of the US Pierce-Arrow 6-66 Raceabout of 1912-18, the US Peerless 6-60 of 1912-14 and the Fageol of 1918. The most powerful current production car is the Lamborghini Countach 5000 Squattro-valvole with a 5167 cc V12 engine developing 455 bhp.

Above: Jay Ohrberg's 'American Dream', the ultimate in long limousines at 60 ft, *18,3 m*.

Left: The most relaxing of the many luxurious features is the hot tub.

Below: No less ingenious—the *lowest* car on the road, Andy Saunder's 34 inch *86,4 cm high* custom-made Mini.

FASTEST CARS — FASTEST CARS — FASTEST CARS — FASTEST CARS — FASTEST CARS

CATEGORY	MPH	KM/H	CAR	DRIVER	PLACE	DATE
Jet Engined (*official*)	633.468	1019,4	Thrust 2	Richard Noble (GB)	Black Rock Desert Nevada, USA	4 Oct 1983
Rocket Engined (*official*)	622.287	1001,473	Blue Flame	Gary Gabelich (US)	Bonneville, Utah, USA	23 Oct 1970
Wheel Driven (*turbine*)	429.311	690,909	Bluebird	Donald Campbell (UK)	Lake Eyre, Australia	17 July 1964
Wheel Driven (*multi piston engines*)	418.504	673,516	Goldenrod	Robert Summers (US)	Bonneville, Utah, USA	12 Nov 1965
Wheel Driven (*single piston engine*)	357.391	575,149	Herda-Knapp-Milodon	Bob Herda	Bonneville, Utah, USA	2 Nov 1967
Rocket Engined (*unofficial*)*	739.666	1190,377	Budweiser Rocket	Stan Barrett (US)	Edwards Air Force Base, California, USA	17 Dec 1979

* This published speed of Mach 1.0106 is *not* officially sanctioned by the USAF whose Digital Instrumented Radar was not calibrated or certified. The radar information was *not* generated by the vehicle directly but by an operator aiming the dish by means of a TV screen. To claim a speed to 6 significant figures appears quite unsustainable.

The most expensive used car. The multi-colour Rolls-Royce previously owned and driven by John Lennon. (Sotheby's).

Engine change record

The fastest time recorded for removing a car engine and replacing it is 42 sec for a Ford Escort by a Royal Marine team of five from Portsmouth, on 21 Nov 1985 on the BBC *Record Breakers* programme.

Petrol consumption

On 9 July 1985 the Mechanical Engineering Department of King's College, London won the Shell-*Motor* magazine prize at Silverstone, Northants with 4010 miles per gallon *1419 km/litre.*

Longest fuel range

The greatest distance driven without refuelling on a tank full of fuel (19.41 galls *88,12 l*) is 1150.3 miles *1851,2 km* by an Audi 100 turbo diesel driven by Stuart Bladon with his son Bruce (navigator) and Bob Proctor (RAC observer) from Land's End to John O'Groats and back to West Falkirk in 22 hrs 28 min in July 1984. The average speed was 51.17 mph *82,33 km/h* giving 59.27 mpg *4.77 l/100 km.*

Most durable car

The highest recorded mileage for a car was 1,184,880 authenticated miles *1 906 879 km* by August 1978 for a 1957 Mercedes 180 D owned by Robert O'Reilly of Olympia, Washington State, USA. Its subsequent fate is unknown. R. L. Bender of Madison, Wisconsin claimed 1,020,000 miles *1 641 530 km* for his car in December 1983. R. L. Bender's car reached 1,021,041 miles *1 643 206 km* on 9 June 1984. He has been driving it since 1958.

Taxis

The largest taxi fleet is that in Mexico City, Mexico with 60,000 'normal' taxis, pesaros (communal fixed route taxis) and settas (airport taxis) in mid 1984. On 1 Apr 1986 there were 14,500 cabs and 19,000 drivers in London. The longest fare on record is one of 7533 miles *12 133 km* through 10 countries from Marble Arch, London on 19 Sept–18 Oct 1981. The trip was sponsored for charity. The driver was Stephen Tillyer. Francis Edward Kenyon (b. 1904) was continuously licensed as a cab driver in Manchester for 57 years 36 days in 1924–81.

MOST EXPENSIVE CARS

Special

The most expensive car to build has been the US Presidential 1969 Lincoln Continental Executive delivered to the US Secret Service on 14 Oct 1968. It has an overall length of 21 ft 6.3 in *6,56 m* with a 13 ft 4 in *4,06 m* wheel-base and with the addition of 2 tons *2,03 tonnes* of armour plate, weighs 5.35 tons *5,43 tonnes* (12,000 lb *5443 kg*). The estimated research, development and manufacture cost was $500,000 (*then £208,000*) but it is rented at $5000 (*now £2300*) per annum. Even if all four tyres were shot out it can travel at 50 mph *80 km/h* on inner rubber-edged steel discs. Carriage House Motor Cars Ltd of New York City in March 1978 completed 4 years work on converting a 1973 Rolls Royce including lengthening it by 30 in *76,2 cm*. The price tag was $500,000 (*then £263,157*).

Standard

The most expensive British standard car is the Rolls-Royce 8 cylinder 6750 cc Silver Spur Limousine quoted in 1986 at £159,467 (including tax). More expensive are custom built models. Jack Barclay Ltd of Berkeley Square, London W1 quote £350,000 for an armour-plated Rolls-Royce Phantom VI (including tax).

The unrivalled collector of Rolls-Royces was Bhagwan Shri Rajneesh (b. 1931), the Indian mystic of Rajneeshpuram, Oregon, USA. His disciples bestowed 93 of these upon him before his deportation in November 1985.

Used

The greatest price paid for any used car is $2,229,000 (*then £1,768,000*) for John Lennon's 1965 Phantom V Rolls Royce, by Jim Pattison, Chairman of the Expo '86 World Fair in Vancouver, Canada, at Sotheby's New York on 29 June 1985. In Great Britain £440,000 was paid in acution at Sotheby's for a Bugatti Type 55 roadster. The greatest collection of vintage cars is the William F. Harrah Collection of 1700, estimated to be worth more than $4 million (*£2.3 million*), at Reno, Nevada, USA. Mr Harrah was still looking for a Chalmer's Detroit 1909 Tourabout, an Owen car of 1910–12 and a Nevada Truck of 1915 at the time of his death in 1978.

Most inexpensive

The cheapest car of all-time was the 1922 Red Bug Buckboard, built by Briggs and Stratton Co of Milwaukee, Wisconsin, USA listed at $150–$125. It had a 62 in *1,57 m* wheel base and weighed 245 lb *111 kg*. The early models of the King Midget cars were sold in kit form for self-assembly for as little as $100 (*then £24 16s*) as late as 1948. By May 1986 the cheapest quoted new car price in Britain was £2431 for a Fiat 126, 652 cc 2 door car.

Longest production

The longest any car has been in mass production is 47 years (1938 to date), including wartime interruptions, in the case of the Volkswagen 'Beetle' series, originally designed by Ferdinand Porsche. The 20 millionth car came off the final production line in Mexico on 15 May 1981, and 20,630,000 had been built by January 1986. Residual production continues in South America. Britain's all-time champion is the Morgan series 4/4 from 27 Dec 1935 from the Morgan Motor Car of Malvern (founded 1910). Britain's champion seller has been the Mini which originally sold for £496 19s 2d in August 1959. Sales reached 5,000,000 on 19 Feb 1986. Bernard Ferriman, 83, sold his own preproduction model, the first ever built, for £2500 on 5 Aug 1985. The off-white vehicle, which he bought for £296 in 1962, went to car distributors Penta of Reading.

LONG DISTANCE DRIVING

Round the world driving

The fastest circumnavigation embracing more than an equator's length of driving (24,901.47 road miles *40 075,0 km*) is one in 74 days 1 hr 11 min by Garry Sowerby (driver) and Ken Langley (navigator) of Canada from 6 Sept to 19 Nov 1980 in a Volvo 245 DL westwards from Toronto, Canada through 4 continents and 23 countries. The distance covered was 43 030 km *26,738 miles* (see below for their Cape to Cape record). Between 30 Mar 1964 and 23 Apr 1984 the folk-singers Manfred Müller and Paul-Ernst Luhrs drove round the world covering 78 countries and 250 000 km *174,000 miles*. They started and finished in Bremerhaven, West Germany.

The 1932 Bugatti which set a UK and European auction record of £440,000. (Sotheby's).

Cape to Cape

The first traverse of the world's greatest land mass (Afro-Eurasia) was achieved by Richard Pape, who left the North Cape in an Austin A90 on 28 July and arrived in Cape Town on 22 Oct 1955 with the milometer recording 17,500 miles *28 160 km* after 86 days. The speed record was set by Ken Langley and Garry Sowerby of Canada driving north in 28 days 13 hr 10 min for 12,531 miles *20 166 km* on 4 Apr—2 May 1984.

Round Britain economy driving

A team consisting of nine members of the Yarm & District Round Table (No 1115) drove the Round Britain course covering a distance of 3777 miles *6078 km.*

They drove an Austin Metro 1.3L supplied by Dutton Forshaw of Middlesborough, Cleveland, which consumed a total of 71.35 gallons *324,35 litres* of petrol and which therefore returned an average of 52.93 mpg *18,73 km/l.*

Driving on behalf of the Royal National Lifeboat Institution's Teesmouth Lifeboat Appeal they left Redcar, Cleveland, at 10 am on Thursday 8 May 1986 returning there at 9 pm on the following Tuesday, 13 May.

Mountain driving

Cars have been driven up Ben Nevis, Highland, Scotland (4406 ft *1343 m*) on five occasions. The record times are 7 hr 23 min (ascent) and 1 hr 55 min (descent) by George F. Simpson in an Austin 7 on 6 Oct 1928. Henry Alexander accomplished the feat twice in May 1911 (Model T Ford) and on 13 Sept 1928 (Model A Ford). The most recent ascent was on 5 June 1984 by a 33 year old Land Rover.

Driving in reverse

Charles Creighton (1908–70) and James Hargis of Maplewood, Missouri, USA, drove their Ford Model A 1929 roadster in reverse from New York City 3340 miles *5375 km* to Los Angeles, California on 26 July–13 Aug 1930 without once stopping the engine. They arrived back in New York in reverse on 5 Sept so completing 7180 miles *11 555 km* in 42 days. The highest average speed attained in any non-stop reverse drive exceeding 500 miles *800 km* was achieved by Gerald Hoagland who drove a 1969 Chevrolet Impala 501 miles *806,2 km* in 17 hr 38 min at Chemung Speed Drome, New York, USA on 9–10 July 1976 to average 28.41 mph *45,72 km/h.*

Brian 'Cub' Keene and James 'Wilbur' Wright drove their Chevrolet Blazer 9,031 miles *14 533 km* in 37 days (1 Aug–6 Sept 1984) through 15 US States and Canada. Though it was prominently named 'Stuck in Reverse' law enforcement in Oklahoma refused to believe it and insisted they drove in reverse reverse, i.e. forwards, out of the State.

Battery powered vehicle

John W. Owen and Roy Harvey travelled 919 miles *1479 km* from John O'Groats to Land's End in a Sinclair C5 in 103 hr 15 min on 30 Apr–4 May 1985. David Turner and Tim Pickhard of Turners of Boscastle Ltd, Cornwall, travelled 875 miles *1408 km* from Land's End to John O'Groats in 63 hours in a Freight Rover Leyland Sherpa powered by a Lucas electric motor on 21–23 Dec 1985.

Two wheel driving

The longest recorded distance for driving on 2 wheels is 209,2 km *129.9 miles* in an Opel Kadett by Michael Signoret at the Paul Ricard circuit in Provence, France on 14 Mar 1985.

Kenneth Eriksson of Äppelbo, Sweden, achieved 122,86 km/h *76.34 mph* on 2 wheels

only at the Anderstorp Circuit, Sweden, on 28 Sept 1985 driving a standard Opel Kadett 1986 GSI 1.8 litre.

Oldest driver

Roy M. Rawlins (b. 10 July 1870) of Stockton, California, USA, was warned for driving at 95 mph *152 km/h* in a 55 mph *88,5 km/h* zone in June 1974. On 25 Aug 1974 he was awarded a California State licence valid till 1978 by Mr John Burrafato, but Mr Rawlins died on 9 July 1975, one day short of his 105th birthday. Mrs Maude Tull of Inglewood, California, who took to driving aged 91 after her husband died, was issued a renewal on 5 Feb 1976 when aged 104. Britain's only recorded centenarian driver was Herbert Warren (1874–1975) of Whatlington, Norfolk, who drove a 1954 Standard 10. Major Geoffrey Chance CBE (b. 16 Dec 1893) of Braydon, Wiltshire who began driving in 1908 successfully took a driving test to re-qualify after a 'minor bump' aged 90 years 90 days at Swindon, Wiltshire on 15 March 1984. The oldest age at which a woman has passed the Department of Transport driving test has been 88 years 5 months by Mrs Harriet Emma Jack (*née* Morse) (b. 9 Dec 1887) on 18 May 1976 in Bognor Regis, West Sussex. She was still driving aged 98.

The holder of the earliest driving licence to be issued in Britain is Mr Gerry Bond (b. July 1889) of Bournemouth, Dorset whose first licence is dated Oct 1907.

Youngest driver

Instances of drivers have been recorded in HM Armed Forces much under 17 years. Mrs P. L. M. Williams (b. 3 Feb 1926), now of Risca, Gwent, as Private Patterson in the ATS drove a 5 ton truck in 1941 aged 15. Mark Blackbourn of Lincoln, having passed his driving test the day after his 17th birthday, went on to pass the advanced test less than 48 hours later on 7 Aug 1985. Mark Collins Hall of Otley, W. Yorks passed his test on 24 July 1985 aged 16 years 103 days.

Most durable

The Goodyear Tire and Rubber Co test driver Weldon C. Kocich drove 3,141,946 miles *5 056 470 km* from 5 Feb 1953 to 28 Feb 1986 so averaging 95,210 miles *153 226 km* per year.

Driving tests

The record for persistence in taking the Ministry of Transport's Learner's Test is held by Mrs Miriam Hargrave (b. 3 Apr 1908) of Wakefield, West Yorkshire, who failed her 39th driving test in eight years on 29 Apr 1970 after 'crashing' a

The car and instructor Rick Chattaway, responsible for the fastest driving test failure. At 1 second and 18 inches—this unenviable record was set in the Australian town of Modbury, Adelaide on 19 Nov 1984.

set of red lights. She triumphed at her 40th attempt after 212 lessons on 3 Aug 1970. The examiner was alleged not to have known about her previous 39 tests. In 1978 she was reported to still disdain right-hand turns. The world's easiest tests have been those in Egypt in which the ability to drive 6 m *19.64 ft* forward and the same in reverse has been deemed sufficient. In 1979 it was reported that accurate reversing had been added between two rubber traffic cones. 'High cone attrition' soon led to the substitution of white lines. Mrs Fannie Turner (b. 1903) of Little Rock, Arkansas, USA passed her *written* test for drivers on her 104th attempt in October 1978.

Most expensive lesson

On 20 June 1985 Mike Collins, Chief Driving Examiner of RoSPA Advanced Drivers Association was flown to Paris from Birmingham to give a 1½ hour driving lesson at a cost of £266.

CAR PARKS

Largest *World*

The world's largest car park is for 20,000 cars at the West Edmonton Mall, Edmonton, Alberta, Canada. There are overflow facilities with an adjoining lot for 10,000 more cars.

Great Britain

The largest parking area in Great Britain is that for 15,000 cars and 200 coaches at the National Exhibition Centre, Birmingham (see p. 104).

Great Britain's highest capacity underground car park is that under the Victoria Centre, Nottingham with a capacity of 1650 cars, opened in June 1972.

Private

The largest private garage is one of two storeys built outside Bombay for the private collection of 176 cars owned by Pranlal Bhogilal (b. 1939).

Filling stations

Little America, west of Cheyenne, Wyoming, USA, at the junction of Interstate Routes 80 and 25 claims to be the world's biggest gas station with 52 diesel and gas pumps—none self-service. The highest in the world is at Leh, Ladakh,

'Big Muskie' is the most massive automotive land vehicle. A full-sized bulldozer can be gobbled up comfortably in its grabbing bucket. (Alan Russell).

India at 3658 m *12,001 ft* operated by Indiaoil. The largest filling station of the 36,000 in the United Kingdom is the Esso service area on the M4 at Leigh Delamere, Wiltshire, opened on 3 Jan 1972. It has 48 petrol and diesel pumps and extends over 43 acres *17,4 ha*.

Buses *Earliest*

The first municipal motor omnibus service in the world was inaugurated on 12 Apr 1903 between Eastbourne railway station and Meads, East Sussex, England. A steam-powered bus named *Royal Patent* ran between Gloucester and Cheltenham for 4 months in 1831.

Largest fleet

In 1983 the world's largest bus fleet is the 6580 single-deck buses in Rio de Janeiro, Brazil. Of London Transport's 5572 fleet, 5020 are double-deckers.

Longest

The longest buses in the world are the 10.72 ton *10 870 kg*, 76 ft *23,16 m* long articulated buses, with 121 passenger seats and room also for 66 'strap-hangers' built by the Wayne Corporation of Richmond, Indiana, USA for use in the Middle East.

Longest route

The longest regularly scheduled bus route is by 'Across Australia Coach Lines', who inaugurated a regular scheduled service between Perth and Brisbane on 9 Apr 1980. The route is 5455 km *3389 miles* taking 75 hr 55 min. The longest bus service in Great Britain is 654 miles *1052 km* between Perth and Eastbourne operated by Midland Scottish.

Largest garage

The KMB Overhaul Centre operated by the Kowloon Motor Bus Co (1933) Ltd, Hong Kong, is the world's largest multi-storeyed service centre. Purpose built for double deck buses, its 4 floors occupy in excess of 47,000 m² *11.6 acres*.

Trolleybuses

The last trolleybus in Britain, owned by Bradford Corporation, ran in 1972. Plans have been made to reintroduce trolleybuses by both West Yorkshire and South Yorkshire Passenger transport Executives.

Caravans *Longest journey*

The longest continuous motor caravan journey is one of 143,716 miles *231 288 km* by Harry B.

The longest load transported in the UK was this gas storage vessel pictured completing its ½ mile *0,8 km* journey on 10 July 1985.

Coleman and Peggy Larson in a Volkswagen Camper from 20 Aug 1976 to 20 Apr 1978 through 113 countries. Saburo Ouchi (b. 7 Feb 1942) of Tokyo, Japan drove 270 000 km *167,770 miles* in 91 countries from 2 Dec 1969 to 10 Feb 1978.

Largest

The largest caravans built in Britain are the £300,000 'State Super Caravans', 18 m *59 ft 0¼ in* in length and 3,5 m *11 ft 5¾ in* wide built by Coventry Steel Caravans Ltd of Newport Pagnell, Buckinghamshire since 1977.

Fastest

The world speed record for a caravan is 124.91 mph *201,02 km/h* by an Alpha 14 towed by a Le Mans Aston Martin V8 saloon driven by Robin Hamilton at RAF Elvington, North Yorkshire on 14 Oct 1980.

Vehicles *Most massive*

The most massive vehicle ever constructed is the Marion eight-caterpillar crawler used for conveying *Saturn V* rockets to their launching pads at Cape Canaveral, Florida, USA. (*see* Chapter 4, Most powerful rocket). It measures 131 ft 4 in *40 m* by 114 ft *34,7 m* and the two built cost $12,300,000 (*then £5,125,000*). The loaded train weight is 8036 tons *8165 tonnes*. Its windscreen wipers with 42 in *106 cm* blades are the world's largest.

The most massive automotive land vehicle is 'Big Muskie' the 10,700 ton *10 890 tonnes* mechanical shovel built by Bucyrus Erie for the Musk mine. It is 487 ft *148,43 m* long; 151 ft *46,02 m* wide and 222 ft *67,66 m* high with a grab capacity of 325 tons.

The longest vehicle ever built is the Arctic Snow Train owned by the world famous wire-walker Steve McPeak (US). This 54 wheeled 572 ft *174,3 m* long vehicle was built by R G Le Tourneau Inc of Longview, Texas for the US Army. Its gross train weight is 400 tons with a top speed of 20 mph *32 km/h* and it was driven by a crew of 6 when used as an 'Overland Train' for the military. McPeak repaired it and every punctured wheel lonehanded in often sub-zero temperatures in Alaska. It generates 4680 shp and has a capacity of 6522 Imperial gallons *29 648 litres*.

Wrecker *Most powerful*

The world's most powerful wrecker is the Vance Corporation 25 ton *25,4 tonne* 30 ft *9,14 m* long Monster No. 2 stationed at Hammond, Indiana, USA. It can lift in excess of 160 tons *163 tonnes* on its short boom.

Earth mover *Largest*

The world's largest earth mover is the 100 tonne T-800 built at the Lenin Tractor Works in Chelyabinsk, USSR, announced in Sept 1984.

Dumper truck *Largest*

The world's largest dump truck is the Terex Titan 33–19 manufactured by the Terex Division of General Motors Corporation. It has a loaded weight of 539.9 tons *548,6 tonnes* and a capacity of 312½ tons *317,5 tonnes*. When tipping its height is 56 ft *17,06 m*. The 16 cylinder engine delivers 3300 hp. The fuel tank holds 1300 Imperial gallons *5904,6 litres*. It went into service in November 1974.

Tractor *Largest and most powerful*

The world's largest tractor is the $459,000 (*then £285,000*) US Department of Agriculture Wide Tractive Frame Vehicle completed by Ag West of Sacramento, California in June 1982. It measures 33 ft *10,05 m* between its wheels which are designed to run on permanent paths and weighs 21.87 tons *22,22 tonnes*.

The sport of tractor-pulling was put on a national US championship basis in 1967 at Bowling Green, Ohio where the winner was 'The Purple Monster' built and driven by Roger E. Varns. Today there are 12 classes ranging up to '12,200 lb unlimited'.

Fire engine *Most powerful*
The world's most powerful fire appliance is the 860 hp 8-wheel Oshkosh firetruck used for aircraft fires. It can discharge 41,600 gal *190 000 l* of foam through two turrets in just 150 sec. It weighs 59.0 tons *60 tonnes*. The fastest on record is the Jaguar XJ12 – 'Chubb Firefighter', which, in Nov 1982, attained a speed of 130.57 mph *210,13 km/h* in tests when servicing the *Thrust 2* land speed record trials (see pp. 125 & 157–8).

Ambulance *Largest*
The world's largest ambulances are the 18 m *59 ft 0½ in* long articulated Alligator Jumbulances Mark VI, VII and VIII, operated by The Across Trust to convey the sick and handicapped on holidays and pilgrimages to the Continent. They are built by Van Hool of Belgium with Fiat engines, cost £176,000 and convey 44 patients and staff.

ROAD LOADS

Load heaviest *World*
On 14–15 July 1984 John Brown Engineers & Contractors BV moved the Conoco Kotter Field production deck with a roll out weight of 3805 tonnes for the Continental Netherlands Oil Company of Leidsenhage, Netherlands.

Great Britain
The heaviest road load moved in the United Kingdom has been a 1305 tonne *1284 ton* module for the semi-submersible drilling rig *Ocean Alliance 2002*. It measured 70 ft *21 m* high by 100 ft *30,5 m* long by 90 ft *27,4 m* and was drawn by four tractor units developing a total of 1625 hp over half a mile *0,8 km* of public road on its journey from the River Tees to the River Clyde on 5 Nov 1985. The longest item moved has been a 275 ft *83,8 m* long high pressure steel gas storage vessel weighing 233 tonnes *229 tons* transported to a new site at Beckton gasworks in east London on 10 July 1985. The overall train length was 325 ft *99 m*.

Tyres *Largest*
The world's largest tyres are manufactured in Topeka, Kansas by the Goodyear Co for giant dumper trucks. They measure 12 ft *3,65 m* in diameter, weigh 12,500 lb *5670 kg* and cost $74,000 (*£49,000*). A tyre 17 ft *5,18 m* in diameter is believed to be the limitation of what is practical.

Skid marks *Longest*
The longest recorded skid marks on a public road have been those 950 ft *290 m* long left by a Jaguar car involved in an accident on the M1 near Luton, Bedfordshire, on 30 June 1960. Evidence given in the High Court case *Hurlock* v. *Inglis and others* indicated a speed 'in excess of 100 mph *160 km/h* before the application of the brakes. The skid marks made by the jet-powered *Spirit of America*, driven by Norman Craig Breedlove, after the car went out of control at Bonneville Salt Flats, Utah, USA, on 15 Oct 1964, were nearly 6 miles *9,6 km* long.

Amphibious vehicle circumnavigation
The only circumnavigation by an amphibious vehicle was achieved by Ben Carlin (Australia) (d. 7 Mar 1981) in an amphibious jeep 'Half-Safe'. He completed the last leg of the Atlantic crossing (the English Channel) on 24 Aug 1951. He arrived back in Montreal, Canada on 8 May

1958 having completed a circumnavigation of 39,000 miles *62 765 km* over land and 9600 miles *15 450 km* by sea and river. He was accompanied on the trans Atlantic stage by his ex-wife Elinore (US) and on the long trans Pacific stage (Tokyo to Anchorage) by Broye Lafayette De-Mente (b. Missouri, 1928).

Snowmobiles
Richard and Raymond Moore and Loren Matthews drove their snowmobile 5876 miles *9456 km* from Fairbanks, Alaska to Fenton, Michigan, USA, in 39 days from 3 Feb–13 Mar 1980.

Solar Powered Vehicle
The highest speed attained under IHPVA (International Human Powered Vehicle Association) rules by a solely solar powered vehicle is 24.74 mph *39,81 km/h* at Bellflower, California on 1 July 1984 by *Sunrunner*, designed by Joel Davidson and Greg Johanson of Photovoltaic Power Systems.

Tow *Longest*
The longest tow on record was one of 4759 miles *7658 km* from Halifax, Nova Scotia to Canada's Pacific Coast, when Frank J. Elliott and George A. Scott of Amherst, Nova Scotia, Canada, persuaded 168 passing motorists in 89 days to tow their Model T Ford (in fact engineless) to win a $1000 bet on 15 Oct 1927.

Lawn mowers
The widest gang mower in the world is the 5 ton 60 ft *18,28 m* wide 27 unit Big Green Machine used by the sod farmer Jay Edgar Frick of Monroe, Ohio. It mows an acre in 60 sec. The greatest distance covered in the annual 12 hour Lawn Mower Race (under the rules of the BLMRA, the British Lawn Mower Racing Association) is 276 miles *444,1 km* by Tony Hazelwood, Derek Bell, Tony Smith and Ray Kilminster at Wisborough Green, W. Sussex on 21–22 June 1980. A 12-hour run behind record of 101.15 miles *162,7 km* was set at Wisborough Green on 8–9 July 1984 by the 'Super Gnome' team.

Go-Karting
The highest mileage recorded in 24 hours on a closed twisting circuit for go-karts driven by a 4 man team is 1018 laps of a mile *1638,3 km* at Erbsville Kartway, Waterloo, Ontario, Canada. The 5 h.p. 140 cc Honda engined kart was driven by Owen Nimmo, Gary Ruddock, Jim Timmins and Danny Upshaw on 4–5 Sept 1983.

MOTORCYCLES

Earliest (see also Chapter 12)
The earliest internal combustion-engined motorised bicycle was a wooden-framed machine built at Bad Cannstatt in Oct–Nov 1885 by Gottlieb Daimler (1834–1900) of Germany and first ridden by Wilhelm Maybach (1846–1929). It had a top speed of 12 mph *19 km/h* and developed one-half of one horsepower from its single-cylinder 264 cc four-stroke engine at 700 rpm. Known as the 'Einspur', it was lost in a fire in 1903. The first motorcycles of entirely British production were the 1046 cc Holden flat-four and the 2¾ hp Clyde single both produced in 1898. The earliest factory which made motorcycles in quantity was opened in 1894 by Heinrich and Wilhelm Hildebrand and Alois Wolfmüller at Munich, West Germany. In its first two years this factory produced over 1000 machines, each having a water-cooled 1488 cc twin-cylinder four-stroke engine developing about 2.5 bhp at 600 rpm—the highest capacity motor cycle engine ever put into production.

Michael J. Waller, Wallasey, Merseyside, who between 9–11 July 1985 covered the four extreme points of the compass of mainland Britain; (N—Dunnet Head, E—Lowestoft, S—Lizard Point, W—Ardnamurchan) plus Land's End and John O'Groats in 25 hr 26 min. His Kawasaki GPZ 1100 motorcycle covered 1405.6 miles *2262 km*.

Fastest road machine
The 115 bhp Japanese Honda V65 Magna with a liquid-cooled, in line V-4, 16 valve DoHC engine of 1098 cc capacity has a design speed of 173 mph *278,4 km/h*.

Fastest racing machine
There is no satisfactory answer to the identity of the fastest track machine other than to say that the current Kawasaki, Suzuki and Yamaha machines have all been geared to attain speeds marginally in excess of 300 km/h *186.4 mph* under race conditions.

Duration record
The longest time a solo motorcycle has been kept in nonstop motion is 500 hr by Owen Fitzgerald, Richard Kennett and Don Mitchell who covered 8432 miles *13 570 km* in Western Australia on 10–31 July 1977.

Most on One Machine
The record for most people on a single machine is 35 members of the Brisbane Police Traffic Branch who travelled 506 metres *553 yards* at 25 km/h *15,5 mph* at Surfer's Paradise, Queensland, Australia, on a Yamaha 1100 cc on 22 June 1984.

'Wheelie'
Doug Domokos on the Alabama International Speedway, Talladega, USA on 27 June 1984 covered 145 miles *233,34 km* non-stop on the rear wheel of his Honda XR 500. He stopped only when the gas ran out. The first recorded case of bettering 100 mph *160,9 km/h* on one wheel was by Ottis Lance at Penwell Raceway Park, Texas, USA on 21 May 1983 with 112 mph *180,2 km/h* over 440 yds *402 m* on a Suzuki GS-1000.

Terry McGauran motor-cycled up the 1760 steps of the CN Tower, Toronto, Canada, on 26 June 1984.

The two-seater double-decker tandem built by Kesaichiro Tagawa, Osaka, Japan. It measures 5 metres *16.4 feet* in length and is 3.4 metres *11.1 feet* to the upper storey handlebars.

Most expensive

The most expensive road motorcycle available in Britain is the Harley Davidson, FLHTC Electra Glide Classic (Liberty) with a 1340 cc engine and priced at £8739. In June 1980 a 1912 Henderson Model A was auctioned in the US for $18,000 (*then £7825*).

Round Britain

Richard Parkhouse of Gwynedd covered all 62 mainland counties of Great Britain by motor cycle (Suzuki 6SX 750 EFE) on a 1634 mile *2629 km* route on 11–12 June 1984 in 28 hours 52 min, averaging 56.6 mph *91,0 km/h*.

BICYCLES

Earliest

The first design for a machine propelled by cranks and pedals, with connecting rods has been attributed to Leonardo da Vinci (1452–1519), or one of his pupils, dated *c.* 1493. The earliest such design actually built was in 1839–40 by Kirkpatrick Macmillan (1810–78) of Dumfries, Scotland. It is now in the Science Museum, Kensington and Chelsea, Greater London. The first practical bicycle was the *vélocipède* built in March 1861 by Pierre and his son Ernest Michaux of Rue de Verneuil, Paris. In 1870, James Starley, in Coventry, constructed the first 'penny farthing' or Ordinary bicycle. It had wire-spoked wheels for lightness and was available with an optional speed gear.

Longest

The longest true tandem bicycle ever built (i.e. without a third stabilizing wheel) is one of 20,40 m *66 ft 11 in* for 35 riders built by the Pedaalstompers Westmalle of Belgium. They rode *c.* 60 m *195 ft* in practice on 20 Apr 1979. The machine weighs 1100 kg *2425 lb*.

Smallest

The world's smallest wheeled rideable bicycle is one with 3,5 cm *1.37 in* wheels weighing 700 g *24.6 oz* built and ridden by Jacques Puyoou of Pau, Pyrénées-Atlantiques, France in 1983. He has also built a tandem 36 cm *14.1 in* long to accommodate Madame Puyoou.

Largest

A classic Ordinary bicycle with wheels of 65¼ in *165,7 cm* diameter front and 18 in *45,7 cm* back was constructed by the Coventry Machinists Co in 1881. It is now owned by Paul Foulkes-Halbard of Crowborough, Sussex.

A bicycle with an 8 ft 2½ in *2,50 m* front wheel with pedal extenders was built in 1878 for circus demonstrations.

Fastest *World and British*

The world speed records for human powered vehicles (HPV's) are 61.94 mph *99,68 km/h* (single rider) by John Seibert at La Garita, Colorado on 27 Oct 1980; and 62.92 mph *101,25 km/h* (multiple riders) by Dave Grylls and Leigh Barczewski at the Ontario Speedway, California on 4 May 1980. A British 200 m record was set by S. Poulter in 'Poppy Flyer', in 9.10 sec at Greenham Common, Berkshire on 2 Aug 1981.

Endurance

On 10–21 July 1983, 24 City and Guilds College, London students drove an HPV round Great Britain on a 3675 mile *5914 km* route to average 14.41 mph *23,19 km/h*.

Unicycle records

The tallest unicycle ever mastered is one 101 ft 9 in *31,01 m* tall ridden by Steve McPeak (with a safety wire or mechanic suspended to an overhead crane) for a distance of 376 ft *114,6 m* in Las Vegas in October 1980. The freestyle riding of ever taller unicycles (that is without any safety harness) must inevitably lead to serious injury or fatality. Deepak Lele of Maharashtra, India unicycled 3963 miles *6 378 km* from New York to Los Angeles on 6 June–25 Sept 1984. Brian Davis, 33 of Tillicoultry, Clackmannan, Scotland rode 901 miles *1450 km* from Land's End to John O'Groats on 16 May to 4 June 1980 in 19 days 1 hr 45 min. Takayuki Koike of Kanagawa, Japan set a record for 100 miles *160,9 km* in 7 hr 49 min 12 sec on 16 Sept 1985. The sprint record from a standing start over 100 metres is 14.89 sec by Floyd Grandall of Pontiac, Michigan, USA, in Tokyo, Japan on 24 Mar 1980.

'Wheelie'

A world record duration record of 1 hr 16 min 54 sec was set by Craig Strong (GB) at Picketts Lock, Edmonton, north London on 7 Jan 1983.

Penny-farthing record

The record for riding from Land's End to John O'Groats on Ordinary bicycles, more commonly known in the 1870s as Penny-farthings, is 10 days 7 hr 12 min by James Richard Moir, 37 of St Leonards-on-Sea, East Sussex on 5–15 June 1977. G. P. Mills (Anfield BC) rode this course in 5 days 1 hr 45 min on a 53 inch Humber on 4–10 July 1886.

Underwater cycling

Thirty-two certified Scuba divers in 60 hours on 27–29 Nov 1981 rode a submarine tricycle 64.96 miles *104,54 km* on the bottom of Amphi High School pool, Tucson, Arizona, USA, in a scheme devised by Lucian Spataro to raise money for the Casa De Los Ninos Nursery.

A team of 32 in 72 underwater hours achieved 87.81 miles *141,322 km* in Norvik, Norway on 28–31 Mar 1984.

TRAINS

Earliest

Wagons running on wooden rails were used for mining as early as 1550 at Leberthal, Alsace, and in Britain for conveying coal at Wollaton near Nottingham from 1603–15 and at Broseley colliery, Shropshire, in October 1605. The earliest commercially successful steam locomotives worked on the Middleton Colliery Railway to Leeds, Yorkshire, authorised by Britain's first Railway Act on 9 June 1758. Richard Trevithick (1771–1883) built his first steam locomotive for the 3 ft *914 mm* gauge iron plateway at Coalbrookdale, Shropshire, in 1803, but there is no evidence that it ran. His second locomotive drew wagons in which men rode on a demonstration run at Penydarren, Mid Glamorgan, Wales, on 22 Feb 1804, but it broke the plate rails. The first permanent public railway to use steam traction was the Stockton & Darlington, from its opening on 27 Sept 1825 from Shildon to Stockton via Darlington, in Cleveland. The 7 ton/*tonne Locomotion* could pull 48 tons/*tonnes* at a speed of 15 mph *24 km/h*. It was designed and driven by George Stephenson (1781–1848). The first regular steam passenger service was inaugurated over a one mile section (between Bogshole Farm and South Street in Whitstable) on the 6¼ mile *10,05 km* Canterbury & Whitstable Railway in Kent on 3 May 1830, hauled by the engine *Invicta*. The first practical electric railway was Werner von Siemens' oval metre-gauge demonstration track about 300 m *328 yd* long at the Berlin Trades Exhibition on 31 May 1879.

Fastest

The highest speed attained by a railed vehicle is 6121 mph *9851 km/h* or Mach 8 by an unmanned rocket sled over the 9½ mile *15,2 km* long rail track at White Sands Missile Range, New Mexico, USA on 5 Oct 1982. The world's fastest rail speed with passengers is 517 km/h *321.2 mph* by the Maglev (magnetic levitation) ML-500 test train over the 7 km *4.3 mile* long JNR experimental track at Miyazaki, Japan in December 1979. The highest speed recorded on any national rail system is 236 mph *380 km/h* by the French SNCF high speed train TGV-PSE on trial near Tonnerre on 26 Feb 1981. The TGV (Train à

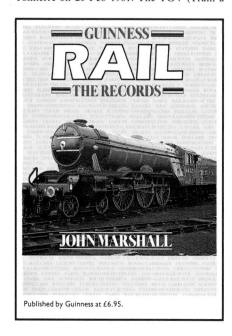

GUINNESS RAIL THE RECORDS

JOHN MARSHALL

Published by Guinness at £6.95.

Grande Vitesse) inaugurated on 27 Sept 1981 by Sept 1983 had reduced its scheduled time for the Paris–Lyon run of 425 km *264 miles* to 2 hr exactly, so averaging 212,5 km/h *132 mph*. The peak speed attained is 270 km/h *168 mph*.

Steam

The highest speed ever ratified (over 440 yards) for a steam locomotive was 125 mph *201 km/h* over 440 yd *402 m* by the LNER 4–6–2 No. 4468 *Mallard* (later numbered 60022), which hauled seven coaches weighing 240 tons *243 tonnes* gross, down Stoke Bank, near Essendine, between Grantham, Lincolnshire, and Peterborough, Cambridgeshire, on 3 July 1938. Driver Joseph Duddington was at the controls with Fireman Thomas Bray. The engine suffered some damage. On 12 June 1905 a speed of 127.06 mph *204,48 km/h* was claimed for the 'Pennsylvania Special' near Elida, Ohio, USA. This claim has never been accepted by leading railway experts.

Great Britain

British Rail inaugurated their HST (High Speed Train) daily services between London–Bristol and South Wales on 4 Oct 1976. The electric British Rail APT-P (Advanced Passenger Train-Prototype) attained 162 mph *261 km/h*, between Glasgow and Carlisle on its first revenue-earning run on 7 Dec 1981. It covered the 400 miles *644 km* from Glasgow to London in 4¼ hr.

The fastest point-to-point schedule in Britain is that from Paddington to Bristol Parkway on British Rail's Western Region HST Service at 103.15 mph *166 km/h* in 65 min over 111.75 miles *179,8 km*. On 27 Sept 1985 the Tees-Tyne Pullman made the 268¾ mile *432,5 km* journey from Newcastle in 2 hr 19 min 37 sec at an average speed of 115.4 mph *185,7 km/h*.

Longest non-stop

The longest run on British Rail without any advertised stop is the Night Motorail Service from Inverness to Euston. The distance is 567.75 miles *913,7 km* and the time taken is 11 hr 4 min. The longest passenger journey without a stop is the re-inaugurated Flying Scotsman's 268.5 mile *432,1 km* run from Kings Cross to Newcastle en route to Edinburgh.

Most powerful *World*

The world's most powerful steam locomotive, measured by tractive effort, was No. 700, a triple articulated or triplex 2–8–8–8–4, 6-cylinder engine built by the Baldwin Locomotive Works in 1916 for the Virginian Railroad. It had a tractive force of 166,300 lb *75 434 kg* working compound and 199,560 lb *90 520 kg* working simple.

Probably the heaviest train ever hauled by a single engine was one of 15,300 tons *15 545 tonnes* made up of 250 freight cars stretching 1.6 miles *2,5 km* by the *Matt H. Shay* (No. 5014), a 2–8–8–8–2 engine which ran on the Erie Railroad from May 1914 until 1929.

Great Britain

On 16 Feb 1986, a single locomotive, No 59001, one of four diesels built by General Motors and privately owned by the quarry company Foster Yeoman of Minehead, Somerset, hauled a 4639 tonne *4565 ton* train, the heaviest on record, during trials at Savernake Bank, Wiltshire.

Longest freight train

The longest and heaviest freight train on record was about 4 miles *6 km* in length consisting of 500 coal cars with three 3600 hp diesels pulling and three more in the middle, on the Iaeger, West Virginia, to Portsmouth, Ohio, USA stretch of 157 miles *252 km* on the Norfolk and

Western Railway on 15 Nov 1967. The total weight was nearly 42,000 tons *42 674 tonnes*. British Rail's heaviest freight train began its regular run on 16 Sept 1983 from Merehead Quarry, Somerset to Acton, West London with 3300 tonnes of limestone in 43 wagons and 2 engines stretching nearly ½ mile *800 m*.

Greatest load

The heaviest single pieces of freight ever conveyed by rail are limited by the capacity of the rolling stock. The world's strongest rail carrier with a capacity of 807 tonnes is the 336 tonne 36 axle 92 m *301 ft 10 in* long 'Schnabel' built for a US railway by Krupp, W. Germany, in March 1981.

The heaviest load carried by British Rail was a 122 ft *37,1 m* long boiler drum, weighing 275 tons *279 tonnes* which was carried from Immingham Dock to Killingholme, Humberside, in September 1968.

The heaviest load ever moved on rails is the 10,700 ton Church of the Virgin Mary built in 1548 in the village of Most, Czechoslovakia, in October–November 1975 because it was in the way of coal workings. It was moved 800 yd *730 m* at 0.0013 mph *0,002 km/h* over 4 weeks at a cost of £9 million.

TRACKS

Longest line

The world's longest run is one of 9438 km *5864½ miles* on the Trans-Siberian line from Moscow to Nakhodka, USSR, in the Soviet Far East. There are 97 stops in the journey which takes 8 days 4 hr 25 min. The 3102 km *1927 miles* Baykal-Amur northern main line (BAM), begun with forced labour in 1938, was restarted in 1974 and put into service on 27 Oct 1984. A total of 10,000 million ft³ *283 million m³* of earth had to be moved and 1,987 bridges built in this £8000 million project.

Longest straight

The longest straight in the world is on the Commonwealth Railways Trans-Australian line over the Nullarbor Plain from Mile 496 between Nurina and Loongana, Western Australia, to Mile 793 between Ooldea and Watson, South Australia, 297 miles *478 km* dead straight although not level. The longest straight on British Rail is the 18 miles *29 km* between Barlby Junction and Brough on the 'down' line on the Selby, North Yorkshire, to Kingston-upon-Hull, Humberside, line.

Widest and narrowest

The widest gauge in standard use is 5 ft 6 in *1,676 m*. This width is used in Spain, Portugal, India, Pakistan, Bangladesh, Sri Lanka, Argentina and Chile. The narrowest gauge on which public services are operated is 10¼ in *260 mm* on the Wells Harbour (0.7 mile *1,12 km*) and Wells–Walsingham Railways (4 miles *6,5 km*) in Norfolk, England.

Highest *World*

The world's highest standard gauge (4 ft 8½ in *1,43 m*) track is on the Peruvian State Railways at La Cima, on the Morococha Branch at 15,806 ft *4817 m* above sea-level. The highest point on the main line is 15,688 ft *4781 m* in the Galera tunnel.

Great Britain

The highest point of the British Rail system is at the pass of Drumochter on the former Perth–Inverness border, where the track reaches an altitude of 1484 ft *452 m* above sea-level. The highest railway in Britain is the Snowdon Mountain Railway, which rises from Llanberis,

Gwynedd to 3493 ft *1064 m* above sea-level, just below the summit of Snowdon (*Yr Wyddfa*). It has a gauge of 2 ft 7½ in *800 mm*.

Lowest

The lowest point on British Rail is in the Severn Tunnel—144 ft *43,8 m* below sea-level.

Steepest gradient *World*

The world's steepest standard gauge gradient by adhesion is 1 : 11 between Chedde and Servoz on the metre gauge SNCF Chamonix line, France.

Great Britain

The steepest sustained adhesion-worked gradient on main line in the United Kingdom is the 2 mile *3,2 km* Lickey incline of 1:37.7 just south west of Birmingham. From the tunnel bottom to James Street, Liverpool, on the former Mersey Railway, there is a stretch of 1:27; and between Folkestone Junction and Harbour a mile *1,6 km* of 1:30.

Slightest gradient

The slightest gradient posted on the British Rail system is one indicated as 1 in 14,400 between Pirbright Junction and Farnborough, Hampshire. This could be described alternatively as England's most obtuse summit.

Busiest rail system

The world's most crowded rail system is the Japanese National Railways, which in 1985 carried 18,860,000 passengers daily. Among articles lost in 1985 were 522,704 umbrellas, 309,446 clothing items, 228,925 books and stationery items, 193,289 accessories and 185,390 purses.

RAIL TRAVEL

Calling All Stations

Alan M. Witton (b. 1943) of Chorlton, Manchester visited every open British Rail station (2362) in a continuous tour for charity of 16,592¾ miles *26 703 km* in 27,136 minutes on 13 July–28 Aug 1980.

Colin M. Mulvany and Seth N. Vafiadis of London W12, visited every British Rail station (2,378) embracing also the Tyne and Wear, Strathclyde and London Underground systems (333 stations) for charity in 31 days 5 hr 8 min 58 sec over 15,527⅜ miles *24 989 km* to average 38.05 mph *61,2 km/h* on 4 June–5 July 1984.

John E. Ballenger of Dunedin, Florida, USA has logged 76,485 miles *123 090 km* of unduplicated rail routes in North and South America. Using Amtrak's All Aboard America $299 ticket, valid for a month, James J. Brady of Wilmington, Ohio travelled through 442 (out of 498) stations over 21,485 unduplicated miles of track (out of 23,000) on 11 Feb–11 Mar 1984.

Carl Lombardelli of Romford, London traversed the extreme points of the compass for stations in Great Britain—Thurso (north), Lowestoft (east), Penzance (south) and Arisaig (west) in 48 hrs 15 mins on 8–10 Sept 1985.

Most Countries in 24 hours

The record number of countries travelled through entirely by train in 24 hours is 10 by W. M. Elbers and R. G. Scholten on 9, 10 Sept 1985. They started in Yugoslavia *via* Austria, Italy, Leichtenstein, Switzerland, France, Luxembourg, Belgium, Netherlands arriving in West Germany 22 hr 47 min later.

Handpumped railcars

A speed of 20 mph was first surpassed at Port Moody, British Columbia, Canada over 300 m *985 ft* by the 5 man team (1 pusher, 4 pumpers) from Port Moody Motors with 33.54 sec on 27 June 1982.

Longest Journey

The longest journey on the British Rail system is from Penzance, Cornwall to Wick, Caithness, Scotland, *via* London, Glasgow, Aberdeen and Inverness, a round trip of 2229¼ miles *3587,6 km*. It was travelled by John Shaw of Huddersfield for charity on 22–24 Sept 1983 in 50 hr 20 mins.

The highest mileage on British Rail within 24 hours is 1622¼ miles *2610,75 km* on 9–10 May 1986 by David Wakefield of London.

STATIONS

Largest *World*

The world's largest railway station is Grand Central Terminal, Park Avenue and 43rd Street, New York City, NY, USA, built 1903–13. It covers 48 acres *19 ha* on two levels with 41 tracks on the upper level and 26 on the lower. On average more than 550 trains and 180,000 people per day use it, with a peak of 252,288 on 3 July 1947.

Great Britain

The largest railway station in extent on the British Rail system is the 17-platform Clapham Junction, London, covering 27¾ acres *11,22 ha* with a total face of 11,185 ft *3409 m*. The station with the largest number of platforms is Waterloo, London (24½ acres *9,9 ha*), with 21 main and two Waterloo and City Line platforms, with a total face of 15,352 ft *4679 m*. Victoria Station (21¾ acres *8,80 ha*) with 17 platforms has, however, a total face length of 18,412 ft *5611 m*.

Oldest

The oldest station in the world is Liverpool Road Station, Manchester, England first used on 15 Sept 1830. It is now part of a museum.

Busiest

The busiest railway junction in Great Britain is Clapham Junction, Wandsworth, London, on the Southern Region of British Rail, with an average of 2200 trains passing through each 24 hr.

Highest

The highest station in the world is Condor, Bolivia at 15,705 ft *4786 m* on the metre gauge Rio Mulato to Potosi line. The highest passenger station on British Rail is Corrour, Highland, at an altitude of 1347 ft *410,5 m* above sea-level.

Waiting rooms

The world's largest waiting rooms are the four in Peking Station, Chang'an Boulevard, Peking, China, opened in September 1959, with a total standing capacity of 14,000.

Longest platform

The longest railway platform in the world is the Khargpur platform, West Bengal, India, which measures 2733 ft *833 m* in length. The State Street Center subway platform staging on 'The Loop' in Chicago, Illinois, USA, measures 3500 ft *1066 m* in length.

The longest platform in the British Rail system is the 1977 ft 4 in *602,69 m* long platform at Gloucester.

UNDERGROUND RAILWAYS

Most extensive

The earliest (first section between Faringdon St. and Edgware Road, opened 10 Jan 1863) and one of the most extensive underground or rapid transit railway systems of the 67 in the world is that of the London Underground with 251 miles *404 km* of route, of which 82 miles *131 km* is bored tunnel and 20 miles *32 km* is 'cut and cover'. This whole system is operated by a staff of 11,000 serving 272 stations. The 453 trains comprising 3875 cars carried 672,000,000 passengers in 1984. The greatest depth is 221 ft *67,3 m* near Hampstead on the Northern Line. The longest journey without a change is Epping to West Ruislip—34.1 miles *54,8 km*. The record for touring the 272 stations including Heathrow Terminal 4 station opened 12 Apr 1986 is 19 hr 51 min 14 sec set by a team of four: Robert Andrew Robinson, his son Peter David Robinson, John Garde and Timothy John Clark on 14 Apr 1986. Peter Robinson (b. 19 July 1974) was the youngest to tour all stations on 22 July 1982 aged 8.

The subway with most stations in the world is the New York City Transport Authority (first section opened on 27 Oct 1904) with a total of 231.73 route miles *372,93 km* and 1,096,006,529 passengers in 1979. The 458 stations are closer set than London's. The record for travelling the whole system was 21 hr 8½ min by Mayer Wiesen and Charles Emerson on 8 Oct 1973.

Busiest

The world's busiest metro system is that in Greater Moscow with as many as 6½ million passengers per day. To mid-1985 it had 123 stations and 198 km *123 miles* of track. The record transit (with 18 changes) in 1982 (115 stations) was 8 hr 10 min 22 sec by Eric Rudkin of Chaddesden, Derbyshire.

MODEL RAILWAYS

The non-stop duration record for a model train (loco plus 6 coaches) is 864 hr 30 min from 1 June–7 July 1978, covering 678 miles *1091 km*, organised by Roy Catton at 'Pastimes' Toy Store, Mexborough, S. Yorkshire. The longest recorded run by a model *steam* locomotive is 144 miles *231,7 km* in 27 hr 18 min by the 7¼ inch *18,4 cm* gauge 'Winifred' built in 1974 by Wilf Grove at Thames Ditton, Surrey on 8–9 Sept 1979. 'Winifred' works on 80 lb/in² *5,6 kg/cm²* pressure and is coal-fired with cylinders 2⅛ in *54 mm* in diameter and 3⅛ in *79 mm* stroke. The most miniature model railway ever built is one of 1:1000 scale by Jean Damery (b. 1923) of Paris. The engine ran on a 4½ volt battery and measures 5/16 in *7,9 mm* overall.

TRAMS

Longest tram journey

The longest tramway journey now possible is from Krefeld St Tönis to Witten Annen Nord, W. Germany. With luck at the 8 inter-connections the 105,5 km *65.5 mile* trip can be achieved in 5½ hr. By late 1977 there were still some 315 tramway systems surviving of which the longest is that of Leningrad, USSR with 2500 cars on 53 routes. The last in Britain is at Blackpool, Lancashire.

Oldest

The oldest trams in revenue service in the world are Motor cars 1 and 2 of the Manx Electric Railway dating from 1893.

4. AIRCRAFT

EARLIEST FLIGHTS

World

The first controlled and sustained power-driven flight occurred near the Kill Devil Hill, Kitty Hawk, North Carolina, USA, at 10.35 a.m. on 17 Dec 1903, when Orville Wright (1871–1948) flew the 12 hp chain-driven *Flyer I* for a distance of 120 ft *36,5 m* at an airspeed of 30 mph *48 km/h*, a ground speed of 6.8 mph *10,9 km/h* and an altitude of 8–12 ft *2,5–3,5 m* for about 12 sec watched by his brother Wilbur (1867–1912) 4 men and a boy. Both brothers, from Dayton, Ohio, were bachelors because, as Orville put it, they had not the means to 'support a wife as well as an aeroplane'. The *Flyer* is now in the National Air and Space Museum at the Smithsonian Institution, Washington DC.

The first hop by a man-carrying aeroplane entirely under its own power was made when Clément Ader (1841–1925) of France flew in his *Eole* for about 50 m *164 ft* at Armainvilliers, France, on 9 Oct 1890. It was powered by a lightweight steam engine of his own design which developed about 20 hp (15 kW). The earliest 'rational design' for a flying machine, according to the Royal Aeronautical Society, was that published by Emanuel Swedenborg (1688–1772) in Sweden in 1717.

Great Britain

The first officially recognised flight in the British Isles was made by the US citizen Samuel Franklin Cody (1861–1913) who flew 1390 ft *423 m* in his own biplane at Farnborough, Hampshire, on 16 Oct 1908. Horatio Frederick Phillips (1845–1924) almost certainly covered 500 ft *152 m* in his Phillips II 'Venetian blind' aeroplane at Streatham, in 1907. The first Briton to fly was George Pearson Dickin (1881–1909), a journalist from Southport, Lancashire as a passenger to Wilbur Wright at Auvóur, France on 3 Oct 1908. The first resident British citizen to fly in Britain was J. T. C. Moore-Brabazon (later Lord Brabazon of Tara PC, GBE, MC) (1884–1964) with 3 short but sustained flights on 30 Apr–2 May 1909.

Cross-Channel

The earliest cross-Channel flight by an aeroplane was made on Sunday, 25 July 1909 when Louis Blériot (1872–1936) of France flew his *Blériot XI* monoplane, powered by a 23 hp Anzani engine, 26 miles *41,8 km* from Les Baraques, France, to Northfall Meadow near Dover Castle, England, in 36½ min, after taking off at 4.41 a.m.

Jet-engined *World*

Proposals for jet propulsion date back to Captain Marconnet (1909) of France, and Henri Coanda (1886–1972) of Romania, and to the turbojet proposals of Maxime Guillaume in 1921. The earliest tested run was that of the British Power Jets Ltd's experimental WU (Whittle Unit) on 12 Apr 1937, invented by Flying Officer (now Air Commodore Sir) Frank Whittle OM, KBE (b. Coventry, 1 June 1907), who had applied for a patent on jet propulsion in 1930. The first flight by an aeroplane powered by a turbojet engine was made by the Heinkel He 178, piloted by Flug Kapitan Erich Warsitz, at Marienehe, Germany, on 27 Aug 1939. It was powered by a Heinkel He S3b engine (834 lb *378 kg* as installed with long tailpipe) designed by Dr Hans 'Pabst' von Ohain and first tested in August 1937.

Great Britain

The first British jet flight occurred when Fl Lt P. E. G. 'Jerry' Sayer, OBE (k. 1942) flew the Gloster-Whittle E.28/39 (wing span 29 ft *8,84 m*, length 25 ft 3 in *7,70 m*) fitted with an 860 lb *390 kg* s. t. Whittle W-1 engine for 17 min at Cranwell, Lincolnshire, on 15 May 1941. The maximum speed was c. 350 mph *560 km/h*.

Supersonic flight

The first supersonic flight was achieved on 14 Oct 1947 by Capt. (later Brig.-Gen) Charles ('Chuck') Elwood Yeager, USAF retd (b. 13 Feb 1923), over Edwards Air Force Base, Muroc, California, USA, in a Bell XS-1 rocket plane ('Glamorous Glennis') with Mach 1.015 (670 mph *1078 km/h*) at an altitude of 42,000 ft

12 800 m. The first British aircraft to attain Mach 1 in a dive was the de Havilland D. H. 108 tailless research aircraft on 6 Sept 1948, piloted by John Derry.

Trans-Atlantic

The first crossing of the North Atlantic by air was made by Lt-Cdr (later Rear Admiral) Albert Cushion Read (1887–1967) and his crew (Stone, Hinton, Rodd, Rhoads and Breese) in the 84 knot *155 km/h* US Navy/Curtiss flying-boat NC-4 from Trepassey Harbour, Newfoundland, *via* the Azores, to Lisbon, Portugal, on 16–27 May 1919. The whole flight of 4717 miles *7591 km* originating from Rockaway Air Station, Long Island, NY on 8 May, required 53 hr 58 min, terminating at Plymouth, England, on 31 May. The Newfoundland–Azores flight of 1200 miles *1930 km* took 15 hr 18 min at 81.7 knots *151,4 km/h.*

Non-stop

The first non-stop trans-Atlantic flight was achieved 18 days later from 4.13 p.m. GMT on 14 June 1919, from Lester's Field, St John's, Newfoundland, 1960 miles *3154 km* to Derrygimla bog near Clifden, County Galway, Ireland, at 8.40 a.m. GMT, 15 June, when the pilot, Capt John William Alcock, DSC (1892–1919), and the navigator Lt Arthur Whitten Brown (1886–1948) flew across in a Vickers *Vimy*, powered by two 360 hp Rolls-Royce *Eagle VIII* engines. Both men were created civil KBE's on 21 June 1919 when Alcock was aged 26 years 227 days, and shared a *Daily Mail* prize of £10,000. On 6 Aug 1945, two USAF B-47 bombers of 308th Bombardment Wing flew nonstop from Hunter Air Force Base, Georgia, USA to simulated targets in southern Europe and return. The 10,000 mile *10 693 km* flights which were crewed by V. Cammack, O. Bernhoff, D. Kepplinger, G. Stockton, A. Guidotti, D. Lutz, J. Terpening and J. Watson, took a total elapsed time of 25 hr 23 min and involved four mid-air refuellings, two in complete darkness.

Solo

The 79th man to achieve a trans-Atlantic flight but the first to do so solo was Capt (later Brig) Charles Augustus Lindbergh (Hon AFC) (1902–74) who took off in his 220 hp Ryan monoplane *Spirit of St. Louis* at 12.52 p.m. GMT on 20 May 1927 from Roosevelt Field, Long Island, NY, USA. He landed at 10.21 p.m. GMT on 21 May 1927 at Le Bourget airfield, Paris, France. His flight of 3610 miles *5810 km* lasted 33 hr 29½ min and he won a prize of $25,000 (*then £5300*).

Most Flights

Between March 1948 and his retirement on 1 Sept 1984 TWA Captain Charles M. Schimpf logged a total of 2,880 Atlantic crossings—at the rate of 6.4 per month.

Trans-Pacific

The first non-stop Pacific flight was by Major Clyde Pangborn and Hugh Herndon in the Bellanca cabin 'plane *Miss Veedol* from Sabishiro Beach, Japan 4558 miles *7335 km* to Wenatchee, Washington, USA in 41 hr 13 min on 3–5 Oct 1931. (For earliest crossing see *Circumnavigational flights* below).

(*Top*) '*The Battle of the "B's"*'. Donald R. Stits' *Baby Bird* with a length of 11 feet *3.35 metres* and a wing span of 6 feet 3 inches *1.91 metres* vying for the title 'Smallest Plane' with Robert H. Starr's *Bumble Bee*. (*Bottom*), length 9 feet 4 inches *2.84 metres*—wing span 6 feet 6 inches *1.98 metres*.

Circumnavigational flights

Strict circumnavigation requires passing through two antipodal points thus with a minimum distance of 24,859.75 miles *40 007,89 km.* The FAI permits flights which exceed the length of the Tropic of Cancer or Capricorn *viz* 22,858.754 miles *36 787,599 km.*

The earliest such flight of 26,345 miles *42 398 km* was by two US Army Douglas DWC amphibians in 57 'hops'. The *Chicago* was piloted by Lt Lowell H. Smith and Lt Leslie P. Arnold and the *New Orleans* was piloted by Lt Erik H. Nelson and Lt John Harding between 6 Apr and 28 Sept 1924 beginning and ending at Seattle, Washington, USA.

The earliest solo claim was by Wiley Hardemann Post (1898–1935) (US) in the Lockheed Vega 'Winnie Mae' starting and finishing at Floyd Bennett Field, New York City on 15–22 July 1933 in 10 'hops'. The distance of 15,596 miles *25 099 km* with a flying time of 115 hr 36 min was however at too high a latitude to qualify.

An attempt to fly round the world without refuelling is expected to be mounted by Dick Rutan and Jeana Yeager from the Mojave airfield, California, USA in September 1986. Their specially designed Voyager aircraft, with a 110 ft 9½ in *33,77 m* wing span, will take off with 3.99 tons of fuel. The existing longest unrefuelled flight was 12,532 miles *20,168 km* by a USAF B-52-H from Okinawa, Japan to Madrid, Spain on 11 Jan 1962.

The first non-stop round-the-world flight completed on 2 Mar 1949 was made by the USAF's Boeing B-50 Superfortress *Lucky Lady II* piloted by Capt James Gallagher from Carswell AFB,

Texas in 94 hr 1 min. The aircraft was refuelled 4 times on its 23,452 mile *37 742 km* flight.

The fastest flight has been the non-stop eastabout flight of 45 hr 19 min by three flight-refuelled USAF B-52's led by Maj-Gen Archie J. Old Jr. They covered 24,325 miles *39 147 km* on 16–18 Jan 1957 finishing at March Air Force Base, Riverside, California, having averaged 525 mph *845 km/h* with four in-flight refuellings by KC-97 aerial tankers.

The first circum-polar flight was solo by Capt Elgen M. Long, 44, in a Piper Navajo on 5 Nov–3 Dec 1971. He covered 38,896 miles *62 597 km* in 215 flying hours. The cabin temperature sank to −40°F *−40°C* over Antarctica.

Circumnavigation *Smallest aircraft*

The smallest aircraft to complete a circumnavigation is the 20 ft 11 in *6,38 m* single-engined 180 hp Thorp T-18 built in his garage by its pilot Donald P. Taylor of Sage, California. His 26,190 mile *42 148 km* flight in 37 stages took 176 flying hours ending at Oshkosh, Wisconsin on 30 Sept 1976.

Largest wing span

The aircraft with the largest wing span ever constructed is the $40 million Hughes H.4 Hercules flying-boat ('Spruce Goose'), which was raised 70 ft *21,3 m* into the air in a test run of 1000 yd *914 m*, piloted by Howard Hughes (1905–76), off Long Beach Harbor, California, USA, on 2 Nov 1947. The eight-engined 190 ton *193 tonnes* aircraft had a wing span of 319 ft 11 in *97,51 m* and a length of 218 ft 8 in *66,64 m* and never flew again. In a brilliant engineering feat she was moved bodily by Goldcoast Corp aided by the US Navy barge crane YD-171 on 22 Feb 1982 to her final resting place 6 miles *9,6 km* across the harbour under a 700 ft *213,4 m* diameter dome.

Heaviest

The highest recorded gross take off weight of any aircraft has been 379.9 tons *386,0 tonnes* in the case of a Boeing 747-200B 'Jumbo' jet during certification tests of its Pratt & Whitney JT9D-7Q engines on 23 May 1979. Some versions are certified for standard airline operation at a maximum take-off weight of 371.9 tons *377,9 tonnes*.

A Boeing 747 (Capt. Eric Moody) became the 'worlds heaviest glider' when all 4 engines stopped at 37,000 ft *11 275 m* due to volcanic ash from Mt. Galunggung, Indonesia on 24 June 1982 on Flight BA.009 with 263 aboard. The crew got the engines restarted after 13 min and landed the plane at Djakarta.

The $40 million Piasecki Heli-Stat, comprising a framework of light-alloy and composite materials to mount four Sikorsky SH-34J helicopters and the envelope of a Goodyear ZPG-2 patrol airship, was exhibited on 26 Jan 1984 at Lakehurst, New Jersey, USA. Designed for use by the US Forest Service and designated Model 94-37J Logger, it has an overall length of 343 ft *104,55 m* and is intended to carry a payload of 21.4 tons.

Solar powered

The solar-powered *Solar Challenger*, designed by a team led by Dr Paul MacCready, was flown for the first time entirely under solar power on 20 Nov 1980. On 7 July 1981, piloted by Steve Ptacek (USA), the *Solar Challenger* became the first aircraft of this category to achieve a crossing of the English Channel. Taking off from Pontois-Cormeilles, Paris, the 163 mile *262,3 km* journey to Manston, Kent was completed in 5 hr 23 min at a maximum altitude of 3353 m *11,000 ft*. The aircraft has a wingspan of 47 ft *14,3 m*.

Ultralight

On 3 Aug 1985 Anthony A. Cafaro (b. 30 Nov 1951) flew a ULA (max weight 245 lb *111 kg*, max speed 65 mph *104,6 km/h*, capacity 5 US gal *18,93 l*) single seater Gypsey Skycycle for 7 hr 31 min at Dart Field, Detroit, Michigan. Nine fuel 'pick-ups' were completed during the flight.

Smallest

The smallest aeroplane ever flown is the 'Baby Bird', designed and built by Donald R. Stits. It is 11 ft *3,35 m* long, with a wing span of 6 ft 3 in *1,91 m*, and weighs 252 lb *114,3 kg* empty. It is powered by a 55 hp 2 cylinder Hirth engine, giving a top speed of 110 mph *177 km/h*. It was first flown by Harold Nember on 4 Aug 1984 at Camarillo, California. The smallest jet is the 280 mph *450 km/h Silver Bullet* weighing 432 lb *196 kg* with a 17 ft *5,18 m* wing span built by Bob Bishop (USA).

Bombers *Heaviest*

The world's heaviest bomber is the eight-jet swept-wing Boeing B-52H Stratofortress, which has a maximum take-off weight of 488,000 lb (217.86 tons *221,35 tonnes*). It has a wing span of 185 ft *56,38 m* and is 157 ft 6¾ in *48,02 m* in length, with a speed of over 650 mph *1046 km/h*. The B-52 can carry twelve SRAM thermonuclear short range attack missiles or twenty-four 750 lb *340 kg* bombs under its wings and eight more SRAM's or eighty-four 500 lb *226 kg* bombs in the fuselage. The ten-engined Convair B-36J, weighing 183 tons *185 tonnes*, had a greater wing span, at 230 ft *70,10 m* but it is no longer in service. Its top speed was 435 mph *700 km/h*.

Fastest

The world's fastest operational bombers are the French Dassault Mirage IV, which can fly at Mach 2.2 (1450 mph *2333 km/h*) at 36,000 ft *11 000 m*; the American General Dynamics FB-111A, with a maximum speed of Mach 2.5; and the Soviet swing-wing Tupolev Tu-22M known to NATO as 'Backfire', which has an estimated over-target speed of Mach 2.0 but which may be as fast as Mach 2.5 and a combat radius of up to 3570 miles *5745 km*.

Airliner largest *World*

The highest capacity jet airliner is the Boeing 747 'Jumbo Jet', first flown on 9 Feb 1969 (see Heaviest aircraft) and has a capacity of from 385 to more than 500 passengers with a maximum speed of 602 mph *969 km/h*. Its wing span is 195.7 ft *59,64m* and its length 231.8 ft *70,7m*. It entered service on 22 Jan 1970. The Boeing 747-300 with lengthened upper deck allowing extra 37 passengers, entered service in March 1983.

The greatest passenger load recorded was one which carried 306 adults, 328 children and 40 babies (total 674) from the cyclone-devastated Darwin to Sydney, New South Wales, Australia on 29 Dec 1974.

Great Britain
The largest ever British aircraft was the experimental Bristol Type 167 Brabazon, which had a maximum take-off weight of 129.4 tons *131,4 tonnes*, a wing span of 230 ft *70,10 m* and a length of 177 ft *53,94 m*. This eight-engined aircraft first flew on 4 Sept 1949. The Concorde (see below) has a maximum take-off weight of 408,000 lb *185 065 kg* (182.14 tons).

Airliner fastest
The supersonic BAC/Aérospatiale Concorde, first flown on 2 Mar 1969, with a capacity of 128 passengers, cruises at up to Mach 2.2 (1450 mph *2333 km/h*). It flew at Mach 1.05 on 10 Oct 1969, exceeded Mach 2 for the first time on 4 Nov 1970 and became the first supersonic airliner used on passenger services on 21 Jan 1976 when Air France and British Airways opened services simultaneously between, respectively, Paris–Rio de Janeiro and London–Bahrain. Services between London–New York and Paris–New York began on 22 Nov 1977. The New York–London record is 2 hr 56 min 35 sec set on 1 Jan 1983.

Most capacious
The Aero Spacelines Guppy-201 has a cargo hold with a usable volume of 39,000 ft³ *1104,4 m³* and a maximum take-off weight of 75.9 tons *77,1 tonnes*. Wing span is 156.2 ft *47,63 m*, length 143.8 ft *43,84 m* and overall height 48.5 ft *14,78 m*. The Soviet Antonov AN-124 Ruslan has a cargo hold with a usable volume of 35,800 ft³ *1014 m³* and a maximum take-off weight of 398.6 tons *405 tonnes*. It is powered by four Lotarev D-18T turbofans giving a cruising speed of up to 528 mph *850 km/h* at 39,370 ft *12 000 m* and a range of 2796 miles *4500 km*.

Largest propeller
The largest aircraft propeller ever used was the 22 ft 7½ in *6,9 m* diameter Garuda propeller, fitted to the Linke-Hofmann R II built in Breslau, Germany (now Wroclaw, Poland), which flew in 1919. It was driven by four 260 hp Mercedes engines and turned at only 545 rpm.

Scheduled flights *Longest*
The longest distance scheduled non-stop flight is the weekly Pan-Am Sydney–San Francisco non-stop 13 hr 25 min Flight 816, in a Boeing 747 SP, opened in December 1976, over 7475 statute miles *12 030 km*. The longest delivery flight by a commercial jet is 8936 nautical miles or 10,290 statute miles *16 560 km* from Seattle, Washington, USA to Cape Town, South Africa by the South African Airway's Boeing 747 SP (Special performance) 'Matroosberg' with 178 400 kg *175.5 tons* of pre-cooled fuel in 17 hr 22½ min on 23–24 Mar 1976.

Shortest
The shortest scheduled flight in the world is that by Loganair between the Orkney Islands of Westray and Papa Westray which has been flown with Britten-Norman Islander twin-engined 10-seat transports since September 1967. Though scheduled for 2 min, in favourable wind conditions it has been accomplished in 58 sec by Capt Andrew D. Alsop.

Gary W. Rovetto of Island Air on 21 Mar 1980 flew on the scheduled flight from Center Island to Decatur Island, Washington, USA in 41 sec.

Paris–London
The fastest time to travel the 214 miles *344 km* from central Paris to central London (BBC TV

centre) is 38 min 58 sec by David Boyce of Stewart Wrightson (Aviation) Ltd on 24 Sept 1983 by motorcycle-helicopter to Le Bourget; Hawker Hunter jet (pilot Michael Carlton) to Biggin Hill, Kent; helicopter to the TV centre car park.

London–New York
The record for central London to downtown New York City by helicopter and Concorde is 3 hr 59 min 44 sec and the return in 3 hr 40 min 40 sec both by David J. Springbett, 1981 Salesman of the Year, and David Boyce (see above) on 8 and 9 Feb 1982.

HIGHEST SPEED

Official record
The official air speed record is 2193.167 mph *3529,56 km/h* by Capt Eldon W. Joersz and Maj George T. Morgan, Jr, in a Lockheed SR-71A near Beale Air Force Base, California, USA over a 15 to 25 km course on 28 July 1976.

Air-launched record
The fastest fixed-wing aircraft in the world was the US North American Aviation X-15A-2, which flew for the first time (after modification from X-15A) on 25 June 1964 powered by a liquid oxygen and ammonia rocket propulsion system. Ablative materials on the airframe once enabled a temperature of 3000°F to be withstood. The landing speed was 210 knots (242 mph *389,1 km/h*) momentarily. The highest speed attained was 4520 mph *7274 km/h* (Mach 6.7) when piloted by Maj William J. Knight, USAF (b. 1930), on 3 Oct 1967. An earlier version piloted by Joseph A. Walker (1920–66), reached 354,200 ft *107 960 m* (67.08 miles) also over Edwards Air Force Base, California, USA, on 22 Aug 1963. The programme was suspended after the final flight of 24 Oct 1968.

The US NASA Rockwell International Space Shuttle Orbiter *Columbia* was launched from the Kennedy Space Center, Cape Canaveral, Florida commanded by Cdr John W. Young USN and piloted by Robert L. Crippen on 12 Apr 1981 after the expenditure of $9900 million since 1972. *Columbia* broke all records for space by a fixed wing craft with 16,600 mph *26 715 km/h* at main engine cut-off. After re-entry from 400,000 ft *122 km*, experiencing temperatures of 2160°C *3920°F*, she glided home weighing 97 tonnes/tons with the highest ever landing speed of 216 mph *347 km/h* on Rogers Dry Lake, California on 14 Apr 1981. Under a new FAI Category P for Aerospacecraft, the *Columbia* is holder of the current absolute world record for duration of 8 days 00 hr 04 min 45 sec, with two astronauts, but *Challenger* (launched 18 June 1983) has since set a duration record of 6 days 02 hr 23 min 59 sec with five astronauts including Sally K. Ride, the first female Space Shuttle astronaut, and on a previous mission set a new record altitude of 206.36 miles *332,1 km*. *Columbia* also holds the current absolute world record for the greatest mass lifted to altitude, a figure of 235,634 lb *106 882 kg* or 105.2 tons.

Fastest jet
The world's fastest jet aircraft is the USAF Lockheed SR-71 reconnaissance aircraft (see Official record) which was first flown on 22 Dec 1964 and is reportedly capable of attaining an altitude ceiling of close to 100,000 ft *30 480 m*. The SR-71 has a wing span of 55.6 ft *16,94 m* and a length of 107.4 ft *32,73 m* and weighs 170,000 lb (75.9 tons *77,1 tonnes*) at take-off. Its reported range is 2982 miles *4800 km* at Mach 3 at 78,750 ft *24 000 m*. At least 30 are believed to have been built. The fastest combat aircraft in the world is the USSR Mikoyan MiG-25 fighter (code name 'Foxbat'). The reconnaissance 'Fox-

bat-B' has been tracked by radar at about Mach 3.2 (2110 mph *3395 km/h*). When armed with four large underwing air-to-air missiles known to NATO as 'Acrid', the fighter 'Foxbat-A' is limited to Mach 2.8 (1845 mph *2969 km/h*). The single-seat 'Foxbat-A' spans 45 ft 9 in *13,95 m*, is 78 ft 2 in *23,82 m* long and has an estimated maximum take-off weight of 82,500 lb *37 421 kg*.

Fastest biplane
The fastest recorded biplane was the Italian Fiat C.R.42B, with a 1010 hp Daimler-Benz DB601A engine, which attained 323 mph *520 km/h* in 1941. Only one was built.

Fastest piston-engined aircraft
The fastest speed at which a piston-engined aeroplane has ever been measured was for a cut-down privately owned Hawker Sea Fury which attained 520 mph *836 km/h* in level flight over Texas, USA, in August 1966 piloted by Mike Carroll (k. 1969) of Los Angeles. The FAI accredited record for a piston-engined aircraft is 517.055 mph *832,12 km/h* over Mojave, California by Frank Taylor (US) in a modified North American P-51D Mustang powered by a 3000 hp Packard Merlin, over a 15 to 25 km course, on 30 July 1983.

Fastest propeller-driven aircraft
The Soviet Tu-114 turboprop transport is the world's fastest propeller-driven aeroplane. It achieved a recorded speed 545.076 mph *877,212 km/h* carrying heavy payloads over measured circuits. It is developed from the Tupolev Tu-95 bomber, known in the West as the 'Bear', and has four 14,795 hp engines. The turboprop-powered Republic XF-84H prototype US Navy fighter which flew on 22 July 1955 had a top *design* speed of 670 mph *1078 km/h* but was abandoned.

Fastest trans-Atlantic flight
The trans-Atlantic flight record is 1 hr 54 min 56.4 sec by Maj James V. Sullivan, 37, and Maj Noel F. Widdifield, 33 flying a Lockheed SR-71A eastwards on 1 Sept 1974. The average speed, slowed by refuelling by a KC-135 tanker aircraft, for the New York–London stage of 3461.53 miles *5570,80 km* was 1806.963 mph *2908,026 km/h*. The solo record (Gander to Gatwick) is 8 hr 47 min 32 sec by Capt John J. A. Smith in a Rockwell 685 on 12 Mar 1978.

Altitude *Official record*
The official world altitude record by an aircraft taking off from the ground under its own power is 123,524 ft (23.39 miles *37 650 m*) by Aleksandr Fedotov (USSR) in a Mikoyan E.266M, (MiG-25) aircraft, powered by two 30,865 lb *14 000 kg* thrust turbojet engines, on 31 Aug 1977.

Duration
The flight duration record is 64 days 22 hr 19 min and 5 sec, set up by Robert Timm and John Cook in a Cessna 172 'Hacienda'. They took off from McCarran Airfield, Las Vegas, Nevada, USA, just before 3.53 p.m. local time on 4 Dec 1958, and landed at the same airfield just before 2.12 p.m. on 7 Feb 1959. They covered a distance equivalent to six times round the world with continued refuellings, without landing.

The record for duration without refuelling is 84 hr 32 min, set by Walter E. Lees and Frederic A. Brossy in a Bellanca monoplane with a 225 hp Packard Diesel engine, at Jacksonville, Florida, USA on 25–28 May 1931. The longest non-stop flight without refuelling was a 12,532 mile *20 169 km* flight from Okinawa to Madrid, Spain by a USAF B-52H on 10–11 Jan 1962.

The longest non-stop solo flight without refuelling was 73 hours 21 min 36 secs by Jerry D. Mullens in a Class C-1 Phoenix on 5–8 Dec 1981 over a closed circuit between Oklahoma City and Jacksonville, Florida. He covered a total distance of 10,007.1 miles *16 104,4 km*.

AIRPORTS

Largest *World*

The world's largest airport is the £2100 million King Khalid International Airport outside Riyadh, Saudi Arabia covering an area of 86 miles² *221 km²*, opened on 14 Nov 1983. It has the world's largest control tower 243 ft *74 m* in height. The Hajj Terminal at the £2800 million King Abdul-Aziz airport near Jeddah is the world's largest roofed structure covering 1,5 km² *370 acres*. The present 6 runways and 5 terminal buildings of the Dallas/Fort Worth Airport, Texas, USA are planned to be extended to 9 runways and 13 terminals with 260 gates with an ultimate capacity for 150 million passengers. The world's largest airport terminal is Hartsfield Atlanta International Airport opened on 21 Sept 1980 with floor space covering 50.50 acres *20,43 ha*. It has 138 gates handling nearly 50 million passengers a year but has a capacity for 75 million.

Great Britain

Seventy-one airline companies from 62 countries operate scheduled services into Heathrow Airport—London (2958 acres *1197 ha*), and during 1985 there was a total of 283,433 air transport movements handled by a staff of 45,500 employed by the various companies and the British Airports Authority. The total number of passengers, both incoming and outgoing, was 31,289,252. The most flights yet handled by Heathrow in a day was 1,022 on 27 Sept 1985 and the largest number of passengers yet handled in a day was 118,257 on 1 Sep 1985. Aircraft fly to 213 destinations direct in 82 countries.

Busiest

The world's busiest airport is the Chicago International Airport, O'Hare Field, Illinois, USA with a total of 746,376 movements and 49,954,362 passengers in the year 1985. This represents a take-off or landing every 42.25 sec round the clock. Heathrow Airport, London handles more *international* traffic than any other. The busiest landing area ever has been Bien Hoa Air Base, south Vietnam, which handled more than 1,000,000 take-offs and landings in 1970. The world's largest 'helipad' was An Khe, south Vietnam.

Highest and lowest

The highest airport in the world is La Sa (Lhasa) Airport, Tibet at 14,315 ft *4363 m*.

The highest landing ever made by a fixed-wing 'plane is 19,947 ft *6080 m* on Dhaulagiri, Himalaya by a Pilatus Porter, named 'Yeti', supplying the 1960 Swiss Expedition. The lowest landing field is El Lisan on the east shore of the Dead Sea, 1180 ft *360 m* below sea-level, but during World War II BOAC Short C-class flying boats operated from the surface of the Dead Sea 1292 ft *394 m* below sea level. The lowest international airport is Schiphol, Amsterdam, at 13 ft *3,9 m* below sea-level. Rotterdam's airport is fractionally lower at 15 ft *4,5 m*.

Farthest and nearest to city or capital centres

The airport farthest from the city centre it allegedly serves is Viracopos, Brazil, which is 60 miles *96 km* from São Paulo. The Gibraltar airport is 880 yd *800 m* from the centre.

Longest runway *World*

The longest runway in the world is one of 7 miles *11 km* in length (of which 15,000 ft *4572 m* is concreted) at Edwards Air Force Base on the bed of Rogers Dry Lake at Muroc, California, USA. The whole test centre airfield extends over 65 miles² *168 km²*. In an emergency an auxiliary 12 mile *19 km* strip is available along the bed of the Dry Lake. The world's longest civil airport runway is one of 16,076 ft (3.04 miles *4,89 km*) at Pierre van Ryneveld Airport Upington, South Africa constructed in five months from August 1975 to January 1976. A paved runway 20,500 ft (3.88 miles *6,24 km*) long appears on maps of Jordan at Abu Husayn. The longest runway available normally to civil aircraft in the United Kingdom is No. 1 at Heathrow Airport—London, measuring 12,800 ft (2.42 miles *3,90 km*). The most southerly major runway (1.6 miles *2,57 km*) in the world is at Mount Pleasant, East Falkland (Lat 51° 50′S) built in 16 months to May 1985.

HELICOPTERS

Fastest

The official world speed record for a pure helicopter is 228.9 mph *368,4 km/h* set by Gourguen Karapetyan in a Mil A-10 on a 15 to 25 km course near Moscow, USSR on 21 Sept 1978.

Largest

The world's largest helicopter is the Soviet Mil Mi-12 ('Homer'), also known as the V-12. It is powered by four 6500 hp turboshaft engines and has a span of 219 ft 10 in *67 m* over its rotor tips with a length of 121 ft 4½ in *37,00 m* and weighs 103.3 tons *105 tonnes*.

Greatest load

On 3 Feb 1982 at Podmoscovnoé in the Soviet Union, a Mil Mi-26 heavy-lift helicopter, crewed by G. V. Alfeurov and L. A. Indeev (co-pilot), lifted a total mass of 125,153.8 lb *56 768,8 kg* (55.87 tons *56,77 tonnes*) to 2000 m *6560 ft*.

Smallest

The Aerospace General Co one-man rocket assisted minicopter weighs about 160 lb *72,5 kg* cruising 250 miles *400 km* at 85 mph *137 km/h*.

Highest

The altitude record for helicopters is 40,820 ft *12 442 m* by an Aérospatiale SA315B *Lama*, over France on 21 June 1972. The highest recorded landing has been at 23,000 ft *7000 m* below the South-East face of Everest in a rescue sortie in May 1971. The World Trade Center helipad is 1385 ft *422 m* above street level in New York City on the South Tower.

Circumnavigation

H. Ross Perot, 23 and Jay Coburn both of Dallas, Texas made the first helicopter circumnavigation in 'Spirit of Texas' on 1–30 Sept 1982. The first solo round-the-world flight in a helicopter was completed by Dick Smith (Australia) on 22 July 1983. Flown from and to the Bell Helicopter facility at Fort Worth, Texas, in a Bell Model 206L Long Ranger III, his unhurried flight began on 5 Aug 1982 and covered a distance of 35,258 miles *56 742 km*.

AUTOGYROS

Earliest

The autogyro or gyroplane, a rotorcraft with an unpowered rotor turned by the airflow in flight, preceded the practical helicopter with engine-driven rotor. Juan de la Cierva (Spain), made the first successful autogyro flight with his model C.4 (commercially named an *Autogiro*) at Getafe, Spain, on 9 Jan 1923.

Speed, altitude and distance records

Wing Cdr Kenneth H. Wallis (GB) holds the straight-line distance record of 543.27 miles *874,32 km* set in his WA-116F autogyro on 28 Sept 1975 non-stop from Lydd, Kent to Wick, Highland. Wg Cdr Wallis flew his WA-116, with 72 hp McCulloch engine, to a record speed of 111.2 mph *179 km/h* over a 3 km *1.86 mile* straight course on 12 May 1969. On 20 July 1982, flying from Boscombe Down, Wiltshire, he established a new autogyro altitude record of 18,516 ft *5643,7 m* in his WA-121/Mc. This, the smallest and lightest Wallis autogyro to date, is powered by a 100 hp Wallis/McCulloch engine.

FLYING-BOAT

Fastest

The fastest flying-boat ever built has been the Martin XP6M-1 Seamaster, the US Navy 4-jet engined minelayer flown in 1955–9 with a top speed of 646 mph *1040 km/h*. In September 1946 the Martin JRM-2 Mars flying-boat set a payload record of 68,327 lb *30 992 kg.* The official flying-boat speed record is 566.69 mph *912 km/h,* set up by Nikolai Andrievsky and crew of two in a Soviet Beriev M-10, powered by two AL-7 turbojets, over a 15 to 25 km course on 7 Aug 1961. The M-10 holds all 12 records listed for jet-powered flying-boats, including an altitude of 49,088 ft *14 962 m* set by Georgiy Buryanov and crew over the Sea of Azov on 9 Sept 1961.

AIRSHIPS

Earliest
The earliest flight in an airship was by Henri Giffard from Paris in his steam-powered coal-gas 88,300 ft³ *2500 m³* 144 ft *43,8 m* long airship on 24 Sept 1852. The earliest British airship was a 20,000 ft³ *566 m³* 75 ft *22,8 m* long craft built by Stanley Spencer whose maiden flight was from Crystal Palace, Bromley, London on 22 Sept 1902. The latest airship to be built in Britain is the 235,400 ft³ *6666 m³* 193.6 ft *59 m* long Skyship 600 designed and built by Airship Industries. This 20 passenger dirigible (G-SKSC) was flown for the first time at RAE Cardington, Bedfordshire on 6 Mar 1984.

Largest *Rigid*
The largest rigid airship ever built was the 210.5 ton *213,9 tonne* German *Graf Zeppelin II* (LZ 130), with a length of 245 m *803.8 ft* and a capacity of 7,062,100 ft³ *199 981 m³.* She made her maiden flight on 14 Sept 1938 and in May and August 1939 made radar spying missions in British air space. She was dismantled in April 1940. Her sister ship *Hindenburg* was 5.6 ft *1,70 m* longer.

British
The largest British airship was the R101 built by the Royal Airship Works, Cardington, Bedfordshire, which first flew on 14 Oct 1929. She was 777 ft *236,8 m* in length and had a capacity of 5,508,800 ft³ *155 995 m³.* She crashed near Beauvais, France, killing 48 aboard on 5 Oct 1930.

Non-Rigid
The largest non-rigid airship ever constructed was the US Navy ZPG 3-W which had a capacity of 1,516,300 ft³ *42 937 m³,* was 403.4 ft *122,9 m* long and 85.1 ft *25,93 m* in diameter, with a crew of 21. She first flew on 21 July 1958, but crashed into the sea in June 1960.

Hot-Air
The world altitude, duration and distance records, of 10,365 ft *3159 m,* 1 hr 26 min 52 sec, and 23.03 miles *37,07 km* respectively, are held by the Cameron D-38 hot-air airship flown at Cunderdin, W. Australia on 27 Aug 1982 by R. W. Taaffe (Australia).

Greatest passenger load
The most people ever carried in an airship was 207 in the US Navy *Akron* in 1931. The trans-Atlantic record is 117 by the German *Hindenburg* in 1937.

Distance records
The FAI accredited straight line distance record for airships is 3967.1 miles *6384,5 km,* set up by the German *Graf Zeppelin,* captained by Dr Hugo Eckener, between 29 Oct and 1 Nov 1928. The German Zeppelin L59 flew from Yambol, Bulgaria to south of Khartoum, Sudan and returned on 21–25 Nov 1917 to cover a minimum of 4500 miles *7250 km.*

Duration record
The longest recorded flight by a non-rigid airship (without refuelling) is 264 hr 12 min by a US Navy Goodyear-built ZPG-2 class ship (Cdr J. R. Hunt USN) from South Weymouth NAS, Massachusetts, USA on 4–15 Mar 1957 landing back at Key West, Florida, USA having flown 9448 miles *15 205 km.*

BALLOONING

Earliest
I. William Deiches (b. 1934) of Brentwood, Essex, has adduced that the 'mace-head' of the Scorpion King *c.* 3100 BC found at Hierakonpolis, Egypt is in reality a depiction of a pannelled hot-air balloon of papyrus construction. The earliest recorded ascent was by a model hot-air balloon invented by Father Bartolomeu de Gusmão (*né* Lourenço) (b. Santos, Brazil, 1685), which was flown indoors at the Casa da India, Terreiro do Paço, Portugal on 8 Aug 1709 (for earliest man-carrying flights see Chapter 10).

Distance record (*Great-circle distance between take-off and first landing point*)
The record distance travelled by a balloon is 5208.68 miles *8382,54 km* by the Raven experimental helium-filled balloon *Double Eagle V* (capacity 11 300 m³ *399,053 ft³*) on 9–12 Nov 1981, from Nagashima, Japan to Covello, California. The crew for this first manned balloon crossing of the Pacific Ocean was Ben L. Abruzzo, 51, Rocky Aoki, 43 (Japan), Ron Clark, 41 and Larry M. Newman, 34.

Ex-USAF Colonel Joe Kittinger (see Parachuting Chapter 10) became the first man to complete a solo trans-Atlantic crossing by balloon. Accomplished in the 3000 m³ helium-filled balloon *Rosie O'Grady* between 14–18 Sept 1984, Kittinger lifted-off from Caribou, Maine and completed a distance of approximately 3543 miles *5701 km* before landing at Montenotte, Italy in 86 hr. The first balloon crossing of the North Atlantic had been made during 12–17 Aug 1978 in the gas balloon *Double Eagle II* crewed by Ben L. Abruzzo, Maxie L. Anderson and Larry M. Newman.

The first crossing of the United States was by the helium-filled balloon *Super Chicken III* (pilots Fred Gorell and John Shoecraft) from Costa Mesa, California, 2515 miles *4047 km* to Blackbeard's Island, Georgia on 9–12 Oct 1981.

Highest *Unmanned*
The highest altitude attained by an unmanned balloon was 170,000 ft *51 815 m* by a Winzen balloon of 47.8 million ft³ *1,35 million m³* launched at Chico, California in October 1972.

Manned
The greatest altitude reached in a manned balloon is the unofficial 123,800 ft (23.45 miles *37 735 m*) by Nicholas Piantanida (1933–66) of Bricktown, New Jersey, USA, from Sioux Falls, South Dakota, USA, on 1 Feb 1966. He landed in a cornfield in Iowa but did not survive. The official record is 113,740 ft *34 668 m* by Cdr Malcolm D. Ross, USNR and the late Lt-Cdr Victor A. Prother, USN in an ascent from the deck of USS *Antietam* on 4 May 1961, over the Gulf of Mexico.

Largest
The largest balloon built is one with an inflatable volume of 70 million ft³ *2 million m³* by Winzen Research Inc, Minnesota, USA.

Ballooning (*Hot-air*)
(Modern revival began in USA in 1961. First World Championships 10–17 Feb 1973 at Albuquerque, New Mexico, USA.)

The world's distance record for hot-air balloons is 717.52 miles *1154,74 km,* set by French balloonists Michel Arnould and Hélène Dorigny on 25–26 Nov 1981 in the Cameron Type A-530 *Semiramis* from Ballina, County Mayo, Eire to St Christophe-en-Boucherie, France. This flight has also been homologated by the FAI as a new world duration record for hot-air balloons of 29 hr 5 min 48 sec, and in addition the *Semiramis* is now the largest hot-air balloon ever built with a volume of 530,000 ft³ *15 008 m³.* On 31 Oct 1980 Julian Nott (GB) attained an altitude, which has been ratified by the FAI, of 55,137 ft *16 805 m,* taking off from Longmont, near Denver, Colorado, USA, in the Cameron-built ICI balloon *Innovation.* The FAI endurance and distance record for a gas and hot-air balloon is 96 hr 24 min and 2074.817 miles *3339,086 km* by *Zanussi* crewed by Donald Allan Cameron (GB) and Major Christopher Davey which failed by only 103 miles *166 km* to achieve the first balloon crossing of the Atlantic on 30 July 1978.

The record altitude in an open basket is 53,000 ft *16 154,4 m* by Chauncey M. Dunn (US) on 1 Aug 1979. He wore a pressure suit.

The immense *Graf Zeppelin II* airship (245 metres *803.8 feet* length) compared in size with a Boeing 747 'Jumbo Jet'. (Artwork: Eddie Botchway).

PERSONAL AVIATION RECORDS

Oldest and youngest passengers
Airborne births are reported every year. The oldest person to fly has been Mrs Jessica S. Swift (b. Anna Stewart 17 Sept 1871) aged 110 yrs 3 months, from Vermont to Florida, USA in Dec 1981. The oldest Briton to fly was probably Mrs Julia Caroline Black (b. 24 Feb 1874 d. 12 May 1980) on a British Caledonian flight from Abbotsinch to Gatwick on 17 Nov 1978 when aged 104 years 8 months.

Youngest and oldest pilots
The youngest age at which anyone has ever qualified as a military pilot is 15 yr 5 months in the case of Sgt Thomas Dobney (b. 6 May 1926) of the RAF. He had overstated his age (14 yr) on entry. The youngest solo pilot has been Cody A. Locke in a Cessna 150 aircraft near Mexiculi, Mexico on 24 Feb 1983, when aged 9 years 316 days. The wholly untutored James A. Stoodley aged 14 years 5 months took his 13 year old brother John on a 29 minute joy ride in an unattended US Piper Cub trainer aircraft near Ludgershall, Wiltshire in December 1942.

The world's oldest pilot is Ed McCarty (b. 18 Sept 1885) of Kimberly, Idaho, USA, who in 1979 was flying his rebuilt 30-year-old Ercoupe aged 94. The oldest British pilot is Air Commodore Harold 'Daddy' Probyn CB, CBE, DSO (b. 8 Dec 1891), who first flew with the RFC in 1916 and was flying in Kenya on his 92nd birthday 67 years later in 1983.

Most flying hours
Max Conrad (1903–79) (USA) between 1928 and mid-1974 totalled 52,929 hr 40 min logged flight—more than 6 years airborne. He com-

pleted 150 trans-Atlantic crossings in light aircraft. The record as a supersonic passenger is by Mr Fred Finn who made his 604th Concorde crossing in June 1986.

Most take-offs and landings from airports
Al Yates and Bob Phoenix of Texas, USA made 193 take-offs and daylight landings at unduplicated airfields in 14 hr 57 min in a Piper Seminole, on 15 June 1979.

E. K. Coventry (pilot) and D. Bullen (navigator) made full stop landings in a Piper Arrow in all England's 45 counties between dawn and dusk on 24 July 1984.

Human-powered flight
The world distance record for human powered flight was set on 12 June 1979 by Dr Paul MacCready's man powered aircraft *Gossamer Albatross*, piloted and pedalled by Bryan Allen. The *Albatross* took off from Folkestone at 05.51 hrs and landed 22.26 miles *35,82 km* distant at Cap Gris Nez, France at 08.40 hrs. The duration was 2 hr 49 min, and this achievement won the £100,000 prize offered by Henry Kremer for the first man-powered crossing of the English Channel. The 70 lb *31,75 kg Gossamer Condor* (96 ft *29,26 m* wing-span) designed by Dr Paul MacCready, flew the figure-of-8 course between pylons 880 yd *804,6 m* apart, powered by the 9¾ stone *61,2 kg* Bryan Allen at Shafter Airport, California on 23 Aug 1977 to win the £50,000 Kremer prize. The flight lasted 7 min 27.5 sec.

MODEL AIRCRAFT

Altitude, speed and duration
Maynard L. Hill (US) flying radio-controlled models established the World record for altitude of 26,929 ft *8208 m* on 6 Sept 1970 and on 4 July 1983 set a closed circuit distance record of 1231 miles *765 km*. The free flight speed record is 213.70 mph *343,92 km/h* by V. Goukoune and V. Myakinin (both USSR) with a radio-controlled model at Klementyeva, USSR, on 21 Sept 1971. The record duration flight is one of 32 hr 7 min 40 sec by Eduard Svoboda (Czechoslovakia), flying a radio controlled glider on 23–24 Aug 1980. An indoor model with a rubber motor designed by J. Richmond (USA) set a duration record of 52 min 14 sec on 31 Aug 1979.

Cross-channel
The first cross-channel model helicopter flight was achieved by an 11 lb *5,00 kg* model Bell 212 radio-controlled by Dieter Zeigler for 32 miles *52 km* between Ashford, Kent and Ambleteuse, France on 17 July 1974.

Smallest
The smallest model aircraft to fly is one weighing 0.004 oz *0,1 g* powered by attaching a horsefly and designed by the insectonaut Don Emmick of Seattle, Washington, USA on 24 July 1979. One flew for 5 minutes at Kirkland, Washington, USA.

Paper aircraft
The flight duration record for a paper aircraft is 16.89 sec by Ken Blackburn in the Reynolds Coliseum, North Carolina State University, USA on 29 Nov 1983. The indoor record with a 12 ft *3,65 m* ceiling is 1 min 33 sec set in the Fuji TV studios, Tōkyō, Japan on 21 Sept 1980. A paper plane was reported and witnessed to have flown 1¼ miles *2,0 km* by 'Chick' C. O. Reinhart from a 10th storey office window at 60 Beaver Street, New York City across the East River to Brooklyn in August 1933, helped by a thermal from a coffee-roasting plant. An indoor distance of 193 ft *58,82 m* was recorded by Tony Felch at the La Crosse Center, Wisconsin, USA on 21 May 1985.

5. POWER PRODUCERS

Steam engines
The oldest steam engine in working order is the 1812 Boulton & Watt 26 hp 42 in *1066 mm* bore beam engine on the Kennet & Avon Canal at Great Bedwyn, Wiltshire. It was restored by the Crofton Society in 1971 and still runs periodically.

The largest single cylinder steam engine ever built was that designed by Matthew Loam of Cornwall and made by the Hayle Foundry Co in 1849 for installation for land draining at Haarlem Netherlands. The cylinder was 12 ft *3,65 m* in diameter such that each stroke also of 12 ft *3,65 m* lifted 13,440 gallons *61 096 l* or 60 tons of water.

The most efficient steam engine recorded was Taylor's engine built by Michael Loam for the United Mines, Gwennap, Cornwall in 1840. It registered only 1.7 lb of coal per horsepower per hour.

Earliest atomic pile
The world's first atomic pile was built in a disused squash court at Stagg Field, University of Chicago, Illinois, USA. It went 'critical' at 3.25 pm on 2 Dec 1942.

Power plant *Largest World*
Currently, the world's most powerful installed power station is the Grand Coulee, Washington State, USA with 9.7 million kilowatt hours (ultimately 10,080 MW) which began operating in 1942.

The $11 billion Itaipu power station on the Paraná river by the Brazil-Paraguay border began generating power formally on 25 Oct 1984 and will by 1988/89 attain 12,600,000 kW from 18 turbines. Construction began in 1975 with a force reaching 28,000 workers. A 20,000 MW power station project on the Tunguska River, USSR was announced in February 1982.

The world's largest coal-fired power complex at Ekibastuz, Kazakhstan, USSR began generating in May 1982.

Great Britain
The power station with the greatest installed capacity in Great Britain is Drax, North Yorkshire, with 5 of its 6 660 MW sets yielding 3300 MW in mid 1985. The sixth set will be operational in early 1986. A 3300 MW oil-fired installation is under construction on the Isle of Grain, Kent.

The largest hydroelectric plant in the UK is the North of Scotland Hydroelectricity Board's Power Station at Loch Sloy, Strathclyde. The installed capacity of this station is 130 MW. The Ben Cruachan Pumped Storage scheme was opened on 15 Oct 1965 at Loch Awe, Strathclyde, Scotland. It has a capacity of 400 MW and cost £24,000,000. The 1880 MW underground pumped storage scheme at Dinorwig, Gwynedd is the largest built in Europe with a head of 1739 ft *530 m* and a capacity of 13,770 ft³/sec *390 m³/sec*. The £425 million plant was completed in 1984 and the capacity is 1681 MW.

Nuclear power station *Largest*
The world's largest atomic power station with 9 reactors giving 7747 MW (net) is the station in Fukushima, Japan. An additional unit with 1067 MW (net) is scheduled to be in operation before 1987.

Nuclear reactor *Largest*
The largest single nuclear reactor in the world is

the 1450 MW (net) reactor at the Ignalina station, Lithuania, USSR, put on full power in Jan 1984. The largest under construction is the CHOOZ-B1 reactor in France which is scheduled for operation in 1991 and will have a net capacity of 1457 MW.

Fusion power
Tokamak-7, the prototype thermonuclear reactor was declared in January 1982 by USSR academician Velikhov to be operating 'reliably for months on end'. The world's largest experimental station is the Joint European Torus at Culham, Oxfordshire built in 1979–84.

Solar power plant
The largest solar furnace in the world is the $141 million 10 megawatt 'Solar I', 12 miles *19,3 km* southeast of Barstow, California first tested in April 1982. It comprises 1818 mirrors in concentric circles focused on a boiler atop a 255 ft *77,7 m* high tower. Sunlight from 222 heliostats is concentrated on a target 114 ft *34,7 m* up in the power tower. The $30 million thermal solar energy system at Pakerland Packing Co, Bellevue Plant, Green Bay, Wisconsin, USA completed in Jan 1984 comprises 9750 4 × 8 ft *1,21 × 2,43 m* collectors covering 7.16 acres *or 28 985 m²*. It will yield up to 8000 million BTU's a month.

Tidal power station
The world's first major tidal power station is the *Usine marèmotrice de la Rance*, officially opened on 26 Nov 1966 at the Rance estuary in the Golfe de St Malo, Brittany, France. It was built in five years at a cost of 420,000,000 francs (£34,685,000), and has a net annual output of 544,000,000 kWh. The 880 yd *804 m* barrage contains 24 turbo alternators. The $1000 million (£540 million) Passamaquoddy project for the Bay of Fundy in Maine, USA, and New Brunswick, Canada, remains a project. A $46 million (*then £25.5 million*) pilot Annapolis River project for the Bay of Fundy was begun in 1981.

Boiler *Largest*
The largest boilers ever designed are those ordered in the United States from the Babcock & Wilcox Company (USA) with a capacity of 1330 MW so involving the evaporation of 9,330,000 lb *4 232 000 kg* of steam per hour. The largest boilers now being installed in the United Kingdom are the five 660 MW units for the Drax Power Station designed and constructed by Babcock & Wilcox Ltd.

The water-powered Priston corn mill in Avon dates from pre-Norman times and has had just four owners, including the Hopwood family, the present occupiers. (Colin Smith).

Generator Largest
Generators in the 2,000,000 kW (or 2000 MW) range are now in the planning stages both in the UK and the USA. The largest operational is a turbo-generator of 1450 MW (net) being installed at the Ignalina Atomic Power Station in Lithuania (see p. 138).

Turbines Largest
The largest hydraulic turbines are those rated at 815,000 kW (equivalent to 1.1 million hp), 32 ft *9,7 m* in diameter with a 401 ton *407 tonnes* runner and a 312½ ton *317,5 tonnes* shaft installed by Allis-Chalmers at the Grand Coulee 'Third Powerplant', Washington, USA.

Pump
The world's largest reversible pump-turbine is that made by Allis-Chalmers for the Bath County project, Virginia, USA. It has a maximum rating of 457 MW as a turbine and maximum operating head of 393 m *1289 ft*. The impeller/runner diameter is 6349 mm *20 ft 9 in* with a synchronous speed of 257.1 rpm.

Longest Lasting Battery
The zinc foil and sulfur dry pile batteries made by Watlin and Hill of London in 1840 have powered ceaseless tintinnabulation inside a bell jar at the Clarendon Laboratory, Oxford since 1840.

Gasworks Largest
The flow of natural gas from the North Sea is diminishing the manufacture of gas by the carbonisation of coal and the reforming process using petroleum derivatives. Britain's largest ever gasworks, 300 acres *120 ha*, were at Beckton, Newham, Greater London. Currently, the largest gasworks in the UK are the Breakwater Works at Oreston, Plymouth, Devon which opened in 1966–7 and cover an area of 19 acres *7,6 ha*. They convert complex hydrocarbons into methane and produce 50 million ft³ *1 415 850 m³* per day.

Biggest black-out
The greatest power failure in history struck seven north-eastern US States and Ontario, Canada, on 9–10 Nov 1965. About 30,000,000 people in 80,000 miles² *207 200 km²* were plunged into darkness. Only two were killed. In New York City the power failed at 5.27 pm and was not fully restored for 13½ hr. The total consequential losses in the 52 min New York City power failure of 13 July 1977 including looting was put at $1 billion (*then £580 million*).

Windmill Earliest
The earliest recorded windmills are those used for grinding corn in Iran (Persia) in the 7th century AD.

The earliest date attributed to a windmill in England is 1185 for one at Weedley, near Hull, Humberside. The oldest Dutch mill is the towermill at Zeddam, Gelderland built in *c.* 1450. The oldest working mill in England is the post-mill at Outwood, Surrey, built in 1665, though the Ivinghoe Mill in Pitstone Green Farm, Buckinghamshire, dating from 1627, has been restored. The postmill in North Ronaldsay, Orkney Islands operated until 1905.

Windmill *Largest conventional*
The largest Dutch windmill is the Dijkpolder in Maasland built in 1718. The sails measure 95¾ ft *29 m* from tip to tip. The tallest windmill in the Netherlands is De Walvisch in Schiedam built to a height of 108 ft *33 m* in 1794. The tallest windmill still standing in Britain is the 9 storey Sutton mill, Norfolk built in 1853 which before being struck by lightning in 1941 had sails 73 ft *22,2 m* in diameter with 216 shutters.

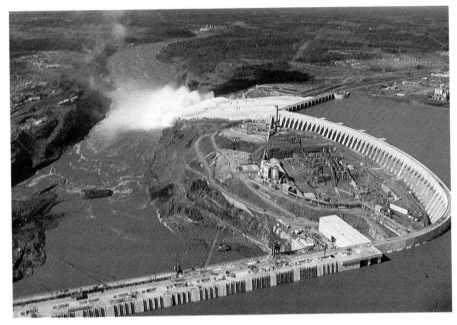

The giant Itaipu power station on the Panama River by the Brazil–Paraguay border with a dam height of 175 metres *580 feet*. It took a work force of 28,000 nine years before finally beginning to generate power on 25 Oct 1984.

Windmill Largest
The world's most powerful wind generator is the 3000 kW 150 m *492 ft* tall turbine, built by Grosse Wind energie–Anlage which was set up in 1982 on the Friesian coast of West Germany. A £10.5 million 3000 kW aerogenerator with 60 m *196 ft 10 in* blades on Burgar Hill, Evie, Orkney planned for completion by Taylor Woodrow end 1986. It should yield 9 million kW/hours per annum. The $14.2 million GEC MOD-5A installation on the North shore of Oahu, Hawaii, USA will produce 7300 kW when the wind reaches 32 mph *51,5 km/h* with 400 ft *122 m* rotors. Installation started in March 1984.

Water Mills
There has been a water-powered corn-mill at Priston Mill near Bath, Avon since pre-Norman times. The earliest record is dated AD 931.

6. ENGINEERING

Blast furnace *Largest*
The world's largest blast furnace is one with an inner volume of 5070 m³ *179,040 ft³* and a 14,8 m *48 ft 6½ in* diameter hearth at the Oita Works, Kyūshū, Japan completed in October 1976 with an annual capacity of 4,380,000 tons *4 451 500 tonnes*.

Cat cracker *Largest*
The world's largest catalyst cracker is the Exxon Co's Bayway Refinery plant at Linden, New Jersey, USA with a fresh feed rate of 5,040,000 US gal *19 077 000 litres* per day.

Conveyor belt *Longest*
The world's longest single flight conveyor belt is one of 18 miles *29 km* in Western Australia by Cable Belt Ltd of Camberley, Surrey. The longest installation in Great Britain is also by Cable Belt and of 5½ miles *8,9 km* underground at Longannet Power Station, Fife, Scotland. The world's longest multi-flight conveyor is one of 100 km *62 miles* between the phosphate mine near Bucraa and the port of El Aaiun, Morocco, built by Krupps and completed in 1972. It has 11 flights of between 9 and 11 km *5.6–6.8 miles* and was driven at 4,5 m/sec *10.06 mph* but has been closed down due to Polisario Front guerrilla activity.

The longest conveyor belt in the world is the Compagnie Minière de l'Ogooué or COMILOG installation built in 1959–62 for the Moanda manganese mine in Gabon which extends 76 km *47.2 miles*. It has 858 towers and 2800 buckets with 155 km *96.3 miles* of wire rope running over 6000 idler pulleys.

Crane Most Powerful *World*
The world's most powerful cranes are those aboard the semi-submersible vessel *Balder* (105,000 tonnes displacement) operated by Heerema Marine Contractors, Switzerland. Each has one 3000 and one 2000 tonne capacity crane which, working in tandem, could raise a 4000 tonne piece. The *Balder* set a record with a 3412 tonne lift in Aug 1983 and in March 1984 was refitted to raise her capacity to close to 6000 tonnes. The American company Brown & Root announced the building of a 140 000 tonne crane-ship with lifting capacity of 6500 tonnes in December 1983.

Gantry crane *Most powerful*
The 92.3 ft *28,14 m* wide Rahco (R. A. Hanson Disc. Ltd) gantry crane at the Grand Coulee Dam Third Powerplant was tested to lift a load of 2232 long tons *2268 tonnes* in 1975. It lowered a 3,944,000 lb *1789 tonne* generator rotor with an accuracy of $\frac{1}{32}$ in *0,8 mm*.

Crane *Tallest mobile*
The tallest mobile crane in the world is the 810 tonnes Rosenkranz K10001 with a lifting capacity of 1000 tonnes *984 tons*, a combined boom and jib height of 202 m *663 ft*. It is carried on 10 trucks each limited to 75 ft 8 in *23,06 m* and an axle weight of 118 tonnes *116 tons*. It can lift 30 tonnes *29.5 tons* to a height of 160 m *525 ft*.

Dragline *Largest World* (see also p. 128)
The Ural Engineering Works at Ordzhonikidze, USSR, completed in March 1962, has a dragline known as the ES-25(100) with a boom of 100 m *328 ft* and a bucket with a capacity of 31.5 yd³ *24 m³*. The world's largest walking dragline is 'Big Muskie', the Bucyrus-Erie 4250W with an

all-up weight of 12,000 tons *12 192 tonnes* and a bucket capacity of 220 yd³ *168 m³* on a 310 ft *94,4 m* boom. This machine, the world's largest mobile land machine, is now operating on the Central Ohio Coal Company's Muskingum site in Ohio, USA.

Great Britain

The largest dragline excavator in Britain is 'Big Geordie', the Bucyrus-Erie 1550W 6250 gross hp, weighing 3000 tons *3048 tonnes* with a forward mast 160 ft *48,7 m* high. On open-cast coal workings at Butterwell, Northumberland in September 1975, it proved able to strip 100 tons *101 tonnes* of overburden in 65 sec with its 65 yd³ *49,7 m³* bucket on a 265 ft *80,7 m* boom. It is owned by Derek Crouch (Contractors) Ltd of Peterborough, Cambridgeshire.

Escalator *Longest*

The term was registered in the US on 28 May 1900 but the earliest 'Inclined Escalator' was installed by Jesse W. Reno on the pier at Coney Island, New York in 1896. The first installation in Britain was at Harrods, Knightsbridge, London in November 1898. The escalators on the Leningrad Underground, USSR at Lenin Square have 729 steps and a vertical rise of 59,68 m *195 ft 9¼ in*. The longest escalators in Britain are the four in the Tyne Tunnel, Tyne and Wear installed in 1951. They measure 192 ft 8 in *58,7 m* between combs with a vertical lift of 85 ft *25,9 m* and a step speed of up to 1.7 mph *2,7 km/h*. The world's longest 'moving sidewalks' are those installed in 1970 in the Neue Messe Centre, Dusseldorf, W. Germany which measure 225 m *738 ft* between comb plates. The longest in Great Britain is the 375 ft *114,3 m* long Dunlop Starglide at London Airport Terminal 3 installed in March-May 1970.

The world's longest *ride* is on the 4-section outdoor escalator at Ocean Park, Hong Kong which has an overall length of 745 ft *227 m* and a total vertical rise of 377 ft *115 m*.

Excavator *Largest*

The world's largest excavator is the 13,000 tonne bucket wheel excavator being assembled at the open cast lignite-mine of Hambach, W. Germany with a rating of 200 000 m³ *260,000 yd³* per 20 hr working day. It is 210 m *690 ft* in length and 82 m *269 ft* tall. The wheel is 67,88 m *222 ft* in circumference with 5 m³ *6.5 yd³* buckets.

Forging *Largest*

The largest forging on record is one of a 450,600 lb *204,4 tonnes* 55 ft *16,76 m* long generator shaft for Japan, forged by the Bethlehem Steel Corp, Pennsylvania in October 1973.

Fork lift truck *Largest World*

Kalmar LMV of Sweden manufactured in 1985 ten counterbalanced fork lift trucks capable of lifting loads up to 80 tonnes *78.7 tons* at a load centre of 2300 mm *90.5 in*. They were built to handle the large diameter pipeline in the Libyan Great Man-made River Project.

Lathe *Largest*

The world's largest lathe is the 126 ft *38,4 m* long 416,2 tonne giant lathe built by Waldrich Siegen of Germany in 1973 for the South African Electricity Supply Commission at Rosherville. It has a capacity for 300 tonne work pieces and a swing-over bed of 5 m *16 ft 5 in* in diameter.

Greatest lift

The heaviest lifting operation in engineering history was the 41,000 short ton (36,607 long tons *37 194 tonnes*) roof of the Velodrome in Montreal, Canada in 1975. It was raised by jacks some 4 in *10 cm* to strike its centering.

Manure drier

The largest manure drier in the world is one measuring 12,8 × 4,2 × 2,75 m *42 × 13.8 × 9 ft* built by Swedrier, Sweden and delivered to the Gulf Agricultural Development Co in the United Arab Emirates.

Oldest machinery *World*

The earliest machinery still in use is the *dâlu*—a water-raising instrument known to have been in use in the Sumerian civilization which originated *c.* 3500 BC in Lower Iraq thus even earlier than the *Saqiyas* on the Nile.

Great Britain

The oldest piece of machinery (excluding clocks) operating in the United Kingdom is the snuff mill driven by a water wheel at Messrs Wilson & Co's Sharrow Mill in Sheffield, South Yorkshire. It is known to have been operating in 1797 and more probably since 1730.

Slowest machine

A nuclear environmental machine for testing stress corrosion has been developed by Nene Instruments of Wellingborough, Northants that can be controlled at a speed as slow as one million millionth of a millimetre per minute, or one metre *3,28 ft* in about 2000 million years.

Nut *Largest*

The largest nuts ever made weigh 5,3 tonnes *104.3 cwt* each and have an outside diameter of 52 in *132 cm* and a 25 in *63,5 cm* thread. Known as 'Pilgrim Nuts', they are manufactured by Doncasters Moorside Ltd of Oldham, Lancashire for use on the columns of a large forging press.

Oil tank *Largest*

The largest oil tanks ever constructed are the five Aramco 1½ million barrel storage tanks at Ju'aymah, Saudi Arabia. The tanks are 72 ft *21,94 m* tall with a diameter of 386 ft *117,6 m* and were completed in March 1980.

Passenger lift Fastest *World*

The fastest domestic passenger lifts in the world are the express lifts to the 60th floor of the 240 m *787.4 ft* tall 'Sunshine 60' building, Ikebukuro, Tōkyō, Japan completed 5 Apr 1978. They were built by Mitsubishi Corp and operate at a speed of 2000 ft/min *609,6 m/min* or 22.72 mph *36,56 km/h*. Much higher speeds are achieved in the winding cages of mine shafts. A hoisting shaft 6800 ft *2072 m* deep, owned by Western Deep Levels Ltd in South Africa, winds at speeds of up to 40.9 mph *65,8 km/h* (3595 ft *1095 m* per min). Otitis-media (popping of the ears) presents problems much above even 10 mph *16 km/h*.

Great Britain

The longest lift in the United Kingdom is one 930 ft long inside the B.B.C. T.V. tower at Bilsdale, West Moor, North Yorkshire, built by J. L. Eve Construction Co Ltd. It runs at 130 ft/min *39,6 m/min*. The longest fast lifts are the two 15-passenger cars in the Post Office Tower, Maple Street, London W1 which travel 540 ft *164 m* at up to 1000 ft/min *304 m/min*.

Graham Coates established an involuntary duration record when trapped in a lift for 62 hr in Brighton, England on 24–26 May 1986.

Pipelines *Oil*

The world's earliest pipeline of 2 in *5 cm* cast iron laid at Oil Creek, Pennsylvania, USA in 1863 was torn up by trade unionists.

The longest crude oil pipeline in the world is the Interprovincial Pipe Line Company's installation from Edmonton, Alberta, Canada to Buf-falo, New York State, USA, a distance of 1775 miles *2856 km*. Along the length of the pipe 13 pumping stations maintain a flow of 6,900,000 gal *31 367 145 litres* of oil per day. The eventual length of the Trans-Siberian Pipeline will be 2319 miles *3732 km*, running from Tuimazy through Omsk and Novosibirsk to Irkutsk. The first 30 mile *48 km* section was opened in July 1957.

Submarine pipelines

The world's longest submarine pipeline is that of 425 km *264 miles* for natural gas from the Union Oil Platform to Rayong, Thailand opened on 12 Sept 1981. The longest North Sea pipeline is the Ekofisk–Emden line stretching 260 miles *418 km* and completed in July 1975. The deepest North Sea pipeline is that from the Cormorant Field to Firths Voe, Shetland at 530 m *162 m*.

Natural gas

The longest natural gas pipeline in the world is the Trans-Canada Pipeline which by 1974 had 5654 miles *9099 km* of pipe up to 42 in *106,6 cm* in diameter. The Tyumen–Chelyabinsk–Moscow–Brandenburg gasline stretches 4330 km *2690 miles*.

The large calibre Urengoi-Uzhgorod line to Western Europe began in November 1982 stretches 4451 km *2765 miles* and was completed on 25 July 1983. It has a capacity of 32,000 million m³ *42,000 million yd³* per annum.

Water

The world's longest water pipeline runs a distance of 350 miles *563 km* to the Kalgoorlie gold fields from near Perth in Western Australia. Engineered in 1903, the system has since been extended five-fold by branches.

Pipeline *Most expensive*

The world's most expensive pipeline is the Alaska pipeline running 798 miles *1284 km* from Prudhoe Bay to Valdez. By completion of the first phase in 1977 it had cost at least $6000 million (£3250 million). The pipe is 48 in *1,21 m* diameter and will eventually carry up to 2 million barrels of crude oil per day.

Press *Largest*

The world's two most powerful production machines are forging presses in the USA. The Loewy closed-die forging press, in a plant leased from the US Air Force by the Wyman-Gordon Company at North Grafton, Massachusetts, USA weighs 9469 tons *9620 tonnes* and stands 114 ft 2 in *34,79 m* high, of which 66 ft *20,1 m* is sunk below the operating floor. It has a rated capacity of 44,600 tons *45 315 tonnes*, and went into operation in October 1955. The other similar press is at the plant of the Aluminium Company of America at Cleveland, Ohio. There has been a report of a press in the USSR with a capacity of 75 000 tonnes *73,800 tons* at Novo Kramatorsk. The Bêché and Grohs counter-blow forging hammer, manufactured in W. Germany are rated at 60,000 tonnes/*tons*. The most powerful press in Great Britain is the closed-die forging and extruding press installed in 1967 at the Cameron Iron Works, Livingston, Lothian. The press is 92 ft *28 m* tall (27 ft *8,2 m* below ground) and exerts a force of 30,000 tons *30 481 tonnes*.

Printer *Fastest*

The world's fastest printer is the Radiation Inc electro-sensitive system at the Lawrence Radiation Laboratory, Livermore, California. High speed recording of up to 30,000 lines each containing 120 alphanumeric characters per minute is attained by controlling electronic pulses through chemically impregnated recording paper which is rapidly moving under closely spaced fixed styli. It can thus print the wordage of the whole Bible (773,692 words) in 65 sec—3333 times as fast as the world's fastest typist.

Radar installation *Largest*
The largest of the three installations in the US Ballistic Missile Early Warning System (BMEWS) is that near Thule, in Kalaatdlit Nunaat, 931 miles *1498 km* from the North Pole, completed in 1960 at a cost of $500,000,000 (*then £178.5 million*). Its sister stations are one at Cape Clear, Alaska, USA, completed in 1961, and a $115,000,000 (*then £41.07 million*) installation at Fylingdales Moor, North Yorkshire, completed in June 1963. The largest scientific radar installation is the 21 acre *84 000 m²* ground array at Jicamarca, Peru.

Ropeway or telepherique Highest *World*
The highest and longest aerial ropeway in the world is the Teleférico Mérida (Mérida téléphérique) in Venezuela, from Mérida City (5379 ft *1639,5 m*) to the summit of Pico Espejo (15,629 ft *4763,7 m*), a rise of 10,250 ft *3124 m*. The ropeway is in four sections, involving 3 car changes in the 8 mile ascent in 1 hr. The fourth span is 10,070 ft *3069 m* in length. The two cars work on the pendulum system—the carrier rope is locked and the cars are hauled by means of three pull ropes powered by a 230 hp *233 cv* motor. They have a maximum capacity of 45 persons and travel at 32 ft *9,7 m* per sec (21.8 mph *35,08 km/h*). The longest single span ropeway is the 13,500 ft *4114 m* span from the Coachella Valley to Mt San Jacinto (10,821 ft *3298 m*), California, USA, inaugurated on 12 Sept 1963.

Great Britain
Britain's longest cabin lift is that at Llandudno, Gwynedd, opened in June 1969. It has 42 cabins with a capacity of 1000 people per hour and is 5320 ft *1621 m* in length.

Transformer *Largest*
The world's largest single phase transformers are rated at 1,500,000 kVA of which eight are in service with the American Electric Power Service Corporation. Of these five stepdown from 765 to 345 kV. Britain's largest transformers are those rated at 1,000,000 kVA 400/275 kV built by Hackbridge & Hewittic Co Ltd, Walton-on-Thames, Surrey first commissioned for the CEGB in October 1968.

Transmission lines *Longest*
The longest span between pylons of any power line in the world is that across the Sogne Fjord, Norway, between Rabnaberg and Fatlaberg. Supplied in 1955 by the Whitecross Co Ltd of Warrington, Cheshire, and projected and erected by A. S. Betonmast of Oslo as part of the high-tension power cable from Refsdal power station at Vik, it has a span of 16,040 ft *4888 m* and a weight of 12 tons/*tonnes*. In 1967 two further high tensile steel/aluminium lines 16,006 ft *4878 m* long, and weighing 33 tons *33,5 tonnes*, manufactured by Whitecross and BICC were erected here. The longest in Britain are the 5310 ft *1618 m* lines built by J. L. Eve Co across the Severn with main towers each 488 ft *148 m* high.

Highest
The world's highest are those across the Straits of Messina, with towers of 675 ft *205 m* (Sicily side) and 735 ft *224 m* (Calabria) and 11,900 ft *3627 m* apart. The highest lines in Britain are those made by BICC at West Thurrock, Essex, which cross the Thames estuary suspended from 630 ft *192 m* tall towers at a minimum height of 250 ft *76 m*, with a 130 ton *132 tonnes* breaking load. They are 4500 ft *1371 m* in length.

Highest voltages
The highest voltages now carried are 1,330,000 volts 1224 miles *1970 km* on the DC Pacific Inter-tie in the United States. The Ekibastuz DC transmission lines in Kazakhstan, USSR are planned to be 2400 km *1490 miles* long with 1,500,000 volt capacity.

Valve *Largest*
The world's largest valve is the 32 ft *9,75 m* diameter, 170 ton/*tonne* butterfly valve designed by Boving & Co Ltd of London for use at the Arnold Airforce Base engine test facility in Tennessee, USA.

Wire ropes *Longest, Strongest and Heaviest*
The longest wire ropes in the world are the 4 made at British Ropes Ltd, Wallsend, Tyneside each measuring 24 000 m *14.9 miles*. The ropes are 35 mm *1.3 in* in diameter, weigh 108,5 tonnes *106.8 tons* each and were ordered by the CEGB for use in the construction of the 2000 MW cross-Channel power cable. The thickest ever made are spliced crane strops from wire ropes 28,2 cm *11¼ in* thick made of 2392 individual wires in March 1979 by British Ropes Ltd of Doncaster at Willington Quay, Tyneside, designed to lift loads of up to 3000 tons/*tonnes*. The heaviest ever wire ropes (4 in number) each of 130 tonnes/*tons*, made for the twin shaft system of Western Deep Levels Gold Mine, South Africa, by Haggie Rand Ltd of Johannesburg.

One of the cable cars at Teleferico Merida in Venezuela used to give passengers the longest and highest aerial ride in the world. (South American Pictures).

TIME PIECES

Clock *Oldest*
The earliest mechanical clock, that is one with an escapement, was completed in China in AD 725 by I Hsing and Liang Lingtsan.

The oldest surviving working clock in the world is the faceless clock dating from 1386, or possibly earlier, at Salisbury Cathedral, Wiltshire, which was restored in 1956 having struck the hours for 498 years and ticked more than 500 million times. Earlier dates, ranging back to *c.* 1335, have been attributed to the weight-driven clock in Wells Cathedral, Somerset, but only the iron frame is original. A model of Giovanni de Dondi's heptagonal astronomical clock of 1348–64 was completed in 1962.

Clock Largest *World*
The world's most massive clock is the Astronomical Clock in the Cathedral of St Pierre, Beauvais, France, constructed between 1865

and 1868. It contains 90,000 parts and measures 40 ft *12,1 m* high, 20 ft *6,09 m* wide and 9 ft *2,7 m* deep. The Su Sung clock, built in China at K'aifeng in 1088–92, had a 20 ton *20,3 tonnes* bronze armillary sphere for 1½ tons, *1,52 tonnes* of water. It was removed to Peking in 1126 and was last known to be working in its 40 ft *12,1 m* high tower in 1136.

The world's largest clock face is that of the floral clock at Tokachigaoka Park, Otofuke, Hokkaido, Japan, completed on 1 Aug 1982 with a diameter of 18 m *59 ft 0⅜ in*.

Public
The largest four-faced clock in the world is that on the building of the Allen-Bradley Company of Milwaukee, Wisconsin, USA. Each face has a diameter of 40 ft 3½ in *12,28 m* with a minute hand 20 ft *6,09 m* in overall length. The largest single-faced clock is the octagonal Colgate clock in Jersey, New Jersey, USA with a diameter of 15,24 m *50 ft* and a minute hand 8,31 m *27 ft 3 in* in length. The tallest four-faced clock in the world is that of the Williamsburgh Savings Bank in Brooklyn, New York City, NY, USA. It is 430 ft *131 m* above street level.

Great Britain
The largest clock in the United Kingdom is that on the Royal Liver Building (built 1908–11) with dials 25 ft *7,62 m* in diameter and the 4 minute hands each 14 ft *4,26 m* long. The mechanism and dials weigh 22 tons and are 220 ft *67 m* above street level.

Longest stoppage 'Big Ben'
The longest stoppage of the clock in the House of Commons clock tower, London since the first tick on 31 May 1859 has been 13 days from noon 4 Apr to noon 17 Apr 1977. In 1945 a host of starlings slowed the minute hand by 5 min.

Clock *Most accurate*
The most accurate and complicated clockwork in the world is the Olsen clock, installed in the Copenhagen Town Hall, Denmark. The clock, which has more than 14,000 units, took 10 years to make and the mechanism of the clock functions in 570,000 different ways. The celestial pole motion of the clock will take 25,753 years to complete a full circle and is the slowest moving designed mechanism in the world. The clock is accurate to 0.5 sec in 300 years—50 times more accurate than the previous record.

Clock *Most expensive*
The highest price paid for any English-made clock is £500,000 for a Thomas Tompion (1639–1713) bracket clock bought by the British Museum by private treaty on 15 July 1982.

Pendulum *Longest*
The longest pendulum in the world is 22,5 m *73 ft 9¾ in* on the water-mill clock installed by Hattori Tokeiten Co. in the Shinjuku NS Building, Tokyo, Japan in 1983.

Watch *Oldest*
The oldest watch (portable clockwork timekeeper) is one made of iron by Peter Henlein in Nürnberg (Nüremberg), Bavaria, Germany, in *c.* 1504. The earliest wrist watches were those of Jacquet-Droz and Leschot of Geneva, Switzerland, dating from 1790.

Watch *Largest*
A facsimile 'Swatch' watch was draped from the roof of the Comme Bank building, Frankfurt, West Germany in December 1985. It was 469 ft *143 m* long, weighed 13 tonnes and had a face 54 ft *16,45 m* in diameter.

Watch *Smallest*
The smallest watches in the world are produced by Jaeger Le Coultre of Switzerland. Equipped

Lawrence D. Kavanagh, Jr, standing inside a 48 foot *14,6 m* high cylindrical sundial he constructed out of a concrete silo at the Louisa Country Club, Louisa, Virginia, USA. Sunlight casts a pattern on the north interior wall in the form of a parabola. Using the base of this parabola as a pointer, the shadows on the walls are then read to give both time and date.

with a 15-jewelled movement they measure just over ½ in *1,2 cm* long and ³⁄₁₆ in *0,476 cm* in width. The movement, and case, weighs under 0,25 oz *7 g*.

Watch *Thinnest*
The world's thinnest wrist watch is the Swiss Concord Delirium IV. It measures 0,98 mm *0.0385 in* thick and retailed for $16,000 *£6800* (including 18 carat gold strap) in June 1980.

Watch *Most expensive*
Excluding watches with jewelled cases, the most expensive standard men's pocket watch is the Swiss *Grande Complication* by Audemars-Piguet which retailed for £72,000 in January 1985. The *Kallista* watch with 130 carats of precious stones by Vacheron et Constantin of Geneva was valued in April 1981 at $5 million (*then £2,272,000*). The record price for an antique watch is SwFr1,870,000 (*£670,250*) paid at Christie's, Geneva on 13 May 1986 by a European collector for a gold enamelled and diamond set pocket watch with a movement *c.*1650 by the Parisian maker Jehan Cremfdorff. At the same auction SwFr286,000 (*£102,500*) was paid for a 1955 Patek Philippe wrist watch, one of only three. It includes a perpetual calendar and records the phases of the moon.

Time measurer *Most accurate*
The most accurate time-keeping devices are the twin atomic hydrogen masers installed in 1964 in the US Naval Research Laboratory, Washington, DC. They are based on the frequency of the hydrogen atom's transition period of 1,420,450,751,694 cycles/sec. This enables an accuracy to within 1 sec in 1,700,000 years.

Sundial Largest
The world's largest sundial is one with a 28 ft 4 in *8,64 m* gnomon and a vertical height of 17 ft 1 in *5,2 m* dedicated on 10 Oct 1913 in San Francisco, California, USA.

COMPUTERS

A geared calculator date *c.* 80 BC was found in the sea by Antikythera Island off northwest Crete in April 1900.

The earliest programmable electronic computer was the 1500 valve Colossus formulated by Prof Max H. A. Newman FRS (b. 1897) and built by T. H. Flowers MBE. It was run in December 1943 at Bletchley Park, Buckinghamshire to break the German coding machine Enigma. It arose from the concept published in 1936 by Dr Alan Mathison Turing OBE, FRS (1912–54) in his paper *On Computable Numbers with an Application to the Entscheidungsproblem*. Colossus was declassified on 25 Oct 1975. The world's first stored-programme computer was the Manchester University Mark I which incorporated the Williams storage cathode ray tube (pat. 11 Dec 1946). It ran its first programme, by Prof Tom Kilburn CBE FRS (b. 1921) for 52 min on 21 June 1948.

Computers were greatly advanced by the invention of the point-contact transistor by John Bardeen and Walter Brattain announced in July 1948, and the junction transistor by R. L. Wallace, Morgan Sparks and Dr William Bradford Shockley (b. 1910) in early 1951. The concept of the integrated circuit, which has enabled micro-miniaturization, was first published on 7 May 1952 by Geoffrey W. A. Dummer MBE (b. 1909) in Washington DC. The Microcomputer was achieved in 1969–73 by M. E. Hoff Jr of Intel Corporation with the production of the microprocessor chip '4004'.

The computer planned to be the world's biggest by a factor of 40 is the $50 million NASF (Numerical Aerodynamic Simulation Facility) at NASA's Ames Research Center, Palo Alto, California. The tenders from CDC and Burroughs called for a capacity of 12.8 giga-flops (12,800 million complex calculations per second).

Most powerful and fastest *World*
The world's most powerful and fastest computer is the liquid-cooled CRAY-2, named after Seymour R. Cray of Cray Research, Inc, Minneapolis, Minnesota USA. Its memory has a capacity of 256 million 64-bit words, resulting in a capacity of 32 million bytes of main memory. (N.B. a 'byte' is a unit of storage compressing 8 'bits' collectively equivalent to one alphabetic symbol or two numericals.) It attains speeds of 250 million floating point operations per second. The cost of a mid-range system was quoted in October 1985 at $17 million. The most powerful British computer is the International Computer's Distribution Array Processor—the ICL DAP.

Control Data Corporation announced the CYBER Model 205-444 system from Arden Hills, Minnesota, USA on 2 June 1980 which has a memory of 4 million 64-Bit words and cost $16.5 million (*£7 million*) at delivery in January 1981. In a test on 19 Nov 1982 the CYBER model 205-424 achieved 791,860,000 calculations in a second.

The CRAY–1/S system, introduced in 1981, has an additional 8 million words of buffer memory and a storage capacity of 19 gigabytes or 1.55136×10^{11} bits with a system cost of up to $17 million for the maximum configuration.

Smallest word processor
The world's smallest word processor, the Easi-Text 1350, was introduced by Minimicro of Huntington, Yorkshire, in April 1986. It is based on the Sharp PC-1350 computer which measures $182 \times 72 \times 16$ mm *7.2 × 2.8 × 0.6 in* and the entire system including an A4 size Epson P-80 printer fits into an executive briefcase.

Megabits
The megabit barrier was broken in February 1984, with the manufacture of a 1024K bit integrated circuit, the size of a drawing pin head and as thin as a human hair, by 4 Japanese companies, Hitachi, NEC, NTT Atsugi Electrical Communications and Toshiba. Toshiba announced that manufacture of an 80 picosecond LSI (large scale integration) chip of gallium arsenide would start in 1985–86.

IBM had announced the first 512K bit 120 nanosecond dynamic access memory chip ⅜ in *9,5 mm* square from Essex Junction, Vermont, USA, on 15 Sept 1983.

CHAPTER NINE

THE
BUSINESS WORLD

At a press conference in New York, USA, on 6 May 1986, it was announced that Michael Joseph Jackson (*see pp. 96–7*) had completed a transaction to endorse the soft drink Pepsi Cola. It has been indicated that the deal is worth over $50 million, the biggest individual endorsement agreement in history.

Oldest industry

The oldest known industry is flint knapping, involving the production of chopping tools and hand axes, dating from 2.4 million years ago. The earliest evidence of trading in exotic stone and amber dates from *c.* 28000 BC in Europe. Agriculture is often described as 'the oldest industry in the world', whereas in fact there is no evidence yet that it was practised before *c.* 11,000 BC.

Oldest company *World*

The oldest company in the world is the Faversham Oyster Fishery Co, referred to in the Faversham Oyster Fishing Act 1930, as existing 'from time immemorial', *i.e.* in English law from before 1189.

Great Britain

The Royal Mint has origins going back to AD 287. The Oxford University Press celebrated a 500th anniversary in 1978 not of itself but of the earliest origin of printing in Oxford in 1478. The Shore Porters' Society of Aberdeen, a haulier, shipping and warehouse partnership, is known to have been established before 4 June 1498. The Whitechapel Bell Foundry of White-chapel Road, London, E1, has been in business since *c.* 1570. It has through Master Founder Thomas Mears II indirect successions, since 1810, *via* Rudhalls of Gloucester back to 1270. The retail business in Britain with the oldest history is the Oxford ironmonger Gill & Co. of 127–8, High Street founded by Abel Smythe *c.* 1530. R. Durtnell & Sons, builders, of Brasted, Kent, has been run by the same family since 1591. Mr Richard Durtnell is of the 12th generation. The first bill of adventure signed by the English East India Co, was dated 21 Mar 1601.

Greatest assets *World all-time*

The business with the greatest amount in physical assets has been the Bell System, which comprised the American Telephone and Tele-graph Company, and its subsidiaries. The Bell System's total assets on the consolidated balance sheet at the time of its divestiture and break-up into 8 companies on 31 Dec 1983 reached $149,529 million *£106,800 m.* The plant involved included more than 142 million telephones. The number of employees was 1,036,000. The com-pany's market value of $47,989 million (*then £30,960 million*) was held among 3,055,000 share-holders. A total of 20,109 shareholders had attended the Annual Meeting in April 1961, thereby setting a world record.

Currently the largest assets of any corporation are the $69,160,000,000 (*£49,400 million*) of Exxon Corporation, the world's largest oil company, on 1 Jan 1986. They have 146,000 employees. The first company to have assets in excess of $1 billion was the United States Steel Corporation with $1400 million (*then £287.73 million*) at the time of its creation by merger in 1917.

Great Britain

The biggest British manufacturing company is Imperial Chemical Industries plc with assets employed of £8317 million as at 1 Jan 1986. Its staff and payroll averaged 118,600 during the year. The company, which has more than 300 UK and overseas subsidiaries, was formed on 7 Dec 1926 by the merger of four concerns— British Dyestuffs Corporation Ltd; Brunner, Mond & Co Ltd; Nobel Industries Ltd and United Alkali Co Ltd. The first chairman was

The '$(US) has in this chapter been converted generally at a fixed mean rate of $1.40 to the £ Sterling for mid-1985 and at the rates relevant to other years.

Sir Alfred Moritz Mond (1868–1930), later the 1st Lord Melchett.

The net assets of The 'Shell' Transport and Trading Company, plc, at 31 Dec 1985 were £9,374,000,000, comprising mainly its 40 per cent share in the net assets of the Royal Dutch/Shell Group of Companies which stood at £23,435 million. Group companies employ 156,000. 'Shell' Transport was formed in 1897 by Marcus Samuel (1853–1927), later the 1st Viscount Bearsted.

Greatest profit and loss

The greatest net profit ever made by any corporation in 12 months is $7647 million (*£4933 million*) by American Telephone and Telegraph Co from 1 Oct 1981 to 30 Sept 1982.

The Argentine petroleum company YPF (Yacimientos Petroliferos) (Government owned) lost a trading record US $4,643,995,000 in 1983. The greatest loss ever recorded by private enterprise has been $4900 million (*£3500 million*) for the 4th quarter of 1983 by American Telephone & Telegraph Co due to extraordinary charges relating to its divestiture (see above). The loss for the National Coal Board in the tax year ending on 31 Mar 1985 was £2225 million.

Largest employer

The world's largest employer is Indian Railways with 1,600,000 staff in 1984. Europe's largest employer is Britain's National Health Service with 1,011,872 staff in 1983. The increase since 1970 was declared by Ralph Howell MP to exceed the increase in the whole population.

Greatest sales

The first company to surpass the $1 billion (US) mark in annual sales was the United States Steel Corporation in 1917. Now there are 570 corporations with sales exceeding £1000 million including 272 from the United States. The *Fortune 500 List* of April 1986 is headed by the General Motor Corporation of Detroit with $96,371,700,000 (*£68,837 million*) for 1985.

The top gross profits in the United Kingdom in *The Times 1000 1985–86* was British Petroleum with £7021 million. The biggest loss maker was the National Coal Board with £391 Million.

Largest take-over

The largest corporate take-over agreement in commercial history is by Chevron (formerly Standard Oil Co. of California) which on 15 June 1984 bought Gulf Oil Corporation for $13,231,253,000 (*then £9450 million*). The fees of the financial intermediaries were estimated by *Fortune* to be $63.9 million.

The biggest takeover in Britain took place when Guinness PLC gained control of The Distillers Company PLC on 18 April 1986 with a bid in excess of £2.7 billion. The Hanson Trust take-over of the Imperial Group on 11 Apr 1986 was reported to be £2.66 billion.

Biggest write off

The largest reduction of assets in the history of private enterprise was the $800 million (*£347 million*) write-off of Tristar aircraft development costs announced on 23 Nov 1974.

Greatest bankruptcy

Rajendra Sethia (b. 1950) was arrested in New Delhi on 2 Mar 1985 on charges including criminal conspiracy and forgery. He had been declared bankrupt by the High Court in London on 18 Jan 1985 when Esal Commodities was stated to be in debt for a record £170 million. His personal debts were estimated at £140 million. William G. Stern (b. Hungary, 1936) of Golders Green, north London, a US citizen since 1957, who set up Wilstar Group Holding Co in the London property market in 1971 was declared bankrupt for £104,390,248 in February 1979. This figure rose to £142,978,413 by Feb 1983. He was discharged for £500,000 suspended for 2½ years on 28 Mar 1983.

Companies

The number of companies on the register in Great Britain at 31 Dec 1985 was 1,044,106 of which 7186 were public and the balance private companies.

Most directorships

The record for directorships was set in 1961 by Hugh T. Nicholson (1914–1985), formerly senior partner of Harmood Banner & Sons, London who, as a liquidating chartered accountant, became director of all 451 companies of the Jasper group in 1961 and had 7 other directorships.

Accountancy firms *Largest*

The largest firm of accountants worldwide is Arthur Andersen & Co. with 1985 revenues of $1574 million, of which about $1180 million was in the US. The largest in the UK is Peat Marwick Mitchell & Co. with $1445 million world wide of which £98,300,000 is in the UK in 1985.

Advertising agency

The largest advertising agency in the world is Saatchi & Saatchi Compton Ltd of London. Following their acquisition of the American agency Ted Bates Worldwide announced on 12 May 1986, *Advertising Age* lists the new group's billings at about $7500 million (*£5000 million*).

Biggest advertiser

The world's biggest advertiser is Sears, Roebuck and Co, with $975,300,000 (*£696 million*) in 1985 excluding its catalogue.

Aerospace company

The world's largest aerospace company is United Technologies of Hartford, Connecticut with 1984 sales of $16,331,757,000 (*£13,609 million*) and assets of $9,904 million (*£8,253 million*). They have a work force of 205,000. Cessna Aircraft Company of Wichita, Kansas, USA, in the year 1985, had a total sales of $718,100,000 (*£513 million*). The company has produced more than 176,300 aircraft since Clyde Cessna's first was built in 1911.

Airline *Largest*

The largest airline in the world is the USSR State airline 'Aeroflot', so named since 1932. This was instituted on 9 Feb 1923, with the title of Civil Air Fleet of the Council of Ministers of the USSR, abbreviated to 'Dobrolet'. It operates 1300 aircraft over about 620,000 miles *1,000,000 km* of routes, employs 500,000 people and carried 112 million passengers to 104 countries in 1984. Most luggage is 'self-handled'. Smoking is allowed only after 4 hours flying. The commercial airline carrying the greatest number of passengers (Dec 1984) was United Airlines Inc. of Illinois, USA with 41,273,000 passengers. The company had 47,900 employees and a fleet of 319 jet planes. On 1 Apr 1986 British Airways were operating a fleet of 189 aircraft (including 31 helicopters). Staff employed on airline activities totalled 37,412 and 18,397,000 passengers were carried in 1985/6 on 323,122 miles *520,900 km* of unduplicated routes.

Oldest

The oldest existing national airline is Koninklijke-Luchtvaart-Maatschappij NV (KLM) of the Netherlands, which opened its first scheduled service (Amsterdam–London) on 17 May 1920, having been established on 7 Oct 1919. One of the original constituents of BOAC, Handley-Page Transport Ltd, was founded in May 1919 and merged into Imperial Airways in 1924. Delag (Deutsche Luftschiffahrt AG) was founded at Frankfurt am Main on 16 Nov 1909 and started a scheduled airship service in June 1910. Chalk's International Airline has been flying amphibians between Miami, Florida and the Bahamas since July 1919. Albert 'Pappy' Chalk flew from 1911 to 1975.

Aluminium producer

The world's largest producer of primary alumin-

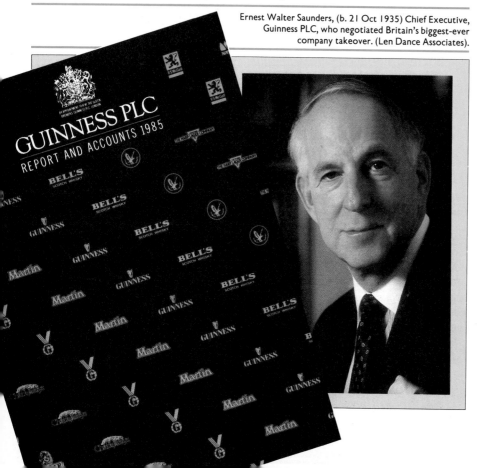

Ernest Walter Saunders, (b. 21 Oct 1935) Chief Executive, Guinness PLC, who negotiated Britain's biggest-ever company takeover. (Len Dance Associates).

ium is the Alcan Aluminium Ltd of Montreal, Canada with its affiliated companies. The company had an output of 2,218,000 tonnes *2 183 000 tons* in 1985.

Art auctioneering

The largest and oldest firm of art auctioneers in the world is the Sotheby Group of London and New York, founded in 1744. The turnover in 1984–85 was $678.7 million (*£485 million*). The highest total for any house sale auction was theirs on 18–27 May 1977 at the 6th Earl of Rosebery's home at Mentmore, Buckinghamshire which reached £6,389,933 or *$10.9 million.* The total realized at the art sale at Sotheby Parke, Bernet, New York on 14 May 1985 was $39,286,500 (*then £28,100,000*). This sale of impressionist and modern paintings saw eleven works selling for over $1 million each.

Bank

The International Bank for Reconstruction and Development (founded 27 Dec 1945), the 'World Bank', a United Nations specialised agency, at 1818 H Street NW, Washington, DC, USA, has an authorized share capital of $75 billion (*£53,571 million*). There were 146 members with a subscribed capital of $58,000 million (*£41,429 million*) at 30 June 1985. The International Monetary Fund in Washington, DC, USA has 149 members with total quotas of SDR 89,305.1 million (*$100,861.2 million* or *£70,291.3 million*) at April 1986.

The USSR State Bank was claimed by Tass to be the world's largest on 15 Jan 1983 incorporating 'nearly 4500 banking institutions within its single system'. No asset figures were disclosed. The commercial bank with the greatest assets is Citicorp of New York with $129,900 million (*£83,800 million*) at 31 Dec 1982. Its operating income was $747 million (*£482 million*). The Barclays Group had some 5300 branches and offices in over 75 countries (some 3000 in the United Kingdom) in December 1985. Deposits totalled £55,127 million and assets £65,193 million. The bank with the largest network in the United Kingdom is the National Westminster with consolidated total assets of £72,468,000,000 and 3200 branches as at 31 Dec 1985. The bank with most branches is The State Bank of India with 10,838 on 1 Jan 1986 with assets of $25,596 million *£18,283 million.*

Bank building

The world's tallest bank building is the Bank of Montreal's First Bank Tower, Toronto, Canada which has 72 storeys and stands 935 ft *284,98 m.* The largest bank vault in the world, measuring 350 × 100 × 8 ft *106,7 × 30,4 × 2,4 m* and weighing 879 tons *893 tonnes* is in the Chase Manhattan Building, New York City, completed in May 1961. Its six doors weigh up to 40 tons *40,6 tonnes* apiece but each can be closed by the pressure of a forefinger.

Bank bail out *Biggest*

On 26 July 1984 the Federal Deposit Insurance Corp bought $4.5 billion in bad loans from the Continental Illinois National Bank for $3.5 billion and also 'gave' $1 billion cash in return for preferred stock.

Banquet Greatest *Outdoors*

It was estimated that some 30,000 attended a military feast at Radewitz, Poland on 25 June 1730 thrown by King August II (1709–33).

Indoors

The greatest number of people served indoors at a single sitting was 18,000 municipal leaders at the Palais de l'Industrie, Paris on 18 Aug 1889. At the wedding of cousins Menachem Teitel-

baum, 18, and Brucha Sima Melsels, 18, conducted by their grandfather Grand Rabbi Moses at Uniondale, Long Island, New York on 5 Dec 1984 the attendance of the Satmar sect of Hasidic Jews was estimated at 17,000 to 20,000. Meal Mart of Brooklyn, a kosher caterer, provided the food including 2 tons of gefilte fish.

Most expensive

The menu for the main 5½ hr banquet at the Imperial Iranian 2500th Anniversary gathering at Persepolis in October 1971 was probably the most expensive ever compiled. It comprised quail eggs stuffed with Iranian caviar, a mousse of crayfish tails in Nantua sauce, stuffed rack of roast lamb, with a main course of roast peacock stuffed with *foie gras,* fig rings and raspberry sweet champagne sherbet, with wines including *Château Lafite-Rothschild* 1945 at £40 (now £215) per bottle from Maxime's, Paris.

Book shop

The book shop with most titles and the longest shelving (30 miles *48 km*) in the world is W. & G. Foyle Ltd, City of Westminster, London. First established in 1904 in a small shop in Islington, the company is now at 113–119 Charing Cross Road. The area on one site is 75,825 ft² *7044 m²*. The most capacious individual bookstore in the world measured by square footage is Barnes & Noble Bookstore of Fifth Ave at 18th Street, New York City, USA with 154,250 ft² *14 330 m²* and with 12.87 miles *20,71 km* of shelving.

Brewer *Oldest*

The oldest brewery in the world is the Weihenstephan Brewery, Freising, near Munich, W. Germany, founded in AD 1040.

Largest World

The largest single brewing organisation in the world is Anheuser-Busch, Inc based in St Louis, Missouri, USA, with 11 breweries in the US. In 1985 the company sold 68,000,000 US barrels, equivalent to *14,040 million Imp. pints,* the greatest annual volume ever produced by a brewing company. The company's St Louis plant covers 100 acres *40,5 ha* and after completion of current modernization projects will have an annual capacity in excess of 13,000,000 US barrels *2684 million Imp. pints.* The largest brewery on a single site is Adolph Coors Co of Golden, Colorado, USA where 14,738,000 barrels *3043 million Imp. pints* were sold in 1985.

Great Britain

The largest brewing company in the United Kingdom based on its 7404 public houses, 830 off-licences and over 100 hotels, is Bass plc. The company has net assets of £1,688,400,000, controls 13 breweries and has 71,260 employees. Its sales figure for the year ending 30 Sept 1985 was £2,410,800,000. The company also has substantial leisure and betting interests.

Brickworks

The largest brickworks in the world is the London Brick Company Limited plant at Stewartby, Bedfordshire. The works, established in 1898, now cover 221 acres *90 ha* and have a production capacity of 13,000,000 bricks and brick equivalent each week.

Building contractors

The largest construction company in the United Kingdom is George Wimpey plc (founded 1880), of London, which undertakes building, civil, offshore, process and marine engineering work worldwide employing 23,000 staff. The turnover of work was £1581 million in over 30 countries in 1985.

Building societies

The biggest building society in the world is the

Halifax Building Society of Halifax, West Yorkshire. It was established in 1853 and has total assets exceeding £24,360,000,000. It has 12,510 employees and over 3300 offices. The world's biggest lender is the Japanese Government-controlled House Loan Corporation.

Chemist shop chain

The largest chain of chemist shops in the world is Boots The Chemists, which has 1024 retail branches. The firm was founded by Jesse Boot (b. Nottingham, 1850), later the 1st Baron Trent, who died in 1931.

Chocolate factory

The largest chocolate and confectionery factory is that built by Hershey Chocolate Company in Hershey, Pennsylvania, USA in 1903–5. It has 2,000,000 ft² *185,800 m²* of floor space.

Computer company

The world's largest computer firm is International Business Machines (IBM) Corporation of New York. In Dec 1985 assets were $52,634,000 (*£37,595,000*) and gross income was $50,056,000 (*£35,755,000*). In Oct 1979 it made the largest borrowing in corporate history with $1 billion. Its worldwide employees numbered 394,930 and there are 792,506 stockholders.

Department stores *World*

F. W. Woolworth, who celebrated their centenary year in 1979, now operate a total of 5822 stores world wide. Frank Winfield Woolworth opened his first Five and Ten Cent Store in Utica, New York State on 22 Feb 1879. The 1985 income from continuing operations was $177 million (*£100,714,280*).

Great Britain

The largest department store in the United Kingdom is Harrods Ltd of Knightsbridge, Royal Borough of Kensington and Chelsea, Greater London named after Henry Charles Harrod (1800–85), who opened a grocery in Knightsbridge Village in 1849. It has a total selling floor space of 20 acres *80 940 m²*, employs 4000 people and achieved record sales of £304 million for the year ending 1 Feb 1986. The record for a day is £5.5 million. The record time from the opening of the doors to the crockery counter is 43 secs.

Highest sales per unit area

The department store with the fastest-moving stock in the world is the Marks & Spencer premier branch, known as 'Marble Arch' at 458 Oxford Street, City of Westminster, London. The figure of £1600 worth of goods per square foot of selling space per year is believed to be an understatement. The selling area is 92,400 ft² *8584 m²*. The company has 269 branches in the UK and operates on over 6.5 million ft² *603 850 m²* of selling space and has stores on the Continent and in Canada.

Longest wait for a sale

Kevin Melish (b. 2 Aug 1948), queued for 18 days 1 hr outside Selfridges, Oxford Street, London from 9–27 Dec 1985. He collected £2000 for the Rainer Foundation but purchased nothing.

Distillery

The world's largest distilling company is The Seagram Company Ltd, of Canada. Its sales in the year ending 31 Jan 1986 totalled US $2,970,669,000 (*£2122 million*). The group employs about 14,300 people, including about 5000 in the United States.

The largest establishment for blending and bottling Scotch whisky is owned by John Walker & Sons Limited at Kilmarnock, Strathclyde, where there is a capacity to fill over 3 million bottles each week. 'Johnnie Walker' is the world's largest-selling brand of Scotch whisky. The world's largest-selling brand of gin is Gordon's. Old Bushmills Distillery, County Antrim, Northern Ireland licensed in 1608 claims to have been in production in 1276.

Fisheries

The greatest catch ever recorded with a single throw is 2471 tonnes by the purse seine-net boat M/S *Flømann* from Hareide, Norway in the Barents Sea·on 28 Aug 1983. It was estimated that more than 120 million fish were caught in this shoal.

Grocery stores

The largest grocery chain in the world is Safeway Stores, Incorporated of Oakland, California, USA with sales in 1985 of $19,650,542,000 (*£14,036 million*) and total current assets valued at $2,026,481,000 (*£1,447 million*) as at 28 Dec 1985. The company has 2365 stores totalling 70,272,000 ft² *6 528 270 m²*. The total number of employees is 164,385.

Hotelier

The top revenue-earning hotel business is the Holiday Inn hotel system, with a 1985 total revenue of $5.9 billion (*£4214 million*), from 1688 hotels (317,628 rooms) at 31 Dec 1985 in 53 countries. The business was founded by Charles Kemmons Wilson with his first Holiday Inn hotel on Summer Avenue, Memphis, Tennessee, USA in 1952.

Insurance

It was estimated in 1978 that the total premiums paid in the United States first surpassed $100 billion (*then £52,600 million*) or $1400 *£736* per household. The company with the highest volume of insurance in force in the world is the Prudential Insurance Company of America of Newark, New Jersey with $580.9 billion at 31 Dec 1985, which is more than 2½ times the UK National Debt figure. The admitted assets are $91,706 million.

The largest single association in the world is the Blue Cross and Blue Shield Association, the US-based hospital insurance organization with a membership of 77,496,584 on 30 Sept 1985. Benefits paid out in 1985 totalled $37,862,000,000 (*£27,044 million*).

Like a beached whale, the vast oil tanker Amoco Cadiz goes down off the French coastline. The resulting insurance claim recorded an all-time high for consequential losses. (Colorific).

Great Britain

The largest life assurance group in the United Kingdom is the Prudential Corporation plc. At 1 Jan 1986 the tangible assets were £20,002,900,000 and the total amount assured was £89,532,400,000.

Life policies Largest

The largest life assurance policy ever written was one for $44 million (*£24.4 million*) for a Calgary land developer Victor T. Uy in February 1982 by Transamerica Occidental Life Assurance Co. The salesman was local manager Lorenzo F. Reyes. The highest pay-out on a single life has been some $18 million (*then £7.5 million*) to Mrs Linda Mullendore, wife of an Oklahoma rancher, reported on 14 Nov 1970. Her murdered husband had paid $300,000 in premiums in 1969.

Marine

The largest ever marine insurance loss was £46 million for the self-propelled semi-submersible drilling platform Ocean Ranger (14,914 tons gross) built for Ocean Drilling & Exploration Co of New Orleans in 1976. On 15 Feb 1982 she was lost with 84 lives in the Hibernia Field, off Newfoundland. One of the most expensive vessels afloat is the British passenger ship *Royal Princess*, 44,348 tons gross, built in 1984, quoted at $140,800,000.

The largest sum claimed for consequential losses is $1700 million (*£890 million*) against owning, operating and building corporations, and Claude Phillips resulting from the 66 million gallon oil spill from M. T. *Amoco Cadiz* on the Brittany Coast on 16 Mar 1978.

Land *Owner*

The world's largest landowner is the United States Government, with a holding of 732,000,000 acres (1,143,800 miles² *2 962 400 km²*) which is more than the area of the world's 8th largest country Argentina and 12.8 times

larger than the United Kingdom. The world's largest *private* landowner is reputed to be International Paper Co with 9 million acres *3,64 million ha*. The United Kingdom's greatest ever private landowner was the 3rd Duke of Sutherland, George Granville Sutherland-Leveson-Gower, KG (1828–92), who owned 1,358,000 acres *549 560 ha* in 1883. Currently the largest landholder in Great Britain is the Forestry Commission (instituted 1919) with 2,918,186 acres *1 180 974 ha*. The landowner with the largest known acreage is the 9th Duke of Buccleuch (b. 1923) with 336,000 acres *136,035 ha*. The longest tenure is that by St Paul's Cathedral of land at Tillingham, Essex, given by King Ethelbert before AD 616.

Value Highest

The world's most expensive land is in the central Giza district of Tokyo, Japan, where the site of the 'Crown' nightclub was bought on 28 Oct 1985 for £13,072 per square foot. The freehold price for a grave site with excellent *Fung Shui* in Hong Kong may cost HK$200,000 for 4 ft × 10 ft *1,21 × 3,04 m* or *£19,400 per ft²*. The real estate value per square metre of the two topmost French vineyards, Grande and Petite Cognac vineyards in Bordeaux, has not been recently estimated. The China Square Inch Land Ltd at a charity auction on 2 Dec 1977 sold 1 cm² *0.155 in²* of land at Sha Tau Kok for HK$2000 (the equivalent of US$17,405,833,737 per acre). The purchasers were Stephen and Tony Nicholson. The most expensive land in Britain is that in the City of London. The freehold price on small prime sites reached £1950/ft² (*£21,230/m²*) in mid 1973.

Highest price

The record price per acre for agricultural land in Great Britain is £12,000 at Elm Road, March, Cambridgeshire. It was sold by J. Collingwood & Son of March on 31 Dec 1973. In Jersey a record of £10,454 per acre (where 2¼ vergées equal 1 acre) was paid at Les Landes, St. Martin on 5 July 1984.

Highest rent

The highest rentals in the world in Nov 1984 for prime sites, according to *World Rental Levels* by Richard Ellis of London, are on Manhattan, New York at £42.41 and London (City) £32 per square foot. With added service charges and rates London is top at £54.72.

Greatest auction
The greatest auction was of the Hughes Aircraft Co for $5,000 million (*£4,166 million*) by General Motors of Detroit, Michigan on 5 June 1985.

Greatest barter deal
The biggest barter in trading history was 36 million barrels of oil valued at £900 million exchanged for 10 Boeing 747's for the Royal Saudi Airline in July 1984.

Mineral water
The world's largest mineral water firm is Source Perrier, near Nîmes, France with an annual production of more than 2,300,000,000 bottles, of which 1,300,000,000 now come from Perrier and Contrexeville. The French drink about 60 litres *105½ pt* of mineral water per person per year.

Motor car manufacturer *Largest World*
In 1980 Japan with 11,043,000 vehicles overtook the USA as the world's No 1 motor manufacturer. The largest manufacturing company in the world is General Motors Corporation of Detroit, Michigan, USA. During 1985 worldwide sales totalled $96,371,700,000 (*£68,837 million*). Its assets at 31 Dec 1985 were valued at $63,832,800,000 (*£45,595 million*). Its total 1985 payroll was $25,639,100,000 (*£18,314 million*) to an average of 811,000 employees. Dividends paid in 1985 were $1,616,900,000 (*£1,154,930,000*).

Great Britain
The largest British manufacturer was BL plc with 557,000 vehicles produced and a sales turnover of £3412 million of which £1062 million was overseas sales in 1985. Direct exports were £764 million.

Largest plant
The largest single automobile plant in the world is the Volkswagenwerk, Wolfsburg, West Germany, with 58,000 employees and a capacity for 4056 vehicles daily. The surface area of the factory buildings is 371 acres *150 ha* and that of the whole plant 4892 acres *1980 ha* with 43.5 miles *70 km* of rail sidings.

Salesmanship
The all-time record for automobile salesmanship in units sold individually is 1425 in 1973 by Joe Girard of Michigan, USA, author of *How to Sell Anything to Anybody*, winner of the No. 1 Car Salesman title each year in 1966–77. His lifetime total of one-at-a-time 'belly to belly' selling was 13,001 sales, all retail with a record 174 in a month. He retired on 1 Jan 1978 to teach others his art and has published also *How to Sell Yourself*.

Oil refineries *Largest*
The world's largest refinery has been the Amerada Hess refinery in St Croix, Virgin Islands with an annual capacity of 28 million tonnes *27.55 million tons*. The largest oil refinery in the United Kingdom is the Esso Refinery at Fawley, Hampshire. Opened in 1921 and much expanded in 1951, it has a capacity of *15,6 million tonnes* per year. The total investment together with the associated chemical plant, on the 1300 acre *526 ha* site is in excess of one billion pounds. The area occupied by the Shell Stanlow Refinery at Ellesmere Port, Cheshire, founded in 1922, and now with a capacity of 18 million tonnes per year, is 2000 acres *810 ha*.

Paper company
The world's largest company in paper, fibre and wood products is Georgia-Pacific of Atlanta, Georgia with sales in 1985 of $6,716 million (*£5,550 million*) and 40,000 workers. The largest paper mill in the United Kingdom is the Bowaters Kemsley Mill near Sittingbourne, Kent with a complex covering an area of 260 acres *105 ha* and a capacity in excess of 300,000 tons/*tonnes* a year.

Pharmaceuticals
The world's largest pharmaceutical company is Johnson & Johnson of New Brunswick, New Jersey with sales of $6,124,500,000 (*£5103 million*) in 1984. Britain's largest pharmaceutical turnover in 1984–85 was by Glaxo with £1,400 million.

Photographic store
The photographic store with the largest selling area is Jessop of Leicester Ltd's Photo Centre, Hinckley Road, Leicester opened in June 1979 with an area now of 27,000 ft² *2508 m²*.

Public relations
The world's largest public relations firm is Burson Marsteller with headquarters in New York and a 1985 net fee income of $104,667,000 (*£74,762,000*). Hill and Knowlton Inc. have most offices worldwide with 56 including one in Beijing, China.

The world's pioneer public relations publication is *Public Relations News,* founded by Mrs Denny Griswold in 1944 and which now circulates in 97 countries.

Publishing
The publishing company generating most net revenue is Time Inc of New York City with $3404 million (*£2430 million*) in 1985. The largest educational book publishing concern in the world is the Book Division of McGraw-Hill Inc of New York with sales of $460,222,000 (*£328.7 million*) in 1985 with 1300 new books and educational products.

Restaurateurs
The largest restaurant chain in the world is that operated by McDonald's Corporation of Oak Brook, Illinois, USA, founded on 15 April 1955 in Des Plaines, Chicago by Ray A. Kroc BH (Bachelor of Hamburgerology). By 31 December 1985 the number of McDonald's restaurants licensed and owned in 41 countries and territories around the world reached 8901, with an aggregate throughput of 55 billion 100 per cent pure beef hamburgers under the motto 'Q.S.C. & V.'—for quality, (fast) service, cleanliness and value. Sales systemwide in 1985 surpassed $11 billion (*£7612 million*). Britain's largest hotel and catering group is Trusthouse Forte which employs up to 45,000 full and part-time staff in the UK, 10,300 overseas, and which had a turnover of £1,244,500,000 in 1984–85. It has 800 hotels world-wide.

Fish and chip restaurant
The world's largest fish and chip shop is Harry Ramsden's, White Cross, Guiseley, West Yorkshire with 160 staff serving 1,400,000 customers per annum, who consumed 270 tons of fish and 430 tons of potatoes. Britain's oldest fryer, Jack Simpson (b. 1885) of Axminster, Devon recalls that a portion with peas plus tea in 1927 cost only 2p.

Retailer
The largest retailing firm in the world is Sears, Roebuck and Co (founded by Richard Warren Sears in North Redwood railway station, Minnesota in 1886) of Chicago, Illinois, USA. World-wide revenues were $26,500,000,000 (*£22.08 billion*) in the year ending 31 Dec 1984 when Sears Merchandise Group had 796 retail stores, 1119 sales offices and 1700 independent catalogue merchants in the USA. Their total assets were valued at $38,800,000,000 (*Then £32.33 billion*).

Ship-building
In 1985 there was 18,156,526 gross tonnage of ships, excluding sailing ships, non-propelled vessels and vessels of less than 100 gross tonnage, completed throughout the world. The figures for Romania and People's Republic of China are incomplete. Japan completed 9,502,831 gross tonnage (52.34 per cent of the world total). The United Kingdom completions totalled 171,940 gross tonnage. The world's leading shipbuilder firm in 1985 was Hyundai of Korea (South), who completed 44 vessels of 1,385,607 gross tonnage. Physically the largest ship yard in the United Kingdom is Harland and Wolff Ltd of Queen's Island, Belfast, which covers some 300 acres *120 ha*.

Shipping line
The largest shipping owners and operators are Exxon Corporation (see p. 143) whose fleets of owned/managed and chartered tankers in 1985 totalled a daily average of 12,700,000 deadweight tons.

A haven and oasis to all fish and chip lovers, Harry Ramsden's shop can accommodate over 1 million 'afishienados' annually.

Shopping centre

The world's largest shopping centre is the $900 million West Edmonton Mall, Alberta, Canada first opened on 15 Sept 1981 and completed four years later which covers 5 million ft² *464 515 m²* on a 110 acre *44,5 ha* site. It encompasses 828 stores and services as well as 6 major department stores. Parking is provided for 30,000 vehicles for more than 500,000 shoppers per week. The world's first shopping centre was Roland Park Shopping Center, Baltimore, Maryland, USA built in 1896. The world's largest wholesale merchandise mart is the Dallas Market Center, located on Stemmons Freeway, Dallas, Texas, USA with nearly 9.3 million ft² *864 000 m²* in 8 buildings. The complex covers 150 acres *60 ha* with some 3400 permanent showrooms displaying merchandise of more than 26,000 manufacturers. The Center attracts 600,000 buyers each year to its 38 annual markets and trade shows. The largest covered shopping centre in Britain is the Manchester Arndale Centre which has a floor area of 2,246,200 ft² *208 672 m²* including the 481,300 ft² *44 713 m²* car park for 1800 cars. It was built in 1976–79, has a gross shopping area of 1,187,000 ft² *110 270 m²* and is the first such centre in Europe with its own radio station. The £40 million centre at Milton Keynes, Buckinghamshire opened in August 1979 has the longest mall in the world—650 m *2132 ft*.

Soft drinks

The world's most popular soft drink is Coca-Cola with over 301,000,000 drinks sold per day by early 1985 in more than 155 countries. Coke was launched as a tonic by Dr John S. Pemberton of Atlanta, Georgia in 1886. The Coca-Cola Company was formed in 1892. The secret '7X' formula was unchanged until 1985 when Coca-Cola had 21.7% of the $28 billion market to Pepsi's 18.8%. Pepsi Co's overall 1985 sales of $8.47 billion were $340 million higher than Coca-Cola.

Steel company *World*

The non-communist world's largest producer of steel has been Nippon Steel of Tōkyō, Japan which produced 28,56 million tonnes *28.11 million tons* of crude steel in 1985. The Fukuyama Works of Nippon Kokan has a capacity of more than 16 000 000 tonnes/*tons* per annum. Its work force is 76,000.

STOCK EXCHANGES

The oldest Stock Exchange of the 138 listed throughout the world is that of Amsterdam, in the Netherlands, founded in 1602.

Most bargains

The highest number of equity bargains in one day on the London Stock Exchange was 47,481 on 4 Apr 1986. The record for a year is 5,567,798 bargains in the year ending 31 Dec 1985. There were 6886 securities (*cf.* 9749 peak in June 1973) listed at 31 Dec 1985. Their total nominal value was £288,348 million (gilt-edged £126,036 million) and their market value was £1,152,120 million (gilt-edged £126,625 million).

The highest closing figure of *The Financial Times* Industrial Ordinary share index (1 July 1935 = 100) was 1425.9 on 3 Apr 1986. The lowest figure was 49.4 on 26 June 1940. The greatest rise in a day has been 25.6 points to 1415.1 on 20 Mar 1986 in continued response to the Chancellor's 18 Mar Budget Statement, and the greatest fall in a day was 28.5 to 1370.8 on 15 Apr 1986, on continued worries of the Libyan crises.

Most highly valued UK Co

The stock valuation of British Telecom in June 1985 was £14,200 million at 236 pence (40 pence uncalled) per share.

Highest par value

The highest denomination of any share quoted in the world is a single share in F. Hoffmann-La Roche of Basel worth Sw. Fr 101,000 (£21,992) on 23 Apr 1976.

U.S. records

The highest index figure on the Dow Jones average (instituted 8 Oct 1896) of selected industrial stocks at the close of a day's trading was 1855.90 on 21 Apr 1986. The record day's trading was 236,565,110 shares on 3 Aug 1984. The old, record trading volume in a day on the New York Stock Exchange of 16,410,030 shares on 29 Oct 1929, the 'Black Tuesday' of the famous 'crash' was unsurpassed until April 1968. The Dow Jones industrial average, which reached 381.71 on 3 Sept 1929, plunged 30.57 points on 29 Oct 1929, on its way to the Depression's lowest point of 41.22 on 8 July 1932. The largest decline in a day, 39.10 points, occurred on 8 Jan 1986. The total lost in security values from 1 Sept 1929 to 30 June 1932 was $74,000 million (*then £23,000 million*). The greatest paper loss in a year was $209,957 million (*then £87,500 million*) in 1974. The record daily increase of 28.40 on 30 Oct 1929 was most recently bettered on 3 Nov 1982 with 43.41 points to 1065.49. The percentage record was 15.34% between 3 Mar (53.84) and the next opening on 15 Mar 1933 (62.10). The largest stock trade in the history of the New York Exchange was a 48,788,800 share block of Navistar International Corporation stock at $10 in a $487,888,000 (*then £348,491,420*) transaction on 10 Apr 1986. The highest price paid for a seat on the NY Stock Exchange was $515,000 (*then £214,580*) in 1969. The lowest 20th century price was $17,000 in 1942. The market value of stocks listed on the New York Stock Exchange reached an all-time high at the end of March 1986—$2,204,114,975,745.

Dr John S. Pemberton, the chemist who invented a tonic containing cola nut extract in the back room of his shop in Atlanta, Georgia, USA, in 1886 which today is the world's most popular drink–Coke.

Largest and smallest equity

The greatest aggregate market value of any corporation at year end was $32.0 billion (*then £26 million*) for IBM on 31 Dec 1985.

Britain's smallest public listed company is Dura Mill Ltd of Whitworth, Lancashire, producers of very high quality yarn with a capitalization of £85,000 in 30 p shares.

Greatest personal loss

The highest recorded personal paper losses on stock values have been those of Ray A. Kroc, Chairman of McDonald's Corporation with $64,901,718 (*then £27 million*) on 8 July 1974 and Edwin H. Land, President of Polaroid Corporation with $59,397,355 on 28–29 May 1974, when Polaroid stock closed $12.12 down at 43¼ on that day.

Largest new issue

The American Telegraph & Telephone Company offered $1375 million's worth of shares in a rights offer on 27,500,000 shares of convertible preferred stock on the New York market on 2 June 1971. The largest offering on the London Stock Exchange by a United Kingdom company was the £624 million rights offer of British Petroleum Co plc on 23 June 1981.

Greatest flotation

The largest equity offering in history was £3,915,600,000 or 50.2 per cent of British Telecom on behalf of H.M. Government by Kleinwort, Benson Ltd in Nov 1984. It is mooted that with the privatizing of British Gas an offering of £8,000 million may be made in 1987–88.

Largest investment house

The largest securities company in the US, and once the world's largest partnership with 124 partners, before becoming a corporation in 1959, is Merrill, Lynch, Pierce, Fenner & Smith Inc (founded 6 Jan 1914) of New York City, USA. Its parent, Merrill, Lynch and Co, has assets of $51.6 billion, approximately 45,000 employees, 1116 offices and 4.9 million customer accounts. The firm is referred to in the United States stock exchange circles as a 'Breed Apart'.

Largest store

The world's largest store is R. H. Macy & Co Inc at Broadway and 34th Street, New York City, NY, USA. It covers 50.5 acres *20,3 ha* and employs 14,000 who handle 400,000 items. The sales of the company and its subsidiaries in 1984–85 were $4,368,386,000 (*£2993 million*). Mr Rowland Hussey Macy's sales on his first day at his fancy goods store on 6th Avenue, on 27 Oct 1858, were recorded as $11.06 (*then £2.20*).

Sugar mill

The highest recorded output for any sugar mill was set in 1966–67 by Ingenio de San Cristobal y Anexas, S.A., Veracruz, Mexico with 247,900 tonnes refined from 2,886,074 tonnes of cane ground. The world's largest cane sugar plant is the California & Hawaii Sugar Co plant founded in 1906 at Crockett, California with an output of 8 million lb per day.

Largest supermarket

The world's largest supermarkets (self-service with check-outs) were the Piggly Wiggly chain started in 1916 by Clarence Saunders (1881–1953) in Memphis, Tennessee, USA. Above 25,000 ft² or *2500 m²* net shopping area, stores are usually termed superstores and above 50,000 ft² or *5000 m²*—hypermarkets. The largest such in Britain is the 104,500 ft² *9660 m²* Tesco hypermarket at Weston Favell, Northampton opened in Nov 1978 with a parking capacity for 1300 cars.

Tobacco company

Subsidiary and affiliates of B.A.T. Industries (founded in London in 1902 as British-American Tobacco Co.) comprise the world's largest tobacco concern. They operate 116 tobacco factories in 52 countries: consolidated turnover in 1985 was £12,696 million and total assets were £8840 million at 31 Dec 1985. The Group's sales in 1985 topped 567,000 million cigarettes.

The world's largest cigarette plant is the $300 million Philip Morris plant at Richmond, Virginia, USA opened in October 1974. Employing 5500 people the factory produces more than 530 million cigarettes a day.

Toy shop
The world's biggest toy shop is Hamleys of Regent Street Ltd, founded in 1760 in Holborn and removed to Regent Street, London, W1 in 1901. It has selling space of 45,000 ft² *4180 m²* on 6 floors with over 300 employees during the Christmas season.

Undertaker (or Mortician)
The world's largest undertaking business is the SCI (Service Corporation International) with 279 funeral homes and 40 flower shops with associated limousine fleets and cemeteries. Their annual revenue in the most recession-proof of industries in the year ending 30 Apr 1983 was $208,536,000 (*£1,345,400*).

Vintners
The oldest champagne firm is Ruinart Père et Fils founded in 1729. The oldest cognac firm is Augier Frères & Co, established in 1643.

Part of one of the six floors that make up the world's biggest toy shop—Hamleys of Regent Street Ltd.

2. MANUFACTURED ARTICLES

Antique *Largest*
The largest antique ever sold has been London Bridge in March 1968. The sale was made by Mr Ivan F. Luckin of the Court of Common Council of the Corporation of London to the McCulloch Oil Corporation of Los Angeles, California, USA for $2,460,000 (*then £1,029,000*). The 10,000 tons/*tonnes* of façade stonework were re-assembled at a cost of £3 million, at Lake Havasu City, Arizona and 're-dedicated' on 10 Oct 1971.

Armour *Most expensive*
The highest auction price paid for a suit of armour is £1,925,000 by B. H. Trupin (US) on 5 May 1983 at Sotheby's, London for the suit made in Milan by Giovanni Negroli in 1545 for Henri II, King of France from the Hever Castle Collection in Kent, England.

Heaviest
The armour of William Somerset, 3rd Earl of Worcester made at the Royal Workshop, Greenwich *c.* 1570 weighed 81 lb 9 oz *37,0 kg*. If his five bullet-proof exchange elements were substituted the total weight reaches 133 lb 13 oz *60,7 kg*.

Beds *Largest functional*
In Bruges, Belgium, Philip, Duke of Burgundy had a bed 12½ ft wide and 19 ft long *3,81 × 5,79 m* erected for the perfunctory *coucher officiel* ceremony with Princess Isabella of Portugal in 1430. The largest bed in Great Britain is the Great Bed of Ware, dating from *c.* 1580, from the Crown Inn, Ware, Hertfordshire, now preserved in the Victoria and Albert Museum, London. It is 10 ft 8½ in wide, 11 ft 1 in long and 8 ft 9 in tall *3,26 × 3,37 × 2,66 m*. The largest bed currently marketed in the United Kingdom is a Super Size Diplomat bed, 9 ft wide by 9 ft long, *2,74 m²* from The London Bedding Centre, Sloane Street, SW1 which costs more than £4000.

Heaviest
The heaviest bed is a water bed 9 ft 7 in × 9 ft 10 in *2,92 × 2,99 m* owned by Milan Vacek of Canyon County, California since 1977. The thermostatically heated water alone weighs 4205 lb *1907 kg*.

Beer cans
Beer cans date from a test marketing by Krueger Beer of Newark, New Jersey at Richmond, Virginia in 1935. The largest collection has been made by John F. Ahrens of Mount Laurel, New Jersey, USA with nearly 15,000 different cans. A Rosalie Pilsner can sold for $6000 (*then £2700*) in the US in April 1981.

Beer mat collections (*Tegestology*)
The world's largest collection of beer mats is owned by Leo Pisker of Vienna, who had collected over 113,500 different mats from 149 countries by April 1985. The largest collection of purely British mats is 32,650 by Timothy J. Stannard of Birmingham.

Beer tankard *Largest*
The largest pewter tankard was made by the Selangor Pewter Co, Kuala Lumpur, Malaysia and unveiled on 30 Nov 1985. It measures 198,7 cm *6 ft 6 in* in height and has a capacity 2796 litre *738,6 gal*.

Blanket
The largest blanket ever made measured 68 × 100 ft *20,7 × 30,48 m* weighing 600 lb *272 kg*. It was knitted in 20,160 squares in 10 months (October 1977–July 1978) by *Woman's Weekly* readers for Action Research for The Crippled Child. It was shown on BBC TV *Record Breakers* in October 1978. The most expensive was a Churro hand-spun serape sold for $115,500 (*then £79,000*) at Sotheby's, New York on 22 Oct 1983.

Bottle caps
Since 1950 Helge Friholm (b. 1910) of Søborg, Denmark has amassed 38,570 different bottle caps (to April 1986) from 145 countries.

Cans
At Maizuru Playground, Nagoya, Japan on 4 Nov 1985 to celebrate the International Youth Year a pyramid consisting of 210,479 empty beverage cans was built in 28 hr.

Candle
A candle 80 ft *24,38 m* high and 8½ ft *2,59 m* in

diameter was exhibited at the 1897 Stockholm Exhibition by the firm of Lindahls. The overall height was 127 ft *38,70 m*. Currently the largest is that made from 1967 to 1985 by Jean-Paul Schwob of Wesserling, Alsace, France, standing 10½ ft *3,20 m* and weighing 1372 lb *622 kg*.

Carpets and rugs *Earliest*
The earliest carpet known is a woollen pile-knotted carpet, red on white ground excavated at Pazyryk, USSR in 1947, dated to the 5th century BC and now preserved in Leningrad.

Largest
Of ancient carpets the largest on record was the gold-enriched silk carpet of Hashim (dated AD 743) of the Abbasid caliphate in Baghdad, Iraq. It is reputed to have measured 180 by 300 ft *54,86 × 91,44 m*. A 52,225 ft² *4851 m²* or 1.23 acre 28 ton red carpet was laid on 13 Feb 1982, by the Allied Corporation, from Radio City Music Hall to the New York Hilton along the Avenue of the Americas.

Most finely woven
The most finely woven old carpet known is one with more than 2193 knots per in² *340 per cm²* from a fragment of an Imperial Mughal prayer carpet of the 17th century now in the Altman collections in the Metropolitan Museum of Art, New York City, NY, USA. The Bikaner Woollen Mills, India announced in March 1985 that they had achieved 2600 knots per in² *403 per cm²*. The most magnificent carpet ever made was the Spring carpet of Khusraw made for the audience hall of the Sassanian palace at Ctesiphon, Iraq. It was about 7000 ft² *650 m²* of silk, gold thread and encrusted with emeralds. It was cut up as booty by military looters in AD 635 and from the known realization value of the pieces must have had an original value of some £100,000,000.

Chair *Largest*
The world's largest chair is the 2000 lb *907 kg* 33 ft 1 in *10,08 m* tall, 19 ft 7 in *5,96 m* wide chair constructed by Anniston Steel & Plumbing Co. Inc for Miller Office Furniture in Anniston, Alabama, USA and completed in May 1981.

Chamber pot
The 33 oz *935 g* silver pot, made by David Willaume and engraved for the 2nd Earl of Warrington made £9,500 at Sotheby's, London on 14 June 1984.

The practical record of George Anastapolis's cigar smoking over 24 years.

Chandelier *Largest*

The world's largest set of chandeliers (ten) were built for the palace of H.M. Sir Muda Hassanal Bolkiah of Brunei in 1983. His palace or Istana Nurul Iman is in the capital Bandar Seri Begawan. Britain's largest is in the Chinese Room at the Pavilion, Brighton.

Chocolates

The most expensive chocolates are by Charbonel et Walker of Old Bond Street, London at £10.00 per pound *453 g* box.

Christmas cracker

The largest functional cracker ever constructed was one 63.97 ft *19,5 m* in length and 10.8 ft *3,3 m* in diameter made by Fowey School, Cornwall and pulled by 800 pupils on 18 Dec 1984.

Cigars *largest*

The largest cigar ever made measures 5,095 m *16 ft 8½ in* in length and weighs 262 kg *577 lb 9 oz* (over ¼ ton) taking 243 hours and using 3330 full tobacco leaves. It was made by Tinus Vinke and Jan Weijmer in Feb 1983 and is in the Tobacco Museum in Kampen, Holland. The largest marketed cigar in the world is the 14 in *35,5 cm* Valdez Emperado by San Andres Cigars.

Most expensive

The most expensive standard cigar in the world is the 11½ in *29,2 cm* long Don Miguel 'Cervantes', which retails in Britain at £15.00.

Cigar bands

Joseph Hruby of Lyndhurst, Ohio has the largest known collection of cigar bands with 175,391 different examples dating from *c.* 1895.

Most voracious smokers

Jim Purol and Mike Papa each smoked 135 cigarettes simultaneously for 5 min on 5 Oct 1978 at Rameys Lounge, Detroit, Michigan, USA. On 3 Sept 1979 at the same venue, they each smoked 27 cigars simultaneously for 5 min and in 1983 Purol smoked 38 pipes. Simon Argevitch of Oakland, California, USA raised his old record to 17 standard size cigars, whilst

simultaneously emitting bird calls or singing, on Fishermans Wharf, San Francisco on 3 July 1982. George Anastassopoulos (b. Patras, Greece 20 Aug 1911) kept account of smoking 40,730 cigars from Jan 1950 to June 1984.

Cigarettes *Consumption*

The heaviest smokers in the world are the people of the United States, where 640,000 million cigarettes (an average of 3750 per adult) were consumed at a cost of some $21,200 million (*£11,700 million*) in 1981. The people of China, however, were estimated to consume 725,000 million in 1977. In Senegal 80% of urban males smoke. The peak consumption in the United Kingdom was 3230 cigarettes per adult in 1973. The peak volume was 243,100,000 lb *110,2 million kg* in 1961, compared with 81.1 million kg *179 million lb* in 1985 when 97,750 million cigarettes were sold. In the United Kingdom 46.5 per cent of adult men and 35 per cent of adult women smoked in 1985.

Tar/Nicotine content

Of the 140 brands most recently analysed for the Dept of Health and Social Security, the one with highest tar/nicotine content is *Capstan Full Strength* with 25/2.6 mg per cigarette. *Silk Cut Ultra Low King Size*, *Embassy Ultra Mild King Size* and *John Player King Size Ultra Mild* with <4/0.3 are at the lower risk end of the league table. In the Philippines there is a brand with 71 mg nicotine per cigarette.

Most popular

The world's most popular cigarette is 'Marlboro', a filter cigarette made by Phillip Morris, which sold 237,000 million units in 1982. The largest selling British cigarette in 1985 was *Benson and Hedges Special Filter*. The Wills brand 'The Three Castles' was introduced in 1878.

Longest and shortest

The longest cigarettes ever marketed were 'Head Plays', each 11 in *27,9 cm* long and sold in packets of 5 in the United States in about 1930, to save tax. The shortest were 'Lilliput' cigarettes, each 1¼ in *31,7 mm* long, and ⅛ in *3 mm* in diameter, made in Great Britain in 1956.

Largest collection

The world's largest collection of cigarettes is that of Robert E. Kaufman, MD, of 950 Park Avenue, New York City 10028, NY, USA. In April 1986 he had 7945 different cigarettes made in 172 countries. The oldest brand represented is 'Lone Jack', made in the USA in *c.* 1885. Both the longest and shortest (see above) are represented.

Cigarette cards

The earliest known tobacco card is 'Vanity Fair' dated 1876 issued by Wm S. Kimball & Co., Rochester, New York. The earliest British example appeared *c.* 1883 in the form of a calendar issued by Allen & Ginter, of Richmond, Virginia, trading from Holborn Viaduct, City of London. The largest known collection is that of Mr Edward Wharton-Tigar, MBE (b. 1913) of London with a collection of more than 1,000,000 cigarette and trade cards in about 45,000 sets.

Cigarette lighter *Most expensive*

The Dunhill Lighthouse Table Lighter is made in 18 ct gold—designed in the shape of a lighthouse set on an island base of amethyst which alone weighs 1 cwt *50 kg*. It weighs 51.4 oz troy *1600 g* and the windows on the lighthouse stem are amethyst. Priced at £37,500 and sold by Alfred Dunhill, St. James's, London.

Cigarette packets

The earliest surviving cigarette packet is the

Finnish 'Petit Canon' packet for 25, made by Tollander & Klärich in 1860, from the Ventegodt Collection. The rarest is the Latvian 700-year anniversary (1201–1901) Riga packet, believed to be unique, from the same collection. The largest verified private collection is one of 60,955 from over 150 countries owned by Vernon Young of Farnham, England.

Credit card collection

The largest collection of valid credit cards at 16 May 1986 is one of 1189 (all different) by Walter Cavanagh (b. 1943) of Santa Clara, California, USA. The cost of acquisition to 'Mr. Plastic Fantastick' was nil, and he keeps them in the world's longest wallet—250 ft *76,2 m* long weighing 35 lb *15,87 kg* worth more than $1.25 million in credit.

Curtain

The largest curtain ever built has been the bright orange-red 4 ton *4064 kg* 185 ft *56 m* high curtain suspended 1350 ft *411 m* across the Rifle Gap, Grand Hogback, Colorado, USA by the Bulgarian-born sculptor Christo, (*né* Javacheff) on 10 Aug 1971. It blew apart in a 50 mph *80 km/h* gust 27 hr later. The total cost involved in displaying this work of art was $750,000 (*then £312,500*).

The world's largest functional curtain is one 550 ft long × 65 ft high *167,6 × 19,8 m* in the Brabazon hanger at British Aerospace Filton, Bristol used to enclose aircraft in the paint spraying bay. It is electrically drawn.

Dolls *Largest*

The most outsize 'doll' ever paraded was made by the Belgian student body KSA on 15 May 1983 in Ostend. It measured 51,07 m *167 ft 6 in* overall. The most massive 'guy' built was one 62 ft 4 in *19 m* high by the Fermain Youth Club, Macclesfield on 5 Nov 1983.

Dress *Most expensive*

The EVA suits for extra-vehicular activity worn by space shuttle crews from 1982 had a unit cost of $2.3 million (*then £1,437,000*). The dress with the highest price tag ever exhibited by a Paris fashion house was one in the Schiaparelli spring/summer collection on 23 Jan 1977. 'The Birth of Venus' designed by Serge Lepage with 512 diamonds was priced at Fr. 7,500,000 (*then £880,000*).

The coronation robe for Emperor Field Marshall Jean-Bédel Bokassa with a 39 ft *11,8 m* long train was encrusted with 785,000 pearls and 1,220,000 crystal beads by Guiselin of Paris for £77,125. It was used at Bangui, Central African Empire (now Republic) on 4 Dec 1977.

Fabrics *Earliest and Most expensive*

The oldest surviving fabric discovered from Level VI A at Çatal Hüyük, Turkey has been radio-carbon dated to 5900 BC.

The most expensive fabric obtainable is Vicuña cloth manufactured by Fuji Keori Ltd of Osaka, Japan at US$3235 (*£2087*) per metre in July 1983. The most expensive evening wear fabric was that designed by Alan Hershman of Duke Street, London at £650 per metre. Each square metre, despite 155,000 hand sewn sequins, weighs less than 7 oz *198 g*.

Finest cloth

The most expensive cloth, the brown-grey throat hair of Indian goats, is Shatoosh (or Shatusa), finer, and more expensive than Vicuña. It was sold by Neiman-Marcus of Dallas, Texas, USA, at $1000 (£555) per yard but supplies have now dried up.

Firework

The largest firework ever produced has been

Universe I exploded for the Lake Toya Festival, Hokkaido, Japan on 28 Aug 1983. The 421 kg *928 lb* shell was 108 cm *42.5 in* in diameter and burst to a diameter of 860 m *2830 ft*, with a 5 colour display. The longest firework 'waterfall' was produced for the Yonago-Gaina Festival in Tottori, Japan and ignited at 8.50 pm on 4 Aug 1985. It measured 1500 m *4920 ft* in length.

Flags *Oldest*

The oldest known flag is one dated to *c.* 3000 BC found in 1972 at Khablis, Iran. It is of metal and measures 23 × 23 cm *9 × 9 in* and depicts an eagle, lions and goddesses.

Largest

The largest flag in the world, the 'Great American Flag', was displayed at Evansville, Indiana on 22 Mar 1980 measuring 411 ft *125 m* by 210 ft *64 m* with a weight of 7 tons/*tonnes*. It was donated to the White House and was the brainchild of Len Silverfine. The largest Union Flag (or Union Jack) was one 240 × 108 ft *73,15 × 32,91 m* displayed at the Royal Tournament, Earl's Court, London in July 1976. It weighed more than a ton and was made by Form 4Y at Bradley Rowe School, Exeter, Devon. The largest flag *flown* from a flagstaff is a Brazilian national flag measuring 70 × 100 m *229 ft 8 in × 328 ft 1 in* in Brasilia. The study of flags is known as vexillology from Latin *vexillum*, a flag, and was coined by Dr Whitney Smith of Winchester, Mass., USA.

Float

The largest float is the 150 ft *45,7 m* long, 22 ft *6,7 m* wide 'Agree' Float bearing 51 All-American Homecoming 'Queens' used at the Orange Bowl parade, Miami, Florida, USA on 29 Dec 1977.

Furniture *Oldest British*

The oldest surviving piece of British furniture is a three-footed tub with metal bands found at Glastonbury, Somerset, and dating from between 300 and 150 BC.

Largest Piece

The largest item of furniture in the world is the wooden bench in Green Park, Obihiro, Hokkaido, Japan which seats 1282 people and measures 400 m *1312 ft 4 in* long. It was completed by a team of 770 on 19 July 1981.

Garden gnome

The earliest recorded garden gnome was one placed in the rockery at Lamport Hall, Northamptonshire, England by Sir Charles Isham Bt. (1819–1903).

Glass

The most priceless example of the art of glassmaking is usually regarded as the glass Portland Vase which dates from late in the 1st century BC or 1st century AD. It was made in Italy and was in the possession of the Barberini family in Rome from at least 1642. It was eventually bought by the Duchess of Portland in 1792 but smashed while in the British Museum by William Lloyd on 7 Feb 1845. The thinnest glass made is 0.003 in *0,076 mm* thick for liquid crystal display (LCD) watches by Corning Glass Works, New York, USA.

The highest price paid for a piece of glass and for any antiquity is £520,000 (hammer price) or £572,000 (with premium) for the Roman cage cup from AD 300 (see Table on p 152).

Gold plate

The gold coffin of the 14th century BC Pharaoh Tutankhamun discovered by Howard Carter on 16 Feb 1923 in the Valley of the Kings, western Thebes, Egypt weighed 110,4 kg *243 lb*. The

exhibition at the British Museum attracted 1,656,151 people (of whom 45.7 per cent bought catalogues) from 30 Mar to 30 Dec 1972, resulting in a profit of £657,731.22.

Jig-saw *Earliest and largest*

The earliest jig-saws were made as 'dissected maps' by John Spilsbury (1739–69) in Russell Court off Drury Lane, London *c.* 1762. The largest jig-saw ever made is *Rose-Petal Place*, sponsored by Hallmark Cards Inc, outside Macy's Store on 34th Street, New York City on 19 Aug 1984. It measured 76 × 48 ft *23,16 × 14,63 m* with 14,000 pieces. Fujisankei Communications Group of Japan commissioned Yanoman Co. to produce a puzzle 3,24 × 5,88 m *10.63 × 19.29 ft* with 61,752 pieces. Each piece was sold for charity. Custom-made Stave puzzles made by Steve Richardson of Vermont, USA of 2300 pieces cost $3700 (*then £2430*) in Jan 1983.

The British record is of the cover of 'BEEB' magazine at ,73 ft 2½ in × 45 ft 3 in *22,31 × 13,79 m* with 1500 interlocking wooden pieces assembled by 100 school children in Canterbury, Kent on 2 Feb 1985 for BBC TV's *Saturday Superstore* show.

Matchbox labels

The oldest match label of accepted provenance is that of Samuel Jones *c.* 1830. The finest collection of trade mark labels (excluding any bar or other advertising labels) is some 280,000 pieces collected by the phillumenist Robert Jones of Indianapolis, USA. The greatest British prize is a Lucifer & Congreve label of *c.* 1835.

Needles

The earliest needles were made of bone. The largest recorded needle is one 6 ft 1 in *185,5 cm* long made by George Davies of Thomas Somerfield, Bloxwich for stitching on mattress buttons lengthways. One is preserved in the National Needle Museum, Forge Mill, Redditch, Worcestershire.

Nylon *Sheerest*

The lowest denier nylon yarn ever produced is the 6 denier used for stockings exhibited at the Nylon Fair in London in February 1956. The sheerest stockings normally available are 9 denier. A hair from the average human head is about 50 denier.

Penknife

The penknife with the greatest number of blades is the Year Knife made by the cutlers, Joseph Rodgers & Sons Ltd, of Sheffield, England, whose trade mark was granted in 1682. The knife was built in 1822 with 1822 blades but had to halt at 1973 because there was no further space. It was acquired by Britain's largest hand tool manufacturers, Stanley Works (Great Britain) Ltd of Sheffield, South Yorkshire in 1970.

Pens *Most expensive*

The most expensive writing pens were the 18 carat pair of pens (one fibre-tipped and one ballpoint) capped by diamonds of 3.88 carats sold by Alfred Dunhill (see Cigarette lighter) for £9943 the pair (incl. VAT). The most expensive fountain pen was the Mont Blanc 18 carat gold and platinum nibbed Meisterstück made by Dunhill in Hamburg, West Germany and which retailed in 1984 for $4250 (*then £3035*).

Pistol

In December 1983 it was reported that Mr Ray Bily (US) owned an initialled gold pistol made for Hitler which was valued for insurance purposes at $375,000 (*£267,850*).

Post cards

Deltiology is claimed to be the third largest

collecting hobby next only to stamps and coins. Austria issued the first cards in 1869 followed by Britain in 1872. The highest price paid for a postcard was $4400 *£3143* for one of the five known Mucha Waverly Cycle post cards. It was sold by Susan Brown Nicholson of Lisle, Illinois, USA in Sept 1984.

Quilting

The world's largest quilt, designed by A. Platteau, was made by the people of Kortrijk-Rollegem, Belgium. It comprises 16,240 squares measuring 21,24 × 30,35 m *69.6 × 99.5 ft*. On 28 Aug 1982 it was hoisted by two cranes.

Ropes *Largest and Longest*

The largest rope ever made was a coir fibre launching rope with a circumference of 47 in *119 cm* made in 1858 for the British liner *Great Eastern* by John and Edwin Wright of Birmingham. It consisted of four strands, each of 3780 yarns. The longest fibre rope ever made without a splice was one of 10,000 fathoms or 11.36 miles *18 288 m* of 6½ in *16,5 cm* circumference manila by Frost Brothers (now British Ropes Ltd) in London in 1874.

The strongest cable-laid wire rope strop made is one 282 mm *11.1 in* in diameter with a breaking strain of 3250 tonnes.

Shoes

James Smith, founder of James Southall & Co of Norwich, England introduced sized shoes in 1792. The firm began making 'Start-rite' children's shoes in 1923.

Emperor Bokassa of the Central African Empire (now Republic) commissioned pearl-studded shoes from the House of Berluti, Paris for his self-coronation in Dec 1977 at a cost of $85,000 (*then £38,800*).

The most expensive standard shoes obtainable are mink-lined golf shoes with 18 carat gold embellishments and ruby-tipped spikes made by Stylo Matchmakers International Ltd, of Northampton, England which retail for £8250, or $12,000 per pair in the USA.

Largest

Excluding cases of elephantiasis, the largest shoes ever sold are a pair size 42 built for the giant Harley Davidson of Avon Park, Florida, USA. The normal limit is size 14. For advertising and display purposes facsimiles of shoes weighing up to 1,5 tonnes have been constructed.

Silver

The largest single pieces of silver are the pair of water jugs of 10,408 troy oz 4.77 cwt *242,7 kg* made in 1902 for the Maharaja of Jaipur (1861–1922). They are 160 cm *5 ft 3 in* tall, with a circumference of 2,48 m *8 ft 1½ in*, and have a capacity of 1800 gallons *8182 litres*. They are now in the City Palace, Jaipur. The silversmith was Gorind Narain.

Snuff *Most expensive*

The most expensive snuff obtainable in Britain is 'Café Royale' sold by G. Smith and Sons (est. 1869) of 74, Charing Cross Road, City of Westminster, Greater London. The price was £2.06 per oz. in April 1986.

Sofa *Longest*

The longest standard sofa manufactured for market is the King Talmage Sofa, 12 ft 2 in *3,7 m* in length made by the Talmageville Furniture Manufacturers, California, USA. Barton Grange Hotel, near Preston, Lancashire bought a 14 ft *4,26 m* long pink leather settee for £3250 on 4 Oct 1984.

Table *Longest*

A buffet table 1007,3 m *3304 ft 10 in* long was

set up for the 400th anniversary of Hudiksvall, Sweden on 19 June 1982. Some 4000 people including HM The King of Sweden were seated.

Table cloth
The world's largest table cloth is one 219 yd *200 m* long by 2 yd *1,8 m* wide double damask made by John S. Brown & Sons Ltd of Belfast in 1972 and shipped to a royal palace in the Middle East. There was also an order for matching napkins for 450 places.

Tapestry *Earliest*
The earliest known examples of tapestry woven linen are three pieces from the tomb of Thutmose IV, the Egyptian pharaoh and dated to 1483–1411 BC.

Largest
The largest single piece of tapestry ever woven is 'Christ in His Majesty', measuring 72 ft by 39 ft *21,94 × 11,88 m* designed by Graham Vivian Sutherland OM (1903–80) for an altar hanging in Coventry Cathedral, West Midlands. It cost £10,500, weighs ¾ ton *760 kg* and was delivered from Pinton Frères of Felletin, France, on 1 Mar 1962.

Longest embroidery
The famous Bayeux *Telle du Conquest, dite tapisserie de la reine Mathilde*, a hanging 19½ in *49,5 cm* wide by 231 ft *70,40 m* in length depicts events of the period 1064–6 in 72 scenes and was probably worked in Canterbury, Kent, in *c.* 1086. It was 'lost' for 2½ centuries from 1476 until 1724. The Overlord Embroidery of 34 panels each 8 × 3 ft *2,43 × 0,91 m*, commissioned by Lord Dulverton CBE, TD (b. 1915) from the Royal School of Needlework, London, was completed in 1979 after 100 man years of work and is 41 ft *12,49 m* longer than the Bayeux and has the largest area of any embroidery with 816 ft² *75,8 m²*. An uncompleted 8 in *20,3 cm* deep 1280 ft *390,14 m* embroidery of scenes from C. S. Lewis's Narnia children's stories has been worked by Mrs Margaret S. Pollard of Truro, Cornwall to the order of Mr Michael Maine.

Tartan *Earliest*
The earliest evidence of tartan is the so-called Falkirk tartan, found stuffed in a jar of coins in Bells Meadow, Falkirk, Scotland. It is of a dark and light brown pattern and dates from *c.* AD 245. The earliest reference to a specific named tartan has been to a Murray tartan in 1618 although Mackay tartan was probably worn earlier. There are 1300 tartans known to the Museums of Scottish Tartans at Cumrie, Perthshire. HRH Prince of Wales is eligible to wear 11 including the Balmoral which has been exclusive to the Royal Family since 1852.

Tea towels
The largest reported collection of unduplicated tea towels was 5967 by Mr Tony Judkin of Luton, Bedfordshire. In April 1986 a fire destroyed 'over a thousand' of them.

Time capsule
The world's largest time capsule is the Tropico Time Tunnel of 10,000 ft³ *283 m³* in a cave in Rosamond, California, USA, sealed by the Kern Antelope Historical Society on 20 Nov 1966 and intended for opening in AD 2866.

Typewriters
The first patent for a typewriter was by Henry Mill in 1714 but the earliest known working machine was made by Pellegrine Turri (Italy) in 1808.

Vase *Largest*
The largest vase on record is one 8 ft *2,78 m*, in height, weighing 650 lb *294,8 kg*, thown by Sebastiano Maglio at Haeger Potteries of Dun-

dee, Illinois, USA (founded 1872) during August 1976. The Chinese ceramic authority Chingwah Lee of San Francisco was reported in Aug 1978 to have appraised a unique 39 in *99 cm* Kang Hsi 4-sided vase then in a bank vault in Phoenix, Arizona, USA at '$60 million' (*then £30 million*).

Wallet
The most expensive wallet ever made is a platinum-cornered, diamond studded crocodile creation made by Louis Quatorze of Paris and Mikimoto of Tokyo selling at £56,000 in Sept 1984.

Wreath *Most expensive*
The most expensive wreath on record was that presented to Sri Chinmoy in New York City, USA on 11 July 1983 by Ashrita Furman and Pahar Meltzer. It was handled by the Garland of Divinity's Love Florist, contained 10,000 flowers, and cost $3500 (*£2260*).

Zip-fastener
The world's longest zip-fastener is 632,45 m *2074 ft* long made for covers of aquatic cables by RIRI of Mendrisio, Italy in Jan 1985. It has 119,007 nylon teeth.

ART NOUVEAU
The highest auction price for any piece of art nouveau is $360,000 (*then £163,600*) for a spider-web leaded glass mosaic and bronze table lamp by L. C. Tiffany at Christie's, New York on 8 Apr. 1980.

BED
A 1930 black lacquer kingsize bed made by Jean Durand was auctioned at Christie's, New York City on 2 Oct 1983 for £49,668.

BLANKET
The most expensive blanket was a Navajo Churro handspun serape of *c.* 1852 sold for $115,500 (*then £79,500*) with premium at Sotheby's, New York City on 22 Oct 1983.

CARPET
In 1946 the Metropolitan Museum, New York, privately paid $1 million (*then £248,138*) for the 26.5 × 13.6 ft *807 × 414 cm* Anhalt Medallion carpet made in Tabriz or Kashan, Persia *c.* 1590. The highest price ever paid at auction for a carpet is £231,000 for a 17th century 'Polonaise' silk and metal thread carpet at Sotheby's, London on 13 Oct 1982.

CERAMICS
The Greek urn painted by Euphronios and thrown by Euxitheos in *c.* 530 was bought by private treaty by the Metropolitan Museum of Art, New York, for $1.3 million (*then £541,666*) in August 1972.

CHAIR
The highest price ever paid for a single chair is $275,000 (*then £177,500*) with premium on 23 Oct 1982 at Sotheby's in Manhattan, for the Chippendale side chair attributed to Thomas Affleck of Philadelphia, USA and made in *c.* 1770.

CIGARETTE CARD
The most valuable card is one of the 6 known baseball series cards of Honus Wagner, who was a non-smoker, which was sold in New York in December 1981 for $25,000 (*then £13,900*).

DOLLS
The highest price at auction for a doll is £24,200 for a 'dimple-cheeked' "Character doll" from Kammer & Reinhart in 1909 at Sotheby's, London on 20 May 1984.

FURNITURE
The highest price ever paid for a single piece of furniture is £1,300,000 (*FF 15 million*) at Ader Picard Tajan, Monaco on 11 Nov 1984 for a mahogany and ebony collector's chest of drawers thought to have been made for Queen Marie-Antoinette (1755–1793) by G. Benneman.
The English furniture record was set by a black-japanned bureau-bookcase of *c.* 1705. Formerly owned by Queen Mary, it made $860,000 (*then £463,366*) at Christie's, New York on 18 Oct 1981. The record in the UK was set on 10 Apr 1986 when twin silver Chippendale mirrors were sold at Christie's, London for £280,000 to Roy Miles, the London dealer.

GLASS
The auction record is £520,000 for a Roman glass cage-cup of *c.* AD 300 measuring 7 in *17,78 cm* in diameter and 4 in *10,16 cm* in height, sold at Sotheby's, London, on 4 June 1979 to Robin Symes.

GOLD PLATE
The highest price for any gold artefact is £950,400 for the 22 carat font made by Paul Storr to the design of Humphrey Repton in 1797. It was sold by Lady Anne Cavendish-Bentinck and bought by Armitage of London at Christie's on 11 July 1985.

GUNS
The highest price ever paid for a single gun is £125,000 given by the London dealers F. Partridge for a French flintlock fowling piece made for Louis XIII, King of

France in *c.* 1615 and attributed to Pierre le Bourgeoys of Lisieux, France (d. 1627). This piece was included in the collection of the late William Goodwin Renwick of the United States sold by Sotheby's, London on 21 Nov 1972 (see also Pistols). It is now in the Metropolitan Museum, New York, USA.

HAT
The highest price ever paid for a hat is $66,000 (*then £34,750*) by the Alaska State Museum at a New York City auction in Nov 1981 for a Tlingit Kiksadi ceremonial frog helmet from *c.* 1600.

ICON
The record auction price for an icon is $150,000 (*then £67,500*) paid at Christie's, New York on 17 Apr 1980 for the *Last Judgement* (from the George R. Hann collection, Pittsburgh, USA) made in Novgorod in the 16th century.

JADE
The highest price ever paid for an item in jade is $396,000 (*£270,307*) (with premium) at Sotheby's, New York on 6 Dec 1983 for a mottled brownish-yellow belt-hook and pendant mask of the Warring States Period of Chinese history.

JEWELS
The highest auction price for any jewels is £2,825,000 (or £3.1 million with the buyer's premium) for two pear-shaped diamond drop earings of 58.6 and 61 carats at Sotheby's, Geneva on 14 Nov 1980. Neither the buyer nor seller was disclosed.

MUSICAL BOX
The highest price paid for a musical box is £20,900 (with premium) for a Swiss-made box made for a Persian prince in 1901, sold at Sotheby's, London on 23 Jan 1985.

PAPERWEIGHT
The highest price ever paid for a glass paperweight is £143,000 (*£97,278*) with premium at Sotheby's, New York City, USA on 2 Dec 1983 for a blue glass weight made at Pantin, Paris *post* 1850.

PISTOL
The highest price paid at auction for a pistol is £110,000 at Christie's London on 8 July 1980 for a Sadeler wheel-lock holster pistol from Munich dated *c.* 1600.

PLAYING CARDS
The highest price paid for a deck of playing cards is $143,352 (*£98,850*) (with premium) by the New York Metropolitan Museum at Sotheby's, London on 6 Dec 1983.

PORCELAIN AND POTTERY
The highest auction price for any ceramic or any Chinese work of art is £792,000 (with premium) for a blue and white Ming vase of 1426–35 bought by Hirano of Japan at Sotheby's, London on 15 Dec 1981.

POT LID
The highest price paid for a pot lid is £3300 for a seaweed patterned 'Spanish Lady' lid sold at Phillips, London on 19 May 1982.

SILVER
The highest price ever paid for silver is £612,500 for the pair of Duke of Kingston tureens made in 1735 by Meissonnier and sold by Christie's, Geneva on 8 Nov 1977. The English silver record was £484,000 at Sotheby's, London on 3 May 1984 for the Duke of Northumberland's 630 troy oz. Shield of Achilles, made in 1822 by Rundell, Bridge and Rundell. The 100 piece Paul de Lamerie service made for the seventh Earl of Thanet *c.* 1745 was sold by Lord Hothfield at Sotheby's, London on 22 Nov 1984 for £825,000 also with premium.

Antiques

RECORD AUCTION PRICES

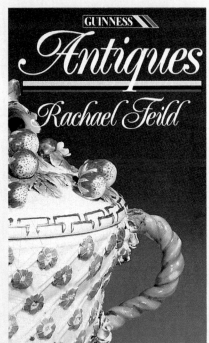

This Ming vase, over 500 years old, fetched a record price for any ceramic. Unusually tall at 20 ins *50,8 cm*, it was probably made for the then Emperor of China, Hsuan Tsung.

The record price paid for a gold artefact is 'going, going, gone'. This christening font, set on a pedestal 13¾ in *34.9 cm* square, effectively fetched £4281 per ounce. It was made for the christening of William Henry Cavendish-Gott-Bentinck in 1797. (Christies).

SNUFF BOX
The highest price ever paid for a snuff box is Sw. Fr. 1,540,000 (*then £435,028*) in a sale at Christie's, Geneva on 11 May 1982 for a gold snuff box dating from 1760–65 and once owned by Frederick the Great of Prussia. It was purchased by S. J. Phillips, the London dealers, for stock.

SPOONS
A Wiener werkstaffe spoon by Josef Hoffmann, Austria *c.* 1905, was sold at Sotheby's, London for £17,600 (with premium) on 28 Apr 1983. A set of 13 Henry VIII Apostle spoons owned by Lord Astor of Hever were sold for £120,000 on 24 June 1981 at Christie's, London.

STUFFED BIRD
The highest price ever paid for a stuffed bird is £9000. This was given on 4 Mar 1971 at Sotheby's, London, by the Iceland Natural History Museum for a specimen of the Great Auk (*Alca impennis*) in summer plumage, which was taken in Iceland *c.* 1821; this particular specimen stood 22½ in *57 cm* high. The Great Auk was a flightless North Atlantic seabird, which was finally exterminated on Eldey, Iceland in 1844, becoming extinct through hunting. The last British sightings were at Co. Waterford in 1834 and St Kilda, Western Isles *c.* 1840.

SWORD
The highest price paid for a sword is the $145,000 (*then £85,800*) paid for the gold sword of honour, presented by the Continental Congress of 1779 to General Marie Jean Joseph Lafayette, at Sotheby Parke Bernet, New York City, USA on 20 Nov 1976.

TAPESTRY
The highest price paid for a tapestry is £550,000 for a Swiss Medieval tapestry frieze in two parts dated 1468–1476 at Sotheby's, Geneva, on 10 Apr 1981 by the Basle Historische Museum.

THIMBLE
The record auction price for a thimble is £8000 paid by the London dealer Winifred Williams at Christie's, London on 3 Dec 1979 for a Meissen dentil-shaped porcelain piece of *c.* 1740.

TOY
The auction record for a toy is £25,500 for a model train set of Stephenson's *Rocket* made by Marklin of Germany in tin plate in 1909 at Sotheby's, London on 29 May 1984.

TYPEWRITER
The highest price paid for an antique machine is £3000 for an 1886 Daw and Tait machine auctioned at Sotheby's, London on 12 Dec 1980.

WALKING STICK
The highest auction price for a walking stick has been $24,200 (*then £17,285*) at Sotheby Parke Bernet, New York in 1983 for an octagonal whale ivory nobbed stick decorated by Scrimshanders in 1845.

GUINNESS

Antiques
Rachael Feild

The Antiques Pocket Price Guide is published by Guinness at £6.95.

3. AGRICULTURE

Origins

It has been estimated that only 21 per cent of the world's land surface is cultivable and that only 7.6 per cent is actually under cultivation. Evidence adduced in 1971 from Nok Nok Tha and Spirit Cave, Thailand tends to confirm plant cultivation and animal domestication was part of the Hoabinhian culture *c.* 11,000 BC. Goats were herded on Mount Carmel, Palestine as early as 16,000 BC.

Goat was domesticated at Asiab, Iran by *c.* 8050 BC and dog at Star Carr, North Yorkshire by *c.* 7700 BC: the earliest definite date for sheep is *c.* 7200 BC at Argissa-Magula, Thessaly, Greece and for pig and cattle *c.* 7000 BC at the same site. The earliest date for horse is *c.* 4350 BC from Dereivka, Ukraine, USSR. Ancient trackings sighted by a US space shuttle in 1982 indicate perhaps an even earlier domestication of draft animals.

FARMS

Earliest

The earliest dated British farming site is a Neolithic one, enclosed within the Iron Age hill-fort at Hembury, Devon, excavated during 1934–5 and now dated to 4210–3990 BC. Pollen analysis from two sites Oakhanger, Hampshire, and Winfrith Heath, Dorset (Mesolithic *c.* 5000 BC) indicates that Mesolithic man may have had herds which were fed on ivy during the winter months.

Largest *World*

The largest farms in the world are collective farms (*sovkhozes*) in the USSR. These have been reduced in number from 235,500 in 1940 to only 18,000 in 1980 and have been increased in size so that units of over 60,000 acres *25 000 ha* are not uncommon. The pioneer farm owned by Laucidio Coelho near Campo Grande, Mato Grosso, Brazil in *c.* 1901 was 3358 miles² *8700 km² 2.15 million* acres with 250,000 head of cattle at the time of his death in 1975.

Great Britain

The largest farms in the British Isles are Scottish hill farms in the Grampians. The largest arable farm is that of Elveden, Suffolk, farmed by the Earl of Iveagh. Here 11,207 acres *4535 ha* are farmed on an estate of 22,918 acres *9275 ha*, the greater part of which was formerly derelict land. The 1985 production included 10 081 tonnes *9,921 tons* of grain and 60 298 tonnes *59,345 tons* of sugar beet. The livestock includes 316 beef cattle, 1030 ewes and 5878 pigs.

Cattle station

The world's largest cattle station is the Anna Creek station of 30 113.5 km² *11,626.8 miles²*, South Australia owned by the Kidman family. It is thus 23 per cent the size of England. The biggest component is Strangway at 14 114 km² *5449 miles²*. Until 1915 the Victoria River Downs Station, Northern Territory had an area of 22,400,000 acres (35,000 miles² *90 650 km²*), the same as England's 20 largest counties put together.

Sheep station

The largest sheep station in the world is Commonwealth Hill, in the north-west of South Australia. It grazes between 60,000 and 70,000 sheep, *c.* 100 cattle and 54,000 uninvited kangaroos in an area of 4080 miles² *10 567 km²*, i.e. larger than the combined area of Norfolk and Suffolk. The head count on Sir William Stevenson's 30,000 acre *12 140 ha* Lochinver Station in New Zealand was 117,500 on 1 Jan 1983 on 21,000 acres *8500 ha*. The largest sheep move on record occurred when 27 horsemen moved a mob of 43,000 sheep 40 miles *64 km* from Barcaldine to Beaconsfield Station, Queensland, Australia, in 1886.

Rice farming

The largest contiguous wild rice (*Zizania aquatica*) farm in the world is Clearwater Rice Inc. at Clearbrook, Minnesota, USA with 2000 acres *809 ha*. In 1985 it yielded 497,563 lb *225 695 kg* the largest to date.

Turkey farm

The world's largest turkey farm is that of Bernard Matthews plc, centred at Gt Witchingham, Norfolk, with 2500 workers tending 7,900,000 turkeys.

Chicken ranch

The world's largest chicken ranch is the Croton Egg Farm, Ohio, USA which has 4.8 million hens laying some 3.7 million eggs daily.

Piggery

The world's largest piggery is the Sljeme pig unit in Yugoslavia which is able to process 300,000 pigs in a year. Even larger units may exist in Romania but details are at present lacking.

Cow shed

The longest cow shed in Britain is that of the Yorkshire Agricultural Society at Harrogate, North Yorkshire. It is 456 ft *139 m* in length with a capacity of 686 cows. The National Agricultural Centre, Kenilworth, Warwickshire, completed in 1967, has, however, capacity for 782 animals.

Foot-and-mouth disease

The worst outbreak of foot-and-mouth disease in Great Britain was that from Shropshire on 25 Oct 1967 to 25 June 1968 in which there were 2364 outbreaks and 429,632 animals slaughtered at a direct and consequential loss of £150,000,000. The outbreak of 1871, when farms were much smaller, affected 42,531 farms. The disease first appeared in Great Britain at Stratford, East London in August 1839.

Sheep shearing

The highest recorded speed for sheep shearing in a working day was that of John Fagan who machine-sheared 804 lambs (average 89.3 per hour) in 9 hr at Hautora Rd, Pio Pio, New Zealand on 8 Dec 1980. Peter Casserly of Christchurch, New Zealand, achieved a solo blade (i.e. hand-shearing) record of 353 lambs in 9 hours on 13 Feb 1976. In a shearing marathon, four men machine-shore 2519 sheep in 29 hr at Stewarts Trust, Waikia, Southland, New Zealand on 11 Feb 1982.

An earth-shattering record as Robert Dee sets the fastest time for ploughing an acre to a 9 in *22 cm* depth.

Mr Lavor Taylor (b. 27 Feb 1896) of Ephraim, Utah claims to have sheared 515,000 sheep to May 1984.

Great Britain

British records for 9 hr have been set at 555 by Roger Poyntz-Roberts (300) and John Savery (255) on 9 June 1971 (sheep caught *by* shearers), and 610 by the same pair (sheep caught *for* shearers) in July 1970.

Sheep *Survival*

The longest recorded survival by a sheep buried in snow is 50 days when Alex Maclennan uncovered 15 dead and 1 live sheep near the River Skinsdale on Mrs Tyser's, Gordonbush Estate, Sutherland, Scotland on 24 Mar 1978 during the great January blizzard.

Mushroom farm

The largest mushroom farm in the world is the Butler County Mushroom Farm, Inc, founded in 1937 in a disused limestone mine near West Winfield, Pennsylvania, USA. It employs over 1000 in a maze of underground galleries 110 miles *177 km* long, producing over 24,000 short tons *21 770 tonnes* of mushrooms per year. The French annual consumption is 7 lb *3,17 kg* per caput.

Wheat field *Largest*

The largest single fenced field sown with wheat was one of 35,000 acres *14 160 ha* sown in 1951 south west of Lethbridge, Alberta, Canada.

Vineyard *Largest*

The world's largest vineyard is that extending over the Mediterranean façade between the Rhône and the Pyrenees in the *départments* Hérault, Gard, Aude, and Pyrenées-Orientales in an area of 840 000 ha *2,075 685 acres* of which 52.3 per cent is *monoculture viticole*.

Hop field *Largest*

The largest hop field in the world is one of 1836 acres *743 ha* near Toppenish, Washington State, USA. It is owned by John I. Haas, Inc, the world's largest hop growers, with hop farms in Idaho, Oregon and Washington State, with a total net area of 3560 acres *1441 ha*.

Community garden *Largest*

The largest recorded community garden project is that operated by the City Beautiful Council, and the Benjamin Wegerzyn Garden Center, Dayton. Ohio, USA. It comprises 1173 allotments each of 812¼ ft² *74,45 m²*.

CROP YIELDS

Wheat

Crop yields for highly tended small areas are of little significance. The British record is 111.4 cwt/acre *13,99 tonnes/ha* at 15.5% moisture on a field of 43.24 acres *17,49 ha* by Gordon Rennie of Clifton Mains, Newbridge, Lothian, Scotland.

Barley

A yield of 93.7 cwt/acre *11 762 kg/ha* of Gerbel Winter Barley was achieved in Aug 1984 by the Brewster family farm at Kirknewton, Midlothian, Scotland from a 20.48 acre *8,29 ha* field.

Potato

The greatest number of US barrels picked in a 9½ hr day is 235 by Walter Sirois (b. 1917) of Caribou, Maine, USA on 30 Sept 1950.

Corn

A yield of 352.64 US bushels (15½ per cent moisture) from an acre, using De Kalb XL-54, was achieved by Roy Lynn, Jr near Kalamazoo, Michigan, USA on 30 Sept 1977.

Sugar beet

The highest recorded yield for sugar beet is 62.4 short tons (55.71 long tons) per acre *139,9 tonnes/ ha* by Andy Christensen and Jon Giannini in the Salinas Valley, California, USA.

Field-to-Loaf Record

The fastest time for producing loaves from growing wheat is 40 min 44 sec at O. S. North's Bakery at Heydon, near Royston, Hertfordshire on 10 Sept 1983.

Ploughing

The world championship (instituted 1953) has been staged in 18 countries and won by ploughmen of 11 nationalities of which the United Kingdom has been most successful with 8 championships. The only man to take the title three times has been Hugh B. Barr of Northern Ireland in 1954–5–6. The 1984 champion was Desmond Wright, 48 (Northern Ireland).

The fastest recorded time for ploughing an acre *0,404 ha* (minimum 32 right-hand turns and depth 9 in *22 cm*) is 11 min 21.8 sec by Robert Dee using a Fiat 180-90 DT tractor at Hodstock Priory Farm, Blythe, Nottinghamshire on 1 Nov 1984.

The greatest recorded acreage ploughed with a 6 furrow plough to a depth of 7 in *17,7 cm* in 24 hr is 123.4 acres *49,9 ha* by David Griffiths and Pat Neylan using a Lamborghini R-1056 DT tractor in the Nakuru District, Kenya on 6– 7 July 1978. Frank Allinson of Leyburn, N Yorks, ploughed for 250 hr 9 min 50 sec on 14– 24 Nov 1981. DMI Inc. of Goodfield, Illinois, USA marketed a 'Hydrawide' plough with 21 furrows in 1978.

Largest rick

A rick of 40,400 bales of straw was completed from 22 July to 3 Sept 1982 by Nick and Tom Parsons with a gang of 8 at Cuckoo-pen Barn Farm, Birdlip, Gloucestershire. It measured 150 × 30 × 60 ft high *45,7 × 9,1 × 18,2 m high* and weighed some 700 tons *711 tonnes*. They baled, hauled and ricked 24,200 bales in 7 consecutive days on 22–29 July.

LIVESTOCK

> Note: Some exceptionally high livestock auction sales are believed to result from collusion between buyer and seller to raise the ostensible price levels of the breed concerned. Others are marketing and publicity exercises with little relation to true market prices.

Highest Priced *Bull*

The highest price ever paid for a bull is $2,500,000 (*then £1,087,000*) for the beefalo (a ⅜ bison, ⅜ charolais, ¼ Hereford) 'Joe's Pride' sold by D. C. Basalo of Burlingame, California to the Beefalo Cattle Co of Canada, of Calgary, Alberta, Canada on 9 Sept 1974. The young 14 month old Canadian Holstein bull 'Pickland Elevation B. ET' was bought by Premier Breeders of Stamfordham, Northumberland for £233,000.

The highest price ever paid for a bull in Britain is 60,000 guineas (£63,000), paid on 5 Feb 1963 at Perth, Scotland, by James R. Dick (1928–74) co-manager of Black Watch Farms, for 'Lindertis Evulse', an Aberdeen-Angus owned by Sir Torquil and Lady Munro of Lindertis, Kirriemuir, Tayside, Scotland. This bull failed a fertility test in August 1963, thus becoming the world's most expensive piece of beef.

Cow

The highest price ever paid for a cow is $1,025,000 (*then £640,625*) for the Holstein Allendairy Glamorous Ivy by Albert Cormier of Georgetown, Ontario, Canada at Doeberiener dispersal sale at Jamestown, Pennsylvania on 20 Nov 1982. The British record is £33,600 for 'Ullswater Beatexus 8th', a British Friesian sold to The British Livestock Embryo Syndicate of Royston, Hertfordshire by Sir Keith and Lady Showering of West Horrington, Wells, Somerset on 9 May 1981 (auctioneers: Hobsons).

Sheep

The highest price ever paid for a ram is $A79,000 (*£49,500*) by the Gnowangerup Animal Breeding Centre, Western Australia for a Merino ram from the Colinsvale Stud, South Australia at the Royal Adelaide Show on 10 Sept 1981.

The British auction record is £21,000 paid by Mr W. Sheddon of Brighouse, Balmaclellan, Kirkcudbright, Scotland for A. W. Carswell & Son's Blackface ram on 4 Oct 1978.

The highest price ever paid for wool is $A187 per kg greasy (*then £111*) for a bale of Saxon Merino wool from the Launceston, Tasmania sales on 28 Feb 1986 by Fujii Keori Ltd of Osaka. This Japanese firm has been top bidders each year from 1973 to 1986 inclusive. It was sold by Jim McEwan of Trefusis, nr Ross.

Pig

The highest price ever paid for a pig is $56,000 (*then £38,356*) for a cross-bred barrow named 'Bud' owned by Jeffrey Roemisch of Hermleigh, Texas and bought by E. A. 'Bud' Olson and Phil Bonzio on 5 Mar 1983. The UK record is 3300 guineas (£3465), paid by Malvern Farms for the Swedish Landrace gilt 'Bluegate Ally 33rd' owned by Davidson Trust in a draft sale at Reading, Berkshire on 2 Mar 1955.

Horse

The highest price for a draught horse is $47,500 (*£9970*) paid for the 7-year-old Belgian stallion 'Farceur' by E. G. Good at Cedar Falls, Iowa, USA on 16 Oct 1917. A Welsh mountain pony stallion 'Coed Cock Bari' was sold to an Australian builder in Wales in September 1978 for 21,000 guineas (*then £22,050*).

Donkey

Perhaps the lowest ever price for livestock was at a sale at Kuruman, Cape Province, South Africa in 1934 where donkeys were sold for less than 2p each.

Heaviest *Cattle*

Of heavyweight cattle the heaviest on record was a Holstein-Durham cross named 'Mount Katahdin' exhibited by A. S. Rand of Maine, USA in 1906–10 and frequently weighed at an even 5000 lb *2267 kg*. He was 6 ft 2 in *1,88 m* at the shoulder with a 13 ft *3,96 m* girth and died in a barn fire *c.* 1923. The British record is the 4480 lb *2032 kg* of 'The Bradwell Ox' owned by William Spurgin of Bradwell, Essex. He was 15 ft *4,57 m* from nose to tail and had a girth of 11 ft *3,35 m* when 6 years old in 1830. The largest breed of heavyweight cattle is the Chianini, brought to Italy from the Middle East in pre-Roman times. Mature bulls average 5 ft 8 in *1,73 m* at the forequarters and weigh 2865 lb *1300 kg*. The Airedale Heifer of East Riddlesdon, nr. Keighley, South Yorkshire *c.* 1820 was 11 ft 10.6 in *3,62 m* long and weighed 2640 lb *1197,5 kg*.

The highest recorded birthweight for a calf is 225 lb *102 kg* from a British Friesian cow at Rockhouse Farm, Bishopston, Swansea, West Glamorgan, in 1961.

Pigs

The heaviest hog recorded was the Poland-China hog 'Big Bill' of 2552 lb *22¾ cwt 1157,5 kg* measuring 9 ft *2,75 m* long with a belly on the ground, owned by Burford Butler of Jackson,

Tennessee, USA and chloroformed in 1933. Raised by W. J. Chappall he was mounted and displayed in Weekly County, Tennessee until 1946. The British record is held by a Gloucester Old Spot hog of 12 cwt 66 lb *639,5 kg* bred by Joseph Lawton and possibly owned by Joseph Bradbury of Little Haywood, Staffordshire. In 1774 it stood 4 ft 8½ in *1,43 m* in height and was 9 ft 8 in *2,94 m* long. The highest recorded weight for a piglet at weaning (8 weeks) is 81 lb *36,7 kg* for a boar, one of nine piglets farrowed on 6 July 1962 by the Landrace gilt 'Manorport Ballerina 53rd', *alias* 'Mary', and sired by a Large White named 'Johnny' at Kettle Lane Farm, West Ashton, Trowbridge, Wiltshire.

Sheep
The highest recorded birthweight for a lamb in the world is 38 lb *17,2 kg* at Clearwater, Sedgwick County, Kansas, USA in 1975, but neither this lamb nor the ewe survived.

Broiler growth
The record for growth for flocks of at least 2400 at 56 days is 2,901 kg *6.396 lb* with a conversion rate of 2.17 by D. B. Marshall (Newbridge) Ltd of Newbridge, Midlothian, Scotland reported in October 1981.

Prolificacy *Cattle*
On 25 Apr 1964 it was reported that a cow named 'Lyubik' had given birth to seven calves at Mogilev, USSR. Five live and one dead calf were recorded from a Fresian at Te Puke, North Island, New Zealand on 27 July 1980 but none survived. A case of five live calves at one birth was reported in 1928 by T. G. Yarwood of Manchester. The life-time prolificacy record is 30 in the case of a cross-bred cow owned by G. Page of Warren Farm, Wilmington, East Sussex, which died in November 1957, aged 32. A cross-Hereford calved in 1916 and owned by A. J. Thomas of West Hook Farm, Marloes, Dyfed, Wales, produced her 30th calf in May 1955 and died in May 1956, aged 40.

'Soender Jylland's Jens' a Danish black and white bull left 220,000 surviving progeny by artificial insemination when he was put down aged 11 in Copenhagen in September 1978. 'Bendalls Adema', a Friesian bull, died aged 14 at Clondalkin, County Dublin, Ireland on 8 Nov 1978 having sired an estimated 212,000 progeny by artificial insemination.

Pigs
The highest recorded number of piglets in one litter is 34, thrown on 25–26 June 1961 by a sow owned by Aksel Egedee of Denmark. In February 1955 a Wessex sow owned by Mrs E. C. Goodwin of Paul's Farm, Leigh, near Tonbridge, Kent, had a litter of 34, of which 30 were born dead. The highest reported number of live births in Britain is 30 by W. Ives of Dane End Fruit Farm, near Ware, Hertfordshire from a white Welsh sow in September 1979. A sow, 'Gertie' (Large White × Landrace) owned by John Caley of Selby, North Yorkshire farrowed 3 litters of 19, 19 and 23 in under 12 months (18 July 1982–20 May 1983). 55 were live born.

Sheep
A case of eight lambs at a birth was reported by D. T. Jones of Priory Farm, Gwent, in June 1956 and by Ken Towse of Buckton near Bridlington in March 1981 but none lived. A Border Leicester-Merino crossbred sheep owned by Roger Saunders gave birth to 4 ram and 3 ewe live lambs at Strathdownie, Victoria, Australia on 19 June 1984. A case of a sheep living to 26 years was recorded in flock book records by H. Poole, Wexford, Ireland.

Egg-laying
The highest authenticated rate of egg-laying is

by a white leghorn chicken hen, no. 2988 at the College of Agriculture, University of Missouri, USA, with 371 eggs in 364 days in an official test conducted by Professor Harold V. Biellier ending on 29 Aug 1979. The UK record is 353 eggs in 365 days in a National Laying Test at Milford, Surrey in 1957 by a Rhode Island Red 'Wonderful Lady' owned by W. Lawson of Welham Grange, Retford, Nottinghamshire.

The heaviest egg reported is one of 16 oz *454 g*, with double yolk and double shell, laid by a white Leghorn at Vineland, New Jersey, USA, on 25 Feb 1956. The largest recorded was one of 'nearly 12 oz' for a 5 yolked egg 12¼ in *31 cm* around the long axis and 9 in *22,8 cm* around the shorter laid by a Black Minorca at Mr Stafford's Damsteads Farm, Mellor, Lancs in 1896.

The highest recorded annual average for a flock is 313 eggs in 52 weeks from a flock of 1000 Warren-Stadler SSL layers (from 21 weeks of age) by Eric Savage, White Lane Farm, Albury, Surrey, England in 1974–5.

Most yolks
The highest claim for the number of yolks in a chicken's egg is 9 reported by Mrs Diane Hainsworth of Hainsworth Poultry Farms, Mount Morris, New York, USA in July 1971 and also from a hen in Kirghizia, USSR in August 1977.

Chicken egg
A chicken egg of 1,47 g *0.05 oz* (27 × 22 mm *1.06 × 0.86 in*) was laid by a Leghorn/Ranger cross named 'Obedience' owned by Miss Verity Nicholson of Adstock Fields Farm House, Buckingham, Bucks on 12 Mar 1986.

Goose egg
The white goose 'Speckle' owned by Donny Brandenberg, of Goshen, Ohio, USA, on 3 May 1977 laid a 24 oz *680 g* egg measuring 13½ × 9½ in *34 × 24 cm* in circumferences.

Duck
An Aylesbury duck belonging to Annette and Angela Butler of Princes Risborough, Bucks before she died on 7 Feb 1986 laid 457 eggs in 463 days including an unbroken run of 375 in as many days.

Milk yields *Cows*
The highest recorded world lifetime yield of milk is 465,224 lb (207.68 tons *211 025 kg*) by the unglamorously named cow No 289 owned by M. G. Maciel & Son of Hanford, California, USA to 1 May 1984. The greatest yield of any British cow was that given by Winton Pel Eva 2 owned by John Waring of Glebe House, Kilnwick near Pocklington with 165 tonnes. The greatest recorded yield for one lactation (maximum 365 days) is 55,661 lb *25 247 kg* by the Holstein 'Beecher Arlinda Ellen' owned by Mr and Mrs Harold L. Beecher of Rochester, Indiana, USA in 1975. The British lactation record (305 days) was set by Michaelwood Holm Emoselle 25 (b. 1 Aug 1973), a Friesian, owned by Mr & Mrs M. T. Holder of Aylesmore Farm, Newent, Gloucestershire 19 400 kg *42,769 lb* in 1984–5. The highest reported milk yield in a day is 241 lb *109,3 kg* by 'Urbe Blanca' in Cuba on or about 23 June 1982.

Hand milking
Andy Faust at Collinsville, Oklahoma, USA in 1937 achieved 120 US gal *99.92 UK gal* in 12 hr.

Goats
The highest recorded milk yield for any goat is 7714 lb *3499 kg* in 365 days by 'Osory Snow-Goose' owned by Mr and Mrs G. Jameson of Leppington, N.S.W., Australia in 1977. A 15 year old goat owned by Mrs Nanbui Meghani of

Bhuj, Gujarat, India was reported in Nov 1984 to have lactated continuously for 12 years.

Butter fat yield
The world record lifetime yield is 16,370 lb *7425 kg* by the US Holstein 'Breezewood Patsy Bar Pontiac' in 3979 days (see left also for yield record). Her lactation record for 365 days of 2230 lb *1011 kg* was reported on 8 Oct 1976. The British record butter fat yield in a lifetime is 12,166 lb *5518 kg* by the Ayrshire cow 'Craighead Welma' owned by W. Watson Steele from 273,072 lb at 4.45 per cent. The British record for 365 days is 761 kg *1677.7 lb* by 'Crookgate Aylwinia 7' a Friesian, owned by J. V. Machin of Hill Farm, Penley near Wrexham, Clwyd, set on 5 May 1973. The United Kingdom record for butter fat in one day is 9.30 lb *4,218 kg* (79 lb *35,8 kg* milk at 11.8 per cent) by Queens Letch Farms' Guernsey Cow 'Thisbe's Bronwen of Trewollack'.

Cheese
The most active cheese-eaters are the people of France, with an annual average in 1983 of 19,8 kg *43.6 lb* per person. The world's biggest producer is the United States with a factory production of 4,773,500,000 lbs (2,165,000 tons *2 200 000 tonnes*) in 1980. The UK cheese consumption in 1984 was 6,2 kg *13.67 lb* per head.

Oldest
The oldest and most primitive cheeses are the Arabian *kishk*, made of dried curd of goats' milk. There are today 450 named cheeses in 18 major varieties, but many are merely named after different towns and differ only in shape or the method of packing. France has 240 varieties.

Most expensive
The world's most expensive cheese in its home market is Le Leruns made from Ewes milk at 90 francs per kilo (now *£3.40 per lb*). Cheese made to the Liederkranz formula in Van Wert, Ohio, USA retails for $2.25 per 4 oz; equivalent to $9.00 (*£6.40*) per lb. Britain's most costly traditional cheese is Blue Wensleydale which has no fixed price but is obtainable from some shops for between £2.80 and £3.90 per lb.

Largest
The largest cheese ever made was a cheddar of 34,591 lb *15 190 kg* made in 43 hr on 20–22 Jan 1964 by the Wisconsin Cheese Foundation for exhibition at the New York World's Fair, USA. It was transported in a specially designed tractor trailer 'Cheese Mobile' 45 ft *13,71 m* long.

CHICKEN PLUCKING
Ernest Hausen (1877–1955) of Fort Atkinson, Wisconsin, USA, died undefeated after 33 years as a champion. On 19 Jan 1939 he was timed at 4.4 sec and reputedly twice did 3.5 sec a few years later.

The record time for plucking 12 chickens clean by a team of 4 women at the annual Chicken Plucking Championship at Masaryktown, Florida, USA is 32.9 sec set on 9 Oct 1976 by Doreena Cary, Diane Grieb, Kathy Roads and Dorothy McCarthy.

TURKEY PLUCKING
Vincent Pilkington of Cootehill, County Cavan, Ireland killed and plucked 100 turkeys in 7 hr 32 min on 15 Dec 1978. His record for a single turkey is 1 min 30 sec on RTE Television in Dublin on 17 Nov 1980.

On 23 May 1983 Joe Glaub (USA) killed 7300 turkeys in a 'working' day. Mrs Madge Colenso gutted 94 turkeys in 60 mins at Rivington Farm, Burstow, Horley, Surrey on 20 Dec 1984.

CHAPTER TEN

HUMAN
ACHIEVEMENTS

Not exactly 'look no hands' as 16 members of the Mito Cycle Club travelled 50 m *164 ft* on one bicycle; 14 are visible here, including the human crossbar. (*See p. 165*).

(*See p. 165*)

1. ENDURANCE AND ENDEAVOUR

Lunar conquest

Neil Alden Armstrong (b. Wapakoneta, Ohio, USA of Scottish (*via* Ireland) and German ancestry, on 5 Aug 1930), command pilot of the Apollo XI mission, became the first man to set foot on the Moon on the Sea of Tranquility at 02.56 and 15 sec GMT on 21 July 1969. He was followed out of the Lunar Module *Eagle* by Col. Edwin Eugene Aldren, Jr, USAF (b. Glen Ridge, New Jersey, USA of Swedish, Dutch and British ancestry, on 20 Jan 1930), while the Command Module *Columbia* piloted by Lt Col Michael Collins, USAF (b. Rome, Italy, of Irish and pre-Revolutionary American ancestry, on 31 Oct 1930) orbited above.

Eagle landed at 20.17 and 42 sec GMT on 20 July and lifted off at 17.54 GMT on 21 July, after a stay of 21 hr 36 min. The Apollo XI had blasted off from Cape Canaveral, Florida at 13.32 GMT on 16 July and was a culmination of the US space programme which, at its peak, employed 376,600 people and attained in the year 1966–7 a peak budget of $5,900,000,000 (*then £2460 million*).

There is evidence that Pavel Belyayev was the cosmonaut selected by the USSR for a manned circumlunar flight in *Zond 7* on 9 Dec 1968, 12 days before the Apollo VIII flight but no launch took place.

Altitude *Man*

The greatest altitude attained by man was when the crew of the ill-fated Apollo XIII were at apocynthion (*i.e.* their furthest point) 158 miles *254 km* above the lunar surface and 248,655 miles *400 187 km* above the Earth's surface at 1.21 a.m. BST on 15 Apr 1970. The crew were Capt. James Arthur Lovell, Jr USN (b. Cleveland, Ohio, 25 Mar 1928), Fred Wallace Haise Jr (b. Biloxi, Miss., USA, 14 Nov 1933) and the late John L. Swigert (1931–82).

Altitude *Woman*

The greatest altitude attained by a woman is 340 km *211 miles* by Pilot-Cosmonaut of the USSR Svetlana Savitskaya (b. 1948) during her flight in *Soyuz T7* on 19–27 Aug 1982. The record in an aircraft is 24 336 m *79,842 ft* by Natalia Prokhanova (USSR) (b. 1940) in an E-33 jet, on 22 May 1965.

Speed *Man*

The fastest speed at which humans have travelled is 24,791 mph *39 897 km/h* when the Command Module of Apollo X carrying Col (*now* Brig Gen) Thomas Patten Stafford, USAF (b. Weatherford, Okla. 17 Sept 1930), and Cdr Eugene Andrew Cernan (b. Chicago, 14 Mar 1934) and Cdr (*now* Capt) John Watts Young, USN (b. San Francisco, 24 Sept 1930), reached this maximum value at the 400,000 ft *121,9 km* altitude interface on its trans-Earth return flight on 26 May 1969.

Speed *Woman*

The highest speed ever attained by a woman is 28 115 km/h *17,470 mph* by Jnr Lt (now Lt Col) Valentina Vladimirovna Tereshkova-Niko-layev (b. 6 Mar 1937) of the USSR in *Vostok 6* on 16 June 1963. The highest speed ever achieved by a woman aircraft pilot is 2687,42 km/h *1669.89 mph* by Svetlana Savitskaya (USSR) reported on 2 June 1975.

Land speed *Man*

The highest reputed land speed is 739.666 mph *1190,377 km/h* or Mach 1.0106 by Stan Barrett (US) in *The Budweiser Rocket*, a rocket engined 3 wheeled car at Edwards Air Force Base, California on 17 Dec 1979 (see also p. 125).

The *official* one mile land speed record is 633.468 mph *1019,467 km/h* set by Richard

Noble OBE (b. 1946) on 4 Oct 1983 over the Black Rock Desert, north Nevada, USA in his 17 000 lb thrust Rolls Royce Avon 302 jet powered *Thrust 2*, designed by John Ackroyd.

The highest land speed attained in Britain is 263.92 mph *424,74 km/h* by Richard Noble in *Thrust 2* at Greenham Common, Berkshire on 25 Sept 1980.

Land speed *Women*
The highest land speed recorded by a woman is 524.016 mph *843,323 km/h* by Mrs Kitty Hambleton *née* O'Neil (US) in the 48,000 hp rocket-powered 3-wheeled S.M.1 *Motivator* over the Alvard Desert, Oregon, USA on 6 Dec 1976. Her official two-way record was 512.710 mph *825,126 km/h* and she probably touched 600 mph *965 km/h* momentarily.

Water speed *Man*
The highest speed ever achieved on water is an estimated 300 knots (345 mph *556 km/h*) by Kenneth Peter Warby, MBE, (b. 9 May 1939) on the Blowering Dam Lake, NSW, Australia on 20 Nov 1977 in his unlimited hydroplane *Spirit of Australia*. The official world water speed record is 514,389 km/h *319.627 mph 277.57 knots* set on 8 Oct 1978 by Warby on Blowering Dam Lake.

Woman
The fastest woman on water is Mary Rife (USA), who has driven her drag boat *Proud Mary* at more than 190 mph *305 km/h*.

Water speed *Propeller driven*
The highest speed recorded by a propeller-driven boat is 229.00 mph *368,54 km/h* by *The Texan*, a Kurtis Top Fuel Hydro Drag Boat, driven by Eddie Hill on 5 Sept 1982 at Chowchilla, California, U.S.A.

Most travelled *Man*
The man who had visited more countries than anyone was Jesse Hart Rosdail (1914–77) of Elmhurst, Illinois, USA, a 5th grade teacher. Of all the separately administered countries and territories listed in the *UN Population Report*, he had visited all excepting only North Korea and French Antarctic Territories. He estimated his mileage to visit 215 countries was 1,626,605 statute miles *2 617 766 km*.

Fred Jurgen Specovius (b. 1942) (West Germany) and Georgio Ricatto (b. 1934) (Italy)

have both visited all 170 sovereign countries. Specovius has also visited all the non-sovereign territories except 6, 3 more than Ricatto.

The most travelled member of the Travellers Century Club of Los Angeles (limited to those who have visited 100 or more countries) is G. Parke Thompson of Akron, Ohio. His blanket coverage of the world lacks only Pitcairn Is. and the four Antarctic territories.

Horseback
The most travelled man in the horseback era was probably the Methodist preacher Francis Asbury (b. Birmingham, England), who travelled 264,000 miles *424 850 km* in North America from 1771 to 1815 preaching 16,000 sermons.

After an initial trial with a rope attached, the first free flight in a hot air balloon, in November 1783, lasted 22 minutes. The pioneer pilot de Rozier was killed two years later attempting to cross the channel. (Mary Evans).

Most isolated *Man*
The farthest any human has been removed from his nearest living fellow man is 2233.2 miles *3596,4 km* in the case of the Command Service Module pilot Alfred M. Worden on the US Apollo XV lunar mission of 30 July–1 Aug 1971.

Passport Records
The world's most expensive passports are those from the USSR. In Feb 1982 an emigration permit was 220 roubles (£172) or up to 3500 roubles (over £2700) on the black market. If applications involved a whole family or travel to the West, the necessary accompanying visa was refused 996 times in each 1000 applications.

Round the World
The fastest time for a round the world trip on scheduled flights for a circumnavigation is 44 hr 6 min by David J. Springbett (b. 2 May 1938) of Taplow, Buckinghamshire, from Los Angeles eastabout *via* London, Bahrain, Singapore, Bangkok, Manila, Tokyo and Honolulu on 8–10 Jan 1980 over a 23,068 mile *37 124 km* route.

The FAI rates any flight taking off and landing at the same point, which is as long as the Tropic of Cancer (viz 22,858.754 miles 36 787,599 km) as a circumnavigational flight.

LONGEST WALKS
The first person reported to have 'walked round the world' is George Matthew Schilling (USA) from 3 Aug 1897 to 1904, but the first verified achievement was by David Kunst (b. 1939) (USA) from 10 June 1970 to 5 Oct 1974. Tomas Carlos Pereira (b. Argentine, 16 Nov 1942) spent ten years, 6 Apr 1968–8 Apr 1978, walking 29,825 miles *48,000 km* around all five continents. George Meegan (b. 2 Oct 1952) from Rainham, Kent, England walked 19,019 miles *30 431 km* from Ushuaia, the southern tip of South America to Prudhoe Bay in Northern Alaska, taking 2426 days from 26 Jan 1977 to 18 Sept 1983, and thus completed the first traverse of the Western Hemisphere. Sean Eugene Maguire (b. USA 15 Sept 1956) walked 7327 miles *11791 km* from the Yukon River, north of Livengood, Alaska, to Key West, Florida, USA, in 307 days, 6 June 1978–9 April 1979. The Trans-Canada (Halifax to Vancouver) record walk of 3764 miles *6057 km* is 96 days by Clyde McRae, 23, from 1 May to 4 Aug 1973.

MILESTONES IN ABSOLUTE HUMAN ALTITUDE RECORDS

Altitude Ft	m	Pilot	Vehicle	Place	Date	
80*	24	Jean François Pilâtre de Rozier (1757–1785) (France)	Hot Air Balloon (tethered)	Fauxbourg, Paris	15 & 17 Oct	1783
c.330	c.100	de Rozier and the Marquis d'Arlandes (1742–1809) (France)	Hot Air Balloon (free flight)	LaMuette, Paris[1]	21 Nov	1783
c.3000	c.900	Dr Jacques-Alexander-Cesar Charles (1746–1823) and Ainé Robert (France)	Charliere Hydrogen Balloon	Tuileries, Paris	1 Dec	1783
c.9000	c.2750	Dr J.-A.-C. Charles (France)	Hydrogen Balloon	Nesles, France	1 Dec	1783
c.13,000	c.4000	James Sadler (GB)	Hydrogen Balloon	Manchester	May	1785
25,400[2]	7740	James Glaisher (1809–1903) (UK)	Hydrogen Balloon	Wolverhampton	17 July	1862
31,500	9615	Prof. A. Berson (Germany)	Hydrogen Balloon Phoenix	Strasbourg, France	4 Dec	1894
36,565	11 145	Sadi Lecointe (France)	Nieuport Aircraft	Issy-les-Moulineaux, France	30 Oct	1923
51,961	15 837	Prof. Auguste Piccard and Paul Kipfer (Switzerland)	FNRS I Balloon	Augsburg, Germany	27 May	1931
72,395	22 066	Capts Orvill A. Anderson and Albert W. Stevens (US Army Air Corps)	US Explorer II Helium Balloon	Rapid City, South Dakota, USA	11 Nov	1935
79,600	24 262	William Barton Bridgeman (USA)	US Douglas D558—11 Skyrocket	California, USA	15 Aug	1951
126,200	38 465	Capt Iven C. Kincheloe, Jr (USAF)	US Bell X-2 Rocket 'plane	California, USA	7 Sept	1956
169,600	51 694	Joseph A. Walker (USA)	US X-15 Rocket 'plane	California, USA	30 Mar	1961
Statute miles	**Km**					
203.2	327	Flt-Major Yuriy A. Gagarin (USSR) (1934–68)	USSR Vostok I Capsule	Orbital flight	12 Apr	1961
234,672		Col Frank Borman, USAF, Capt James Arthur Lovell, Jr, USN and Major William A. Anders, USAF	US Apollo VIII Command Module	Circum-lunar flight	25 Dec	1968
248,655	400 171	Capt James Arthur Lovell Jr, USN, Frederick Wallace Haise Jr and John L. Swigert Jr (1931–82)	US Apollo XIII	Abortive lunar landing mission	15 Apr	1970

* There is some evidence that Father Bartolomeu de Gusmo flew in his hot-air balloon in his 4th experiment post August 1709 in Portugal.
* There is some evidence that Father Bartolomeu de Gusmo flew in his hot-air balloon in his 4th experiment post August 1709 in Portugal.
[2] Glaisher, with Henry Tracey Coxwell (1819–1900) claimed 37,000 ft 11 275 m from Wolverhampton on 5 Sept 1862. Some writers accept 30,000 ft 9145 m.
Note: A complete progressive table comprising entries from 1783 to date was published in the 23rd edition of 1977.

PROGRESSIVE SPEED RECORDS

Speed m.p.h.	Km/h	Person and Vehicle	Place	Date	
25	40	Sledging	Heinola, Finland	c. 6500 BC	
35	55	Horse-riding	Anatolia, Turkey	c. 1400 BC	
45	70	Mountain Sledging	Island of Hawaii (now USA)	ante AD	1500
50	80	Ice Yachts (earliest patent)	Netherlands	AD	1600
56.75	95	Grand Junction Railway 2–2–2: *Lucifer*	Madeley Banks, Staffs, England	13 Nov	1830
87.8	141,3	Tommy Todd, downhill skier	La Porte, California, USA	Mar	1873
90.0	144,8	Midland Railway 4–2–2 7 ft 9 in *2,36 m* single	Ampthill, Bedford, England	Mar	1897
130.61	210,2	Siemens and Halske electric engine	Marienfeld-Zossen, near Berlin	27 Oct	1903
c.150	c.257,5	Frederick H. Marriott (fl. 1957) Stanley Steamer *Wogglebug*	Ormond Beach, Florida, USA	26 Jan	1907
210.64	339	Sadi Lecointe (France) Nieuport-Delage 29	Villesauvage, France	25 Sept	1921
415.2	668,2	Flt Lt (Later Wing Cdr) George Hedley Stainforth AFC *Supermarine S.6B*	Lee-on-Solent, England	29 Sept	1931
623.85	1004	Flugkapitan Heinz Dittmar *Me. 163V–1*	Peenemunde, Germany	2 Oct	1941
670	1078	Capt Charles Elwood Yeager, USAF *Bell XS–1*	Muroc Dry Lake, California, USA	14 Oct	1947
967	1556	Capt Charles Elwood Yeager, USAF *Bell XS–1*	Muroc Dry Lake, California, USA	26 Mar	1948
2905	4675,1	Major Robert M. White, North American *X–15*	Muroc Dry Lake, California, USA	7 Mar	1961
c.17,560	c.28 260	Flt Maj Yuriy Alekseyevich Gagarin, *Vostok I*	Earth orbit	12 Apr	1961
24,226	38 988	Col Frank Borman, USAF, Capt James Arthur Lovell, Jr, USN, Major William A. Anders, USAF *Apollo VIII*	Trans-lunar injection	21 Dec	1968
24,790.8	39 897,0	Cdrs Eugene Andrew Cernan and John Watts Young, USN and Col Thomas P. Stafford, USAF *Apollo X*	Re-entry after lunar orbit	26 May	1969

Note: *A complete progressive table comprising entries from pre-historic times to date was published in the 23rd edition of 1977.*

John Lees (b. 23 Feb 1945) of Brighton, East Sussex, England between 11 Apr and 3 June 1972, walked 2876 miles *4628 km* across the USA from City Hall, Los Angeles to City Hall, New York City in 53 days 12 hr 15 min (average 53.75 miles *86,49 km* a day).

The longest continuous walk in Britain is one of 6824 miles *10 982 km*, around the British coast by John N. Merrill (b. 19 Aug 1943), from 3 Jan to 8 Nov 1978. The feminine record was set over 3524 miles *5671 km* by Mrs Vera Andrews of Clacton-on-Sea, Essex on 31 Mar–8 Nov 1984.

North Pole conquest
The claims of neither of the two US Arctic explorers, Dr Frederick Albert Cook (1865–1940) nor Cdr (later Rear Ad.) Robert Edwin Peary (1856–1920), of the US Naval Civil Engineering branch in reaching the North Pole are subject to positive proof. Cook accompanied by the Eskimos, Ah-pellah and Etukishook, two sledges and 26 dogs, struck north from a point 60 miles *96,5 km* north of Svartevoeg, on Axel Heiberg I., Canada, 460 miles *740 km* from the Pole on 21 Mar 1908, allegedly reaching Lat. 89° 31′ N on 19 Apr and the Pole on 21 Apr. Peary, accompanied by his Negro assistant, Matthew Alexander Henson (1866–1955) and the four Eskimos, Ooqueah, Eginwah, Seegloo and Ootah (1875–1955), struck north from his Camp Bartlett (Lat. 87° 44′ N.) at 5 a.m. on 2 Apr 1909. After travelling another 134 miles *215 km*, he allegedly established his final camp, Camp Jessup, in the proximity of the Pole at 10 a.m. on 6 Apr and marched a further 42 miles *67,5 km* quartering the sea-ice before turning south at 4 p.m. on 7 Apr. On excellent pack ice and modern sledges Wally Herbert's 1968–9 Expedition (see below) attained a best day's route mileage of 23 miles *37 km* in 15 hr. Cook claimed 26 miles *41,8 km* twice while Peary claimed a surely unsustainable average of 38 miles *61 km* for 8 consecutive days.

The earliest indisputable attainment of the North Pole over the sea-ice was at 3 p.m. (Central Standard Time) on 19 Apr 1968 by Ralph Plaisted (US) and three companions after a 42-day trek in four Skidoos (snow-mobiles). Their arrival was independently verified 18 hr later by a US Air Force weather aircraft. The sea bed is 13,410 ft *4087 m* below the North Pole.

Naomi Uemura (1941–1984) the Japanese explorer and mountaineer became the first person to reach the North Pole in a solo trek across the Arctic Ice Cap at 4.45 a.m., GMT on 1 May 1978. He had travelled 450 miles 725 km setting out on 7 Mar from Cape Edward, Ellesmere Island in northern Canada. He averaged nearly 8 miles *13 km* per day with his sled 'Aurora' drawn by 17 huskies.

The first women to set foot on the North Pole was Mrs Fran Phipps, wife of the Canadian bush pilot Weldy Phipps on 5 Apr 1971. Galina Aleksandrovna Lastovskaya (b. 1941) and Lilia Vladislavovna Minina (b. 1959) were crew members of the USSR atomic icebreaker *Arktika* which reached the Pole on 17 Aug 1977.

The soviet scientist Dr Pavel A. Gordienko and 3 companions were arguably the first ever to stand on the exact point Lat. 90° 00′ 00″ N (+ 300 metres) on 23 Apr 1948.

South Pole conquest
The first men to cross the Antarctic circle (Lat. 66° 33′ S.) were the 193 crew of the *Resolution* (462 tons/*tonnes*) (Capt James Cook RN (1728–79) and *Adventure* (336 tons/*tonnes*) (Lt T. Furneaux) on 17 Jan 1773 in 39° E. The first person known to have sighted the Antarctic ice shelf was Capt. F. F. Bellinghausen (Russian) (1778–1852) on 27 Jan 1820 from the vessels *Vostock* and *Mirnyi*. The first known to have sighted the mainland of the continent was Capt William Smith (1790–1847) and Master Edward Bransfield, RN, in the brig *Williams*. They saw the peaks of Trinity Land 3 days later on 30 Jan 1820.

The South Pole (alt. 9186 ft *2779 m* on ice and 336 ft *102 m* bed rock) was first reached at 11 a.m. on 16 Dec 1911 by a Norwegian party led by Capt. Roald Engebereth Gravning Amundsen (1872–1928), after a 53-day march with dog sledges from the Bay of Whales, to which he had penetrated in the *Fram*. Subsequent calculations showed that Olav Olavson Bjaaland (the last survivor, dying in June 1961, aged 88) and Helmer Hanssen probably passed within 400–600 m of the exact pole. The other two members were Sverre H. Hassell (d. 1928) and Oskar Wisting (d. 1936).

Women
The first woman to set foot on Antarctica was Mrs Karoline Mikkelsen on 20 Feb 1935. No woman stood on the South Pole until 11 Nov 1969. On that day Lois Jones, Eileen McSaveney, Jean Pearson, Terry Lee Tickhill (all US), Kay Lindsay (Australia) and Pam Young (NZ) arrived by air.

First on both Poles
Dr Albert P. Crary (USA) reached the North Pole in a Dakota aircraft on 3 May 1952. On 12 Feb 1961 he arrived at the South Pole by Sno Cat on a scientific traverse party from the McMurdo Station. He thus pre-empted David Porter by 18 years.

Arctic crossing
The first crossing of the Arctic sea-ice was achieved by the British Trans-Arctic Expedition which left Point Barrow, Alaska on 21 Feb 1968 and arrived at the Seven Island Archipelago north-east of Spitzbergen 464 days later on 29 May 1969 after a haul of 2920 statute miles *4699 km* and a drift of 700 miles *1126 km* compared with the straight line distance of 1662 miles *2674 km*. The team was Wally Herbert (leader), 34, Major Ken Hedges, 34, RAMC, Allan Gill, 38, and Dr Roy Koerner, 36 (glaciologist), and 40 huskies. The only crossing achieved in a single season was that by Fiennes and Burton (see below) from Alert via the North Pole to the Greenland Sea in open snowmobiles.

Antarctic crossing
The first surface crossing of the Antarctic continent was completed at 1.47 p.m. on 2 Mar 1958, after a trek of 2158 miles *3473 km* lasting 99 days from 24 Nov 1957, from Shackleton Base to Scott Base *via* the Pole. The crossing party of twelve was led by Dr (now Sir) Vivian Ernest Fuchs (born 11 Feb 1908). The 2600 mile *4185 km* trans-Antarctic leg from Sanae to Scott Base of the 1980–82 Trans-Globe Expedition was achieved in 66 days from 26 Oct 1980 to 11 Jan 1981 having passed through the South Pole on 23 Dec 1980. The 3 man party on snowmobiles comprised Sir Ranulph Fiennes (b. 1944), Oliver Shepard and Charles Burton.

Polar Circumnavigation (First)
Sir Ranulph Fiennes, Bt and Charles Burton of the British Trans-Globe Expedition travelled South from Greenwich (2 Sept 1979), via the South Pole (17 Dec 1980) and the North Pole (11 Apr 1982), and back to Greenwich arriving after a 35,000 mile *56 325 km* trek on 29 Aug 1982.

GUINNESS BOOK OF RECORDS HALL OF FAME

1986

TRANS-ATLANTIC AND PACIFIC MARINE RECORDS

(Compiled by Sq Ldr D. H. Clarke, DFC, AFC)

TRANS-ATLANTIC MARINE RECORDS

CATEGORY	NAME	VESSEL	START	FINISH	DURATION	DATE
Earliest Canoe	'Finn-Man' (Eskimo)	Kayak 11 ft 10 in 3,6 m	Greenland	Humber, England	Time not known	1613
Earliest Rowing	John Brown + 5 British deserters from garrison	Ship's boat c. 20 ft 6,1 m	St Helena (10 June)	Belmonte, Brazil (fastest ever row)	28 days (83 mpd)	1799
Earliest Crossing (2 men)	C. R. Webb + 1 crew (US)	Charter Oak 43 ft 13,1 m	New York	Liverpool	35 days 15 hr	1857
Earliest Trimaran (Raft)	John Mikes + 2 crew (US)	Non Pareil, 25 ft 7,62 m	New York	Southampton	51 days	1868
Earliest Solo Sailing (E–W)	Josiah Shackford (US)	15 ton gaff sloop	Bordeaux, France	Surinam (Dutch Guiana)	35 days	1786
Earliest Solo Sailing (W–E)	Alfred Johnson (US)	Centennial 20 ft 6,09 m	Glos., Mass	Wales	46 days	1876
Earliest Woman (with US husband)	Mrs Joanna Crapo (b. Scotland)	New Bedford 20 ft 6,09 m (Bermudan ketch)	Chatham, Mass.	Newlyn, Cornwall	51 days (Earliest with Bermudan rig)	1877
Earliest Single-handed race	J. W. Lawlor (US) (winner)	Sea Serpent 15 ft 4,57 m	Boston (21 June)	Coverack, Cornwall	45 days	1891
Earliest Rowing by 2 men	Georg Harboe and Frank Samuelsen (Nor)	Fox 18⅓ ft 5,58 m	New York City (6 June)	Isles of Scilly (1 Aug)	55 days (56 mpd)	1897
Fastest Solo Sailing (W–E)	J. V. T. McDonald (GB)	Inverarity 38 ft 11,58 m	Nova Scotia	Ireland	16 days (147 mpd)	1922
Earliest Canoe (with sail)	Franz Romer (Germany)	Deutscher Sport 21½ ft 6,55 m	Las Palmas	St Thomas	58 days (47 mpd)	1928
Earliest Woman Solo (East–West)	Ann Davison (GB)	Felicity Ann 23 ft 7,01 m	Portsmouth Las Palmas	Dominica (20 Nov 1952)	65 days	1952–3
Earliest Woman Solo (W–E)	Gladys Gradeley (US)	Lugger 18 ft 5,5 m	Nova Scotia	Hope Cove, Devon	60 days	1903
Earliest Woman Solo (across 2 oceans)	Anna Woolf (SA)	Zama Zulu 43 ft 13,1 m (Ferroconcrete)	Cape Town	Bowling, Scotland	8920 miles in 109 days	1976
Fastest Woman solo	Naomi James DBE	Kriter Lady 53 ft 16,15 m	Plymouth	Newport, R.I.	25 days 19 hr 12 min	1980
Fastest 2-woman crew	Annick Martin (Fr) Annie Cordelle (Fr)	Super Marches Bravo 45 ft 13,7 m	Plymouth	Newport, R.I.	21 days 4 hr 28 min	1981
Smallest West–East	Wayne Dickinson (US)	God's Tear 8 ft 11 in 2,71 m	Allerton, Mass (30 Oct)	Aranmore Is NW Eire (20 Mar)	142 days	1982–3
Smallest (East–West) (Southern)	Eric Peters (GB)	Toniky-Nou 5 ft 10½ in 1,79 m barrel	Las Palmas (25 Dec)	St Francoise, Guadaloupe (8 Feb)	46 days	1982–3
Fastest Crossing Sailing (multihull) (East–West)	Eric Tabarly (France) + 2 crew	Pen Duick IV 67 ft 20,42 m	Tenerife	Martinique	251.4 miles 404,5 km/ day (10 days 12 hours)	1968
Fastest Crossing Sailing (monohull) (East–West)	Wilhelm Hirte & crew (Ger)	Kriter II 80 ft 24,38 m	Canary Is.	Barbados	13 days 8 hr	1977
Fastest Crossing (multihull) (West–East)	Patrick Morvan (Fr) (3 crew)	Jet Services II 60 ft 18,3 m BM Sloop—Catamaran	Sandy Hook, NJ	Land's End	8 days 16 hr 36 min 375.16 mpd	1984
Fastest Crossing monohull (West–East)	Wilson Marshall (US) & crew	Atlantic 185 ft 56,38 m	Sandy Hook, NJ	Lizard, Cornwall (3054 miles)	12 days 4 hr (fastest noon to noon 341 miles)	1905
Fastest Crossing Sailing Ship (West–East)	A. Eldridge (US) and crew	Red Jacket (Clipper) 260 ft 79,24 m	Sandy Hook, NJ	Liverpool Bar	12 days 00 hr 00 min 277.7 mpd	1854
Fastest Solo East–West (Northern) (monohull)	Kazimierz Jaworski (Poland)	Spaniel II 56 ft 17,06 m	Plymouth	Newport, R.I.	19 days 13 hr 25 min	1980
Fastest East–West (Northern) monohull	Bruno Bacilieri (It) Marc Vallin	Faram Serenissima 66½ ft 20,27 m	Plymouth	Newport, R.I.	16 days 1 hr 25 min	1981
Fastest Solo East–West (Northern) (multihull)	Philip Weld (US)	Moxie 51 ft 15,54 m (Tri)	Plymouth	Newport, R.I.	17 days 23 hr 12 min	1980
Fastest Solo East–West (Southern) (monohull)	Sir Francis Chichester KBE (GB)	Gipsy Moth V 57 ft 17,37 m	Portuguese Guinea	Nicaragua	179.1 miles 288,2 km/ day (22.4 days)	1970
Fastest Ever Yacht Sail (N. route) (East–West)	Chay Blyth (GB) Rob James (GB)	Brittany Ferries GB 65½ ft 20 m (Tri)	Plymouth	Newport, R.I.	14 days 13 hr 54 min 212.1 mpd	1981
Fastest 24 Hour Run	Michael Birch (Can) +8 crew	Formula Tag (BM Sloop—Cat)	Quebec	St Malo	512.3 miles in 23 hr 42 min on 27 Aug	1984
Fastest Solo Rowing East–West	Sidney Genders, (51 years) (GB)	Khaggavisana 19¾ ft 6,02 m	Penzance, Cornwall	Miami, Florida via Antigua	37.8 miles 60,8 km/day 160 days 8 hr	1970
Fastest Solo Rowing West–East	Gérard d'Aboville (Fr)	Capitaine Cook 5,60 m 18 ft 4 in	Chatham, Mass 10 July	Ushant, France 20 Sept	71 days 23 hr 72 km 44.8 mpd	1980
Earliest Solo Rowing East–West	John Fairfax (GB)	Britannia 22 ft 6,70 m	Las Palmas (20 Jan)	Ft Lauderdale, Florida (19 July)	180 days	1969
Earliest Solo Rowing West–East	Tom McClean (Ireland)	Super Silver 20 ft 6,90 m	St John's, Newfoundland	Black Sod Bay, Ireland (27 July)	70.7 days	1969
Youngest Solo Sailing	David Sandeman (17½ years) (GB)	Sea Raider 35 ft 10,67 m	Jersey, C.I.	Newport, R.I.	43 days	1976
Oldest Solo Sailing	Monk Farnham (74 years 276 days)	Seven Bells 28 ft 8,53 m	Shannon, Ireland	Rhode Is.	72 days (3 stops)	1983
Earliest by Sailboard	Christian Marty (Fr) (Escorted by yacht Assiduous)	Sodim (type)	Dakar Senegal	Kourou Fr Guiana	37 days 16 hr 4 min (slept on board)	1981–2

TRANS-PACIFIC MARINE RECORDS

CATEGORY	NAME	VESSEL	START	FINISH	DURATION	DATE
Fastest (Trans Pac)	Bob Hanel (US) + 6 crew	Double Bullet (BM Sloop—Cat)	Los Angeles	Hawaii	7 days 7 hr 31 min 325.5 mpd	1983
Fastest Yacht (Australia–Horn)	O. K. Pennendreft (Fr) + 13 crew	Kriter II 80 ft 24,38 m	Sydney	Cape Horn	21 days (275 mpd)	1975–6
Fastest Clipper (Australia–Horn)	Capt J. N. Forbes (GB) + crew	Lightning 244 ft 74,36 m	Melbourne	Cape Horn	19 days 1 hr (315 mpd)	1854
Fastest Solo Monohull (Australia–Horn)	Philippe Jeantot (Fr)	Credit Agricole 56 ft 17,07 m	Sydney	Cape Horn	29 days 23 hr (5709 miles, = 190.6 mpd)	1982–3
Fastest seven days solo run	Philippe Jeantot (Fr)	Credit Agricole 56 ft 17,07 m	As above 8 Feb	On passage 15 Feb	Covered 1552 miles	1983
Earliest Solo (Woman)	Sharon Sites Adams (US)	Sea Sharp II 31 ft 9,45 m	Yokohama, Japan	San Diego, Cal	75 days (5911 miles)	1969
Earliest Rowing	John Fairfax (GB) Sylvia Cook (GB)	Britannia II 35 ft 10,66 m	San Francisco, Cal. 26 Apr 1971	Hayman I., Australia 22 Apr 1972	362 days	1971–2
Earliest Rowing Solo	Peter Bird, 36 (GB)	Hele-on-Britannia 32 ft 9,75 m	San Francisco 23 Aug 1982	Gt. Barrier Reef Australia 14 June 1983	294 days 9000 miles 14 480 km	1982–3
Earliest Solo (Totally Blind)	Hank Dekker (US)	Dark Star 25 ft 7 in (BM Sloop)	San Francisco	Honolulu	23 days (Braille charts, Compass and Loran)	1983
Earliest raft (shore to shore)	Vital Alsar (Sp) and 3 crew	La Balsa (Balsa logs) 42 ft 12,8 m	Guayaquil Ecuador	Mooloolaba Australia	160 days	1970

N.B.—The earliest single-handed Pacific crossings were achieved East–West by Bernard Gilboy (US) in 1882 in the 18 ft 5,48 m double-ender Pacific to Australia and West–East by Fred Rebel (Latvia) in the 18 ft 5,48 m Elaine, (from Australia) and Edward Miles (US) in the 36¾ ft 11,2 m Sturdy II (from Japan) both in 1932, the latter via Hawaii.

MARINE CIRCUMNAVIGATION RECORDS
(Compiled by Sq Ldr D. H. Clarke, DFC, AFC)

A *true* circumnavigation entails passing through two antipodal points which are at least 12,429 statute miles *20 000 km* apart. A non-stop circumnavigation is entirely self-maintained; no water supplies, equipment or replacements of any sort may be taken aboard en route.

CATEGORY	VESSEL	NAME	START	FINISH
Earliest	*Vittoria* Expedition of Fernão de Magalhães, *c.* 1480–k. 1521	Juan Sebastián de Elcano or del Cano (d. 1526) and 17 crew	Seville, Spain 20 Sept 1519	San Lucar, 6 Sept 1522 30,700 miles *49 400 km*
Earliest British	*Golden Hind* (ex *Pelican*) 100 tons/*tonnes*	Francis Drake (*c.* 1540–96) (Knighted 4 April 1581)	Plymouth, 13 Dec 1577	26 Sept. 1580
Earliest Woman	*Etoile*	Crypto-female valet of M. de Commerson, named Baré	St Malo, 1766	1769
Earliest fore-and-aft rigged vessel	*Union* 98 tons (Sloop)	John Boit Junior, 19–21, (US) and 22 crew	Newport, RI 1794 (via Cape Horn westabout)	Newport, RI 1796
Earliest Yacht	*Sunbeam* 170 ft *51,8 m* 3 Mast Topsail schooner	Lord and Lady Brassey (GB) passengers and crew	Cowes, Isle of Wight 1876	Cowes, Isle of Wight 1877
Earliest Solo	*Spray* 36¾ ft *11,20 m* gaff yawl	Capt Joshua Slocum, 51, (US) (a non-swimmer) (No 1 solo circum)	Newport, RI, *via* Magellan Straits, 24 Apr 1895	3 July 1898 46,000 miles *74 000 km*
Earliest Motor Boat	*Speejacks* 98 ft *29,87 m*	Albert Y. Gowen (US) wife and crew	New York City 1921	New York City 1922
Earliest Motor Boat (Solo)	*Mabel E. Holland* 42 ft *12,8 m* (no sails)	David Scott Cowper (GB)	Plymouth 1984 (via Panama Canal)	Plymouth 170 days 2 hr 15 min (165.7 mpd)
Earliest Woman Solo	*Mazurek* 31 ft 2 in *9,5 m* Bermudan Sloop	Krystyna Chojnowska-Liskiewicz (Poland) (No 58 solo circum)	Las Palmas 28 Mar 1976 westabout *via* Panama	Tied knot 21 Mar 1978
Earliest Woman Solo (*via* Cape Horn)	*Express Crusader* 53 ft *16,15 m* Bermuda Sloop	Naomi James (NZ/GB) (later DBE) (No 59 solo circum)	Dartmouth 9 Sept 1977 (Cape Horn 19 Mar 1978)	Dartmouth 8 June 1978 (266 days 19 hr)
Smallest Boat	*Super Shrimp* 18 ft 4 in *5,58 m* Bermuda Sloop	Shane Acton (GB) Iris Derungs (Swiss)	Cambridge, England August 1972	Cambridge, England August 1980 (E–W *via* Panama Canal)
Earliest Submerged	*US Submarine Triton*	Capt Edward L. Beach USN plus 182 crew	New London, Connecticut 16 Feb 1960	10 May 1960 39,708 miles *49 422 km*
Earliest non-stop Solo (Port to Port)	*Suhaili* 32.4 ft *9,87 m* Bermudan Ketch	Robin Knox Johnston CBE (b. 1939) (No 25 solo circum)	Falmouth, 14 June 1968	22 Apr 1969 (312 days)
Longest non-stop alone at sea	*Dar Przemysla* 46 ft 7 in *14,2 m* Ketch	Henryk Jaskula (Poland) (No 68 solo circum)	Gdynia 1979 (W–E via Cape Horn)	Gdynia 1980 (344 days)
Fastest Solo (speed)	*Manureva* (ex *Pen Duick IV*) 70 ft *21,33 m* Trimaran	Alain Colas (France) (No 40 solo circum)	Saint Malo *via* Sydney	29 Mar 1974 30,067 miles *48 387 km* in 169 days 4 hr 11 min = 177.7 mpd
Earliest solo in both directions	*Solitaire* 34 ft *10,36 m* Bermudan Sloop	Leslie Thomas Powles (GB) (No 62 & 71 solo circum)	Falmouth 1975 (E–W) Lymington 1980 (W–E)	(via Panama) Lymington 1978 (via Horn) Lymington 1981
Earliest solo in both directions (*via* Horn)	*Ocean Bound* 41 ft 1 in *12,52 m* Bermudan Sloop	David Scott Cowper (GB) (No 66 & 78 solo circum)	Plymouth 1979 (W–E) Plymouth 1981 (E–W)	Plymouth 1980 Plymouth 1982 (see below)
Fastest Solo non-stop (Time and speed)	*American Promise* 60 ft *18,3 m* Bermudan Sloop	Dodge Morgan (US)	Bermuda 12 Nov 1985 (W–E *via* Horn)	Bermuda 11 Apr 1986 25,671 miles *41 312 km* in 150 days 1 hr 6 min = 171.1 mpd
Fastest time and fastest speed (yacht)	*Flyer* 76 ft *23,1 m* Bermudan Sloop	Cornelis von Rietschoten (Dutch) (and 15 crew)	Portsmouth 29 Aug 1981 (W–E *via* Cape Horn)	29 Mar 1982 120 days 6 hr 35 min (220.7 mpd)
Fastest (clipper)	*James Baines* 266 ft *81,07 m*	Capt C. McDonald (GB) and crew	Liverpool to Melbourne (58 days) 1854	Melbourne to Liverpool (69 days) 1855
Fastest Solo Westabout (*via* Cape Horn)	*Ocean Bound* 41 ft 1 in *12,52 m* Bermudan sloop	David Scott Cowper (GB) (No 78 solo circum)	Plymouth 22 Sept 1981 (south of 5 capes)	Plymouth 17 May 1982 (221 sailing days) 31,350 miles *50 451 km* av 141.85 mpd
Fastest-ever time (yacht)	*Awahnee II* 53 ft *16,15 m* Bermuda Cutter	Bob Griffith (US) (5 crew)	Bluff, NZ. 1970 (W–E *via* Horn)	Bluff, NZ, 1971 (88 sailing days plus 23 days stopovers)
Fastest-ever time (clipper)	*Red Jacket* 260 ft *79,24 m*	Capt S. Reid (GB) and crew	From/to Lat 26° 25′ W (*via* Horn)	62 days 22 hr 1854
Earliest Solo Double circumnavigation	*Perie Banou* 33 ft 7 in *10,24 m* Bermudan Sloop	Jon Sanders (Australia) (No 75 & 81 solo circum)	Fremantle 1981 (W–E) (continuously at sea but not non-stop)	(via Horn) Fremantle 1982 (via Plymouth) 420 days 1982

* Eduard Roditi, author of *Magellan of the Pacific*, advances the view that Magellan's slave, Enrique, was the first circumnavigator. He had been purchased in Malacca and it was shown that he already understood the Filipino dialect Vizayan, when he reached the Philippines from the east. He 'tied the knot' off Limasawa on 28 Mar 1521. The first to circumnavigate in both directions was Capt Tobias Furneaux, RN (1735–81) as second lieutenant aboard the *Dolphin* from/to Plymouth east to west *via* the Magellan Straits in 1766–68 and as captain of the *Adventure* from/to Plymouth west to east *via* Cape Horn in 1772–4.

Longest sledge journeys

The longest totally self-supporting Polar sledge journey ever made was one of 1080 miles *1738 km* from West to East across Greenland on 18 June to 5 Sept 1934 by Capt M. Lindsay (1905–1981) (later Sir Martin Lindsay of Dowhill, Bt, CBE, DSO), ever later Sir Arthur S. T. Godfrey, RE, (later Lt Col, k. 1942), Andrew N. C. Croft (later Col, DSO) and 49 dogs. The Ross Sea Party of 10 (3 died) sledged over 2000 miles *3220 km* in the period of 300 days from 6 May 1975.

Greatest ocean descent

The record ocean descent was achieved in the Challenger Deep of the Marianas Trench, 250 miles *400 km* south-west of Guam, in the Pacific Ocean, when the Swiss-built US Navy bathyscaphe *Trieste*, manned by Dr Jacques Piccard (b. 1914) (Switzerland) and Lt Donald Walsh, USN, reached the ocean bed 35,820 ft (6.78 miles *10 917 m*) down, at 1.10 p.m. on 23 Jan 1960 (see page 58). The pressure of the water was 16,883 lbf/in² *1183 kgf/cm²* and the temperature 37.4° F *3° C*. The descent required 4 hr 48 min and the ascent 3 hr 17 min.

Deep diving records

The record depth for the extremely dangerous activity of breath-held diving is 105 m *344 ft* by Jacques Mayol (France) off Elba, Italy, in December 1983 for men and 147½ ft *45 m* by Giuliana Treleani (Italy) off Cuba in September 1967 for women. Mayol descended on a sled in 104 sec and ascended in 90 sec. The record dive with Scuba (self-contained under-water breathing apparatus) is 437 ft *133 m* by John J. Gruener and R. Neal Watson (USA) off Freeport, Grand Bahama on 14 Oct 1968. The record dive utilizing gas mixtures (nitrogen, oxygen and helium) is a simulated dive of 2250 ft *685,8 m* in a dry chamber by Stephen Porter, Len Whitlock and Erik Kramer at the Duke University

The controversial Reverend Moon officiated over the largest mass wedding ceremony involving 5837 couples from 83 different countries. Few details are known of the 'honeymoonies'. (Rex Features).

Medical Center in Durham, North Carolina on 3 Feb 1981 in a 43 day trial in a sphere of 8 ft *2,43 m*. Patrick Raude and 5 Comex divers left and returned to the bell 'Petrel' at 501 m *1643 ft*, off Cavalaire, France, in 1982.

Deepest underwater escapes
The deepest underwater rescue achieved was of the *Pisces III* in which Roger R. Chapman, 28 and Roger Mallinson, 35 were trapped for 76 hr when it sank to 1575 ft *480 m* 150 miles *240 km* south-east of Cork, Ireland on 29 Aug 1973. She was hauled to the surface by the cable ship *John Cabot* after work by Pisces V, Pisces II and the remote control recovery vessel US CURV on 1 Sept. The greatest depth of an actual escape without any equipment has been from 225 ft *68,58 m* by Richard A. Slater from the rammed submersible *Nekton Beta* off Catalina Island, California, USA on 28 Sept 1970.

Deepest salvage
The greatest depth at which salvage has been achieved is 16,500 ft *5029 m* by the bathyscaphe *Trieste II* (Lt Cdr Mel Bartels, USN) to attach cables to an 'electronic package' on the sea bed 400 miles *645 km* north of Hawaii on 20 May 1972. Project Jennifer by USS *Glomar Explorer* in June/July 1974 to recover a Golf class USSR submarine, 750 miles *1200 km* NW of Hawaii, cost $550 million but was not successful.

Flexible dress divers
The deepest salvage operation ever achieved with divers was on the wreck of HM Cruiser *Edinburgh* sunk on 2 May 1942 in the Barents Sea off Northern Norway inside the Arctic Circle in 803 ft *244,7 m* of water. Twelve divers dived on the wreck in pairs using a bell from the *Stephaniturm* (1423 tons) over 32 days under the direction of former RN officer and project director Michael Stewart from 17 Sept to 7 Oct 1981.

The 431 gold ingots were divided; £14.6 million to the USSR, £7.3 million to HM Government and some £18 million to the salvage contractors, Jessop Marine Recoveries Ltd (10%) and Wharton Williams Ltd (90%). John Rossier, 28 was the first to touch the gold. The longest decompression time was 7 days 10 hr 27 min. The £39.9 million is an all-time record but 34 bars worth £4 million were believed unrecovered.

Greatest penetration into the earth
The deepest penetration made into the ground by man is in the Western Deep Levels Mine at Carletonville, Transvaal, South Africa where a record depth of 3777 m *12,500 ft* (2.36 miles) has been attained. The rock temperature at this depth is 131° F *55° C*.

Longest on a raft
The longest recorded survival alone on a raft is 133 days (4½ months) by Second Steward Poon Lim BEM (b. Hong Kong) of the UK Merchant Navy, whose ship, the SS *Ben Lomond*, was torpedoed in the Atlantic 565 miles *910 km* west of St Paul's Rocks in Lat. 00° 30′ N Long. 38° 45′ W at 11.45 a.m. on 23 Nov 1942. He was picked up by a Brazilian fishing boat off Salinópolis, Brazil, on 5 Apr 1943 and was able to walk ashore. In July 1943, he was awarded the BEM and now lives in New York City.

Maurice and Maralyn Bailey survived 118⅓ days in an inflatable dinghy 4½ ft *1,37 m* in diameter in the north-east Pacific from 4 Mar to 30 June 1973.

Shaft sinking record
The one month (31 days) world record is 1251 ft *381,3 m* for a standard shaft 26 ft *7,92 m* in diameter at Buffelsfontein Mine, Transvaal, South Africa, in March 1962. The British record of 131,2 m *430 ft* of 7,92 m *26 ft* diameter shaft was set in No 2 Shaft of the NCB's Whitemoor Mine near Selby, North Yorkshire in 31 days (15 Nov–16 Dec 1982).

Most marriages *World*
The greatest number of marriages accumulated in the monogamous world is 27 by the former Baptist minister Glynn 'Scotty' Wolfe (b. 25 July 1908) of Blythe, California, who first married in 1927. His latest wife is Daisy Delgado (b. 29 Dec 1970), a Filipino from Liloan, Cebu. His previous oldest wife was 38. His total number of children is, he says, 41. He suffered only 25 mothers-in-law because two of his 25 wives were the subject of re-marriages.

Mrs Beverly Nina Avery, then aged 48, a barmaid from Los Angeles, California, USA, set a monogamous world record in October 1957 by obtaining her sixteenth divorce from her fourteenth husband, Gabriel Avery. She alleged outside the court that five of the 14 had broken her nose.

The record for bigamous marriages is 104 by Giovanni Vigliotto, one of some 50 aliases used by either Fred Jipp (b. New York City, 3 Apr 1936) or Nikolai Peruskov (b. Siracusa, Sicily, 3 Apr 1929) over the span 1949–1981 in 27 US States and 14 other countries. Four victims were aboard one ship in 1968 and two in London. On 28 Mar 1983 in Phoenix, Arizona he was sentenced to 28 years for fraud, 6 years for bigamy and fined $336,000.

Great Britain
The only monogamous citizen married eight times is Olive Joyce Wilson of Marston Green, Birmingham. She has consecutively been Mrs John Bickley; Mrs Don Trethowan; Mrs George Hundley; Mrs Raymond Ward; Mrs Harry Latrobe; Mrs Leslie Harris; Mrs Ray Richards and now Mrs John Grassick. All were divorced except Mr Hundley, who died.

Oldest bride and bridegroom
The oldest recorded bridegroom has been Harry Stevens, 103, who married Thelma Lucas, 84, at the Caravilla Retirement Home, Wisconsin on 3 Dec 1984.

The British record was set by Sir Robert Mayer CH, KCVO (1879–1985) who married Jacqueline Noble, 51 in London on 10 Nov 1980 when aged 101 years.

Mrs Winifred Clark (b. 13 Nov 1871) became Britain's oldest recorded bride when she married Albert Smith, 80, at St. Hugh's Church, Cantley, South Yorkshire the day before her 100th birthday.

Longest engagements
The longest engagement on record was between Octavio Guillen, and Adriana Martinez. They finally took the plunge after 67 years in June 1969 in Mexico City, Mexico. Both were then 82.

Longest marriage *World*
The longest recorded marriages are of 86 years between Sir Temulji Bhicaji Nariman and Lady Nariman from 1853 to 1940 resulting from a cousin marriage when both were five. Sir Temulji (b. 3 Sept 1848) died, aged 91 years 11 months, in August 1940 at Bombay. Lazurus Rowe (b. Greenland, New Hampshire, 1725) and Molly Webber were recorded as marrying in 1743. He died first in 1829 after 86 years of marriage.

Great Britain
James Frederick Burgess (born 3 March 1861, died 27 Nov 1966) and his wife Sarah Ann, *née* Gregory (born 11 July 1865, died 22 June 1965) were married on 21 June 1883 at St James's, Bermondsey, London, and celebrated their 82nd anniversary.

Golden Weddings
Despite the advent of the computer, records on golden (or 50 year long) weddings remain still largely uncollated. Unusual cases reported include that of Mrs Agnes Mary Amy Mynott (b. 25 May 1887) who attended the golden wedding of her daughter Mrs Violet Bangs of St Albans on 20 Dec 1980, 23 years after her own. The 3 sons and 4 daughters of Mr and Mrs J. Stredwick of East Sussex *all* celebrated golden weddings between May 1971 and April 1981. Triplets Lucille (Mrs Vogel), Marie (Mrs McNamara) and Alma (Mrs Prom) Pufpaff all celebrated their golden weddings on 12 Apr 1982 having all married in Cleveland, Minnesota in 1932.

Britain's most durable marriage reached an 81st anniversary with Sam Loveridge, 104 (1880–1984) and Annie (*née* Pocock), 100 (b. Taunton, 1884).

Most married
Jack V. and Edna Moran of Seattle, Washington, USA have married each other 40 times since the original and only really necessary occasion on 27 July 1937 in Seaside, Oregon. Subsequent ceremonies have included those at Banff, Canada (1952), Cairo, Egypt (1966) and Westminster Abbey, London (1975).

Mass ceremony
The largest mass wedding ceremony was one of 5837 couples from 83 countries officiated over by Sun Myung Moon (b. 1920) of the Holy Spirit Association for the Unification of World Christianity in the Chamsil Gymnasium, Seoul, South Korea on 14 Oct 1982. The response to the

question 'Will you swear to love your spouse for ever?' is 'Ye'.

Most Expensive Wedding

The wedding of Mohammed, son of Shaik Zayid ibn Sa'id al-Makhtum, to Princess Salama in Abu Dhabi in May 1981 lasted 7 days and cost an estimated £22 million in a purpose built stadium for 20,000.

Oldest Divorced

In March 1980 a divorce was reported in the Los Angeles Superior Court, California between Bernardine and Leopold Delpes in which both parties were aged 88. The British record age is 101 years by Harry Bidwell at Brighton, Sussex on 21 Nov 1980.

Dining out

The world champion for eating out is Fred E. Magel of Chicago, Illinois, USA who since 1928 has dined out 46,000 times in 60 nations as a restaurant grader (to 21 June 1983). He asserts the one which served largest helpings was Zehnder's Hotel, Frankenmuth, Michigan, USA. Mr Magel's favourite dishes are South African rock lobster and mousse of fresh English strawberries.

Party giving

The 'International Year of the Child' children's party in Hyde Park, London was attended by the Royal Family and 160,000 children on 30–31 May 1979. The longest street party ever staged was for 5500 children by the Oxford Street Association to celebrate the Royal Wedding of TRH The Prince and Princess of Wales on 25 July 1981 along the entire length from Park Street to St. Giles Circus, London.

The largest Christmas Party ever staged was that thrown by The Boeing Company in the 65,000 seat Kingdome, Seattle, Washington, USA, in two shows totalling 103,152 people on 15 Dec 1979. During St. Patrick's week of 11–17 Mar 1985, Houlihan's Old Place hosted St. Pat's Parties at the 48 Kansas City, Missouri-based Gilbert/Robinson restaurants for a total of 206,854 documented guests.

Toastmasters

The Guild of Professional Toastmasters (founded 1962) has only 12 members. Its founder and President, Ivor Spencer, once had to listen to a speech in excess of 2 hr by the maudlin guest of honour of a retirement luncheon. The Guild also elects the most boring speaker of the year, but for professional reasons, will not publicize the winners' names until a decent interval has elapsed. Red coats were introduced by the pioneer professional, William Knight-Smith (d. 1932) c. 1900.

Lecture agency

In 1980 Bob Jones of Wellington, New Zealand addressed a seminar of 1048 people in Auckland on property. He received $NZ200,000 or $NZ16,666 per hour. In March 1981 it was reported that both Johnny Carson and Bob Hope commanded fees of $40,000 (then £18,000).

Working week

A case of a working week of 142 hours was recorded in June 1980 by Dr Paul Ashton, 32 the anaesthetics registrar at Birkenhead General Hospital, Merseyside. This left an average each day of 3 hr 42 min 51 sec for sleep. Some non-consultant doctors are actually contracted to work 110 hours a week or be available for 148 hours. Some contracts for fully salaried University lecturers call for a 3 hr week or a 72 hr year spread over 24 weeks.

Working career

The longest working life has been that of 98 years by Mr Izumi (see pp. 11–12), who began work goading draft animals at a sugar mill at Isen, Tokunashima, Japan in 1872. He retired as a sugar cane farmer in 1970 aged 105.

The longest working life recorded in the UK was that of Susan O'Hagan (1802–1909) who was in domestic service with 3 generations of the Hall family of Lisburn, near Belfast, Northern Ireland for 97 years from the age of 10 to light duties at 107.

The longest recorded industrial career in one job in Britain was that of Miss Polly Gadsby who started work with Archibald Turner & Co of Leicester aged 9. In 1932, after 86 years service, she was still at her bench wrapping elastic, at the age of 95. Mr Theodore C. Taylor (1850–1952) served 86 years with J. T. & T. Taylor of Batley, West Yorkshire including 56 years as chairman. The longest serving chairman (appointed July 1926) of any board of directors was Mrs Mary Henrietta Anne Moody (b. 7 Apr 1881) of Mark & Moody Ltd, printers and booksellers of Stourbridge, West Midlands. She had completed 59 years at the time of her death on 5 Aug 1985. Edward William Beard (1878–1982), a builder of Swindon, Wiltshire retired in October 1981 from the firm he founded in 1896 after 85 years. Commissioner Catherine Bramwell-Booth (b. 1883) has been serving the Salvation Army since 1903. Richard John Knight (b. 2 Apr 1881) was Company Secretary to 7 companies at the time of his death on 12 Nov 1984 aged 103 years.

Most durable coal miner

George Stephenson (b. 21 Apr 1833) worked at William Pit, a Whitehaven Colliery, Cumbria from 1840 (aged 7) for 82 years until his retirement in 1922. He died on 18 Mar 1926 aged 92 years 10 months having received a testimonial of £54 12s.

Longest pension

Miss Millicent Barclay, daughter of Col William Barclay was born posthumously on 10 July 1872 and became eligible for a Madras Military Fund pension to continue until her marriage. She died unmarried on 26 Oct 1969 having drawn the pension for every day of her life of 97 years 3 months.

Medical families

The 4 sons and 5 daughters of Dr Antonio B. Vicencio of Los Angeles all qualified in 1964–82. Eight sons of John Robertson of Benview, Dumbarton, Scotland graduated as medical doctors between 1892 and 1914. Henry Lewis Lutterloh and Elizabeth Grantham of Chatham County, North Carolina, USA were the grandparents of 19 medical doctors. From 1850 to 1962 they practised a total of 704 man-years. The Maurice family of Marlborough, Wiltshire have had the same practice for 6 generations since 1792.

2. MISCELLANEOUS ENDEAVOURS

ACCORDION PLAYING

Tom Luxton of Oldbury, West Midlands, played an accordion for 84 hr from 4–7 Aug. 1982.

APPLE PEELING

The longest single unbroken apple peel on record is one of 172 ft 4 in *52,51 m* peeled by Kathy Wafler, of Wolcott, NY, USA in 11 hr 30 min at Long Ridge Mall, Rochester, NY on 16 Oct 1976. The apple weighed 20 oz *567 g*.

APPLE PICKING

The greatest recorded performance is 365½ US

Pure genius . . . Norwegian Jan Solberg managed to collect 218,600 different beer labels from around the world. See p. 164.

bushels (354.1 Imperial bushels *128,80 hectolitres*) picked in 8 hr by George Adrian, 32 of Indianapolis, Indiana, USA, on 23 Sept 1980.

AUCTIONEERING

The longest one man auction on record is for 40 hr 7 min by Reg Coates in Gosport, Hampshire from 26–28 Apr 1985.

BAG-CARRYING

The greatest non-stop bag-carrying feat carrying 1 cwt *50,8 kg* of household coal in an open bag is 32 miles *51,5 km* by Brian Newton in 10 hr 18 min from Leicester to the Nottingham border on 27 May 1983.

The record for the 1012,5 m *1107.2 yd* course annual Gawthorpe, West Yorkshire race is 4 min 19 sec by Terry Lyons, 36 on 16 Apr 1979.

BAG-PIPES

The longest duration pipe has been one of 100 hr by Neville Workman, Clive Higgins, Patrick Forth and Paul Harris, playing two at a time in shifts, of Churchill School Pipe Band, Harare, Zimbabwe on 9–13 July 1976.

BALANCING ON ONE FOOT

The longest recorded duration for balancing on one foot is 34 hr by Shri N. Ravi in Sathyaman-galam City, Tamil Nadu, India on 17–18 Apr 1982. The disengaged foot may not be rested on the standing foot nor may any object be used for support or balance.

BALLOON FLIGHTS

The longest reported toy balloon flight is one of 10,000 miles *16 090 km* from Dobbs Ferry, New York, USA to Wagga Wagga, Australia. It was helium-filled and released by 11-year old Justin Fiore on 19 Apr 1982. The longest recorded hydrogen-filled balloon flight from the geographical British Isles is one of 5880 miles *9460 km* from Jersey which was returned from Camps Bay, Cape Province, South Africa on 28 Apr 1974, 43 days after release by Gerard Wankling.

Multi-musician Rory Blackwell in action blowing his own trumpet as well as a host of different horn instruments. (See Band, One-Man.)

BALLOON RELEASE

The largest mass balloon release ever achieved was one of 1,121,448 balloons at the Skyfest's One Million Balloon Salute to Walt Disney at Anaheim, California, USA on 5 Dec 1985.

BAND MARATHONS

The longest recorded 'blow-in' is 100 hr 2 min by the Du Val Senior High School, Lanham, Maryland, USA on 13–17 May 1977. The minimum number of musicians is 10.

BAND ONE-MAN

Rory Blackwell, aided by his left-footed perpen-dicular percussion-pounder and his right-footed horizontal four pronged differential beater, played 24 (4 melody, 20 percussion) instruments in Plymouth, Devon on 2 May 1985. He also played in a single rendition 314 instruments in 1 min 23.07 sec at Dawlish, Devon on 27 May 1985. Dave Sheriff of Rugby, Warwickshire played his one-man band (which must include at least 3 instruments played simultaneously) for 100 hr 20 min on 24-28 Mar 1986 at the Hotel Leofric, Coventry, West Midlands. Nicki Clarke of Chester, Cheshire created the women's record of the same time *at* the same time at the same place.

BARREL JUMPING *on Ice Skates*

The official distance record is 29 ft 5 in *8,99 m* over 18 barrels by Yvon Jolin at Terrebonne, Quebec, Canada on 25 Jan 1981. The feminine record is 20 ft 4½ in *6,21 m* over 11 barrels by Janet Hainstock in Michigan, USA, on 15 Mar 1980.

BARREL ROLLING

The record for rolling a full 36 gallon metal beer barrel over a measured mile is 8 min 7.2 sec by Phillip Randle, Steve Hewitt, John Round, Trevor Bradley, Colin Barnes and Ray Glover of Haunchwood Collieries Institute and Social Club, Nuneaton, Warwickshire on 15 Aug 1982. A team of 10 rolled a 63½ kg *140 lb* barrel 240,35 km *150 miles* in 30 hr 31 min in Chlum-cany, Czechoslovakia on 27–28 Oct 1982.

BARROW PUSHING

The heaviest loaded one-wheeled barrow pushed for a minimum 200 level feet *60,96 m* is one loaded with bricks weighing a gross 7,750 lb *3,51 tonnes* through 237 ft *72,23 m* by Gary Windebank at Romsey, Hampshire on 12 Oct 1985.

BARROW RACING

The fastest time attained in a 1 mile *1,609 km* wheelbarrow race is 4 min 50.29 sec by John Coates and Brian Roades of Richmond, BC, Canada on 9 July 1983 at the Ladner Sports Festival, Delta, B.C. Brothers-in-law Malcolm Shipley and Adrian Freeburg pushed each other from John O'Groats to Land's End for charity in 30 days from 28 July–26 Aug 1981.

BATH TUB RACING

The record for the annual international 36 miles *57,9 km* Nanaimo to Vancouver, British Col-umbia bath tub race is 1 hr 29 min 40 sec by Gary Deathbridge (Australia) on 30 July 1978. Tubs are limited to 75 in *1,90 m* and 6 hp motors. The greatest distance for paddling a hand propelled bath tub in 24 hr is 90.5 miles *145,6 km* by 13 members of Aldington Prison Officers Social Club, nr. Ashford, Kent on 28–29 May 1983.

BATON TWIRLING

Victor Cerda, Sol Lozano, Harry Little III (leader) and Manuel Rodriguez, twirled batons for 122½ hours on 24–29 June 1984 in El Seveno, California.

BEARD OF BEES

The ultimate beard of bees was achieved by Max Beck, 21, of Arcola, Pennsylvania, USA with 70,000 bees weighing 20 lb *9 kg* reported in October 1985.

BED MAKING

The record time set under the rigorous rules of the Australian Bedmaking Championships is 28.2 sec solo by Wendy Wall, 34, of Hebersham, Sydney, NSW on 30 Nov 1978. The British pair record with 1 blanket, 2 sheets, an undersheet, an uncased pillow, 1 counterpane and 'hospital' corners is 19.0 sec by Sisters Jill Bradbury and Chris Humpish of Hammersmith Hospital, London on 8 Oct 1985 on BBC TV *Record Breakers* programme.

BED OF NAILS

The duration record for lying on a bed of nails (sharp 6-inch *15,2 cm*; 2 in *5 cm* apart) is 274 hr 2 min by Inge Widar Svingen ending on TV's 'Good Morning Norway' programme on 3 Nov 1984. Much longer durations are claimed by uninvigilated *fakirs*—the most extreme case being *Silki* who claimed 111 days in São Paulo, Brazil ending on 24 Aug 1969.

BED PUSHING

The longest recorded push of a normally sessile object is of 3233 miles 1150 yd *5204 km* in the case of a wheeled hospital bed by a team of 9 employees of Bruntsfield Bedding centre, Edin-burgh on 21 June–26 July 1979.

BED RACE

The record time for the annual Knaresborough Bed Race (established 1966) in North Yorkshire is 12 min 36 sec for the 2 mile 63 yd *3,27 km* course crossing the River Nidd by the Beavers' Team on 9 June 1984. The course record for the 10 mile *16,09 km* Chew Valley Lake race (inst. 1977). in Avon, England is 50 min by the Westbury Harrier 3-man bed team.

BEER LABEL COLLECTING

Jan Solberg of Oslo, Norway has amassed 218,600 different labels from around the world.

The greatest collection of different British Beer labels is 29,500 (to April 1986) by Keith Osborne, Hon Sec of The Labologists Society (founded by Guinness Exports Ltd in 1958). His oldest is one from D. B. Walker & Co, Warrington of *c.* 1846.

BEER MAT FLIPPING

At the inaugural Ind Coope British Champion-ships Darren Ault, 18, flipped and caught a pile of 67 mats (1.2 mm thick 490 gsm wood pulp board) through 180 degrees at Brewery Vaults, Burton-on-Trent, Staffs on 31 May 1985.

BEER STEIN CARRYING

Barmaid Rosie Schedelbauer covered 15 m *49 ft 2½ in* in 4.0 sec with 5 full steins in each hand in a televised contest at Königssee, West Germany on 29 June 1981.

BEST MAN

The world's champion 'best man' is Mr Wally Gant, a bachelor fishmonger from Wakefield,

West Yorkshire, who officiated for the 50th time since 1931 in December 1964.

BICYCLE *Most mounting simultaneously*

On 2 Apr 1984 at Mito, Ibaragi, Japan 16 members of the Mito-Itomi Unicycle Club mounted and rode a single bicycle a distance of 50 m *164 ft.*

BILLIARD TABLE JUMPING

Joe Darby (1861–1937) cleared a full-sized 12 ft *3,65 m* billiard table lengthwise, taking off from a 4 in *10 cm* high solid wooden block, at Wolverhampton, West Midlands on 5 Feb 1892.

BOMB DEFUSING

The highest reported number of unexploded bombs defused by any individual is 8000 by Werner Stephan in West Berlin, Germany, in the 12 years from 1945 to 1957. He was killed by a small grenade on the Grunewald blasting site on 17 Aug 1957. Britain's two most highly decorated bomb disposal officers were the late Cdr H. Syme GC GM* and Lt-Cdr J. Bridge GC GM*.

BOOMERANG THROWING

The earliest mention of a word similar to *boomerang* is *wo-murrang* in Collins *Acct. N.S. Wales Vocab.* published in 1798. The earliest certain Australian account of a returning boomerang (term established, 1827) was in 1831 by Major (later Sir Thomas) Mitchell. Curved throwing sticks for wild fowl hunting were found in the tomb of Tutankhamun dating from the mid 14th century BC.

World championships and codified rules were not established until 1970. The Boomerang Association of Australia's championship record for distance reached from the thrower before the boomerang returns is 111 m *364.1 ft* diameter by Bob Burwell in November 1981 at Albury. The longest unofficial out and return record on record is one of 375 ft *114,3 m* by Peter Ruhf (US) at Randwick, Sydney, NSW, Australia on 28 June 1982. The longest flight duration (with self-catch) is one of 28.9 sec by Bob Burwell at Alberg, NSW on 7 Apr 1984. The greatest number of consecutive two handed catches on record is 653 by Bob Croll (Victoria) on the same occasion.

BREATHING APPARATUS

The continuous duration record for wearing self-contained breathing apparatus is 342 hr 10 min on 4–18 Aug 1984 by a team of four firemen from Chertsey, Surrey.

BRICK CARRYING

The greatest distance achieved for carrying a brick 8 lb 15 oz *4,053 kg* in a nominated un-gloved hand in an uncradled downward pincher grip is 45 miles *72,4 km* by David and Kym Barger of Lamar, Missouri, USA on 21 May 1977. The British record is 61¾ miles *99,37 km* by Reg Morris of Walsall with a 9 lb *4,08 kg* brick in the West Midlands on 16 July 1985.

The feminine record for a 9 lb 12 oz *4,422 kg* brick is 22½ miles *36,2 km* by Wendy Morris of Walsall, West Midlands, on 28 Apr 1986. The British feminine record for a 6 lb 9 oz *2,97 kg* smooth-sided brick is 6 miles *9,6 km* by Karen Stevenson of Wallasey, Merseyside on 17 Aug 1984.

BRICKLAYING

Ralph Charnock of Benfleet, Essex broke The Brick Development Association Bricklaying

Championship record at Colindale, north-west London which he himself set on 30 Sept 1981. He laid 725 bricks in 60 min on 17 June 1983 at Wiggins Construct, Thundersley, Essex.

BRICKLIFTING

Alan Keates of Cheadle, Staffordshire lifted 26 8½ in *21,6 cm* bricks of 5 lb *2,26 kg* weight horizontally in Cheadle on 15 May 1984. The span was 66½ in *168,9 cm* and 130 lb *59 kg.*

BRICK RACING

The record times recorded at the Annual NFBTE Young Builders Dry-brick championship in Leicester are 100 metres: 1 min 7.0 sec + 11 penalty points giving a gross 1 min 18.0 sec by Ian Jones on 3 June 1979, and 1 mile (team): 21 min 25 sec + 118 penalties giving an overall time of 23 min 23 sec by William Davis & Company (Leicester) Ltd, on 15 June 1980.

BRICK THROWING

The greatest reported distance for throwing a standard 5 lb *2,268 kg* building brick is 44,54 m *146 ft 1 in* by Geoff Capes at Braybrook School, Orton Goldhay, Cambridgeshire on 19 July 1978.

BUBBLE GUM BLOWING

The greatest reported diameter for a bubble gum bubble is 22 in *55,8 cm* by Susan Montgomery Williams of Fresno, Calif, USA in June 1985. The British record also using 'Bubble Yum' is 16½ in *42 cm* by Nigel Fell, 13 from Derriaghy, N. Ireland in November 1979. This was equalled by John Smith of Willingham, Cambridgeshire on 25 Sept 1983.

BURIAL ALIVE

Voluntary burial alive (for which claims up to 217 days have been published) are inadmissible unless the depth of the coffin is a minimum 2 m *6 ft 6¾ in* below ground; the coffin has a maximum cubic capacity of 1,5 million cc or *54 ft³* and the single aperture for communication and feeding has a maximum dimension of 10 cm or *4 inches.* 'Country' Bill White, 50, was so buried from 31 July to 19 Dec 1981 (141 days) in Killeen, Texas, USA.

CAMPING OUT

The silent Indian *fakir* Mastram Bapu 'contented father' has remained on the same spot by the roadside in the village of Chitra for 22 years 1960–82.

CANAL JUMPING (DYKE VAULTING)

In the sport of Fierljeppen at Winsam, Friesland, Netherlands, the record is 18.61 m *61 ft 0¾ in* across the water with a 40 ft *12,2 m* aluminium pole set by Aarth de Wit in Aug 1983.

CARD THROWING

Kevin St Onge threw a standard playing card 185 ft 1 in *56,41 m* at the Henry Ford Community College Campus, Dearborn, Michigan, USA on 12 June 1979.

CARRIAGE DRIVING

The only man to drive 48 horses in a single hitch is Dick Sparrow of Zearing, Iowa, USA in 1972–77. The lead horses were on reins 135 ft *41 m* long.

CAR WRECKING

The greatest number of cars wrecked in a

Un-stung hero—extraordinary sight of Max Beck covered by 70,000 bees. The bees are attracted by strapping boxes containing queen bees to parts of his body including his chin. (George Bilyk).

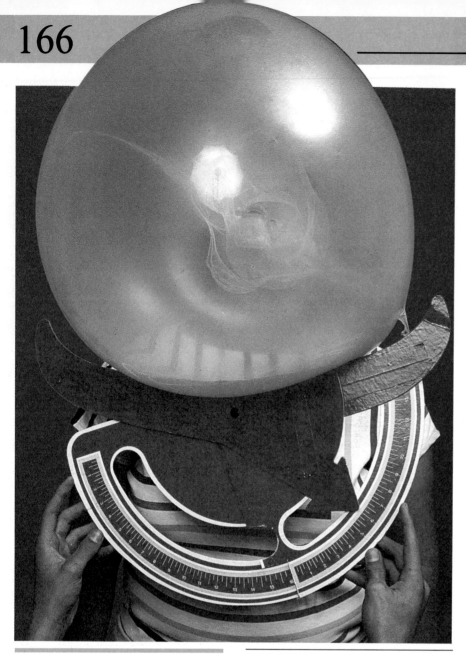

Blown out of all proportion . . . Susan
Montgomery's bubble measured 55,8 cm *22 in* in
diameter. *See p. 165.*

stunting career is 1859 to 1 June 1986 by Dick
Sheppard of Gloucester, England.

CATAPULTING

The greatest recorded distance for a catapult
shot is 1362 ft *415 m* by James M. Pfotenhauer
using a patented 17 ft 1½ in *5,22 m* 'Monarch IV
Supershot' and a 53 calibre lead musket ball on
Ski Hill Road, Escanaba, Michigan, USA on 10
Sept 1977.

CHAMPAGNE FOUNTAIN

The greatest number of storeys achieved in a
champagne fountain, successfully filled from the
top and using 10,404 traditional long-stem
glasses, is 44 (height 24.7 ft *7,52 m*) achieved by
Pascal Leclerc at the Biltmore Hotel, Los
Angeles, USA on 18 June 1984.

CLAPPING

The duration record for continuous clapping
(sustaining an average of 160 claps per min
audible at 120 yd *109,7 m*) is 54 hr by V.
Jeyaraman of Tamil Nadu, India from 13–15
Dec 1985.

CLUB SWINGING

Albert Rayner set a world record of 17,512
revolutions (4.9 per sec) in 60 min at Wakefield,
W Yorkshire on 27 July 1981. M. Dobrilla
swung continuously for 144 hr at Cobar, NSW
finishing on 15 Sept 1913.

COAL CUTTING

The most productive coal mine in Britain has
been Bagworth Colliery, Leicestershire with 5.8
tonnes per man shift in the 41 weeks from April
to 31 Dec 1980. The colliery dates from 1829.
The individual record for filling is 218 tons in a
week of 5 shifts by Jim Marley (b. 1914) at East
Walbottle Colliery, Tyne and Wear, England in
1949. This included 47½ tons in 6 hr. The NCB
record for a week's production by a 48 man team
is 32,333 tonnes at the biggest pit at Kellingley
Colliery, Knottingley, West Yorkshire in the
pre-Christmas 'Bull Week' in December 1982.

COAL SHOVELLING

The record for filling a ½-ton *508 kg* hopper with
coal is 29.4 sec by Piet Groot at the Inangahua
A. and P. Show, New Zealand on 1 Jan 1985.

COIN BALANCING

The tallest column of coins ever stacked on the
edge of a coin is 205 Canadian 25 cent pieces on
top of a Canadian Olympic commemorative

coin which was freestanding vertically on the
base of a coin flat on the surface by Bruce
McConachy (b. 1963) of West Vancouver, BC,
for Fuji-TV in Tōkyō, Japan on 24 Feb 1985.
Alex Chervinsky (b. 22 Feb 1908) of Lock
Haven, Pennsylvania, USA achieved a pyramid
of 390 coins on his 75th birthday.

COIN SNATCHING

The greatest number of 10p pieces clean caught
from being flipped from the back of a forearm
into the same palm is 85 by Andrew Gleed at
The Guinness World of Records permanent
exhibition at the Trocadero, Piccadilly, London
on 29 May 1986. *This category is now retired in
favour of the international style in which the coins
must be caught palm down in a single downward
sweep.*

COMPETITION WINNINGS

The largest individual competition prize win on
record is $307,500 (*then £109,821*) by Herbert J.
Idle, 55, of Chicago in an encyclopaedia contest
run by Unicorn Press Inc on 20 Aug 1953. The
highest value first prize offered in Britain has
been a £50,000 new house in a £100,000
competition sponsored by Lever Brothers, British Gas and the New Homes Marketing Board
from Mar–Oct 1985.

COW CHIP TOSSING

The record distances in the country sport of
throwing dried cow chips depends on whether
or not the projectile may or may not be 'moulded
into a spherical shape'. The greatest distance
achieved under the 'non-sphericalization and
100% organic' rule (established in 1970) is 266 ft
81,07 m by Steve Urner at the Mountain Festival,
Tehachapi, California, USA on 14 Aug 1981.

CRAWLING

The longest continuous voluntary crawl (pro-
gression with one or other knee in unbroken
contact with the ground) on record is 27 miles
43,45 km by Chris Lock at Durdham Downs,
Bristol, England on 18–19 Aug 1984. Over a
space of 15 months ending on 9 Mar 1985
Jagdish Chander, 32, crawled 1400 km *870 miles*
from Aligarh to Jamma, India to propitiate his
favourite Hindu goddess Mata.

CROCHET

Mrs Barbara Jean Sonntag (b. 1938) of Craig,
Colorado, USA crocheted 330 shells plus 5
stitches (equivalent to 4412 stitches) in 30 min
at a rate of 147 stitches a minute on 13 Jan 1981.
She also set a record for a crochet chain on 31
Oct 1981 with a strand measuring 34.9 miles
56,16 km. Mrs Sybille Anthony completed a
120 hr crochet marathon at Toombul Shopping-
town, Queensland, Australia on 7 Oct 1977.

CUCUMBER SLICING

Norman Johnson of Blackpool College of Art
and Technology set a record of 13.4 sec for
slicing a 12 in *30,48 cm* cucumber 1½ in *3,81 cm*
diameter at 22 slices to the inch (total 244 slices)
on West Deutscher Rundfunk in Cologne on 3
Apr 1983.

CUSTARD PIE THROWING

The most times champion in the annual World
Custard Pie Championships now at Ditton,
Maidstone, Kent (instituted 1968) have been the
'The Birds', ('The Bashers') and the 'Coxheath
Men' ('Custard Kings') each with 3 wins. The
target (face) must be 8 ft 3⅞ in *2,53 m* from the
thrower who must throw a pie no more than
10¼ in *26,03 cm* in diameter. Six points are scored
for a square hit full in the face.

DANCING

Largest and longest dances
An estimated 25,000 attended a 'Moonlight Serenade' outdoor evening of dancing to the music of the Glen Miller Orchestra in Buffalo, New York, USA on 20 July 1984. An estimated total of 20,000 dancers took part in the National Square Dance Convention at Louisville, Kentucky, USA on 26 June 1983.

Marathon dancing must be distinguished from dancing mania, or tarantism, which is a pathological condition. The worst outbreak of this was at Aachen, Germany, in July 1374, when hordes of men and women broke into a frenzied and compulsive choreomania in the streets. It lasted for hours till injury or complete exhaustion ensued.

Will Kemp in 1599 Morris danced his way from London to Norwich in 9 days.

The most severe marathon dance staged as a public spectacle was one by Mike Ritof and Edith Boudreaux who logged 5148 hr 28½ min to win $2000 at Chicago's Merry Garden Ballroom, Belmont and Sheffield, Illinois, USA from 29 Aug 1930 to 1 Apr 1931. Rest periods were progressively cut from 20 to 10 to 5 to nil minutes per hour with 10 inch steps and a maximum of 15 seconds for closure of eyes.

Ballet
In the *entrechat* (a vertical spring from the fifth position with the legs extended criss-crossing at the lower calf), the starting and finishing position each count as one such that in an *entrechat douze* there are *five* crossings and uncrossings. This was performed by Wayne Sleep for the BBC *Record Breakers* programme on 7 Jan 1973. He was in the air for 0.71 sec.

Most turns
The greatest number of spins called for in classical ballet choreography is the 32 *fouettés rond de jambe en tournant* in 'Swan Lake' by Pyotr Ilyich Chaykovskiy (Tschaikovsky) (1840–93). Miss Rowena Jackson (later Chatfield), MBE (b. Invercargill, NZ, 1925) achieved 121 such turns at her class in Melbourne, Victoria, Australia, in 1940.

Most Curtain Calls
The greatest recorded number of curtain calls ever received is 89 by Dame Margaret Evelyn Arias, DBE *née* Hookham (born Reigate, Surrey, 18 May 1919) *alias* Margot Fonteyn, and Rudolf Hametovich Nureyev (born on a train near Irkutsk, USSR, 17 Mar 1938) after a performance of 'Swan Lake' at the Vienna Staatsoper, Austria, in October 1964.

Largest Cast
The largest number of ballet dancers used in a production in Britain has been 2000 in the London Coster Ballet of 1962, directed by Lillian Rowley, at the Royal Albert Hall, London.

Marathon
The indivual continuous world record for ballroom dancing is 120 hr 30 min by Alain Dumas on 28 June–3 July 1983 at the Disco-Shop, Granby, Quebec, Canada. Nine girls worked shifts as his partner.

Champions
The world's most successful professional ballroom dancing champions have been Bill Irvine, MBE and Bobbie Irvine, MBE, who won 13 world titles between 1960 and 1972. The oldest competitive ballroom dancer is Albert J. Sylvester

CBE, JP (b. 24 Nov 1889) of Corsham, Wiltshire. In 1977 he won the topmost amateur Alex Moore award for a 10 dance test with his partner Paula Smith in Bath on 26 Apr 1977. By 1981 he had won nearly 50 medals and trophies since he began dancing in 1964.

Belly dancing
The longest recorded example was one of 106 hr by Eileen Foucher at Rush Green Hospital, Romford, Essex on 30 July–3 Aug 1984.

Charleston
The Charleston duration record is 110 hr 58 min by Sabra Starr of Lansdowne, Pennsylvania, USA on 15–20 Jan 1979.

Conga
The longest recorded conga was one comprising a 'snake' of 8659 people from the South Eastern Region of the Camping and Caravanning Club of Great Britain and Ireland on 4 Sept 1982.

Disco
The longest recorded disco dancing marathon is one of 371 hr by John Sharples of Preston, Lancashire on 18 Jan–3 Feb 1982.

Flamenco
The fastest flamenco dancer ever measured is Solero de Jerez aged 17 who in Brisbane, Australia in September 1967 in an electrifying routine attained 16 heel taps per second.

High kicking
The world record for high kicks (heel to ear level) is 10,376 in 6 hr 5 min 55 sec by Alagarajah Srikandarajah at Aubigney, France on 22 July 1984. Tara Hobbs, 13, set a speed record of 95 kicks in 1 min on BBC TV's *Record Breakers* on 2 Sept 1984. Veronica Evans set a speed record for 50 in Manchester on 24 Dec 1931 with 25.0 sec.

Jiving
The duration record for non-stop jiving is 97 hr 42 min by Richard Rimmer (with a relay of partners) of Caterham, Surrey on 11–16 Nov 1979. Under the strict rules of the European Rock n' Roll Association the duration pair record is 22 hr by Mirco and Manuela Catalono in Munich on 6–7 Feb 1981.

Limbo
The lowest height for a bar (flaming) under which a limbo dancer has passed is 6⅛ in *15,5 cm* off the floor by Marlene Raymond, 15 at the Port of Spain Pavilion, Toronto, Canada on 24 June 1973. Junior J. Renaud (b. 7 June 1954), Australia, became the first Official World Limbo Champion at the inaugural International Limbo competition on 19 Feb 1974 at Port of Spain, Trinidad and Tobago. The record on roller skates is 5¼ in *13,33 cm* by Tracey O'Callaghan on 2 June 1984 and Sandra Siviour on 30 Mar 1985 both at Bexley North, NSW, Australia to equal Denise Culp of Rock Hill, South Carolina, USA on 22 Jan 1984.

Tap
The fastest *rate* ever measured for tap dancing is 1440 taps per min (24 per sec) by Roy Castle on BBC TV *Record Breakers* programme on 14 Jan 1973. On 31 Oct–1 Nov 1985 Roy achieved one million taps in 23 hr 44 min at the Guinness World of Records, London. The greatest ever assemblage of tap dancers in a single routine is 3565 outside Macy's Store in New York City, USA on 8 Sept 1985.

DEBATING *Most protracted*
The Oxford Union Society, Oxford University, debated the motion '. . . Heineken refreshes the parts' for 193 hr 49 min on 21–29 May 1986. The debate, with 175 formal speakers included a 2½ hour joke and raised £2500 for charity.

DEMOLITION WORK
Fifteen members of the Black Leopard Karate Club demolished a 7-room wooden farmhouse west of Elnora, Alberta, Canada in 3 hr 18 min by foot and empty hand on 13 June 1982.

DOMINO TOPPLING
The greatest number of dominoes (set up singlehanded) toppled is 281,581 out of 320,236 set up, by Klaus Friedrich, 22, in Bayern, West Germany on 27 Jan 1984. The dominoes fell within 12 min 57.3 sec having taken 31 days (10 hours daily) to set up.

DRUMMING
The world's duration drumming record is 42 days 1 hr 6 min 20 sec by Laurent Rebboah of Cupertino, California, USA, on 22 Sept–3 Nov 1983.

Four hundred separate drums were played in 58 seconds by rock star Cozy Powell on BBC TV *Record Breakers* at TV Centre, London on 5 Nov 1985.

DUCKS AND DRAKES
The best accepted ducks and drakes (stone-skipping) record is 29 skips (14 plinkers and 15 pitty-pats) by Arthur Ring, 69, on 4 Aug 1984. Forty skips are alleged to be possible with 2 inch wide artificial discs with central dimples.

EGG HUNT
The greatest egg hunt on record involved 72,000 hard-boiled eggs and 40,000 candy eggs at the 26th annual Garrison egg hunt at Homer, Georgia, USA on 7 Apr 1985.

EGG AND SPOON RACING
Chris Riggio of San Francisco, California, USA completed a 28.5 mile *45,86 km* fresh egg and dessert spoon marathon in 4 hr 34 min on 7 Oct 1979.

EGG SHELLING
Two kitchen hands, Harold Witcomb and Gerald Harding, shelled 1050 dozen eggs in a 7¼ hr shift at Bowyers, Trowbridge, Wiltshire on 23 Apr 1971. Both were blind.

EGG THROWING
The longest authenticated distance for throwing a fresh hen's egg without breaking is 96,90 m *317 ft 10 in* by Risto Antikainen to Jyrki Korhonen at Siilinjarvi, Finland on 6 Sept 1982.

ESCAPOLOGY
The most renowned of all escape artists has been Ehrich Weiss *alias* Harry Houdini (1874–1926), who pioneered underwater escapes from locked, roped and weighted containers while handcuffed and shackled with irons.

One of the major manufacturers of strait-jackets acknowledges that an escapologist 'skilled in the art of bone and muscle manipulation' could escape from a standard jacket in seconds. There are however methods by which such circumvention can itself be circumvented. Nick Janson of Benfleet, Essex has demonstrated his ability to escape from handcuffs locked on him by more than 1000 different police officers.

FAMILY TREE *Longest*

The farthest back the lineage of any family has been traced is that of K'ung Ch'iu or Confucius (551–479 BC). His 4 greats grandfather K'ung Chia is known from the eighth century BC. This man's 85th lineal descendants Wei-yi (b. 1939) and Wei-ning (b. 1947) live today in Taiwan (Formosa).

FASHION SHOW *Longest*

The longest distance covered by girl models is 71.1 miles *114,4 km* on 19–21 Sept 1983 by Roberta Brown and Lorraine McCourt at Parke's Hotel, Dublin, Ireland. The male model Eddie Warke covered a further 11.9 miles *19,1 km* on the catwalk. The compère throughout was Marty Whelan of Radio 2.

FAUX PAS

If measuring by financial consequence, the greatest *faux pas* on record was that of the young multi-millionaire, James Gordon Bennett, committed on 1 Jan 1877 at the family mansion of his demure fiancée one Caroline May, in Fifth Avenue, New York City. Bennett arrived in a two-horse cutter late and obviously in wine. By dint of intricate footwork, he gained the portals to enter the withdrawing room where he was the cynosure of all eyes. He mistook the fireplace for a plumbing fixture more usually reserved for another purpose. The May family broke the engagement and Bennett (1841–1918) was obliged to spend the rest of his foot-loose and fancy-free life based in Paris with the resultant non-collection of millions of tax dollars by the US Treasury.

York firemen pumped an average 998,4 litres *219.6 gallons* per hour during their fire pumping marathon which lasted over 3 days.

FEMININE BEAUTY

Female pulchritude being qualitative rather than quantitative does not lend itself to records. It has been suggested that, if the face of Helen of Troy (*c.* 1200 BC) was capable of launching 1000 ships, a unit of beauty sufficient to launch one ship should be a millihelen.

The earliest international beauty contest was that staged by P. T. Barnum (with the people to be the judges) in the United States in June 1855. The Miss America contest was staged at Atlantic City, New Jersey, USA in 1921 and was won by a thin blue-eyed blonde with a 30 in *76,2 cm* chest, Margaret Gorman. The world's largest annual beauty pageants are Miss World (inaugurated 1951) and Miss Universe (1952) contests. The most successful country in the latter contest has been the USA with winners in 1954–56–60–67–70–80. The number of countries represented has reached 80. The United Kingdom is the only country to have produced five winners in the Miss World contest. They were Rosemarie Frankland (1961); Ann Sidney (1964); Lesley Langley (1965); Helen Morgan (1974), who resigned and Sarah-Jane Hutt (1983). The maximum number of contestants was 72 in November 1983. The shortest reign was 18 hours by Miss Germany (Gabriella Brum) in 1980.

FIRE PUMPING

The greatest gallonage stirrup-pumped by a team of 8 in an 80 hr charity pump is 17,570 gal *79 863 litres* by the York Fire Station team of the North Yorkshire Fire Brigade on 26–29 Mar 1986.

FIRE PUMP MANHANDLING

The longest unaided tow of a fire appliance in excess of 10 cwt *508 kg* in 24 hr on a closed circuit is 211 miles *339,5 km* by a 32 man team of the Dublin Fire Brigade with an 11 cwt *558,8 kg* fire pump on 18–19 June 1983.

FLUTE MARATHON

The longest recorded marathon by a flautist is 50 hr 44 min by Ken Munson, Las Vegas, Nevada, USA on 30–31 Dec 1984.

FLYING DISC THROWING *Formerly Frisbee*

The World Flying Disc Federation indoor records are Men: 121,6 m *399 ft* by Van Miller at Flagstaff, Arizona on 18 Sept 1982; and Women: 229.6 ft *69,9 m* by Suzanne Fields at Cedar Falls, Iowa on 26 Apr 1981. The outdoor records are: Men: 166,42 m *546 ft* by Morten Sandorff, 21 May 1983, Farum, Denmark; and Women: 401.5 ft *122,3 m* by Lizzie Reeve, 14 June 1980, Surrey, England. The throw, run and catch record is 83,10 m *272 ft 7 in* by Steve Bentley on 8 Apr 1982 at Sacramento, California. The group marathon record is 1198 hr by Prince George's Community College Flying High Club on 1 June–22 July 1983 (see Throwing p. 175).

FOOTBAG

The world record for keeping a footbag airborne is 17,872 consecutive kicks or hacks by Andy Linder (US) in Portland, Oregon on 16 Aug 1983 and 6,184 consecutive kicks by Tricia Sullivan, 22, (US) at the BBC TV Centre, London on *Record Breakers* on 21 Oct 1984. The sport originated in Oregon, USA in 1972 and was invented by John Stalberger (US).

GIRNING

The only girner to have won 6 national titles is Ron Looney of Egremont, Cumberland in 1979–84.

GLADIATORIAL COMBAT

Emperor Trajan of Rome (AD 98–117) staged a display involving 4941 pairs of gladiators over 117 days. Publius Ostorius, a freed-man, survived 51 combats in Pompeii.

GOLD PANNING

The fastest time recorded for 'panning' 8 planted gold nuggets in a 10 in *25,4 cm* diameter pan is 9.23 sec by Bob Box of Ahwahnee, California, and the female record is 10.03 sec by Susan Bryeans of Fullerton, California both in the 23rd World Gold Panning Championship on 6 Mar 1983 at Knotts Berry Farm, Buena Park, California, USA.

GOLF BALL BALANCING

Lang Martin balanced 7 golf balls vertically without adhesive at Charlotte, North Carolina, USA on 9 Feb 1980.

GRAPE CATCHING

The greatest distance at which a grape thrown from level ground has been caught in the mouth is 319 ft 8 in *97,43 m* by Arden Chapman at Northeast Louisiana University, Monroe, USA on 18 July 1980.

GRAVE DIGGING

It is recorded that Johann Heinrich Karl Thieme, sexton of Aldenburg, Germany, dug 23,311 graves during a 50-year career. In 1826 his understudy dug *his* grave.

GUITAR PLAYING

The longest recorded solo guitar playing marathon is one of 264 hr by Ron Woodley of Raymore, Missouri, USA on 19–30 June 1984.

GUM BOOT THROWING

The longest recorded distance for 'Wellie wang-

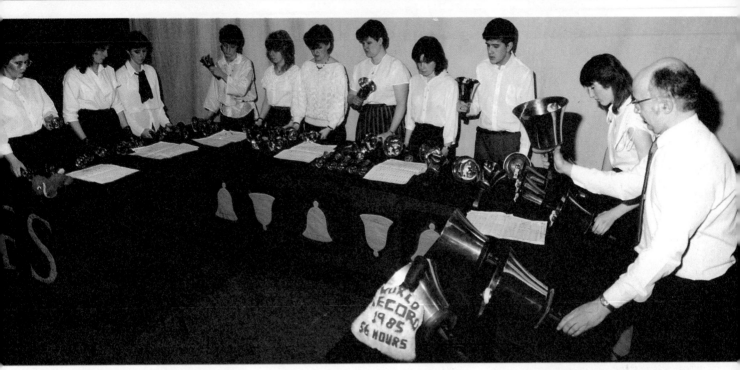

ing' (a size 8 Challenger Dunlop Boot) is 173 ft *52,73 m* by Tony Rodgers of Warminster, Wilts on 9 Sept 1978. Rosemary Payne established the feminine record at Cannon Hill Park, Birmingham on 21 June 1975 with 129 ft 11 in *39,60 m*.

GUN RUNNING

The record for the Royal Tournament Naval Field Gun competition (instituted 1907, with present rules since 1913) is 2 min 40.6 sec by the Portsmouth Command Field Gun crew at Earl's Court, Kensington & Chelsea, London on 19 July 1984. The barrel alone weighs 8 cwt *406 kg*. The wall is 5 ft *1,52 m* high and the chasm 28 ft *8,53 m* across.

HAGGIS HURLING

The longest recorded distance for throwing a haggis (min. weight 1 lb 8 oz *680 g*) is 180 ft 10 in *55,11 m* by Alan Pettigrew on Inchmoran, Loch Lomond, Scotland on 24 May 1984.

HAIR-DRESSING

Hugo Vanpe cut, set and styled hair continuously for 366 hr on 8–23 June 1984 in Kensington, Johannesburg, South Africa.

HAIR SPLITTING

The greatest reported achievement in hair splitting has been that of the former champion cyclist and craftsman Alfred West (1901–1985) who succeeded in splitting a human hair 17 times into 18 parts on eight occasions.

HANDBELL RINGING

The longest recorded handbell ringing recital has been one of 56 hr 3 min by the 12 Handbell Ringers of Ecclesfield School, Sheffield on 21–23 July 1985.

HANDSHAKING

A world record for handshaking was set up by Theodore Roosevelt (1858–1919), President of the USA, when he shook hands with 8513 people at a New Year's Day, White House Presentation in Washington, DC, USA on 1 Jan 1907. Peter Hargrave of Tesco's Supermarket, Brent Park,

(*Above*) The Ecclesfield School ring the changes for the record books with a 56 hr 3 min marathon. (Dave Muscroft).

London shook 12,500 different hands in 9 hr 20 min on 7 June 1986. *Many record claims have been rendered meaningless because aspirants merely tend to arrange circular queues or wittingly or unwittingly shake the same hands repetitively.*

HIGH DIVING

The highest regularly performed head first dives are those of professional divers from La Quebrada ('the break in the rocks') at Acapulco, Mexico, a height of 87½ ft *26,7 m*. The leader of the 27 divers in the Club de Clavadistas is Raul Garcia (b. 1928) with more than 35,000 dives. The first feminine accomplishment was by Mrs Barbara Winters (b. 12 Nov 1953), *née* Mayer, on 7 Dec 1976. The base rocks, 21 ft *6,40 m* out from the take-off, necessitate a leap of 27 ft *8,22 m* out. The water is 12 ft *3,65 m* deep.

Hurling a burly haggis—Alan Pettigrew in action performing his record breaking throw of 180 ft 10 in *55,11 m*.

The world record high dive is 174 ft 8 in *53,23 m* by Randal Dickison (US) at Ocean Park, Hong Kong on 6 Apr 1985. The feminine record is 120 ft *36,57 m* by Lucy Wardle (US) at the same exhibition. The highest witnessed in Britain is one of 108 ft *32,9 m* into 8 ft *2,43 m* of water at the Aqua show at Earl's Court, London on 22 Feb 1946 by Roy Fransen (1915–85).

On 8 May 1885, Sarah Ann Henley, aged 24, jumped from the Clifton Suspension Bridge, which crosses the Avon, England. Her 250 ft *76 m* fall was slightly cushioned by her voluminous dress and petticoat acting as a parachute. She landed, bruised and bedraggled, in the mud on the north bank and was carried to hospital by four policemen. On 11 Feb 1968 Jeffrey Kramer, 24, leapt off the George Washington Bridge 250 ft *76 m* above the Hudson River, New York City, NY and survived. Of the 696 (to 1 Jan 1980) identified people who have made 240 ft *73 m* suicide dives from the Golden Gate Bridge, San Francisco, California, USA since 1937, twelve survived of whom Todd Sharratt, 17, was the only one who managed to swim ashore unaided.

Col Harry A. Froboess (Switzerland) jumped 110 m *360 ft* into the Bodensee from the airship *Graf Hindenburg* on 22 June 1936.

The greatest height reported for a dive into an air bag is 326 ft *99,36 m* by the stuntman Dan Koko from the top of Vegas World Hotel and Casino into a 20 × 40 × 14 ft *6,1 × 12,2 × 4,2 m* target on 13 Aug 1984. His impact speed was 88 mph *141 km/h*. Kitty O'Neill dived 180 ft *54,8 m* from a helicopter over Northridge, California on 9 Sept 1979 onto an air cushion measuring 30 × 60 ft *9,14 × 18,28 m* for a TV film stunt.

HIGHEST SHALLOW DIVE

Henri La Mothe (b. 1904) set a record diving 28 ft *8,53 m* into 12⅜ in *31,43 cm* of water in a child's paddling pool in Northridge, California, on 7 Apr 1979. He struck the water chest first at a speed of 28.4 mph *45,7 km/h*.

HIGH-WIRE ACT

The greatest height above street level of any

high wire performance has been from a 140 ft *42,6 m* wire between the 1350 ft *411 m* twin towers of the World Trade Center, New York City by Philippe Petit, 24 of Nemours, France on 7 Aug 1974. He was charged with criminal trespass after a 75 min display of at least 7 crossings. The police psychiatrist opined 'Anyone who does this 110 storeys up can't be entirely right'.

HITCH-HIKING

The title of world champion hitch-hiker is claimed by Bill Heid of Allen Park, Mich, USA who from 1964 to 1985 obtained free rides of 305,870 miles *492,248 km*. Stephen Burns of Melbourne, Australia hitched round all 48 coterminous states of the USA in 26 days 6 hr in an 11,438 mile *18,407 km* trip in 56 vehicles on 8 Sept–4 Oct 1984. The hitch-hiking record for the 874 miles *1406 km* from Land's End, Cornwall, to John O'Groats, Highland, Scotland, is 17 hr 50 min by Andrew Markham of Brigg, S Humbs. on 3–4 Sept 1979. The time before the first 'hitch' on the first day is excluded. The fastest time recorded for the round trip is 41 hr 42 min by Anthony D. Sproson of Wolverhampton on 17–19 Sept 1984.

HOD CARRYING

Jim Ford of Bury, Lancs carried bricks totalling 355 lb *161 kg* up the minimum 12 foot *3,65 m* ladder (17 rungs) on 28 June 1984 at Hever Castle, Kent on the International Guinness TV Show presented by David Frost. Eric Stenman of Jakobstad, Finland carried 74 bricks of 4 kg *8.8 lb* each so totalling 651 lb *296 kg* in a 4 kg *8.8 lb* hod 5 metres *16.4 ft* on the flat before ascending up a runged ramp to a height of 7 ft *2,13 m* on 25 July 1939.

HOOP ROLLING

In 1968 it was reported that Zolilio Diaz (Spain)

'Human Fly' Daniel Goodwin practising here on the Bonnadventure Building, Los Angeles, literally scales the heights using only clamps and suction cups. (Anne Marie Weber. T.K.O. Images).

had rolled a hoop 600 miles *965 km* from Mieres to Madrid and back in 18 days.

HOP SCOTCH

The longest recorded hop scotch marathon is one of 101 hr 15 min by Mark Harrison and Tony Lunn at the Studio Night Club, Leicester on 30 Sept–4 Oct 1985.

HOUSE OF CARDS

The greatest number of storeys achieved in building freestanding houses of standard playing cards is 68 to a height of 12 ft 3 in *3,73 m* built by John Sain, 15, of South Bend, Indiana, USA in May 1984.

HULA HOOPING

The highest claim for sustaining gyrating hoops between shoulders and hips is 81 by William Kleeman 'Chico' Johnson (b. 8 July 1939) on BBC TV *Record Breakers* on 18 Sept 1983. Three complete gyrations are mandatory. The feminine record is 65 by Melody Howe (US) on BBC TV *Pebble Mill* on 27 Feb 1985. The longest recorded marathon for a single hoop is 72 hr by Kym Coberly in Denton, Texas, USA on 17–20 Oct 1984.

HUMAN CANNONBALL

The first human cannonball was Emilio Onra *né* Maitrejean at Cirque, D'Hiver, Paris on 21 Nov 1875. The record distance for firing a human from a cannon is 175 ft *53,3 m* in the case of Emanuel Zacchini, son of the pioneer Hugo

Zacchini in the Ringling Bros and Barnum & Bailey Circus, Madison Square Gardens, New York City, USA, in 1940. His muzzle velocity has been estimated at 54 mph *86,9 km/h*. On his retirement the management were fortunate in finding that his daughter Florinda was of the same calibre. An experiment on Yorkshire TV on 17 Aug 1978 showed that when Miss Sue Evans, 17 was fired she was ⅜ in *9,5 mm* shorter on landing.

HUMAN FLY

The longest climb achieved on the vertical face of a building occurred on 25 May 1981 when Daniel Goodwin, 25, scaled the outside of the 1454 ft *443 m* Sears Tower, Chicago in 7 hr 25 min at the rate of 3.2 ft/min *99 cm/min* using 'T' clamps and suction cups. The name of the masked 'human fly', who has ridden at 380 km/h *240 mph* atop a DC-8 jetliner in April 1977 has not been disclosed. It is however believed unlikely that he is a member of the jet set. Lead climber Jean-Claude Droyer (b. 8 May 1946) of Paris and Pierre Puiseux (b. 2 Dec 1953) of Pau, France climbed up the outside of the Eiffel Tower to a height of 300 m *984 ft* with no dynamic mechanical assistance on 21 July 1980. Jean-Claude took 2 hr 18 min 15 sec to complete the climb.

Jaromir Wagner (b. Czechoslovakia 1941) became the first man to fly the Atlantic standing on the wing of an aircraft. He took off from Aberdeen, Scotland on 28 Sept 1980.

JOKE CRACKING

T. R. (Tim) Benker of Chicago told jokes unremittingly for 48 hr at the Mt Prospect Snuggery, Illinois on 27–29 Dec 1984. The duo record is 52 hr by Wayne Malton and Mike Hamilton at the Howard Johnson Motor Hotel, Toronto airport, Ontario, Canada on 13–16 Nov 1975.

JUMBLE SALE

Britain's largest Jumble Sale was 'Jumbly '79' sponsored by *Woman's Own* at Alexandra Palace, London on 5–7 May 1979 in aid of Save The Children Fund. The attendance was 60,000 and the gross takings in excess of £60,000. The Winnetka Congregational Church, Illinois, USA raised $147,378.74 (*then £98,253*) in their 54th one-day rummage sale on 8 May 1986.

The Cleveland Convention Center, Ohio, White Elephant Sale (inst. 1933) on 18–19 Oct 1983 raised $427,935.21 (*then £305,668*).

KARATE CHOP

Claims for breaking bricks and wooden slats etc. are unsatisfactory because of the lack of any agreed standards upon which comparisons can be made of friability and the spacing of fulcrums.

KISS OF LIFE

Five members of the St John Ambulance NSW District at Pier One, Sydney maintained a 'Kiss of Life' for 315 hr with 232,150 inflations on 27 Aug–9 Sept 1984. The 'patient' was a dummy. Robert Stanbury and Wyatt Pace completed a 53 hour CPR (cardiopulmonary resuscitation—15 compressions alternating with 2 breaths) between 15–18 May 1984 in Omaha, Nebraska, USA.

KISSING

The most prolonged osculatory marathon in cinematic history is one of 185 sec by Regis Toomey and Jane Wyman, born Sarah Jane Faulks 4 Jan 1914, (later Mrs Ronald Reagan) in *You're In the Army Now* released in 1940. Eddie Leven and Delphine Crha celebrated the breaking of the record for the longest ever kiss of 17 days 10¼ hr in Chicago, USA on 24 Sept 1985 with a kiss. John McPherson kissed 4444 women in 8 hr in Eldon Square, Newcastle-upon-Tyne on 8 Mar 1985, a rate of 1 each 6.48 sec. The most protracted kiss underwater was one of 2 min 18 sec by Toshiaki Shirai and Yukiko Nagata on Channel 8, Fuji TV, in Tokyo, Japan on 2 Apr 1980.

KITE FLYING *Largest*

The largest kite flown is the Thai Snake flown by Herman van den Broek and Jan Pieter Kuil for 22 min 50 sec at Uithuizen, Netherlands on 11 Aug 1984. It measured 650 m *2133 ft* in length, with an area of 770 m² *8288ft²*.

KITE FLYING *Greatest number*

The most kites flown on a single line is 5581 by Kazuhiko Asaba, 60 at Kamakura, Japan on 8 Nov 1983.

KITE FLYING *Altitude*

The classic record is 9740 m *31,955 ft* by a chain of 8 kites over Lindenberg, East Germany on 1 Aug 1919. The record for a single kite is 22,500 ft (min)–28,000 ft (max) *6860–8530 m* by Prof. Philip R. and Jay P. Kunz of Laramie, Wyoming, USA on 21 Nov 1967. *Kite Lines* magazine of Baltimore, Maryland, USA does not accept triangulation by line angle and length but only range-finder sightings or radar.

KITE FLYING *Duration*

The longest recorded flight is one of 180 hr 17 min by the Edmonds Community College team at Long Beach, Washington, USA on 21–29 Aug 1982. Managing the flight of the J-25 parafoil was Harry N. Osborne.

KNITTING

The world's most prolific hand-knitter of all time has been Mrs Gwen Matthewman of Featherstone, West Yorkshire. She had attained a speed of 111 stitches per min in a test at Phildar's Wool Shop, Central Street, Leeds on 29 Sept 1980. Her technique has been filmed by the world's only Professor of Knitting—a Japanese.

KNOT-TYING

The fastest recorded time for tying the six Boy Scout Handbook Knots (square knot, sheet bend, sheep shank, clove hitch, round turn and two half hitches and bowline) on individual ropes is 8.1 sec by Clinton R. Bailey Sr, 52, of Pacific City, Oregon, USA, on 13 Apr 1977.

LEAP FROGGING

Fourteen members of the Phi Gamma Delta Club at the University of Washington, Seattle, USA, covered 602 miles *968,8 km* in 114 hr 46 min on 20–25 Mar 1983. (Total leaps 108,463—one every 9.77 yd.)

LIFE SAVING

In November 1974 the City of Galveston, Texas and the Noon Optimist Club unveiled a plaque to the deaf-mute lifeguard Leroy Colombo (1905–74) who saved 907 people from drowning in the waters around Galveston Island from 1917 to his death.

LIGHTNING MOST TIMES STRUCK

The only man in the world to be struck by lightning 7 times is ex-Park Ranger Roy C. Sullivan (US) the human lightning conductor of Virginia. His attraction for lightning began in 1942 (lost big toe nail), and was resumed in July 1969 (lost eyebrows), in July 1970 (left shoulder seared), on 16 Apr 1972 (hair set on fire), on 7 Aug 1973 (new hair refired and legs seared), on 5 June 1976 ankle injured, and sent to Waynesboro Hospital with chest and stomach burns on 25 June 1977 after being struck while fishing. In September 1983 he died by his own hand reportedly rejected in love.

LION-TAMING

The greatest number of lions mastered and fed in a cage by an unaided lion-tamer was 40, by 'Captain' Alfred Schneider in 1925. Clyde Raymond Beatty handled more than 40 'cats' (mixed lions and tigers) simultaneously. Beatty (b. Bainbridge, Ohio, 10 June 1903, d. Ventura, California, USA, 19 July 1965) was the featured attraction at every show he appeared with for more than 40 years. He insisted upon being called a lion-trainer. More than 20 lion-tamers have died of injuries since 1900.

LOG ROLLING

The record number of International Championships is 10 by Jubiel Wickheim (of Shawnigan Lake, British Columbia, Canada) between 1956 and 1969. At Albany, Oregon on 4 July 1956 Wickheim rolled on a 14 in. *35,5 cm* log against Chuck Harris of Kelso, Washington USA for 2 hr 40 min before losing. The youngest international log rolling champion is Cari Ann Hayer (b. 23 June 1977), who won her first championship on 15 July 1984 at Mayward, Wisconsin, USA.

MAGICIAN MOST VERSATILE

Under the surveillance of two officers of the British Magical Society, Paul Scott (b. 1937) performed 49 separate tricks in 4 min at the National Agricultural Centre, Stoneleigh, Warwicks on 9 Sept 1984.

MERRY GO ROUND

The longest merry go round marathon on record is one of 312 hr 43 min by Gary Mandau, Chris Lyons and Dana Dover in Portland, Oregon, USA on 20 Aug–2 Sept 1976.

MESSAGE IN A BOTTLE

The longest recorded interval between drop and pick-up is 72 years in the case of a message thrown from the *SS Arawatta* out of Cairns, Queensland on 9 June 1910 in a lotion bottle and reported to be found on Moreton Island on 6 June 1983.

METEOROLOGICAL BALLOON INFLATION

The inflation of a standardized 1000 gramme meteorological balloon to a diameter of 8 ft *2,43 m* against time was achieved by Nicholas Berkeley Mason in 57 min 7 sec for a Fiji TV programme in Tokyo, Japan on 9 Mar 1986.

MILK BOTTLE BALANCING

The greatest distance walked by a person continuously balancing a full pint milk bottle on the head is 24 miles *38,6 km* by Ashrita Furman of Jamaica, NY, USA on 10 July 1983.

MORSE

The highest recorded speed at which anyone has received morse code is 75.2 words per minute—over 17 symbols per second. This was achieved by Ted R. McElroy of the United States in a tournament at Asheville, North Carolina, USA on 2 July 1939. The highest speed recorded for hand key transmitting is 475 symbols a minute by Harry A. Turner of the US Army Signal Corps at Camp Crowder, Missouri on 9 Nov 1942. Thomas Morris, a GPO operator, is reputed to have been able to send at 39–40 wpm in *c.* 1919 but this is not verifiable.

MUSICAL CHAIRS

The largest game on record was one starting with 5151 participants and ending with Bill Bronson on the last chair at University of Notre Dame, Indiana, USA on 6 Sept 1985.

NEEDLE THREADING

The record number of times a strand of cotton can be threaded through a number 13 needle (eye ½ in × 1/16 in, *12,7 mm × 1,6 mm*) in 2 hr is 3795 by Miss Brenda Robinson of the College of Further Education, Chippenham, Wiltshire on 20 Mar 1971.

NOODLE MAKING

Mark Pi of the China Gate Restaurant, Columbus, Ohio, USA made 2048 noodle strings (over 5 ft *1,52 m*) in 34.5 sec on 12 Feb 1983.

OMELETTE MAKING

The greatest number of two-egg omelettes made in 30 min is 315 by John Elkhay at the City Lights Restaurant in Providence, Rhode Island, USA on 29 June 1985.

ONION PEELING

The record for peeling 50 lb *22,6 kg* of onions is 3 min 18 sec by Alain St. John in Plainfield, Conn., USA, on 6 July 1980. Under revised rules stipulating a minimum of 50 onions, Alfonso Salvo of York, Pennsylvania, USA peeled 50 lb *22,67 kg* of onions (52 onions) in 5 min 23 sec on 28 Oct 1980.

PARACHUTING
Longest fall without

Vesna Vulovic, 22, a Jugoslavenski Aerotransport hostess, survived when her DC–9 blew up at 33,330 ft *10 160 m* over the Czechoslovak village of Serbska Kamenice on 26 Jan 1972. She was in hospital for 16 months after emerging from a 27 day coma.

GUINNESS BOOK OF RECORDS HALL OF FAME

1986

ORGAN

The longest recorded electric organ marathon is one of 411 hr by Vince Bull at the Comet Hotel, Scunthorpe, South Humberside on 2–19 June 1977. The longest church organ recital ever sustained has been 110 hr by Angie Thompson at St. Stephen's Church, Newport, Brough, Humberside on 16–20 Apr 1985.

PADDLE BOATING

The longest recorded voyage is 2226 miles *3582 km* in 103 days by the foot power of Mick Sigrist and Brad Rud down the Mississippi

River from the headwaters in Minnesota to the Gulf of Mexico on 4 Aug–11 Nov 1979.

PARACHUTING *Longest fall without*

It is estimated that the human body reaches 99 per cent of its low level terminal velocity after falling 1880 ft *573 m* which takes 13–14 secs. This is 117–125 mph *188–201 km/h* at normal atmospheric pressure in a random posture, but up to 185 mph *298 km/h* in a head down position.

The British record is 18,000 ft *5485 m* by Flt-Sgt Nicholas Stephen Alkemade, aged 21, who jumped from a blazing RAF *Lancaster* bomber over Germany on 23 Mar 1944. His headlong fall was broken by a fir tree near Oberkürchen and he landed without a broken bone in a snow bank 18 in *45 cm* deep.

PIANO-PLAYING

The longest piano-playing marathon has been one of 1218 hr (50 days 18 hr) playing 22 hr every day (with 5 min intervals each playing hour) from 7 May to 27 June 1982 by David Scott at Wagga Wagga Leagues Football Club, NSW, Australia. *Category now discontinued.*

PIANO SMASHING

The record time for demolishing an upright piano and passing the entire wreckage through a circle 9 in *22,8 cm* in diameter is 1 min 37 sec by six members of the Tinwald Rugby Football

PARACHUTING
Longest delayed drop

Joseph Kittinger, a Captain in the US Air Force achieved the longest delayed drop on 16 Aug 1960. He jumped from a balloon 19.47 miles *31,33 km* above the earth at Tularosa, New Mexico and fell for 4 min 36 sec (16.04 miles *25,81 km*) before deploying his parachute. During the fall, he broke the sound barrier.

GUINNESS BOOK OF RECORDS HALL OF FAME

1986

Club, Ashburton, New Zealand led by David Young on 6 Nov 1977. Messrs Anthony Fukes, Mike Newman and Terry Cullington smashed a piano with bare hands and feet in 2 min 53 sec in Nottingham on 25 Aug 1979. (All wreckage was passed through the circle.)

PIANO TUNING

The record time for pitch raising (one semi-tone or 100 cents) and then returning a piano to a musically acceptable quality is 4 min 20 sec by Steve Fairchild at the Piano Technicians Guild contest at the Dante Piano Co factory, NY, USA on 5 Feb 1980.

PARACHUTING RECORDS

Category	Name		Place	Date
First from Tower[1]	Louis-Sébastian Lenormand (1757–1839)	quasi-parachute	Montpellier France	1783
First from Balloon	André-Jacques Garnerin (1769–1823)	2230 ft *680 m*	Monceau Park, Paris	22 Oct ... 1797
Earliest Mid-air Rescue	Miss Dolly Shepherd brought down Miss Louie May on her single 'chute	from balloon at 11,000 ft *3350 m*	Longton, Staffordshire	9 June ... 1908
First from Aircraft (man)	'Captain' Albert Berry	Aerial exhibitionist	St. Louis, Missouri	1 Mar ... 1912
(woman)	Mrs Georgina 'Tiny' Broadwick (b. 1893)		Griffith Park, Los Angeles	21 June ... 1913
Lowest Escape	S/Ldr Terence Spencer, DFC, RAF	30–40 ft *9–12 m*	Wismar Bay, Baltic	19 April ... 1945
Longest Duration Fall	Lt Col Wm H. Rankin, USMC	40 min due to thermals	North Carolina	26 July ... 1956
Highest Escape	Flt Lt J. de Salis and Fg Off P. Lowe, RAF	56,000 ft *17 068 m*	Monyash, Derby	9 April ... 1958
Longest Delayed Drop (man)	Capt Joseph W. Kittinger[2]	84,700 ft 16.04 miles *25 816 m* from balloon at 102,800 ft *31 333 m*	Tularosa, New Mexico	16 Aug ... 1960
(woman)	O. Kommissarova (USSR)	14 100 m *46,250 ft.*	over USSR	21 Sept ... 1965
(civilian, over UK)	P. Halfacre, R. O'Brien, R. James	27,300 ft *8321 m* from 30,000 ft *9144 m*	Sibson, Peterborough	27 Aug ... 1983
(civilian, world)	R. W. K. Beckett (GB) Harry Ferguson (GB)	30,000 ft *9144 m* from 32,000 ft *9754 m*	D. F. Malan Airport, Capetown	23 Nov ... 1969
(group, U.K.)	S/Ldr J. Thirtle, AFC; Fl Sgt A. K. Kidd, AFM; Sgts L. Hicks (d. 1971), P. P. Keane, AFM BEM, K. J. Teesdale, AFM	39,183 ft *11 943 m* from 41,383 ft *12 613 m*	Boscombe Down, Wiltshire	16 June ... 1967
Longest Base Jump[3]	Carl Ronald Boenische; Jean K. Campbell Boenische	5784 ft *1763 m*	Trollveggan Spire, Romsdal, Norway	4 July ... 1984
Most Southerly	T/Sgt Richard J. Patton (d. 1973)	Operation Deep Freeze	South Pole	25 Nov ... 1956
Most Northerly	Dr Jack Wheeler (US); pilot Capt. Rocky Parsons	− 25° F (− 31,6° C)	In Lat. 90° 00' N	15 Apr ... 1981
Cross Channel (Lateral fall)	Sgt. Bob Walters with 3 soldiers and 2 Royal Marines	22 miles *35,4 km* from 25,000 ft *7600 m*	Dover to Sangatte, France	31 Aug ... 1980
Career total (man)	Yuri Baranov and Anatolyi Osipov (USSR)	10,000	over USSR	to Sept ... 1980
(woman)	Valentina Zakoretskaya (USSR)	8000	over USSR	1964–Sept 1980
Highest Landing	Ten USSR parachutists[4]	23,405 ft *7133 m*	Lenina Peak	May ... 1969
Heaviest Load	US Space Shuttle *Columbia* external rocket retrieval	80 ton capacity, triple array, each 120 ft *36,5 m* diameter	Atlantic off Cape Canaveral, Florida	12 Apr ... 1981
Highest from Bridge	Donald R. Boyles	1053 ft *320 m*	Royal Gorge, Colorado	7 Sept ... 1970
Highest Tower Jump	Herbert Leo Schmidtz (US)	KTUL-TV Mast 1984 ft *604 m*	Tulsa, Oklahoma	4 Oct ... 1970
Biggest Star (17 sec hold)	99 man team	Formation held 17 sec (US Parachuting Assc. rules)	Freeport, Illinois	3 Apr ... 1985
Highest column (world)	28 USA team		United Parachute Club, Gilbertsville, Pennsylvania	22 Sept ... 1985
(Great Britain)	23 Royal Marine Team		Netheravon, Wilts	17 Dec ... 1985
Lowest Indoor Jump	Andy Smith and Phil Smith	192 ft *58,5 m*	Houston Astrodome, Texas	16–17 Jan. ... 1982
Most travelled	Kevin Seaman from a Cessna Skylane (pilot Charles E. Merritt)	12,186 miles *19 611 km*	Jumps in all 50 US States	26 July–15 Oct 1972
Oldest Man	Edwin C. Townsend	89 years	Vermillion Bay, Louisiana, USA	5 Feb ... 1986
Woman	Mrs. Stella Davenport (GB)	75 years 8 months	Bridlington Aerodrome, Humberside	27 June ... 1981
24 Hr Total	David Huber (US)	250	Issaquah, Washington, USA	3–4 July ... 1985

[1] The king of Ayutthaya, Siam in 1687 was reported to have been diverted by an ingenious athlete parachuting with two large umbrellas. Faustus Verancsis is reputed to have descended in Hungary with a framed canopy in 1617.
[2] Maximum speed in rarefied air was 625.2 mph 1006 km/h. at 90,000 ft *27 430 m*—marginally supersonic.
[3] 'Base' is an acronym for jumping from fixed objects—Building, Antenna, Span and Earth. Carl Boenische was killed on 7 July 1984.
[4] Four were killed.

PILLAR BOX MOUNTING

The record number to pile on top of or hang from a pillar box (oval top of 6 ft² *0,55 m²*) is 32, all students of Wentworth College, York University in Parliament St., York on 27 Feb 1985.

PIPE SMOKING

The duration record for keeping a pipe (3,3 g *0.1 oz* of tobacco) continuously alight with only an initial match under IAPSC (International Association of Pipe Smokers Clubs) rules is 126 min 39 sec by the five-time champion William Vargo of Swartz Creek, Michigan at the 27th World Championships in 1975. The only other 5-time champion is Paul T. Spaniola (USA) (1951–66–70–73–77). On 18 Aug 1984 Joe Oetli achieved 130 min 11 sec at the 15th Iowa State Fair contest using *two* matches. Longer durations have been recorded in less rigorously invigilated contests in which the foul practices of 'tamping' and 'gardening' are not unknown.

PLANE PULLING

Dave Gauder, 30, frustrated the take-off of two Piper Cherokees by holding two tow ropes despite a pull of 612 kg *1349 lb* at Bobbington, Staffs on 16 July 1985.

PLATE SPINNING

The greatest number of plates spun simultaneously is 72 by Shukuni Sasaki of Takamatsu, Japan at Nio Town Taiyo Exhibition, Kagawa, on 16 July 1981. The British record is 54 set by Holley Gray set during BBC *Record Breakers* on 6 May 1980.

POGO STICK JUMPING

The greatest number of jumps achieved is 130,077 by Gary Stewart in Reading, Ohio, USA on 8–9 Mar 1985. Ashrita Furman set a distance record of 11.1 miles *17.8 km* in New York, USA on 8 Jan 1986.

POLE-SQUATTING

Modern records do not, in fact, compare with that of St Simeon the Younger, (c. 521–597 AD) called Stylites, a monk who spent his last 45 years up a stone pillar on The Hill of Wonders, near Antioch, Syria. This is probably the longest lasting example of record setting.

There being no international rules, the 'standards of living' atop poles vary widely. Mark Sutton, finally descended from his pole on 1 July 1985 in Victoria, B.C., Canada after 488 days.

Robert 'Rob' C. Roy (b. 1961) stayed in a barrel (max. capacity 108 gallons) atop a pole (30 ft *9,14 m*) outside The Black Horse, Darlaston, Staffordshire for 34 days 22 hrs 10 mins on 28 July–1 Sept 1984.

POP GROUP

The duration record for a 4-man group is 147 hr by the 'Decorators' at Becketts Bar, Bexhill-on-Sea, East Sussex on 8–14 Jan 1984.

POTATO PEELING

The greatest amount of potatoes peeled by 5 people to an institutional cookery standard with standard kitchen knives in 45 min is 266,5 kg *587 lb 8 oz* by J. Mills, M. McDonald, P. Jennings, E. Gardiner and V. McNulty at Bourke Street Hall, Melbourne, Vic, Australia on 17 Mar 1981.

PRAM PUSHING

The greatest distance covered in pushing a pram in 24 hr is 345.25 miles *555,62 km* by Runner's Factory of Los Gatos, California, USA with an All-Star team of 57 California runners on 23–24 June 1979. A 10 man Royal Marine team from the Commando Training Centre, Lympstone, Devon, with an adult 'Baby', covered 252.65 miles *406.60 km* in 24 hr on 31 Mar–18 Apr 1984.

'PSYCHIATRIST' FASTEST

The world's fastest 'psychiatrist' was Dr Albert L. Weiner of Erlton, New Jersey, USA, who was trained solely in osteopathy but who dealt with up to 50 psychiatric patients a day in four treatment rooms. He relied heavily on narco-analysis, muscle relaxants and electro-shock treatments. In December 1961 he was found guilty on 12 counts of manslaughter from using unsterilized needles.

QUIZZES

The highest number of participants was 80,977 in the All Japan High School Quiz Championship televised by NTV on 31 Dec 1983. The most protracted contest was that lasting 110 hrs in Long Hanborough, Oxfordshire on 27 Mar–1 Apr 1986. The two teams correctly answered 22,483 of the 37,310 questions.

QUOIT THROWING

The world's record for rope quoit throwing is an unbroken sequence of 4002 pegs by Bill Irby, Snr of Australia in 1968.

RAMP JUMPING

The longest distance ever achieved for motor cycle long jumping is *64,60 m* 212 ft over 16 buses by Alain Jean Prieur (b. 4 July 1939) of France at Montlhéry near Paris on 6 Feb 1977. The pioneer of this form of exhibition—Evel Knievel (b. Robert Craig Knievel, 17 Oct 1938 at Butte, Montana, USA) had suffered 433 bone fractures by his 1975 season. His abortive attempt to cross the 1600 ft *485 m* wide and 600 ft *180 m* deep Snake River Canyon, Idaho on 8 Sept 1974 in a rocket reputedly increased his life-time earnings by $6 million (*then £2¼ million*). The longest jump in Britain is 208 ft *63,30 m* by Chris Bromham at Bromley Common, South London on 29 Aug 1983. The longest ramp jump in a car by a professional stunt driver is 232 ft *70,73 m* by Jacqueline De Creed (*née* Creedy) in a 1967 Ford Mustang at Santa Pod Raceway, Bedfordshire on 3 Apr 1983.

RAPPELING (or Abseiling)

On 26 July 1982 Jim Bridwell and John N. Long (both USA) descended down the face of the precipice adjacent to the Angel Falls in Venezuela on an 1800 ft *548 m* nylon rope. The longest descent down the side of a skyscraper is one of 580 ft *176,7 m* (52 storeys) in Hong Kong by Capt. Martin Fuller (1st Bn Cheshire Regt.) on 1 Sept 1984.

RIDING IN ARMOUR

The longest recorded ride in full armour (8 stone *50,8 kg*) is one of 167 miles *268,7 km* from Edinburgh to Dumfries in 3 days (riding time 28 hr 30 min) by Dick Brown, 48, on 13–15 June 1979.

RIVETING

The world's record for riveting is 11,209 in 9 hr by J. Moir at the Workman Clark Ltd shipyard, Belfast, Northern Ireland, in June 1918. His peak hour was his seventh with 1409, an average of nearly 23½ per min.

ROCKING CHAIR

The longest recorded 'Rockathon' is 444 hr by Linda Kennedy at the IKEA store, Calgary, Alberta, Canada on 16 Jan–3 Feb 1984.

ROLLING PIN

The record distance for a woman to throw a 2 lb *907 g* rolling pin is 175 ft 5 in *53,4 m* by Lori La Deane Adams, 21 at Iowa State Fair, Iowa, USA, on 21 Aug 1979.

SAND SCULPTURING

The longest sand sculpture was an 8498 ft *2590 m* long representation of a 19th century train along Virginia Beach, Virginia, USA on 2 Oct 1983 organized by Louise Lowenthal. The tallest sculpture is by Sand Sculpture International who built the 'Lost City of Atlantis' on Treasure Island, Florida, USA on 21–26 Apr 1986. It measures 16,08 m *52 ft 9 inches* in height.

SCOOTER RIDING

The greatest distance covered by a team of 25 in 24 hr is 336.11 miles *540,93 km* by Wimmera Young Farmers, Victoria, Australia on 22–23 Mar 1980.

SEARCH *Longest*

Walter Edwin Percy Zillwood (b. Deptford, London SE8, Dec 1900) traced his missing sister Lena (Mrs Elizabeth Eleanor Allen, b. Nov 1897, d. Jan 1982) after 79 years through the agency of the Salvation Army on 3 May 1980.

SEE-SAW

George Partridge and Tamara Marquez of Auburn High School, Washington, USA on a suspension see-saw completed 1101 hr 40 min (indoor) on 28 Mar–13 May 1977. Georgia Chaffin and Tammy Adams of Goodhope Jr. High School, Cullman, Alabama, USA completed 730 hr 30 min (outdoor) on 25 June–25 July 1975.

SERMON

The longest sermon on record was delivered by the Rev. Ronald Gallagher at the Baptist Temple, Lynchburg, Virginia, USA for 120 hr on 26 June–1 July 1983. From 31 May to 10 June 1969 the 14th Dalai Lama (b. 6 July 1934 as Tenzin Gyalto) the exiled ruler of Tibet, completed a sermon on Tantric Buddhism for 5–7 hr per day to total 60 hr in India.

SHAVING

The fastest demon barber on record is Gerry Harley, who shaved 987 men in 60 min with a safety razor in Gillingham, Kent on 28 Apr 1983 taking a perfunctory 3.64 sec per volunteer. On 13 Aug 1984 he shaved 235 even braver volunteers with a cutthroat razor in a less perfunctory 15.3 sec per face. He drew blood only once.

SHEAF TOSSING

The world's best performance for tossing a 3,63 kg *8 lb* sheaf for height is 19,77 m *64.86 ft* by Trond Ulleberg of Skolleborg, Norway on 11 Nov 1978. Such pitchfork contests date from 1914.

SHOESHINE BOYS

In this category (limited to a team of 4 teenagers; duration of 8 hr; shoes 'on the hoof') the record is 6780 pairs by the Sheffield Citadel Band of Salvation Army, S. Yorkshire, on 27 Feb 1982.

Going solo . . . for over 8 days. Jorge Chamorro records the world's longest singing marathon in Barcelona. Certainly a record of note(s)!

SHORTHAND FASTEST

The highest recorded speeds ever attained under championship conditions are: 300 words per min (99.64 per cent accuracy) for 5 min and 350 wpm (99.72 per cent accuracy, that is, two insignificant errors) for 2 min by Nathan Behrin (USA) in tests in New York in December 1922. Behrin (b. 1887) used the Pitman system invented in 1837. Morris I. Kligman, official court reporter of the US Court House, New York has taken 50,000 words in 5 hr (a sustained rate of 166.6 wpm). Rates are much dependent upon the nature, complexity and syllabic density of the material. Mr. G. W. Bunbury of Dublin, Ireland held the unique distinction of writing at 250 wpm for 10 min on 23 Jan 1894.

Mr Arnold Bradley achieved a speed of 309 words per minute without error using the Sloan-Duployan system with 1545 words in 5 minutes in a test in Walsall, West Midlands on 9 Nov 1920.

SHOUTING

The greatest number of wins in the national town criers' contest is 11 (between 1939–73) by Ben Johnson of Fowey, Cornwall. The first national feminine champion has been Mrs Henrietta Sargent, town-crier, of The Three Horse Shoes, Cricklade, Wiltshire in 1980. On being told she had beaten the other 31 contestants she said 'I'm speechless'. In the seventh International Town Criers Championships in Halifax, Nova Scotia, Canada on 15 Sept 1984, Donald H. Burns of St George's Bermuda won the Loudest Cry Trophy with 113 decibels. (See also Longest-ranged voice, Chapter 1 page 17.)

SHOWERING

The most prolonged continuous shower bath on record is one of 340 hr 40 min by Kevin

McCartney of State University College at Buffalo, New York, USA, on 29 Mar to 12 Apr 1985. The feminine record is 121 hr 1 min by Lisa D'Amato on 5–10 Nov 1981 at Harpur College, Binghamton, New York, USA. Desquamation can be a positive danger.

SINGING

The longest recorded solo singing marathon is one of 200 hr 20 min by Jorge Antonio Hidalgo Chamorro at the Piano Bar, Barcelona, Spain, on 7–11 Nov 1985. The marathon record for a choir has been 72 hr 2 min by the combined choir of Girls' High School and Prince Edward School, Salisbury (now Harare), Zimbabwe on 7–10 Sept 1979. Acharya Prem Bhikuji started chanting the Akhand Rama-Dhoon since 31 July 1964 and devotees have continued these devotions which were still in progress in 23 Dec 1985.

SKATE BOARDING

'World' championships have been staged intermittently since 1966. David Frank, 25 covered 270.483 miles *435,3 km* in 36 hr 43 min 40 sec in Toronto, Canada on 11–12 Aug 1985.

The highest speed recorded on a skate board under USSA rules is 71.79 mph *115,53 km/h* on a course at Mt Baldy, California in a prone position by Richard K. Brown, 33, on 17 June 1979. The stand-up record is 53.45 mph *86,01 km/h* by John Hutson, 23 at Signal Hill, Long Beach, California on 11 June 1978. The high jump record is 5 ft 5.7 in *1,67 m* by Trevor Baxter (b. 1 Oct 1962) of Burgess Hill, East Sussex at Grenoble, France on 14 Sept 1982. At the 4th US Skateboard Association championship, at Signal Hill on 25 Sept 1977, Tony Alva, 19, jumped 17 barrels (17 ft *5,18m*).

SLINGING

The greatest distance recorded for a sling-shot is 1434 ft 2 in *437,13 m* using a 51 in *129,5 cm* long sling and a 2 oz *56,5 g* stone by Lawrence L. Bray at Loa, Utah, USA on 21 Aug 1981.

SMOKE RING BLOWING

The highest recorded number of smoke rings formed from the lips from a single pull of a cigarette (cheek-tapping is disallowed) is 355 by Jan van Deurs Formann of Copenhagen achieved in Switzerland in August 1979.

SNOW SHOEING

The U.S.S.A. record for covering a mile *1609,34 m* is 7 min 56 sec by Mark Lessard at Corinth, New York, USA in 1979.

SPEAR THROWING

The greatest distance achieved throwing a spear with the aid of a woomera is 326 ft 6 in *99,51 m* (or 17 ft 4 in *5,29 m* beyond the Javelin record) by Bailey Bush on 27 June 1982 at Camden, NSW, Australia.

SPINNING BY HAND

The duration record for spinning a clock balance wheel by unaided hand is 5 min 26.8 sec by Philip Ashley, 16, of Leigh, Lancashire on 20 May 1968. The record using 36 in *91,4 cm* of string with a 7¼ oz *205,5 g* top is 58 min 20 sec by Peter Hodgson at Southend-on-Sea, Essex on 4 Feb 1985.

SPITTING

The greatest distance achieved at the annual tobacco spitting classic (instituted 1955) at Raleigh, Mississippi, USA, is 33 ft 7½ in *10,24 m*

by Jeff Barber on 25 July 1981. (In 1980 he reached 45 ft *13,71 m* at Fulton, Miss. and on 29 June 1985 he won a record 13th National Spitting title at Raleigh, Miss.). In the 3rd International Spittin', Belchin' and Cussin' Triathlon, Harold Fielden reached 34 ft 0¼ in *10,36 m* at Central City, Colorado, USA, on 13 July 1973. Distance is dependent on the quality of salivation, absence of cross wind, the two finger pucker and coordination of the back arch and neck snap. Sprays or wads smaller than a dime are not measured. Randy Ober of Bentonville, Arkansas, USA spat a tobacco wad 47 ft 7 in *14,50 m* at the Calico 5th Annual Tobacco Chewing and Spitting Championships north of Barstow, California, USA on 4 Apr 1982. The record for projecting a melon seed under WCWSSCA rules is 65 ft 4 in *19,91 m* by John Wilkinson in Luling, Texas, USA, on 28 June 1980. The furthest reported distance for a cherry stone is 65 ft 2 in *19,86 m* by Rick Krause, at Eau Claire, Michigan, USA on 5 July 1980. Spitters who care about their image wear 12 in *30,4 cm* block-ended boots so practice spits can be measured without a tape.

SQUARE DANCE CALLING

Alan Covacic called continuously for 24 hr 2 min for the Wheelers and Dealers SDC at St. John's Hospital, Stone, Buckinghamshire on 23–24 Nov 1984.

STAIR CLIMBING

The 100 storey record for stair climbing was set by Dennis W. Martz in the Detroit Plaza Hotel, Detroit, Michigan, USA, on 26 June 1978 at 11 min 23.8 sec. Dale Neil, 22, ran a vertical mile on the stairs of the Peachtree Plaza Hotel, Atlanta, Georgia in continuous action of 2 hr 1 min 24 sec on 9 Mar 1984. *These records can only be attempted in buildings with a minimum of 70 storeys.*

The record for the 1760 steps (vertical height 1122 ft *342 m*) in the world's tallest free-standing structure, Toronto's CN Tower, is 10 min 10 sec by Michael Round on 9 Aug 1980. Robert C. Jezequel ran 17 round trips in 11 hr 20 min on 18 Oct 1985 without use of the elevator for a vertical height of 15 708 ft *4787 m*.

Pete Squires raced up the 1575 steps of the Empire State Building, New York City on 12 Feb 1981 in 10 min 59 sec.

In the line of duty Bill Stevenson mounted 334 of the 364 steps of the tower in the Houses of Parliament, 4000 times in the 15 years (1968–83)—equivalent to 24.9 ascents of Everest.

STANDING

The longest period on record that anyone has continuously stood is for more than 17 years in the case of Swami Maujgiri Maharij when performing the *Tapasya* or penance from 1955 to November 1973 in Shahjahanpur, Uttar Pradesh, India. When sleeping he would lean against a plank. He died aged 85 in Sept 1980.

STAMP LICKING

Paul Robinson (using the GPO London rules) licked and affixed 175 definitive stamps in 4 minutes at Christchurch, New Zealand on 30 Aug 1985.

STILT-WALKING

Hop stringers use stilts up to 15 ft *4.57 m*. In 1892 M. Garisoain of Bayonne stilt-walked 8 km *4.97 miles* into Biarritz in 42 min to average 11,42 km/h *7.10 mph*. In 1891 Sylvain Dornon stilt-walked from Paris to Moscow *via* Vilno in

50 stages for the 1830 miles *2945 km*. Another source gives his time as 58 days. Even with a safety or Kirby wire very high stilts are *extremely dangerous*—25 steps are deemed to constitute 'mastery'. Eddy Wolf (also known as Steady Eddy) of Loyal, Wisconsin, USA mastered stilts measuring 40 ft 6½ in *12,36 m* from ground to ankle over a distance of 27 steps without touching his safety handrail wires, at Yokohama Dreamland Park, Yokohama on 9 Mar 1986. His aluminium stilts weighed 55 lb *25 kg* each. Joe Long (b. Kenneth Caesar), who has suffered 5 fractures, mastered 56 lb *25,4 kg* 24 ft *7,31 m* stilts at the BBC TV Centre, London on 8 Dec 1978. The endurance record is 3008 miles *4804 km* from Los Angeles, California to Bowen, Kentucky, USA, from 20 Feb to 26 July 1980 by Joe Bowen. Masaharu Tatsushiro, 28, (Japan) ran 100 m *328 ft* on 1 ft *30,48 cm* high stilts in 14.15 sec in Tōkyō on 30 Mar 1980.

STOWAWAY

The most rugged stowaway was Socarras Ramirez who escaped from Cuba on 4 June 1969 by stowing away in an unpressurized wheel well in the starboard wing of a Douglas DC8 from Havana to Madrid in a 5600 mile *9010 km* Iberian Airlines flight. He survived 8 hr at 30,000 ft *9145 m* where temperatures were −8° F *−22° C*.

STRETCHER BEARING

The longest recorded carry of a stretcher case with a 10 st *63,5 kg* 'body' is 127 miles *204,34 km* in 45 hr 45 min by two four man teams from the Sri Chinmoy marathon team of Jamaica, NY, USA, on 17–19 Apr 1981.

The record limited to Youth Organizations (under 20 years of age) and 8 hr carrying is 42.02 miles *67,62 km* by 8 members of the Henry Meoles School, Moreton, Wirral, Cheshire on 13 July 1980.

STRING BALL LARGEST

The largest ball of string on record is one of 12 ft 9 in *3,88 m* in diameter, 40 ft *12,19 m* in circumference and weighing 10 tons/*tonnes* amassed by Francis A. Johnson of Darwin, Minnesota, USA, between 1950–78.

SUBMERGENCE

The most protracted underwater endurance record (excluding the use of diving bells) is 147 hr 15 min established by Robert Ingolia in tests in which the US Navy was the beneficiary of all data in 1961.

The *continuous* duration record (i.e. no rest breaks) for 'Scuba' (i.e. self-contained and without surface air hoses) is 212 hr 30 min by Michael Stevens of Birmingham in a Royal Navy tank at the National Exhibition Centre, Birmingham on 14–23 Feb 1986. Measures have to be taken to reduce the risk of severe desquamation in such endurance trials.

SUGGESTION BOXES

The most prolific example on record of the use of any suggestion box scheme is that of John Drayton (b. 18 Sept 1907) of Newport, Gwent who has plied British Rail system with a total of 31,215 suggestions from 1924 to May 1986 of which over 100 have been accepted. In 1983 he was presented with a chiming clock by British Rail to mark almost 60 years of suggestions.

SWINGING

The record duration for continuous swinging in a hammock is 196 hr by Patrick Galvin and Mark Ungar of San Mateo, California on 31 July–8 Aug 1984.

SWITCHBACK RIDING

The endurance record for rides on a roller coaster is 503 hr by M. M. Daniel Glada and Normand St-Pierre at Parc Belmont, Montreal, Canada on 18 July–10 Aug 1983. The minimum qualifying average speed required is 25 mph *40 km/h*.

TAILORING

The highest speed in which the manufacture of a 3 piece suit has been made from sheep to finished article is 1 hr 34 min 33.42 sec by 65 members of the Melbourne College of Textiles, Pascoe Vale, Victoria, Australia on 24 June 1982. The catching and fleecing took 2 min 21 sec, and the carding, spinning, weaving and tailoring occupied the remaining time.

TALKING

The world record for non-stop talking has been 7 days 15 min by Hugh Porter at the Queensland Government Travel Center, Brisbane from 24 Sept–10 Oct 1984. A feminine non-stop talking record was set by Mrs Mary E. Davis, who on 2–7 Sept 1958 started at a radio station in Buffalo, New York, USA and did not draw breath until 110 hr 30 min 5 sec later in Tulsa, Oklahoma, USA. (See also Filibusters, Chap 11.)

Historically the longest recorded after-dinner speech with unsuspecting victims was one of 3 hr by the Rev. Henry Whitehead (d. March 1896) at the Rainbow Tavern, Fleet Street, London on 16 Jan 1874. At a dinner at St. George's Hotel, Lime Street, Liverpool Paul Osgood (b. 11 Jan 1964) replied to the toast to the guests for 16 hr 6 min on 21–22 Mar 1985.

T-BONE DIVE

The so-called T-bone dives or Dive Bomber crashes by cars off ramps over and on to parked cars are often measured by the number of cars, but owing to their variable size and that their purpose is purely to cushion the shock, distance is more significant.

Jean-Pierre Vignan attained 59,86 m *196 ft 5 in* in a Ford Capri at Montlhéry, Paris on 20 July 1980.

TEETH-PULLING

The man with 'the strongest teeth in the world' is 'Hercules' John Massis (b. Wilfried Oscar Morbée, 4 June 1940) of Oostakker, Belgium, who raised a weight of 233 kg *513¾ lb* 15 cm *6 in* from the ground with a teeth bit at Evrey, France on 19 Mar 1977. Massis prevented a helicopter from taking off using only a tooth-bit harness in Los Angeles, California, USA on 7 Apr 1979 for a *Guinness Spectacular* TV Show.

THROWING

The greatest distance any inert object heavier than air has been thrown is 1298 ft *395,63 m*, in the case of the Skyro flying ring by Tom McRann, 35, of Menlo Park, California, USA on 21 May 1986 at Santa Clara, California. The ring made of plastic and rubber weighs 3.21 oz *91 g* and has a diameter of 11½ in *29,21 cm*.

TIGHTROPE WALKING

The greatest 19th century tightrope walker was Jean François Gravelet, *alias* Charles Blondin (1824–97), of France, who made the earliest crossing of the Niagara Falls on a 3 in *76 mm* rope, 110 ft *335 m* long, 160 ft *48,75 m* above the Falls on 30 June 1859. He also made a crossing with Harry Colcord, pick-a-back on 15 Sept 1860. Though other artists still find it difficult to believe, Colcord was his agent. The oldest wirewalker was 'Professor' William Ivy Baldwin (1866–1953), who crossed the South Boulder Canyon, Colorado, USA on a 320 ft *97,5 m* wire with a 125 ft *38,1 m* drop on his 82nd birthday on 31 July 1948.

TIGHTROPE WALKING *Endurance*

The world tightrope endurance record is 185 days by Henri Rochetain (b. 1926) of France on a wire 394 ft *120 m* long, 82 ft *25 m* above a supermarket in Saint Etienne, France, on 28 Mar–29 Sept 1973. His ability to sleep on the wire has left doctors puzzled. Steven G. Wallenda, 33, walked 2.36 miles *3,81 km* on a wire 250 ft *76,2 m* long 32 ft *9,75 m* high at North Port, Florida, USA on 26 Mar 1983 in 3 hr 31 min.

TIGHTROPE WALKING *Highest and Steepest*

Steve McPeak (b. 21 April 1945) of Las Vegas, Nevada, USA ascended the 46,6 mm *1.83 in* diameter Zugspitzbahn cable for a vertical height of 705 m *2313 ft* in 3 stints aggregating 5 hr 4 min on 24/25/28 June 1981. The maximum gradient over the stretch of 2282 m *7485 ft* was above 30 degrees. Earlier on 28 June 1981 he had walked on a thinner stayed cable 181 steps across a gorge at the top of the 2963 m *9721 ft* mountain with a sheer drop of 960 m *3150 ft* below him.

The first crossing of the River Thames was achieved by Charles Elleano (b. 1911) of Strasbourg, France on a 1050 ft *320 m* wire 60 ft *18,2 m* above the river in 25 min on 22 Sept 1951.

TREE-CLIMBING

The fastest speed climb up a 100 ft *30,4 m* fir spar pole and return to the ground is one of 27.16 sec by Ed Johnson of Victoria, BC, Canada in July 1982 at the Lumberjack World Championships in Hayward, Wisconsin.

The fastest time up a 9 m *29.5 ft* coconut tree barefoot is 4.88 sec by Fuatai Solo, 17, in Sukuna Park, Fiji on 22 Aug 1980.

TREE-SITTING

The duration record for sitting in a tree is 431 days by Timothy Roy at Golf N'Stuff Amusement Park, Norwalk, Calif., USA from 4 July 1982–8 Sept 1983.

TYPEWRITING *Longest*

The world duration record for typewriting on an electric machine is 264 hr by Violet Gibson Burns at The Royal Easter Show, Sydney, Australia on 29 Mar–9 Apr 1985.

The longest duration typing marathon on a manual machine is 120 hr 15 min by Mike Howell, a 23-year-old blind office worker from Greenfield, Oldham, Greater Manchester on 25–30 Nov 1969 on an Olympia manual typewriter in Liverpool. In aggregating 561,006 strokes he performed a weight movement of 2482 tons *2521 tonnes* plus a further 155 tons *157 tonnes* on moving the carriage for line spacing. Les Stewart of Mudjimba Beach, Qld, Australia has typed the numbers 1 to 417,000 in *words* on 8230 quarto sheets as of 26 Feb 1986. His target is to become a "millionaire".

TYPEWRITING *fastest*

The highest recorded speeds attained with a ten-word penalty per error on a manual machine are:

Five Min: 176 wpm net Mrs Carole Forristall Waldschlager Bechen at Dixon, Illinois on 2 Apr 1959. One Hour: 147 words (net rate per min) Albert Tangora (US) (Underwood Standard), 22 Oct 1923.

The official hour record on an electric machine is 9316 words (40 errors) on an IBM machine, giving a net rate of 149 words per min, by Margaret Hamma, now Mrs Dilmore (US), in Brooklyn, New York City, NY, USA on 20 June 1941. Mary Ann Morel (South Africa) set a numerical record at the CABEX '85 Exhibition in Johannesburg, South Africa on 6 Feb 1985 by typing spaced numbers from 1 to 781 in 5 min.

In an official test in 1946 Stella Pajunas, now Mrs Garnard, attained a rate of 216 words in a minute on an IBM machine.

TYRE SUPPORTING

The greatest number of motor tyres supported in a free-standing 'lift' is 96 by Gary Windebank of Romsey, Hants in Feb 1984. The total weight was 1440 lb *653 kg*. The tyres used were Michelin XZX 155 × 13.

UNSUPPORTED CIRCLE

The highest recorded number of people who have demonstrated the physical paradox of all being seated without a chair is an unsupported circle of 10,323 employees of the Nissan Motor Company at Komazawa Stadium, Tokyo, Japan on 23 Oct 1982.

WAITERS MARATHON

Beverly Hills restaurateur Roger Bourban, Switzerland, *Le garçon rapide*, ran a full marathon in full uniform in London on 9 May 1982 carrying a free standing open bottle of mineral water on a tray in the same hand (gross weight 3 lb 2 oz *1,42 kg*) in 2 hr 47 min.

WALKING ON HANDS

The duration record for walking on hands is 1400 km *871 miles* by Johann Hurlinger, of Austria, who in 55 daily 10 hr stints, averaged 1.58 mph *2,54 km/h* from Vienna to Paris in 1900. Thomas P. Hunt of USAF Academy, Colorado Springs, completed a 50 m *54.68 yd* inverted sprint in 18.4 sec in Tokyo on 22 Sept 1979. Four men (Bob Sutton, Danny Scannell, Phil Johnson and John Hawkins) relayed a mile in Oak Ridge, Tennessee, USA on 13 Mar 1983 in 31 min 15.8 sec.

WALKING ON WATER

Using outsize shoes-cum-floats Fritz Weber walked on the Main from Beyreuth over 300 km *185 miles* to Mainz on 1 Sept to 15 Oct 1983.

WALL OF DEATH

The greatest endurance feat on a wall of death was 6 hr 7 min 38 sec by Hugo Dabbert (b. Hildesheim, 24 Sept 1938) at Rüsselsheim, West Germany on 14 Aug 1980. He rode 6841 laps on the 10 m *32.8 ft* diameter wall on a Honda CM 400T averaging 35,2 km/h *21.8 mph* for the 214,8 km *133.4 miles*.

WHIP CRACKING

The longest stock whip ever 'cracked' (*i.e.* the end made to travel above the speed of sound— 760 mph *1223 km/h*) is one of 140 ft *42,67 m* (excluding the handle) wielded by Garry Brophy at Adelaide, Australia on 31 Oct 1985.

WHISTLING *Loudest and Longest*

Roy Lomas achieved 122.5 decibels at 2½ metres in the Deadroom at the BBC Manchester Studios on 19 Dec 1983. The whistling marathon record is by David Frank of Toronto, Canada, who completed 30 hr 10 min non-stop at the Annapurnn Vegetarian Restaurant, Toronto, on 23–24 Nov 1985.

WINDOW CLEANING

On 19 Oct 1984 at the Clearview Challenge Cup contest, Sydney, Australia Roy Ridley achieved 18.92 sec without a smear for three standard *40.94 × 45.39 in* 1040 × 1153 mm office windows with a *11.8 in* 300 mm long squeegee and *15.83 pts* 9 litres of water.

WIRE SLIDE

The greatest distance recorded in a wire slide is from a height of 175 ft *53,3 m* over a distance of 300 ft *91,44 m* by Grant Page with Bob Woodham over his shoulder across the Australian landmark known as 'The Gap' for the filmed episode in 'The Stunt Men' in 1972.

WOOD-CUTTING

The earliest competitions date from Tasmania in 1874. The records set at the Lumberjack World Championships at Hayward, Wisconsin, USA, (founded 1960) are:

Power Saw		8.73 sec
Sven Johnson (US)		1983
One-Man Bucking		21.70 sec
Merv Jensen (NZ) (d. Apr 1983)		1982
Standing Block Chop		25.38 sec
Mel Lentz (US)		1982
Underhand Block Chop		18.66 sec
Mel Lentz (US)		1982
Two-Man Bucking		9.44 sec
Merv Jensen (NZ) Cliff Hughes (NZ)		1982
Hand Splitting a cord into quarters*		
		53 min 40 sec
Richard Sawyer (US)		1982

White pine logs 14 in *35,5 cm* diameter are used for chopping and 20 in *50,8 cm* for sawing.
* Hardwood (white ash) cord of 128 ft³ *3,62 m³* using a quartering wedge at Sag Harbour, NY, on 2 July 1982.

WRITING MINISCULE

In 1926 an account was published of Alfred McEwen's pantograph record in which the 56 word version of the Lord's Prayer was written by diamond point on glass in the space of 0.0016 × 0.0008 in *0,04 × 0,02 mm*. Frank C. Watts of Felmingham, Norfolk demonstrated for photographers on 24 Jan 1968, his ability, without mechanical or optical aid, to write the Lord's Prayer 34 times (9452 letters) within the size of a definitive UK postage stamp (viz.) 0.84 × 0.71 in *21,33 × 18,03 mm*. Tsutomu Ishii of Tokyo demonstrated the ability to write the names of 44 countries (184 letters) on a single grain of rice and TOKYO JAPAN in Japanese on a human hair in April 1983. In Dec 1980 Michael Isaacson, Associate Professor of the School of Applied and Engineering Physics, Cornell University, Ithaca, New York, succeeded in etching the 16 letters in 'molecular devices' on a sodium chloride crystal with a 100,000 volt electron beam. The 'writing' was 2 nanometers wide.

Mary Ann Morel soaks her weary fingers after typing spaced numbers from 1 to 781 in 5 minutes. Quite a speedy type!

WRITING UNDER HANDICAP

The ultimate feat in 'funny writing' appears to be the ability to write extemporaneously and decipherably backwards, upside down, laterally inverted (mirror-style) while blindfolded with both hands simultaneously. Three claims to this ability with both hands and feet simultaneously, by Mrs Carolyn Webb of Thirlmere, NSW, Australia, Mrs Judy Hall of Chesterfield, Virginia, USA, and Robert Gray of Toronto, Ontario, Canada are outstanding but have not been witnessed in the act by our staff.

YODELLING

The most protracted yodel on record was that of Errol Bird for 26 hr in Lisburn, Northern Ireland on 27–28 Sept 1984. Yodelling has been defined as 'repeated rapid changes from the chest-voice to falsetto and back again'. The most rapid recorded is 5 tones (3 falsetto) in 1.9 sec by Donn Reynolds of Canada on 25 July 1984.

YO-YO

A Yo-yo was a toy in Grecian times and is depicted on a bowl dated 450 B.C. It was also a Filipino jungle fighting weapon recorded in the 16th century weighing 4 lb *1,81 kg* with a 20 ft *6 m* thong. The word means 'come-come'. Though illustrated in a book in 1891 as a bandalore the craze did not begin until it was started by Donald F. Duncan of Chicago, USA in 1926. The most difficult modern yo-yo trick is the 'Whirlwind' incorporating both inside and outside horizontal loop-the-loops. The individual continuous endurance record is 120 hr by John Winslow of Gloucester, Virginia, USA on 23–28 Nov 1977. Dr Allen Bussey in Waco, Texas, USA on 23 Apr 1977 completed 20,302 loops in 3 hr (including 6886 in a single 60 min period). He used a Duncan Imperial with a 34½ in *87,6 cm* nylon string. Spins of 8000 rpm have been recorded.

The largest yo-yo ever constructed was one by Dr Tom Kuhn weighing 256 lb *116,11 kg* test launched from a 150 ft *52,2 m* crane in San Francisco, California, USA, on 13 Oct 1979.

GLUTTONY RECORDS

Records for eating and drinking by trenchermen do not match those suffering from the rare disease of bulimia (morbid desire to eat) and polydipsia (pathological thirst). Some bulimics exceed 20,000 calories a day and others eat all their waking hours. An extreme consumption of 384 lb 2 oz *174,236 kg* of food in six days by Matthew Daking, aged 12 (known as Mortimer's case) was reported in 1743. Fannie Meyer of Johannesburg, after a skull fracture, was stated in 1974 to be unsatisfied by less than 160 pints of water a day. By October 1978 he was down to 52 pints. Miss Helge Andersson (b. 1908) of Lindesberg, Sweden was reported in January 1971 to have been drinking 40 pints *22,73 litres* of water a day since 1922—a total of 87,600 gal *3982 hectolitres*.

The world's greatest trencherman has been Edward Abraham ('Bozo') Miller (b. 1909) of Oakland, California, USA. He consumes up to 25,000 calories per day or more than 11 times that recommended. He stands 5 ft 7½ in *1,71 m* tall but weighs from 20 to 21½ st *127–139 kg* with a 57 in *144 cm* waist. He had been undefeated in eating contests since 1931 (see below). He ate 27 (2 lb *907 g*) pullets at a sitting in Trader Vic's, San Francisco in 1963. Phillip Yadzik (b. 1912)

CIRCUS RECORDS

The world's largest permanent circus is Circus Circus, Las Vegas, Nevada, USA opened on 18 Oct 1968 at a cost of $15,000,000 (*then £6,250,000*). It covers an area of 129,000 ft² *11 984 m²* capped by a tent-shaped flexiglass roof 90 ft *27,43 m* high. The largest travelling circus is the Circus Vargas in the USA which can accommodate 5000 people under its Big Top.

Flying Trapeze

Downward circles or 'Muscle grinding'—1350 by Sarah Denu (age 14) (US) Madison, Wisconsin, USA, 21 May 1983. Single heel hang on swinging bar, Angela Revelle (Angelique), Australia, 1977.

Highest Aerial Act

Ian Ashpole (b. 15 Jan 1956) of Ross-on-Wye, Hereford and Worcester performed a trapeze act suspended from a hot air balloon between St. Neots, Cambridgeshire and Newmarket, Suffolk at 16,420 ft *5004,8 m* on 16 May 1986.

Triple Twisting Double Somersault

Tom Robin Edelston to catcher John Zimmerman, Circus World, Florida, 20 Jan 1981.

Full Twisting Triple and the Quadruple Somersault

Vasquez Troupe. Miguel Vasquez to catcher Juan Vasquez at Ringling Bros, Amphitheatre, Chicago, USA in Nov 1981. On 20 Sept 1984 he performed a triple somersault in a layout position (no turn) to catcher Juan Vasquez at the Sports Arena, Los Angeles, California, USA.

Triple Back Somersault with 1½ Twists

Terry Cavaretta Lemus (now Mrs. St Jules). At Circus Circus, Las Vegas, Nevada, USA in 1969.

Teeter Board

Six man high perch pyramid, Emilia Ivanova (Bulgaria) of the Kehaiovi Troupe at Inglewood, California, USA, 21 July 1976.

Trampoline

Septuple twisting back somersault to bed and quintuple twisting back somersault to shoulders by Marco Canestrelli to Belmonte Canestrelli at Madison Square, NY, USA on 5 Jan and 28 Mar 1979. Richard Tison (France) performed a triple twisting triple back somersault for television near Berchtesgaden, West Germany on 30 June 1981.

Flexible Pole

Double full twisting somersault to a 2 in *5,08 cm* diameter pole by Roberto Tabak (aged 11) in Sarasota, Florida, USA in 1977. Triple full twisting somersault by Corina Colonelu Mosoiann (aged 13) at Madison Square Gardens, New York, USA on 17 Apr 1984.

Human Pyramid (or Tuckle)

Twelve (3 high) supported by a single understander. Weight 771 kg *1700 lb* or 121.4 stone by Tahar Douis of the Hassani Troupe at BBC TV Pebble Mill Studio, Birmingham, England, on 17 Dec 1979.

Nine high by top-mounter Josep-Joan Martínez Lozano, 10, of the Colla Vella dels Xiquets 12 m *39 ft* tall on 25 Oct 1981 in Valls, Spain.

Clown, Oldest

Charlie Revel (b. Andrea Lassere in Spain 24 Apr 1896) performed for 82 years (1899–1981).

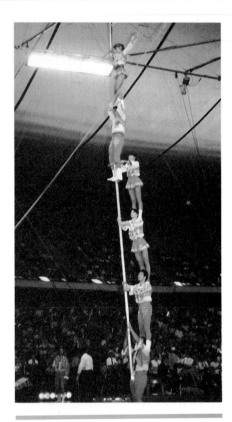

Perched on top of five people, Corina Colonelu Mosoiann performed a full twisting triple somersault to a flexible pole.

JUGGLING RECORDS

7 clubs

Albert Petrovski (USSR), 1963; Sorin Munteanu (Romania), 1975; Jack Bremlov (Czech), currently

8 plates

Enrico Rastelli (Italy), 1896–1931

10 balls

Enrico Rastelli (Italy), 1896–1931

11 rings

Albert Petrovski (USSR), 1963–66; Eugene Belaur (USSR), 1968; Sergei Ignatov (USSR), 1973

Pirouettes with 3 cigar boxes

Kris Kremo (Swiss) (quadruple turn with 3 boxes in mid-air), 1977

Duration 5 clubs

16 min 20 sec, Ignatov in USSR, 1977

3 clubs while running—Joggling

Albert Lucas, USA, 100 m in 12.67 sec, 1984. Scott Damgaard, USA, 1 mile *1,6 km* in 4 min 37 sec, 1981. Marty Gardella, USA, 5 km *3.1 miles* in 18 min 47.95 sec, 1982.

5 ping-pong balls with mouth

Gran Picaso (Spain), 1971

5 balls inverted

Bobby May (USA), since 1953

of Chicago in 1955 ate 77 large hamburgers in 2 hours and in 1957 101 bananas in 15 min. The bargees on the Rhine are reputed to be the world's heaviest eaters with 5200 calories a day. However the New Zealand Sports Federation of Medicine reported in December 1972 that a long-distance road runner consumed 14,321 calories in 24 hr.

While no healthy person has been reported to have succumbed in any contest for eating non-toxic food or drinking non-alcoholic drinks, such attempts, from a medical point of view, must be regarded as *extremely* inadvisable, particularly among young people. Gluttony record attempts should aim at improving the *rate* of consumption rather than the volume. The Guinness Book of Records will not list any records involving the consumption of more than 2 litres *3.52 Imperial pints* of beer nor any at all involving spirits. Nor will records for such potentially dangerous categories as live ants, chewing gum, marsh mallow or raw eggs with shells be published. The ultimate in stupidity—the eating of a bicycle—has however been recorded since it is unlikely to attract competition.

Liquidising, processing or puréeing foodstuffs is not permitted. However drinking during attempts is permissible.

Specific records have been claimed as follows:

BAKED BEANS
2780 cold baked beans one by one with a cocktail stick in 30 min by Karen Stevenson, of Wallasey, Merseyside on 4 Apr 1981.

BANANAS
17 (edible weight minimum 4½ oz *128 g* each) in 2 min by Dr Ronald L. Alkana at the University of California, Irvine on 7 Dec 1973.

BEER
Steven Petrosino drank one litre of beer in 1.3 sec on 22 June 1977 at 'The Gingerbreadman', Carlisle, Pennsylvania.
Peter G. Dowdeswell (b. London 29 July 1940) of Earls Barton, Northants holds the following records:
2 pints—2.3 sec Zetters Social Club, Wolverton, Bucks, 11 June 1975.
2 litres—6.0 sec Carriage Horse Hotel, Higham Ferrers, Northants, 7 Feb 1975.
Yards of Ale
2⅓ pints—5.0 sec RAF Upper Heyford, Oxfordshire, 4 May 1975.
3 pints—5.00 sec Royal Oak, Bishop's Cleeve, Gloucestershire, 6 July 1985.
3½ pints—5.44 sec Easby Street, Nottingham, 5 July 1985.

Upsidedown
2 pints—6.4 sec Top Rank Club, Northants, 25 May 1975.

CHAMPAGNE
1000 bottles per annum by Bobby Acland of the 'Black Raven', Bishopsgate, City of London.

CHEESE
16 oz *453 g* of Cheddar in 1 min 13 sec by Peter Dowdeswell (see above) in Earls Barton, Northants on 14 July 1978.

CHICKEN
2.1 kg *4 lb 10 oz* in 10 min 37 sec by Valentin Florentino Muñoz Muñoz at Kortezubi, Vizcaya, Spain on 27 Apr 1986.

CLAMS
424 (Littlenecks) in 8 min by Dave Barnes at Port Townsend Bay, Washington, USA on 3 May 1975.

COCKLES
2 pints *113,5 centilitres* in 60.8 sec by Tony Dowdeswell at Kilmarnock, Ayrshire on 1 June 1984.

DOUGHNUTS
12¾ (51 oz *1,445 kg*) in 5 min 46 sec by James Wirth, and 13 (52 oz *1,474 kg*) in 6 min 1.5 sec by John Haight, both at the Sheraton Inn, Canandaigua, New York on 3 Mar 1981.

EELS
1 lb *453 g* of elvers in 13.7 sec by Peter Dowdeswell at Reeves Club, Bristol on 20 Oct 1978.

EGGS
(Hard Boiled) 14 in 58 sec by Peter Dowdeswell (see above) at the Stardust Social Club, Corby, Northants on 18 Feb 1977.
(Soft Boiled) 38 in 75 sec by Peter Dowdeswell in Kilmarnock, Ayrshire on 28 May 1984.
(Raw) 13 in 1.0 sec by Peter Dowdeswell at Kilmarnock, Ayrshire on 16 May 1984.

FRANKFURTERS
23 (2 oz *56,6 g*) in 3 min 10 sec by Lynda Kuerth, 21, at the Veterans Stadium, Philadelphia, on 12 July 1977.

GHERKINS
1 lb *453 g* in 41.60 sec by Peter Dowdeswell at Ronelles Discoteque on 8 Feb 1986.
1 lb *453 g* (liquidized) in 35.2 sec by Peter L. Citron on TV in San Francisco, USA on 1 Apr 1983. *This category has now been retired.*

GRAPES
3 lb 1 oz of grapes in 34.6 sec by Jim Ellis of Montrose, Michigan, USA on 30 May 1976.

HAGGIS
26 oz *737 g* in 49 sec by Peter Dowdeswell at The Grand Hotel, Hartlepool on 21 Feb 1983.

HAMBURGERS
21 hamburgers (each weighing 3½ oz *100 g* totalling *2,07 kg* of meat) and buns in 9 min 42 sec by Peter Dowdeswell at Cockshut Hill School, Yardley, Birmingham on 30 June 1984.

ICE CREAM
3 lb 6 oz *1,530 kg* in 50.04 sec by Tony Dowdeswell at the Cardinal Wolsey Hotel, East Molesey, Surrey on 26 Jan 1984. The ice cream must be unmelted.

JELLY
20 fl oz *56,8 centilitres* in 13.11 sec by Peter Dowdeswell at Stoke Mandeville, Buckinghamshire on 27 June 1984. The jelly must be gelatinous.

KIPPERS
27 (self-filleted) in 60 min by Karen Stevenson of Wallasey, Merseyside on 5 Mar 1982.

LEMONS
12 quarters (3 lemons) whole (including skin and pips) in 15.3 sec by Bobby Kempf of Roanoke, Virginia, USA on 2 May 1979.

MEAT
One whole roast ox in 42 days by Johann Ketzler of Munich, Germany in 1880.

MEAT PIES
22 (each weighing 5½ oz *156 g*) in 18 min 13 sec by Peter Dowdeswell of Earls Barton, Northants on 5 Oct 1978.

MILK
2 pt (1 Imperial quart or *113,5 centilitres*) in 3.2 sec by Peter Dowdeswell (see above) at Dudley Top Rank Club, West Midlands on 31 May 1975.

OYSTERS (*Eating, Opening*)
6 lb *2,72 kg* (edible mass of 288) in 1 min 33 sec by Tommy Greene in Annapolis, Maryland on 6 July 1985. The record for opening oysters is 100 in 2 min 45.5 sec by W. Heath Jr at Babson Park, Florida, USA on 28 Oct 1983.

PANCAKES
(6 inch *15,2 cm* diameter buttered and with syrup) 62 in 6 min 58.5 sec by Peter Dowdeswell (see above) at The Drapery, Northampton on 9 Feb 1977.

PEANUTS
100 (whole unshelled) singly in 46 sec by Jim Kornitzer, 21 at Brighton, Sussex on 1 Aug 1979.

PEAS
7175 petit pois one by one in 60 min using chopsticks by Mrs Janet Harris, Seal Hotel, Selsey, West Sussex on 16 Aug 1984.

PICKLED ONIONS
91 pickled onions (total weight 30 oz *850 g*) in 1 min 8 sec by Pat Donahue in Victoria, British Columbia on 9 Mar 1978.

PIZZA
825 g *1.8 lb* in 5 min 23 sec by Geir Storvann of Drammen, Norway on 24 Aug 1984 at Karl Johans Gate, Oslo, Norway.

POTATOES
3 lb *1,36 kg* in 1 min 22 sec by Peter Dowdeswell in Earls Barton, Northants on 25 Aug 1978.

POTATO CRISPS
Thirty 2 oz *56,6 g* bags in 24 min 33.6 sec, without a drink, by Paul G. Tully of Brisbane University in May 1969.

Valentin Florentino Muñoz Muñoz of Spain didn't chicken out from eating his way to a world record—4 lb 10 oz of roast chicken in just 10 min 37 sec. (E Prieto, Maeva, SA).

PRUNES
144 in 34 sec by Peter Dowdeswell at Easy Street Nightclub, Nottingham on 26 Apr 1985.

RAVIOLI
5 lb *2,25 kg* (170 squares) in 5 min 34 sec by Peter Dowdeswell at Pleasurewood Hills American Theme Park, Lowestoft, Suffolk on 25 Sept 1983.

SANDWICHES
40 in 17 min 53.9 sec (jam 'butties' 6 × 3¾ × ½ in *15,2 × 9,5 × 1,2 cm*) by Peter Dowdeswell on 17 Oct 1977 at The Donut Shop, Reedley, California, USA.

SAUSAGE MEAT
2630 g *5 lb 12¾ oz* (96 pieces) in 4 min 29 sec by Peter Dowdeswell on Fuji TV, Tōkyō, Japan on 24 Feb 1985. No 'Hot Dog' contest results have been remotely comparable.

SHRIMPS
3 lb *1,36 kg* in 3 min 10 sec by Peter Dowdeswell at Weymouth, Dorset on 7 Aug 1985.

SNAILS
1,1 kg *38.8 oz* in 1 min 5.6 sec by Andoni Basterrechea Dominguez at Kortezubi, Vizcaya, Spain on 27 Apr 1986.

SPAGHETTI
100 yd *91,44 m* in 21.7 sec by Peter Dowdeswell at The Globe Hotel, Weedon, Northants on 25 Feb 1983.

STRAWBERRIES
2 lb *907 g* in 12.95 sec by Peter Dowdeswell at Easby Street, Nottingham on 5 July 1985.

SUSHI
680 g *1½ lb* of nigiri-sushi in 1 min 13.5 sec in Tōkyō, Japan by Peter Dowdeswell on 22 February 1985.

TORTILLA
74 (total weight 4 lb 1½ oz *1,85 kg*) in 30 min by Tom Nall in the 2nd World Championship at Mariano's Mexican Restaurant, Dallas, Texas, USA on 16 Oct 1973.

TREE
11 ft *3,35 m* Birch (4.7 in *12 cm* diameter trunk) in 89 hr by Jay Gwaltney, 19 on WKQX's 'Outrageous Contest', Chicago, 11–15 Sept 1980.

WHELKS
100 (unshelled) in 5 min 17 sec by John Fletcher at The Apples and Pears Public House, Liverpool Street Station, London on 18 Aug 1983.

WINKLING
50 shells picked (with a straight pin) in 3 min 15 sec by Mrs B. Charles at Eastbourne, East Sussex on 4 Aug 1982.

GREATEST OMNIVORE
Michel Lotito (b. 15 June 1950) of Grenoble, France, known as Monsieur Mangetout, has been eating metal and glass since 1959. Gastroenterologists have X-rayed his stomach and have described his ability to consume 2 lb *900 g* of metal per day as unique. His diet since 1966 has included 10 bicycles, a supermarket trolley in 4½ days, 7 TV sets, 6 chandeliers and a low calorie Cessna light aircraft which he ate in Caracas, Venezuela. He is said to have provided the only example in history of where a coffin (handles and all) ended up inside a man.

WEALTH AND POVERTY

The comparison and estimations of extreme personal wealth are beset with intractable difficulties. Quite apart from reticence and the element of approximation in the valuation of assets, as Jean Paul Getty (1892–1976) once said 'if you can count your millions you are not a billionaire'. The term millionaire was invented c. 1740 and billionaire (in the American sense of one thousand million) in 1861. The earliest dollar centi-millionaire was Cornelius Vanderbilt (1794–1877) who left $100 million in 1877. The earliest billionaires were John Davison Rockefeller (1839–1937); Henry Ford (1863–1947) and Andrew William Mellon (1855–1937). In 1937, the last year in which all 3 were alive, a billion US dollars were worth £205 million but that amount of sterling would today have a purchasing power exceeding £5000 million.

Richest men *World*

Many of the riches of most of the world's 29 remaining monarchs are national rather than personal assets. The least fettered and most monarchical is H.M. Sir Muda Hassanal Bolkiah Mu'izzaddin Waddaulah Hon GCMG (b. 15 July 1946) of Brunei. He appointed himself Prime Minister, Finance and Home Affairs Minister on 1 Jan 1984. Brunei's annual oil revenue is £3000 million and its foreign reserves are £10,000 million all of which is effectually at his disposal.

The richest man in the United States has been Gordon Peter Getty (b. 1930), fourth son of Jean Paul Getty by his fourth wife Ann Rork, and sole trustee of the Sarah C. Getty Trust valued in Sept 1984 at $4100 million (*£3400 million*) but reduced by taxes and an estate split to under $1 billion by 1986.

The annual rankings in *Forbes Magazine* for 1985 list 13 billionaires headed by Sam Moore Walton, 67 of Wal-Mart Stores of Bentonville, Arkansas, USA.

Richest man *Great Britain*

The richest man in Great Britain is reputed to be Sir John Moores, CBE the co-founder of Littlewoods football pools in 1924. In 1973 he was estimated to be worth about £400 million (hence £1600 million in 1986). His first job after leaving school at 14 was as a telephone operator. He was born in Eccles, Lancashire on 25 Jan 1896. He reassumed the chairmanship of Littlewoods on 17 Oct 1980 and finally retired in February 1982.

Highest incomes

The greatest incomes derive from the collection of royalties per barrel by rulers of oil-rich sheikhdoms, who have not abrogated personal entitlement. Shaikh Zayid ibn Sultan an-Nuhayan (b. 1918) head of state of the United Arab Emirates arguably has title to some $9000 million of the country's annual gross national product.

The highest gross income ever achieved in a single year by a private citizen is an estimated $105,000,000 (*then £21¼ now £390 million*) in 1927 by the Neopolitan born Chicago gangster Alphonse ('Scarface Al') Capone (1889–1947). This was derived from illegal liquor trading and alky-cookers (illicit stills), gambling establishments, dog tracks, dance halls, 'protection' rackets and vice in which there were in 1925–27 nil convictions from 915 murders by his 'Italian Mob' in South Chicago. On his business card the former 'bouncer' and brothel-keeper described himself as a 'Second hand Furniture Dealer'. The highest gross earned income in a year by a UK subject is reputedly in excess of £25 million earned by Paul McCartney MBE in the years since 1979.

Proved wills and death duties

Sir John Reeves Ellerman, 2nd Bt, (1909–73) left £53,238,370 on which all-time record death duties were payable. This is the highest value will ever proved in the United Kingdom. On 29 Apr 1985 the estate of Sir Charles Clore (1904–1979) was agreed at £123 million. The Inland Revenue claimed £84 million but settled for £67 million. The greatest will proved in Ireland was that of the 1st Earl of Iveagh (1847–1927), who left £13,486,146.

Most millionaires

The United States was estimated to have some 832,500 millionaire families in early 1985 with the million mark expected by December 1986. Most work 6 days a week for an average $121,000 (*£79,000*) per annum.

Millionairesses

The world's wealthiest woman was probably Princess Wilhelmina Helena Pauline Maria of Orange-Nassau (1880–1962), formerly Queen of the Netherlands from 1890 to her abdication, 4 Sept 1948, with a fortune which was estimated at over £200 million. The largest amount proved in the will of a woman in the United Kingdom has been the £7,607,168 of the Rt. Hon Countess of Sefton in 1981. Mrs. Anna Dodge (later Mrs. Hugh Dillman) who was born in Dundee, Scotland, died on 3 June 1970 in the United States, aged 103, and left an estate of £40,000,000.

The cosmetician Madame C. J. Walker *née* Sarah Breedlove (b. Delta, Louisiana, USA 23 Dec 1867, d. 1919) is reputed to have become the first self-made millionairess. She was an uneducated Negro orphan scrub-woman whose fortune was founded on a hair straightener.

Millionaire and millionairess *Youngest*

The youngest person ever to accumulate a million dollars was the child film actor Jackie Coogan (b. Los Angeles, 26 Oct 1914) co-star with Sir Charles Chaplin (1889–1977) in 'The Kid' made in 1920. Shirley Temple (b. Santa Monica, California 23 Apr 1928), formerly Mrs John Agar, Jr, now Mrs Charles Black, accumulated wealth exceeding $1,000,000 (*then £209,000*) before she was 10. Her child actress career spanned the years 1934–9.

Richest families

It has been tentatively estimated that the combined value of the assets nominally controlled by the du Pont family of some 1600 members may be of the order of $150,000 million. The family arrived in the USA from France on 1 Jan 1800. Capital from Pierre du Pont (1730–1817) enabled his son Eleuthère Irénée du Pont to start his explosives company in the United States. It was estimated in 1985 that both sons and both daughters of Haroldson Lafayette Hunt were billionaires.

Largest dowry

The largest recorded dowry was that of Elena Patiño, daughter of Don Simón Iturbi Patiño (1861–1947), the Bolivian tin millionaire, who in 1929 bestowed £8,000,000 from a fortune at one time estimated to be worth £125,000,000.

Greatest miser

If meanness is measurable as a ratio between expendable assets and expenditure then Henrietta (Hetty) Howland Green (*née* Robinson) (1835–1916), who kept a balance of over $31,400,000 (*then £6.2 million*) in one bank alone, was the all-time world champion. Her son had to have his leg amputated because of her delays in finding a *free* medical clinic. She herself ate cold porridge because she was too thrifty to heat it. Her estate proved to be of $95 million (*then £19 million [and now worth £270 million]*).

Return of cash

The largest amount of *cash* ever found and returned to its owners was $500,000 (US) found by Lowell Elliott, 61 on his farm at Peru, Indiana, USA. It had been dropped in June 1972 by a parachuting hi-jacker. Jim Priceman, 44, assistant cashier at Doft & Co Inc returned an envelope containing $37.1 million (*then £20.6 million*) in *negotiable* bearer certificates found outside 110 Wall Street to A G Becker Inc of New York City on 6 April 1982. In announcing a reward of $250 (*then £140*) Beckers were acclaimed as 'being all heart'.

Greatest bequests

The greatest bequests in a life-time of a millionaire were those of the late John Davison Rockefeller (1839–1937), who gave away sums totalling $750,000,000 (*now £350 million*). The greatest benefactions of a British millionaire were those of William Richard Morris, later the Viscount Nuffield, GBE, CH (1877–1963), which totalled more than £30,000,000 between 1926 and his death on 22 Aug 1963. The Scottish-born US citizen Andrew Carnegie (1835–1919) is estimated to have made benefactions totalling £70 million during the last 18 years of his life. These included 7689 church organs and 2811 libraries. He had started life in a bobbin factory at $1.20 per week.

The largest bequest made in the history of philanthropy was the $500,000,000 (*then £178,570,000*) gift, announced on 12 Dec 1955, to 4157 educational and other institutions by the Ford Foundation (established 1936) of New York City, NY, USA.

Salary Highest *World*

The highest reported remuneration of any US businessman was $51,544,000 (*£33¼ million*) in salary, bonus and stock options received by Mr Frederick W. Smith, board chairman of Federal Express in 1982. The highest amount in salary in 1985 was $12.7 million (*£8.8 million*) paid by DWG Corporation of Miami Beach, Florida to Victor Posner, their Chairman of the Board.

Highest Fees

The highest paid investment consultant in the world is Harry D. Schultz, who operates from Western Europe. His standard consultation fee for 60 minutes is $2400 on weekdays and $3400 at weekends. His quarterly retainer permitting calls on a daily basis is $28,125. He edits an information packed International Newsletter instituted in 1964 now sold at $50 or *£35* per copy.

Salary Highest *Great Britain*

The highest salary paid by any public company in 1986 was £883,000 to Mr Richard Giordano (b. New York 1931), Chairman and Chief Executive of BOC (British Oxygen) International.

Share options

The record profit on a share option is £1,010,000 for Sir Francis Tombs (b. 17 May 1924) on 500,000 Turner & Newall shares. He had been appointed chairman in 1982.

Golden handshake

The highest carat handshake reported was one of 'nearly £700,000' on 20 Jan 1983 attributed to Mr Bill Fieldhouse CBE (b. 1 Jan 1932) from Letraset of which he had been a director since 1969.

Lowest incomes

The poorest people in the world are the Tasaday tribe of cave-dwellers of central Mindanao, Philippines, who were 'discovered' in 1971 without any domesticated animals, agriculture, pottery, wheels or clothes.

3. HONOURS, DECORATIONS AND AWARDS

Oldest Order

The earliest honour known was the 'Gold of Honour' for extraordinary valour awarded in the 18th dynasty c. 1440–1400 BC. A statuette was found at Qan-el-Kebri, Egypt. The order which can trace its origins furthest back is the Military Hospitaller Order of St Lazarus of Jerusalem founded by St Basil the Great in the 4th Century AD. A date as early as AD 809 has been attributed to the Most Ancient Order of the Thistle but is of doubtful provenance. The Order of St John in Scotland, founded in 1124, was suppressed in the 16th century but revived in 1947. The prototype of the princely Orders of Chivalry is the Most Noble Order of the Garter founded by King Edward III in c. 1348.

Eponymous record

The largest object to which a human name is attached is the universe itself—in the case of three different cosmological models devised in 1922 by the Russian mathematician Aleksandr Aleksandrovitch Friedman (1888–1925).

Most titles

The most titled person in the world is the 18th Duchess of Alba (Alba de Tormes), Doña Maria del Rosario Cayetana Fitz-James Stuart y Silva. She is 8 times a duchess, 15 times a marchioness, 21 times a countess and is 19 times a Spanish grandee.

Versatility

The only person to win a Victoria Cross and an Olympic Gold Medal has been Lt Gen Sir Philip Neame, VC, KBE, CB, DSO (1888–1978). He won the VC in 1914 and was an Olympic gold medallist for Britain for rifle shooting in 1924 though under the illusion at the time that he was shooting for the British Empire. The only George Cross holder who was also a Fellow of the Royal Society was Prof Peter Victor Danckwerts, GC, MBE, FRS F Eng (1916–1985) who defused 16 parachute mines in under 48 hr in the London docks during the Battle of Britain as a Sub Lt RNVR in August 1940.

Victoria Cross *Double awards*

The only three men ever to have been awarded a bar to the Victoria Cross (instituted 29 Jan 1856) are:

Surg-Capt (later Lt-Col) Arthur Martin-Leake, VC*, VD, RAMC (1874–1953) (1902 and bar 1915).
Capt Noel Godfrey Chavasse, VC*, MC, RAMC (1884–1917) (1916 and bar posthumously 14 Sept 1917).
Second Lieut (later Capt) Charles Hazlitt Upham, VC*, NZMF (b. 21 Sept 1908) (1941 and bar 1942).

The most VC's awarded in a war were the 634 in World War I (1914–18). The greatest number won in a single action was 11 at Rorke's Drift in the Zulu War on 22–23 Jan 1879. The school with most recipients is Eton College, Col H. H. Jones being the 36th in the Falklands Campaign.

Victoria Cross *Youngest*

The lowest established age for a VC is 15 years 100 days for Hospital Apprentice Andrew (wrongly gazetted as Arthur) Fitzgibbon (born at Peteragurh, northern India, 13 May 1845) of the Indian Medical Services for bravery at the Taku Forts in northern China on 21 Aug 1860. The youngest living VC is Capt Rambahadur Limbu (b. 1 Nov 1939, Chyangthapu, Nepal) of the 10th Princess Mary's Own Gurkha Rifles. The award was for his courage as a L/Cpl while fighting in the Bau district of Sarawak, East

Malaysia, on 21 Nov 1965. He retired on 25 Mar 1985.

Victoria Cross *Longest lived*

The longest lived of all the 1351 winners of the Victoria Cross has been Lt Col Harcus Strachan VC. He was born in Bo'ness, Scotland on 7 Nov 1884 and died in Vancouver, Canada on 1 May 1982 aged 97 years 175 days.

Most highly decorated

The six living persons to have been twice decorated with any of the United Kingdom's topmost decorations are Capt C. H. Upham VC and bar; the Viscount De L'Isle VC, KG; HM the Queen Mother CI, GCVO, GBE, who is a Lady of the Garter and a Lady of the Thistle; HRH the Duke of Edinburgh KG, KT, OM, GBE; HRH Prince Charles KG, KT, GCB and HM King Olaf V of Norway KG, KT, GCB, GCVO. Lord De L'Isle is the only person who has both the highest military and highest civil honour. Britain's most highly decorated woman is the World War II British agent Mrs Odette Hallowes GC, MBE, Légion d'Honneur, Ordre St George (Belge), who survived imprisonment and torture at the hands of the Gestapo in 1943–45. Violette Reine Elizabeth Szabo (*née* Bushnell) GC (1921–45) lost her husband in the French Legion at El Alamein in 1942. He was Etienne Szabo, Médaille Militaire, Legion d'Honneur and Croix de Guerre.

Top jet ace

The greatest number of kills in jet to jet battles is 16 by Capt Joseph Christopher McConnell, Jr, USAF (b. Dover, New Hampshire, 30 Jan 1922) in the Korean war (1950–3). He was killed on 25 Aug 1954. It is possible that an Israeli ace may have surpassed this total in the period 1967–70 but the identity of pilots is subject to strict security.

Top woman ace

The record score for any woman fighter pilot is 12 by Jnr Lt Lydia Litvak (USSR) (b. 1921) on the Eastern Front between 1941 and 1943. She was killed in action on 1 Aug 1943.

Top Scoring Air Aces (World Wars I and II)

The 'scores' of air aces in both wars are *still* hotly disputed. The highest figures officially attributed have been:

World	United Kingdom
World War I	
75[1] Col René Paul Fonck (France) Gr Cordon Ld'H, C de G (26 palms), Méd. Mil., MC*, C de G (Belge) (d. 1953)	73 Major Edward Mannock, VC, DSO**, MC*
World War II	
352 Major Erich Hartmann (Germany)	38 Wg Cdr (now AVM) James Edgar Johnson, CB, CBE, DSO**, DFC*[2]

[1] A total of 80 was attributed to Rittmeister Manfred Freiherr (Baron) von Richthofen (Germany) but fewer than 60 of these could subsequently be verified from German records, leaving Col-Gen. Ernst Udet (d. 1941) Ordre pour le Mérite, Iron Cross with the highest number of victories at 62.

[2] The greatest number of successes against flying bombs (V.1's) was by Sqn Ldr Joseph Berry, DFC** (b. Nottingham, 1920, killed 2 Oct 1944) who brought down 60 in 4 months. The most successful fighter pilot in the RAF was Sqn Ldr Marmaduke Thomas St John Pattle, DFC*, of South Africa, with a known total of at least 40. In the Battle of Leyte Gulf, Cdr David McCampbell USN shot down 9 aircraft in one mission on 24 Oct 1944.

The maximum number of bars (repeat awards) ever awarded to the Air Force Cross (AFC) is two. Second bars have been awarded only to the following:

Sqn Ldr W. R. Read MC DFC AFC**
Flt Lt P. W. S. Bulman CBE MC* AFC*
AVM T. A. Langford-Sainsbury CB OBE DFC AFC**
Group Capt H. J. Wilson CBE AFC**
Group Capt T. W. Kean CBE AFC**
Wg Cdr A. H. Humphrey OBE DFC AFC**
AVM M. D. Lyne CB AFC**
Wg Cdr P. D. Thorne OBE AFC**
Air Cdre R. L. Topp AFC**
AVM F. L. Dodd CBE DSO DFC AFC** AE
Wg Cdr L. G. Press OBE AFC**
Group Capt H. P. R. Smith AFC**

NOBEL PRIZES

Earliest 1901 for Physics, Chemistry, Medicine and Physiology, Literature and Peace

Most Prizes USA outright or shared 117 including most for Medicine–Physiology (33); Physics (31); Peace (13); Economics (12); Chemistry (21). France has most for Literature (11). The United Kingdom total is 75 (all classes) comprising Physics (18); Chemistry (20); Medicine (16); Peace (9); Literature (7) and Economics (5)

Oldest Laureate Prof. Francis Peyton Rous (US) (1879–1970) in 1966 shared in Medicine prize aged 87

Youngest Laureates *At time of award:* Prof Sir William Bragg CH OBE MC (1890–1971) 1915 Physics prize at 25 *At time of work:* Bragg and Theodore W Richards (US) (1868–1928) 1914 Chemistry prize at 23 *Literature:* Rudyard Kipling (UK) (1865–1936) 1907 prize at 41 *Peace:* Mrs Mairead Corrigan-Maguire (b. 27 Jan 1944) 1976 Prize (shared) at 32

Most Three Awards: International Committee for Red Cross (founded 1863) (1917, 1944 and 1963 (shared)); Two Awards: Dr Linus Carl Pauling (US) (b. 28 Feb 1901) Chemistry, 1954 and Peace 1962; Mde Marja Sklodowska Curie (Polish-French) (1867–1934) Physics, 1903 (shared) Chemistry 1911; Prof John Bardeen (US) (b. 23 May 1908) Physics 1956 (shared), 1972 (shared); Prof. Frederick Sanger CBE FRS (b. 13 Aug 1918) Chemistry 1958 (shared) and 1980 (shared)

Highest Prize Sw Kr 1,650,000 (for 1984) equivalent to £152,800

Lowest Prize Sw Kr 115,000 (1923) equivalent to £6,620

The maximum number of bars ever awarded to the Air Force Medal (AFM) is one. Bars have been awarded only to the following:

Ch Mech Mate E. S. Rhoads AFM* USN
Sgt J. M. Bennett AFM*
Sgt W. H. Shiers AFM*
SMII W. R. Mayes DSM AFM*
Flt Sgt S. J. Heath AFM*
Flt Sgt G. W. Hunt AFM*
Flt Sgt G. Aklam AFM*
Flt Sgt A. W. Card AFM*
Flt Sgt J. W. Allen AFM*
Sgt J. Donnelly AFM*

Anti-submarine successes

The highest number of U-boat kills attributed to one ship in the 1939–45 war was 15 to HMS *Starling* (Capt Frederic John Walker, CB, DSO***, RN). Captain Walker was in command at the sinking of a total of 25 U-boats between 1941 and the time of his death on 9 July 1944. The US Destroyer Escort *England* sank six Japanese submarines in the Pacific between 18 and 30 May 1944.

Most successful submarine captains

The most successful of all World War II submarine commanders was Leutnant Otto Kretschmer, captain of the U.23 and U.99 who up to March 1940 sank one destroyer and 44 Allied merchantmen totalling 266,629 gross registered tons.

In World War I Kapitän-Leutnant (later Vize-admiral) Lothar von Arnauld de la Périère, in the U.35 and U.139, sank 195 allied ships totalling 458,856 gross tons. The most successful boats were U.35, which in World War I sank 54 ships of 90,350 grt in a single voyage and 224 ships of 539,711 grt all told, and U.48 which sank 51 ships of 310,007 grt in World War II. The largest target ever sunk by a submarine was the Japanese aircraft carrier *Shinano* (59,000 tons) by USS *Archerfish* (Cdr Joseph F. Enright, USN) on 29 Nov 1944.

Youngest Award

The youngest age at which an official gallantry award has ever been won is 8 years in the case of Anthony Farrer who was given the Albert Medal on 23 Sept 1916 for fighting off a cougar at Cowichan Lake, Vancouver Island, Canada to save Doreen Ashburnham. She was also awarded the AM which in 1971 was exchanged for the George Cross.

Record Price

The highest ever paid for a VC group has been £110,000 for the medals of the Battle of Britain fighter pilot Wing Cdr J. B. Nicholson VC, DFC, AFC (k. 1944), one of the only 3 men ever to win the VC actually defending Britain. The auction was at Christie's, London on 8 May 1983.

The record for a George Cross is £20,250 for that of Sgt Michael Willets (3rd Battalion Parachute Regiment), killed in Ulster in 1971, at Christie's on 14 Mar 1985.

Order of Merit

The Order of Merit (instituted on 23 June 1902) is limited to 24 members. The longest lived holder has been the Rt Hon. Bertrand Arthur William Russell, 3rd Earl Russell, who died on 2 Feb 1970 aged 97 years 260 days. The oldest recipient was Admiral of the Fleet the Hon. Sir Henry Keppel, GCB, OM, (1809–1904), who

received the Order aged 93 years 56 days on 9 Aug 1902. The youngest recipient has been HRH the Duke of Edinburgh, KG, KT, OM, GBE, who was appointed on his 47th birthday on 10 June 1968.

Most mentions in despatches

The record number of 'mentions' is 24 by Field Marshal the Rt Hon Sir Frederick Sleigh Roberts Bt, the Earl Roberts, VC, KG, PC, KP, GCB, OM, GCSI, GCIE, VD (1832–1914).

Most post-nominal letters

Lord Roberts, who was also a privy counsellor, was the only non-royal holder of 8 sets of *official* post-nominal letters. Currently the record number is seven by Marshal of the RAF the Rt Hon Lord Elworthy KG, GCB, CBE, DSO, LVO, DFC, AFC (b. 23 Mar 1911) of New Zealand. HRH the Duke of Windsor (1894–1972) when Prince of Wales had 10 sets and was also a privy counsellor *viz*: KG, PC, KT, KP, GCB, GCSI, GCMG, GCIE, GCVO, GBE, MC. He later appended the ISO but never did so in the case of the OM, CH or DSO of which orders he had also been sovereign.

Civilian gallantry

Reginald H. Blanchford of Guernsey, received the MBE for Gallantry in 1950; the Queen's Commendation in 1957; the George Medal in 1958; the OBE for Gallantry in 1961 for saving life from cliff tops. He was also awarded the Life Saving Medal in Gold 1957 with golden bar 1963 and was made a Knight of Grace of the Order of St John in 1970.

USSR

The USSR's highest award for valour is the Gold Star of a Hero of the Soviet Union. Over 10,000 were awarded in World War II. Among

Reginald Blanchford whose history of cliff-top life-saving has earned him most medals for Gallantry including the MBE and George Medal.

the 109 awards of a second star were those to Marshal Iosif Vissarionovich Dzhugashvili, *alias* Stalin (1879–1953) and Lt-General Nikita Sergeyevich Khrushchyov (1894–1971). The only war-time triple awards were to Marshal Georgiy Konstantinovich Zhukov, Hon GCB (1896–1972) (subsequently awarded a fourth Gold Star) and to the leading air aces Guards' Colonel (later Marshal of Aviation) the late Aleksandr Ivanovich Pokryshkin and Aviation Maj Gen Ivan Nikitovich Kozhedub. Zhukov also uniquely had the Order of Victory, twice, the Order of Lenin (6 times) and the Order of the Red Banner, (thrice). Leonid Brezhnev (1907–1982) was 4 times Hero of the Soviet Union; Hero of Socialist Labour, Order of Victory, Order of Lenin (8 times) and Order of the Red Banner (twice).

Germany

The Knight's Cross of the Iron Cross with swords, diamonds and golden oak-leaves was uniquely awarded to Col Hans Ulrich Rudel (1916–1982) for 2530 operational flying missions on the Eastern Front in 1941–5. He destroyed 519 Soviet armoured vehicles.

USA

The highest US military decoration is the Medal of Honor. Five marines received both the Army and Navy Medals of Honor for the same acts in 1918 and 14 officers and men from 1863 to 1915 have received the medal on two occasions. Maj. Audie Murphy received in World War II the

Medal of Honor, the Distinguished Service Cross, the Silver Star, the Legion of Merit, the Bronze Star Medal and the Purple Heart with 2 oak leaf clusters.

AWARDS

Most Valuable Annual Prize

The Templeton Foundation Prize for Progress in Religion inaugurated in 1972 by Mr John M. Templeton (b. 1912) has at times been more than Nobel Prizes. The awards of £170,000 in 1986 was won by Dr James McCord, 66, founder in 1982 of the Centre for Theological Inquiry at Princeton University, USA.

Most statues

The world record for raising statues to oneself was set by Generalissimo Dr Rafael Leónidas Trujillo y Molina (1891–1961), former President of the Dominican Republic. In March 1960 a count showed that there were 'over 2000'. The country's highest mountain was named Pico Trujillo (now Pico Duarte). One province was called Trujillo and another Trujillo Valdez. The capital was named Ciudad Trujillo (Trujillo City) in 1936, but reverted to its old name of Santo Domingo de Guzmán on 23 Nov 1961. Trujillo was assassinated in a car ambush on 30 May 1961, and 30 May is now celebrated annually as a public holiday. The man to whom most statues have been raised is Buddha. The 20th century champion is Vladimir Ilyich Ulyanov, *alias* Lenin (1870–1924), busts of whom have been mass-produced as also has been the case with Mao Tse-tung (1893–1976) and Ho Chi Minh (1890–1969).

PEERAGE

Most ancient

The oldest extant peerage is the premier Earldom of Scotland, held by the Rt Hon Margaret of Mar, the Countess of Mar and 31st holder of this Earldom (b. 19 Sept 1940), who is the heir-at-law of Roderick or Rothri, 1st Earl (or Mormaer) of Mar, who witnessed a charter in 1114 or 1115 as 'Rothri *comes*'.

Oldest creation

The greatest age at which any person has been raised to the peerage is 93 years 337 days in the case of Sir William Francis Kyffin Taylor, GBE, KC (b. 9 July 1854), created Baron Maenan of Ellesmere, County Shropshire, on 10 June 1948, and died, aged 97, on 22 Sept 1951. The oldest elevation to a Life Peerage has been that of Emmanuel Shinwell PC, CH (b. 18 Oct 1884) on 2 June 1970 when aged 85 years 227 days. He died on 8 May 1986.

Longest lived peer

The longest lived peer ever recorded was the Rt Hon Emanuel Shinwell, PC, CH (b. 18 Oct 1884) created a life baron in 1970. He died in London aged 101 years 202 days on 8 May 1986. The oldest peeress recorded was the Countess Desmond, who was alleged to be 140 when she died in 1604. This claim is patently exaggerated but it is accepted that she may have been 104. Currently the oldest peer is Rt Hon Lord Brockway (b. Calcutta 1 Nov 1888).

Youngest peers

Twelve Dukes of Cornwall became (in accordance with the grant by the Crown in Parliament) peers at birth as the eldest son of a Sovereign; and the 9th Earl of Chichester posthumously inherited his father's (killed 54 days previously) earldom at his birth on 14 Apr 1944. The youngest age at which a person has had a peerage conferred on him is 7 days old in the case of the Earldom of Chester on HRH the Prince George (later George IV) on 19 Aug 1762. The youngest

to be created a life peer is Baroness Masham of Ilton, Countess of Swinton (b. 19 Apr 1935) aged 34 in 1970.

Longest and shortest peerages

The longest tenure of a peerage has been 87 years 10 days in the case of Charles St Clair, Lord Sinclair, b. 30 July 1768, succeeded 16 Dec 1775 and died aged 94 years 243 days on 30 Mar 1863.

The shortest enjoyment of a peerage was the 'split second' by which the law assumes that the Hon Wilfrid Carlyl Stamp (b. 28 Oct 1904), the 2nd Baron Stamp, survived his father, Sir Josiah Charles Stamp, GCB, GBE, the 1st Baron Stamp, when both were killed as a result of German bombing of London on 16 Apr 1941. Apart from this legal fiction, the shortest recorded peerage was one of 30 min in the case of Sir Charles Brandon, KB, the 3rd Duke of Suffolk, who died, aged 13 or 14, just after succeeding his brother, Henry, when both were suffering a fatal illness, at Buckden, Cambridgeshire, on 14 July 1551.

Highest numbering

The highest succession number borne by any peer is that of the present 35th Baron Kingsale (John de Courcy, b. 27 Jan 1941), who succeeded to the then 746-year-old Barony on 7 Nov 1969. His occupations have included barman, bingo-caller and plumber.

Most creations

The largest number of new hereditary peerages created in any year was the 54 in 1296. The record for all peerages (including 40 life peerages) is 55 in 1964. The greatest number of extinctions in a year was 16 in 1923 and the greatest number of deaths was 44 in 1935.

Most prolific

The most prolific peers of all time are believed to be the 1st Earl Ferrers (1650–1717) and the 3rd Earl of Winchilsea (*c.* 1620–89) each with 27 legitimate children. In addition, the former reputedly fathered 30 illegitimate children. Currently the peer with the largest family is the Rt Hon Bryan Walter Guinness, 2nd Baron Moyne (b. 27 Oct 1905) with 6 sons and 5 daughters. The most prolific peeress is believed to be Mary Fitzgerald, wife of Patrick, 19th Baron Kingsale who bore 23 children (no twins) who survived to baptism. She died in 1663.

Baronets

The greatest age to which a baronet has lived is 101 years 188 days, in the case of Sir Fitzroy Donald Maclean, 10th Bt., KCB (1835–1936). He was the last survivor of the Crimean campaign of 1853–56. Capt Sir Trevor Wheler, 13th Baronet (b. 20 Sept 1889) entered his 83rd year as a baronet on 11 Aug 1984 but died aged 96 on 14 Jan 1986. The only baronetess is Dame Maureen Dunbar of Hempriggs, who succeeded in her own right as 8th in line of a 1706 baronetcy in 1965.

Knights

The greatest number of knights dubbed in a single day was 432 by James I in the Royal Garden, Whitehall on 23 July 1603. On his coronation day two days later, he appointed 62 Knights of the Garter.

Youngest and oldest

The youngest age for the conferment of a knighthood is 29 days for HRH the Prince George (b. 12 Aug 1762) (later George IV) by virtue of his *ex officio* membership of the Order of the Garter (KG) consequent upon his creation as Prince of Wales on 17 or 19 Aug 1762. The

greatest age for the conferment of a knighthood is on a 100th birthday, in the case of the knight bachelor Sir Robert Mayer (1879–1985), additionally made a KCVO by the Queen at the Royal Festival Hall, London on 5 June 1979.

Most brothers

George and Elizabeth Coles of Australia had 5 sons knighted—Sir George, CBE (1885–1977); Sir Arthur (b. 1892); Sir Kenneth (b. 1896); Sir Edgar (b. 1899) and Sir Norman (b. 1907).

Most freedoms

Probably the greatest number of freedoms ever conferred on any man was 57 in the case of Andrew Carnegie (1835–1919), who was born in Dunfermline, Fife but emigrated to the United States in 1848. The most freedoms conferred upon any citizen of the United Kingdom is 42, in the case of Sir Winston Churchill (1874–1965).

Most honorary degrees

The greatest number of honorary degrees awarded to any individual is 96, given to Rev Father Theodore M. Hesburgh (b. 1918), president of the University of Notre Dame, Indiana, USA. These were accumulated from 1954 to May 1984.

Greatest vote

The largest monetary vote made by Parliament to a subject was the £400,000 given to the 1st Duke of Wellington (1769–1852) on 12 Apr 1814. He received in all £864,000. The total received by the 1st, 2nd and 3rd Dukes to January 1900 was £1,052,000.

The Royal Society (founded 1662)

The longest term as an FRS (Fellow of the Royal Society) has been 61 years in the case of Bertrand Russell, 3rd Earl (1872–1970), who had been elected in 1908. The longest lived FRS has been Sir Rickard Christophers CIE, OBE (1873–1978) aged 104 years 84 days. John Lubbock (1834–1913), later 1st Baron Avebury, was elected at the age of 23 in 1857.

Erasmus Darwin was elected on 9 Apr 1761 and was followed by his son Robert (1788 to 1848), *his* son Charles (1879 to 1881), his sons Sir George (1879 to 1912), Francis (1882–1925) and Horace (1903 to 1928) and Sir George's son Sir Charles (1922 to 1962) so spanning over 200 years with 5 generations.

Who's Who

The longest entry in *Who's Who* (founded 1848) was that of the Rt Hon Sir Winston Leonard Spencer Churchill, KG, OM, CH, TD (1874–1965), who appeared in 67 editions from 1899 (18 lines) and had 211 lines by the 1965 edition. Currently the longest entry in its wider format is that of Barbara Cartland, the romantic novelist, with 130 lines. Apart from those who qualify for inclusion by hereditary title, the youngest entry has been Sir Yehudi Menuhin, KBE (b. New York City, USA 22 Apr 1916), the concert violinist, who first appeared in the 1932 edition aged 15. The longest entry of the 66,000 entries in *Who's Who in America* is that of Dr Glenn T. Seaborg (b. 19 Apr 1912) whose all-time record of 100 lines compares with the 9 line entry on President Reagan.

Oxford and Cambridge Unions

Four brothers were Presidents of the Union in the case of the sons of the Rt Hon Isaac Foot. Sir Dingle Foot (Balliol, 1927–8); John (Lord Foot) (Balliol, 1930–1) and Rt Hon Michael (Wadham, 1933–4) at Oxford and Hugh (Lord Caradon) (St John's, 1929) at Cambridge. The last named's son Paul was President at Oxford (University College, 1960–1).

CHAPTER ELEVEN

THE
HUMAN
WORLD

A scene from the extraordinary Live Aid concert at Wembley. 1.6 billion saw the event on television, one third of the world's population, and the appeals raised a record sum for charity in aid of famine relief. *See p. 205.* (Duncan Raban).

See p. 205.

1. POLITICAL AND SOCIAL

Largest political division

The British Commonwealth of Nations, a free association of 49 sovereign independent states together with 27 non-sovereign states and dependencies administered by them covers an area of 13,095,000 miles² *33 915 000 km²* with a population which in 1980 surpassed 1,000,000,000. The British Empire began to expand when Henry VII patented trade monopolies to John Cabot in March 1496 and when the East India Co. was incorporated on 31 Dec 1600.

COUNTRIES

The world comprises 170 sovereign countries and 59 separately administered non-sovereign territories making a total of 229. The United Nations still lists the *de jure* territories of East Timor (now incorporated into Indonesia), Western Sahara (now in Morocco) and the uninhabited Canton and Enderbury Islands (now disputed between the US and Kiribati) but does not list the three Baltic States of Estonia, Latvia and Lithuania though their forcible incorporation into the USSR in 1940 has never been internationally recognized. Neither does it list the *de facto* territories of Taiwan, Mayotte or Spanish North Africa, the 4 Antarctic Territories or the Australian Territory of Coral Sea Islands and Heard and McDonald Islands.

Largest

The country with the greatest area is the Union of Soviet Socialist Republics (the Soviet Union), comprising 15 Union (constituent) Republics with a total area of 22 402 200 km² *8,648,500 miles²*, or 15.0 per cent of the world's total land area, and a total coastline (including islands) of 106 360 km *66,090 miles*. The country measures 8980 km *5580 miles* from east to west and 4490 km *2790 miles* from north to south and is 91.8 times the size of the United Kingdom. Its population in mid-1984 was 275,500,000 (est.).

The United Kingdom covers 94,221 miles² *244 030 km²* (including 1197 miles² *3100 km²* of inland water), or 0.16 per cent of the total land area of the world. Great Britain is the world's eighth largest island, with an area of 84,186 miles² *218 040 km²* and a coastline 4928 miles *7930 km* long, of which Scotland accounts for 2573 miles *4141 km*, Wales 426 miles *685 km* and England 1929 miles *3104 km*.

Smallest

The smallest independent country in the world is the State of the Vatican City or Holy See (Stato della Città del Vaticano), which was made an enclave within the city of Rome, Italy on 11 Feb 1929. The enclave has an area of 44 hectares *108.7 acres*. The maritime sovereign country with the shortest coastline is Monaco with 3.49 miles *5,61 km* excluding piers and break-waters. The world's smallest republic is Nauru, less than 1 degree south of the equator in the Western Pacific, which became independent on 31 Jan 1968, has an area of 5263 acres *2129 ha* and a population of 7000 (latest estimate mid-1984).

The smallest colony in the world is Gibraltar (since 1969, the City of Gibraltar) with an area of 2½ miles² *5,8 km²*. However, Pitcairn Island, the only inhabited (58 people at 31 Dec 1985) island of a group of 4 (total area 18½ miles² *48 km²*) has an area of 1½ miles² or 960 acres *388 ha*.

The official residence, since 1834, of the Grand Master of the Order of the Knights of Malta totalling 3 acres *1,2 ha* and comprising the Villa del Priorato di Malta on the lowest of Rome's seven hills, the 151 ft *46 m* Aventine, retains certain diplomatic privileges as does 68 Via Condotti. The Order has accredited representatives to foreign governments and is hence sometimes cited as the smallest 'state' in the world.

Flattest and Most Elevated

The country with the lowest highest point is the Republic of the Maldives which attains 8 ft

Available at £7.95

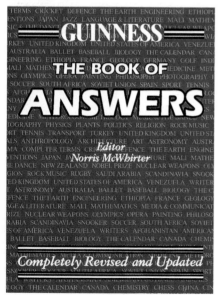

2,4 m. The country with the highest lowest point is Lesotho. The egress of the Senqu (Orange) river-bed is 4530 ft *1381 m* above sea level.

Most impenetrable boundary

The 'Iron Curtain' (858 miles *1380 km*) dividing the Federal Republican (West) and the Democratic Republican (East) parts of Germany, utilizes 2,230,000 land mines and 50,000 miles *80 500 km* of barbed wire, much of it of British manufacture, in addition to many watch-towers containing detection devices. The last of 55,000 SM-70 scatter guns was removed on 30 Nov 1984. The whole strip of 270 yd *246 m* wide occupies 133 miles² *344 km²* of East German territory and cost an estimated $7000 million to build and maintain. It reduced the westward flow from more than 200,000 in 1961 to a trickle of 30 (including 8 guards) in 1985. The death toll has been 184 since 1962. Construction of the second wall (the 'anti-fascist defensive barrier') began in East Berlin in March 1984.

Longest and Shortest frontier

The longest *continuous* frontier in the world is that between Canada and the United States, which (including the Great Lakes boundaries) extends for 3987 miles *6416 km* (excluding 1538 miles *2547 km* with Alaska). The frontier which is crossed most frequently is that between the United States and Mexico. It extends for 1933 miles *3110 km* and there are more than 120,000,000 crossings every year. The Sino-Soviet frontier, broken by the Sino-Mongolian border, extends for 4500 miles *7240 km* with no reported figure of crossings. The 'frontier' of the Holy See in Rome measures 2.53 miles *4,07 km*. The land frontier between Gibraltar and Spain at La Linea, closed in June 1969, measures 1672 yd *1,53 km*. It was opened again at midnight on 4–5 Feb 1985. Zambia, Zimbabwe, Botswana and Namibia (South West Africa) almost merge.

Most frontiers

China has the most land frontiers with 13— Mongolia, USSR, North Korea, Hong Kong, Macau, Vietnam, Laos, Burma, India, Bhutan, Nepal, Pakistan and Afghanistan. These extend for 24 000 km *14,900 miles*. France, if all her *Départements d'outre-mer* are included, may, on extended territorial waters, have 20. The United Kingdom's frontier with the Republic of Ireland measures 223 miles *358 km*.

POPULATIONS
World

The daily increase in the world's population is 215,850, or 149.9 per minute. For past, present and future estimates (see table).

Most populous country

The largest population of any country is that of China, which in *pinyin* is written Zhongguo (meaning central land). The census of July 1982 was 1,008,175,288 (excluding Taiwan, Hong Kong and Macau). The rate of natural increase in the People's Republic of China is now estimated to be 38,700 a day or 14.1 million per year. The mid-year 1986 estimate would then be close to 1065 million. The census required 5,100,000 enumerators to work for 10 days. India is set to overtake China during the next century.

Least populous

The independent state with the smallest population is the Vatican City or the Holy See (see Smallest country, above), with 1008 inhabitants in 1984 and a nil return for births.

Most densely populated

The most densely populated territory in the world is the Portuguese province of Macau (or Macao), on the southern coast of China. It has

an estimated population of 343,000 (mid-1984) in an area of 6.2 miles² *16,05 km²* giving a density of 55,300 per mile² *21 360 per km²*.

The Principality of Monaco, on the south coast of France, has a population of 27,000 (mid-1984) in an area of 473 acres *189 ha* giving a density of 38,179/mile² *14,741/km²*. The above acreage is inclusive of marine infilling which has increased the land area by some 20 per cent. Singapore has 2,558,000 (end-1984) people in an inhabited area of 73 miles² *189 km²*.

Of territories with an area of more than 1000 km², Hong Kong (405 miles² *1049 km²*) contains 5,579,000 (estimated March 1985), giving the territory a density of 13,775/mile² *5318/km²*. Hong Kong is now the most populous of all colonies. The transcription of the name is from a local pronunciation of the Peking dialect version of Xiang gang (a port for incense). The 1976 by-census showed that the West Area of the urban district of Mong Kok on the Kowloon Peninsula had a density of 252,090/km² *652,910/mile²*. In 1959, at the peak of the housing crisis, it was reported that in one house designed for 12 people the number of occupants was 459, including 104 in one room and 4 living on the roof.

Of countries over 1000 miles² *2589 km²* the most densely populated is Bangladesh with a population of 96,730,000 (mid-1984 estimate) living in 55,126 miles² *142 775 km²* at a density of 1754/mile² *677/km²*. The Indonesian island of Java (with an area of 48,763 miles² *126 295 km²*) had a population of 94,693,000 (1981 estimate), giving a density of 1941/mile² *750/km²*.

The United Kingdom (94,221 miles² *244 030 km²*) had an estimated population of 56,487,800 at mid-1984, giving a density of 598 persons/mile² *231/km²*. The population density for the Royal Borough of Kensington and Chelsea, London is 11 250.3/km² *29,138.4/mile²*.

Most sparsely populated

Antarctica became permanently occupied by relays of scientists from October 1956. The population varies seasonally and reaches 2000 at times.

The least populated territory, apart from Antarctica, is Kalaallit Nunaat (formerly Greenland), with a population of 52,000 (estimated mid-1983) in an area of 840,000 miles² *2 175 000 km²* giving a density of one person to every ·16.15 miles² *41,83 km²*. Some 84.3 per cent of the island comprises an ice-cap.

The lowest population densities in the United Kingdom are in the Scottish Highlands and Islands with 13,1/km² *33.9/mile²*. The most sparsely populated county in England is Northumberland with 154.15/mile² *59,51/km²*.

Emigration

More people emigrate from Mexico than from any other country. An estimated 800,000 emigrated illegally into the USA in 1980 alone. A total of 163,900 emigrated from the UK in 1984. Her largest number of emigrants in any one year was 360,000 in 1852, mainly from Ireland.

Immigration

The country which regularly receives the most legal immigrants is the United States. It has been estimated that in the period 1820–1984, the USA has received 51,950,349 *official* immigrants. One in 24 of the US population is however an *illegal* immigrant to which another 700,000 were added in 1980. The peak year for immigration into the United Kingdom was the 12 months from 1 July 1961 to 30 June 1962, when about 430,000 Commonwealth citizens arrived. The number of new Commonwealth

WORLD POPULATION *Progressive estimates*

Date	Millions	Date	Millions
10 000 BC	c. 5	1960	3049
AD 1	c. 200	1970	3704
1000	c. 275	1975	4033
1250	375	1980	4453
1500	420	1981	4530
1650	550–600	1982	4607
1700	615	1983	4685
1750	720	1984	4763
1800	900	1985	4845
1900	1625	1986	4925
1920	1862	2000†	6100
1930	2070	2025	8200
1940	2295	2100	10,500
1950	2513		

† *The UN publication 'State of World Population, 1984' forecast that the world population will not stabilize until 2095 at c. 10,500 million and will reach 6100 million by 31 Dec 2000.*
Note The all-time peak annual increase of 2.0% c. 1958–1962 had declined to 1.73% by 1975–1980. By 1990 this should decline to 1.5%. This, however, produces an annual increment c. 80 million to even higher figures in the 1990s. The French demographer Biraben has calculated that 60,000 million people died between 40,000 BC and AD 1980. This indicates that there have thus been some 65,000 million specimens of Homo sapiens sapiens who ever lived.

and Pakistani immigrants in the year to March 1985 was 24,800 added to an estimated total of 2,200,000 or 4.0% of the population.

Most patient 'Refusenik'
The USSR citizen who has waited longest for an exit visa is Benjamin Bogomolny (b. 7 Apr 1946) who first applied in 1966.

Tourism
In 1985 the United Kingdom received 14,577,000 visitors who spent an estimated £5473 million excluding fares to British carriers.

Birth rate *Highest and Lowest*
The rate for the whole world was 27.5 per 1000 in 1982. The highest estimated by the UN is 54.6 per 1000 for Kenya in 1980. A world wide survey published in 1981 showed only Nepal (48.9) with a still rising birth rate.

Excluding Vatican City, where the rate is negligible, the lowest recorded rate is 9.5 (1984) for the Federal Republic of Germany. The fastest falling is in Thailand where the 3.3 average number of children per family has fallen to 1.8 in 10 years.

The 1985 rate in the United Kingdom was 13.3/1000 (13.1 in England and Wales, 12.3 in Scotland and 17.1 in Northern Ireland), while the 1986 rate for the Republic of Ireland was 17.5 registered births per 1000. The highest number of births in England and Wales (since the first full year of 463,787 in 1838) has been 957,782 in 1920 and the lowest this century 569,259 in 1977. After falling each year since 1964 (875,972) the figure started rising again at the end of 1977 with the 1985 figure being 656,417 or 1798 per day or 1.25 per minute.

Death rate *Highest and Lowest*
The death rate for the whole world was 10.7 per 1000 in 1982. The highest of the latest available estimated death rates is 40.0 deaths per 1000 of the population in Kampuchea in 1975–80.

The lowest of the latest available recorded rates is 3.3 deaths/1000 in Tonga in 1983.

The 1984 rate in the United Kingdom was 11.5/1000 (11.5 in England and Wales, 12.1 in Scotland and 10.3 in Northern Ireland). The highest SMI (Standard Mortality Index where the national average is 100) is in Salford, Manchester with a figure of 133. The 1984 rate for the Republic of Ireland was 9.1 registered deaths per 1000.

Natural increase
The rate of natural increase for the whole world

is estimated to be 27.5–10.7 = 16.8 per 1000 in 1982 compared with a peak 22 per 1000 in 1965. The highest of the latest available recorded rates is 40.4 (54.6 – 14.2) in Kenya in 1980.

The 1984 rate for the United Kingdom was 1.5 (0.9 in England and Wales, 0.1 in Scotland and 7.2 in Northern Ireland). The rate for the first time in the first quarter of 1975 became one of natural decrease. The figure for the Republic of Ireland was 9.7/1000 in 1983.

The lowest rate of natural increase in any major independent country is in Federal Republic of Germany with a negative figure of −1.8 per 1000 (9.5 births and 11.3 deaths) for 1984.

Marriage ages
The lowest average age for marriage is India, with 20.0 years (males) and 14.5 years (females). At the other extreme is Ireland, with 26.8 (males) and 24.7 (females). In the mid 16th century the average age for first marriages by women in England was 26.7 years. In the People's Republic of China the *recommended* age for marriage for men has been 28 and for women 25. In England and Wales the peak (mode) ages for marriage are 23 years (male) and 21 years (female). The average ages in 1985 are 27.5 (women) and 30.2 (men).

Divorces
The country with most divorces is the United States with a total of 1,155,000 in 1984—a rate of 46.49 per cent on the then current annual total of marriages (all time high of 1,213,000—49.75 per cent in 1981).

Sex ratio
There were estimated to be 1006.7 men in the world for every 1000 women (1981). The country with the largest recorded shortage of males is the USSR, with 1145.9 females to every 1000 males (1981 census). The country with the largest recorded woman shortage is Pakistan, with 906 to every 1000 males in 1981. The figures are, however, probably under-enumerated due to *purdah*. The ratio in the United Kingdom was 1056 females to every 1000 males at mid-1982, and is expected to be 1014.2/1,000 by AD 2000.

Infant mortality
The world rate in 1978 was 91 per 1000 live births. Based on deaths before one year of age, the lowest of the latest available recorded rates is 6.2 in Finland and Iceland in 1983.

The highest recorded infant mortality rate reported has been 195 to 300 for Burma in 1952 and 259 for Zaïre in 1950. In Ethiopia the infant mortality rate was unofficially estimated to be

nearly 550/1000 live births in 1969. Many Third World countries have ceased to make returns.

The United Kingdom figure for 1984 was 9.4/1000 live births (England and Wales 9.2, Scotland 10.1, Northern Ireland 13). The Republic of Ireland figure for 1984 was 10.1.

Life expectation
World expectation of life is rising from 47.4 years (1950–55) towards 64.5 years (1995–2000). There is evidence that life expectation in Britain in the 5th century AD was 33 years for males and 27 years for females. In the decade 1890–1900 the expectation of life among the population of India was 23.7 years.

Based on the latest available data, the highest recorded expectation of life at age 12 months is 74.54 years in Japan for males and 80.18 years for females in Japan (1985).

The lowest recorded expectation of life at birth is 27 years for both sexes in the Vallée du Niger area of Mali in 1957 (sample survey, 1957–8). The figure for males in Gabon was 25 years in 1960–1 but 45 for females.

The latest available figures for England and Wales (1982–84) are 71.6 years for males and 77.6 years for females, 69.9 and 75.9 in Scotland, 69.8 and 76.0 in Northern Ireland, and Republic of Ireland (1980) 69.5 years for males and 75 for females. The British figure for 1901–10 was 48.53 years for males and 52.83 years for females.

Housing
For comparison, dwelling units are defined as a structurally separated room or rooms occupied by private households of one or more people and having separate access or a common passageway to the street.

The first country to surpass 100,000,000 housing units was India, with 100,251,000 occupied by 1972.

Great Britain had a stock of 21,894,000 dwellings as at 1 Jan 1986, of which 62.0% was owner-occupied. The record number of permanent houses built in a year has been 413,715 in 1968.

Physicians
The country with the most physicians is the USSR, with 831,300, or one to every 307 persons. China had an estimated 1.4 million para-medical personnel known as 'bare foot doctors' by 1981. In the United Kingdom there were 126,448 doctors filling or provisionally registered in the list published by the General Medical Council.

Dentists
The country with the most dentists is the United States, where 145,000 were registered members of the American Dental Association in 1985.

Psychiatrists
The country with the most psychiatrists is the United States. The registered membership of the American Psychiatric Association (inst. 1894) was 27,000 in 1984. The membership of the American Psychological Association (inst. 1892) was 66,000 in 1985.

Hospital Largest *World*
The largest mental hospital in the world is the Pilgrim State Hospital, West Brentwood, Long Island, NY, USA, with 3618 beds. It formerly contained 14,200 beds. The largest psychiatric institute is at the University of California, Los Angeles.

The busiest maternity hospital in the world was the Mama Yemo Hospital, Kinshasa, Zaïre with 41,930 deliveries in 1976. The record 'birth-quake' occurred on a day in May 1976 with 175 babies born. It had 599 beds.

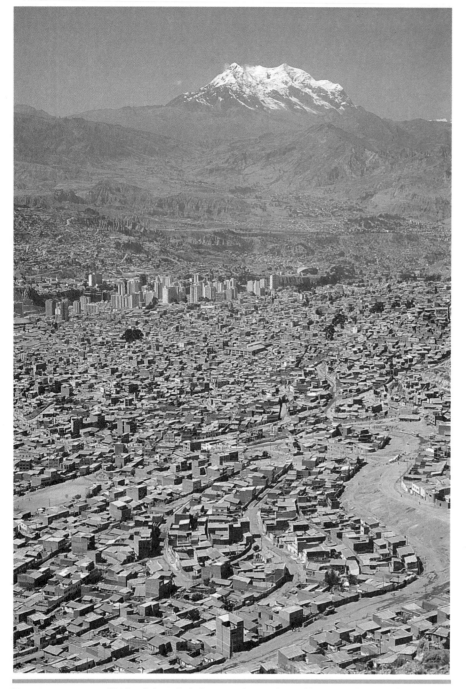

The picturesque siting of La Paz, Bolivia, the highest capital city in the world, just 30 miles *48 km* from Lake Titicaca, the highest lake in the world that is plied by shipping. (Tony Morrison).

Great Britain

The largest hospitals of any kind in Great Britain are Hartwood Hospital near Shotts, Lanarkshire with 1600 staffed beds for mentally ill patients and Winwick Hospital near Warrington, which has 1469 staffed beds.

The largest general hospital in Great Britain is the St James's University Hospital (which is also a teaching hospital), Leeds, West Yorkshire, with 1424 staffed beds.

The largest maternity hospital in Great Britain is the Simpson Memorial Maternity Pavilion, Edinburgh with 181 staffed beds.

The largest children's hospital in Great Britain is Queen Mary's Hospital for Children, at Carshalton, Sutton, Surrey, with 401 staffed beds.

Longest stay in hospital

Miss Martha Nelson was admitted to the Columbus State Institute for the Feeble-Minded in Ohio, USA in 1875. She died in January 1975 aged 103 years 6 months in the Orient State Institution, Ohio after spending more than 99 years in institutions.

CITIES

Oldest *World*

The oldest known walled town in the world is Arīhā (Jericho). The latest radio-carbon dating on specimens from the lowest levels reached by archaeologists indicate habitation there by perhaps 3000 people as early as 7800 BC. The settlement of Dolní Věstonice, Czechoslovakia, has been dated to the Gravettian culture *c.*

27000 BC. The oldest capital city in the world is Dimashq (Damascus), the capital of Syria. It has been continuously inhabited since *c.* 2500 BC.

Great Britain

The oldest town in Great Britain is often cited as Colchester, the old British Camulodunum, headquarters of Belgic chiefs in the 1st century BC. However, the name of the tin trading post Salakee, St Mary's, Isles of Scilly, is derived from pre-Celtic roots and hence *ante* 550 BC. The oldest borough in Britain is reputed to be Barnstaple, Devon whose charter was granted by King Athelstan (927–939) in AD 930.

The only one of the United Kingdom's 58 cities with a Saxon charter is Ripon, North Yorkshire which was a bishopric in 672 and had a charter dated 886.

Most populous *World*

The most populous 'urban agglomeration' in the world is the 'Keihin Metropolitan Area' (Tōkyō-Yokohama Metropolitan Area) of 1081 miles² *2800 km²* containing an estimated 29,002,000 people in 1981. The municipal population of Tōkyō in 1985 was 11,903,900. The population of the metropolitan area of Greater Mexico City in 1981 was published as 16,248,500 with the city proper at 8,389,800 (1984 est).

Great Britain

The largest conurbation in Britain is London, with a population of 6,754,000 (1984 est.). The residential population of the City of London (677.3 acres *274 ha* plus 61.7 acres *24,9 ha* foreshore) is 5800 (1986 estimate) compared with 128,000 in 1801. The daytime figure is 285,000. The peak figure for London was 8,615,050 in 1939.

Largest in area

The world's largest town, in area, is Mount Isa, Queensland, Australia. The area administered by the City Council is 15,822 miles² *40 978 km²*. The largest conurbation in the United Kingdom is Greater London with an area of 609.8 miles² *1579,5 km²*.

Towns, villages and hamlets *Great Britain*

The smallest place with a town council is Llanwrtyd Wells, Powys (pop 614 in 1979). The smallest town with a Royal Charter (granted in 1290) is Caerwys, Clwyd, Wales with a population of 801. The strongest claimant to be Britain's oldest village is Thatcham, Berkshire. The earliest Mesolithic settlement there has been dated to 7720 BC.

Highest *World*

The highest capital in the world, before the domination of Tibet by China, was Lhasa, at an elevation of 12,087 ft *3684 m* above sea-level. La Paz, the administrative and *de facto* capital of Bolivia, stands at an altitude of 11,916 ft *3631 m* above sea-level. El Alto airport is at 4080 m *13,385 ft*. The city was founded in 1548 by Capt Alonso de Mendoza on the site of an Indian village named Chuquiapu. It was originally called Ciudad de Nuestra Señora de La Paz (City of Our Lady of Peace), but in 1825 was renamed La Paz de Ayacucho, its present official name. Sucre, the legal capital of Bolivia, stands at 9301 ft *2834 m* above sea-level. The new town of Wenchuan, founded in 1955 on the Chinghai–Tibet road, north of the Tangla range, is the highest in the world at 5100 m *16,732 ft* above sea-level.

Great Britain

The highest village in Britain is Flash, in northern Staffordshire, at 1518 ft *462 m* above sea-level. The highest in Scotland is Wanlockhead, in Dumfries and Galloway at 1380 ft *420 m* above sea-level.

Lowest
The settlement of Ein Bokek, which has a synagogue, on the shores of the Dead Sea is the lowest in the world at 1291 ft *393,5 m* below sea-level.

Northernmost
The world's most northerly town with a population of more than 10,000 is the Arctic port of Dikson, USSR in 73° 32′ N. The northernmost village is Ny Ålesund (78° 55′ N.), a coalmining settlement on King's Bay, Vest Spitsbergen, in the Norwegian territory of Svalbard, inhabited only during the winter season. The northernmost capital is Reykjavik, the capital of Iceland, in 64° 08′ N. Its population was estimated to be 80,000 (1985).

Southernmost
The world's southernmost village is Puerto Williams (population about 350), on the north coast of Isla Navarino, in Tierra del Fuego, Chile, 680 miles *1090 km* north of Antarctica. Wellington, the North Island, New Zealand is the southernmost capital city on 41° 17′ S. The world's southernmost administrative centre is Port Stanley (51° 43′ S.), in the Falkland Islands, off South America.

Most remote from the sea
The largest town most remote from the sea is Ürümqi in Xinjiang (formerly Tihwa, Sinkiang), capital of the Uighur Autonomous Region of China, at a distance of about 1400 miles *2250 km* from the nearest coastline. Its population was estimated to be 320,000 in 1974.

2. ROYALTY & HEADS OF STATE

WORLD'S MOST POPULOUS *Urban Settlements*
Progressive List

Population	Name		Date
> 100	**Dolní Věstonice**	Czechoslovakia	c.27000 BC
c. 150	**Chemi Shanidar**	Iraq	8900 BC
27,000	**Jericho (Ariḥā)**	Occupied Jordan	7800 BC
c. 5000	**Çatal Huyuk, Anatolia**	Turkey	c.6800 BC
50,000	**Uruk (Erech) (now Warka) from 7000 to 3800 BC**	Iraq	3000 BC
250,000	**Greater Ur (now Tell Muqayyar)**	Iraq	2200 BC
350,000	**Babylon (now al-Hillah)**	Iraq	600 BC
500,000	**Pataliputra (Patna) Bihār**	India	400–185 BC
600,000	**Seleukia (near Baghdad)**	Iraq	300 BC–165 AD
1,100,000	**Rome (founded c. 510 BC)**	Italy	133 BC
1,500,000	**Angkor**	Cambodia	900 AD
1.0–1.5 million	**Hangchow (now Hangzhou)**	China	1279
707,000	**Peking (Cambaluc), (now Beijing)**	China	1578
1,117,290	**London**	United Kingdom	1801
8,615,050	**London (peak)**	United Kingdom	1939
11,600,069	**Tokyo**	Japan	1985

Note: The UN projections for AD 2000 for Greater Mexico City is 31,616,000.

Oldest ruling house and Longest Reign
The Emperor of Japan, Hirohito (born 29 Apr 1901), is the 124th in line from the first Emperor, Jimmu Tenno or Zinmu, whose reign was traditionally from 660 to 581 BC, but more probably from c. 40 BC to c. 10 BC. The present Emperor, who succeeded on 25 Dec 1926 is currently the world's longest reigning monarch.

Her Majesty Queen Elizabeth II (b. 21 Apr 1926) represents dynasties historically traceable at least back until the 4th century AD; in the case Tegid, great grandfather of Cunedda, founder of the House of Gwynedd in Wales; she is 54th in line. If the historicity of some early Scoto-Irish and Pictish kings were acceptable, the lineage could be extended to about 70 generations.

Reigns *Longest All Time*
The longest recorded reign of any monarch is that of Phiops II or Neferkare, a Sixth Dynasty Pharaoh of ancient Egypt. His reign began in c. 2281 BC, when he was aged 6, and is believed to have lasted c. 94 years. Minhti, King of Arakan (Burma) is reputed to have reigned for 95 years between 1279 and 1374. Musoma Kanijo, chief of the Nzega district of western Tanganyika (now part of Tanzania), reputedly reigned for more than 98 years from 1864, when aged 8, until his death on 2 Feb 1963. The longest reign of any European monarch was that of Afonso I Henrigues of Portugal who ascended the throne on 30 Apr 1112 and died on 6 Dec 1185 after a reign of 73 years 220 days, first as a Count and then as King.

Roman Occupation
During the 369 year long Roman occupation of England, Wales and parts of southern Scotland there were 40 sole and 27 co-Emperors of Rome. Of these the longest reigning was Constantinus

---

BRITISH MONARCHY RECORDS

	Kings	Queens Regnant	Queens Consort
LONGEST REIGN OR TENURE	59 years 96 days[1] George III 1760–1820	63 years 216 days Victoria 1837–1901	57 years 70 days Charlotte 1761–1818 (Consort of George III)
SHORTEST REIGN OR TENURE	77 days[2] Edward V 1483	13 days[3] Jane, 6–19 July 1553	154 days Yoleta (1285–6) (second consort of Alexander III)
LONGEST LIVED	81 years 239 days George III (b. 1738–d. 1820)	81 years 243 days Victoria (b. 1819–d. 1901)	85 years 303 days Mary of Teck (b. 1867–d. 1953) (Consort of George V)
MOST CHILDREN (LEGITIMATE)[5]	18 Edward I 1272–1307	9[6] Victoria (b. 1819–d. 1901)	15 Eleanor (c. 1244–90) and Charlotte (b. 1744–d. 1818)
OLDEST TO START REIGN OR CONSORTSHIP	64 years 10 months William IV 1830–7	37 years 5 months Mary I 1553–8	56 years 53 days Alexandra (b. 1844–d. 1925) (Consort of Edward VII)
YOUNGEST TO START REIGN OR CONSORTSHIP	269 days Henry VI in 1422	6 or 7 days Mary, Queen of Scots in 1542	6 years 11 months Isabella (second consort of Richard II in 1396)
MOST MARRIED	6 times Henry VIII 1509–47	3 times Mary, Queen of Scots 1542–67 (executed 1587)	4 times Catherine Parr (b. c. 1512–d. 1548) (sixth consort of Henry VIII)
MOST ALIVE SIMULTANEOUSLY	Between 30 Oct 1683 (birth of George Augustus of Hanover, later George II) and 6 Feb 1685 (death of Charles II) there were 8 heads of state living simultaneously (Charles II, James II, William and Mary, Anne, George I and II) and also Richard Cromwell (d. 1712) the 2nd Lord Protector and *de facto* Head of State in 1658–59.		

Notes (Dates are dates of reigns or tenures unless otherwise indicated).

[1] *James Francis Edward, the Old Pretender, known to his supporters as James III, styled his reign from 16 Sept 1701 until his death 1 Jan 1766 (i.e. 64 years 109 days).*

[2] *There is the probability that in pre-Conquest times Sweyn 'Forkbeard', the Danish King of England, reigned for only 40 days in 1013–14.*

[3] *She accepted the allegiance of the Lords of the Council (9 July) and was proclaimed on 10 July so is often referred to as the '9 (or 10) day Queen'.*

[4] *Richard Cromwell (b. 4 Oct 1626), the 2nd Lord Protector from 3 Sept 1658 until his abdication on 24 May 1659, lived under the alias John Clarke until 12 July 1712 aged 85 years 9 months and was thus the longest lived Head of State.*

[5] *Henry I (b. 1068–d. 1135) in addition to one (possibly two) legitimate sons and a daughter had at least 20 bastard children (9 sons, 11 daughters), and possibly 22, by six mistresses.*

[6] *Queen Anne (b. 1665–d. 1714) had 17 pregnancies, which produced only 5 live births.*

I (The Great) from 31 Mar 307 to 22 May 337–30 years 2 months.

Shortest

The Crown Prince Luis Filipe of Portugal was mortally wounded at the time that his father was killed by a bullet, which severed his carotid artery, in the streets of Lisbon on 1 Feb 1908. He was thus technically King of Portugal (Dom Luis III) for about 20 minutes.

Highest post-nominal numbers

The highest post-nominal number ever used to designate a member of a Royal House was 75 briefly enjoyed by Count Heinrich LXXV Reuss (1800–1). All male members of this branch of this German family are called Heinrich and are successively numbered from I upwards *each* century.

British regnal numbers date from the Norman conquest. The highest is 8, used by Henry VIII (1509–1547) and by Edward VIII (1936) who died as HRH the Duke of Windsor, on 28 May 1972. Jacobites liked to style Henry Benedict, Cardinal York (b. 1725), the grandson of James II, as Henry IX in respect of his 'reign' from 1788 to 1807 when he died as last survivor in the male line of the House of Stuart.

Longest lived 'Royals'

The longest life among the Blood Royal of Europe has been that of the late HSH Princess Elizabeth Maria Auguste of Ysenburg and Büdingen, West Germany. She was born on 12 Nov 1883 and died, as Duchess of Vandières, on 10 Oct 1982 aged 98 years 332 days. The greatest age among European Royal Consorts is the 101 years 268 days of HSH Princess Leonilla Bariatinsky (b. Moscow, 9 July 1816), who married HSH Prince Louis of Sayn-Wittgenstein-Sayn and died in Ouchy, Switzerland on 1 Feb 1918. The longest-lived Queen on record has been the Queen Grandmother of Siam, Queen Sawang (b. 10 Sept 1862), 27th daughter of King Mongkut (Rama IV); she died on 17 Dec 1955 aged 93 years 3 months.

HRH Princess Alice Mary, VA, GCVO, GBE, Countess of Athlone (b. 25 Feb 1883) became the longest ever lived British 'royal' on 15 July 1977 and died aged 97 years 313 days on 3 Jan 1981. She fulfilled 20,000 engagements, including the funerals of five British monarchs.

Youngest King and Queen

Forty-six of the world's 169 sovereign states are not republics. They are lead by 1 Emperor, 14 Kings, 3 Queens, 4 princely rulers, 1 Sultan, 3 Amirs, the Pope, a Shaik, a Ruler and one elected monarch. Queen Elizabeth II is Head of State of 16 other Commonwealth countries. That with the youngest King is Swaziland where King Mswati III was crowned on 25 Apr 1986 aged 18. He was born Makhosetive, the 67th son of King Subhusa II. That with the youngest Queen is Denmark with Queen Margrethe II (b. 16 Apr 1940).

Heaviest monarch

The world's heaviest monarch is the 6 ft 3 in *1,90 m* tall King Taufa'ahau of Tonga who in Sept 1976 was weighed on the only adequate scales in the country at the airport recording 33 st (462 lb) *209,5 kg*. By 1985 he was reported to have slimmed down to 22 st (308 lb) *139,7 kg*. His embassy car in London has the number plate '1 TON'.

Most prolific

The most prolific monogamous 'royals' have been Prince Hartmann of Liechtenstein (1613–86) who had 24 children, of whom 21 were live born, by Countess Elisabeth zu Salm-Reiffer-

scheidt (1623–88). HRH Duke Roberto I of Parma (1848–1907) also had 24 children but by two wives. One of his daughters HIM Empress Zita of Austria (b. 9 May 1892) was exiled on 23 Mar 1919 but visited Vienna, her titles intact on 17 Nov 1982 reminding republicans that her father succeeded to the throne of Parma in 1854.

Head of State *Oldest and Youngest*

The oldest head of state in the world is the Emperor of Japan (b. 29 Apr 1901). The youngest is King Mswati III of Swaziland (b. 19 Apr 1968).

Earliest Elected Female

President Vigdis Finnbogadottir (b. 1930) of Iceland became the first democratically elected female head of state on 30 June 1980.

---

3. LEGISLATURES

PARLIAMENTS—WORLD

Earliest and Oldest

The earliest known legislative assembly or *ukkim* was a bicameral one in Erech, Iraq *c.* 2800 BC. The oldest legislative body is the *Althing* of Iceland founded in AD 930. This body, which originally comprised 39 local chieftains at Thingvellir, was abolished in 1800, but restored by Denmark to a consultative status in 1843 and a legislative status in 1874. The legislative assembly with the oldest continuous history is the Court of Tynwald in the Isle of Man, which celebrated its millenium in 1979.

Largest

The largest legislative assembly in the world is the National People's Congress of the People's Republic of China. The fifth Congress, when convened in 1978, had 3497 members. Its standing committee has 197 members.

Smallest quorum

The House of Lords has the smallest quorum, expressed as a percentage of eligible voters, of any legislative body in the world, namely less than one-third of 1 per cent. To transact business there must be three peers present, including the Lord Chancellor or his deputy. The House of Commons quorum of 40 MPs, including the Speaker or his deputy, is 20 times as exacting.

Highest paid legislators

The most highly paid of all the world's legislators are Members of the US Congress whose basic annual salary was raised on 1 Jan 1985 to $72,600 (*then £60,500*) and limited honoraria to $20,940 (*£17,550*). In addition up to $1,021,167 (*£850,000*) per annum is allowed for office help, with a salary limit of $50,000 (*now £41,660*) for any one staff member (limited to 16 in number). Senators are allowed up to $143,000 (*£119,200*) per annum for an official office expense account from which official travel, telegram, long distance telephone, air mail, postage, stationery, subscriptions to newspapers, and office expenses in home state are paid. They also command very low rates for filming, speech and radio transcriptions and, in the case of women senators, beauty treatment. When abroad they have access to 'counterpart funds'. A retiring President electing to take also his congressional pension would enjoy an annual pension of $103,500 (*£66,774*).

Longest membership

The longest span as a legislator was 83 years by József Madarász (1814–1915). He first attended the Hungarian Parliament in 1832–6 as *oblegatus absentium* (*i.e.* on behalf of an absent deputy). He was a full member in 1848–50 and from 1861 until his death on 31 Jan 1915.

UN Speech *Longest*

The longest speech made in the United Nations has been one of 4 hr 29 min by President Dr Fidel Castro Ruz (b. 13 Aug 1927) of Cuba on 26 Sept 1960.

Filibusters

The longest continuous speech in the history of the United States Senate was that of Senator Wayne Morse (1900–74) of Oregon on 24–25 Apr 1953, when he spoke on the Tidelands Oil Bill for 22 hr 26 min without resuming his seat. Interrupted only briefly by the swearing-in of a new senator, Senator Strom Thurmond (b. 1902) (South Carolina, Democrat) spoke against the Civil Rights Bill for 24 hr 19 min on 28–29 Aug 1957. The United States national record duration for a filibuster is 43 hr by Texas State senator Bill Meier against nondisclosure of industrial accidents in May 1977.

Treaty *Oldest*

The world's oldest treaty is the Anglo-Portuguese Treaty of Alliance signed in London over 613 years ago on 16 June 1373. The text was confirmed 'with my usual flourish' by John de Banketre, Clerk.

Constitutions

The world's oldest constitution is that of the United States of America ratified by the necessary Ninth State (New Hampshire) on 21 June 1788 and declared to be in effect on 4 Mar 1789. The only countries without one document constitutions are Israel, Libya, New Zealand, Oman, and the United Kingdom.

Women's suffrage

The earliest legislature with female voters was the Territory of Wyoming, USA in 1869, followed by the Isle of Man in 1881. The earliest country to have universal suffrage was New Zealand in 1893. The vote of Mrs Lily Maxwell in Manchester on 26 Nov 1867 was declared illegal on 9 Nov 1868.

PARLIAMENTS
UNITED KINGDOM

Earliest

The earliest known use of the term 'parliament' is an official English royal document, in the meaning of a summons to the King's (Henry III's) council, dates from 19 Dec 1241.

The Houses of Parliament of the United Kingdom in the Palace of Westminster, London, had 1826 members (House of Lords 1176, House of Commons 650) in June 1986.

Longest

The longest English Parliament was the 'Pensioners' Parliament of Charles II, which lasted from 8 May 1661 to 24 Jan 1679, a period of 17 years 8 months and 16 days. The longest United Kingdom Parliament was that of George V, Edward VIII and George VI, lasting from 26 Nov 1935 to 15 June 1945, a span of 9 years 6 months and 20 days.

Shortest

The parliament of Edward I, summoned to Westminster for 30 May 1306, lasted only 1 day. The parliament of Charles II at Oxford from 21–28 Mar 1681 lasted 7 days. The shortest United Kingdom Parliament was that of George III, lasting from 15 Dec 1806 to 29 Apr 1807, a period of only 4 months and 14 days.

Sittings *Longest*

The longest sitting in the House of Commons was one of 41½ hr from 4 p.m. on 31 Jan 1881 to 9.30 a.m. on 2 Feb 1881, on the question of better Protection of Person and Property in

Ireland. The longest sitting of the Lords has been 19 hr 16 min from 2.30 p.m. on 29 Feb to 9.46 a.m on 1 Mar 1968 on the Commonwealth Immigrants Bill (Committee stage). The longest sitting of a Standing Committee occurred from 10.30 a.m. 11 May to 12.08 p.m. 13 May 1948 when Standing Committee D considered the Gas Bill through two nights for 49 hr 38 min.

Speech *Longest*

The longest recorded continuous speech in the Chamber of the House of Commons was that of Henry Peter Brougham (1778–1868) on 7 Feb 1828, when he spoke for 6 hr on Law Reform. He ended at 10.40 p.m. and the report of this speech occupied 12 columns of the next day's edition of *The Times*. Brougham, created the 1st Lord Brougham and Vaux on 22 Nov 1830, then set the House of Lords record, also with 6 hours on 7 Oct 1831, when speaking on the second reading of the Reform Bill and 'fortified by 3 tumblers of spiced wine'.

The longest back bench speech under present, much stricter, Standing Orders has been one of 4 hr 23 min by Ivan John Lawrence QC MP (b 24 Dec 1936) Conservative member for Burton opposing the Water (Fluoridation) Bill on 6 Mar 1985. John Golding MP (b. 9 Mar 1931) (Labour, Newcastle-under-Lyme) spoke for 11 hr 15 min in committee on small amendments to the British Telecommunications Bill on 8–9 Feb 1983.

The longest speech in Stormont, Northern Ireland was one of 9 hr 26 min by Thomas Gibson Henderson MP (1887–1970) on the Appropriations Bill from 6.32 p.m. on 26th to 3.58 a.m. on 27th May 1936.

Greatest parliamentary petition

The greatest petition has been supposed to be the Great Chartist Petition of 1848 but of the 5,706,000 'signatures' only 1,975,496 were valid. The largest of all time was for the abolition of Entertainment Duty with 3,107,080 signatures presented on 5 June 1951.

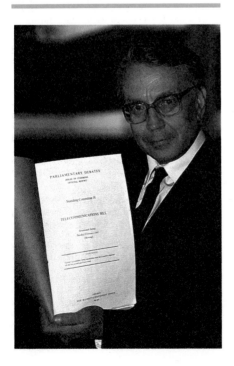

A slow motion . . . John Golding MP spoke in committee for 11 hr 15 min on amendments to the Telecommunications Bill.

(*Top*) Cuban President Fidel Castro made the longest speech in the history of the United Nations since it was formed in 1945. (Astral Photo). (*Above*) George Washington presides over the United States' constitution, the oldest in the world, in 1788. (Virginia Museum of Fine Arts).

Most and least time consuming legislation

The most profligate use of parliamentary time was on the Government of Ireland Bill of 1893–4, which required 82 days in the House of Commons of which 46 days was in Committee. The record for a standing committee is 59 sessions for the Police and Criminal Evidence Bill from 17 Nov 1983 to 29 Mar 1984.

The Abdication Bill (of King Edward VIII) passed all its stages in the Commons (2 hr) and the Lords (8 min) on 11–12 Dec 1936 and received the Royal Assent at 1.52 a.m. on the latter date.

Private Members' Bills

Balloting by private members for parliamentary time was in being at least as early as 1844. The highest recorded number of public bills intro-

duced by private members was 226 in 1908 but the highest number to receive Royal Assent was 27 in the Commons and 7 in the Lords in 1963–64. The worst session was 1973–74 with nil from 42 presented in the Commons and nil from 10 in the Lords.

Divisions

The record number of divisions in the House of Commons is 64 on 23–24 Mar 1971 including 57 in succession between midnight and noon. The largest division was one of 350–310 on the vote of no confidence on 11 Aug 1892.

ELECTIONS—WORLD

Largest

The largest elections in the world were those beginning on 24 Dec 1984 for the Indian *Lok*

Election day in India, 1984, the largest election in the world. Nearly 8 per cent of the entire population of the world were eligible to vote. (Rex Features).

Sabha (Lower House) which has 542 elective seats. The government of Rajiv Gandhi was returned in polls in which 379,000,000 electors were eligible to vote for 5,301 candidates at 480,000 polling stations manned by 2½ million staff. In Maduranthkam (electorate 120,021) there were 90 candidates.

Closest
The ultimate in close general elections occurred in Zanzibar (now part of Tanzania) on 18 Jan 1961, when the Afro-Shirazi Party won by a single seat, after the seat of Chake-Chake on Pemba Island had been gained by a single vote.

The narrowest recorded percentage win in an election would seem to be for the office of Southern District highway commissioner in Mississippi State, USA on 7 Aug 1979. Robert E. Joiner was declared the winner over W. H. Pyron with 133,587 votes to 133,582. The loser got more than 49.9999 per cent of the votes.

Most decisive
North Korea recorded a 100 per cent turn-out of electors and a 100 per cent vote for the Worker's Party of Korea in the general election of 8 Oct 1962. The next closest approach was in Albania on 14 Nov 1982 when a single voter spoiled national unanimity for the official (and only) Communist candidates, who thus obtained only 99.99993 per cent of the poll in a 100 per cent turn out of 1,627,968.

Most bent
In the Liberian presidential election of 1927 President Charles D. B. King (1875–1961) was returned with a majority over his opponent, Mr Thomas J. R. Faulkner of the People's Party, officially announced as 234,000. President King thus claimed a 'majority' more than 15½ times greater than the entire electorate.

Highest personal majority
The highest ever personal majority by any politician has been 424,545 by Ram Bilas Paswan, 30, the Janata candidate for Hajipur in Bihar, India in March 1977. The electorate was 625,179.

Communist parties
The largest national Communist party outside the USSR (19,000,000 members in 1986) and Communist states has been the Partito Comunista Italiano, with a membership of 2,300,000 in 1946. The total was 1,600,000 in 1986. The membership in mainland China was estimated to be 39,000,000 in 1986. The Communist Party of Great Britain, formed on 31 July 1920 in Cannon Street Station Hotel, London, attained its peak membership of 56,000 in December 1942, compared with 12,711 in 1985 of whom not more than 8000 had been re-registered. The decline has been caused by divisions over relations with the USSR and doctrine leading to expulsions and the formation of new parties or groups within the Labour movement.

Largest Ballot Paper
On 5 Mar 1985 in the State Assembly (Vidha Sabha) elections in Karnataka, India there were 301 candidates for Belguum City.

Voting age Extremes
The eligibility for voting is 15 years of age in the Philippines and 25 years in Andorra.

Most Coups
Statisticians contend Bolivia, since it became a sovereign country in 1825, had its 190th coup on 30 June 1984 when President Hernan Siles Zuazo, 70, was kidnapped from his official residence by more than 60 armed men.

PRIME MINISTERS AND STATESMEN

Oldest *World*
The longest lived Prime Minister of any country was Christopher Hornsrud, Prime Minister of Norway from 28 Jan to 15 Feb 1928. He was born on 15 Nov 1859 and died on 13 Dec 1960, aged 101 years 28 days. The Hon. Richard Gavin Reid (b. Glasgow 17 Jan 1879), Premier of Alberta, Canada in 1934–35 died on 17 Oct 1980 aged 101 years 274 days.

El Hadji Muhammad el Mokri, Grand Vizier of Morocco, died on 16 Sept 1957, at a reputed age of 116 Muslim (*Hijri*) years, equivalent to 112.5 Gegorian years. The oldest age of first appointment has been 81 by Morarji Ranchhodji Desai of India (b. 29 Feb 1896) in March 1977.

Longest term of office *World*
The longest serving current prime minister is Lee Kuan Yew, Hon GCMG, Hon CH (b. 16 Sept 1923) of the former Crown Colony Republic of Singapore who entered his 28th year in office on 5 June 1986.

Enver Hoxha (b. 16 Oct 1908), First Secretary of the Central Committee of the Albania Party of Labour, ruled from Oct 1944 to his death on 11 Apr 1985.

Andrei Andreyevich Gromyko (b. 6 July 1909) had been Minister of Foreign Affairs of the USSR since 15 Feb 1957, having been Deputy Foreign Minister since 1946, until he was elected President of the USSR on 2 July 1985. Pyotr Lomako (b. 1904) has served in the government of the USSR as Minister for Non-Ferrous Metallurgy from 1940. He was still in place in June 1986, having served on the Central Committee of the CPSU Union since 1952

EUROPEAN ASSEMBLY ELECTION RECORDS

In the European Assembly elections of 14 June 1984 the highest majority in the 81 U.K. constituencies was 95,557 (L. Smith, Lab) in Wales South-East. Lowest was 2,625 (Sir Peter Vanneck, Con) in Cleveland and Yorkshire North. Largest and smallest electorates were 574,022 in Essex North-East and 307,265 in Highlands and Islands. Highest turnout was 42.4 per cent in Wales North. Lowest was 25.2 per cent in London North-East. Northern Ireland voted by proportional representation.

MAJORITIES—UNITED KINGDOM

Party
The largest party majorities were those of the Liberals, with 307 seats and a record of 66.7% of the vote in 1832. In 1931 the Coalition of Conservatives, Liberals and National Labour candidates had a majority of 491 seats and 60.5% of the vote. The narrowest party majority was that of the Whigs in 1847, with a single seat. The highest popular vote for a single party was 13,948,883 for Labour in 1951.

The largest majority on a division was one of 463 (464 votes to 1), on a vote of confidence in the conduct of World War II, on 29 Jan 1942. Since the war the largest has been one of 461 (487 votes to 26) on 10 May 1967, during the debate on the government's application for Britain to join the European Economic Community (the 'Common Market').

HOUSE OF LORDS

Oldest member
The oldest member ever was the Rt Hon Lord Shinwell PC CH (1884–1986) who first sat in the Lower House in November 1922 and lived to be 101 years 202 days. The oldest peer to make a maiden speech was Lord Maenan (1854–1951) aged 94 years 123 days (see Oldest creation, p. 182).

Youngest member
The youngest present member of the House of Lords has been HRH the Prince Charles Philip Arthur George, KG, PC, KT, GCB, the Prince of Wales (b. 14 Nov 1948). All Dukes of Cornwall, of whom Prince Charles is the 24th, are technically eligible to sit, regardless of age—in his case from his succession on 6 Feb 1952, aged 3. The 20th and 21st holders, later King George IV (b. 1762) and King Edward VII (b. 1841), were technically entitled to sit from birth. The youngest creation of a life peer or peeress under the Peerage Act 1958 has been that of Lady Masham (b. 14 Apr 1935) who was created Baroness Masham of Ilton at 34 years 262 days.

PRIME MINISTERIAL RECORDS

Though given legal warrant in the instrument of the Congress of Berlin in 1878 and an established place in the orders of Precedence in England and Scotland in 1904, the office of Prime Minister was not statutorily recognised until 1917. All previous acknowledged First Ministers had tenure as First Lords of the Treasury with the exception of No. 12, William Pitt, Earl of Chatham, who controlled his ministers as Secretary of State of the Southern Department or as Lord Privy Seal. The first to preside over his fellow King's ministers was Walpole from 1721.

LONGEST SERVING	20 years 326 days	1st	Sir Robert Walpole KG (1676–1745)	3 Apr 1721–12 Feb 1742
LONGEST SERVING (20th century)	8 years 243 days	38th	Earl of Oxford and Asquith, KG (1852–1928)	8 Apr 1908–7 Dec 1916
MOST MINISTERIES	5 times	41st	Earl Baldwin, KG (1867–1947)	22 May 1923–28 May 1937
SHORTEST SERVING IN OFFICE	120 days	22nd	George Canning (1770–1827)	10 Apr–8 Aug 1827
YOUNGEST TO ASSUME OFFICE	24 years 205 days	17th	Hon. William Pitt (1759–1806)	19 Dec 1783 (declined when 23 yr 275 days)
OLDEST TO FIRST ASSUME OFFICE	70 years 109 days	31st	Viscount Palmerston, KG, GCB (1784–1865)	6 Feb 1855
GREATEST AGE IN OFFICE	84 years 64 days	33rd	William Gladstone (1809–1898)	3 Mar 1894 (elected at 82 yr 171 days)
LONGEST LIVED	91 + years	47th	Earl of Stockton, OM (b. 10 Feb 1894)	from 6 Apr 1984 (so surpassing No 44)
LONGEST SURVIVAL AFTER OFFICE	41 years 45 days	13th	Duke of Grafton, KG (1735–1811)	from 28 Jan 1770
SHORTEST LIVED	44 years	7th	Duke of Devonshire, KG (1720–1764)	d. 2 Oct 1764 (exact birth date unknown)
SHORTEST MINISTRY	22 days	24th	Duke of Wellington, KG, GCB, GCH (1769–1852)	17 Nov–9 Dec 1834
SHORTEST POSSESSION OF SEALS	c. 48 hours	4th	Earl of Bath (1684–1764)	10–12 Feb 1746
SHORTEST PRIOR SERVICE AS MP	2 years 11 months	17th	Hon. William Pitt (1759–1806)	–19 Dec 1783
LONGEST PRIOR SERVICE AS MP	47 years	31st	Viscount Palmerston, KG, GCB (1784–1865)	1807–6 Feb 1855
LONGEST SUBSEQUENT SERVICE AS MP	22 years 156 days	39th	Earl Lloyd George, OM (1863–1945)	22 Oct 1922–26 Mar 1945
LONGEST SPAN AS MP	63 years 360 days	44th	Sir Winston Churchill, KG, OM, CH (1874–1965)	1 Oct 1900–25 Sep 1964
RICHEST	£7¼ million (now say £190 million)	29th	Earl of Derby, KG, GCMG (1799–1869)	Annual rent roll in 1869 £170,000
POOREST	£40,000 (now > £1 million) in debt	17th	Hon. William Pitt (1759–1806)	Level of personal debt by 1800
TALLEST	6 ft 1½ in 1,83 m	51st	James Callaghan (b. 27 Mar 1912)	
SHORTEST	5 ft 4¾ in 1,64 m	28th	Lord John Russell, KG (1792–1878)	Seven month baby: max. wt. 8 stone 50,7 kg
MOST CHILDREN (fathered)	15 or 16	13th	Duke of Grafton, KG (1735–1811)	Twice married
MOST CHILDREN (uniquely mothered)	2	52nd	Mrs Margaret Thatcher (b. 13 Oct 1925)	Twins born, 21 Aug 1953
MOST LIVING SIMULTANEOUSLY	18	9th–27th	Peel (b. 5 Feb 1788) to death of 9th Earl of Bute (d. 10 Mar 1792)	1788–1792
MOST LIVING EX PRIME MINISTERS	5	9th, 13–16th	Bute, Grafton, North, Shelburne, Portland.(Pitt) till Bute died	19 Dec 1783–10 Mar 1792
	5	46–50th	Eden, Macmillan, Home, Wilson, Heath (Callaghan) till Eden died	5 Apr 1976–14 Jan 1977
	5	47–51st	Macmillan, Home, Wilson, Heath, Callaghan (Mrs Thatcher)	from 4 May 1979

Some of the record breaking Prime Ministers; (Above left) The Duke of Wellington whose ministry lasted just 22 days; (centre top) Robert Walpole, the first Prime Minister, who was also the longest serving at just short of 21 years.

(Above right) Sir Winston Churchill, who served in Parliament longer than anyone else, nearly 64 years, was Prime Minister twice, from 1940–45 and from 1951–55. (Left) Stanley Baldwin, later Earl of Bewdley, formed five ministries between 1923 and 1937.

Artwork: Don Roberts

POLITICAL OFFICE HOLDERS

Chancellorship *Longest and shortest tenures*
The Rt Hon Sir Robert Walpole, KG, later the 1st Earl of Orford (1676–1745), served 22 years 5 months as Chancellor of the Exchequer, holding office continuously from 12 Oct. 1715 to 12 Feb 1742, except for the period from 16 Apr 1717 to 2 Apr 1721. The briefest tenure of this office was 26 days in the case of the Baron (later the 1st Earl of) Mansfield (1705–93), from 11 Sept to 6 Oct 1767. The only man with four terms in this office was the Rt Hon William Ewart Gladstone (1809–98).

The longest budget speech was that of Rt Hon David (later Earl) Lloyd George, PC, OM (1863–1945) on 29 Apr 1909 which lasted 4 hr 51 min but was interrupted by a 30 min larygeal tea break. He announced *inter alia* the introduction of car tax and petroleum duty. Mr Gladstone spoke for 4¾ hours on 18 Apr 1853.

Foreign Secretaryship *Longest tenures*
The longest continuous term of office of any Foreign Secretary has been the 10 years 360 days of Sir Edward Grey, KG, MP (later Viscount Grey of Fallodon) from 10 Dec 1905 to 5 Dec 1916. The Rt Hon Sir Henry John Temple, 3rd Viscount Palmerston, KG, PC, GCB, in three spells in 1830–34, 1835–41 and 1846–51 aggregated 15 years 296 days.

Colonial Secretaryship *Longest tenures*
The longest term of office has been 19 years 324 days by the Rt Hon Henry Bathurst, Earl Bathurst (1762–1834), who was Secretary of State for the Colonial and War Department from 11 June 1812 to 1 May 1827. The longest tenure this century has been the 5 years 78 days of the Rt Hon Alan Tindal Lennox-Boyd, Viscount Boyd of Merton, PC CH (1904–82) from 28 July 1954 to 13 Oct 1959.

Speakership *Longest*
Arthur Onslow (1691–1768) was elected Mr Speaker on 23 Jan 1728, at the age of 36. He held the position for 33 years 43 days, until 18 Mar 1761 allowing for the 'lost' 11 days (3–13 Sept 1752).

MPs *Youngest*
The youngest ever woman M.P. has been Josephine Bernadette Devlin now Mrs Michael McAliskey (b. 23 Apr 1947) elected for Mid Ulster (Ind. Unity) aged 21 yr 359 days on 17 Apr 1969. Henry Long (1420–90) was returned for an Old Sarum seat also at the age of 15. His precise date of birth is unknown. Minors were debarred in law in 1695 and in fact in 1832.

Oldest
The oldest of all members was Samuel Young (b. 14 Feb 1822), Nationalist MP for East Cavan (1892–1918), who died on 18 Apr 1918, aged 96 years 63 days. The oldest 'Father of the House' in Parliamentary history was the Rt Hon Charles Pelham Villiers (b. 3 Jan 1802), who was the member for Wolverhampton South when he died on 16 Jan 1898, aged 96 years 13 days. He was a Member of Parliament for 63 years 6 days, having been returned at 17 elections. The oldest member is Robert Edwards MP (Lab) for Wolverhampton South East (b. 16 Jan 1905).

Longest span
The longest span of service of any MP is 63 years 11 months (1 Oct 1900 to 25 Sept 1964) by the Rt Hon Sir Winston Leonard Spencer-Churchill, KG, OM, CH, TD (1874–1965), with breaks only in 1908 and 1922–24. The longest continuous span was that of C. P. Villiers (see above). The longest span in the Palace of Westminster (both Houses of Parliament) has been 72 years by the 10th Earl of Wemyss and March GCVO, who, as Sir Francis Wemyss-Charteris-Douglas, served as MP for East Gloucestershire (July 1841–6) and Haddingtonshire (1847–83) and then took his seat in the House of Lords, dying on 30 June 1914, aged 95 years 330 days.

Briefest span
There are two 18th century examples of posthumous elections. Capt the Hon Edward Legge RN (1710–47) was returned unopposed for Portsmouth on 15 Dec 1747. News came later that he had died in the West Indies 87 days before polling. In 1780 John Kirkman standing for the City of London expired before polling had ended but was nonetheless duly returned.

The 'Hundred Years War' between England and France, the longest in history, actually lasted 115 years, from 1338 to 1453. Below is a picture depicting the Battle of Poitiers in 1356. (Mary Evans).

A. J. Dobbs (Lab, Smethwick) elected on 5 July 1945 was killed on the way to take his seat at Westminster.

Women MPs *Earliest*
The first woman to be elected to the House of Commons was Mme. Constance Georgine Markievicz (*née* Gore Booth). She was elected as member (Sinn Fein) for St Patrick's Dublin, on 28 December 1918. The first woman to take her seat was the Viscountess Astor, CH (1879–1964) (b. Nancy Witcher Langhorne at Danville, Virginia, USA; formerly Mrs Robert Gould Shaw), who was elected Unionist member for the Sutton Division of Plymouth, Devon, on 28 Nov 1919, and took her seat three days later. The first woman to take her seat from the island of Ireland was Lady Fisher *née* Patricia Smiles as unopposed Ulster Unionist for North Down on 15 Apr 1953 as Mrs Patricia Ford.

The first woman cabinet minister was Rt Hon Margaret Grace Bondfield, PC, CH, appointed Minister of Labour in 1929.

Heaviest and Tallest
The heaviest MP of all-time is believed to have been Cyril Smith MBE, Liberal member for Rochdale since October 1972, when in January 1976 his peak reported weight was 29 st 12 lb *189,60 kg*. Sir Louis Gluckstein GBE, TD, QC (1897–1979), Conservative member for East Nottingham (1931–45), was an unrivalled 6 ft 7½ in *2,02 m*. Currently the tallest is the Hon. Archie Hamilton, Conservative member for Epsom and Ewell at 6 ft 6 in *1,98 m*.

Mayoralties
The longest recorded mayoralty was that of Edmond Mathis (1852–1953) *maire* of Ehuns, Haute-Saône, France for 75 years (1878–1953). The mayoralty of the City of London dates from 1192 with the 20 year term of Henry Fitz Ailwyn till 1212. The most elections, since these became annual in 1215, has been 8 by Gregory de Rokesley (1274/5 to 1280/1). The earliest recorded mayor of the City of York, Nigel, dates from 1142. Alderman G. T. Paine served as Mayor of Lydd, Kent for 29 consecutive years in 1931 to 1961. The first recorded all-female mayoral team was the Mayor, Mayoress and Deputy Mayor of Lancaster city council in May 1972. On Hyndburn Borough Council in May 1981 there was a fourth lady with the appointment of a Deputy Mayoress.

Local Government Service Duration Records
The office of reeve was first mentioned in AD 787 and evolved to that of shire reeve hence sheriff.

Major Sir Philip Barber Bt, DSO, TD, DL (1876–1961) served as county councillor for Nottinghamshire for 63 years 41 days from 8 Mar 1898 to 18 Apr 1961. Henry Winn (1816–1914) served as parish clerk for Fulletby near Horncastle, Lincolnshire for 76 years.

Clifford Tasker (1906–1980) of Pontefract, West Yorkshire was appointed as presiding officer for elections in 1921 when aged 15, and served for 59 years until March 1980.

Weight of Legislation
The greatest amount of legislation in a year has been 11,453 pages (83 Public general acts and 2251 Statutory Instruments) in 1975. This compares with 46 Acts and 1130 Instruments of 1998 pages in 1928. Most Acts were 123 in 1939 and fewest 39 in 1929 and 1942. The peak for Statutory Instruments was 2916 in 1947.

4. MILITARY AND DEFENCE

WAR

Earliest Conflict
The oldest known offensive weapon is a broken wooden spear found in April 1911 at Clacton-on-Sea, Essex by S. Hazzledine Warren. This is much beyond the limit of carbon-dating and is estimated to have been fashioned before 200,000 BC.

Longest
The longest of history's countless wars was the 'Hundred Years War' between England and France, which lasted from 1338 to 1453 (115 years), although it may be said that the nine Crusades from the First (1096–1104) to the Ninth (1270–91), extending over 195 years comprised a single Holy War. The Swiss Jean Jacques Babel estimated that since c. 3500 BC there have only been 292 years without recorded warfare.

Shortest
The shortest war on record was that between the United Kingdom and Zanzibar (now part of Tanzania) from 9.02 to 9.40 a.m. on 27 Aug 1896. The UK battle fleet under Rear-Admiral (later Admiral Sir) Harry Holdsworth Rawson (1843–1910) delivered an ultimatum to the self-appointed Sultan Sa'īd Khalid to evacuate his palace and surrender. This was not forthcoming until after 38 minutes of bombardment. Admiral Rawson received the Brilliant Star of Zanzibar (first class) from the new Sultan Hamud ibn Muhammad. It was proposed at one time that elements of the local populace should be compelled to defray the cost of the ammunition used.

Bloodiest
By far the most costly war in terms of human life was World War II (1939–45), in which the total number of fatalities, including battle deaths and civilians of all countries, is estimated to have been 54,800,000 assuming 25 million USSR fatalities and 7,800,000 Chinese civilians killed. The country which suffered most was Poland with 6,028,000 or 22.2 per cent of her population of 27,007,000 killed. The total combatant death roll from World War I was 9,700,000 compared with the 15,600,000 of World War II.

In the case of the United Kingdom, however, the heaviest armed forces fatalities occurred in World War I (1914–18), with 765,399 killed out of 5,500,000 engaged (13.9 per cent), compared with 265,000 out of 5,896,000 engaged (4.49 per cent) in World War II.

In the Paraguayan war of 1864–70 against Brazil, Argentina and Uruguay, their population was reduced from 1,400,000 to 220,000 of whom only 30,000 were adult males.

Surgeon Major William Brydon CB (1811–1873) was the sole survivor of the 7 day retreat of 16,000 soldiers and camp followers from Kabul, Afghanistan. His horse died two days after his arrival at Jellalabad, India on 13 Jan 1842.

Bloodiest civil
The bloodiest civil war in history was the T'ai-p'ing ('Great Peace') rebellion, in which peasant sympathizers of the Southern Ming dynasty fought the Manchu Government troops in China from 1851 to 1864. The rebellion was led by the deranged Hung Hsiu-ch'üan (executed) who imagined himself to be a younger brother of Jesus Christ. His force was named T'ai-p'ing T'ien Kuo (Heavenly Kingdom of Great Peace).

According to the best estimates, the loss of life was between 20,000,000 and 30,000,000 including more than 100,000 killed by Government forces in the sack of Nanking on 19–21 July 1864.

Most costly
The material cost of World War II far transcended that of the rest of history's wars put together and has been estimated at $1.5 million million. The total cost to the Soviet Union was estimated in May 1959 at 2,500,000,000,000 roubles (£100,000 million) while a figure of $530,000 million has been estimated for the USA. In the case of the United Kingdom the cost of £34,423 million was over five times as great as that of World War I (£6700 million) and 158.6 times that of the Boer War of 1899–1902 (£217 million).

Last battle on British soil
The last pitched land battle in Britain was at Culloden Field, Drummossie Moor, near Inverness, Highland, on 16 Apr 1746. The last Clan battle in Scotland was between Clan Mackintosh and Clan MacDonald at Mulroy, Highland in 1689. The last battle on English soil was the Battle of Sedgemoor, Somerset, on 6 July 1685, when the forces of James II defeated the supporters of Charles II's illegitimate son, James Scott (formerly called Fitzroy or Crofts), the Duke of Monmouth (1649–85). During the Jacobite rising of 1745–6, there was a skirmish at Clifton Moor, Cumbria, on 18 Dec 1745, when the British forces under Prince William, the Duke of Cumberland (1721–65), brushed with the rebels of Prince Charles Edward Stuart (1720–88) with about 12 killed on the King's side and 5 Highlanders. This was a tactical victory for the Scots under Lord George Murray.

Bloodiest battle *Modern*
The battle with the greatest recorded number of *military* casualties was the First Battle of the Somme, France from 1 July to 19 Nov 1916, with 1,043,896—Allied 623,907 (of which 419,654 were British) and 419,989 German. The published German figure of c. 670,000 is not now accepted. The gunfire was heard on Hampstead Heath, London. The greatest death roll in a battle has been estimated at c. 2,100,000 in the Battle of Stalingrad ending with the German surrender on 2 Feb 1943 by Field Marshal Friedrich von Paulus (d. 1957). The Soviet garrison commander was Gen Vassilyi Chuikov. Additionally 1,515 civilians from a pre-war population of more than 500,000 were found alive after the battle. The final investment of Berlin by the Red Army on 16 Apr–2 May 1945 involved 3,500,000 men; 52,000 guns and mortars; 7750 tanks and 11,000 aircraft on both sides.

Ancient
Modern historians give no credence, on logistic grounds, to the casualty figures attached to ancient battles, such as the 250,000 reputedly killed at Plataea (Greeks v Persians) in 479 BC or the 200,000 allegedly killed in a single day at Châlons, France (Huns v Romans) in AD 451.

British
The bloodiest battle fought on British soil was the Battle of Towton, in North Yorkshire, on 29 Mar 1461, when 36,000 Yorkists defeated 40,000 Lancastrians. The total loss has been estimated at between 28,000 and 38,000 killed. A figure of 80,000 British dead was attributed by Tacitus to the battle of AD 61 between Queen Boudicca (Boadicea) of the Iceni and the Roman Governor of Britain Suetonius Paulinus, for the reputed loss of only 400 Romans in an army of 10,000. The site of the battle is unknown but may have been near Borough Hill, Daventry, Northamp-

tonshire, or more probably near Hampstead Heath, Greater London. Prior to this battle the Romans had lost up to 70,000 in Colchester and London.

Greatest naval battle
The greatest number of ships and aircraft ever involved in a sea-air action was 231 ships and 1996 aircraft in the Battle of Leyte Gulf, in the Philippines. It raged from 22 to 27 Oct 1944, with 166 Allied and 65 Japanese warships engaged, of which 26 Japanese and 6 US ships were sunk. In addition 1280 US and 716 Japanese aircraft were engaged. The greatest purely naval battle of modern times was the Battle of Jutland on 31 May 1916, in which 151 Royal Navy warships were involved against 101 German warships. The Royal Navy lost 14 ships and 6097 men and the German fleet 11 ships and 2545 men. The greatest of ancient naval battles was the Battle of Salamis, Greece on 23 Sept 480 BC. There were an estimated 800 vessels in the defeated Persian fleet and 310 in the victorious Greek fleet with a possible involvement of 190,000 men. The death roll at the Battle of Lepanto on 7 Oct 1571 has been estimated at 33,000.

Invasion Greatest *Seaborne*
The greatest invasion in military history was the Allied land, air and sea operation against the Normandy coasts of France on D-day, 6 June 1944. Thirty-eight convoys of 745 ships moved in on the first three days, supported by 4066 landing craft, carrying 185,000 men and 20,000 vehicles, and 347 minesweepers. The air assault comprised 18,000 paratroopers from 1087 aircraft. The 42 available divisions possessed an air support from 13,175 aircraft. Within a month 1,100,000 troops, 200,000 vehicles and 750,000 tons of stores were landed. The Allied invasion of Sicily on 10–12 July 1943 involved the landing of 181,000 men in 3 days.

Airborne
The largest airborne invasion was the Anglo-American assault of three divisions (34,000 men), with 2800 aircraft and 1600 gliders, near Arnhem, in the Netherlands, on 17 Sept 1944.

Last on the soil of Great Britain
The last invasion of Great Britain occurred on 12 Feb 1797, when the Irish-American adventurer General Tate landed at Carreg Gwastad with 1400 French troops. They surrendered near Fishguard, Dyfed, to Lord Cawdor's force of the Castlemartin Yeomanry and some local inhabitants armed with pitchforks. The UK Crown Dependency of the Falkland Islands were invaded by Argentine troops on 2 Apr 1982. British troops re-landed at San Carlos on 21 May and accepted the surrender of Brig Gen Mario Menéndez on 14 June 1982.

Greatest evacuation
The greatest evacuation in military history was that carried out by 1200 Allied naval and civil craft from the beach-head at Dunkerque (Dunkirk), France, between 27 May and 4 June 1940. A total of 338,226 British and French troops were taken off.

Worst sieges
The worst siege in history was the 880-day siege of Leningrad, USSR by the German Army from 30 Aug 1941 until 27 Jan 1944. The best estimate is that between 1.3 and 1.5 million defenders and citizens died. The longest recorded siege was that of Azotus (now Ashdod), Israel which according to Herodotus was invested by Psamtik I of Egypt for 29 years in the period 664–610 BC.

Longest Range Attack
The longest range attacks in air history were

from Ascension Island to Port Stanley, Falkland Is. by refuelled RAF Vulcan bombers carrying 1000 lb *453,5 kg* bombs in a round trip of more than 8000 miles *12 875 km* in May 1982.

ARMED FORCES

Largest
Numerically the largest regular armed force in the world is that of the USSR with 5,300,000 (1985). China's People's Liberation Army of 3,900,000 will lose 1 million by 1987. Her reserves number 10¾ million and her para-military forces of armed and unarmed militias are estimated by the International Institute of Strategic Studies at 'some 12 million'. The USA's military manpower is 2,151,568 (1985) and that of the United Kingdom 327,100 (1986).

Navies *Largest*
The largest navy in the world in terms of manpower is the United States Navy, with a manpower of 568,780 and 196,240 Marines in mid-1985. The active strength in 1985 included 4 nuclear powered aircraft carriers, with 10 others, 2 battleships, 95 attack nuclear submarines and 4 diesel attack submarines, 29 cruisers, 68 destroyers, 101 frigates and 61 amphibious warfare ships. The USSR navy has a larger submarine fleet of 371 vessels (121 nuclear, 250 diesel). It has 6 aircraft carriers, 39 cruisers, 47 nuclear armed and 22 gun destroyers.

The strength of the Royal Navy in mid-1985 included 4 nuclear submarines with strategic atomic missiles, 13 other nuclear and 15 diesel attack submarines and 4 anti-submarine commando carriers, 15 guided weapon destroyers, and 39 frigates. The uniformed strength was 70,600 including Royal Naval Air Service and Royal Marines (7800) in 1985/86. In 1914 the Royal Navy had 542 warships including 72 capital ships with 16 building thus being the largest navy in the world.

Admiral *Longest serving*
Admiral of the Fleet Sir Provo Wallis GCB (1791–1892) first served on *HMS Cleopatra* in Oct 1804. Because of his service on *HMS Cleopatra* in 1805 against the French he was kept on the active list in 1870 for life. He thus was 87 years 4 months on paid active service though he was earlier on the books as a volunteer from 1795–1804 for a further 9 years—a system by which even infants could gain seniority on joining.

Armies *Oldest*
The oldest army in the world is the 83-strong Swiss Guard in the Vatican City, with a regular foundation dating back to 21 Jan 1506. Its origins, however, extend back before 1400.

Largest
Numerically, the world's largest army is that of the People's Republic of China, with a total

---

DEFENCE SPENDING
The estimated level of spending on armaments throughout the world in 1984 was in excess of $700,000 million *£583,000 million*. This represents £107 per person per annum, or 10 per cent of the world's total production of goods and services. Also in 1985 there were 27.2 million full-time armed force regulars or conscripts.

The budgeted expenditure on defence by the US government for the fiscal year 1986 was $302.5 billion (*£216 billion*).

The defence burden on the USSR has been variously estimated as a percentage of GNP to be between 12 and 17% and thus may be nearly treble that of the US.

---

strength of some 2,975,000 in mid-1985. The total size of the USSR's army in mid-1985 was estimated by the International Institute of Strategic Studies at 1,995,000 men, believed to be organised into 199 divisions. The strength of the British Army was 163,000 in 1985/86. The The basic strength maintained in Northern Ireland is some 9000. Between 1969 and 1 Jan 1984, 2365 people have been killed.

Oldest soldiers
The oldest old soldier of all time was probably John B. Salling of the army of the Confederate States of America and the last accepted survivor of the US Civil War (1861–5). He died in Kingsport, Tennessee, USA on 16 Mar 1959, aged 113 years 1 day. The oldest Chelsea pensioner, based *only* on the evidence of his tombstone, was the 111-year-old William Hiseland (b. 6 Aug 1620, d. 7 Feb 1732). The longest serving British soldier has been Field Marshal Sir William Maynard Gomm GCB (1784–1875), who was an ensign in 1794 and the Constable of the Tower at his death aged 91.

Youngest soldiers
Marshal Duke of Caxias (b. 25 Aug 1803, d. 7 May 1880), Brazilian military hero and states-man, entered his infantry regiment at the age of 5 in 1808.

Dr Kenneth Vernon Bailey MC (b. 14 Dec 1897) served as a 2nd Lieutenant in the 2/8th Btn Manchester Regt. for some 6 weeks before his 17th birthday. Probably the youngest enlistment in the 20th century was of William Frederick Price, (b. 1 June 1891), who was enlisted into the Army at Aldershot on 23 May 1903, aged 11 years 356 days.

Youngest conscripts
President Francisco Macias Nguema of Equatorial Guinea decreed in March 1976 compulsory military service for all boys between 7 and 14. The edict stated that any parent refusing to hand over his or her son 'will be imprisoned or shot'.

Tallest soldiers
The tallest soldier of all time was Väinö Myllyrinne (1909–63) who was inducted into the Finnish Army when he was 7 ft 3 in *2,21 m* and later grew to 8 ft 3 in *251,4 cm*. The British Army's tallest soldier was Benjamin Crow who was signed on at Lichfield in November 1947 when he was 7 ft 1 in *2,15 m* tall. Edward Evans (1924–58), who later grew to 7 ft 8½ in *235 cm*, was in the Army when he was 6 ft 10 in *2,08 m*.

British regimental records
The oldest regular regiment in the British Army is the Royal Scots, raised in French service in 1633, though the Buffs (Royal East Kent Regiment) can trace back their origin to independent companies in Dutch pay as early as 1572. The Coldstream Guards, raised in 1650, were, however, placed on the establishment of the British Army before the Royal Scots and the Buffs. The oldest armed body in the United Kingdom is the Queen's Bodyguard of the Yeomen of the Guard formed in 1485. The Honourable Artillery Company, formed from the Fraternity of St. George, Southwark, received its charter from Henry VIII in 1537 but this lapsed until re-formed in 1610. The infantry regiment with most battle honours is The Queen's Lancashire Regiment with 188.

The most senior regiment of the Reserve Army is The Royal Monmouthshire Royal Engineers (Militia) formed on 21 Mar 1577 and never disbanded, with battle honours at Dunkirk, 1940 and Normandy, 1944.

Greatest mutiny
In the 1914–18 War 56 French divisions com-

---

prising some 650,000 men and their officers refused orders on the Western Front sector of General Robert Nivelle in April 1917 after the failure of his offensive.

Longest march
The longest march in military history was the famous Long March by the Chinese Communists in 1934–5. In 368 days, of which 268 days were days of movement, from October to October, their force of 90,000 covered 6000 miles *9650 km* from Kiangsi to Yenan in Shensi *via* Yünnan. They crossed 18 mountain ranges and six major rivers and lost all but 22,000 of their force in continual rear-guard actions against Nationalist Kuo-min-tang (KMT) forces.

On the night of 12–13 Sept 1944 a team of nine from B Company 4th Infantry Battalion of the Irish Army made a night march of 42 miles *67,59 km* in full battle order carrying 40 lb *18,1 kg* in 11 hr 49 min. The record road march (11 men with 40 lb *18,14 kg* packs) over a marathon (26 miles 385 yds *42 195 m*) in 6 hr 26 min 23.22 sec by Company D, 1st Battn US Army Intelligence School, Fort Devens, Mass. on 30 June 1983.

Air Forces *Oldest*
The earliest autonomous air force is the Royal Air Force whose origin began with the Royal Flying Corps (created 13 May 1912); the Air Battalion of the Royal Engineers (1 Apr 1911) and the Corps of Royal Engineers Balloon Section (1878) which was first operational in Botswana (then Bechuanaland) in 1884. The Prussian Army used a balloon near Strasbourg, France as early as 24 Sept 1870.

Largest
The greatest Air Force of all time was the United States Army Air Corps (now called the US Air Force), which had 79,908 aircraft in July 1944 and 2,411,294 personnel in March 1944. The US Air Force including strategic air forces had 603,900 personnel and 4000 combat aircraft in mid-1985. The USSR Air Force is undergoing massive reorganisation but best estimates indicate 465,000 men in mid-1984. It had 5950 combat aircraft and 2300 armed helicopters. In addition, the USSR's Offensive Strategic Rocket Forces had about 325,000 operational personnel in mid-1983. The strength of the Royal Air Force was 93,500 with 599 combat aircraft in 1985/86.

BOMBS

Heaviest
The heaviest conventional bomb ever used operationally was the Royal Air Force's 'Grand Slam', weighing 22,000 lb *9975 kg* and measuring 25 ft 5 in *7,74 m* long, dropped on Bielefeld railway viaduct, Germany, on 14 Mar 1945. In 1949 the United States Air Force tested a bomb weighing 42,000 lb *19 050 kg* at Muroc Dry Lake, California, USA. The heaviest known nuclear bomb has been the 4 tonne 9 megatonne carried by US B-52 bombers. These bombs 3,67 m *12 ft 0¼ in* in length were phased out by Jan 1984.

Atomic
The first atom bomb dropped on Japan by the United States in 1945 had an explosive power equivalent to that of 12,500 short tons *12.5 kilotons* of trinitrotoluene ($C_7H_5O_6N_3$), called TNT. Code-named 'Little Boy' it was 10 ft *3,04 m* long and weighed 9000 lb *4080 kg* and burst 1670 ft *509 m* above Hiroshima. The most powerful thermo-nuclear device so far tested is one with a power equivalent of 57,000,000 short tons of TNT, or 57 megatons, detonated by the USSR in the Novaya Zemlya

area at 8.33 a.m. GMT on 30 Oct 1961. The shock wave was detected to have circled the world three times, taking 36 hr 27 min for the first circuit. Some estimates put the power of this device at between 62 and 90 megatons. The largest US H-Bomb tested was the 18–22 megaton 'Bravo' at Bikini Atoll, Marshall Islands on 1 Mar 1954. On 9 Aug 1961, Nikita Khrushchyov, then the Chairman of the Council of Ministers of the USSR, declared that the Soviet Union was capable of constructing a 100-megaton bomb, and announced the possession of one in East Berlin, Germany, on 16 Jan 1963. Such a device could make a crater in rock 355 ft *107 m* deep and 1.8 miles *2,9 km* wide and a fireball 46,000 ft or 8.7 miles *13,9 km* in diameter.

Atom bomb theory began with Einstein's publication of the $E = mc^2$ formula in *Annalen der Physik* in Leipzig on 14 May 1907. This postulated that the latent energy of 1 gram of matter was 89,875,517,873.781 dynes. It became a practicality with the mesothorium experiments of Otto Hahn (1879–1968), Fritz Strassman (b. 1902) and Lise Meitner (1878–1968) on 17 Dec 1938. Work started in the USSR on atomic bombs in June 1942 although their first chain reaction was not achieved until December 1945 by Dr Igor Vasilyevich Kurchatov (1903–1960). The concept of a thermo-nuclear fusion bomb was that of Edward Teller (b. 1908) in 1942. Development was ordered by President Truman on 30 Jan 1950 and code-named 'Super'. The bomb only became practical as a result of a calculation by the Polish born American Stanislaw Ulam (1909–1984).

Largest nuclear weapons
The most powerful ICBM are the USSR's SS–18s (Model 5) believed to be armed with ten 750 kiloton MIRVs (multiple independently-targetable re-entry vehicles). Models 1 and 3 have a single 20 megaton warhead. The US Minuteman III has 3 MIRVs each of 335 kiloton force.

No official estimate has been published of the potential power of the device known as Doomsday, but this far surpasses any tested weapon. If it were practicable to construct, it is mooted that a 50,000 megaton cobalt-salted device could wipe out the entire human race except people deep underground and who did not emerge for at least five years.

'Star Wars'
The first reported successful 'high frontier' interception test in outer space by the United States Strategic Defence Initiative occurred over the Pacific on 10 June 1984.

Largest 'conventional' explosion
The largest use of conventional explosive was for the demolition of the fortifications and U Boat pens at Heligoland on 18 Apr 1947. A net charge of 3797 tons *4061 tonnes* (7122 tonnes gross) was detonated by Commissioned Gunner E. C. Jellis of the RN team headed by Lt F. T. Woosnam RN aboard *HMS Lasso* lying 9 miles *14,5 km* out to sea.

Most bombed country
The most heavily bombed country in the world has been Laos. It has been estimated that between May 1964 and 26 Feb 1973 some 2½ million tons of bombs of all kinds were dropped along the North to South Ho Chi Minh Trail supply route to South Vietnam.

TANKS
Earliest
The first tank was 'No 1 Lincoln' modified to become 'Little Willie' built by William Foster & Co Ltd of Lincoln. It first ran on 6 Sept 1915.

Tanks were first taken into action by the Heavy Section, Machine-Gun Corps, which later became the Royal Tank Corps, at the battle of Flers-Courcelette in France, on 15 Sept 1916. The Mark I Male tank, armed with a pair of 6-pounder guns and 4 machine-guns, weighed 28 tons *28,4 tonnes* and was driven by a motor developing 105 hp which gave it a maximum road speed of 3 to 4 mph *4,8–6,4 km/h.*

Heaviest and fastest
The heaviest tank ever constructed was the German Panzer Kampfwagen Maus II, which weighed 189 tons *192 tonnes*. By 1945 it had reached only the experimental stage and was not proceeded with.

Scientists Otto Hahn (Germany) and Edward Teller (USA) who were at the forefront of bomb technology during the initial stages of World War II. Nicknamed the father of the Hydrogen Bomb, Teller (*top*) was responsible for the concept of a thermo-nuclear fusion bomb. Otto Hahn (*below*), pictured on his 100th birthday, was one of three eminent scientists working on mesothorium experiments. (Photos: Central Press/Keystone Press).

The heaviest operational tank used by any army was the 74 ton *75,2 tonnes* 13-man French Char de Rupture 2C bis of 1922. It carried a 155 mm howitzer and had two 250 hp engines giving a maximum speed of 8 mph *12 km/h.* The world's most heavily armed tank since 1972 has been the Soviet T-72 with a 125 mm *4.92 in* high velocity gun. The British AVRE 'Centurion' has a 165 mm *6.5 in* low velocity demolition gun. The world's fastest tank is the British Scorpion AFV which can touch 50 mph *80,5 km/h* with 75% payload.

The heaviest British armoured vehicle ever built was the 78-ton *79 tonnes* prototype 'Tortoise'. With a crew of seven and a designed speed of 12 mph *19 km/h,* this tank had a width 2 in *5 cm* less than that of the one-time operational 65-ton *66 tonnes* 'Conqueror'.

GUNS
Earliest
Although it cannot be accepted as proved, the best opinion is that the earliest guns were constructed in North Africa, possibly by Arabs, in *c.* 1250. The earliest representation of an English gun is contained in an illustrated manuscript dated 1326 at Oxford. The earliest anti-aircraft gun was an artillery piece on a high angle mounting used in the Franco-Prussian War of 1870 by the Prussians against French balloons.

Largest
The two most massive guns ever constructed were used by the Germans in the siege of Sevastopol on the Eastern Front. They were of a calibre of 800 mm *31.5 in* with barrels 28,87 m *94 ft 8¼ in* long and named *Dore* and *Gustav*. Their remains were discovered, one near Metzenhof, Bavaria in Aug 1945 and the other in the Soviet zone. They were built by Krupp as railway guns carried on 24 cars two of which had 40 wheels each. The whole assembly of the gun was 42,9 m *141 ft* long and weighed 1323 tons *1344 tonnes* with a crew of 1500. The range for an 8¼ ton projectile was 29 miles *46,67 km.*

During the 1914–18 war the British Army used a gun of 18 in *457 mm* calibre. The barrel alone weighed 125 tons *127 tonnes*. In World War II the 'Bochebuster', a train-mounted howitzer with a calibre of 18 in *457 mm* firing a 2500 lb *1133 kg* shell to a maximum range of 22,800 yd *20 850 m,* was used from 1940 onwards as part of the Kent coast defences.

Greatest range
The greatest range ever attained by a gun was achieved by the HARP (High Altitude Research Project) gun consisting of two 16.5 in *419 mm* calibre barrels in tandem 36,4 m *119.4 ft* long weighing 150 tonnes/tons at Yuma, Arizona, USA. On 19 Nov 1966 an 84 kg *185 lb* projectile was fired to an altitude of 180 km *111.8 miles* or *590,550 ft.* The static V3 underground firing tubes built in 50 degree shafts near Mimoyecques, near Calais, France to bombard London were never operative.

The famous long range gun, which shelled Paris in World War I, was the *Kaiser Wilhelm geschütz* with a calibre of 220 mm *8.66 in,* a designed range of 79.5 miles *127,9 km* and an achieved range of 76 miles *122 km* from the Forest of Cérpy in March 1918. The Big Berthas were mortars of 420 mm *16.53 in* calibre and with a range of less than 9 miles *14 500 m.*

Mortars
The largest mortars ever constructed were Mallets mortar (Woolwich Arsenal, London, 1857), and the 'Little David' of World War II,

made in the USA. Each had a calibre of 36¼ in *920 mm*, but neither was ever used in action. The heaviest mortar used was the tracked German 600 mm *23.6 in* siege piece known as 'Karl' before Stalingrad, USSR.

Largest cannon
The highest calibre cannon ever constructed is the *Tsar Puchka* (King of Cannons), now housed in the Kremlin, Moscow, USSR. It was built in the 16th century with a bore of 920 mm *36.2 in* and a barrel 10 ft 5 in *3,18 m* long. It weighs 2400 *pouds* (*sic*) or 40 tonnes. The Turks fired up to seven shots per day from a bombard 26 ft *7,92 m* long, with an internal calibre of 42 in *1066 mm* against the walls of Constantinople (now Istanbul) from 12 Apr to 29 May 1453. It was dragged by 60 oxen and 200 men and fired a 1200 lb *543 kg* stone cannon ball.

Military engines
The largest military catapults, or onagers, could throw a missile weighing 60 lb *27 kg* a distance of 500 yd *457 m*.

Conscientious Objector *Most Obdurate*
The only Conscientious Objector to be 6 times court martialled in World War II was Gilbert Lane of Wallington, Surrey. He served 31 months detention and 183 days imprisonment.

Nuclear Delivery Vehicles
As of 1 Jan 1985 the USSR deployed 2547 strategic nuclear delivery vehicles or 297 above the SALT II contractual ceiling. The USA on the same date deployed 1814 vehicles or 436 below the 2250 SALT II limit. The comparative number of warheads has been estimated at USSR 9990 and USA 10,174.

5. JUDICIAL

LEGISLATION AND LITIGATION

Statutes *Oldest*
The earliest surviving judicial code was that of King Ur-Hammu during the third dynasty of Ur, Iraq, in *c*. 2110 BC. The oldest English statute in the Statute Book is a section of the Statute of Marlborough of 1267, retitled in 1948 'The Distress Act, 1267'. Some statutes enacted by Henry II (d. 1189) and earlier kings are even more durable as they have been assimilated into the Common Law. An extreme example is Ine's Law concerning the administration of shires. Ine reigned 689–726 AD.

Longest in the United Kingdom
Measured in bulk the longest statute of the United Kingdom, is the Income Corporation Taxes Act, 1970, which ran to 540 sections, 15 schedules and 670 pages. It is 1½ in *37 mm* thick. However, its 540 sections are surpassed in number by the 748 of the Merchant Shipping Act, 1894. Of old statutes, 31 George III XIV, the Land Tax Act of 1791, written on parchment, consists of 780 skins forming a roll 1170 ft *360 m* long.

Shortest
The shortest statute is the Parliament (Qualification of Women) Act, 1918, which runs to 27 operative words—'A woman shall not be disqualified by sex or marriage from being elected to or sitting or voting as a Member of the Commons House of Parliament'. Section 2 contains a further 14 words giving the short title.

Most inexplicable
Certain passages in several Acts have always defied interpretation and the most inexplicable

must be a matter of opinion. A Judge of the Court of Session of Scotland once sent the Editor his candidate which reads, 'In the Nuts (unground), (other than ground nuts) Order, the expression nuts shall have reference to such nuts, other than ground nuts, as would but for this amending Order not qualify as nuts (unground) (other than ground nuts) by reason of their being nuts (unground).'

Earliest English patent
The earliest of all known English patents was that granted by Henry VI in 1449 to Flemish-born John of Utyman for making the coloured glass required for the windows of Eton College. The peak number of applications for patents filed in the United Kingdom in any one year was 63,614 in 1969. The shortest, concerning a harrow attachment, of 48 words was filed on 14 May 1956 while the longest, comprising 2318 pages of text and 495 pages of drawings, was filed on 31 Mar 1965 by IBM to cover a computer.

An artist's impression of the character at the centre of the longest trial in the annals of British justice. The trial spanned 1025 days. The jury took 30 minutes to pass a verdict. Arthur Orton was sentenced to 14 years imprisonment with hard labour. (Mary Evans).

Most protracted litigation
The longest contested law suit ever recorded ended in Poona, India on 28 Apr 1966, when Balasaheb Patloji Thorat received a favourable judgement on a suit filed by his ancestor Maloji Thorat 761 years earlier in 1205. The points at issue were rights of presiding over public functions and precedences at religious festivals.

The dispute over the claim of the Prior and Convent (now the Dean and Chapter) of Durham Cathedral to administer the spiritualities of the diocese during a vacancy in the See grew fierce in 1283. It flared up again in 1672 and 1890; an attempt in November 1975 to settle the issue, then 692 years old, was unsuccessful. Neither side admit the legitimacy of writs of appointment issued by the other even though identical persons are named.

Fastest trial
The law's shortest delay occurred in Duport Steel and Others *v.* Sirs and Others heard in the High Court on 25 Jan 1980; the appeal was heard on 26 Jan and the appeal heard in the House of Lords on 1 Feb (am) with the decision given pm.

Longest trial
The longest trial in criminal history was *People of the State of California v Angelo Buono, Jr.* involving 10 charges of the Hillside murders of young women from 18 Oct 1977 to Feb 1978. The jury trial took 345 trial days over 2 years 2 days (16 Nov 1981–18 Nov 1983) with a 57,079 page transcript, 400 witnesses and 2000 exhibits. Judge Ronald M. George imposed nine sentences of life without parole on 9 Jan 1984.

Longest British trials
The longest trial in the annals of British justice was the Tichborne personation case. The civil trial began on 11 May 1871, lasted 103 days and collapsed on 6 Mar 1872. The criminal trial went on for 188 days, resulting in a sentence on 28 Feb 1874 for two counts of perjury (two 7 year consecutive terms of imprisonment with hard labour) on the London-born Arthur Orton, *alias* Thomas Castro (1834–98), who claimed to be Roger Charles Tichborne (1829–54), the elder brother of Sir Alfred Joseph Doughty-Tichborne, 11th Bt (1839–66). The whole case thus spanned 1025 days. The jury were out for only 30 minutes.

The impeachment of Warren Hastings (1732–1818), which began in 1788, dragged on for seven years until 23 Apr 1795, but the trial lasted only 149 days. He was appointed a member of the Privy Council in 1814.

The fraud case *R v Bouzaglo and others* ended before Judge Brian Gibbens (1912–1985) on 1 May 1981 having lasted 274 days. They appealed on 10 Dec 1981. Trial costs were estimated at £2.5 million.

The fluoridation case *McColl v Strathclyde Regional Council* before Lord Jauncey lasted 204 days ending on 27 July 1982.

The longest case in the House of Lords was *Armstrong Patents v British Leyland*—seven weeks ending on 27 Feb 1986.

Murder
The longest murder trial in Britain was that at the Old Bailey, London of Reginald Dudley, 51, and Robert Maynard, 38 in the Torso Murder of Billy Moseley and Micky Cornwall which ran before Mr Justice Swanwick from 11 Nov 1976 to 17 June 1977 with 136 trial days. Both men were sentenced to life (minimum 15 years) imprisonment. The costs were estimated to exceed £500,000 and the evidence 3,500,000 words.

Longest Tribunal
Divorce
The longest trial of a divorce case in Britain was *Gibbons v. Gibbons and Roman and Halperin*. On 19 Mar 1962, after 28 days, Mr Alfred George Boyd Gibbons was granted a decree *nisi* against his wife Dorothy for adultery with Mr John Halperin of New York City, NY, USA.

Shortest trials
The shortest recorded British murder hearings were *R. v. Murray* on 28 Feb 1957 and *R. v. Cawley* at Winchester assizes on 14 Dec 1959. The proceedings occupied only 30 sec on each occasion.

Litigants in Person
Since the Union of the Parliaments in 1707 the

only Scot to win an appeal in person before the House of Lords has been Mr Jack Malloch, an Aberdeen Schoolmaster. In 1971 he was restored to his employment with costs under the dormant but operative Teachers Act, 1882 securing also a professional status in law for all qualified Scottish teachers.

Dr Mark Feldman, a podiatric surgeon, of Lauderhill, Florida became the first litigant in person to secure 7 figures ($1 million) before a jury in compensatory and punitive damages in Sept 1980. The case concerned conspiracy and fraud alleged against 6 other doctors.

Longest address
The longest address in a British court was in *Globe and Phoenix Gold Mining Co. Ltd. v. Amalgamated Properties of Rhodesia.* Mr William Henry Upjohn, KC (1853–1941) concluded his speech on 22 Sept 1916, having addressed the court for 45 days.

Highest bail *World*
The highest amount ever demanded as bail was $46,500,000 (*then £16,608,333*) against Antonio De Angelis in a civil damages suit by the Harbor Tank Storage Co. filed in the Superior Court, Jersey City, New Jersey, USA on 16 Jan 1964 in the Salad Oil Swindle. He was released on 4 June 1973. Hassen Ebtehaj, later Chairman of the Iranian Bank in Teheran, was in 1967 granted bail in excess of $50 million.

Great Britain
The highest bail figure in a British court is £325,000 each, granted to Roy Garner and Kenneth Howard of North London by the High Court on 31 Mar 1983. They had been in custody after arrest at Gatwick Airport in connection with alledged trading in Krugerrands.

Longest arbitration
The longest arbitration (under the 1950 Act) on record has been the Royce Arbitration. It lasted 239 days and concerned the Milchell Construction Co. and the East Anglian Regional Hospital Board over the building of Peterborough Hospital.

The longest case before an Industrial Tribunal has been 44 days during more than 13 months (2 May 1977–29 June 1978) when the columnist C. Gordon Tether contested the fairness of his dismissal by *The Financial Times* in person.

Longest Inquiry
The longest and most expensive public inquiry has been that over the projected £1,200 million Sizewell B nuclear power station, Suffolk under Sir Frank Layfield, QC. It began on 11 Jan 1983 and finished after 340 days of hearings on 7 Mar 1985 in The Snape Maltings, Aldeburgh. Shorthand writers transcribed 16 million words from 195 witnesses. The cost to public funds was £2,407,000.

Best attended trial
The greatest attendance at any trial was that of Major Jesús Sosa Blanco, aged 51, for an alleged 108 murders. At one point in the 12½ hr trial (5.30 p.m. to 6 a.m., 22–23 Jan 1959), 17,000 people were present in the Havana Sports Palace, Cuba. He was executed on 18 Feb 1959.

Greatest damages *Personal injury World*
The greatest personal injury damages ever awarded were to a male child of undisclosed identity born in 1979 at the US Army's Le Herman General Hospital in a medical malpractice suit. If the child which had 'total cerebral palsy' lives out his expectation of life the potential US federal government payment will reach $70 million. Reports of 30 Sept 1983 did not disclose the name of the US Army doctor.

On 24 Nov 1983 a jury in Corpus Christi, Texas, USA awarded punitive damages of $106 million *£75 million* against the Ford Motor Co for alleged design faults in the Ford Mustang II in which Bevary Durrill, 20, died in 1974. An appeal is pending.

Great Britain
On 20 Dec 1985 Mrs Linda Thomas (b 1958) *née* Maffey was awarded £679,000 in damages by Mr Justice Hutchison at Cardiff Crown Court for severe brain damage in University Hospital, Cardiff. The award was against the anaesthetist Prof. John Wignall and the South Glamorgan Health Authority, who did not admit liability for 94 months.

Civil damages
The largest damages awarded in legal history were $11,120 million (*£7500 million*) to Pennzoil Co against Texaco concerning the latter's alledgedly unethical tactics to break up a merger between Pennzoil and Getty Oil Co, by Judge Solomon Casseb Jr in Houston, Texas on 10 Dec 1985. The two leading counsel were Joe Jamail (Pennzoil) and Richard Miller (Texaco).

Breach of promise
The largest sum involved in a breach of promise suit in the United Kingdom was £50,000, accepted in 1913 by Miss Daisy Markham, *alias* Mrs Annie Moss (d. 20 Aug 1962, aged 76), in settlement against the 6th Marquess of Northampton DSO (1885–1978).

Defamation *World*
A sum of $16,800,000 (*£6,720,000*) was awarded to Dr John J. Wild, 58, at the Hennepin District Court, Minnesota, USA, on 30 Nov 1972 against The Minnesota Foundation and others for defamation, bad-faith termination of a contract, interference with professional business relationship and $10.8 million in punitive damages. The Supreme Court of Minnesota granted an option of a new trial or a $1.5 million *remittitur* to Dr Wild on 10 Jan 1975. There was a no-disclosure clause in the settlement. The $39.6 million awarded in Columbus, Ohio on 1 Mar 1980 to Robert Guccione, publisher of *Penthouse*, for defamation against Lowry Flynt, publisher of *Hustler* was reduced by Judge Craig Wright to $4 million on 17 Apr 1980. The hearing ended in May 1982 with *Penthouse* being cleared of libel.

The greatest damages for defamation ever awarded in the United Kingdom have been £327,000 in the Courts in Edinburgh in favour of Capital Life Assurance Co against the *Scottish Daily Record* and the *Sunday Mail* for articles published in the latter in 1975.

The most expensive defamation trial in Great Britain has been the 87 day long case of *Gee v British Broadcasting Corporation* which ran before Rt Hon Lord Justice Croom-Johnson, PC. DSC, from 22 Oct 1984 to 2 May 1985. The costs have been estimated at £1.5 million excluding the BBC's internal costs over the 681 days from the offending transmission of *That's Life* on 26 June 1983. Dr Gee, who was in the witness stand for 27 days, received a record settlement of £100,007.

A $640 million libel suit was brought by the California resort La Costa against *Penthouse* and its publisher in March 1975. In May 1982 a jury found for the magazine. In July their verdict was set aside by a California judge, who then removed the case. Costs exceed $10 million to date.

Greatest compensation for Wrongful Imprisonment
William De Palma (b. 1938) of Whittier, Cali-

fornia, agreed to a $750,000 (*then £340,000*) settlement for 16 months wrongful imprisonment in McNeil Island Federal Prison, on 12 Aug 1975 after a 15 year sentence for armed robbery in Buena Park on forged fingerprint evidence in 1968.

The greatest Crown compensation in Britain for wrongful imprisonment has been £17,500 paid to Laszlo Virag, 35, who had been sentenced to 10 years imprisonment at Gloucester assizes in 1969 for theft and shooting and wounding a police officer. His acceptance of this sum was announced on 23 Dec 1974 after he was released in April 1974 on grounds of mistaken identification.

Greatest Alimony
The highest alimony awarded by a court has been $2,261,000 (*then £983,000*) against George Storer Sr, 74, in favour of his third wife Dorothy, 73, in Miami, Florida on 29 Oct 1974. Mr Storer, a broadcasting executive, was also ordered to pay his ex-wife's attorney $200,000 (*then £86,950*) in fees.

Greatest Alimony Suit
Belgian born Sheika Dena Al-Fassi, 23, filed the highest ever alimony claim of $3000 million (*then £1666 million*) against her former husband Sheik Mohammed Al-Fassi, 28, of the Saudi Arabia royal family in Los Angeles, California in February 1982. Mr Marvin Mitchelson explaining the size of the settlement claim alluded to the Sheik's wealth which included 14 homes in Florida alone and numerous private aircraft. On 14 June 1983 she was awarded $81 million (*then £52 million*) and declared she would be 'very very happy' if she was able to collect.

Greatest divorce settlement
The highest High Court divorce award received was £700,000 on 13 Nov 1980 for 'Mrs P' after 23 years of marriage against her former husband from Jersey from whom she had been receiving £6000 per annum. In *Edgar v Edgar* in 1980, £750,000 was awarded but this was set aside on appeal when Mrs Edgar accepted a much lesser figure.

Patent case
The greatest settlement ever made in a patent infringement suit is $55.8 million (*£37.2 million*) in Pfizer Inc v International Rectifier Corp. and Rochelle Laboratories over the antibiotic dioxycycline on 5 July 1983.

Largest suit
The highest amount of damages ever sought to date is $675,000,000,000,000 (then equivalent to 10 times the US national wealth) in a suit by Mr I. Walton Bader brought in the US District Court, New York City on 14 Apr 1971 against General Motors and others for polluting all 50 states.

Largest Law firm
The world's largest law firm is Baker & McKenzie with 815 lawyers in 35 offices in 25 countries. It was founded in Chicago in 1949.

Highest costs
The 119 day trial of 7 servicemen from Cyprus under the Official Secrets Act, 1911 ending at the Old Bailey, London on 29 Oct 1985 cost an esimated £3½–£5 million.

The most expensive man-hunt in police history was one costing £4 million terminated on 13 June 1981 with the arrest of Peter William Sutcliffe, known as the Yorkshire Ripper, in Sheffield, South Yorkshire. His trial at the Old Bailey, London, cost £250,000 and resulted in his being sentenced to a minimum of 30 years for 13 murders and 7 attempted murders which orphaned 25 children.

Longest lease
The longest lease on record is one concerning a plot for a sewage tank adjoining Columb Barracks, Mullinger, County Meath, Ireland signed on 3 Dec 1868 for 10,000,000 years. It is to be assumed that a future civil servant will bring up the matter for review early in AD 10,001,868.

Greatest lien
The greatest lien ever imposed by a court is 40,000 million lire (*then £27 million*) on 9 Apr 1974 upon Vittorio and Ida Riva in Milan for back taxes allegedly due on a chain of cotton mills around Turin, Italy.

Wills *Shortest*
The shortest valid will in the world is 'Vše zene', the Czech for 'All to wife', written and dated 19 Jan 1967 by Herr Karl Tausch of Langen, Hesse, Germany. The shortest will contested but subsequently admitted to probate in English law was the case of *Thorne v. Dickens* in 1906. It consisted of the three words 'All for Mother' in which 'mother' was not his mother but his wife. The smallest will preserved by the Record Keeper is an identity disc 1½ in *3.8 cm* in diameter belonging to A.B. William Skinner killed aboard HMS Indefatigable at Jutland in 1916. It had 40 words engraved on it including the signatures of two witnesses and was proved on 24 June 1922.

Longest
The longest will on record was that of Mrs Frederica Evelyn Stilwell Cook proved at Somerset House, London on 2 Nov 1925. It consisted of four bound volumes containing 95,940 words.

Judges *Most Durable*
The oldest recorded active judge was Judge Albert R. Alexander (1859–1966) of Plattsburg, Missouri, USA. He was the magistrate and probate judge of Clinton County until his retirement aged 105 years 8 months on 9 July 1965.

United Kingdom
The greatest recorded age at which any British judge has sat on a bench was 93 years 9 months in the case of Sir William Francis Kyffin Taylor, GBE, KC (*later* Lord Maenan), who was born on 9 July 1854 and retired as presiding judge of the Liverpool Court of Passage in April 1948, having held that position since 1903. Sir Salathiel Lovell (1619–1713) was, however, still sitting when he died on 3 May 1713 in his 94th or 95th year. The greatest age at which a House of Lords judgement has been given is 92 in the case of the 1st Earl of Halsbury (b. 3 Sept 1823) in 1916. Lord Chief Baron of Exchequer in Ireland, the Rt. Hon. Christopher Palles (1831–1920) served for 42 years from 17 Feb 1874 till 1916.

Master of the Rolls
The longest tenure of the Mastership of the Rolls since the office was inaugurated in 1286 has been 24 years 7 months by David de Wollore from 2 July 1346 to 27 March 1371. The longest tenure since the Supreme Court Judicature Act, 1881 has been that of 20 years by Rt Hon Lord Denning PC (b. 23 Jan 1899) from 1962 to 30 Sept 1982. He had been first appointed a high court judge in 1944. William Morland held the office for 77 days while in 1629 Sir Humphrey May died 'soon after' his appointment on 10 April.

Judge *Youngest*
No collated records on the ages of judicial appointments exist. However David Elmer Ward had to await the legal age of 21 before taking office after nomination in 1932 as Judge of the County Court at Fort Myers, Florida, USA.

The youngest certain age at which any English judge has been appointed is 28, in the case of Sir Ernest Wild, KC (b. 1 Jan 1869) who was appointed Judge of the Norwich Guildhall Court of Record in 1897 aged 28. The lowest age of appointment this century has been 42 years 2 months of Lord Hodson in 1937.

Most Judges
Lord Balmerino was found guilty of treason by 137 of his peers on 28 July 1746. In *R* v. *Canning* at the Old Bailey in 1754 Elizabeth Canning was deported to Connecticut for wilful perjury by 19 judges voting 10 to 9. In *Young, James and Webster* v. *United Kingdom*, the British Rail 'Closed Shop' case, before the European Court of Human Rights in Strasbourg on 3–4 Mar 1981, Mr David Calcutt QC won a judgement for the railwaymen by 18 to 3.

Youngest English QC
The earliest age at which a barrister has taken silk this century is 33 years 8 months in the case of Mr (later the Rt Hon Sir) Francis Raymond Evershed (1899–1966) in April 1933. He was later Lord Evershed, Master of the Rolls. Buller was nepotistically given silk aged 31, being a nephew of the then Lord Chancellor, Lord Bathurst.

Multimillionaire Melvin M. Belli (b. 30 July 1907) took display advertisements in the press on his 77th birthday to celebrate his 'unparalleled 50-year career in law defending the injured and the poor'.

Most successful
Sir Lionel Luckhoo KCMG CBE, senior partner of Luckhoo and Luckhoo of Georgetown, Guyana succeeded in getting his 245th successive murder charge acquittal by 1 Jan 1985.

Most Durable Solicitors
William George (1865–1967), brother of David Lloyd George, passed his preliminary law examination in May 1880 and was practising until December 1966 aged 101 years 9 months. The most durable firm is Thomson, Snell & Passmore of Tonbridge, Kent begun by the Rev Nicholas Hooper, a part-time scrivener in 1570.

CRIME

Mass Killings *China*
The greatest massacre ever imputed by the government of one sovereign nation against the government of another is that of 26,300,000 Chinese during the regime of Mao Tse-tung between 1949 and May 1965. This accusation was made by an agency of the USSR Government in a radio broadcast on 7 Apr 1969. The broadcast broke down the figure into four periods:—2.8 million (1949–52); 3.5 million (1953–7); 6.7 million (1958–60); and 13.3 million (1961–May 1965). The highest reported death figures in single monthly announcements on Peking radio were 1,176,000 in the provinces of Anhwei, Chekiang, Kiangsu, and Shantung, and 1,150,000 in the Central South Provinces. Po I-po, Minister of Finance, is alleged to have stated in the organ *For a lasting peace, for a people's democracy* 'in the past three years (1950–2) we have liquidated more than 2 million bandits'. General Jacques Guillermaz, a French diplomat, estimated the total executions between February 1951 and May 1952 at between 1 million and 3 million. In April 1971 the Executive cabinet or *Yuan* of the implacably hostile government of The Republic of China in Taipei, Taiwan announced its official estimate of the mainland death roll in the period 1949–69

as 'at least 39,940,000'. This figure, however, excluded 'tens of thousands' killed in the Great Proletarian Cultural Revolution, which began in late 1966. The Walker Report published by the US Senate Committee of the Judiciary in July 1971 placed the parameters of the total death roll within China since 1949 between 32.25 and 61.7 million. An estimate of 63.7 million was published by Jean-Pierre Dujardin in *Figaro* magazine of 19–25 Nov 1978.

USSR
The total death roll in the Great Purge, or *Yezhovshchina*, in the USSR, in 1936–8 has, not surprisingly, never been published. Evidence of its magnitude may be found in population statistics which show a deficiency of males from *before* the outbreak of the 1941–5 war. The reign of terror was administered by the *Narodny Kommissariat Vnutrennykh Del* (NKVD), or People's Commissariat of Internal Affairs, the Soviet security service headed by Nikolay Ivanovich Yezhov (1895–1939), described by Nikita Khrushchev in 1956 as a 'degenerate'. S. V. Utechin, regarded estimates of 8,000,000 or 10,000,000 victims as 'probably not exaggerations'. On 17 Aug 1942 Stalin indicated to Churchill in Moscow that 10 million *kulaks* had been liquidated for resisting the collectivization of their farms. Nobel Prize winner Alexander Solzhenitsyn estimated the loss of life from State repression and terrorism from October 1917 to December 1959 under Lenin, Stalin and Khrushchev at 66,700,000.

Nazi Germany
The best estimate of the number of Jewish victims of the Holocaust or the genocidal 'Final Solution' or *Endlösung* ordered by Adolf Hitler (1889–1945) in April 1941 and continued into May 1945 is 5.8 million. Obersturmbannführer (Lt-Col) Karl Adolf Eichmann (b. Solingen, W. Germany 19 Mar 1906) of the SS was hanged in a small room inside Ramleh Prison, near Tel Aviv, Israel, at just before midnight (local time) on 31 May 1962, for his complicity in the deaths of an indeterminably massive number of Jews.

At the SS (*Schutzstaffel*) extermination camp (*Vernichtungslager*) known as Auschwitz-Birkenau (Oświęcim-Brzezinka), near Oświęcim (Auschwitz), in southern Poland, where a minimum of 920,000 people (Soviet estimate is 4,000,000) were exterminated from 14 June 1940 to 18 Jan 1945, the greatest number killed in a day was 6000. The man who operated the release of the 'Zyklon B' cyanide pellets into the gas chambers there during this time was Sgt Major Moll (variously Mold). The Nazi (*Nationalsozialistische Deutsche Arbeiterpartei*) Commandant during the period 1940–3 was Rudolph Franz Ferdinand Höss who was tried in Warsaw from 11 Mar to 2 Apr 1947 and hanged, aged 47, at Oświęcim on 15 Apr 1947.

Forced labour
No official figures have been published of the death roll in Corrective Labour Camps in the USSR, first established in 1918. The total number of such camps was known to be more than 200 in 1946 but in 1956 many were converted to less severe Corrective Labour Colonies. An estimate published in the Netherlands puts the death roll between 1921 and 1960 at 19,000,000. The camps were administered by the *Cheka* until 1922, the OGPU (1922–34), the NKVD (1934–46), the MVD (1946–53) and the KGB (Komitet Gosudarstvennoi Bezopasnostc) since 1953. A study published in 1985 estimated that there are 289 labour camp zones with a population of 4½ million.

In China there are no published official statistics on the numbers undergoing *Lao Jiao* (Education through Labour) nor *Lao Dong Gai Zao* (Reform through manual labour). An estimate published by Bao Ruo-wang, who was released in 1964 due to his father having been a Corsican, was 16,000,000 which then approached 3 per cent of the population.

Genocide

As a percentage of a nation's total population the worst genocide appears to be that in Kampuchea, formerly Cambodia, according to the Khmer Rouge foreign minister Ieng Sary, more than a third of the 8 million Khmers were killed between 17 Apr 1975 and January 1979. The highest 'class' ideals induced indifference to individual suffering to the point of serving as a warrant for massacre. Under the rule of Saloth Sar *alias* Pol Pot, a founder member of the CPK (Communist Party of Kampuchea, formed in September 1960) towns, money and property were abolished and economical execution by bayonet and club introduced for such offences as falling asleep during the day, asking too many questions, playing non-Communist music, being old and feeble, being the offspring of an 'undesirable' or being too well educated. Deaths at the Tuol Sleng interrogation centre reached 582 in a day.

In Chinese history of the 13th–17th centuries there were three periods of wholesale massacre. The numbers of victims attributed to these events are assertions rather than reliable estimates. The figure put on the Mongolian invasions of northern China in 1210–19 and in 1311–40 are both of the order of 35 million while the number of victims of the bandit leader Chang Hsien-Chung (*c.* 1605–47), known as the Yellow Tiger, in 1643–47 in the Zechuan province has been put at 40 million.

Saving of Life

The greatest number of people saved from extinction by one man is an estimated 90,000 Jews in Budapest, Hungary from July 1944 to January 1945 by the Swedish diplomat Raoul Wallenberg (b. 4 Aug 1912). After escaping an assassination attempt by the Nazis, he was imprisoned without trial by the Soviet Union. On 6 Feb 1957 Mr Gromyko said Prisoner 'Walenberg' had died in a cell in Lubyanka Jail, Moscow on 16 July 1947. Sighting reports within the Gulag system have persisted for 40 years after his disappearance. He was made an Honorary Citizen of the USA on 5 Oct 1981 and in March 1984 there was an agitation in Hungary to restore his removed statue to St Stephan's Park, in Budapest.

Largest criminal organization

The largest syndicate of organized crime is the Mafia or La Cosa Nostra, which has infiltrated the executive, judiciary and legislature of the United States. It consists of some 3000 to 5000 individuals in 25 'families' federated under 'The Commission', with an annual turnover in vice, gambling, protection rackets, tobacco, bootlegging, hijacking, narcotics, loan-sharking and prostitution estimated in a US News & World Report of Dec 1982 at $200 billion and a profit estimated in March 1986 by the Attorney Rudolph Giuliani at $75 billion. The origin in the US dates from 1869 in New Orleans. The biggest Mafia (derived from an arabic expression connoting beauty, excellence allied with bravery) killing was on 11–13 Sept 1931 when 40 mafiosi were liquidated following the murder in New York of Salvatore Maranzano, *Il Capo di Tutti Capi*, on 10 Sept. The greatest breaches of *omerta* (the vow of silence) were by Joseph Valachi who 'sang like a canary' in 1963 and by the much bereaved Tommaso Buschetta, 56, in 1984.

The Italian equivalent of a 'Supergrass' Tommaso Buschetta enters the court to give evidence against the largest criminal organisation—the Mafia. (Rex Features).

Murder rate *Highest*

The country with the highest recorded murder rate is Brazil, with 104 homicides for each 100,000 of the population in 1983, or 370 per day. A total of 592 deaths was attributed to one Colombian bandit leader, Teófilo ('Sparks') Rojas, aged 27, between 1948 and his death in an ambush near Armenia on 22 Jan 1963. Some sources attribute 3500 slayings to him during La Violencia of 1945–62.

The highest homicide rates recorded in New York City have been 58 in a week in July 1972 and 13 in a day in August 1972. In 1973 the total for Detroit, Michigan (pop. then 1.5 million) was 751. The Chicago Crime Commission published in March 1983 a list of 1081 unsolved gang slayings since 1919.

Lowest

The country with the lowest officially recorded rate in the world is The Maldives with a nil rate among its naturals since its independence in July 1965. In the Indian state of Sikkim, in the Himalayas, murder is, however, practically unknown, while in the Hunza area of Kashmir, in the Karakoram, only one definite case by a Hunzarwal has been recorded since 1900.

Great Britain

In Great Britain the total number of homicides and deaths from injuries purposely inflicted by other persons in the year 1981 was 612. This figure compares with a murder total of 124 in 1937 and 125 in 1958.

Terrorist Outrages

The greatest civilian death toll from a terrorist bomb was 329 killed when an Air-India Boeing 747 was destroyed by a bomb over the North Atlantic approaching Shannon, Ireland on 23 June 1985.

Most prolific murderers *World*

It was established at the trial of Behram, the Indian thug, that he had strangled at least 931 victims with his yellow and white cloth strip or *ruhmal* in the Oudh district between 1790 and 1840. It has been estimated that at least 2,000,000 Indians were strangled by Thugs (*burtotes*) during the reign of the Thugee (pronounced tugee) cult from 1550 until its final suppression by the British *raj* in 1853. The greatest number of victims ascribed to a murderess has been 650 in the case of Countess Erzsebet Bathory (1560–1614) of Hungary. At her trial which began on 2 Jan 1611 a witness testified to seeing a list of her victims in her own handwriting totalling this number. All were alleged to be young girls from the neighbourhood of her castle at Csejthe where she died on 21 Aug 1614. She had been walled up in her room for the 3½ years after being found guilty.

20th century

Pedro Alonso López (b. Columbia, 1949) known as the 'Columbian Monster', was reported captured by the villagers of Ambato, Ecuador in early March 1980. He admitted to more than 300 murders of pre-teen girls in Colombia, Peru and Ecuador since 1973. The remains of 53 victims of the 110 admitted to in Ecuador were rapidly detected after his confession.

In drunken rampage lasting 8 hours on 26–27 Apr 1982 Policeman Wou Bom-Kon, 27, killed 57 people and wounded 35 with 176 rounds of rifle ammunition and hand grenades in the Kyong Sang-Namdo province of South Korea. He blew himself up with a grenade.

United Kingdom

Six men were each charged with 21 murders at Lancaster Crown Court on 9 June 1975 concerning the bombing of the two Birmingham public houses Mulberry Bush and Tavern in the Town on 21 Nov 1974. They were John Walker, Patrick Hill, Robert Hunter, Noel McIlkenny, William Power and Hugh Callaghan. The Home Office began, in February 1981, to investigate the attribution of 26 deaths between 1973 and 1979 to the self-confessed arsonist Bruce Lee. In January 1981 he was sent to a mental hospital by Leeds Crown Court, but on 14 Mar 1982 he retracted his confessions and on 2 Dec 1983 the Court of Appeal quashed charges of causing 11 of the deaths.

Judith Minna Ward, 25, of Stockport, Cheshire was convicted on 11 separate murder charges on 4 Nov 1974 making 12 in all arising from the explosion in an army coach on the M.62 near Drighlington, West Yorkshire on 4 Feb 1974. Mary Ann Cotton (*née* Robson) (b. 1832, East Rainton, County Durham), hanged in Durham Jail on 24 Mar 1873 is believed to have poisoned 14, possibly 20, people.

Dennis Andrew Nilsen (b. 1948) then of 23 Cranley Gardens, Muswell Hill, north London

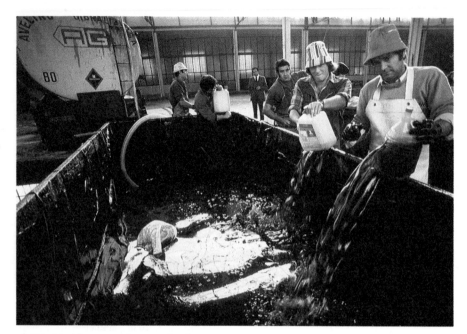

Hundreds of litres of deadly cooking oil are destroyed to prevent further death following the Spanish tragedy which has now claimed over 350 victims. (Rex Features).

admitted to 15 one-at-a-time murders between Dec 1978 and Feb 1983. He was sentenced to life with a 25 year minimum on 4 Nov 1983 at the Old Bailey by Rt Hon Lord Justice Croom-Johnson PC, DSC for 6 murders and 2 attempted murders both there and at Cricklewood.

Dominic McGlinchey (b. 1955) in November 1983 admitted in a press interview to at least 30 killings in Northern Ireland. He was jailed for 10 years at Dublin's Special Criminal Court on 11 Mar 1986 for shooting with intent to resist arrest in County Clare on 17 May 1984. On 7 May 1981 John Thompson of Hackney, London was found guilty at the Old Bailey of the 'specimen' murder by arson of Archibald Campbell and jailed for life. There were 36 other victims at the Spanish Club, Denmark St, London.

'Smelling out'
The greatest 'smelling out' recorded in African history occurred before Shaka (1787–1828) and 30,000 Nguni subjects near the River Umhlatuzana, Zululand (now Natal, South Africa) in March 1824. After 9 hr, over 300 were 'smelt out' as guilty of smearing the Royal *Kraal* with blood, by 150 witch-finders led by the hideous female *isangoma* Nobela. The victims were declared innocent when Shaka admitted to having done the smearing himself to expose the falsity of the power of his diviners. Nobela poisoned herself with atropine ($C_{17}H_{23}NO_3$), but the other 149 witch-finders were thereupon skewered or clubbed to death.

Suicide
The estimated daily rate of suicides throughout the world surpassed 1000 in 1965. The country with the highest suicide rate is Hungary, with 46 per 100,000 of the population in 1984. The country with the lowest recorded rate is Jordan with a single case in 1970 and hence a rate of 0.04 per 100,000. In England and Wales there were 4315 suicides in 1984, or an average of 11.7 per day. In the northern hemisphere April and May tend to be peak months.

Mass Suicide
The total number of victims of the mass cyanide poisoning of the People's Temple cult near Port Kaituma, Guyana on 18 Nov 1978 was 913. The leader was the paranoid 'Rev.' Jim Jones of San Francisco, who had deposited 'millions of dollars' overseas.

The volcanic crater of Mt Mihara on an island in Sagami Bay, south of Yokohama was the scene of more than 1000 suicides in 1933–36.

Mass Poisonings
On 1 May 1981 the first victim of the Spanish cooking oil scandal fell ill. On 12 June it was discovered that his cause of death was the use of 'denatured' industrial colza from rape seed. By May 1984 the death toll was over 350 dead with thousands maimed. The manufacturers Ramon and Elias Ferrero await trial in Carabanchel Jail, Madrid.

Robbery
The greatest robbery on record was that of the Reichsbank following Germany's collapse in April/May 1945. The Pentagon in Washington described the event first published in the *Guinness* Book in 1957 as 'an unverified allegation'. *Nazi Gold* by Ian Sayer and Douglas Botting published in 1984 however finally revealed full details and estimated the total haul at current values as £2500 million.

On 26 Nov 1983 six masked men removed 6,800 bars of gold and platinum in 76 boxes together with diamonds and travellers' cheques worth £26,369,778 from the Brinks-Mat Ltd Unit 7 warehouse at the Heathrow Trading Estate. Michael McAvoy, 32 of East Dulwich and Brian Robinson, 41 of Lewisham were each sentenced to 25 years at the Old Bailey on 3 Dec 1984.

Art
It is arguable that the *Mona Lisa*, though never valued, is the most valuable object ever stolen. It disappeared from The Louvre, Paris on 21 Aug 1911. It was recovered in Italy in 1913 when Vincenzo Perruggia was charged with its theft.

On 27 Oct 1985 paintings valued at 100 million Francs (*£9.3 million*) were removed from the Mermotte Museum, Paris. On 25 Dec 1985 140 'priceless' gold, jade and obsidian artefacts were stolen from the National Anthropology and History Institute, Mexico City, Mexico.

Bank
During the extreme civil disorder prior to 22 Jan 1976 in Beirut, Lebanon, a guerilla force blasted the vaults of the British Bank of the Middle East in Bab Idriss and cleared out safe deposit boxes with contents valued by former Finance Minister, Lucien Dahadah, at $50 million and by another source as an 'absolute minimum' of $20 million.

Train
The greatest recorded train robbery occurred between about 3.03 a.m. and 3.27 a.m. on 8 Aug 1963, when a General Post Office mail train from Glasgow, Scotland, was ambushed at Sears Crossing and robbed at Bridego Bridge near Mentmore, Buckinghamshire. The gang escaped with about 120 mailbags containing £2,631,784 worth of bank notes being taken to London for destruction. Only £343,448 was recovered.

Jewels
The greatest recorded theft of jewels was from the bedroom of the 'well-guarded' villa of Prince Abdel Aziz Bin Ahmed Al-Thani near Cannes, France on 24 July 1980 valued at $16,000,000 (*then £7¼ million*). The haul from Bond Jewellers, Conduit St, London W1 on 20 June 1983 was estimated to be £6 million.

Greatest kidnapping ransom
Historically the greatest ransom paid was that for Atahualpa by the Incas to Francisco Pizarro in 1532–3 at Cajamarca, Peru which constituted a hall full of gold and silver worth in modern money some $170 million (*£95 million*).

The greatest ransom ever reported in modern times is 1500 million pesos (*£25,300,000*) for the release of the brothers Jorge Born, 40 and Juan Born, 39, of Bunge and Born, paid to the left wing urban guerila group Montoneros in Buenos Aires, Argentina on 20 June 1975.

The youngest person kidnapped has been Carolyn Wharton born at 12.46 p.m. on 19 Mar 1955 in the Baptist Hospital, Texas, USA and kidnapped, by a woman disguised as a nurse, at 1.15 p.m. aged 29 min.

Greatest hijack ransom
The highest amount ever paid to aircraft hijackers has been $6 million (*then £3.42 million*) by the Japanese government in the case of a JAL DC-8 at Dacca Airport on 2 Oct 1977 with 38 hostages. Six convicted criminals were also exchanged. The Bangladesh government had refused to sanction any retaliatory action.

Largest narcotics haul
In Oct 1983 it was estimated that the narcotics crime in the USA was running at $80,000 million per annum with cocaine dealers turning a profit of $35,000 million and illegal domestic 'green collar' marijuana growers netting $13,900 million.

The greatest drug haul ever achieved was 12,500 kg *12.3 tons* of cocaine with a street value of $1,200 million (£860 million) taken in the Caqueta jungle province of Colombia on 10 Mar 1984 in 10 processing plants protected by the armed wing of the Colombian Communist Party FARC (Fuerzas Armadas Revolucionarias Columbias).

The bulkiest haul was 2850 long tons *2 903 000 kg* of Colombian marijuana in the 14 month long 'Operation Tiburon' concluded by the DEA with the arrest of 495 people and the seizure of 95 vessels announced on 5 Feb 1982.

In Britain, the Home Office disclosed on 23 Dec 1977 that 13 million LSD tablets with a street value approaching £100 million had been destroyed on the conclusion of 'Operation Julie'.

Greatest banknote forgery
The greatest forgery was the German Third Reich government's forging operation, code name 'Bernhard', engineered by SS Sturmbann-fuhrer Alfred Naujocks of the Technical Dept of the German Secret Service Amt VI F in Berlin in 1940–1. It involved £150,000,000 worth of £5 notes.

Biggest bank fraud
The largest amount of money named in a defalcation case has been a gross SwF 222 million then £33,000,000 at the Lugano branch of Lloyd's Bank International Ltd in Switzerland on 2 Sept 1974. Mark Colombo was arrested pending charges including falsification of foreign currency accounts and suppression of evidence.

Computer fraud
Between 1964 and 1973, 64,000 fake insurance policies were created on the computer of the Equity Funding Corporation involving $2000 million.

Stanley Mark Rifkin (b. 1946) was arrested in Carlsbad, California by the FBI on 6 Nov 1978 charged with defrauding a Los Angeles bank of $10.2 million (*then £4.85 million*) by manipulation of a computer system. He was sentenced to 8 years in June 1980.

Theft
It was estimated in Nov 1983 that the greatest theft in the world is running at $160,000 million per annum. This is the value of 'bosses time' paid for but not worked in the United States in 1983/84.

The government of the Philippines announced on 23 Apr 1986 that they had succeeded in identifying $860.8 million 'salted' by the former President Ferdinand Edralin Marcos (b. 11 Sept 1917) and his wife Imelda. It was asserted that the total since November 1965 was believed to be between $5 and $10 billion.

Welfare swindle
The greatest welfare swindle yet worked was that of the gypsy Anthony Moreno on the French Social Security in Marseille. By forging birth certificates and school registration forms, he invented 197 fictitious families and 3000 children on which he claimed benefits from 1960 to mid-1968. Moreno, nicknamed 'El Chorro' (the fountain), was later reported free of extradition worries and living in luxury in his native Spain having absquatulated with an estimated £2,300,000.

Largest object ever stolen by a single man
On a moonless night at dead calm high water on 5 June 1966 armed with only a sharp axe, N William Kennedy slashed free the mooring lines at Wolfe's Cove, St Lawrence Seaway, Quebec, Canada, of the 10,639 dwt S S *Orient Trader* owned by Steel Factors Ltd of Ontario. The vessel drifted to a waiting blacked out tug thus escaping a ban on any shipping movements during a violent wild-cat waterfront strike. She sailed for Spain.

Maritime fraud
A cargo of 180 000 tonnes of Kuwaiti crude oil on the supertanker *Salem* at Durban was sold without title to the South African government in Dec 1979. The ship mysteriously sank off Senegal on 17 Jan 1980 leaving the government to pay £148 million (*$305 million*) to Shell International who owned the shipment.

Ex-President and Mrs Marcos who were, according to the Philippine government, allegedly responsible for a theft of enormous proportions. (John Hillelson Agency).

CAPITAL PUNISHMENT

Capital punishment is known to have dated at least from the Iron Age as evidenced by the finding of Tollund man in Denmark. The countries in which capital punishment is still prevalent include China (hundreds of shootings per annum); South Africa (about 100 hangings for rape, robbery and murder); Turkey; Iran; USA (re-introduced in 38 States for the most heinous murders); USSR (23 capital offences including profiteering, speculation and currency offences for which some 400 persons have been reportedly shot annually).

Capital punishment was first abolished *de facto* in 1798 in Liechtenstein. The death penalty for murder was formally abolished in Britain on 18 Dec 1969. Between the 5–4 Supreme Court decision against capital punishment in June 1972 and January 1983, 38 of the 50 States of the USA voted to restore it.

Capital punishment in the British Isles dates from AD 450, but was abolished by William I and re-imposed by Henry I, reaching a peak in the reign of Edward VI (1547–53), when an average of 560 persons were executed annually at Tyburn alone. Even into the 19th century, there were 223 capital crimes, but these resulted in only 25 hangings. Between 1830 and 1964 the most murderers hanged in a year was 27 (24 men, 3 women) in 1903. While in 1956 there were no executions.

Largest hanging
The most people hanged from one gallows was 38 Sioux Indians by William J. Duly outside Mankato, Minnesota, USA for the murder of unarmed citizens on 26 Dec 1862. The Nazi Feldkommandant simultaneously hanged 50 Greek resistance men as a reprisal in Athens on 22 July 1944.

The last publicly-guillotined French citizen was Eugene Weidmann, seen leaving St Pierre Prison for his execution in 1939. (Photo Source/Keystone).

Last hangings
The last public execution in England took place outside Newgate Prison, London at 8 a.m. on 26 May 1868, when Michael Barrett was hanged for his part in the Fenian bomb outrage on 13 Dec 1867, when 12 were killed outside the Clerkenwell House of Detention, London. The earliest non-public execution was of the murderer Thomas Wells on 13 Aug 1868. The last public hanging in Scotland was that of the murderer Robert Smith outside Dumfries Gaol on 12 May 1868 by the hangman Mr Askern. The last in the United States occurred at Owensboro, Kentucky in 1936. The last hangings in the United Kingdom were those of Peter Anthony Allen (b. 4 Apr 1943) hanged at Walton Prison, Liverpool by Mr Leslie Stewart, and John Robson Walby (b. 1 Apr 1940), *alias* Gwynne Owen Evans, at Strangeways Gaol, Manchester both on 13 Aug 1964. They had been found guilty of the capital murder of John Alan West, on 7 Apr 1964. The 15th, youngest and last woman executed this century was Mrs Ruth Ellis (*née* Neilson), 28, for the murder of David Blakely, 25, shot outside the Magdala, Hampstead, on 10 Apr 1955. She was executed on 13 July at Holloway. The last hanging in the Republic of Ireland was in 1954.

Last from yard-arm
The last naval execution at the yard-arm was the hanging of Private John Dalliger, Royal Marines, aboard HMS *Leven* in Victoria Bay near Lu-ta, China, on 13 July 1860. Dalliger had been found guilty of two attempted murders.

Youngest
On 26 June 1885 James Arcene was executed for a crime he committed when aged 10. In Britain the hanging of persons under 18 was expressly excluded only in the Children's and Young Person's Act, 1933 (Sec. 33). No person under that age was, in fact, executed more recently than 1887. The lowest satisfactorily recorded age was of a boy aged 8 'who had malice, cunning and revenge' in firing two barns and who was hanged at Abingdon, Oxfordshire in the 17th century. The youngest persons hanged since 1900 have been six 18 year olds, the most recent of whom was Francis Robert George ('Flossie') Forsyth on 10 Nov 1960.

Oldest
The oldest person hanged in the United Kingdom since 1900 was a man of 71 named Charles Frembd (*sic*) at Chelmsford Gaol on 4 Nov 1914, for the murder of his wife at Leytonstone, Waltham Forest, Greater London. In 1822 John Smith, said to be 80, of Greenwich, south-east London, was hanged for the murder of a woman.

Last guillotinings
The last person to be publicly guillotined in France was the murderer Eugene Weidmann before a large crowd at Versailles, near Paris, at 4.50 a.m. on 17 June 1939. The executioner was Henri Desfourneaux, who was succeeded by his nephew André Obrecht in 1951 who was in turn succeeded by his niece's husband Marcel Chevalier in January 1978. Dr Joseph Ignace Guillotin (1738–1812) died a natural death. He had advocated the use of the machine designed by Dr Antoine Louis in 1789 in the French constituent assembly. The last use before abolition on 9 Sept 1981 was on 10 Sept 1977 at Baumettes Prison, Marseilles for the torturer and murderer Hamida Djandoubi, 28.

Death row
The longest sojourn on Death Row is the 37 years of Sadamichi Hirasawa (b. 18 Feb 1893) in Sendai Jail, northern Japan. He was convicted in 1948 of poisoning 12 bank employees with potassium cyanide to effect a theft of £100. The longest stay in the US is since 1 Mar 1960 by Henry R. Anderson, an attorney, at the Kentucky State Penitentiary in Eddyville. In October 1985 there were 1590 prisoners (including 18 women) in 38 US states on 'Death Row'.

Executioners
The longest period of office of a Public Executioner was that of William Calcraft (1800–79), who was in action from 1828 to 25 May 1874 and officiated at nearly every hanging outside and later inside Newgate Prison, London. On 2 Apr 1868 he hanged the murderess Mrs Frances Kidder, 25, outside Maidstone Jail, Kent—the last public execution of a woman.

For 56 years from 1900 to the retirement of Albert in February 1956, the Pierrepoint family largely monopolized the task of executing murderers and war criminals. Henry Albert (1876–1922) officiated from 1900–1911 with a record 20 executions in Britain in 1909 and the last double female execution (the baby farmers Mrs Amelia Sachs and Mrs Annie Walters) on 3 Feb 1903. The longest serving executioner has been his eldest brother Thomas Pierrepoint from 1903 to 1948. Albert Pierrepoint, son of Henry Albert, officiated at the hanging of 530 men and 20 women in his career in 9 countries including a record 27 war criminals in a day in Germany. Britain's 9th and last chief prison hangman was Henry B. Allen who was on call until abolition of hanging for murder in 1969.

Lynching
The worst year in the 20th century for lynchings in the United States has been 1901, with 130 lynchings (105 Negroes, 25 Whites), while the first year with no reported cases was 1952. The last lynching recorded in Britain was that of Panglam Godolan, a suspected murderer, in London on 27 Oct 1958.

Corporal punishment
The last use of corporal punishment in one of HM Prisons was on 26 June 1962 and it was abolished in the United Kingdom by the Criminal Justice Act, 1967. The treadmill which 14 prisons operated in 1878 was finally suspended on 1 Apr 1902. Men on the 36-man wheel at Northallerton, Yorkshire raised themselves 9639 ft *2937 m* in an 8-hr day, equivalent to reaching within 111 ft *33,8 m* of the summit of Everest in 3 days.

PRISON SENTENCES

Longest sentences *World*
A 10,000 year sentence was imposed on Deuel Wilhelm Davies, 40 on 4 Dec 1981 in Tuscaloosa, Alabama, USA for a triple murder (including his mother-in-law) in 1976. A sentence of 384,912 years was *demanded* at the prosecution of Gabriel March Grandos, 22, at Palma de Mallorca, Spain on 11 Mar 1972 for failing to deliver 42,768 letters or 9 years per letter.

Juan Corona, a Mexican-American, was sentenced to 25 consecutive life terms, for murdering 25 farm workers in 1970–1 around Feather River, Yuba City, California, at Fairfield on 5 Feb 1973. His 20th century record was surpassed by Dean Corll (27) in 1974 and John Wayne Gacy (33 victims) in 1980.

United Kingdom
Kevin Mulgrew from the Ardoyne district of Belfast was sentenced on 5 Aug 1983 to life imprisonment for the murder of Sergeant Julian Connolley of the UDR, in addition he was given a further 963 years to be served concurrently on 84 other serious charges including 13 conspiracies to murder and 8 attempted murders.

The longest single period served by a reprieved murderer in Great Britain this century was 40 years 11 months by John Watson Laurie, the Goat Fell or Arran murderer, who was reprieved on the grounds of insanity in November 1889. He died in Perth Penitentiary on 4 Oct 1930.

On 23 June 1986 the 'Brighton bomber', Patrick Joseph Magee, 35, of Belfast was sentenced to 8 life terms with a recommended minimum of 35 years by Mr Justice Boreham.

The longest specific minimum period recommended by a judge under the Murder (Abolition of Death Penalty) Act 1965 has been 35 years in the case of Patrick Armstrong and Michael Hill on 22 Oct 1975 for pub bombings (7 killed, 99 injured) at Guildford and Woolwich in 1974.

The longest prison sentence ever passed under British law was one of three consecutive and two concurrent terms of 14 years, thus totalling 42 years, imposed on 3 May 1961 on George Blake *né* Behar (b. Rotterdam, 11 Nov 1922), for treachery. Blake, formerly UK vice-consul in Seoul, South Korea, had been converted to Communism during 34 months' internment there from 2 July 1950 to April 1953. It had been alleged that his betrayals may have cost the lives of up to 42 British agents. He was 'sprung' from Wormwood Scrubs Prison, London, on 22 Oct 1966.

The longest single sentence passed on a woman under English law was 20 years for Mrs Lona Teresa Cohen née Petra (b. 1913) at the Old Bailey, City of London on 2 Mar 1961 for conspiring to commit a breach of the Official Secrets Act, 1911. The sentence of this KGB agent was remitted by the Foreign Secretary on no known lawful authority on 24 July 1969. Ward (see Most Prolific Murderers) was sentenced to 20 years for a single offence and an aggregate 30 years on 4 Nov 1974.

Longest time served
Paul Geidel, (b. 21 Apr 1894) was convicted of second degree murder on 5 Sept 1911 as a 17 year old porter in a New York Hotel. He was released from the Fishkill Correctional Facility, Beacon, New York aged 85 on 7 May 1980 having served 68 years 8 months and 2 days—the longest recorded term in US history. He first refused parole in 1974. Rudolf Hess was captured at Eaglesham on 10 May 1941 and in 1986 entered his 46th year in prison.

The longest serving prisoner in Britain is John Straffen (b. 1930) now in his 31st year behind bars for 3 child murders.

Longest in Broadmoor Special Hospital
The longest period for which any person has been detained in the Broadmoor hospital for the criminally insane, near Crowthorne, Berkshire, is 76 years in the case of William Giles. He was admitted as an insane arsonist at the age of 11 and died there on 10 Mar 1962, at the age of 87.

The first patient from Broadmoor to subsequently hold public office and to be accepted on any party's parliamentary candidates list is Peter Thompson.

Most appearances
A record for arrests was set by Tommy Johns, 60, in Brisbane, Queensland, Australia on 9 Sept 1982 when he faced his 2000th conviction for drunkenness since 1957.

Greatest mass arrests
The greatest mass arrest reported in a democratic country was of more than 13,000 people in an anti-war demonstration designed to block rush-hour traffic in Washington DC, USA on 3-5 May 1971. The largest in the United Kingdom occurred on 17 Sept 1961, when 1314 demonstrators supporting unilateral nuclear disarmament were arrested for obstructing highways leading to Parliament Square, London, by sitting down. As a consequence of the 1926 General Strike there were 3149 prosecutions: incitement (1760) and violence (1389).

FINES

Heaviest *World*
It was reported in January 1979 that Carlo Ponti, husband of Sophia Loren, was to be fined the equivalent of $26.4 million by the Italian courts in connection with claims for tax alleged to be due but unpaid.

UK
The heaviest fine ever imposed by a United Kingdom Court is £525,000 on the National Graphical Association (NGA) for illegal picketing the *Messenger* newspaper plant, Warrington, Cheshire owned by Mr Eddie Shah on 10 Dec 1983.

On 6 Feb 1985 Lloyd's of London fined Peter Dixon, chairman of the PCW (Peter Cameron-Webb) Syndicate, £1,000,000 in connection with alleged misappropriation of £38.17 million. A High Court judgment of £8.2 million against Mr Dixon was also made in chambers.

The highest fine ever imposed on a U.K. company is 10 million Ecus (equivalent to £5.7 million) on ICI by the EEC for irregular trading arrangements concerning polypropylene in 1977-83 on 24 Apr 1986.

Rarest prosecution
There are a number of crimes in English law for which there have never been prosecutions. Among unique prosecutions are *Rex v. Crook* in 1662 for the praemunire of disputing the King's title and *Rex v. Gregory* for selling honours under the Honours (Prevention of Abuses) Act, 1924, on 18 Feb 1933. John Maundy Gregory (d. 3 Oct 1941 in France as 'Sir' 'Arthur' Gregory) was an honours broker during 6 administrations from 1919 to 1932 and was sentenced to two months in Wormwood Scrubs, London.

PRISONS

Largest *Great Britain*
The most capacious prison in Great Britain is Wormwood Scrubs, West London, with 1208 cells. The highest prison walls in Great Britain are those of Lancaster Prison measuring 36-52 ft *11-15,85 m*. The Maze Prison, opened in 1974, covers 133 acres *53,8 ha* with seven 100 cell blocks surrounded by a 30 ft *9,1 m* wall.

The largest prison in Scotland is Barlinnie, Glasgow, with 753 single cells. Ireland's largest prison is Mountjoy Prison, Dublin, with 808 cells.

Penal camps
The largest penal camp systems in the world have been those near Kolyma, in the USSR, with a population of 500,000 and a death roll in 1932-54 of six fold that figure. The largest labour camp is now said to be the Dubrovlag Complex of 15 camps centred on Pot'ma, Mordovian SSR. The official NATO estimate for all Soviet camps was 'more than one million' in March 1960 compared with a peak of probably 12 million during the Stalinist era.

Devil's Island
The largest French penal settlement was that of St Laurent du Maroni, which comprised the notorious Îles du Diable, Royale and St Joseph (for incorrigibles) off the coast of French Guiana, in South America. It remained in operation for 99 years from 1854 until the last group of

repatriated prisoners, including Théodore Rouselle, who had served 50 years, was returned to Bordeaux on 22 Aug 1953. It has been estimated that barely 2000 *bagnards* (ex-convicts) of the 70,000 deportees ever returned. These, however, included the executioner Ladurelle (imprisoned 1921-37), who was murdered in Paris in 1938.

Highest population
The peak prison population, including Borstals and detention centres, for England and Wales was the figure for March 1980 with 44,223. In Scotland the prison population record was 5400 in 1972 and in Northern Ireland 2934 on 16 Nov 1975.

Most secure prison
After it became a maximum security Federal prison in 1934, no convict was known to have lived to tell of a successful escape from the prison of Alcatraz Island in San Francisco Bay, California, USA. A total of 23 men attempted it but 12 were recaptured, 5 shot dead, one drowned and 5 presumed drowned. On 16 Dec 1962, just before the prison was closed on 21 Mar 1963, one man reached the mainland alive, only to be recaptured on the spot. John Chase held the record with 26 years there.

Most expensive prison
Spandau Prison, Berlin, built 100 years ago for 600 prisoners is now used solely for the person widely and officially purported to be Nazi war criminal Rudolf Hess (b. 26 Apr 1894). The cost of maintenance of the staff of 105 has been estimated at $415,000 (£245,000) per annum.

Longest escape
The longest recorded escape by a recaptured prisoner was that of Leonard T. Fristoe, 77, who escaped from Nevada State Prison, USA, on 15 Dec 1923 and was turned in by his son on 15 Nov 1969 at Compton, California. He had had 46 years of freedom under the name of Claude R. Willis. He had killed two sheriff's deputies in 1920. The longest period of freedom achieved by a British gaol breaker is more than 30 years by Irish-born John Patrick Hannan, who escaped from Verne Open Prison at Portland, Dorset, on 22 Dec 1955 and was still at large in June 1986. He had served only 1 month of a 21-month term for car-stealing and assaulting two policemen.

Of the eleven escapers from Alcatraz Island none ever lived to tell the tale, therefore enhancing its reputation as the most secure prison in the world. (Photographers' Library).

Greatest gaol break

In February 1979 a retired US Army Colonel Arthur 'Bull' Simons led a band of 14 to break into Gasre prison, Tehran, Iran to rescue two fellow Americans. Some 11,000 other prisoners took advantage of this and the Islamic revolution in what became history's largest ever gaol break.

In July 1971, Raoul Sendic and 105 other Tupamaro guerrillas escaped from a Uruguayan prison through a tunnel 91 m *298 ft* long.

The greatest gaol break in the United Kingdom was that from the Maze Prison, on 25 Sept 1983 when 38 IRA prisoners escaped from Block H-7. By June 1986 12 were still at large. The Provisional IRA had been first set up in Ballinamore, County Leitrim, Ireland in 1967.

6. ECONOMIC

MONETARY AND FINANCE

Largest budget *World*

The greatest governmental expenditure ever made by any country has been $979,900 million (*£699,930 million*) by the United States government for the fiscal year 1986. The highest ever revenue figure was $771,100 million (*£550,785 million*) in this same U.S. fiscal year.

The world's greatest fiscal surplus was $8,419,469,844 in the United States in 1947–8. The worst deficit was the $212,300 million in the U.S. fiscal year ending 30 Sept 1985.

Largest budget *United Kingdom*

The greatest budgeted government expenditure has been £149,273 million for the fiscal year 1985–86. The highest budgeted government receipts have been £139,107 million for the same fiscal year, showing a General Government Borrowing Requirement of £10,166 million.

Foreign aid

The total net foreign aid given by the United States government between 1 July 1945 and 1 Jan 1985 was $243,481 million. The country which received most US aid in 1986 was Israel with $3750 million. US foreign aid began with $50,000 to Venezuela for earthquake relief in 1812.

Least taxed

The lowest income-taxed sovereign countries in the world are Bahrain, Brunei, Kuwait and Qatar where the rate regardless of income is nil. No tax is levied on the Sarkese (inhabitants of Sark) in the Channel Islands or the inhabitants of Tristan da Cunha.

Highest taxation rates

The country with the most confiscatory taxation is Norway where in January 1974 the Labour Party and Socialist Alliance abolished the 80 per cent limit. Some 2000 citizens were then listed in the *Lignings Boka* as paying more than 100 per cent of their taxable income. The shipping magnate Hilmer Reksten (1898–1980) was assessed at 491 per cent. In the United Kingdom the former top earned and unearned rates of 83 per cent and 98 per cent were reduced to 60 per cent and 75 per cent in the budget on 12 June 1979. The all-time record ruled in 1967–8, when a 'special charge' of up to 9s. (45p) in the £ additional to surtax brought the top rate to 27s. 3d. (or 136%) in the £ on investment income.

Balance of Payments

The record deficit for any country is $124,289 million (*then £102.5 billion*) in 1985 by the USA. The record surplus was 8,358 billion yen (*£35,120 million*) by Japan in the calendar year 1985.

The most favourable current balance of payments figure for the United Kingdom has been

a surplus of £7,272 million in 1981 (best quarter Jan–Mar £2,698 million). The worst figure was a deficit of £3,591 million in 1974. Monthly figures are regarded as too erratic to be of great significance.

Tax demands highest

The highest recorded personal tax demand is one for $336 million (*then £164 million*) for 70 per cent of the estate of Howard Hughes. The highest disclosed UK personal income tax demand raised is one for £5,371,220 against the international merchant banker Nicholas Van Hoogstraten, 34, for 1981.

Highest and lowest rates in Great Britain

Income tax was first introduced in Great Britain in 1799 for incomes above £60 per annum. It was discontinued in 1815, only to be reintroduced in 1842 at the rate of 7d. (2.91p) in the £. It was at its lowest at 2d. (0.83p) in the £ in 1875, gradually climbing to 1s. 3d. (6.24p) by 1913. From April 1941 until 1946 the record peak of 10s. (50p) in the £ was maintained to assist in the financing of World War II.

National Debt

The largest national debt of any country in the world is that of the United States, where the gross federal public debt of the Federal Government supassed the 'trillion' (10^{12}) dollar mark on 30 Sept 1981. By May 1986 it had reached $2,112 billion.

The National Debt in Great Britain was less than £1 million during the reign of James II in 1687. It was £158,251 million or £2,798 per person at 31 Mar 1985. This amount placed in a pile of brand new £1 notes would be 8685.8 miles *13 978 km* in height.

Most Foreign Debt

The country most heavily in overseas debt is Brazil with $103 billion by mid-1985. The highest *per caput* is that of Chile with $17,000 million for a population of 11.5 million in mid-1983 or $1478 per person.

Gross National Product

The country with the largest Gross National Product is the United States reaching $3 trillion ($3 \times 10^{12}$) in 1981. By 31 Dec 1985 this was running at $3,988.5 billion. The GNP of the United Kingdom at factor cost was £351,400 million for 1985.

National wealth

The richest nation, measured by average per caput, is Nauru with $21,400 in 1983. The USA which had taken the lead in 1910 was 6th behind Nauru, UAE, Qatar, Brunei and Kuwait. The United Kingdom stood 26th with $8970 (*then £5790*) per head. It has been estimated that the value of all physical assets in the USA on 1 Jan 1983 was $12.5 trillion ($10^{12}$) or $53,800 per caput. The figure for private wealth in the United Kingdom was £325,000 million (1976) or £5811 per head.

Poorest country

The lowest published annual income per caput of any country in the world is Chad with $59 (then £29) in 1983 but the World Bank has no publishable data for 17 Marxist countries.

Gold reserves *World*

The country with the greatest monetary gold reserve is the United States, whose Treasury had 262.66 million fine oz of the world's 950 million fine oz on hand in March 1986. Valued at $315 per fine oz, these amounts translate to $82,780 million and $300,000 million respectively. The United States Bullion Depository at Fort Knox, 30 miles *48 km* south-west of Louisville, Ken-

tucky, USA has been the principal Federal depository of US gold since Dec 1936. Gold is stored in 446,000 standard mint bars of 400 troy ounces *12,4414 kg* measuring $7 \times 3\frac{5}{8} \times 1\frac{5}{8}$ in, *17,7 × 9,2 × 4,1 cm*.

Gold and foreign currency reserves *Great Britain*

The lowest published figure for the sterling area's gold and convertible currency reserves was $298,000,000 (*then £74 million*) on 31 Dec 1940. The valuation on 1 Apr 1981 was a peak $28,212 million and the peak figure for gold was $7334 million on 31 Dec 1981. The figure for 1 Feb 1986 was $17,817 million of which $1,903 million was in gold.

Minimum Lending Rate

The highest ever figure for the British bank rate (since 13 Oct 1972, the Minimum Lending Rate) has been 17 per cent from 15 Nov 1979 to 3rd July 1980. The longest period without a change was the 12 years 13 days from 26 Oct 1939 to 7 Nov 1951, during which time the rate stayed at 2 per cent. This lowest ever rate had been first attained on 22 Apr 1852.

Worst inflation *World*

The world's worst inflation occurred in Hungary in June 1946, when the 1931 gold pengö was valued at 130 trillion (1.3×10^{20}) paper pengös. Notes were issued for 'Egymillard billion' (one milliard billion or 10^{21}) pengös on 3 June and withdrawn on 11 July 1946. Vouchers for 1000 billion billion (10^{27}) pengös were issued for taxation payment only. On 6 Nov 1923 the circulation of Reichsbank marks reached 400,338,326,350,700,000,000 and inflation was755,700 million fold on 1913 levels. The country with the highest current rate of inflation for 1985 was Bolivia with 8000 plus %. It peaked in October with >24,000%, a year rate of 23,503%, September 1984–September 1985.

Worst inflation *Great Britain*

The United Kingdom's worst rate in a year has been for August 1974 to August 1975 when inflation ran at a rate of 26.9 per cent compared with 2.8 per cent for the 12 months to May 1986. The Tax and Price Index (allowing for tax reliefs) for the 12 months to May 1986 was 0.9%. The peak TPI extrapolated figure was 31.9 per cent in August 1975.

PAPER MONEY

Earliest

Paper money is an invention of the Chinese first tried in AD 910 and prevalent by AD 970. The world's earliest bank notes (*banco-sedler*) were issued in Stockholm, Sweden, in July 1661. The oldest surviving banknote is one of 5 dalers dated 6 Dec 1662. The oldest surviving printed Bank of England note is one for £555 to bearer, dated 19 Dec 1699 ($4\frac{1}{2} \times 7\frac{1}{2}$ in, *11,4 × 19,6 cm*).

Largest and smallest

The largest paper money ever issued was the one kwan note of the Chinese Ming dynasty issue of 1368–99, which measured 9×13 in *22,8 × 33,0 cm*. In Oct 1983 one sold for £340. The smallest national note ever issued was the 10 bani note of the Ministry of Finance of Romania, in 1917. It measured (printed area) 27,5 × 38 mm *1.09 × 1.49 in*. Of German *notgeld* the smallest are the 1–3 pfg of Passau (1920–21) measuring 18 × 18,5 mm *0.70 × 0.72 in*.

Highest denominations *World*

The highest denomination notes in circulation are US Federal Reserve Bank notes for $10,000 (*£5260*). They bear the head of Salmon Portland Chase (1808–73). None has been printed since July 1944 and the US Treasury announced in 1969 that no further notes higher than $100 would be issued. Only 348 $10,000 bills remain in circulation or unretired.

Great Britain

Two Bank of England notes for £1,000,000 still exist, dated before 1812 but these were used only for internal accounting. In November 1977 the existence of a Treasury £1 million note dated 30 Aug 1948 came to light and was sold by private treaty for $A18,500 (then £11,300) in Australia.

The highest issued denominations have been £1000 notes, first printed in 1725, discontinued on 22 Apr 1943 and withdrawn on 30 Apr 1945. At least 16 of these notes were still unretired up to Nov 1979 (last data to be published). Of these perhaps 10 are in the hands of collectors or dealers.

Lowest denomination *World*
The lowest denomination legal tender bank note is the 1 sen (or 1/100th of a rupiah) Indonesian note. Its exchange value in mid-1984 was 140 to the new penny.

Great Britain
The lowest denomination Bank of England notes ever printed were the black on pale blue half-crown (now 12½p) notes in 1941, signed by the late Sir Kenneth Peppiatt. Very few examples have survived and they are now valued at from £750.

Highest circulation
The highest ever Bank of England note circulation in the United Kingdom was £14,071,000,000 as at 31 Dec 1985—equivalent to a pile of £5 notes 139.86 miles *225,09 km* high.

CHEQUES AND COINS

Largest *World*
The greatest amount paid by a single cheque in the history of banking has been one for Rs. 16,640,000,000 equivalent to £852,791,660 handed over by Hon. Daniel P. Moynihan, US Ambassador to India in New Delhi on 18 Feb 1974. An internal US Treasury cheque for $4,176,969,623.57 was drawn on 30 June 1954.

Largest *Great Britain*
The largest cheque drawn in Britain was one for £604,604,115 drawn on 1 Sept 1982 by British Petroleum Oil Development Ltd, payable to the Inland Revenue against BP's North Sea Oil tax bill. If converted to pound notes this would comprise a stack 36.84 miles *59,28 km* high.

Greatest collection
The highest price paid for a coin collection has been $7,300,000 (then £3,550,000) for a hoard of 407,000 US silver dollars from the La Vere Redfield estate in a courtroom auction in Reno, Nevada on 27 Jan 1976 by Steven C. Markoff of A-Mark Coin Co. Inc. of Beverley Hills, Cal.

Largest hoards
The largest hoard was one of about 80,000 aurei in Brescello near Modena, Italy in 1814 believed to have been deposited *c.* 37 BC. The numerically largest hoard ever found was the Brussels hoard of 1908 containing *c.* 150,000 coins. A hoard of 56,000 Roman coins was found at Cunetio near Marlborough, Wiltshire on 15 Oct 1978.

On 20 July 1985 two sons of Mel Fisher found the main cargo of the Spanish *Nuestra Senhora de Atocha* sunk off Key West, Florida in 1622. The value of the cargo already recovered was $80 million but is now expected to attain close to $400 million, mainly in silver bars.

The greatest discovery of treasure is the estimated $2000 million of gold coins and platinum ingots from the sunken Tsarist battleship *Admiral Nakhimov* 8524 tons/tonnes 200 ft *60 m* down off the Japanese island of Tsushima. She sank

Pete Townshend, George Michael, Bob Geldof (Hon KBE), Paul Weller, Bono and Freddie Mercury bring to a close the 1985 Live Aid Concert from Wembley—the record-breaking charity fund-raising event. (Duncan Raban).

COINS

Oldest
World: c. 670 BC electrum staters of King Gyges of Lydia, Turkey[1]

British: c. 95 BC Westerham type gold stater (51 known)[2]

Earliest Dated
Samian silver tetradrachm struck in Zankle (now Messina), Sicily dated year 1 *viz* 494 BC—shown as 'A'

Christian Era: MCCXXXIIII (1234) Bishop of Roskilde coins, Denmark (6 known)

British: 1539 James V of Scotland silver 'bonnet piece'

Heaviest
World: 19,71 kg *43 lb 7¼ oz* Swedish 10 daler copper plate 1644[3]

British: 39,94 g *1.4066 oz* Gold £5 piece. The latest mintages are dated 1980, 1981 and 1982. (Legal tender record)[4]

Lightest and Smallest
World: 0.002 g or 14,000 to the oz Nepalese silver ¼ Jawa *c.* 1740

British: 7.27 grains or 61 to the oz Maundy silver one penny piece since 1822

Most Expensive
World: Agrigentum decadrahm sold by private treaty to Nelson Bunker Hunt (US) for $900,000 in Oct 1980

British: £71,500 (including premium) bid for a Henry III gold 20 pence (6 known) at Spink's, London on 13 June 1985 (see below). 20th century record: £40,000 bid for Edward VIII proof sovereign of 1937 at Spink's, London on 7 Dec 1984

Rarest
World: Many 'singletons' known e.g. Only 700 Axumite coins known of which only one of bronze and gold of Kaleb I *c.* AD 500

British: Unique: 1952 George VI half-crown; 1954 Elizabeth II 1d sold in March 1978 for £23,000

---

[1] Chinese uninscribed 'spade' money of the Chou dynasty has been dated to *c.* 770 BC.
[2] Bellovaci type gold staters circulated as early as *c.* 130 BC but were struck in Northern France and not in Britain.
[3] The largest coin-like medallion was completed on 21 Mar 1986 for the World Exposition in Vancouver, BC, Canada, Expo 86—a $1,000,000 gold piece. Its dimensions were 37.5 in *95,25 cm* diameter and ⅜ in *19,05 mm* thick and weighing 166 kg *365 lb 15 oz* or 5337 oz (troy) of gold.
[4] The George III 'Cartwheel' Copper 2d coin of 1797 weighed 2.04 oz *58,0 g*. The 5 guinea gold pieces.

---

on 27 May 1905. A figure of $2000 million has also been ascribed to the *San Jose* which sank in 700–1200 ft *210–365 m* of water off Colombia in 1708. Diving began in Aug 1984.

Largest mint
The largest mint in the world is the US Treasury's mint built in 1965–9 on Independence Mall, Philadelphia, covering 11½ acres *4,65 ha* with an annual capacity on a 3 shift 7-day week production of 8000 million coins. A single stamping machine can produce coins at a rate of 10,000 per hour.

Charity Fund Raising
The globally televised 'Live Aid' concerts, organised by Bob Geldof and Bill Graham, with 60 rock acts in Philadelphia and London on 20 July 1985, raised £35 million within two weeks with an estimated further £60 million to come for famine relief. The estimated viewership, via a record 12 satellites, 1.6 billion or one-third of the world's population. The 'Sport Aid' event, conceived by Chris Long and organised by Bob Geldof (Hon KBE), took place in 277 cities in 78 countries on 25 May 1986 and raised a world wide figure of over £67 million (*$100 million*).

The greatest recorded amount raised by a charity walk or run is (Can)$24.7 million by Terry Fox (1958–81) of Canada who ran from St John's, Newfoundland to Thunder Bay, Ontario with an artificial leg in 143 days from 12 Apr–2 Sept 1980. He covered 5373 km *3339 miles*.

Longest and Most Valuable Line of Coins
The most valuable column of coins amassed for charity was worth £13,628 knocked over by Frankie Vaughan at Mecca's Club, Bolton, Lancashire on 18 Aug 1984. The longest and highest value line of coins was 10 miles, 5 feet, 7 inches (*16,12 km*) made-up of 662,353 US quarters to a value of $165,788 (*£138,155*) on 16 Mar 1985 at Central City Park, Atlanta, Georgia, USA, sponsored by the National Kidney Foundation of Georgia Inc. The Copper Mountain, devised by Terry Pitts Fenby for the NSPCC at Selfridges, Oxford Street amassed over 3 million coins in 350 days (24 May 1984–7 May 1985) valued at £57,051.34.

LABOUR

Trade union Oldest *Great Britain*
The oldest of the 105 trade unions affiliated to the Trades Union Congress (founded 1868) is the National Society of Brushmakers and General Workers (current membership 725) founded in 1747. The oldest union currently affiliated to the TUC under its original name is the Educational Institute of Scotland (EIS) founded in 1847.

Trade union Largest World

The world's largest union has been Solidar- ność (Solidarity) founded in Poland in Nov 1980 which by October 1981 was reported to have 8,000,000 members. The union with the longest name is the International Association of Marble, Slate and Stone Polishers, Rubbers and Sawyers, Tile and Marble Setters' Helpers and Marble Mosaic and Terrazzo Workers Helpers or IAMSSPRSTMSHMMTWH of Washington DC, USA.

Trade union Largest Great Britain

The largest union in the United Kingdom is the Transport and General Workers' Union, with 1,434,005 members at March 1986. Their peak membership was 2,086,281 in 1979.

Trade union Smallest

The smallest Trade Union Congress affiliated union is the Sheffield Wool Shear Workers' Union with a membership of just 27. The unaffiliated London Handforged Spoon and Fork Makers' Society instituted in July 1874, has a last reported membership of 6. The Unión de Pilotos de la Autoridad de Energía Eléctrica of Puerto Rico in 1984 boasted 3 members.

Labour dispute Earliest

A labour dispute concerning monotony of diet and working conditions was recorded in 1153 BC in Thebes, Egypt. The earliest recorded strike was one by an orchestra leader from Greece named Aristos in Rome c. 309 BC. The cause was meal breaks.

Labour dispute Largest

The most serious single labour dispute in the United Kingdom was the General Strike of 4– 12 May 1926, called by the Trades Union Congress in support of the Miners' Federation. During the nine days of the strike 1,580,000 people were involved and 14,500,000 working days were lost.

During the year 1926 a total of 2,750,000 people were involved in 323 different labour disputes and the working days lost during the year amounted to 162,300,000, the highest figure ever recorded. The figures for 1985 were 6,372,000 working days involving 855 stoppages with 737,000 workers involved.

Britain's most protracted national strike was called by the National Union of Mineworkers from 8 Mar 1984 to 5 Mar 1985. H.M. Treasury estimated the cost to be £2625 million or £46.50 per head of the population.

Labour dispute Longest

The world's longest recorded strike ended on 4 Jan 1961, after 33 years. It concerned the employment of barbers' assistants in Copen- hagen, Denmark. The longest recorded major strike was that at the plumbing fixtures factory of the Kohler Co. in Sheboygan, Wisconsin, USA, between April 1954 and October 1962. The strike is alleged to have cost the United Automobile Workers' Union about $12,000,000 (then £4.8 million) to sustain.

Unemployment Highest

The highest recorded percentage unemployment in Great Britain was on 23 Jan 1933, when the total of unemployed persons on the Employment Exchange registers was 2,903,065, representing 22.8% of the insured working population. The peak figure for the post-war period has been 14.1% (3,407,729) in Jan 1986.

Unemployment Lowest

In Switzerland in December 1973 (pop. 6.6 million), the total number of unemployed was reported to be 81. The lowest recorded peace- time level of unemployment in Britain was 0.9

per cent on 11 July 1955, when 184,929 persons were registered. The peak figure for the Em- ployed labour force in the United Kingdom has been 25,520,000 in December 1979.

ASSOCIATION

Oldest Club

Britain's oldest gentleman's club is White's, St James', London, opened c. 1697 by Francis White (d. 1711), as a Chocolate House, and moved to its present site in 37 St. James's in 1755. This has been described as an 'oasis in a desert of democracy'. Britain's oldest known dining club is the Charterhouse School Foun- der's Day Dinner held each Twelfth of Decem- ber. The 1984 dinner to commemorate Old Etonian coal-owner Thomas Sutton (1532–1611) was the 358th.

CONSUMPTION

Prohibition

The longest lasting imposition of prohibition has been 26 years in Iceland (1908–34). Other prohibitions have been Russia, later USSR (1914–24) and USA (1920–33). The Faeroe Islands have had a public (as opposed to private licensed) prohibition since 1918. By way of contrast the Northern Territory of Australia's annual intake has been estimated to be as high as 416 pints *236 litres* per person. A society for the prevention of alcoholism in Darwin had to disband in June 1966 for lack of support. It is perhaps noteworthy that the only parliamentary candidate on record in Britain ever to receive a nil vote was in 1860 at Ripon, North Yorkshire by Mr F. R. Lees, who described himself as a Temperance Chartist.

Biggest round

The largest round of drinks ever recorded was one for 1501 people stood by Paul Deer at U- Zoo & Co., Atlanta, Georgia, USA on 14 July 1982.

Largest dish

The largest menu item in the world is roasted camel, prepared occasionally for Bedouin wed- ding feasts. Cooked eggs are stuffed in fish, the fish stuffed in cooked chickens, the chickens stuffed into a roasted sheep carcass and the sheep stuffed into a whole camel.

Most expensive food

The most expensively priced food (as opposed to spice) is First Choice Black Périgord truffle (*Tuber melanosporum*) retailed at £8.50 per 12.5 g *0.44 oz* tin. However, in January 1985 in the Hafr El-Baten market, Riyadh, Saudi Arabia local truffles sold for SR 5000 for 3 kg equivalent to £50.16 for 12.5 g.

Longest banana split

The longest banana split ever made was one of 4 miles *6,43 km* in length made by the Zeta Beta Tau Fraternity of Bowling Green State Univer- sity, Ohio, USA on 25 Aug 1985.

Largest barbecue

On 31 Jan 1981, 46,386 chicken halves supplied by Ernie Morgado were barbecued for 15,000 people at Iolani School, Honolulu, Hawaii. At the 1982 holding of the annual Fancy Farm Picnic, Kentucky (est. 1880) on 6 August the consumption of mutton, pork and chicken meat reached 15,000 lb *6,80 tonnes*. The cook was Harold Carrico.

At the Sertoma Club Barbecue, New Port Richey, Florida, USA 21,112 lb *9576 kg* of beef was sold on 7–9 Mar 1986.

Largest hamburger

The largest hamburger on record is one of 2270,66 kg *5005 lb 13.8 oz* made on 13 Oct 1985

by Spur Steak Ranches (Pty) Ltd at Three Anchor Bay, Cape Town, South Africa. The burger had a diameter of 7,10 m *23 ft 3⅓ in* and was cut into over 15,750 portions after grilling.

Largest cake

The largest cake ever created weighed 90,000 lb *40,82 tonnes*, included 30,000 lb *13,61 tonnes* of vanilla icing, was 110 × 80 ft *33,5 × 24,3 m* in size and was baked in 32 hours by Chef Franz Eichenauer at the City Coliseum, Austin, Texas, USA on 20 Feb 1986. It was cut by HRH the Prince of Wales and the Governor of Texas, Mark White Jr. The tallest recorded free- standing cake is one of 71 tiers, 45 ft 5 in *13,84 m* completed by the management and staff of the Hyatt Central Plaza Bangkok Hotel, Thailand on 12 Sept 1985.

Largest Christmas Pudding

One of 617 lb *279,8 kg* was made for charity at Burton-on-Trent, Staffordshire, England on 14 Dec 1985.

Largest chocolate

The largest chocolate model was one measuring 10 × 5 m *32 ft 9⅓ in × 16 ft 4¾ in* and 73 cm *28.7 in* high of the 1992 Olympic Centre, Barcelona, Spain by Gremi Provincial de Pastig- eria i Confiteria School in November 1985.

Heaviest and Largest Easter eggs

The heaviest Easter egg ever made was one weighing 3430 kg *7561 lb 13½ oz*, measuring 10 ft *3,04 m* high, by Siegfried Berndt at 'Macopa' Patisserie, Leicester, England and completed on 7 Apr 1982. An egg 5,42 m *17 ft 9⅜ in* tall weighing 2323 kg *5121 lb* was exhibited by Patisserie Eueen Lauwers at Schelle, Belgium on 19 Mar 1983.

Largest haggis

The largest haggis (encased in 7 ox stomach linings) on record was one weighing 541¼ lb *245,6 kg* made for the CWS Hypermarket of Glasgow, Scotland by David A. Hall Ltd. of Broxburn Lothian, Scotland in January 1980. The cooking time was 12 hr.

Longest loaf

The longest loaf ever baked was a rosca de Reyes 649,90 m *2132 ft 2⅓ ins* in length and 1173 kg *1.15 tons* in weight at the Exelaris Hyatt Regency Hotel, Acapulco, Mexico on 6 Jan 1985. If a consumer of the rosca (twisted loaf) finds the embedded bread doll he has to throw the next rosca party.

The longest pan loaf baked was one of 2 cwt *101,6 kg* measuring 1,7 m × 70 cm × 90 cm *5 ft 6¾ m × 2 ft 3¼ in × 2ft 11¾ in* at San Lameer Complex, Natal, South Africa on 26 May 1984.

Largest apple pie

The largest apple pie ever baked was that by the ITV Chef Glynn Christian in a 40 ft × 23 ft *12 m × 7 m* dish at Hewitts Farm, Chelsfield, Kent on 25–27 Aug 1982. Over 600 bushels of apples were included in the pie which weighed 30,115 lb *13,66 tonnes*. It was cut by Rear Admiral Sir John Woodward.

Largest cherry pie

The largest cherry pie ever made was one weighing a total of 6¼ tons *6350 kg* and contain- ing 4950 lb *2245 kg* of cherries. It measured 14 ft 4 in *4,36 m* in diameter, 24 in *60,96 cm* in depth, and was baked in the grounds of the Medusa Cement Corporation, Charlevoix, Michigan on 15 May 1976, as part of the town's contribution to America's Bicentennial celebrations.

Largest meat pie

The largest meat pie ever baked weighed 5¾ tons, measuring 18 × 6 ft 18 in deep *5,48 × 1,83 × 0,45 m*, the eighth in the series of Denby Dale, West Yorkshire pies, to mark four royal births, baked on 5 Sept 1964. The first was in 1788 to celebrate King George III's return to sanity, but the fourth (Queen Victoria's Jubilee, 1887) went a bit 'off' and had to buried in quick-lime.

Largest mince pie
The largest mince pie recorded was one of 2260 lb *1025 kg* 20 × 5 ft *6,09 × 1,52 m*, baked at Ashby-de-la-Zouch, Leicestershire on 15 Oct 1932.

Largest omelette
The largest omelette in the world was one made of 45,000 eggs in a pan 10 × 43 ft *3,05 × 13,11 m* cooked by the Kinsman's Mothers' March of British Columbia, Canada at the Hotel Meridien, Vancouver on 27 Jan 1986.

Largest pancake
The largest pancake of 20 ft diameter 4 in thick weighing 2107 lb containing 900 lb pancake mix, 1600 lb maple syrup, 15 blocks of butter and 100 gal of milk was made in Highgate, Franklin Co, Vt on 18 Aug 1984.

Longest pastry
The longest pastry in the world is the 'record' pastry 489,87 m *1607 ft 2 in* in length made by the Gothenburg Patissiers Association of Sweden (organiser Sven Gustavsson) at The Liseberg Amusement Park on 15 June 1983.

Largest pizza pie
The largest pizza ever baked was one measuring 26,4 m *86 ft 7 in* in diameter, hence 547 m² *5895 ft²* in area completed by Marco Cagnazzo at Norwood Hypermarket, Johannesburg, South Africa on 31 Mar 1984.

Largest potato crisps
Charles Chip Inc of Mountville, Pennsylvania, produced crisps 4 × 7 in *10 × 17,5 cm* from outsize potatoes in February 1977.

Potato mash
A single serving of 18,260 lb *8,26 tonnes* of potato mash was prepared in a concrete mixer for the 17th Annual Potato Bowl at Grand Forks, North Dakota, USA on 4 Sept 1982.

Largest iced lollipop
The world's largest iced lollipop was one of 5750 lb *2608 kg* constructed for the Westside Assembly of God Church, Davenport, Iowa, USA on 7 Sept 1975. The largest 'regular' lollipop was one of 400 lb *181,4 kg* (220 lb of

A contender for the world's largest paella record is this vegetarian variety made in August 1985 at Torré Del Mar, Malaga, Spain. It had the same diameter (10 m *32 ft 9 in*) as the one made in Barcelona in 1984. *See page 208.*
(*Below*) The icing on the cake . . . 30,000 lb *1,36 tonnes*. The world's largest cake measured 110 ft × 80 ft *33,5 m × 24,3 m* and was big enough for 300,000 people to have their cake and eat it.

A lot of roast beef was needed to go with this Yorkshire Pudding. The largest of its kind in the world, it measured over 25 ft × 4 ft *7,6 m × 1,2 m* and was made, of course, in Yorkshire, on 'Yorkshire Day'. (*Right*) A 71 tier cake built in Thailand, towers over spectators at the Hyatt Central Plaza Bangkok Hotel where it was made by the management and staff.

sugar and 180 lb of corn syrup) made by American Candy Co, Selma, Alabama for the World's Fair, Knoxville, Tennessee, USA on 28 Apr 1982.

Largest Paella
The largest paella ever made was one with a diameter of 10 m *32 ft 9 in* and a depth of 45 cm *1 ft 5¾ in* built in the Plaza de Catalunya, Cornella de Llobregat, Barcelona, Spain on 24 June 1984 for 15,000 people. It included 750 kg *1650 lb* of meat and 300 kg *660 lb* of pimientos.

Blackpool rock
The mightiest piece of Blackpool lettered rock ever produced was a piece weighing more than 3 cwt *152 kg* delivered on 16 Apr 1975 to the Royal Variety Club of Great Britain in London by Ashton Candy Co. Ltd. of Blackpool.

Largest salami
The largest salami on record was one 8,91 m *29 ft 2¾ in* long with a circumference of 71 cm *28 in*, weighing 333 kg *734.13 lb* made by Don Smallgoods for Australian Safeway Stores at Broadmeadows, Vic on 23 Apr 1982.

Longest sausage
The longest continuous sausage ever made was one of 5.54 miles *8,91 km* weighing 2.38 tons *2418 kg* by Rex's Sausage Manufacturing Co of Stirchley, Birmingham, on 22 June 1983.

Smörgåstårta Largest
On 9 Mar 1985 in Köping, Sweden a *smör-* (butter)-*gås*(goose)-*tårta*(cake) 510,69 m *1675 ft 6 in* long was set up by Hans Pettersson and a team. It was demolished in short order.

Strawberry Bowl
The largest bowl of strawberries with a net weight of 513 lb *232,7 kg* was weighed on 4 July 1985 at Battle, E. Sussex.

Largest sundae
The largest ice cream sundae ever concocted is one of 27,102 lb *12,293 kg* with strawberries, nuts and whipped topping constructed at St. Albans, Vermont, USA on 15 Apr 1983.

Largest Yorkshire pudding
The largest Yorkshire pudding is one measuring 105.8 ft² *9,82 m²* made on the Knavesmire, York with 44 dozen eggs, 87 lb *39,4 kg* of flour and 29 gal *131,8 l* of milk on 1 Aug 1985.

Top selling sweet
The world's top selling sweets (candies) are Life Savers with 29,651,840,000 rolls between 1913 and 30 June 1980. A tunnel formed by the holes in the middle placed end to end would stretch to the moon and back 3 times. Thomas Syta of Van Nuys, California, USA made one last 7 hr 10 min (with hole intact) on 15 Jan 1983.

Spice *Most expensive*
Prices for wild gingseng (root of *Panax quinque-folius*), from the Chan Pak Mountain area of China thought to have aphrodisiac qualities were reported in November 1977 to be as high as $23,000 (*then £10,454*) per ounce in Hong Kong. Total annual shipments from Jilin Province do not exceed 4 kg *140 oz* a year. A leading medical journal in the USA has likened its effects to 'corticosteroid poisoning'.

Spice *'Hottest'*
The hottest of all spices is claimed to be Siling labuyo from the Philippines.

The chili pepper or Capsicum known as Tepin from the south west of the USA comes in pods ⅜ in *7 mm* in diameter. A single dried gram will produce detectable 'heat' in 68.3 lb *31 kg* of bland sauce.

Most Expensive fruit
On 5 Apr 1977 John Synnott of Ashford, Co. Wicklow, Ireland sold 1 lb *453 g* of strawberries (a punnet of 30 berries) to the restaurateur, Mr Leslie Cooke, at auction by Walter L. Cole Ltd.

in the Dublin Fruit Market for £530 or £17.70 a berry.

Rarest condiment

The world's most prized condiment is Cà Cuong, a secretion recovered in minute amounts from beetles in northern Vietnam. Owing to war conditions, the price had risen to $100 (*now £57*) per ounce *28 g* before supplies virtually ceased in 1975.

Largest Trifle

The largest sherry trifle on record was one weighing 300 lb including 11 gallons *50 l* of sherry organised by Mrs Judy Fraser for St. Andrew's Hospice, Cleethorpes, Humberside on 19 Aug 1984.

ENERGY CONSUMPTION

To express the various forms of available energy (coal, liquid fuels and water power, etc., but omitting vegetable fuels and peat), it is the practice to convert them all into terms of coal.

The highest consumption in the world is in the United States, with an average of 13 240 kg *260.1 cwt* per person. With only 5.3 per cent of the world's population the US consumes 28.6 per cent of the world's gasoline and 32.9 per cent of the world's electric power. The United Kingdom average was 5527 kg *108.7 cwt* per person in 1984. The lowest recorded average for 1974 was 13 kg *28.6 lb* per person in Rwanda.

MASS COMMUNICATIONS

Airline

The country with the busiest airlines system is the United States of America where 277,182,916,000 revenue passenger miles were flown on larger US certificated air carriers in domestic operations in 1985. This was equivalent to an annual trip of 1168 miles *1880 km* for every one of the inhabitants of the USA. The United Kingdom airlines flew 614,116,000 km *381,604,410 miles* and carried 41,912,917 passengers on all services excluding Air Taxi operations in 1985.

The longest air ticket record was one of 12 m *39 ft 4¼ in* issued for $4500 to M. Bruno Leunen of Brussels, Belgium in December 1984 for a 85 623 km *53,203 miles* air trip on 80 airlines involving 109 stopovers.

Merchant shipping

The world total of merchant shipping, excluding vessels of less than 100 tons gross, sailing vessels and barges, was 76,395 vessels of 416,268,534 tons gross on 1 July 1985. The largest merchant fleet in the world as at mid-1985 was that under the flag of Liberia with 1808 ships of 58,179,717 tons gross. The UK figure for mid-1985 was 2378 ships of 14,343,512 tons gross.

Largest and busiest ports

Physically, the largest port in the world is the Port of New York and New Jersey, USA. The port has a navigable waterfront of 755 miles *1215 km* (295 miles *474 km* in New Jersey) stretching over 92 miles² *238 km²*. A total of 261 general cargo berths and 130 other piers give a total berthing capacity of 391 ships at one time. The total warehousing floor space is 422.4 acres *170,9 ha*. The world's busiest port and largest artificial harbour is Rotterdam-Europoort in the Netherlands which covers 38 miles² *100 km²* with 76 miles *122,3 km* of quays. It handled 31,457 sea-going vessels carrying a total of 251 million tonnes of sea-going cargo, and about 182,000 barges in 1985. It is able to handle 310 sea-going vessels simultaneously of up to 318,000 tonnes and 72 ft *21,96 m* draught.

Railways

The country with the greatest length of railway is the United States, with 184,235 miles *296 489 km* of track at 1 Jan 1980. The farthest anyone can get from a railway on the mainland island of Great Britain is 110 miles *177 km* by road in the case of Southend, Mull of Kintyre.

The number of journeys made on British Rail in 12 months to Mar 1985 was 700,700,000 (average 26.4 miles *42,4 km*) compared with the peak year of 1957, when 1101 million journeys (average 20.51 miles *33 km*) were made.

Road *Mileages*

The country with the greatest length of road is the United States (all 50 States), with 3,891,781 miles *6 263 043 km* of graded roads at 1 Jan 1985. Regular driving licences are issuable at 15, without a driver education course only in Hawaii and Mississippi. Thirteen US States issue restricted juvenile licences at 14.

Great Britain has 213,555 miles *343 685 km* of road including 1659 miles *2671 km* of motorway at April 1983 and 21,030,120 vehicles in 1986.

The first sod on Britain's first motorway, the M6 Preston By-Pass, was cut by bulldozer driver Fred Hackett on 12 June 1956 on the section between junctions 29 and 32 opened in December 1958. Britain's longest uninterrupted dual carriageway is from Plymouth to Exeter (A38) and thence by the M5 and M6 for 515 miles *829 km* terminating at Dunblane Fourways Restaurant, Stirling, Scotland.

Traffic volume *Highest*

The highest traffic volume of any point in the world is at the East Los Angeles interchange (Santa Ana, Pomona, Golden State, Santa Monica, Hollywood and San Bernardino Freeways), California, USA with a 24-hr average of 458,060 vehicles in 1983—318 per minute. The most heavily travelled stretch of road is between 43rd and 47th Street on the Dan Ryan Expressway, Chicago with an average daily volume of 254,700 vehicles.

The territory with the highest traffic density in the world is Hong Kong. By 1 Jan 1984 there were 302,118 motor vehicles on 778.9 miles *1253 km* of serviceable roads giving a density of 4.53 yd *4,14 m* per vehicle. The comparative figure for the United Kingdom in 1984 was

21.44 yd *19,60 m*. The world's busiest bridge is the Howrah Bridge across the river Hooghly in Calcutta. In addition to 57,000 vehicles a day it carries an incalculable number of pedestrians across its 1500 ft *457 m* long 72 ft *21,9 m* wide span.

The greatest traffic density at any one point in Great Britain is at Hyde Park Corner, London. The flow (including the underpass) for 24 hours in 1982 was 214,000 vehicles. The busiest Thames bridge in 1982 was Putney Bridge, with a 24-hr average of 57,700 vehicles compared with 72,500 for the Blackwall Tunnel. Britain's busiest and most heavily travelled motorway is the M25 (see By Pass Largest) on which more than 100,000 vehicles have been registered in 24 hours.

Traffic jams *Largest*

The longest traffic jam ever reported was that of 16 Feb 1980 which stretched northwards from Lyon 176 km *109.3 miles* towards Paris. The longest traffic jam reported in Britain was one of 40 miles *64,3 km* on the M1 from Junction 13 (Milton Keynes) to Junction 18 (Rugby) on 5 Apr 1985.

Road *Widest*

The widest street in the world is the Monumental Axis running for 1½ miles *2,4 km* from the Municipal Plaza to the Plaza of the Three Powers in Brasilia, the capital of Brazil. The six-lane Boulevard was opened in April 1960 and is 250 m *273.4 yd* wide. The San Francisco-Oakland Bay Bridge Toll Plaza has 23 lanes (17 west bound) serving the Bridge in Oakland, California.

The only instance of 17 carriageway lanes side by side in Britain occurs on the M61 at Linnyshaw Moss, Worsley, Greater Manchester.

Road *Narrowest*

The world's narrowest street is in the village of Ripatransone in the Marche region of Italy. It is called Vicolo della Virilita-Virility Alley and is 43 cm *16.9 in* wide.

The central reservation and intersection of the world's widest dual carriageway 'The Monumental Axis' in Brasilia. (Duncan Raban/Daily Telegraph).

Road *Longest*

The longest motorable road in the world is the Pan-American Highway, from North West Alaska to Santiago, Chile, thence eastward to Buenos Aires, Argentina and terminating in Brasília, Brazil. There remains a gap known as the Tapon del Darién, in Panama and the Atrato Swamp, Colombia. This was first traversed by the land rover La Cucaracha Cariñosa (The Affectionate Cockroach) of the Tran's-Darien Expedition 1959–60 crewed by former SAS man Richard E Bevir (UK) and engineer Terence John Whitfield (Australia). They left Chepo, Panama on 3 Feb 1960 and reached Quibdó, Colombia on 17 June averaging 220 yd *201 m* per hour of indescribable difficulty. The Range Rover VXC 868K of the British Trans-Americas Expedition was the first vehicle to traverse the American continent end-to-end, leaving Alaska on 3 Dec 1971 and arriving in Tierra del Fuego on 9 June 1972 after a journey of 17,018 miles *27 387 km*.

Most complex interchange

The most complex interchange on the British road system is that at Gravelly Hill, north of Birmingham on the Midland Link Motorway section of the M6 opened on 24 May 1972. There are 18 routes on 6 levels together with a diverted canal and river, which consumed 26,000 tons/ *tonnes* of steel, 250,000 tons/*tonnes* of concrete, 300,000 tons/*tonnes* of earth and cost £8,200,000.

Bypass *Longest World*

The longest bypass in the world is the M25 6-lane London Orbital Motorway at 121½ miles *195,5 km* begun in 1972 and due for completion in October 1986 at an estimated cost of £909 million.

WORLD'S LONGEST TELEPHONE CALL

1. LONDON . 28 DEC . 15:50
2. SYDNEY . 29 DEC . 02:50
3. MONTREAL . 28 DEC . 10:50

A telephone call around the world, over an estimated 98,700 miles *158 845 km* was made on 28 Dec 1985 from and back to, the Royal Institution, London, during one of the Christmas lectures given by David Pye, Professor of Zoology, Queen Mary College, London. The international telecommunications 'rule', that only one communication satellite be used at a time, was suspended for the demonstration so that both geostationary Intelsats, one over the Indian Ocean and one over the Pacific could be employed.

From London, the call was connected to the Earth Station at Madley, Hereford and Worcester (200 miles *320 km*) and then to Ceduna, South Australia via the Indian Ocean satellite (44,600 miles *71 775 km*). It went on to the Earth Station at Moree, New South Wales by landline (1000 miles *1610 km*), thence to Lake Cowichan, Vancouver Island, Canada, via the Pacific Ocean satellite (44,600 miles *71 775 km*) across Canada to Montreal by microwave link (4000 miles *6440 km*) and finally to Widemouth Bay, Cornwall, by submarine cable, Cantat 2 (4000 miles *6440 km*) from where final connection was made back to London (300 miles *485 km*). The two 'telephonists', Anieka Russell (*right*) and Alison Risk (*far right*) experienced a delay in their conversation of 530 milliseconds.

Artwork: Rob Burns

Street *Longest World*

The longest designated street in the world is Yonge Street running north and west from Toronto, Canada. The first stretch completed on 16 Feb 1796 ran 34 miles 53 chains *55,783 km*. Its official length now extended to Rainy River at the Ontario–Minnesota border is 1178.3 miles *1896,2 km*.

Longest *Great Britain and Commonest Name*

The longest designated road in Great Britain is the A1 from London to Edinburgh of 404 miles *650 km*. The longest Roman roads were Watling Street, from Dubrae (Dover) 215 miles *346 km* through Londinium (London) to Viroconium (Wroxeter), and Fosse Way, which ran 218 miles *350 km* from Lindum (Lincoln) through Aquae Sulis (Bath) to Isca Dumnoniorum (Exeter). However, a 10 mile *16 km* section of Fosse Way between Ilchester and Seaton remains indistinct. The commonest street name in Greater London is High Street (122) followed by Station Road (100).

Shortest

The title of 'The Shortest Street in the World' has been claimed for Bacup, Lancashire where 'Elgin Street', by the old market ground, measures 17 ft 0 in *5,18 m*. It is not a carriageable but a railed close.

Steepest

The steepest street in the world is Baldwin Street, Dunedin, New Zealand which has been surveyed to have a maximum gradient of 1 in 1.266. Britain's steepest motorable road is the unclassified Chimney Bank which is signposted '1 in 3' at Rosedale Abbey, North Yorkshire. The County Surveyor states it is 'not quite' a 33 per cent gradient. Of the five unclassified roads with 1 in 3 gradients the most severe is Hard Knott Pass between Boot and Ambleside, Cumbria.

Longest hill

The longest steep hill on any road in the United Kingdom is on the road westwards from Lochcarron towards Applecross in Highland, Scotland. In 6 miles *9,6 km* this road rises from sealevel to 2054 ft *626 m* with an average gradient of 1 in 15.4, the steepest part being 1 in 4.

Road *Highest World*

The highest trail in the world is an 8 mile *13 km* stretch of the Kang-ti-suu between Khaleb and Hsin-chi-fu, Tibet which in two places exceeds 20,000 ft *6080 m*. The highest carriageable road in the world is one 1180 km *733.2 miles* long between Tibet and south western Sinkiang, completed in October 1957, which takes in passes of an altitude up to 18,480 ft *5632 m* above sea-level. Europe's highest pass (excluding the Caucasian passes) is the Col de Restefond (9193 ft *2802 m*) completed in 1962 with 21 hairpins between Jausiers and Saint Etienne-de-Tinée, France. It is usually closed between early October and early June. The highest motor road in Europe is the Pico de Veleta in the Sierra Nevada, southern Spain. The shadeless climb of 36 km *22.4 miles* brings the motorist to 11,384 ft *3469 m* above sea-level and became, on completion of a road on its southern side in Summer 1974, arguably Europe's highest 'pass'.

Highest Great Britain

The highest road in the United Kingdom is the A6293 unclassified tarmac, private extension at Great Dun Fell, Cumbria, (2780 ft *847 m*) leading to a Ministry of Defence and Air Traffic Control installation. A permit is required to use it. The highest public classified road in England is the A689 at Killhope Cross (2056 ft *626 m*) on the Cumbria–Durham border near Nenthead.

The highest classified road in Scotland is the A93 road over the Grampians through Cairnwell, a pass between Blairgowrie, Tayside, and Braemar, Grampian, which reaches a height of 2199 ft *670 m*. The highest classified road in Wales is the Rhondda-Afan Inter-Valley road (A4107), which reaches 1750 ft *533 m* 2½ miles *4 km* east of Abergwynfi, Mid Glamorgan. An estate track exists to the summit of Ben a'Bhuird (3860 ft *1176 m*) in Grampian, Scotland. The highest motorway in Great Britain is the trans-Pennine M62, which, at the Windy Hill interchange, reaches an altitude of 1220 ft *371 m*. Its Dean Head cutting is the deepest roadway cutting in Europe at 183 ft *55,7 m*.

Lowest

The lowest road in the world is that along the Israeli shores of the Dead Sea, 1290 ft *393 m* below sea-level. The lowest surface roads in Great Britain are just below sea-level in the Holme Fen area of Cambridgeshire. The world's lowest 'pass' is Rock Reef Pass, Everglades National Park, Florida which is 3 ft *91 cm* above sea-level.

Longest viaduct

The longest elevated road viaduct on the British road system is the 2.97 mile *4779 m* Gravelly Hill to Castle Bromwich section of the M6. It was completed in May 1972.

Biggest square

The Tian an men (Gate of Heavenly Peace) Square in Peking, described as the navel of China, extends over 98 acres *39,6 ha*. The Maiden e Shah in Isfahan, Iran extends over 20.1 acres *8,1 ha*. The oldest London Square is Lincoln's Inn Fields dating to the mid 17th century. The largest is the 6.99 acre *2,82 ha* Ladbroke Square (open to residents only) constructed in 1842–45 while Lincoln's Inn Fields measures 6.84 acres *2,76 ha*.

Traffic lights

Semaphore-type traffic *signals* had been set up in Parliament Square, London in 1868 with red and green gas lamps for night use. It was not an offence to disobey traffic signals until assent was given to the 1930 Road Traffic Bill. Traffic *lights* were introduced in Great Britain with a one-day trial in Wolverhampton on 11 Feb 1928. They were first permanently operated in Leeds, West Yorkshire on 16 Mar and in Edinburgh, Scotland on 19 Mar 1928. The first vehicle-actuated lights were installed by Plessey at the Cornhill–Gracechurch junction, City of London in April 1932.

Parking meters

The earliest parking meters ever installed were those put in the business district of Oklahoma City, Oklahoma, USA, on 19 July 1935. They were the invention of Carl C. Magee (USA) and reached London in 1958.

Worst driver

It was reported that a 75-year-old *male* driver received 10 traffic tickets, drove on the wrong side of the road four times, committed four hit-and-run offences and caused six accidents, all within 20 minutes, in McKinney, Texas, USA on 15 Oct 1966. The most heavily banned driver in Britain was John Hogg, 28, who, in the High Court, Edinburgh on 27 Nov 1975, received 5¾ years in gaol and his 3rd, 4th and 5th life bans for drunken driving in a stolen car while disqualified. For his previous 40 offences he had received bans of 71½ years plus two life bans.

Milestone

Britain's oldest milestone *in situ* is a Roman stone dating from AD 150 on the Stanegate, at Chesterholme, near Bardon Mill, Northumberland.

Longest ford

The longest ford in any classified road in England is the Longwater Ford near Wookey, Somerset, which measures more than 105 yards, *96 m*.

Inland waterways

The country with the greatest length of inland waterways is Finland. The total length of navigable lakes and rivers is about 50 000 km *31,000 miles*. In the United Kingdom the total length of navigable rivers and canals is 3940 miles *6340 km*.

Longest navigable river

The longest navigable natural waterway in the world is the River Amazon, which sea-going vessels can ascend as far as Iquitos, in Peru, 2236 miles *3598 km* from the Atlantic seaboard. On a National Geographic Society expedition ending on 10 Mar 1969, Helen and Frank Schreider navigated downstream from San Francisco, Peru, a distance of 3845 miles *6187 km* to Bélem.

TELECOMMUNICATIONS

Telephones

The country with the greatest number of telephone lines is the United States, with 114,349,000 lines, equivalent to 483 for every 1000 people. This compares with the United Kingdom figure of 20,921,000 (31 Mar 1985) (sixth largest in the world to the USA, Japan, USSR, West Germany and France), or 371 per 1000 people. The territory with fewest reported telephone lines is Pitcairn Island with 24.

The greatest total of calls made in any country is in the United States, with 434,569 million (1837 calls per person) in 1984. The United Kingdom telephone service connected 24,842,400,000 calls, an average of 440 per person (1984/85).

The city with most telephones is New York City, NY, USA, with 5,808,145 (821 per 1000 people) at 1 Jan 1981. In 1981 Washington DC reached the level of 1727 telephones per 1000 people.

Telephones *Longest telephone cable*

The world's longest submarine telephone cable is the Commonwealth Pacific Cable (COMPAC), which runs for 9340 miles *15 032 km* from Sydney, Australia, *via* Norfolk Is, Fiji and the Hawaiian Islands to Port Alberni, Canada. It cost about £35,000,000 and was inaugurated on 2 Dec 1963. The final splice was made on 24 Mar 1984.

Telephone Directories

The world's most difficult directory to tear in half was that for Houston, Texas which runs to 2889 pages for 939,640 listings. It is now issued in 2 sections. The easiest would be that for Knippa, Texas—221 listings on 2 pages. The directory for Anguilla in 1972 was of 26 numbers in typescript.

Switchboard *largest*

The world's biggest switchboard is that in the Pentagon, Washington DC with 25,000 lines and an annual phone bill of $8.7 million.

Optical Fibre Record

The longest distance at which signals have been transmitted without repeaters is 251,6 km *156,3 miles* at the British Telecom research laboratory at Martlesham Heath, Suffolk in February 1985. The laser wavelength was 1525 nm and the rate was 35 mega bits/sec.

Postal services

The country with the largest mail in the world is the United States, whose population posted 140.1 billion letters and packages in 1985 when the US Postal Service employed 744,490 people with the world's largest civilian vehicle fleet of 200,811 cars and trucks. The United Kingdom total was 11,400 million letters and 203 million parcels in the year ending 31 Mar 1985.

The United States also takes first place in the average number of letters which each person posts during one year. The figure was 589 in 1985. The United Kingdom figure was 204 per head in 1985.

Postal address *Highest numbering*

The practice of numbering houses began on the Pont Notre Dame, Paris, France in 1463. The highest numbered house in Britain is No 2679 Stratford Road, Hockley Heath, West Midlands, owned since 1964 by Mr and Mrs Howard Hughes. The highest numbered house in Scotland is No 2629 London Road, Mount Vernon, Glasgow, which is part of the local police station.

Pillar-boxes *Oldest*

The oldest pillar-box still in service is one dating from 8 Feb 1853 in Union Street, St Peter Port, Guernsey. It was cast by John Vaudin in Jersey and was restored to its original maroon livery in October 1981. The oldest box in mainland Britain is at Barnes Cross, Holwell (postally in Bishop's Caundle), Dorset, dating from probably later in 1853. The hexagonal roof pillar box in Kent Railway Station, Glanmere, Cork dates from 1857.

Post Offices

The Post Office's northernmost post office is at Haroldswick, Unst, Shetland Islands. The most southerly in the British Isles is at Samarès,

The oldest pillar box still in service is posted in Union Street, St Peter Port, Guernsey. It has seen over 130 years of correspondence, dating back to February 1853. (Jersey Tourist Board).

Jersey. The oldest is at Sanquhar, Dumfries and Galloway which was first referred to in 1763. In England the Post Office at Shipton-Under-Wychwood, Oxon dates back to April 1845. The highest Post Office in England is at Flash, Staffordshire at 1518 ft *462,6 m.*

The longest counter in Britain was one of 185 ft *56,38 m* with 33 positions when opened in 1962 at Trafalgar Square, London. The longest in 1985 is at George Square, Glasgow, being 157 ft *47,8 m* long with 27 positions.

7. EDUCATION

Compulsory education was first introduced in 1819 in Prussia. It became compulsory in the United Kingdom in 1870.

University Oldest *World*

The Sumerians had scribal schools or *É-Dub-ba* soon after 3500 BC. The oldest existing educational institution in the world is the University of Karueein, founded in AD 859 in Fez, Morocco. The University of Bologna was founded in 1088.

University Oldest *Great Britain*

The oldest university in the United Kingdom is the University of Oxford, which came into being in *c.* 1167. The oldest of the existing colleges is probably University College (1249), though its foundation is less well documented than that of Merton College in 1264. The earliest college at Cambridge University is Peterhouse, founded in 1284. The largest college at either university is Trinity College, Cambridge. It was founded in 1546. The oldest university in Scotland is the University of St. Andrews, Fife. Established as a university in 1411, theology and medicine may have been taught there since *c.* 900 AD.

University *Greatest enrolment*

The university with the greatest enrolment in the world is the State University of New York, USA, with 156,175 students enrolled in 1984–1985. Its oldest college at Potsdam, New York was founded in 1816. Britain's largest university is the University of London with 40,274 internal students and 24,498 external students (in 1984–

POSTAGE STAMPS

EARLIEST	Put on sale at GPO 1 May 1840	1d Black of Great Britain, Queen Victoria, 68,158,080 printed. Available for prepayment of postage on 6 May 1840.
HIGHEST PRICE (TENDER) (WORLD)	$1 million (*then £495,000*)	5 cent Blue Alexandria USA cover, Nov 25 1846 by George Normann *via* David Feldmans of Geneva on 9 May 1981.
HIGHEST PRICE (AUCTION) (WORLD)	£615,000	Baden 9 kr black on blue-green, colour error 1851 from the John R. Boker collection sold by Heinrich Köhler in Weisbaden, West Germany on 16 Mar 1985.
HIGHEST PRICE (ERROR)	$500,000 (*£227,500*)	US 1918 24 cent airmail invert of Jenny biplane 'Princeton' block of 4, by Myron Kaller syndicate on 19 July 1979. A single example reached $180,000 at auction in New York City in May 1982.
HIGHEST PRICE (AUCTION) (UK)	£105,000	Norwegian 4 Skilling Blue, 1855 block of 39 used—found in Trondheim railway station *c.* 1923 sold by Phillips, New Bond St, London on 5 Mar 1981.
LARGEST PHILATELIC PURCHASE	$11,000,000 (*then £4,945,000*)	Marc Haas collection of 3000 US postal and pre-postal covers to 1869 by Stanley Gibbons International Ltd of London in August 1979.
LARGEST (SPECIAL PURPOSE)	9¾ × 2¾ in *247,5 × 69,8 mm*	Express Delivery of China, 1913.
(STANDARD POSTAGE)	6.3 × 4.33 in *160 × 110 mm*	Marshall Islands 75 cents issued 30 Oct 1979.
SMALLEST	0.31 × 0.37 in *8 × 9,5 mm*	10 cent and 1 peso Colombian State of Bolivar, 1863–6.
HIGHEST DENOMINATION (WORLD)	£100	Red and black, George V, of Kenya, 1925–7.
(UK)	£5	Orange, Victoria, issued 21 Mar 1882. Pink and Blue Elizabeth II definitive 2 Feb 1977.
LOWEST DENOMINATION	3,000 pengö of Hungary	Issued 1946 when 150 million million pengö = 1p.
RAREST (WORLD)	Unique examples include	British Guiana (now Guyana) 1 cent black on magenta of 1856 (see above); Swedish 3 skilling banco yellow colour error of 1855. Gold Coast provisional of 1885 and the US post-master stamp from Boscowen, New Haven and Lockport, NY.
RAREST (UK) (Issued for postal use)	11 or 12	6d dull purple Inland Revenue Edward VII, issued and withdrawn on 14 May 1904. Only unused specimen in private hands from W. H. Harrison-Cripps sold by Stanley Gibbons for £10,000 on 27 Oct 1972.

85) so totalling 64,772. The Open University, first called the University of the Air (Royal Charter 30 May 1969) at Walton Hall near Milton Keynes has 5520 part-time tutors and 126,750 students.

University *Largest*
Tenders for the $3.4 billion (*£1790 million*) University of Riyadh, Saudi Arabia closed in June 1978. The University will house 15,000 families and have its own mass transport system.

The largest existing university building in the world is the M. V. Lomonosov State University on the Lenin Hills, south of Moscow, USSR. It stands 240 m *787.4 ft* tall, has 32 storeys and 40,000 rooms. It was constructed in 1949–53.

University *Most northerly*
The world's most northerly university is Inupiat University of the Arctic Barrow, Alaska, USA in *Lat* 71° 16′ N. Eskimo subjects feature in the curricula.

Largest court or quadrangle
The largest College quadrangle at any Oxford or Cambridge college is the Great Court, Trinity College, Cambridge completed in 1605. It averages 325 ft × 273 ft *99,06 m × 83,2 m.*

Professor *Youngest*
The youngest at which anybody has been elected to a chair in a university is 19 years in the case of Colin MacLaurin (1698–1746), who was elected to Marischal College, Aberdeen as Professor of Mathematics on 30 Sept 1717. In 1725 he was made Professor of Mathematics at Edinburgh University on the recommendation of Sir Isaac Newton who was a professor at Cambridge aged 26.

Professors *Most durable*
Dr Joel Hildebrand (1881–1983), Professor Emeritus of Physical Chemistry at the University of California, Berkeley, became first an Assistant Professor in 1913 and published his 275th research paper 68 years later in 1981. The longest period of which any professorship has been held in Britain is 63 years in the case of Thomas Martyn (1735–1825), Professor of Botany at Cambridge University from 1762 until his death. The last professor-for-life was the pathologist Professor Henry Roy Dean (1879–1961) for his last 39 years at Cambridge.

Senior Wranglers
Since 1910 the Wranglers (first class honours students in the Cambridge University mathematical Tripos, part 2) have been placed in alphabetical order only. In 1890 Miss Philippa Garrett Fawcett (d. 1948) in Newnham was placed 'above the Senior Wrangler'.

Most Graduates in Family
Mr & Mrs Albert Kunz of Bloomington, Indiana, USA saw all their 8 daughters and 5 sons graduate from Indiana University between 1932 and 1956.

Youngest undergraduate and graduate
The most extreme recorded case of undergraduate juvenility was that of William Thomson (1824–1907), later Lord Kelvin, OM, GCVO, who entered Glasgow University aged 10 years 4 months in October 1834 and matriculated on 14 Nov 1834. Dr Merrill Kenneth Wolf (b. 28 Aug 1931) of Cleveland, Ohio took his B.A. in music from Yale University in September 1945 in the month of his 14th birthday. Ruth Lawrence (b. 1971) of Huddersfield, West Yorkshire passed Pure Mathematics O level at the age of 9 and Pure Mathematics A level and Grade 1 S level in June 1981 aged 10. She was accepted for entrance to Oxford at the age of 12 and graduated from St. Hugh's with a first class degree, top of 191 entrants, on 4 July 1985.

Youngest Doctorate
On 13 Apr 1814 the mathematician Carl Witte of Lochau was made a Doctor of Philosophy of the University of Giessen, Germany when aged 12.

Schools *Oldest in Britain*
The title of the oldest existing school in Britain is contested. It is claimed that King's School in Canterbury, Kent, was a foundation of Saint Augustine, some time between his arrival in Kent in AD 597 and his death in *c.* 604. Cor Tewdws (College of Theodosius) at Llantwit Major, South Glamorgan, reputedly burnt down in AD 446, was refounded, after an elapse of 62 years, by St Illtyd in 508 and flourished into the 13th century. Winchester College, Hampshire was founded in 1382. Lanark Grammar School, Strathclyde claims to have been referred to in a papal bull drawn up in 1183 by Lucius III.

School Largest *World*
In 1983/84 South Point High School, Calcutta, India (founded 1954) had an enrolment of 12,350 regular students.

Great Britain
The school with the most pupils in Great Britain was Exmouth Comprehensive, Devon with 2599 (1983–84). The highest enrolment in Scotland has been at Our Lady's Roman Catholic High School, Motherwell, Strathclyde with a peak of 2325 in August 1977. The total in Holy Child School, Belfast, Northern Ireland reached 2752 in 1973 before being split up. The highest enrolment in 1983/84 is 2329 at the Methodist College, Belfast.

School Most Expensive *World*
The annual cost of keeping a pupil at Le Rosey, Gstaad, Switzerland in 1983/84 was reputed to be $20,000.

Great Britain
In the academic year 1985–86 St. Andrew's Private Tutorial Centre, Cambridge, England (Director C. T. Easterbrook) charged £11,928 for full-time science students (tuition and accommodation). The most expensive school in Great Britain is Millfield (founded 1935) in Street, Somerset (headmaster C. R. M. Atkinson). The annual fee for boarding entries in 1985–6 is £7710. The most expensive girls' school in 1985 was Cobham Hall (founded 1960), Kent (headmistress Miss Susan Cameron), with annual fees of £5121.

Earliest Comprehensive School
Lakes School, Cumbria, formed from an intake from Windermere Grammar School and other Westmorland schools adopted the non-selective comprehensive principle as early as 1945. Calder High School was established after formal rejection of the 11 plus examinations from two West Riding schools in 1950. The earliest purpose-built was Kidbrooke Comprehensive for Girls, London SE opened in 1954.

Oldest old school tie
The practice of wearing distinctive neckties bearing the colours of registered designs of schools, universities, sports clubs, regiments, etc., appears to date from *c.* 1880. The practice originated in Oxford University, where boater bands were converted into use as 'ribbon ties'. The earliest definitive evidence stems from an order from Exeter College for college ties, dated 25 June 1880.

PTA Oldest
The Parent-Teacher Association with the earliest foundation date in Britain is St. Christopher School, Letchworth, Parents' Circle formed in 1919.

Most schools
The greatest documented number of schools attended by a pupil is 265 by Wilma Williams, now Mrs R. J. Horton, from 1933–43 when her parents were in show business in the USA.

Most 'O' and 'A' levels
Dr Francis L. Thomason of Hammersmith, London, had by March 1986 accumulated 69 O and O/A, 12 A and 1 S levels making a total of 82 of which 36 were in the top grade. A. F. Prime, a prisoner in HM Open Prison Sudbury, accumulated a total of 1 S, 14 A's and 34 O's between 1968 and 1982. Environmental difficulties tend to make study harder in prison than elsewhere.

Stephen Murrell of Crown Woods School, Eltham passed 8 A levels at one sitting in June 1978 achieving 7 at grade A. Robert Pidgeon (b. 7 Feb 1959) of St Peter's School, Bournemouth, secured 13 O level passes at grade A at one sitting in the summer of 1975. Subsequently he passed 3 A levels at grade A and 2 S levels with firsts. Andrew Maclaren (b. 1963) of Chelmsford, Essex passed 14 O levels, 5 A levels all at grade A and 3 S levels at grade one—making 22 top grades. At Queens' College, Cambridge he obtained first class honours in 1983.

Youngest headmaster
The youngest headmaster of a major public school was Henry Montagu Butler (b. 2 July 1833), appointed Headmaster of Harrow School on 16 Nov 1859, when aged 26 years 137 days. His first term in office began in January 1860.

Most durable don
Dr Martin Joseph Routh (b. Sept 1755) was President of Magdalen College, Oxford, from April 1791 for 63 years 8 months, until his death in his 100th year on 22 Dec 1854. He had previously been a fellow for 16 years and was thus a don for a span of 79 years.

Most durable teachers
David Rhys Davies (1835–1928) taught as a pupil teacher and latterly as teacher and headmaster of Dame Anna Child's School, Whitton, Powys (1879–1928) for a total of 76 years 2 months. Col Ernest Achey Loftus CBE, TD, DL (b. 11 Jan 1884) served as a teacher over a span of 73 years from May 1901 in York, England until 18 Feb 1975 in Zambia retiring as the world's oldest civil servant aged 91 years 38 days. His father William was born in Hull in the reign of William IV in 1832.

Elsie Marguerite Touzel (1889–1984) of Jersey began her teaching career aged 16 in 1905 and was teaching at Les Alpes School, Faldonet until her retirement 75 years later on 30 Sept 1980.

Most successful teacher
Cyril Leonard Mapley (b. 22 May 1923), Head of the Drawing Office at Tunbridge Wells Technical High School, Kent, has achieved an 'A' level pass rate unmatched by others. In 1981 49 out of 53 (91%) in his classes in their fifth year gained 'A' levels in one-eighth normal time and thus two years in advance of the entry age.

Highest Endowment
The greatest single gift in the history of higher education has been $125 million to Louisiana State University by C. B. Pennington in 1983.

8. RELIGIONS

Oldest
Human burial, which has religious connotations, is known from *c.* 60,000 BC among *Homo sapiens neanderthalensis* in the Shanidar cave, N. Iraq. The earliest named prophet was Zoroaster

(Zarathushtra) dated to *c.* 1600 BC. He has 250,000 followers today.

Largest

Religious statistics are necessarily only approximate. The test of adherence to a religion varies widely in rigour, while many individuals, particularly in the East, belong to two or more religions.

Christianity is the world's prevailing religion, with some 1,070,000,000 adherents in 1985. The Vatican statistics office reported that in 1983 there were 825,592,000 Roman Catholics.

The largest non-Christian religion is Islam (Muslim) with some 560,000,000 followers.

In the United Kingdom the Anglicans comprise members of the Established Church of England, the Dis-established Church in Wales, the Episcopal Church in Scotland and the Church of Ireland. The Church of England has two provinces (Canterbury and York), 44 dioceses, 10,643 full time diocesan clergymen and 13,369 parishes (1 Jan 1986).

In Scotland the most numerous group is the Church of Scotland (12 Synods, 47 Presbyteries), which had 870,527 members as at 1 Jan 1985.

Largest clergies

The world's largest religious organization is the Roman Catholic Church, with 152 Cardinals, 716 archbishops, 3076 bishops, 406,376 priests and 935,221 nuns in 1985. There are about 420,000 churches.

Jews

The total of world Jewry was estimated to be 16 million in 1985. The highest concentration is in North America, with 7.3 million, of whom 2.0 million are in the New York area. The total in Israel is 3,255,000. The total of British Jewry is 385,000 of whom 259,100 are in Greater London, and 11,000 in Glasgow, the largest concentration in Scotland. The total in Tōkyō, Japan, is only 400.

PLACES OF WORSHIP

Earliest *World*

A sculpted stone face, half primate/half feline, discovered by Dr Leslie Freeman of the University of Chicago in the El Juyo cave shrine, Northern Spain, is claimed to be the oldest known religious shrine and is dated to *c.* 12,000 BC. The oldest surviving Christian church in the world is a converted house in Douro-Europos now Qal'at es Salihiye in eastern Syria, dating from AD 232.

Oldest *Great Britain*

The oldest ecclesiastical building in the United Kingdom is a 6th century cell built by St Brendan in AD 542 on Eileachan Naoimh (pronounced Noo), Garvelloch Islands, Strathclyde. The Church in Great Britain with the oldest origins is St Martin's Church in Canterbury, Kent. It was built in AD 560 on the foundations of a 1st century Roman church. The chapel of St Peter on the Wall, Bradwell-on-Sea, Essex was built in AD 654–660. The oldest church in Ireland is the Gallerus Oratory, built in *c.* 750 at Ballyferriter, near Kilmalkedar, County Kerry. Britain's oldest nunnery is St Peter and Paul Minster, on the Isle of Thanet, Kent. It was founded in *c.* 748 by the Abbess Eadburga of Bugga. The oldest catholic church is St Etheldreda, Ely Place, Holborn, London founded in 1251. The oldest non-conformist chapel is the thatched chapel at Horningsham, Wiltshire dated 1566.

Temple Largest

The largest religious structure ever built is Angkor Wat (City Temple), enclosing 402 acres *162,6 ha* in Kampuchea, south-east Asia. It was built to the Hindu god Vishnu by the Khmer King Suryavarman II in the period 1113–50. Its curtain wall measures 1400 × 1400 yd *1280 × 1280 m* and its population, before it was abandoned in 1432, was 80,000. The whole complex of 72 major monuments begun *c.* AD 900 extends over 15 × 5 miles *24 × 8 km*. The largest Buddhist temple in the world is Borobudur, near Jogjakarta, Indonesia built in the 8th century. It is 103 ft *31,5 m* tall and 403 ft *123 m* square.

The largest Mormon temple is the Salt Lake Temple, Utah, USA dedicated on 6 Apr 1893 and with a floor area of 253,015 ft² or 5.80 acres *23 505 m²*.

Cathedral Largest *World*

The world's largest cathedral is the cathedral church of the Diocese of New York, St John the Divine, with a floor area of 121,000 ft² *11 240 m²* and a volume of 16,822,000 ft³ *476 350 m³*. The cornerstone was laid on 27 Dec 1892, and work on the Gothic building was stopped in 1941. Work re-started in earnest in July 1979. In New York it is referred to as 'Saint John the Unfinished'. The nave is the longest in the world, 601 ft *183,18 m* in length, with a vaulting 124 ft *37,79 m* in height.

The cathedral covering the largest area is that of Santa Mariá de la Sede in Sevilla (Seville), Spain. It was built in Spanish Gothic style between 1402 and 1519 and is 414 ft *126,18 m* long, 271 ft *82,60 m* wide and 100 ft *30,48 m* high to the vault of the nave.

Cathedral Largest *Great Britain*

The largest cathedral in the British Isles is the Cathedral Church of Christ in Liverpool. Built in modernized Gothic style, work was begun on 18 July 1904, and it was finally consecrated on 25 Oct 1978 after 74 years (*cf.* Exeter 95 years) using ½ million stone blocks and 12 million bricks at an actual cost of some £6 million. The building encloses 104,275 ft² *9687 m²* and has an overall length of 636 ft *193,85 m*. The Vestey Tower is 331 ft *100,88 m* high. It contains the highest vaulting in the world—175 ft *53,34 m* maximum at undertower and the highest Gothic arches ever built being 107 ft *32,61 m* at apices.

Cathedral Smallest

The smallest church in the world designated as a cathedral is that of the Christ Catholic Church, Highlandville, Missouri, USA. Consecrated in July 1983 it measures 14 × 17 ft *4,26 × 5,18 m* and has seating for 18 people. The smallest cathedral in use in the United Kingdom (of old foundation) is St Asaph in Clwyd, Wales, it is 182 ft *55,47 m* long, 68 ft *20,72 m* wide and has a tower 100 ft *30,48 m* high. Oxford Cathedral in Christ Church (College) is 155 ft *47,24 m* long. The nave of the Cathedral of the Isles on the Isle of Cumbrae, Strathclyde measures only 40 × 20 ft *12,19 × 6,09 m*. The total floor area is 2,124 ft² *197,3 m²*.

Church Largest *World*

The largest church in the world is the basilica of St Peter, built between 1492 and 1612 in the Vatican City, Rome. The length of the church, measured from the apse, is 611 ft 4 in *186,33 m*. The area is 162,990 ft² *15 142 m²*. The inner diameter of the famous dome is 137 ft 9 in *41,98 m* and its centre is 119 m *390 ft 5 in* high. The external height is 457 ft 9 in *139,52 m*.

The elliptical Basilique of St Pie X at Lourdes, France, completed in 1957 at a cost of £2,000,000 has a capacity of 20,000 under its giant span arches and a length of 200 m *656 ft*.

The crypt of the underground Civil War Memorial Church in the Guadarrama Mountains, 45 km *28 miles* from Madrid, Spain, is 260 m *853 ft* in length. It took 21 years (1937–58) to build, at a reported cost of £140,000,000, and is surmounted by a cross 150 m *492 ft* tall.

Church Largest *Great Britain*

The largest Church in the United Kingdom is the Collegiate Church of St Peter at Westminster built AD 1050–1745. Its maximum dimensions are overall: length 530 ft *161,5 m*; breadth across transept 203 ft *61,87 m* and internal height 101 ft 8 in *30,98 m*. The largest parish church is the Parish Church of the Most Holy and Undivided Trinity at Kingston-upon-Hull covering 27,235 ft² *2530 m²* and with an external length and width of 288 ft × 124 ft *87,7 × 37,7 m*. It is also believed to be the country's oldest brick building serving its original purpose, dating from *c.* 1285. Both the former Cathedral of St Mungo, Glasgow and Beverley Minster, Hum-

---

berside are now used as parish churches. The largest school chapel is that of the 150 ft *45,7 m* high Lancing College, West Sussex with a capacity of 600.

Church Smallest *World*

The world's smallest church is the Union Church at Wiscasset, Maine, USA, with a floor area of 31½ ft² *2,92 m²* (7 × 4½ ft *2,13 × 1,37 m*). St. Gobban's Church, Portbradden, County Antrim, Northern Ireland measures 12 ft 1½ in by 6 ft 6 in *3,7 × 2,0 m*.

Church Smallest *Great Britain*

The smallest church in use in England is Bremilham Church, Cowage Farm, Foxley near Malmesbury, Wiltshire which measures 12 × 12 ft *3,65 × 3,65 m* and is used for service once a year. The smallest completed medieval English church in regular use is that at Culbone, Somerset, which measures 35 × 12 ft *10,66 × 3,65 m*. The smallest Welsh chapel is St Trillo's Chapel, Rhôs-on-Sea (Llandrillo-yn-Rhôs), Clwyd, measuring only 12 × 6 ft *3,65 × 1,83 m*. The smallest chapel in Scotland is St Margaret's, Edinburgh, measuring 16½ × 10½ ft *5,02 × 3,20 m*, giving a floor area of 173¼ ft² *16,09 m²*.

Synagogue Largest *World*

The largest synagogue in the world is the Temple Emanu-El on Fifth Avenue at 65th Street, New York City, NY, USA. The temple, completed in September 1929, has a frontage of 150 ft *45,72 m* on Fifth Avenue and 253 ft *77,11 m* on 65th Street. The Sanctuary proper can accommodate 2500 people, and the adjoining Beth-El Chapel seats 350. When all the facilities are in use, more than 6000 people can be accommodated.

Synagogue Largest *Great Britain*

The largest synagogue in Great Britain is the Edgware Synagogue, Barnet, Greater London, completed in 1959, with a capacity of 1630 seats. That with highest registered membership is Ilford Synagogue with 2492 at 1 Jan 1983.

Mosque Largest

The largest mosque ever built was the now ruinous al-Malawiya mosque of al-Mutawakil in Samarra, Iraq built in AD 842–52 and measuring 9.21 acres *3,72 ha* with dimensions of 784 × 512 ft *238,9 × 156,0 m*. The world's largest mosque in use is the Umayyad Mosque in Damascus, Syria built on a 2000-year-old religious site measuring 157 × 97 m *515 × 318 ft* thus covering an area of 3.76 acres *1,52 ha*. The largest mosque will be the Merdeka Mosque in Djakarta, Indonesia, which was begun in 1962. The cupola will be 45 m *147.6 ft* in diameter and the capacity in excess of 50,000 people.

Minaret *Tallest*

The tallest minarets in the world are the 4 of 105 m *344 ft 5 in* being built for a new mosque in Shah Alam, Selangor, Malaysia. The Qutb Minar, south of New Delhi, India, built in 1194 is 238 ft *72,54 m* tall.

Pagoda *Tallest and Oldest*

The world's tallest pagoda is the Phra Pathom Chedi at Nakhon Pathom, Thailand, which was built for King Mongkut in 1853–70. It rises to 115 m *377 ft*. The oldest pagoda in China is Sung-Yo Ssu in Honan built with 15 12-sided storeys, in AD 523 though the 326 ft *99,3 m* tall Shwedagon Pagoda, Rangoon, Burma is built on the site of a 27 ft *8,2 m* tall pagoda of 585 BC.

Sacred Object *Most Valuable*

The sacred object with the highest intrinsic value is the 15th century gold Buddah in Wat Trimitr Temple in Bangkok, Thailand. It is 10 ft *3,04 m* tall and weighs an estimated 5½ tonnes.

At $500 per fine ounce its intrinsic worth has been put at £28½ million. The gold under the plaster exterior was only found in 1954.

Nave *Longest*

The longest nave in the United Kingdom is that of St Albans Cathedral, Hertfordshire, which is 285 ft *86,86 m* long. The central tower of Liverpool's Anglican Cathedral (internal overall length 636 ft *193,85 m*) interrupts the nave with an undertower space.

Spire Tallest *World*

The tallest cathedral spire in the world is that of the Protestant Cathedral of Ulm in Germany. The building is early Gothic and was begun in 1377. The tower, in the centre of the west façade, was not finally completed until 1890 and is 160,90 m *528 ft* high. The world's tallest church spire is that of the Chicago Temple of the First Methodist Church on Clark Street, Chicago, Illinois, USA. The building consists of a 22-storey skyscraper (erected in 1924) surmounted by a parsonage at 330 ft *100,5 m*, a 'Sky Chapel' at 400 ft *121,92 m* and a steeple cross at 568 ft *173,12 m* above street level.

Great Britain

The highest spire in Great Britain is that of the church of St Mary, called Salisbury Cathedral, Wiltshire. The Lady Chapel was built in the years 1220–5 and the main fabric of the cathedral was finished and consecrated in 1258. The spire was added later, *ante* 1305, and reaches a height of 404 ft *123,13 m*. The central spire of Lincoln Cathedral completed in *c.* 1307 and which fell in 1548 was 525 ft *160,02 m* tall.

Stained glass *Oldest*

Pieces of stained glass dated before 850 AD possibly some even to the 7th century excavated nearby by Prof. Rosemary Cramp were placed into a window of that date in St Paul's Church, Jarrow, County Durham.The oldest complete stained glass in the world represents the Prophets in a window of the cathedral of Augsburg, Bavaria, Germany, dating from the second half of the 11th century. The oldest datable stained glass in the United Kingdom has been represented by a figure of St Michael in All Saints Church, Dalbury, Derbyshire of the late 11th century.

Stained glass *Largest*

The largest stained glass window is the complete mural of The Resurrection Mausoleum in Justice, Illinois, measuring 22,381 ft² *2079 m²* in 2448 panels completed in 1971. The back-lit glass mural installed in 1979 in the atrium of the Ramada Hotel, Dubai is 135 ft *41,14 m* high. The largest single stained glass window in Great Britain is the East window in Gloucester Cathedral measuring 72 × 38 ft *21,94 × 11,58 m*, set up to commemorate the Battle of Crécy (1346), while the largest area of stained glass is 128 lights, totalling 25,000 ft² *2 322 m²* in York Minster.

Brasses

The world's oldest monumental brass is that commemorating Bishop Yso von Wölpe in Andreaskirche, Verden, near Hanover, W. Germany, dating from 1231. An engraved coffin plate of St Ulrich (d. 973), laid in 1187, was found buried in the Church of SS Ulrich and Afra, Augsburg, W. Germany in 1979. The oldest brass in Great Britain is of Sir John D'Abernon (d. 1277) at Stoke D'Abernon, near Leatherhead, Surrey, dating from *c.* 1320.

A dedication brass dated 24 Apr 1241 in Ashbourne church, Derbyshire has been cited as the earliest arabic writing extant in Britain.

The oldest complete stained glass window in the United Kingdom dates back to the late 11th century and can still be seen in the Church of St Mary the Virgin, Brabourne, Kent. (Martin of Smeeth).

CHURCH PERSONNEL

Saints

There are 1848 'registered' saints (including 60 St Johns) of whom 628 are Italians, 576 French and 271 from the United Kingdom and Ireland. Of these 8 came from Cambridge and 7 from Oxford between 1535 and 1645 but none from the House of Commons. Britain's first Christian martyr was St Alban executed *c.* AD.209. The first US born saint is Mother Elizabeth Ann Bayley Seton (1774–1821) canonized 14 Sept 1975. The total includes 76 Popes.

Most rapidly canonized

The shortest interval that has elapsed between the death of a Saint and his canonization was in the case of St Anthony of Padua, Italy, who died on 13 June 1231 and was canonized 352 days later on 30 May 1232. For the other extreme of 857 years see Papal table.

Bishopric *Longest tenure*

The longest tenure of any Church of England bishopric is 57 years in the case of the Rt Rev. Thomas Wilson, who was consecrated Bishop of Sodar and Man on 16 Jan 1698 and died in office on 7 Mar 1755. Of English bishoprics the longest tenures, if one excludes the unsubstantiated case of Aethelwulf, reputedly Bishop of Hereford from 937 to 1012, are those of 47 years by Jocelin de Bohun (Salisbury) 1142–89 and Nathaniel Crew or Crewe (Durham) 1674–1721.

Bishop *Oldest*

The oldest serving bishop (excluding Suffragans and Assistants) in the Church of England as at April 1986 was the Right Reverend Richard David Say, Bishop of Rochester, who was born on 4 Oct 1914.

The oldest Roman Catholic bishop in recent years has been Bishop Angelo Teutonico, formerly Bishop of Aversa (b. 28 Aug 1874), who died aged 103 years 276 days on 31 May 1978. He had celebrated Mass about 24,800 times. Bishop Herbert Welch of the United Methodist Church, who was elected a bishop for Japan and Korea in 1916, died on 4 Apr 1969 aged 106.

Bishop *Youngest*

The youngest bishop of all time was HRH The Duke of York and Albany, KG, GCB, GCH, the second son of George III, who was elected Bishop of Osnabrück, through his father's influence as Elector of Hanover, at the age of 196 days on 27 Feb 1764. He resigned after 39 years' enjoyment. The youngest serving bishop (excluding Suffragans and Assistants) in the Church of England is the Rev Dr David Hope (b. 14 Apr 1940) whose appointment to the See of Wakefield was announced on 2 July 1985. The Bishop Suffragen of Taunton The Ven. Nigel McCulloch was born 17 Jan 1942.

Oldest parish priest

Father Alvaro Fernandez (b. 8 Dec 1880) served as a parish priest at Santiago de Abres, Spain from 1919 and continued into his 105th year. The oldest Anglican clergyman the Rev Clement Williams (b. 30 Oct 1879) died aged 106 years 3 months on 3 Feb 1986. He lined the route at Queen Victoria's funeral and was ordained in 1904.

Longest incumbency

The longest Church of England incumbency on record is one of 75 years 357 days by the Rev. Bartholomew Edwards, Rector of St Nicholas, Ashill, Norfolk from 1813 to 1889. There appears to be some doubt as to whether the Rev. Richard Sherinton was installed at Folkestone from 1524 or 1529 to 1601. If the former is correct it would surpass the Norfolk record. The parish of Farrington, Hampshire had only two incumbents in a 122 year period *viz* Rev. J. Benn (28 Mar 1797 to 1857) and Rev. T. H. Massey (1857 to 5 Apr 1919). From 1675 to 1948 the incumbents of Rose Ash, Devon were from 8 generations of the family of Southcomb.

Longest serving chorister

Harry Phillips (1884–1983) joined the choir of St Michael and All Angels West Felton, Shropshire in 1893 aged 8. He was still serving as a chorister 90 years later in April 1983. Having become a chorister in 1876 at the age of 9, Thomas Rogers was appointed vicar's warden in 1966 at Montacute, Somerset.

Sunday School

Sunday Schools were established by Congregationalists in Neath and Tirdwyncyn, Wales in 1697. Roland E. Daab (b. 25 Mar 1914) now of St. Paul United Church of Christ, Columbia, Illinois, USA has attended for 3486 consecutive Sundays without a miss for 67 years to 15 Sept 1985.

Parishes *Largest and Smallest*

The smallest parish in the United Kingdom is The Scares which consists of rocky islets in Luce Bay with an area of 1.10 acres *0.44 ha* and included in Wigtown, Dumfries and Galloway. In 1982 the parish of Dallinghoo Wield, Suffolk boasted a population of nil and an area of 38 acres *14,6 ha*. The largest parish is Kilmonivaig in Inverness, Highland with an area of 267,233.03 acres *108 145,46 ha*.

Oldest parish register

The oldest part of any parish register surviving in England contains entries from the summer of 1538. There is a sheet from that of Alfriston, East Sussex recording a marriage on 10 July 1504 but this is amid entries from 1547. Scotland's oldest surviving register is that for Anstruther-Wester, Fife, with burial entries from 1549.

Crowds *Largest*

The greatest recorded number of human beings assembled with a common purpose was an estimated 12,700,000 at the Hindu festival of Kumbh-Mela, which was held at the confluence of the Yamuna (formerly called the Jumna), the Ganges and the invisible 'Sarasvati' at Allahabad, Uttar Pradesh, India, on 19 Jan 1977. The holiest time during this holiest day since 1833 was during the planetary alignment between 9.28 and 9.40 a.m. during which only 200,000 achieved immersion to wash away the sins of a lifetime. The queue at the grave of the chansonier and guitarist Vladimir Visotsky (died 28 July 1980), stretched 10 km *6.2 miles*.

Largest funerals

The funeral of the charismatic C. N. Annadurai (died 3 Feb 1969) Madras Chief Minister was, according to a police estimate attended by 15 million. The longest funeral in Britain was probably that of Vice Admiral Viscount Nelson on 9 Jan 1806. Ticket-holders were seated in St Paul's Cathedral by 8.30 a.m. Many were unable to leave until after 9 p.m.

Biggest demonstrations

A figure of 2.7 million was published from China for the demonstration against the USSR in Shanghai on 3–4 Apr 1969 following the border clashes, and one of 10 million for the May Day celebrations of 1963 in Peking.

A reported 15 million attended the funeral of C. N. Annadurai in February 1969. As Chief Minister of Madras, he gained his immense popularity for starting a people's movement. (The Hindu/Camera Press).

9. ACCIDENTS AND DISASTERS

WORST IN THE WORLD

DISASTER	NUMBER KILLED	LOCATION	DATE
Pandemic	75,000,000	Eurasia: The Black Death (bubonic, pneumonic and septicaemic plague)	1347–51
Genocide	c. 35,000,000	Mongol extermination of Chinese Peasantry	1311–40
Famine	c. 30,000,000[1]	Northern China	1959–61
Influenza	21,640,000	Worldwide: Influenza	April–Nov 1918
Earthquake	1,100,000	Near East and E. Mediterranean (see p. 53)	c. July 1201
Circular Storm[2]	1,000,000	Ganges Delta Islands, Bangladesh	12–13 Nov 1970
Flood	900,000	Hwang-ho River, China	Oct 1887
Landslide	180,000	Kansu Province, China	16 Dec 1920
Atomic Bomb	141,000	Hiroshima, Japan	6 Aug 1945
Conventional Bombing[3]	c. 140,000	Tokyo, Japan	10 Mar 1945
Volcanic Eruption	92,000	Tambora Sumbawa, Indonesia	5–7 April 1815
Avalanches	c. 18,000[4]	Yungay, Huascarán, Peru	31 May 1970
Marine (single ship)	c. 7700	Wilhelm Gustloff (25,484 tons) German Liner torpedoed off Danzig by USSR submarine S-13	30 Jan 1945
Dam Burst	c. 5000[5]	Manchhu River Dam, Morvi, Gujarat, India	11 Aug 1979
Panic	c. 4000[6]	Chungking (Zhong qing) China air raid shelter	c. 8 June 1941
Smog	2,850	London fog, England (excess deaths)	5–13 Dec 1951
Tunnelling (Silicosis)	c. 2500	Hawk's Nest hydroelectric tunnel, W. Virginia, USA	1931–35
Industrial (Chemical)	c. 2500[7]	Union Carbide Methylisocyanate plant, Bhopal, India	2–3 Dec 1984
Explosion	1963[8]	Halifax, Nova Scotia, Canada	6 Dec 1917
Fire[9] (single building)	1670	The Theatre, Canton, China	May 1845
Mining[10]	1572	Hinkeiko Colliery, China (coal dust explosion)	26 April 1942
Riot	c. 1200	New York anti-conscription riots	13–16 July 1863
Road[11]	c. 1100	Petrol tanker explosion inside Salang Tunnel, Afghanistan	2 or 3 Nov 1982
Mass Suicide	913	People's Temple cult by cyanide, Jonestown, Guyana	18 Nov 1978
Crocodiles	c. 900	Japanese soldiers, Ramree I., Burma (disputed)	19–20 Feb 1945
Railway	>800	Bagmati River, Bihar state, India	6 June 1981
Fireworks	>800	Daupine's Wedding, Seine, Paris	16 May 1770
Tornado	689	South Central States, USA (3 hours)	18 Mar 1925
Aircraft (Civil)[12]	583	KLM-Pan Am Boeing 747 ground crash, Tenerife	27 Mar 1977
Man-eating Animal	436	Champawat district, India, tigress shot by Col. Jim Corbet (d. 1955)	1907
Terrorism	329	Bomb aboard Air-India Boeing 747, crashed into Atlantic south of Ireland. Sikh extremists suspected	23 June 1985
Bacteriological & Chemical Warfare	c. 300	Novosibirsk B & CW plant, USSR	April–May 1979
Hail	246	Moredabad, Uttar Pradesh, India	20 April 1888
Off-Shore Oil Plant	123	Alexander L. Kielland 'Flotel' (10,105 tons), North Sea	27 Mar 1980
Submarine	130	Le Surcouf rammed by US merchantman Thomas Lykes in Caribbean	18 Feb 1942
Helicopter	54	Israel military 'Sea Stallion', West Bank	10 May 1977
Ski Lift (Cable car)	42	Cavalese resort, Northern Italy	9 Mar 1976
Mountaineering	40[13]	USSR Expedition on Mount Everest	Dec 1952
Nuclear Reactor	28[14]	Chernobyl No 4, Ukraine, USSR	25 Apr 1986
Elevator (Lift)	23	Vaal Reefs Gold mine lift fell 1.2 miles 1,93 km.	27 Mar 1980
Lightning	21	Hut in Chinamasa Krael nr. Umtali, Zimbabwe (single bolt)	23 Dec 1975
Yacht Racing	19	28th Fastnet Race—23 boats sank or abandoned in Force 11 gale	13–15 Aug 1979
Space Exploration	3	Apollo oxygen fire, Cape Kennedy, Fla., USA	27 Jan 1967
	3	Soyuz II re-entry over USSR	29 June 1971
Nuclear Waste Accident	high but undisclosed[15]	Venting of plutonium extraction wastes, Kyshtym, USSR	c. Dec 1957

WORST IN THE UNITED KINGDOM

DISASTER	NUMBER KILLED	LOCATION	DATE
Famine	1,500,000[1]	Ireland (famine and typhus)	1846–51
Pandemic	800,000	The Black Death (bubonic, pneumonic and septicaemic plague)	1347–50
Influenza	225,000	Influenza	Sept–Nov 1918
Circular Storm	c. 8000	'The Channel Storm'	26 Nov 1703
Smog	2,850	London fog (excess deaths)	5–13 Dec 1951
Flood	c. 2000[2]	Severn Estuary	20 Jan 1606
Conventional bombing	1436	London	10–11 May 1941
Marine (single ship)	c. 800[3]	HMS Royal George, off Spithead	29 Aug 1782
Riot	565 (min)	London anti-Catholic Gordon riots	2–13 June 1780
Mining	439	Universal Colliery, Senghenydd, Mid Glamorgan	14 Oct 1913
Dam Burst	250	Bradfield Reservoir, Dale Dyke, near Sheffield, South Yorkshire (embankment burst)	12 Mar 1864
Railway	227[4]	Triple collision, Quintins Hill, Dumfries & Galloway	22 May 1915
Fire (single building)	188[5]	Theatre Royal, Exeter	5 Sept 1887
Panic	183	Victoria Hall, Sunderland, Tyne and Wear	16 June 1883
Landslide	144	Pantglas coal tip No 7, Aberfan, Mid Glamorgan	21 Oct 1966
Explosion	134[6]	Chilwell, Notts. (explosive factory)	1 July 1918
Aircraft (Civil)	118[7]	BEA Trident 1C, Staines, Surrey	18 June 1972
Submarine	99	HMS Thetis, during trials, Liverpool Bay	1 June 1939
Tornado	75	Tay Bridge collapsed under impact of two tornadic vortices	28 Dec 1879
Nuclear Reactor	39	Excess cancer deaths to 1977 Winscale (now Sellafield), Cumbria	10 Oct 1957
Road	33	Coach crash, River Dibb, nr Grassington, North Yorks	27 May 1975
Lightning	31	(Annual total) Worst year on record (annual av. 12)	1914
Off-Shore Oil Plant	24	Alexander L. Kielland 'Flotel' (10,105 tons), North Sea	27 Mar 1980
Terrorism	21	Birmingham Pub bombs (IRA)	21 Nov 1974
Yacht Racing	19	28th Fastnet Race—23 boats sank or abandoned in Force 11 gale. Of 316 starters only 128 finished	13–15 Aug 1979
Avalanches	8	Lewes, East Sussex	27 Dec 1836
Mountaineering	6	On Cairngorm, Scotland (4084 ft)	21 Nov 1971
Earthquake	2	London Earthquake, Christ's Hospital (Newgate)	6 April 1580

WORST IN WORLD FOOTNOTES

[1] It has been estimated that more than 5 million died in the post-World War I famine of 1920–1 in the USSR. The USSR government in July 1923 informed Mr (later President) Herbert Hoover that the ARA (American Relief Administration) had since August 1921 saved 20 million lives from famine and famine diseases.

[2] This figure published in 1972 for the Bangladeshi disaster was from Dr Afzal, Principal Scientific Officer of the Atomic Energy Authority Centre, Dacca. One report asserted that less than half of the population of the 4 islands of Bhola, Charjabbar, Hatia and Ramagati (1961 Census 1.4 million) survived. The most damaging hurricane recorded was Hurricane Gloria on 26–28 Sept 1985 with estimated insurance losses of £3,500 million.

[3] The number of civilians killed by the bombing of Germany has been put variously as 593,000 and 'over 635,000' including 550,000 deaths in the raids of Dresden, Germany on 13–15 Feb 1945. Total Japanese fatalities were 600,000 (conventional) and 220,000 (nuclear).

[4] A total of 18,000 Austrian and Italian troops were reported to have been lost in the Dolomite valleys of Northern Italy on 13 Dec 1916 in more than 100 snow avalanches. Some of the avalanches were triggered by gun-fire.

[5] The dynamiting of a Yangtze Kiang dam at Huayuan Kow by the KMT during the Sino-Japanese war in 1938 is reputed to have resulted in 900,000 deaths.

[6] It was estimated that some 5000 people were trampled to death in the stampede for free beer at the coronation celebration of Czar Nicholas II in Moscow in May 1896.

[7] Final death roll obscured by litigation.

[8] Some sources maintain that the final death roll was over 3000 on 6–7 Dec. Published estimates of the 11,000 killed at the BASF chemical plant explosion at Oppau, W. Germany on 21 Sept 1921 were exaggerated. The best estimate is 561 killed.

[9] > 200,000 killed in the sack of Moscow, freed by the Tartars in May 1571. Worst ever hotel fire 162 killed, Hotel Daeyungak, Seoul, South Korea 25 Dec 1971. Worst Circus fire 168 killed Hartford, Conn. USA 6 July 1944.

[10] The worst gold mining disaster in South Africa was 152 killed due to flooding in the Witwatersrand Gold Mining Co. Gold Mine in 1909.

[11] Some estimates ran as high as 2700 victims from carbon monoxide asphyxiation after Soviet military sealed both ends of the 1.7 mile 2,7 km long tunnel. The worst ever years for road deaths in the USA and the UK were respectively 1969 (56,400) and 1941 (9169). The global aggregate death roll was put at 25 million by September 1975. The world's highest death rate is 29 per 100,000 in 1978 in Luxembourg and Portugal. The greatest pile-up on British roads was on the M6 near Lymm Interchange, near Thelwell, involving 200 vehicles on 13 Sept 1971 with 11 dead and 60 injured.

[12] The crash of JAL's Boeing 747, flight 123, near Tokyo on 12 Aug 1985, in which 520 passengers and crew perished, was the worst single plane crash in aviation history.

[13] According to Polish sources, not confirmed by the USSR. Also 23 died on Mount Fuji, Japan, in blizzard and avalanche on 20 Mar 1972.

[14] Explosion at 0123 hrs Soviet European time 26 Apr 1986. The total excess cancer deaths from Chernobyl will not become apparent for many years but are certain to constitute the worst ever such disaster.

[15] More than 30 small communities in a 1200 km^2 460 mile^2 area eliminated from USSR maps since 1958. Possibly an ammonium nitrate-hexone explosion.

WORST IN UK FOOTNOTES

[1] Based on the net rate of natural increase between 1841 and 1851, a supportable case for a loss of population of 3 million can be made out if rates of under-enumeration of 25 per cent (1841) and 10 per cent (1851) are accepted. Potato rot (Phytophthora infestans) was first reported on 13 Sept 1845.

[2] Death rolls of 100,000 were reputed in England and Holland in the floods of 1099, 1421 and 1446.

[3] c. 2800 were lost on HM Troopship Lancastria 16,243 tons off St. Nazaire on 17 June 1940. The Princess Alice collision in the Thames with the Bywell Castle off Woolwich on 3 Sept 1878 killed 786.

[4] The 213 yd 194.7 m long troop train was telescoped to 67 yd 61,2 m. Signalmen Meakin and Tinsley were sentenced for manslaughter. Britain's worst underground train disaster was the Moorgate Tube disaster of 28 Feb 1975 when 43 were killed.

[5] In July 1212, 3000 were killed in the crush, burned or drowned when London Bridge caught fire at both ends. The death roll in the Great Fire of London of 1666 was only 8. History's first 'fire storm' occurred in the Quebec Yard, Surrey Docks, Southwark, London during the 300-pump fire in the Blitz on 7–8 Sept 1940. Dockland casualties were 306 killed. Britain's most destructive fire was the £165 million loss at the Army Ordnance depot, Donnington, Shropshire in June 1982.

[6] HM Armed Cruiser Natal blew up off Invergordon killing 428 on 30 Dec 1915.

[7] The worst crash by a UK operated aircraft was that of the Dan-Air Boeing 727 from Manchester which crashed into a mountain in the Canary Islands on 25 Apr 1980 killing 146 people. There were no survivors.

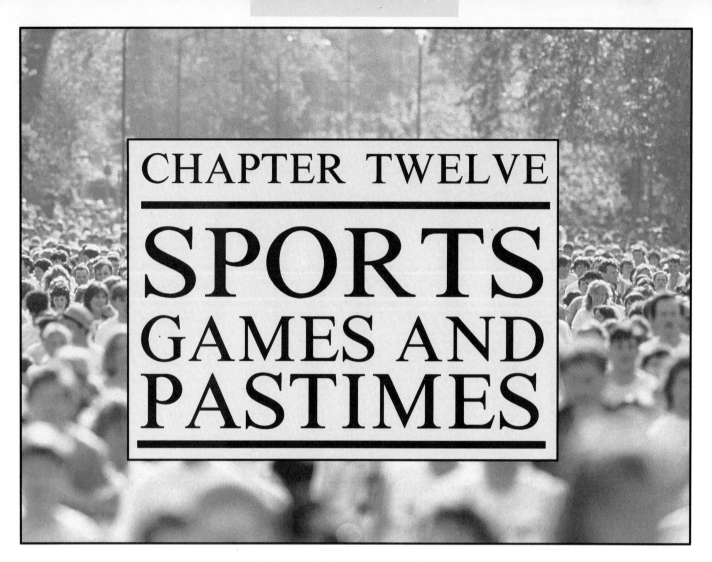

CHAPTER TWELVE
SPORTS GAMES AND PASTIMES

Earliest

The origins of sport stem from the time when self-preservation ceased to be the all-consuming human preoccupation. Archery was a hunting skill in mesolithic times (by *c.* 8000 BC), but did not become an organised sport until later, certainly *c.* AD 300, among the Genoese and possibly as early as the 12th century BC, as an archery competition is described in Homer's Iliad. The earliest dated evidence for sport is *c.* 2750–2600 BC for wrestling. Ball games by girls depicted on Middle Kingdom murals at Beni Hasan, Egypt have been dated to *c.* 2050 BC.

Fastest

The highest speed reached in a non-mechanical sport is in sky-diving, in which a speed of 185 mph *298 km/h* is attained in a head-down free falling position, even in the lower atmosphere. In delayed drops speeds of 625 mph *1005 km/h* have been recorded at high rarefied altitudes. The highest projectile speed in any moving ball game is *c.* 188 mph *302 km/h* in pelota. This compares with 170 mph *273 km/h* (electronically-timed) for a golf ball driven off a tee.

Slowest

In wrestling, before the rules were modified towards 'brighter wrestling', contestants could be locked in holds for so long that a single bout once lasted for 11 hr 40 min. In the extreme case of the 2 hr 41 min pull in the regimental tug o' war in Jubbulpore, India, on 12 Aug 1889, the winning team moved a net distance of 12 ft *3,6 m* at an average speed of 0.00084 mph *0,00135 km/h*.

Longest

The most protracted sporting contest was an automobile duration test of 222,621 miles

358 273 km (equivalent to 8.93 times around the equator) by Appaurchaux and others in a Ford Taunus at Miranas, France. This was contested over 142 days in July–Nov 1963.

The most protracted non-mechanical sporting event is the *Tour de France* cycling race. In 1926 this was over 3569 miles *5743 km* lasting 29 days but is now reduced to 23 days.

Largest pitch

The largest pitch of any ball game is that of polo, with 12.4 acres *5,0 ha*, or a maximum length of 300 yd *274 m* and a width, without side boards, of 200 yd *182 m*. With boards the width is 160 yd *146 m*. Twice a year in the Parish of St Columb Major, Cornwall, a game called Hurling (not to be confused with the Irish game) is played on a 'pitch' which consists of the entire Parish, approximately 25 square miles *64,7 km²*.

Youngest and oldest world record breakers

The youngest at which anybody has broken a non-mechanical world record is 12 yr 298 days for Gertrude Caroline Ederle (USA) (b. 23 Oct 1906) with 13 min 19.0 sec for women's 880 yd freestyle swimming at Indianapolis, USA, on 17 Aug 1919. Gerhard Weidner (W. Germany) (b. 15 Mar 1933) set a 20 mile walk record on 25 May 1974, aged 41 yr 71 days.

Youngest and oldest champions

The youngest successful competitor in a world title event was a French boy, whose name is not recorded, who coxed the Netherlands' Olympic pair at Paris on 26 Aug 1900. He was not more than ten and may have been as young as seven.

The youngest individual Olympic winner was Marjorie Gestring (USA) (b. 18 Nov 1922), who took the springboard diving title at the age of 13 yr 268 days at the Olympic Games in Berlin on 12 Aug 1936. Oscar Gomer Swahn (Sweden) (1847–1927) was aged 64 yr 258 days when he won a gold medal in the 1912 Olympic Running Deer team shooting competition.

Youngest and oldest internationals

The youngest age at which any person has won international honours is eight years in the case of Joy Foster, the Jamaican singles and mixed doubles table tennis champion in 1958. The youngest British international has been diver Beverley Williams (b. 5 Jan 1957), who was 10 yr 268 days old when she competed against the USA at Crystal Palace, London, on 30 Sept 1967. It would appear that the greatest age at which anyone has actively competed for his country was 72 yr 280 days in the case of Oscar Swahn (see above) who won a silver medal for shooting in the Olympic Games at Antwerp on 26 July 1920. He qualified for the 1924 Games but was unable to participate due to illness. Britain's oldest international was Hilda Lorna Johnstone (b. 4 Sept 1902) who was 70 yr 5 days when she was placed twelfth in the Dressage competition at the 1972 Games.

Most versatile

Charlotte 'Lottie' Dod (1871–1960) won the Wimbledon Singles tennis title five times between 1887 and 1893, the British Ladies' Golf Championship in 1904, an Olympic silver medal for archery in 1908, and represented England at hockey in 1899. She also excelled at skating and tobogganing. Mildred 'Babe' Zaharias (*née* Didrikson) (1914–56) (USA) won two gold medals (80 m hurdles and javelin) and a silver (high jump) at the 1932 Olympic Games.

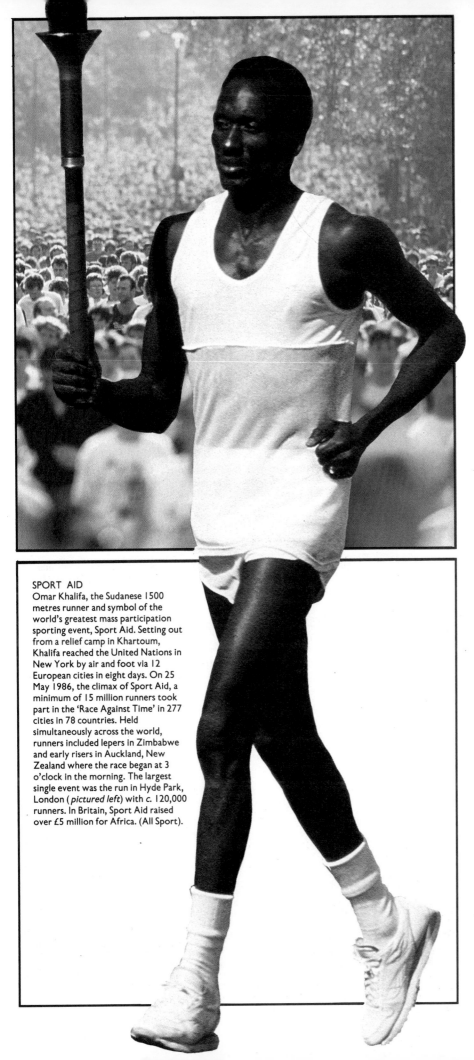

SPORT AID
Omar Khalifa, the Sudanese 1500 metres runner and symbol of the world's greatest mass participation sporting event, Sport Aid. Setting out from a relief camp in Khartoum, Khalifa reached the United Nations in New York by air and foot via 12 European cities in eight days. On 25 May 1986, the climax of Sport Aid, a minimum of 15 million runners took part in the 'Race Against Time' in 277 cities in 78 countries. Held simultaneously across the world, runners included lepers in Zimbabwe and early risers in Auckland, New Zealand where the race began at 3 o'clock in the morning. The largest single event was the run in Hyde Park, London (*pictured left*) with *c.* 120,000 runners. In Britain, Sport Aid raised over £5 million for Africa. (All Sport).

She set world records at those three events in 1930–32. She was an All-American basketball player for three years and set the world record for throwing the baseball 296 ft *90,22 m*. Switching to golf she won the US Women's Amateur title in 1946 and the US Women's Open in 1948, 1950 and 1954. She also excelled at several other sports. Charles Burgess Fry (GB) (1872–1956) was probably the most versatile male sportsman at the highest level. On 4 Mar 1893 he equalled the world long jump record of 23 ft 6½ in *7,17 m*. He represented England *v.* Ireland at soccer (1901) and played first-class rugby for the Barbarians. His greatest achievements were at cricket, where he headed the English batting averages in six seasons and captained England in 1912. He was also an excellent angler and tennis player.

Most prolific record breaker
Between 24 Jan 1970 and 1 Nov 1977 Vasili Alexeyev (USSR) (b. 7 Jan 1942) broke 80 official world records in weightlifting.

Longest reign
The longest reign as a world champion is 33 years (1829–62) by Jacques Edmond Barre (France) (1802–73) at real tennis. The longest reign as a British champion is 41 years by the archer Alice Blanche Legh (1855–1948) who won 23 national titles between 1881 and 1922, when she was aged 67.

Shortest reign
Olga Rukavishnikova (USSR) (b. 13 Mar 1955) held the pentathlon world record for 0.4 sec at Moscow on 24 July 1980. That is the difference between her second place time of 2 min 04.8 sec in the final 800 m event of the Olympic five-event competition, and that of third-placed Nadyezhda Tkachenko (USSR), whose overall points were better, 5083 to 4937.

Heaviest sportsman
The heaviest sportsman of all-time was the professional wrestler William J. Cobb of Macon, Georgia, USA, who in 1962 was billed as the 802 lb (57 st 4 lb *363 kg*) 'Happy Humphrey'. The heaviest player of a ball-game was the 487 lb *221 kg* Bob Pointer, the US Football tackle formerly on the 1967 Santa Barbara High School Team, California, USA.

Greatest earnings
The greatest fortune amassed by an individual in sport is an estimated $69 million by the boxer Muhammad Ali (USA) in 1960–81. The highest paid woman athlete in the world is tennis player Martina Navratilova (b. Prague, Czechoslovakia, 18 Oct 1956) (USA) whose official career earnings passed $10 million on 8 Mar 1986. (*See Tennis section*).

Biggest sports contract
In March 1982, the National Football League concluded a deal worth $2000 million for five years coverage of American Football by the three major TV networks, ABC, CBS and NBC. This represents $14.2 million for each league team.

Largest crowd
The greatest number of live spectators for any sporting spectacle is the estimated 2,500,000 who annually line the route of the New York Marathon. However, spread over 23 days, it is estimated that more than 10,000,000 see the annual *Tour de France* cycling race along the route.

The total attendance at the 1984 summer Olympic Games was given at 5,797,923 for all sports, including 1,421,627 for soccer and 1,129,465 for track and field athletics.

The largest crowd travelling to any single sporting venue is 'more than 400,000' for the annual *Grand Prix d'Endurance* motor race on the Sarthe circuit near Le Mans, France. The record stadium crowd was one of 199,854 for the Brazil *v.* Uruguay soccer match in the Maracaña Municipal Stadium, Rio de Janeiro, Brazil, on 16 July 1950.

Most participants
An estimated 85,000 runners, of whom 67,000 finished, contested the 76th annual Examiner Bay to Breakers 7.6 mile race in San Francisco in 1985. The 1983 Women's International Bowling Congress Championship tournament attracted 75,480 bowlers for the 83-day event held 7 Apr—1 July at Showboat Lanes, Las Vegas, Nevada, USA.

Largest television audience
The largest television audience for a single sporting event, excluding Olympic events, was an estimated 1500 million who saw the final of the 1982 soccer World Cup.

Worst disasters
The worst sports disaster in recent history was when an estimated 604 were killed after some stands at the Hong Kong Jockey Club racecourse collapsed and caught fire on 26 Feb 1918. During the reign of Antoninus Pius (AD 138–161) the upper wooden tiers in the Circus Maximus, Rome, collapsed during a gladiatorial combat killing some 1112 spectators. Britain's worst sports disaster was when 66 were killed and 145 injured at the Rangers *v.* Celtic football match at Exit 13 of Ibrox Park stadium, Glasgow on 2 Jan 1971.

AEROBATICS

Earliest
The first aerobatic 'manoeuvre' is generally considered to be the sustained inverted flight in a Bleriot of Célestin-Adolphe Pégoud (1889–1915), at Buc, France on 21 Sept 1913, but Lieut. Peter Nikolayevich Nesterov (1887–1914), of the Imperial Russian Air Service, performed a loop in a Nieuport Type IV monoplane at Kiev, USSR on 27 Aug 1913.

World Championships
Held biennially since 1960 (excepting 1974), scoring is based on the system devised by Col. José Aresti of Spain. The competition consists of two compulsory and two free programmes. The men's team competition has been won a record five times by the USSR. Igor Egorov (USSR) in 1976 and Petr Jirmus (Czechoslovakia) in 1984 won three out of four programmes. Betty Stewart (USA) won the women's competition in 1980 and 1982. Lidia Leonova (USSR) won a record three medals: first in 1976, second in 1978 and third in 1972. The only medal achieved by Britain has been a bronze in the team event at Kiev, USSR in 1976. The highest individual placing by a Briton is fourth by Neil Williams (1935–77) in 1976.

Inverted flight
The duration record for inverted flight is 4 hr 9 min 5 sec by John 'Hal' McClain in a Swick Taylorcraft on 23 Aug 1980 over Houston International Raceways, Texas, USA.

Loops
On 21 June 1980, R. Steven Powell performed 2315⅜ inside loops in a Bellanca Decathlon over Almont, Michigan, USA. John McClain achieved 180 outside loops in a Bellanca Super Decathlon on 2 Sept 1978 over Houston, Texas, USA.

Ken Ballinger completed 155 consecutive inside loops in a Bellanca Citabria on 6 Aug 1983 over Staverton Airport, Cheltenham, Gloucestershire.

AMERICAN FOOTBALL

Origins
American Football, a direct descendant of the British games of soccer and rugby, evolved at American Universities in the 19th century. The first match under the Harvard Rules was played by Harvard against McGill University of Montreal at Cambridge, Mass., in 1874. The Intercollegiate Football Association was founded in 1876. The professional game dates from August 1895 when Latrobe played Jeanette at Latrobe, Pennsylvania. The American Professional Football Association was formed in 1919. This became the National Football League (NFL) in 1922 and the American Football League (AFL) was formed in 1960; they merged in 1970. The USFL was formed in 1982.

Super Bowl
First held in 1967 between the winners of the NFL and the AFL. Since 1970 it has been contested by the winners of the National and American Conferences of the NFL. Pittsburgh Steelers have most wins, four, 1975–6 and 1979–80. The highest aggregate score was in 1979

Super Bowl XX, where the Chicago Bears set a new scoring record with 46 points. It was also the most one-sided final in the history of the event, a record margin of 36 points. (All Sport).

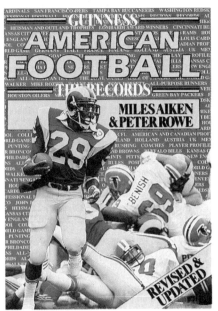

Published by Guinness at £7.95

when Pittsburgh beat Dallas Cowboys 35–31. The highest team score and record victory margin was when the Chicago Bears beat the New England Patriots 46–10 at New Orleans, Louisiana on 26 Jan 1986. The Green Bay Packers won a record 11 NFL titles between 1929 and 1967.

College Football *Highest team score*
Georgia Tech, Atlanta, Georgia scored 222 points, including a record 32 touchdowns, against Cumberland University, Lebanon, Tennessee (nil) on 7 Oct 1916.

PROFESSIONAL RECORDS—AMERICAN FOOTBALL
(NFL 1920–86, AFL 1960–9)

MOST POINTS	career	2002	George Blanda (Chicago Bears, Baltimore, Houston, Oakland)	1949–75
	season	176	Paul Hornung (Green Bay)	1960
	game	40	Ernie Nevers (Chicago Cardinals)	28 Nov 1929
MOST TOUCHDOWNS	career	126	Jim Brown (Cleveland)	1957–65
	season	24	John Riggins (Washington Redskins)	1983
	game	6	Ernie Nevers (Chicago Cardinals)	28 Nov 1929
		6	William 'Dub' Jones (Cleveland)	25 Nov 1951
		6	Gale Sayers (Chicago)	12 Dec 1965
MOST YARDS GAINED RUSHING	career	14,860	Walter Payton (Chicago Bears)	1975–85
	season	2105	Eric Dickerson (Los Angeles Rams)	1984
	game	275	Walter Payton (Chicago Bears)	20 Nov 1977
MOST YARDS GAINED PASSING	career	47,003	Fran Tarkentin (Minnesota, New York Giants)	1961–78
	season	5084	Dan Marino (Miami Dolphins)	1984
	game	554	Norm Van Brocklin (Los Angeles Rams)	28 Sept 1951
MOST PASSES COMPLETED	career	3686	Fran Tarkenton (Minnesota, New York Giants)	1961–78
	season	362	Dan Marino (Miami Dolphins)	1984
	game	42	Richard Todd (New York Jets)	21 Sept 1980
PASS RECEPTIONS	career	716	Charley Joiner (Houston, Cincinnati, San Diego)	1969–85
	season	106	Art Monk (Washington Redskins)	1984
	game	18	Tom Fears (Los Angeles Rams)	3 Dec 1950
FIELD GOALS	career	373	Jan Stenerud (Kansas City, Green Bay, Minnesota)	1967–85
	season	35	Ali Haji-Sheikh (New York Giants)	1983
	game	7	Jim Bakken (St Louis Cardinals)	24 Sept 1967

SUPER BOWL INDIVIDUAL GAME RECORDS

POINTS	18	Roger Craig (San Francisco 49ers)	1985
TOUCHDOWNS	2	by many players	
YARDS GAINED RUSHING	191	Marcus Allen (Los Angeles Raiders)	1984
YARDS GAINED PASSING	331	Joe Montana (San Francisco 49ers)	1985
PASSES COMPLETED	29	Dan Marino (Miami Dolphins)	1985
PASS RECEPTIONS	11	Dan Ross (Cincinnati Bengals)	1982
FIELD GOALS	4	Don Chandler (Green Bay Packers)	1968
	4	Ray Wersching (San Francisco 49ers)	1982

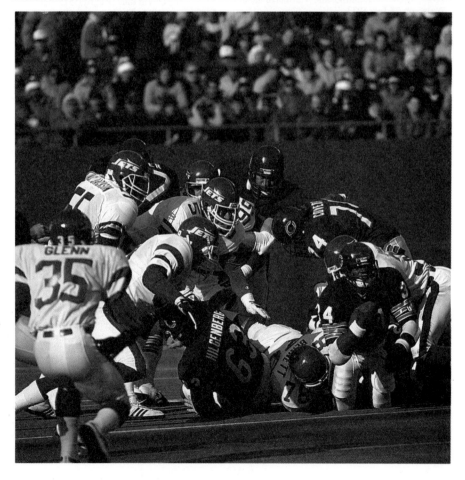

(*Above*) Miami quarter back Dan Marino who broke two season's passing records in 1984. (*Right*) Walter Payton (14), one of the greatest running backs, broke Jim Brown's long standing NFL rushing record. (All Sport).

ANGLING

Oldest existing club
The Ellem fishing club was formed by a number of Edinburgh and Berwickshire gentlemen in 1829. Its first Annual General Meeting was held on 29 April 1830.

Catch *Largest Single*
The largest officially ratified fish ever caught on a rod is a man-eating Great white shark (*Carcharodon carcharias*) weighing 2664 lb *1208 kg* and measuring 16 ft 10 in *5,13 m* long, caught on a 130 lb *58 kg* test line by Alf Dean at Denial Bay, near Ceduna, South Australia, on 21 Apr 1959. A Great white shark weighing 3388 lb *1537 kg* was caught by Clive Green off Albany, Western Australia, on 26 Apr 1976 but will remain unratified as whale meat was used as bait. The biggest ever rod-caught fish by a British angler is a 1260 lb *571,5 kg* Black marlin, by Edward A. Crutch off Cairns, Queensland, Australia on 19 Oct 1973.

In June 1978 a Great white shark measuring 29 ft 6 in *9,00 m* in length and weighing over 10,000 lb *4536 kg* was harpooned and landed by fishermen in the harbour of San Miguel, Azores.

The largest marine animal ever killed by *hand* harpoon was a Blue whale 97 ft *29,56 m* in length, by Archer Davidson in Twofold Bay, New South Wales, Australia, in 1910. Its tail flukes measured 20 ft *6,09 m* across and its jaw bone 23 ft 4 in *7,11 m.*

The largest officially ratified fish ever caught in a British river was a 388 lb *176 kg* sturgeon (9 ft 2 in *2,79 m* long) landed by Alec Allen (1895–1972), helped by David Price, from the River Towy, between Llandilo and Carmarthen, S. Wales, on 25 July 1933.

Catch *Smallest*
The smallest fish to win a competition is a smelt, weighing $\frac{1}{16}$ oz *1 dram*, caught by Peter Christian at Buckenham Ferry, Norfolk, England on 9 Jan 1977, in defeating 107 other competitors.

Spear fishing
The largest fish ever taken underwater was an 804 lb *364 kg* Giant black grouper or jewfish by Don Pinder of the Miami Triton Club, Florida, USA, in 1955. The British spear-fishing record is 89 lb *40,36 kg* for an Angler fish by James Brown (Weymouth Association Divers) in 1969.

Championship records *World freshwater*
The *Confédération Internationale de la Pêche Sportive* championships were inaugurated as European championships in 1953 and recognised as World Championships in 1957. France won twelve times between 1956 and 1981 and Robert Tesse (France) took the individual title uniquely three times, in 1959–60, 1965. The record weight (team) is 76 lb 8 oz 8 dr *34,71 kg* in 3 hr by West Germany on the Neckar at Mannheim, West Germany on 21 Sept 1980. The individual record is 37 lb 7 oz 3 dr *16,99 kg* by Wolf-Rüdiger Kremkus (West Germany) at Mannheim on 20 Sept 1980. The most fish caught is 652 by Jacques Isenbaert (Belgium) at Dunajvaros, Yugoslavia on 27 Aug 1967.

World flyfishing
World flyfishing championships were inaugurated by the CIPS in 1981. The first British winner was Henry Anthony 'Tony' Pawson (b. 22 Aug 1921) at Salamanca, Spain in 1984.

Championship records *British*
The National Angling Championship (instituted 1906) has been won seven times by Leeds (1909–10, 1914, 1928, 1948–9, 1952). James H. R. Bazley (Leeds) won the individual title twice (1909, 1927). Since 1972 the event has been split into divisions. Eddie Townsin (Cambridge) won the national title in 1967 and Div. 4 in 1982; Charlie Hibbs (Leigh) won Div. 2 in 1974 and 1984. The record catch is 76 lb 9 oz *34,72 kg* by David Burr (Rugby) in the Huntspill, Somerset in 1965. The largest single fish caught in the Championships is a carp of 14 lb 2 oz *6,41 kg* by John C. Essex on 13 Sept 1975 on the River Nene, Peterborough. The team champi-

onship is determined on points earned by team members in each section. The points record in Division 1, where there are 80 teams of 12 anglers, is 883 by Nottingham Federation in 1980 on the lower Trent. The winning team in 1983, Nottingham Federation, produced a team weight of 63,99 kg *141.07 lbs* of fish.

Match fishing
In a sweepstake on the Sillees River, a tributary of the Erne, Co. Fermanagh, Ulster, on 14 May 1981, Peter Burrell weighed in 258 lb 9½ oz *117,29 kg* of fish in the five hour open event.

Casting records
The longest freshwater cast ratified under ICF (International Casting Federation) rules is 175,01 m *574 ft 2 in* by Walter Kummerow (W. Germany), for the Bait Distance Double-Handed 30 g event held at Lenzerheide, Switzerland in the 1968 Championships. The British National record is 148,78 m *488 ft 1 in* by Andy Dickison on the same occasion. The longest Fly Distance Double-Handed cast is 78,38 m *257 ft 2 in* by Sverne Scheen (Norway), also at Lenzerheide in September 1968. Peter Anderson set a British National professional record of 70,50 m *231 ft 3 in* on water at Scarborough on 11 Sept 1977, and Hugh Newton cast 80,47 m *264 ft* on land at Stockholm, Sweden on 20 Sept 1978. The UK Surfcasting Federation record (150 gr *5¼ oz* weight) is 248 m *815 ft* by Neil Mackellow on 4 Sept 1983 at Norwich.

IGFA WORLD RECORDS
The International Game Fish Association (IGFA) recognise world records for game fish—both Freshwater and Saltwater—for a large number of species of fish. Their thousands of categories include all-tackle, various line classes and tippet classes for fly fishing. The IGFA recognised 1074 new world records in 1984 and 694 in 1985.

Freshwater All-Tackle records
The heaviest category recognised by the IGFA is for the sturgeon—468 lb *212,28 kg* by Joey Pallotta on 9 July 1983 off Benicia, California, USA.

BRITISH RECORDS—NATIONAL COARSE FISH
As recognised by the National Coarse Fish Record Committee

Species	Weight lb. oz. dr	kg	Name of Angler	Location	Date
Barbel	14 6 –	6,52	A. D. Tryon	Royalty Fishery, Hants Avon	1934
Bleak	4	0,120	B. Derrington	River Monnow, Wye Mouth	1982
Bream, common	15 10 –	7,08	J. Knowles	Queenford Lagoon, Oxfordshire	1985
Carp	51 8 –	23,36	C. Yates	Redmire Pool	1980
Carp, crucian	5 10 8	2,56	G. Halls	Lake near Kings Lynn, Norfolk	1976
Catfish (Wels)	43 8 –	19,73	R. J. Bray	Wilstone Res., Tring, Herts	1970
Chub	8 4 –	3,74	G. F. Smith	Royalty Fishery, Hants Avon	1913
Dace	1 4 4	0,57	J. L. Gasson	Little Ouse, Thetford, Norfolk	1960
Eel	11 2 –	5,04	S. Terry	Kingfisher Lake, Ringwood, Hants	1978
Gudgeon	4 4	0,120	M. J. Brown	Fish Pond, Ebbw Vale, Gwent	1977
Orfe, golden	5 6 –	2,44	M. Foot	Kingsley, Hants	1978
Perch	5 9 –	2,52	J. Shayler	Private water, Kent	1985
Pike	42 2 –	19,11	D. Amies	River Thurne, Norfolk	1985
Roach	4 1 –	1,84	R. G. Jones	Gravel pit, Notts	1975
Rudd	4 8 –	2,04	Rev. E. C. Alston	Thetford, Norfolk	1933
Ruffe	5 4	0,148	R. J. Jenkins	West View Farm, Cumbria	1980
Tench	12 8 11	5,69	A. Wilson	Wilstone Res., Tring, Herts	1985
Walleye	11 12 –	5,33	F. A. Adams	The Delph, Welney, Norfolk	1934
Zander	17 12 –	8,05	D. Litton	Great Ouse, Relief Channel, Norfolk	1977

WORLD RECORDS—FRESHWATER AND SALTWATER

Records ratified by the International Game Fish Association as at June 1986

Species	Weight lb. oz.	kg/g	Name of Angler	Location	Date
Barracuda, great	83 0...	37,64	K. J. W. Hackett	Lagos, Nigeria	13 Jan 1952
Bass, largemouth	22 4...	10,09	George W. Perry	Montgomery Lake, Georgia, USA	2 June 1932
Bass, smallmouth	11 15...	5,41	David L. Hayes	Dale Hollow Lake, Kentucky, USA	9 July 1955
Bass, striped	78 8...	35,60	Albert R. McReynolds	Atlantic City, New Jersey, USA	21 Sept 1982
Bluefish	31 12...	14,40	James M. Hussey	Hatteras, North Carolina, USA	30 Jan 1972
Dolphin	87 0...	39,46	Manuel Salazar	Papagalio Gulf, Costa Rica	25 Sept 1976
Jack, crevalle	54 7...	24,69	Thomas F. Gibson, Jr	Port Michel, Gabon	15 Jan 1982
Jewfish	680 0...	308,44	Lynn Joyner	Fernandina Beach, Florida, USA	20 May 1961
Mackerel, king	90 0...	40,82	Norton I. Thornton	Key West, Florida, USA	16 Feb 1976
Marlin, black	1 560 0...	707,61	Alfred C. Glassell, Jr	Cabo Blanco, Peru	4 Aug 1953
Marlin, blue (Atlantic)	1 282 0...	581,51	Larry Martin	St. Thomas, Virgin Islands	6 Aug 1977
Marlin, blue (Pacific)	1 376 0...	624,14	Jay Wm. de Beaubien	Kaaiwi Point, Kona Coast, Hawaii, USA	31 May 1982
Marlin, striped	455 4...	206,50	Bruce Jenkinson	Mayor Island, New Zealand	8 Mar 1982
Marlin, white	181 14...	82,49	Evando Luiz Coser	Vitoria, Brazil	8 Dec 1979
Muskellunge	69 15...	31,72	Arthur Lawton	St. Lawrence River, New York, USA	22 Sept 1957
Permit	51 8...	23,35	William M. Kenney	Lake Worth, Florida, USA	28 Apr 1978
Sailfish (Atlantic)	128 1...	58,10	Harm Steyn	Luanda, Angola	27 Mar 1974
Sailfish (Pacific)	221 0...	100,24	C. W. Stewart	Santa Cruz Island, Ecuador	12 Feb 1947
Salmon, Atlantic	79 2...	35,89	Harm Steyn	Luanda, Angola	27 Mar 1974
Salmon, chinook	97 4...	44,11	Les Anderson	Kenia River, Alaska, USA	17 May 1985
Salmon, coho	31 0...	14,06	Mrs. Lee Halberg	Cowichan Bay, B.C., Canada	11 Oct 1947
Shark, hammerhead	991 0...	449,50	Allen Ogle	Sarasota, Florida, USA	30 May 1982
Shark, mako	1 080 0...	489,88	James L. Melanson	Montauk, New York, USA	26 Aug 1979
Shark, porbeagle	465 0...	210,92	Jorge Potier	Padstow, Cornwall, England	23 July 1976
Shark, thresher	802 0...	363,80	Dianne North	Tutukaka, New Zealand	8 Feb 1981
Shark, tiger	1 780 0...	807,40	Walter Maxwell	Cherry Grove, S. Carolina, USA	14 June 1964
Shark, white	2 664 0	1208,38	Alfred Dean	Ceduna, South Australia	21 Apr 1959
Snapper, cubera	121 8...	55,11	Mike Hebert	Cameron, Louisiana, USA	5 July 1982
Snook	53 10...	24,32	Gilbert Ponzi	Rio de Parasmina, Costa Rica	18 Oct 1978
Sturgeon	468 0...	212,28	Joey Pallotta, III	Benicia, California, USA	9 July 1983
Swordfish	1 182 0...	536,15	L. Marron	Iquique, Chile	17 May 1953
Tarpon	283 0...	128,36	M. Salazar	Lake Maracaibo, Venezuela	19 Mar 1956
Trout, brook	14 8...	6,57	Dr. W. J. Cook	Nipigon River, Ontario, Canada	July 1916
Trout, brown	35 15...	16,30	Eugenio Cavaglia	Nahuel Huapi, Argentina	16 Dec 1952
Trout, lake	65 0...	29,48	Larry Daunis	Great Bear Lake, N.W.T., Canada	8 Aug 1970
Trout, rainbow	42 2...	19,10	David Robert White	Bell Island, Alaska, USA	22 June 1970
Tuna, bigeye (Pacific)	435 0...	197,31	Dr. Russel V. A. Lee	Cabo Blanco, Peru	17 Apr 1957
Tuna, bluefin	1 496 0...	679,00	Ken Fraser	Aulds Cove, Nova Scotia, Canada	26 Oct 1979
Tuna, yellowfin	388 12...	176,35	Curt Wiesenhutter	San Benedicto I. Mexico	1 Apr 1977
Wahoo	149 0...	67,58	John Pirovano	Cat Cay, Bahamas	15 June 1962
Walleye	25 0...	11,34	Mabry Harper	Old Hickory Lake, Tennessee, USA	1 Apr 1960

An 834 lb *378,30 kg* sturgeon was landed (not by rod) by Garry Oling on 11 Aug 1981 from the Fraser River at Albion, British Columbia, Canada.

Longest fight
The longest recorded individual fight with a fish is 32 hr 5 min by Donal Heatley (b. 1938) (New Zealand) with a black marlin (estimated length 20 ft *6,09 m* and weight 1500 lb *680 kg*) off Mayor Island off Tauranga, North Island on 21–22 Jan 1968. It towed the 12 ton/*tonnes* launch 50 miles *80 km* before breaking the line.

ARCHERY

Earliest references
Though the earliest evidence of the existence of bows is seen in the Mesolithic cave paintings in Spain, archery as an organized sport appears to have developed in the 3rd century AD. Competitive archery may however date back to the 12th century BC. The oldest archery body in the British Isles is the Royal Company of Archers, the Sovereign's bodyguard for Scotland, dating from 1676, though the Society of Kilwinning Archers, in Scotland, have contested the Papingo Shoot since 1488. The world governing body is the *Fédération Internationale de Tir à l'Arc* (FITA), founded in 1931.

Highest Championship scores
The highest scores achieved in either a world or Olympic championship for Double FITA rounds are: men, 2617 points (possible 2880) by Darrell Pace (b. 23 Oct 1956) (USA) and Richard McKinney (b. 20 Oct 1963) (USA); and women, 2616 points by Kim Jin Ho (S. Korea), all at Long Beach, California, USA on 21–22 Oct 1983.

World Records
Single FITA rounds

Event	Points	Name and Country	Possible	Year
MEN				
FITA	1341	Darrell Pace (USA)	1440	1979
90 m	322	Vladimir Yesheyev (USSR)	360	1980
70 m	342	Richard McKinney (USA)	360	1985
50 m	345	Richard McKinney (USA)	360	1982
30 m	356	Darrell Pace (USA)	360	1978
Team	3912	USA (Richard McKinney, Darrell Pace, Jerry Pylpchuk)	4320	1985
WOMEN				
FITA	1325	Lyudmila Arshanikova (USSR)	1440	1984
70 m	328	Natalia Butuzova (USSR)	360	1979
60 m	338	Lyudmila Arshanikova (USSR)	360	1984
50 m	335	Yanzhina Tsyrenzhapova (USSR)	360	1985
30 m	353	Valentina Radionova (USSR)	360	1981
Team	3925	USSR (Lyudmila Arshanikova, Natalia Butuzova, Sebinsio Rustamova)	4320	1983

Indoor Double FITA rounds at 25 m

MEN	589	Darrell Pace (USA)	600	1984
WOMEN	588	Elena Marfel (USSR)	600	1985

British records
York Round—possible 1296 pts: Single Round, 1160 Steven Hallard at Meriden on 26 June 1983; Double Round, 2240 Steven Hallard at Stoneleigh on 14 Aug 1983.

Hereford (Women)—possible 1296 pts: Single Round, 1182 Elaine Tomkinson at Bingley on 10 Aug 1980; Double Round, 2331 Sue Willcox at Oxford on 27–28 June 1979.

FITA Round (Men): Steven Hallard, 1300 Single Round and 2566 Double Round, both at Castle Ashby, Nottinghamshire on 20 May 1983.

FITA Round (Women's): Single Round, 1273 Pauline Edwards at Worcester on 23 July 1983. Double Round, 2520 Rachel Fenwick at Brussels, Belgium on 12–13 Aug 1978.

Most titles *World*
The greatest number of world titles (instituted 1931) ever won by a man is four by Hans Deutgen (b. 28 Feb 1917) (Sweden) in 1947–50. The greatest number won by a woman is seven by Janina Spychajowa-Kurkowska (b. 8 Feb 1901) (Poland) in 1931–4, 1936, 1939 and 1947. Oscar Kessels (Belgium) (1904–68) participated in 21 world championships.

Most titles *Olympic*
Hubert van Innis (1866–1961) (Belgium) won six gold and three silver medals at the 1900 and 1920 Olympic Games.

Most titles *British*
The greatest number of British Championships is 12 by Horace Alfred Ford (1822–80) in 1849–59 and 1867, and 23 by Alice Blanche Legh (1855–1948) in 1881, 1886–92, 1895, 1898–1900, 1902–9, 1913 and 1921–2. Miss Legh was inhibited from winning from 1882 to 1885—because her mother was champion—and for four further years 1915–8 because there were no Championships during the First World War.

Flight shooting
The longest recorded distance ever shot is 1 mile 268 yd *1854,40 m* in the unlimited footbow class by Harry Drake (b. 7 May 1915) (USA) at 3000 ft *915 m* altitude at Ivanpah Dry Lake, California, USA on 24 Oct 1971. The female footbow record is 1113 yd 2 ft 6 in *1018,48 m* by Arlyne Rhode (b. 4 May 1936) at Wendover, Utah, USA on 10 Sept 1978. Alan Webster

(England) set the flight record for the handbow with 1231 yd 1 ft 10 in *1126,19 m* on 2 Oct 1982 and April Moon (USA) set a women's record of 1039 yd 1 ft 1 in *950,39 m* on 13 Sept 1981, both at Ivanpah Dry Lake. Drake holds the crossbow flight record with 1359 yd 2 ft 5 in *1243,4 m* on 14 Oct 1967 and the regular footbow record with 1542 yd 2 ft 10 ins *1410,87 m* on 6 Oct 1979 both at Ivanpah Dry Lake. Compound bow world records are—men: 977 yd 2 in *893,42 m* by Bruce Odle (USA); women: 612 yd 1 ft 5 in *560,04 m* by Arlyne Rhode (USA), both at the Bonneville Flight Range, Utah, USA in 1976.

Greatest draw
Gary Sentman, of Roseberg, Oregon, USA drew a longbow weighing a record 176 lb *79,83 kg* to the maximum draw on the arrow of 28¼ in *72 cm* at Forksville, Penn., on 20 Sept 1975.

24 Hours—target archery
The highest recorded score over 24 hours by a pair of archers is 51,633 during 48 Portsmouth Rounds by Jimmy Watt and Gordon Danby at the Epsom Showgrounds, Auckland NZ, on 18–19 Nov 1977.

24 Hours—field archery
The highest recorded score at field archery is 123,724 by six members of the Holland Moss Field Archery Club at Holland Moss Field, Pimbo, Lancashire on 28–29 Apr 1983. Bill Chambers set an individual record score of 30,506.

On target . . . Richard McKinney, part of the American World Championship-winning team, also holds world individual records. (US National Archery Association).

Origins
A similar game was played in China in the 2nd millennium BC. The modern game may have evolved c 1870 at Badminton Hall in Avon, the seat of the Dukes of Beaufort, or from a game played in India. The first modern rules were codified in Poona in 1876.

MOST INTERNATIONAL APPEARANCES

	Times	Men	
England	137	Michael G. Tredgett	1970–85
Scotland	80	William A. Gilliland	1975–86
Ireland	81	Bill Thompson	1975–86
Wales	54	Philip Sutton	1977–86
	Times	Women	
England	108	Gillian Gilks (née Perrin)	1966–85
Wales	63	Sue Brimble	1969–84
Ireland	68	Barbara Beckett	1971–85
Scotland	69	Pamela Hamilton	1975–86

Shortest game
In the 1969 Uber Cup in Tōkyō, Japan, Noriko Takagi (later Mrs Nakayama) (Japan) beat Poppy Tumengkol (Indonesia) in 9 min.

Longest hit
Frank Rugani drove a shuttlecock 79 ft 8½ in *24,29 m* in indoor tests at San José, California, USA, on 29 Feb 1964.

Thomas Cup
The International Championship or Thomas Cup (instituted 1948) has been won eight times by Indonesia (1958, 1961, 1964, 1970, 1973, 1976, 1979 and 1984).

Uber Cup
The Ladies International Championship or Uber Cup (instituted 1956) has been won five times by Japan (1966, 1969, 1972, 1978 and 1981).

Most titles
The All-England Championships were instituted in 1899. The men's singles have been won a record eight times by Rudy Hartono Kurniawan (Indonesia) (b. 18 Aug 1948) in 1968–74 and 1976. The greatest number of titles won (including doubles) is 21 by George Alan Thomas (1881–1972) between 1903 and 1928. The women's singles were won ten times by Judy Hashman (née Devlin) (USA) (b. 22 Oct 1935) in 1954, 1957–8, 1960–4, 1966–7. She also equalled the greatest number of titles won of 17 by Meriel Lucas (later Mrs King Adams) from 1899 to 1910.

Earliest game
The Rev Thomas Wilson, of Maidstone, Kent, England, wrote disapprovingly, in 1700, of baseball being played on Sundays. The earliest baseball game under the Cartwright (Alexander Joy Cartwright Jr 1820–92) rules was at Hoboken, New Jersey, USA, on 19 June 1846, with the New York Nine beating the Knickerbockers 23–1 in four innings.

Home runs *Most*
Henry Louis 'Hank' Aaron (Milwaukee and Atlanta Braves) (b. 5 Feb 1934) holds the major league career home run record of 755, from 1954

BASEBALL

to 1976. Joshua Gibson (1911–47) of Homestead Grays and Pittsburgh Crawfords, Negro League clubs, achieved a career total of nearly 800 homers including an unofficial total of 75 in 1931. The US major league record for home runs in a season is 61 by Roger Eugene Maris (1934–85) for New York Yankees in 162 games in 1961. George Herman 'Babe' Ruth (1895–1948) hit 60 in 154 games in 1927. The most official home runs in minor leagues is 72 by Joe Bauman of Rosewell, New Mexico in 1954.

Longest home run
The longest home run ever measured was one of 618 ft *188,4 m* by Roy Edward 'Dizzy' Carlyle (1900–56) in a minor league game at Emeryville Ball Park, California, USA, on 4 July 1929. In 1919 Babe Ruth hit a 587 ft *178,9 m* homer in a Boston Red Sox *v.* New York Giants exhibition match at Tampa, Florida.

Longest throw
The longest throw (ball weighs 5–5¼ oz *141–148 g*) is 445 ft 10 in *135,88 m* by Glen Edward Gorbous (b. Canada 8 July 1930) on 1 Aug 1957. The longest throw by a woman is 296 ft *90,2 m* by Mildred Ella 'Babe' Didrikson (later Mrs Zaharias) (US) (1914–56) at Jersey City, New Jersey, USA on 25 July 1931.

Fastest base runner
The fastest time for circling bases is 13.3 sec by Ernest Evar Swanson (1902–73) at Columbus, Ohio, in 1932, at an average speed of 18.45 mph *29,70 km/h.*

Fastest pitcher
The fastest recorded pitcher was Lynn Nolan Ryan (then of the California Angels) (b. 31 Jan 1947) who, on 20 Aug 1974 at Anaheim Stadium, California, USA, was measured to pitch at 100.9 mph *162,3 km/h.*

Youngest player
The youngest major league player of all time was the Cincinnati pitcher, Joseph Henry Nuxhall (b. 30 July 1928) who started his career in June 1944, aged 15 yr 314 days.

Record attendances and receipts
The World Series record attendance is 420,784 (six games) when the Los Angeles Dodgers beat the Chicago White Sox 4–2 on 1–8 Oct 1959. The single game record is 92,706 for the fifth game at the Memorial Coliseum, Los Angeles, California, on 6 Oct 1959. The highest seating capacity in a baseball stadium is now 74,208 in

Pete Rose broke Ty Cobb's record for career base hits in September 1985, 57 years after its establishment. (All-Sport).

the Cleveland Municipal Stadium, Ohio, USA. The all-time season record for attendances for both leagues has been 46,828,819 in 1984/5.

An estimated 114,000 spectators watched a game between Australia and an American Services team in a 'demonstration' event during the Olympic Games at Melbourne, 1 Dec 1956.

BASKETBALL

Origins
The game of 'Pok-ta-Pok' was played in the 10th century BC by the Olmecs in Mexico, and closely resembled basketball in its concept. 'Ollamalitzli' was a variation of this game played by the Aztecs in Mexico as late as the 16th century. If the solid rubber ball was put through a fixed stone ring the player was entitled to the clothing of all the spectators. Modern basketball (which may have been based on the German game *Korbball*) was devised by the Canadian-born Dr James A. Naismith (1861–1939) at the Training School of the International YMCA College at Springfield, Massachusetts, USA, in mid-December 1891. The first game played under modified rules was on 20 Jan 1892. The International Amateur Basketball Federation (FIBA) was founded in 1932, and the English Basketball Association in 1936.

Most titles *Olympic*
The USA have won nine men's Olympic titles. From the time the sport was introduced to the Games in 1936 until 1972 in Munich they won 63 consecutive matches in the Olympic Games until they lost 50–51 to the USSR in the disputed Final match. They won eighth and ninth titles in 1976 and 1984. The women's title was won by the USSR in 1976 and 1980 and by the USA in 1984.

Most titles *World*
The USSR have won most titles at both the men's World Championships (inst. 1950) with three (1967, 1974 and 1982) and women's (inst. 1953) with six (1959, 1964, 1967, 1971, 1975 and 1983).

Most titles *European*
The most European Champions Cup (instituted 1957) wins is seven by Real Madrid, Spain. The women's title has been won 18 times by Daugawa, Riga, Latvia, USSR. The most wins in the European Nations Championships for

---

US MAJOR LEAGUE RECORDS AL American League, NL National League

——— BATTING ———

Batting av., career	.367	Tyrus Raymond Cobb (AL)	1905–28
Batting av., season	.438	Hugh Duffy (Boston, NL)	1894
Runs, career	2244	Tyrus Raymond Cobb	1905–28
RBIs, career	2297	Henry 'Hank' Aaron (Milwaukee NL, Atlanta NL, Milwaukee AL)	1954–76
„ season	190	Lewis Rober 'Hack' Wilson (Chicago, NL)	1930
„ game	12	James LeRoy Bottomley (St Louis, NL)	16 Sept 1924
„ innings	7	Edward Cartwright (St Louis, AA)	23 Sept 1890
Base hits, career	4204	Pete Rose	1963–86
„ season	257	George Harold Sisler (St Louis, AL)	1920
Total bases, career	6856	Henry 'Hank' Aaron	1954–76
„ season	457	George H. 'Babe' Ruth (New York, AL)	1921
Hits, consecutive	12	Michael Franklin 'Pinky' Higgins	19–21 June 1938
„ „	12	Walter 'Moose' Dropo	14–15 July 1952
Consecutive games batted safely	56	Joseph Paul DiMaggio (New York, AL)	15 May–16 July 1941
Stolen bases, career	938	Louis Clark Brock	1961–79
„ „ season	130	Rickey Henderson (Oakland, AL)	1982
Consecutive games played	2130	Henry Louis 'Lou' Gehrig	1 June 1925–30 April 1939

——— PITCHING ———

Games won, career	511	Denton True 'Cy' Young	1890–1911
„ season	60	Charles Gardner Radbourne (Providence, NL)	1884
Consecutive games won	24	Carl Owen Hubbell (New York, NL)	1936–37
Shutouts, career	113	Walter Perry Johnson	1907–27
„ season	16	George W. Bradley (St Louis, NL)	1876
	16	Grover Cleveland Alexander (Philadelphia, NL)	1916
Strikeouts, career	4083	Lynn Nolan Ryan (New York, NL; California, AL; Houston, NL)	1968–86
„ season	383	Lynn Nolan Ryan (California, AL)	1973
No-hit games, career	5	Lynn Nolan Ryan	1966–81
Earned run av., season	0.90	Ferdinand Schupp (140 inn) (New York, NL)	1916
„ „	1.01	Hubert 'Dutch' Leonard (222 inn) (Boston, AL)	1914
„ „	1.12	Robert Gibson (305 inn) (St Louis, NL)	1968
Complete games, career	751	Denton True 'Cy' Young	1890–1911

BASEBALL WORLD SERIES RECORDS AL American League, NL National League

Most wins	22	New York Yankees (AL)	1923–78
Most series played	14	Lawrence P. 'Yogi' Berra (New York, AL) (10 wins)	1947–63
Most home runs in a game	3	George H. 'Babe' Ruth (New York, AL)	6 Oct 1926
	3	Reginald M. Jackson (New York, AL)	18 Oct 1977
Only perfect pitch (in 9 innings)		Donald J. Larson (New York, AL) *v* Brooklyn	8 Oct 1956

JAPANESE LEAGUE RECORDS Superior to those in US major leagues:

Home runs, career	868	Sadaharu Oh (Yomuiri)	1959–80
Stolen bases, career	939	Yutaka Fukumoto (Hankyu)	1969–83

men is 13 by the USSR, and in the women's event 17 also by the USSR.

Most titles *American Professional*

The most National Basketball Association (NBA) titles (instituted 1947), played for between the leading professional teams in the United States, have been won by the Boston Celtics with 16 victories between 1957 and 1986.

Most titles *English*

The most English National Championship titles (instituted 1936) have been won by London Central YMCA, with eight wins in 1957–8, 1960, 1962–4, 1967 and 1969. The English National League title has been won seven times by Crystal Palace 1974, 1976–8, 1980 and 1982–3. Most English Women's Cups (instituted 1965) have been won by Tigers with eight wins, 1972–3, 1976–80 and 1982.

Highest score *International*

The highest score recorded in a senior international match is 251 by Iraq against Yemen (33) at New Delhi in November 1982 at the Asian Games. The highest in a British Championship is 125 by England *v.* Wales (54) on 1 Sept 1978. England beat Gibraltar 130–45 on 31 Aug 1978.

Highest score *Match*

The highest aggregate score in an NBA match is 370 when the Detroit Pistons (186) beat the Seattle Nuggets (184) in Denver on 13 Dec 1983. Overtime was played after a 145–145 tie in regulation time.

Highest score *United Kingdom*

The highest score recorded in a match is 250 by the Nottingham YMCA Falcons *v.* Mansfield Pirates at Nottingham, on 18 June 1974. It was

(*Left*) Scaling the heights . . . 7 ft 4 in *2,24 m* Kareem Abdul-Jabbar has scored over 35,000 points in his NBA career. (All-Sport). (*Below*) Martin Clark, the only player in the English National League to have scored 50 points in three successive games. (All-Sport).

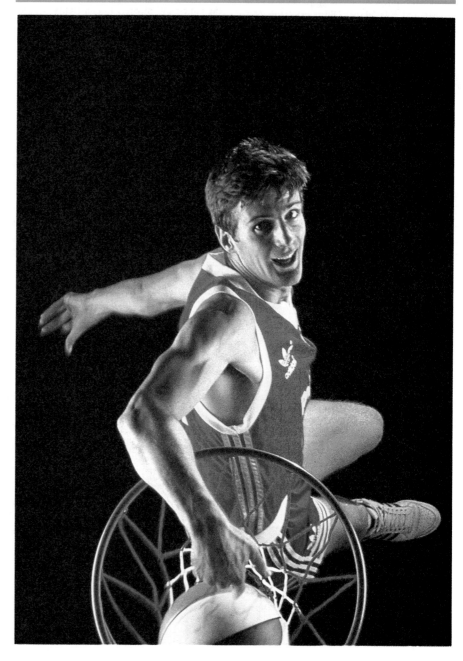

a handicap competition and Mansfield received 120 points towards their total of 145. The highest score in a senior National League match is 167 by West Bromwich Kestrels v. Milton Keynes (69) on 13 Feb 1983. The highest in the National Cup is 146 by Doncaster v. Cleveland (109) on 11 Feb 1976.

Highest score *Individual*
Mats Wermelin, 13, (Sweden) scored all 272 points in a 272–0 win in a regional boys' tournament in Stockholm, Sweden on 5 Feb 1974. The highest single game score in an NBA game is 100 points by Wilton Norman Chamberlain (b. 21 Aug 1936) for Philadelphia v. New York on 2 Mar 1962. The most in a college game is 113 points by Clarence 'Bevo' Francis, for Rio Grande College, Ohio v. Hillsdale at Jackson, Ohio on 2 Feb 1954. The record score by a woman is 156 points by Marie Boyd (now Eichler) of Central HS, Lonaconing, Maryland, USA in a 163–3 defeat of Ursaline Academy, Cumberland on 25 Feb 1924.

The highest score by a British player is 124 points by Paul Ogden for St Albans School, Oldham (226) v. South Chadderton (82) on 9 Mar 1982. The highest individual score in a League match in Britain is 108 by Lewis Young for Forth Steel in his team's 154–74 win over Stirling in the Scottish League Division One at Stirling on 2 Mar 1985. The record in an English National League (Div. One) or Cup match is 73 points by Terry Crosby (USA) for Home Spare Bolton in his team's 120–106 defeat by Cottrills Manchester Giants at Altrincham, Cheshire on 26 Jan 1985.

Most points
Kareem Abdul-Jabbar (formerly Lewis Ferdinand Alcindor) (b. 16 Apr 1947) has scored a career record 35,004 points from 1969 to 31 Mar 1986 for the Milwaukee Bucks and Los Angeles Lakers. The previous record holder, Wilt Chamberlain had a record average of 30.1 points per game for his total of 31,419. He set a season's record 4029 for Philadelphia in 1962. The record for the most points scored in a college career is (women): 4061, Pearl Moore of Francis Marion College, Florence, S. Carolina, 1975–9, (men): 4045 by Travis Grant for Kentucky State in 1969–72. In the English National League, Ian Day (b. 16 May 1953) has scored 3456 points in 203 games, 1973–84.

Tallest players
The tallest player of all time is reputed to be Suleiman Ali Nashnush (b. 1943) who played for the Libyan team in 1962 when measuring 2,45 m *8 ft.* Aleksandr Sizonenko of Kuibyshev Stroitel and USSR is 2,39 m *7 ft 10 in* tall. The tallest woman player was Iuliana Semenova (USSR) (b. 9 Mar 1952) at a reported 7 ft 2 in *2,18 m* and weighing 281 lb *127,4 kg.* The tallest British player has been the 7 ft 6¼ in *2,29 m* tall Christopher Greener of London Latvians whose international debut for England was v. France on 17 Dec 1969.

Most accurate—Free Throws
The greatest goal shooting demonstration has been by Ted St Martin of Jacksonville, Florida, who, on 25 June 1977, scored 2036 consecutive free throws.

In 24 hours Jeff Liles scored 15,138 free throws from a total of 17,862 taken (84.75%) at Lakeland Christian School, Lakeland, Florida, USA on 11–12 Apr 1986.

Longest recorded goal
The longest recorded field goal in a match is a measured 92 ft 5¼ in *28,17 m* by Bruce Morris for Marshall University v. Appalachian State University at Huntington, West Virginia, USA

on 8 Feb 1985. A British record of 75 ft 9½ in *23,10 m* is claimed by David Tarbatt (b. 23 Jan 1949) of Altofts Aces v. Harrogate Demons at Featherstone, West Yorkshire on 27 Jan 1980.

Largest ever gate
The Harlem Globetrotters (USA) played an exhibition in front of 75,000 in the Olympic Stadium, West Berlin, Germany, in 1951. The largest indoor basketball attendance was 67,596, including 64,682 tickets sold at the box office, for the Indiana Olympic Basketball Tribute at the Hoosier Dome, Indianapolis, Indiana, USA on 9 July 1984. They saw victories by the US men's and women's Olympic teams over All-Star opposition.

BILLIARDS

Earliest mention
The earliest recorded mention of billiards was in France in 1429, while Louis XI, King of France 1461–83, is reported to have had a billiard table. The first recorded public billiards room in England was the Piazza, Covent Garden, London, in the early part of the 19th century. Rubber cushions were introduced in 1835 and slate beds in 1836.

Most titles *Professional*
The greatest number of world championships (instituted 1870) won by one player is eight by John Roberts, Jnr (1847–1919) (England) in 1870 (twice), 1871, 1875 (twice), 1877 and 1885 (twice). The greatest number of United Kingdom titles (instituted 1934) won is seven (1934–39 and 1947) by Joe Davis (1901–78) (England), who also won four world titles (1928–30 and 1932). William F. Hoppe (USA) (1887–1959) won 51 'world' titles in the United States variant of the game between 1906 and 1952.

Most titles *Amateur*
The record for world amateur titles is four by Robert James Percival Marshall (Australia) (b. 10 Apr 1910) in 1936, 1938, 1951 and 1962. The greatest number of English Amateur Championships (instituted 1888) ever won is 15 by Norman Dagley (b. 27 June 1930) in 1965–66, 1970–75, 1978–84. The record number of women's titles is eight by Vera Selby (b. 13 Mar 1930) 1970–8.

Highest breaks
Tom Reece (1873–1953) made an unfinished break of 499,135, including 249,152 cradle cannons (two points each) in 85 hr 49 min against Joe Chapman at Burroughes' Hall, Soho Square, London, between 3 June and 6 July 1907. This was not recognized because press and public were not continuously present. The highest certified break made by the anchor cannon is 42,746 by William Cook (England) from 29 May to 7 June 1907. The official world record under the then baulk-line rule is 1784 by Joe Davis in the United Kingdom Championship on 29 May 1936. Walter Albert Lindrum (Australia) (1898–1960) made an official break of 4137 in 2 hr 55 min against Joe Davis at Thurston's on 19–20 Jan 1932, before the baulk-line rule was in force. Davis had an unofficial personal best of 2502 (mostly pendulum cannons) in a match against Tom Newman (1894–1943) (England) in Manchester in 1930. The highest break recorded in amateur competition is 1149 by Michael Ferreira (India) at Calcutta, India on 15 Dec 1978. On 1 Jan 1983 the more stringent 'two pot' rule under which Robert Marshall (Aus) made a break of 702 at Brisbane on 17 Sept 1953 was restored. Ferreira's 962 unfinished in a tournament at Bombay, India on

29 Apr 1986 is the highest break since the restoration of the rule.

Fastest century
Walter Lindrum made an unofficial 100 break in 27.5 sec in Australia on 10 Oct 1952. His official record is 100 in 46.0 sec set in Sydney in 1941.

3 CUSHION
This pocketless variation dates back to 1878. The world governing body, the *Union Mondiale de Billiard* (UMB) was formed in 1928. The most successful exponent spanning the pre and post international era from 1906 to 1952 was Willie Hoppe who won 51 billiards championships in all forms. Most UMB titles have been won by Raymond Ceulemans (Belgium) (b. 12 July 1935) with 18 (1963–6, 1968–73, 1975–81, 1983).

BAR BILLIARDS

Highest scoring rate
The record scoring rate in a league game has been 28,530 in 19 min 5 sec by Keith Sheard at the Crown and Thistle, Headington, Oxford on 9 July 1984.

24 hours
The highest bar billiards score in 24 hr by a team of five is 1,506,570 by John Burrows, Kent Murray, Ray Hussey, Roy Buckle and Brian Ray of 'The Hour Glass', Sands, High Wycombe, Buckinghamshire on 26–27 Nov 1983.

BOARD GAMES

BACKGAMMON
Forerunners of the game have been traced back to a dice and a board game found in excavations at Ur, dated to 3000 BC. Later the Romans played a game remarkably similar to the modern one. The name 'Backgammon' is variously ascribed to Welsh "little battle", or Saxon "back game".

Alan Malcolm Beckerson (b. 21 Feb 1938) devised the shortest game of 16 throws in 1982.

CHESS

Origins
The game originated in ancient India under the name Chaturanga (literally 'four-corps'—an army game). The name chess is derived from the Persian word *shah* (a king or ruler). The earliest reference is from the Middle Persian Karnamak (*c.* AD 590–628), though in December 1972, two ivory chessmen were found in the Uzbek Soviet Republic dateable to AD 200. It reached Britain in *c.* 1255. The *Fédération Internationale des Echecs* was established in 1924.

Most World titles
World champions have been generally recognised since 1886. The longest undisputed tenure was 27 years by Dr Emanuel Lasker (1868–1941) of Germany, from 1894 to 1921. The women's world championship was held by Vera Menchik-Stevenson (1906–44) (USSR, later GB) from 1927 till her death, and was successfully defended a record seven times. Nona Gaprindashvili (USSR) (b. 3 May 1941) held the title from 1962 to 1978 and defended successfully four times. Robert J. 'Bobby' Fischer (b. Chicago, Illinois, USA, 9 March 1943) is reckoned on the officially adopted Elo System to be the greatest Grand Master of all-time with a 2785 rating. Gary Kimovich Kasparov (USSR) (b. 13 Apr 1963), at 2720 is currently the highest ranked player. The highest rated woman player is Maya

Taking the strain . . . the youngest-ever women's world chess champion, Maya Chiburdanidze, watched by her coach Eduard Gufeld. (Novosti).

Chiburdanidze (USSR) (b. 17 Jan 1961) at 2455. The USSR has won the men's team title a record 15 times and the women's title ten times to 1984.

The most active world champion was Anatoliy Yevgenyevitch Karpov (USSR) (b. 23 May 1951) who in his tenure as champion, 1975–85, averaged 45.2 competitive games per year, played in 32 tournaments and finished first in 26.

Youngest and oldest world champions
The youngest world champion is Gary Kasparov, who won the title on 9 Nov 1985 at 22 yr

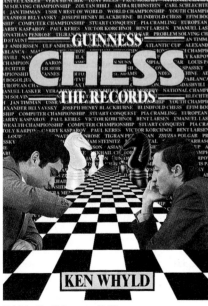

GUINNESS' CHESS THE RECORDS

KEN WHYLD

Published by Guinness at £7.95

210 days. The oldest was Wilhelm Steinitz (Czechoslovakia) (1836–1900) who was 58 yr old when he lost his title to Lasker in 1894.

Maya Chiburdanidze won the women's title in 1978 when only 17.

Most British titles
Most British titles have been won by Dr Jonathan Penrose (b. 7 Oct 1933) with ten titles in 1958–63, 1966–9. Rowena Mary Bruce (*née* Dew) (b. 15 May 1919) won 11 women's titles between 1937 and 1969. The first British player to attain official International Grand Master status was Anthony Miles (b. 23 Apr 1955), on 24 Feb 1976. Miles ranks as the top British player at 2610 on the Elo list of 1 Jan 1986.

Least games lost by a world champion
José Raúl Capablanca (Cuba) (1888–1942) lost only 34 games in his adult career, 1909–39. He was unbeaten from 10 Feb 1916 to 21 Mar 1924 and was world champion 1921–7.

Most opponents
Vlastimil Hort (b. 12 Jan 1944) (Czechoslovakia), in Seltjarnes, Iceland on 23–24 Apr 1977, played 550 opponents including 201 simultaneously; he only lost ten games. Eric Knoppert (West Germany) played 500 games of 10-minute chess against opponents averaging 2002 on the Elo scale on 13–16 Sept 1985. He scored 413 points (1 for win, $\frac{1}{2}$ for draw), a success rate of 82.6%. The record for most consecutive games played is 663 by Vlastimil Hort over $32\frac{1}{2}$ hours at Porz, W. Germany on 5–6 Oct 1984. He played 60–100 opponents at a time, scoring over 80% wins and averaging 30 moves per game.

Slowest and longest games
The slowest reported moving (before modern rules) in an official event is reputed to have been by Louis Paulsen (Germany) (1833–91) against Paul Charles Morphy (USA) (1837–84) on 29 Oct 1857. The game ended in a draw on move 56 after 15 hours of play of which Paulsen used most of the allotted time. Grandmaster Friedrich Sämisch (1896–1975) (Germany) ran out of the allotted time (2 hr 30 min for 45 moves) after only 12 moves, in Prague, Czechoslovakia, in 1938.

The Master game with most moves on record was when Yedael Stepak (Israel) (b. 21 Aug 1940) beat Yaakov Mashian (Iran, later Israel) (b. 17 Dec 1943) in 193 moves in Tel Aviv, Israel on 23 Mar–16 Apr 1980. The total playing time was a record 24 hr 30 min.

DRAUGHTS
Draughts, known as checkers in North America, has origins earlier than chess. It was played in Egypt in the second millennium BC. The earliest book on the game was by Antonio Torquemada of Valencia, Spain in 1547. There have been four US v. Great Britain internationals (crossboard) 1905, 1927, 1973 and 1983, three won by the United States and one by Great Britain.

Walter Hellman (USA) (1916–75) won a record six world championships, 1948–67. Melvin Pomeroy (US) was internationally undefeated from 1914 until his death in 1933.

The British Championship (biennial) was inaugurated in 1886. A record six titles were won by Samuel Cohen (London), 1924, 1927, 1929, 1933, 1937 and 1939. John McGill (Kilbride) won six Scottish titles between 1959 and 1974. William Edwards of Abercynon, Wales won the English open title on a record four successive occasions—1979, 1981, 1983 and 1985.

Most opponents
Con McCarrick (Ireland) was reported as having

MAH-JONGG
The tile game of Mah-Jongg is of 19th century Chinese origin, where it was played in varying forms according to province and dialect. The name derives from various transliterations signifying 'sparrow' or 'bird of 100 intelligences', and a bird appears on one of the tiles, the 'one-bamboo'. Mah-Jongg is the western version, the name having been coined and copyrighted by Joseph P Babcock, a US resident in Shanghai, shortly after World War One. The National Mah-Jongg League was founded in the United States in 1937 and today has over 150,000 members. An International Championship held 20 years ago, then for women only, is to be revived in December 1986.

played a record 154 games simultaneously, winning 136, drawing 17 and losing one, in 4 hr 30 min at Dundalk, Co. Louth, Ireland on 14 Mar 1982. Newell W. Banks (b. Detroit, USA, 10 Oct 1887) played 140 games simultaneously, winning 133 and drawing seven, in Chicago, Illinois in 1933. His playing time was 145 min, so averaging about one move per sec. In 1947 he played blindfold for 4 hr per day for 45 consecutive days, winning 1331 games, drawing 54 and losing only two, while playing six games at a time.

Longest and shortest games
In competition the prescribed rate of play is not less than 30 moves per hour with the average game lasting about 90 min. In 1958 a match between Dr Marion Tinsley (US) and Derek Oldbury (GB) lasted 7 hr 30 min. The shortest possible game is one of 20 moves composed by Alan Malcolm Beckerson (GB) in 1977.

SCRABBLE ® Crossword Game

Origins
The crossword game was invented by Alfred M. Butts in 1931 and was developed, refined and trademarked as Scrabble ® Crossword Game by James Brunot in 1948. He sold the North American rights to Selchow & Richter Company, New York, the European rights to J. W. Spear & Sons, London, and the Australian rights to Murfett Pty Ltd, Melbourne.

Highest scores
The highest competitive league game score is 849 by Maurice Rocker (GB) at Sheffield on 6 July 1985. The highest competitive single turn score recorded is 392 by Dr Saladin Karl Khoshnaw (of Kurdish origin) in Manchester in April 1982. He laid down 'CAZIQUES', which means 'native chiefs of West Indian aborigines'.

The greatest margin of victory in a league game was achieved by Ron Hendra when he beat Amber Sturdy 730–180 in a London League match in 1983.

Most titles

British National Championships were instituted in 1971. Olive Behan, 1972 and 1975, and Philip Nelkon, 1978 and 1981, have both won twice. The highest score in the Championship has been 1843 (three games total) by Viraf Mehta in 1986.

BIGGEST BOARD GAME

The world's biggest board game, called Heartopoly, involved 4317 participants and stretched around the ¼ mile *403 metres* Flagler Dog Track in Miami, Florida, USA on 14–15 Sept 1985.

BOBSLEIGH AND TOBOGGANING

BOBSLEDDING

Origins

The oldest known sledge is dated *c.* 6500 BC and came from Heinola, Finland. The first known bobsleigh race took place at Davos, Switzerland in 1889. The International Federation of Bobsleigh and Tobogganing was formed in 1923, followed by the International Bobsleigh Federation in 1957.

Most titles *Olympic*

The Olympic four-man bob title (inst. 1924) has been won four times by Switzerland (1924, 1936, 1956 and 1972). The USA (1932, 1936), Switzerland (1948, 1980), Italy (1956, 1968), W. Germany (1952, 1972) and GDR (1976, 1984) have won the Olympic two-man bob (inst. 1932) event twice. The most gold medals won by an individual is three by Meinhard Nehmer (GDR) (b. 13 June 1941) and Bernhard Germeshausen (GDR) (b. 21 Aug 1951) in the 1976 two-man, 1976 and 1980 four-man events. The most medals won is six (two gold, two silver, two bronze) by Eugenio Monti (Italy) (b. 23 Jan 1928), 1956 to 1968. The only British victory was at two-man bob in 1964 by Hon. Robin Thomas Valerian Dixon (b. 21 Apr 1935) and Anthony James Dillon Nash (b. 18 Mar 1936).

Most titles *World*

The world four-man bob title (inst. 1924) has been won 15 times by Switzerland (1924, 1936, 1939, 1947, 1954–7, 1971–3, 1975, 1982–3, 1986). Italy won the two-man title 14 times (1954, 1956–63, 1966, 1968–9, 1971 and 1975). Eugenio Monti was a member of eleven world championship crews, eight two-man and three four-man in 1957–68.

TOBOGGANING

The word toboggan comes from the Micmac American Indian word *tobaakan*. The St Moritz Tobogganing Club, Switzerland, founded in 1887 is the oldest toboggan club in the world. It is unique in being the home of the Cresta Run, which dates from 1884, and for the introduction of the one-man racing toboggan skeleton. The course is 3977 ft *1212,25 m* long with a drop of 514 ft *157 m* and the record is 51.31 sec (av. 52.85 mph *85,05 km/h*) by Franco Gansser of Switzerland on 16 Feb 1986. On 21 Feb 1986 Nico Baracchi (Switzerland) set a record from Junction (890,2 m *2920 ft*) of 41.58 sec.

The greatest number of wins in the Grand National (inst. 1885) is eight by the 1948 Olympic champion Nino Bibbia (Italy) (b. 9 Sept 1924) in 1960–4, 1966, 1968 and 1973. The greatest number of wins in the Curzon Cup (inst. 1910) is eight by Bibbia in 1950, 1957–8, 1960, 1962–4, and 1969, who hence won the double in 1960 and 1962–4.

LUGEING

In lugeing the rider adopts a sitting, as opposed to a prone, position. Official international competition began at Klosters, Switzerland, in 1881. The first European championships were at Reichenberg, E. Germany, in 1914 and the first world championships at Oslo, Norway, in 1953. The International Luge Federation was formed in 1957. Lugeing became an Olympic sport in 1964.

Fastest speed

The highest recorded, photo-timed, speed is 137,4 km/h *85.38 mph* by Asle Strand (Norway) at Tandådalens Linbane, Sälen, Sweden on 1 May 1982.

Most titles *World and Olympic*

The most successful rider in the world championships is Thomas Köhler (GDR) (b. 25 June 1940), who won the single-seater title in 1962, 1964 (Olympic), 1966 and 1967 and shared the two-seater title in 1967 and 1968 (Olympic). Margit Schumann (GDR) (b. 14 Sept 1952) has won five women's titles, 1973–5, 1976 (Olympic) and 1977.

BOWLING (TENPIN)

Origins

The ancient German game of nine-pins (*Heidenwerfen*—knock down pagans) was exported to the United States in the early 17th century. In 1841 the Connecticut State Legislature prohibited the game and other states followed. Eventually a tenth pin was added to evade the ban;

Pat Duggan, the only Briton to achieve two maximum single game scores. A 'perfect' game requires 12 consecutive strikes. (Brian Morrison).

but there is some evidence of ten pins being used in Suffolk, UK about 300 years ago. The first body to standardize rules was the American Bowling Congress (ABC), established in New York on 9 Sept 1895.

The world's largest bowling centre is the Fukuyama Bowl, Osaka, Japan which has 144 lanes. The Tōkyō World Lanes Centre, Japan, now closed, had 252 lanes. The largest in Europe is the Nottingham Bowl at Nottingham, England, where the game was introduced in 1960, with 48 lanes on two floors.

World championships

The world (Fédération Internationale des Quilleurs) championships were instituted for men in 1954 and for women in 1963. The highest pinfall in the individual men's event is 5963 (in 28 games) by Ed Luther (US) at Milwaukee, Wisconsin, on 28 Aug 1971. For the current schedule of 24 games the men's record is 5242 by Mats Karlsson (Sweden) and the women's is 4806 by Bong Coo (Philippines) both at Caracas, Venezuela in Nov 1983.

Highest scores *World*

The highest individual score for three sanctioned games (possible 900) is 886 by Albert 'Allie' Brandt of Lockport, New York, USA, on 25 Oct 1939. The record by a woman is 859 by Patty Ann of New Ulm, Minnesota, USA on 2 Apr 1985. The record for consecutive strikes in sanctioned match play is 33, first achieved by John Pezzin (b. 1930) at Toledo, Ohio, USA on 4 Mar 1976. The highest number of sanctioned 300 games is 27 (to 1986) by Elvin Mesger of Sullivan, Missouri, USA; the women's record is nine by Jeanne Maiden of Solon, Ohio.

The highest average for a season attained in sanctioned competition is 242 by John Ragard of Susquehanna, Pa., USA for 66 games in 1981–82. The women's record is 232 by Patty Ann in 1983–84.

Highest scores *Great Britain*

The British record for a three-game series is 802 by Simon Brown (b. 22 Oct 1963) of Havant, Hampshire in April 1986. Army Sergeant Michael Langley scored 835 at S.H.A.P.E., Belgium on 15 Apr 1985. The maximum score for a single game of 300 has been achieved on several occasions. The first man to do so was Albert Kirkham (b. 1931) of Burslem, Staffordshire, on 5 Dec 1965. The first woman was Georgina Wardle at the Sheffield Bowl, S. Yorkshire on 20 Jan 1985. The first person to achieve the feat twice is Patrick Duggan, in 1972 and 1986. The three-game series record for a woman player is 740 by Elizabeth Cullen at the Astra Bowl, RAF Brize Norton, Oxfordshire on 15 Mar 1983.

Highest earnings

Earl Anthony (b. 1938) won a record $1,257,021 in Professional Bowlers Association (PBA) competition including a record 41 PBA titles to 1986.

Highest score—24 Hours

A team of six from Portsmouth Polytechnic scored 37,934 in 24 hours at AMF Humber Bowling Centre, Portsmouth on 1–2 Mar 1986.

BOWLS

OUTDOOR

Origins

Whilst bowling games date back some 7000 years, the game of Bowls in recognisable form can be traced back to the 13th century in England. The Southampton Town Bowling was formed in 1299. A green dating back to 1294 is claimed by the Chesterfield Bowling Club. After falling into disrepute, the game was rescued by the bowlers of Scotland who, headed by William W. Mitchell (1803–84), framed the modern rules in 1848–9.

Most titles *World*
The only man to win two singles titles is David John Bryant (b. 27 Oct 1931) (England) in 1966 and 1980. At Johannesburg, South Africa, in February 1976, the South African team achieved an unprecedented clean sweep of all four titles plus the team competition (Leonard Trophy).

Elsie Wilke (New Zealand) won two women's singles titles, 1969 and 1974. Merle Richardson (Australia) has won three women's gold medals: fours 1977, singles and pairs 1985.

Most titles *International Championship*
In the annual International Championships (inst. 1903) Scotland have won a record 34 times including 11 consecutive wins, 1965 to 1975.

Most titles *English & British*
The record number of English Bowls Association (founded 8 June 1903) championships is 16 won or shared by David Bryant, including six singles (1960, 1966, 1971–3, 1975), three pairs (1965, 1969, 1974), three triples (1966, 1977, 1985) and four fours championships (1957, 1968, 1969 and 1971). He has also won six British Isles titles (four singles, one pairs, one fours) in the period 1957–74.

Highest score
The highest score achieved in an international bowls match is the 63–1 victory by Swaziland *v* Japan during the World Championships at Melbourne, Australia on 16 Jan 1980.

Most eights
Freda Ehlers and Linda Bertram uniquely scored three consecutive eights in the Southern Transvaal pairs event at Johannesburg, South Africa on 30 Jan 1978.

International appearances
The greatest number of international appearances outdoors by any bowler is 78 reached by Syd Thompson (b. 29 Aug 1912) for Ireland 1947–73. He also has had 50 indoor caps. The youngest bowler to represent England was Gerard Anthony Smyth (b. 29 Dec 1960) at 20 yr

196 days on 13 July 1981. The youngest ever EBA singles champion was David J. Cutler (b. 1 Aug 1954) at 25 yr 16 days in 1979. He had been a member of the winning triples team at 18 yr 18 days in 1972.

INDOOR
The English Indoor Bowling Association became an autonomous body in 1971. Prior to that it was part of the English Bowling Association.

Most titles
The four-corner international championship was first held in 1936. England have won most titles with 22 wins. The National Singles title (inst. 1960) has been won most often by David Bryant with nine wins between 1964 and 1983. David Bryant has won the World Indoor Championship (inst 1979) three times, 1979–81.

The youngest EIBA singles champion, John Dunn (b. 6 Oct 1963) was 17 yr 117 days when he won in 1981.

Highest score
The highest score in a British International match is 52 by Scotland *v.* Wales (3) at Teeside in March 1972.

C. Hammond and B. Funnell of The Angel, Tonbridge beat A. Wise and C. Lock 55–0 over 21 ends in the second round of the EIBA National Pairs Championships on 17 Oct 1983 at The Angel, Tonbridge, Kent.

BOXING

Earliest references
Boxing with gloves was depicted on a fresco from the Isle of Thera, Greece which has been dated 1520 BC. The earliest prize-ring code of rules was formulated in England on 16 Aug 1743 by the champion pugilist Jack Broughton (1704–89), who reigned from 1734 to 1750. Boxing, which had, in 1867, come under the Queensberry Rules formulated for John Sholto Douglas, 8th Marquess of Queensberry (1844–1900), was not established as a legal sport in Britain until after the ruling, R. *v.* Roberts and Others, of Mr Justice Grantham, following the death of Billy Smith (Murray Livingstone) due to a fight on 24 Apr 1901.

Longest fights
The longest recorded fight with gloves was between Andy Bowen of New Orleans (1867–94) and Jack Burke in New Orleans, Louisiana, USA, on 6–7 Apr 1893. The fight lasted 110 rounds and 7 hr 19 min (9.15 p.m.–4.34 a.m.), and was declared a no contest (later changed to a draw). Bowen won an 85 round bout on 31 May 1893. The longest bare knuckle fight was 6 hr 15 min between James Kelly and Jack Smith at Fiery Creek, Dalesford, Victoria, Australia on 3 Dec 1855. The longest bare knuckle fight in Britain was 6 hr 3 min (185 rounds) between Bill Hayes and Mike Madden at Edenbridge, Kent, on 17 July 1849. The greatest number of rounds was 276 in 4 hr 30 min when Jack Jones beat Patsy Tunney in Cheshire in 1825.

Shortest fights
There is a distinction between the quickest knock-out and the shortest fight. A knock-out in 10½ sec (including a 10 sec count) occurred on 23 Sept 1946, when Al Couture struck Ralph Walton while the latter was adjusting a gum shield in his corner at Lewiston, Maine, USA. If the time was accurately taken it is clear that Couture must have been more than half-way

across the ring from his own corner at the opening bell. The shortest fight on record appears to be one in a Golden Gloves tournament at Minneapolis, Minnesota, USA, on 4 Nov 1947 when Mike Collins floored Pat Brownson with the first punch and the contest was stopped, without a count, 4 sec after the bell.

The fastest officially timed knock-out in British boxing is 11 sec (including a doubtless fast 10 sec count) when Jack Cain beat Harry Deamer, both of Notting Hill, London at the National Sporting Club on 20 Feb 1922. More recently, Hugh Kelly knocked out Steve Cook with the first punch of their contest at the Normandy Hotel, Glasgow on 14 May 1984, again in 11 sec, including the 10 sec count.

The shortest world title fight was the James J. Jeffries (1875–1953)–Jack Finnegan heavyweight bout on 6 Apr 1900, won by Jeffries in 55 sec. The shortest ever British title fight was one of 40 sec (including the count), when Dave Charnley knocked out David 'Darkie' Hughes in a lightweight championship defence in Nottingham on 20 Nov 1961.

Most British titles
The most defences of a British heavyweight title is 14 by 'Bombardier' Billy Wells (1889–1967) from 1911 to 1919. The only British boxer to win three Lonsdale Belts outright was Henry William Cooper (b. 3 May 1934), heavyweight champion (1959–69, 1970–1). He retired after losing to Joe Bugner (b. Hungary, 13 Mar 1950), having held the British heavyweight title from 12 Jan 1959 to 28 May 1969 and from 24 Mar 1970 to 16 Mar 1971.

Tallest
The tallest boxer to fight professionally was Gogea Mitu (b. 1914) of Romania in 1935. He was 7 ft 4 in *233 cm* and weighed 23 st 5 lb (327 lb) *148 kg*. John Rankin, who won a fight in New Orleans, Louisiana, USA, in November 1967, was reputedly also 7 ft 4 in *233 cm*.

Longest career
The heavyweight Jem Mace (GB) (1831–1910), known as 'the gypsy', had a career lasting 35 years from 1855 to 1890, and had an exhibition bout in 1896 but his career is not fully documented. Kid Azteca (b. Luis Villanuera Paramo 1915 in Mexico City) started boxing profession-

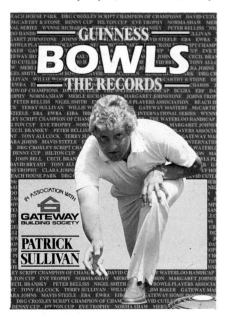

Published by Guinness at £7.95

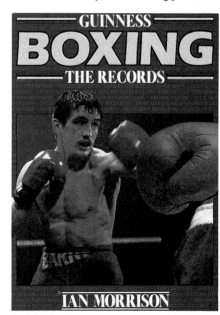

IAN MORRISON

Published by Guinness at £7.95

ally in 1929 and has a published record that includes at least one bout per year 1932–61.

Most fights without loss
Edward Henry (Harry) Greb (USA) (1894–1926) was unbeaten in 178 bouts, but these included 117 'No Decision', of which five were unofficial losses, in 1916–23. Of boxers with complete records Packey McFarland (USA) (1888–1936) had 97 fights (five draws) in 1905–15 without a defeat. Pedro Carrasco (Spain) (b. 7 Nov 1943) won 83 consecutive fights from 22 April 1964 to 3 Sept 1970, drew once and had a further nine wins before his loss to Armando Ramos in a WBC lightweight contest on 18 Feb 1972.

Most knock-outs
The greatest number of finishes classed as 'knock-outs' in a career (1936–63) is 145 (129 in professional bouts) by Archie Moore (USA) (b. Archibald Lee Wright, 13 Dec 1913 or 1916). The record for consecutive KO's is 44 by Lamar Clark (b. 1 Dec 1934) (USA) from 1958 to 11 Jan 1960. He knocked out six in one night (five in the first round) at Bingham, Utah, on 1 Dec 1958.

Largest purse
The total purse for the world middleweight fight between 'Marvelous' Marvin Hagler (b. 23 May 1954) and Thomas Hearns (USA) at Las Vegas on 16 Apr 1985, was estimated as $17 million (including a guaranteed $11 million). Hagler won in the third round.

Highest earnings in career
The largest fortune made in a fighting career is an estimated $69 million (including exhibitions) by Muhammad Ali from October 1960 to December 1981 in 61 fights comprising 549 rounds.

Attendances *Highest*
The greatest paid attendance at any boxing fight has been 120,757 (with a ringside price of $27.50) for the Tunney v. Dempsey world heavyweight title fight at the Sesquicentennial Stadium, Philadelphia, Pennsylvania, USA, on 23 Sept 1926. The indoor record is 63,350 at the Ali v. Leon Spinks fight in the Superdrome, New Orleans, Louisiana, on 15 Sept 1978. Record receipts of $7,293,600 were reported for the WBC world heavyweight title fight at Las Vegas on 11 June 1982 when Larry Holmes (USA) (b. 3 Nov 1949) beat Gerry Cooney (USA) (b. 24 Aug 1956). The British attendance record is 82,000 at the Len Harvey v. Jock McAvoy fight at White City, London, on 10 July 1939.

The highest non-paying attendance is 135,132 at the Tony Zale v. Billy Pryor fight at Juneau Park, Milwaukee, Wisconsin, USA, on 16 Aug 1941.

Attendances *Lowest*
The smallest attendance at a world heavyweight title fight was 2434 at the Clay v. Liston fight at Lewiston, Maine, USA, on 25 May 1965.

WORLD HEAVYWEIGHT CHAMPIONS

Earliest title fight
The first world heavyweight title fight, with gloves and 3 min rounds, was that between John Lawrence Sullivan (1858–1918) and 'Gentleman' James John Corbett (1866–1933) in New Orleans, Louisiana, USA, on 7 Sept 1892. Corbett won in 21 rounds.

Longest and shortest reigns
The longest reign of any world heavyweight champion is 11 years 252 days by Joe Louis

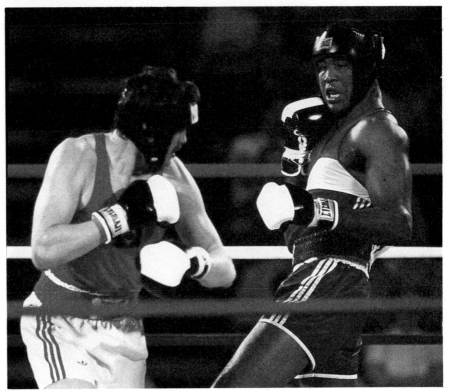

Veteran amateur heavyweight Teofilo Stevenson (*right*), triple World and Olympic champion, who has persistently turned down the financial carrot of professional status. George Foreman said of him, 'He could be world champion any time he chose'. (All-Sport).

(USA) (b. Joseph Louis Barrow, 1914–81), from 22 June 1937, when he knocked out James Joseph Braddock in the eighth round at Chicago, Illinois, USA, until announcing his retirement on 1 Mar 1949. During his reign Louis made a record 25 defences of his title. The shortest reign was by Greg Page (USA) (b. 25 Oct 1958) for 150 days from 1 Dec 1984 to 29 Apr 1985. Ken Norton (USA) (b. 9 Aug 1945) was recognised by the WBC as champion for 83 days from 18 Mar–9 June 1978. The longest lived world heavyweight champion was Jack Dempsey who died on 31 May 1983 aged 87 yr 341 days.

Most recaptures
Muhammad Ali (b. Cassius Marcellus Clay Jr. 17 Jan 1942) is the only man to regain the heavyweight championship twice. Ali first won the title on 25 Feb 1964 defeating Sonny Liston. He defeated George Foreman on 30 Oct 1974 having been stripped of the title by the world boxing authorities on 28 Apr 1967. He won the WBA title from Leon Spinks on 15 Sept 1978 having previously lost to him on 15 Feb 1978.

Undefeated
Rocky Marciano (b. Rocco Francis Marchegiano) (1923–69) is the only world heavyweight champion to have been undefeated during his entire professional career (1947–56). He won all his 49 fights, 43 by knockouts or stoppages.

Oldest and Youngest
The oldest man to win the heavyweight crown was Jersey Joe Walcott (USA) (b. Arnold Raymond Cream, 31 Jan 1914) who knocked out Ezzard Mack Charles (1921–75) on 18 July 1951 in Pittsburgh, Pennsylvania, when aged 37 yr 168 days. Walcott was the oldest holder at 38 yr 236 days, losing his title to Rocky Marciano (1923–69) on 23 Sept 1952. The youngest age at which the world title has been won is 21 yr 331 days by Floyd Patterson (USA) (b. 4 Jan 1935), when he won the vacant title by beating Archie Moore in Chicago, Illinois, USA, on 30 Nov 1956.

Heaviest and lightest
The heaviest world champion was Primo Car-

nera (Italy) (1906–67), the 'Ambling Alp', who won the title from Jack Sharkey in six rounds in New York City, NY, USA, on 29 June 1933. He scaled 267 lb *121 kg* for this fight but his peak weight was 270 lb *122 kg*. He had an expanded chest measurement of 53 in *134 cm* and the longest reach at 85½ in *217 cm* (finger tip to finger tip). The lightest champion was Robert James 'Bob' Fitzsimmons (1863–1917), from Helston, Cornwall, who at a weight of 167 lb *75 kg*, won the title by knocking out James Corbett in 14 rounds at Carson City, Nevada, USA, on 17 Mar 1897.

The greatest differential in a world title fight was 86 lb *39 kg* between Carnera (270 lb *122 kg*) and Tommy Loughran (184 lb *83 kg*) of the USA, when the former won on points at Miami, Florida, USA, on 1 Mar 1934.

Tallest and shortest
The tallest world champion according to measurements by the Physical Education Director of the Hemingway Gymnasium, Harvard University, was Carnera at 6 ft 5.4 in *196,6 cm* although he was widely reported and believed to be up to 6 ft 8½ in *204 cm*. Jess Willard (1881–1968), who won the title in 1915, often stated to be 6 ft 6¼ in *199 cm* was in fact 6 ft 5¼ in *196 cm*. The shortest was Tommy Burns, world champion from 23 Feb 1906 to 26 Dec 1908, who stood 5 ft 7 in *170 cm* and weighed between 168 and 180 lb *76–81 kg*.

WORLD CHAMPIONS *Any weight*

Longest reign
Joe Louis's heavyweight duration record of 11 years 252 days stands for all divisions.

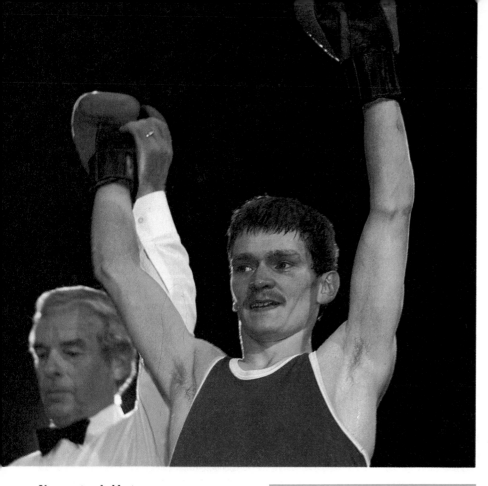

BOXING

Most titles *Great Britain*
The greatest number of ABA titles won by any boxer is six by Joseph Steers at middleweight and heavyweight between 1890 and 1893. Alex 'Bud' Watson (b. 27 May 1914) of Leith, Scotland won the Scottish heavyweight title in 1938, 1942–3, and the light-heavyweight championship 1937–9, 1943–5 and 1947, making ten in all. He also won the ABA light-heavyweight title in 1945 and 1947.

Longest span
The greatest span of ABA title-winning performances is that of the heavyweight Hugh 'Pat' Floyd (b. 23 Aug 1910), who won in 1929 and gained his fourth title 17 years later in 1946.

CANOEING

Origins
The acknowledged pioneer of canoeing as a modern sport was John Macgregor (1825–92), a British barrister, in 1865. The Canoe Club was formed on 26 July 1866.

Most titles *Olympic*
Gert Fredriksson (b. 21 Nov 1919) of Sweden has won most Olympic gold medals with six in 1948, 1952, 1956 and 1960. The most by a woman is three by Ludmila Pinayeva (*née* Khvedosyuk) (b. 14 Jan 1936) (USSR), in 1964, 1968 and 1972. The most gold medals at one Games is three by Vladimir Parfenovich (b. 2 Dec 1958) (USSR) in 1980 and by Ian Ferguson (b. 20 July 1952) (New Zealand) in 1984.

Most titles *World*
Thirteen titles have been won by Rüdiger Helm (GDR) (b. 6 Oct 1956), ten world and three Olympic between 1976 and 1983. Birgit Schmidt

Richard Fox, winner of three world titles in the slalom event. (All-sport).

Youngest and oldest
The youngest age at which any world championship has been won is 17 yr 176 days by Wilfred Benitez (b. New York, 12 Sept 1958) of Puerto Rico, who won the WBA light welterweight title in San Juan, PR, on 6 Mar 1976. The oldest world champion was Archie Moore who was recognised as a light heavyweight champion up to 10 Feb 1962 when his title was removed. He was then believed to be between 45 and 48. Bob Fitzsimmons had the longest career of any official world titleholder with over 31 years from 1883 to 1914. He had his last world title bout on 20 Dec 1905 at the age of 42 yr 208 days.

Longest fight
The longest world title fight (under Queensberry Rules) was that between the lightweights Joe Gans (1874–1910), of the USA, and Oscar Matthew 'Battling' Nelson (1882–1954), the 'Durable Dane', at Goldfield, Nevada, USA, on 3 Sept 1906. It was terminated in the 42nd round when Gans was declared the winner on a foul.

Most recaptures
The only boxer to win a world title five times at one weight is 'Sugar' Ray Robinson (USA) (b. Walker Smith, Jr, 3 May 1921), who beat Carmen Basilio (USA) in the Chicago Stadium on 25 Mar 1958, to regain the world middleweight title for the fourth time. The record number of title bouts in a career is 37, of which 18 ended in 'no decision' by three-time world welterweight champion, Jack Britton (USA) (1885–1962) in 1915–22.

Greatest weight span
The only man to hold world titles at three weights *simultaneously* was Henry 'Homicide Hank' Armstrong (b. 12 Dec 1912), now the Rev Henry Jackson, of the USA, at featherweight, lightweight and welterweight from August to December 1938.

Greatest 'tonnage'
The greatest 'tonnage' recorded in any fight is 700 lb *317 kg* when Claude 'Humphrey' Mc-

---

In 1986 John Lyon won his fifth ABA flyweight title, a record for that division. (All-Sport).

Bride (Oklahoma) 340 lb *154 kg* knocked out Jimmy Black (Houston), who weighed 360 lb *163 kg* in the third round at Oklahoma City on 1 June 1971. The greatest 'tonnage' in a world title fight was 488¾ lb *221½ kg*, when Carnera, then 259½ lb *117½ kg* fought Paolino Uzcudun 229¼ lb *104 kg* of Spain in Rome on 22 Oct 1933.

Most knock-downs in Title fights
Vic Toweel (South Africa) (b. 12 Jan 1929) knocked down Danny O'Sullivan of London 14 times in ten rounds in their world bantamweight fight at Johannesburg on 2 Dec 1950, before the latter retired.

AMATEUR

Most Olympic titles
Only two boxers have won three Olympic gold medals: southpaw László Papp (b. 25 Mar 1926) (Hungary), middleweight 1948, light-middleweight 1952 and 1956; Teofilo Stevenson (b. 23 Mar 1952) (Cuba), heavyweight 1972, 1976 and 1980. The only man to win two titles in one celebration was Oliver L. Kirk (USA), who won both bantam and featherweight titles in St Louis, Missouri, USA, in 1904, but he only needed one bout in each class.

Oldest gold medallist
Richard Kenneth Gunn (1871–1961) (GB) won the Olympic featherweight gold medal on 27 Oct 1908 in London aged 37 yr 254 days.

World Championships
Two boxers have won three world championships (inst. 1974): Teofilo Stevenson (Cuba), heavyweight 1974, 1978 and 1986, and Adolfo Horta (b. 3 Oct 1957) (Cuba) bantam 1978, feather 1982 and lightweight 1986.

(née Fischer) (b. 25 Feb 1962) won 13 women's world titles 1979–85, including the Olympic kayak singles in 1980. The most individual titles by a British canoeist is three by Alan Emus, canoe sailing 1961, 1965 and 1969 and by Richard Fox at K1 slalom in 1981, 1983 and 1985.

Most titles *British*
The most British Open titles (instituted 1936) ever won is 32 by John Laurence Oliver (Lincoln Canoe Club) (b. 12 Jan 1943) from 1966 to 1976 including 12 individual events. David Mitchell (Chester S&CC) won eight British slalom titles in 1963–8, 1970–1.

Highest speed
The Olympic 1000 m best performance of 3 min 02.70 sec set in a heat by the USSR K4 at Moscow on 31 July 1980, represents an average speed of 12.24 mph *19,70 km/h*. They achieved 13.14 mph *21,15 km/h* for the first 250 m.

Longest journey
The longest journey ever made by canoe is 12,181 miles *19 603 km* by father and son Dana and Donald Starkell from Winnipeg, Manitoba, Canada by ocean and river to Belem, Brazil from 1 June 1980 to 1 May 1982. All portages were human powered.

The longest journey without portages or aid of any kind is one of 6102 miles *9820 km* by Richard H. Grant and Ernest 'Moose' Lassy circumnavigating the eastern USA via Chicago, New Orleans, Miami, New York and the Great Lakes from 22 Sept 1930 to 15 Aug 1931.

Longest open sea voyage
Beatrice and John Dowd, Ken Beard and Steve Benson (Richard Gillett replaced him midjourney) paddled 2170 miles *3491 km* (of a total 2192 miles *3527 km*) from Venezuela to Miami, Florida, USA, via the West Indies, 11 Aug 1977–29 Apr 1978 in two Klepper Aerius 20 kayaks.

Cross-Channel
The singles record across the English Channel is 3 hr 33 min 47 sec by Andrew William Dougall Samuel (b. 12 July 1937) of Glasgow, from Shakespeare Bay, Dover, to Wissant, France, on 5 Sept 1976. The doubles record is 2 hr 54 min 54 sec by Andrew Samuel and Sgt John David Anderson (RAF) (b. 18 Mar 1957) in a K2 *Accord*, from Shakespeare Bay, Dover to Cap Gris Nez, France on 22 Aug 1980.

The record for a double crossing is 12 hr 47 min in K1s by nine members of the Canoe Camping Club, GB, on 7 May 1976.

North Sea
On 22–23 June 1986, a team of five in the 'Canadian Club Challenge' paddled K1s from Zeebrugge, Belgium to Felixstowe, England, over 110 miles *177 km* across open sea, in 28 hr 56 min 12 sec.

Loch Ness
The fastest time for a K1 from Fort Augustus to Lochend (22.7 miles *36,5 km*) is 3 hr 13 min 47 sec by Flt. Lt. John David Anderson (RAF) in a Jaguar K1 on 22 Oct 1985.

Highest altitude
In September 1976 Dr Michael Leslie Jones (1951–78) and Michael Hopkinson of the British Everest Canoe Expedition canoed down the River Dudh Kosi, Nepal from an altitude of 17,500 ft *5334 m*.

24 Hours
The solo 24-hour canoe record is 230,65 km *143.32 miles* by Dr. Chris L. Greeff (S. Africa) in a Jaguar K1 canoe on Breede River, Robert-

Frank Palmer and Bob Cope, who set a two-man downstream record for the River Rhine (1139 km *707.7 miles*) in May 1986. It took them 11 days 8 hr.

son to Cape Infanta, Cape Province, South Africa on 11–12 Aug 1985. The women's record was set at 156,4 km *97.2 miles* by Lydia Formentin on the Swan River, Western Australia in 1979.

Greatest lifetime distance
Fritz Lindner of Berlin, W. Germany, totalled 91 486 km *56,847 miles* from 1928 to 1983.

Eskimo Rolls
Steve Flint achieved 1000 eskimo rolls in 44 min 7 sec at Larkfield Leisure Centre, Maidstone, Kent on 18 July 1985. Julian Dean achieved 1555 continuous rolls at Casterton Swimming Pool, Cumbria, taking 1 hr 49 min 45 sec on 6 Dec 1983. A 'hand-rolling' record of 100 rolls in 2 min 39.35 sec was set by Colin Hill at Crystal Palace, London on 23 Feb 1986.

CARD GAMES

CONTRACT BRIDGE

Bridge (a corruption of Biritch, a now-obsolete Russian word whose meanings include 'declarer') is thought to be either of Levantine origin, similar games having been played there in the early 1870s, or to have come from India.

Auction Bridge (highest bidder names trump) was invented *c.* 1902. The contract principle, present in several games (notably the French game *Plafond, c.* 1917) was introduced to Bridge by Harold Sterling Vanderbilt (USA) on 1 Nov 1925 during a Caribbean voyage aboard the SS *Finland*. It became a world-wide craze after the USA *v.* Great Britain challenge match between Romanian-born Ely Culbertson (1891–1955) and Lt-Col Walter Thomas More Buller (1887–1938) at Almack's Club, London, in September 1930. The USA won the 200-hand match by 4845 points.

Biggest tournament
The Epson World Bridge Championship, held on 14 June 1986, was contested by 66,000 players playing simultaneously worldwide.

Most World titles
The World Championship (Bermuda Bowl) has been won most often by Italy's Blue Team (*Squadra Azzura*), 1957–9, 1961–3, 1965–7, 1969, 1973–5. Italy also won the Olympiad in 1964, 1968 and 1972. Giorgio Belladonna (b. 7 June 1923) was in all these winning teams.

Most master points
In the latest ranking list based on Master Points

awarded by the World Bridge Federation, the leading male player in the world was Giorgio Belladonna (Italy) with 1766¼ points. The leading Briton is Boris Schapiro (b. 22 Aug 1909) in 22nd place with 353 points. The world's leading woman player is Dorothy Hayden Truscott (USA) with 331¼ points. Third ranked Rika 'Rixi' Markus is the leading British woman and was first woman Grand Master (1973), with 281 points.

Barry Crane of Los Angeles led the American Contract Bridge League rankings from 1968 to his murder in 1985. He amassed a record total of 35,137.6 master points. The current leader is Paul Suloway with 23,848.1. The most master points scored in a year is 3270 by Grant Baze (USA) in 1984.

The first man to win 10,000 master points was Oswald Jacoby (USA) (1902–84) in October 1967. He had been a member of the winning World Championship team in 1935 and on 4 Dec 1983 became the oldest member of a winning team of a major open team championship in the Curtis Reisinger Trophy.

Youngest Life Master
Dougie Hsieh (b. 23 Nov 1969) of New York City became the world's youngest ever Life Master in 1981 at 11 yr 306 days. The youngest ever female Master is Patricia Thomas (b. 10 Oct 1968) at 14 yr 28 days in 1982.

Perfect deals
The mathematical odds against dealing 13 cards of one suit are 158,753,389,899 to 1, while the odds against receiving a 'perfect hand' consisting of all 13 spades are 635,013,559,596 to 1. The odds against each of the four players receiving a complete suit (a 'perfect deal') are 2,235,197,406,895,366,368,301,559,999 to 1.

CRIBBAGE

The invention of the game (once called Cribbidge) is credited to the English dramatist Sir John Suckling (1609–42).

Rare hands
William E. Johnson of Waltham, Mass., USA had four maximum 29 point hands, 1974–81. Paul Nault of Athol, Mass, USA had two such hands within eight games in a tournament on 19 Mar 1977.

WHIST

Whist, first referred to in 1529 (as trump), was the world's premier card game until 1930. The rules were standardised in 1742.

Highest score
The highest score claimed for 24 hands is 214 by Mrs Margaret Shipley of Dorset Social Club, South Shields, Tyne & Wear.

CAVING

See also page 59

The world depth record was set by the Groupe Vulcain in the Gouffre Jean Bernard, France at 1535 m *5035 ft* in October 1983. However this cave, explored via multiple entrances has never been entirely descended, so the 'sporting' record for the greatest descent into a cave is recognised as 1370 m *4495 ft* in the Snezhnaya–Mezhonnogo, USSR by a team led by A. Morozov in 1984. The deepest cave explored through a single entrance is the 1338 m *4391 ft* Sima de la Puerta de Illamina in Spain by F. Vergier in August 1981.

The spearhead of the brilliant West Indian pace attack, Malcolm Marshall has achieved the unprecedented feat of taking 20 wickets in seven successive Test series. (All-Sport).

CRICKET

Origins

The earliest evidence of a game similar to cricket is from a drawing depicting two men playing with a bat and ball dated *c*. 1250. The game was played in Guildford, Surrey, at least as early as 1550. The earliest major match of which the full score survives was one in which a team representing England (40 and 70) was beaten by Kent (53 and 58 for 9) by one wicket at the Artillery Ground in Finsbury, London, on 18 June 1744. Cricket was played in Australia as early as 1803. The first international match was played between Canada and USA in 1844. Fifteen years later those countries were host to the first English touring team. The first touring team to visit England was an Australian Aborigine XI in 1868.

FIRST-CLASS CRICKET (1815 to 1985)

A substantial reduction in the English first-class cricket programme since 1968 has rendered many of the record aggregates for a season unassailable.

BATTING RECORDS—TEAMS

Highest innings

The highest recorded innings by any team was one of 1107 runs in 10 hr 30 min by Victoria against New South Wales in an Australian Sheffield Shield match at Melbourne on 27–28 Dec 1926.

The highest innings in Test cricket and the highest made in England is 903 runs for 7 wickets declared in 15 hr 17 min, by England against Australia at Kennington Oval, London, on 20, 22 and 23 Aug 1938. The highest innings in a county championship match is 887 in 10 hr 50 min by Yorkshire v. Warwickshire at Edgbaston, Birmingham on 7–8 May 1896.

Lowest innings

The lowest recorded innings is 12 made by Oxford University *v.* the Marylebone Cricket Club (MCC) at Cowley Marsh, Oxford on 24 May 1877, and 12 by Northamptonshire *v.* Gloucestershire at Gloucester on 11 June 1907. On the occasion of the Oxford match, however, the University batted a man short. The lowest in modern times is 14 by Surrey v. Essex at Chelmsford on 30 May 1983. The lowest score in a Test innings is 26 by New Zealand *v.* England in the second innings at Auckland on 28 Mar 1955.

The lowest aggregate for two innings is 34 (16 in first and 18 in second) by Border *v.* Natal in the South African Currie Cup at East London on 19 and 21 Dec 1959.

Greatest victory

The greatest recorded margin of victory is an innings and 851 runs, when Pakistan Railways (910 for 6 wickets declared) beat Dera Ismail Khan (32 and 27) at Lahore on 2–4 Dec 1964. The largest margin in England is an innings and 579 runs by England over Australia at The Oval on 20–24 Aug 1938 when Australia scored 201 and 123 with two men short in both innings. The most one-sided county match was when Surrey (698) defeated Sussex (114 and 99) by an innings and 485 runs at The Oval on 9–11 Aug 1888.

Most runs in a day

The greatest number of runs scored in a day is 721 all out (ten wickets) in 5 hr 48 min by the Australians *v.* Essex at Southchurch Park, Southend-on-Sea on 15 May 1948. The Test record for runs in a day is 588 at Old Trafford, Manchester, on 27 July 1936 when England added 398 and India were 190 for 0 in their second innings by the close.

BATTING RECORDS *Individuals*

Highest innings

The highest individual innings recorded is 499

INDIVIDUAL CAREER RECORDS
All First-Class Cricket (FC) and Test Cricket (Test)

			Name	Team	Year
BATTING					
Most runs	FC	61,237	Sir John Berry 'Jack' Hobbs (1882–1963) (av 50.65)	Surrey/England	1905–34
	Test	9192	Sunil Manohar Gavaskar (b. 10 July 1949) (av 51.35)	India (112 Tests)	1971–86
Most centuries	FC	197	Sir Jack Hobbs (in 1315 innings)	Surrey/England	1905–34
	Test	32	Sunil Gavaskar	India	1971–86
Highest average	FC	95.14	Sir Donald George Bradman (b. 27 Aug 1908) (28,067 runs in 338 innings)	NSW/South Australia/Australia	1927–49
	Test	99.94	Sir Don Bradman (6996 runs in 80 innings)	Australia (52 Tests)	1928–48
BOWLING					
Most wickets	FC	4187	Wilfred Rhodes (1877–1973) (av 16.70)	Yorkshire/England	1898–1930
	Test	355	Dennis Keith Lillee (b. 18 July 1949) (av 23.92)	Australia (70 Tests)	1971–84
Most hat-tricks	FC	7	Douglas Vivian Parson Wright (b. 21 Aug 1914)	Kent	1932–57
	Test	2	Hugh Trumble (1867–1938)	Australia	1890–1904
		2	Thomas James Matthews (1884–1943)	Australia (in same match)	1912
Lowest average (min 15 wkts)	Test	10.75	George Alfred Lohmann (1865–1901) (112 wkts)	England (18 Tests)	1886–96
WICKET-KEEPING					
Most dismissals	FC	1646	Robert William Taylor (b. 17 July 1941)	Derbyshire/England	1960–84
	Test	355	Rodney William Marsh (b. 11 Nov 1947)	Australia (96 Tests)	1970–84
Most catches	FC	1471	Robert Taylor	Derbyshire/England	1960–84
	Test	343	Rodney Marsh	Australia	1970–84
Most stumpings	FC	415	Leslie Ethelbert George Ames (b. 3 Dec 1905)	Kent/England	1926–51
	Test	52	William Albert Stanley Oldfield (1894–1976)	Australia (54 Tests)	1920–37
FIELDING					
Most catches	FC	1018	Frank Edward Woolley (1887–1978)	Kent/England	1906–38
	Test	122	Gregory Stephen Chappell (b. 7 Aug 1948)	Australia (87 Tests)	1970–84
MOST MATCHES					
First class		1107	Wilfred Rhodes	Yorkshire/England	1898–1930
Test		115	Sunil Gavaskar	India	1971–86

in 10 hr 35 min by Hanif Mohammad (b. 21 Dec 1934) for Karachi v. Bahawalpur at Karachi, Pakistan, on 8, 9 and 11 Jan 1959. The highest score in England is 424 in 7 hr 50 min by Archibald Campbell MacLaren (1871–1944) for Lancashire v. Somerset at Taunton on 15–16 July 1895. The record for a Test match is 365 not out in 10 hr 14 min by Sir Garfield St Aubrun Sobers (b. 28 July 1936) playing for West Indies against Pakistan at Sabina Park, Kingston, Jamaica, on 27 Feb–1 Mar 1958. The England Test record is 364 by Sir Leonard Hutton (b. 23 June 1916) v. Australia at The Oval on 20, 22 and 23 Aug 1938.

Longest innings

The longest innings on record is one of 16 hr 10 min for 337 runs by Hanif Mohammad (Pakistan) v. West Indies at Bridgetown, Barbados, on 20–23 Jan 1958. The English record is 13 hr 17 min by Len Hutton in his record Test score of 364.

Most runs *Off an over*

The first batsman to score 36 runs off a six-ball over was Sir Garfield Sobers (Nottinghamshire) off Malcolm Andrew Nash (b. 9 May 1945) (Glamorgan) at Swansea on 31 Aug 1968. His feat was emulated by Ravishankar Jayadritha Shastri (b. 27 May 1962) for Bombay v. Baroda at Bombay, India on 10 Jan 1985 off the bowling of Tilak Raj.

Most runs *Off a ball*

The most runs scored off a single hit is ten by Albert Neilson Hornby (1847–1925) off James Street (1839–1906) for Lancashire v. Surrey at The Oval on 14 July 1873, and ten by Samuel Hill Wood (later Sir Samuel Hill Hill-Wood) (1872–1949) off Cuthbert James Burnup (1875–1960) in the Derbyshire v. MCC match at Lord's, London, on 26 May 1900.

Most sixes *In an innings*

The highest number of sixes hit in an innings is 15 by John Richard Reid (b. 3 June 1928), in an innings of 296, lasting 3 hr 40 min, for Wellington v. Northern Districts in the Plunket Shield Tournament at Wellington, New Zealand, on 14–15 Jan 1963. The Test record is ten by Walter Hammond in an innings of 336 not out for England v. New Zealand at Auckland on 31 Mar and 1 Apr 1933.

Most sixes *In a match*

William James Perver Stewart (b. 31 Oct 1934) hit a record 17 sixes (ten in the first innings and seven in the second) for Warwickshire v. Lancashire at Blackpool on 29–31 July 1959. His two innings were of 155 and 125.

		Name	Team	Year
BATTING				
Most runs	3816	Denis Charles Scott Compton (b. 23 May 1918) (av 90.85)	Middlesex/England	1947
Most centuries	18	Denis Compton (in 50 innings with 8 not outs)	Middlesex/England	1947
Highest average	115.66	Sir Donald Bradman (2429 runs in 26 innings, with 5 not outs)	Australians	1938
BOWLING				
Most wickets	304	Alfred Percy 'Tich' Freeman (1888–1965) (1976.1 overs) (av 18.05)	Kent	1928
Lowest average (min 100 wkts)	8.54	Alfred Shaw (1842–1907) (186 wkts)	Nottinghamshire	1880
WICKET-KEEPING				
Most dismissals	127	Leslie Ames (79 caught, 48 stumped)	Kent	1929
Most catches	96	James Graham Binks (b. 5 Oct 1935)	Yorkshire	1960
Most stumpings	64	Leslie Ames	Kent	1932
FIELDING				
Most catches	78	Walter Reginald Hammond (1903–65)	Gloucestershire	1928

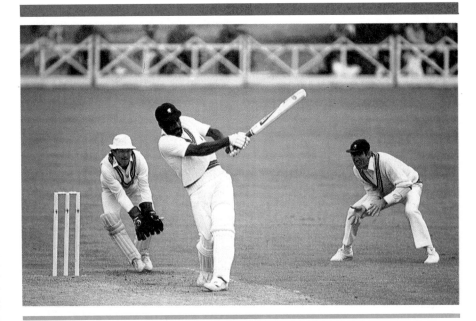

The mercurial Viv Richards in action. His 56-ball century against England in Antigua was the fastest in Test history. (All-Sport).

Most boundaries in an innings

The highest number of boundaries was 68 (all in fours) by Percival Albert Perrin (1876–1945) in an innings of 343 not out for Essex v. Derbyshire at Chesterfield on 18–19 July 1904.

Double hundreds

The only batsman to score double hundreds in both innings is Arthur Edward Fagg (1915–77), who made 244 and 202 not out for Kent v. Essex at Colchester on 13–15 July 1938. Sir Donald Bradman scored a career record 37 double hundreds 1927–49.

'Carrying bat'

Cecil John Burditt Wood (1875–1960), of Leicestershire, is the only batsman to carry his bat through both completed innings of a match, and score a hundred in both innings, (107 not out, 117 not out) on 12–14 June 1911 v. Yorkshire at Bradford.

Fastest scoring

The fastest 50 was completed off 13 balls in 8 min (1.22 to 1.30 p.m.) and in 11 scoring strokes by Clive Clay Inman (b. 29 Jan 1936) in an innings of 57 not out for Leicestershire v. Nottinghamshire at Trent Bridge, Nottingham on 20 Aug 1965. Full tosses were bowled to expedite a declaration.

The fastest hundred was completed in 35 min off between 40 and 46 balls by Percy George Herbert Fender (b. 22 Aug 1892), when scoring 113 not out for Surrey v. Northamptonshire at

INDIVIDUAL RECORDS IN A TEST SERIES

		Name	Team	Year
BATTING				
Most runs	974	Sir Donald Bradman (av 139.14)	Australia v. England (5 T)	1930
Most centuries	5	Clyde Leopold Walcott (b. 17 Jan 1926)	West Indies v. Australia (5 T)	1954–55
Highest average	563.00	Walter Reginald Hammond (563 runs in 2 innings, 1 not out)	England v. New Zealand (2 T)	1932–33
BOWLING				
Most wickets	49	Sydney Francis Barnes (1873–1967) (av 10.93)	England v. South Africa (4 T)	1913–14
Lowest average (min 20 wkts)	5.80	George Alfred Lohmann (35 wkts)	England v. South Africa (3 T)	1895–96
WICKET-KEEPING				
Most dismissals	28	Rodney Marsh (all caught)	Australia v. England (5 T)	1982–83
Most stumpings	9	Percy William Sherwell (1880–1948)	South Africa v. Australia (5 T)	1910–11
FIELDING				
Most catches	15	Jack Morrison Gregory (1895–1973)	Australia v. England (5 T)	1920–21
ALL-ROUND				
400 runs/ 30 wickets	475/34	George Giffen (1859–1927)	Australia v. England (5 T)	1894–95

Northampton on 26 Aug 1920. Steven Joseph O'Shaughnessy (b. 9 Sept 1961) also scored a hundred in 35 minutes for Lancashire v. Leicestershire at Old Trafford, Manchester off 54 balls on 13 Sept 1983. In all he scored 105 and with Graeme Fowler (b. 20 Apr 1957) put on 201 runs for the 1st wicket in 45 mins. The match was 'dead' and irregular bowlers were used.

The hundred in fewest recorded deliveries was by David William Hookes (b. 3 May 1955) in 34 balls, in 43 min, for South Australia v. Victoria at Adelaide on 25 Oct 1982. In all he scored 107 from 40 balls in this the second innings, following 137 in the first innings. The most prolific scorer of hundreds in an hour or less was Gilbert Laird Jessop (1874–1955), with 11 between 1897 and 1913. The fastest Test hundred was one off 56 balls by Isaac Vivian Alexander Richards (b. 7 Mar 1952) for West Indies v. England at St John's, Antigua on 15 Apr 1986. His final score was 110 in 81 minutes. Edwin Boaler Alletson (1884–1963) scored 189 runs in 90 min for Nottinghamshire v. Sussex at Hove on 20 May 1911.

A HUNDRED 100's

Don Bradman

A select group of top batsmen have scored 100 hundreds in first-class cricket. The last to do so was Zaheer Abbas (Pakistan) on 11 Dec 1982. In 1986 Dennis Amiss moves closer to this group scoring his 99th in June.

The table shows all those to have reached this milestone, with their career total and the number of innings taken to reach the 100th century.

BATSMAN/Career	100s	Innings
Jack Hobbs 1905–34	197	821
'Patsy' Hendren 1907–38	170	740
Walter Hammond 1920–51	167	679
Philip Mead 1905–36	153	892
Geoffrey Boycott 1962–85	149	645
Herbert Sutcliffe 1919–45	149	700
Frank Woolley 1906–38	145	1031
Len Hutton 1934–60	129	619
W. G. Grace 1865–1908	126	1100
Denis Compton 1936–64	123	552
Tom Graveney 1948–72	122	940
Don Bradman (Aus) 1927–49	117	295
Colin Cowdrey 1950–76	107	1035
Andrew Sandham 1911–38	107	871
Zaheer Abbas (Pak) 1965–85	107	662
Tom Hayward 1893–1914	104	1076
John Edrich 1956–78	103	945
Glenn Turner (NZ) 1964–83	103	779
Leslie Ames 1926–51	102	915
Ernest Tyldesley 1909–36	102	919

Don Bradman has much the highest incidence of centuries, with one every 2.9 innings.

The youngest was Walter Hammond, who was 31 years 359 days old when he scored his 100th in 1935.

Both Geoffrey Boycott (in 1977) and Zaheer Abbas (in 1982) scored their 100th hundred in a Test match.

A double hundred in 113 min was scored by Ravi Shastri for Bombay v. Baroda at Bombay on 10 Jan 1985 (see most runs off an over). He received 123 balls. Clive Hubert Lloyd (b. 31 Aug 1944), for West Indians v. Glamorgan at Swansea on 9 Aug 1976, and Gilbert Jessop (286), for Gloucestershire v. Sussex at Hove on 1 June 1903, both scored 200 in 120 min. Lloyd received 121 balls but the figure for Jessop is not known.

The fastest treble hundred was completed in 181 min by Denis Compton, who scored 300 for the MCC v. North-Eastern Transvaal at Benoni on 3–4 Dec 1948.

Slowest scoring

The longest time a batsman has ever taken to score his first run is 1 hr 37 min by Thomas Godfrey Evans (b. 18 Aug 1920), who scored 10 not out for England v. Australia at Adelaide on 5–6 Feb 1947. The longest innings without scoring is 87 minutes by Vincent Richard Hogg (b. 3 July 1952) for Zimbabwe–Rhodesia 'B' v. Natal 'B' at Pietermaritzburg in the South African Castle Bowl competition on 20 Jan 1980.

The slowest hundred on record is by Mudassar Nazar (b. 6 Apr 1956) of Pakistan v. England at Lahore on 14–15 Dec 1977. He required 9 hr 51 min for 114, reaching the 100 in 9 hr 17 min. The slowest double hundred recorded is one of 10 hr 52 min (426 balls) by Anshuman Dattajirao Gaekwad (b. 23 Sept 1952) during an innings of 201 for India v. Pakistan at Jullundur on 25–29 Sept 1983.

Highest partnership

The record partnership for any wicket is the fourth wicket stand of 577 by Gul Mahomed (b. 15 Oct 1921), who scored 319, and Vijay Samuel Hazare (b. 11 Mar 1915) 288 in the Baroda v. Holkar match at Baroda, India, on 8–10 Mar 1947. The highest stand in English cricket is the first-wicket partnership of 555 by Percy Holmes (1886–1971) (224 not out) and Herbert Sutcliffe (1894–1978) (313) for Yorkshire v. Essex at Leyton on 15–16 June 1932.

The highest Test partnership is 451 for the second wicket by William Harold Ponsford (b. 19 Oct 1900) (266) and Sir Donald Bradman (244) for Australia v. England at the Oval on 18 Aug 1934, and 451 for the third wicket by Mudassar Nazar (231) and Javed Miandad Khan (b. 12 Jun 1957) (280 not out) for Pakistan v. India at Hyderabad, Pakistan on 14–15 Jan 1983.

BOWLING

Most wickets *In an innings*

The taking of all ten wickets by a single bowler has been recorded many times but only one bowler has achieved this feat on three occasions—Alfred Freeman of Kent, against Lancashire at Maidstone on 24 July 1929, against Essex at Southend on 13–14 Aug 1930 and against Lancashire at Old Trafford on 27 May 1931. The fewest runs scored off a bowler taking all ten wickets is ten, when Hedley Verity (1905–43) of Yorkshire dismissed (eight caught, one lbw, one stumped) Nottinghamshire at Leeds on 12 July 1932. The only bowler to bowl out all ten was John Wisden (1826–84) of Sussex, playing for North v. South at Lord's in 1850.

Most wickets *Match*

James Charles Laker (1922–86) of Surrey took 19 wickets for 90 runs (9–37 and 10–53) for England v. Australia in the Fourth Test at Old Trafford, on 27–31 July 1956. No other bowler has taken more than 17 wickets in a first-class match.

Most wickets *In a day*

The greatest number of wickets taken in a day's play is 17 (for 48 runs) by Colin Blythe (1879–1917), for Kent v. Northamptonshire at Northampton on 1 June 1907; by Hedley Verity for 91 runs, for Yorkshire v. Essex at Leyton on 14 July 1933; and by Thomas William John Goddard (1900–66) for 106 runs, for Gloucestershire v. Kent at Bristol on 3 July 1939.

Most consecutive wickets

No bowler in first-class cricket has yet achieved five wickets with five consecutive balls. The nearest approach was that of Charles Warrington Leonard Parker (1882–1959) (Gloucestershire) in his own benefit match against Yorkshire at Bristol on 10 Aug 1922, when he struck the stumps with five successive balls but the second was called as a no-ball. The only man to have taken four wickets with consecutive balls more than once is Robert James Crisp (b. 28 May 1911) for Western Province v. Griqualand West at Johannesburg on 24 Dec 1931 and against Natal at Durban on 3 Mar 1934.

Patrick Ian Pocock (b. 24 Sep 1946) took five wickets in six balls, six in nine balls and seven in eleven balls for Surrey v. Sussex at Eastbourne on 15 Aug 1972. In his own benefit match at Lord's on 22 May 1907, Albert Edwin Trott (1873–1914) of Middlesex took four Somerset wickets with four consecutive balls and then later in the same innings achieved a 'hat trick'.

Most consecutive maidens

Hugh Joseph Tayfield (b. 30 Jan 1929) bowled 16 consecutive eight-ball maiden overs (137 balls without conceding a run) for South Africa v. England at Durban on 25–26 Jan 1957. The greatest number of consecutive six-ball maiden overs bowled is 21 (131 balls) by Rameshchandra Gangaram 'Bapu' Nadkarni (b. 4 Apr 1932) for India v. England at Madras on 12 Jan 1964. The English record is 17 overs (105 balls) by Horace Leslie Hazell (b. 30 Sept 1909) for Somerset v. Gloucestershire at Taunton on 4 June 1949. Alfred Shaw (1842–1907) of Nottinghamshire bowled 23 consecutive four-ball maiden overs (92 balls) for North v. South at Trent Bridge on 17 July 1876.

Most balls

The most balls bowled in a match is 917 by Cottari Subbanna Nayudu (b. 18 Apr 1914), 6–153 and 5–275, for Holkar v. Bombay at Bombay on 4–9 Mar 1945. The most balls bowled in a Test match is 774 by Sonny Ramadhin (b. 1 May 1929) for West Indies v. England, 7–49 and 2–179, at Edgbaston on 29 May–4 June 1957. In the second innings he bowled a world record 588 balls (98 overs).

Most expensive bowling

The greatest number of runs hit off one bowler in one innings is 362, scored off Arthur Alfred Mailey (1886–1967) in the New South Wales v. Victoria match at Melbourne on 24–28 Dec 1926. The greatest number of runs ever conceded by a bowler in one match is 428 by Cottari Subbanna Nayudu in the Holkar v. Bombay match above. The most runs conceded in a Test innings is 298 by Leslie O'Brien 'Chuck' Fleetwood-Smith (1910–71) for Australia v. England at the Oval on 20–23 Aug 1938.

Fastest

The highest electronically measured speed for a ball bowled by any bowler is 99.7 mph *160,45 km/h* by Jeffrey Robert Thomson (b. 16 Aug 1950) (Australia) during the Second Test v. the West Indies in December 1975. Albert Cotter (1884–1917) of New South Wales, Australia, is reputed to have broken a stump on more than 20 occasions.

ALL-ROUNDERS

The Double
The 'double' of 1000 runs and 100 wickets in the same season was performed a record number of 16 times by Wilfred Rhodes between 1903 and 1926. The greatest number of consecutive seasons in which a player has performed the 'double' is 11 (1903–13) by George Herbert Hirst (1871–1954), of Yorkshire and England. Hirst is also the only player to score 2000 runs (2385) and take 200 wickets (208) in the same season (1906).

Test Cricket
The best all-round Test career record is that of Ian Terrence Botham (b. 24 Nov 1955) with 4577 runs (av. 34.67), 354 wickets (av. 27.06) and 96 catches in 84 matches to 1 June 1986. Botham is the only player to score a hundred and take eight wickets in a single innings in the same Test, with 108 and eight for 34 for England v. Pakistan at Lord's on 15–19 June 1978. He scored a hundred (114) and took more than ten wickets (6–58 and 7–48) in a Test, for England v. India in the Golden Jubilee Test at Bombay on 15–19 Feb 1980. This feat was emulated by Imran Khan Niazi (b. 25 Nov 1952) with 117, 6–98 and 5–82 for Pakistan v. India at Faisalabad on 3–8 Jan 1983. Botham completed the double of 1000 runs and 100 wickets in the fewest Test matches (21) on 30 Aug 1979. Kapil Dev Nikhanj (b. 6 Jan 1959) of India achieved this double in the shortest time span, 1 year 107 days and at the youngest age, 21 yr 27 days, in his 25th Test. The double of 2000 runs and 200 wickets was achieved in fewest matches (42) by Botham and at the youngest age by Kapil Dev at 24 yr 68 days. Botham completed 3000 runs and 300 wickets in 72 Tests at 28 yr 259 days.

WICKET-KEEPING

Most dismissals *Innings*
The most dismissals by a wicket-keeper in an innings is eight (all caught) by Arthur Theodore Wallace 'Wally' Grout (1927–68) for Queensland v. Western Australia at Brisbane on 15 Feb 1960 and by David Edward East (b. 27 July 1959) for Essex v. Somerset at Taunton on 27 July 1985. The most stumpings in an innings is six by Henry 'Hugo' Yarnold (1917–74) for Worcestershire v. Scotland at Broughty Ferry, Tayside, on 2 July 1951. The Test record is seven (all caught) by Wasim Bari (b. 23 Mar 1948) for Pakistan v. New Zealand at Auckland on 23 Feb 1979, and by Robert Taylor for England v. India at Bombay on 15 Feb 1980.

Most dismissals *Match*
The greatest number of dismissals by a wicket-keeper in a match is 12 by Edward Pooley (1838–1907), eight caught, four stumped, for Surrey v. Sussex at The Oval on 6–7 July 1868; nine caught, three stumped by both Donald Tallon (1916–84) of Australia for Queensland v. New South Wales at Sydney on 2–4 Jan 1939, and by Hedley Brian Taber (b. 29 Apr 1940) for New South Wales v. South Australia at Adelaide 13–17 Dec 1968. The record for catches is 11 by Arnold Long (b. 18 Dec 1940), for Surrey v. Sussex at Hove on 18 and 21 July 1964, by Rodney Marsh for Western Australia v. Victoria at Perth on 15–17 Nov 1975 and by David Leslie Bairstow (b. 1 Sept 1951) for Yorkshire v. Derbyshire at Scarborough on 8–10 Sept 1982. The most stumpings in a match is nine by Frederick Henry Huish (1869–1957) for Kent v. Surrey at The Oval on 21–23 Aug 1911. The Test record for dismissals is ten, all caught, by Robert Taylor for England v. India at Bombay, 15–19 Feb 1980.

FIELDING

Most catches *Innings and Match*
The greatest number of catches in an innings is seven, by Michael James Stewart (b. 16 Sept 1932) for Surrey v. Northamptonshire at Northampton on 7 June 1957, and by Anthony Stephen Brown (b. 24 June 1936) for Gloucestershire v. Nottinghamshire at Trent Bridge on 26 July 1966.

The most catches in a Test match is seven by Greg Chappell for Australia v. England at Perth on 13–17 Dec 1974, and by Yajurvindra Singh (b. 1 Aug 1952) for India v. England at Bangalore on 28 Jan–2 Feb 1977.

Walter Hammond held a match record total of ten catches (four in the first innings, six in the second) for Gloucestershire v. Surrey at Cheltenham on 16–17 Aug 1928. The record for a wicket-keeper is 11 (see wicket-keeping).

John Lever of Essex, holder of two career records for one-day cricket. One of the most consistent wicket-takers in England, he has taken 100 wickets in a season four times. (All-Sport).

Longest throw
A cricket ball ($5\frac{1}{2}$ oz *155 g*) was reputedly thrown 140 yd 2 ft *128,6 m* by Robert Percival, a left-hander, on Durham Sands racecourse on Easter Monday, 18 Apr 1881.

OTHER TEST RECORDS

Test appearances
The most appearances as Test Captain is 74 by Clive Lloyd of West Indies from 1974 to 1985. Sunil Gavaskar played in a record 99 consecutive Tests from 1975 to 1986. The English record for consecutive Tests is 65 by Alan Philip Eric Knott (b. 9 Apr 1946), 1971–77 and by Ian Botham, 1978–84.

Longest match

The lengthiest recorded cricket match was the 'timeless' Test between England and South Africa at Durban on 3–14 Mar 1939. It was abandoned after ten days (eighth day rained off) because the boat taking the England team home was due to leave. The total playing time was 43 hr 16 min and a record Test match aggregate of 1981 runs were scored.

Largest crowds

The greatest attendance at a cricket match is about 394,000 for the Test between India and England at Eden Gardens, Calcutta on 1–6 Jan 1982. The record for a Test series is 933,513 for Australia and England (5 matches) in 1936–37. The greatest recorded attendance at a cricket match on one day was 90,800 on the second day of the Test between Australia and West Indies at Melbourne on 11 Feb 1961. The English record is 159,000 for the Test between England and Australia at Headingley, Leeds, on 22–27 July 1948, and the record for one day probably a capacity of 46,000 for a match between Lancashire and Yorkshire at Old Trafford on 2 Aug 1926. The English record for a Test series is 549,650 for the series against Australia in 1953. The highest attendance for a limited-overs game is 84,153 at the Benson & Hedges World Series Cup match between Australia and England at Melbourne on 23 Jan 1985.

Most successful Test captain

Clive Hubert Lloyd (b. 31 Aug 1944), led the West Indies in a record 74 Test matches from 22 November 1974 to 2 January 1985. Of these 74, 36 were won, 12 lost and 26 were drawn. His team set records for most successive Test wins, 11 in 1984, and most Tests without defeat, 27, between losses to Australia in December 1981 and January 1985 (through injury Lloyd missed one of those matches, when West Indies were captained by Vivian Richards).

ENGLISH COUNTY CHAMPIONSHIP

The greatest number of victories since 1890, when the championship was officially constituted, has been secured by Yorkshire with 29 outright wins (the last in 1968), and one shared (1949). The most 'wooden spoons' have been won by Northamptonshire, with eleven since 1923. They did not win a single match between May 1935 and May 1939. The record number of consecutive title wins is seven by Surrey from 1952 to 1958. The greatest number of appearances in county championship matches is 763 by Wilfred Rhodes for Yorkshire between 1898 and 1930, and the greatest number of consecutive appearances is 423 by Kenneth George Suttle (b. 25 Aug 1928) of Sussex between 1954 and 1969. James Graham 'Jimmy' Binks (b. 5 Oct 1935) played in every county championship match for Yorkshire between his debut in 1955 and his retirement in 1969—412 matches. The seven sons of the Rev Henry Foster, of Malvern, uniquely all played county cricket for Worcestershire between 1899 and 1934.

OLDEST AND YOUNGEST

The oldest man to play in a Test match was Wilfred Rhodes, aged 52 yr 165 days, when he played for England v. West Indies at Kingston,

ONE-DAY INTERNATIONALS

The first 'Limited Overs' International was played at Melbourne Cricket Ground on 5 Jan 1971 after the Third Test of the Australian–England series had been abandoned due to rain. The Prudential Trophy series of one-day internationals began in England in 1972, matches being of 55 overs per side. The Benson and Hedges World Cup Series has been held annually in Australia since 1979–80.

World Cup

The Prudential World Cup was first held in England in 1975. It was held again in 1979 and 1983, and in 1987 will be staged in India and Pakistan. The West Indies won in 1975 and 1979, India in 1983. Matches are played at 60 overs per side.

One-Day International Records

Highest score: 338–5 Pakistan v. Sri Lanka, Swansea 9 June 1983
Lowest completed innings: 45 Canada v. England, Old Trafford 14 June 1979
Victory margin: 232 Australia v. Sri Lanka (323–2 to 91), Adelaide 28 June 1985

Individual match records

Highest score: 189* Isaac Vivian Alexander Richards (b. 7 Mar 1952), West Indies v. England, Old Trafford 31 May 1984
Best bowling: 7–51 Winston Walter Davis (b. 18 Sept 1958), West Indies v. England, Headingley 12 June 1983
Most dismissals: 5 by four men
Best partnership: 224* Dean Mervyn Jones (b. 24 Mar 1961) & Allan Robert Border (b. 27 July 1955), Australia v. Sri Lanka, Adelaide 28 Jan 1985

Career records

Most runs: 4265 Vivian Richards (West Indies) 1975–86
Most wickets: 125 Joel Garner (West Indies) (b. 16 Dec 1952) 1977–86
Most dismissals: 123 (119 ct, 4 st) Rodney Marsh (Australia) 1971–84
(* not out)

ENGLISH ONE-DAY CRICKET RECORDS

GC/NWT—Gillette Cup (inst. 1963)/Nat West Bank Trophy (from 1981)—60 overs matches
JPL—John Player League (inst. 1969)—40 overs matches
B & H—Benson & Hedges Cup (inst. 1972)—55 overs matches

MOST WINS
GC/NWT—4 Lancashire 1970–2, 1975
JPL —3 Kent 1972–3, 1976; Essex 1981, 1984–5
B & H —3 Kent 1973, 1976, 1978; Leicestershire 1972, 1975, 1985

HIGHEST INDIVIDUAL INNINGS
GC/NWT—206 Alvin Isaac Kallicharan (b. 21 Mar 1949) Warwickshire v. Oxfordshire, Edgbaston, 1984
JPL —176 Graham Alan Gooch (b. 23 July 1953) Essex v. Glamorgan, Southend, 1983
B & H —198* Graham Gooch, Essex v. Sussex, Hove, 1982

BEST INDIVIDUAL BOWLING
GC/NWT—7–15 Alan Leonard Dixon (b. 27 Nov 1933) Kent v. Surrey, The Oval, 1967
JPL —8–26 Keith David Boyce (b. 11 Oct 1943) Essex v. Lancashire, Old Trafford, 1971
Alan Ward (b. 10 Aug 1947) took 4 wickets in 4 balls, Derbyshire v. Sussex, Derby, 1970
B & H —7–12 Wayne Wendell Daniel (b. 16 Jan 1956) Middlesex v. Minor Counties (East), Ipswich, 1978

MOST DISMISSALS IN INNINGS
GC/NWT—6 Robert William Taylor (b. 17 July 1941) Derbyshire v. Essex, Derby, 1981
JPL —7 Bob Taylor, Derbyshire v. Lancashire, Old Trafford, 1975
B & H —8 Derek John Somerset Taylor (b. 12 Nov 1942) Somerset v. Cambridge University, Taunton, 1982

HIGHEST INNINGS TOTAL
GC/NWT—392–5 Warwickshire v. Oxfordshire, Edgbaston, 1984
JPL —310–5 Essex v. Glamorgan, Southend, 1983
B & H —350–3 Essex v. Oxford & Cambridge Universities, Chelmsford, 1979

LOWEST COMPLETED INNINGS TOTAL
GC/NWT—39 Ireland v. Sussex, Hove, 1985
JPL —23 Middlesex v. Yorkshire, Headingley, 1974
B & H —56 Leicestershire v. Minor Counties, Wellington, 1982

RUNS IN CAREER
GC/NWT—1774 Dennis Leslie Amiss (b. 7 Apr 1943) Warwickshire 1963–85
JPL —6486 Dennis Amiss, Warwickshire 1969–85
B & H —2743 Graham Gooch, Essex 1973–85

WICKETS IN CAREER
GC/NWT—81 Geoffrey Graham Arnold (b. 3 Sept 1944) Surrey, Sussex 1963–80
JPL —329 John Kenneth Lever (b. 24 Feb 1949) Essex 1969–85
B & H —122 John Lever, Essex 1972–85

DISMISSALS IN CAREER
GC/NWT—66 Bob Taylor, Derbyshire 1963–84
JPL —236 Bob Taylor, Derbyshire 1969–84
B & H —96 David Leslie Bairstow (b. 1 Sept 1951), Yorkshire 1972–85

*Not out

Jamaica on 12 April 1930. Rhodes made his Test debut in the last Test of William Gilbert Grace (1848–1915), who at 50 yr 320 days at Nottingham on 3 June 1899 was the oldest ever Test Captain. The youngest Test captain was the Nawab of Pataudi (later Mansur Ali Khan) at 21 yr 77 days on 23 Mar 1962 for India *v.* West Indies at Bridgetown, Barbados. The youngest Test player was Mushtaq Mohammad (b. 22 Nov 1943), aged 15 yr 124 days, when he played for Pakistan *v.* West Indies at Lahore on 26 March 1959. England's youngest player was Dennis Brian Close (b. 24 Feb 1931) aged 18 yr 149 days *v.* New Zealand at Old Trafford on 23 July 1949.

The oldest player in first-class cricket was Col Cottari Kanakaiya Nayudu (1895–1967) (India), aged 68 yr 4 days, when he played for the Maharashtra Governor's XI *v.* Chief Minister's XI at Nagpur, India on 4 Nov 1963. The youngest is reputed to be Qasim Feroze (Pakistan) (b. 21 Jan 1958) who played for Bahawalpur *v.* Karachi Whites on 19 Jan 1971 aged 12 yr 363 days. The oldest Englishman was George Robert Canning, the 4th Lord Harris (1851–1932) who played for Kent *v.* All India at Catford on 4 July 1911 aged 60 yr 151 days. The youngest English first-class player was Charles Robertson Young when he played for Hampshire against Kent at Gravesend on 13 June 1867, aged 15 yr 131 days.

WOMEN'S CRICKET

Earliest
The first recorded women's match took place at Gosden Common, Surrey, England on 26 July 1745. *Circa* 1807 Christina Willes is said to have introduced the roundarm bowling style. The first Test match was Australia *v.* England at Brisbane on 28–31 Dec 1934. The International Women's Cricket Council was formed in 1958.

Batting *Individual*
The highest individual innings recorded is 224 not out by Mabel Bryant for Visitors *v.* Residents at Eastbourne, East Sussex, in August 1901. The highest innings in a Test match is 189 by Elizabeth Alexandra 'Betty' Snowball for England *v.* New Zealand at Christchurch, NZ on 16 Feb 1935. The highest Test innings in England is 179 by Rachel Flint (*née* Heyhoe) (b. 11 June 1939) for England *v.* Australia at The Oval, London on 27–28 July 1976. Rachel Flint also has scored the most runs in Test cricket with 1814 (av. 49.02) in 25 matches from December 1960 to July 1979.

Batting *Team*
The highest innings score by any team is 567 by Tarana *v.* Rockley, at Rockley, NSW Australia in 1896. The highest Test innings is 503 for five wickets declared by England *v.* New Zealand at Christchurch, NZ on 16 and 18 Feb 1935. The most in a Test in England is 379 by Australia *v.* England at The Oval, London on 26–27 July 1976. The highest innings total by any team in England is 410 for two wickets declared by the South *v.* East at Oakham, Leicestershire on 29 May 1982.

The lowest innings in a Test is 35 by England *v.* Australia at St Kilda, Melbourne, Australia on 22 Feb 1958. The lowest in a Test in England is 63 by New Zealand at Worcester on 5 July 1954.

Bowling
The greatest number of wickets taken in Test matches is 77 (av. 13.49) by Mary Beatrice Duggan (England) (1925–73) in 17 Tests from 1949 to 1963. She recorded the best Test analysis with seven wickets for six runs for England *v.* Australia at St Kilda, Melbourne on 22 Feb 1958.

Dennis Amiss' one-day career records for Warwickshire date to 1963; from 1966–77 he also scored 3612 runs for England at an average of 46.30. (All-Sport).

On 26 June 1931 Rubina Winifred Humphries (b. 19 Aug 1915), for Dalton Ladies *v.* Woodfield SC, took all ten wickets for no runs. (She also scored all her team's runs.) This bowling feat was equalled by Rosemary White (b. 22 Jan 1938) for Wallington LCC *v.* Beaconsfield LCC in July 1962.

World Cup
Three women's World Cups have been staged. Australia won in 1978 and 1982 and England in 1973. The highest individual score in this series is 138 not out by Janette Ann Brittin (b. 4 July 1959) for England *v.* International XI at Hamilton, New Zealand on 14 Jan 1982.

MINOR CRICKET RECORDS
(where excelling those in First Class Cricket)

Highest individual innings
In a Junior House match between Clarke's House (now Poole's) and North Town, at Clifton College, Bristol, 22–23, 26–28 June 1899, Arthur Edward Jeune Collins (1885–1914) scored an unprecedented 628 not out in 6 hr 50 min, over five afternoons' batting, carrying his bat through the innings of 836. The scorer, E. W. Pegler, gave the score as '628—plus or minus 20, shall we say'.

Fastest individual scoring
Stanley Keppel 'Shunter' Coen (South Africa) (1902–67) scored 50 runs (11 fours and one six) in 7 min for Gezira *v.* the RAF in 1942. The fastest hundred by a prominent player in a minor match was by Vivian Frank Shergold Crawford (1879–1922) in 19 min at Cane Hill, Surrey on 16 Sept 1899. David Michael Roberts Whatmore (b. 6 Apr 1949) scored 210 (including 25 sixes and 12 fours) off 61 balls for Alderney *v.* Sun Alliance at Alderney on 19 June 1983. His first 100 came off 33 balls and his second off 25 balls.

Successive sixes
Cedric Ivan James Smith (1906–79) hit nine successive sixes for a Middlesex XI *v.* Harrow and District at Rayner's Lane, Harrow in 1935. This feat was equalled by Arthur Dudley Nourse (1910–81) in a South African XI *v.* Military Police match at Cairo, Egypt in 1942–3. Nourse's feat included six sixes in one over.

Fastest and Slowest scoring rates
In the match Royal Naval College, Dartmouth *v.* Seale Hayne Agricultural College in 1923, Kenneth Anderson Sellar (now Cdr 'Monkey' Sellar, DSO, DSC, RN) (b. 11 Aug 1906) and Leslie Kenneth Allen Block (later Judge Block, DSC) (1906–80) were set to score 174 runs in 105 min but achieved this total in 33 min, so averaging 5.27 runs per min. Playing for Gentlemen of Leicestershire CC *v.* Free Foresters, at Oakham, Rutland, on 19 Aug 1963, Ian H. S. Balfour batted for 100 min without adding to his score of five. He went on to make 39.

Consecutive not out hundreds
Gerald Vivian William Lukehurst (b. 5 Oct 1917), hit six consecutive not out hundreds for Gore Court and F. Day's XI between 3 July and 20 July 1955.

Consecutive ducks
A unique distinction of scoring two ducks (known as 'a pair of spectacles') in less than 60 seconds was 'achieved' by Peter Judge (Glamorgan) in the match *v.* India at Cardiff Arms Park, South Wales on 11 June 1946. Glamorgan had reversed their batting order for the second innings and India had agreed to waive the interval between innings.

Most runs off a ball
A scoring stroke of 11 (all run, with no overthrows) was achieved by Lt (later Lt-Col)

Philip Mitford (1879–1946), QO Cameron Highlanders, in a Malta Governor's Cup match on 28 May 1903.

Most runs off an over
H. Morely scored 62, nine sixes and two fours, off an eight-ball over from R. Grubb which had four no-balls in a Queensland country match in 1968–9.

Greatest stand
T. Patten and N. Rippon made 641 for the third wicket for Buffalo v. Whorouly at Gapsted, Victoria, Australia, on 19 Mar 1914.

Bowling
Stephen Fleming, bowling for Marlborough College 'A' XI, New Zealand v. Bohally Intermediate at Blenheim, New Zealand in December 1967 took nine wickets in nine consecutive balls. In February 1931 in South Africa, Paul Hugo also took nine wickets with nine consecutive balls for Smithfield School v. Aliwal North. In the Inter-Divisional Ships Shield at Purfleet, Essex, on 17 May 1924, Joseph William Brockley (b. 9 Apr 1907) took all ten wickets, clean bowled, for two runs in 11 balls—including a triple hat trick. Jennings Tune took all ten wickets, all bowled, for 0 runs in five overs for Cliffe v. Eastrington in the Howden and District League at Cliffe, Yorkshire on 6 May 1922.

In 1881 Frederick Robert Spofforth (1835–1926) at Bendigo, Victoria, Australia clean bowled all ten wickets in *both* innings. J. Bryant for Erskine v. Deaf Mutes in Melbourne on 15 and 22 Oct 1887, and Albert Rimmer for Linwood School v. Cathedral GS at Canterbury, New Zealand in December 1925 repeated the feat. In 1910, H. Hopkinson, of Mildmay CC London, took 99 wickets for 147 runs.

Maurice Hanes bowled 107 consecutive balls (17 overs and five balls) for Bedworth II v. A P Leamington II at Bedworth, Warwickshire on 16 June 1979, without conceding a run.

All-rounders
Guy Stephenson scored 144 not out and took all ten wickets (for 22 runs in 11 overs) for Stanton 2nd XI v. Clay Cross Works on 13 June 1953 in Nottinghamshire.

Ian H. S. Balfour (b. 8 Jan 1934) took all 20 wickets in a Stamford School Junior League match on 18 June 1948, and on 9 Aug 1950 scored a century and took all 10 wickets in an innings for Stamford Youth XI v. Rutland Youth XI; a unique combination of these rare feats.

Wicket-keeping
Welihinda Badalge Bennett (b. 25 Jan 1933) caught four and stumped six batsmen in one innings, on 1 March 1953 for Mahinda College v. Galle CC, at the Galle Esplanade, Sri Lanka.

Fielding
In a Wellington, New Zealand secondary schools 11-a-side match on 16 Mar 1974, Stephen Lane, 13, held 14 catches in the field (seven in each innings) for St Patrick's College, Silverstream v. St Bernard's College, Lower Hutt.

CROQUET

Earliest references
Croquet was probably derived from the French game *Jeu de Mail* first mentioned in the 12th century. In its present-day form, it originated as a country-house lawn game in Ireland in the 1830s when it was called 'crokey' and was introduced to Hampshire 20 years later. The first club was formed in the Steyne Gardens, Worthing, West Sussex in 1865.

Most championships
The greatest number of victories in the Open Croquet Championships (instituted at Evesham, Hereford & Worcester, 1867) is ten by John William Solomon (b. 1932) (1953, 1956, 1959, 1961, 1963–8). He also won ten Men's Championships (1951, 1953, 1958–60, 1962, 1964–5, 1971 and 1972), ten Open Doubles (with Edmond Patrick Charles Cotter) (1954–5, 1958–9, 1961–5 and 1969) and one Mixed Doubles (with Freda Oddie) in 1954, making a total of 31 titles. Solomon has also won the President's Silver Cup (inst. 1934) on nine occasions (1955, 1957–9, 1962–4, 1968 and 1971), and was Champion of Champions on all four occasions that this competition has been run (1967–70).

Dorothy Dyne Steel (1884–1965), fifteen times winner of the Women's Championship (1919–39), won the Open Croquet Championship four times (1925, 1933, 1935–36). She had also five Doubles and seven Mixed Doubles for a total of 31 titles.

International trophy
The MacRobertson International Shield (instituted 1925) has been played for eleven times. Great Britain have a record seven wins (in 1925, 1937, 1956, 1963, 1969, 1974 and 1983). Five international appearances were made by J. C. Windsor (Australia) in 1925, 1928, 1930, 1935 and 1937 and John Solomon (GB) in 1951, 1956, 1963, 1969 and 1974.

Lowest handicap
Historically the lowest playing handicap has been that of Humphrey Osmond Hicks (Devon) (b. 1904) with minus 5½. In 1974 the limit was however fixed at minus 5. The player holding the lowest handicap is G. Nigel Aspinall with minus 5.

CROSS-COUNTRY RUNNING

WORLD CHAMPIONSHIPS

The earliest recorded international cross-country race took place over 14,5 km *9 miles 18 yd* from Ville d'Avray, outside Paris, on 20 Mar 1898 between England and France (England won by 21 points to 69). The inaugural International Cross-Country Championships took place at the Hamilton Park Racecourse, Scotland, on 28 Mar 1903. The greatest margin of victory is 56 sec or 390 yd *356 m* by John 'Jack' Thomas Holden (England) (b. 13 Mar 1907) at Ayr Racecourse, Scotland, on 24 Mar 1934. Since 1973 the events have been official world championships under the auspices of the International Amateur Athletic Federation.

The greatest men's team wins have been those of England, with a minimum of 21 points (the first six runners to finish) on two occasions, at Gosforth Park, Newcastle, Tyne and Wear, on 22 Mar 1924, and at the Hippodrome de Stockel, Brussels, Belgium, on 20 Mar 1932.

Most appearances
Marcel Van de Wattyne (Belgium) (b. 7 July 1924) ran in a record 20 races, 1946–65. The women's record is 16 by Jean Lochhead (Wales) (b. 24 Dec 1946), 1967–79, 1981, 1983–4.

Most wins
The greatest number of team victories have been by England with 45 for men, 11 for junior men and 7 for women. The USA also have seven women's team victories.

The greatest number of men's individual vic-

tories is four by Jack Holden (England) in 1933–5 and 1939, by Alain Mimoun-o-Kacha (France) (b. 1 Jan 1921) in 1949, 1952, 1954 and 1956 and by Gaston Roelants (Belgium) (b. 5 Feb 1937) in 1962, 1967, 1969 and 1972. The women's race has been won five times by Doris Brown-Heritage (USA) (b. 17 Sept 1942) 1967–71, and by Grete Waitz (*née* Andersen) (Norway) (b. 1 Oct 1953), 1978–81 and 1983.

English championship
The English Cross-Country Championship was inaugurated at Roehampton, Wandsworth, London, in 1877. The most individual titles won is four by Percy H. Stenning (1854–92) (Thames Hare and Hounds) and Alfred E. Shrubb (1878–1964) (South London Harriers) in 1901–4. The most successful club in the team race has been Birchfield Harriers from Birmingham with 27 wins and one tie between 1880 and 1953. The largest field was the 1907 starters and 1806 finishers in the senior race in 1985 at Milton Keynes, Buckinghamshire.

Largest field
The largest recorded field in any cross-country race was 11,763 starters (10,810 finished) in the 30 km *18.6 miles* Lidingöloppet, near Stockholm, Sweden, on 3 Oct 1982.

CURLING

Origins
Although a 15th century bronze figure in the Florence Museum appears to be holding a curling stone, the earliest illustration of the sport was in one of the Flemish painter Pieter Bruegel's winter scenes *c.* 1560. The game was probably introduced into Scotland by Flemings in the 15th century. The earliest documented club is Muthill, Tayside, Scotland, formed in 1739. Organized administration began in 1838 with the formation in Edinburgh of the Grand (later Royal) Caledonian Curling Club, the international legislative body until the foundation of the International Curling Federation in 1966. The first indoor ice rink to introduce curling was in Montreal, Canada in 1807, and the first in Britain was at Southport, Merseyside in 1878.

The USA won the first Gordon International Medal series of matches, between Canada and the USA, at Montreal in 1884. Curling has been a demonstration sport at the Olympic Games of 1924, 1932 and 1964 and will be again in 1988.

Most titles
The record for World Championships (inst. 1959) for the Air Canada Silver Broom is 17 wins by Canada, in 1959–64, 1966, 1968–72, 1980, 1982–3, 1985–6. The most Strathcona Cup (inst. 1903) is seven by Canada (1903, 1909, 1912, 1923, 1938, 1957, 1965) against Scotland. The most Women's World Championships (inst. 1979) is three titles by Canada (1980, 1984–5).

'Perfect' games
Stu Beagle, of Calgary, Alberta, Canada, played a perfect game (48 points) against Nova Scotia in the Canadian championships (Brier) at Fort William (now Thunder Bay), Ontario, on 8 Mar 1960. Bernice Fekete, of Edmonton, Alberta, Canada, skipped her rink to two consecutive eight-enders on the same ice at the Derrick Club, Edmonton, on 10 Jan and 6 Feb 1973. Two eight-enders in one bonspiel were scored at the Parry Sound Curling Club, Ontario, Canada on 6–8 Jan 1983. Andrew McQuistin, of Stranraer, skipped a Scotland rink to a 1–0 win over Switzerland, scoring in the tenth end after nine consecutive blank ends, in the Uniroyal World

Junior Championships at Kitchener-Waterloo, Ontario, Canada on 16 Mar 1980.

Largest bonspiel

The largest bonspiel in the world is the Manitoba Curling Association Bonspiel held annually in Winnipeg, Canada. In 1985, there were 848 teams of four men, a total of 3392 curlers, using 171 sheets of curling ice.

Largest rink

The world's largest curling rink is the Big Four Curling Rink, Calgary, Alberta, Canada, opened in 1959. 96 teams and 384 players are accommodated on two floors each with 24 sheets of ice.

CYCLING

Earliest race

The earliest recorded bicycle race was a velocipede race over 2 km *1.24 miles* at the Parc de St Cloud, Paris, on 31 May 1868, won by Dr James Moore (GB) (1847–1935) (later Chevalier de la Legion d'Honneur).

Highest speed

The highest speed ever achieved on a bicycle is 152.284 mph *245,077 km/h* by John Howard (USA) behind a wind-shield at Bonneville Salt Flats, Utah, USA on 20 July 1985. It should be noted that considerable help is provided by the slipstreaming effect of the lead vehicle. The British speed record is 98.21 mph *158,05 km/h* over 200 metres by David Le Grys on a closed section of the M42 at Alvechurch, Warwickshire on 28 Aug 1985. Fred Markham recorded an official unpaced 6.832 sec for 200 m (65.484 mph

PLACE TO PLACE RECORDS

(British) as recognised by the Road Records Association

	MEN					WOMEN				
	hr	min	sec	Name	Date	hr	min	sec	Name	Date
London to Edinburgh (380 miles *610 km*)	18	49	42	Cliff Smith	2 Nov 1965	20	11	35	Eileen Sheridan	3–4 June 1954
London to Bath and back (212 miles *341 km*)	9	03	07	John Woodburn	13 June 1981	10	41	22	Eileen Sheridan	26 Aug 1952
London to York (197 miles *317 km*)	7	41	13	Bob Addy	6 Aug 1972	9	05	20	Eileen Sheridan	15 Aug 1953
London to Birmingham (112.8 miles *181,5 km*)	4	19	13	Phil Bayton	7 Nov 1982	5	12	18	Kathy Bellingham	18 Oct 1980
London to Brighton and back (107 miles *172 km*)	4	15	8	Phil Griffiths	20 July 1977	4	55	28	Gill Clapton	15 July 1972
Land's End to London (287 miles *461 km*)	12	34	.0	Robert Maitland	17 Sept 1954	13	43	33	Ann Horswell	8 Sept 1970

105,386 km/h) on a streamlined bicycle on Highway 120, California, USA, on 11 May 1986.

The greatest distance ever covered in one hour is 122,771 km *76 miles 504 yd* by Leon Vanderstuyft (Belgium) (1890–1964) on the Montlhery Motor Circuit, France, on 30 Sept 1928, achieved from a standing start paced by a motorcycle. The 24 hr record behind pace is 860 miles 367 yd *1384,367 km* by Hubert Ferdinand Opperman (later Hon Sir) (b. 29 May 1904) in Melbourne, Australia on 23 May 1932.

Most titles *Olympic*

The most gold medals won is three by Paul Masson (France) (1874–1945) in 1896, Francisco Verri (Italy) (1885–1945) in 1906 and Robert Charpentier (France) (1916–66) in 1936. Daniel Morelon (France) won two in 1968, and a third in 1972. He also won a bronze medal in 1964. In the 'unofficial' 1904 cycling programme, Marcus Hurley (USA) (1884–1950) won four events.

Most titles *World*

World championships are contested annually. They were first staged for amateurs in 1893 and for professionals in 1895. The most wins at a particular event is nine by Koichi Nakano (Japan) (b. 14 Nov 1955), professional sprint 1977–85. The most wins at a men's amateur event is seven by Daniel Morelon (France) (b. 28 July 1944), sprint 1966–7, 1969–71, 1973, 1975; and Leon Meredith (UK) (1882–1930), 100 km motor paced 1904–5, 1907–9, 1911, 1913. The most women's titles is seven by Beryl Burton (UK) (b. 12 May 1937) pursuit 1959–60, 1962–3, 1966 and road 1960, 1967; and by Yvonne Reynders (Belgium) pursuit 1961, 1964–5 and road 1959, 1961, 1963, 1966.

Most titles *British*

Beryl Burton (b. 12 May 1937), 25 times British all-round time trial champion (1959–83), has won 71 individual road TT titles, 14 track pursuit

John Howard broke the speed cycling record reaching an extraordinary speed of over 150 mph *240 km/h*. The official land speed record only passed this mark in 1926, and any deviation from behind the windshield would have meant certain death. (Al Gross).

titles and 12 road race titles to 1986. Mrs Burton's career overshadows all male achievements. Ian Hallam (b. 24 Nov 1948) won a record 25 men's titles, 1969–82.

Tour de France

The greatest number of wins in the Tour de France (inaugurated 1903) is five by Jacques Anquetil (France) (b. 8 Jan 1934), 1957, 1961–4, Eddy Merckx (Belgium) (b. 17 June 1945), 1969–72 and 1974 and Bernard Hinault (France) (b. 14 Nov 1954) 1978–9, 1981–2 and 1985. The closest race ever was in 1968 when after 4665 km *2898.7 miles* over 25 days (27 June–21 July) Jan Janssen (Netherlands) (b. 19 May 1940) beat Herman van Springel (Belgium) in Paris by 38 sec. The fastest average speed was 37,84 km/h *23.51 mph* by Bernard Hinault in 1981. The longest race was 5745 km *3569 miles* in 1926, and most participants were 170 starters in 1982 and 1984. The longest ever stage was the 486 km from Les Sables d'Olonne to Bayonne in 1919. The longest in 1984 was 338 km from Nantes to Bordeaux.

Tour of Britain (Milk Race)

Four riders have won the Tour of Britain twice each—Bill Bradley (1959–60), Les West (1965, 1967), Fedor den Hertog (Netherlands) (1969, 1971) and Yuri Kashurin (USSR) (1979, 1982). The closest race ever was in 1976 when after 1035 miles *1665,67 km* over 14 days (30 May–12 June) Bill Nickson (GB) (b. 30 Jan 1953) beat Joe Waugh (GB) by 5 sec. The fastest average speed is 26.213 mph *42,185 km/h* by Joey McLoughlin (GB) (b. 3 Dec 1964) in the 1986 race (1065 miles *1714 km*). Malcolm Elliott (b. 1 July 1961) won a record six stages in 1983 and had taken his total to 12 by 1986. The longest Milk Race was in 1969 (1515 miles *2438,16 km*) although the longest ever Tour of Britain was in 1953 (1631 miles *2624,84 km* starting and finishing in London).

Six-day races

The most wins in 6-day races is 88 out of 233 events by Patrick Sercu (b. 27 June 1944), of Belgium, 1964–83.

Longest one-day race

The longest single-day 'massed start' road race is the 551–620 km *342–385 miles* Bordeaux–Paris, France, event. Paced over all or part of the route, the highest average speed was in 1981 with 47,186 km/h *29.32 mph* by Herman van Springel (Bel) (b. 14 Aug 1943) for 584,5 km *363.1 miles* in 13 hr 35 min 18 sec.

Land's End to John o' Groats

The 'end to end' record for the 847 miles *1363 km* is 1 day 21 hr 3 min 16 sec (average speed 18.80 mph *30,25 km/h*) by John Woodburn (b. 22 Dec 1936) on 14–15 Aug 1982. The women's record is 2 days 11 hr 7 min by Eileen Sheridan (b. 18 Oct 1923) on 9–11 July 1954. She completed 1000 miles *1609 km* in 3 days 1 hr.

Endurance

Thomas Edward Godwin (1912–75) (GB) in the 365 days of 1939 covered 75,065 miles *120 805 km* or an average of 205.65 miles *330,96 km* per day. He then completed 100,000 miles *160 934 km* in 500 days to 14 May 1940.

Jay Aldous and Matt DeWaal cycled 14,290 miles *22 997 km* on a round trip from Place Monument, Salt Lake City, Utah, USA in 106 days, 2 Apr–16 July 1984.

Nicholas Mark Sanders (b. 26 Nov 1957) of Glossop, Derbyshire, circumnavigated the world (13,035 road miles *20 977,8 km*) in 78 days 3 hr 30 min between 5 July and 21 Sept 1985. He cycled 4802 miles *7728 km* around Britain in 22 days, 10 June–1 July 1984. Jonathan Boyer cycled across America in a record 9 days 2 hr 6 min in July 1985.

WORLD RECORDS

(In events contested by professional and amateur riders only the better mark is given)

OPEN AIR TRACKS

MEN

Distance	min sec	Name and Country	Place	Date
Professional unpaced standing start:				
5 km	5:45.646	Hans-Henrik Oersted (Denmark) (b. 13 Dec 1954)	Bassano del Grappa, Italy	19 July 1985
10 km	11:39.720	Francesco Moser (Italy)	Mexico City	19 Jan 1984
20 km	23:21.592	Francesco Moser (Italy)	Mexico City	23 Jan 1984
100 km	2 hr 14:02.51	Ole Ritter (Denmark) (b. 29 Aug 1941)	Mexico City	18 Nov 1971
1 hour	51,151.35 km *31 miles 1380 yd*	Francesco Moser (Italy)	Mexico City	23 Jan 1984
Amateur unpaced standing start:				
1 km	1:02.547	Marc Malchow (GDR)	Mexico City	14 Oct 1980
4 km	4:37.824	Umaras Gintautas (USSR)	Medellín, Colorado, USA	14 Sept 1985
Amateur unpaced flying start:				
200 metres	10.190	Lutz Hesslich (GDR)	Colorado Springs, USA	4 July 1985
500 metres	26.993	Rory O'Reilly (USA) (b. 25 Jun 1955)	La Paz, Bolivia	23 Nov 1985
1 km	58.510	Rory O'Reilly	La Paz, Bolivia	23 Nov 1985
Professional motor-paced:				
100 km	1 hr 12:04.115	Max Hurzeler (Swi)	Zürich, Switzerland	21 Aug 1984
Amateur motor-paced:				
50 km	35:35.248	Aleksandr Romanov (USSR)	Tbilisi, USSR	11 May 1984
100 km	1 hr 11:29.374	Aleksandr Romanov (USSR)	Tbilisi, USSR	11 May 1984
1 hour	83,873 km *52 miles 204 yd*	Aleksandr Romanov (USSR)	Tbilisi, USSR	11 May 1984

WOMEN

Unpaced standing start:				
1 km	1:14.249	Erika Salumyae (USSR)	Tashkent, USSR	17 May 1984
3 km	3:49.780	Rebecca Twigg (USA)	Barcelona, Spain	29 Aug 1984
5 km	6:41.75	Amanda Jones (GB)	Leicester, England	31 July 1982
10 km	13:34.39	Keetie Van Oostenhage (Netherlands)	Munich, W. Germany	16 Sept 1978
20 km	27:26.66	Keetie Van Oostenhage (Netherlands)	Munich, W. Germany	16 Sept 1978
100 km	2 hr 31:28.374	Francesco Galli (Italy)	Milan, Italy	8 Aug 1985
1 hour	43,082 km *26 miles 1355 yd*	Keetie Van Oostenhage (Netherlands)	Munich, W. Germany	16 Sept 1978
Unpaced flying start:				
200 metres	11.393	Connie Paraskevin (USA)	Colorado Springs, USA	6 July 1985
500 metres	31.70	Galina Tsareva (USSR)	Tbilisi, USSR	6 Oct 1978
1 km	1:10.463	Erika Salumyae (USSR)	Tashkent, USSR	15 May 1984

INDOOR TRACKS

MEN

Amateur unpaced standing start:				
1 km	1:02.955	Lothar Thoms (GDR) (b. 18 May 1956)	Moscow, USSR	22 July 1980
4 km	4:34.103	Umaras Gintautas (USSR)	Moscow, USSR	6 Feb 1986
5 km	5:48.256	Umaras Gintautas (USSR)	Moscow, USSR	3 Aug 1984
10 km	12:06.29	Hans-Henrik Oersted (Denmark)	Copenhagen, Denmark	28 Nov 1978
20 km	24:41.197	Aleksandr Stepanov (USSR)	Moscow, USSR	29 Oct 1985
100 km	2 hr 22:50.230	Ercole Mores (Italy)	Zürich, Switzerland	14 Dec 1985
1 hour	48,448 km *30 miles 185 yd*	Vyacheslav Yekimov (USSR)	Moscow, USSR	28 Oct 1985
Amateur unpaced flying start:				
200 metres	10.249	Sergey Kopylov (USSR)	Moscow, USSR	6 Aug 1985
500 metres	27.469	Aleksandr Panfilov (USSR)	Moscow, USSR	5 Aug 1984
1 km	1:00.279	Sergey Kopylov (USSR)	Moscow, USSR	30 July 1982
Amateur motor-paced:				
50 km	33:05.568	Aleksandr Romanov (USSR)	Moscow, USSR	30 Oct 1985
100 km	1 hr 06:25.739	Aleksandr Romanov (USSR)	Moscow, USSR	30 Oct 1985
1 hour	90,488 km *56 miles 399 yd*	Aleksandr Romanov (USSR)	Moscow, USSR	30 Oct 1985

WOMEN

Unpaced standing start:				
1 km	1:13.377	Erika Salumyae (USSR)	Moscow, USSR	21 Sept 1983
5 km	6:29.606	Jeannie Longo (France) (b. 31 Oct 1958)	Paris, France	15 Nov 1985
10 km	13:41.519	Galina Tsareva (USSR)	Moscow, USSR	18 Jan 1983
20 km	27:46.73	Galina Tsareva (USSR)	Moscow, USSR	28 Apr 1983
100 km	2 hr 31:30.43	Mieke Havik (Netherlands)	Rotterdam, Netherlands	19 Sept 1983
1 hour	42,319 km *26 miles 522 yd*	Barbara Ganz (Switzerland)	Zürich, Switzerland	25 Nov 1985
Unpaced flying start:				
200 metres	11.494	Erika Salumyae (USSR)	Moscow, USSR	14 May 1985
500 metres	30.580	Isabelle Nicoloso (France)	Paris, France	16 Nov 1985
1 km	1:07.189	Isabelle Nicoloso (France)	Paris, France	17 Nov 1985

LONG DISTANCE BESTS

24 hr	830,79 km *516.24 miles*	Michael L. Secrest (USA) (b. 20 Jan 1953)	Montreal, Canada	13–14 Mar 1985
1 000 km	32 hr 4 min	Herman de Munck (Belgium)	Keerbergen, Belgium	23–24 Sept 1983
1 000 miles	51 hr 12 min 32 sec	Herman de Munck (Belgium)	Keerbergen, Belgium	23–25 Sept 1983

Connie Paraskevin (USA), whose world record 200 metres took under $11\frac{1}{2}$ seconds. (All-Sport).

Cheryl Marek and Estelle Gray completed a tandem ride across the USA from Santa Monica Pier, Cal. to New York, 2925 miles *4707 km*, in 10 days 22 hr 48 min in 1985. The Trans-Canada record is 14 days 22 hr 47 min by Wayne Phillips of Richmond, BC, 3800 miles *6115 km* from Vancouver, BC to Halifax, Nova Scotia, on 13–28 June 1982.

Carlos Vieira cycled for 191 hr 'non-stop' at Leira, Portugal on 8–16 June 1983. The distance covered was 2407,64 km *1496.04 miles* and he was moving 98.7% of the time.

Cycle touring

The greatest mileage amassed in a cycle tour was more than 402,000 miles *643 700 km* by the itinerant lecturer Walter Stolle (b. Sudetenland, 1926) from 24 Jan 1959 to 12 Dec 1976. He visited 159 countries starting from Romford, Essex, England. From 1922 to 25 Dec 1973 Tommy Chambers (1903–84) of Glasgow, rode a verified total of 799,405 miles *1 286 517 km*.

Visiting every continent, John W. Hathaway (b. England, 13 Jan 1925) of Vancouver, Canada covered 50,600 miles *81 300 km* from 10 Nov 1974 to 6 Oct 1976. Veronica and Colin Scargill, of Bedford, travelled 18,020 miles *29 000 km* around the world, on a tandem, 25 Feb 1974–27 Aug 1975.

The most participants in a bicycle tour was 27,220 in the 56 mile *90 km* London to Brighton Bike Ride on 15 June 1986.

Highest

Nicholas and Richard Crane cycled their mountainbikes to the summit of Mount Kilimanjaro, Tanzania 5894 m *19 340 ft* on 31 Dec 1984.

CYCLO-CROSS

The greatest number of world championships (inst. 1950) have been won by Eric de Vlaeminck (Belgium) (b. 23 Aug 1945) with the amateur and Open in 1966 and six professional titles in 1968–73. British titles (inst. 1955) have been won most often by John Atkins (b. 7 Apr 1942) with five amateur (1961–2, 1966–8), seven professional (1969–75) and one Open title in 1977.

Pennine Way

John North (b. 18 Aug 1943) of Rawtenstall, Lancashire, cycled or carried his machine along the 271 miles *436 km* Pennine Way from Edale, Derbyshire to Kirk Yetholm, Borders in 2 days 8 hr 45 min on 9–11 June 1978.

CYCLE SPEEDWAY

First mention of the sport is at Coventry in 1920 and it was first organised in 1945. The sport's governing body, the Cycle Speedway Council, was formed in 1973. Most British senior team championships (inst. 1950) is six by Wednesfield, Wolverhampton (1974, 1976–8, 1981 and 1983) and by Offerton, Cheshire (1962, 1964–5, 1969, 1972–3). The most individual titles is four by Derek Garnett (b. 16 July 1937) (1963, 1965, 1968 and 1972).

ROLLER CYCLING

Paul Swinnerton (GB) achieved a record 164 km/h *102 mph* for 200 m on rollers on 12 Feb 1982 at Stoke-on-Trent. The greatest dis-

BRITISH RECORDS

OPEN AIR TRACKS

MEN

Distance	min sec	Name	Place	Date
Professional unpaced standing start:				
5 km	6:20.90	Ian Hallam (b. 24 Nov 1948)	Leicester, Leicestershire	30 July 1979
Amateur unpaced flying start:				
500 m	30.5	Paul McHugh	Leicester, Leicestershire	12 June 1984
Amateur unpaced standing start:				
1 km	1:08.3	Mark Barry (b. 13 May 1964)	Leicester, Leicestershire	10 July 1982
10 km	13:01.08	David Lloyd (b. 12 Oct 1949)	Leicester, Leicestershire	14 July 1981
20 km	26:01.05	David Lloyd	Leicester, Leicestershire	14 July 1981
1 hour	28 miles 513 yd *45,531 km*	David Lloyd	Leicester, Leicestershire	26 July 1981
Amateur motor-paced standing start:				
50 km	41:46.00	Michael Coles	Leicester, Leicestershire	12 Aug 1981
1 hour	43 miles 1426 yd *70,506 km*	Rik Notley	Leicester, Leicestershire	31 July 1976

WOMEN
unpaced standing start:

Distance	min sec	Name	Place	Date
1 km	1:16.893	Brenda Atkinson	Leicester, Leicestershire	4 Aug 1981
3 km	3:59.701	Amanda Jones (b. 24 Mar 1962)	Leicester, Leicestershire	31 July 1982
5 km	6:41.75	Amanda Jones	Leicester, Leicestershire	31 July 1982
10 km	14:01.1	Amanda Jones	Leicester, Leicestershire	30 June 1981
20 km	28:31.30	Amanda Jones	Leicester, Leicestershire	30 June 1981
1 hour	25 miles 1190 yd *41,322 km*	Amanda Jones	Leicester, Leicestershire	30 June 1981

ROAD CYCLING RECORDS

(British) as recognised by the Road Time Trials Council (out-and-home records)

MEN

Distance	hr min sec	Name	Course area	Date
10 miles	19 11	David Lloyd	Tonbridge, Kent	5 Sept 1981
25 miles	49 24	Alf Engers (b. 1941)	Kelvedon, Essex	5 Aug 1978
30 miles	1 00 11	Martin Pyne	Kelvedon, Essex	30 May 1981
50 miles	1 39 51	Ian Cammish (b. 1 Oct 1956)	Boroughbridge, North Yorkshire	25 June 1983
100 miles	3 31 53	Ian Cammish	Brentwood, Essex	24 July 1983
12 hours	287.282 miles *462,32 km*	Glenn Longland	Ringwood, Hampshire	14 Aug 1983
24 hours	507.00 miles *815,93 km*	Roy Cromack	Cheshire	26–27 July 1969

WOMEN

Distance	hr min sec	Name	Course area	Date
10 miles	21 25	Beryl Burton (b. 12 May 1937)	Blyth, Nottinghamshire	29 Apr 1973
25 miles	53 21	Beryl Burton	Catterick, North Yorkshire	17 June 1976
30 miles	1 08 36	Beryl Burton	Kelvedon, Essex	3 Oct 1981
50 miles	1 51 30	Beryl Burton	Boroughbridge, North Yorkshire	25 July 1976
100 miles	3 55 05	Beryl Burton	Essex	4 Aug 1968
12 hours	277.25 miles *446,19 km*	Beryl Burton	Wetherby, West Yorkshire	17 Sept 1967
24 hours	438.16 miles *705,15 km*	Anne Mann	Abbess Roding, Essex	25–26 June 1983

ROAD RECORDS ASSOCIATION'S STRAIGHT-OUT DISTANCE RECORDS

	MEN				WOMEN			
Distance	hr min sec	Name	Date		hr min sec	Name	Date	
25 miles	42 37	David Lloyd	21 Sept 1982		56 05	Pauline Strong	4 Oct 1981	
50 miles	1 35 45	David Lloyd	26 Oct 1974		1 55 00	Eileen Sheridan	10 Oct 1954	
100 miles	3 28 40	Ray Booty	28 Sept 1956		4 16 01	Eileen Sheridan	18 June 1952	
1000 miles	2 days 10 40 00	Reg Randell	19–21 Aug 1960		3 days 1 00 00	Eileen Sheridan	9–12 July 1954	

Sticking together . . . Cheryl Marek and Estelle Gray crossed America cycling an average 267 miles *429,9 km* per day.

tance achieved in 24 hr is 2511,74 km *1560.73 miles* by Piet Vitten (Netherlands) at Midden, Beemster, Netherlands on 8–9 March 1980.

STATIONARY CYCLING

Rudi Jan Jozef De Greef (b. 28 Dec 1955) stayed stationary without support for 10 hr at Meensel-Kiezegem, Belgium on 19 Nov 1982.

DARTS

Origins

The origins of darts date from the use by archers of heavily weighted ten-inch throwing arrows for self-defence in close quarters fighting. The 'dartes' were used in Ireland in the 16th century and darts was played on the *Mayflower* by the Plymouth pilgrims in 1620. The modern game dates from at least 1896 when Brian Gamlin of Bury, Lancashire, is credited with inventing the present numbering system on the board. The first recorded score of 180 was by John Reader at the Highbury Tavern in Sussex in 1902. Today there are an estimated 6,000,000 darts players in the British Isles.

Most titles

Eric Bristow (b. 25 Apr 1957) has most wins in the World Masters Championship (inst. 1974) with five, in 1977, 1979, 1981 and 1983–4, and in the World Professional Championship (inst. 1978) with five, in 1980–1 and 1984–6. Bristow completed a unique treble in 1983 by also winning the World Cup singles. Six men have won the annual *News of the World* individual Championship twice; most recently Eric Bristow in 1983 and 1984 and Bobby George in 1978 and 1986. John Lowe (b. 21 July 1945) is the only other man to have won each of the four major titles: World Masters, 1976 and 1980; World Professional, 1979; World Cup Singles, 1981; and *News of the World*, 1981.

The National Darts Association of Great Britain individual title was won by Tom O'Regan (b. 28

Feb 1939) of the Northern Star, New Southgate, Greater London in 1970–2. Maureen Flowers (b. 6 Dec 1946), in 1979 and 1980, is the only double winner of the NDA women's individual title.

World Cup

The first World Cup was held at the Wembley Conference Centre, London in 1977. Wales were the inaugural champions and England won in 1979, 1981 and 1983.

Record prize

John Lowe won £102,000 for achieving the first 501 scored with the minimum nine darts in a major event on 13 Oct 1984 at Slough in the quarter-finals of the World Match-play Championships. His darts were six successive treble 20s, treble 17, treble 18 and double 18.

DARTS SCORING RECORDS

24 HOUR SCORES

Men (8 players)	1,722,249 by Broken Hill Darts Club at Broken Hill, New South Wales, Australia on 28–29 Sept 1985.
Women (8 players)	547,647 by a team (including seven Oxfordshire county players) from the Globe Inn, Oxford on 10–11 May 1986.
Individual	424,100 by Paul Glet at the Welsh Tavern, Stone, nr. Dartford, Kent on 1 Dec 1985.
Bulls and 25s (8 players)	419,900 (3182 bulls, 10,432 inners) by a team from Farringdon Community Centre in March 1986.

TEN HOUR SCORES

Most trebles	3056 (from 7992 darts) by Paul Taylor at the Woodhouse Tavern, Leytonstone, London on 19 Oct 1985.
Most doubles	3085 (from 9945 darts) by David Broad at Blantyre Sports Club, Malawi on 17 Mar 1984.
Highest score (retrieving own darts)	374,588 by Ian Knowles and Gary Johns at St Austell's Railway Club, St Austell, Cornwall on 28 Mar 1986.
Highest score (without retrieving)	494,796 by Raymond Jones (GB) and Leo Beerens (Netherlands) in Weert, Netherlands on 24 Aug 1985. Note: category now discontinued.

SIX HOUR HIGHEST SCORES

Men	189,153 by Daniel Tryner at St. Joseph's Catholic Club, Nottingham on 9 Feb 1986.
Women	89,697 by Karen Heavey at the Rose Inn, Gillingham, Kent on 25 Apr 1986.

MILLION AND ONE UP

Men (8 players)	37,809 darts by a team from the Gardener's Arms, Ipswich on 28 Feb–2 Mar 1986 (their attempt included 180 180s).
Women (8 players)	70,066 darts by The Delinquents darts team at the Top George, Combe Martin, Devon on 18–20 Apr 1986.

Mike Gregory broke the record for scoring 3001 in the fewest darts, with 75. The score is technically possible with 51. (Sporting Pictures).

EQUESTRIANISM

The women's record for 3001 was broken by Linda Batten (*left*), who finished on a double after 117 darts—an average of 25.65 per dart. (*Right*) Conrad Homfeld, the only person to win the World Cup twice. In 1985 he rode on *Abdullah*, pictured here, on whom he also won the 1984 Olympic silver medal. (Kit Houghton).

Longest unbeaten run

Mike Bowell (b. 31 May 1947) of Paulton Darts League, Avon, won 152 consecutive competition games from 9 Feb 1971 to 29 Nov 1974. The White Horse Inn, Ashton-under-Lyne, Manchester, were undefeated in a total of 169 matches from 31 May 1979 to 9 Feb 1981.

Fastest three 301s

The fastest time taken to complete three games of 301, finishing on doubles, is 1 min 47 sec by Keith Deller on BBC TV's *Record Breakers* on 22 Oct 1985.

Fastest 'Round the board'

The record time for going round the board clockwise in 'doubles' at arm's length is 9.2 sec by Dennis Gower at the Millers Arms, Hastings, East Sussex on 12 Oct 1975 and 14.5 sec in numerical order by Jim Pike (1903–60) at the Craven Club, Newmarket in March 1944. The record for this feat at the 9 ft *2,7 m* throwing distance, retrieving own darts, is 2 min 13 sec by Bill Duddy (b. 29 Sept 1932) at The Plough, Haringey, London on 29 Oct 1972.

Least darts

Scores of 201 in four darts, 301 in six darts, 401 in seven darts and 501 in nine darts, have been achieved on various occasions. The lowest number of darts thrown for a score of 1001 is 19 by Cliff Inglis (b. 27 May 1935) (160, 180, 140, 180, 121, 180, 40) at the Bromfield Men's Club, Devon on 11 Nov 1975. A score of 2001 in 52 darts was achieved by Alan Evans (b. 14 June 1949) at Ferndale, Glamorgan on 3 Sept 1976. 3001 in 75 darts was thrown by Mike Gregory (b. 16 Dec 1956) at the Stones Cross Hotel, Midsomer Norton, Somerset in Sept 1985. Linda Batten (b. 26 Nov 1954) set a women's 3001 record of 117 darts at The Old Wheatsheaf, Enfield, Middlesex on 2 Apr 1986.

EQUESTRIAN SPORTS

Origins

Evidence of horse-riding dates from a Persian engraving dated *c.* 3,000 BC. Pignatelli's academy of horsemanship at Naples dates from the 16th century. The earliest jumping competition was at the Agricultural Hall, Islington, London, in 1869. Equestrian events have been included in the Olympic Games since 1912.

Most Olympic medals

The greatest number of Olympic gold medals is five by Hans-Günter Winkler (b. 24 July 1926) (W. Germany) who won four team gold medals as captain in 1956, 1960, 1964 and 1972 and won the individual Grand Prix in 1956. The most team wins in the Prix des Nations is five by Germany in 1936, 1956, 1960, 1964 and 1972. The lowest score obtained by a winner is no faults by Frantisek Ventura (1895–1969) (Czechoslovakia) on *Eliot*, 1928 and Alwin Schockemöhle (b. 29 May 1937) (W. Germany) on *Warwick Rex*, 1976. Pierre Jonqueres d'Oriola (b. 1 Feb 1920) (France) uniquely won the individual gold medal twice, 1952 and 1964. Richard John Hannay Meade (b. 4 Dec 1938) (Great Britain) is the only British rider to win three gold medals—as an individual in 1972 and team titles in 1968 and 1972, all in the 3-day event.

Most titles *World*

The men's world championships (inst. 1953) have been won twice by Hans-Günter Winkler (W. Germany) (1954–5) and Raimondo d'Inzeo (Italy) (1956 and 1960). The women's title (1965–74) was won twice by Jane 'Janou' Tissot (*née* Lefebvre) (France) (b. Saigon, 14 May 1945) on *Rocket* (1970 and 1974).

The man from Wombat Forest, Mollongghip, Australia . . . Henry Perry used six horses to ride around Australia, the longest ride in history.

World Cup

Instituted in 1969, the only double winner is Conrad Homfeld (USA) (b. 25 Dec 1951), 1980 and 1985.

King George V Gold Cup and Queen Elizabeth II Cup

David Broome (b. 1 Mar 1940) has won the King George V Gold Cup (first held 1911) a record five times, 1960 on *Sunsalve*, 1966 on *Mister Softee*, 1972 on *Sportsman*, 1977 on *Philco* and 1981 on *Mr Ross*. The Queen Elizabeth II Cup (first held 1949), for women, has been won five times by his sister Elizabeth Edgar (b. 28 Apr 1943), 1977 on *Everest Wallaby*, 1979 on *Forever*, 1981 and 1982 on *Everest Forever*, 1985 on *Everest Rapier*. The only horse to win both these trophies is *Sunsalve* in 1957 (with Elisabeth Anderson) and 1960.

The Prince Philip Trophy (World Team Championship)

Instituted in 1965 as the President's Trophy, and renamed in 1985, it has been won a record eleven times by Great Britain, 1965, 1967, 1970, 1972–4, 1977–9, 1983 and 1985.

Three-day event

The Badminton Three-Day Event (inst. 1949) has been won six times by Lucinda Green (*née* Prior-Palmer) (b. 7 Nov 1953) in 1973 (on *Be Fair*), 1976 (*Wide Awake*), 1977 (*George*), 1979 (*Killaire*), 1983 (*Regal Realm*) and 1984 (*Beagle Bay*)

Jumping records

The official *Fédération Equestre Internationale* records are: high jump 8 ft 1¼ in *2,47 m* by *Huasó*, ridden by Capt Alberto Larraguibel Morales (Chile) at Viña del Mar, Santiago, Chile, on 5 Feb 1949; long jump over water 27 ft 6¾in *8,40 m* by *Something*, ridden by André Ferreira (S. Africa) at Johannesburg on 26 Apr 1975.

The British high jump record is 7 ft 7$\frac{5}{16}$ in *2,32 m* by the 16.2 hands *167 cm* grey gelding *Lastic* ridden by Nick Skelton (b. 30 Dec 1957) at Olympia, London, on 16 Dec 1978. On 25 June 1937, at Olympia, the Lady Wright (*née* Margery Avis Bullows) set the best recorded height for a British equestrienne on her liver chestnut *Jimmy Brown* at 7 ft 4 in *2,23 m*.

The greatest recorded height reached bareback is 7 ft *2,13 m* by Michael Whitaker (b. 17 Mar 1960) on *Red Flight* at Dublin on 14 Nov 1982.

Driving

The most wins at the biennial World Driving Championships (inst. 1972) is three, by Great Britain in 1972, 1974 and 1980 (George Bowman was a member of each of those teams); and Hungary, 1976, 1978 and 1984.

Longest ride

Henry G. Perry, a stockman from Mollongghip, Victoria, Australia rode 22 565 km *14,021 miles* around Australia in 157 days, 1 May to 4 Oct 1985, with six horses.

Origins

'Fencing' (fighting with single sticks) was practised as a sport, or as a part of a religious ceremony, in Egypt as early as *c.* 1360 BC. The first governing body for fencing in Britain was the Corporation of Masters of Defence founded by Henry VIII before 1540 and fencing has been practised as sport, notably in prize fights, since that time. The modern foil was introduced in France as a practice weapon for the short court sword in the mid-17th century. In the late 19th century the épée was developed in France and the light fencing sabre in Italy.

Most titles *World*

The greatest number of individual world titles won is five by Aleksandr Romankov (USSR) (b. 7 Nov 1953), at foil 1974, 1977, 1979, 1982 and 1983, but Christian d'Oriola (France) won four world foil titles, 1947, 1949, 1953–4 as well as two individual Olympic titles. Four women foilists have won three world titles: Helène Mayer (Germany) (1910–53) 1929, 1931, 1937; Ilona Schacherer-Elek (Hungary) (b. 17 May 1907) 1934–5, 1951; Cornelia Hanisch (W. Germany) (b. 12 June 1952) 1979, 1981, 1985. Of these only Ilona Schacherer-Elek also won two individual Olympic titles (1936 and 1948).

Most titles *Olympic*

The most individual Olympic gold medals won is three by Ramón Fonst (Cuba) (1883–1959) in 1900 and 1904 (two) and by Nedo Nadi (Italy) (1894–1952) in 1912 and 1920 (two). Nadi also won three team gold medals in 1920 making a then unprecedented total of five gold medals at one celebration. Edoardo Mangiarotti (Italy) (b. 7 Apr 1919) with six gold, five silver and two bronze, holds the record of 13 Olympic medals. He won them for foil and épée from 1936 to 1960. The most gold medals by a woman is four (one individual, three team) by Elena Novikova-Belova (USSR) (b. 28 July 1947) from 1968 to

Cornelia Hanisch shows great poise in defending an advance. She has collected a record three world titles. (All-Sport).

FENCING

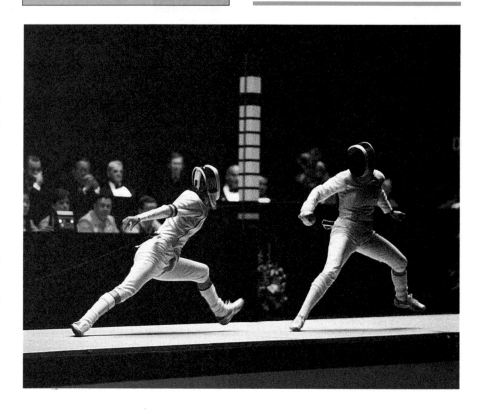

1976, and the record for all medals is seven (two gold, three silver, two bronze) by Ildikó Sagi-Retjö (formerly Ujlaki-Retjö) (Hungary) (b. 11 May 1937) from 1960 to 1976.

British Olympic records

The only British fencer to win a gold medal is Gillian Mary Sheen (b. 21 Aug 1928) in the 1956 foil. A record three Olympic medals were won by Edgar Seligman (1867–1958) with silver medals in the épée team event in 1906, 1908 and 1912. Henry William Furse Hoskyns (b. 19 Mar 1931) has competed most often for Great Britain with six Olympic appearances, 1956–76.

Amateur Fencing Association titles

The most won at one weapon is ten at women's foil by Gillian Sheen (now Donaldson), 1949, 1951–8, 1960.

FIELD SPORTS

FOXHUNTING

Earliest references

Hunting the fox in Britain became popular from the second half of the 18th century though it is mentioned very much earlier. Prior to that time hunting was confined principally to the deer and the hare.

Pack *Oldest*

The Old Charlton Hunt (later the Goodwood) in West Sussex (now extinct), the Duke of Monmouth and Lord Grey of Werke at Charlton, Sussex, and the Duke of Buckingham in north Yorkshire, owned packs which were entered to fox only during the reign (1660–85) of Charles II.

Pack *Largest*

The pack with the greatest number of hounds has been the Duke of Beaufort's hounds maintained at Badminton, Avon, since 1786. At times hunting six days a week, this pack once had 120 couples at hounds. It now meets four days a week.

Longest span

Jean Bethel 'Betty' McKeever (*née* Dawes) (b. 26 Feb 1901) has been Master of the Blean Beagles in Kent since 1909. The 10th Duke of Beaufort (1900–84) was Master of Foxhounds from 1924 until his death in 1984 and hunted on 3895 days from 1920–67.

Longest hunt

The longest recorded hunt was one held by Squire Sandys which ran from Holmbank, northern Lancashire to Ulpha, Cumbria, a total of nearly 80 miles *128 km* in reputedly only 6 hr, in January or February 1743. The longest duration hunt was one of 10 hr 5 min by Charlton Hunt of West Sussex, which ran from East Dean Wood at 7.45 am to a kill over 57¼ miles *92 km* away at 5.50 pm on 26 Jan 1738.

Most Widespread Hunting

Between 1969 and 1986, J. N. P. Watson, Hunting Correspondent to Country Life, hunted with 228 different packs of foxhounds, staghounds and harehounds in Britain, Ireland, USA and Europe.

GAME SHOOTING

Record heads

The world's finest head is the 23-pointer stag in the Maritzburg collection, E. Germany. The outside span is 75½ in *191 cm*, the length 47½ in *120 cm* and the weight 41⅓ lb *18,824 kg*. The greatest number of points is probably 33 (plus

29) on the stag shot in 1696 by Frederick III (1657–1713), the Elector of Brandenburg, later King Frederick I of Prussia.

Largest tally to a single sportsman

556,813 head of game fell to the guns of the 2nd Marquess of Ripon between 1867 and when he dropped dead on a grouse moor after shooting his 52nd bird on the morning of 22 Sept 1923. This figure included 241,234 pheasants, 124,193 partridge and 31,900 hares. (His game books are held by the gunmakers, James Purdey and Sons.)

Thomas, 6th Baron Walsingham bagged 1070 grouse, a one-day record for a single gun, in Yorkshire on 30 Aug 1888.

FIVES

ETON FIVES

A handball game against the buttress of Eton College Chapel was first recorded in 1825. New courts were built at Eton in 1840, the rules were codified in 1877, rewritten laws were introduced three times and last amended in 1981.

Most titles

One pair has won the Amateur Championship (Kinnaird Cup) eight times—Anthony Hughes and Arthur James Gordon Campbell (1958, 1965–8, 1971, 1973 and 1975). Hughes was also in the winning pair in 1963 and has played in 16 finals. The Clubs' knock-out championship (the Alan Barber Cup) has been won a record twelve times by Old Cholmeleians (1969–70, 1975, 1977–85). The Douglas Keeble Cup for the National League has been won a record eight times by Old Edwardians (1975–7, 1981–5).

RUGBY FIVES

As now known, this game dates from *c.* 1850 with the first inter-public school matches recorded in the early 1870s. The Oxford *v.* Cambridge contest was inaugurated in 1925 and the Rugby Fives Association was founded in the home of Dr Edgar Cyriax (1874–1954), in Welbeck Street, London, on 29 Oct 1927. The dimensions of the Standard Rugby Fives court were approved by the Association in 1931.

Most titles

The greatest number of Amateur Singles Championships (instituted 1932) ever won is twelve by Wayne Enstone in 1973–8 and 1980–5. The record for the Amateur Doubles Championship (instituted 1925) is seven shared by John Frederick Pretlove (1952, 1954, 1956–9, 1961) and David E. Gardner (1960, 1965–6, 1970–2, 1974).

The invitation World Championships was first held in 1983. On the first three occasions Wayne Enstone won the singles and Enstone and S. Ashton won the doubles.

FOOTBALL (ASSOCIATION)

Origins

A game with some similarities termed *Tsu-chu* was played in China in the 4th and 3rd centuries BC. One of the earliest references to the game in England is a Royal Proclamation by Edward II in 1314 banning the game in the City of London. The earliest clear representation of football is an Edinburgh print dated 1672–3. The game was standardised with the formation of the

Football Association in England on 26 Oct 1863. The oldest club is Sheffield FC, formed on 24 Oct 1857. The oldest in the Football League is Notts County, founded in 1862. Eleven per side became standard in 1870.

PROFESSIONAL

Longest match

The duration record for first class fixtures is 3 hr 30 min (with interruptions) in the Copa Libertadores in Santos, Brazil, on 2–3 Aug 1962, when Santos drew 3–3 with Penarol FC of Montevideo, Uruguay.

The longest British match on record was one of 3 hr 23 min between Stockport County and Doncaster Rovers in the second leg of the Third Division (North) Cup at Edgeley Park, Stockport, Greater Manchester on 30 Mar 1946.

Longest unbeaten streak

Nottingham Forest were undefeated in 42 consecutive Division I matches from 20 Nov 1977 to 9 Dec 1978. In Scottish Football Glasgow Celtic were undefeated in 62 matches (49 won, 13 drawn), 13 Nov 1915–21 April 1917.

Most postponements

The Scottish Cup tie between Inverness Thistle and Falkirk during the winter of 1978–9 was postponed a record 29 times due to weather conditions. Finally Falkirk won the game 4–0.

GOAL SCORING

Teams

The highest score recorded in a first-class match is 36. This occurred in the Scottish Cup match between Arbroath and Bon Accord on 12 Sept 1885, when Arbroath won 36–0 on their home ground. But for the lack of nets and the consequent waste of retrieval time the score must have been even higher. Seven further goals were disallowed for offside.

The highest margin recorded in an international match is 17, when England beat Australia 17–0 at Sydney on 30 June 1951. This match is not listed by England as a *full* international. The highest in the British Isles was when England beat Ireland 13–0 at Belfast on 18 Feb 1882.

The highest score between English clubs in any major competition is 26, when Preston North End beat Hyde 26–0 in an FA Cup tie at Deepdale, Lancashire on 15 Oct 1887. The biggest victory in an FA Cup Final is six when Bury beat Derby County 6–0 at Crystal Palace on 18 Apr 1903, in which year Bury did not concede a single goal in the five Cup matches.

The highest score by one side in a Football League (Division I) match is 12 goals when West Bromwich Albion beat Darwen 12–0 at West Bromwich, West Midlands on 4 Apr 1892; when Nottingham Forest beat Leicester Fosse by the same score at Nottingham on 21 Apr 1909; and when Aston Villa beat Accrington 12–2 at Perry Barr, W. Midlands on 12 Mar 1892.

The highest aggregate in League Football was 17 goals when Tranmere Rovers beat Oldham Athletic 13–4 in a Third Division (North) match at Prenton Park, Merseyside, on Boxing Day, 1935. The record margin in a League match has been 13 in the Newcastle United 13, Newport County 0 (Division II) match on 5 Oct 1946 and in the Stockport County 13, Halifax 0 (Division III (North)) match on 6 Jan 1934.

The highest number of goals by any British team in a professional league in a season is 142 in 34 matches by Raith Rovers (Scottish Division II) in the 1937–8 season. The English League record is 134 in 46 matches by Peterborough United (Division IV) in 1960–1.

Individual

The most scored by one player in a first-class match is 16 by Stephan Stanis (*né* Stanikowski, b. Poland, 15 July 1913) for Racing Club de Lens *v.* Aubry-Asturies, in Lens, France, in a wartime French Cup game on 13 Dec 1942.

The record number of goals scored by one player in an international match is ten by Sofus Nielsen (1888–1963) for Denmark *v.* France (17–1) in the 1908 Olympics and by Gottfried Fuchs (1889–1972) for Germany who beat Russia 16–0 in the 1912 Olympic tournament (consolation event) in Sweden.

Season

The most goals in a League season is 60 in 39 games by William Ralph 'Dixie' Dean (1907–80) for Everton (Division I) in 1927–8 and 66 in 38 games by James Smith (1902–76) for Ayr United (Scottish Division II) in the same season. With three more in Cup ties and 19 in representative matches Dean's total was 82.

Career

Artur Friedenreich (1892–1969) (Brazil) scored an undocumented 1329 goals in a 43 year first class football career. The most goals scored in a specified period is 1216 by Edson Arantes do Nascimento (Brazil) (b. 23 Oct 1940), known as Pelé, from 7 Sept 1956 to 2 Oct 1974 in 1254 games. His best year was 1959 with 126, and the *milesimo* (1000th) came in a penalty for his club Santos in the Maracaña Stadium, Rio de Janeiro on 19 Nov 1969 when playing his 909th first-class match. He later played for New York Cosmos and on his retirement on 1 Oct 1977 his total had reached 1281, in 1363 games. He added two more goals later in special appearances. Franz 'Bimbo' Binder (b. 1 Dec 1911) scored 1006 goals in 756 games in Austria and Germany between 1930 and 1950.

The international career record for England is 49 goals by Robert 'Bobby' Charlton (b. 11 Oct 1937). His first was *v.* Scotland on 19 Apr 1958 and his last on 20 May 1970 *v.* Colombia.

The greatest number of goals scored in British first-class football is 550 (410 in Scottish League matches) by James McGrory of Glasgow Celtic (1922–38). The most scored in League matches is 434, for West Bromwich Albion, Fulham, Leicester City and Shrewsbury Town, by George Arthur Rowley (b. 21 Apr 1926) between 1946 and April 1965. Rowley also scored 32 goals in the F.A. Cup and one for England 'B'.

Fastest goals

The fastest Football League goals on record were scored in 6 sec by Albert E. Mundy (b. 12 May 1926) (Aldershot) in a Division IV match *v.* Hartlepool United at Victoria Ground, Hartlepool, Cleveland on 25 Oct 1958, by Barrie Jones (b. 31 Oct 1938) (Notts Co) in a Division III match *v.* Torquay United on 31 Mar 1962, by Keith Smith (b. 15 Sept 1940) (Crystal Palace) in a Division II match *v.* Derby County at the Baseball Ground, Derby on 12 Dec 1964 and by Tommy W. Langley (b. 8 Feb 1958) (Queen's Park Rangers) in a Division II match *v.* Bolton Wanderers on 11 Oct 1980.

The fastest confirmed hat-trick is in 2½ minutes by Ephraim 'Jock' Dodds (b. 7 Sept 1915) for Blackpool *v.* Tranmere Rovers on 28 Feb 1943, and by Jimmy Scarth (b. 26 Aug 1920) for Gillingham *v.* Leyton Orient in Div III (Southern) on 1 Nov 1952. A hat-trick in 1 min 50 sec is claimed for Maglioni of Independiente *v.* Gimnasia y Escrima de la Plata in Argentina on 18 Mar 1973. John McIntyre (Blackburn Rovers) scored four goals in 5 min *v.* Everton at Ewood Park, Blackburn, Lancashire on 16 Sept 1922.

BRITISH GOAL SCORING RECORDS

SCOTTISH CUP

13 John Petrie for Arbroath v Bon Accord on 5 Sept 1885

FOOTBALL LEAGUE

10 Joe Payne (1914–77) for Luton Town v Bristol Rovers (Div 3S) at Luton on 13 Apr 1936

F. LEAGUE DIV I

7 Ted Drake (b. 16 Aug 1912) for Arsenal v Aston Villa at Birmingham on 14 Dec 1935; James David Ross for Preston NE v Stoke at Preston on 6 Oct 1888

FA CUP (PRELIM)

10 Chris Marron for South Shields v Radcliffe at South Shields on 20 Sept 1947

FA CUP

9 Edward 'Ted' MacDougall (b. 8 Jan 1947) for Bournemouth v Margate at Bournemouth on 20 Nov 1971

SCOTTISH DIV I

8 James Edward McGrory (1904–82) Celtic v Dunfermline at Celtic Park, Glasgow on 14 Jan 1928

HOME INTERNATIONAL

6 Joe Bambrick (b. 3 Nov 1905) for Ireland v Wales at Belfast on 1 Feb 1930

AMATEUR INTERNATIONAL

6 William Charles Jordan (1885–1949) for England v France at Park Royal, London on 23 Mar 1908; Vivian John Woodward (1879–1954) for England v Holland at Stamford Bridge, London on 11 Dec 1909; Harold A. Walden for Great Britain v Hungary at Stockholm, Sweden on 1 July 1912

William 'Ginger' Richardson (West Bromwich Albion) scored four goals in 5 min from the kick-off against West Ham United at Upton Park on 7 Nov 1931. Frank Keetley scored six goals in 21 min in the 2nd half of the Lincoln City *v.* Halifax Town league match on 16 Jan 1932. The international record is three goals in 3½ min by Willie Hall (Tottenham Hotspur) for England against Ireland on 16 Nov 1938 at Old Trafford, Greater Manchester.

Fastest own goal

Torquay United's Pat Kruse (b. 30 Nov 1953) equalled the fastest goal on record when he

Published by Guinness at £6.95

headed the ball into his own net only 6 sec after kick-off *v.* Cambridge United on 3 Jan 1977.

GOALKEEPING

Individual record

The longest that any goalkeeper has succeeded in preventing any goals being scored past him in international matches is 1142 min for Dino Zoff (Italy), from September 1972 to June 1974. The Football League record is 1103 min by Steve Death (b. 19 Sept 1949) for Reading in Division IV from 24 March to 18 Aug 1979.

FA CHALLENGE CUP AND SCOTTISH FA CUP

Most wins

The greatest number of FA Cup wins is seven by Aston Villa, 1887, 1895, 1897, 1905, 1913, 1920 and 1957 (nine final appearances) and by Tottenham Hotspur, 1901, 1921, 1961, 1962, 1967, 1981 and 1982 (seven appearances). Newcastle United and Arsenal have been in the final 11 times. The highest aggregate scores have been 6–1 in 1890 and 4–3 in 1953.

The greatest number of Scottish FA Cup wins is 27 by Celtic in 1892, 1899, 1900, 1904, 1907–8, 1911–12, 1914, 1923, 1925, 1927, 1931, 1933, 1937, 1951, 1954, 1965, 1967, 1969, 1971, 1972, 1974, 1975, 1977, 1980 and 1985.

Youngest player

The youngest player in a FA Cup Final was Paul Allen (b. 28 Aug 1962) of West Ham United, who played against Arsenal on 10 May 1980 aged 17 years 256 days. Derek Johnstone (Rangers) (b. 4 Nov 1953) was 16 years 11 months old when he played in the Scottish League Cup Final against Celtic on 24 Oct 1970. The youngest goal scorer in the FA Cup Final was Norman Whiteside (b. 7 May 1965) for Manchester United *v.* Brighton at 18 yr 19 days on 26 May 1983. The youngest player ever in the FA Cup competition was Scott Endersby (b. 20 Feb 1962) who was only 15 years 288 days old when he played in goal for Kettering *v.* Tilbury on 26 Nov. 1977.

Most medals

Three players have won five FA Cup winner's medals: James Forrest (Blackburn Rovers) (1884–6, 1890–1); the Hon Sir Arthur Fitzgerald Kinnaird, KT (Wanderers) (1873, 1877–8) and Old Etonians (1879, 1882); and Charles H. R. Wollaston (Wanderers) (1872–3, 1876–8).

The most Scottish Cup winners' medals won is eight by Charles Campbell (Queen's Park) in 1874–6, 1880–2, 1884 and 1886.

Longest tie

The most protracted FA Cup tie in the competition proper was that between Stoke City and Bury in the third round with Stoke winning 3–2 in the fifth meeting after 9 hr 22 min of play in January 1955. The matches were at Bury (1–1) on 8 Jan; Stoke on Trent on 12 Jan (abandoned after 22 min of extra time with the score 1–1); Goodison Park (3–3) on 17 Jan; Anfield (2–2) on 19 Jan; and finally at Old Trafford on 24 Jan. In the 1972 final qualifying round Alvechurch beat Oxford City after five previous drawn games (total playing time 11 hours).

FOOTBALL LEAGUE/MILK CUP

Instituted in 1960–1, the most wins is four by Liverpool, 1981–4.

SCOTTISH LEAGUE CUP

Instituted in 1946–7, the most wins is 12 by Rangers between 1947 and 1984.

European Champion Clubs Cup

The European Cup for the League champions of the respective nations was approved by FIFA on 8 May 1955 and was run by the European governing body UEFA (Union of European Football Associations) which came into being in the previous year. Real Madrid won the first final, and have won a record six times (including five times consecutively) 1956–60, 1966. The highest score in a final was Real Madrid's 7–3 win over Eintracht Frankfurt at Hampden Park, Glasgow on 18 May 1960.

Albert Mundy, scorer of the fastest goal in League history—after just six seconds.

LEAGUE CHAMPIONSHIPS

World

The record number of successive national League championships is nine by Celtic (Scotland) 1966–74, CSKA, Sofia (Bulgaria) 1954–62 and MTK Budapest (Hungary) 1917–25. The Sofia club hold a European postwar record of 23 league titles.

English

The greatest number of League Championships (Division I) is 16 by Liverpool in 1901, 1906, 1922, 1923, 1947, 1964, 1966, 1973, 1976–7, 1979–80, 1982–84, and 1986. The record number of wins in a season is 33 from 42 matches by Doncaster Rovers in Division III (North) in 1946–7. The Division I record is 31 wins from 42 matches by Tottenham Hotspur in 1960–1. In 1893–4 Liverpool won 22 and drew 6 in 28 Division II games. They also won the promotion match. The most points in a season under the current scoring system is 102 by Swindon in Division IV in 1985–6. In 1985–6 Wimbledon gained promotion to the First Division only nine seasons after playing non-league football.

'Double'

The only FA Cup and League Championship 'doubles' are those of Preston North End in 1889, Aston Villa in 1897, Tottenham Hotspur in 1961, Arsenal in 1971 and Liverpool in 1986. Preston won the League without losing a match and the Cup without having a goal scored against them throughout the whole competition.

Scottish

Glasgow Rangers have won the Scottish League Championship 36 times between 1899 and 1978 and were joint champions on another occasion. Their 76 points in the Scottish Division I in 1920–1 represents a record in any division.

Closest win

In 1923–4 Huddersfield won the Division I championship over Cardiff by 0.02 of a goal with a goal average of 1.81.

TOURNAMENT RECORDS

World Club Championship

This club tournament was started in 1960 between the winners of the European Cup and the Copa Libertadores, the South American equivalent. The most wins is three by Penarol, Uruguay in 1961, 1966 and 1982. Independiente, Argentina won in 1973 and 1984 and reached the final in 1975, but couldn't agree dates for the matches with Bayern Munich.

European Championship (*Nations Cup*)

The European equivalent of the World Cup started in 1958 and is staged every four years. West Germany are the only country to have won twice, in 1972 and 1980. They also lost in the 1976 final, to Czechoslovakia.

THE FIFA WORLD CUP

The Fédération Internationale de Football Association (FIFA), which was founded on 21 May 1904, instituted the first World Cup on 13 July 1930, in Montevideo, Uruguay. It is now held quadrennially. Three wins have been achieved by Brazil 1958, 1962 and 1970, and by Italy 1934, 1938 and 1982.

Goal scoring and Appearances

Antonio Carbajal (b. 1923) (Mexico) is the only player to have appeared in five World Cup final tournaments, keeping goal for Mexico in 1950, 1954, 1958, 1962 and 1966, playing 11 games in all. Uwe Seeler (b. 5 Nov 1936) (West Germany) holds the record for the most appearances in final tournaments, playing as a centre forward in 21 games in the 1958–1970 events, whilst Pelé is the only player to have been with three World Cup winning teams, in 1958, 1962 and 1970. The youngest ever to play in the World Cup is Norman Whiteside who played for Northern Ireland *v.* Yugoslavia aged 17 yr 42 days on 17 June 1982. The record goal scorer is Just Fontaine (b. Marrakesh, Morocco, 18 Aug 1933) of France who scored 13 goals in six matches in the final stages of the 1958 competition in Sweden. Gerd Müller (b. 3 Nov 1945) (West Germany) scored 10 goals in 1970 and four in 1974 for the highest aggregate of 14 goals. Fontaine and Jairzinho (Brazil) are the only two players to have scored in every match in a final series, as Jairzinho scored seven in six games in 1970.

The most goals scored in a final is three by Geoff Hurst (b. 8 Dec 1941) for England *v.* West Germany on 30 July 1966. Three players have scored in two finals, Vava (real name Edwaldo Izito Neto) (Brazil) in 1958 and 1962, Pelé in 1958 and 1970, and Paul Breitner (West Germany) in 1974 and 1982. The fastest goal in World Cup competition was one in 27 sec by Bryan Robson (b. 11 Jan 1957) for England *v.* France in Bilbao on 16 June 1982.

The highest score in a World Cup match occurred in a qualifying match in Auckland on 15 Aug 1981 when New Zealand beat Fiji 13–0. The highest score during the final stages is 10, scored by Hungary in a 10–1 win over El Salvador at Elche, Spain on 15 June 1982. The highest match aggregate in the finals tournament is 12, when Austria beat Switzerland in 1954.

The highest scoring team in a final tournament has been West Germany who scored 25 in six matches in 1954, for the highest average of 4.17 goals per game.

The best defensive record belongs to England, who in six matches in 1966 conceded only three goals. Curiously, no team has ever failed to score in a World Cup Final.

MEXICO 1986

The 13th World Cup Final was won by Argentina at the Azteca Stadium, Mexico City, Mexico on 29 June 1986, when they beat West Germany 3–2.

Only six nations have won the World Cup. Argentina became the third to have won it twice, along with Uruguay (1930 and 1950) and West Germany (1954 and 1974), who were making a record fifth appearance in the final.

The attendance in the Azteca, 114,590, was the second highest ever for a final. (*See Page 250— Attendances.*) Gary Lineker (England) (b. 30 Nov 1960) was the tournament's highest scorer with six, whilst the goals-per-game average was 2.54 (excluding penalty shoot outs), the lowest in the history of the tournament.

Wladyslaw Szmuda (Poland) (b. 6 June 1954) equalled Uwe Seeler's record (*see opposite*) for the most appearances in World Cup finals with his 21st *v.* Brazil on 16 June 1986. He made his first appearance in 1974.

Diego Maradona, captain of the world champions. (All-Sport).

Glasgow Celtic became the first British club to win the Cup beating Inter-Milan 2–1 in Lisbon, Portugal, on 25 May 1967. They also became the first British club to win the European Cup and the two senior domestic tournaments (League and Cup) in the same season. Liverpool, winners in 1977, 1978, 1981 and 1984, have been the most successful British club and in the 1983–4 season emulated Celtic by also winning two domestic competitions—League and Milk Cup.

European Cup Winners Cup
A tournament for the national Cup winners started in 1960–1. Clubs to win twice have been AC Milan 1968 and 1973, Anderlecht 1976 and 1978, Barcelona 1979 and 1982, and Dynamo Kiev 1975 and 1986. Tottenham Hotspur were the first British club to win the trophy, beating Atlético Madrid 5–1 in Rotterdam in 1963.

UEFA Cup
Originally known as the International Inter-City Industrial Fairs Cup, this club tournament began in 1955. The first competition lasted three years, the second two years. In 1960–1 it became an annual tournament and since 1971–2 has been replaced by the UEFA Cup. The first British club to win the trophy was Leeds United in 1968. The most wins is three by Barcelona in 1958, 1960 and 1966.

PLAYERS

Most durable player
The most durable player in League history has been Terence Lionel Paine (b. 23 Mar 1939) who

Zavarov scores for Dynamo Kiev in their electrifying 3–0 win over Atlético Madrid in the 1986 Cup Winners Cup Final. They became the fourth club to win the competition twice. (All-Sport).

made 824 league appearances from 1957 to 1977 playing for Southampton and Hereford Utd. Norman John Trollope (b. 14 June 1943) made 770 League appearances for one club, Swindon Town, between 1960 and 1980.

Transfer fees
The greatest transfer fee quoted for a player is 15,895 million lire (£6.9 million) by Napoli in 1984 for Diego Maradona (Argentina) (b. 30 Oct 1960) from Barcelona. This exceeded the c. £5 million that Barcelona paid for Maradona in 1982.

The record fee between British clubs was £1,500,000 (incl VAT and other levies) paid by Manchester United to West Bromwich Albion for Bryan Robson on 3 Oct 1981.

The highest transfer fee for a British player is the estimated £3.2 million paid by Juventus of Italy to Liverpool for Ian Rush in June 1986.

Heaviest goalkeeper
The biggest goalkeeper in representative football was the England international Willie J. 'Fatty' Foulke (1874–1916), who stood 6 ft 3 in *1,90 m* and weighed 22 st 3 lb *141 kg*. His last games were for Bradford City, by which time he was

26 st *165 kg*. He once stopped a game by snapping the cross bar.

ATTENDANCES

Greatest crowds
The greatest recorded crowd at any football match was 205,000 (199,589 paid) for the Brazil *v.* Uruguay World Cup match in the Maracaña Municipal Stadium, Rio de Janeiro, Brazil on 16 July 1950. The record attendance for a European Cup match is 136,505 at the semi-final between Glasgow Celtic and Leeds United at Hampden Park, Glasgow on 15 Apr 1970.

The British record paid attendance is 149,547 at the Scotland *v.* England international at Hampden Park, Glasgow, on 17 Apr 1937. It is, however, probable that this total was exceeded (estimated 160,000) at the FA Cup Final between Bolton Wanderers and West Ham United at Wembley Stadium on 28 Apr 1923, when the crowd broke in on the pitch and the start was delayed 40 min until the pitch was cleared. The counted admissions were 126,047.

The Scottish Cup record attendance is 146,433 when Celtic played Aberdeen at Hampden Park on 24 Apr 1937. The record attendance for a League match in Britain is 118,567 for Rangers *v.* Celtic at Ibrox Park, Glasgow on 2 Jan 1939.

The highest attendance at an amateur match has been 120,000 in Senayan Stadium, Jakarta, Indonesia, on 26 Feb 1976 for the Pre-Olympic Group II final, North Korea *v.* Indonesia.

Smallest crowd

The smallest crowd at a full home international was 2315 for Wales v. Northern Ireland on 27 May 1982 at the Racecourse Ground, Wrexham, Clwyd. The smallest paying attendance at a Football League fixture was for the Stockport County v. Leicester City match at Old Trafford, Greater Manchester, on 7 May 1921. Stockport's own ground was under suspension and the 'crowd' numbered 13 but an estimated 2000 gained free admission. When West Ham beat Castilla of Spain (5–1) in the European Cup Winners Cup at Upton Park, Greater London, on 1 Oct 1980 and when Aston Villa beat Besiktas of Turkey (3–1) in the European Cup at Villa Park on 15 Sept 1982, there were no paying spectators due to disciplinary action by the European Football Union.

INTERNATIONAL CAPS

Oldest and youngest caps

The oldest cap has been William Henry 'Billy' Meredith (1874–1958) (Manchester City and United) who played outside right for Wales v. England at Highbury, London, on 15 Mar 1920 when aged 45 yr 229 days. He played internationally for a record span of 26 years (1895–1920).

The youngest British international was Norman Whiteside, who played for Northern Ireland v. Yugoslavia, at 17 yr 42 days on 17 June 1982.

England's youngest international was Duncan Edwards (1936–58) of Manchester United v. Scotland at Wembley on 2 Apr 1955, at 18 yr 183 days. The youngest Welsh cap was John Charles (b. 27 Dec 1931), of Leeds United v. Ireland at Wrexham on 8 Mar 1950, aged 18 yr 71 days. Scotland's youngest international has been Johnny Lambie of Queen's Park, at 17 yr 92 days v. Ireland on 20 Mar 1886. The youngest for the Republic of Ireland was James Holmes (b. 11 Nov 1953) of Coventry City, at 17 yr 200 days v. Austria in Dublin on 30 May 1971.

Most international appearances

The greatest number of appearances for a national team is 150 by Hector Chumpitaz (b. 12 Apr 1943) (Peru) from 1963 to 1982. This includes all matches played by the national team. The record for full internationals against other national teams is 119 by Pat Jennings of Northern Ireland (as above).

The most women's internationals is 56 (49 as captain) by Carol Thomas (b. 5 June 1955) for England, 1974–86.

OLYMPIC GAMES

The only country to have won the Olympic football title three times is Hungary in 1952, 1964 and 1968. The United Kingdom won the unofficial tournament in 1900 and the official tournaments of 1908 and 1912. The highest Olympic score is Denmark (17) v. France 'A' (1) in 1908.

OTHER MATCHES

Highest scores Teams

In a Felixstowe Sunday League match on 11 Mar 1984 Ipswich Exiles beat Seaton Rovers 45–0.

In an under-14 league match between Midas FC and Courage Colts, in Kent, on 11 Apr 1976, the full time score after 70 min play was 59–1. Top scorer for Midas was Kevin Graham with 17 goals. Courage had scored the first goal.

Needing to improve their goal 'difference' to gain promotion in 1979, Ilinden FC of Yugoslavia, with the collusion of the opposition,

INTERNATIONAL APPEARANCES

WORLD RECORD

Pat Jennings, playing in his 119th appearance against Brazil on his 41st birthday.

BRITISH RECORD HOLDERS

Kenny Dalglish

Joey Jones

NORTHERN IRELAND....119
Patrick A. Jennings (b. 12 June 1945) .... Watford/Tottenham H/Arsenal 1964–86
ENGLAND....108
Robert Frederick 'Bobby' Moore (b. 12 Apr 1941) ..... West Ham U/Fulham 1962–73
SCOTLAND....100
Kenneth M. Dalglish (b. 4 Mar 1951) .... Celtic/Liverpool 1971–86
WALES....68
Ivor Allchurch (b. 29 Dec 1929) .... Swansea C/Newcastle/Cardiff C/Worcester C 1950–68
Joseph P. 'Joey' Jones (b. 4 Mar 1955) .... Wrexham, Liverpool, Chelsea, Huddersfield T. 1972–86
REPUBLIC OF IRELAND....60
Michael J. 'Johnny' Giles (b. 6 Jan 1940) .... Manchester U/Leeds U/West Bromwich A 1960–79

Mladost, and the referee, won their final game of the season by 134–1. Their rivals in the promotion race won their match, under similar circumstances by 88–0.

Highest scores *Individual*

Dean Goodliff scored 26 goals for Deleford Colts *v.* Iver Minors in the Slough Boys Soccer Combination Under 14 League at Iver, Buckinghamshire in his team's 33–0 win on 22 Dec 1985. The women's record is 22 goals by Linda Curl of Norwich Ladies in a 40–0 league victory over Milton Keynes Reserves at Norwich on 25 Sept 1983.

Highest scores *Season*

The greatest number of goals in a season reported for an individual player in junior professional league football is 96 by Tom Duffy (b. 7 Jan 1937), who played centre forward for Ardeer Thistle FC, Strathclyde in 1960–1. Paul Anthony Moulden (b. 6 Sept 1967) scored 289 goals in 40 games for Bolton Lads Club in Bolton Boys Federation intermediate league and cup matches in 1981–2. An additional 51 goals scored in other tournaments brought his total to 340, the highest season figure reported in any class of competitive football for an individual. He made his Football League debut for Manchester City on 1 Jan 1986 and has played for the England Youth team.

Fastest goals

Wind-aided goals in 3 sec after kick-off have been scored by a number of players. Tony Bacon, of Schalmont HS scored three goals *v.* Icabod Crane HS in 63 sec at Schenectady, New York, USA on 8 Oct 1975.

Fastest own goal

The fastest own goals on record have been in 5 sec, 'scored' by Peter Johnson of Chesham United *v.* Wycombe Wanderers on 21 Feb 1976 and by John Smythe of Vernon Carus. *v.* Duke Williams Reserves in March 1986.

Longest ties

The aggregate duration of ties in amateur soccer have not been collated but it is recorded that in the London FA Intermediate Cup first qualifying round Highfield FC Reserves had to meet Mansfield House FC on 19 and 26 Sept and 3, 10 and 14 Oct 1970 to get a decision after 9 hr 50 min play with scores of 0–0, 1–1, 1–1, 3–3, and 0–2. In the Hertfordshire Intermediate Cup, London Colney beat Leavesden Hospital after 12 hr 41 min play and seven ties from 6 Nov to 17 Dec 1971.

Largest tournament

The Metropolitan Police 5-a-side Youth Competition in 1981 attracted an entry of 7008 teams, a record for an FA sanctioned competition.

Most and Least successful teams

The Home Farm FC, Dublin, Ireland, between 12 Oct 1968 and 10 Oct 1970 won 79 consecutive matches. Winlaton West End FC, Tyne and Wear, completed a run of 95 league games without defeat between 1976 and 1980. Penlake Junior Football Club remained unbeaten for 153 games (winning 152) in the Warrington Hilden Friendly League from 1981 till a defeat finally in 1986. Stockport United FC, of the Stockport Football League, lost 39 consecutive League and Cup matches, September 1976 to 18 Feb 1978.

Most indisciplined

In the local Cup match between Tongham Youth Club, Surrey and Hawley, Hampshire, on 3 Nov 1969 the referee booked all 22 players including one who went to hospital, and one of the linesmen. The match, won by Tongham 2–0, was described by a player as 'A good, hard game'.

In a Gancia Cup match at Waltham Abbey, Essex on 23 Dec 1973, the referee, Michael J. Woodhams, sent off the entire Juventus-Cross team and some club officials. Glencraig United, Faifley, nr Clydebank, had all 11 team members and two substitutes for their match against Goldenhill Boys' Club on 2 Feb 1975 booked in the dressing room before a ball was kicked. The referee, Mr Tarbet of Bearsden, took exception to the chant which greeted his arrival. It was not his first meeting with Glencraig. The teams drew 2–2.

Ball control

Mikael Palmquist (Sweden) juggled a regulation soccer ball for 14 hr 14 min non-stop with feet, legs and head without the ball ever touching the ground at Göteborg, Sweden on 6 Apr 1986. Palmquist also headed a regulation football non-stop for 4½ hr at Göteborg, Sweden in 1984. Uno Lindström of Boden, Sweden kept a football up while he travelled a distance of 21,097 km *13.110 miles* in 2 hr 55 min 49 sec on 10 Aug 1985.

(*Above*) Dean Goodliff's net profit amounted to 26 goals in a match for Deleford Colts. (*Right*) The travelling skills of Uno Lindström, who went over 13 miles *21 km* without letting the ball drop.

GAELIC FOOTBALL

Earliest references

The game developed from inter-parish 'free for all' with no time-limit, no defined playing area nor specific rules. The earliest reported match was Meath *v.* Louth, at Slane in 1712. Standardisation came with the formation of the Gaelic Athletic Association in Thurles, Ireland, on 1 Nov 1884.

Most titles

The greatest number of All Ireland Championships won by one team is 29 by Ciarraidhe (Kerry) between 1903 and 1985. The greatest number of successive wins is four by Wexford (1915–18) and Kerry twice (1929–32, 1978–81). Leinster has won most Inter-provincial championships (Railway Cup) with 18 between 1928 and 1974. Sean O'Neill (Down) holds the record of eight medals with Ulster (1960–71).

Cheers!
The first single
payout of over £1 million, to
members of Roundway
Hospital in Devizes, Wiltshire.

Highest scores

The highest team score in an All-Ireland final was when Dublin, 27 (5 goals, 12 points) beat Armagh, 15 (3 goals, 6 points) on 25 Sept 1977. The highest combined score was 45 points when Cork (26) beat Galway (19) in 1973. A goal equals three points. The highest individual score in an All-Ireland final has been 2 goals, 6 points by Jimmy Keaveney (Dublin) *v.* Armagh in 1977, and by Michael Sheehy (Kerry) *v.* Dublin in 1979.

Lowest scores

In four All-Ireland finals the combined totals have been 7 points; 1893 Wexford (1 goal, till 1894 worth 5 points, 1 point) *v.* Cork (1 point); 1895 Tipperary (4 points) *v.* Meath (3 points); 1904 Kerry (5 points) *v.* Dublin (2 points); 1924 Kerry (4 points) *v.* Dublin (3 points).

Most appearances

The most All-Ireland finals contested is ten by Dan O'Keeffe (Kerry) of which seven (a record) were on the winning side.

Largest crowd

The record crowd is 90,556 for the Down *v.* Offaly final at Croke Park, Dublin, in 1961.

GAMBLING

World's biggest win

The world's biggest individual gambling win is $40 million by Mike Wittkowski in the Illinois State Lottery, announced on 3 Sep 1984. From $35 worth of 'Lotto' tickets bought by his family, the winning six numbers bring him $2 million annually for 20 years.

World's biggest loss

An unnamed Italian industrialist was reported to have lost £800,000 in 5 hr at roulette in Monte Carlo, Monaco on 6 Mar 1974. A Saudi Arabian prince was reported to have lost more than $1 million in a single session at the Metro Club, Las Vegas, USA in December 1974.

Largest casino

The largest casino in the world is the Resorts International Casino, Atlantic City, NJ, USA. It reported a record month in July 1983 with winnings of $29.3 million. The Casino comprises 60,000 ft^2 *5574 m^2*, containing 127 gaming tables and 1640 slot machines. Attendances total over 35,000 daily at peak weekends.

BINGO

Bingo is a lottery game which, as keno, was developed in the 1880s from lotto, whose origin is thought to be the 17th century Italian game *tumbule*. It has long been known in the British Army (called Housey-Housey) and the Royal Navy (called Tombola). The winner was the first to complete a random selection of numbers from 1 to 90. The USA version called Bingo differs in that the selection is from 1 to 75. There are six million players in the United Kingdom.

Largest house

The largest 'house' in Bingo sessions was 15,756 at the Canadian National Exhibition, Toronto on 19 Aug 1983. Staged by the Variety Club of Ontario Tent #28, there was total prize money of $C250,000 with a record one-game payout of $C100,000.

Earliest and latest Full House

A 'Full House' call occurred on the 15th number by Norman A. Wilson at Guide Post Working-men's Club, Bedlington, Northumberland on 22 June 1978, by Anne Wintle of Brynrethin, Mid Glamorgan, on a coach trip to Bath on 17 Aug 1982 and by Shirley Lord at Kahibah Bowling Club, New South Wales, Australia on 24 Oct 1983. 'House' was not called until the 86th number at the Hillsborough Working Men's Club, Sheffield, S. Yorkshire on 11 Jan 1982. There were 32 winners.

ELECTIONS

The highest ever individual bet was £90,000 to win £20,000 for the Conservative party to return the most MPs in the 1983 General Election, by an unnamed man. A bet of £5000 at 200–1 was placed by Frank Egerton in April 1975 that his political Centre Party would win the next General Election. It didn't.

FOOTBALL POOLS

Two unnamed punters won *c.* £1.5 million each in November 1972 on the state run Italian pools. The winning dividend paid out by Littlewoods Pools in their first week in February 1923 was £2 12s 0d (*£2.60*). In 1984–5 the three British Pools companies which comprise the Pool Promoters Association (Littlewoods, Vernons and Zetters) had a total record turnover of £519,554,000 of which Littlewoods contributed over 70%.

Biggest win

The record payout from the British Pools—which is also the biggest ever prize paid in any British competition—is £1,017,890 paid on 30 Apr 1986 to nursing sister Margaret Francis and ten colleagues from the Roundway Hospital, Devizes, Wiltshire, by Littlewoods Pools, making them the first ever Pools Millionaires. The largest amount won by a single person is £953,874.10 by brewery worker David Preston, 47, of Burton-on-Trent, Staffs, on 23 Feb 1980. This total comprised £804,573.35 from Littlewoods Pools and £149,300.75 from Vernons Pools.

The record double payout is £1,565,873.20 by Littlewoods on 7 May 1986. The winners were Trevor Myers and two friends, all warehousemen with Marks & Spencer in Newcastle-upon-Tyne, with £807,358.30 and a Southampton man who collected £758,514.90. On 27 March 1985, Littlewoods paid a record treble—the first time three people each won over £½ million each. They were: Mrs. Patricia Samways, of Dorchester, Dorset, who collected £574,847.55; Kevin Adams and seven friends, of Sunderland, Tyne & Wear, with £513,805.23 and George Pinnock, of Colchester, Essex, who received £512,138.19—a record total of £1,600,790.97. Littlewoods record total payout in one week is £2,472,722 on 15 Mar 1986.

The odds for selecting 8 draws (if there are only 8 draws) from 55 matches for an all-correct line are 1,217,566.350 to 1 against. (In practice, the approximate odds of winning a dividend of any size on Littlewoods Pools are 80 to 1.)

HORSE RACING

Highest ever odds
The highest secured odds were 1,670,759 to 1 by George Rhodes of Aldershot, Hampshire. For a 5p bet, with a 10% bonus for the ITV Seven, less tax, he was paid £86,056.42 by the William Hill Organisation on 30 Sept 1984. Edward Hodson of Wolverhampton landed a 3,956,748 to 1 bet for a 55p stake on 11 Feb 1984, but his bookmaker had a £3000 payout limit. The world record odds on a 'double' are 31,793 to 1 paid by the New Zealand Totalisator Agency Board on a five shilling tote ticket on *Red Emperor* and *Maida Dillon* at Addington, Christchurch, in 1951.

Greatest pay-out
A group of punters won $764,283 for a $1 bet at Sportsman's Park, Chicago in March 1985. The bet involved selecting the first two horses in order in two races and the first three in a third. The largest payout by a British bookmaker is £185,640 by Corals, paid to Ernie Platt for a £10 Ante-Post Accumulator (tax paid) placed on 14 Dec 1984 and collected on 4 May 1985.

Biggest tote win
The best recorded tote win was one of £341 2s 6d to 2s (*£341.12½ to 10p*) representing odds of 3,410¼ to 1, by Catharine Unsworth of Blundellsands, Liverpool at Haydock Park on a race won by *Coole* on 30 Nov 1929. The highest odds in Irish tote history were £289.64 for 10p unit on *Gene's Rogue* at Limerick on 28 Dec 1981.

Largest bookmaker
The world's largest bookmaker is Ladbrokes of London with a turnover from gambling in 1984 of £787 million. The largest chain of betting shops is that of Ladbrokes with 1416 shops in the United Kingdom at the end of 1984.

Topmost tipster
The only recorded instance of a racing correspondent forecasting ten out of ten winners on a race card was at Delaware Park, Wilmington, Delaware, USA on 28 July 1974 by Charles Lamb of the *Baltimore News American*.

JAI-ALAI
The highest parimutuel payout in the USA was for a group of punters who won $988,326 (less $197,664 paid to the Internal Revenue) for a $2 ticket naming six consecutive winning Jai-Alai players at Palm Beach, Florida on 1 Mar 1983.

ROULETTE
The longest run on an ungaffed (*i.e.* true) wheel reliably recorded is six successive coups (in No. 10) at El San Juan Hotel, Puerto Rico on 9 July 1959. The odds with a double zero were 1 in 38^6 or 3,010,936,383 to 1.

SLOT MACHINES
The biggest beating handed to a 'one-armed bandit' was $2,478,716.15 by Rocco Dinubilo from Fresno, California at Harrah's Tahoe Casino, Nevada, USA on 31 Dec 1983.

GLIDING

Origins
Isadore William Deiches has researched evidence of the use of gliders in Ancient Egypt *c.* 2500–1500 BC. Emanuel Swedenborg (1688–1772) of Sweden made sketches of gliders *c.* 1714. The earliest man-carrying glider was designed by Sir George Cayley (1773–1857) and carried his coachman (possibly John Appleby) about 500 yd *457 m* across a valley in Brompton Dale, North Yorkshire in the summer of 1853.

Most titles *World*
The most World individual championships (inst. 1948) won is three by Helmut Reichmann (b. 1942) (W. Germany) in 1970 and 1974 (Standard class), 1978 (15 metre class), Douglas George Lee (GB) (b. 7 Nov 1945) in 1976, 1978 and 1981 (all Open class) and by Ingo Renner (Australia) in 1976 (Standard class), 1983 and 1985 (Open).

Altitude Records *Women*
The women's single-seater world record for absolute altitude is 12 637 m *41,449 ft* by Sabrina Jackintell (USA) in an Astir GS on 14 Feb 1979. The British single-seater record is 10 550 m *34,612 ft* by Anne Burns in a Skylark 3B over South Africa on 13 Jan 1961, when she set a world record for height gain of 9119 m *29,918 ft.*

HANG GLIDING
Origins
In the eleventh century the monk, Eilmer, is reported to have flown from the 60 ft *18,3 m* tower of Malmesbury Abbey, Wiltshire. The earliest modern pioneer was Otto Lilienthal (1848–96) (Germany) with about 2500 flights in gliders of his own construction between 1891 and 1896. In the 1950s Professor Francis Rogallo of the National Space Agency, USA, developed a flexible 'wing' from his space capsule re-entry researches.

World Championships
The World Team Championships have been won most often by Great Britain (1978–9, 1981, 1985).

Greatest distance
The official FAI record is 300,62 kms *186.80 miles* by John Pendry (GB) flying an Airwave Magic 3 from Horseshoe Meadows, Owens Valley, California to Summit Mtn., Monitop Range, Nevada, USA on 13 July 83. The Womens official FAI record is 233,90 km *145.34 miles* by Judy Leden (GB) flying a Wills Wing Duck 160 from Horseshoe Meadows, Owens Valley, California to Luning, Nevada, USA on 13 July 1983. The record set in Britain is 213,16 km *132.46 miles* by Peter Hargreaves from Wether Fell to Skegness on 9 Sept 1985.

Greatest ascent
The official FAI height gain record is 4343,4 m *14,250 ft* by Larry Tudor (USA) at Horseshoe Meadows, Ca., USA on 4 Aug 1985. The British record is 3230 m *10,600 ft* by John Stirk at Wether Fell, North Yorkshire on 6 July 1984.

Greatest descent
John Bird piloted a hang glider from a height of 39,000 ft *11,887.2 m* when he was released from a hot-air balloon, to the ground, landing in Edmonton, Alberta, Canada on 29 Aug 1982. He touched down 50 miles *80,4 km* from his point of departure.

GLIDING—WORLD RECORDS (Single-seaters)

STRAIGHT DISTANCE	1460.8 km *907.7 miles*	Hans-Werner Grosse (W. Germany) in an ASW-12 on 25 Apr 1972 from Lübeck to Biarritz
DECLARED GOAL DISTANCE	1254,26 km *779.4 miles*	Bruce Drake, David Speight, S. H. 'Dick' Georgeson (all NZ) all in Nimbus 2s, Te Anau to Te Araroa, 14 Jan 1978
GOAL AND RETURN	1646,68 km *1023.2 miles*	Tom Knauff (USA) in a Nimbus 3 from Williamsport, Pennsylvania to Knoxville, Tennessee on 25 April 1983
ABSOLUTE ALTITUDE	14 102 m *46,266 ft*	Paul F. Bikle, Jr (USA) in a Schweizer SGS 1–23E over Mojave, California on 25 Feb 1961
HEIGHT GAIN	12 894 m *42,303 ft*	Paul Bikle on 25 Feb 1961 (see above)

SPEED OVER TRIANGULAR COURSE		
100 km	195,30 km/h *121.35 mph*	Ingo Renner (Australia) in a Nimbus 3 on 14 Dec 1982
300 km	176,99 km/h *109.98 mph*	B. Bünzli (Switzerland) in a DG–LOO over South Africa on 14 Nov 1985
500 km	159,64 km/h *99.20 mph*	Hans-Werner Grosse (W. Germany) in an ASW-22 on 20 Dec 1983
750 km	158,40 km/h *98.43 mph*	Hans-Werner Grosse (W. Germany) in an ASW-22 over Australia on 8 Jan 1985
1000 km	145,32 km/h *90.29 mph*	Hans-Werner Grosse (W. Germany) in an ASW-17 over Australia on 3 Jan 1979
1250 km	133,24 km/h *82.79 mph*	Hans-Werner Grosse (W. Germany) in an ASW-17 over Australia on 9 Dec 1980

BRITISH RECORDS[1] (Single-seaters)

949,7 km *589.9 miles*	Karla Karel in a LS-3 over Australia on 20 Jan 1980
579,36 km *360 miles*	H. C. N. Goodhart in a Skylark 3, Lasham, Hants, to Portmoak, Scotland on 10 May 1959
1127,68 km *700.72 miles*	Alan Sands (USA) in a Nimbus 3, Lock Haven, Pa. to Bluefield, Va., USA on 7 May 1985
11 500 m *37,729 ft*	H. C. N. Goodhart in a Schweizer 1-23 over California, USA on 12 May 1955
10 065 m *33,022 ft*	D. Benton in a Nimbus 2 on 18 Apr 1980

143,3 km/h *88.99 mph*	E. Paul Hodge in a Standard Cirrus over Rhodesia on 30 Oct 1976
146,8 km/h *91.2 mph*	Edward Pearson in a Nimbus 2 over S.W. Africa on 30 Nov 1976
141,3 km/h *87.8 mph*	Bradley James Grant Pearson in an ASW-20 over South Africa on 28 Dec 1982
109,8 km/h *68.2 mph*	Michael R. Carlton in a Kestrel 19 over South Africa on 5 Jan 1975

[1] British National Records may be set up by British pilots in any part of the world.

GOLF

Origins

Although a stained glass window in Gloucester Cathedral, dating from 1350, portrays a golfer-like figure, the earliest mention of golf occurs in a prohibiting law passed by the Scottish Parliament in March 1457 under which 'goff be utterly cryit doune and not usit'. The Romans had a cognate game called *paganica* which may have been carried to Britain before AD 400. The Chinese Nationalist Golf Association claim the game is of Chinese origin ('Ch'ui Wan—the ball hitting game') in the 3rd or 2nd century BC. There were official ordinances prohibiting a ball game with clubs in Belgium and Holland from 1360. Gutta percha balls succeeded feather balls in 1848 and by 1902 were in turn succeeded by rubber-cored balls, invented in 1899 by Coburn Haskell (USA). Steel shafts were authorised in the USA in 1925 and in Britain in 1929.

Club *Oldest*

The oldest club of which there is written evidence is the Gentlemen Golfers (now the Honourable Company of Edinburgh Golfers) formed in March 1744—ten years prior to the institution of the Royal and Ancient Club of St Andrews, Fife. However the Royal Burgess Golfing Society of Edinburgh claim to have been founded in 1735.

Course *Highest*

The highest golf course in the world is the Tuctu Golf Club in Morococha, Peru, which is 4369 m *14,335 ft* above sea-level at its lowest point. Golf has, however, been played in Tibet at an altitude of over 4875 m *16,000 ft*.

The highest golf course in Great Britain is one of nine holes at Leadhills, Strathclyde, 1500 ft *457 m* above sea-level.

Longest hole

The longest hole in the world is the 7th hole (par-7) of the Sano Course, Satsuki GC, Japan, which measures 831 m *909 yd*. In August 1927 the sixth hole at Prescott Country Club in Arkansas, USA, measured 838 yd *766 m*. The longest hole on a championship course in Great Britain is the sixth at Troon, Strathclyde, which stretches 577 yd *528 m*.

Largest green

Probably the largest green in the world is that of the par-6 695 yd *635 m* fifth hole at International GC, Bolton, Massachusetts, USA, with an area greater than 28,000 ft² *2600 m²*.

Biggest bunker

The world's biggest bunker (called a trap in the USA) is Hell's Half Acre on the 585 yd *535 m* seventh hole of the Pine Valley course, Clementon, New Jersey, USA, built in 1912 and generally regarded as the world's most trying course.

Longest course

The world's longest course is the par-77 8325 yd *7612 m* International GC, (*see also above*), from the 'Tiger' tees, remodelled in 1969 by Robert Trent Jones. Floyd Satterlee Rood used the United States as a course, when he played from the Pacific surf to the Atlantic surf from 14 Sept 1963 to 3 Oct 1964 in 114,737 strokes. He lost 3511 balls on the 3397.7 mile *5468 km* trail.

Longest drives

In long-driving contests 330 yd *300 m* is rarely surpassed at sea-level. In officially regulated long driving contests over level ground the greatest distance recorded is 392 yd *358 m* by William

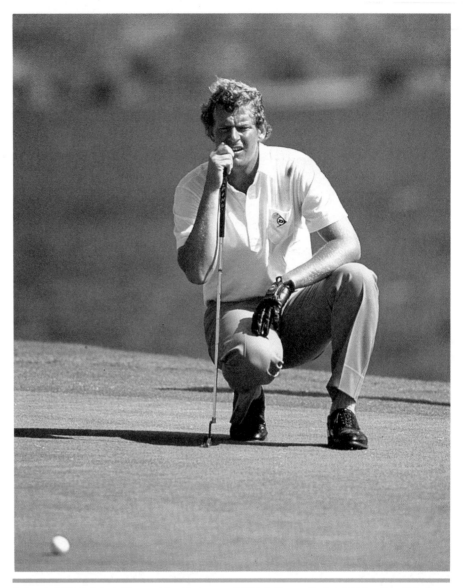

A thoughtful Sandy Lyle. In his record-breaking season of 1985, he became the first British golfer to win the Open Championship since Tony Jacklin in 1969.

Thomas 'Tommie' Campbell (b. 24 July 1927) (Foxrock Golf Club) at Dun Laoghaire, Co. Dublin, in July 1964.

On an airport runway Liam Higgins (Ireland) drove a Spalding Top Flite ball 579,8 m *634.1 yd* at Baldonnel military airport, Dublin, Ireland on 25 Sept 1984. The greatest recorded drive on an ordinary course is one of 515 yd *471 m* by Michael Hoke Austin (b. 17 Feb 1910) of Los Angeles, California, USA, in the US National Seniors Open Championship at Las Vegas, Nevada, on 25 Sept 1974. Austin, 6 ft 2 in *1,88 m* tall and weighing 210 lb *92 kg* drove the ball to within a yard of the green on the par-4 450 yd *412 m* fifth hole of the Winterwood Course and it rolled 65 yd *59 m* past the flagstick. He was aided by an estimated 35 mph *56 km/h* tailwind.

A drive of 2640 yd (1½ miles) *2414 m* across ice was achieved by an Australian meteorologist named Nils Lied at Mawson Base, Antarctica, in 1962. Arthur Lynskey claimed a drive of 200 yd *182 m* horizontal and 2 miles *3200 m* vertical off Pikes Peak, Colorado (14,110 ft *4300 m*) on 28 June 1968. On the moon the

energy expended on a mundane 300 yd *274 m* drive would achieve, craters permitting, a distance of 1 mile *1,6 km*.

Longest putt

The longest recorded holed putt in a major tournament was one of 86 ft *26 m* on the vast 13th green at the Augusta National, Georgia by Cary Middlecoff (b. 6 Jan 1921) (USA) in the 1955 Masters' Tournament. Robert Tyre 'Bobby' Jones Jr (1902–71) was reputed to have holed a putt in excess of 100 ft *30 m* at the fifth green in the first round of the 1927 Open at St. Andrews. Bob Cook (USA) sunk a putt measured at 140 ft 2¾ in *42,74 m* on the 18th at St. Andrew's in the International Fourball Pro Am Tournament on 1 Oct 1976.

SCORES

Lowest 9 holes and 18 holes *Men*

At least four players are recorded to have played a long course (over 6000 yd *5486 m*) in a score of 58, most recently Monte Carlo Money (USA) (b. 3 Dec 1954) the par-72, 6607 yd *6041 m* Las Vegas Municipal GC, Nevada, USA on 11 Mar 1981. The lowest recorded score on a long course in Britain is 58 by Harry Weetman (1920–72)

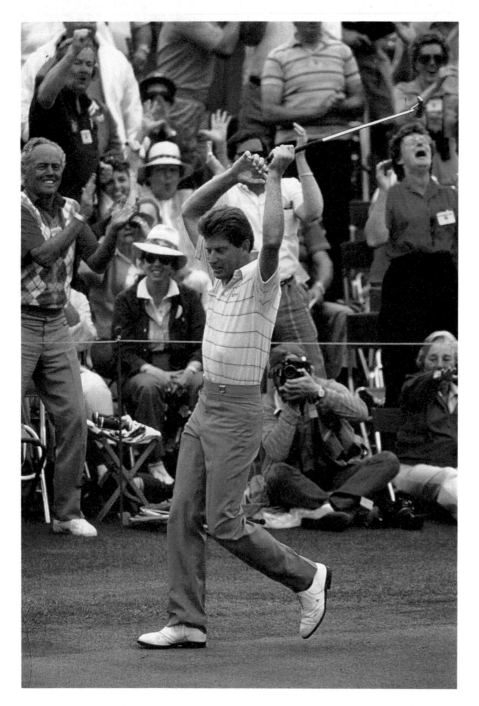

Lowest 18 holes *Women*

The lowest recorded score on an 18-hole course (over 6000 yd *5486 m*) for a woman is 62 (30 + 32) by Mary 'Mickey' Kathryn Wright (b. 14 Feb 1935) (USA) on the Hogan Park Course (par-71, 6286 yd *5747 m*) at Midland, Texas, USA, in November 1964. Wanda Morgan (b. 22 Mar 1910) recorded a score of 60 (31 + 29) on the Westgate and Birchington Golf Club course, Kent, over 18 holes (5002 yd *4573 m*) on 11 July 1929.

Lowest 18 holes *Great Britain*

The lowest score recorded in a first class professional tournament on a course of more than 6000 yd *5486 m* in Great Britain is 61 (29 + 32), by Thomas Bruce Haliburton (1915–75) of Wentworth GC in the Spalding Tournament at Worthing, West Sussex, in June 1952, and 61 (32 + 29) by Peter J. Butler (b. 25 Mar 1932) in the Bowmaker Tournament on the Old Course at Sunningdale, Berkshire, on 4 July 1967.

Lowest 36 holes

The record for 36 holes is 122 (59 + 63) by Sam Snead in the 1959 Sam Snead Festival on 16–17 May 1959. Horton Smith (1908–1963), twice US Masters Champion, scored 121 (63 + 58) on a short course on 21 Dec 1928 (*see 72 holes*). The lowest score by a British golfer has been 124 (61 + 63) by Alexander Walter Barr 'Sandy' Lyle (b. 9 Feb 1958) in the Nigerian Open at the 6024 yd *5508 m* (par-71) Ikoyi Golf Club, Lagos in 1978.

(*Left*) Nick Price and supporters celebrate his record round of 63 in the 1986 US Masters. (*Below*) Nancy Lopez, record prize money winner in a season. (All-Sport).

the British Ryder Cup golfer, for the 6171 yd *5642 m* Croham Hurst Course, Croydon, Surrey, on 30 Jan 1956. Alfred Edward Smith (1903–85) achieved an 18-hole score of 55 (15 under bogey 70) on his home course on 1 Jan 1936. The course measured 4248 yd *3884 m*. The detail was 4, 2, 3, 4, 2, 4, 3, 4, 3 = 29 out, and 2, 3, 3, 3, 3, 2, 5, 4, 1 = 26 in.

Nine holes in 25 (4, 3, 3, 2, 3, 3, 1, 4, 2) was recorded by A. J. 'Bill' Burke in a round in 57 (32 + 25) on the 6389 yd *5842 m* par-71 Normandie course St Louis, Missouri, USA on 20 May 1970. The tournament record is 27 by Mike Souchak (USA) (b. 10 May 1927) for the second nine (par-35) first round of the 1955 Texas Open (*see 72 holes*), Andy North (USA) (b. 9 Mar 1950) second nine (par-34), first round, 1975 BC Open at En-Joie GC, Endicott, NY, José Maria Canizares (Spain) (b. 18 Feb 1947), first nine, third round, in the 1978 Swiss Open on the 6811 yd *6228 m* Crans-Sur course and by Robert Lee (GB) (b. 12 Oct 1961) first nine, first round, in the Monte Carlo Open on the 5714 m *6249 yd* Mont Agel course on 28 June 1985.

The United States PGA tournament record for 18 holes is 59 (30 + 29) by Al Geiberger (b. 1 Sept 1937) in the second round of the Danny Thomas Classic, on the 72-par 7249 yd *6628 m* Colonial GC course, Memphis, Tennessee on 10 June 1977. Three golfers have recorded 59 over 18 holes in non-PGA tournaments; Samuel Jackson Snead (b. 27 May 1912) in the third round of the Sam Snead Festival at White Sulphur Springs, West Virginia, USA on 16 May 1959; Gary Player (South Africa) (b. 1 Nov 1935) in the second round of the Brazilian Open in Rio de Janeiro on 29 Nov 1974, and David Jagger (GB) (b. 9 June 1949) in a Pro-Am tournament prior to the 1973 Nigerian Open at Ikoyi Golf Club, Lagos.

Lowest 72 holes

The lowest recorded score on a first-class course is 255 (29 under par) by Leonard Peter Tupling (b. 6 Apr 1950) (GB) in the Nigerian Open at Ikoyi Golf Club, Lagos in February 1981, made up of 63, 66, 62 and 64 (average 63.75 per round).

The lowest 72 holes in a US professional event is 257 (60, 68, 64, 65) by Mike Souchak in the 1955 Texas Open at San Antonio.

The lowest 72 holes in an Open championship in Europe is 262 (67, 66, 66, 63) by Percy Alliss (GB) (1897–1975) in the 1932 Italian Open at San Remo, and by Lu Liang Huan (Taiwan) (b. 10 Dec 1935) in the 1971 French Open at Biarritz. Kelvin D. G. Nagle (b. 21 Dec 1920) of Australia shot 261 in the Hong Kong Open in 1961. The lowest for four rounds in a British first class tournament is 262 (66, 63, 66 and 67) by Bernard Hunt in the Piccadilly tournament on the par-68 6184 yd 5655 m Wentworth East Course, Virginia Water, Surrey on 4–5 Oct 1966.

Horton Smith scored 245 (63, 58, 61 and 63) for 72 holes on the 4700 yd 4297 m course (par-64) at Catalina Country Club, California, USA, to win the Catalina Open on 21–23 Dec 1928.

World one-club record

Thad Daber (USA), with a 6-iron played the 6037 yd 5520 m Lochmore GC, Cary, N. Carolina, USA in 73 on 10 Nov 1985 to win the world one-club championship.

Highest score

It is recorded that Chevalier von Cittern went round 18 holes in 316, averaging 17.55 per hole, at Biarritz, France in 1888. Steven Ward took 222 strokes for the 6212 yd 5680 m Pecos Course, Reeves County, Texas, USA, on 18 June 1976—but he was only aged 3 years 286 days.

Most shots for one hole

A woman player in the qualifying round of the Shawnee Invitational for Ladies at Shawnee-on-Delaware, Pennsylvania, USA, in c. 1912, took 166 strokes for the short 130 yd 118 m 16th hole. Her tee shot went into the Binniekill River and the ball floated. She put out in a boat with her exemplary but statistically minded husband at the oars. She eventually beached the ball 1½ miles 2,4 km downstream but was not yet out of the wood. She had to play through one on the home run. In a competition at Peacehaven, Sussex, England in 1890, A. J. Lewis had 156 putts on one green without holing out.

The highest score for a single hole in the British Open is 21 by a player in the inaugural meeting at Prestwick in 1860. Double figures have been recorded on the card of the winner only once, when Willie Fernie (1851–1924) scored a ten at Musselburgh, Lothian, in 1883. Ray Ainsley of Ojai, California, took 19 strokes for the par-4 16th hole during the second round of the US Open at Cherry Hills Country Club, Denver, Colorado, on 10 June 1938. Most of the strokes were used in trying to extricate the ball from a brook. Hans Merell of Mogadore, Ohio, took 19 strokes on the par-3 16th (222 yd 203 m) during the third round of the Bing Crosby National Tournament at Cypress Point Club, Del Monte, California, USA, on 17 Jan 1959.

Rounds fastest *Individual*

With such variations in lengths of courses, speed records, even for rounds under par, are of little comparative value. Rick Baker completed 18 holes (6142 yd 5616 m) in 25 min 48.47 sec at Surfer's Paradise, Queensland, Australia on 4 Sept 1982, but this test permitted the striking of the ball whilst still moving. The record for a still ball is 28.09 min by Gary Shane Wright (b. 27 Nov 1946) at Tewantin-Noosa Golf Club, Queensland (18 holes, 6039 yd 5522 m) on 9 Dec 1980. Roger Sanders set a British record of 31 min 50 sec at East Berkshire Golf Club, Berkshire on 11 May 1986.

Rounds fastest *Team*

Seventy-seven players completed the 18-hole 6502 yd 5945 m Kern City course, California, USA in 10 min 30 sec on 24 Aug 1984 using only one ball. They scored 80!

Rounds slowest

The slowest stroke play tournament round was one of 6 hr 45 min taken by South Africa in the first round of the 1972 World Cup at the Royal Melbourne GC, Australia. This was a four-ball medal round, everything holed out.

Most rounds

The greatest number of rounds played on foot in 24 hr is 22 rounds and five holes (401 holes) by Ian Colston, 35, at Bendigo GC, Victoria (par-73, 6061 yd 5542 m) on 27–28 Nov 1971. The British record is 360 holes by Antony J. Clark at Childwall GC, Liverpool on 18 July 1983. Using golf carts for transport Charles Stock played 702 holes in 24 hr at an average 72.12 per round at Boston Hills Country Club, Hudson, Ohio, USA on 7–8 July 1985. Terry Zachary played 391 holes in 12 hours on the 6706 yd 6132 m course at Connaught Golf Club, Alberta, Canada on 16 June 1986. The most holes played on foot in a week (168 hr) is 1128 by Steve Hylton at the Mason Rudolph Golf Club (6060 yd 5541m), Clarkesville, Tennessee, USA, from 25–31 Aug 1980.

Throwing the golf ball

The lowest recorded score for throwing a golf ball round 18 holes (over 6000 yd or 5500 m) is 82 by Joe Flynn (USA), 21, at the 6228 yd 5694 m Port Royal Course, Bermuda, on 27 Mar 1975.

CHAMPIONSHIP RECORDS

The Open

The Open Championship was inaugurated in 1860 at Prestwick, Strathclyde, Scotland. The lowest score for 9 holes is 28 by Denis Durnian (b. 30 June 1950), at Royal Birkdale, Southport, Lancashire in the second round on 15 July 1983.

The lowest round in The Open is 63 by Mark Hayes (b. 12 July 1949) (USA) at Turnberry, Strathclyde, on 7 July 1977, and by Isao Aoki (b. 31 Aug 1942) (Japan) at Muirfield, East Lothian, on 19 July 1980. Thomas Henry Cotton (b. 26 Jan 1907) at Royal St George's, Sandwich, Kent completed the first 36 holes in 132 (67 + 65) on 27 June 1934. The lowest 72-hole aggregate is 268 (68, 70, 65, 65) by Tom Watson (b. 4 Sept 1949) (USA) at Turnberry, ending on 9 July 1977.

US Open

The United States Open Championship was inaugurated in 1895. The lowest 72-hole aggregate is 272 (63, 71, 70, 68) by Jack Nicklaus (b. 21 Jan 1940) on the Lower Course (7015 yd 6414 m) at Baltusrol Country Club, Springfield, New Jersey, on 12–15 June 1980. The lowest score for 18 holes is 63 by Johnny Miller (b. 29 Apr 1947) on the 6921 yd 6328 m par-71 Oakmont Country Club course, Pennsylvania on 17 June 1973; by Jack Nicklaus (*see above*) and by Tom Weiskopf (USA) (b. 9 Nov 1942), both on 12 June 1980.

US Masters'

The lowest score in the US Masters' (instituted on the par-72 6980 yd 6382 m Augusta National Golf Course, Georgia, in 1934) has been 271 by Jack Nicklaus in 1965 and Raymond Floyd (b. 4 Sept 1942) in 1976. The lowest round is 63 by Nick Price (b. 28 Jan 1957, Zimbabwe) in 1986.

World Cup (formerly Canada Cup)

The World Cup (instituted as the Canada Cup in 1953) has been won most often by the USA with 16 victories between 1955 and 1983. The only men to have been on six winning teams have been Arnold Palmer (b. 10 Sept 1929) (1960, 1962–4, 1966–7) and Jack Nicklaus (1963–4, 1966–7, 1971 and 1973). Only Nicklaus has taken the individual title three times (1963–4, 1971). The lowest aggregate score for 144 holes is 544 by Australia, Bruce Devlin (b. 10 Oct 1937) and David Graham (b. 23 May 1946), at San Isidro, Buenos Aires, Argentina on 12–15 Nov 1970. The lowest individual score has been 269 by Roberto de Vicenzo (Argentina) (b. 14 Apr 1923), also in 1970.

Ryder Cup

The biennial Ryder Cup professional match between USA and Europe (British Isles or Great Britain prior to 1979) was instituted in 1927. The USA have won 21½ to 4½ to date. William Earl 'Billy' Casper (b. San Diego, California, USA, 24 June 1931) has the record of winning most matches in the Trophy with 20 in 1961–75. Christy O'Connor Sr (b. 21 Dec 1924) (Ireland) played in ten matches, 1955–73.

Walker Cup

The USA v. GB & Ireland series instituted in 1921 (for the Walker Cup since 1922 and now held biennially) has been won by the USA 27½–2½ to date. Joseph Boynton Carr (GB&I) (b. 18 Feb 1922) played in ten contests, 1947–67.

Curtis Cup

The biennial ladies' Curtis Cup match between USA and Great Britain and Ireland was first held in 1932. The USA have won 19, GB&I two and two matches have been tied. Mary McKenna (GB&I) (b. 29 Apr 1949) played in a record eighth match in 1984.

Richest prizes

The greatest first place prize money was $500,000 (total purse $1,100,000) won by Johnny Miller in 1982 and Raymond Floyd in 1983, at Sun City, Bophuthatswana, S. Africa. Both won in play-offs, from Severiano Ballesteros and Craig Stadler respectively.

Highest earnings *US PGA and LPGA circuits*

The all time professional money-winner is Jack Nicklaus, with $4,857,494 to 25 May 1986. The record for a year is $530,808 by Tom Watson in 1980. The record career earnings for a woman is by Pat Bradley (b. 24 Mar 1951) with $2,096,497 to 8 July 1986. Nancy Lopez (b. 6 Jan 1957) won a season's record $416,472 in 1985.

Highest earnings *European circuit*

Sandy Lyle won a European record £162,352 in European Order of Merit tournaments (£199,020 in all European events) plus a £25,000 bonus in 1985.

Most tournament wins

The record for winning tournaments in a single season is 18 (plus one unofficial), including a record 11 consecutively, by John Byron Nelson (b. 4 Feb 1912) (USA), from 8 Mar–4 Aug 1945. Sam Snead won 84 official US PGA Tour events 1936–65, and has been credited with a total 134 tournament victories since 1934. The Ladies PGA record is 88 by Kathy Whitworth (b. 27 Sept 1939) from 1962 to 1985.

Biggest winning margin

The greatest margin of victory in a major

tournament is 21 strokes by Jerry Pate (b. 16 Sept 1953) (USA) in the Colombian Open with 262 on 10–13 Dec 1981. Cecilia Leitch won the Canadian Ladies Open Championship in 1921 by the biggest margin for a major title, 17 up and 15 to play.

Youngest and oldest champions

The youngest winner of The Open was Tom Morris, Jr. (1851–75) at Prestwick, Strathclyde in 1868 aged 17 yr 249 days. The youngest winners of The Amateur title were John Charles Beharrell (b. 2 May 1938) at Troon, Strathclyde, on 2 June 1956, and Robert 'Bobby' E. Cole (b. 11 May 1948) (South Africa) at Carnoustie, Tayside, on 11 June 1966, both aged 18 yr 1 month. The oldest Open Champion was 'Old Tom' Morris (1821–1908), aged 46 yr 99 days when he won at Prestwick in 1867. In recent times the 1967 champion, Roberto de Vicenzo was aged 44 yr 93 days. The oldest winner of The Amateur was the Hon Michael Scott (1878–1959) at Hoylake, Merseyside in 1933, when 54 yr 297 days. The oldest United States Amateur Champion was Jack Westland (1904–82) at Seattle, Washington, on 23 Aug 1952, aged 47 yr 253 days. The oldest US Open champion was Raymond Floyd (b. 4 Sept 1942) at 43 yr 284 days on 15 June 1986. Isabella 'Belle' Robertson (b. 11 Apr 1936) won the 1986 Scottish Women's Championship aged 50 yr 43 days.

Longest span

Jacqueline Ann Mercer (née Smith) (b. 5 Apr 1929) won her first South African title at Humewood GC, Port Elizabeth in 1948, and her fourth at Port Elizabeth GC on 4 May 1979, 31 years later.

Most club championships

Bernard Charles Cusack (b. 24 Jan 1920) has won a record total of 34 Club championships, including 33 consecutively, at the Narembeen GC, Western Australia, between 1943 and 1982. The women's record is 31 by Molly St John Pratt (b. 19 Oct 1912) at the Stanthorpe GC, Queensland, Australia from 1931 to 1979, and also by 67 year old Helen Gray at Todmorden GC, Lancashire between 1951 and 1985. The record for consecutive wins is 22 (1959–80) by Patricia Mary Shepherd (b. 7 Jan 1940) at Turriff GC, Aberdeenshire, Scotland.

Record tie

The longest delayed result in any National Open Championship occurred in the 1931 US Open at Toledo, Ohio. George von Elm (1901–61) and Billy Burke (1902–72) tied at 292, then tied the first replay at 149. Burke won the second replay by a single stroke after 72 extra holes.

Largest tournament

The Volkswagen Grand Prix Open Amateur Championship in the United Kingdom attracted a record 321,779 (206,820 men and 114,958 women) competitors in 1984.

HOLES IN ONE

Longest

The longest straight hole ever holed in one shot is the tenth (447 yd *408 m*) at Miracle Hills Golf Club, Omaha, Nebraska, USA by Robert Mitera (b. 1944) on 7 Oct 1965. Mitera stood 5 ft 6 in *1,68 m* tall and weighed 165 lb *75 kg* (11 st 11 lb). He was a two handicap player who normally drove 245 yd *224 m*. A 50 mph *80 km/h* gust carried his shot over a 290 yd *265 m* drop-off. The longest 'dog-leg' hole achieved in one is the 480 yd *439 m* fifth at Hope Country Club, Arkansas by L. Bruce on 15 Nov 1962. The women's record is 393 yd *359 m* by Marie Robie on the first hole of the Furnace Brook Golf Club,

Jack Nicklaus has contested 98 major championships since turning professional in 1962; he has won 18 and placed second another 18 times. In 1986 he produced a storming finish to take a record sixth US Masters title. (All Sport).

Wollaston, Mass., USA, on 4 Sept 1949. The longest hole in one performed in the British Isles is the seventh (par-4, 393 yd *359 m*) at West Lancashire GC by Peter Richard Parkinson (b. 26 Aug 1947) on 6 June 1972.

Most

The greatest number of holes-in-one in a career is 68 by Harry Lee Bonner from 1967 to 1985, most at his home 9-hole course of Las Gallinas, San Rafael, California, USA. The British record is 31 by Charles T. Chevalier (1902–73) of Heaton Moor Golf Club, Stockport, Greater Manchester between 20 June 1918 and 1970.

The most holes-in-one in a year is 28 by Scott Palmer from 5 June 1983 to 31 May 1984, all on par –3 or par –4 holes between 130 yd *119 m* and 350 yd *320 m* in length at Ballboa Park, San Diego, California, USA.

Consecutive

There are at least 16 cases of 'aces' being achieved in two consecutive holes, of which the greatest was Norman L. Manley's unique 'double albatross' on the par-4 330 yd *301 m* seventh and par-4 290 yd *265 m* eighth holes on the Del Valle Country Club Course, Saugus, California, on 2 Sept 1964. The first woman to record consecutive 'aces' was Sue Prell, on the 13th and 14th holes at Chatswood Golf Club, Sydney, Australia on 29 May 1977.

The closest to achieving three consecutive holes in one was the late Dr Joseph Boydstone on the 3rd, 4th and 9th at Bakersfield GC, California, USA, on 10 Oct 1962 and the Rev Harold Snider (b. 4 July 1900) who aced the 8th, 13th and 14th holes of the par-3 Ironwood course, Arizona, USA on 9 June 1976.

Youngest and oldest

The youngest golfer recorded to have shot a hole-in-one was Coby Orr (5 years) of Littleton, Colorado on the 103 yd *94 m* fifth at the Riverside Golf Course, San Antonio, Texas in 1975. The oldest golfers to have performed this feat are: (men) 99 yr 244 days Otto Bucher (Switzerland) (b. 12 May 1885) on the 130 yd *100 m* 12th at La Manga GC, Spain on 13 Jan 1985; (women) 96 yr Erna Ross on the 112 yd *102 m* 17th at The Everglades Club, Palm Beach, Florida, USA on 25 May 1986. The British record was set by Samuel Richard Walker (b. 6 Jan 1892) at the 156 yd *143 m* 8th at West Hove GC, E. Sussex at the age of 92 yr 169 days on 23 June 1984.

The oldest player to score his age is C. Arthur Thompson (1869–1975) of Victoria, British Columbia, Canada, who scored 103 on the Uplands course of 6215 yd *5682 m* aged 103 in 1973.

GREYHOUND RACING

Earliest meeting

In September 1876 a greyhound meeting was staged at Hendon, North London with a railed hare operated by a windlass. Modern greyhound racing originated with the perfecting of the mechanical hare by Owen Patrick Smith at Emeryville, California, USA, in 1919. St. Petersburg Kennel Club located in St. Petersburg, Florida, USA which opened on 3 Jan 1925, is the oldest greyhound track in the world still in operation on its original site. The earliest greyhound race behind a mechanical hare in the British Isles was at Belle Vue, Manchester, opened on 24 July 1926.

MOST TITLES *World's major championships:*

The Open	Harry Vardon (1870–1937)	6	...1896, 1898–9, 1903, 11,14
The Amateur	John Ball (1861–1940)	8	...1888, 90, 92, 94, 99, 1907, 10, 1912
US Open	Willie Anderson (1880–1910)	4	...1901, 03–5
	Robert Tyre Jones, Jr. (1902–71)	4	...1923, 26, 29–30
	William Ben Hogan (b. 13 Aug 1912)	4	...1948, 50–1, 53
	Jack William Nicklaus (b. 21 Jan 1940)	4	...1962, 67, 72, 80
US Amateur	Robert Tyre Jones, Jr. (1902–71)	5	...1924–25, 27–8, 30
PGA Championship (USA)	Walter Charles Hagan (1892–1969)	5	...1921, 24–7
	Jack William Nicklaus (b. 21 Jan 1940)	5	...1963, 71, 73, 75, 80
Masters' Championship (USA)	Jack William Nicklaus (b. 21 Jan 1940)	6	...1963, 65–6, 72, 75, 86
US Women's Open	Elizabeth 'Betsy' Earle-Rawls (b. 4 May 1928)	4	...1951, 53, 57, 60
	'Mickey' Wright (b. 14 Feb 1935)	4	...1958–59, 61, 64
US Women's Amateur	Glenna C. Vare (née Collett) (b. 20 June 1903)	6	...1922, 25, 28–30, 35
British Women's	Charlotte Cecilia Pitcairn Leitch (1891–1977)	4	...1914, 20–1, 26
	Joyce Wethered (b. 17 Nov 1901) (Now Lady Heathcoat-Amory)	4	...1922, 24–5, 29

Note: Nicklaus is the only golfer to have won five different major titles (The Open, US Open, Masters, PGA and US Amateur titles) twice and a record 20 all told (1959–86). His remarkable record in The US Open is four firsts, eight seconds and two thirds. In 1930 Bobby Jones achieved a unique 'Grand Slam' of the US and British Open and Amateur titles.

Derby
The only two greyhounds to have won the English Greyhound Derby (instituted 1927, now over 500 m *546 yd*) are *Mick the Miller* (whelped in Ireland, June 1926 and died 1939) on 25 July 1929, when owned by Albert H. Williams, and on 28 June 1930 (owned by Mrs Arundel H. Kempton), and *Patricia's Hope* on 24 June 1972 (when owned by Gordon and Basil Marks and Brian Stanley) and 23 June 1973 (when owned by G. & B. Marks and J. O'Connor). The highest prize was £35,000 to *Indian Joe* for the Derby on 28 June 1980. The only greyhounds to win the English, Scottish and Welsh Derby 'triple' are *Trev's Perfection*, owned by Fred Trevillion, in 1947, *Mile Bush Pride*, owned by Noel W. Purvis, in 1959, and *Patricia's Hope* in 1972. The only two greyhounds to have won the American Derby, at Taunton, Mass., twice are *Real Huntsman* in 1950–51 and *Dutch Bahama* in 1984–5.

Grand National
The only greyhound to have won the Grand National (inst. 1927 over 525 yd *480 m*, now 500 m, and five flights) three times is *Sherry's Prince*, a 75 lb *32 kg* dog (whelped in April 1967, died July 1978) owned by Mrs Joyce Mathews of Sanderstead, Surrey, in 1970, 1971 and 1972.

Fastest greyhound
The highest speed at which any greyhound has been timed is 41.72 mph *67,14 km/h* (410 yd *374 m* in 20.1 sec) by *The Shoe* on the then straightaway track at Richmond, NSW, Australia on 25 Apr 1968. It is estimated that he covered the last 100 yd *91,44 m* in 4.5 sec or at 45.45 mph *73,14 km/h*. The highest speed recorded for a greyhound in Great Britain is 39.13 mph *62,97 km/h* by *Beef Cutlet*, when covering a straight course of 500 yd *457 m* in 26.13 sec at Blackpool, Lancashire, on 13 May 1933.

Fastest speeds for four-bend tracks
The fastest automatically timed speed recorded for a full 4-bend race is 38.89 mph *62,59 km/h* at Brighton, E. Sussex by *Glen Miner* on 4 May 1982 with a time of a 29.62 sec for 515 m *563 yd*. The fastest over hurdles is 37.64 mph *60.58 km/h* at Brighton by *Wotchit Buster* on 22 Aug 1978.

Most wins
The most career wins is 143 by the American greyhound, *JR's Ripper* in 1982–6. The world record for consecutive victories is 31 by an American greyhound *Joe Dump* from 18 Nov 1978 to 1 June 1979. *Ballyregan Bob*, owned by Cliff Kevern and trained by George Curtis, set a British record of 28 consecutive wins in 1985–6.

Highest earnings
The career earnings record is held by *Marathon Hound* with over $225,000 in the USA, 1981–4. The richest first prize for a greyhound race is $100,000 won by *DD's Jackie* in the 1982 Greyhound Grand Prix at Hollywood, Florida, USA.

Longest odds
Apollo Prince won at odds of 250–1 at Sandown GRC, Springvale, Queensland, Australia on 14 Nov 1968.

GYMNASTICS

Earliest references
A primitive form of gymnastics was practised in ancient Greece and Rome during the period of the ancient Olympic Games (776 BC to AD 393) but Johann Friedrich Simon was the first teacher of modern gymnastics at Basedow's School, Dessau, Germany in 1776.

Ballyregan Bob attracted tremendous interest as he smashed track records around England and extended his superlative sequence of wins. (Alf Baker).

Most titles *World*
The greatest number of individual titles won by a man in the World Championships is ten by Boris Shakhlin (b. 27 Jan 1932) (USSR) between 1954 and 1964. He also won three team titles. The female record is ten individual wins and five team titles by Larissa Semyonovna Latynina (b. 27 Dec 1934) of the USSR, between 1956 and 1964. Japan has won the men's team title a record five times (1962, 1966, 1970, 1974, 1978) and the USSR the women's team title on nine occasions (1954, 1958, 1962, 1970, 1974, 1978, 1981, 1983 and 1985).

The most overall titles in Modern Rhythmic Gymnastics is three by Maria Gigova (Bulgaria) in 1969, 1971 and 1973 (shared). Galina Shugurova (USSR) (b. 1955) won eight apparatus titles from 1969–77.

Most titles *Olympic*
Japan (1960, 1964, 1968, 1972 and 1976) have won the men's team title most often. The USSR have won the women's title eight times (1952–80). The most men's individual gold medals is six by Boris Shakhlin (USSR), one in 1956, four (two shared) in 1960 and one in 1964, and Nikolai Andrianov (USSR) (b. 14 Oct 1952), one in 1972, four in 1976 and one in 1980.

Vera Caslavska-Odlozil (b. 3 May 1942) (Czechoslovakia), has won most individual gold medals with seven, three in 1964 and four (one shared) in 1968. Larissa Latynina won six individual gold medals and was in three winning teams in 1956–64 making nine gold medals. She also won five silver and four bronze making 18 in all—an Olympic record. The most medals for a male gymnast is 15 by Nikolai Andrianov (USSR), 7 gold, 5 silver and 3 bronze in 1972–80. Aleksander Ditiatin (USSR) (b. 7 Aug 1957) is the only man to win a medal in all eight categories in the same Games, with 3 gold, 4 silver and 1 bronze at Moscow in 1980.

Highest score *Olympics*
Nadia Comaneci (Romania) (b. 12 Nov 1961) was the first to achieve a perfect score, with seven of 10.00 at the Montreal Olympics in July 1976.

Youngest International and World Champion
Pasakevi 'Voula' Kouna (b. 6 Dec 1971) was aged 9 yr 299 days at the start of the Balkan Games at Serres, Greece on 1–4 Oct 1981, when she represented Greece. Olga Bicherova (USSR) (b. 26 Oct 1966) won the women's world title at 15 yr 33 days on 28 Nov 1981. The youngest male world champion was Dmitri Belozerchev (USSR) (b. 17 Dec 1966) at 16 years 315 days at Budapest, Hungary on 28 Oct 1983.

Most titles *British*
The British Gymnastic Championship was won ten times by Arthur John Whitford (b. 2 July 1908) in 1928–36 and 1939. He was also in four winning teams. Wray 'Nik' Stuart (b. 20 July 1927) equalled the record of nine successive wins, 1956–64. The women's record is eight by Mary Patricia Hirst (b. 18 Nov 1918) (1947, 1949–50 and 1952–6). The most overall titles in Modern Rhythmic Gymnastics is by Sharon Taylor with five successive, 1977–81.

Most titles *World Cup*
In the first World Cup Competition, in London in 1975, Ludmilla Tourischeva (now Mrs Valeriy Borzov) (b. 7 Oct 1952) (USSR) won all five gold medals available.

Somersaults
Ashrita Furman performed 7400 forward rolls over 12 miles 390 yards *19,67 km* from Boston to Lexington in April 1986. Corporal Wayne Wright of the Royal Engineers made a successful dive and tucked somersault over 37 men at Old Park Barracks, Dover, Kent on 30 July 1980. Shigeru Iwasaki (b. 1960) backwards somersaulted over 50 m *54.68 yd* in 10.8 sec at Tokyo, Japan on 30 Mar 1980.

Largest gymnasium
The world's largest gymnasium is Yale University's nine-storey, Payne Whitney Gymnasium at New Haven, Connecticut, USA, completed in 1932 and valued at $18,000,000 (*£10,285,000*).

The remarkable 8-year-old from Hong Kong, Chung Kwun Ying, who performed 1985 consecutive hand stand push-ups in an hour.

EXERCISES—SPEED AND STAMINA

From this year, records are accepted for the most repetitions of the following activities within the given time span.

CHINS ONE ARM (FROM DEAD HANG POSITION)—**CONSECUTIVE** 170 Lee Chin Yong (b. 15 Aug 1925) at Backyon Gymnasium, Seoul, Korea on 10 May 1983.

CHINS (FROM A RING)—**CONSECUTIVE** 22 Robert Chisholm (b. 9 Dec 1952) at Queen's University, Kingston, Ontario, Canada on 3 Dec 1982. (Also 18 two-finger chins, 12 one-finger chins).

PARALLEL BAR DIPS—I HOUR 718 Roger Perez (b. 11 July 1962) at Cosumnes River College, Sacramento, California, USA on 14 Dec 1983.

PRESS-UPS (PUSH-UPS)—24 HOURS 25,573 by Paul Lynch (GB) at the Hippodrome Club, London on 18 July 1985.

PRESS-UPS (ONE ARM)—5 HOURS 3856 by Colin Hewick (GB) at Bodyworld Health Club, Hull, Humberside on 13 June 1986.

PUSH-UPS (FINGER TIP)—5 HOURS 4,500 John Decker (GB) at the Congleton Leisure Centre, Cheshire on 28 June 1986.

PUSH-UPS (ONE FINGER)—CONSECUTIVE 100 Harry Lee Welch Jr. at Durham, N. Carolina, USA on 31 Mar 1985.

HAND-STAND PUSH-UPS—I HOUR 1985 by Chung Kwun Ying (Hong Kong) at Government City Hall, Hong Kong on 18 May 1986.

SIT-UPS—24 HOURS 43,418 Louis Scripa Jr. (USA) at Jack La Lanne's American Health & Fitness Spa, Sacramento, Cal., USA on 6–7 Oct 1984.

LEG RAISES—12 HOURS 21,598 Louis Scripa Jr. in 6 hours at Fairfield, Cal., USA on 8 Dec 1983.

JUMPING JACKS—24 HOURS 40,014 August Hoffman Jr. at Van Nuys, Cal., USA on 4 Dec 1982.

PUMMEL HORSE DOUBLE CIRCLES—CONSECUTIVE 75 by Lee Thomas (GB) on BBC television on 12 Dec 1985.

PRESS-UPS IN A YEAR Adam Parsons, a retired Lieutenant Colonel in the US Air Force, achieved a documented 1,293,850 press-ups in Alcron, Ohio, USA in the calendar year of 1985.

SKIPPING

MARATHON
The longest recorded skipping marathon (5 min per hour breaks) was one of 12 hr 34 min by Randall Schneider on 2 Aug 1985 in Janesville, Wisconsin, USA.

Other records made without a break:

MOST TURNS IN 10 SEC 128 by Albert Rayner, Stanford Sports, Birmingham, 19 Nov 1982.

MOST TURNS IN I MIN 330 by Brian D. Christensen, Ridgewood Shopping Center, Tennessee, 1 Sept 1979.

MOST DOUBLES (WITH CROSS) 1664 by Sean Birch at Tralee, Co. Kerry, Ireland, 27 Apr 1984.

DOUBLE TURNS 10,133 by Katsumi Suzuki, Saitama, Japan, 27 Sept 1979.

TREBLE TURNS 381 by Katsumi Suzuki, Saitama, Japan, 29 May 1975.

QUADRUPLE TURNS 51 by Katsumi Suzuki, Saitama, Japan, 29 May 1975.

QUINTUPLE TURNS 6 by Hideyuki Tateda (b. 1968), Aomori, Japan, 19 June 1982.

DURATION 1264 miles *2034 km* by Tom Morris, Brisbane-Cairns, Queensland, 1963.

MOST ON SINGLE ROPE (minimum 12 turns obligatory) 160 (50 m rope) by Shimizu Iida Junior High School, Shizuoka-ken, Japan, 10 Dec 1982.

MOST TURNS ON SINGLE ROPE (team of 90) 121 by Ohyanocho-Kami Elementary School of Amakusa, Kumamoto, Japan on 9 Mar 1986.

ON A TIGHTROPE 58 (consecutive) by Bryan Andro (né Dewhurst) TROS TV, Holland, 6 Aug 1981.

Origins
Handball, similar to association football with hands substituted for feet, was first played *c.* 1895 in Germany. It was introduced into the Olympic Games at Berlin in 1936 as an 11-a-side outdoor game with Germany winning, but when re-introduced in 1972 it was an indoor game with seven-a-side, the standard size of team since 1952.

The International Handball Federation was founded in 1946. The first international match was held at Halle/Saale on 3 Sept 1925 when Austria beat Germany 6–3.

Most Championships
Three Olympic titles have been won by the USSR—men 1976, women 1976 and 1980 and by Yugoslavia—men 1972 and 1984, women 1984. The most victories won in world championship (inst. 1938) competition are by Romania with four men's and three women's titles from 1956 to 1974. The Super Cup is contested by men's Olympic and World Champions. First held in 1979, West Germany and the USSR have each won once.

The most European Cup titles is eleven in the women's event by Spartak Kiev, USSR between 1970 and 1986. FC Barcelona became the first men's team to win the European Cup three times in succession, 1984–6.

Highest score
The highest score in an international match was recorded when the USSR beat Afghanistan 86–2 in the 'Friendly Army Tournament' at Miskolc, Hungary in August 1981.

Nihilator, the champion pacer. In harness racing, pacers move with left legs in unison and then right legs, and wear hopples, leather or plastic straps that connect front and rear legs on the same sides.

Origins
Trotting races were held in Valkenburg, Netherlands in 1554. In England the trotting gait (the simultaneous use of the diagonally opposite legs) was known in the 16th century. The sulky first appeared in harness racing in 1829. Pacers thrust out their fore and hind legs simultaneously on one side.

Most successful driver
The most successful sulky driver in North American harness racing history has been Herve Filion (b. 1 Feb 1940) of Quebec, Canada with a record 9327 wins and $47,977,237 in purse money to 1 Jan 1986. He won his 13th North American championship in 1982. The most wins in a year is 637 by Herve Filion in 1974. The greatest earnings in a year is $10,207,372 by William O'Donnell (b. 4 May 1948) when he won 419 races in 1985.

Highest price
The highest price ever paid for a pacer is $19.2 million for *Nihilator* who was syndicated by Wall Street Stable and Almahurst Stud Farm in 1984. The highest price paid for a trotter is $5.25 million for *Mystic Park* by Lana Lobell Farms from Gerald & Irving Wechter of New York and Robert Lester of Florida, announced on 13 July 1982.

Greatest winnings
The greatest winnings for any harness horse is $3,225,653 by the pacer *Nihilator,* who won 35 of 38 races in 1984–5. The greatest amount won by a trotting horse is $2,753,666 by *Ideal du Gazeau* (France) to July 1983. The single season record is $1,864,286 by *Nihilator* in 1985.

The largest ever purse was £2,161,000 for the Woodrow Wilson two-year-old race over 1 mile at the Meadowlands, New Jersey on 16 Aug 1984. Of this sum a record $1,080,500 went to the winner *Nihilator,* driven by Bill O'Donnell.

HARNESS RACING *Records against time*

TROTTING

World race record (mile)	...1:53.4	......*Prakas* (driver, William O'Donnell) at Du Quoin, Illinois, USA	....	31 Aug 1985
British record (mile)	........2:06.8	......*Ted Trot* (driver, John Blisset) at Chasewater, West Midlands	....	21 June 1975

PACING

World (mile track)	............1:49.2	......*Niatross* (driver, Clint Galbraith) (US) at Lexington, Kentucky, USA	....	1 Oct 1980
World race record (mile)	...1:49.6	......*Nihilator* (driver, William O'Donnell) (US) at East Rutherford, New Jersey, USA		3 Aug 1985
British record (mile)	........2:02.1	......*Lydia M* (driver, James Pickard) at York	....	10 July 1982

HOCKEY

Origins
A representation of two players with curved snagging sticks apparently in an orthodox 'bully' position was found in Tomb No. 17 at Beni Hasan, Egypt and has been dated to c. 2050 BC. There is a British reference to the game in Lincolnshire in 1277. The modern game evolved in South London in the 1870s. An English Hockey Association was founded in 1875, but the current English men's governing body, the Hockey Association was formed on 18 Jan 1886. The All-England Women's Hockey Association was founded in 1895. The Fédération Internationale de Hockey was formed on 7 Jan 1924.

The first organised club was the Blackheath Rugby and Hockey Club founded in 1861. The oldest club with a continuous history is Teddington HC formed in the autumn of 1871. They played Richmond on 24 Oct 1874 and used the first recorded circle *versus* Surbiton at Bushey Park on 9 Dec 1876. The first international match was the Wales *v.* Ireland match at Rhyl on 26 Jan 1895. Ireland won 3–0.

Most Olympic medals
The Indians were Olympic Champions from the re-introduction of Olympic hockey in 1928 until 1960, when Pakistan beat them 1–0 at Rome. They had their eighth win in 1980. Of the seven Indians who have won three Olympic team gold medals two have also won a silver medal—Leslie Walter Claudius (b. 25 Mar 1927) in 1948, 1952, 1956 and 1960 (silver) and Udham Singh (b. 4 Aug 1928) in 1952, 1956, 1964 and 1960 (silver). A women's tournament was added to the Olympic Games in 1980, and the winners have been Zimbabwe in 1980 and the Netherlands in 1984.

World Cup
The World Cup for men was first held in 1971, and for women in 1974. Three wins have been achieved by: Pakistan (men): 1971, 1978 and 1982; and Netherlands (women): 1974, 1978 and 1983.

MEN

Highest international score
The highest score in international hockey was when India defeated the USA 24–1 at Los Angeles, California, USA, in the 1932 Olympic Games. The greatest number of goals in a home international match was when England defeated France 16–0 at Beckenham on 25 Mar 1922.

Most international appearances
Michael Peter (b. 7 May 1949) represented West Germany over 250 times between 1969 and 1984, indoors and out. The most by a home countries player is 144 by Terry Gregg (b. 23 Nov 1950) with 102 for Ireland and 42 for Great Britain. H. David Judge (b. 19 Jan 1936) played a record 124 times for Ireland, 1957–78.

Greatest scoring feats
The greatest number of goals scored in international hockey is 150 by Paul Litjens (Netherlands) (b. 9 Nov 1947) in 112 games to 1979. M. C. Marckx (Bowden 2nd XI) scored 19 goals against Brooklands 2nd XI (score 23–0) on 31 Dec 1910. He was selected for England in March 1912 but declined due to business priorities. Between 1923 and 1958, Fred H. Wagner scored 1832 goals for Beeston HC, Nottingham Casuals and the Nottinghamshire county side. David Ashman has scored 1473 goals for one club, Hamble Old Boys, Southampton, from 1958 to 1986.

The fastest goal in an international was in 7 sec by John French for England *v.* West Germany at Nottingham, on 25 Apr 1971.

Greatest goalkeeping
Richard James Allen (b. 4 June 1902) (India) did not concede a goal during the 1928 Olympic Tournament and only a total of three in the following two Olympics of 1932 and 1936. In these three Games India scored a total of 102 goals.

Longest game
The longest international game on record was one of 145 min (into the sixth period of extra time), when Netherlands beat Spain 1–0 in the Olympic tournament at Mexico City on 25 Oct 1968. Club matches of 205 min have twice been recorded: The Hong Kong Football Club beat Prison Sports Dept as the first to score in 'sudden death' play-off after 2–2 at full time on 11 Mar 1979 and Gore Court beat Hampstead in the first round of the English Club Championships in 1983.

WOMEN

Origins
The earliest women's club was East Molesey in Surrey, England formed in c. 1887. Two Ladies Hockey Clubs, Wimbledon and Ealing, each founded one year later are still in existence. The first national association was the Irish Ladies' Hockey Union founded in 1894. The All England Women's Hockey Association held its first formal meeting in Westminster Town Hall, London, on 23 Nov 1895. The first international match was an England *v.* Ireland game in Dublin in 1896. Ireland won 2–0.

Most international appearances
Valerie Robinson made a record 144 appearances for England in 1963–84.

Highest scores
The highest score in a women's international match was when England beat France 23–0 at Merton, Greater London, on 3 Feb 1923. In club hockey, Ross Ladies beat Wyeside, at Ross-on-Wye, Herefordshire, 40–0 on 24 Jan 1929, when Edna Mary Blakelock (b. 22 Oct 1904) scored a record 21 goals.

Highest attendance
The highest attendance at a women's hockey match was 65,165 for the match between England and the USA at Wembley, London, on 11 Mar 1978.

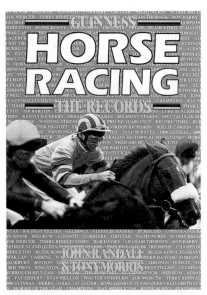

Published by Guinness at £6.95.

HORSE RACING

Origins
Horsemanship was an important part of the Hittite culture of Anatolia, Turkey dating from 1400 BC. The 33rd ancient Olympic Games of 648 BC in Greece featured horse racing. The earliest races recorded in England were those held in about AD 200 at Netherby, Cumbria, between Arab horses imported by the Romans.

Racecourse *Largest*
The world's largest racecourse is at Newmarket. It now comprises the Rowley Mile Course and the July Course, whose grandstands are about a mile apart, although a portion of the course is common to both. The Beacon Course of 4 miles 397 yd *6,80 km*, is no longer in use. The course is situated in the middle of Newmarket Heath, c 2500 acres, the largest training area in the world.

Largest prizes
The highest prize money for a day's racing is $10 million for the Breeders' Cup series of seven races staged at Hollywood Park, Los Angeles, USA on 10 Nov 1984, and at Aqueduct, New York, on 2 Nov 1985. Included was a record $3 million for the Breeders' Cup Classic.

A record $2.6 million for one race was won by *Spend A Buck*, in the Jersey Derby, Garden State Park, NJ, USA on 27 May 1985. This included a $2 million bonus for also winning the Kentucky Derby and two preparatory races at Garden State Park.

Most runners
The most horses in a race is 66 in the Grand National on 22 Mar 1929. The record for the Flat is 58 in the Lincolnshire Handicap at Lincoln on 13 Mar 1948. The most runners at a Flat meeting was 214 in seven races at Newmarket on 15 June 1915, and at a jump meeting—229 in eight races at Worcester on 13 Jan 1965.

Dead-heats
There is no recorded case in Turf history of a quintuple dead-heat. The nearest approach was in the Astley Stakes at Lewes, Sussex, on 6 Aug 1880 when *Mazurka, Wandering Nun* and *Scobell* triple dead-heated for first place a head in front of *Cumberland* and *Thora*, who dead-heated for fourth place. Each of the five jockeys thought he had won. The only three known examples of a quadruple dead-heat were between *Honest Harry, Miss Decoy, Young Daffodil* and *Peteria* at Bogside on 7 June 1808, between *Defaulter, The Squire of Malton, Reindeer* and *Pulcherrima* in the Omnibus Stakes at The Hoo, Hertfordshire, on 26 Apr 1851, and between *Overreach, Lady Golightly, Gamester* and *The Unexpected* at Newmarket on 22 Oct 1855. Since the introduction of the photo-finish, the highest number of horses dead-heating has been three, on several occasions.

Horses *Most successful*
The horse with the best win-loss record was *Kincsem*, a Hungarian mare foaled in 1874, who was unbeaten in 54 races (1876–9) throughout Europe, including the Goodwood Cup of 1878. The longest winning sequence is 56 races by *Camarero*, foaled in 1951, in Puerto Rico from 19 Apr 1953 to 17 Aug 1955. (In his career to 1956 he won 73 of 77 races). The most wins in a career is 137 from 159 starts by *Galgo Jr* (foaled 1928) in Puerto Rico between 1930 and 1936; in 1931 he won a record 30 races in one year.

The only horse to win the same race in seven successive years was *Doctor Syntax* (foaled 1811) in the Preston Gold Cup, 1815–21.

Triple Crown winners

The English Triple Crown (2000 Guineas, Derby, St Leger) has been won 15 times, most recently by *Nijinsky* in 1970. The fillies' equivalent (1000 Guineas, Oaks, St Leger) has been won 9 times, most recently by *Oh So Sharp* in 1985. Two of these fillies also won the 2000 Guineas: *Formosa* (in a dead-heat) 1868 and *Sceptre* in 1902. The American Triple Crown (Kentucky Derby, Preakness Stakes, Belmont Stakes) has been achieved 11 times, most recently by *Affirmed* in 1978.

Horse *Highest price*

The most expensive horse ever is *Shareef Dancer* syndicated for $40 million in August 1983 by his owner Sheikh Mohammed Bin Rashid Al Maktoum. Forty shares were issued at $1 million each. The most paid for a yearling is $13.1 m on 23 July 1985 at Keeneland, Kentucky, by Robert Sangster and partners for *Seattle Dancer*.

Horses *Greatest winnings*

The career earnings record is $6,597,947 by the gelding *John Henry* (foaled 1975) with 39 wins from 83 races, 1977–84. The leading money-winning mare is *All Along* (foaled 1979) with $3,018,420 in France and the USA, 1981–4.

Horses *Biggest weight*

The biggest weight ever carried is 30 stone *190 kg* by both Mr Maynard's mare and Mr Baker's horse in a match won by the former over a mile at York on 21 May 1788.

Horses *Oldest winners*

The oldest horses to win on the Flat have been the 18-year-olds *Revenge* at Shrewsbury in September 1790, *Marksman* at Ashford, Kent in September 1826 and *Jorrocks* at Bathurst, Australia in February 1851. At the same age *Wild Aster* won three hurdle races in six days in March 1919 and *Sonny Somers* won two steeple-chases in February 1980.

World speed records

The highest race speed recorded is 69,62 km/h *43.26 mph* by *Big Racket*, 20.8 sec for ¼ mile *409,26 m*, at Mexico City, Mexico on 5 Feb 1945. The 4-year-old carried 114 lb *51,7 kg*. The record for 1½ miles *2414 m* is 60,76 km/h *37.76 mph* by *Fiddle Isle* (carrying 124 lb *56,2 kg*) on 21 Mar 1970 and by *John Henry* (carrying 126 lb *57,1 kg*) on 16 Mar 1980, both at Santa Anita, Arcadia, California, USA in a time of 2 min 23 sec.

Jockeys *Most successful*

The most successful jockey of all time has been William Lee 'Bill' Shoemaker (USA) (b. weighing 2½ lb *1,1 kg*, 19 Aug 1931) now weighing 94 lb *43 kg* and standing 4 ft 11 in *1,50 m*. He rode 8514 winners from 38,201 mounts, earning $103,848,268 from his first ride on 19 Mar 1949 and first winner on 20 Apr 1949 to 29 Jan 1986. Laffitt Pincay Jr. (b. 29 Dec 1946, Panama City) has earned a record $106,595,202 from over 6000 winners, 1966–86.

The greatest amount ever won by any jockey in a year is $12,038,213 by Chris McCarron (USA) (b. 1955) in the USA in 1984. The most winners ridden in a year is 546, from a record 2199 mounts, by Chris McCarron in 1974.

Jockeys *Wins on one card*

The most winners ridden on one card is eight by Hubert S. Jones, 17, from 13 rides at Caliente, Cal., USA on 11 June 1944, by Oscar Barattuci, at Rosario City, Argentina, on 15 Dec 1957, by Dave Gall, from ten rides at Cahokia Downs, East St Louis, Illinois, USA on 18 Oct 1978 and by Chris Loseth, from ten rides at Exhibition Park, Vancouver, BC, Canada on 9 Apr 1984.

The longest winning streak is 12 by Sir Gordon Richards (b. 5 May 1904) (one race at Nottingham on 3 Oct, six out of six at Chepstow on 4 Oct and the first five races next day at Chepstow) in 1933.

Jockeys *Youngest and oldest*

The youngest jockey was Australian-born Frank Wootton (1893–1940) (English champion jockey 1909–12), who rode his first winner in South Africa aged 9 years 10 months. The oldest jockey was Harry Beasley, who rode his last race at Baldoyle, Co. Dublin, Ireland on 10 June 1935 aged 83.

Jockey *Lightest*

The lightest recorded jockey was Kitchener (d. 1872), who won the Tradesmen's Plate (Chester Cup) on *Red Deer* in 1844 at 3 st 7 lb *22 kg*. He was said to have weighed only 2 st 7 lb *16 kg* in 1840.

Trainers

Jack Van Berg (USA) has the greatest number of wins in a year, 496 in 1976, and in a career, 4400 to 1986. The greatest amount won in a year is $11,802,701 by D. Wayne Lukas (USA) in 1985.

The only trainer to saddle the first five finishers in a championship race is Michael Dickinson in the 1983 Cheltenham Gold Cup; on 27 Dec 1982 he won a record 12 races in one day.

Owners

The most lifetime wins by an owner is 4775 by Marion Van Berg in North America in the 35 years up to his death in 1971. The most winners in a year is 494 by Dan R. Lasater (USA) in 1974. The greatest amount won in a year is $3,070,225 by John Franks in 1984.

Sheikh Mohammed of the United Arab Emirates, whose enthusiastic support of British racing has returned him a record season's prize money. (All Sport).

BRITISH TURF RECORDS

Horses *Most successful*

Eclipse (foaled 1764) still has the best win-loss record, being unbeaten in a career of 18 races between May 1769 and October 1770. The longest winning sequence is 21 races by *Meteor* (foaled 1783) between 1786 and 1788. The most races won in a season is 23 by three-year-old *Fisherman* in 1856. *Catherina* (foaled 1830) won a career record 79 out of 176 races, 1832–41. The most successful sire was *Stockwell* (foaled 1849) whose progeny won 1153 races (1858–76) and in 1866 set a record of 132 races won. The greatest amount ever won by an English-trained horse is $1,182,140 by the filly *Pebbles* (foaled 1981) in 1983–5. In 1985 she won a record $1,012,611 in one season, including the Breeders Cup Turf in New York. The biggest winning margin in a Classic is 20 lengths by *Mayonaise* in the 1000 Guineas in 1859.

Jockeys *Most successful*

Sir Gordon Richards won 4870 races from 21,834 mounts from his first mount at Lingfield on 16 Oct 1920 to his last at Sandown on 10 July 1954. His first win was on 31 Mar 1921. In 1953, at his 28th and final attempt, he won the Derby, six days after his knighthood. He was champion jockey 26 times between 1925 and 1953 and won a record 269 races in 1947.

The most Classic races won by a jockey is 29 by Lester Piggott (b. 5 Nov 1935) from his first on *Never Say Die*, in the 1954 Derby to the 1985 2000 Guineas on *Shadeed*. (Derby—9, St Leger—8, Oaks—6, 2000 Guineas—4, 1000 Guineas—2). He retired in 1985.

Trainers *Most successful*

The record first-prize money earned in a season is £1,148,189 by Henry Cecil in 1985. The most Classics won by a trainer is 40 by John Scott (1794–1871) of Malton, Yorkshire between 1827 and 1863. James Croft of Middleham, Yorkshire trained the first four horses in the 1822 St Leger. Alec Taylor of Manton, Wiltshire headed the trainers' list for a record 12 seasons between 1907 and 1925. In 1867 John Day jr. of Danebury, Hampshire won 146 races.

Owners *Most successful*

H H Aga Khan III (1877–1957) was leading owner a record 13 times between 1924 and 1952. The record first-prize money won in a season is £1,082,502 by Sheikh Mohammed Bin Rashid Al Maktoum. The most wins in a season is 115 by David Robinson in 1973. The most Classics won is 20 by the 4th Duke of Grafton (1760–1844) between 1813 and 1831 and by the 17th Earl of Derby (1865–1948) between 1910 and 1945.

THE DERBY

The greatest of England's five Classics is the Derby Stakes, inaugurated on 4 May 1780, and named after the 12th Earl of Derby (1752–1834). The distance was increased in 1784 from a mile to 1½ miles *2414 km*. The race has been run at Epsom Downs, Surrey, except for the two war periods, when it was run at Newmarket, and is for three-year-olds only. Since 1884 the weights have been: colts 9 st *57 kg*, fillies 8 st 9 lb *55 kg*. Geldings were eligible until 1904.

Largest and smallest winning margins

Shergar, ridden by Walter R. Swinburn, won the Derby by a record ten lengths in 1981. There have been two dead-heats: in 1828 when *Cadland* beat *The Colonel* in the run-off, and in 1884 between *St Gatien* and *Harvester* (stakes divided).

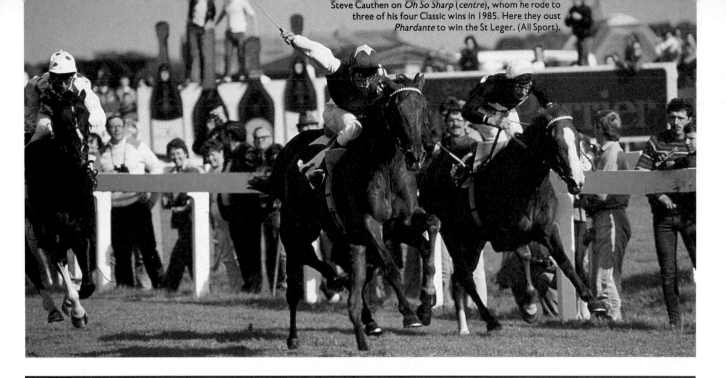

Steve Cauthen on *Oh So Sharp* (*centre*), whom he rode to three of his four Classic wins in 1985. Here they oust *Phardante* to win the St Leger. (All Sport).

MAJOR RACE RECORDS

RACE	RECORD TIME	MOST WINS			LARGEST FIELD
		Jockey	Trainer	Owner	

FLAT

RACE	RECORD TIME	Jockey	Trainer	Owner	LARGEST FIELD
Derby (1780) 1½ miles *2414 m* Epsom	2 min 33.8 sec *Mahmoud* 1936	9—Lester Piggott 1954, 57, 60, 68, 70, 72, 76, 77, 83	7—Robert Robson 1793, 1802, 09, 10, 15, 17, 23 7—John Porter 1868, 82, 83, 86, 90, 91, 99 7—Fred Darling 1922, 25, 26, 31, 38, 40, 41	5—3rd Earl of Egremont 1782, 1804, 05, 07, 26 5—H. H. Aga Khan III 1930, 35, 36, 48, 52	34 (1862)
2000 Guineas (1809) 1 mile *1609 m* Newmarket	1 min 35.8 sec *My Babu* 1948	9—Jem Robinson 1825, 28, 31, 33, 34, 35, 36, 47, 48	7—John Scott 1842, 43, 49, 53, 56, 60, 62	5—4th Duke of Grafton 1820, 21, 22, 26, 27 5—5th Earl of Jersey 1831, 34, 35, 36, 37	28 (1930)
1000 Guineas (1814) 1 mile *1609 m* Newmarket	1 min 36.85 sec *Oh So Sharp* 1985	7—George Fordham 1859, 61, 65, 68, 69, 81, 83	9—Robert Robson 1818, 19, 20, 21, 22, 23, 25, 26, 27	8—4th Duke of Grafton 1819, 20, 21, 22, 23, 25, 26, 27	29 (1926)
Oaks (1779) 1½ miles *2414 m* Epsom	2 min 34.21 sec *Time Charter* 1982	9—Frank Buckle 1797, 98, 99, 1802, 03, 05, 17, 18, 23	12—Robert Robson 1802, 04, 05, 07, 08, 09, 13, 15, 18, 22, 23, 25	6—4th Duke of Grafton 1813, 15, 22, 23, 28, 31	26 (1848)
St Leger (1776) 1 m 6 f 127 yd *2932 m* Doncaster	3 min 01.6 sec *Coronach* 1926 *Windsor Lad* 1934	9—Bill Scott 1821, 25, 28, 29, 38, 39, 40, 41, 46	16—John Scott 1827, 28, 29, 32, 34, 38, 39, 40, 41, 45, 51, 53, 56, 57, 59, 62	7—9th Duke of Hamilton 1786, 87, 88, 92, 1808, 09, 14	30 (1825)
King George VI and Queen Elizabeth Diamond Stakes (1951) 1½ miles *2414 m* Ascot	2 min 26.98 sec *Grundy* 1975	7—Lester Piggott 1965, 66, 69, 70, 74, 77, 84	4—Dick Hern 1972, 79, 80, 85	2—Nelson Bunker Hunt 1973, 74	19 (1951)
Prix de l'Arc de Triomphe (1920) 2400 metres *1 mile 864 yd* Longchamp, France	2 min 28 sec *Detroit* 1980	4—Jacques Doyasbère 1942, 44, 50, 51 4—Frédéric 'Freddy' Head 1966, 72, 76, 79 4—Yves Saint-Martin 1970, 74, 82, 84	4—Charles Semblat 1942, 44, 46, 49 4—Alec Head 1952, 59, 76, 81 4—François Mathet 1950, 51, 70, 82	6—Marcel Boussac 1936, 37, 42, 44, 46, 49	30 (1967)
VRC Melbourne Cup (1861) 3200 metres *1 mile 1739 yd* Flemington, Victoria, Australia	3 min 19.1 sec *Rain Lover* 1968	4—Bobby Lewis 1902, 15, 19, 27 4—Harry White 1974, 75, 78, 79	7—Bart Cummings 1965, 66, 67, 74, 75, 77, 79	4—Etienne de Mestre 1861, 62, 67, 78	39 (1890)
Kentucky Derby (1875) 1¼ miles *2012 m* Churchill Downs, USA	1 min 59.4 sec *Secretariat* 1973	5—Eddie Arcaro 1938, 41, 45, 48, 52 5—Bill Hartack 1957, 60, 62, 64, 69	6—Ben Jones 1938, 41, 44, 48, 49, 52	8—Calumet Farm 1941, 44, 48, 49, 52, 57, 58, 68	23 (1974)
Irish Derby (1866) 1½ miles *2414 m* The Curragh	2 min 28.8 sec *Tambourine* 1962	6—Morny Wing 1921, 23, 30, 38, 42, 46	6—Vincent O'Brien 1953, 57, 70, 77, 84, 85	5—H. H. Aga Khan III 1925, 32, 40, 48, 49	24 (1962)

JUMPING

RACE	RECORD TIME	Jockey	Trainer	Owner	LARGEST FIELD
Grand National (1839) 4½ miles *7242 m* Liverpool	9 min 01.9 sec *Red Rum* 1973	5—George Stevens 1856, 63, 64, 69, 70	4—Fred Rimell 1956, 61, 70, 76	3—James Machell 1873, 74, 76 3—Sir Charles Assheton-Smith 1893, 1912, 13 3—Noel Le Mare 1973, 74, 77	66 (1929)
Cheltenham Gold Cup (1924) 3¼ miles *5230 m* Cheltenham	6 min 23.4 sec *Silver Fame* 1951	4—Pat Taaffe 1964, 65, 66, 68	5—Tom Dreaper 1946, 64, 65, 66, 68	7—Dorothy Paget 1932, 33, 34, 35, 36, 40, 52	22 (1982)
Champion Hurdle (1927) 2 miles *3218 m* Cheltenham	3 min 51.7 sec *See You Then* 1985	4—Tim Molony 1951, 52, 53, 54	5—Peter Easterby 1967, 76, 77, 80, 81	4—Dorothy Paget 1932, 33, 40, 46	24 (1964)

Pebbles, whose money-earning record included over £1 million in the Breeders' Cup Turf at the world's richest meeting. (All Sport).

Longest and shortest odds

Three winners have been returned at odds of 100–1: *Jeddah* (1898), *Signorinetta* (1908) and *Aboyeur* (1913). The shortest priced winner was *Ladas* (1894) at 2–9 and the hottest losing favourite was *Surefoot*, fourth at 40–95 in 1890.

Largest prize

The richest prize on the British Turf was £239,260 in the 207th Derby on 4 June 1986, won by H. H. Aga Khan IV's *Shahrastani*.

JUMPING

Horse *Greatest winnings*

The greatest amount earned by a British or Irish-trained jumper is £247,344 in 1982–86 by the mare *Dawn Run* (k. 1986), the first horse ever to win both Champion Hurdle (1984) and Cheltenham Gold Cup (1986).

Horses *Most successful*

Triple champion hurdler *Sir Ken* (foaled 1947) won a record 16 hurdle races in succession, April 1951 to March 1953.

Jockeys *Most successful*

John Francome (b. 13 Dec 1952) won a career record 1138 races over jumps (from 5061 mounts), from 1970 to 1985.

The record number of wins in a season is 149 by John 'Jonjo' O'Neill (b. 13 Apr 1952) in 1977–8. The most wins in a day is six by amateur Charlie Cunningham at Rugby on 29 Mar 1881. The record number of successive wins is ten by John Alnam 'Johnny' Gilbert (b. 26 July 1920), 8–30 Sept 1959. The record number of championships is seven by Gerald 'Gerry' Wilson (1903–68) 1933–8 and 1941, and by John Francome (one shared) in 1976, 1979, 1981–5.

Trainers *Most successful*

The most first-prize money earned in a season is £358,837 from a record 120 winners by Michael Dickinson in 1982–3. Fred Winter won a record eight trainers' championships, 1971–5, 1977–8 and 1985.

GRAND NATIONAL

The first Grand National Steeple Chase may be regarded as the Grand Liverpool Steeple Chase of 26 Feb 1839 though the race was not given its present name until 1847. It became a handicap in 1843. Until 1930 five-year-olds were eligible, but since then it has been for six-year-olds and above. Except for 1916–8, and 1941–5 when no race was held, the race has been run at Aintree, near Liverpool, over 30 fences.

Most wins

The only horse to win three times is *Red Rum* (foaled 1965) in 1973, 1974 and 1977, from five runs. He came second in 1975 and 1976. *Manifesto* ran a record eight times (1895–1904). He won in 1897 and 1899, came third three times and fourth once.

Highest prize

The highest prize and the richest ever over jumps in Great Britain was £60,647 won by *West Tip* on 5 Apr 1986.

Highest weight

The highest weight ever carried to victory is 12 st 7 lb *79,4 kg* by *Cloister* (1893), *Manifesto* (1899), *Jerry M.* (1912) and *Poethlyn* (1919).

Earliest reference

A game of very ancient origin, hurling was included in the Tailteann Games (inst 1829 BC). It only became standardised with the formation of the Gaelic Athletic Association in Thurles, Ireland, on 1 Nov 1884. The Irish Hurling Union was formed on 24 Jan 1879.

Most titles *All-Ireland*

The greatest number of All-Ireland Championships won by one team is 24 by Cork between 1890 and 1978. The greatest number of successive wins is four by Cork (1941–4).

Most titles *Inter-provincials*

Munster holds the greatest number of inter-provincial (Railway Cup) championships with 34 (1928–77).

Most appearances

The most appearances in All-Ireland finals is ten shared by Christy Ring (Cork and Munster) and John Doyle (Tipperary). They also share the record of All-Ireland medals won with eight each. Ring's appearances on the winning side were in 1941–4, 1946 and 1952–4, while Doyle's were in 1949–51, 1958, 1961–2 and 1964–5. Ring also played in a record 22 inter-provincial finals (1942–63) and was on the winning side 18 times.

Highest and lowest scores

The highest score in an All-Ireland final (60 min) was in 1896 when Tipperary (8 goals, 14 points) beat Dublin (no goals, 4 points). The record aggregate score was when Cork (6 goals, 21 points), defeated Wexford (5 goals, 10 points) in the 80 min final of 1970. A goal equals three points. The highest recorded individual score was by Nick Rackard (Wexford), who scored 7 goals and 7 points against Antrim in the 1954

All-Ireland semi-final. The lowest score in an All-Ireland final was when Tipperary (1 goal, 1 point) beat Galway (nil) in the first championship at Birr in 1887.

Longest stroke
The greatest distance for a 'lift and stroke' is one of 129 yd *117 m* credited to Tom Murphy of Three Castles, Kilkenny, in a 'long puck' contest in 1906. The record for the annual *An Poc Fada* (Long Puck) contest (instituted 1961) in the ravines of the Cooley Hills, north of Dundalk, County Louth, is 65 pucks (drives) plus 87 yd *79 m* over the course of 3 miles 320 yd *5120 km* by Fionnbar O'Neill (Cork) in 1966. This represents an average of 84.8 yd *77,5 m* per drive.

Largest crowd
The largest crowd was 84,865 for the final between Cork and Wexford at Croke Park, Dublin, in 1954.

ICE HOCKEY

Origins
There is pictorial evidence that a hockey-like game (*Kalv*) was played on ice in the early 16th century in The Netherlands. The game was probably first played in North America on 25 Dec 1855 at Kingston, Ontario, Canada, but Halifax also lays claim to priority. The International Ice Hockey Federation was founded in 1908. The National Hockey League (NHL) of North America was inaugurated 1917.

World Championships and Olympic Games
World Championships were first held for amateurs in 1920 in conjunction with the Olympic Games, which were also considered as World Championships up to 1968. From 1977 World Championships have been open to professionals. The USSR have won 20 world titles between 1954 and 1986, including the Olympic titles of 1956, 1964 and 1968. They have won three further Olympic titles in 1972, 1976 and 1984. Canada won 19 titles, between 1920 and 1961, including 6 Olympic titles (1920, 1924, 1928, 1932, 1948 and 1952). The longest Olympic career is that of Richard Torriani (b. 1 Oct 1911) (Switzerland) from 1928 to 1948. The most gold medals won by any player is three achieved by USSR players Vitaliy Davidov, Anatoliy Firssov, Viktor Kuzkin and Aleksandr Ragulin in 1964, 1968 and 1972, and by Vladislav Tretyak in 1972, 1976 and 1984.

Stanley Cup
The Stanley Cup, presented by the Governor-General, Lord Stanley (original cost $48.67), became emblematic of National Hockey League supremacy 33 years after the first contest at Montreal in 1893. It has been won most often by the Montreal Canadiens with 23 wins in 1916, 1924, 1930–1, 1944, 1946, 1953, 1956–60, 1965–6, 1968–9, 1971, 1973, 1976–9, 1986.

British Competitions
The English National (later British) League championship (inst. 1935) has been won by the Wembley Lions four times in 1936–7, 1952 and 1957 and by Streatham (now Redskins) in 1950, 1953, 1960 and 1982. Murrayfield Racers have won the Northern League (inst. 1966) seven times, 1970–2, 1976, 1979–80 and 1985. The Icy Smith Cup (first held 1966), emblematic of British club supremacy until 1981, was won by Murrayfield Racers nine times, 1966, 1969–72, 1975 and 1979–81. The British club championship (inst. 1982) was won by Dundee Rockets in 1982, 1983 and 1984.

Most goals *Team*
The greatest number of goals recorded in a world championship match was when Canada beat Denmark 47–0 in Stockholm, Sweden on 12 Feb 1949. The NHL record is 21 goals when Montreal Canadiens beat Toronto St Patrick's, at Montreal, 14–7 on 10 Jan 1920.

Most goals and points *Individual*
The most goals scored in a season in the NHL is 92 in the 1981–2 season by Wayne Gretzky (b. 26 Jan 1961) (Edmonton Oilers). He scored a record 215 points, including a record 163 assists in 1985–6. In 1981–2 in all games, adding Stanley Cup playoffs and for Canada in the World Championship he scored 238 points (103 goals, 135 assists). The North American career record for goals is 1071 (801 in the NHL) by Gordie Howe (b. 31 Mar 1928) (Detroit Red Wings, Houston Aeros, New England Whalers and Hartford Whalers) from 16 Oct 1946 in 32 seasons ending in 1979–80. He took 2204 games to achieve the 1000th goal, but Robert Marvin 'Bobby' Hull (b. 3 Jan 1939) (Chicago Black Hawks and Winnipeg Jets) scored his 1000th in 1600 games on 12 Mar 1978.

Most goals and points *British*
The highest score and aggregate in a British League match was set when Medway Bears beat Richmond Raiders 48–1 at Gillingham in a Second Division fixture on 1 Dec 1985, when Kevin McNaught scored a record 25 points from seven goals and 18 assists. In a Midland League match at Solihull on 29 Dec 1985, Solihull Barons defeated Oxford City Stars 50–0. After conceding 28 goals, the Oxford goalminder was carried off with exhaustion, and was replaced by a member of Oxford's women's team.

The most individual goals scored in a senior game is 14 by Ron Halpin (Canada) (b. 18 Oct 1955) for Dundee Rockets in a 24–1 win over Durham Wasps at Dundee on 4 April 1982. Tim Salmon (Canada) (b. 27 Nov 1964) set British senior records of 312 points and 183 assists in 47 games for Ayr Bruins in the 1985–86 season. Dave Stoyanovich (Canada) (b. 1959) scored 162 goals for Fife Flyers in 51 games in 1984–5.

Most points one game
The North American major league record for most points scored in one game is ten (3 goals, 7 assists) by Jim Harrison (b. 9 July 1947) (for Alberta, later Edmonton Oilers) in a World Hockey Association match at Edmonton on 30 Jan 1973, and by Darryl Sittler (b. 18 Sept 1950) (6 goals, 4 assists) for Toronto Maple Leafs in a NHL match at Toronto on 7 Feb 1976.

Fastest scoring *World*
In the NHL the fastest goal was after 4 sec in the second period by Joseph Antoine Claude Provost (b. 17 Sept 1933) (Montreal Canadiens) *v.* Boston Bruins at Montreal on 9 Nov 1957. Doug Smail of the Winnipeg Jets scored 5 sec from the opening whistle against St Louis on 20 Dec 1981. Canadian Bill Mosienko (Chicago Black Hawks) (b. 2 Nov 1921) scored three goals in 21 sec *v.* New York Rangers on 23 Mar 1952. Toronto scored eight goals in 4 min 52 sec *v.* New York Americans on 19 Mar 1938.

In minor leagues, Kim D. Miles scored in 3 sec for Univ of Guelph *v.* Univ of W Ontario on 11 Feb 1975. Three goals in 12 sec was achieved by Steve D'Innocenzo for Holliston *v.* Westwood in a high school match in Massachusetts, USA on 9 Jan 1982. The Skara Ishockeyclubb, Sweden, scored three goals in 11 sec against Örebro IK at Skara on 18 Oct 1981. The Vernon Cougars scored five goals in 56 sec against Salmon Arm Aces at Vernon, BC, Canada on 6 Aug 1982. The Kamloops Knights of Columbus

scored seven goals in 2 min 22 sec *v.* Prince George Vikings on 25 Jan 1980.

Fastest scoring *Great Britain*
The fastest goal in the Heineken League was scored by Steve Johnson for Durham Wasps after four seconds *v.* Ayr Bruins at Ayr, Scotland on 6 Nov 1983. Kenny Westman (Nottingham Panthers) scored a hat trick in 30 sec *v.* Brighton Tigers on 3 Mar 1955.

In an English Junior League (under-16) game Jonathan Lumbis scored a hat-trick in 13 sec for Nottingham Cougars *v.* Peterborough Jets on 4 Nov 1984.

Most successful goaltending
The most matches played by a goaltender in an NHL career without conceding a goal is 103 by Terrance 'Terry' Gordon Sawchuck (1929–70) of Detroit, Boston, Toronto, Los Angeles and New York Rangers, between 1950 and 1967. Gerry Cheevers (b. 2 Dec 1940), Boston Bruins, went a record 33 successive games without a defeat in 1971–2.

Longest match
The longest match was 2 hr 56 min 30 sec (playing time) when Detroit Red Wings beat Montreal Maroons 1–0 in the sixth period of overtime at the Forum, Montreal, at 2.25 a.m. on 25 Mar 1936. Norm Smith, the Red Wings goaltender, turned aside 92 shots for the NHL's longest single shutout.

ICE SKATING

Origins
The earliest reference to ice skating is in early Scandinavian literature referring to the 2nd century though its origins are believed, on archaeological evidence, to be ten centuries earlier still. The earliest English account of 1180 refers to skates made of bone. The earliest skating club was the Edinburgh Skating Club formed in about 1742. The first recorded race was from Wisbech to Whittlesea, East Anglia, in 1763. The earliest artificial rink in the world was opened at the Baker Street Bazaar, Portman Square, London, on 7 Dec 1842, although the surface was not of ice. The first artificial ice rink was opened in the King's Road, Chelsea, London on 7 Jan 1876. The National Skating Association of Great Britain was founded in 1879. The International Skating Union was founded at Scheveningen, Netherlands in 1892.

FIGURE SKATING

Most titles *Olympic*
The most Olympic gold medals won by a figure skater is three by Gillis Grafström (1893–1938) of Sweden in 1920, 1924, and 1928 (also silver medal in 1932); by Sonja Henie (1912–69) of Norway in 1928, 1932 and 1936; and by Irina Rodnina (b. USSR 12 Sept 1949) with two different partners in the Pairs event in 1972, 1976, and 1980.

Most titles *World*
The greatest number of individual world figure skating titles (instituted 1896) is ten by Ulrich Salchow (1877–1949) of Sweden, in 1901–5 and 1907–11. The women's record (inst. 1906) is also ten individual titles by Sonja Henie between 1927 and 1936. Irina Rodnina has won ten pairs titles (inst. 1908), four with Aleksey Ulanov (b. 4 Nov 1947) 1969–72, and six with her husband Aleksandr Zaitsev (b. 16 June 1952) 1973–8. The most ice dance titles (inst. 1952) won is six by Ludmila Pakhomova (1946–86) and her husband Aleksandr Gorshkov (b. 8 Oct 1946)

(USSR) 1970–4 and 1976. They also won the first ever Olympic ice dance title in 1976.

Most titles British
The most individual British titles is 11 by Jack Ferguson Page (1900–47) (Manchester SC) in 1922–31 and 1933, and six by Cecilia Colledge (b. 28 Nov 1920) (Park Lane FSC, London) in 1935–7 (two), 1938 and 1946. Page and Ethel M. Muckelt (1885–1953) won nine pairs titles, 1923–31. The most by an ice dance couple is six by Jayne Torvill (b. 7 Oct 1957) and Christopher Dean (b. 27 July 1958), 1978–83.

Triple Crown
The only British skaters to win the 'Grand Slam' of World, Olympic and European titles in the same year are John Anthony Curry (b. 9 Sept 1949) in 1976 and the ice dancers Jayne Torvill and Christopher Dean in 1984. Karl Schäfer (Austria) (1909–76) and Sonja Henie achieved double 'Grand Slams', both in the years 1932 and 1936.

Highest marks
The highest tally of maximum six marks awarded in an international championship was 29 to Jayne Torvill and Christopher Dean (GB) in the World ice dance championships at Ottawa, Canada on 22–24 Mar 1984. This comprised seven in the compulsory dances, a perfect set of nine for presentation in the set pattern dance and 13 in the free dance including

SPEED SKATING WORLD RECORDS
MEN

Metres	min sec	Name (Country)	Place	Date
500	36.49*	Igor Zhelezovsky (USSR)	Moscow, USSR	21 Dec 1985
1000	1.12.58	Pavel Pegov (USSR)	Medeo, USSR	25 Mar 1983
1500	1.53.00	Igor Zhelezovsky (USSR)	Medeo, USSR	15 Dec 1985
3000	4.03.22	Viktor Shasherin (USSR)	Davos, Switzerland	19 Jan 1986
5000	6.49.15	Viktor Shasherin (USSR)	Medeo, USSR	23 Mar 1984
10,000	14.12.14	Geir Karlstad (Norway)	Inzell, W. Germany	16 Feb 1986

WOMEN

Metres	min sec	Name (Country)	Place	Date
500	39.52	Karin Kania (née Enke) (GDR)	Medeo, USSR	21 Mar 1986
1000	1.18.84	Karin Kania	Karuizawa, Japan	23 Feb 1986
1500	1.59.30	Karin Kania	Medeo, USSR	22 Mar 1986
3000	4.18.02	Karin Kania	Medeo, USSR	21 Mar 1986
5000	7.20.99	Andrea Ehrig (née Schöne) (GDR)	Medeo, USSR	22 Mar 1986

* represents an average speed of 49.33 km/hr *30.65 mph*.
Note that Medeo, Alma Ata, USSR is situated at an altitude of 1691 m above sea level.

WORLD SHORT TRACK SPEED SKATING RECORDS
MEN

Metres	min sec	Name (Country)	Place	Date
500	45.08	Louis Grenier (Canada)	Amsterdam, Netherlands	16 Mar 1985
1000	1.34.79	Guy Daignealt (Canada)	Chamonix, France	6 Apr 1986
1500	2.25.66	Tatsuyoshi Ishihara (Japan)	Chamonix, France	5 Apr 1986
3000	5.04.24	Tatsuyoshi Ishihara (Japan)	Amsterdam, Netherlands	17 Mar 1985

WOMEN

Metres	min sec	Name (Country)	Place	Date
500	48.12	Bonnie Blair (USA)	Chamonix, France	5 Apr 1986
1000	1.41.80	Marie Perrault (Canada)	Chamonix, France	6 Apr 1986
1500	2.35.21	Bonnie Blair	Chamonix, France	5 Apr 1986
3000	5.32.31	Sylvie Daigle (Canada)	Kobe, Japan	17 Apr 1983

another perfect set from all nine judges for artistic presentation. They previously gained a perfect set of nine sixes for artistic presentation in the free dance at the 1983 World Championships in Helsinki, Finland and at the 1984 Olympic Games in Sarajevo, Yugoslavia. In their career Torvill and Dean received a record total of 136 sixes.

The most by a soloist was seven to Donald Jackson (b. 2 Apr 1940) (Canada) in the world men's championship at Prague, Czechoslovakia, in 1962.

Karin Kania (*above*) of East Germany, double gold-medallist at the 1984 Winter Olympics, regained four of her world speed skating records in 1986. (All Sport). (*Right*) Wilf O'Reilly, who holds all four British records for short track speed skating. (J. Gooch).

Distance
Robin Cousins (GB) (b. 17 Mar 1957) achieved 19 ft 1 in *5,81 m* in an Axel jump and 18 ft *5,48 m* with a back flip at Richmond Ice Rink, Surrey on 16 Nov 1983.

Largest rink
The world's largest indoor ice rink is in the Moscow Olympic arena which has an ice area of 8064 m² *86,800 ft²*. The five rinks at Fujikyu Highland Skating Centre, Japan total 26 500 m² *285,243 ft²*.

SPEED SKATING
Most titles *Olympic*
The most Olympic gold medals won in speed skating is six by Lidia Skoblikova (b. 8 Mar 1939) of Chelyabinsk, USSR, in 1960 (two) and 1964 (four). The male record is by Clas Thunberg (1893–1973) (Finland) with five gold (including one tied), and also one silver and one tied bronze in 1924 and 1928. Eric Heiden (USA) (b. 14 June 1958) also won five gold medals, all at Lake Placid, NY, USA, in 1980.

Most titles *World*
The greatest number of world overall titles (inst. 1893) won by any skater is five by Oscar Mathisen (Norway) (1888–1954) in 1908–9 and 1912–14, and Clas Thunberg in 1923, 1925, 1928–9 and 1931. The most titles won in the women's events (inst. 1936) is four by Inga Voronina (*née* Artomonova) (1936–66) (USSR) in 1957, 1958, 1962 and 1964 and Atje Keulen-Deelstra (b. 31 Dec 1938) (Netherlands) 1970, 1972–4.

The record score achieved in the world overall title is 160.807 points by Viktor Shasherin (USSR) (b. 23 July 1962) at Medeo, USSR, 23–24 Mar 1984. The record women's score is 171.760 points by Andrea Schöne (GDR) (b. 1 Dec 1960) at Medeo, 23–24 Mar 1984.

Longest race
The 'Elfstedentocht' ('Tour of the Eleven Towns') was held in the Netherlands from the 1800s to 1963 and again in 1985, covering 200 km *124 miles 483 yd*. It was transferred first to Lake Vesijärvi, near Lahti, Finland and in 1984 to Canada as the International Race of 11 Cities on the Ottawa River. The record time for 200 km is 6 hr 5 min 12 sec by Jan-Roelof Kruithof (Netherlands) (b. 1936) on 25 Feb 1979 at Oulu, Finland. Kruithof won the race eight times, 1974, 1976–7, 1979–83. An estimated 16,000 skaters took part in 1986.

24 hours
Ton Smits (Netherlands) skated 506,375 km *314.65 miles* in 24 hours in Eindhoven, Netherlands on 15–16 Dec 1984.

ICE AND SAND YACHTING

Origins
The sport originated in the Low Countries from the year 1600 (earliest patent granted) and along the Baltic coast. The earliest authentic record is Dutch, dating from 1768. Land or sand yachts of Dutch construction were first reported on beaches (now in Belgium) in 1595. The earliest International championship was staged in 1914.

Largest yacht
The largest ice yacht was *Icicle*, built for Commodore John E. Roosevelt for racing on the Hudson River, New York, in 1869. It was 68 ft 11 in *21 m* long and carried 1070 ft² *99 m²* of canvas.

Highest speeds *Ice*
The highest speed officially recorded is 143 mph *230 km/h* by John D. Buckstaff in a Class A stern-steerer on Lake Winnebago, Wisconsin, USA, in 1938. Such a speed is possible in a wind of 72 mph *115 km/h.*

Highest speeds *Sand*
The official world record for a sand yacht is 107 km/h *66.48 mph* set by Christian-Yves Nau (b. 1944) (France) in *Mobil* at Le Touquet, France on 22 Mar 1981, when the wind speed reached 120 km/h *75 mph*. A speed of 88.4 mph *142,26 km/h* was attained by Nord Embroden (USA) in *Midnight at the Oasis* at Superior Dry Lake, California, USA on 15 Apr 1976.

JUDO

Origins
Judo is a modern combat sport which developed out of an amalgam of several old Japanese fighting arts, the most popular of which was ju-jitsu (jiu-jitsu), which is thought to be of Chinese origin. Judo has greatly developed since 1882, when it was first devised by Dr Jigoro Kano (1860–1938). The International Judo Federation was founded in 1951.

Most titles *World and Olympic*
World championships were inaugurated in Tōkyō in 1956. Women's championships were first held in 1980 in New York. Yashiro Yamashita won nine consecutive Japanese titles 1977–85, four world titles; Heavyweight 1979, 1981 and 1983 and Open 1981, and the Olympic Open category in 1984. He retired undefeated after 203 successive wins, 1977–85. Two other men have won four world titles, Wilhelm Ruska (b. 29 Aug 1940) (Netherlands), 1967, 1971 Heavyweight and the 1972 Olympic Heavyweight and Open titles, and Shozo Fujii (Japan) (b. 12 May 1950), the Middleweight title 1971, 1973, 1975, and 1979. Ingrid Berghmans (Belgium) with six, has won most medals by a woman in world championships, gold (Open) and bronze (72 kg) in 1980, gold (Open) and silver (72 kg) in 1982 and two golds (both 72 kg and Open) in 1984.

Most titles *British*
The greatest number of titles (inst. 1966) won is nine by David Colin Starbrook (b. 9 Aug 1945) (6th dan); Middleweight 1969–70, Light-heavyweight 1971–5 and the Open division 1970–1. A record six titles in the women's events (inst. 1971) were won by Christine Child (now Mrs Gallie) (b. 1946) (6th dan): Heavyweight 1971–5 and the Open division in 1973. Neil Adams (b. 27 Sept 1958) has the most successful international record of any British player. He won two junior (1974 and 1977) and five senior (1979–80, 1983–5) European titles; four World championships medals (one gold, one silver, two bronze) and two Olympic silver medals. To 1985 he has won eight British senior titles.

Highest grades
The efficiency grades in Judo are divided into pupil (*kyu*) and master (*dan*) grades. The highest awarded is the extremely rare red belt *Judan* (10th dan), given only to 13 men so far. The Judo protocol provides for an 11th dan (*Juichidan*) who also would wear a red belt, a 12th dan (*Junidan*) who would wear a white belt twice as wide as an ordinary belt and the highest of all, *Shihan*, but these have never been bestowed. The highest British native Judo grade is 8th dan by Charles Stuart Palmer (b. 1930). Christine Gallie (née Child) was awarded her 6th Dan in 1983.

KARATE

Origins
Based on techniques devised from the sixth century Chinese art of Shaolin boxing (Kempo), Karate was developed by an unarmed populace in Okinawa as a weapon against armed Japanese oppressors *c.* 1500. Transmitted to Japan in the 1920s by Funakoshi Gichin, this method of combat was refined into Karate and organised into a sport with competitive rules. The five major styles of Karate in Japan are: *Shotokan*, *Wado-ryu*, *Goju-ryu*, *Shito-ryu* and *Kyokushinkai*, each of which place different emphasis on speed and power, etc. Other styles include *Sankukai*, *Shotokai* and *Shukokai*. *Wu shu* is a comprehensive term embracing all Chinese martial arts. *Kung fu* is one aspect of these arts popularised by the cinema. (*See also p. 175*).

The Governing Body for the sport in Britain is the Martial Arts Commission upon which all the martial arts are represented.

World championships
Great Britain have won a record three world titles (inst 1970) at the Kumite team event, 1975, 1982 and 1984.

Top exponents
The leading exponents among karatekas are a number of 10th dans in Japan. The leading exponents in the United Kingdom are Tatsuo Suzuki (8th dan, *Wado-ryu*) (b. 27 Apr 1928) chief instructor to the European Karatedo Wadokai; Keinosuke Enoeda (8th dan, *Shotokan*), resident instructor to the Karate Union of Great Britain; Steve Arneil (7th dan, *Kyokushinkai*), British national born in South Africa; and national coach David Donovan (7th dan, *Ishinryu*).

LACROSSE

MEN'S LACROSSE

The game is of American Indian origin, derived from the inter-tribal game *baggataway*, and was played before 1492 by Iroquois Indians in lower Ontario, Canada and upper New York State, USA. The French named it after their game of *Chouler à la crosse*, known in 1381. It was introduced into Great Britain in 1867. The English Lacrosse Union was formed in 1892. Lacrosse was included in the Olympic Games of 1908 and featured as an exhibition sport in the 1928 and 1948 Games.

Most titles *World*
The United States have won three of the four World Championships, in 1967, 1974 and 1982 and also won the pre-Olympic tournament in 1984. Canada won the other world title in 1978 beating the USA 17–16 after extra time—this was the first drawn international match.

Most titles *English*
The English Club Championship (Iroquois Cup—inst. 1890), has been won most often by Stockport with 15 wins between 1897 and 1934. The record score in a final was set by Sheffield University, 30–5 *v.* Hampstead in 1982 and 30–1 *v.* Kenton in 1983.

Most international appearances
The record number of international representations is 33 for England by James Michael 'Mike' Roberts (Urmston) (b. 22 Feb 1946), to 1982. He is the only man to play in four World Championships.

PE teacher Barbara Dootson of Weybridge, who has appeared more times than anyone else for England and Great Britain. She keeps a goal 1,83 m by 1,83 m (6 ft × 6 ft) wide.

Highest scores

The highest score in an international match was the United States' 28–4 win over Canada at Stockport, Greater Manchester on 3 July 1978. England's highest score was their 19–11 win over Canada at Melbourne in 1974.

Fastest scoring

Rod Burns scored only 4 sec into the game for South Manchester and Wythenshawe v. Sheffield Univ. on 6 Dec 1975.

WOMEN'S LACROSSE

The first reported playing of lacrosse by women was in 1886. The All-England Women's Lacrosse Association was formed in 1912. The game has evolved from the men's game so that the rules now differ considerably.

World Championships

World Cup competitions have been won by USA in 1982 and Australia in 1986.

Most international appearances

Barbara Dootson (b. 24 Aug 1955) has played in 55 internationals (13 for Great Britain and 42 for England).

Highest score

The highest score by an international team was by Great Britain and Ireland with their 40–0 defeat of Long Island during their 1967 tour of the USA.

MARBLES

Origins

Marbles may have been a children's game in Ancient Egypt, and was introduced into Britain by the Romans in the 1st Century AD. It became a competitive sport under the British Marbles Board of Control at the Greyhound Hotel, Tinsley Green, Crawley, West Sussex in 1926.

Most championships

The British Championship (established 1926) has been won most often by the Toucan Terribles with 20 consecutive titles (1956–75). Three founder members, Len Smith, Jack and Charlie Dempsey played in every title win. They were finally beaten in 1976 by the Pernod Rams, captained by Len Smith's son, Paul. Len Smith (b. 13 oct 1917) has won the individual title 15 times (1957–64, 1966, 1968–73) but lost in 1974 to his son Alan.

Speed record

The record for clearing the ring (between 5¾ and 6¼ ft 1,75–1,90 m in diameter) of 49 marbles is 2 min 57 sec by the Toucan Terribles at Worthing, West Sussex in 1971.

MICROLIGHTING

Altitude

An FAI world record flight of 7906,5 m 25,939.64 ft was set by R Rowley (USA) on 17 Sept 1983. Bob Calvert set a British record of 5791,27 m 19,000 ft on 19 Feb 1983 at Pleasington, Lancashire.

Distance

Jean Paul Mathias (France) set a distance record of 694,8 km 431.74 miles from Maeux, France to Biarritz on 7 July 1984. Peter Davies set a British record of 545,52 km 338.98 miles on 3 Mar 1984 from Parham, Sussex to St Just, Cornwall.

Speed

Dave Cook (GB) set an FAI world speed record (3 km 1.86 miles course, restricted altitude) of 126,356 km/h 78.51 mph on 4 Aug 1982 in Covehithe, Suffolk.

MODERN PENTATHLON & BIATHLON

Points scores in riding, fencing, cross country and hence overall scores have no comparative value between one competition and another. In shooting and swimming (300 m) the scores are of record significance and the best achievements are shown.

The Modern Pentathlon (Riding, Fencing, Swimming, Shooting and Running) was inaugurated into the Olympic Games at Stockholm in 1912. The Modern Pentathlon Association of Great Britain was formed in 1922. L'Union Internationale de Pentathlon Moderne et Biathlon (UIPMB) was founded in 1948. Originally the UIPM, the administration of Biathlon (cross-country skiing and shooting) was added in 1957, and the name modified accordingly.

MODERN PENTATHLON

Most titles *World* (Inst. 1949)

András Balczó (Hungary) (b. 16 Aug 1938) won the record number of world titles, six individual and seven team. He won the world individual title in 1963, 1965–7 and 1969 and the Olympic title in 1972. His seven team titles (1960–70) comprised five world and two Olympic.

Women's world championships were first held in 1981. Great Britain won three team titles 1981–83, with Sarah Parker (b. 16 July 1956) a member of each of those teams. Wendy Johana Norman (b. 20 Feb 1965) won the individual title in 1982 and team golds in 1981–2. She also won the individual world cup title in 1980 and Great Britain won three world cup team titles, 1978–80.

Most titles *Olympic*

The greatest number of Olympic gold medals won is three by András Balczó, a member of the winning team in 1960 and 1968 and the 1972 individual champion. Lars Hall (b. 30 Apr 1927) (Sweden) has uniquely won two individual Championships (1952 and 1956). Pavel Lednev (USSR) (b. 25 Mar 1943) won a record seven medals (two gold, two silver, three bronze), 1968–80. The best British performance is the team gold medal at Montreal, Canada 18–22 July 1976 by Jim Fox, Adrian Philip Parker and Daniel Nightingale. The best individual placing is fourth by Jeremy Robert 'Jim' Fox (b. 19 Sept 1941) at Munich in 1972.

Probably the greatest margin of victory was by William Oscar Guernsey Grut (b. 17 Sept 1914) (Sweden) in the 1948 Games in London, when he won three events and was placed fifth and eighth in the other two events.

Most titles *British*

The pentathlete with most British titles is Jim Fox, with ten (1963, 1965–8, 1970–4). Wendy Norman won a record four women's titles, 1978–80 and 1982.

BIATHLON

The biathlon, which combines cross-country skiing and rifle shooting was first included in the Olympic Games in 1960, and world championships were first held in 1958.

Most titles *Olympic Games*

Magnar Solberg (Norway) (b. 4 Feb 1937), in 1968 and 1972, is the only man to have won two

MODERN PENTATHLON HIGHEST SCORES
In major competition

	Performance	Points	Name and Place	Date and Venue
WORLD				
Shooting	200/200	—[1]	Charles Leonard (USA) (b. 23 Feb 1913)	3 Aug 1936, Berlin, Germany
	200/200	1132	Daniele Masala (Italy) (b. 12 Feb 1955)	21 Aug 1978, Jönkoping, Sweden
	200/200	1132	George Horvath (Sweden) (b. 14 Mar 1960)	22 July 1980, Moscow, USSR
Swimming	3 min 08.22 sec	1368	John Scott (USA) (b. 14 Apr 1962)	27 Aug 1982, London, England
BRITISH				
Shooting	198/200	1088	Timothy Kenealy (b. 3 Mar 1950)	Helsinki, Finland, 4 June 1979
Swimming	3 min 14 sec	1320	Richard Lawson Phelps (b. 19 Apr 1961)	5 July 1986, Milton Keynes, England

[1] points not given in 1936 Olympic Games.

Olympic individual titles. The USSR have won all five 4 × 7,5 km relay titles, 1968–84. Aleksandr Tikhonov (b. 2 Jan 1947) who was a member of the first four teams also won a silver in the 1968 20 km.

Most titles *World Championship*
Frank Ullrich (GDR) (b. 24 Jan 1958) has won a record six individual world titles, four at 10 km, 1978–81, including the 1980 Olympics, and two at 20 km 1982–3. Aleksandr Tikhonov was in ten winning USSR relay teams, 1968–80 and won four individual titles.

The biathlon world cup (inst 1979) was won three times by Frank Ullrich, 1980–2. He was 2nd in 1979 and 3rd in 1983.

MOTORCYCLE RACING

Earliest race
The first motorcycle race was held over a mile *1,6 km* on an oval track at Sheen House, Richmond, Surrey, on 29 Nov 1897, won by Charles Jarrott (1877–1944) on a Fournier. The oldest motorcycle races in the world are the Auto-Cycle Union Tourist Trophy (TT) series, first held on the 15.81 mile *25,44 km* 'Peel' ('St John's') course in the Isle of Man on 28 May 1907, and still run in the island on the 'Mountain' circuit.

Fastest circuits
The highest average lap speed attained on any closed circuit is 160.288 mph *257,958 km/h* by Yvon du Hamel (Canada) (b. 1941) on a modified 903 cc four-cylinder Kawasaki Z1 at the 31 degree banked 2.5 mile *4,02 km* Daytona International Speedway, Florida, USA, in March 1973. His lap time was 56.149 sec.

The fastest road circuit was the Francorchamps circuit near Spa, Belgium, then 8.74 miles *14,12 km* in length. It was lapped in 3 min 50.3 sec (average speed 137.150 mph *220,721 km/h*) by Barry Stephen Frank Sheene (GB) (b. 11 Sept 1950) on a 495 cc four-cylinder Suzuki during the Belgian Grand Prix on 3 July 1977. The world's fastest now is the Portstewart-Coleraine-Portrush circuit in Londonderry, N. Ireland. The lap record (10.1 mile *16,26 km* lap) is 4 min 53.2 sec (average speed 124.060 mph *199,655 km/h*) by John Glyn Williams (1946–78) on a 747 cc four-cylinder Yamaha on lap five of the 750cc event of the North West 200, on 21 May 1977. Minor circuit changes prior to 1986 have resulted in slower times.

The lap record for the outer circuit (2.767 miles *4,453 km*) at the Brooklands Motor Course, near Weybridge, Surrey (open between 1907 and 1939) was 80.0 sec (average speed 124.51 mph *200,37 km/h*) by Noel Baddow 'Bill' Pope (later Major) (1909–71) of the United Kingdom on a Brough Superior powered by a supercharged 996 cc V-twin '8-80' JAP engine developing 110 bhp, on 4 July 1939.

Fastest race *World*
The fastest road race is the 500 cc Belgian Grand Prix held on the Francorchamps circuit (*see above*). The record time for this ten lap (87.74 mile *141,20 km*) race is 38 min 58.5 sec (average speed 135.068 mph *217,370 km/h*) by Barry Sheene, on a 495 cc four-cylinder Suzuki, on 3 July 1977.

Fastest race *United Kingdom*
The fastest race in the United Kingdom is the

750 cc event of the North-West 200 held on the Londonderry circuit (*see above*). The record lap speed is 127.63 mph *205,395 km/h* by Tom Herron (1949–79) on a 747 cc Yamaha in 1978.

Longest race
The longest race was the Liège 24 hr, run on the old Francorchamps circuit. The greatest distance ever covered is 2761.9 miles *4444,8 km* (average speed 115.08 mph *185,20 km/h*) by Jean-Claude Chemarin and Christian Leon, both of France, on a 941 cc four-cylinder Honda on the Francorchamps circuit on 14–15 Aug 1976.

Longest circuit
The 37.73 mile *60,72 km* 'Mountain' circuit on the Isle of Man, over which the principal TT races have been run since 1911 (with minor amendments in 1920), has 264 curves and corners and is the longest used for any motorcycle race.

Most successful riders *Tourist Trophy*
The record number of victories in the Isle of Man TT races is 14 by Stanley Michael Bailey Hailwood (1940–81) between 1961 and 1979. The first man to win three consecutive TT events in two events was James A. Redman (Rhodesia) (b. 8 Nov 1931). He won the 250 cc and 350 cc events in 1963–5. Mike Hailwood won three events in one year, in 1961 and 1967 and this feat was emulated by Joey Dunlop (Ireland) in 1985.

The TT circuit speed record is 118.47 mph *190,66 km/h* by Joey Dunlop on a Honda on 4 June 1984.

Most successful riders
World championships
The most world championship titles (instituted by the *Fédération Internationale Motocycliste* in 1949) won are 15 by Giacomo Agostini (Italy) (b. 16 June 1942), the 350 cc in 1968–74, and 500 cc in 1966–72, 1975. He is the only man to win two world championships in five consecutive years (350 and 500 cc titles 1968–72).

Agostini won 122 races in the world championship series between 24 Apr 1965 and 29 Aug 1976, including a record 19 in 1970, also achieved by Mike Hailwood in 1966. Klaus Enders (W. Germany) (b. 1937) won six world side-car titles, 1967, 1969–70, 1972–4.

In 1985 Freddie Spencer (USA), riding for Honda, became the first man ever to win the 250 cc and 500 cc titles in the same year.

Trials
A record three World trials championships have been won by Yrjö Vesterinen (Finland), 1976–8 and by Eddie Lejeune (Belgium), 1982–4.

Moto-cross
Joël Robert (Belgium) (b. 11 Nov 1943) won six 250 cc moto-cross world championships (1964, 1968–72). Between 25 Apr 1964 and 18 June 1972 he won a record fifty 250 cc Grands Prix. He became the youngest moto-cross world champion on 12 July 1964 when he won the 250 cc title aged 20 yr 244 days.

Most successful machines
Italian MV-Agusta machines won 37 world championships between 1952 and 1973, and 276 world championship races between 1952 and 1976.

Youngest and oldest world champions
Alberto 'Johnny' Cecotto (Venezuela) (b. 25 Jan 1956) is the youngest to win a world championship. He was 19 yr 211 days when he won the 350 cc title on 24 Aug 1975. The oldest was Hermann-Peter Müller (1909–76) of W. Germany, who won the 250 cc title in 1955 aged 46.

Highest speeds
Official world speed records must be set with two runs over a measured distance made in opposite directions within a time limit—1 hr for FIM records and 2 hr for AMA records.

Donald A. Vesco (USA) (b. 8 Apr 1939) riding his 21 ft *6,4 m* long *Lightning Bolt* streamliner, powered by two 1016 cc Kawasaki engines on Bonneville Salt Flats, Utah, USA on 28 Aug 1978 set AMA and FIM absolute records with an overall average of 318.598 mph *512,733 km/h* and had a fastest run at an average of 318.66 mph *513,165 km/h*.

The highest speed achieved over two runs in the UK is 191.897 mph *308.82 km/h* by Roy Francis Daniel (b. 7 Dec 1938) on his 998 cc supercharged twin-engined RDS Triumph at Elvington, N. Yorks on 29 July 1978. His average time for the flying 440 yd *402 m* was 4.69 sec.

The world record for 1 km *1,093.6 yd* from a standing start is 16.68 sec by Henk Vink (b. 24 July 1939) (Netherlands) on his supercharged 984 cc four-cylinder Kawasaki, at Elvington Airfield, North Yorkshire on 24 July 1977. The faster run was made in 16.09 sec.

Freddie Spencer, the 1983 500 cc world champion, returned in 1985 after injury to pull off the unique double of both 'junior' and 'senior' titles, the 250 cc and 500 cc. (All Sport).

The world record for 440 yd *402 m* from a standing start is 8.805 sec by Henk Vink on his supercharged 1132 cc four-cylinder Kawasaki at Elvington Airfield, North Yorkshire on 23 July 1977. The faster run was made in 8.55 sec.

The fastest time for a single run over 440 yd *402 m* from a standing start is 7.08 sec by Bo O'Brechta (USA) riding a supercharged 1200 cc Kawasaki-based machine at Ontario, California, in 1980. The highest terminal velocity recorded at the end of a 440 yd *402 m* run from a standing start is 199.55 mph *321,14 km/h* by Russ Collins (USA) at Ontario on 7 Oct 1978.

MOTOR RACING

Earliest races

There are various conflicting claims, but the first automobile race was the 201 mile *323 km* Green Bay to Madison, Wisconsin, USA run in 1878 won by an Oshkosh steamer. In 1887 Count Jules Felix Philippe Albert de Dion de Malfiance (1856–1946) won the *La Velocipede* 19.3 miles *31 km* race in Paris in a De Dion steam quadricycle in which he is reputed to have exceeded 37 mph *59 km/h*. The first 'real' race was from Paris to Bordeaux and back (732 miles *1178 km*) on 11–13 June 1895. The first to finish was Emile Levassor (1844–97) of France, in a Panhard-Levassor two-seater, with a 1.2 litre Daimler engine developing 3½ hp. His time was 48 hr 47 min (average speed 15.01 mph *24,15 km/h*). The first closed circuit race was held over five laps of a mile *1,6 km* dirt track at Narragansett Park, Cranston, Rhode Island, USA, on 7 Sept 1896, won by A. H. Whiting, driving a Riker electric.

The oldest race in the world, still regularly run, is the RAC Tourist Trophy, first staged on 14 Sept 1905, in the Isle of Man. The oldest continental race is the French Grand Prix first held on 26–27 June 1906. The Coppa Florio, in Sicily, has been irregularly held since 1900.

Fastest circuits

The highest average lap speed attained on any closed circuit is 250.958 mph *403,878 km/h* in a trial by Dr Hans Liebold (b. 12 Oct 1926) (Germany) who lapped the 7.85 mile *12,64 km* high-speed track at Nardo, Italy in 1 min 52.67 sec in a Mercedes-Benz C111-IV experimental coupé on 5 May 1979. It was powered by a V8 engine with two KKK turbochargers with an output of 500 hp at 6,200 rpm.

The highest average race lap speed for a closed circuit is 214.158 mph *344,654 km/h* by Mario Gabriele Andretti (USA) (b. Trieste, Italy, 28 Feb 1940) driving a 2.6 litre turbocharged Viceroy Parnelli-Offenhauser on the 2 mile *3,2 km*, 22 degree banked oval at Texas World Speedway, College Station, Texas, USA on 6 Oct 1973.

The fastest road circuit was the Francorchamps circuit near Spa, Belgium, then 8.761 miles *14,10 km* in length which was lapped in 3 min 13.4 sec (average speed 163.086 mph *262,61 km/h*) on 6 May 1973, by Henri Pescarolo (France) (b. 25 Sept 1942) driving a 2993 cc V12 Matra-Simca MS670 Group 5 sports car. The race lap average speed record at Berlin's AVUS track was 171.75 mph *276,38 km/h* by Bernd Rosemeyer (Germany) (1909–38) in a 6-litre V16 Auto Union in 1937.

The General Motors' High Speed Circuit (2.03 mile *3,27 km* with a 21.4 degree banking all round), at Millbrook, Bedfordshire, was lapped in 41.48 secs (average speed 176.16 mph *283,49 kph*) by Tom Walkinshaw (b. 1947) and partnered by Michael Scarlett driving a 5343 cc V12 Jaguar XJS Group A racing saloon in June 1985.

Fastest pit stop

Robert William 'Bobby' Unser (USA) (b. 20 Feb 1934) took 4 sec to take on fuel on lap 10 of the Indianapolis 500 on 30 May 1976.

Fastest race

The fastest race is the Busch Clash at Daytona, Florida over 125 miles *201 km* on a 2½ miles 31 degree banked track. In 1979 Elzie Wylie 'Buddy' Baker (b. 25 Jan 1941) averaged 194.384 mph *312,831 km/h* in an Oldsmobile. Bill Elliott set the world record for a 500 mile *805 km* race in 1985 when he won at Talladega, Alabama at an average speed of 186.288 mph *299,793 km/h*. The NASCAR (National Association for Stock Car Automobile Racing) qualifying record is 212.229 mph *341,549 km/h* by Bill Elliott (b. 8 Oct 1955) in a Ford Thunderbird at Alabama International Motor Speedway, Talladega, Alabama, USA, a 2.66 mile *4,28 km* oval speedway with 33° banked turns, on 1 May 1986.

Ayrton Senna in the Lotus and Nigel Mansell in the Honda Williams were just 0.014 seconds apart—representing less than a metre—after a couple of hours driving in the Spanish Grand Prix. (Sporting Pictures).

NASCAR records

Richard Lee Petty (USA) (b. 2 July 1937) won 200 NASCAR Winston Cup races in 1000 starts, 1958–86. His best season was 1967 with 27 wins. Petty, on 1 Aug 1971 was the first driver to pass $1 million career earnings. The NASCAR career money record is $6,703,305 to 4 June 1986 by Darrell Waltrip (b. 5 Feb 1949). Bill Elliott won a year's record $2,044,468 in NASCAR events in 1985. Geoff Bodine (b. 18 Apr 1949) won 55 races in NASCAR Modified racing in 1978.

WORLD CHAMPIONSHIP GRAND PRIX MOTOR RACING

Drivers *Most successful*

The World Drivers' Championship, inaugurated in 1950, has been won a record five times by Juan-Manuel Fangio (Argentina) (b. 24 June 1911) in 1951, 1954–7. He retired in 1958, after having won 24 Grand Prix races (two shared).

The most Grand Prix victories is 27 by John Young 'Jackie' Stewart (GB) (b. 11 June 1939) between 12 Sept 1965 and 5 Aug 1973. The most Grand Prix points is 418½ by Niki Lauda (Austria) (b. 22 Feb 1949) in 171 Grands Prix, with 25 wins from 1971 to 1985. The most Grand Prix victories in a year is seven by James 'Jim' Clark (GB) (1936–68) in 1963 and by Alain Prost (France) (b. 24 Feb 1955) in 1984. The most Grand Prix starts is 176 (out of a possible 184) between 18 May 1958 and 26 Jan 1975 by Norman Graham Hill (GB) (1929–75). Between 20 Nov 1960 and 5 Oct 1969 he took part in 90 consecutive Grands Prix.

Oldest and youngest

The youngest world champion was Emerson Fittipaldi (Brazil) (b. 12 Dec 1946) who won his first world championship on 10 Sept 1972 aged 25 yr 273 days. The oldest world champion was Juan-Manuel Fangio who won his last world championship on 18 Aug 1957 aged 46 yr 55 days.

The youngest Grand Prix winner was Bruce Leslie McLaren (1937–70) of New Zealand, who won the United States Grand Prix at Sebring, Florida, on 12 Dec 1959 aged 22 yr 104 days. The oldest Grand Prix winner (in pre-World Championship days) was Tazio Giorgio Nuvolari (Italy) (1892–1953), who won the Albi Grand Prix at Albi, France on 14 July 1946 aged 53 yr 240 days. The oldest Grand Prix driver was Louis Alexandre Chiron (Monaco) (1899–1979), who finished 6th in the Monaco Grand Prix on 22 May 1955 aged 55 yr 292 days. The youngest driver to qualify for a Grand Prix was Michael Christopher Thackwell (New Zealand) (b. 30 Mar 1961) at the Canadian GP on 28 Sept 1980, aged 19 yr 182 days.

Manufacturers

Ferrari have won a record eight manufacturers' world championships, 1961, 1964, 1975–7, 1979, 1982–3. Ferrari have 91 race wins in 392 Grands Prix, 1950–85.

Fastest race

The fastest overall average speed for a Grand Prix race on a circuit in current use is 235.405 km/h *146.274 mph* by Alain Prost (France) in a McLaren at Silverstone in the British Grand Prix on 21 July 1985. The qualifying lap record was set on this occasion by Keke Rosberg (Finland) at 1 min 05.59 sec, an average speed of 258.803 km/h *160.817 mph*, in a Williams-Honda on 20 July 1985.

Closest finish

The closest finish to a World Championship race was when Ayrton Senna (Brazil) in a Lotus beat Nigel Mansell (GB) in a Williams by 0.014 sec in the Spanish Grand Prix at Jerez de la Frontera on 13 Apr 1986. In the Italian Grand Prix at Monza on 5 Sept 1971, 0.61 sec separated winner Peter Gethin (GB) from the fifth placer.

BRITISH GRAND PRIX

First held in 1926 as the RAC Grand Prix, and held annually with the above name since 1949, the venue has alternated between Brands Hatch, Kent and Silverstone, Northants.

Bill Elliott driving a Ford Thunderbird in which he set an American stock car speed record of over 212 mph *340 km/h*. Elliott also has record earnings of over $2 million. (NASCAR).

Fastest speed

The fastest race time is 1 hr 18 min 10.436 sec, when Alain Prost won in 1985. See Fastest race (above).

Most wins

The most wins by a driver is five by Jim Clark, 1962–65 and 1967, all in Lotus cars. Ferrari have most wins with ten, 1951–4, 1956, 1958, 1961, 1976, 1978 and 1983.

LE MANS

The greatest distance ever covered in the 24 hour *Grand Prix d'Endurance* (first held on 26–27 May 1923) on the old Sarthe circuit at Le Mans, France is 5333,724 km *3314.222 miles* by Dr Helmut Marko (Austria) (b. 27 Apr 1943) and Jonkheer Gijs van Lennep (Netherlands) (b. 16 Mar 1942) in a 4907 cc flat-12 Porsche 917K Group 5 sports car, on 12–13 June 1971.

The record for the current circuit is 5088,507 km *3161.938 miles* (av. speed 212,021 km/h *131.747 mph*) by Klaus Ludwig (W. Germany), Paulo Barillo (Italy) and John Winter (W. Germany) in a Porsche 956 on 15–16 June 1985.

The race lap record (8.475 mile *13,64 km* lap) is 3 min 25.1 sec (average speed 148.61 mph *239,16 km/h* by Jacky Ickx (Belgium) in a Porsche 962C in 1985. The practice lap record is 3 min 14.8 sec (av. speed 156.62 mph *252,05 km/h*) by Hans Stuck (W. Germany) in a Porsche 962c on 14 June 1985.

Most wins

The race has been won by Porsche cars eleven times, in 1970–1, 1976–7, 1979, 1981–6. The most wins by one man is six by Jacques Bernard 'Jacky' Ickx (Belgium) (b. 1 Jan 1945), 1969, 1975–7 and 1981–2.

The race has been won 13 times by British cars: Bentley in 1924 and 1927–30, Lagonda in 1935, Jaguar in 1951, 1953 and 1955–7, Aston Martin in 1959 and a Gulf-Ford in 1975.

INDIANAPOLIS 500

The Indianapolis 500 mile *804 km* race (200 laps) was inaugurated in the USA on 30 May 1911. The most successful driver has been Anthony Joseph 'A.J.' Foyt, Jr (USA) (b. 16 Jan 1935) who won in 1961, 1964, 1967 and 1977. The record time is 2 hr 55 min 42.48 sec (average speed 170.72 mph *274,75 km/h*) by Bobby Rahal (USA) driving a Penske March-Cosworth on 31 May 1986. The qualifying record average speed is 216.828 mph *348,951 km/h* for four laps, including a one lap record 217.581 mph *350,162 km/h*, by Rick Mears (USA) in a March-Cosworth on 10 May 1986. The record prize fund is $3,271,025 and the individual prize record $581,062 by Bobby Rahal, both in 1986.

RALLIES

Earliest

The earliest long rally was promoted by the Parisian daily *Le Matin* in 1907 from Peking, China to Paris over about 7500 miles *12 000 km* on 10 June. The winner, Prince Scipione Borghese (1872–1927) of Italy, arrived in Paris on 10 Aug 1907 in his 40 hp Itala accompanied by his chauffeur, Ettore, and Luigi Barzini.

Longest

The longest ever rally was the *Singapore Airlines* London–Sydney Rally over 19,329 miles *31 107 km* from Covent Garden, London on 14 Aug 1977 to Sydney Opera House, won on 28 Sept 1977 by Andrew Cowan, Colin Malkin and Michael Broad in a Mercedes 280E. The longest held annually is the Safari Rally (first run 1953 through East Africa (now only Kenya)) which has been up to 3874 miles *6234 km* long, as in the 17th Safari held between 8 and 12 Apr 1971. It has been won a record five times by Shekhar Mehta (b. Uganda 1945) in 1973, 1979–82.

Monte Carlo

The Monte Carlo Rally (first run 1911) has been won a record four times by Sandro Munari (b. 1940) (Italy) in 1972, 1975, 1976 and 1977 and by Walter Röhrl (b. 7 Mar 1947) (with co-driver Christian Geistdorfer) in 1980, 1982–84, each time in a different car. The smallest car to win was an 851 cc Saab driven by Erik Carlsson (Sweden) (b. 5 Mar 1929) and Gunnar Häggbom (Sweden) on 25 Jan 1962, and by Carlsson and Gunnar Palm on 24 Jan 1963.

Britain

The RAC Rally (first held 1932) has been recognised by the FIA since 1957. Hannu Mikkola (Finland) (b. 24 May 1942) (with co-driver Arne Hertz) has a record four wins in a Ford Escort, 1978–9 and an Audi Quatro, 1981–2.

World Championship

Walter Röhrl is the only man to win two drivers' world championships (inst. 1979), 1980 and 1982.

DRAGGING

Piston engined

The lowest elapsed time recorded by a piston-engined dragster is 5.391 sec from a standing start for 440 yd *402 m* by Gary Beck (USA) in qualifying for the World Finals at Irvine, California, USA on 15 Oct 1983. The highest terminal velocity recorded at the end of a 440 yd run is 268.01 mph *431,320 km/h* by Donald Glenn Garlits (USA) (b. 1932) at Pomona, California on 17 Oct 1985 in qualifying for the World Finals.

The world record for two runs in opposite directions over 440 yd *402 m* from a standing start is 6.70 sec by Dennis Victor Priddle (b. 1945) of Yeovil, Somerset, driving his 6424 cc supercharged Chrysler dragster developing 1700 bhp using nitromethane and methanol, at Elvington Airfield, North Yorkshire on 7 Oct 1972. The faster run was made in 6.65 sec.

Rocket or jet-engined

The highest terminal velocity recorded by any dragster is 392.54 mph *631,732 km/h* by Kitty O'Neil (USA) at El Mirage Dry Lake, California, USA on 7 July 1977. The lowest elapsed time was 3.72 sec also by Kitty O'Neil on the same occasion.

Highest speeds *See also pp. 157–8*

The most successful land speed record breaker was Major Sir Malcolm Campbell (1885–1948) of the United Kingdom. He broke the official record nine times between 25 Sept 1924, with 146.157 mph *235,216 km/h* in a Sunbeam, and 3 Sept 1935, when he achieved 301.129 mph *480,620 km/h* in the Rolls-Royce engined *Bluebird*.

'Big Daddy' Don Garlits set a terminal velocity record of over 268 mph *431 km/h*. Drag cars are designed for high speeds over short distances—usually just 440 yd *402 m*. (All Sport).

Duration record

The greatest distance ever covered in one year is 400 000 km *248,548.5 miles* by François Lecot (1879–1949), an innkeeper from Rochetaillée, near Lyon, France, in a 1900 cc 66 bhp Citroën 11 sedan, mainly between Paris and Monte Carlo, from 22 July 1935 to 26 July 1936. He drove on 363 of the 370 days allowed.

MOUNTAINEERING

Origins

Although bronze-age artifacts have been found on the summit of the Riffelhorn, Switzerland (9605 ft *2927 m*), mountaineering as a sport has a continuous history dating back only to 1854. Isolated instances of climbing for its own sake exist back to the 13th century. The Atacamenans built sacrificial platforms near the summit of Llullaillaco (22,058 ft *6723 m*) in late pre-Columbian times c. 1490. The earliest recorded rock climb in the British Isles was of Stac na Biorrach, St Kilda (236 ft *71,9 m*) by Sir Robert Moray in 1698.

Mount Everest

Mount Everest (29,028 ft *8848 m*) was first climbed at 11.30 a.m. on 29 May 1953, when the summit was reached by Edmund Percival Hillary (b. 20 July 1919), created KBE, of New Zealand, and the Sherpa, Tenzing Norgay (1914–86, formerly called Tenzing Khumjung Bhutia), who was awarded the GM. The successful expedition was led by Col (later Hon Brigadier) Henry Cecil John Hunt, CBE, DSO (b. 22 June 1910), who was created a Knight Bachelor in 1953, a life Baron on 11 June 1966 and KG on 23 Apr 1979.

The Sherpa, Sundare (or Sungdare) has climbed Everest a record four times in 1979, 1981, 1982 and 1985. Ang Rita Sherpa, with ascents in 1983, 1984 and 1985, is the first person to scale Everest three times without the use of bottled oxygen. Reinhold Messner (Italy) was the first to make the entire climb solo on 20 Aug 1980. Messner and Peter Habeler (b. 22 July 1942) (Austria) made the first entirely oxygen-less ascent on 8 May 1978. The first Britons to reach the summit were Douglas Scott (b. 29 May 1941) and Dougal Haston (1940–77) on 24 Sept 1975. The first woman to reach the summit was Junko Tabei (b. 22 Sept 1939) (Japan) on 16 May 1975. The oldest person was Richard Daniel Bass (b. 21 Dec 1929) aged 55 yr 130 days on 30 Apr 1985.

Reinhold Messner (b. 17 Sept 1944), with his ascent of Kangchenjunga in 1982, became the first person to climb the world's three highest mountains, having earlier reached the summits of Everest and K2. He has successfully scaled a record 12 of the world's 14 mountains of over 8000 m *26,250 ft*, all without oxygen.

Greatest walls

The highest final stage in any wall climb is that on the south face of Annapurna I (26,545 ft *8091 m*). It was climbed by the British expedition led by Christian John Storey Bonington (b. 6 Aug 1934) when from 2 Apr to 27 May 1970, using 18,000 ft *5500 m* of rope, Donald Whillans (b. 9 Aug 1933) and Dougal Haston scaled to the summit. The longest wall climb is on the Rupal-Flank from the base camp at 3560 m *11,680 ft* to the South Point 8042 m *26,384 ft* of Nanga Parbat—a vertical ascent of 4482 m *14,704 ft*. This was scaled by the Austro-German-Italian Expedition led by Dr Karl Maria Herrligkoffer in April 1970.

Europe's greatest wall is the 6,600 ft *2000 m* north face of the Eigerwand (Ogre wall) first climbed by Heinrich Harrer and Fritz Kasparek of Austria and Anderl Heckmair and Wiggerl

Vörg of Germany on 21–24 July 1938. The north-east face of the Eiger had been climbed on 20 Aug 1932 by Hans Lauper, Alfred Zurcher, Alexander Graven and Josef Knubel. The greatest alpine solo climb was that of Walter Bonatti (b. Bergamo, Italy, 22 June 1930) of the South West Pillar of the Dru, Montenvers now called the Bonatti Pillar, with five bivouacs in 126 hr 7 min on 17–22 Aug 1955.

The most demanding free climbs in the world are those rated at 5.13, the premier location for these being in the Yosemite Valley, California, USA. The top routes in Britain are graded E7.7b, which relates closely to 5.13.

Highest bivouac

Two Japanese, Hironobu Kamuro (1951–83) and Hiroshi Yoshino (1950–83), bivouacked at 8800 m *28,870 ft* on Everest on the night of 8/9 Oct 1983. Yoshino died on 9 Oct while Kamuro died either during the bivouac night or also next day.

MOUNTAIN RACING

Mount Cameroun

Timothy Leku Lekunze (Cameroun) descended from the summit 13,353 ft *4070 m* to Buea at 3000 ft *914 m* in 1 hr 9 min 26 sec on 26 Jan 1986, achieving a vertical rate of 45 m *149 ft* per min. He also set the record for the race to the summit and back of 3 hr 47 min 57 sec. The record time for the ascent is 2 hr 34 min 27 sec by Michael Short (GB) in 1985.

Ben Nevis

The record time for the race from Fort William Town Park to the Cairn on the summit of Ben Nevis (4418 ft *1346,6 m*) and return is 1 hr 25 min 34 sec by Kenneth Stuart (b. 25 Feb 1957) and the feminine record is 1 hr 43 min 25 sec by Pauline Haworth (b. 1 Aug 1956), both on 1 Sept 1984. The full course by the bridle path is about 14 miles *22 km* but distance is saved by crossing the open hillside. The mountain was first climbed *c.* 1720 and the earliest run, by William Swan in 2 hr 41 min, was in 1895.

Snowdon

The Snowdon Race (Ras Yr Wyddfa) has been run annually since 1976 from Llanberis to the summit of Snowdon and back. The fastest time is 1 hr 3 min 46 sec by Fausto Bonzi (Italy) on 21 July 1984. On the same date Pauline Haworth set a ladies record of 1 hr 24 min 3 sec.

FELL RUNNING

In the 1972 Skiddaw Fell Race (3053 ft to 250 ft *930 to 107m*) a vertical descent rate of 128 ft *39m* per min was achieved by George Jeffrey Norman (b. 6 Feb 1945) (Altrincham AC).

Joss Naylor (b. 10 Feb 1936) won the Ennerdale mountain race (23 miles *37 km*) nine times, 1968–1977. The fastest time is 3 hr 20 min 57 sec by Kenny Stuart (b. 25 Feb 1957) of Keswick AC in 1985.

The Yorkshire three peak record for the current 24 mile course is 2 hr 49 min 13 sec by Hugh Symonds of Kendal AC in 1985. The record for the former 23 mile course was 2 hr 37 min 30 sec by John Wild on 25 Apr 1982.

The Lakeland 24-hr record is 72 peaks achieved by Joss Naylor, on 22–23 June 1975. He covered 105 miles *168 km* with 37,000 ft *11 227 m* of ascents and descents in 23 hr 11 min.

The record for the Bob Graham Round of 42 Lakeland Peaks covering a total distance of 72 miles *116 km* and 27,000 ft *8230 m* of ascent and descent, is 13 hr 54 min by Billy Bland, 34, on 19 June 1982. Ernest Roger Baumeister (Dark Peak Fell Runners Club) (b. 17 Dec 1941) ran the double Bob Graham Round in 46 hr 34½ min on 30 June–1 July 1979.

The record for traversing the 85 mile *136.79 km* cross-country route of the nine 4000 ft *1219,2 m* Scottish peaks is 22 hr 33 min by J. S. 'Stan' Bradshaw (Clayton-le-Moors Harriers) on 30 May 1982.

The 'Three Thousander' record over the 14 Welsh peaks of over 3000 ft *914 m* is 4 hr 46 min 22 sec, by Joss Naylor on 17 June 1973.

The Ten Peaks run is from Burnthwaite Farm, Wasdale Head, Cumbria to the top of Skiddaw *via* England's nine other highest mountains and tops. The record time is 6 hr 56 min by Joss Naylor, wholly on foot, in May 1975.

Three Peaks record

The Three Peaks route from sea level at Fort William, Inverness-shire, to sea level at Caernarvon, *via* the summits of Ben Nevis, Scafell Pike and Snowdon, was walked by Arthur Eddleston (1939–84) (Cambridge H) in 5 days 23 hr 37 min on 11–17 May 1980. Peter and David Ford, David Robinson, Kevin Duggan and John O'Callaghan, of Luton and Dunstable, ran the distance in relay in 54 hr 39 min 14 sec on 7–9 Aug 1981. The fastest individual total time for climbing the three mountains is 4 hr 16 min by Joss Naylor on 8–9 July 1971.

On 23 June 1984 a team of 3 from the Greater Manchester Police Tactical Aid Group covered the distance in 8 hrs 22 min, being transported between the peaks by helicopter. Their running time was 5 hr 4 min.

A total climbing time of 7 hr 47 min was achieved by Brian Stadden on 13–15 Aug 1982 for Five Peaks, adding the highest points in Northern Ireland—Slieve Donard (2796 ft *852 m*) and in the Republic of Ireland—Carrauntaul (3414 ft *1041 m*) to the Three Peaks.

Ray Ewry, who had suffered from polio as a child, won a record ten Olympic gold medals at the standing jumps. The three events (standing high, long and triple jump) were only included at the Games between 1900 and 1912.

Pennine Way

The record for traversing the 271 mile *436 km* long Pennine Way is 2 days 21 hr 55 min by Michael Cudahy, 43, on 1–3 June 1984.

Multiple Peaks

Three members of the 'Climathon' team, Mick Cottam, Matthew Beresford and Andrew Curson, completed a climb of all 349 peaks in England over 2000 ft *609,6 m* (walking a distance of 402.5 miles *647,76 km*) from 21 July–11 Aug 1985.

NETBALL

Origins

The game was invented in the USA in 1891 and introduced into England in 1895 by Dr Toles. The All England Women's Netball Association was formed in 1926. The oldest club in continuous existence is the Polytechnic Netball Club of London founded in 1907.

Most titles *World*

Australia have won the World Championships (inst. 1963) a record five times, 1963, 1971, 1975, 1979 and 1983.

Most titles *English*

The National Club's Championships (inst. 1966) have been won eight times by Sudbury Netball Club (1968–69, 1970–1 (both shared), 1973, 1983–5).

Surrey have won the County Championships (inst. 1932) a record 19 times (1949–64, 1966, 1981; 1969 and 1986 (both shared)).

Most international appearances

The record number of internationals is 90 by June Wightman (b. 28 June 1946) for Northern Ireland, 1964–85. Lesley Owen (b. 16 Oct 1942) played 73 times for Wales 1968–80. The record for England is 80 by Jillean Hipsey, 1978–85.

Highest scores

The World Tournament record score was in Auckland, New Zealand in 1975 when England beat Papua New Guinea 114 goals to 16. The record number of goals in the World Tournament is 402 by Judith Heath (England) (b. 1942) in 1971.

OLYMPIC GAMES

Note: These records include the Games held at Athens in 1906.

Origins

The earliest celebration of the ancient Olympic Games of which there is a certain record is that of July 776 BC, when Coroibos, a cook from Elis, won the foot race, though their origin dates from perhaps as early as *c.* 1370 BC. The ancient Games were terminated by an order issued in Milan in AD 393 by Theodosius I, 'the Great' (*c.* 346–95), Emperor of Rome. At the instigation of Pierre de Fredi, Baron de Coubertin (1863–1937), the Olympic Games of the modern era were inaugurated in Athens on 6 Apr 1896.

Ever present

Four countries have never failed to be represented at the 21 celebrations of the Summer Games: Australia, Greece, Great Britain and Switzerland. Of these only Great Britain has been present at all Winter celebrations as well.

Largest crowd

The largest crowd at any Olympic site was 150,000 at the 1952 ski-jumping at the Holmeŋkøllen, outside Oslo, Norway. Estimates of the number of spectators of the marathon race through Tōkyō, Japan on 21 Oct 1964 were 500,000 to 1,500,000. The total spectator attendance at Los Angeles in 1984 was given as 5,797,923 (see All Sports).

Most medals *Individual gold*

In the ancient Olympic Games victors were given a chaplet of wild olive leaves. Leonidas of Rhodos won 12 running titles 164–152 BC. The most individual gold medals won by a male competitor in the modern Games is ten by Raymond Clarence Ewry (USA) (1874–1937) (see Track and Field Athletics). The female record is seven by Vera Caslavska-Odlozil (Czechoslovakia) (see Gymnastics). The most gold medals won by a British competitor is four by Paul Radmilovic (1886–1968) in water polo, 1908, 1912 and 1920 and the 4 × 200 m freestyle relay in 1908, and swimmer Henry Taylor (1885–1951) in 1906 and 1908. The Australian swimmer Iain Murray Rose, who won four gold medals, was born in Birmingham, England on 6 Jan

1939. The only Olympian to win four consecutive individual titles in the same event has been Alfred A. Oerter (b. 19 Sept 1936) of the USA, who won the discus in 1956–68.

Swimmer Mark Andrew Spitz (USA) (b. 10 Feb 1950) won a record seven golds at one celebration, at Munich in 1972, including three in relays. The most won in individual events at one celebration is five by speed skater Eric Heiden (USA) (b. 14 June 1958) at Lake Placid, USA, in 1980.

The only man to win a gold medal in both the Summer and Winter Games is Edward F. Eagan (USA) (1898–1967) who won the 1920 Light-Heavyweight boxing title and was a member of the winning four-man bob in 1932.

Most medals Individual
Gymnast Larissa Latynina (USSR) (b. 27 Dec 1934) won a record 18 medals (see Gymnastics). The record at one celebration is eight by gymnast Aleksandr Ditiatin (USSR) (b. 7 Aug 1957) in 1980.

Youngest and oldest gold medallists
The youngest ever winner was a French boy (whose name is not recorded) who coxed the Netherlands pair in 1900. He was 7–10 years old and he substituted for Dr Hermanus Brockmann, who coxed in the heats but proved too heavy. The youngest ever female champion is Marjorie Gestring (USA) (b. 18 Nov 1922, now Mrs Bowman), aged 13 yr 267 days, in the 1936 women's springboard event. Oscar Swahn (see p. 218) was in the winning Running Deer shooting team in 1912 aged 64 yr 258 days.

Youngest and oldest Great Britain
The youngest competitor to represent Britain in the Olympic Games was Magdalena Cecilia Colledge (b. 28 Nov 1920) aged 11 yr 73 days when she skated in the 1932 Games. The oldest was Hilda Lorna Johnstone (b. 4 Sept 1902) aged 70 yr 5 days in the Equestrian Dressage in the 1972 Games.

Longest span
The longest span of an Olympic competitor is 40 years by Dr Ivan Osiier (Denmark) (1888–1965) in fencing, 1908–32 and 1948, and Magnus Konow (Norway) (1887–1972) in yachting, 1908–20, and 1936–48. The longest feminine span is 24 years (1932–56) by the Austrian fencer Ellen Müller-Preis (b. 6 May 1912). Raimondo d'Inzeo (b. 8 Feb 1925) competed for Italy in equestrian events at a record eight celebrations from 1948 to 1976, gaining one gold, two silver and three bronze medals. Janice Lee York Romary (b. 6 Aug 1928) the US fencer, competed in all six Games from 1948 to 1968, and Lia Manoliu (Romania) (b. 25 Apr 1932) competed from 1952 to 1972 winning the discus in 1968.

The longest span of any British competitor is 28 years by Enoch Jenkins (b. 6 Nov 1892) who appeared in the 1924 and the 1952 Games in the clay pigeon shooting event, and the longest feminine span by Dorothy Jennifer Beatrice Tyler (née Odam) (b. 14 Mar 1920) who high-jumped from 1936 to 1956. The record number of appearances for Great Britain is six by fencer Bill Hoskyns from 1956 to 1976. Durward Randolph Knowles (b. 2 Nov 1917) competed in yachting for Britain in 1948 and in the following six Games for the Bahamas.

ORIENTEERING

Origins
Orienteering as now known was invented by Major Ernst Killander in Sweden in 1918. It was based on military exercises of the 1890s. The term was first used for an event at Oslo, Norway on 7 Oct 1900. World championships were instituted in 1966. Annual British championships were instituted in 1967 following the formation of the British Orienteering Federation.

Most titles World
Sweden has won the men's relay six times between 1966 and 1979 and the women's relay seven times, 1966, 1970, 1974, 1976, 1981, 1983 and 1985. Three women's individual titles have been won by Annichen Kringstad-Svensson (Sweden) (b. 15 July 1960), 1981, 1983 and 1985. The men's title has been won twice by Åge Hadler (Norway) (b. 14 Aug 1944) in 1966 and 1972, Egil Johansen (Norway) (b. 18 Aug 1954) 1976 and 1978, and Ogvin Thon (Norway) (b. 25 Mar 1958) in 1979 and 1981.

Most titles British
The men's relay has been won twice by Oxford University, 1975, 1979, and the women's relay three times by Derwent Valley Orienteers, 1975, 1979 and 1980. Geoffrey Peck (b. 27 Sept 1949) has won the men's individual title a record five times, 1971, 1973, 1976–7 and 1979 as well as the over-35s title in 1985. Carol McNeill (b. 20 Feb 1944) has won the women's title six times, 1967, 1969, 1972–76. She also won the over-35s title in 1984 and 1985.

Lorna Collett (b. 2 Sept 1922) of South Ribble O.C. and Terry Dooris (b. 22 Sept 1926) of Southern Navigators have both completed in all 20 British individual championships 1967–86.

Most competitors
The most competitors at an event in one day is 22,510 on the first day of the Swedish O-Ringen at Småland on 18 July 1983.

PARACHUTING

See also page 172
Origins
Parachuting became a regulated sport with the institution of world championships in 1951. A team title was introduced in 1954 and women's events were included in 1956.

Most titles World
The USSR won the men's team titles in 1954, 1958, 1960, 1966, 1972, 1976, and 1980, and the women's team title in 1956, 1958, 1966, 1968, 1972, and 1976. Nikolai Ushamyev (USSR) has won the individual title twice, 1974 and 1980.

Most titles British
Sgt Ronald Alan 'Scotty' Milne (b. 5 Mar 1952) of the Parachute Regiment has won the British title five times in 1976–7, 1979–81. Rob Colpus and Geoff Sanders have each shared ten British titles for Relative Work parachuting, the 4 Way and 8 Way titles won by their team 'Symbiosis' in 1976–7, 1979, 1981–2.

Greatest accuracy
Jacqueline Smith (GB) (b. 29 Mar 1951) scored ten consecutive dead centre strikes (10 cm 4 in disc) in the World Championships at Zagreb, Yugoslavia, 1 Sept 1978. At Yuma, Arizona, USA, in March 1978, Dwight Reynolds scored a record 105 daytime dead centres, and Bill Wenger and Phil Munden tied with 43 nighttime DCs, competing as members of the US Army team, the Golden Knights. With electronic measuring the official FAI record is 50 DCs by Alexander Aasmiae (USSR) at Ferghana, USSR, Oct 1979.

The Men's Night Accuracy Landing Record on an electronic score pad is 27 consecutive dead centres by Cliff Jones (USA) in 1981.

Parascending
Andrew Wakelin (UK) at Artesia Airport, New Mexico, USA on a Sorcerer 33 canopy on a 1600 ft 488 m line on 1 Aug 1985 set records for distance: 7300 m 23,950 ft, and height gain: 400 m 1312 ft. The duration record is 21 min 8 sec by Pat Sugrue on a Paramount 9 in South Wales on 12 Apr 1986.

Nigel Horder scored four successive dead centres at the Dutch Open, Flevhof, Netherlands on 22 May 1983.

PELOTA VASCA (Jaï Alaï)

Origins
The game, which originated in Italy as longue paume and was introduced into France in the 13th century, is said to be the fastest of all ball games. The glove or gant was introduced c. 1840 and the chistera was invented by Jean 'Gantchiki' Dithurbide of Ste Pée, France. The grand chistera was invented by Melchior Curuchague of Buenos Aires, Argentina in 1888. The world's largest frontón (enclosed stadium) is the World Jaï Alaï at Miami, Florida, USA, which had a record attendance of 15,052 on 27 Dec 1975.

World Championships
The Federacion Internacional de Pelota Vasca stage world championships every four years (first in 1952). The most successful pair have been Roberto Elias and Juan Labat (Argentina), who won the Trinquete Share four times, 1952, 1958, 1962 and 1966. Labat won a record seven world titles in all. The most wins in the long court game Cesta Punta is three by Hamuy of Mexico, with two different partners, 1958, 1962 and 1966.

Highest speed
An electronically measured ball velocity of 302 km/h 188 mph was recorded by José Ramon Areitio at the Newport Jai Alai, Rhode Island, USA on 3 Aug 1979.

Longest domination
The longest domination as the world's No. 1 player was enjoyed by Chiquito de Cambo (né Joseph Apesteguy) (France), (1881–1955) from the beginning of the century until succeeded in 1938 by Jean Urruty (France) (b. 19 Oct 1913).

PÉTANQUE

Origins
The origins of pétanque or boules can be traced back over 2000 years, but it was not until 1945 that the Fédération Français de Pétanque et Jeu Provençal was formed, and subsequently the Fédération Internationale (FIPJP). The first recognised British club was formed on 30 Mar 1966 as the Chingford Club de Pétanque and the British Pétanque Association was founded in 1974.

World Championships
Winner of the most world championships (inst. 1959) has been France with eight titles to 1985.

PIGEON RACING

Earliest references
Pigeon racing developed from the use of homing

pigeons for carrying messages. The sport originated in Belgium from commercial services and the earliest long-distance race was from London to Antwerp in 1819, involving 36 pigeons.

Longest flights
The greatest recorded homing flight by a pigeon was made by one owned by the 1st Duke of Wellington (1769–1852). Released from a sailing ship off the Ichabo Islands, West Africa, on 8 April, it dropped dead a mile from its loft at Nine Elms, Wandsworth, London on 1 June 1845, 55 days later, having flown an airline route of 5400 miles *8700 km*, but an actual distance of possibly 7000 miles *11 250 km* to avoid the Sahara Desert. The official British duration record (into Great Britain) is 1173 miles *1887 km* in 15 days by C.S.O. (owned by Rosie and Bruce of Wick) in the 1976 Palamos Race. In the 1975 Palamos Race, *The Conqueror*, owned by Alan Raeside, homed to Irvine, Strathclyde, 1010 miles *1625 km*, in 43 hr 56 min. The greatest number of flights over 1000 miles flown by one pigeon is that of *Dunning Independence* owned by D. Smith which annually flew from Palamos to Dunning, Perthshire, Scotland 1039 miles *1662 km* between 1978 and 1981.

Highest speeds
In level flight in windless conditions it is very doubtful if any pigeon can exceed 60 mph *96 km/h*. The highest race speed recorded is one of 3229 yd *2952 m* per min (110.07 mph *177,14 km/h*) in the East Anglian Federation race from East Croydon on 8 May 1965 when the 1428 birds were backed by a powerful south southwest wind. The winner was owned by A. Vigeon & Son, Wickford, Essex.

The highest race speed recorded over a distance of more than 1000 km *621.37 miles* is 2432.7 yd *2224,5 m* per min (82.93 mph *133,46 km/h*) by a hen in the Central Cumberland Combine race over 683 miles 147 yd *1099,316 km* from Murray Bridge, South Australia to North Ryde, Sydney on 2 Oct 1971.

24 hr records
The world's longest reputed distance in 24 hr is 803 miles *1292 km* (velocity 1525 yd *1394 m* per min) by E. S. Petersen's winner of the 1941 San Antonio R.C. event in Texas, USA.

The best 24 hr performance into the United Kingdom is 724 miles 219 yd *1165,3 km* by E. Cardno's *Mormond Lad*, on 2 July 1977, from Nantes, France to Fraserburgh, Grampian. Average speed was 1648 yd *1507 m* per min (56.18 mph *90,41 km/h*).

Most first prizes
Owned by R. Green, of Walsall Wood, West Midlands, *Champion Breakaway* won 59 first prizes from 1972 to May 1979.

Highest priced bird
The highest recorded price paid for a pigeon is approximately £25,000 by a Japanese fancier for *De Wittslager* to Georges Desender (Belgium) in October 1978.

POLO

Earliest games
Polo is usually regarded as being of Persian origin having been played as *Pulu c.* 525 BC. Other claims have come from Tibet and the Tang Dynasty of China AD 250. The earliest polo club of modern times was the Cachar Club (founded in 1859) in Assam, India. The oldest still existing club is the Calcutta Polo Club (1862). The game was introduced into England from India in 1869 by the 10th Hussars at

The brothers Hipwood—Julian (*right*) of The Maple Leafs and Howard of Kennelot Stables—are the highest handicapped British polo players, with nine goals. By comparison, Prince Charles has a four-goal handicap. (Mike Roberts).

Aldershot, Hampshire and the earliest match was one between the 9th Lancers and the 10th Hussars on Hounslow Heath, Greater London, in July 1871. The earliest international match between England and the USA was in 1886.

Most titles
The British Open Championship for the Cowdray Park Gold Cup was first held in 1956. The most wins is five by Stowell Park, 1973–4, 1976, 1978 and 1980.

Highest handicap
The highest handicap based on eight 7½-min 'chukkas' is ten goals introduced in the USA in 1891 and in the United Kingdom and in Argentina in 1910. A total of 42 players have received ten-goal handicaps. The only two currently playing in Britain are the Mexicans Guillermo and Carlos Gracida. The latter, with Ernesto Trotz (Argentina) in 1985 is the most recent recipient of this handicap. The last (of six) ten-goal handicap players from Great Britain was Gerald Balding in 1939. A match of two 40-goal teams was staged for the only time, at Palermo, Buenos Aires, Argentina, in 1975.

The highest handicaps of current United Kingdom players are nine by Julian Hipwood (b. 23 June 1946) and by Howard Hipwood (b. 24 Mar 1950). Claire J. Tomlinson of Gloucestershire has a handicap of four, the highest ever attained by a woman.

Highest score
The highest aggregate number of goals scored in an international match is 30, when Argentina beat the USA 21–9 at Meadow Brook, Long Island, New York, USA, in Sept 1936.

POOL

Pool or championship pocket billiards with numbered balls began to become standardized *c.* 1890. The greatest exponents were Ralph Greenleaf (USA) (1899–1950) who won the 'world' professional title 19 times (1919–37) and

William Mosconi (USA) (b. 27 June 1913) who dominated the game from 1941 to 1957.

The longest consecutive run in an American straight pool match is 625 balls by Michael Eufemia at Logan's Billiard Academy, Brooklyn, NY, on 2 Feb 1960. The greatest number of balls pocketed in 24 hr is 15,780 by Vic Elliott at the Royal George, Lincoln on 2–3 Apr 1985.

The record time for potting all 15 balls in a speed competition is 40.06 sec by Ross McInnes (b. 19 Jan 1955) at Clacton, Essex on 11 Sept 1983.

A record break of 132 for 14–1 pool was set by Ross McInnes at Pontin's, Heysham, Lancashire on 3 Oct 1984.

POWERBOAT RACING

Origins
A petrol engine was first installed in a boat by Jean Joseph Etienne Lenoir (1822–1900) on the River Seine, Paris in 1865. Actual powerboat racing started in about 1900, the first prominent race being from Calais to Dover in 1903. International racing was largely established by the presentation of a Challenge Trophy by Sir Alfred Harmsworth in 1903. Thereafter racing developed mainly as a 'circuit' or short, sheltered course type competition. Offshore or sea passage races also developed, initially for displacement (non-planing) cruisers. Offshore events for fast (planing) cruisers began in 1958 with a 170 mile *273 km* passage race from Miami, USA to Nassau, Bahamas. Outboard motor, i.e. the combined motor/transmission detachable propulsion unit type racing began in the USA in about 1920. Both inboard and outboard motor boat engines are mainly petrol fuelled, but since 1950 diesel (compression ignition) engines have appeared and are widely used in offshore sport.

Highest Speeds (*For the world water speed record see page 158.*)
The highest speed recorded by a propeller-driven boat is 229.00 mph *368,54 km/h* by *The Texan*, a Kurtis Top Fuel Hydro Drag Boat, driven by Eddie Hill on 5 Sept 1982 at Chowchilla, California, USA. He also set a 440 yd *402 m* elapsed time record of 5.16 seconds in this boat at Firebird Lake, Arizona, USA on 13 Nov 1983. The official American Drag Boat Association record is 223.88 mph *360,29 km/h*

by *Final Effort* a Blown Fuel Hydro boat driven by Bob Burns at Creve Coeur Lake, St Louis, Missouri, USA on 15 July 1985 over a ¼ mile *402 m* course.

The fastest speed recognised by the Union Internationale Motonautique for an outboard powered boat is in the Class OZ unlimited, circuit boat: 169.531 mph *272,833 km/h* by a Carlson hydroplane powered by an Evinrude V8 engine, driven by Bob Hering (USA); he also set the world Formula One record at 165.338 mph *266,085 km/h*, both at Parker, Arizona on 21 Apr 1986.

The fastest speed recognised for an offshore boat was set by *Innovation*, a 35 ft *10,7 m* Maelstrom boat powered by three Johnson Evinrude outboard engines each of 214 cu in *3507 cc*, driven by Mike Drury at a mean speed for two runs of 131.088 mph *210,966 km/h* at New Orleans, Louisiana, USA on 31 March 1984.

The fastest speed recorded for a diesel (compression ignition) boat is 218,26 km/h *135.62 mph* by the hydroplane *Iveco World Leader*, powered by an Aifo-Fiat engine, driven by Carlo Bonomi at Venice, Italy in 1985.

Highest race speeds
The highest speed recorded in an offshore race is 103.29 mph *166,22 km/h* by Tony Garcia (USDA) in a Class I powerboat at Key West, Florida, USA in November 1983.

Longest races
The longest offshore race has been the Port Richborough London to Monte Carlo Marathon Offshore International event. The race extended over 2947 miles *4742 km* in 14 stages on 10–25 June 1972. It was won by *H.T.S.* (GB) driven by Mike Bellamy, Eddie Chater and Jim Brooker in 71 hr 35 min 56 sec for an average of 41.15 mph *66,24 km/h*. The longest circuit race is the 24 hour race held annually since 1962 on the River Seine at Rouen, France. The 1983 winners Francois Greens, Jan van Brockels and Roger Robin of Belgium drove a Johnson outboard engined Piranha boat at an average speed of 75,02 km/h *46.63 mph*.

Longest Jetboat Jumps
The longest ramp jump achieved by a jetboat has been 120 ft *36,57 m* by Peter Horak (USA) in a Glastron Carlson CVX 20 Jet Deluxe with a 460 Ford V8 engine (take-off speed 55 mph *88 km/h*) for a documentary TV film, at Salton Sea, California, USA on 26 Apr 1980. The longest leap on to land is 172 ft *38,7 m* by Norm Bagrie (NZ) from the Shotover River on 1 July 1982 in the 1½ ton jetboat *Valvolene*.

RACKETS

Origins
There is record of the sale of a racket court at Southernhay, Exeter, Devon dated 12 Jan 1798. The game which is of 17th century origin was played by debtors in the Fleet Prison, London in the middle of the 18th century, and an inmate, Robert Mackay, claimed the first 'world' title in 1820. The first closed court champion was Francis Erwood at Woolwich in 1860. A new court was constructed at the Seacourt Club, Hayling Island, Hampshire in 1979.

Longest reign
Of the 22 world champions since 1820 the longest reign is by Geoffrey Willoughby Thomas Atkins (b. 20 Jan 1927) who held the title after beating the professional James Dear (1910–81) in 1954 and retired, after defending it four times, in April 1972.

Most Amateur titles
Since the Amateur singles championship was instituted in 1888 the most titles won by an individual is nine by Edgar Maximilian Baerlein (1879–1971) between 1903 and 1923. Since the institution of the Amateur doubles championship in 1890 the most shares in titles has been eleven by David Sumner Milford (1905–84), between 1938 and 1959 and John Ross Thompson (b. 10 May 1918) between 1948 and 1966. Milford also won seven Amateur singles titles (1930–51), an Open title (1936) and held the World title from 1937 to 1946. Thompson has additionally won an Open singles title and five Amateur singles titles.

RACKETBALL

Racquetball using a 40 ft by 20 ft court was invented in 1950 by Joe Sobek at the Greenwich YMCA, Connecticut, USA, originally as Paddle Rackets. The International Racquetball Association was founded in 1968 by Bob Kendler (USA). John Treharne won three British titles, 1981–83.

Racketball using a 32 ft by 21 ft court (as for squash) was introduced to Britain by Ian Wright in 1976. The British Racketball Association was formed and staged inaugural British National Championships in 1984. Men's and women's champions were Denis Secher and Greer Batty respectively.

RODEO

Origins
Rodeo which developed from 18th century *fiestas* came into being in the early days of the North American cattle industry. The sport originated in Mexico and spread from there into the cattle regions of the USA. Steer wrestling came in with Bill Pickett (1870–1932) of Texas, in 1900.

The largest rodeo in the world is the Calgary Exhibition and Stampede at Calgary, Alberta, Canada. In 1981 the total paid attendance for the rodeo events over ten days was 122,268. The National Finals Rodeo is organised annually by the Professional Rodeo Cowboys Association (PRCA). In 1985 a record $1,790,000 prize money was offered for the event, staged in Las Vegas, Nevada, USA.

Most world titles
The record number of all-around titles in the PRCA world championships is six by Larry Mahan (USA) (b. 21 Nov 1943) in 1966–70 and 1973 and, consecutively, 1974–9 by Tom Ferguson (b. 20 Dec 1950). Tom Ferguson had record career earnings of $978,809 to 1985. Jim Shoulders (b. 1928) of Henryetta, Oklahoma, USA has won a record 16 world championships between 1949 and 1959. The record figure for prize money in a single season is $153,391 by Roy Cooper (b. 13 Nov 1955) of Durant, Oklahoma, USA in 1983. The record for one rodeo is $30,677 by Dee Pickett at the National Finals Rodeo, Oklahoma City in December 1984.

Youngest champion
The youngest winner of a world title is Metha Brorsen, of Oklahoma, USA, who won the International Rodeo Association Cowgirls barrel-racing event in 1975 at 11 years old. The youngest champion in Professional Rodeo Cowboys Association/Women's Professional Rodeo Association competition is Jackie Jo Perrin of Antlers, Oklahoma, USA, who won the barrel-racing title in 1977 at age 13.

Time records
Records for PRCA timed events, such as calf-roping and steer-wrestling, are not always comparable, because of the widely varying conditions due to the size of arenas and amount of start given the stock. The fastest time recorded for roping a calf is 5.7 sec by Lee Phillips at Assiniboia, Saskatchewan, Canada in 1978, and the fastest time for overcoming a steer is 2.4 sec by James Bynum, at Marietta, Oklahoma, USA, in 1955, by Carl Deaton at Tulsa, Oklahoma, USA in 1976 and by Gene Melton at Pecatonica, Illinois, USA, in 1976.

The highest score in bull riding was 98 points out of a possible 100 by Denny Flynn on *Red Lightning* at Palestine, Illinois, USA in 1979.

Champion bull
The top bucking bull was probably *Tornado*, who bucked out of the chute 220 times before Freckles Brown, in 1967, became the first cowboy to ride him to the eight-second bell. *Tornado* retired a year later after a 14-year career.

Champion bronc
Traditionally a bronc called *Midnight* owned by Jim McNab of Alberta, Canada was never ridden in 12 appearances at the Calgary Stampede.

ROLLER SKATING

Origins
The first roller skate was devised by Jean Joseph Merlin (1735–1803) of Huy, Belgium, in 1760 and demonstrated by him in London but with disastrous results. James L. Plimpton of New York produced the present four-wheeled type and patented it in January 1863. The first indoor rink was opened in the Haymarket, London, in about 1824.

Most titles *Speed*
Most world speed titles have been won by Alberta Vianello (Italy) with 16 between 1953 and 1965. Most British national individual men's titles have been won by Michael Colin McGeogh (b. 30 Mar 1946) with 19 in 1966–85. Chloe Ronaldson (b. 30 Nov 1939) has won 40 individual and 14 team ladies' senior titles from 1958 to 1985.

Most titles *Figure*
The records for figure titles are five by Karl Heinz Losch in 1958–9, 1961–2 and 1966, and four by Astrid Bader, both of W. Germany, in 1965–8. Most world pair titles have been taken by Dieter Fingerle (W. Germany) with four in 1959, 1965–7 with two different partners.

Speed skating
The fastest speed put up in an official world record is 25.78 mph *41,48 km/h* when Giuseppe Cantarella (Italy) (b. 13 Aug 1944) recorded 34.9 sec for 440 yd *402 m* on a road at Catania, Sicily on 28 Sept 1963. The world mile record on a rink is 2 min 25.1 sec by Gianni Ferretti (Italy) (b. 11 May 1948) at Inzell, W. Germany on 28 Sept 1968. The greatest distance skated in 1 hr on a rink by a woman is 37,097 km *23.051 miles* by Annie Lambrechts (Belgium) at Louvain, Belgium on 1 July 1985 during a 50 km record of 1 hr 21 min 25 sec. The men's record on a track is 37,230 km *23.133 miles* by Alberto Civolani (Italy) (b. 16 Mar 1933) at Inzell, W. Germany on 28 Sept 1968. He went on to skate 50 miles *80,46 km* in 2 hr 20 min 33.1 sec.

Largest rink
The greatest indoor rink ever to operate was

located in the Grand Hall, Olympia, London. Opened 1890 and closed in 1912 it had an actual skating area of 68,000 ft² *6 300 m²*. The current largest is the main arena of 34,981 ft² *3250 m²* at Guptill Roll-Arena, Boght Corner, New York, USA. The total rink area is 41,380 ft² *3844 m²*.

Endurance

Theodore James Coombs (b. 1954) of Hermosa Beach, California, skated 5193 miles *8357 km* from Los Angeles to New York and back to Yates Center, Kansas from 30 May to 14 Sept 1979.

Land's End to John o'Groats

Steve Fagan, 20, roller skated the distance, 925 miles *1488 km*, in 9 days 10 hr 25 min on 1–10 May 1984, averaging 157 km *98 miles* a day.

ROLLER HOCKEY

Roller hockey (previously known as Rink Hockey in Europe) was introduced to Britain as Rink Polo, at the old Lava rink, Denmark Hill, London in the late 1870s. The Amateur Rink Hockey Association was formed in 1908, and in 1913 became the National Rink Hockey (now Roller Hockey) Association. Britain won the inaugural World Championship in 1936 since when Portugal has won most titles with 12 between 1947 and 1982. The European Championship (inst. 1926) was won by Portugal a record 15 times between 1947 and 1977.

ROWING

Oldest race

The Sphinx stela of Amenhotep II (1450–1425 BC) records that he *stroked* a boat for some three miles. The earliest established sculling race is the Doggett's Coat and Badge, which was first rowed on 1 Aug 1716 from London Bridge to Chelsea and is still contested annually. Although rowing regattas were held in Venice in 1300 the first English regatta probably took place on the Thames by the Ranelagh Gardens, near Putney in 1775.

Kenton Grua, Rudi Petschek and Steve Reynolds broke the record for rowing the Grand Canyon along the Colorado river in northern Arizona, USA. The 277 mile *445,8 km* distance was first navigated in 1869 by John Wessley Powell; Messrs Grua, Petschek and Reynolds completed it in 36 hr 38 min 29 sec in 1983.

Most Olympic medals

Six oarsmen have won three gold medals: John B. Kelly (USA) (1889–1960), father of the late HSH Princess Grace of Monaco, in the sculls (1920) and double sculls (1920 and 1924); his cousin Paul Vincent Costello (USA) (b. 27 Dec 1899) in the double sculls (1920, 1924 and 1928); Jack Beresford, Jr (GB) (1899–1977) in the sculls (1924), coxless fours (1932) and double sculls (1936), Vyacheslav Ivanov (USSR) (b. 30 July 1938) in the sculls (1956, 1960 and 1964) and Siegfried Brietzke (GDR) (b. 12 June 1952) in the coxless pairs (1972) and coxless fours (1976, 1980) and Pertti Karpinen (Finland) (b. 17 Feb 1953) in the sculls 1976, 1980 and 1984.

World Championships

World rowing championships distinct from the Olympic Games were first held in 1962, at first four-yearly, but from 1974 annually, except in Olympic years.

The most gold medals won is five by Ulrich Diessner (GDR) (b. 27 Dec 1954), four at coxed fours 1977–9 and 1982 and one at coxed pairs in 1983. He also won an Olympic gold medal at coxed fours in 1980. Four single sculls titles have been won by Peter-Michael Kolbe (W. Germany) (b. 2 Aug 1953), 1975, 1978, 1981 and 1983 and in the women's events by Christine Hahn (née Schieblich) (GDR) (b. 31 Dec 1954), 1974–5, 1977–8 (as well as the 1976 Olympic title). Crews to win four gold medals have been the twins Bernd and Jörg Landvoigt (GDR) (b. 23 Mar 1951), coxless pairs 1974–5, 1978–9 (and the Olympic titles of 1976 and 1980), and Siegfried Brietzke, Andreas Decker, Stefan Sempler and Wolfgang Mager (GDR), coxless fours 1974–5, 1977, 1979 (and the 1976 Olympic title).

Boat Race

The earliest University Boat Race, which Oxford won, was from Hambledon Lock to Henley Bridge on 10 June 1829. Outrigged eights were first used in 1846. In the 132 races to 1986, Cambridge won 69 times, Oxford 62 times and there was a dead heat on 24 Mar 1877.

The race record time for the course of 4 miles 374 yd *6779 km* (Putney to Mortlake) is 16 min 45 sec by Oxford on 18 Mar 1984. This represents an average speed of 15.09 mph *24,28 km/h*. The smallest winning margin has been by a canvas by Oxford in 1952 and 1980. The greatest margin (apart from sinking) was Cambridge's win by 20 lengths in 1900.

Boris Rankov (Oxford, 1978–83) rowed in a record six winning boats. Susan Brown (b. 29 June 1958), the first woman to take part, coxed the winning Oxford boats in 1981 and 1982. Daniel Topolski coached Oxford to ten successive victories 1976–85.

The heaviest man ever to row in a University boat has been Stephen G. H. Plunkett (Queen's) the No. 5 in the 1976 Oxford boat at 229 lb *104 kg*. The 1983 Oxford crew averaged a record 204.3 lb *92,5 kg*. The lightest oarsman was the 1882 Oxford Stroke, Alfred Herbert Higgins, at 9 st 6½ lb *60 kg*. The lightest coxes, Francis Henry Archer (Cambridge) (1843–89) in 1862 and Hart Parker Vincent Massey (Oxford) (b. Canada, 30 Mar 1918) in 1939, were both 5 st 2 lb *32,6 kg*.

Head of the River

A processional race for eights instituted in 1926, the Head has an entry limit of 420 crews (3780 competitors). The record for the course Mortlake–Putney (the reverse of the Boat race) is 17 min 10.42 sec by the ARA National Squad in 1982.

Henley Royal Regatta

The annual regatta at Henley-on-Thames, Oxfordshire, was inaugurated on 26 Mar 1839. Since then the course, except in 1923, has been about 1 mile 550 yd *2112 m* varying slightly according to the length of boat. In 1967 the

FASTEST TIMES OVER 2000 m COURSE

(STILL WATER) MEN

	min sec	Country	Place	Date	
Single Sculls	6:48.08	Pertti Karppinen, Finland	Willebroek, Belgium	1 Sept	1985
Double Sculls	6:12.48	Norway	Montreal, Canada	23 July	1976
Coxed Pairs	6:49.75	GDR	Duisberg, W Germany	4 Sept	1983
Coxless Pairs	6:32.63	GDR	Lucerne, Switzerland	23 Aug	1982
Coxed Fours	6:05.21	GDR	Lucerne, Switzerland	17 June	1984
Coxless Fours	5:53.65	GDR	Montreal, Canada	23 July	1976
Quadruple Sculls	5:45.97	GDR	Duisberg, W. Germany	4 Sept	1983
Eights	5:27.14	USA	Lucerne, Switzerland	17 June	1984

(STILL WATER) WOMEN

	min sec	Country	Place	Date	
Single Sculls	7:39.83	Cornelia Linse, GDR	Lucerne, Switzerland	14 July	1985
Double Sculls	6:58.80	GDR	Willebroek, Belgium	1 Sept	1985
Coxless Pairs	7:25.08	Romania	Willebroek, Belgium	1 Sept	1985
Coxed Fours	6:50.08	GDR	Willebroek, Belgium	1 Sept	1985
Quadruple Sculls	6:16.31	GDR	East Berlin, GDR	14 June	1986
Eights	6:14.00	GDR	Willebroek, Belgium	1 Sept	1985

Note that the standard distance for women's international rowing was increased from 1000 m to 2000 m from January 1985.

shorter craft were 'drawn up' so all bows start level.

The most wins in the Diamond Challenge Sculls (inst. 1844) is six consecutively by Stuart A. Mackenzie (b. 5 Apr 1937) (Australia and GB) 1957–62. The record time is 7 min 40 sec by Sean Drea (Neptune RC, Ireland) on 5 July 1975. The Grand Challenge Cup (inst. 1839) for eights, has been won 27 times by Leander crews between 1840 and 1953. The record time for the event is 6 min 13 sec by Harvard Univ, USA, and a combined Leander/Thames Tradesmen crew, both on 5 July 1975.

Sculling
The record number of wins in the Wingfield Sculls (Putney to Mortlake) (instituted 1830) is seven by Jack Beresford, Jr. from 1920 to 1926. The fastest time for the course has been 21 min 11 sec by Leslie Frank 'Dick' Southwood (b. 18 Jan 1906) in winning the Wingfield Sculls on 12 Aug 1933.

Highest speed
The highest recorded speed on non-tidal water for 2000 m *2187 yd* is by an American eight in 5 min 27.14 sec (22,01 km/h *13.68 mph*) at Lucerne, Switzerland on 17 June 1984. A crew from Penn AC, USA, was timed in 5 min 18.8 sec (14.03 mph *22,58 km/h*) in the FISA Championships on the River Meuse, Liege, Belgium, on 17 Aug 1930.

24 hours
The greatest distance rowed in 24 hrs (upstream and downstream) by a crew of eight is 130 miles *209 kms* by members of the Renmark Rowing Club, South Australia, on 20–1 Apr 1984.

Cross Channel
Ivor Lloyd sculled across the English Channel in a record 3 hr 35 min 1 sec on 4 May 1983.

River Thames
A crew of five from Poplar Fire Station, London Fire Brigade rowed the navigable length of the Thames, 185.88 miles *299,14 km*, from Lechlade Bridge, Gloucestershire to Southend Pier, Essex in 45 hr 32 min in a 22 ft 10 in *6,96 m* skiff on 16–18 Apr 1984.

The fastest time from Folly Bridge, Oxford to Westminster Bridge, London (112 miles *180 km*) is 14 hr 25 min 15 sec by an eight from Kingston Rowing Club on 1 Feb 1986.

Longest race
The longest annual rowing race is the annual Tour du Lac Leman, Geneva, Switzerland for coxed fours (the five man crew taking turns as cox) over 160 km *99 miles*. The record winning time is 12 hr 52 min by LAGA Delft, Netherlands on 3 Oct 1982.

International Dragon Boat Races
Instituted in 1975 and held annually in Hong Kong, the fastest time achieved for the 640 metres *700 yd* course is 2 min 27.45 sec by the Chinese Shun De team on 30 June 1985. The best time for a British team was 2 min 51.8 sec by an Amateur Rowing Association team in 1984. Teams have 28 members—26 rowers, one steersman and one drummer.

RUGBY LEAGUE

There have been four different scoring systems in rugby league football. For the purpose of these records all points totals remain as they were under the system in operation at the time they were made.

Origins
The Rugby League was formed on 29 Aug 1895 at the George Hotel, Huddersfield, W. Yorks. Twenty one clubs from Yorkshire and Lancashire were present and all but one agreed to resign from the Rugby Union and form the 'Northern Rugby Football Union'. Though payment for loss of wages was the major cause of the breakaway the 'Northern Union' did not embrace full professionalism until 1898. A reduction in the number of players per team from 15 to 13 took place in 1906. The title 'Rugby Football League' was adopted in 1928.

Most titles
There have been seven World Cup Competitions. Australia have most wins, with four, 1957, 1968, 1970 and 1977 as well as a win in the International Championship of 1975.

The Northern Rugby League was formed in 1901. The word 'Northern' was dropped in 1980. Wigan have won the League Championship a record nine times (1909, 1922, 1926, 1934, 1946, 1947, 1950, 1952 and 1960).

In the Rugby League Challenge Cup (inaugurated 1896–7 season) Leeds have most wins with ten, 1910, 1923, 1932, 1936, 1941–2 (wartime), 1957, 1968, 1977–8. Oldham is the only club to appear in four consecutive Cup Finals (1924–7).

Since 1974 there have been five major competitions for RL clubs: Challenge Cup, League Championship, Premiership, John Player Trophy and County Cup. Over this period only Widnes have won three in one season (Challenge Cup, John Player Trophy and Lancashire Cup) in 1978–79. Wigan has a record 36 wins in these five competitions.

Three clubs have won all possible major Rugby League trophies in one season: Hunslet, 1907–8 season, Huddersfield, 1914–15 and Swinton, 1927–8, all won the Challenge Cup, League Championship, County Cup and County League (now defunct).

HIGHEST SCORES

Senior match
The highest aggregate score in a game where a senior club has been concerned was 121 points, when Huddersfield beat Swinton Park Rangers by 119 (19 goals, 27 tries) to 2 (one goal) in the first round of the Northern Union Cup on 28 Feb 1914. The highest score in League football is 112 points by Leeds v. Coventry (nil) on 12 Apr 1913.

Challenge Cup Final
The highest score in a Challenge Cup Final is 38 points (8 tries, 7 goals) by Wakefield Trinity v. Hull (5) at Wembley on 14 May 1960. The record aggregate is 52 points when Wigan beat Hull 28–24 at Wembley on 4 May 1985. The greatest winning margin was 34 points when Huddersfield beat St Helens 37–3 at Oldham on 1 May 1915.

International match
The highest score in an international match is Australia's 63–13 defeat of England at Paris, France on 31 Dec 1933. The highest score in a World Cup match is the 53–19 win by Great Britain over New Zealand at Hameau, Paris on 4 Nov 1972.

Touring teams
The record score for a British team touring Australasia is 101 points by England v. South Australia (nil) at Adelaide in May 1914. The record for a touring team in Britain is 92 (10 goals, 24 tries) by Australia against Bramley's 7 (2 goals, 1 try) at the Barley Mow Ground, Bramley, near Leeds, on 9 Nov 1921.

Most points *Season*
Leigh scored a record 1436 points (258 tries, 199 goals, 6 drop goals) in the 1985–6 season, playing in 43 Cup and League games.

HIGHEST INDIVIDUAL SCORES

Most points, goals and tries in a game
George Henry 'Tich' West (1882–1927) of Hull Kingston Rovers scored 53 points (10 goals and a record 11 tries) in a First Round Challenge Cup-tie v. Brookland Rovers on 4 Mar 1905.

The most goals in a Cup match is 22 kicked by Jim Sullivan (1903–77) for Wigan v. Flimby and Fothergill on 14 Feb 1925. The most goals in a League match is 15 by Mick Stacey for Leigh v. Doncaster on 28 Mar 1976. The most tries in a League match is 10 by Lionel Cooper (b. Australia 1922) for Huddersfield v. Keighley on 17 Nov 1951.

Most points *League*
Jimmy Lomas (Salford) scored a record 39 points (5 tries, 12 goals) against Liverpool City (78–0) on 2 Feb 1907.

Most points *Season & career*
The record number of points in a season was 496 by Benjamin Lewis Jones (Leeds) (b. 11 Apr 1931) 194 goals, 36 tries, in 1956–7.

Neil Fox scored 6220 points (2575 goals, 358

Keith Elwell hanging onto the ball in the 1984 Challenge Cup Final. In his career he has gained more winners or runners'-up medals in major competitions than anyone else; in this instance a winners' as Widnes defeated Wigan. (Colorsport).

tries, 4 drop goals) in a senior Rugby League career from 10 Apr 1956 to the end of the 1979–80 season.

Most tries *Season & career*
Albert Aaron Rosenfeld (1885–1970) (Huddersfield), an Australian-born wing-threequarter, scored 80 tries in 42 matches in the 1913–14 season.

Brian Bevan (b. Australia, 24 Apr 1924), a wing-threequarter, scored 796 tries in 18 seasons (16 with Warrington, two with Blackpool Borough) from 1946 to 1964. He scored 740 for Warrington, 17 for Blackpool and 39 in representative matches.

Most goals *Season & career*
The record number of goals in a season is 221 by David Watkins (b. 5 Mar 1942) (Salford) in the 1972–3 season.

Jim Sullivan (Wigan) kicked 2859 goals in his club and representative career, 1921–46.

Most consecutive scores
David Watkins (Salford) played and scored in every club game during seasons 1972–3 and 1973–4; contributing 41 tries and 403 goals—a total of 929 points, in 92 games.

Individual international records
Jim Sullivan (Wigan) played in most internationals (60 for Wales and Great Britain) kicked most goals (160) and scored most points (329).

Mick Sullivan (no kin) (b. 12 Jan 1934) of Huddersfield, Wigan, St Helens and York played in 51 international games for England and Great Britain and scored a record 45 tries.

Most Challenge Cup Finals
Eric Batten (Leeds, Bradford Northern and Featherstone Rovers) played in a record eight Challenge Cup Finals including war-time guest appearances between 1941 and 1952 and was on four winning sides.

Seven players have been in four Challenge Cup winning sides—Alan Edwards, Eric Batten, Alex Murphy, Brian Lockwood, Mick Adams, Keith Elwell and Eric Hughes. Alan Edwards was the only one to do so with four different clubs, Salford 1938, Leeds 1942, Dewsbury 1943, Bradford Northern 1949.

Youngest and oldest players
Harold Wagstaff (1891–1939) played his first League game for Huddersfield at 15 yr 175 days, for Yorkshire at 17 yr 141 days, and for England at 17 yr 228 days.

The youngest player in a Cup Final was Shaun Edwards (b. 17 Oct 1966) at 17 yr 201 days for Wigan when they lost 6–19 to Widnes at Wembley on 5 May 1984. He became the youngest Great Britain international when he played against France at Headingley, Leeds on 1 Mar 1985 at 18 yr 135 days.

The oldest player for Great Britain was Jeff Grayshon (b. 4 Mar 1949) at 36 yr 243 days *v.* New Zealand at Wigan on 2 Nov 1985.

Most durable player
The most appearances for one club is 769 by Jim Sullivan for Wigan, 1921–46. He played a record 921 first class games in all. The longest continuous playing career is that of Augustus John 'Gus' Risman (b. Cardiff 21 Mar 1911) who played his first game for Salford on 31 August 1929 and his last for Batley on 27 December 1954.

Keith Elwell (b. 12 Feb 1950) played in 239 consecutive games for Widnes from May 1977 to September 1982. In his career, 1972–85, he received a record 28 winners' or runners-up medals in the major competitions.

Most and least successful teams
Wigan won 31 consecutive league games from February 1970 to February 1971. Hull are the only club to win all League games in a season, 26 in Division II 1978–9. Doncaster hold the record of losing 40 consecutive League games from 16 Nov 1975 to 21 Apr 1977.

Record transfer fee
The highest RL transfer fee is £100,000 paid to Widnes for winger Joe Lydon (b. 26 Nov 1963) by Wigan on 20 Jan 1986.

Greatest crowds
The greatest attendance at any Rugby League match is 102,569 for the Warrington *v.* Halifax Challenge Cup Final replay at Odsal Stadium, Bradford, on 5 May 1954.

The record attendance for any international match is 70,204 for the Test between Australia and England on the Sydney Cricket Ground on 6 June 1932. The highest international attendance in Britain is 43,500 for the Test between Great Britain and Australia at Odsal Stadium, Bradford on 29 January 1949.

AMATEUR RUGBY LEAGUE

The British Amateur Rugby League Association (BARLA) was formed in 1973 'to foster, develop, extend and control amateur rugby league football in Great Britain'. Prior to that year the ultimate control of amateurs as well as professionals rested with the Rugby Football League.

National Cup
Pilkington Recreation (St Helens, Merseyside) have won the National Cup four times (1975, 1979, 1980, 1982).

Highest score *Major competition*
Humberside beat Carlisle by 138 points to nil in the second round of the National Inter-league Competition on 20 Oct 1984.

RUGBY UNION

Records are determined in terms of present day scoring values, i.e. a try at 4 points; a dropped goal, penalty or goal from a mark at 3 points; and a conversion at 2 points. The *actual* score, in accordance with which ever of the eight earlier systems was in force at the time, is also given, in brackets.

Origins
Though there are records of a game with many similarities to Rugby dating back to the Roman occupation, the game is traditionally said to have originated from a breach of the rules of the football played in November 1823 at Rugby School by William Webb Ellis (later the Rev) (*c.* 1807–72). This handling code of football evolved gradually and was known to have been played at Cambridge University by 1839. The Rugby Football Union was founded on 26 Jan 1871. The International Rugby Football Board (IRFB) was founded in 1886.

INTERNATIONAL CHAMPIONSHIP

The International Championship was first contested by England, Ireland, Scotland and Wales in 1884. France first played in 1910.

Most wins

Wales have won a record 21 times outright and tied for first a further ten times. Since 1910 Wales have 15 wins and 9 ties and England 15 wins and 7 ties.

Highest team score

The highest score in an International Championship match was set at Swansea in 1910 when Wales beat France 49–14 or 59–16 on present day scoring values (8 goals, 1 penalty goal, 2 tries to 1 goal, 2 penalty goals, 1 try).

Season's scoring

Jean-Patrick Lescarboura (France) (b. 12 Mar 1961) scored a record 54 points (10 penalty goals, 6 conversions, 4 dropped goals) in 1984.

Individual match records

W. J. Bancroft kicked a record 9 goals (8 conversions and 1 penalty goal) for Wales v. France at Swansea on 1910.

HIGHEST TEAM SCORES

Internationals

The highest score in any full International was when France beat Spain by 92 points (including 19 tries) to nil at Oléron, France on 4 Mar 1979.

The highest aggregate score for any International match between the Four Home Unions is 69 when England beat Wales by 69 points (7 goals, 1 drop goal and 6 tries) to 0 at Blackheath, London in 1881. (Note: there was no point scoring in 1881).

The highest score by any Overseas side in an International in the British Isles is 53 points (7 goals, 1 drop goal and 2 tries) to 0 when South Africa beat Scotland at Murrayfield, Edinburgh, on 24 Nov 1951 (44–0).

Tour match

The record score for any international tour match is 125–0 (17 goals, 5 tries and 1 penalty goal) (103–0) when New Zealand beat Northern New South Wales at Quirindi, Australia, on 30 May 1962. The highest under scoring in use for the game is 117–6 for New Zealand's defeat of South Australia on 1 May 1974.

Match

In Denmark, Comet beat Lindo by 194–0 on 17 Nov 1973. The highest British score is 174–0 by 7th Signal Regiment v. 4 Armoured Workshop, REME, on 5 Nov 1980 at Herford, W. Germany. Scores of over 200 points have been recorded in school matches, for example Radford School beat Hills Court 214 points (31 goals and 7 tries) to 0 (200–0) on 20 Nov 1886.

Season

The highest number of points accumulated in a season by a rugby club is 1607 points by Pontypool, Gwent in 1983–4. The record number of tries is 269 by Bridgend, Mid-Glamorgan, 1983–4.

HIGHEST INDIVIDUAL SCORES

Internationals

Colin Mair scored 30 points (9 conversions, 4 penalty goals) for Scotland v. Japan at Tokyo on 18 Sept 1977. The highest individual points score in any match between members of the International Board is 26 by Alan Hewson (b. 1953) (1 try, 2 conversions, 5 penalty goals and a drop goal) for New Zealand against Australia at Auckland on 11 Sept 1982.

Ian Scott Smith (Scotland) (1903–72) scored a record six consecutive international tries in 1925; comprised of the last three v. France and two weeks later, the first three v. Wales. His 24 tries, 1924–33, is the record for an international career.

The most points scored in an international career is 301 by Andrew Robertson Irvine (Heriots) (b. 16 Sept 1951), 273 for Scotland (including 12 v. Romania) and 28 for the British Lions, from 1973 to 1982.

Season

The first class rugby scoring record for a season is 581 points by Samuel Arthur Doble (1944–77) of Moseley, in 52 matches in 1971–2. He also scored 47 points for England in South Africa out of season.

Career

William Henry 'Dusty' Hare (b. 29 Nov 1952) scored 5926 points in first class games from 1971–86, comprising 1800 for Nottingham, 3202 for Leicester, 240 for England, 88 for the British Lions and 596 in other representative matches.

Match

Jannie van der Westhuizen scored 80 points (14 tries, 9 conversions, 1 dropped goal, 1 penalty goal) for Carnarvon (88) v. Williston (12) at North West Cape, S. Africa on 11 March 1972.

In a junior house match in February 1967 at William Ellis School, Edgware, Greater London, between Cumberland and Nunn, Thanos Morphitis, 12, contributed 90 points (13 tries and 19 conversions) (77) to Cumberland's winning score.

Paul Thorburn, who scored 52 points for Wales in the 1986 season. He twice scored 5 penalties in a game and spectacularly drop-kicked from over 70 yd *64 m* against Scotland. (Colorsport).

All-rounder

Canadian international, Barrie Burnham, scored all possible ways—try, conversion, penalty goal, drop goal, goal from mark—for Meralomas v. Georgians (20–11) at Vancouver, BC, on 26 Feb 1966.

Most International Appearances

Cameron Michael Henderson Gibson (b. 3 Dec 1942) played in 69 internationals for Ireland, 1964–79, a record for matches between the seven member countries of the 'International Rugby Football Board' and France. Including 12 appearances for the British Lions, he played in a total of 81 international matches. Willie John McBride (b. Co. Antrim, 6 June 1940) made a record 17 appearances for the British Lions, as well as 63 for Ireland.

Youngest International

Edinburgh Academy pupils Ninian Jamieson Finlay (1858–1936) and Charles Reid (1864–1909) were both 17 yr 36 days old when they played for Scotland v. England in 1875 and 1881 respectively. However, as Finlay had one less leap year in his lifetime up to his first cap, the outright record must be credited to him. Daniel Brendan Carroll (b. 17 Feb 1892) was aged only 16 yr 149 days when he played for Australia in the 1908 Olympic Games Rugby tournament — not considered to be a 'full' international.

County Championships

The County Championships (inst. 1889) have been won most often by Gloucestershire with 15 titles (1910, 1913, 1920–2, 1930–2, 1937, 1972, 1974–6 and 1983–4). The most individual appearances is 104 by Richard Trickey (Sale) (b. 6 Mar 1945) for Lancashire between 1964 and 1978.

Club Championships

The most outright wins in the RFU Club Competition (John Player Cup, inst. 1971–2) is three by Leicester, 1979–81 and Bath, 1984–6. Gloucester won in 1972 and 1978 and shared the Cup in 1982.

The most wins in the Welsh Rugby Union Challenge Cup (Schweppes Welsh Cup, inst. 1971–2) is five by Llanelli, 1973–6 and 1985. The most wins in the Scottish League Division One (inst. 1973–4) is nine by Hawick, 1973–4 to 1977–8, 1981–2 and 1983–6.

Seven-a-sides *Origins*

Seven-a-side rugby dates from 28 Apr 1883 when Melrose RFC Borders, in order to alleviate the poverty of a club in such a small town, staged a seven-a-side tournament. The idea was that of Ned Haig, the town's butcher.

Middlesex Seven-a-sides

The Middlesex Seven-a-sides were inaugurated in 1926. The most wins is nine by Richmond (inc. once by their second Seven) (1951, 1953, 1955, 1974–5, 1977, 1979–80, 1983).

Greatest crowd

The record paying attendance is 104,000 for Scotland's 12–10 win over Wales at Murrayfield, Edinburgh, on 1 Mar 1975.

Highest posts

The world's highest Rugby Union goal posts are 110 ft $\frac{1}{2}$ in *33,54 m* high at the Roan Antelope Rugby Union Club, Luanshya, Zambia. The posts at Brixham RFC, Devonshire, are 57 ft *17,37 m* high with an additional 1 ft *0,30 m* spike.

Longest kicks

The longest recorded successful drop-goal is 90 yd *82 m* by Gerald Hamilton 'Gerry' Brand (b. 8 Oct 1906) for South Africa v. England at Twickenham, Greater London, on 2 Jan 1932. This was taken 7 yd *6 m* inside the England 'half' 55 yd *50 m* from the posts and dropped over the dead ball line.

The place kick record is reputed to be 100 yd *91 m* at Richmond Athletic Ground, Greater London, by Douglas Francis Theodore Morkel (b. 1886) in an unsuccessful penalty for South Africa v. Surrey on 19 Dec 1906. This was not measured until 1932. In the match Bridlington School 1st XV v. an Army XV at Bridlington, Humberside on 29 Jan 1944, Ernie Cooper (b. 21 May 1926), captaining the school, landed a penalty from a measured 81 yd *74 m* from the post with a kick which carried over the dead ball line. The international record was set at 70 yd 8½ in *21,55 m* by Paul Thorburn (b. 24 Nov 1962) for Wales v. Scotland on 1 Feb 1986.

Fastest try
The fastest try in an international game was when H. L. 'Bart' Price scored for England v. Wales at Twickenham on 20 Jan 1923 less than 10 sec after kick off.

Most tries
Alan Morley (b. 25 June 1950) has scored 473 tries in senior rugby in 1968–86 including 378 for Bristol, a record for one club. John Huins scored 85 tries in 1953–4, 73 for St Luke's College, Exeter and 12 more for Neath and in trial games.

Longest try
The longest 'try' ever executed is by a team of 15, from Power-House RUFC, Victoria, Australia, who ran a try of 1470.6 miles *2366,7 km* on 4–13 Mar 1983 around Albert Park Lake, Victoria. There were no forward passes or knock-ons, and the ball was touched down between the posts in the prescribed manner (Law 12).

Most successful team
The Leamington Spa junior team played 92 successive games without defeat from 6 Oct 1980 to 13 Apr 1984.

Shinty

Origins
Shinty (from the Gaelic *sinteag*, a bound) has roots reaching back more than 2000 years to the ancient game of *camanachd*, the sport of the curved stick, the diversion of the heroes of Celtic history and legend. It was effective battle training, exercising speed and co-ordination of eye and arm along with aggression and cool self-control. In spite of the break up of the clan system in the Highlands of Scotland, the "ball plays", involving whole parishes, without limit in number or time except the fall of night, continued in areas such as Lochaber, Badenoch and Strathglass. Whisky and the inspiration of the bagpipes were important ingredients of these occasions. The ruling body of this apparently ungovernable game was established in 1893 when the Camanachd Association was set up at Kingussie, Highland.

Most titles
Newtonmore, Highland has won the Camanachd Association Challenge Cup (instituted 1896) a record 28 times, 1896–1986. Johnnie Campbell, David Ritchie and Hugh Chisholm, all of Newtonmore have won a record 11 winners' medals. In 1923 the Furnace Club, Argyll won the cup without conceding a goal throughout the competition.

In 1984 Kingussie Camanachd Club won all five senior competitions, including the Camanachd Cup final. This feat was equalled by Newtonmore in 1985.

Highest scores
The highest Scottish Cup Final score was in 1909 when Newtonmore beat Furnace 11–3 at Glasgow, Dr Johnnie Cattanach scoring eight hails or goals. In 1938 John Macmillan Mactaggart scored ten hails for Mid-Argyll in a Camanachd Cup match.

Shooting

Earliest club
The Lucerne Shooting Guild (Switzerland) was formed c.1466 and the first recorded shooting match was at Zurich in 1472.

SHOOTING—INDIVIDUAL WORLD RECORDS
World records are accepted only when set at major international championships.

MEN

FREE RIFLE Three positions 3 × 40 shots at 300 m

1164/1200	Malcolm Cooper (GB)	Zürich, Switzerland	9 June 1985
	Prone 60 shots at 300 m		
595/600	Kalle Leskinen (Finland)	Olso, Norway	18 June 1983
595/600	Toni Müller (Switzerland)	Oslo, Norway	18 June 1983
595/600	Malcolm Cooper (GB)	Zürich, Switzerland	9 June 1985

STANDARD RIFLE Three positions 3 × 20 shots at 300 m

583/600	Malcolm Cooper (GB)	Zürich, Switzerland	8 June 1985

SMALLBORE RIFLE Three positions 3 × 40 shots at 50 m

1175/1200	Kiril Ivanov (USSR)	Osijek, Yugoslavia	11 Sept 1985
	Prone 60 shots at 50 m		
600/600	Alistair Allan (GB)	Titograd, Yugoslavia	21 Sept 1981
600/600	Ernest van de Zande (USA)	Rio de Janeiro, Brazil	10 Nov 1981

FREE PISTOL 60 shots at 50 m

581/600	Aleksandr Melentev (USSR)	Moscow, USSR	20 July 1980

RAPID FIRE PISTOL 60 shots at 25 m

599/600	Igor Puzryev (USSR)	Titograd, Yugoslavia	21 Sept 1981

CENTRE FIRE PISTOL 60 shots at 25 m

597/600	Thomas D. Smith (USA)	Sao Paulo, Brazil	20 Apr 1963

STANDARD PISTOL 60 shots at 25 m

584/600	Eric Buljong (USA)	Caracas, Venezuela	20 Aug 1983

RUNNING GAME TARGET 60 shots at 50 m with small-bore rifle

595/600	Igor Sokolov (USSR)	Miskulc, Hungary	9 Aug 1981

OLYMPIC TRAP 200 birds

200/200	Danny Carlisle (USA)	Caracas, Venezuela	21 Aug 1983

OLYMPIC SKEET 200 birds

200/200	Matthew Dryke (USA)	Sao Paulo, Brazil	11 Nov 1981
200/200	Jan Hula (Czechoslovakia)	Zaragossa, Spain	16 June 1984

AIR RIFLE 60 shots at 10 m

594/600	Ralf Westerlund (Finland)	Varna, Bulgaria	3 Mar 1985

AIR PISTOL 60 shots at 10 m

591/600	Vladas Tourla (USSR)	Caracas, Venezuela	20 Aug 1983

WOMEN

STANDARD RIFLE Three positions 3 × 20 shots at 50 m

592/600	Marlies Helbig (GDR)	Titograd, Yugoslavia	17 Sept 1981
	Prone 60 shots at 50 m		
598/600	Eulalia Rolinska (Poland)	Suhl, GDR	28 Aug 1971
598/600	Margaret Murdock (USA)	Thun, Austria	21 Sept 1974
598/600	Nonka Matova (Bulgaria)	Osijek, Yugoslavia	8 Sept 1985

SMALLBORE SPORT PISTOL 60 shots at 25 m

594/600	Silvia Kaposztai (Romania)	Osijek, Yugoslavia	6 Sept 1985

OLYMPIC TRAP 200 birds

195/200	Susan Nattrass (Canada)	Seoul, S. Korea	4 Oct 1978

OLYMPIC SKEET 200 birds

197/200	Svetlana Yakimova (USSR)	Zaragossa, Spain	16 June 1984

AIR RIFLE 40 shots at 10 m

395/400	Anna Malekhova (USSR)	The Hague, Netherlands	18 Mar 1982
395/400	Marlies Helbig (GDR)	Innsbruck, Austria	22 Sept 1983

AIR PISTOL 40 shots at 10 m

387/400	Nina Stolyarova (USSR)	Enschede, Netherlands	23 Feb 1974
387/400	Marina Dobrancheva (USSR)	Varna, Bulgaria	2 Mar 1985

Most Olympic medals
The record number of medals won is 11 by Carl Townsend Osburn (USA) (1884–1966) in 1912, 1920 and 1924, consisting of five gold, four silver and two bronze. Six other marksmen have won five gold medals. The only marksman to win three individual gold medals has been Gudbrand Gudbrandsönn Skatteboe (Norway) (1875–1965), in 1906. Separate events for women were first held in 1984.

Bisley

The National Rifle Assocation was instituted in 1859. The Queen's (King's) Prize has been shot since 1860 and has only once been won by a woman—Marjorie Elaine Foster (1894–1974) (score 280) on 19 July 1930. Arthur George Fulton (1887–1972) won a record three times (1912, 1926, 1931). Both his father and his son also won the Prize.

The highest score (possible 300) for the final of the Queen's Prize is 295 by Lindsay Peden (Scotland) on 24 July 1982. The record for the Silver Medals is 150 (possible 150) by Martin John Brister (City Rifle Club) (b. 1951) and the Lord Swansea on 24 July 1971. This was equalled by John Henry Carmichael (WRA Bromsgrave RC) on 28 July 1979 and Robert Stafford on 26 July 1980, with the size of the bullseyes reduced.

Small-Bore

The National Small-Bore Rifle Association, of Britain, was formed in 1901. The British team record (1966 target) is 1988×2000 by Lancashire in 1968–9 and London in 1980–1. The British individual small-bore rifle record for 60 shots prone is 600×600, first achieved by John Palin (b. 16 July 1934) in Switzerland in 1972. Richard Hansen shot 5000 bullseyes in 24 hr at Fresno, Cal, USA on 13 June 1929.

Clay Pigeon

Most world titles have been won by Susan Nattrass (Canada) (b. 5 Nov 1950) with six in 1974–5, 1977–9, 1981. The record number of clay birds shot in an hour is 2215 by Joseph Kreckman at the Paradise Shooting Centre, Cresco, Pennsylvania, USA on 28 Aug 1983 (from 3176 shots from the hip). Graham Douglas Geater (b. 21 July 1947) shot 2264 targets in an hour on a Trapshooting range at the NILO Gun Club, Papamoa, New Zealand on 17 Jan 1981.

The maximum 200/200 was achieved by Ricardo Ruiz Rumoroso at the Spanish clay pigeon championships at Zaragoza on 12 June 1983.

Noel D. Townend achieved the maximum 200 consecutive Down the Line targets at Nottingham on 21 Aug 1983.

Bench rest shooting

The smallest group on record at 1000 yd *914 m* is 5.093 in *12,94 cm* by Rick Taylor with a 300 Weatherby at Williamsport, Penn., USA on 24 Aug 1980.

Highest score in 24 hr

The Easingwold Rifle and Pistol Club team of John Smith, Edward Kendall, Phillip Kendall and Paul Duffield scored 120,242 points (averaging 95.66 per card) on 6–7 Aug 1983.

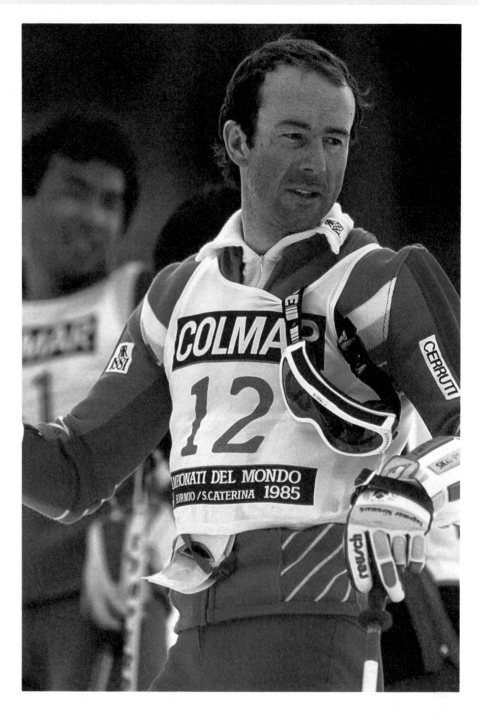

Most World Cup titles: ALPINE

MEN

OVERALL	4	Gustavo Thoeni (Italy)	1971–3, 1975
DOWNHILL	5	Franz Klammer (Austria)	1975–8, 1983
SLALOM	9	Ingemar Stenmark (Sweden)	1975–81, 1983–4
GIANT SLALOM	7	Ingemar Stenmark	1975–6, 1978–81, 1984

Jean-Claude Killy (France) (b. 30 Aug 1943) is the only person to win all four titles—downhill, slalom, giant slalom and overall. He won them all in 1967.

WOMEN

OVERALL	6	Annemarie Moser (Austria)	1971–5, 1979
DOWNHILL	7	Annemarie Moser	1971–5, 1978–9
SLALOM	4	Erika Hess (Switzerland)	1981–3, 1985
GIANT SLALOM	3	Annemarie Moser	1971–2, 1975

NORDIC

MEN

JUMPING	3	Matti Nykänen (Finland)	1983, 1985–6
CROSS-COUNTRY	3	Gunde Svan (Sweden)	1984–6

WOMEN

CROSS-COUNTRY	2	Marja-Liisa Kirvesniemi (née Hämäläinen) (Finland)	1983–4

SKIING

Origins

The most ancient ski in existence was found well preserved in a peat bog at Hoting, Sweden, dating from *c.* 2500 BC. The earliest recorded military use of skiing was at the Battle of Isen, near Oslo, Norway in 1200. The Trysil Shooting and Skiing Club, founded in Norway in 1861, claims it is the world's oldest. The oldest ski competitions are the Holmenkøllen Nordic events which were first held in 1866. The first downhill races were staged in Australia in the 1850s. The International Ski Federation (FIS) was founded on 2 Feb 1924, succeeding the International Skiing Commission, founded at Christiania (Oslo), Norway on 18 Feb 1910. The Ski Club of Great Britain was founded on 6 May

(*Left*) Ingemar Stenmark, whose 83 World Cup wins in slalom events far surpasses anyone else; unusually, he has never raced downhill. (*Right*) Franz Weber, aerodynamically-attired for speed skiing records, and in contrast (*bottom right*), Gunde Svan, triple cross-country world champion. Cross-country events are held at 15,30 and 50 km. (All Sport).

1903. The National Ski Federation of Great Britain was formed in 1964 and changed its name to the British Ski Federation in 1981.

Most titles *World Championships—Alpine*
The world Alpine championships were inaugurated at Mürren, Switzerland, in 1931. The greatest number of titles won has been by Christel Cranz (b. 1 July 1914) of Germany, with seven individual—four Slalom (1934, 1937–9) and three Downhill (1935, 1937, 1939), and five Combined (1934–5, 1937–9). She also won the gold medal for the Combined in the 1936 Olympics. The most won by a man is seven by Anton 'Toni' Sailer (b. 17 Nov 1935) (Austria) who won all four in 1956 (Giant Slalom, Slalom, Downhill and the non-Olympic Alpine Combination) and the Downhill, Giant Slalom and Combined in 1958.

Most titles *World Championships—Nordic*
The first world Nordic championships were those of the 1924 Winter Olympics in Chamonix, France. The greatest number of titles won is nine by Galina Kulakova (b. 29 Apr 1942) (USSR) in 1968–78. She also won four silver and four bronze medals for a record 17 in total. The most won by a man is eight, including relays, by Sixten Jernberg (b. 6 Feb 1929) (Sweden) in 1956–64. Johan Grøttumsbraaten (1899–1942) of Norway won six individual titles (two 18 km cross-country, four Nordic combined) in 1926–32. The record for a jumper is five by Birger Ruud (b. 23 Aug 1911) of Norway, in 1931–2 and 1935–7. Ruud is the only person to win Olympic events in each of the dissimilar Alpine and Nordic disciplines. In 1936 he won the ski-jumping and the Alpine downhill (which was not then a separate event, but only a segment of the combined event).

WORLD CUP

The World Cup was introduced for Alpine events in 1967 and for Nordic events in 1981. The most individual event wins is 83 by Ingemar Stenmark (Sweden) (b. 18 Mar 1956) in 1974–86, including a record 14 in one season in 1979. Franz Klammer (Austria) (b. 3 Dec 1953) won a record 35 downhill races, 1974–85. Annemarie Moser (née Pröll) (Austria) (b. 27 Mar 1953) won a women's record 62 individual event wins, 1970–9. She had a record 11 consecutive downhill wins from Dec 1972 to Jan 1974.

Most titles *British*
The most British skiing overall titles won is four by Stuart Fitzsimmons (b. 28 Dec 1956) in 1973, 1975–6 and 1979. The most ladies' titles won is four by Isobel M. Roe, 1938–9, 1948–9, Gina Hathorn (b. 6 July 1949) 1966, 1968–70, and Valentina Iliffe (b. 17 Feb 1956) 1975–6, 1979–80.

Ski-jumping
The longest ski-jump ever recorded is one of 191 m *626 ft* by Matti Nykänen (b. 17 July 1963) (Finland) at Planica, Yugoslavia on 15 Mar 1985 and by Andreas Felder (Austria) at Bad Mitterndorf, Austria on 9 Mar 1986. The female record is 110 m *361 ft* by Tiina Lehtola (b. 3 Aug 1962) (Finland) at Ruka, Finland on 29 Mar 1981. The

longest dry ski-jump is 92 m *302 ft* by Hubert Schwarz (W. Ger.) at Berchtesgarten, W. Germany on 30 June 1981.

Highest speed—downhill

The highest speed claimed for a skier is 208,936 km/h *129.827 mph* by Franz Weber (Austria) and the fastest by a woman is 200,780 km/h *124.759 mph* by Melissa Dimino (USA) both at Les Arcs, France on 19 Apr 1984. The British record is 201,34 km/h *125.11 mph* by John Clark at La Clupaz, France on 28 Mar 1986. The highest average speed in the Olympic downhill race was 104,53 km/h *64.95 mph* by William D. Johnson (USA) (b. 30 Mar 1960) at Sarajevo, Yugoslavia on 16 Feb 1984. The fastest in a World Cup downhill is 107,82 km/h *67.00 mph* by Harti Weirather (Austria) (b. 25 Jan 1958) at Kitzbühl, Austria on 15 Jan 1982.

Highest speed—cross country

Bill Koch (USA) (b. 13 Apr 1943) on 26 March 1981 skied ten times round a 5 km *3.11 miles* loop on Marlborough Pond, near Putney, Vermont, USA. He completed the 50 km in 1 hr 59 min 47 sec, an average speed of 25,045 km/h *15.57 mph*. A race includes uphill and downhill sections; the record time for a 50 km race is 2 hr 10 min 49.9 sec by Gunde Svan (Sweden) (b. 12 Jan 1962) in the 1985 World Championships, an average speed of 22,93 km/h *14.25 mph*. The record for a 15 km Olympic or World Championship race is 38 min 52.5 sec by Oddvar Braa (Norway) (b. 16 Mar 1951) at the 1982 World Championships, an average speed of 23,15 km/h *14.38 mph*.

Closest Verdict

The narrowest winning margin in a championship ski race was one hundredth of a second by Thomas Wassberg (Sweden) over Juha Mieto (Finland) (b. 20 Nov 1949) in the Olympic 15 km Cross-country race at Lake Placid, USA on 17 Feb 1980. His winning time was 41 min 57.63 sec.

Highest altitude

Jean Afanassieff and Nicolas Jaeger skied from 8200 m *26,900 ft* to 6200 m *20,340 ft* on the 1978 French Expedition on Mt Everest.

Steepest descent

The steepest descents in alpine skiing history have been by Sylvain Saudan. At the start of his descent from Mont Blanc on the north-east side down the Couloir Gervasutti from 4248 m *13,937 ft* on 17 Oct 1967 he skied to gradients of c. 60°.

Longest run

The longest all-downhill ski run in the world is the Weissfluhjoch-Küblis Parsenn course, near Davos, Switzerland, which measures 12,23 km *7.6 miles*. The run from the Aiguille du Midi top of the Chamonix lift (vertical lift 2759 m *9052 ft*) across the Vallée Blanche is 20,9 km *13 miles*.

Longest races

The world's greatest Nordic ski race is the Vasaloppet, which commemorates an event of 1521 when Gustav Vasa (1496–1560), later King Gustavus Eriksson, fled 85,8 km *53.3 miles* from Mora to Sälen, Sweden. He was overtaken by loyal, speedy scouts on skis, who persuaded him to return eastwards to Mora to lead a rebellion and become the king of Sweden. The re-enactment of this return journey is now an annual event at 89 km *55.3 miles*, contested by about 12,000 skiers. The fastest time is 3 hr 48 min 55 sec by Bengt Hassis (Sweden) on 2 Mar 1986.

The longest downhill race is the *Inferno* in Switzerland, 14 km *8.7 miles* from the top of the

---

Schilthorn to Lauterbrunnen. In 1981 there was a record entry of 1401, with Heinz Fringer (Switzerland) winning in a record 15 min 44.57 sec.

Long Distance Nordic skiing records

In 24 hr Teuvo Rantanen covered 315 km *195 miles* at Jyväskylä, Finland on 24–25 Mar 1984. The women's record is 197,83 km *122.9 miles* by Marlene Severs at East Burke, Vermont, USA on 7–8 Mar 1985.

In 48 hr Bjørn Løkken (Norway) (b. 27 Nov 1937) covered 513,568 km *319 miles 205 yd* on 11–13 Mar 1982.

Ski-Bob *Origins*

The ski-bob was invented by J. C. Stevenson of Hartford, Connecticut, USA in 1891, and patented (No. 47334) on 19 Apr 1892 as a 'bicycle with ski-runners'. The Fédération Internationale de Skibob was founded on 14 Jan 1961 in Innsbruck, Austria and the first world championships were held at Bad Hofgastein, Austria in 1967. The Ski-Bob Association of Great Britain was registered on 23 Aug 1967. The highest speed attained is 166 km/h *103.4 mph* by Erich Brenter (b. 1940) (Austria) at Cervinia, Italy, in 1964.

Ski-Bob *World Championships*

The only ski-bobbers to retain a world championship are: men—Alois Fischbauer (Austria) (b. 6 Oct 1951), 1973 and 1975, Robert Mühlberger (W. Germany), 1979 and 1981; women—Gerhilde Schiffkorn (Austria) (b. 22 Mar 1950), 1967 and 1969, Gertrude Geberth (Austria) (b. 18 Oct 1951), 1971 and 1973.

Snowmobile

A record speed of 148.6 mph *239,1 km/h* was set by Tom Earhart (USA) in a Budweiser-Polaris snowmobile designed and owned by Bob Gaudreau at Lake Mille Lacs, Minnesota, USA on 25 Feb 1982. (*See also p. 129*).

Longest lift

The longest gondola ski lift is 6239 m *3.88 miles* long at Grindelwald-Männlichen, Switzerland (in two sections, but one gondola). The longest chair lift in the world was the Alpine Way to Kosciusko Châlet lift above Thredbo, near the Snowy Mountains, New South Wales, Australia. It took from 45 to 75 min to ascend the 3.5 miles *5,6 km*, according to the weather. It has now collapsed. The highest is at Chacaltaya, Bolivia, rising to 5029 m *16,500 ft*.

GRASS SKIING

Grass skis were first manufactured by Josef Kaiser (W. Ger.) in 1963. World Championships (awarded for giant slalom, slalom and combined) were first held in 1979. The most titles won is seven by Ingrid Hirschhofer (Austria) to 1985. The most by a man is four by Erwin Gansner (Switzerland), two each in 1981 and 1983.

The speed record is 86,88 km/h *53.99 mph* by Erwin Gansner on 5 Sept 1982; the British record is 79,49 km/h *43.39 mph* by Laurence Beck on 8 Sept 1985, both at Owen, West Germany.

SKITTLES

24 Hours

Eight players from the Alkies skittle team knocked down 83,440 West Country skittles on 30–31 Mar 1985 at Torquay, Devon. The highest hood skittle score in 24 hr is 118,951 pins by 12 players from the White Hart, Grafton Regis, Northamptonshire on 9–10 April 1986. The highest long alley score is 59,140 by a team of 8 from the British Institute for Brain Injured Children in Bridgwater, Somerset on 28 Feb–1 Mar 1986. The highest table skittle score in 24 hr is 90,446 skittles by 12 players at the Finney Gardens Hotel, Hanley, Staffs on 27–28 Dec 1980.

SNOOKER

Origins

Research shows that snooker was originated by Colonel Sir Neville Francis Fitzgerald Chamberlain (1856–1944) as a hybrid of 'black pool', 'pyramids' and billiards, in Jubbulpore, India in 1875. It did not reach England until 1885, where the modern scoring system was adopted in 1891. Championships were not instituted until 1916. The World Professional Championship was instituted in 1927.

Most titles *World*

The world professional title (inst 1927) was won a record 15 times by Joe Davis, 1927–40 and 1946. The most wins in the amateur championships (inst 1963) have been two by Gary Owen

Joe Johnson, who in 1978 set a world amateur record break of 140, became the surprise winner of the professional World Championships in 1986.

(England) in 1963 and 1966, and Ray Edmonds (England) 1972 and 1974.

Most titles *Women*
Maureen Baynton (*née* Barrett) won a record eight women's amateur championships between 1954 and 1968, as well as seven at billiards.

World Championships *Youngest*
The youngest player to win a world title is Jimmy White (GB) (b. 2 May 1962) who was 18 yr 191 days when he won the World Amateur Snooker championship in Launceston, Tasmania, Australia on 9 Nov 1980.

Highest breaks
Over 100 players have achieved the 'maximum' break of 147. The first to do so was E. J. 'Murt' O'Donoghue (b. New Zealand 1901) at Griffiths, NSW, Australia on 26 Sept 1934. The first officially ratified 147 was by Joe Davis against Willie Smith at Leicester Square Hall, London on 22 Jan 1955. The first maximum achieved in a major tournament was by John Spencer (b. 18 Sept 1935) at Slough, Berkshire on 13 Jan 1979, but the table had oversized pockets. Steve Davis (b. 22 Aug 1957) had a ratified break of 147 against John Spencer in the Lada Classic at Oldham on 11 Jan 1982. The first 147 scored in the World Championships was by Cliff Thorburn (Canada) (b. 16 Jan 1948) against Terry Griffiths at the Crucible Theatre, Sheffield on 23 April 1983, thereby winning a £10,000 jackpot prize.

The official world amateur record break is 140 set by Joe Johnson (England) (b. 29 July 1952) in the TUC Club, Middlesbrough, Cleveland in 1978. David Taylor (b. 29 July 1943) made three consecutive frame clearances of 130, 140, and 139 at Minehead, Somerset, on 1 June 1978. Jim Meadowcroft (b. 15 Dec 1946) made four consecutive frame clearances of 105, 115, 117 and 125 at Connaught Leisure Centre, Worthing on 27 Jan 1982.

The first century break by a woman in competitive play was 114 by Stacey Hillyard in a league match at Bournemouth on 15 Jan 1985.

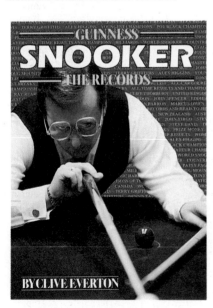

GUINNESS
SNOOKER
THE RECORDS

BY CLIVE EVERTON

Published by Guinness at £6.95.

SOFTBALL

Origins
Softball, the indoor derivative of baseball, was invented by George Hancock at the Farragut Boat Club of Chicago, Illinois in 1887. Rules were first codified in Minneapolis, Minnesota, USA in 1895 as Kitten Ball. The name Softball was introduced by Walter Hakanson at a meeting of the National Recreation Congress in 1926. The name was adopted throughout the USA in 1930. Rules were formalised in 1933 by the International Joint Rules Committee for Softball and adopted by the Amateur Softball Association of America. The International Softball Federation was formed in 1950 as governing body for both fast pitch and slow pitch. It was re-organised in 1965.

Most titles
The USA has won the men's world championship (inst. 1966) four times, 1966, 1968, 1976 (shared), and 1980. The USA won the women's title (inst. 1965) in 1974, 1978 and 1986.

SPEEDWAY

Origins
Motorcycle racing on large dirt track surfaces has been traced back to 1902 in the United States. The first organized 'short track' races were at the West Maitland (New South Wales, Australia) Agricultural Show in November 1923. The sport evolved in Great Britain with small diameter track racing at Droylsden, Greater Manchester on 25 June 1927 and a cinder track event at High Beech, Essex, on 19 Feb 1928.

British championships
The National League was contested from 1932 to 1964. The Wembley Lions who won in 1932, 1946–7, 1949–53, had a record eight victories. In 1965 it was replaced by the British League which Belle Vue have won four times, including three times in succession (1970–2). Wimbledon are the only club to have competed every year since 1929 in Southern, National and British Leagues. Belle Vue (Manchester) had a record nine victories (1933–7, 1946–7, 1949 and 1958)

SOFTBALL WORLD CHAMPIONSHIP RECORDS

MEN

MOST RUNS SCORED	14	Takayuki Ietke (Japan)	1984
MOST HOME RUNS	4	Robert 'Bob' Burrows (Canada)	1976
MOST HITS	17	Basil McLean (New Zealand)	1976
RBIs	14	Chuck Teuscher (USA)	1966
	14	Robert 'Bob' Burrows (Canada)	1976
HIGHEST AVERAGE	.583	Takayuki Ietke (Japan)	1984
MOST WINS (PITCHING)	6	Owen Walford (New Zealand)	1976
	6	Owen Walford (USA, formerly NZ)	1980
MOST INNINGS PITCHED	59	Ty Stofflet (USA)	1976
MOST STRIKEOUTS	98	Ty Stofflet (USA)	1976
MOST PERFECT GAMES	1	By seven men	—

WOMEN

MOST RUNS SCORED	13	Kathy Elliott (USA)	1974
MOST HITS	17	Miyoko Naruse (Japan)	1974
MOST DOUBLES	4	Vicki Murray (New Zealand)	1982
	4	Suh-Chiung Ju (Taiwan)	1982
MOST TRIPLES	6	Miyoko Naruse (Japan)	1974
	6	Yug-Feng Yang (Taiwan)	1982
RBIs	11	Miyoko Naruse (Japan); Keiko Usui (Japan); Kathy Elliott (USA)	1974
HIGHEST AVERAGE	.550	Tamara Bryce (Panama)	1978
MOST WINS (PITCHING)	6	Lorraine Wooley (Australia)	1965
	6	Nancy Welborn (USA)	1970
MOST INNINGS PITCHED	50	Nancy Welborn (USA)	1970
MOST STRIKEOUTS	76	Joan Joyce (USA)	1974
MOST PERFECT GAMES	2	Joan Joyce (USA)	1974

All Sport

in the National Trophy Knock-out Competition (held 1931–64). This was replaced in 1965 by the Knock Out Cup, which has been won four times by Cradley Heath and Ipswich.

World championships

The World Speedway Championship was inaugurated at Wembley, London on 10 Sept 1936. The most wins have been six by Ivan Gerald Mauger (New Zealand) (b. 4 Oct 1939) in 1968–70, 1972, 1977 and 1979. Barry Briggs (New Zealand) (b. 30 Dec 1934) made a record 17 consecutive appearances in the finals (1954–70) and won the world title in 1957–8, 1964 and 1966. He also scored a record 201 points in world championship competition from 87 races.

England have most wins in the World Team Cup (inst. 1960) with eight, and the World Pairs Championship (inst. 1968) with seven. Poland uniquely competed in 21 successive World Team Cup finals, 1960–80 and in a 22nd in 1984. The maximum 30 points were scored in the World Pairs Championship by Jerzy Szczakiel (b. 28 Jan 1949) and Andrzej Wyglenda (Poland) at Rybnik, Poland in 1971 and by Arthur Dennis Sigalos (b. 16 Aug 1959) and Robert Benjamin 'Bobby' Schwartz (b. 10 Aug 1956) (USA) at Liverpool, New South Wales, Australia on 11 Dec 1982.

Ivan Mauger also won four World Team Cup, two World Pairs and two world long track titles. Ove Fundin (Sweden) (b. 23 May 1933) won twelve world titles: five individual, one Pairs, and six World Team Cup medals in 1956–70. Erik Gundersen (Denmark) (b. 8 Oct 1959) became in 1985 the first man to hold simultaneously world titles at individual, pairs, team and long-track events.

League racing

In League racing the highest score recorded was when Crayford beat Milton Keynes 76–20 in the then 16-heat formula for the National League on 26 Oct 1982. A maximum possible score was achieved by Bristol when they defeated Glasgow (White City) 70–14 on 7 Oct 1949 in the National League Division Two. The highest number of League points scored by an individual in a season was 516 by Stephen Faulder Lawson (b. 11 Dec 1957) for Glasgow in the National League in 1982. The League career record is 6471 points by Nigel Boocock (b. 17 Sept 1937), 1955–80.

Tests—*maximum points*

The only rider to have scored maximum points in every match of a Test series was Arthur 'Bluey' Wilkinson (b. 27 Aug 1911) in five matches for Australia v. England in Sydney in 1937–8.

SQUASH RACKETS

Earliest champion

Although rackets (US spelling racquets) with a soft ball was played in 1817 at Harrow School, Harrow, Greater London, there was no recognised champion of any country until John A.

Miskey of Philadelphia won the American Amateur Singles Championship in 1907.

World Championships

Jahangir Khan (b. 10 Dec 1963) (Pakistan) has won five World Open (inst. 1976) titles, 1981–5, and the ISRF World individual title (formerly World Amateur, inst. 1967) in 1979 and 1983. The last man to defeat Jahangir (in the 1981 British Open), was Geoffrey B. Hunt (b. 11 Mar 1947) (Australia) who won four World Open titles, 1976–7 and 1979–80 and three World Amateur, 1967, 1969 and 1971.

Australia, 1967, 1969, 1971 and 1973, and Pakistan, 1977, 1981, 1983 and 1985 have each won four men's team titles and Australia have won three women's, 1976, 1981 and 1983.

Most titles *Open Championship*

The most wins in the Open Championship (amateurs or professionals), held annually in Britain, is eight by Geoffrey Hunt in 1969, 1974, 1976–81. Hashim Khan (Pakistan) (b. 1915) won seven times, 1950–5 and 1957, and also won the Vintage title six times in 1978–83.

The most British open women's titles is 16 by Heather Pamela McKay (*née* Blundell) (Australia) (b. 31 July 1941) from 1961 to 1977. She also won the World Open title in 1976 and 1979. In her career from 1959 to 1980 she only lost two games (one in 1960, one in 1962).

Most titles *Amateur Championship*

The most wins in the Amateur Championship is six by Abdelfattah Amr Bey (Egypt) (b. 14 Feb 1910), who won in 1931–3 and 1935–7. Norman Francis Borrett (b. 1 Oct 1917) of England won in 1946–50.

Erik Gundersen set a unique record in 1985 by becoming the first man to hold simultaneously world championship titles at individual, pairs, team and long-track. (All Sport).

Longest and shortest championship matches

The longest recorded competitive match was one of 2 hr 45 min when Jahangir Khan beat Gamal Awad (Egypt) (b. 8 Sept 1955) 9–10, 9–5, 9–7, 9–2, the first game lasting a record 1 hr 11 min, in the final of the Patrick International Festival at Chichester, West Sussex, England on 30 Mar 1983. Suzanne Burgess beat Carolyn Mett in just 8 min (9–2, 9–0, 9–0) in the British Under-23 Open Championship at The Oasis Club, Marlow, Buckinghamshire on 20 Jan 1986.

Most international appearances

The men's record is 110 by David Gotto for Ireland. The women's record is 71 by Geraldine Barniville for Ireland, 1973–83.

Largest crowd and tournament

The finals of the Hi-Tec British Open Squash Championships at Wembley Conference Centre, London had a record attendance for squash of 2948 on 22 Apr 1986.

The InterCity National Squash Challenge was contested by 7236 players in 1985–6, a knock-out tournament record.

SURFING

Origins

The traditional Polynesian sport of surfing in a canoe (*ehorooe*) was first recorded by Captain James Cook, RN, FRS (1728–79) on his first voyage at Tahiti in December 1771. Surfing on a board (*Amo Amo iluna ka lau oka nalu*) was first described 'most perilous and extraordinary . . . altogether astonishing and is scarcely to be credited' by Lt (later Capt) James King, RN, FRS in March 1779 at Kealakekua Bay, Hawaii Island. A surfer was first depicted by this voyage's official artist John Webber. The sport was revived at Waikiki by 1900. Hollow boards were introduced in 1929 and the light plastic foam type in 1956.

Most titles

World Amateur Championships were inaugurated in May 1964 at Sydney, Australia; two titles have been won by Joyce Hoffman (US) in 1965 and 1966 and by Mike Novakov (Australia) who won the Kneeboard event in 1982 and 1984. A World Professional series was started in 1975 and Mark Richards (Australia) has won the men's title four times, 1979–82.

Highest waves ridden

Makaha Beach, Hawaii provides the reputedly highest consistently high waves often reaching the rideable limit of 30–35 ft *9–10 m*. The highest wave ever ridden was the *tsunami* of 'perhaps 50 ft *15,24 m*', which struck Minole, Hawaii on 3 Apr 1868, and was ridden to save his life by a Hawaiian named Holua.

Longest ride *Sea wave*

About four to six times each year rideable surfing waves break in Matanchen Bay near San Blas, Nayarit, Mexico which makes rides of *c.* 5700 ft *1700 m* possible.

Longest ride *River bore*

The longest recorded rides on a river bore have been set on the Severn bore, England. The official British Surfing Association record for riding a surfboard in a standing position is 0.8 mile *1,3 km* by Nick Hart (b. 11 Dec 1958) from Lower Rea to Hempsted on 26 Oct 1984. The longest ride on a surfboard standing or lying down is 2.94 miles *4,73 km* by Colin Kerr Wilson (b. 23 June 1954) on 23 May 1982.

SWIMMING

Earliest references

In Japan, swimming in schools was ordered by Imperial edict of Emperor Go-Yozei (1586–1611) in 1603 but competition was known from 36 BC. Sea water bathing was fashionable at Scarborough, North Yorkshire as early as 1660. In Great Britain competitive swimming originated from at least 1791. The earliest pool was Pearless Pool, North London, opened in 1743. Swimming races were particularly popular in the 1820s in Liverpool, where the earliest pool opened at St George's Pier Head, Liverpool in 1828.

Largest pools

The largest swimming pool in the world is the sea-water Orthlieb Pool in Casablanca, Morocco. It is 480 m *1574 ft* long and 75 m *246 ft* wide, and has an area of 3.6 ha *8.9 acres*. The largest land-locked swimming pool with heated water was the Fleishhacker Pool on Sloat Boulevard, near Great Highway, San Francisco, California, USA. It measured 1000 × 150 ft *304,8 × 45,7 m* and up to 14 ft *4,26 m* deep and contained 7,500,000 US gal *28 390 hectolitres* of heated water. It was opened on 2 May 1925 but has now been abandoned. The greatest spectator accommodation is 13,614 at Osaka, Japan. The largest in use in the United Kingdom is the Royal Commonwealth Pool, Edinburgh, completed in 1970 with 2000 permanent seats, but the covered over and unused pool at Earls Court, London (opened 1937) could seat some 12,000 spectators.

Fastest swimmer

The fastest speed measured in a 50 m pool is by the world record holders for 50 metres (see table): *men*: Matt Biondi 8,06 km/h *5.01 mph* and *women*: Tamara Costache 7,10 km/h *4.41 mph*.

Most world records

Men: 32, Arne Borg (Sweden) (b. 18 Aug 1901), 1921–9. Women: 42, Ragnhild Hveger (Denmark) (b. 10 Dec 1920), 1936–42. Under modern conditions (only metric distances in 50 m pools) the most is 26 by Mark Andrew Spitz (USA) (b. 10 Feb 1950), 1967–72, and 23 by Kornelia Ender (GDR) (b. 25 Oct 1958), 1973–6.

Most world titles

In the world championships (inst 1973) the most medals won is ten by Kornelia Ender with eight gold and two silver in 1973 and 1975. The most by a man is eight by Ambrose 'Rowdy' Gaines (USA) (b. 17 Feb 1959), five gold and three

American Matt Biondi who has broken the world record for 100 metres three times in 1985–86—remarkable progress taking the record down from 49.36 to 48.74 sec. (All Sport).

silver, in 1978 and 1982. The most gold medals is six by James Montgomery (USA) (b. 24 Jan 1955) in 1973 and 1975. The most medals in a single championship is six by Tracy Caulkins (USA) (b. 11 Jan 1963) in 1978 with five golds and a silver.

OLYMPIC RECORDS

Most medals *Men*

The greatest number of Olympic gold medals won is nine by Mark Spitz (USA): 100 m and 200 m freestyle 1972; 100 m and 200 m butterfly 1972; 4 × 100 m freestyle 1968 and 1972; 4 × 200 m freestyle 1968 and 1972; 4 × 100 m medley 1972. *All but one of these performances (the 4 × 200 m freestyle of 1968) were also new world records.* He also won a silver (100 m butterfly) and a bronze (100 m freestyle) in 1968 for a record eleven medals.

Most medals *Women*

The record number of gold medals won by a woman is four shared by Patricia McCormick (*née* Keller) (USA) (b. 12 May 1930), the high and springboard diving double in 1952 and 1956 (also the female record for individual golds), Dawn Fraser (Australia) (b. 4 Sept 1937), the 100 m freestyle (1956, 1960 and 1964) and the 4 × 100 m freestyle (1956) and Kornelia Ender (GDR) the 100 and 200 m freestyle, 100 m butterfly and 4 × 100 m medley in 1976. Dawn Fraser is the only swimmer to win the same event on three successive occasions.

The most medals won by a woman is eight by Dawn Fraser, who in addition to her four golds won four silvers (400 m freestyle 1956, 4 × 100 m freestyle 1960 and 1964, 4 × 100 m medley 1960), Kornelia Ender who in addition to her four golds won four silvers (200 m individual medley 1972, 4 × 100 m medley 1972, 4 × 100 m freestyle 1972 and 1976) and Shirley Babashoff (USA) (b. 3 Jan 1957), who won two golds (4 × 100 m freestyle 1972 and 1976) and six silvers (100 m freestyle 1972, 200 m freestyle 1972 and 1976, 400 m and 800 m freestyle 1976, 4 × 100 m medley 1976).

Most individual gold medals

The record number of individual gold medals won is four by Charles M. Daniels (USA) (1884–1973) (100 m freestyle 1906 and 1908, 220 yd freestyle 1904, 440 yd freestyle 1904); Roland Matthes (GDR) (b. 17 Nov 1950) with 100 m and 200 m backstroke 1968 and 1972; Mark Spitz and Pat McCormick. The most individual golds by a British swimmer is three by Henry Taylor.

Most medals *British*

The record number of gold medals won by a British swimmer (excluding Water Polo, *q.v.*) is four by Henry Taylor (1885–1951) in the mile freestyle (1906), 400 m freestyle (1908), 1500 m freestyle (1908) and 4 × 200 m freestyle (1908).

Henry Taylor won a record eight medals in all with a silver (400 m freestyle 1906) and three bronzes (4 × 200 m freestyle 1906, 1912, 1920). The most medals by a British woman is four by M. Joyce Cooper (now Badcock) (b. 18 Apr 1909) with one silver (4 × 100 m freestyle 1928) and three bronze (100 m freestyle 1928, 100 m backstroke 1928, 4 × 100 m freestyle 1932).

Closest verdict

The closest verdict in the Olympic Games was in Los Angeles on 29 July 1984, when Nancy Hogshead (b. 17 Apr 1962) and Carrie Steinsiefer (b. 12 Feb 1968) (both USA) dead-heated for the women's 100 m freestyle gold medal in 55.92 sec.

In the 1972 men's 400 m individual medley Gunnar Larsson (Sweden) (b. 12 May 1951) beat Tim McKee (USA) (b. 14 Mar 1953) by just 2/1000th second, just 3 mm. Now timings are determined to hundredths.

DIVING

Most Olympic medals *World*

The most medals won by a diver are five (three gold, two silver) by Klaus Dibiasi (b. Austria, 6 Oct 1947) (Italy) in four Games from 1964 to 1976. He is also the only diver to win the same event (highboard) at three successive Games (1968, 1972 and 1976). Pat McCormick (*see above*) won four gold medals.

Most Olympic medals *British*

The highest placing by a Briton has been the silver medal by Beatrice Eileen Armstrong (later Purdy) (1894–1981) in the 1920 highboard event. The best placings by male divers are the bronze medals by Harold Clarke (b. 1888) (plain high diving, 1924) and Brian Phelps (b. 21 Apr 1944) (highboard, 1960).

Most world titles

Phil Boggs (USA) (b. 29 Dec 1949) won three springboard gold medals, in 1973, 1975 and 1978

but Klaus Dibiasi (Italy) won four medals (two gold, two silver) in 1973 and 1975. Irina Kalinina (USSR) (b. 8 Feb 1959) has won five medals (three gold, one silver, one bronze) in 1973, 1975 and 1978. Greg Louganis (USA) (b. 29 Jan 1960), won one world title in 1978 and two in 1982, as well as two Olympic gold medals in 1984.

Highest scores

Greg Louganis achieved record scores at the 1984 Olympic Games in Los Angeles, with 754.41 points for the 11-dive springboard event and 710.91 for the highboard. At the world championships in Guayaquil, Ecuador in 1984 he was awarded a perfect score of 10.0 by all seven judges for his highboard inward 1.5 somersault in the pike position.

The first diver to be awarded a score of 10.0 by all seven judges was Michael Finneran (b. 21 Sept 1948) in the 1972 US Olympic Trials, in Chicago, Illinois, for a backward 1½ somersault, 2½ twist, from the 10 m board.

CHANNEL SWIMMING

Earliest

The first to swim the English Channel from

SWIMMING—WORLD RECORDS (*set in 50 m pools*)

MEN

FREESTYLE

	Min. Sec.	Name, Country and date of birth	Place	Date	
50 metres	22.33	Matthew Biondi (USA) (b. 8 Oct 1965)	Orlando, Florida, USA	26 June	1986
100 metres	48.74	Matthew Biondi (USA)	Orlando, Florida, USA	25 June	1986
200 metres	1:47.44	Michael Gross (W. Germany) (b. 17 June 1964)	Los Angeles, USA	29 July	1984
400 metres	3:47.80	Michael Gross (W. Germany)	Remscheid, W. Germany	27 June	1985
800 metres	7:50.64	Vladimir Salnikov (USSR) (b. 21 May 1960)	Moscow, USSR	4 July	1986
1500 metres	14:54.76	Vladimir Salnikov (USSR)	Moscow, USSR	22 Feb	1983
4 × 100 metres relay	3:17.08	United States (Scott McAdam, Michael Heath, Paul Wallace, Matthew Biondi)	Tokyo, Japan	17 Aug	1985
4 × 200 metres relay	7:15.69	United States (Michael Heath, David Larson, Jeffery Float, Lawrence Bruce Hayes)	Los Angeles, USA	30 July	1984

BREASTSTROKE

100 metres	1:01.65	Steven Lundquist (USA) (b. 20 Feb 1961)	Los Angeles, USA	29 July	1984
200 metres	2:13.34	Victor Davis (Canada) (b. 19 Feb 1964)	Los Angeles, USA	2 Aug	1984

BUTTERFLY

100 metres	52.84	Pedro Pablo Morales (USA) (b. 5 Dec 1964)	Orlando, Florida, USA	24 June	1986
200 metres	1:56.24	Michael Gross (W. Germany)	Hannover, W. Germany	28 June	1986

BACKSTROKE

100 metres	55.19	Richard Carey (USA) (b. 13 Mar 1963)	Caracas, Venezuela	21 Aug	1983
200 metres	1:58.14	Igor Polyanski (USSR) (b. 20 Mar 1967)	Gera, GDR	3 Mar	1985

MEDLEY

200 metres	2:01.42	Alex Baumann (Canada) (b. Prague 21 Apr 1964)	Los Angeles, USA	4 Aug	1984
	2:01.42	Alex Baumann	Montreal, Canada	4 Mar	1986
400 metres	4:17.41	Alex Baumann	Los Angeles, USA	30 July	1984
4 × 100 metres relay	3:38.28	United States (Richard Carey, Pedro Pablo Morales, Matthew Biondi, John Moffet)	Tokyo, Japan	18 Aug	1985

WOMEN

FREESTYLE

50 metres	25.34	Tamara Costache (Romania) (b. 1970)	Bucharest, Romania	14 June	1986
100 metres	54.79	Barbara Krause (GDR) (b. 7 July 1959)	Moscow, USSR	21 July	1980
200 metres	1:57.55	Heike Friedrich (GDR) (b. 1970)	East Berlin, GDR	18 June	1986
400 metres	4:06.28	Tracey Wickham (Australia) (b. 24 Nov 1962)	West Berlin, W. Germany	24 Aug	1978
800 metres	8:24.62	Tracey Wickham (Australia)	Edmonton, Canada	5 Aug	1978
1500 metres	16:04.49	Kim Lineham (USA) (b. 11 Dec 1962)	Fort Lauderdale, Florida, USA	19 Aug	1979
4 × 100 metres relay	3:42.41	GDR (Kristin Otto, Karin Konig, Heike Friedrich, Birgit Meineke)	Moscow, USSR	21 Aug	1984
4 × 200 metres relay	8:02.27	GDR (Kristin Otto, Astrid Strauss, Cornelia Sirch, Birgit Meineke)	Rome, Italy	23 Aug	1983

BREASTSTROKE

100 metres	1:08.29	Sylvia Gerasch (GDR) (b. 16 Mar 1969)	Moscow, USSR	23 Aug	1984
200 metres	2:28.20	Sylvia Gerasch (GDR)	Leningrad, USSR	28 Feb	1986

BUTTERFLY

100 metres	57.93	Mary T. Meagher (USA) (b. 27 Oct 1964)	Milwaukee, Wisconsin, USA	16 Aug	1981
200 metres	2:05.96	Mary T. Meagher	Milwaukee, Wisconsin, USA	13 Aug	1981

BACKSTROKE

100 metres	1:00.59	Ina Kleber (GDR) (b. 29 Sept 1964)	Moscow, USSR	24 Aug	1984
200 metres	2:08.60	Betsy Mitchell (USA) (b. 15 Jan 1966)	Orlando, Florida, USA	27 June	1986

MEDLEY

200 metres	2:11.73	Ute Geweniger (GDR) (b. 24 Feb 1964)	East Berlin, GDR	4 July	1981
400 metres	4:36.10	Petra Schneider (GDR) (b. 11 Jan 1963)	Guayaquil, Ecuador	1 Aug	1982
4 × 100 metres relay	4:03.69	GDR (Ina Kleber, Sylvia Gerasch, Ines Geissler, Birgit Meineke)	Moscow, USSR	24 Aug	1984

shore to shore (without a life jacket) was the Merchant Navy captain Matthew Webb (1848–83) who swam breaststroke from Dover, England to Calais Sands, France, in 21 hr 45 min from 12.56 p.m. to 10.41 a.m., 24–25 Aug 1875. He swam an estimated 38 miles *61 km* to make the 21-mile *33 km* crossing. Paul Boyton (USA) had swum from Cap Gris-Nez to the South Foreland in his patent life-saving suit in 23 hr 30 min on 28–29 May 1875. There is good evidence that Jean-Marie Saletti, a French soldier, escaped from a British prison hulk off Dover by swimming to Boulogne in July or August 1815. The first crossing from France to England was made by Enrico Tiraboschi, a wealthy Italian living in Argentina, in 16 hr 33 min on 12 Aug 1923, to win the *Daily Sketch* prize of £1000.

The first woman to succeed was Gertrude Caroline Ederle (b. 23 Oct 1906) (USA) (*see also p. 220*) who swam from Cap Gris-Nez, France to Deal, England on 6 Aug 1926, in the then overall record time of 14 hr 39 min. The first woman to swim from England to France was Florence Chadwick (b. 1918) (USA) in 16 hr 19 min on 11 Sept 1951. The first Englishwoman to succeed was Mercedes Gleitze (later Carey) (1900–81) who swam from France to England in 15 hr 15 min on 7 Oct 1927.

Fastest

The official Channel Swimming Association (founded 1927) record is 7 hr 40 min by Penny Dean (b. 21 Mar 1955) of California, USA, from Shakespeare Beach, Dover to Cap Gris-Nez, France, on 29 July 1978.

The fastest crossing by a relay team is 7 hr

Reaching new lengths . . . Alyson Gibbons set a women's record for the greatest mileage swum in 24 hours. Her 2707 lengths amounted to 42.05 miles *67,675 km.*

17 min, by six Dover lifeguards, from England to France on 9 Aug 1981.

BRITISH NATIONAL *long course* RECORDS

MEN

Event	Time Min. Sec.	Name and date of birth	Place	Date	
FREESTYLE					
100 metres	51.32	David Lowe (b. 28 Feb 1960)	Rome, Italy	24 Aug	1983
200 metres	1:51.52	Andrew Astbury (b. 29 Nov 1960)	Brisbane, Australia	2 Oct	1982
400 metres	3:53.29	Andrew Astbury	Brisbane, Australia	4 Oct	1982
800 metres	8:12.39	David Stacey (b. 22 Feb 1965)	Los Angeles, USA	3 Aug	1984
1500 metres	15:30.10	David Stacey (b. 22 Feb 1965)	Los Angeles, USA	3 Aug	1984
4 × 100 metres relay	3:23.61	UK (David Lowe, Roland Lee, Paul Easter, Richard Burrell)	Los Angeles, USA	2 Aug	1984
4 × 200 metres relay	7:24.78	UK (Neil Cochran, Paul Easter, Paul Howe, Andrew Astbury)	Los Angeles, USA	30 July	1984
BREASTSTROKE					
100 metres	1:02.89	Adrian Moorhouse (b. 24 May 1964)	Coventry, England	30 May	1986
200 metres	2:15.11	David Andrew Wilkie (b. 8 Mar 1954)	Montreal, Canada	24 July	1976
BUTTERFLY					
100 metres	54.24	Andrew Jameson (b. 19 Feb 1965)	Austin, Texas, USA	7 Dec	1985
200 metres	2:00.21	Philip Hubble (b. 19 July 1960)	Split, Yugoslavia	11 Sept	1981
BACKSTROKE					
100 metres	57.72	Gary Abraham (b. 8 Jan 1959)	Moscow, USSR	24 July	1980
200 metres	2:04.23	Douglas Campbell (b. 30 Sept 1960)	Moscow, USSR	26 July	1980
MEDLEY					
200 metres	2:03.76	Neil Cochran (b. 12 Apr 1965)	Austin, Texas, USA	6 Dec	1985
400 metres	4:24.70	John Darby (b. 29 Dec 1964)	Coventry, England	30 May	1986
4 × 100 metres relay	3:47.39	UK (Neil Harper, Adrian Moorhouse, Andrew Jameson, Richard Burrell)	Los Angeles, USA	4 Aug	1984

WOMEN

Event	Time Min. Sec.	Name and date of birth	Place	Date	
FREESTYLE					
100 metres	56.60	June Croft (b. 17 June 1963)	Amersfoort, Netherlands	31 Jan	1982
200 metres	1:59.74	June Croft	Brisbane, Australia	4 Oct	1982
400 metres	4:10.27	Sarah Hardcastle (b. 9 April 1969)	Los Angeles, USA	31 July	1984
800 metres	8:32.57	Sarah Hardcastle	Sofia, Bulgaria	10 Aug	1985
1500 metres	16:43.95	Sarah Hardcastle	Montreal, Canada	21 Apr	1985
4 × 100 metres relay	3:50.12	UK (June Croft, Nicola Fibbens, Debra Gore, Annabelle Cripps)	Los Angeles, USA	31 July	1984
4 × 200 metres relay	8:15.21	UK (Annabelle Cripps, Sarah Hardcastle, Ruth Gilfillan, June Croft)	Crystal Palace, London	26 Feb	1984
BREASTSTROKE					
100 metres	1.11.05	Susannah 'Suki' Brownsdon (b. 16 Oct 1965)	Split, Yugoslavia	8 Sept	1981
200 metres	2:33.16	Susannah 'Suki' Brownsdon	Cardiff, Wales	4 May	1985
BUTTERFLY					
100 metres	1:01.48	Nicola Fibbens (b. 29 Apr 1964)	Los Angeles, USA	2 Aug	1984
200 metres	2:11.97	Samantha Purvis (b. 24 June 1967)	Los Angeles, USA	4 Aug	1984
BACKSTROKE					
100 metres	1:03.61	Beverley Rose (b. 21 Jan 1964)	Los Angeles, USA	31 July	1984
200 metres	2:14.87	Katharine Read (b. 30 June 1969)	Coventry, England	30 May	1986
MEDLEY					
200 metres	2:17.31	Sharron Davies (b. 1 Nov 1962)	Blackpool, England	20 Apr	1980
400 metres	4:46.83	Sharron Davies	Moscow, USSR	26 July	1980
4 × 100 metres relay	4:12.24	UK (Helen Jameson, Margaret Kelly, Ann Osgerby, June Croft)	Moscow, USSR	20 July	1980

Mary Meagher, who has remained the best in the world at 100 m and 200 m butterfly since 1981. (All Sport).

Earliest and latest

The earliest date in the year on which the Channel has been swum is 6 June by Dorothy Perkins (England) (b. 1942) in 1961, and the latest is 28 Oct by Michael Peter Read (GB) (b. 9 June 1941) in 1979.

Youngest and oldest

The youngest conqueror is Marcus Hooper (GB) (b. 14 June 1967) who swam from Dover to Sangatte, France in 14 hr 37 min on 5–6 Aug 1979, when he was aged 12 yr 53 days. The youngest girl is Samantha Claire Druce (GB) (b. 21 Apr 1971) who was 12 yr 119 days on 18 Aug 1983 when she swam from Dover to Cap Gris-Nez in 15 hr 27 min.

The oldest has been Ashby Harper (b. 1 Oct 1916) of Albuquerque, USA at 65 years 332 days when he swam from Dover to Cap Blanc Nez in 13 hr 52 min on 28 Aug 1982. The oldest woman was Stella Ada Rosina Taylor (b. 20 Dec 1929) aged 45 yr 350 days when she did the swim in 18 hr 15 min on 26 Aug 1975.

Double crossing

Antonio Abertondo (Argentina) (b. 1919), swam from England to France in 18 hr 50 min (8.35 a.m. on 20 Sept to 3.25 a.m. on 21 Sept 1961) and after about 4 min rest returned to England in 24 hr 16 min, landing at St Margaret's Bay at 3.45 a.m. on 22 Sept 1961, to complete the first 'double crossing' in 43 hr 10 min. Kevin Murphy (b. 1949) completed the first double crossing by a Briton in 35 hr 10 min on 6 Aug 1970. The first swimmer to achieve a crossing both ways was Edward Harry Temme (1904–78) on 5 Aug 1927 and 19 Aug 1934.

The fastest double crossing was in 18 hr 15 min by Irene van der Laan (Netherlands) (b. 27 Dec 1960) on 18 Aug 1983. The first British woman to achieve the double crossing was Alison Streeter (b. 29 Aug 1964) in 21 hr 16 min on 4 Aug 1983. The fastest by a relay team is 15 hr 36½ min by the six-man West One International Team (GB) on 24 Sept 1985.

Triple crossing

The first triple crossing was by Jon Erikson (USA) (b. 6 Sept 1954) in 38 hr 27 min on 11–12 Aug 1981.

Most conquests

The greatest number of Channel conquests is 31 by Michael Read (GB) from 24 Aug 1969 to 19 Aug 1984, including a record six in one year. Cindy Nicholas made her first crossing on 29 July 1975 and her nineteenth (and fifth two-way) on 14 Sept 1982.

LONG DISTANCE SWIMMING

Longest swims

The greatest recorded distance ever swum is 1826 miles *2938 km* down the Mississippi, USA between Ford Dam near Minneapolis and Carrollton Ave, New Orleans, Louisiana, by Fred P. Newton, (b. 1903) of Clinton, Oklahoma from 6 July to 29 Dec 1930. He was 742 hr in the water.

The greatest distance covered in a continuous swim is 299 miles *481,5 km* by Ricardo Hoffmann (b. 5 Oct 1941) from Corrientes to Santa Elena, Argentina in the River Parana in 84 hr 37 min on 3–6 Mar 1981.

The longest ocean swim is one of 128.8 miles *207,3 km* by Walter Poenisch Snr (USA) (b. 1914) who started from Havana, Cuba, and arrived at Little Duck Key, Florida, USA (in a shark cage and wearing flippers) 34 hr 15 min later on 11–13 July 1978.

In 1966 Mihir Sen of Calcutta, India uniquely swam the Palk Strait from Sri Lanka to India (in 25 hr 36 min on 5–6 Apr); the Straits of Gibraltar (in 8 hr 1 min on 24 Aug); the length of the Dardanelles (in 13 hr 55 min on 12 Sept), the Bosphorus (in 4 hr on 21 Sept) and the length of the Panama Canal (in 34 hr 15 min on 29–31 Oct).

Irish Channel
The swimming of the 23 mile *37 km* wide North Channel from Donaghadee, Northern Ireland to Portpatrick, Scotland was first accomplished by Tom Blower of Nottingham in 15 hr 26 min in 1947. A record time of 11 hr 21 min was set by Kevin Murphy on 11 Sept 1970. The first Irish-born swimmer to achieve the crossing was Ted Keenan on 11 Aug 1973 in 52–56°F *11–13°C* water in 18 hr 27 min.

Bristol Channel
The first person to achieve a crossing of the Bristol Channel was Kathleen Thomas (now Mrs Day) (b. Apr 1906) who swam from Penarth, South Glamorgan to Weston-super-Mare, Avon in 7 hr 20 min on 5 Sept 1927. The record for the longer swim from Glenthorne Cove, Devon to Porthcawl, Mid-Glamorgan is 10 hr 46 min by Jane Luscombe (b. 13 Jan 1961) of Jersey, CI, on 19 Aug 1976.

Lake swims
The fastest time for swimming the 22.7 mile *36,5 km* long Loch Ness, is 9 hr 57 min by David Morgan (b. 25 Sept 1963) on 31 July 1983. The first successful swim was by Brenda Sherratt (b. 1948) of West Bollington, Cheshire on 26–27 July 1966. David Morgan achieved a unique double crossing of Loch Ness in 23 hr 4 min on 1 Aug 1983. The fastest time for swimming Lake Windermere, 10.5 miles *16,9 km* is 3 hr 49 min 56 sec by Karen Toole, 17, of Darlington on 5 Sept 1981. The fastest time for the Lake Windermere International Championship, 16.5 miles *26,5 km*, is 6 hr 10 min 33 sec by Mary Beth Colpo (USA) (b. 1961) on 5 Aug 1978.

Longest duration
The longest duration swim ever achieved was one of 168 continuous hours, ending on 24 Feb 1941, by the legless Charles Zibbelman, *alias* Zimmy (b. 1894) in a pool in Honolulu, Hawaii, USA. The longest duration swim by a woman was 87 hr 27 min in a salt-water pool by Myrtle Huddleston (USA) at Raven Hall, Coney Island, NY, USA, in 1931.

24 hours
David Goch (USA) swam 55.682 miles *89,611 km* in a 25 yd *22,86 m* pool at the University of Michigan, USA on 17–18 May 1986. The record in a 50 m pool is 87,528 km *54.39 miles* by Bertrand Malègue at St. Etienne, France on 31 May–1 June 1980.

The women's record is 42.05 miles *67,67 km* by Alyson Gibbons (Sutton Coldfield) in the 25 m Aston Newtown Baths, Birmingham on 7–8 Sept 1985.

Greatest lifetime distance
Gustave Brickner (b. 10 Feb 1912) of Charleroi, Pennsylvania, USA in 58 years to November 1985 had recorded 38,162 miles *61 415 km*.

Long distance relays
The New Zealand national relay team of 20 swimmers swam a record 182,807 km *113.59 miles* in Lower Hutt, NZ in 24 hours, passing 160 km *100 miles* in 20 hr 47 min 13 sec on 9–10 Dec 1983. The most participants in a one-day swim relay is 2135, each swimming a length, organised by Syracuse YMCA in Syracuse, New York, USA on 11 Apr 1986. A team

of four from Capalaba State Primary School—Kim Wilson, Tanya Obstoj, Paul Giles, Darren Sheldrick—set an endurance record of 168 hr with one of the team in the water at any time, covering 540,8 km *336 miles* on 12–19 Dec 1983 at Sheldon, Queensland, Australia.

Underwater Swimming
Paul Cryne (UK) and Samir Sawan al Awami of Qatar swam 49.04 miles *78,92 km* in a 24 hr period from Doha, Qatar to Umm Said and back on 21–22 Feb 1985 using subaqua equipment. They were swimming underwater for 95.5% of the time.

Tony Boyle, Eddie McGettigan, Laurence Thermes and Gearoid Murphy swam a relay of 332.88 miles *535,71 km* underwater in 168 hr using subaqua equipment at the Mosney Holiday Centre, Co. Meath, Ireland, 22–29 June 1985.

The first underwater cross-Channel swim was achieved by Fred Baldasare (b. 1924) (USA), who completed a 42 mile *67,5 km* distance from France to England with Scuba equipment in 18 hr 1 min on 10–11 July 1962.

Sponsored swimming
The greatest amount of money collected in a charity swim was £87,173.13 in 'Splash '86' organised by the Royal Bank of Scotland Swimming Club for the 1986 Commonwealth Games Appeal. Held at the Royal Commonwealth Pool, Edinburgh, Scotland on 11–12 Jan 1986, 3559 swimmers took part.

Origins
The earliest evidence relating to a game resembling table tennis has been found in the catalogues of London sports goods manufacturers in the 1880s. The old Ping Pong Association was formed in 1902 but the game proved only a temporary craze until resuscitated in 1921. The English Table Tennis Association was formed on 24 Apr 1927.

Most English titles
The highest total of English men's titles (instituted 1921) is 20 by G. Viktor Barna (1911–72) (b. Hungary, Győző Braun). The women's record is 17 by Diane Rowe (b. 14 Apr 1933), now Mrs Eberhard Scholer. Her twin Rosalind (now Mrs Cornett) has won nine (two in singles).

The most titles won in the English Closed Championships is 22 by Desmond Douglas (b. 20 July 1955), a record nine men's singles, 1976 and 1979–86, nine men's doubles and four mixed doubles. A record seven women's singles were won by Jill Patricia Hammersley (now Parker *née* Shirley) (b. 6 Dec 1951) in 1973–6, 1978–9, 1981.

Internationals
The youngest ever international was Joy Foster, aged 8, when she represented Jamaica in the

TEAM AND INDIVIDUAL TABLE TENNIS CHAMPIONSHIPS

MOST WINS IN WORLD CHAMPIONSHIPS (Instituted 1926–7)

Event	Name and Nationality	Times	Years
Men's Singles (St Bride's Vase)	G. Viktor Barna (Hungary) (1911–72)	5	1930, 1932–5
Women's Singles (G. Geist Prize)	Angelica Rozeanu (Romania) (b. 15 Oct 1921)	6	1950–5
Men's Doubles	G. Viktor Barna (Hungary)	8	1929–35, 1939
Women's Doubles	Maria Mednyanszky (Hungary) (1901–79)	7	1928, 1930–5
Mixed Doubles (Men)	Ferenc Sido (Hungary) (b. 1923)	4	1949–50, 1952–3
Mixed Doubles (Women)	Maria Mednyanszky (Hungary)	6	1927–8, 1930–1, 1933–4

G. Viktor Barna gained a personal total of 15 world titles, while 18 have been won by Maria Mednyanszky.
Note: With the staging of championships biennially the breaking of the above records would now be virtually impossible.

MOST TEAM TITLES

Event	Team	Times	Years
Men's Team (Swaythling Cup)	Hungary	12	1927–31, 1933–5, 1938, 1949, 1952, 1979
Women's Team (Marcel Corbillon Cup)	Japan	8	1952, 1954, 1957, 1959, 1961, 1963, 1967, 1971

MOST WINS IN ENGLISH OPEN CHAMPIONSHIPS (Instituted 1921)

Event	Name and Nationality	Times	Years
Men's Singles	Richard Bergmann (Austria, then GB) (1920–70)	6	1939–40, 1948, 1950, 1952, 1954
Women's Singles	Maria Alexandru (Romania) (b. 1941)	6	1963–4, 1970–2, 1974
Men's Doubles	G. Viktor Barna (Hungary, then GB)	7	1931, 1933–5, 1938–9, 1949
Women's Doubles	Diane Rowe (GB) (now Scholer) (b. 14 Apr 1933)	12	1950–6, 1960, 1962–5
Mixed Doubles (Men)	G. Viktor Barna (Hungary, then GB)	8	1933–6, 1938, 1940, 1951, 1953
Mixed Doubles (Women)	Diane Rowe (GB) (now Scholer)	4	1952, 1954, 1956, 1960

British internationals Desmond Douglas (*left*) and Alan Cooke seen breaking the counter-hitting record on BBC TV's *Record Breakers*. They later set a better mark with 170 hits in a minute—on average a hit every 0.353 sec.

West Indies Championships at Port of Spain, Trinidad in Aug 1958. The youngest ever to play for England was Carl Prean (b. 20 Aug 1967), aged 14 yr 191 days, against Portugal at Lisbon on 27 Feb 1982.

Jill Parker played for England on a record 413 occasions, 1967–83.

Counter hitting

The record number of hits in 60 sec is 170 by English Internationals Alan Cooke (b. 23 Mar 1966) and Desmond Douglas at Scotswood Sports Centre, Newcastle upon Tyne on 28 Feb 1986. The women's record is 163 by the sisters Lisa (b. 9 Mar 1967) and Jackie (b. 9 Sept 1964) Bellinger at Stopsley Sports Centre, Luton, Beds. on 23 June 1985. With a bat in each hand, Gary D. Fisher of Olympia, Wash., USA, completed 5000 consecutive volleys over the net in 44 min 28 sec on 25 June 1979.

Highest speed

No conclusive measurements have been published but in a lecture M. Sklorz (W. Germany) stated that a smashed ball had been measured at speeds up to 170 km/h *105,6 mph*.

Tae Kwon-do

The founder and father of this martial art is General Choi Hong Hi 9th Dan, the highest Dan awarded. Tae Kwon-Do was officially recognised as part of Korean tradition and culture on 11 Apr 1955.

The highest Dan in Britain is Master Rhee Ki Ha 8th Dan, the Chief Instructor of the United Kingdom Tae Kwon-Do Association.

Tennis (Lawn)

Origins

The modern game is generally agreed to have evolved as an outdoor form of the indoor game of Tennis (see separate entry). 'Field Tennis' is mentioned in an English magazine—*Sporting Magazine*—of 29 Sept 1793. The earliest club for such a game, variously called Pelota or Lawn Rackets, was the Leamington Club founded in 1872 by Major Harry Gem. The earliest attempt to commercialise the game was by Major Walter Clopton Wingfield (1833–1912) who patented a form called 'sphairistike' on 23 Feb 1874. It soon became called Lawn Tennis. Amateur players were permitted to play with and against professionals in 'Open' tournaments in 1968.

Grand Slam

The grand slam is to hold at the same time all four of the world's major championship singles: Wimbledon, the United States, Australian and French championships. The first man to have won all four was Frederick John Perry (GB) (b. 18 May 1909) with the French title in 1935. The first man to hold all four championships simultaneously was John Donald Budge (USA) (b. 13 June 1915) with the French title in 1938. The first man to achieve the grand slam twice was Rodney George Laver (Australia) (b. 9 Aug 1938) having won in 1962 as an amateur and again in 1969 when the titles were 'open' to professionals.

Three women have achieved the grand slam: Maureen Catherine Connolly (USA) (1934–69), later Mrs Norman E. Brinker, in 1953; Margaret Jean Court (*née* Smith) (Australia) (b. 16 July 1942) in 1970 and Martina Navratilova (USA) (b. Prague, Czechoslovakia 18 Oct 1956) in 1983–4. Miss Navratilova won six successive grand slam singles titles in 1983–4 and with Pamela Howard Shriver (USA) (b. 4 July 1962) won eight successive grand slam tournament women's doubles titles and 109 successive matches in all events in April 1983 to July 1985.

The most singles championships in 'grand slam' tournaments is 24 by Margaret Court (eleven Australian, five French, five USA, three Wimbledon), 1960–73. The men's record is 12 by Roy Emerson (Australia) (b. 3 Nov 1936) (six Australian, two each French, USA, Wimbledon), 1961–7.

Fastest service

The fastest service timed with modern equipment is 138 mph *222 km/h* by Steve Denton (USA) (b. 5 Sept 1956) at Beaver Creek, Colorado, USA on 29 July 1984. The fastest *ever* measured was one of 163.6 mph *263 km/h* by William Tatem Tilden (1893–1953) (USA) in 1931.

Longest game

The longest known singles game was one of 37 deuces (80 points) between Anthony Fawcett (Rhodesia) and Keith Glass (GB) in the first round of the Surrey championships at Surbiton, Surrey, on 26 May 1975. It lasted 31 min. Noëlle Van Lottum and Sandra Begijn played a game lasting 52 min in the semi-finals of the Dutch Indoor Championships at Ede, Gederland on 12 Feb 1984.

The longest rally in tournament play is one of 643 times over the net between Vicky Nelson and Jean Hepner at Richmond, Virginia, USA in October 1984. The 6 hr 22 min match was won by Nelson 6–4, 7–6. It concluded with a

1 hr 47 min tiebreak, 13–11, for which one point took 29 min.

The longest tiebreaker was 26–24 for the fourth and decisive set of a first round Men's Doubles at the Wimbledon Championships on 1 July 1985. Jan Gunnarsson (Sweden) and Michael Mortensen (Denmark) defeated John Frawley (Australia) and Victor Pecci (Paraguay) 6–3, 6–4, 3–6, 7–6.

Greatest crowd

A record 30,472 people were at the Astrodome, Houston, Texas, on 20 Sept 1973, when Billie-Jean King (*née* Moffitt) (b. 22 Nov 1943) (USA) beat Robert Larimore Riggs (b. 25 Feb 1918) (USA). The record for an orthodox tennis match is 25,578 at Sydney, NSW, Australia on 27 Dec 1954 in the Davis Cup Challenge Round (first day) Australia *v.* USA.

Highest earnings

Ivan Lendl (Czechoslovakia) (b. 7 Mar 1960) won a men's record $2,028,850 in 1982. The record for a woman is $2,173,556 in 1984 (including a $1 million Grand Slam bonus) by Martina Navratilova. Earnings from special restricted events and team tennis are not included. Navratilova's lifetime earnings by 8 July 1986 reached $10,881,986.

The one match record is $500,000 by James Scott Connors (USA) (b. 2 Sept 1952) when he beat John David Newcombe (Australia) (b. 23 May 1944) in a challenge match at Caesar's Palace, Las Vegas, USA on 26 Apr 1975. The highest total prize money is $3,450,800 for the 1986 US Championships.

Longest span as national champion

Walter Westbrook (b. June 1898) won the US National Clay Court men's doubles with Harvey Snodgrass in 1925. Fifty eight years later he won the US National 85-and-over Clay Court men's singles championship. In the final he defeated Kirk Reid, whom he had first defeated to win the Western Clay Court Championships in 1925.

Dorothy May Bundy-Cheney (USA) (b. Sept 1916) won 141 US titles at various age groups from 1941 to 1984.

International Contest *Longest span*

Jean Borotra (France) (b. 13 Aug 1898) played for the 100th time in the match between the International Club of France and the I.C. of Great Britain at Wimbledon 1–3 Nov 1985. The twice yearly contest was first staged in 1929 and Borotra played in every one. Among other matches he played a mixed doubles against Kitty Godfree (GB) (b. 7 May 1896), both former Wimbledon singles champions, and aged 87 and 89 respectively.

INTERNATIONAL TEAM COMPETITIONS

Davis Cup (inst. 1900)

The most wins in the Davis Cup, the men's international team championship, have been (to 1983) by the USA with 28. The most appearances for Cup winners is eight by Roy Emerson (Australia), 1959–62, 1964–7. The British Isles/Great Britain have won nine times in 1903–6, 1912, 1933–6.

Nicola Pietrangeli (b. 11 Sept 1933) (Italy) played a record 163 rubbers, 1954 to 1972, winning 120. He played 109 singles (winning 78) and 54 doubles (winning 42). He took part in 66 ties. The record number of rubbers by a British player is 65 (winning 43) by Michael J. Sangster (b. 9 Sept 1940), 1960–8; the most wins is 45 from 52 rubbers by Fred Perry, including 34 of 38 singles, 1931–6.

Martina Navratilova (*right*) and Pam Shriver, whose extraordinary doubles record of 13 Grand Slam tournament titles includes eight consecutive successes in the 'big four' between 1983 and 1985. (All Sport).

WIMBLEDON
Most titles

Six times singles champion Billie-Jean King (b. 22 Nov 1943) (USA) has won ten women's doubles and four mixed doubles during the period 1961 to 1979, to total a record 20 titles.

Wightman Cup (inst. 1923)
The Wightman Cup has been won 47 times by the United States and 10 times by Great Britain. Virginia Wade (GB) (b. 10 July 1945) played in a record 20 ties and 55 rubbers, 1965–84. Christine Marie Lloyd (*née* Evert) (USA) (b. 21 Dec 1954) won all 26 of her singles matches, 1971 to 1985.

Federation Cup (inst. 1963)
The most wins in the Federation Cup, the women's international team championship, is 11 by the USA. Virginia Wade (GB) played each year from 1967 to 1983, in a record 55 ties, playing 100 rubbers, including 56 singles (winning 36) and 44 doubles (winning 30). Chris Lloyd won all her 28 singles matches and 14 of 15 doubles, 1977 to 1982.

WIMBLEDON CHAMPIONSHIPS

Most wins *Women* (see above)
Elizabeth Montague Ryan (USA) (1892–1979) won a record 19 doubles (12 women's, 7 mixed) titles from 1914 to 1934.

Most wins *Men*
The greatest number of titles by a man has been 13 by Hugh Laurence Doherty (GB) (1875–1919) with five singles titles (1902–6) and a record eight men's doubles (1897–1901, 1903–5) partnered by his brother Reginald Frank (1872–1910).

Most wins *Singles*
The greatest number of singles titles is eight by Helen Newington Moody (*née* Wills) (USA) (b. 6 Oct 1905), who won in 1927–30, 1932–3, 1935 and 1938. The most men's singles wins since the Challenge Round was abolished in 1922 is five consecutively, by Bjorn Borg (Sweden) in 1976–80. William Charles Renshaw (GB) (1861–1904) won seven singles in 1881–6 and 1889.

Most wins *Mixed doubles*
The male record is four titles shared by Elias Victor Seixas (USA) (b. 30 Aug 1923) in 1953–6, Kenneth Norman Fletcher (Australia) (b. 15 June 1940) in 1963, 1965–6, 1968 and Owen Keir Davidson (Australia) (b. 4 Oct 1943) in 1967, 1971, 1973–4. The female record is seven by Elizabeth Ryan (USA) from 1919 to 1932.

Most appearances
Arthur William Charles 'Wentworth' Gore (1868–1928) (GB) made a record 36 appearances at Wimbledon between 1888 and 1927. In 1964, Jean Borotra (b. 13 Aug 1898) of France, made his 35th appearance since 1922. In 1977 he appeared in the Veterans' Doubles aged 78.

Youngest champions
The youngest champion was Charlotte 'Lottie' Dod (1871–1960), who was 15 yr 285 days when she won in 1887. The youngest male champion was Boris Becker (W. Germany) (b. 22 Nov 1967) who won the men's singles title in 1985 at 17 yr 227 days. The youngest ever player at Wimbledon is reputedly Mita Klima (Austria) who was 13 yr in the 1907 singles competition. The youngest player to win a match at Wimbledon is Kathy Rinaldi (b. 24 Mar 1967) (USA), at 14 yr 91 days on 23 June 1981.

Oldest champions
The oldest champion was Margaret Evelyn du Pont (*née* Osborne) (USA) (b. 4 Mar 1918) at 44 yr 125 days when she won the mixed doubles in 1962 with Neale Fraser (Aus). The oldest singles champion was Arthur Gore (GB) in 1909 at 41 yr 182 days.

Greatest crowd
The record crowd for one day is 39,813 on 26 June 1986. The record for the whole championship is 400,032 in 1986.

UNITED STATES CHAMPIONSHIPS

Most wins
Margaret Evelyn du Pont (*née* Osborne) won a record 24 titles between 1941 and 1960. She won a record 13 women's doubles (12 with Althea Louise Brough), eight mixed doubles and three singles. The men's record is 16 by William Tatem Tilden, including seven men's singles, 1920–25, 1929—a record for singles shared with Richard Dudley Sears (1861–1943), 1881–7; William A. Larned (1872–1926), 1901–2, 1907–11, and at women's singles by Molla Mallory (*née* Bjurstedt) (1892–1959), 1915–6, 1918, 1920–2, 1926 and Helen Moody (*née* Wills), 1923–5, 1927–9, 1931.

Youngest and Oldest
The youngest champion was Vincent Richards (1903–59), who was 15 yr 139 days when he won the men's doubles with Bill Tilden in 1918. The youngest singles champion was Tracy Ann Austin (b. 12 Dec 1962) who was 16 yr 271 days when she won the women's singles in 1979. The oldest champion was Margaret du Pont who won the mixed doubles at 42 yr 166 days in 1960. The oldest singles champion was William Larned at 38 yr 242 days in 1911.

FRENCH CHAMPIONSHIPS

Most wins (from International status 1925)
Margaret Court won a record 13 titles, five singles, four women's doubles and four mixed doubles, 1962–73. The men's record is nine by Henri Cochet (France) (b. 14 Dec 1901), four singles, three men's doubles and two mixed doubles, 1926–30. Bjorn Borg won a record six singles, 1974–81.

Youngest and oldest
The youngest champions were the 1981 mixed doubles winners, Andrea Jaeger (b. 4 June 1965) at 15 yr 339 days and Jimmy Arias (b. 16 Aug 1964) at 16 yr 296 days. The youngest singles winner was Mats Wilander (Sweden) (b. 22 Aug 1964) at 17 yr 288 days in 1982. The oldest champion was Elizabeth Ryan who won the 1934 women's doubles with Simone Mathieu (France) at 42 yr 88 days. The oldest singles champion was Andres Gimeno in 1972 at 34 yr 301 days.

Grand Prix Masters
The first Grand Prix Masters Championships were staged in Tokyo, Japan in 1971. They have been held in New York annually from 1977. Qualification to this annual event is by relative success in the preceding year's Grand Prix tournaments. Ilie Nastase (Romania) (b. 19 Aug 1946) won a record four titles, 1971–3, 1975. James Scott Connors (USA) (b. 7 Sept 1952) uniquely qualified for 14 consecutive years, 1972–85. He chose not to play in 1975, 1976 and 1985, and won in 1977.

Kathy Rinaldi, who in 1981 became the youngest player ever to win a match at Wimbledon, turned professional a month later—the youngest ever to do so at 14 years 4 months. (All Sport).

TENNIS (REAL OR ROYAL)

The game originated as *jeu de paume* in French monasteries *c.* 1050. A tennis court is mentioned in the sale of the Hôtel de Nesle, Paris bought by King Philippe IV of France in 1308. The oldest of the surviving active courts in Great Britain is that at Falkland Palace, Fife, Scotland, built by King James V of Scotland in 1539.

Most titles *World*
The first recorded World Tennis Champion was Clerge (France) *c.* 1740. Jacques Edmond Barre (France) (1802–73) held the title for a record 33 yr from 1829 to 1862. Pierre Etchebaster (1893–1980), a Basque, holds the record for the greatest number of successful defences of the title with eight between 1928 and 1952.

The inaugural women's world championship in 1985 was won by Judy Clarke (Australia).

Most titles *British*
The Amateur Championship of the British Isles (instituted 1888) has been won 16 times by Howard Rea Angus (b. 25 June 1944) 1966–80 and 1982. Angus, a left-hander, is also the first British amateur to win a World title, in 1975.

TIDDLYWINKS

National Championships
Alan Dean (Edwinstowe, Notts) (b. 22 July 1949) has won the singles title a record five times, 1971–3, 1976, 1978. He has also won the pairs title five times. Jonathan Mapley (b. 1947) has won the pairs title a record six times, 1972, 1975, 1977, 1980 and 1983–4.

Guinness Trophy
England has been unbeaten against Scotland, Ireland and Wales since the Trophy's inception in 1960. The closest result has been their 59½–52½ win over Wales at Warwick on 7 Apr 1968.

Potting records
The record for potting 24 winks from 18 in *45 cm* is 21.8 sec by Stephen Williams (Altrincham

Grammar School) in May 1966. Allen R. Astles (University of Wales) potted 10,000 winks in 3 hr 51 min 46 sec at Aberystwyth, Cardiganshire in February 1966. The greatest number of winks potted in 3 min by a relay of four is 29 by Paul Light, Paul Hoffman, Andrew James and Geoff Thorpe at 'The Castle', Cambridge on 6 Dec 1974.

High Jump

Jonathan Mapley, Nick Inglis, Tony Brennan and Stewart Sage achieved individually 2,29 m *7 ft 6 in* on BBC Television on 24 Apr 1986.

TRACK AND FIELD ATHLETICS

Origins

Track and field athletics date from the ancient Olympic Games. The earliest accurately known Olympiad dates from July 776 BC, at which celebration Coroibos won the foot race. The oldest surviving measurements are a long jump of 7,05 m *23 ft 1½ in* by Chionis of Sparta in *c.* 656 BC and a discus throw of 100 cubits (about 46.30 m *152 ft*) by Protesilaus.

Earliest landmarks

The first time 10 sec ('even time') was bettered for 100 yd under championship conditions was when John Owen, then aged 30, recorded 9⅘ sec in the AAU Championship at Analostan Island, Washington, DC, USA, on 11 Oct 1890. The first recorded instance of 6 ft *1,83 m* being cleared in the high jump was when Marshall Jones Brooks (1855–1944) jumped 6 ft 0⅛ in *1,832 m* at Marston, near Oxford, on 17 Mar 1876. The breaking of the 'four-minute barrier' in the 1 mile *1609,34 m* was first achieved by Dr (now Sir) Roger Gilbert Bannister, CBE (b. Harrow, London, 23 Mar 1929), when he recorded 3 min 59.4 sec on the Iffley Road track, Oxford, at 6.10 p.m. on 6 May 1954.

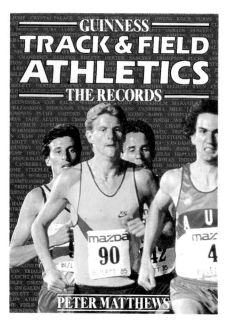

Published by Guinness at £7.95

Willie Banks (*left*), whose ebullient enthusiasm has greatly boosted the popularity of the triple jump. He set his world record after a decade of competition in the event. The supremely versatile Said Aouita (*right*) is the first man in thirty years to hold concurrently world records at 1500 and 5000 metres. (All Sport.)

Fastest speed

The fastest speed recorded in an individual world record is 36,51 km/h *22.69 mph*, but this does not allow for the effects of the delay in reaching peak speed from a standing start. Maximum speeds exceeding 40 km/h *25 mph* for men and 36,5 km/h *22.5 mph* for women have been measured; for instance for Carl Lewis (8.94 sec) and Evelyn Ashford (9.97 sec) respectively for their final 100 metres in the 1984 Olympic sprint relays.

Highest jump above own head

The greatest height cleared above an athlete's own head is 23¼ in *59 cm* by Franklin Jacobs (USA) (b. 31 Dec 1957), who cleared 7 ft 7¼ in *2,32 m* at New York, USA, on 27 Jan 1978. He

is only 5 ft 8 in *1,73 m* tall. The greatest height cleared by a woman above her own head is 30,5 cm *12 in* by Cindy John Holmes (USA) (b. 29 Aug 1960), 5 ft *1,525 m* tall, who jumped 6 ft *1,83 m* at Provo, Utah, USA on 1 June 1982.

Most Olympic titles *Men*

The most Olympic gold medals won is ten (an absolute Olympic record) by Ray C. Ewry (USA) (1874–1937) in the Standing High, Long and Triple Jumps in 1900, 1904, 1906 and 1908.

Most Olympic titles *Women*

The most gold medals won by a woman is four shared by Francina 'Fanny' E. Blankers-Koen (Netherlands) (b. 26 Apr 1918) with 100 m, 200 m, 80 m hurdles and 4 × 100 m relay, 1948;

WORLD RECORDS MEN

World records for the men's events scheduled by the International Amateur Athletic Federation. Fully automatic electric timing is mandatory for events up to 400 metres.

RUNNING

	Min Sec	Name and Country	Place	Date
100 metres	9.93A	Calvin Smith (USA) (b. 8 Jan 1961)	Colorado Springs, Colorado, USA	3 July 1983
200 metres	19.72A	Pietro Mennea (Italy) (b. 28 June 1952)	Mexico City, Mexico	12 Sept 1979
400 metres	43.86A	Lee Edward Evans (USA) (b. 25 Feb 1947)	Mexico City, Mexico	18 Oct 1968
800 metres	1:41.73	Sebastian Newbold Coe (GB) (b. 29 Sept 1956)	Florence, Italy	10 June 1981
1000 metres	2:12.18	Sebastian Newbold Coe (GB)	Oslo, Norway	11 July 1981
1500 metres	3:29.45	Saïd Aouita (Morocco) (b. 2 Nov 1960)	W. Berlin, W. Germany	23 Aug 1985
1 mile	3:46.32	Steven Cram (GB) (b. 14 Oct 1960)	Oslo, Norway	27 July 1985
2000 metres	4:51.39	Steven Cram (GB)	Budapest, Hungary	4 Aug 1985
3000 metres	7:32.1	Henry Rono (Kenya) (b. 12 Feb 1952)	Oslo, Norway	27 June 1978
5000 metres	13:00.40	Saïd Aouita (Morocco)	Oslo, Norway	27 July 1985
10,000 metres	27:13.81	Fernando Mamede (Portugal) (b. 1 Nov 1951)	Stockholm, Sweden	2 July 1984
20,000 metres	57:24.2	Josephus Hermens (Netherlands) (b. 8 Jan 1950)	Papendal, Netherlands	1 May 1976
25,000 metres	1 hr 13:55.8	Toshihiko Seko (Japan) (b. 15 July 1956)	Christchurch, New Zealand	22 Mar 1981
30,000 metres	1 hr 29:18.8	Toshihiko Seko (Japan)	Christchurch, New Zealand	22 Mar 1981
1 hour	20 944 m *13 miles 24 yd 2 ft*	Josephus Hermens (Netherlands)	Papendal, Netherlands	1 May 1976

A *These records were set at high altitude—Mexico City 2240 m 7349 ft, Colorado Springs 2195 m 7201 ft. Best marks at low altitude have been: 100 m: 9.95 sec, Ben Johnson (Can) (b. 30 Dec 1961), Moscow, USSR, 9 July 1986. 200 m: 19.75 sec, Frederick Carlton 'Carl' Lewis (USA) (b. 1 July 1961), Indianapolis, Indiana, USA, 19 June 1983. 400 m: 44.26 sec, Alberto Juantorena (Cuba) (b. 21 Nov 1950), Montreal, Canada, 29 July 1976. Long Jump: 8.79 m 28 ft 10¼ in, Carl Lewis, Indianapolis, Indiana, USA, 19 June 1983.*

HURDLING

		Name and Country	Place	Date
110 metres (3' 6" 106 cm)	12.93	Renaldo Nehemiah (USA) (b. 24 Mar 1959)	Zürich, Switzerland	19 Aug 1981
400 metres (3' 0" 91,4 cm)	47.02	Edwin Corley Moses (USA) (b. 31 Aug 1955)	Koblenz, W. Germany	31 Aug 1983
3000 metres steeplechase	8:05.4	Henry Rono (Kenya)	Seattle, Washington, USA	13 May 1978

RELAYS

		Name and Country	Place	Date
4 × 100 metres	37.83	United States National Team: Sam Graddy, Ronald James Brown, Calvin Smith, Frederick Carlton Lewis	Los Angeles, USA	11 Aug 1984
4 × 200 metres	1:20.26†	University of Southern California, USA: Joel Andrews, James Sanford, William Mullins, Clancy Edwards	Tempe, Arizona, USA	27 May 1978
4 × 400 metres	2:56.16A	United States National Team: Vincent Edward Matthews, Ronald J. Freeman, George Lawrence James, Lee Edward Evans	Mexico City, Mexico	20 Oct 1968
4 × 800 metres	7:03.89	Great Britain: Peter Elliott, Gary Peter Cook, Steven Cram, Sebastian Newbold Coe	Crystal Palace, London	30 Aug 1982
4 × 1500 metres	14:38.8	West Germany: Thomas Wessinghage, Harald Hudak, Michael Lederer, Karl Fleschen	Cologne, W. Germany	17 Aug 1977

† *Texas Christian University ran 1:20.20 at Philadelphia, Pa, USA on 26 Apr 1986. This time could not be ratified as their team was composed of different nationalities: Roscoe Tatum (USA), Andrew Smith (Jamaica), Leroy Reid (Jamaica), Greg Sholars (USA).*
A *Best mark at low altitude: 2:58.65 USA (Herman Frazier, Benny Brown, Fred Newhouse, Maxie Parks) Montreal, Canada, 31 July 1976.*

FIELD EVENTS

	m	ft in	Name and Country	Place	Date
High Jump	2,41	7 10¾	Igor Paklin (USSR) (b. 15 June 1963)	Kobe, Japan	4 Sept 1985
Pole Vault	6,01	19 8¾	Sergey Bubka (USSR) (b. 4 Dec 1963)	Moscow, USSR	8 July 1986
Long Jump	8,90A	29 2½	Robert Beamon (USA) (b. 29 Aug 1946)	Mexico City, Mexico	18 Oct 1968
Triple Jump	17,97	58 11¼	William Augustus 'Willie' Banks (USA) (b. 11 Mar 1956)	Indianapolis, USA	16 June 1985
Shot 7,26 kg 16 lb	22,62*	74 2½	Ulf Timmermann (GDR) (b. 1 Nov 1962)	East Berlin, GDR	22 Sept 1985
Discus 2 kg 4 lb 6.55 oz	74,08	243 0	Jürgen Schult (GDR) (b. 11 May 1960)	Neubrandenburg, GDR	6 June 1986
Hammer 7,26 kg 16 lb	86,66	284 4	Yuriy Georgiyevich Sedykh (USSR) (b. 11 Jun 1955)	Tallinn, USSR	22 June 1986
Javelin 800 g 28.22 oz	104,80†	343 10	Uwe Hohn (GDR) (b. 16 July 1962)	East Berlin, GDR	20 July 1984

* *One professional performance is superior to the IAAF mark, but the same highly rigorous rules as to measuring and weighing were not necessarily applied.*

| | 22,86 | 75 0 | Brian Ray Oldfield (USA) (b. 1 Jan 1945) | El Paso, Texas, USA | 10 May 1975 |

† *Old javelin. A new javelin, with the centre of gravity moved forwards, was introduced in 1986. The best performance at the end of the year will be recognised as the new world record.*

DECATHLON

		Name and Country	Place	Date
8847 points		Francis Morgan 'Daley' Thompson (GB) (b. 30 July 1958)	Los Angeles, USA	8–9 Aug 1984

(1st day: 100 m 10.44 sec, Long Jump 8,01 m 26' 3½", Shot Put 15,72 m 51' 7", High Jump 2,03 m 6' 8", 400 m 46.97 sec) (2nd day: 110 m Hurdles 14.33 sec, Discus 46,56 m 152' 9", Pole Vault 5,00 m 16' 4¾", Javelin 65,24 m 214' 0", 1500 m 4:35.00 sec)

Betty Cuthbert (Australia) (b. 20 Apr 1938) with 100 m, 200 m, 4 × 100 m relay, 1956 and 400 m, 1964; and Bärbel Wöckel (*née* Eckert) (b. 21 Mar 1955) (GDR) with 200 m and 4 × 100 m relay in 1976 and 1980.

Most wins at one Games
The most gold medals at one celebration is five by Paavo Johannes Nurmi (Finland) (1897–1973) in 1924, and the most individual is four by Alvin C. Kraenzlein (USA) (1876–1928) in 1900.

Most Olympic medals *Men*
The most medals won is 12 (nine gold and three silver) by Paavo Nurmi (Finland) in the Games of 1920, 1924 and 1928.

Most Olympic medals *Women*
The most medals won by a woman athlete is seven by Shirley de la Hunty (*née* Strickland) (Australia) (b. 18 July 1925) with three gold, one silver and three bronze in the 1948, 1952 and 1956 Games. A recently discovered photo-finish indicates that she finished third, not fourth, in the 1948 200 metres event, thus unofficially increasing her medal haul to eight. Irena Szewinska (*née* Kirszenstein) (Poland) (b. 24 May 1946) won three gold, two silver and two bronze in 1964, 1968, 1972 and 1976, and is the only woman athlete to win a medal in four successive games.

Most Olympic titles *British*
The most gold medals won by a British athlete (excluding Tug of War and Walking, *q.v.*) is two by: Charles Bennett (1871–1949) (1500 m and 5000 m team, 1900); Alfred Tysoe (1874–1901) (800 m and 5000 m team, 1900); John Rimmer (1879–1962) (4000 m steeplechase and 5000 m team, 1900); Albert G. Hill (1889–1969) (800 m and 1500 m, 1920); Douglas Gordon Arthur Lowe (1902–81) (800 m 1924 and 1928); Sebastian Newbold Coe (b. 29 Sept 1956) (1500 m 1980 and 1984) and Francis Morgan 'Daley' Thompson (b. 30 July 1958) (decathlon 1980 and 1984).

Most Olympic medals *British*
The most medals won by a British athlete is four by Guy M. Butler (1899–1981) gold for the 4 × 400 m relay and silver for 400 m in 1920 and

bronze for each of these events in 1924 and by Seb Coe, who also won silver medals at 800 m in 1980 and 1984. Three British women athletes have won three medals: Dorothy Hyman (b. 9 May 1941) with a silver (100 m, 1960) and two bronze (200 m, 1960 and 4 × 100 m relay, 1964), Mary Denise Rand (now Toomey, *née* Bignal), (b. 10 Feb 1940) with a gold (long jump), a silver (pentathlon) and a bronze (4 × 100 m relay), all in 1964 and Kathryn Jane Cook (née Smallwood) (b. 3 May 1960), all bronze—at 4 × 100 m relay 1980 and 1984, and at 400 m in 1984.

Olympic champions *Oldest and youngest*
The oldest athlete to win an Olympic title was Irish-born Patrick J. 'Babe' McDonald (USA) (1878–1954) who was aged 42 yr 26 days when he won the 56 lb *25,4 kg* weight throw at Antwerp, Belgium on 21 Aug 1920. The oldest female champion was Lia Manoliu (Romania) (b. 25 Apr 1932) aged 36 yr 176 days when she won the discus at Mexico City on 18 Oct 1968. The youngest gold medallist was Barbara Pearl Jones (USA) (b. 26 Mar 1937) who was a member of the winning 4 × 100 m relay team, aged 15 yr 123 days, at Helsinki, Finland on 27 July 1952. The youngest male champion was Robert Bruce Mathias (USA) (b. 17 Nov 1930) aged 17 yr 263 days when he won the decathlon at London on 5–6 Aug 1948.

The oldest Olympic medallist was Tebbs Lloyd Johnson (1900–84), aged 48 yr 115 days when he was third in the 1948 50,000 m walk. The oldest women's medallist was Dana Zátopková aged 37 yr 348 days when she was second in the javelin in 1960.

World record breakers *Oldest and youngest*
For the greatest age at which anyone has broken a world record under IAAF jurisdiction *see p. 218*. The female record is 35 yr 255 days for Dana Zátopková, *née* Ingrova (b. 19 Sept 1922) of Czechoslovakia, who broke the women's javelin record with 55,73 m *182 ft 10 in* at Prague, Czechoslovakia, on 1 June 1958. The youngest individual record breaker is 15 year old Wang Yang (b. 1971) (China) who set a women's 3000 metres walk record with 21 min 33.8 sec at Jian, China on 9 Mar 1986. The male record is 17 yr 198 days by Thomas Ray (1862–1904) when he pole-vaulted 3.42 m *11 ft 2¼ in* on 19 Sept 1879 (prior to IAAF ratification).

Most records in a day
Jesse Owens (1913–80) (USA) set six world records in 45 min at Ann Arbor, Michigan on

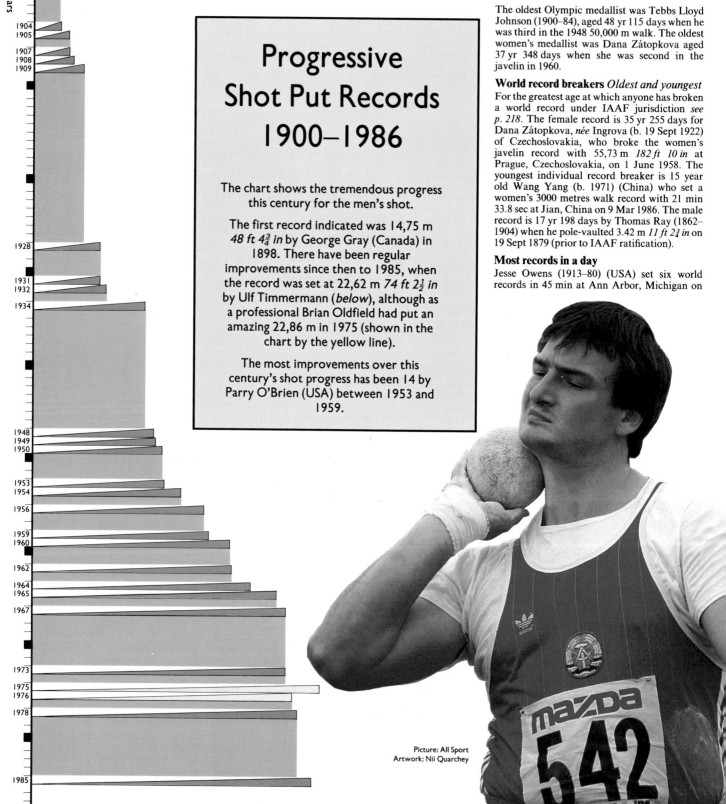

Progressive Shot Put Records 1900–1986

The chart shows the tremendous progress this century for the men's shot.

The first record indicated was 14,75 m *48 ft 4¾ in* by George Gray (Canada) in 1898. There have been regular improvements since then to 1985, when the record was set at 22,62 m *74 ft 2½ in* by Ulf Timmermann (*below*), although as a professional Brian Oldfield had put an amazing 22,86 m in 1975 (shown in the chart by the yellow line).

The most improvements over this century's shot progress has been 14 by Parry O'Brien (USA) between 1953 and 1959.

Picture: All Sport
Artwork: Nii Quarchey

RUNNING	Min sec	Name and Country	Place	Date
100 metres	10.76	Evelyn Ashford (USA) (b. 15 Apr 1957)	Zürich, Switzerland	22 Aug 1984
200 metres	21.71	Marita Koch (GDR) (b. 18 Feb 1957)	Karl Marx Stadt, GDR	10 June 1979
		Marita Koch (GDR)	Potsdam, GDR	21 July 1984
		Heike Drechsler [née Daute] (GDR) (b. 16 Dec 1964)	Jena, GDR	29 June 1986
400 metres	47.60	Marita Koch (GDR)	Canberra, Australia	6 Oct 1985
800 metres	1:53.28	Jarmila Kratochvilova (Czechoslovakia)	Munich, W. Germany	26 July 1983
1000 metres	2:30.6	Tatyana Providokhina (USSR) (b. 26 Mar 1953)	Podolsk, USSR	20 Aug 1978
1500 metres	3:52.47	Tatyana Kazankina (USSR) (b. 17 Dec 1951)	Zürich, Switzerland	13 Aug 1980
1 mile	4:16.71	Mary Slaney [née Decker] (USA) (b. 4 Aug 1958)	Zürich, Switzerland	21 Aug 1985
2000 metres	5:28.69	Maricica Puica (Rumania) (b. 29 July 1950)	Crystal Palace, London	11 July 1986
3000 metres	8:22.62	Tatyana Kazankina (USSR)	Leningrad, USSR	26 Aug 1984
5000 metres	14:48.07	Zola Budd (UK) (b. 26 May 1966)	Crystal Palace, London	26 Aug 1985
10000 metres	30:13.74	Ingrid Kristiansen (née Christensen) (Norway) (b. 21 Mar 1956)	Oslo, Norway	5 July 1986

HURDLING		Name and Country	Place	Date
100 metres (2' 9" 84 cm)	12.36	Grazyna Rabsztyn (Poland) (b. 20 Sept 1952)	Warsaw, Poland	13 June 1980
400 metres (2' 6" 76 cm)	53.55	Sabine Busch (GDR) (b. 21 Nov 1962)	East Berlin, GDR	22 Sept 1985

RELAYS		Name and Country	Place	Date
4 × 100 metres	41.37	GDR: Silke Gladisch, Sabine Rieger, Ingrid Auerswald [née Brestrich], Marlies Göhr [née Oelsner]	Canberra, Australia	6 Oct 1985
4 × 200 metres	1:28.15	GDR: Marlies Göhr [née Oelsner], Romy Müller [née Schneider], Bärbel Wöckel [née Eckert], Marita Koch	Jena, GDR	9 Aug 1980
4 × 400 metres	3:15.92	GDR: Gesine Walther, Sabine Busch, Dagmar Rübsam, Marita Koch	Erfurt, GDR	3 June 1984
4 × 800 metres	7:50.17	USSR: Nadezha Olizarenko, Lyubov Gurina, Lyudmila Borisova, Irina Podyalovskaya	Moscow, USSR	4 Aug 1984

FIELD EVENTS	m	ft in	Name and Country	Place	Date
High Jump	2,08	6 9¾	Stefka Kostadinova (Bulgaria) (b. 25 Mar 1965)	Sofia, Bulgaria	31 May 1986
Long Jump	7,45	24 5½	Heike Drechsler	Tallinn, USSR	21 June 1986
			Heike Drechsler	Dresden, GDR	3 July 1986
Shot 4 kg 8 lb 13 oz	22,53	73 11	Natalya Lisovskaya (USSR) (b. 16 July 1962)	Sochi, USSR	27 May 1984
Discus 1 kg 2 lb 3.27 oz	74,56	244 7	Zdenka Silhava (Czechoslovakia) (b. 15 June 1954)	Nitra, Czechoslovakia	26 Aug 1984
Javelin 600 g 24.74 oz	75,40	247 4	Petra Felke (GDR) (b. 30 July 1959)	Schwerin, GDR	4 June 1985

HEPTATHLON		Name and Country	Place	Date
7148 points		Jacqueline Joyner (USA) (b. 3 Mar 1962)	Moscow, USSR	6–7 July 1986

(100 m hurdles 12.85 sec; High Jump 1,88 m 6 ft 2 in; Shot 14.76 m 48 ft 5¼ in; 200 m 23.00 sec; Long Jump 7,01 m 23 ft; Javelin 49,86 m 163 ft 7 in; 800 m 2 min 10.02 sec

25 May 1935 with a 9.4 sec 100 yd at 3.15 p.m., a 26 ft 8¼ in *8,13 m* long jump at 3.25 p.m., a 20.3 sec *220 yd* (and 200 m) at 3.45 p.m. and a 22.6 sec 220 yd low hurdles (and 200 m) at 4.00 p.m.

Most national titles *Great Britain*
The greatest number of senior AAA titles (excluding those in tug of war events) won by one athlete is 14 individual and one relay title by Emmanuel McDonald Bailey (Trinidad) (b. 8 Dec 1920), between 1946 and 1953. The most won outdoors in a single event is 13 by Denis Horgan (Ireland) (1871–1922) in the shot put between 1893 and 1912. 13 senior titles were also won by Michael Anthony Bull (b. 11 Sept 1946) at pole vault, eight indoor and five out and by Geoffrey Lewis Capes (b. 23 Aug 1949) at shot, six indoor and seven out.

The greatest number of WAAA titles won by one athlete is 14 by Suzanne Allday (*née* Farmer) (b. 26 Nov 1934) with seven each at shot and discus between 1952 and 1962.

Most international appearances
The greatest number of international matches contested for any nation is 89 by Bjørn Bang Andersen (b. 14 Nov 1937) for Norway, 1960–81.

The greatest number of full Great Britain international appearances (outdoors and indoors) is 73 by Verona Marolin Elder (*née* Bernard) (b. 5 Apr 1953) from 1971 to 1983. The men's record is 67 by Geoff Capes, 1969–80. Mike Bull had 66 full internationals or 69 including the European Indoor Games, before these were official internationals. The most outdoors is 61 by Andrew Howard Payne (b. South Africa, 17 Apr 1931) from 1960 to 1974.

Oldest and youngest internationals
The oldest full Great Britain international was Hector Harold Whitlock (1903–85) at the 1952 Olympic Games, aged 48 yr 218 days. The oldest woman was Christine Rosemary Payne (*née* Charters) (b. 19 May 1933) in the Great Britain v. Finland match on 26 Sept 1974, aged 41 yr 130 days. The youngest man was Ross Hepburn (b. 14 Oct 1961) v. the USSR on 26 Aug 1977, aged 15 yr 316 days, and the youngest woman was Janis Walsh (b. 28 Mar 1960) v. Belgium (indoor) at 60 m and 4 × 200 m relay on 15 Feb 1975, aged 14 yr 324 days.

Longest career
Duncan McLean (1884–1980) of Scotland set a world age (92) record of 100 m in 21.7 sec in August 1977, over 73 years after his best ever sprint of 100 yd in 9.9 sec in South Africa in February 1904.

London to Brighton race
Ian Thompson (b. 16 Oct 1949) (Luton United H) won the 54.3 miles *87,4 km* race (inst. 1951) in 5 hr 15 min 15 sec on 28 Sept 1980, averaging 10.33 mph *16,62 km/h*. The most wins is four by Bernard Gomersall (b. 28 Aug 1932) in 1963–6.

'End to end'
The fastest confirmed run from John o'Groats to Land's End is 12 days 1 hr 59 min by Kenneth John Craig (S. Africa) (b. 27 Nov 1935) on 29 Aug–10 Sept 1984. A faster 10 days 3 hr 30 min was claimed by Fred Hicks (GB) for 876 miles *1410 km* on 20–30 May 1977.

Longest non-stop run
Bertil Järläker (Sweden) (b. 1936) ran 352.9 miles *568 km* in 121 hr 54 min at Norrköping, Sweden, 26–31 May 1980. He was moving for 95.04 per cent of the time.

Longest running race
The longest races ever staged were the 1928 (3422 miles *5507 km*) and 1929 (3665 miles *5898 km*) Trans-continental races from New York City, NY, to Los Angeles, California, USA. The Finnish-born Johnny Salo (1893–1931) was the winner in 1929 in 79 days, from 31 Mar to 18 June. His elapsed time of 525 hr 57 min 20 sec (averaging 6.97 mph *11,21 km/h*) left him only 2 min 47 sec ahead of Englishman Pietro 'Peter' Gavuzzi (1905–81).

Longest runs
The longest ever solo run is 10,608 miles *17 072 km* by Robert J. Sweetgall (USA) (b. 8 Dec 1947) around the perimeter of the USA starting and finishing in Washington, DC, 9 Oct 1982–15 July 1983. Ron Grant (Australia) (b. 15 Feb 1943) ran around Australia, 13 383 km *8316 miles* in 217 days 3 hr 45 min, running every day from 28 Mar to 31 Oct 1983. Max Telford (NZ) (b. Hawick, Scotland, 2 Feb 1935) ran 5110 miles *8224 km* from Anchorage, Alaska to Halifax, Nova Scotia, in 106 days 18 hr 45 min from 25 July to 9 Nov 1977. The fastest time for the cross-America run is 46 days 8 hr 36 min by Frank Giannino Jr (USA) (b. 1952) for the 3100 miles *4989 km* from San Francisco to New York on 1 Sept–17 Oct 1980.

Greatest mileage
Douglas Alistair Gordon Pirie (b. 10 Feb 1931) (GB), who set five world records in the 1950s, estimated that he had run a total distance of 216,000 miles *347,600 km* in 40 years to 1981.

Dr. Ron Hill (b. 21 Sept 1938), the 1969 European and 1970 Commonwealth marathon champion, has not missed a day's training since

20 Dec 1964. Since then he has run twice a day, except once on Sundays and missing only 23 Dec 1964. His meticulously compiled training log shows a total of 111,273 miles *179 076 km* from 3 Sept 1956 to 1 June 1986. He has finished 109 marathons, all sub 2:50.

The greatest competitive distance run in a year is 8855 km *5502 miles* by Malcolm Campbell (GB) (b. 17 Nov 1934) in 1985.

Mass relay records
The record for 100 miles *160,9 km* by 100 runners from one club is 7 hr 53 min 52.1 sec by Baltimore Road Runners Club, Towson, Maryland, USA, on 17 May 1981. The women's record is 10 hr 47 min 9.3 sec on 3 Apr 1977 by the San Francisco Dolphins Southend Running Club, USA. The best club time for 100 × 400 metres is 1 hr 29 min 11.8 sec (average 53.5 sec) by the Physical Training Institute, Leuven, Belgium on 19 Apr 1978. The best women's club time for 100 × 100 metres is 23 min 28 sec by Amsterdamse dames athletiek-

vereniging, on 26 Sept 1981 in Amsterdam, Netherlands.

The longest relay ever run was 16 936 km *10,524 miles* by 2660 runners at Trondheim, Norway on 26 Aug–20 Oct 1985. Twenty members of the Melbourne Fire Brigade ran 15 059 km *9357 miles* around Australia on Highway No. 1 in 43 days 23 hr 58 min, 10 July–23 Aug 1983. The most participants is 4800, 192 teams of 25, in the Batavierenrace, 167,2 km *103.89 miles* from Nijmegan to Enschede, Netherlands on 23 Apr 1983.

Highland Games
The weight and height of cabers (Gaelic *cabar*) vary considerably. Extreme values are 25 ft *7,62 m* and 280 lb *127 kg*. The Braemar caber (19 ft 3 in *5,86 m* and 120 lb *54,4 kg*) in Grampian, Scotland, was untossed from 1891 until 1951 when it was tossed by George Clark. The best authentic mark recorded for throwing the 56 lb weight for height, using one hand only is 17 ft 2 in *5,23 m* by Geoffrey Lewis Capes (GB)

(b. 23 Aug 1949) at Lagos, Nigeria on 5 Dec 1982. The best throw recorded for the Scots hammer is 151 ft 2 in *46,08 m* by William Anderson (b. 6 Oct 1938) at Lochearnhead on 26 July 1969.

Highest one-legged jump
One-legged Arnie Boldt (b. 1958), of Saskatchewan, Canada, cleared 2.04 m *6 ft 8¼ in* in Rome, Italy on 3 Apr 1981.

Backwards running
Anthony 'Scott' Weiland, 27, ran the Detroit marathon backwards in 4 hr 7 min 54 sec on 3 Oct 1982. Donald Davis (b. 10 Feb 1960) (USA) ran 1 mile backwards in 6 min 7.1 sec at the University of Hawaii on 21 Feb 1983. Ferdie Adoboe (USA) ran 100 yd backwards in 12.8 sec (100 m in 14.0 sec) at Amherst, Mass. on 28 July 1983.

Arvind Pandya of India ran backwards across America, Los Angeles to New York, in 107 days,

UNITED KINGDOM (NATIONAL) RECORDS *MEN*

RUNNING

	min sec	Name	Place	Date
100 metres	10.04	Linford Christie (b. 10 Apr 1960)	Madrid, Spain	4 June 1986
200 metres	20.21	Allan Wipper Wells	Moscow, USSR	28 July 1980
400 metres	44.82	Derek Antony Redmond (b. 3 Sept 1965)	Oslo, Norway	27 July 1985
800 metres	1:41.73	Sebastian Newbold Coe (b. 29 Sept 1956)	Florence, Italy	10 June 1981
1000 metres	2:12.18	Sebastian Newbold Coe	Oslo, Norway	11 July 1981
1500 metres	3:29.67	Steven Cram (b. 14 Oct 1960)	Nice, France	16 July 1985
1 mile	3:46.32	Steven Cram	Oslo, Norway	27 July 1985
2000 metres	4:51.39	Steven Cram	Budapest, Hungary	4 Aug 1985
3000 metres	7:32.79	David Robert Moorcroft (b. 10 Apr 1953)	London (Crystal Palace)	17 July 1982
5000 metres	13:00.41	David Robert Moorcroft	Oslo, Norway	7 July 1982
10,000 metres	27:30.3 *	Brendan Foster (b. 12 Jan 1948)	London (Crystal Palace)	23 June 1978
20,000 metres	58:39.0	Ronald Hill (b. 25 Sept 1938)	Leicester	9 Nov 1968
25,000 metres	1 hr 15:22.6	Ronald Hill	Bolton, Lancashire	21 July 1965
30,000 metres	1 hr 31:30.4	James Noel Carroll Alder (b. 10 June 1940)	London (Crystal Palace)	5 Sept 1970
1 hour	12 miles 1268 yd *20 472m*	Ronald Hill	Leicester	9 Nov 1968

* *Ratified at 27:30.6*

HURDLING

	min sec	Name	Place	Date
110 metres	13.43	James Mark Holtom (b. 6 Feb 1958)	Brisbane, Australia	4 Oct 1982
400 metres	48.12	David Peter Hemery (b. 18 July 1944)	Mexico City, Mexico	15 Oct 1968
3000 metres Steeplechase	8:13.50	Colin Robert Reitz (b. 5 April 1960)	Budapest, Hungary	4 Aug 1985

RELAYS

	min sec	Name	Place	Date
4 × 100 metres	38.62	United Kingdom: Michael Anthony McFarlane, Allan Wipper Wells, Robert Cameron Sharp, Andrew Emlyn McMaster	Moscow, USSR	1 Aug 1980
4 × 200 metres	1:24.1	Great Britain: Brian William Green, Roger Wilfred Walters, Ralph Banthorpe, Martin Edward Reynolds	Paris, France	2 Oct 1971
4 × 400 metres	2:59.13	United Kingdom: Kriss Akabusi, Gary Peter Cook, Todd Bennett, Phil Brown	Los Angeles, USA	11 Aug 1984
4 × 800 metres	7:03.89	United Kingdom: Peter Elliott, Gary Peter Cook, Steven Cram, Sebastian Newbold Coe	London (Crystal Palace)	30 Aug 1982
4 × 1500 metres	14:56.8	United Kingdom: Alan David Mottershead, Geoffrey Michael Cooper, Stephen John Emson, Roy Wood	Bourges, France	24 June 1979

FIELD EVENTS

	m	ft in	Name	Place	Date
High Jump	2,28*	7 5¾	Geoffrey Peter Parsons (b. 14 Aug 1964)	London (Crystal Palace)	17 May 1986
Pole Vault	5,65	18 6½	Keith Frank Stock (b. 18 Mar 1957)	Oslo, Norway	7 July 1981
Long Jump	8,23	27 0	Lynn Davies (b. 20 May 1942)	Bern, Switzerland	30 June 1968
Triple Jump	17,57	57 7¾	Keith Leroy Connor (b. 16 Sept 1957)	Provo, Utah, USA	5 June 1982
Shot 7.26 kg *16 lb*	21,68	71 1½	Geoffrey Lewis Capes (b. 23 Aug 1949)	Cwmbran, Gwent	18 May 1980
Discus 2 kg *4 lb 6.55 oz*	64,32†	211 0	William Raymond Tancred (b. 6 Aug 1942)	Woodford, Essex	10 Aug 1974
Hammer 7.26 kg *16 lb*	77,54	254 5	Martin Girvan (b. 17 Apr 1960)	Wolverhampton, West Midlands	12 May 1984
Javelin 800 g *28.22 oz*	91,40‡	299 10	Arne-Roald Bradstock (b. 24 Apr 1962)	Arlington, Texas, USA	4 May 1985

* *Also 2,30 m 7 ft 6½ in indoors by Geoff Parsons at Cosford, Shropshire on 25 Jan 1986.*
† *William Raymond Tancred threw 64.94 m 213 ft 1in at Loughborough on 21 July 1974 and Richard Charles Slaney (b. 16 May 1956) threw 65,16 m 213 ft 9 in at Eugene, Oregon, USA on 1 July 1985 but these were not ratified.*
‡ *Old javelin; also 81,74 m 268 ft 1 in with new javelin at Tucson, Arizona on 3 May 1986.*

DECATHLON

		Name	Place	Date
8847 points		Francis Morgan 'Daley' Thompson (b. 30 July 1958)	Los Angeles, USA	8–9 Aug 1984

(1st day: 100 m 10.44 sec, Long Jump 8,01 m *26′ 3¼″*, Shot Put 15,72m *51′ 7″*, High Jump 2,03 m *6′ 8″*, 400 m 46.97 sec)

(2nd day: 110 m Hurdles 14.33 sec, Discus 46,56 m *152′ 9″*, Pole Vault 5,00 m *16′ 4¾″*, Javelin 65,24 m *214′ 0″*, 1500 m 4:35.00 sec)

18 Aug–3 Dec 1984. He also ran backwards from John O'Groats to Land's End, 880 miles *1416,2 km* in 29 days 5 hr 39 min, 2–31 Oct 1985.

Fastest blind sprinting

Graham Henry Salmon (GB) (b. 5 Sept 1952) ran 100 m *109 yd* in 11.4 sec at Grangemouth, Scotland on 2 Sept 1978.

Pancake racing

Dale R. Lyons (b. 26 Feb 1937) (GB) has run several marathons during which he tosses a 2 oz *57 g* pancake repeatedly en route in a 1½ lb *0,68 kg* pan. His fastest time with a pancake is 3 hr 6 min 48 sec in London on 20 Apr 1986.

WALKING

Most Olympic medals

Walking races have been included in the Olympic events since 1906 but walking matches have been known since 1589. The only walker to win three gold medals has been Ugo Frigerio (Italy) (1901–68) with the 3000 m and 10,000 m in 1920 and 1924. He also holds the record of most medals with four (he won the bronze medal at 50,000 m in 1932) a total shared with Vladimir Golubnichiy (USSR) (b. 2 June 1936), who won gold medals for the 20,000 m in 1960 and 1968, the silver in 1972 and the bronze in 1964.

The best British performance has been two gold

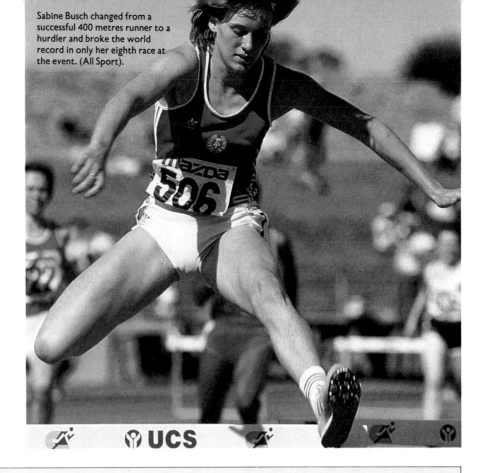

Sabine Busch changed from a successful 400 metres runner to a hurdler and broke the world record in only her eighth race at the event. (All Sport).

UNITED KINGDOM (NATIONAL) RECORDS *WOMEN*

RUNNING

	Min sec			
100 metres	11.10	Kathryn Jane Smallwood [now Cook] (b. 3 May 1960)	Rome, Italy	5 Sept 1981
200 metres	22.10	Kathryn Jane Cook [*née* Smallwood]	Los Angeles, USA	9 Aug 1984
400 metres	49.43	Kathryn Jane Cook [*née* Smallwood]	Los Angeles, USA	6 Aug 1984
800 metres	1:57.42	Kirsty Margaret McDermott [now Wade] (b. 6 Aug 1962)	Belfast, N. Ireland	24 June 1985
1000 metres	2:33.70	Kirsty Margaret McDermott [now Wade]	Gateshead, Tyne and Wear	9 Aug 1985
1500 metres	3:59.96	Zola Budd (b. 26 May 1966)	Brussels, Belgium	30 Aug 1985
1 mile	4:17.57	Zola Budd	Zurich, Switzerland	21 Aug 1985
2000 metres	5:29.58	Yvonne Carol Grace Murray (b. 4 Oct 1964)	London (Crystal Palace)	11 July 1986
3000 metres	8:28.83	Zola Budd	Rome, Italy	7 Sept 1985
5000 metres	14:48.07	Zola Budd	Crystal Palace, London	26 Aug 1985
10000 metres	32:57.17	Kathryn Mary Binns (b. 13 Jan 1958)	Sittard, Netherlands	14 Aug 1980

RELAYS

4 × 100 metres	42.43	United Kingdom: Heather Regina Hunte [now Oakes], Kathryn Jane Smallwood [now Cook], Beverley Lanita Goddard [now Callender], Sonia May Lannaman	Moscow, USSR	1 Aug 1980
4 × 200 metres	1:31.57	United Kingdom: Donna-Marie Louise Hartley [*née* Murray], Verona Marolin Elder [*née* Bernard], Sharon Colyear [now Danville], Sonia May Lannaman	London (Crystal Palace)	20 Aug 1977
4 × 400 metres	3:25.51	United Kingdom: Michelle Scutt, Helen Catherine Barnett, Gladys Taylor, Joslyn Yvonne Hoyte-Smith	Los Angeles, USA	11 Aug 1984
4 × 800 metres	8:23.8	Great Britain: Joan Florence Allison [*née* Page], Sheila Janet Carey [*née* Taylor], Patricia Barbara Lowe [now Cropper], Rosemary Olivia Stirling [now Wright]	Paris, France	2 Oct 1971

HURDLING

100 metres	12.87	Shirley Elaine Strong (b. 18 Nov 1958)	Zürich, Switzerland	24 Aug 1983
400 metres	56.04	Susan Anita Jayne Morley [now Chick] (b. 6 Jan 1960)	Helsinki, Finland	10 Aug 1983

FIELD EVENTS

	m	ft	in			
High Jump	1,95	6	4¾	Diana Clare Elliot (now Davies) (b. 7 May 1961)	Oslo, Norway	26 June 1982
Long Jump	6,90	22	7¾	Beverley Kinch (b. 14 Jan 1964)	Helsinki, Finland	14 Aug 1983
Shot 4 kg *8 lb 13 oz*	19,00*	62	4	Judith Miriam Oakes (b. 14 Feb 1958)	Cwmbran, Gwent	26 May 1986
Discus 1 kg *2 lb 3.27 oz*	67,48	221	5	Margaret Elizabeth Ritchie	Walnut, California, USA	26 April 1981
Javelin 600 g *21.16 oz*	73,58	241	5	Theresa Ione Sanderson (b. 14 Mar 1956)	Edinburgh, Scotland	26 June 1983

HEPTATHLON

6347 points		Judith Earline Veronica Livermore (b. 14 Nov 1960)	Sofia, Bulgaria	10–11 Sept 1983

(100 m hurdles 13.23 sec; High Jump 1,87 m *6' 1½"*; Shot 13,54 m *44' 5¼"*; 200 m 24.75; Long Jump 6,10 m *20' 0¼"*; Javelin 38,60 m *126' 8"*; 800 m 2 min 12.50 sec)

* Venissa Anne Head (b. 1 Sept 1956) achieved 19,06 m *62 ft 6½ in* indoors at St. Athan, Gwent on 7 Apr 1984.

Ian McCombie's British record for one hour walking represents an average speed of 8.9 mph *14,3 km/h*. (All Sport).

MARATHON

The marathon is run over a distance of 26 miles 385 yd *42 195 m*. This distance was that used for the race at the 1908 Olympic Games, run from Windsor to the White City stadium, and which became standard from 1924. The marathon (of 40 km) was introduced to the 1896 Olympic Games to commemorate the legendary run of Pheidippides (or Philippides) from the battlefield of Marathon to Athens in 490 BC. The 1896 Olympic marathon was preceded by trial races that year. The first Boston marathon, the world's longest lasting major marathon, was held on 19 Apr 1897 at 39 km *24 miles 1232 yd* and the first national marathon championship was that of Norway in 1897.

It is only in the past decade that marathon running by women has become widespread, following the pioneering efforts, particularly in the USA, of some determined ladies who had quite a struggle to overcome prejudices against their participation. The first championship marathon for women was organised by the Road Runners Club of America on 27 Sept 1970.

Records

There are as yet no official records for the marathon, and it should be noted that courses may vary in severity. The following are the best times recorded, all on courses whose distance has been verified.

World men: 2:07:12 Carlos Alberto Sousa Lopes (Portugal) (b. 18 Feb 1947) Rotterdam, Netherlands 20 Apr 1985.

World women: 2:21:06 Ingrid Kristiansen (née Christensen) (Norway) (b. 21 Mar 1956) London 21 Apr 1985.

British men: 2:07:13 Stephen Henry Jones (b. 4 Aug 1955) Chicago, USA 20 Oct 1985.

British women: 2:28:04 Marie-Veronique Antoinette Colette Jeannine Marot (b. 16 Sept 1955) Chicago, USA 20 Oct 1985.

Most competitors

The largest field for a marathon is 19,261 starters, of whom 18,175 finished, for the London marathon on 20 Apr 1986. A record 93 men ran under 2 hr 20 min and 29 under 2:15 at London in 1983, and a record 6 men ran under 2:10 at Fukuoka, Japan on 4 Dec 1983. A record 9 women ran under 2:30 in the first Olympic marathon for women at Los Angeles, USA on 5 Aug 1984.

Oldest finishers

The oldest man to complete a marathon was Dimitrion Yordanidis (Greece), aged 98, in Athens, Greece on 10 Oct 1976. He finished in 7 hr 33 min. Thelma Pitt-Turner (New Zealand) set the women's record in August 1985, completing the Hastings, New Zealand marathon in 7 hr 58 min at the age of 82.

medals by George Edward Larner (1875–1949) for the 3500 m and the 10 miles in 1908, but Ernest J. Webb (1872–1937) won three medals being twice 'walker up' to Larner and finishing second in the 10,000 m in 1912.

Most titles

Four time Olympian, Ronald Owen Laird (b. 31 May 1938) of the New York AC, USA, won a total of 65 National titles from 1958 to 1976, plus four Canadian championships. The greatest number of UK National titles won by a British walker is 27 by Vincent Paul Nihill (b. 5 Sept 1939) from 1963 to 1975.

Longest race

The Paris–Colmar, until 1980 Strasbourg–Paris, event (inst. 1926 in the reverse direction), now about 518 km *322 miles* is the world's longest annual race walk.

The fastest performance is by Robert Pietquin (Belgium) (b. 1938) who walked 507 km *315 miles* in the 1980 race in 60 hr 1 min 10 sec (deducting 4 hr compulsory stops). This represents an average speed of 8.45 km/h *5.25 mph*. Gilbert Roger (France) (b. 1914) won six times (1949, 1953–4, 1956–8). The first woman to complete the race was Annie van der Meer (Netherlands) (b. 24 Feb 1947), who was 10th in 1983 in 82 hr 10 min.

Dumitru Dan (1890–1978) of Romania was the only man of 200 entrants to succeed in a contest in walking 100,000 km *62,137 miles* organised by the Touring Club de France on 1 Apr 1910. He covered 96,000 km *59,651 miles* up to 24 Mar 1916 so averaging 43,85 km *27.24 miles* a day.

'End to end'

The fastest Land's End to John o'Groats walk is 12 days 3 hr 45 min for 886.3 miles *1426,4 km* by WO2 Malcolm Barnish of the 19th Regiment, Royal Artillery on 9–21 June 1986. The women's record is 13 days 17 hr 42 min by Ann Sayer (b. 16 Oct 1936) on 20 Sept–3 Oct 1980. The Irish

'End to End' record over the 400.2 miles *644 km* from Malin Head, Donegal to Mizen Head, Cork is 5 days 22 hr 30 min, set by John 'Paddy' Dowling (b. 15 June 1929) on 18–24 Mar 1982.

London to Brighton

The record time for the 53 miles *85 km* walk is 7 hr 35 min 12 sec by Donald James Thompson (b. 20 Jan 1933) on 14 Sept 1957. Richard Esmond Green (b. 22 Apr 1924) completed the course a record 44 times from 1950 to 1980.

TRACK WALKING—WORLD RECORDS

The International Amateur Athletic Federation recognises men's records at 20 km, 30 km, 50 km and 2 hours, and women's at 5 km and 10 km. This table also includes world bests for other standard distances.

Event	Time hr min sec	Name, country and date of birth	Place	Date
MEN				
3 km	10 54.6	Carlo Mattioli (Italy) (23 Oct 1954)	Milan, Italy (indoors)	6 Feb 1980
10 km	38 02.60	Jozef Pribilinec (Czechoslovakia) (6 July 1960)	Banska Bystrica, Czechoslovakia	5 May 1981
20 km	1 18 40.0	Ernesto Canto (Mexico) (18 Oct 1959)	Fana, Norway	5 May 1984
30 km	2 06 07.3	Maurizio Damilano (Italy) (6 Apr 1957)	San Donato Milanese	5 May 1985
50 km	3 41 38.4	Raul Gonzalez (Mexico) (29 Feb 1952)	Fana, Norway	25 May 1979
1 hour	15 253 metres	Ernesto Canto (Mexico)	Fana, Norway	5 May 1984
2 hours	28 565 metres	Maurizio Damilano (Italy)	San Donato Milanese	5 May 1985
WOMEN				
3 km	12 31.57	Giulliana Salce (Italy) (b. 6 June 1955)	Florence, Italy (indoors)	6 Feb 1985
5 km	21 33.8	Wang Yang (China) (b. 1971)	Jian, China	9 Mar 1986
10 km	44 59.2	Xu Yongjiu (China) (b. 29 Oct 1984)	Beijing, China	30 Mar 1986

TRACK WALKING—BRITISH RECORDS

Event	Time hr min sec	Name, country and date of birth	Place	Date
MEN				
3 km	11 35.2	Philip John Vesty (b. 5 Jan 1963)	Melbourne, Australia	13 Feb 1986
	11 28.0	Philip John Vesty (unratified)	Leicester	9 May 1984
10 km	40 53.60	Philip John Vesty	Cwmbran, Gwent	28 May 1984
20 km	1 24 22.0	Ian Peter McCombie (b. 11 Jan 1961)	Southwark Park, London	7 July 1985
30 km	2 19 18	Christopher Lloyd Maddocks (28 Mar 1957)	Birmingham	22 Sept 1984
50 km	4 05 47.3	Christopher Lloyd Maddocks	Birmingham	22 Sept 1984
1 hour	14 324 metres	Ian Peter McCombie	Southwark Park, London	7 July 1985
2 hours	26 037 metres	Ronald Edward Wallwork (26 May 1941)	Stretford, Lancashire	31 July 1971
WOMEN				
3 km	13 25.2	Carol Joan Tyson (15 Dec 1957)	Östersund, Sweden	6 July 1979
5 km	23 11.2	Carol Joan Tyson	Östersund, Sweden	30 June 1979
10 km	47 56.3	Virginia Claire Birch (née Lovell) (b. 1 July 1955)	Borås, Sweden	15 June 1985

MEN

20 km in 1 hr 19 min 29.6 sec, Jozef Pribilinec (Czechoslovakia) (b. 6 July 1960) at Bergen, Norway on 24 Sept 1983.
30 km in 2 hr 03 min 06 sec, Daniel Bautista (Mexico) (b. 4 Aug 1952) at Cherkassy, USSR on 27 Apr 1980.
50 km in 3 hr 38 min 31 sec, Ronald Weigel (GDR) (b. 8 Aug 1950) at East Berlin, GDR on 20 July 1984.

WOMEN

10 km in 44 min 43 sec, Yan Hong (China) (b. 23 Oct 1966) at Jiading, China on 16 Mar 1985.
20 km in 1 hr 33 min 29 sec, Kerry Saxby (Australia) (b. 1961) at Canberra, Australia on 13 Sept 1985.
50 km in 5 hr 01 min 52 sec, Lillian Millen (GB) (b. 5 Mar 1945) at York, GB on 16 Apr 1983.

BRITISH BEST PERFORMANCES

MEN

20 km in 1 hr 22 min 37 sec, Ian Peter McCombie (b. 11 Jan 1961) at Thamesmead, London on 11 May 1985.
30 km in 2 hr 7 min 56 sec, Ian Peter McCombie at Edinburgh on 27 Apr 1986.
50 km in 4 hr 00 min 47 sec, Leslie Morton (b. 1 July 1958) at Madrid, Spain on 16 Mar 1986.

WOMEN

10 km in 47 min 58.3 sec by Beverley Colleen Allen (née Francis) (b. 16 Mar 1959) at Plymouth on 23 June 1986.
20 km in 1 hr 40 min 45 sec, Irene Lillian Bateman at Basildon, Essex on 9 Apr 1983.

Longest non-stop walk

Tom Benson (GB) walked 414.74 miles *667,46 km* in 6 days 12 hr 45 min at Moor Park, Preston, Lancs on 29 Apr–5 May 1986. This was 233 laps of a 1.78 miles *2,86 km* closed circuit. He was not permitted any stops for rest and was moving 98.78 per cent of the time.

24 hours

The greatest distance walked in 24 hr is 226,432 km *140 miles 1229 yd* by Paul Forthomme (Belgium) on a road course at Woluwé, Belgium on 13–14 Oct 1984. The best by a woman is 202,3 km *125.7 miles* by Annie van der Meer at Rouen, France, on 30 Apr–1 May 1984 over a 1,185 km lap road course.

Backwards walking

The greatest ever exponent of reverse pedestrianism has been Plennie L. Wingo (b. 24 Jan 1895) then of Abilene, Texas, who completed his 8000 mile *12 875 km* trans-continental walk from Santa Monica, California to Istanbul, Turkey, from 15 Apr 1931 to 24 Oct 1932. The longest distance recorded for walking backwards in 24 hr is 84.0 miles *135,18 km* by Anthony Thornton (USA) in Minneapolis, Ma., USA on 31 Dec 1985–1 Jan 1986.

TRAMPOLINING

Origins

Trampolines were used in show business at least as early as 'The Walloons' of the period 1910–12. The sport of trampolining (from the Spanish word *trampolin*, a springboard) dates from 1936, when the prototype 'T' model trampoline was developed by George Nissen (USA).

Most titles

Four men have won a world title (instituted 1964) twice; Dave Jacobs (USA) in 1967–8, Wayne Miller (b. 1946) (USA), in 1966 and 1970, Richard Tison (b. 17 Aug 1956) (France) in 1974 and 1976 (shared), and Evgeni Janes (USSR), 1976 (shared) and 1978. Judy Wills (b. 1948) (USA) won the first five women's titles (1964–8). Two European titles (1969 and 1971) have been won by Paul Luxon (b. 1952) (GB), the 1972 world champion. A record seven United Kingdom titles have been won by Wendy Wright (1969–70, 1972–5, 1977). The most by a man have been five by Stewart Matthews (b. 19 Feb 1962) (1976–80).

Youngest international *Great Britain*

Andrea Holmes (b. 2 Jan 1970) competed for Britain at 12 yr 131 days in the World Championships at Montana, USA on 13 May 1982.

Somersaults

Richard Cobbing of Gateshead Metro Trampoline Club performed 1610 consecutive somersaults at Gateshead, Tyne and Wear, on 22 July 1984.

Richard Cobbing and Phil Seaman both achieved 66 completed somersaults in one minute on BBC Televisions's *Record Breakers* on 5 Nov 1985.

ULTRA LONG DISTANCE TRACK WORLD RECORDS

WORLD BESTS—LONG DISTANCE TRACK EVENTS

	hr:min:sec			
50 km	2:48:06	Jeff Norman (UK)	Timperley, Manchester	7 Jun 1980
50 miles	4:51:49	Don Ritchie (UK)	Hendon, London	12 Mar 1983
100 km	6:10:20	Don Ritchie (UK)	Crystal Palace	28 Oct 1978
100 miles	11:30:51	Don Ritchie (UK)	Crystal Palace	15 Oct 1977
200 km	15:11:10	Yiannis Kouros (Gre)	Montauban, France	15–16 Mar 1985
200 miles	27:48:35	Yiannis Kouros (Gre)	Montauban, France	15–16 Mar 1985
500 km	60:23:00	Yiannis Kouros (Gre)	Colac, Australia	26–29 Nov 1984
500 miles	105:42:09	Yiannis Kouros (Gre)	Colac, Australia	26–30 Nov 1984
1000 km	136:17:00	Yiannis Kouros (Gre)	Colac, Australia	26–31 Nov 1984

	kilometres			
24 hours	283,600	Yiannis Kouros (Gre)	Montauban, France	15–16 Mar 1985
48 hours	452,270	Yiannis Kouros (Gre)	Montauban, France	15–17 Mar 1985
6 days	1023,2	Yiannis Kouros (Gre)	Colac, Australia	26 Nov–1 Dec 1984

LONG DISTANCE ROAD BESTS

Where superior to track bests and run on properly measured road courses.

50 miles	4:50:21	Bruce Fordyce (SAf)	London–Brighton	25 Sept 1983
1000 miles	11 d 20 hr 36 min	Stu Mittleman (USA)	Queens, New York, USA	26 Apr–8 May 1986

	kilometres			
24 hours	286,463	Yiannis Kouros (Gre)	New York, USA	28–29 Sept 1985

WORLD BESTS—WOMEN'S LONG DISTANCE TRACK EVENTS

	hr:min:sec			
15 km	49:44.0	Silvana Cruciata (Ita)	Rome	4 May 1981
20 km	1:06:55.5	Rosa Mota (Por)	Lisbon	14 May 1983
25 km	1:31:04.3	Chantal Langlacé (Fra)	Amiens	3 Sep 1983
30 km	1:49:55.7	Chantal Langlacé (Fra)	Amiens	3 Sep 1983
50 km	3:36:58	Ann Franklin (UK)	Barry, Wales	9 Mar 1986
50 miles	6:17:30†	Monika Kuno (W. Germany)	Vogt, W. Germany	8—9 Jul 1983
100 km	8:01:01	Monika Kuno (W. Germany)	Vogt, W. Germany	8—9 Jul 1983
100 miles	15:44:21	Lynn Fitzgerald (UK)	Nottingham	31 Jul–1 Aug 1983
200 km	20:48:36	Eleanor Adams (UK)	Nottingham	4–5 Aug 1985
200 miles	44:44:08	Eleanor Adams (UK)	Montauban, France	15–17 Mar 1985
500 km	86:26:02	Eleanor Adams (UK)	Colac, Australia	24 Feb–2 Mar 1986
500 miles	143:49:00	Eleanor Adams (UK)	Colac, Australia	26 Nov–1 Dec 1984

	kilometres			
1 hour	18,084	Silvana Cruciata (Ita)	Rome	4 May 1981
24 hours	222,8	Eleanor Adams (UK)	Nottingham	4–5 Aug 1985
48 hours	347,420	Arlette Touchard (Fra)	Montauban, France	14–16 Mar 1986
6 days	808,4	Eleanor Adams (UK)	Colac, Australia	24 Feb–2 Mar 1986

† Timed on one running watch only.

LONG DISTANCE ROAD BESTS

Where superior to track bests and run on properly measured road courses.

50 km	3:13:51	Janis Klecker (USA)	Tallahassee	17 Dec 1983
40 miles	4:43:22	Marcy Schwam (USA)	Chicago	3 Oct 1982
50 miles	5:59:26	Marcy Schwam (USA)	Chicago	3 Oct 1982
100 km	7:26:01	Chantal Langlacé (Fra)	Migennes, France	17 Jun 1984
100 miles	15:07:45	Christine Barrett (UK)	Forthampton, Gloucestershire	14 Apr 1984
500 km	82:10§	Annie van der Meer (Hol)	Paris–Colmar	8–11 Jun 1983

§ for 518 km.

It should be noted that road times must be assessed with care as course conditions can vary considerably.

TRIATHLON

The Triathlon combines long distance swimming, cycling and running. Distances for each of the phases can vary, but for the best established event, the Hawaii Ironman (inst. 1978), competitors first swim 3,8 km *2.4 miles*, then cycle 180 km *112 miles*, and finally run a full marathon of 42 195 m *26 miles 385 yards*. Record times for the Hawaii Ironman are: men: 8 hr 50 min 54 sec Scott Tinley (USA) (b. 1956) in 1985; women: 10 hr 25 min 13 sec Sylviane Puntous (Canada) (b. 1960) in 1984. Dave Scott (USA) has won a record three races , 1982–4.

World Championships

The world championships have been held annually in Nice, France from 1982; the distances 3200 m, 120 km and 32 km respectively. In 1985 Mark Allen (USA) won his fourth successive title.

Largest field

The largest field in a triathlon race has been

2060 finishers in the US Triathlon series race at Chicago in July 1985. This series encompasses races over 1500 m, 40 km and 10 km for the three phases.

TUG OF WAR

Though ancient China and Egypt have been suggested as the originators of the sport, it is known that neolithic flint miners in Norfolk, England practised 'rope-pulling'. The first rules were those framed by the New York AC in 1879. Tug of War was an Olympic sport from 1900 until 1920. In 1958 the Tug-of-War Association was formed to administer Britain's 600 clubs. A ladies world championship was held for the first time in 1986.

Most titles

The Wood Treatment team (formerly the Bosley Farmers) of Cheshire have represented England since 1964, winning two World and ten European Championships at 720 kg *1587 lb*. They also won 20 consecutive AAA Catchweight Championships 1959–78. Hilary Brown (b. 13 Apr 1934) was in every team. Trevor Brian Thomas (b. 1943) of British Aircraft Corporation Club is the only holder of three winner's medals in the European Open club competitions.

Longest pulls

The longest recorded pull (prior to the introduction of AAA rules) is one of 2 hr 41 min when 'H' Company beat 'E' Company of the 2nd Battalion of the Sherwood Foresters (Derbyshire Regiment) at Jubbulpore, India, on 12 Aug 1889. The longest recorded pull under AAA Rules (in which lying on the ground or entrenching the feet is not permitted) is one of 11 min 23 sec for the first pull between the Isle of Oxney and St Claret's at Chertsey, Surrey on 26 May 1979. The record time for 'The Pull' (inst. 1898), across the Black River, between freshman and sophomore teams at Hope College, Holland, Mich, USA, is 3 hr 51 min on 23 Sept 1977, but the method of bracing the feet precludes the replacing of the preceding records.

VOLLEYBALL

The game was invented as *Mintonette* in 1895 by William G. Morgan at the YMCA gymnasium at Holyoke, Massachusetts, USA. The International Volleyball Association was formed in Paris in April 1947. The Amateur (now English) Volleyball Association of Great Britain was formed in May 1955.

Most world titles

World Championships were instituted in 1949 for men and 1952 for women. The USSR has won six men's titles (1949, 1952, 1960, 1962, 1978, 1982) and four women's (1952, 1956, 1960 and 1970).

Most Olympic titles

The sport was introduced to the Olympic Games for both men and women in 1964. The USSR have won a record three men's (1964, 1968 and 1980) and three women's (1968, 1972 and 1980) titles. The only player to win four medals is Inna Ryskal (USSR) (b. 15 June 1944), who won silver medals in 1964 and 1976 and golds in 1968 and 1972. The record for men is held by Yuriy Poyarkov (USSR) (b. 10 Feb 1937) who won gold medals in 1964 and 1968 and a bronze in 1972, and by Katsutoshi Nekoda (Japan) (b. 1 Feb 1944) who won gold in 1972, silver in 1968 and bronze in 1964.

Most internationals *Great Britain*
Ucal Ashman (b. 10 Nov 1957) made a record 153 men's international appearances for England, 1976–86. The women's record is 166 by Ann Jarvis (b. 3 June 1955) for England, 1974–86.

WATER POLO

Origins

Water polo was developed in England as 'Water Soccer' in 1869 and first included in the Olympic Games in Paris in 1900.

Most Olympic titles

Hungary has won the Olympic tournament most often with six wins in 1932, 1936, 1952, 1956, 1964 and 1976. Great Britain won in 1900, 1908, 1912 and 1920.

Five players share the record of three gold medals; Britons, George Wilkinson (1879–1946) in 1900, 1908, 1912; Paulo 'Paul' Radmilovic (1886–1968), and Charles Sidney Smith (1879–1951) in 1908, 1912, 1920; and Hungarians Deszo Gyarmati (b. 23 Oct 1927) and György Kárpáti (b. 23 June 1935) in 1952, 1956, 1964. Gyarmati's wife (Eva Szekely) and daughter (Andrea) won gold and silver medals respectively in swimming. Paul Radmilovic also won a gold medal for the 4 × 200 m freestyle relay in 1908.

ASA championships

The greatest number of Amateur Swimming Association titles is 14 between 1956 and 1982, by London Polytechnic, who have also won a record ten National League (formed 1963) titles—1964, 1969–70, 1972–7, 1979.

Most goals

The greatest number of goals scored by an individual in an international is 13 by Debbie Handley for Australia (16) *v* Canada (10) at the World Aquatic Games in Guayaquil, Ecuador in 1982.

Most international appearances

The greatest number of international appearances is 412 by Alexei Barkalov (USSR) (b. 18 Feb 1946), 1965–80. The British record is 126 by Martyn Thomas, of Cheltenham, 1964–78.

WATER SKIING

Origins

The origins of water skiing lie in walking on planks and aquaplaning. A 19th century treatise on sorcerers refers to Eliseo of Tarentum who, in the 14th century, 'walks and dances' on the water. The first report of aquaplaning was on America's Pacific coast in the early 1900s. At Scarborough, Yorkshire, on 15 July 1914, a single plank-gliding contest was won by H. Storry.

The present day sport of water skiing was pioneered by Ralph W. Samuelson (1904–77) on Lake Pepin, Minnesota, USA, on two curved pine boards in the summer of 1922, though claims have been made for the birth of the sport on Lake Annecy (Haute Savoie), France at about the same time. The first world organisation, the United Internationale de Ski Nautique, was formed in Geneva on 27 July 1946. The British Water Ski Federation was founded in London in 1954.

Most titles

World Overall Championships (inst. 1949) have been won three times by one man, Sammy Duvall (USA) in 1981, 1983 and 1985, and by two women, Willa McGuire (*née* Worthington) of the USA in 1949–50 and 1955 and Elizabeth 'Liz' Allan-Shetter (USA) in 1965, 1969 and 1975. Liz Allan-Shetter has won a record eight individual championship events and is the only person to win all four titles—slalom, jumping, tricks and overall in one year, at Copenhagen, Denmark in 1969. The USA has won the team championship on 15 successive occasions 1957–85. The most British Overall titles (instituted 1953) won by a man is seven by Michael Hazelwood (b. 14 Apr 1958) in 1974, 1976–9, 1981, 1983; the most by a woman is nine by Karen Jane Morse (b. 1956) in 1971–6, 1978, 1981, 1984.

Highest speed

The fastest water skiing speed recorded is 230,26 km/h *143.08 mph* by Christopher Michael Massey (Australia) on the Hawkesbury River, Windsor, New South Wales, Australia on 6 Mar 1983. His drag boat driver was Stanley Charles Sainty. Donna Patterson Brice (b. 1953)

WATER SKIING RECORDS

━━━ WORLD RECORDS MEN ━━━

Slalom	...5 buoys on a 10,75 m line	Bob LaPoint (USA)	Shreveport, Florida, USA	1984
	5 buoys on a 10,75 m line	Andy Mapple (GB)	USA	Sept 1985
Tricks	...10,300 points	Cory Pickos (USA)	USA	Sept 1985
Jumping	...61,9 m *203 ft*	Michael Hazelwood (GB)	Birmingham, Alabama, USA	30 June 1986

━━━ WORLD RECORDS WOMEN ━━━

Slalom	...4 buoys on a 11,25 m line	Deena Brush (USA)	Palm Beach, Florida, USA	2 Oct 1983
	4 buoys on a 11.25 m line	Jennifer Leachman (WA)		Aug 1985
Tricks	...8350 points	Ana Maria Carasco (Venezuela)		Sept 1984
Jumping	...45,8 m *150 ft 2 in*	Sue Lipplegoes (Australia)	Kirtons Farm, Reading, Berkshire	31 July 1983

━━━ BRITISH RECORDS MEN ━━━

Slalom	...5 buoys on a 10,75 m line	Andy Mapple (b. 3 Nov 1962)	USA	Sept 1985
Tricks	...8650 points	John Battleday (b. 1 Feb 1957)	Lyon, France	5 Aug 1984
Jumping	...61,9 m *203 ft*	Michael Hazelwood (b. 14 Apr 1958)	Birmingham, Alabama, USA	30 June 1986

━━━ BRITISH RECORDS WOMEN ━━━

Slalom	...4½ buoys at 12 m	Karen Jane Morse (b. 14 Aug 1956)	France	1982
Tricks	...6820 points	Nicola Rasey (b. 6 June 1966)	Martigues, France	27 Oct 1984
Jumping	...44,9 m *147 ft*	Kathy Hulme (b. 11 Feb 1959)	Kirtons Farm, Reading, Berkshire	1 Aug 1982

set a feminine record of 178,81 km/h *111.11 mph* at Long Beach, California on 21 Aug 1977. The fastest recorded speed by a British skier over a measured kilometre is 131,217 km/h *81.535 mph* (average) on Lake Windermere, Cumbria on 18 Oct 1973 by Billy Rixon. The fastest by a British woman is 122,187 km/h *75.92 mph* by Elizabeth Hobbs on Windermere, 14 Oct 1982.

Longest run

The greatest distance travelled is 2099,7 km *1304.6 miles* by Will Coughey on 18–19 Feb 1984 on Lake Tikitapu, New Zealand.

Barefoot

The first person to water ski barefoot is reported to be Dick Pope Jr at Lake Eloise, Florida, on 6 Mar 1947. The barefoot duration record is 2 hr 42 min 39 sec by Billy Nichols (USA) (b. 1964) on Lake Weir, Florida, on 19 Nov 1978. The backward barefoot record is 39 min by Paul McManus (Aust). The British duration record is 67 min 5 sec by John Doherty on 1 Oct 1974. The official barefoot speed record (two runs) is 177,06 km/h *110.02 mph* by Lee Kirk (USA) at Firebird Lake, Phoenix, Ariz, on 11 June 1977. His fastest run was 182,93 km/h *113.67 mph*. The fastest by a woman is 118,56 km/h *73.67 mph* by Karen Toms (Australia) on the Hawkesbury River, Windsor, New South Wales on 31 Mar 1984. The British record is: (men's) 114,86 km/h *71.37 mph* by Richard Mainwaring at Holme Pierrepont, Notts. on 2 Dec 1978; (women's) 70,75 km/h *43.96 mph* by Linda Wright at Holme Pierrepont, Notts. in Sept 1984. The fastest official speed backward barefoot is 100 km/h *62 mph* by Robert Wing (Aus) on 3 Apr 1982.

The barefoot jump record is 20,10 m *65 ft 11¼ in* by Mike Siepel (WA) in 1984. The British record is 18,00 m *59 ft 0½ in* by Chris Harris in Italy in 1985.

WEIGHTLIFTING

Origins

Competitions for lifting weights of stone were held in the ancient Olympic Games. The first championships entitled 'world' were staged at the Café Monico, Piccadilly, London, on 28 Mar 1891 and then in Vienna, Austria on 19–20 July 1898, subsequently recognised by the IWF. Prior to that time, weightlifting consisted of professional exhibitions in which some of the advertised poundages were open to doubt.

The International Weightlifting Federation (IWF) was established in 1920, and their first official championships were held in Tallinn, Estonia on 29–30 Apr 1922.

Most Olympic Medals

Norbert Schemansky (USA) (b. 30 May 1924) won a record four Olympic medals: Gold, middle-heavyweight 1952; Silver, heavyweight 1948; Bronze, heavyweight 1960 and 1964.

Most titles *World*

The most world title wins, including Olympic Games, is eight by John Davis (USA) (1921–84) in 1938, 1946–52; by Tommy Kono (USA) (b. 27 June 1930) in 1952–9; and by Vasili Alexeyev (USSR) (b. 7 Jan 1942) 1970–7.

Youngest world record holder and champion

Naim Suleimanov (now Neum Shalamanov) (Bulgaria) (b. 23 Nov 1967) set 56 kg world records for clean and jerk (160 kg) and total (285 kg) at 15 yr 123 days at Allentown, New Jersey, USA on 26 Mar 1983. On 23 Oct 1983 in

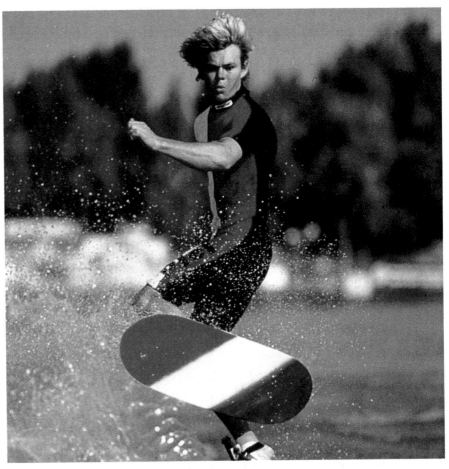

'Tricks' specialist Patrice Martin outpointed Cory Pickos to win the World Championship in 1985. Pickos then took the world record score, whilst Martin's 10,370 points in Florida in May 1986 is probably ineligible for a world record. (All Sport).

Moscow, USSR he became the youngest world champion at 15 yr 334 days.

Most successful British lifter

The only British lifter to win an Olympic title has been Launceston Elliot (1874–1930), the open one-handed lift champion in 1896 at Athens. Louis George Martin (b. Jamaica, 11 Nov 1936) won four World and European mid-heavyweight titles in 1959, 1962–3, 1965. He won an Olympic silver medal in 1964 and a bronze in 1960 and three Commonwealth gold medals in 1962, 1966, 1970. His total of British titles was 12.

Greatest lift

The greatest weight ever raised by a human being is 6270 lb *2844 kg* (2.80 tons *2,84 tonnes*) in a back lift (weight raised off trestles) by the 26 st *165 kg* Paul Anderson (USA) (b. 17 Oct 1932), the 1956 Olympic heavyweight champion, at Toccoa, Georgia, USA, on 12 June 1957. The greatest lift by a woman is 3564 lb *1616 kg* with a hip and harness lift by Josephine Blatt (*née* Schauer) (1869–1923) at the Bijou Theatre, Hoboken, New Jersey, USA, on 15 Apr 1895.

Greatest overhead lifts

The greatest overhead lifts made from the ground are the clean and jerks achieved by super-heavyweights (see world record table). The greatest overhead lift ever made by a woman is 303 lb *137 kg* by Karyn Tarter (b. 1956) in New York in December 1984.

Greatest power lifts

Paul Anderson, as a professional, reportedly achieved 1200 lb *544 kg* in a squat so aggregating, with a 627 lb *284 kg* press and an 820 lb *371 kg* dead lift, a career total of 2647 lb *1200 kg*.

Hermann Görner (1891–1956) (Germany) performed a one-handed dead lift of 734½ lb *333,1 kg* in Dresden on 20 July 1920. Görner also raised 24 men weighing 4123 lb *1870 kg* on a plank on the soles of his feet in London on 12 Oct 1927 and carried on his back a 1444 lb *654 kg* piano for 52½ ft *16 m* at Leipzig on 3 June 1921. Willie Whoriskey achieved a British record one-handed deadlift of 670.9 lb *304,3 kg* at Bloxwich, W. Midlands on 26 Nov 1983. Clive Lloyd (b. 23 Aug 1961) achieved a one-handed straddle lift of 669 lb *303,5 kg* at Grosvenor House, London on 12 Aug 1983. This was a record 3.46 times his body weight of 87,8 kg *193.5 lb*.

The greatest power lift by a woman is a squat of 545½ lb *247,5 kg* by Jan Suffolk Todd (b. 22 May 1952) (USA) (weighing 88,5 kg *195 lb*) at Columbus, Georgia, USA in Jan 1981. Cammie Lynn Lusko (b. 5 Apr 1958) (USA) became the first woman to lift more than her body weight with one arm, with 59,5 kg *131 lbs* at a body weight of 58,3 kg *128.5 lb*, at Milwaukee, Wisconsin, USA on 21 May 1983.

24 Hr and 1 Hr Lifts

A deadlifting record of 2 378 755 kg *5,244,169 lb* in 24 hr was set by a team of ten from ASC Unterwössen at Kreuzheben, W. Germany on 27–28 Jan 1984.

A team of nine from Gymfit Soud (Oman) of Leicester lifted 2 175 865 kg *4,796,955 lb* in 24 hr with bench presses at the Hogarth Club, London on 12–13 Apr 1986.

Jack Atherton, prison officer at HMP Featherstone, achieved 655 repetitions of his body-weight (67,5 kg *148.8 lb*) in one hour by bench presses on 22 Mar 1986. He went on to achieve 3062 repetitions in a 12 hr period.

Body weight feats

Lamar Gant (USA) was the first man to deadlift five times his own bodyweight, lifting 299,5 kg *661 lb* when 59,5 kg *132 lb* in 1985. Stefan Topurov (Bulgaria) clean and jerked 180 kg *396¾ lb*, three times his bodyweight, at Moscow, USSR on 24 Oct 1983.

Strandpulling

The International Steel Strandpullers' Association was founded by Gavin Pearson (Scotland) in 1940. The greatest ratified poundage to date is a super-heavyweight right arm push of 815 lb *369,5 kg* by Malcolm Bartlett (b. 9 June 1955) of Oldham, Lancashire. The record for the Back Press Anyhow is 645 lb *292,5 kg* by Barry Anderson, of Leeds, in 1975. A record 20 British Open titles have been won by Ian Storton (b. 2 Feb 1951) of Morecambe, 1974–86.

BRITISH WEIGHTLIFTING RECORDS (in kg)

Class	Snatch		Date	
52 kg	92,5	Precious McKenzie	25 Jan	1974
56 kg	105	Dean Willey	15 June	1981
60 kg	122,5	Dean Willey	26 Feb	1983
67,5 kg	142,5	Dean Willey	30 Mar	1985
75 kg	150	David Morgan	28 Jan	1984
82,5 kg	160	David Morgan	4 May	1986
90 kg	160	Gary Langford	13 Apr	1980
100 kg	160,5	Gary Langford	7 Mar	1982
110 kg	180	Gary Taylor	30 Mar	1985
Super	162,5	John Burns	5 Sept	1982

Class	Jerk		Date	
52 kg	122,5	Precious McKenzie	25 Jan	1974
56 kg	132,5	Geoff Laws		1982
60 kg	152,5	Dean Willey	26 Mar	1983
67,5 kg	170	Dean Willey	1 Aug	1984
75 kg	185,5	David Morgan	24 Sept	1983
82,5 kg	185	Newton Burrowes	27 Feb	1982
90 kg	201	David Mercer	26 May	1984
100 kg	202,5	Peter Pinsent	17 Sept	1983
110 kg	200	Brian Strange	28 Feb	1976
Super	200	Andrew Kerr	9 Nov	1974

Class	Total		Date	
52 kg	215	Precious McKenzie	25 Jan	1974
56 kg	235	Geoff Laws		1982
60 kg	272,5	Dean Willey	26 Feb	1983
67,5 kg	315	Dean Willey		1985
75 kg	330	David Morgan	24 Sept	1983
82,5 kg	355	David Morgan	4 May	1986
90 kg	352,5	David Mercer	5 Aug	1984
100 kg	362,5	Peter Pinsent	17 Sept	1983
110 kg	375	Gary Taylor	30 Mar	1985
Super	350	Brian Strange	4 Mar	1978

WORLD WEIGHTLIFTING RECORDS

Bodyweight class	Lift	kg	lb	Name and Country	Place	Date
52 kg *114¼ lb* FLYWEIGHT	Snatch	115,5	254½	Neno Terziyski (Bulgaria)	San Marino	9 May 1983
	Jerk	152,5	336	Neno Terziyski (Bulgaria)	Vittoria, Spain	27 Apr 1984
	Total	262,5	578½	Neno Terziyski (Bulgaria)	Vittoria, Spain	27 Apr 1984
56 kg *123¼ lb* BANTAMWEIGHT	Snatch	133	293	Oksen Mirzoyan (USSR)	Varna, Bulgaria	12 Sept 1984
	Jerk	170,5	375¾	Neum Shalamanov (Bulgaria)	Belgrade	12 Sept 1984
	Total	300	661¼	Neum Shalamanov (Bulgaria)	Varna, Bulgaria	11 May 1984
60 kg *132¼ lb* FEATHERWEIGHT	Snatch	145,5	320¾	Neum Shalamanov (Bulgaria)	Karl-Marx-Stadt, GDR	8 May 1986
	Jerk	187,5	413¼	Neum Shalamanov (Bulgaria)	Karl-Marx-Stadt, GDR	8 May 1986
	Total	332,5	733	Neum Shalamanov (Bulgaria)	Karl-Marx-Stadt, GDR	8 May 1986
67.5 kg *148¾ lb* WELTERWEIGHT	Snatch	155,5	342¾	Vladimir Grachev (USSR)	Minsk, USSR	15 Mar 1984
	Jerk	200	440¾	Alexander Varbanov (Bulgaria)	Varna, Bulgaria	13 Sept 1984
	Total	352,5	777	Andreas Behm (GDR)	Schwedr, GDR	20 July 1984
75 kg *165¼ lb* MIDDLEWEIGHT	Snatch	167,5	369¼	Vladimir Kuznytsov (USSR)	Moscow, USSR	26 Oct 1983
	Jerk	212,5	468¼	Alexander Varbanov (Bulgaria)	Karl-Marx-Stadt, GDR	9 May 1986
	Total	377,5	832	Zdravko Stoichkov (Bulgaria)	Varna, Bulgaria	14 Sept 1984
82.5 kg *181¼ lb* LIGHT-HEAVYWEIGHT	Snatch	182,5	402¼	Yuri Vardanyan (USSR)	Varna, Bulgaria	14 Sept 1984
	Jerk	224	493¾	Yuri Vardanyan (USSR)	Varna, Bulgaria	14 Sept 1984
	Total	405	892½	Yuri Vardanyan (USSR)	Varna, Bulgaria	14 Sept 1984
90 kg *198¼ lb* MIDDLE-HEAVYWEIGHT	Snatch	195,5	431	Blagoi Blagoyev (Bulgaria)	Varna, Bulgaria	1 May 1983
	Jerk	233	513½	Viktor Solodov (USSR)	Varna, Bulgaria	15 Sept 1984
	Total	422,5	931¼	Viktor Solodov (USSR)	Varna, Bulgaria	15 Sept 1984
100 kg *220¼ lb*	Snatch	200	440¼	Yuri Zakharevich (USSR)	Odessa, USSR	4 Mar 1983
	Jerk	241,5	532¼	Pavel Kuznyetsov (USSR)	Varna, Bulgaria	15 Sept 1984
	Total	440	970	Yuri Zakharevich (USSR)	Odessa, USSR	4 Mar 1983
110 kg *242¼ lb* HEAVYWEIGHT	Snatch	200,5	442	Yuri Zakharevich (USSR)	Varna, Bulgaria	16 Sept 1984
	Jerk	247,5	545½	Vyacheslav Klokov (USSR)	Moscow, USSR	30 Oct 1983
	Total	442.5	975½	Leonid Taranenko (USSR)	Varna, Bulgaria	16 Sept 1984
Over 110 kg *242½ lb* SUPER-HEAVYWEIGHT	Snatch	211	465	Aleksandr Gunyashev (USSR)	Rheims, France	1 June 1984
	Jerk	265	584	Anatoliy Pisarenko (USSR)	Varna, Bulgaria	16 Sept 1984
	Total	467,5	1030½	Leonid Taranenko (USSR)	Moscow, USSR	6 July 1986

(*Left*) Prison officer Jack Atherton, who bench-pressed his bodyweight 655 times in an hour; (*above left*) Yuri Zakharevich, poised to straighten his legs to complete the snatch. (Bruce Klemens); (*above*) Alexander Varbanov of Bulgaria displays ideal technique in locking his arms under a heavy jerk. (Bruce Klemens). Lifters must hold out for two seconds for world records to be ratified.

WORLD POWERLIFTING RECORDS (All weights in kilograms)

Class	Squat		Bench Press		Deadlift		Total	
MEN								
52 kg	242,5	Joe Cunha (USA) 1981	146,5	Joe Cunha 1982	233	Hideaki Inaba (Jap) 1983	567,5	Hideaki Inaba (Jap) 1980
56 kg	237,5	Hideaki Inaba (Jap) 1982	152,5	Hiroyaki Isagawa (Jap) 1984	289,5	Lamar Gant (USA) 1982	625	Lamar Gant 1982
60 kg	295	Joe Bradley (USA) 1980	180	Joe Bradley 1980	296,5	Lamar Gant 1983	707,5	Joe Bradley 1982
67,5 kg	297	Robert Wahl (USA) 1982	200	Kristoffer Hulecki (Swe) 1985	312,5	Raimo Valineva (Fin) 1981	732,5	Joe Bradley 1981
75 kg	327,5	Mike Bridges (USA) 1980	217,5	James Rouse (USA) 1980	325,5	Eric Coppin (Bel) 1985	850	Rick Gaugler (USA) 1982
82,5 kg	379,5	Mike Bridges 1982	240	Mike Bridges 1981	357,5	Veli Kumpuniemi (Fin) 1980	952,5	Mike Bridges 1982
90 kg	375	Fred Hatfield (USA) 1980	255	Mike MacDonald (USA) 1980	372,5	Walter Thomas (USA) 1982	937,5	Mike Bridges 1980
100 kg	400	Fred Hatfield 1982	262	Francis Silva (USA) 1986	377,5	James Cash (USA) 1982	952,5	James Cash 1982
110 kg	393,5	Dan Wohleber (USA) 1981	270	Jeffrey Magruder (USA) 1982	395	John Kuc (USA) 1980	1000	John Kuc 1980
125 kg	412,5	David Waddington (USA) 1982	278,5	Tom Hardman (USA) 1982	385	Terry McCormick (USA) 1982	1005	Ernie Hackett (USA) 1980
125+ kg	445	Dwayne Fely (USA) 1982	300	Bill Kazmaier (USA) 1981	402	Bill Kazmaier 1981	1100	Bill Kazmaier 1981
WOMEN								
44 kg	140	Anna-Liisa Prinkkala (Fin) 1983	75	Teri Hoyt (USA) 1982	165	Nancy Belliveau (USA) 1985	352,5	Marie Vassart (Belgium) 1985
48 kg	147	Majik Jones (USA) 1983	82,5	Michelle Evris (USA) 1981	182,5	Majik Jones (USA) 1984	390	Majik Jones 1984
52 kg	172,5	Sisi Dolman (Hol) 1984	95	Mary Ryan (USA) 1984	197	Diana Rowell (USA) 1984	427,5	Diana Rowell (USA) 1984
56 kg	190	Vicki Steenrod (USA) 1984	112	Vicki Steenrod 1984	200	Diana Rowell (USA) 1984	482,5	Vicky Steenrod 1984
60 kg	200,5	Ruthi Shafer (USA) 1983	105	Vicki Steenrod 1985	213	Ruthi Shafer 1983	502,5	Vicki Steenrod 1985
67,5 kg	230	Ruthi Shafer 1984	106	Heidi Wittesch (Aus) 1986	244	Ruthi Shafer 1984	565	Ruthi Shafer 1984
75 kg	212,5	Beverley Francis (Aus) 1981	140	Beverley Francis 1981	210	Pam Mathews (Aus) 1982	550	Beverley Francis 1983
82,5 kg	230	Juanita Trujillo (USA) 1986	150	Beverley Francis 1981	227,5	Vicky Gagne (USA) 1981	577,5	Beverley Francis 1983
90 kg	237,5	Lorraine Constanzo (USA) 1986	120,5	Gael Martin 1983	210	Rebecca Waibler (GFR) 1982	550	Lorraine Constanzo (USA) 1986
90+ kg	247,5	Jan Todd (USA) 1981	130	Gael Martin 1982	230	Wanda Sander (USA) 1981	567,5	Gael Martin 1982

BRITISH POWERLIFTING RECORDS (All weights in kilograms)

Class	Squat		Bench Press		Deadlift		Total	
MEN								
52 kg	217,5	P. Stringer 1980	130	P. Stringer 1981	222,5	P. McKenzie 1975	530	P. Stringer 1982
56 kg	235	P. Stringer 1982	137,5	P. Stringer 1983	229	P. McKenzie 1973	567,5	N. Bhairo 1982
60 kg	247,5	A. Galvez 1981	142,5	C. Lewis 1985	275	E. Pengelly 1977	645	E. Pengelly 1979
67,5 kg	275	E. Pengelly 1981	165	H. Salih 1979	295	E. Pengelly 1982	710	E. Pengelly 1982
75 kg	302,5	J. Howells 1979	185	P. Fiore 1981	310	R. Limerick 1984	760	S. Alexander 1983
82,5 kg	337,5	M. Duffy 1984	210	M. Duffy 1981	355	R. Collins 1980	855	R. Collins 1980
90 kg	347,5	D. Caldwell 1985	227,5	J. Chandler 1985	350,5	R. Collins 1980	870	D. Caldwell 1985
100 kg	380	A. Stevens 1984	225	A. Stevens 1985	362,5	A. Stevens 1984	955	A. Stevens 1984
110 kg	372,5	A. Stevens 1984	232,5	J. Neighbour 1985	380	A. White 1982	920	A. White 1982
125 kg	385	S. Spillane 1985	240	S. Spillane 1985	365	S. Zetolofsky 1984	957,5	S. Zetolofsky 1984
125+ kg	380	S. Zetolofsky 1979	258	T. Purdoe 1971	377,5	A. Kerr 1982	982,5	A. Kerr 1983
WOMEN								
44 kg	105	J. White 1984	57,5	J. White 1983	130	A. Brown 1982	277,5	J. White 1984
48 kg	125	S. Smith 1985	75	S. Smith 1985	132,5	M. Green 1984	325	S. Smith 1985
52 kg	142,5	J. Hunter 1985	81	J. Hunter 1986	172,5	J. Hunter 1986	390	J. Hunter 1986
56 kg	140	D. Mears 1983	70	J. Hunter 1985	162,5	J. Hunter 1985	372,5	J. Hunter 1985
60 kg	160	R. Bass 1985	85	R. Bass 1986	177,5	D. Webb 1984	420	R. Bass 1986
67,5 kg	167,5	T. Roberts 1986	85	T. Roberts 1986	176,5	S. Mackness 1986	417,5	R. Bass 1984
75 kg	195	P. Morgan 1984	95	J. Oakes 1981	202,5	J. Oakes 1984	492,5	J. Oakes 1984
82,5 kg	210	J. Oakes 1986	112,5	J. Oakes 1983	210	J. Oakes 1986	532,5	J. Oakes 1986
90 kg	170	J. Pepper 1986	100	J. Kerr 1983	190	J. Pepper 1986	445	J. Pepper 1986
90+ kg	162,5	J. Kerr 1981	112,5	V. Head 1982	185	J. Kerr 1981	440	J. Kerr 1980

WRESTLING

Origins
The earliest depictions of wrestling holds and falls on wall plaques and a statue indicate that organised wrestling dates from *c.* 2750–2600 BC. It was the most popular sport in the ancient Olympic Games and victors were recorded from 708 BC. The Greco-Roman style is of French origin and arose about 1860. The International Amateur Wrestling Federation (FILA) was founded in 1912.

Most titles *Olympic*
Three Olympic titles have been won by: Carl Westergren (1895–1958) (Sweden) in 1920, 1924, 1932; Ivar Johansson (1903–79) (Sweden) in 1932 (two), 1936; and Aleksandr Medved (b. 16 Sept 1937) (USSR) in 1964, 1968, 1972. Four Olympic medals were won by Eino Leino (b. 7 Apr 1891) at freestyle 1920–32 and by Imre Polyák (Hungary) (b. 16 Apr 1932) at Greco-Roman in 1952–64.

Most titles *World*
The freestyler Aleksandr Medved (USSR) (b. 16 Sept 1937) won a record ten world championships at 97 kg in 1962–4 (Olympic) and 1966, 97+ kg 1967–8 (Olympic), and 100+ kg in 1969–72 (Olympic). The only wrestler to win the same title in seven successive years has been Valeriy Rezantsev (b. 2 Feb 1947) (USSR) in the Greco-Roman 90 kg class in 1970–6, including the Olympic Games of 1972 and 1976.

Most titles and longest span *British*
The most British titles won is ten by heavyweight Kenneth Alan Richmond (b. 10 July 1926) between 1949 and 1960. The longest span for BAWA titles is 24 years by George Mackenzie (1890–1957) between 1909 and 1933. He represented Great Britain in five successive Olympiads, 1908 to 1928.

Most wins
In international competition, Osamu Watanabe (b. 21 Oct 1940), of Japan, the 1964 Olympic freestyle 63 kg champion, was unbeaten and unscored-upon in 187 consecutive matches. Wade Schalles (USA) won 821 bouts from 1964 to 1984, with 530 of these victories by pin.

Longest bout
The longest recorded bout was one of 11 hr 40 min when Martin Klein (1885–1947) (Estonia representing Russia) beat Alfred Asikáinen (1888–1942) (Finland) for the Greco-Roman 75 kg 'A' event silver medal in the 1912 Olympic Games in Stockholm, Sweden.

Heaviest heavyweight
The heaviest wrestler in Olympic history is Chris Taylor (1950–79), bronze medallist in the super-heavyweight class in 1972, who stood 6 ft 5 in *1,96 m* and weighed over 420 lb *190 kg*. FILA introduced an upper weight limit of 130 kg *286 lb* for international competition in 1985.

CUMBERLAND AND WESTMORLAND WRESTLING

J. Baddeley (middleweight in 1905–6, 1908–10, 1912) and Ernest Aubrey Bacon (b. 1893) (lightweight in 1919, 1921–3, 1928–9) both won six titles in the British amateur championships (inst. 1904).

PROFESSIONAL WRESTLING

Professional wrestling dates from 1874 in the USA. Georges Karl Julius Hackenschmidt (USSR) (1877–1968), Estonian-born, was undefeated at Greco-Roman contests from 1900 to his retirement in 1911. (*See also p. 95*.)

SUMO WRESTLING

The sport's origins in Japan date from *c.* 23 BC. The heaviest ever *sumotori* is Samoan-American Salevaa Fuali Atisnoe of Hawaii, *alias* Konishiki, who in 1986 had a peak weight of 512 lb *232 kg*. Weight is amassed by over alimentation with a high protein stew called *chankonabe*. The most successful wrestlers have been Sadaji Akiyoshi (b. 1912) *alias* Futabayama, winner of 69 consecutive bouts in the 1930s, Koki Naya (b. 1940) *alias* Taiho ('Great Bird'), who won the Emperor's Cup 32 times up to his retirement in 1971 and the *ozeki* Torokichi *alias* Raiden who in 21 years (1789–1810) won 254 bouts and lost only ten for the highest ever winning percentage of 96.2. Taiho and Futabayama share the record of eight perfect tournaments without a single loss. The youngest of the 59 men to attain the rank of *Yokozuna* (Grand Champion) was Toshimitsu Ogata (b. 16 May 1953) *alias* Kitanoumi, in July 1974 aged 21 years and two months. He set a record in 1978 winning 82 of the 90 bouts that top *rikishi* fight annually and had a career record 956 wins. Hawaiian born Jesse Kuhaulua (b. 16 June 1944), now a Japanese citizen named Daigoro Watanabe, *alias* Takamiyama was the first non-Japanese to win an official tournament in July 1972 and in 1981 set a record of 1231 consecutive top division bouts. He weighed in at 450 lb *204 kg* before his retirement in 1984.

YACHTING

Origins
Yachting in England dates from the £100 stake race between Charles II and his brother James, Duke of York, on the Thames on 1 Sept 1661 over 23 miles from Greenwich to Gravesend. The oldest club in the world is the Royal Cork Yacht Club (formerly the Cork Harbour Water Club), established in Ireland in 1720. The oldest active club in Britain is the Starcross Yacht Club at Powderham Point, Devon. Its first regatta was held in 1772.

Olympic titles *World*
The first sportsman ever to win individual gold medals in four successive Olympic Games was Paul B. Elvström (b. 24 Feb 1928) (Denmark) in the Firefly class in 1948 and the Finn class in 1952, 1956 and 1960. He also won eight other world titles in a total of six classes. The lowest number of penalty points by the winner of any

Ken Black, who completed the 70 miles *112,7 km* windsurf around the Isle of Wight in a record 7 hr 58 min.

class in an Olympic regatta is three points (five wins, one disqualified and one second in seven starts) by *Superdocious* of the Flying Dutchman class (Lt. Rodney Stuart Pattisson RN (b. 5 Aug 1943) and Iain Somerled Macdonald-Smith (b. 3 July 1945)) at Acapulco Bay, Mexico in October 1968.

Olympic titles British
The only British yacht to win two titles was *Scotia* in the Open class and Half-One Ton class at the 1900 Regatta with Lorne Campbell Currie (1871–1926), and John H. Gretton (1867–1947). The only British yachtsman to win in two Olympic regattas is Rodney Pattisson in 1968 (*see above*) and again with *Superdoso* crewed by Christopher Davies (b. 29 June 1946) at Kiel, W. Germany in 1972. He gained a silver medal in 1976 with Julian Brooke Houghton (b. 16 Dec 1946).

Admiral's Cup
The ocean racing series with the most participating nations (three boats allowed to each nation) is the Admiral's Cup held by the Royal Ocean Racing Club. A record 19 nations competed in 1975, 1977 and 1979. Britain has a record eight wins.

America's Cup
The America's Cup was originally won as an outright prize by the schooner *America* on 22 Aug 1851 at Cowes and was later offered by the New York Yacht Club as a challenge trophy. On 8 Aug 1870 J. Ashbury's *Cambria* (GB) failed to capture the trophy from the *Magic*, owned by F. Osgood (USA). Since then the Cup has been challenged by Great Britain in 16 contests, in 2 contests by Canada, and by Australia 7 times, but the United States were undefeated winning 77 races and only losing eight until 1983 when *Australia II*, skippered by John Bertrand and owned by a Perth syndicate headed by Alan Bond beat *Liberty* 4–3, the narrowest series victory, at Newport, RI, USA.

Longest race
The longest regular sailing race is the quadrennial Whitbread Round the World race (inst. Aug 1973) organized by the Royal Naval Sailing Association. The distance is 26,180 nautical miles from Portsmouth, and return with stops and re-starts at Cape Town, Auckland and Mar del Plata. The record (sailing) time is 117 days 14 hr 31 min by *UBS Switzerland*, skipper Pierre Fehlmann (Switzerland), finishing on 9 May 1986 (*see also p. 161*).

Greatest distance
The greatest distance covered in a day's run under sail was set by the 80 foot *24,4 m* catamaran *Formula Tag* (skipper: Michael Birch). During the 1984 Transat TAG Race between Quebec and St Malo she covered 512.55 nautical miles in 23.70 hours for an average of 21.63 knots. She must have achieved at least 518 nm in the full 24 hours. For one period of 24.6 mins she averaged 31.68 knots.

Highest speeds
The official world sailing speed record is 36.04 knots (41.50 mph *66,78 km/h*) by the 73½ ft *22,40 m* proa *Crossbow II* over a 500 m *547 yd* course in Portland Harbour, Dorset, on 17 Nov 1980. The vessel (sail area 1400 ft² *130,06 m²*) was designed by Rod McAlpine-Downie and owned and steered by Timothy Colman. In an unsuccessful attempt on the record in October 1978, *Crossbow II* is reported to have momentarily attained a speed of 45 knots (51 mph *83 km/h*). The fastest 24 hr single-handed run by a sailing yacht was recorded by Nick Keig (b. 13 June 1936), of the Isle of Man, who covered 340 nautical miles in a 37½ ft *11,43 m* trimaran *Three

Legs of Mann I during the Falmouth to Punta, Azores race on 9–10 June 1975, averaging 14.16 knots (16.30 mph *26,23 km/h*). The fastest bursts of speed reached were about 25 knots (28.78 mph *46,32 km/h*).

Marinas, *Largest*
The largest marina in the world is that of Marina Del Rey, Los Angeles, California, USA, which has 7500 berths. The largest in Britain is the Brighton Marina, East Sussex, with 2313 berths.

Most competitors
The most boats ever to start in a single race was 1947, of which 1767 finished in the Round Zealand (Denmark) race on 17–20 June 1983, over a course of 375 km *233 miles*. The greatest number to start in a race in Britain was 1309 keeled yachts and multihulls on 31 May 1986 from Cowes in the Annual Round-the-Island race. The fastest time achieved in this annual event is 3 hr 55 min 28 sec by the trimaran *Paragon*, owned and sailed by Michael Whipp on 31 May 1986.

Highest
The greatest altitude at which sailing has taken place is 4910 m *16,109 ft* on Laguna Huallatani, Bolivia, in Mirror Dinghy 55448, variously by Peter Williams, Gordon Siddeley, Keith Robinson and Brian Barrett, on 19 Nov 1977. The highest for boardsailing is 4970 m *16,300 ft* by Juan Felipe Marti, Juan Ojeda, Fermin Tarres and Philippe Levrel on Tilicho's Lake, Nepal on 20 Oct 1983.

BOARDSAILING

Origins
The High Court ruled on 7 Apr 1982 that Peter Chilvers (when aged 12) had devised a prototype of a boardsailer in 1958 in England. In 1968 Henry Hoyle Schweitzer and Jim Drake pioneered the sport, often termed windsurfing, in California, USA. World championships were first held in 1973 and the sport was added to the Olympic Games in 1984 when the winner was Stephan van den Berg (Netherlands), who also won five world titles 1979–83.

English Channel
The record time for boardsailing across the English Channel is 1 hr 4 min 33 sec by Baron Arnaud de Rosnay (France) on 4 July 1982 from Cap Gris Nez to Dover at an average speed of 16.9 knots (19.5 mph *31,3 km/h*). After 45 mins rest he returned to Wissant, France in 1 hr 4 min 37 sec.

Highest Speed
The record speed for boardsailing is 35.52 knots *65,78 km/h* by Pascal Maka (France) off the Canary Islands in July 1986. Peter Bridgeman set a British record of 31.89 knots *59,10 km/h* at Port-Saint-Louis, Marseille, France on 17 Apr 1985. A women's record of 28.96 knots *53,60 km/h* was set on the same occasion by Paty Whitcombe.

Endurance
Marco Topdemir of France set an endurance record of 87 hr 33 min 52 sec in Brest, France on 10–13 Oct 1985.

The longest wind surf ever made was by Timothy John Batstone (b. 22 Apr 1959) in circumnavigating 1794 miles *2887 kms* round Great Britain on 2 May–10 July 1984. He did 70 miles *112,6 kms* in a single stretch, made 40 sail changes and had zero falls on eight days.

Longest 'snake'
The longest 'snake' of boardsails was set by 60 windsurfers in tandem at the 'International Windsurfing Week' event in Balk, Holland on 2 July 1985.

ENDURANCE MARATHONS

ACTIVITY	TOTAL NO. IN ATTEMPT	DURATION
Backgammon	2	151 hr 11 min

Dick Newcomb and Greg Peterson at Rockford, Illinois, USA, 30 June–6 July 1978

Badminton (*singles*)	2	78 hr 23 min

Cameron McMullen and Michael Patterson at Blessed Edward Jones High School, Rhyl, Clwyd, Wales, 1–4 Apr 1986.

Badminton (*doubles*)	4	77 hr 1 min

Paul Farmer, Andrew Hood, Ben Smith and Loraine Storey at Chilwell, Nottingham, 29 May–1 June 1984

Bar Billiards	2	50 hr

Michael Howell and Kevin Pilcher at the White Hart Hotel, Hythe, Kent, 19–21 July 1985.

Basketball	10	102 hr

Sigma Nu Fraternity at Indiana University, Pennsylvania, USA, 13–17 Apr 1983.

Bingo calling	2	285 hr 24 min

Phillip Carter and Mark Kiely at the Top Rank Club, Kingston, Surrey, 8–20 May 1983.

Bowling (*Ten Pin*)	1	195 hr 1 min

Jim Webb at Gosford City Bowl, New South Wales, Australia, 1984.

Bowls (*outdoor*)	8	100 hr 2 min

Two teams from Taieri Bowling Club, Mosglel, New Zealand, 27–31 Mar 1986.

Bowls (*indoor*)	8	77 hr

Two teams from Sutton Indoor Bowls Club, Sutton, Surrey, 24–27 Apr 1986.

Bridge (*Contract*)	4	180 hr

Four students at Edinburgh University, 21–28 Apr 1972.

Chess	2	200 hr

Roger Long and Graham Croft at Dingles, Bristol, 11–19 May 1984.

Cribbage	4	120 hr

Geoff Lee, Ken Whyatt, Ray Charles and Paul Branson at Mapperley, Nottingham, 16–21 Mar 1982.

Cricket	22	316 hr

Two teams from Belper, Derbyshire, 14–27 Aug 1983.

Cricket (*indoor*)	16	124 hr

Two teams from Seymour Indoor CC, Victoria, Australia, 31 Jan–5 Feb 1986.

Croquet	4	113 hr 25 min

Hilary Lund-Yates, Hilary Cuthbert, Simon Clay and Roger Swift at Birmingham University, 18–23 June 1983.

Curling	4	67 hr 55 min

Capital Winter Club, Fredericton, New Brunswick, Canada, 9–12 Apr 1982.

Curling	2	38 hr

Jim Paul and Chris McCrady at the Brockville Country Club, Ontario, Canada, 26–28 Mar 1962.

Darts	2	134 hr 54 min

Raymond Azzopardi and Alan Alden at the Bank of Valletta Sports & Social Club, Marsa, Malta, 11–17 Dec 1985.

Dominoes	2	150 hr 5 min

Neil Thomas and Tim Beesley at St Anselm's College, Wirral, Merseyside, 5–11 Aug 1985. (A 4-person record of 144 hr was set by Keith Hannard and Alan, Bob and Ray McKeith at the Cyprus Hotel, South Shields, 25–31 Aug 1985).

Draughts	2	138 hr 28 min

Greg Davis and Mark Schumacher at Denny's Restaurant, Nunawading, Victoria, Australia, 26 Aug–1 Sept 1985.

Dungeons & Dragons (*TSR*)	5–9	66 hr

A team of eight (six finished) for Dr. Barnado's at Ilford, Essex, 30 June–3 July 1986.

Fives (*Rugby*)	2	32 hr

Christopher Howard and John Ingham at Giggleswick School, Settle, N. Yorks, 21–22 Mar 1986.

The draughts marathon record of over 5¾ days.

ACTIVITY	TOTAL NO. IN ATTEMPT	DURATION
Football (*Soccer*)	22	64 hr 44 min

Two teams from Stewart's, Lake Park, Florida, USA, 31 Aug–3 Sept 1984.

Football (*outdoor*)	10	74 hr 30 min

Two teams at Liswerry Leisure Centre, Newport, Gwent, Wales, 23–26 June 1983.

Football (*indoor*)	10	104 hr 10 min

Two teams from the A.C.E. '83 group, at Summerhill College, Sligo, Ireland, 27–31 Mar 1983.

Gaelic Football	14	60 hr 5 min

Two teams from Kilcornan G.A.A. Club, Kilcornan, Co. Limerick, Ireland, 23–25 May 1986.

Handball	22	44 hr 20 min

Two teams from the Fancom-Bevo Handball Club, Beringe, Netherlands, 24–25 Aug 1985.

Hockey (*outdoor*)	22	40 hr

Two teams from Maidstone Hockey Club, Kent, 3–4 May 1986.

Hockey (*indoor*)	12	44 hr 43 min

Two teams from Nottingham University Men's Hockey Club, 18–20 Mar 1986.

Horsemanship	1	112 hr 30 min

Ken Nothdurft at Kingsthorpe, Queensland, Australia, 31 Aug–4 Sept 1985.

Ice skating	1	109 hr 5 min

Austin McKinley at Christchurch, New Zealand, 21–25 June 1977.

Judo	6	245 hr 30 min

Five of six people at Smithfield RSL Youth Club, New South Wales, Australia, 3–13 Jan 1984.

Netball	14	38 hr

The 'Pan-Ems' at the Emerton Youth Centre, Mt. Druitt, NSW, Australia, 30 Sept–1 Oct 1984.

Pool	2	300 hr 16 min

Barry Wicks and Derek Shaw; also Paul Haslam and Vincent Moore at the New Inn, Galgate, Lancaster, 21 May–2 June 1984.

Racquetball	2	41 hr 22 min

Jean Gratton and Marc Ouellette (Canada) at St. Antoine, Canada, 18–19 Jan 1986.

Roller Cycling	1	83 hr 29 min

Gilbert Bil at Café Zuid, Almere, Netherlands, 1–4 Dec 1985.

Roller Skating	1	344 hr 18 min

Isamu Furugen at Naha Roller Skate Land, Okinawa, Japan, 11–27 Dec 1983.

Scrabble	2	153 hr

Peter Finan and Neil Smith at St. Anselm's College, Wirral, Merseyside, 18–25 Aug 1984. (Ken Cardozo played for 155 hr 48 min against various opponents at 'Perfect Pizza', Fulham, 5–11 Dec 1984).

Skiing (*Alpine*)	1	138 hr

Luc Labrie at Daie Comeau, Quebec, Canada, 20–25 Feb 1984.

ENDURANCE MARATHONS

ACTIVITY	TOTAL NO. IN ATTEMPT	DURATION
Skiing (*Alpine*)	2	83 hr 17 min

With no waiting for lifts—Dave Phillips and Gerry O'Neill at Grouse Mountain, North Vancouver, Canada, 20–23 Feb 1986.

Skittles	6	168 hr

Gloucester & District Irish Society at Gloucester, 15–22 Aug 1981.

Snakes & Ladders	4	260 hr

Team from Essex Young Farmers Club, West Mersea, Essex, 29 Jan–2 Feb 1982.

Snooker	2	304 hr

Nick Burgess and Mark Sullivan at Sidwell Snooker Club, Exeter, Devon, 28 June–11 July 1986.

Softball (*fast pitch*)	18	57 hr

Two teams from Austin, Minnesota, USA, 24–26 July 1981.

Softball (*slow pitch*)	20	100 hr

Two teams from Alpha Gamma Chi fraternity, Lee College, Cleveland, Tennessee, USA, 1–5 Apr 1986.

Squash	2	122 hr 44 min

Amir Shailch and Phillip Marlowe at Wembley Squash Centre, Wembley, Middlesex, 8–13 Nov 1985.

Table Football	2	60 hr 31 min

Miles Blackford and Simon Gibson at Dakyns' House, Clifton College, Bristol on 22–24 May 1986.

Table Tennis	2	147 hr 47 min

S. Unterslak and J. Boccia at Dewaal Hotel, Cape Town, South Africa, 12–18 Nov 1983.

ACTIVITY	TOTAL NO. IN ATTEMPT	DURATION
Table Tennis (*Doubles*)	4	101 hr 1 min

Lance, Phil and Mark Warren and Bill Weir at Sacramento, Cal., USA, 9–13 Apr 1979.

Tennis (*Lawn*)	2	117 hr

Mark and Jim Pinchoff at the Fitness Resort, Lafayette, Louisiana, USA, 14–19 May 1985.

Tennis (*Doubles*)	4	96 hr 25 min

Ann Wilkinson, Peter Allsopp, John Thorpe and David Dicks at Mansfield Lawn Tennis Club, Notts, 17–21 Aug 1983.

Tiddlywinks	6	300 hr

Southampton University Tiddlywinks Club, 20 Feb–5 Mar 1981.

Trampolining	1	266 hr 9 min

Jeff Schwartz at Glenview, Illinois, USA, 14–25 Aug 1981.

Volleyball	12	84 hr

Two teams from Beta Theta Pi fraternity, Bethany College, Bethany, West Virginia, USA, 27–30 Sept 1984.

Water Polo	14	24 hr 50 min

Two teams from Puyallup High School, Washington, USA, 12–13 Oct 1984.

IMPORTANT

Rest breaks of five minutes for each completed hour played (not calculated according to a running total) are permitted in these endurance marathons. Such breaks are aggregable but at no time can the earned rest period be exceeded. The number of participants in team events is shown in the table, all must be in action throughout the attempt, except that a drop out rate of up to 20% of the people is permitted. No substitutes are allowed. Claims for new records must be accompanied by full authentication.

Edinburgh 24 July–2 August 1986

COMMONWEALTH GAMES

BOWLS

Nell Hunter (b. 3 Feb 1915) was, at 71 years, the oldest Games competitor.

ROWING

Steven Redgrave (b. 23 Mar 1962) won gold medals for England at single sculls, coxless pairs and coxed fours: the first rower ever to win three Commonwealth gold medals at one Games.

SHOOTING

Malcolm Cooper (England), who had won a record six medals, two gold, three silver and one bronze, in 1982, added two gold and two bronze medals this time. Both his 1986 gold medals came in the small-bore rifle three positions, the individual (in a Games record 1170) and the pairs (2278), the latter with his wife Sarah.

Greg Yelavich (New Zealand) won both the free pistol (551) and air pistol (575) gold medals.

SWIMMING

Allison Higson (Canada) (b. 13 Mar 1973) won the 200 m breaststroke on 26 July at the age of 13 years 135 days, **the youngest champion in Games history**.

Three gold medals were won by Alex Baumann: 200 m and 400 m individual medley and for Canada's 4 × 100 m medley relay team.

Commonwealth records were set at women's 800 m freestyle: 8:24.77 Sarah Hardcastle (England); 400 m individual medley: 4:45.82 Suzane Landells (Australia), and for the men's 4 × 200 m freestyle relay team: 7:23.49 Australia (Thomas Stachewicz, Duncan Armstrong, Robert Gleria, Peter Dale).

Other British Records
Men's 100 metres freestyle: 51.21 Andrew Jameson.
Men's 100 metres butterfly: 54.07 Andrew Jameson.
Men's 400 metres individual medley: 4:24.71 Stephen Poulter.
Men's 4 × 100 metres medley: 3:44.85 England (Neil Harper, Adrian Moorhouse, Andrew Jameson, Roland Lee).
Women's 4 × 100 metres freestyle: 3:49.65 England (Caroline Cooper, Nicola Fibbens, Zara Long, Annabelle Cripps).

TRACK AND FIELD ATHLETICS

English athletes Daley Thompson (decathlon) and Kathy Cook (4 × 100 m relay) won third gold medals at their events: a feat achieved by five athletes previously. Kathy Cook also won two silver and one bronze, to bring her medal tally at major championships to 23—a British record.

Two Commonwealth records were set: Lisa Martin (Australia), 2 hr 26 min 7 sec for the women's marathon, and Elizabeth Lynch (Scotland), 31:44.42 for the women's 10,000 metres. British records: Elizabeth Lynch (above), while Geoff Parsons equalled his own record of 2.28 m in the high jump.

Unique doubles were achieved in the women's events by Debbie Flintoff (Australia) 400 m and 400 m hurdles, and Kirsty Wade (Wales) 800 m and 1500 m. Gael Martin (Australia) became the fourth to win the shot and discus double. Steve Cram followed Herb Elliott (1958) and Peter Snell (1962) in winning both 800 m and 1500 m

WEIGHTLIFTING

Commonwealth records were set by the gold medallists at: 67.5 kg Dean Willey (England)—snatch 145, total 315 kg; 82.5 kg David Morgan (Wales)—snatch 160, jerk 190, total 350 kg.

Dean Lukin (Australia) retained his 110 kg+ title with a Games record total of 392.5 kg.

FINAL MEDAL TABLE

	Gold	Silver	Bronze	Total
England	52	42	48	142
Canada	51	34	30	115
Australia	40	46	34	120
New Zealand	8	16	14	38
Wales	6	5	12	23
Scotland	3	12	18	33
N. Ireland	2	4	9	15
Isle of Man	1	0	0	1
Guernsey	0	2	0	2
Swaziland	0	1	0	1
Hong Kong	0	0	2	2
Malawi	0	0	2	2
Botswana	0	0	1	1
Jersey	0	0	1	1
Singapore	0	0	1	1

CHAPTER 1

HUMAN BEING

NATIONAL LONGEVITY (p. 11—table footnote) The claim for the late David Trumble is now acknowledged to be baseless.

MOST VORACIOUS FIRE BREATHERS AND EXTINGUISHERS (p. 19) On 29 May 1986 Roberto Kalin (b. 1961) of Bregenz, Vorarlberg, Austria, extinguished 14,648 torches of flame successively in his mouth in 2 hr at Ried, Innkreis, Austria.

MOST INFECTIOUS DISEASE (p. 18) The US death roll from AIDS is predicted to reach 179,000 by 1991 with care costs possibly reaching $16,000 million.

MOTIONLESSNESS (p. 20) In a mass attack on the motionlessness record in Semerang, Indonesia on 21 July 1986, Reuter reported Sunardi won after 15 hr 25 min.

HEART TRANSPLANT (p. 21) 'Baby Moses' underwent a heart transplant at the Loma Linda Hospital, California, USA in November 1985 aged 4 days.

CHAPTER 2

LIVING WORLD

TOP SHOW DOGS (p. 33) From 27 Apr 1975 to 17 Apr 1984 the German Shepherd bitch 'Ch. Clayfield's Mon Ami' (whelped 7 Feb 1971), owned by Neal, Sharon, Buffy and Holly Leas of West Des Moines, Iowa, USA, won 10 championships on 4 continents.

LARGEST CAT (p. 33) 'Himmy' of Queensland, Australia, died on 12 Mar 1986, weight unchanged.

RAREST BIRDS (p. 35) An Ivory-billed woodpecker (*Campephilus principalis bairdi*) was positively identified in the mountains of eastern Cuba in April 1986. It was last recorded in the island in 1972.

LONGEST FROG JUMP (p. 38) 'Rosie the Ribeter' owned and trained by Lee Giudici of Santa Clara, California, USA, leapt 21 ft 5¾ in *6,55 m* on 18 May 1986 at the annual Calaveras Jumping Jubilee at Angels Camp.

PHILODENDRON (p. 45) Professor F. J. Francis of the University of Massachusetts, USA, has grown a specimen 1114 ft *339,5 m* which is now 31 years old.

LARGEST WREATH (p. 46) The Farm Stand, wholesale nurserymen of Walworth, New York, USA, constructed in November 1985 a free standing wreath 100 ft 8 in *30,68 m* in diameter and weighing 9840 lb *4463 kg*.

LARGEST WATERMELON (p. 47) Jason Bright, 10, of Hope, Arkansas, USA, grew a watermelon reported by Grace's Gardens in September 1985 to weigh 260 lb *118 kg* and overtaking the joint record set by his father and grandfather.

LARGEST CUCUMBER (p. 48) Mrs Eileen Chappel of Bowen Hills, Queensland, Australia, grew a cucumber reported on 13 May 1986 to weigh 22 kg *48,5 lb*.

LARGEST PETUNIA (p. 48) Bert Lawrence of Windham NY, USA, grew a petunia plant measured on 19 Sept 1985 at 13 ft 8 in *4,16 m*.

REMOTEST TREE (p. 49) The tree believed to be the remotest from any other is a Norwegian spruce, the only one on Campbell Island, Antarctica. Its nearest companion would be over 120 miles *195 km* away on the Auckland Islands.

RAREST TREE (p. 49) The Cafe Marron tree *Ramosmania heterophylla* uniquely growing on Rodriguez Island, Indian Ocean was reported in April 1986 to be down to a single specimen.

EARLIEST LIFE FORM (p. 50) The estimated age of Kakabekia was revised in July 1986 to 4000 million years ago.

CHAPTER 3

THE NATURAL WORLD

HEAVIEST HAILSTONES (p. 54) Stones up to 2¼ lb *1,02 kg* are reported to have killed 92 people in the Gopalganj district of Bangladesh on 14 Apr 1986.

ROCKALL (p. 57—picture caption) The person encamped is Tom McClean setting a duration record of 38 days 22 hr 52 min on 25 May–4 July 1985.

CHAPTER 4

THE UNIVERSE & SPACE

MOST SATELLITES (p. 67) With the discovery of new Uranian moons by the US *Voyager 2*, the number in the Solar System now becomes 63.

MOST DISTANT HEAVENLY BODY (p. 68—table) It was announced in February 1986 that using the UK Schmidt telescope C. Hazard, R. G. McMahon and W. L. W. Sargent had identified quasar 1208 + 1011 with a red shift of 3.80 consonant with a recession velocity of 91.7 per cent that of light and to a distance of 14,900 million light years, 8.78 × 1022 miles *1,41 × 1023 km*.

THE UNIVERSE: LARGEST OBJECT (p. 69) Burns and Batuski announced in March 1985 that they had identified a filamentary arrangement of Abell galaxy clusters of length 1000 million light years 5.89 × 10²¹ miles *9,46 × 10²¹ km*.

CHAPTER 5

SCIENTIFIC WORLD

GREATEST PERFUME SHOWER (p. 71) On 9 Feb 1986, Carlos Norberto Varaldo of Cheiro da Terra Perfumes arranged for 900 litre *198 gal* of jasmine essence perfume to be sprayed over the 140,000 who attended a local carnival in Rio de Janeiro.

MOST EXPENSIVE SPIRITS (p. 72) On 17 June 1986 a single bottle of whisky, Lot 402, 'The Macallan Over 50 Years Old', a single malt distilled in 1928, was sold at auction for £1265 to a Scottish wine merchant, Christopher Lynas, at Christie's, Glasgow, Scotland.

CHAPTER 6

THE ARTS & ENTERTAINMENTS

LONGEST DIARY (p. 85) George C. Edler (b. 13 Dec 1889) of Bethesda, Maryland, USA, has kept a diary with no breaks since 1 Jan 1917.

MOST EXPENSIVE BRITISH MANUSCRIPT (p. 85) John Paul Getty II acquired four illustrated leaves from the only known manuscript life of Thomas à Becket for £1,375,000 at Sotheby's, London on 24 Jun 1986.

FASTEST BOOK PUBLISHING (p. 87) The 128-page hardback *Invitation to a Royal Wedding* was on sale at W. H. Smith, Heathrow, London Airport 47 hr 25 min after the commencement of typesetting. Published by William Collins on the occasion of the wedding of HRH Prince Andrew and Miss Sarah Ferguson on 23 July 1986 the book was written by Trevor Hall and compiled by Colour Library Books International.

MOST DURABLE CROSSWORD COMPILER (p. 89) Roger F. Squires has published 27,388 puzzles to August 1986.

FASTEST BAGPIPE PLAYING (p. 91) Sgt Mick Maitland, Pipe Major of No 111 RAF Fighter Squadron played 'Scotland The Brave' on his pipes at a speed of Mach 2.0 and a height of 40,000 ft *12 190 m*. He was flown in Phantom XV 574 by Wing Commander Phil W. Roser, the Squadron Commander. This supersonic performance was given 40 miles *64,3 km* south of RAF Akrotiri, Cyprus on 3 June 1986.

LARGEST ORCHESTRA (p. 91) On 17 Apr 1982, 6179 'musicians' congregated at Bay Shore Mall, Milwaukee, Wisconsin, USA, for a rendering of Sousa's 'Stars and Stripes Forever'. According to one music critic, the 'instruments' included 'kazoos, 7-Up bottles, one-man-band contraptions, coffee cans, bongo drums and anything-you-can-thump-on. At times' the report concludes, 'you could almost tell what they were playing'.

LONGEST RUNS—REVUE (p. 94) There have been, to 6 May 1986, 46,250 performances of The Golden Horseshoe Revue.

LONGEST RUNS—BROADWAY (p. 94) 'The Fantasticks', which opened on 3 May 1960, was scheduled to close after 10,864 performances on 8 Jun 1986.

MOST ROLES (p. 94) Kanzaburo Nakamura, 77, of Tokyo, Japan, has played leading roles in 803 different Kabuki titles from November 1926 to September 1985. As each title lasts 25 days he has therefore made 20,075 performances.

MOST DURABLE ACTRESS (p. 94) Dame Anna Neagle, DBE, died on 3 June 1986.

MOST DURABLE ACTOR (p. 94) David Raven played the part of Major Metcalf in 'The Mousetrap' on 4575 occasions from 22 July 1957 to 23 Nov 1968.

EARLIEST RECORDINGS (p. 96) The voice of Lajos Kossuth, the Hungarian patriot, (b. 9 Sept 1802) was recorded on 20 Sept 1890.

MOST PORTRAYED CINEMA CHARACTER (p. 98) Sherlock Holmes has been portrayed by 68 actors in 187 films between 1900 and 1986.

HIGHEST PAID TV PERFORMER (p. 101) It was reported in July 1986 that Bill Cosby earned £6.5 million in 12 months on US TV shows and concerts and from advertisements and albums.

'MASTERMIND' (p. 101) Jennifer Keaveney equalled her semi-final record score of 40 points when she won the 1986 final with 'the life and works of Elizabeth Gaskell'.

MOST DURABLE TELEVISION BROADCASTER (p. 101) The greatest number of hours on camera on US national commercial television is 9916½ by the TV personality Hugh Downs in over 40 years to 31 July 1985.

FASTEST VIDEO PRODUCTION (p. 101) Tapes of the Royal Wedding of HRH Prince Andrew and Miss Sarah Ferguson on 23 July 1986 were produced by Thames Video Collection. Live filming ended with the departure of the honeymoon couple from Chelsea Hospital by helicopter at 4.42 pm. The first fully edited and packaged VHS tapes were purchased 5 hr 41 min later by Fenella Lee and Lucinda Burland of West Kensington at the Virgin Megastore in Oxford Street, London at 10.23 pm.

CHAPTER 7

STRUCTURES

LONGEST PLEASURE PIER (p. 107) Southend Pier was rammed and sliced in two on 30 July 1986 by the 645 ton coaster *Kings Abbey*, and reopened on 8 Aug 1986. The pier railway, which was reopened on 2 May 1986 by HRH The Princess Anne, was undamaged.

HIGHEST UK PUBLIC HOUSE (p. 108) The 'Tan Hill Inn', Co. Durham is now open all the year round.

LONGEST BRIDGE (p. 109) It was reported on 8 Apr 1986 that the Akashi bridge span would be 6529 ft *1990 m* and would cost $5.5 billion on completion in 1998.

BUSIEST CANAL (p. 111) The ships with the greatest beam to transit the Panama Canal have been four Iowa class battleships of the US Navy with beams of 108 ft 2 in *33 m*.

LARGEST TUNNEL (p. 113) Traffic through the Yerba Buena tunnel is now reported to have reached 80 million by 1986.

LARGEST UK MARQUEE (p. 116) The largest single-unit tent covers a ground area of more than 12 000 m² *129,170 ft²* and is manufactured by Clyde Canvas Ltd of Edinburgh, Scotland.

CHAPTER 8

THE MECHANICAL WORLD

COACHING (p. 124) John Parker changed a team of horses at Wingfield, Norfolk on 29 July 1986 in 25.06 sec.

MOST EXPENSIVE USED CAR (p. 126) A 1931 Bugatti Royale from the collection of the late William F. Harrah made $6.5 million *£4.3 million* at auction on 27 June 1986 at Reno, Nevada, USA .

ROUND BRITAIN ECONOMY DRIVING (p. 127) John Bloxham, Toney Cox and Ian Hughes assisted by Wolverhampton Rotary Club drove the Round Britain course on 14–18 June 1986 in a diesel powered Peugeot 205 GRD. The overall fuel consumption for the 3623 mile *5830,6 km* run was 64.376 mpg *22,79 km/litre*.

CAPE TO LONDON (p. 127) Brig John and his wife, Dr Lucy Hemsley drove the 11,674 mile *18 787 km* route from Cape Town, South Africa to London in 14 days 19 hr 26 min on 8–22 Jan 1983 in a Range Rover.

BATTERY POWERED VEHICLE (p. 127) Joe Schwarzkopf-Bowers, 37, of Watford, Herts drove his modified battery-powered Bond Equipe from 'Heathrow Airport to Crewkerne, Somerset on 16 May 1986, a distance of 132 miles *212,4 km* on a single charge costing an estimated 60p.

TWO WHEEL DRIVING (p. 127) Göran Eliason (b. 7 Dec 1946) of Boras, Sweden achieved 134,9 km/h *83.8 mph* on the two wheels of a standard Volvo 760 at Anderstrop, Sweden on 18 May 1986.

SNOWMOBILES (p. 129) Tony Lenzini of Duluth, Minnesota, USA, drove a 1986 Arctic Cat Cougar snowmobile a total of 7211 miles *11 604,6 km* in 60 riding days between 28 Dec 1985 and 20 Mar 1986.

UNICYCLE (p. 130) Hanspeter Beck of Jindabyne, NSW, Australia, rode from South Hedland, WA, to Melbourne, Vic., a distance of 6237,96 km *3876.08 miles* in 51 days 23 hr 25 min between 30 June–20 Aug 1985.

PENNY-FARTHING (p. 130) Clive Flint, 31, a police officer from Manchester, rode from John O' Groats to Land's End, a distance of 898 miles *1445 km*, in 9 days 6 hr 52 min on 2–10 June 1986.

FLIGHT DURATION (p. 135) The Voyager aircraft flew 11,857 miles *19 081 km* without refuelling in 110 hr on 15 July 1986.

TALLEST WINDMILL (p. 139) De Noord windmill in Schiedam, Netherlands at 33,33 m *109 ft 4 in*, is the tallest in Europe.

HELICOPTER SPEED RECORD (p. 136) Trevor Eggington, 53, averaged 249.10 mph *400.87 kph* over Somerset on 11 Aug 1986 in a Westland's Lynx Company Demonstrator helicopter.

LARGEST WRISTWATCH (p. 141) A 'Swatch' 162 m *531 ft 6 in* long and 20 m *65 ft 7¼ in* in diameter, made by D. Tomas Feliu, was set up on the Bank of Bilbao building, Madrid, Spain from 7–12 Dec 1985.

CHAPTER 9

THE BUSINESS WORLD

LARGEST BRITISH ACCOUNTANCY FEE (p. 144) Coopers and Lybrand reported a fees income of nearly £120 million.

STOCK EXCHANGES—MOST BARGAINS (p. 148) The greatest fall in a day on the London Stock Exchange occurred on 7 Aug 1986 when the Financial Times 30-share index fell 32.1 to 1233.7. Nearly £4 billion was wiped from the value of equities.

CANDLE (p.149) The Atletiek-en Trimvereniging Tegelen Sportsclub of Tegelen, Holland constructed a candle 27,155 m *89 ft 1 in* high on 1 June 1986.

LARGEST JIG-SAW (p. 151) The Monadnock United Way of Keene, New Hampshire, USA, constructed a puzzle at the Keene College gymnasium on 21–23 Sept 1985 measuring 84 ft 10½ in × 55 ft 2¼ in *25,87 × 16,83 m* with 15,520 pieces.

ANTIQUES AT AUCTION (pp. 152–3) A Philadelphia tea table was auctioned at Christie's, New York, on 25 Jan 1986 for $1,045,000 (£697,000).

ENGLISH PORCELAIN (p. 152) A Chelsea polychrome figure of Hogarth's dog 'Trump' (1745–47) from the estate of James Newman was bought for £85,000 at Sotheby's, London on 1 July 1986.

CHAPTER 10

HUMAN ACHIEVEMENTS

NORTH POLE CONQUEST (p. 159) Dr Jean-Louis Etienne, 39, was the first to reach the Pole, solo and without dogs, on 11 May 1986 after 63 days.

FASTEST TRANS-ATLANTIC CROSSING (p. 160) The 72 ft *Virgin Atlantic*

Challenger II owned by Richard Branson and with a crew of 6 made the fastest West to East crossing for a monohull on 26–29 June 1986 in 3 days 8 hr 31 min.

WORKING CAREER—JOURNALIST (p. 163) The writer who has interviewed most heads of state and heads of government in the world is Brian Rossiter Crozier (b. 4 Aug 1918) with 58 in the period 1952–85.

AUCTIONEERING (p. 164) Reg Coates conducted a continuous auction of 53½ hr on 3–5 July 1986 at Guinness World of Records exhibition, the Trocadero, Piccadilly, London.

BAG (COAL) CARRYING (p. 164) Neil Sullivan, 37, of Small Heath, Birmingham, carried a 1 cwt *50,8 kg* bag of coal for 34 miles *54,7 km* in 12¾ hr on 24 May 1986.

BED OF NAILS (p. 164) The Rev Ken Owen, 48, of Pontypridd, Mid-Glamorgan, lay on a bed of nails for a total of 300 hr, including 132 hr 30 min without a break, between 3–14 May 1986 starting at Bridgend Hotel, Pontygwaith, and concluding at the 'The Three Horse Shoes', Tonteg, Pontypridd.

CROCHET (p. 166) Miss Ria van der Honing of Wormerveer, Netherlands, completed a crochet chain 62,50 km *38.83 miles* in length on 14 July 1986.

BALLROOM DANCING MARATHON (p. 167) Scott Michael, 31, dancing instructor of Huntington Beach, California, USA, danced for 126 hr non-stop aided by 27 partners between 20–25 June 1986 at the Dance Masters Ballroom Studio, Stanton, California.

FLUTE MARATHON (p. 168) Flautist Joseph Shury of the Sri Chinmoy Marathon Team, Toronto, Ontario, Canada, played continuously for 61 hr between 21–23 Mar 1986.

FOOTBAG (p. 168) Andy Linder improved his record with 32,598 kicks and Tricia Sullivan hers with 12,838 both on 31 July 1985 at Golden, Colorado, USA.

HEDGE LAYING (p. 169) John Williams of Sennybridge, Brecon and David James of Llanwern, Brecon hedged by the 'stake and pleach' method a total of 264 yd *241,4 m* in 11 hr 24 min.

KNITTING—'SHEEP TO SHOULDER' (p. 171) The Exeter Spinners—Audrey Felton, Christine Heap, Eileen Lancaster, Marjorie Mellis, Ann Sandercock and Maria Scott produced a jumper by hand from raw fleece in 1 hr 55 min 50.2 sec on 25 Sept 1983 at BBC Television Centre, London.

PARACHUTING (p. 172) During the National Skydiving Championships, on 5 July 1986, a team of 100 skydivers led by Guy Manos and Tom Piras of Deland, Florida, USA linked in a cluster formation for 7.67 sec. They jumped at 15,000 ft *4572 m* and took 61 sec to make the formation over Davis Field, Muskogee, Oklahoma, USA.

ROCK BAND (p. 173) Cleveland, a 6-piece band sponsored by WRQC, Cleveland, Ohio, USA played continuous for 100 hr 25 min between 7–11 Apr 1986.

STAMP LICKING (p. 174) Ian Thomas of Brisbane, Australia, licked and affixed 204 stamps at the Sunpex '85 Exhibition, Brisbane on 5 Oct 1985.

TALKING (p. 175) Andy Page, 23, a Methodist lay preacher of Woolton, Liverpool gave an after-dinner speech lasting 24 hr on 1–2 July 1986 at the city's St George's Hotel.

TEETER BOARD (p. 177) A seven-man high perch pyramid was established by the Bulgarian 'Kehaiovi Troupe' at the Tower Circus, Blackpool in 16 July 1986.

CHICKEN (p. 178) Sean Barry ate 3 lb 12 oz *1,7 kg* of chicken in 8 min 5 sec at the 'Royal Oak', Bishops Cleeve, Cheltenham, Gloucestershire on 5 July 1986.

EGGS (p. 178) Peter Dowdeswell consumed 14 hard-boiled eggs in 41.57 sec on 'The Morning Show' in New York, NY, USA on 17 July 1986.

ICE CREAM (p. 178) Tony Dowdeswell ate 3 lb 6 oz *1,53 kg* of unmelted ice cream in 31.67 sec at the Guinness Museum of World Records, New York, NY, USA on 16 July 1986.

JELLY (p. 178) Peter Dowdeswell ate 20 fluid oz *56,8 cl* of solid jelly in 8.25 sec at the 'Royal Oak', Bishops Cleeve, Glos. on 5 July 1986.

KIPPERS (p. 178) Reg Morris of Walsall, West Midlands, ate 27 kippers weighing 16 lb 15 oz *7,68 kg* (self-filleted) in 35 min 24 sec on 31 Oct 1985.

SPAGHETTI (p. 178) Peter Dowdeswell consumed 100 yd *91,44 m* in 12.02 sec at 42nd Street Disco, Halesowen, West Midlands on 3 July 1986.

GREATEST BEQUESTS (p. 179) Ryoichi Sasakawa, Chairman of the Japanese Shipbuilding Industry Foundation, has made total donations of 405,732,907,012 Yen *£1,758,322,430* during the years 1962–84.

CHAPTER 11

THE HUMAN WORLD

HIGHEST PERSONAL MAJORITY (p. 190) S. W. R. D. Bandaranaike in the 1956 general election in Ceylon (Sri Lanka) achieved 91.82 per cent of the total votes polled, 45,016 of 49,025, in his constituency, Attanagalla.

MAYORALTY (p. 192) When Councillor Denis Martineau took office on 20 May 1986 as Lord Mayor of the City of Birmingham he followed his great-great-grandfather Robert, his great-grandfather Thomas, his grandfather Ernest and his father Wilfrid.

GOLD ROBBERY (p. 200) Kenneth Noye, 38, who killed Detective Constable John Fordham by stabbing was sentenced to 14 years for conspiring to handle the gold and fined £250,000 with £200,000 (maximum) for costs on 24 July 1986.

LONGEST LINE OF COINS (p. 205) A line of 1,000,130 one-cent coins 19,782 km *12.29 miles* in length and totalling $10,001.30 was laid by pupils of Blacktown Girls' High School, Blacktown, NSW on 15 Nov 1985 at the local International Peace Park.

LONGEST SAUSAGE (p. 208) Ian Zulic of Hero's Smallgoods, Geelong, Vic., Australia, extruded a sausage 11 km *6.83 miles* in length on 3 Nov 1985 at the local Springding Festival.

YOUNGEST GRADUATE (p. 213) Ruth Lawrence, aged 14, became a double First on 4 July 1986 having completed the 3 year physics course in 12 months.

LONGEST SERVING CHORISTER (p. 216) John Love Vokins (b. 19 Jan 1890) has been a chorister for 91 years. He joined the choir of Christ Church, Heeley, Sheffield in 1895 and that of St Michael's, Hathersage 35 years later.

ACCIDENTS AND DISASTERS (p. 217 table) Chernobyl death total was 31, as of 7 Aug 1986.

CHAPTER 12

SPORTS, GAMES & PASTIMES

ALL SPORTS (p. 219) To June 1986, Sport Aid in Britain raised £8.7 million.

ARCHERY (p. 223) Earliest references—The Society of Archers in Yorkshire date to 14 May 1673.

BOARD GAMES (p. 227–8) Chess—ELO ratings at 1 July 1986: men—Kasparov 2740; women—Zsuzsa Polgar 2455. UK: Nigel Short 2615. Scrabble®—highest three-game score in British Championship: 1843 by Viraf Mehta in 1986.

BOWLING (TEN-PIN) 24-hr (p. 229) A team of six, 'The Cobras', from the 3rd Royal Tank Regiment, scored 53,543 in 24 hr at the Paderborn Bowling Centre, Paderborn, West Germany, on 24–5 July 1986.

BOWLS (p. 229) David Bryant won a further British Isles title at triples in 1986.

CANOEING (p. 233) Canoe Raft—A raft of 285 canoes was held together for over 30 sec by a team from the National Association of Boys Clubs on the River Trent, Nottingham on 28 May 1986.

Cross Channel (p. 233) A doubles record of 2 hr 28 min 18 sec was set by Shaun Rice and Colin Simpkins in a K2 kayak from Shakespeare Beach, Dover to Cap Gris Nez on 19 July 1986.

24 hr (p. 233): Chris Greeff achieved 230,65 km *143.32 miles* on the River Breede, Cape Province, South Africa on 11–12 Aug 1985.

CRICKET (p. 234) Test cricket: Sunil Gavaskar Test career: 9367 runs (ave. 50.63) in 201 innings in 115 tests to July 1986.

A Hundred 100's (p. 236) Dennis Amiss hit his 100th first-class century on 29 July 1986 for Warwicks v. Lancs at Edgbaston. Geoff Boycott 151 centuries to 21 July.

Women's cricket (p. 239): Earliest match: amend to 1745. Highest Test innings score: 190 by Sandhya Aggarwal (India) v. England at Worcester on 14 July 1986.

CROQUET (p. 240) International Trophy—a record six appearances by John Prince (NZ), 1963–86. He was also the youngest international, aged 17 yr 190 days on his debut.

CYCLING Land's End to John O'Groats (p. 242) One-legged cyclist Hugh Culverhouse (GB) completed the 847 miles *1363 km* trip in 77 hr 53:17 on 21–24 Aug 1985.

Most Titles, British (p. 241) Beryl Burton won 72nd title in 1986.

World Record, Indoors (p. 242)—Women's unpaced flying start 200 m: 11.948 sec, Erika Salumyae (USSR), Moscow 7 July 1986.

Richard and Nicholas Crane cycled to the remotest point on Earth (ie the farthest from the sea—see p. 58) after a 3294 mile *5301,2 km* trip from Bangladesh, 1 May–27 June 1986.

Highest altitude (p. 243): Adrian Crane (UK) cycled from the lower summit of Mount Chimborazo, Ecuador, an altitude of 6267 m *20,561 ft*, to the town of Riobamba, Ecuador on 11 May 1986.

FIVES (p. 247) Rugby Fives, most titles: Wayne Enstone won a 13th Championship in 1986.

GAMBLING, LARGEST BOOKMAKER (p. 254) Ladbrokes turnover 1985: £984.4 million; 1496 shops in the UK plus 820 in Belgium.

Bingo (p. 253) The largest simultaneous game of bingo, the National Bingo Game, was held on 19 June 1986; launched by up to half a million people for prize money totalling £100,000. Clubs were linked by computer and the game lasted from 8.25 to 8.40 pm.

GLIDING (p. 254) Absolute Altitude world record: 49,009 ft *14 938 m* by Robert Harris (USA) in a Grob G102 over California City on 17 Feb 1986. Hang gliding—The Britannia Trophy (for 'the most victorious performance in the air') was won for the first time by the British Hang Gliding Team in 1986.

GOLF—The Open (p. 257) Greg Norman (Australia) (b. 10 Feb 1955) scored the lowest scoring round of 63 at Turnberry on 18 July 1986.

Most Rounds (p. 257) Charles Stock played 711 holes in 24 hr (averaging 36.5 per nine holes) at Boston Hills, Hudson, Ohio, USA on 7 July 1986.

Bill Ridge (USA) played 504 holes (28 rounds) on foot in 24 hr at Bob-O-Link Country Club on 26 June 1986.

Curtis Cup (p. 257): First British win since 1956 and their first win in America.

Hole-in-One (p. 258): The odds against 'aceing' have been calculated at 84,000 to 1. Jim Cobb, 69, of Craig, Colorado, USA scored three in 30 hr, per 'USA Today' on 8 Aug 1985.

Gordon McKay and Hamish McAlpine played holes on 101 different courses in Scotland in a 24 hr period, 19–20 June 1986.

GYMNASTICS—Press Ups, 24 Hours (p. 260): 29,601 by Jack Atherton at HMP Featherstone on 11–12 July 1986.

Skipping (p. 260): John Baber (USA) skip-ran the 10 mile *16 km* Purple Classic road race in 78 min 40 sec at Williamstown, Massachusetts, USA on 27 Apr 1986.

MOTOR CYCLING (p. 269) Motorcycle balancing—Vaughan Wilson remained stationary on a bike without touching the floor for 60 min 27 sec at Nackington, Kent on 7 June 1986.

MOUNTAINEERING—Fell Running (p. 273) Martin Stone completed the nine 4000 ft Scottish peaks (85 miles *137 km*) in 21 hr 39 min on 4 July 1986. Joss Naylor ran over the 214 Lakeland Peaks mentioned in the Wainwright Guides, 391 miles *629 km*, in 7 days 14 hr 25 min on 27 June–5 July 1986.

Pennine Way (p. 273) A relay record of 29 hr 7 min 58 sec was set by 24 members of Holmfirth Harriers in June 1986.

PARASCENDING (p. 274) Roy Castle parascended 2¼ nautical miles under ten bridges of the River Thames (Lambeth to Tower Bridge) in 16 min 57 sec, pulled by a Mastercraft Powerslot boat (driven by Brian Tripp) on 22 July 1986.

PIGEON RACING—Highest Priced Bird (p. 275) c. £33,000 for *Sproetekop*, bred and raced by Arthur Leflere of Belgium, paid by a Japanese fancier in 1986.

Most competitive miles—by one pigeon is 20,082 miles by *Nunnies*, a chequer cock owned by Terry Haley (GB). *Nunnies* was bred in 1966 and took part in 102 races until 1978 when he was retired.

POLO (p. 275) Highest handicap: Claire Tomlinson handicap of 5 from 19 Sept 1986.

ROWING—Fastest Times (p. 278) Men: coxed pairs 6:44.92 GB Lucerne, 13 July 1986. Women: Quadruple sculls 6:21.36 GDR Lucerne, 13 July 1986.

Heaviest cox—Geoffrey Dickens JP MP coxed an eight in the Speaker's Regatta on the River Thames over a 500 m course on 16 July 1986. He weighed 21 stone 3 lb *134,7 kg* and completed the course 'having taken on board a great deal of water.'

SKIING (p. 282) A world downhill speed record for blind skiers was set by Mike May of Palo Alto, California, USA at 58 mph *93,34 km/h*.

SWIMMING Channel, Double Crossing (p. 290) Fastest time—17 hr 56 min by Philip Rush (NZ) (b. 6 Nov 1963) on 9 Sept 1985. World record (p. 288) Women 50 m: 25.31 Tamara Costache, Sofia, Bulgaria, 2 Aug 1986.

TENNIS Federation Cup (p. 293) USA achieved 12th win, but in an earlier round Chris Lloyd's unbroken sequence of success ended after 29 wins.

TIDDLYWINKS (p. 293) A new record for winking a distance of one mile *1,6 km* was set by Stephan Hewerdine in a time of 4 hr 5 min at Wyndham Park, Grantham, Lincolnshire on 22 May 1986.

TRACK & FIELD—LAND'S END TO JOHN O' GROATS (p. 297) A relay record of 97 hr 34 min 25 sec was set by a team of ten from Crosby Squash Club, Crosby, Liverpool, 22–26 June 1986.

World Records, Women (p. 297) Heptathlon: Jackie Joyner 7161 pts, Houston, Texas, USA, 1–2 July 1986.

5000 m: Ingrid Kristiansen 14:37.33, Stockholm, Sweden, 5 Aug 1986.

WATERSKIING (p. 302) Men's tricks WR: 10,440 pts Patrice Martin, Giffaumont, France, 27 July 1986.

WEIGHTLIFTING—Greatest power lifts (p. 303) William Whorriskey, 48, reportedly achieved a one-arm dead lift of 771 lb *350,5 kg* (lifting the frame and five waterfilled barrels) in Birmingham, England on 5 May 1986.

World Weightlifting Records (p. 304) 52 kg snatch—116 kg *255½ lb* by He Zhuqqiang (China) at Donaueschingen, West Germany on 26 May 1986.

Body Weight Feats (p. 304) Naum Shalamanov became the second man to clean and jerk three times his body weight; his world record now stands at 187.5 kg. Geoff Capes achieved 107 kg on a grip dynamometer at Gosport in May 1986.

24 hr squat record: 2,168,625 kg *4 780 994 lb* in 24 hr was set by a team of ten from St Albans Weightlifting Club/Ware Boys' Club, Herts on 20–21 July 1985.

YACHTING/BOARDSAILING (p. 306) Highest speed: Pascal Maka improved to 38.86 knots *71,96 km/h* in a wind of 50 knots. (Women): Britt Dunkerbeke—33.77 knots *62,58 km/h* in the Canary Islands, July 1986.

ENDURANCE MARATHONS—DARTS (p. 307–8) 145 hr by two separate teams of four (playing doubles) from the Skyways Bar, Sliema, Malta, 16–23 Dec 1985

Dungeons & Dragons—84 hr by five members of an original nine) of 'Dragon Aid' in London, 22–25 July 1986.

Fives (Winchester)—34 hr 40 min by Steven Humphrey and Spencer Page at Rossall School, Fleetwood, Lancashire, 4–5 July 1986.

Bar Billiards: 53 hr, David and Peter Lillie, Tony Boorman and Steve Richardson at the 'King's Head', Sudbury, Suffolk, 1–3 Aug 1986.

Trivial Pursuits—105 hr 9 min; Cribbage 124 hr 15 min by students of St Anselms College, Merseyside, 14–19 July 1986.

312

315

Chancellorship, longest and shortest tenures, most appointments, Foreign Secretaryship, longest tenures, Colonial Secretaryship, longest tenures, Speakership, longest, M.P.s youngest, oldest, longest briefest span, earliest women, heaviest, tallest, M.P. 192

PARROT, most talkative 37

PARSNIP, heaviest 48

PARTICIPANTS, most (sport) 220

PARTICLE, number, lightest and heaviest sub-nuclear, newest, shortest lived nuclear 71

PARTICLE ACCELERATOR, most powerful 77

PARTY GIVING, most expensive, largest 163

PASS, highest 211

PASSENGER, oldest, youngest air 137

PASSENGER LIFT, fastest world, longest U.K. 140

PASSENGER LINER, largest, longest 121

PASSION PLANT, longest 45

PASSPORT, most expensive 158

PASTRY, longest 207

PATENT, earliest radio 99, television 100, earliest H Bomb 195, earliest English, most applications, shortest, longest 196, greatest infringement damages 197

PEACH, largest 47

PEANUTS, eating record 178

PEAPOD, longest 48

PEAR, heaviest 48

PEARL, largest, most expensive 75

PEAS, eating record 178

PEDIGREE, longest 83

PEELING, records, onion 171, potato 173

PEER, most ancient peerage, oldest creation, longest lived, youngest, longest and shortest, highest succession number, most creations, most prolific 182

PEERAGE, most ancient, oldest creation, longest, shortest, highest numbering, most creations, most prolific 182

PEERESS, most prolific 182

PELOTA VASCA, 254, 274

PENAL CAMPS, largest 203

PENAL SETTLEMENT, largest French 203

PENDULUM, longest 141

PENINSULA, largest 58

PENKNIFE, most blades 151

PENNINE WAY, cycling 243, fell running* 273

PENNY FARTHING, records* 130

PENPALS, most durable 86

PENS, most expensive 151

PENSION, longest 163

PERFECT DEALS (Bridge), 233

PERFECT NUMBERS, lowest, highest 74

PERFORMER, biggest audience 91, highest paid T.V. 101

PERFUME*, most expensive 71

PERIODICAL, oldest world, G.B., largest circulation, world, G.B., annual 89, highest advertising rates 89–90

PERMAFROST, deepest 54

PERSONAL INJURY, highest damages world, G.B. 197

PERSONAL NAMES, earliest, longest pedigree, longest single Christian name, surname, world, U.K., most Christian names, shortest, commonest surname 83, commonest Christian name 83–4, most versions of, most contrived 84

PETANQUE, 274

PETITION, greatest parliamentary 189

PETROL, consumption 126

PETUNIA, tallest* 48

PHARMACEUTICALS, biggest sales 147

PHILODENDRON, largest* 45

PHONE, see Telephone

PHONOGRAPH, see Gramophone

PHOTOGRAPHIC STORE, largest 147

PHOTOGRAPHY, earliest world, U.K., earliest aerial, largest negative 73

PHYSICAL EXTREMES, 76–7

PHYSICIANS, most, highest, lowest proportion 185

PHYSIOLOGY, 15–21

Pi, number of places memorized 16, most accurate, inaccurate version 74

PIANIST, highest paid, greatest span 92

PIANO, earliest, grandest, most expensive 90, highest notes 91

PIANO COMPOSITION, longest 92

PIANO PLAYING, world, U.K. 172

PIANO SMASHING, record 172

PIANO TUNING, record 172

PICKLED ONIONS, eating record 178

PIE, largest apple, cherry 206, meat 206–7, mince, pizza 207

PIER, oldest, longest, most, pleasure*, world, G.B. 107, longest world, G.B. 116

PIG, highest price 155, heaviest 155–6, prolificacy record 156

PIGEON RACING*, 274–5

PIGGERY, largest 154

PILLAR BOX, oldest 212

PILLAR BOX STANDING, record number of people 173

PILLAR OF COINS, 205

PILL-TAKER, greatest 20

PILOT, most flying hours 137–8, most take offs and landings 138, oldest and youngest 137, human powered flight 138, ace 180–81

PINEAPPLE, largest 47

PINNIPEDS, largest world, G.B. 27, smallest 27–8, most abundant, rarest, fastest, deepest dive, longest lived 28

PIPELINE, longest oil, submarine, natural gas, water, most expensive 140

PIPE SMOKING, duration record 173

PISTOLS, most expensive 151, highest auction price 152

PITCH, (sound), highest detectable 17, bat 28, (sport), largest 218

PIZZA PIE, largest 207, eating record 178

PLACE-NAMES, earliest, longest world, G.B., shortest world, G.B., most spellings 84

PLAGUE, most infectious disease 18

PLANE PULLING, 173

PLANET, largest, shortest 'day', smallest, highest orbital speed, hottest, coldest, nearest, surface features 66, brightest and faintest 66–7, densest and least dense, conjunctions, most dramatic, next conjunction 67

PLANETARIUM, first, largest, earliest world, G.B. 74

PLANT KINGDOM, 44–50, oldest 44–5, rarest, northernmost, southernmost, highest, roots, depth, length, worst weeds, most spreading 45, largest blossoming world, G.B., smallest flowering, smallest, most valuable, fastest growth, slowest flowering 46, largest leaves world, G.B. 47, champion collector 46

PLATEAU, greatest 60

PLATE SPINNING, record 173

PLATFORM, Railway, longest 132

PLATINUM, largest refinery 119

PLATINUM DISC, unique award 96

PLAY, longest runs*, shortest runs, longest, Shakespeare 94

PLAYING CARDS, rarest and most expensive 152

PLEASURE BEACH, biggest 107

PLEASURE PIER, earliest, longest*, most 107, 116

PLOUGHING, championship, greatest acreage ploughed, fastest 155

PLUCKING, chicken, turkey record 156

POEM, longest, most successful 87

POET LAUREATE, youngest, oldest 87

POGO-STICK, JUMPING, 173

POISON, most potent 71, (also most poisonous snake, most active frog venom 38, most venomous fish 39, most poisonous spider 40), mass poisoning 200

POLAR CONQUESTS, first North*, South, first on both poles, first circumnavigation 159

POLAR LIGHT, see Aurora

POLDER, largest 112

POLE SQUATTING, records 173

POLICY (Life assurance), largest, highest pay-out 146

POLITICAL DIVISION, largest 183

POLITICAL SPEECH, longest on record 189

POLLEN COUNT, highest 50

POLO*, 275

POOL, 275, 307

POPE, longest, shortest reign, longest lived, oldest, youngest, last non-Italian, last ex-Cardinalate, English, last married, quickest and slowest election 214

POP FESTIVAL, greatest attendance 91

POP GROUP, most successful 96, loudest 97, non-stop playing* 173

POPULATION, world, progressive mid-year estimates 185, largest, smallest, densest, U.K., sparsest 184, cities 186

PORCELAIN, highest price* 152

PORT, largest, busiest 209

PORTRAIT, most expensive miniature 79

PORTRAITIST, most prolific 79

POST OFFICE, northernmost U.K., and southernmost, oldest, longest counter 212

POSTAGE STAMPS, see Stamps

POSTAL SERVICE, largest and highest average letter mail, highest numbered address, oldest pillar-boxes, northernmost and southernmost, oldest post office, longest counter 212

POSTCARDS, 151

POSTER, largest 79

POTATO, record display 47, dimension, weight 50, record yield 155, peeling record 173, eating record 178

POTATO CRISPS, eating record 178, largest 207

POTATO MASH, largest serving 207

POT LID, highest price 152

POT PLANT, largest 45

POTTERY, highest price 152

POWDER, finest 72

POWERBOAT RACING, 275–6

POWER FAILURE, greatest 139

POWERLIFTING*, 303–5

POWER PRODUCERS, 138–9

POWER STATION, largest world, non-hydro-electric, largest G.B., atomic, solar, tidal 138

PRAM PUSHING, record distance 173

PREDATOR, largest 43

PREGNANCY, longest, shortest 13

PREHISTORIC ANIMALS, see Extinct Animals

PREHISTORIC MONUMENT, largest 116

PREMIER, see Prime Minister

PREMIUM (Insurance), largest 146

PRESS, largest 140

PRESS UPS*, 260

PRESSURE, highest, lowest Barometric 54, laboratory 76

PRIMATE, largest, heaviest, smallest, rarest, longest lived, strongest 28, earliest 10, 43

PRIME MINISTER, oldest, longest term of office 190, U.K., records, longest terms of office, shortest, most times, oldest, youngest, other records 191

PRIME NUMBERS, lowest, highest 74

PRINTER, largest 88, fastest 140–41

PRINTING, earliest, earliest books, largest 84, smallest 84–5, most valuable books 85, highest print order 87

PRISON, longest sentences, world, G.B. 202–3, longest time served, longest detention, and escapes from Broadmoor, largest, G.B., highest population, most secure, most expensive, longest escape 203, greatest break 204

PRISONER, oldest, most convictions 203

PRIZE, largest radio 99, T.V. 101, competition 166, most valuable annual 182

PROCARYOTA, 50–51

PRODUCER, youngest Broadway 94, most prolific TV 101

PROFESSOR, youngest, most durable 213

PROFIT AND LOSS, greatest 144

PROHIBITION, longest lasting 206

PROMISE, Breach of, highest damages 197

PROPELLER, largest ship 122, largest aircraft 135

PROPERTY, most valuable 146–7

PROSECUTION, rarest 203

PROTEIN, most and least proteinous fruit 47

PROTISTA, largest, smallest, fastest moving, fastest reproduction 50

PROTOPHYTE, smallest 50

PROTOZOAN, largest, smallest, fastest moving, fastest reproduction 50

PRUNES, eating record 178

PSALM, longest, shortest 85

PSYCHIATRIST, most 185, fastest 185

PSYCHIC FORCES, 21

PUBLICATION, largest 84

PUBLIC HOUSE, oldest, U.K., largest world, G.B., smallest, longest tenure, longest name, shortest name, commonest name, highest*, most visits 108

PUBLIC RELATIONS, largest trim 147

PUBLISHERS, fastest*, oldest 87, most prolific 87–8

PUBLISHING, largest enterprise 147

PULSARS, first, fastest 69

PULSE RATES, highest, lowest 18

PUMPING (FIRE), greatest gallonage 168

PUMPKIN, heaviest 48

PUMP-TURBINE, largest 139

PURGE, greatest 198–9

PYGMIES, smallest 9

PYRAMID, tallest (progressive records) 109, oldest 117, largest 116–17, work force 116

Q.C., see Queen's Counsel

QUADRUPLETS, oldest 12, heaviest, most sets 13

QUARRY, deepest, largest world, England 119

QUARTZ, records 75

QUASAR*, 68, 69

QUAY, longest 116

QUEEN, longest lived, youngest 188, British records 187

QUEEN'S COUNSEL, youngest, most successful 198

QUIETEST PLACE, 77

QUILT, world's largest 151

QUINDECAPLETS, 13

QUINTUPLETS, heaviest 13

QUIZ, largest T.V. prize 101, most participants, most protracted 173

QUOIT THROWING, record 173

QUORUM, smallest parliamentary 188

RABBITS, largest litter 33, largest breed, heaviest specimen, smallest, most prolific, longest ears, oldest 34

RACE (Ethnology), poorest 178

RACKETBALL, 276, 307

RACKETS, 276

RADAR INSTALLATION, largest 141

RADIO, origins, earliest patent, earliest broadcast world, G.B., earliest trans-Atlantic, longest broadcast, topmost prize, most durable programmes, most heard broadcaster, earliest Antipodal reception, most assiduous ham, most stations, highest listnership 99, highest response 99–100, smallest set 101, tallest masts 109

RADIO-MICROPHONES, earliest 99

RADIO TELESCOPE, first fully steerable, largest 74

RADISH, heaviest 48

RAFT, longest survival 162

RAILWAY, longest bridge 110, highest bridge 110–11, tunnel, subway tunnel 113, earliest 130, fastest 130–31, longest non-stop, most powerful engine, longest freight train, greatest load, longest run, straight, widest, narrowest gauge world, G.B., highest, lowest, steepest (world, G.B.), shallowest gradients, busiest rail system, calling all stations, most countries, railroad handcar pumping 131, longest journey, stations, largest world, G.B., oldest, busiest, highest, largest waiting rooms, longest platform, underground most extensive, greatest depth, longest, quickest journey, most stations, busiest subway, model railway duration record, longest run, most miniature 132, country with greatest length, furthest place from in G.B., number of journeys on British Rail 209, disasters 217

RAILWAY DISASTERS, worst world, U.K. 217

RAILWAY ENGINE, see Engine, Railway

RAINBOW, longest lasting 55

RAINFALL, most intense 55, greatest, least 54

RAINY DAYS, most in years 54

RALLY (motor), earliest, longest 271

RAMP JUMPING, longest 173

RANSOM, highest 200

RAPPELING, longest descent 173

RAT, oldest 34

RATTING, record by dog 33

RAVIOLI, eating record 178

REACTION, fastest human 19

REACTOR, largest single atomic 138

REAL ESTATE, most valuable 146–7

REAL TENNIS, 293

RECORD, Gramophone, see Gramophone Record

RECORD, longest held 173

RECORD BREAKERS (sport), youngest and oldest 218, most prolific 219

RECORDED SOUND 95–7; earliest* 95–6, oldest, smallest, jazz records, earliest tape, most successful artist, group, earliest, most golden discs, most recorded song 96, most recordings, biggest sales 98–9, fastest selling album, greatest advance sales, loudest group, Grammy awards 97

RECORDING ARTIST, most successful, earliest golden disc, most golden discs, most recordings, best-selling, charts, fastest sellers, greatest advance sales, Grammy awards 97

RED CABBAGE, heaviest 48

REDWOOD, tallest 49

REED, tallest 47

REEF, longest 58

REFINERY (Oil), largest 147

REFLECTING TELESCOPE, largest and most powerful 73–4

REFLEXES, fastest 19

REFRACTING TELESCOPE, largest 74

'REFUSNIK', most patient 185

REGIMENT, British, oldest, most senior 194

REGISTRATION PLATE, earliest, most expensive 124

Indexing by

Anna Pavord

World Copyright Reserved   Copyright © 1986   Guinness Superlatives Ltd

This book is sold subject to the Standard Conditions of Sale of Net Books and may not be resold in the United Kingdom below the net price fixed by the publishers and ascertainable from their 1986 Catalogue.

British Library Cataloguing in Publication Data

Guinness book of records.—33rd ed.
1. Curiosities and wonders—Periodicals
032'.02   AG240

ISBN 0–85112–439–9

Standard Book Number ISBN: 0–85112–439–9
Standard Book Number ISBN: 0–85112–440–2 (Australian Edition)

'Guinness' is a registered trade mark of Guinness Superlatives Ltd.

Printed in England. Produced by William Clowes Limited, Beccles, Suffolk.
Printed by Jarrold Printing, Norwich, Norfolk.
Litho origination by East Anglian Engraving, Norwich, Norfolk.

The Editor of the

GUINNESS BOOK OF RECORDS

wishes to thank

ASSISTANT EDITORS

Julian Farino
Alex E Reid
Ian R Smith

ART EDITOR

David L Roberts

ASSISTANTS

Sheila Goldsmith
Muriel Ling
Bethan Rees
Colin C Smith
Moira F Stowe

CONTRIBUTORS

C V Appleton; John W Arblaster AIM; Howard Bass; Pat Besford; Robin Bradford; Henry G Button; David Cheslin; Sq Ldr D H Clarke DFC, AFC; Clive Everton; Frank L Forster; Bill Frindall; Tim Furniss; Ian Goold; Stan Greenberg; International Boxing Research Organisation; John Marshall; Peter J Matthews; Andy Milroy; Alan Mitchell BA, BAg(For); Ian Morrison; Susann Palmer; John Randall; Jack Rollin; Graham Snowdon; Donald Steel; Lance Tingay; Nicholas Todd (GRRR Books); Juhani Virola; Dr A C Waltham; Gerry L Wood FZS

OVERSEAS EDITORS

DENMARK Ludwig E Bramsen; **FINLAND** Juhani Stenqvist; **FRANCE** Philippe Scali; **GERMANY** Hans Heinrich Kummel; **GREECE** Athanasios Rigas; **ICELAND** Orlygur Halfdanarson; **ISRAEL** Shay Hausman; **ITALY** Maurizio Orlandi; **JAPAN** H Nishio; **MIDDLE EAST** Sami Naufal; **NETHERLANDS** Klaas de Boer; **NORWAY** Per Damsgaard; **SPAIN** Margarita Jordan; **SWEDEN** Lisbet Ekberg; **USA** David A Boehm

and to

D Richard Bowen (Europe); Bob Burton (Australasia); Ben Matsumoto (Far East)

PRODUCTION/PRINTING

David Browne; John Catchpole; Malcolm Debenham; Derek Driver; Basil Forder; John Hudston; Des Palmer; Bill Thomas; Ted Tuffen

1987 Cover Concept, design and execution: Bernstein Hounsfield Associates, London (with acknowledgements to Pictor International)
Photography: Michael Dunning
Computer graphics: Trademasters Limited
Additional picture research: Lesley Davy

YOU'VE READ THE BOOK, NOW SEE IT BROUGHT TO LIFE.

GUINNESS WORLD OF RECORDS EXHIBITION
·THE TROCADERO · PICCADILLY CIRCUS · LONDON W1V 7FD · 01-439 7331·

Other Guinness Exhibitions already established in: USA – New York City; Myrtle Beach, South Carolina; Gatlinburg and Nashville, Tennessee; San Francisco, California. CANADA – Niagara Falls, Ontario.